MARKETS AND MERCHANTS
OF THE LATE
SEVENTEENTH CENTURY

From *Le Parfait Négociant* by Jacques Savary (1675). Reproduced by kind permission of the British Library.

RECORDS OF SOCIAL AND ECONOMIC HISTORY
NEW SERIES XII

MARKETS AND MERCHANTS OF THE LATE SEVENTEENTH CENTURY

THE MARESCOE-DAVID LETTERS, 1668–1680

SELECTED AND EDITED
WITH AN INTRODUCTION
BY

HENRY ROSEVEARE

Published for THE BRITISH ACADEMY
by THE OXFORD UNIVERSITY PRESS

Oxford University Press, Walton Street, Oxford OX2 6DP

Oxford   New York   Toronto
Delhi   Bombay   Calcutta   Madras   Karachi
Petaling Jaya   Singapore   Hong Kong   Tokyo
Nairobi   Dar es Salaam   Cape Town
Melbourne   Auckland

and associated companies in
Berlin   Ibadan

Oxford is a trade mark of Oxford University Press

Published in the United States
by Oxford University Press, New York

First published 1987
Paperback edition 1991

British Library Cataloguing in Publication Data

Marescoe, Charles
Markets and merchants of the late seventeenth century:
the Marescoe-David letters, 1668–1680.—
(Records of social and economic history. New series; 12)
1. Marescoe, Charles   2. David, Jacob
3. Merchants—Europe—Biography
I. Title   II. David, Jacob   III. Roseveare, Henry
IV. British Academy   V. Series
380.1′092′2   HF3494.6.D3/

ISBN 0-19-726106-X

Printed in Great Britain
at the Alden Press, Oxford

INTRODUCTORY NOTE

Materials published in the Records of Social and Economic History series have normally been homogeneous in form, e.g. account books, diaries or charters, relating to specific families, places or estates. They have only exceptionally been selections from an archive. Dr Roseveare's edition of the Marescoe-David manuscripts is, however, just such an exception. It is based upon a very large deposit in the Chancery Masters' Exhibits in the Public Record Office. Because of its fragile state the collection has been withdrawn from public access, for repair and conservation. The collection is unique in its coverage of the Europe-wide trading activities of inter-related London-based families in the later seventeenth century. It includes ledgers, account books, over 10,000 letters (the majority in Dutch) and large numbers of miscellaneous mercantile and financial documents. Dr Roseveare, who has been given special access to these records, has selected and translated nearly 500 letters, and provided a detailed introduction together with appendices of prices, exchange rates and other financial and commercial data. An ancillary feature of this volume is that the originals of the letters in Dutch and German which Dr Roseveare has translated will be available on microfiche on application to the British Academy (see below p. 220).

D. C. Coleman
Chairman, Records of Social and Economic History Committee

CONTENTS

Contents

THE LETTERS, 1668–1680

APPENDICES A.—I.

INDEXES

LIST OF ILLUSTRATIONS

Frontispiece. From *Le Parfait Négociant* by Jacques Savary (1675). Reproduced by kind permission of the British Library.

Between pp. 10 and 11. Marescoe–David book-keeping.

(a) From Ledger 'F' [Table 1, A.1(b)] f. 97—Marescoe's Profit & Loss account (in Peter Joye's hand) showing some of the firm's large profits during the Second Anglo-Dutch War.

(b) From Invoice Book [B.1] p. 3—entries by CM, PJ and Moses Coulon of sale accounts for copper, wine, brandy and timber received in 1666.

(c) From Receipt Book [E.1]—receipts for payment of freight charges signed by Swedish captains (Andries Biorsen, Elias Johansen, Jolle Tyerdts, etc.) and for lighterage wages for unloading iron from some of the detained Tar Co. vessels in the autumn of 1668, with (centre right) the marks and initials of lightermen.

(d) From Invoice Book [B.1] p. 65—entries by CM and JD of sale-accounts for copper-wire from Jacob Momma and invoices of exports to Hamburg and Venice.

(e) From CM's Memorandum Book [F.1]—entries of shipping and cargo arrivals, August–October, 1669.

(f) From Cash Book [C.4]—entries by JD, counter-signed by LM, with some of her withdrawals for 'household expenses'.

ix

TABLES

FIGURES

MAPS

FOR KARIN

INTRODUCTION

It is to be hoped that the documents presented in this volume will shed light on a peculiarly important epoch in Europe's economic history. Few would dispute that the late seventeenth century witnessed a crucial phase in the evolution of international commerce, with implications of great significance for England, France, Germany, Sweden and the Netherlands. For England, above all, the seventh and eighth decades of that century have been recognized as an age of 'commercial revolution' in which the take-off to subsequent trading ascendancy clearly began. Led by a powerful growth in re-exports to western Europe it was accompanied by a stronger English presence in the Baltic and a continuing penetration of the Mediterranean. The fruits of the Levant, of the East and West Indies now passed through the protected English entrepôt into a Europe where Dutch commercial hegemony was showing faint signs of beginning to wane. In Sweden too, trades and industries which had been largely Dutch-financed and Dutch-managed were turning to markets outside the Dutch sphere. Politically the turn was to France, and for France too these decades of Colbertian reform were a painfully strenuous experience of failure and success—failure for the great chartered companies which sought to rival those of England and the United Provinces, but success for the domestic and colonial expansion of trade, industry and agriculture. The fortunes of many weaker economies followed in the wake of these powers. Spain's silver fleets still gave a strong if irregular pulse to the heartlands of European capital; her markets at home and abroad gave employment in the clothing industries of England, France and the Netherlands. Lille might pass from Spanish to French suzerainty but her textile manufactures still moved prosperously with the demands of New Spain and Central America. Italy too, although almost bereft of her great textile industries, was both an indispensable emporium of luxuries and domestic products and a valuable market for the raw materials and re-exports of the north. Altogether, in a century marked by stagnation and depression, the 1660s and 1670s saw hopeful stirrings of growth.

It will seem improbable that the business papers of any one firm should be capable of illuminating such a broad canvas, yet the essential interest of the Marescoe-David papers lies in the remarkable diversity of their subjects and the considerable geographical range of their correspondence (Map I). At the heart of the business lay strong bonds with Sweden's greatest industrialists—the De Geers, the Momma-Reenstiernas, the Kock-Cronströms—which not only ensured for the firm an intermittent monopoly of England's imports from Sweden's chartered Tar Company but also a large share of her booming iron and copper imports. Marescoe in the 1660s and David in the 1670s may well have monopolized the London copper-wire market, as they claimed, and in both decades the strategic significance of their position roused jealousy and alarm in the City and Whitehall. Yet, at the same time, the firm was capable of shipping through Hamburg perhaps 10 per cent of England's sugar re-exports, and with this went a wide range of other goods—cotton, galls, ginger, indigo, logwood, silk—commissioned by some of Hamburg's leading merchant houses. In Amsterdam, likewise, they corresponded with many of those merchant-princes whose great houses still line the Keizersgracht, Herengracht or Achterburgwal—with Louis Trip, Steven de Geer, Joseph Deutz, Guillaume Bartolotti and Jean and Hendrik van Baerle. In Rouen their correspondents included the immensely wealthy Thomas Legendre and a group of earnest Protestant merchants whose conscientious efforts to maintain a traffic in English lead, tin, cotton and sugar contended unsuccessfully with Colbertian tariffs and prohibitions. In Lille too, political constraints after 1668 stunted, but did not wholly extinguish, the firm's shipments of oil, cotton and dyes destined for the city's industrious *sayetteurs*. In Venice the consortium to which Marescoe belonged was responsible for perhaps 80 per cent of London's exports to that market, though controversially handled for it by a Dutch agency. Only in Spain was the firm's marketing wholly English, selling English cloth and stockings through unimpeachably English factors, and the profits earned here in silver and gold were among the highest gained anywhere in the firm's operations. By 1670, in his early thirties, Charles Marescoe was among London's richest merchants and but for his wife's record of astonishing extravagance Jacob David might have rivalled him.

But who were Charles Marescoe and Jacob David? And why has nothing been heard of them before?

Although these names will mean little or nothing to most English or European scholars, students of Sweden's economic history have had the chance of being better informed. In 1911 Per Sondén identified Marescoe as the London agent of the Momma-Reenstierna brothers, and in 1957 Karl-Gustaff Hildebrand drew on Marescoe's correspondence in the Stockholm Riksarkiv to illustrate Sweden's marketing of iron and copper during the 1650s. Shortly after, Annagreta Hallberg noted Marescoe as the London agent for the Tar Company. Above all, Sven-Erik Åström has the credit for introducing non-Swedish readers to both Charles Marescoe and Jacob David. In his *From Cloth to Iron* he placed Marescoe firmly in the context of Sweden's flourishing trade with England in the 1660s, and in his essay 'The English Navigation Laws and the Baltic Trade, 1660–1700' he uncovered something of Jacob David's role as the London agent for Dutch-financed distribution of pitch and tar in the 1670s.

Regrettably, when Professor Åström was making his pioneering researches in Anglo-Swedish archives, the class of documents in the London Public Record Office known as 'Chancery Masters' Exhibits' had not yet become fully accessible. Dating in some cases from the twelfth century, the documents thus classified had long possessed an anomalous status in limbo between the private and public domain for in large part they consist of private papers placed in evidence before the Court of Chancery and not reclaimed. In 1860 they had been transferred by the Court of Chancery Act (23 & 24 Vict. c. 149, §.9) to the Clerk of Records and Writs of the Court of Chancery. Under the 1877 Public Record Office Act (40 & 41 Vict. c. 55 §.2) they were placed under the charge and superintendence of the Master of the Rolls 'as if they were records within the meaning of [the Public Record Office Acts of 1838 and 1877]' and thus, in effect, in his custody. They were held in the Public Record Office at Chancery Lane, but inspection was subject to the consent of the Master of the Rolls and the Treasury and their contents were so perfunctorily catalogued that no clear idea of their nature could be obtained. This was still the case in 1958 when all restrictions on access were removed by the Public Record Office Act [6 & 7 Elizabeth II c. 51 §.8 (5)].

It was still the case in the autumn of 1963 when I first explored the catalogue. Listed merely as 'late 17th century merchants' papers' the documents then enumerated as C. 114/64–78 'Frederick *v*. David' held out some slight promise of answering questions about the relationship between commercial investment and the counter-attractions of public borrowing, but one could not anticipate the deluge of unsorted documents which now tumbled out. Large oil-cloth bundles contained a completely miscellaneous heap of ledgers, cash-books, letters and commercial documents, largely in Dutch, often fragile, and evidently untouched since their deposit in the late seventeenth century. But it soon became clear that here was a potentially rich source of information about European trade, for all the principal centres seem represented in a commercial dialogue dealing with a wide range of English exports and a highly significant group of Scandinavian imports.

With nothing more than this impression it was enough to bring to the attention of Professor Charles Wilson and Professor Donald Coleman, who in turn secured the interest of the British Academy's Committee for Social and Economic History. In 1973 sabbatical leave from King's College, London allowed me to begin a period of full-time work on this material with the two-fold objective of sorting and arranging the documents and of publishing a selection of their contents. Neither task could be completed without a thorough analysis of what the documents contained and that inevitably entailed a laborious process of deciphering and translating much scarcely legible material. In 1977 the Social Science Research Council endowed the project with funds to enable research among complementary archives in Sweden, Germany and Holland and to provide three years of research assistance. The appointment of Dr E. K. Newman as full-time Research Officer transformed the pace of investigation. Her wide knowledge of the Dutch and German aspects of late seventeenth-century trade ideally equipped her to cope with these sections of the correspondence and the effective digestion of many thousands of these letters is owed to her unflagging industry.

The intention to produce from the 10,500 letters contained within this archive a single-volume selection has inevitably imposed painful problems of choice and presentation. Even if the choice could have extended to 1,000 letters it would have left 90 per cent of the series unrepresented and totally unexplained. A compromise has therefore been struck between explanation and representation by (i) an introductory account in which the whole course and content of Marescoe and David's business operations between 1664 and 1680 are analysed, and (ii) a selection of transcribed and translated letters which illustrates much of that analysis. The 480 letters printed here represent only a modest fraction of the whole but I am confident that any increase in their number at the expense of the introduction would not have produced a commensurate gain in illumination. Had the trading activities of Marescoe and David been confined to one area of Europe the task would have been easier, but instead they dealt with seven or eight during an epoch broken up by wars into three distinct phases, and this has imposed a complex pattern on the structure of the following pages.

ACKNOWLEDGMENTS

In the course of twelve years I have incurred many debts of gratitude. The sponsorship of the British Academy's Social and Economic History Committee and the financial support of the Social Science Research Council have been indispensable in sustaining the project over these years. Nor could it have been carried through without the collaboration of the Public Record Office at Chancery Lane. Past and present members of its staff have been unfailingly helpful—Mr E. K. Timings, Miss Daphne Gifford, Mrs Jane Cox, Dr Michael Jubb, Dr A. J. Hollaender and Dr Edward Higgs have combined assistance with hospitality. King's College London granted me leaves of absence and my colleagues in the Department of History have borne my absence with fortitude. Numerous archives, libraries and institutions have been of assistance—the British Library, the Cambridge University Library, the Institute of Historical Research, the London Library, the London University Library, the British Library of Political and Economic Science, the India Office Library, the City of London Record Office, the Gemeente Archief of Amsterdam, the Staatsarchiv of Hamburg and the Riksarkiv, Stockholm.

My debts to individuals are inadequately discharged in this way but I must record my particular thanks to Professor Donald Coleman for his unfailing patience and encouragement. Many others have provided advice and information—Professor John Bromley, Professor K. N. Chaudhuri, Dr David Clarke, Professor John Elliott, Professor F. J. Fisher,

Dr Robin Gwynn, Professor R. M. Hatton, Professor Jonathan Israel, Professor H. G. Koenigsberger, Mr Robert Latham, Professor Peter Marshall, Professor John McCusker, Mrs Mary Miller, Professor Walter Minchinton, Professor Jacob Price, Professor K. Swart and Professor S.-E. Åström.

The publication of this book has been assisted by a grant from the Twenty-Seven Foundation and a grant from the late Miss Isobel Thornley's Bequest to the University of London.

King's College, London
1987

ABBREVIATIONS

[i] Throughout the footnotes and letter-headings the names of major protagonists are abbreviated thus:

JD = Jacob David
PJ = Peter Joye
JL = [Sir] John Lethieullier
CM = Charles Marescoe
LM = Leonora Marescoe

[ii] Archives and Libraries:
BL = The British Library, London
CLRO = The City of London Record Office
CUL = Cambridge University Library
GA = Gemeente Archief, Amsterdam
PRO = The Public Record Office, London
RA = Riksarkivet, Stockholm
StA = Staatsarchiv, Hamburg

[iii] Weights, measures and money:
@ = asper
c.i.f. = inclusive of customs, insurance, freight
cwt. = hundredweight (112 lb. avoirdupois)
d = penny, denier, pfennig, etc.
d.c.m. = dollar-copper-money, Sweden
d.s.m. = dollar-silver-money, Sweden
D = ducat (Spain, Italy)
f.o.b. = free-on-board, all expenses paid
f = florin, or guilder
g = groot[en] flemish
ggl = gold guilder
£.flem = pound flemish
£.stg = pound sterling
£.t = livre tournois
lb. = pound-weight, pond, pfund, livre, etc.
LD = leeuwendaalder, Lion dollar
ML = Mark Lübeck
mvs = maravedis
RD = rixdollar, rijksdaalder, reichsthaler.
R. pta = real plata
$ = dollar (or piastre) Leghorn
s = shilling, schelling, soldi, sol, etc.
slb = shippound
st = stuiver
W = écu (or crown)

[iv] Books, serial publications, etc.

BMHG   = *Bijdragen en Mededelingen van het Historisch Genootschap te Utrecht*
CJ   = *Journals of the House of Commons*
CSPD   = *Calendar of State Papers, Domestic Series*
CTB   = *Calendar of Treasury Books and Papers*
EcHR   = *The Economic History Review*
RGP   = *Rijks Geschiedkundige Publicatien*
Stiernman = A. A. von Stiernman, *Samling utaf Kongl. bref, stadgar och förordningar, etc,
             angående Sveriges rikes commerce, politie och oeconomie uti gemen* (Stockholm,
             1753)
Wittrock, I = Georg Wittrock, *Karl XI:s förmyndares finanspolitik. Gustaf Bondes finansför-
             valtning och brytningen under bremiska kriget, 1661–1667.* Skrifter utgifna af K.
             Humanistiska Vetenskaps-Samfundet i Uppsala, 15: 3 (Uppsala, 1914)
Wittrock, II = Georg Wittrock, *Karl XI:s förmyndares finanspolitik. Från blå boken till franska
             forbundet, 1668–1672.* Skrifter utgifna af K. Humanistiska Vetenskaps-
             Samfundet i Uppsala, 19:1 (Uppsala, 1917)

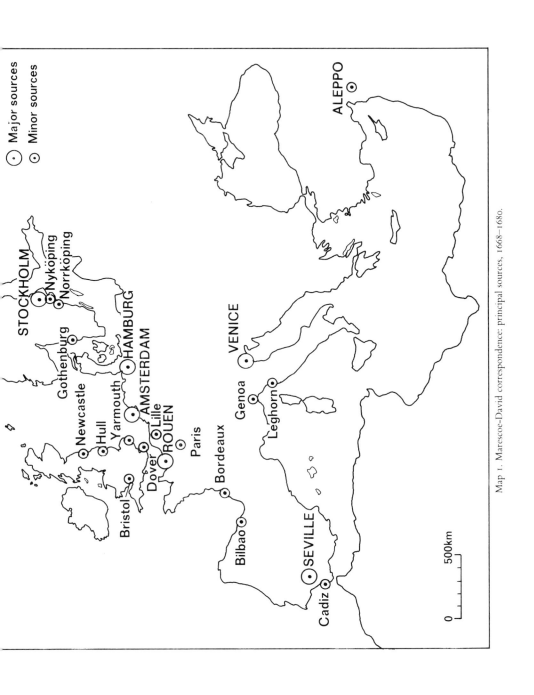

Map 1. Marescoe-David correspondence: principal sources, 1668–1680.

1. THE MARESCOES AND THE DAVIDS

Charles, 'son of James Marescoe and Jane his wife' was born in Lille.[1] One can write with less certainty about the date of his birth, but it was probably some time during 1633,[2] and as early as 1649 it is evident that he was living in London, employed by a Dutch merchant called Jacques Boeve (anglicized as James Bovey).[3] In 1653 Marescoe described his duties: he had custody of Bovey's books and papers, he wrote up his accounts and he answered his correspondence—in other words, he discharged all the normal responsibilities of any young merchant's apprentice.[4] Bovey's identity and interests remain both intriguing and elusive[5] but he was evidently trading to Sweden, as well as between England and the Netherlands, and many years later was to be remembered respectfully by Willem Momma as his earliest English correspondent.[6] Associated with him in this trade was a John Buck, whose origins probably lay in Hamburg,[7] and by 1654, at the age of 22, Charles Marescoe had graduated to a partnership with Buck which was to last until the latter's death in 1661. Their business combined the Swedish trade they inherited from Bovey with an interest in Spain, Portugal and the Mediterranean, and this connection with southern waters can only have been reinforced by Marescoe's marriage in July 1658 to Leonora, daughter of John Lethieullier.[8]

The Lethieulliers, like Marescoe, originated in the Spanish Netherlands.[9] Like him, they were members of the French Protestant church in London, but they could claim a more impressive lineage and a more eminent position in the merchant community. Descended

---

[1] *Letters of Denization and Acts of Naturalization for Aliens in England and Ireland, 1603–1700*, ed. W. A. Shaw (Lymington, 1911) pp. 71, 78.

[2] Marescoe stated his age on nine occasions between 1653 and 1666, appearing as a witness before the Courts of Admiralty and Chancery. Several of these statements are incompatible and could indicate birth at any time between 1630 and 1634, but four are consistent with some date in the course of 1633. PRO, HCA. 13/68; 13/69; 13/70; 13/71; C. 24/765; 24/895; 24/897 (i); 24/911.

[3] 'James Boeve' and Susannah his wife unsuccessfully sought an Act of Naturalization in 1641. (*Letters of Denization and Acts of Naturalization*, ed. Shaw, p. 61.) When administration of his wife's London property was granted to him in 1650 Boeve was described as a citizen of Middelburg. PRO, PROB. 6/25 f. 12; cf. PROB. 6/27 f. 87.

[4] PRO, C. 24/765; evidence on behalf of 'James Bovey', defendant against Lewellin and others, 5 August 1653.

[5] As 'Boeve' and 'Bovey' he figures frequently in the correspondence of Edward Hyde, earl of Clarendon, between 1658 and 1660, acting as a royalist intermediary and informant. As a merchant he suffered some substantial loss for which Clarendon, through Sir George Downing, later sought recompense from the States General between 1661 and 1664. *Calendar of the Clarendon State Papers*, ed. F. J. Routledge (Oxford, 1932, 1970) IV, pp. 64, 112, 132, 160, 163, 172, 180, 226, 257, 277, 283, 334, 346, 379, 395, 397, 415, 420, 423, 471, 599, 607, 663; V, pp. 101, 200, 202, 227, 398. References to Boeve's trading activities figure in *CSPD, 1650*, pp. 37, 445, 524; *CSPD, 1651*, p. 467; *CSPD, 1651–2*, pp. 459, 524, 557. See also *The Diary of Samuel Pepys*, eds. R. Latham & W. Matthews (London, 1971, 1983) IX, p. 206, X, p. 34, where Boeve/Bovey appears in his second career, as a lawyer. As such he occasionally acted as an arbitrator for Marescoe in minor mercantile disputes of the 1660s. See, e.g. PRO, C. 6/185/75, *Marescoe v. Wythers*, 1669).

[6] W. Momma to JD, 30 March 1677.

[7] John Buck, born *c.* 1620, had been an associate of James Bovey for four years by 1653 (PRO, C. 24/765). His will, of 16 April 1661, made bequests to two sisters resident in Hamburg, where the Buck family figures in the seventeenth-century merchant community. PRO, PROB. 11/304 f. 66; M. Reissmann, *Die hamburgische Kaufmannschaft des 17. Jahrhunderts in sozialgeschichtlicher Sicht*, (Hamburg, 1975) pp. 175, 192, 203.

[8] *Registers of the French Church, Threadneedle Street, London*, Publications of the The Huguenot Society, XII ed. W. J. C. Moens (Lymington, 1899) II, p. 40. The marriage was on 7 July 1658.

[9] L. B. Ellis, 'The Lethieullier Family' *The Huguenot Society's Proceedings*, XIX No. 2 (1954) pp. 60–3.

I

from the Huguenot martyr, Jan Le Thieullier, executed at Valenciennes in 1567 or 1568, they had been established in England since 1605 and by 1658 Leonora's father was a prominent London merchant with several thriving sons.[10] The eldest, also named John, was to become a sheriff of London and to be knighted in 1674. In 1658 he was already sufficiently eligible to contract a marriage with the rich and attractive daughter of William Hooker, a future Lord Mayor.[11] In marrying into the Lethieulliers Marescoe was thus allying himself to a close-knit community of prosperous merchants—among them the Houblons, the DuQuesnes and the Burkins—who were to provide London with several civic leaders and great trading companies with many of their directors.[12] For Marescoe it yielded an immediate dividend in the younger John Lethieullier's familiarity with south European markets, and for the rest of his business career he was to enjoy a profitable, if informal, partnership with this extremely capable brother-in-law.

It is less clear that the partnership with Buck prospered. Described as 'factors to the Duke of Courland' the firm of Buck & Marescoe was embroiled in a lengthy dispute with its principal,[13] and its trade to the Baltic can only have suffered from the northern wars of 1658 to 1660. When Buck died in 1661 his will disposed of a comparatively modest estate.[14] Marescoe, on the other hand, was worth over £13,000 by the middle of 1664 and was on the point of realizing even greater wealth from the onset of the second Anglo–Dutch war. By the end of 1667 he was in a position to divide his capital, now grown to nearly £40,000, between two concurrent operations—one conducted solely on his own account, the other in partnership with his new brother-in-law, Peter Joye.

Joye, unlike Marescoe, has already made his mark in the literature of Restoration trade.[15] Born in 1636, he was to long outlive his kinsman and to establish an impressive position as a leading Admiralty contractor, Eastland merchant and director of the Royal African Company.[16] In 1668, however, he was merely Marescoe's junior partner, drawing a 25-percent share from the commissions earned by the firm, and of the partnership's operating capital of £27,000 only £7,000 was his. Indeed, by the time Peter Joye married Marescoe's sister Elizabeth it is evident that the whole Marescoe family was prosperously established in London. Charles had secured his naturalization in 1657 and, more securely, in 1660.[17] His

[10] For JL's City career see J. R. Woodhead, *The Rulers of London, 1660–1689*, London & Middlesex Archaeological Society (London, 1965) p. 107.

[11] For Sir William Hooker, see Woodhead, *Rulers of London*, p. 92; for his daughter, so much admired by Pepys, see *The Diary*, 3, 13 and 25 December 1665, 4 and 13 February 1666.

[12] Woodhead, *Rulers of London*, pp. 41, 62, 93–4. Alderman James Burkin, Master of the Clothworkers Company and an elder of the Dutch Church, Austin Friars, was Marescoe's brother-in-law through his marriage to Leonora Lethieullier's sister. Marescoe was godfather to Burkin's son Charles. Alderman Peter DuCane (Du Quesne) was father-in-law to Christopher Lethieullier (Leonora's brother) and uncle of Aldermen James, John and Peter Houblon.

[13] *CSPD 1656–57*, pp. 300–1; Privy Council Register, 1661, PRO, PC. 2/55, p. 400.

[14] After bequests totalling £170 to his sisters and the poor of his parish and of the French and Dutch Churches in London, he left £2,300 in trust for his daughter Elizabeth, payable on marriage or at twenty-one. The remainder of his goods—no other money or real property is referred to—was left to his widow, Mary Florentia. CM, Nicholas Corsellis and William Boeve (James's brother) were appointed overseers of the will. For Marescoe's custody of the widow Buck's investments see p. 17.

[15] K. G. Davies, *The Royal African Company* (London, 1957) pp. 67, 171–2; S-.E. Åström, *From Cloth to Iron: The Anglo-Baltic Trade in the late Seventeenth Century*, Part I (Helsingfors, 1963) pp. 123, 160 n. 15, 164, 165, 236.

[16] Woodhead, *Rulers of London*, p. 100. PJ and Elizabeth Marescoe (born c. 1640) were married at Low Leyton in 1668. A son, Charles, was baptized in March 1670. Elizabeth died 14 April 1680; Peter died 11 January 1721. A. G. B. West, *The Church and Parish of St Dunstan in the East* (London, 1935) p. 92.

[17] *Letters of Denization*, ed. Shaw, pp. 71, 78. Marescoe's petty-cash book records further expenses concerning his naturalization as late as 1664 and 1665, when he paid £27 5s to the Lord Chancellor and his officials.

parents, James and Jane, are described as residents of Stepney in 1668.[18] His elder brother, Peter, also naturalized in 1658,[19] was a Spitalfields weaver and of his three sisters, Anthoinette was already married to David le Griel and Marie to David Cocqueau, naturalized immigrants from Dieppe.[20] All were members of the French Church in Threadneedle Street where most of their numerous progeny were baptized. Any links they may have retained with Lille must have been weakened by the death, early in 1670, of James Marescoe and the subsequent division of their small property in the Netherlands.[21]

Charles Marescoe's roots were now being developed in London.[22] Until the Great Fire of 1666 he was content to rent a house in Fenchurch Street but with its destruction he was obliged to divide his household, sending wife and children to a country residence he rented at Low Leyton in Essex. This was already sheltering members of the Lethieullier family and in what was probably a reciprocal arrangement Marescoe himself carried on business from a Lethieullier house in London.[23] In 1669, however, he embarked on a series of purchases which for £2,210 placed him in possession of a sizeable building-plot bordered by Thames Street, Tower Street and Bosse Alley—an area close to the Custom House quay and much favoured by well-to-do merchants. Here he started building not one house but several—four of which he quickly leased. At the centre of this construction was a large mansion, designed to house Marescoe and his family.[24]

By 1670 this family had produced seven children. A daughter, Leonora, had been born in 1659 and she was followed by Jane in 1661, Elizabeth in 1663, Mary in 1665 and Anne in 1666. A son, Charles, appeared in April 1668 but was dead in little over a year.[25] A second son, James, was born early in 1670 and it was to this child that Marescoe bequeathed his real estate when, on 5 September 1670, he made his will.[26] The illness which prompted this precaution was brief: on 9 September Charles Marescoe was dead.

With John Lethieullier and Peter Joye among his executors there was little risk of Marescoe's trading estate being seriously impaired by his death, but the possibility of its being enlarged depended largely on the initiative of his widow. Leonora's character is crucial to much that follows and it is difficult to see this spirited young woman as a passive participant in the decision to continue trading. The partnership with Peter Joye was extended and the informal collaboration with her brother was maintained. It was not her fault that profitable Swedish commissions were lost, or that the third Anglo–Dutch war brought smaller rewards

---

    18 Woodhead, *Rulers of London*, p. 100.

    19 *Letters of Denization*, ed. Shaw, p. 71; cf. the erroneous information in D. C. A. Agnew, *Protestant exiles from France in the reign of Louis XIV*, (1886) I, pp. 39, 272.

    20 *Registers of the French Church, Threadneedle Street*, pp. 41a, 155q; *Letters of Denization*, ed. Shaw, p. 78.

    21 Marescoe's Journal records the receipt of £26 16s 2d on 22 July 1670 as a one-fifth share of James Marescoe's estate. A further £8 was recorded on 13 December 1672 for lands sold in Flanders.

    22 Upon the nomination of the new Lord Mayor, Sir John Robinson, Marescoe became a freeman of the City of London by redemption in November 1662, and in 1668 he became a liveryman of his Company, the Clothworkers. CLRO, Repertory 69, f. 14b; Marescoe's Journal, 3 March 1668.

    23 Marescoe leased his house from Sir Abraham Cullen in 1663, for £30 p.a., but the owner was Margaret Towerson who secured surrender of the lease and damages in lieu of rebuilding in June 1668 — *The Fire Court*, ed. P. E. Jones (London, 1970) II, pp. 209 , 210. The house at Low Leyton was rented from William Bowyer, and in June 1668 Marescoe received £100 from JL for one year's expenses of his family. Marescoe in turn paid John £125 for rent, housekeeping and warehousing for himself and servants in 1668.

    24 The original ground-plans of what may have been the mansion, and adjoining houses, survive among Marescoe's papers. When occupied, in 1672, the mansion paid Hearth Tax on 23 hearths.

    25 *The Registers of St Dunstan in the East, London, 1653–1691* ed. R. H. D'Elboux, Harleian Society LXXXIV–V (London, 1954–5) pp. 8, 10, for the baptisms of Leonora II and Jane. Other dates are deduced from ages stated in correspondence or the Chancery suit, see note 45.

    26 PRO, PROB. 11/333 No. 114.

than the second. Leonora Marescoe continued to serve, as best she could, the same extensive clientele as her late husband.

However, there was now a new participant in these arrangements—Jacob David. David, born *c.* 1640, came from Darnetal, near Rouen.[27] Son of a small clothier, he had no ties of kinship with either the Marescoes or the Lethieulliers, but in 1668 his services had been warmly recommended to Charles Marescoe by one of his most reliable Rouen correspondents, Robert Oursel. As his former employer, Oursel could vouch for David's character and abilities as a competent book-keeper, experienced in commerce and quite free of the normal aberrations of youth. Upon Oursel's testimonial, Jacob David was taken into Marescoe's service, joining another young clerk called Moses Coulon, with a salary of £40 p.a. While Coulon—whose handwriting was always execrable—looked after the petty cash and the humbler routines of the counting house, Jacob David brought a new degree of order and elegance to the firm's book-keeping and correspondence. By 1670 he was evidently well-established in the Marescoe household and Charles bequeathed him £25.

Leonora was more generous. In setting up her new partnership with Peter Joye on 10 October 1670 each of them put up £4,000, but to this was joined £1,000 found by Moses Coulon and £1,000 put up by Leonora in Jacob David's name. It is the first indication that he may have been held in the young widow's special esteem. However, there was no formal change in their relationship for some years, although early in 1673 Leonora wound up the partnership with Peter Joye and embarked on a new one with David. As a purely business partnership it was rather one-sided. Notwithstanding the modest dividends he had enjoyed over the last few years Jacob David was still unable to put up his nominal one-quarter share in the Company's capital, and the requisite £1,000 was evidently advanced by Mrs Marescoe.

At this point, any plans which Jacob and Leonora may have had for their own future were put in abeyance by more profitable plans for the eldest of Marescoe's daughters, Leonora II. In February 1675, at 16 years of age, she was married to Thomas Frederick, the 24-year-old son of Alderman Sir John Frederick, a former sheriff of London and Member of Parliament for the City.[28] It was a rich match. Her portion was reckoned at £11,000 and the Fredericks endowed her with £6,500 in cash plus rentals valued at £308 p.a. The wedding banquet at Drapers Hall was a lavish affair, costing the delighted Mrs Marescoe some £500.[29] Nor did her generosity stop there. Having met all the expenses of the wedding and given handsome presents to bride and bridegroom she insisted on the young couple taking up residence in the new Marescoe mansion, with free bed and board and stabling.[30] This cosy honeymoon lasted nine months, the time it took for Jacob David and the widow to decide on their own marriage in October 1675.

To explain the violent quarrel which now erupted between mother and daughter one can only guess at the nature of deep-seated resentments. It is conceivable that young Mrs Frederick, proud of her match to the eminent Alderman's son, should feel herself diminished by her mother's alliance with a man she regarded as a domestic servant. Perhaps she detested David; perhaps she had long hated her mother? Whatever the case, her indignant

[27] JD's background and character were reported on by Robert Oursel in a letter of 11 July 1668. His father, David David, is described there as 'drapier drapant', a status which is scrupulously defined by Jaques Savary des Bruslons, *Dictionnaire Universel de Commerce* (Amsterdam, 1726) I, p. 1733.

[28] *Allegations for Marriage Licences issued by the Dean and Chapter of Westminster, 1558 to 1679*, Harleian Society XXIII, (London, 1886), p. 237. For Sir John Frederick, see Woodhead, *Rulers of London*, p. 73, and *The History of Parliament: The Commons, 1660–1690*, ed. B. D. Henning (London, 1983) II, pp. 363–5.

[29] Evidence given in *Frederick v. David*, PRO, C. 10/137/38; Answer of Thomas Frederick and Leonora, his wife, 17 November 1679. The wedding feast was held on 23 and 24 February and the original bills survive.

[30] PRO, C. 10/137/38.

remonstration against the marriage was met with a furious and vindictive response. Amid the mother's accusations of rank ingratitude, the Fredericks were bundled out of the house and pursued with large bills—£200 for their wedding feast, £300 for their board and £575 9s for the bride's trousseau![31]

It took some time for Thomas Frederick to mount a counter-attack. He had received little over £8,000 of the £11,000 expected as his wife's portion, and when he visited Jacob David for an elucidation of the estate in February 1676 he received a dusty answer.[32] It was not until 1678 that he could press more serious inquiries and even then it was only as a result of a hint dropped by the deposed Peter Joye.[33] His advice was that Frederick should find out what happened to some East India Company shares which had formed part of Charles Marescoe's estate. This seemingly innocent suggestion was to have explosive consequences.

To understand what follows one must return to the history of Charles Marescoe's fortune and its subsequent disposition. As a freeman of the City of London Marescoe and his estate were subject to the 'custom of London' which provided that, where under-age children were involved, the protective jurisdiction of the Aldermen and the Court of Orphans should superintend their customary inheritance of one-third of the estate.[34] This was usually placed on deposit in the City's treasury, the Chamber of the City of London, until the children came of age or, in the case of daughters, married with the Court's approval. Until that time their legacies remained under the City's jurisdiction and they could receive nothing but an appropriate allowance drawn from the accumulating interest. Custom also granted the widow one-third, and this would be wholly at her disposal, but if the final one-third, known as the Testator's third, was also willed to the children that too was placed in the Chamber under control of the Court.

Such was the case with Marescoe's estate. Granting his widow one-third, he left the remainder of his personal estate to his children, reserving the real property for his young son James, if he should live to maturity. When a preliminary inventory of the fortune was registered before the City's Common Serjeant on 22 March 1671 it revealed only £20,005 7s 5d net, and from the testator's third would have to be deducted a further £2,696 0s 10d for bequests, funeral charges and future building costs on the mansion house.[35] But among his assets there were also some 'doubtful' and 'desperate' debts totalling £19,549 17s 1d from which something more might yet be salvaged, and when a final account was presented on 3 October 1672 it revealed that a further £15,179 11s 10d net had actually been realized and that another £6,311 10s 2d had been identified as doubtful or desperate debts.[36] After various deductions, also borne by the testator's third, the children's total share came to £20,039 16s 11½d, and as the executors had already deposited £21,300 in the Chamber of the City on their behalf there seemed to be no imaginable grounds for complaint.

However, the widow had done rather too well out of the settlement. An early over-estimate of her husband's estate had resulted in her receiving £18,850 as her one-third by March 1671. £13,000 of this she quickly reinvested in short-term loans, mostly at 6 per cent, and although she was obliged to disgorge £5,800 as over-payment she had profited well

[31] Ibid. See also PRO, C. 10/138/99, joint answer of JD and Leonora, 12 May 1680.

[32] PRO, C. 24/1060 Part 2, f. 5. 'Town Depositions'; evidence of John Whitehead, Royal Exchange factor, 3 January 1682.

[33] PRO. C. 10/137/38; C. 24/1060 Part 2, ff. 27–31, evidence of PJ, 13 January 1682.

[34] Despite its inaccurate account of the Marescoe-David case, the best introduction to this subject is Charles Carlton's *The Court of Orphans* (Leicester, 1974).

[35] CLRO, Common Serjeant's Book II, f. 240.

[36] Ibid. f. 293b.

when her final share was settled at £13,001 0s 11d. Included in this allocation were £2,250 in East India Company stock, valued at par.

The existence of this asset was not clearly revealed in the inventory. Deceptively, it was presented among 'good debts' as a liability owing by the East India Company, rather than as an asset or investment, currently yielding handsome dividends. This curious oversight, whether deliberate or not, was to be the crux of the ensuing dispute. The widow admitted later that it was 'a great mistake and error of him or them that writt and made up the said inventory' but being a woman and ignorant of financial matters she claimed to be innocent of any deliberate deception.[37] She had always intended to credit the estate with the market value of the shares, currently standing at 170.

Yet in fact she retained the shares until 1672 when, presumably in an attempt to mask their origin and validate her ownership, she 'sold' them to her brother John who immediately 'sold' them back to her, without registering the transfer in the East India Company's records. In October 1675, upon her marriage to Jacob David, she again transferred them to the trusteeship of her Lethieullier brothers, Sir John and Samuel.[38] By October 1677 the stock stood at 245 and had yielded £2,925 in dividends since 1670.

It was Frederick's discovery of these transactions which opened up one line of attack. But there were others. The widow's extravagance since 1670 had been flagrant and had raised serious doubts about the justness of some of the other charges which had been debited against the children's inheritance. For a start, Charles Marescoe's funeral had been extraordinarily expensive, costing over £630 of which all but £100 had been charged to the children's account. Then there had been the costs of the Marescoe household's removal to London from Low Leyton shortly before Christmas 1670—put at another £500. The mansion house and other buildings, on which £3,345 1s 11d had already been spent, were not yet ready and £1,700 had been allocated to the completion, but the widow—after numerous alterations and luxurious additions—had raised this to a total of £3,095 19s 11d, of which £2,320 15s was borne by the children's share.[39] In return, she had procured from the executors a lease of the mansion for a mere £100 p.a.[40] All this, and more, provided Frederick with a *prima facie* case for rousing the Orphans Court to an inquiry, and since his father was a member this was not difficult to arrange. In the course of 1678 Jacob David found himself called upon to render an account of his wife's stewardship and after much prevarication an account was presented to the Court of Aldermen on 14 February 1679. It was found unsatisfactory, as was a second account, and Thomas Frederick was duly given leave to sue the Davids upon the recognizances of £10,000 and £30,000 into which Leonora had entered for the honest discharge of her responsibilities.[41] The Chamberlain of the City, Sir Thomas Player, was joined to the suit as a fellow-plaintiff on behalf of the other children who, like Leonora II, were still minors.[42]

Faced with these heavy odds, the Davids responded with a combination of defiance and

---

[37] PRO, C. 10/137/38, Jacob and Leonora David's bill of complaint, 29 July 1679; C. 10/330/38, Answer of Jacob and Leonora David, 18 March 1682.

[38] The alleged transfer of 1672 does not figure in *A Calendar of the Court Minutes of the East India Company*, ed. E. B. Sainsbury, for that year, but the transfer of £4,500 in November 1675 is noted in the volume for 1674–1676 (Oxford, 1935), p. 401.

[39] PRO, C. 10/330/38: 'a greate parte of itt was in Curiosities & fancies of the Widdow and her now husband'.

[40] PRO, C. 24/1059 Part 1, ff. 1–4, evidence of JL, 5 July 1681.

[41] PRO, C. 24/1059 Part 1, f. 20; C. 24/1060 Part 2, ff. 8–9, evidence of Henry Crispe, Common Serjeant, 13 January 1682.

[42] CLRO, Small suits, Box 1, No. 43, *Frederick v. David*; Large suits, Box 12, No. 17, *Lord Mayor, etc. v. Gansel*. See also PRO, C. 10/330/38, *Lord Mayor, etc. v. Jacob David*, 1681.

cunning which was to characterize the whole of their rearguard action. On the one hand they turned to the Court of Chancery, pleading for an equitable intervention against Frederick's suit. In their petition, dated 29 July 1679, they admitted that 'your Orators, (not haveing strictly observed some small circumstances specified in the condiĉons of the said Recognizances) cannot defend themselves att Law against the penalties thereof', but offered a reasonable settlement if the Fredericks could be brought to discuss terms.[43]

Meanwhile, they sought to shorten the odds against them by dealing with the remaining children. James had died long since in 1671; Elizabeth and Mary in 1673. In 1679 the only unmarried daughters to survive were Jane, now 18, and Anne, aged 13. Consequently it was Jane who was now offered in matrimony with her portion of £7,100. Through intermediaries a bridegroom was found in John Lewknor, son of a leading Sussex family and, at 20, an under-age Member of Parliament for his county. Surviving correspondence shows him to have been an amiably deferential son-in-law and the Davids had no difficulty in getting him to sign a general release, discharging them of any further liability for their daughter's estate after payment of the £7,100 portion.[44]

With their liabilities now diminished by one-third they could now concentrate on their Chancery suit against Frederick. It was heard in November 1679, but failed, and it was superseded by the far more promising suit of 'Frederick *versus* David'.

This suit, to which we owe the survival of the Marescoe-David papers, contributes very little to our appreciation of their significance. It was also a remarkably long case, lasting eleven years and involving no less than 105 hearings before the Court.[45] A detailed account of it would be inappropriate, though intriguing, marked as it was by masterly tactics of prevarication handled by some of the leading lawyers of the day. It took a whole year before Jacob David could be made to surrender the books and papers of Marescoe's partnerships, and another year was dissipated in the assembling of witnesses. Judgment on the side issue of the East India Company shares was not given until 25 October 1682. It found 'that there had been a secret contrivance which is a badge of fraud in the defendants, to deprive the testator's estate of the said stock', and the Davids were ordered to make good the plaintiffs' share in the stock and its dividends.[46]

By this time, however, the situation had become even more complicated by the Davids' attempt to repeat in 1681 the stratagem which had worked so well in 1679. It was now Anne's turn to be disposed of in marriage, and to find a suitably compliant husband Jacob David turned to an old business friend from Rouen, called David Gansel. His correspondence with David reveals that, in addition to being fat and forty, he was also something of a fool, pathetically incapable of making a sensible business decision. It was precisely for this incapacity that David must have selected him. Appealing to Gansel to help safeguard Anne from imaginary kidnappers, he proffered the bait of her £7,100 portion, together with £1,000 from his own pocket, as an inducement to immediate marriage. The only condition was signature of a post-dated document releasing the Davids from any further liability for Anne's estate, and with this requirement Gansel trustingly complied—for he could read no

[43] PRO, C. 10/137/38, Jacob and Leonora David's bill of complaint.
[44] PRO, C. 10/330/38, bill of complaint of Lord Mayor, etc, and Anne Gansel, 4 February 1682; for Lewknor see *The Commons, 1660–1690*, ed. Henning II, p. 743.
[45] In addition to the Chancery Bills and Answers (PRO, C. 10), the case has to be pursued through Chancery Affidavits (C. 31/49), Register of Affidavits (C. 41/22, 23, 24, 25, 26, 27 and 28), Town Depositions (C. 1059 and 1060), Reports and Certificates (C. 38/206, 208, 212, 214, 218, 220, 224, 227, and 231) and Decrees and Orders (C. 33/247, 251, 253, 255, 257, 259, 261, 263, 265, 267, 269, 271 and 273).
[46] PRO, C. 33/259 f. 53.

English.[47] The clandestine marriage—without the permission of the Court of Orphans—was in early July 1681, but its existence was soon known and by the 28th of that month Jacob David was in Newgate, sentenced to a £2,000 fine and subjected to all the obloquy of a francophobe public.[48] Gansel, helpless and friendless in the hands of an incomprehensible legal system, suffered a similar fate.

Yet, released after only two months and the payment of a small fraction of his fine, Jacob David found his position still far from hopeless. Thanks to the ingenuity of his lawyers, he managed to spin out the proceedings for several more years. The Fredericks had still seen nothing of their money in February 1684 when a detailed analysis of the estate's concealed profits put them at £11,187 4s 1d.[49] The Frederick's share, £2,486 0s 10d (i.e. one-third of the children's two-thirds) was still being defiantly withheld eighteen months later.[50] But, after six years of evasion, time was finally running out for Jacob and Leonora David. A writ of execution was served on them on 4 August 1685 and, after another brief interlude under arrest, they fled the country on 9 October.[51]

From their refuge in Amsterdam they fought out the remaining stages of the battle, helped by their loyal book-keeper, Thomas Vieroot, who held on to what remained of their property. The final reckoning was deferred until 1687. On 22 April, the Lord Chancellor gave final judgment in favour of the plaintiffs and awarded them costs. The detailed bill was ready in November. At best, it was found that the Davids still owed the Fredericks £4,257 5s 3d which they were now ordered to pay. At worst, the Court's analysis established that they owed the children, for concealed assets, accumulated profits and arrears of interest, sums totalling nearly £20,000. In due course, £5,675 13s 1d of this was awarded to the Gansels.[52]

Pursued in vain by 'writs of rebellion' the Davids were now irretrievably committed to exile. The children of their marriage, a daughter Isabella, born in November 1676, and a son born in June 1678, were brought to them in May 1686 and within months were happily speaking Dutch and learning to skate.[53] A letter from Jacob David speaks cheerfully of relatives and good friends, new and old, gathered about them in Amsterdam. But his wife, ever stubborn and passionate, was still consumed with resentments. 'Pierced to the very heart' by the ingratitude of her daughters, bitterly reflecting 'on the injustice they have done her in her Estate and reputation, against natural affection and justice, having never wronged them of a peny' she paced the house day after day, eating little, 'nothing but skin and bon'.[54] By 1689 she had more substantial griefs. The children died of smallpox within months of each and other and in May 1689, after a violent illness, her broken-hearted husband followed them.[55]

The remaining years of Leonora David are illuminated by only a handful of letters written by her to the antiquarian John Strype, the resident minister of Low Leyton. The friendship of

---

[47] PRO, C. 10/225/54, 'The further answer of David Gansel', 9 December 1686.

[48] PRO, C. 33/255 f. 739, 20 October 1681; also PRO, ADM./77/1, No. 114, f. 194, (Newsletters to Sir Francis Radclyffe, 28 July 1681). I am indebted to Dr Robin Gwynn for the latter reference.

[49] PRO, C. 33/261 ff. 268, 621; C. 38/214.

[50] PRO, C. 33/261, f. 649.

[51] PRO, C. 33/265 f. 583; C. 38/227.

[52] PRO, C. 33/267 ff. 642–4; C. 38/227, 21 November 1687. The plaintiffs' costs were claimed at £1,885 8s 5d, but were taxed at £1,285 6s 8d.

[53] Cambridge University Library, Strype MSS, Vol. I (Part 1) Add 1, No. 102, JD to John Strype, 28 January 1687. I am indebted to the late Professor James Cargill-Thompson for suggesting this source.

[54] Ibid.

[55] CUL, Strype MSS, Vol. I (Part 1) Add 1, Nos. 103, 104; Leonora David to John Strype, 16 March and 31 May 1689.

this distinguished and amiable man does something to redeem the Davids' reputation, and the letters Leonora wrote to him are charged with a very plausible spirit of Christian charity towards her persecuting sons-in-law. The news that Frederick had fallen heavily from his horse moved her to pious hopes for his penitence and change of heart.[56] Reports of David Gansel's ruinous expenditure on building and litigation elicited only tender solicitude for her daughters Anne and Jane.[57] Thanking God that 'I have enough and to spare, but not to spend prodigally' she busied herself with plans for a more fitting church monument to 'dear Mr Marescoe' and the long-dead children of that earlier marriage.[58] But by February 1703, arthritic or gouty, she was unable to leave her rooms and found it difficult to write. The letters cease, and by 1715 it is clear that she was dead.[59]

Charles Marescoe's line now lay with the Fredericks, the Lewknors and the Gansels. But Jane Lewknor disgraced herself by a very public adultery and, after eloping with her lover in 1685, was duly divorced.[60] Anne Gansel's marriage may have been a little happier. Her husband, after tormented years in the clutches of Chancery, seems to have retained a fortune sufficient for them to live in some grandeur at Low Leyton, where he built a fine house.[61] As for Leonora Frederick, her destiny remained prosperous, if not entirely happy. Her husband, immersed in the affairs of the East India Company, of which he became Deputy Governor (1698–1700), seems to have harboured little warmth for his children and in his will was to divert £9,000 to London hospitals on the grounds of their disaffection.[62] But if the quarrel with his mother-in-law still rankled, Leonora II's own pride in her family was undiminished and, as a widow after 1721, she commissioned a 'famille verte' porcelain service with the armorial bearings of Frederick impaling Marescoe, with Marescoe arms repeated twice.[63] It was a fitting gesture. The Marescoe blood now ran in distinguished veins. Her eldest son secured the baronetcy of his house and her daughter Jane, in a crowning triumph, became Duchess of Atholl.[64]

[56] CUL, Strype MSS, Vol. III (Part 1) Add 4, No. 69; Leonora David to John Strype, 15 February 1704.

[57] CUL, Strype MSS, Vol. I (Part 2) Add 2, No. 236, Leonora David to John Strype, 7 August 1699.

[58] Ibid. The monument, described by John Strype in his edition of John Stow's *Survey of London* (1720), did not survive to this century. See A. Hills, 'The Marescoe slab in Leyton Church', *Essex Review*, LI (1942), p. 221; references also in *Essex Review*, XLI (1932), p. 194. The information in the note, 'The Marescoe Mansion', *Essex Review*, LIII (1944), p. 69, is largely erroneous.

[59] CUL, Strype MSS, Vol. IV (Part 2) Add 8, No. 158; Gottfried Bohlen and John Scheers [Leonora's executors] to John Strype, 10 December 1715.

[60] See *The Commons, 1660–1690*, ed. Henning, II. p. 743; III, p. 90 for 'Lewknor, John II (1658–1707)' and 'Montagu, William (1652–91)' with whom Jane eloped in December 1685.

[61] See Thomas Wright, *The History and Topography of the County of Essex* (London, 1831) II, p. 497; *The Victoria County History: Essex* (London, 1973) VI, p. 179; G. O. Rickword, 'The Story of a Short-Lived County Family: Gansel of Leyton Grange and East Donyland Hall, Essex', *Essex Review*, LIII (1944), pp. 81–5. David Gansel I (d. 1714) built Leyton House, *c.* 1706; his son, David Gansel II (d. 1753) built Leyton Grange, *c.* 1720. Anne Gansel (née Marescoe) died in November 1718.

[62] Woodhead, *Rulers of London*, p. 73.

[63] A. Hills, 'Lethieullier Family China', *Essex Review*, L (1941), pp. 204–8. Marescoe arms are described as 'blue and three doves close proper'. Charles Marescoe appears to have obtained licence to bear his arms in 1663—Petty-Cash Book, 27 February 1663.

[64] *The Complete Peerage . . .*, ed. G. E. C[okayne] (London, 1910) I, p. 319. Jane was the widow of James Lannoy when she married James Murray, Duke of Atholl, on 28 April 1726. She died 13 June 1748, having borne 2 sons (who died in infancy) and 2 daughters, one of whom became wife of the 3rd Duke of Atholl.

2. THE MARESCOE-DAVID PAPERS

It will be clear enough from the foregoing saga why the papers of Charles Marescoe and Jacob David came to remain in the custody of Chancery. Although judgment was given in the case, its enforcement was never properly completed and the respective claims of Frederick, Gansel, the City of London and (no doubt) of the Davids' counsel remain unsatisfied in perpepuity. There could be no undisputed owner of these documents, and after 1687 there was little chance of Jacob David claiming them. Thus they remained in limbo as 'Chancery Masters' Exhibits' until liberated for public inspection by the 1958 Public Record Office Act 6 & 7 Elizabeth II c. 51.

At the time of writing they still remain outside the normal scope of accessibility at the Public Record Office, being under arrangement and—in portions—unfit for production, but a definitive schedule of their contents and arrangement is now possible and the sounder portions will be made accessible under supervision. What follows is therefore merely a description of the main characteristics of the documents, grouped under three broad headings either as (1) books, (2) letters or (3) papers.

1. BOOKS. Under this heading I include all the bound volumes which served Marescoe and David in their business accounting. The major items are matching pairs of journals and ledgers of the kind which, in any well-conducted counting-house, formed the summit of the book-keeping system. Although the series here is not complete and is complicated by the successive partnerships and divisions of capital it provides a reasonably full picture of the firm's trading activities from 1664 to 1680.

The journal and ledger 'F', which were opened on 27 June 1664, served to record (in Dutch) all Marescoe's business until 2 April 1668, when he began to transfer selected commission accounts to a new journal and ledger 'G', devoted to his new partnership with Peter Joye. The remaining accounts, reserved for his sole account, continued for a while in 'F' but at the end of 1668 were transferred into another pair, journal and ledger 'M', of which only the journal survives. At his death in September 1670 the balances due to Marescoe from 'G' were incorporated in 'M' where they were absorbed in his total estate and gradually wound up over the years 1670 to 1677.

Meanwhile, in September and October 1670, the widow Leonora had opened two pairs of books—one pair, called 'B', devoted to her own personal estate and recorded in French; the other, called 'A', recording in Dutch her business in partnership with Peter Joye. Both pairs were penned by Jacob David, who had taken over the firm's higher book-keeping tasks since late 1668. Of Leonora's four volumes, the journal of 'A' is missing. Both pairs were wound up during 1673, preparatory to her partnership with Jacob David, and Leonora's aggregate capital was then transferred to a new series, called optimistically 'No. 1', of which the journal for 1673–7 is missing. But the ledger, covering the period to August 1679 survives and it is joined by a journal opened on 28 August 1677 and terminating on 4 August 1679. A diagram and table will help to clarify these relationships (Table 1, Figure 1).

It will be seen that all phases of the various Marescoe-David partnerships are covered, either by a journal or a ledger, from mid-1664 to mid-1679, but it is regrettable that two journals should be lacking, for while it is comparatively easy to reconstruct a missing ledger from its surviving journal the reverse process is extremely laborious and unsatisfactory.

MARESCOE-DAVID BOOK-KEEPING

(Plates reproduced by kind permission of the Public Record Office)

(a) From Ledger 'F' [Table 1, A.1(b)] f. 97—Marescoe's Profit & Loss account (in Peter Joye's hand) showing some of the firm's large profits during the Second Anglo-Dutch War.

(b) From Invoice Book [B.1] p. 3—entries by CM, PJ and Moses Coulon of sale accounts for copper, wine, brandy and timber received in 1666.

(c) From Receipt Book [E.1]—receipts for payment of freight charges signed by Swedish captains (Andries Biorsen, Elias Johansen, Jolle Tyerdts, etc) and for lighterage wages for unloading iron from some of the detained Tar Co. vessels in the autumn of 1668, with (centre right) the marks and initials of lightermen.

(d) From Invoice Book [B.1] p. 65—entries by CM and JD of sale-accounts for copper-wire from Jacob Momma and invoices of exports to Hamburg and Venice.

(e) From CM's Memorandum Book [F.1]—entries of shipping and cargo arrivals, August–October, 1669.

(f) From Cash Book [C.4]—entries by JD, counter-signed by LM, with some of her withdrawals for 'household expenses'.

Credit.

1664					£		
August	18	p⁰ Isex gecoomen mit de Mars Smaland & Gryp voor Intendt van £800 ...	91	£	22	—	—
	29	p⁰ Herman Boetteken voor Intendt van verschoote penn:	101	£	2	5	—
Sepr	1	p⁰ Laurence de Geer voor Rabatt van £400 ...	83	£	10	—	—
	2	p⁰ Laurence de Geer voor Intendt van £800 voor 1½ maenden ...	83	£	6	13	4
	3	p⁰ Cattou Taxne geaduant op de Isel partye uit de voorg aend Colctie ...	74	£	50	—	—
	27	p⁰ Thomas Rudham en Daniel Mercer voor bij twisten moet⁰ Debit⁰ 17098½	59	£	—	—	—
8ber	5	p⁰ Robert Fickx voor Intendt van £450 voor t̃ nabij dien te vall⁰ den 27 78	26	£	13	10	—
	12	p⁰ Daniel Mathew voor Intendt van verschoten penn: op Casta en ongeuijt	52	£	9	17	10
	25	p⁰ Robert Fickx voor Intendt van penn: uijt Journal	26	£	6	17	6
9ber	10	p⁰ Ant Upton en Benjamin Bathurst voor cort gewonden in 2 block: &	80	£	5	19	7
	16	p⁰ Jochim Potter en Hendrick Thuin myn R⁺ voor Intendt van £1000	16	£	15	—	—
	29	p⁰ Casa Outfanger van Edward Backwell voor Intendt van £500 ...	110	£	18	15	—
Xber	19	p⁰ Humphry Brown voor myn R⁺ op 35 sacken peeper ...	100	£	27	10	6
	20	p⁰ Cooperdrael voor myn R⁺ op die keek⁰ geadvan ± ...	118	£	156	18	—
	27	p⁰ Willem Momma voor Rabatt van £177, 6. 6 R op Latoen	119	£	3	10	—
	28	p⁰ Actie in d'oostinsche Comp⁺ voor soo veel Ick estimeert myn Intendt	12	£	450	—	—
	30	p⁰ boyagie naer Cadix onder directie van San Lethulier daerop gew⁰	42	£	52	14	1
1664/5 Jan⁰	2	p⁰ Laurence de Geer voor rabatt van penn: en Intendt	116	£	20	—	—
		p⁰ John Berry uitstaent voor £150. betij 2 p⁰ ± op den verliet. onder den stock	66	£	108	—	—
	17	p⁰ diverse als Swinock Bateman en Lipart voor £400: passen ± a 7.2. &⁰	72-114	£	288	—	—
Meert	2	p⁰ Cooperdrael voor myn R⁺ voor rabatt £313. 17 β voor ⁵⁄ₘ	67	£	3	10	—
	13	p⁰ Guillm Huwe voor kabatt van £359. 1. 4 R voor ⁵⁄ₘ a 6 p⁺	118	£	7	14	6
		p⁰ Inwaeten voor rabatt van £957. 17. 4 R voor ⁵⁄ₘ a 6 p⁺	31	£	13	16	4
1665	29	p⁰ San Lethulier geadvan ± op 34 ½ p⁰ Laeckens	88	£	32	—	—
			44	£	5	7	1
Aprill	6	p⁰ Ant Upton en Benjamin Bathurst om R⁺ te ballanceeren	80	£	52	17	8
	12	p⁰ Guill Huwe voor Intendt van penn:	31	£	11	15	—
	26	p⁰ Pieter Juncker myn Oude R⁺ d'daerop Gott Loff gewonden	15	£	85	10	—
May	6	p⁰ Jonas Franckmoet geadvan ± Godt Loff op £150: geleent op Boden	4	£	37	17	4
	9	p⁰ Eustachius Ettmult voor rabat van penn: en de drees ±	96	£	2	13	—
Juny	2	p⁰ Thomas Heger myn R⁺ geadvan ± op de Rednctie Gott Loff	68	£	5	15	7
	22	p⁰ John Hanson voor myn R⁺ voor rabat van £338. 17. 9 R	136	£	8	5	9
	24	p⁰ Fickx en Teer voor myn R⁺ voor op geadvan ± Gott Loff	140	£ 1699	12	8
Jully	25	p⁰ Fickx en Teer voor R⁺ van de Teer Comp⁺ voor rabat van	5	£	31	16	3
Sepr	20	p⁰ Actie in d'oostinsche Comp⁺ voor 25 p⁰ ± die myn Capitall	12	£	187	10	—
	21	p⁰ Inwaeten voor soo veel geadvan ± op 5 packen Linnen	88	£	20	15	—
Octobr	11	p⁰ Isex voor myn R⁺ voor soo veel daerop gewonden Godt Loff	57	£ 1047	1	10
		p⁰ Isex gecoomen gecoomen mit de Mars Smaland & Gryp Gott Loff	91	£	596	11	5
	12	p⁰ Isex gecoomen mit Hendrick Brandt voor myn R⁺ daerop ghw⁰	112	£	810	—	3
	16	p⁰ Committie Reeckeningh voor soo veel gewonden Godt Loff	124	£ 1839	9	6
	24	p⁰ Wesell R⁺ voor soo veel Godt Loff daerop gewonden	144	£	37	7	10
	18	p⁰ Indigno om soo veel daerop gewonden Godt Loff	103	£	186	2	6
	30	p⁰ Herman Wetteken voor Intendt van penn:	158	£	3	—	—
Novr	16	p⁰ Abraham Muyssart Vader en Soon myn Oud R⁺ gewonden	13	£	102	8	3
Xber	6	p⁰ d'oostinsche Comp⁺ voor Intendt van £600 voor ⁵⁄ₘ	160	£	18	—	—
	15	p⁰ Thomas Player voor Intendt om £100: 17. 4/₄ maenden ...	2	£	8	17	4
		p⁰ Latoen voor rabat van penn:	1	£	5	4	10
	16	p⁰ d'oostinsche Comp⁺ Intendt van £600: voor ⁵⁄ₘ	160	£	18	—	—
	28	p⁰ Joan Backman Leyonbergh voor Intendt van t'valle penn:	53	£	8	—	—
1665/6 Jan⁰	1	p⁰ Actie in d'oostinsche Comp⁺ voor 15 p⁰ ± gebetent van £750	12	£	112	10	—
	2	p⁰ Edward Palmer en Robert Isaack Gott Loff geadvan ±	47	£	7	—	—
	3	p⁰ Fickx en Teer voor R⁺ van de Teer Comp⁺ voor rabat van penn:	5	£	33	14	8
	24	p⁰ d'oostinsche Comp⁺ voor Intendt van £800: voor ⁵⁄ₘ	160	£	20	—	—
	25	p⁰ decora van Kuyff voor rabat van penn:	148	£	14	3	—
	29	p⁰ Peter Simons voor rabat van penn:	149	£	16	10	10
		J Chanspenter 1670	166	£ 8358	17	11

Jan 25 ob *t* getrocken . . . . £ 200 — —

feb 1 ob *t* getrocken . . . . £ 49 — —

16 ob *t* getrocken . . . . £ 51 10 —

mert 2 ob *t* Luedens getrocken *en* Ballance . . . . £ 300 10 —
                                               £ 63 3 10

Door *d* gesonden adij 22 marty *e* *d* boeck gesloeten
                                               £ 363 13 10

f transport van daer door over voor 170 eengen toepor . . . . . £ 293 10 8

Volgen d'oncosten daerop:

                                         £ 18:14:6
                                         £ —:14:2
                                         £ —:8:—
                                       £ 6:12:—
                                       £ 2:16:8
                                       £ 1:15:—
                                       £ 5:15:—
Comissie &c. &c *f* fl 1:16:8 *f* provisie 2 *fl* £ 5:12:9 *d* . . . . . . £ 7:14:—
                                         £ 44 9 4

Door *d* gesonden *en* *d* boeck gesloten adij 5 april 1667
                                         £ 249 1 4

1666 marty 1. Schip Swon Pieterson opt schip Leopart moed hebben voor vraght van mon' massus . . . . £ 986 — —
                                        £ 29 10 10
                                        £ 1015 10 10

1667 april 5 . . . .

Door *d* boeck gesloet *e* gesonden aen Philips Poel Emanuell *e* Daniel Loyanan &c
adij 5 april 1667 . . . . £ 1015 10 10

Sans *deo* in London *e* 19 April A° 1667

Reckeningh van dreg *e* coop van £ 83: d *e* *ℓ* 14 *6/10* Tonnen (of load Balckh ortt van een schip Mongaar *e* *e* schip *f* Salomon Johnson gelaed *e* tot in noerweg &c voor R *e* van Sr: Salmon potter &c Hendrick Thuele van t'achthelms . tot *d* positie van Sr peter Simons tynd gelocht aen peter Rich als volgt *e* £ 83: d *e* *ℓ* tot £ 4:15 *1/16* *fl* . . . . £ 394 5 —
14 Tonnen *e* *fo* van *d* Tonnen of lead van 50 voet tot 40 *fl* *fl* Tonne . . . . £ 33 18 — | £ 428 3 —
Betaelt voor 2 lichters *e* party *e* dalck te losen tot mondt *e* *d* *Jacop* . . . . . . £ 2 16 — | £ 9 10 —
fl *f* eert *e* 2 gemeldingen *d* Stelcolt coopen *e* *e* *d* water te gaen . . . . £ 18 — — | £ 437 13 —
Betaelt a *d* schip *e* Salamon Johnson *e* schipsvolck van syn schip
van 14 *d* *e* *f* geent *f* etc *e* quart *f* voet van *d* *Jacop* te 5/8 *fl* *e* *fl* . . . . . . £ 100 — —
voor my *f* premie van den *Jacop* a *f* *fl* . . . . £ 8 15 — | £ 116 3 8

Door *d* boeck gesloet adij 26 april 1667. *e* gesonden den 26 *dito*
                                       £ 321 9 4

Sans *deo* in London adij 19 April A° 1667

Reckeningh van den *Jacop* van S *e* 197 Tonnen Balckh ortt van £ 23: — 33: d *e* *ℓ* &c *e* 94 stucke eijck Stolpitt ortt *e* van *e* het schip *e* Guilaud Broun *e* schip *f* Claus Leewt *e* de Diken *e* *e* gelaad *e* tot in noerweg &c voor R *e* van Sr Topkin potter &c Hendrick Thuele te positie van Sr peter Simons: tynd gelocht als volgt aen John Slick 197 Tonnen Balckh *f* *e* *e* *e* 50 do *e* *ℓ* int bit cent voor *d* Tonne *e* tot *f* 21: 6 *fl* *d* Tonne van 50 voet . . . . £ 496 19 6
£ 23 — 23: deelin a £ 5: 17: 6 *fl* *f* . . . . £ 136 5 —
94 eijcke Stolpitt tot *fl* 2 *fl* stuck . . . . £ 9 8 — | £ 642 12 6

Volgen d'oncosten daerop:
Betaelt voor 2 lichters in *d* deelingh Balckh legge *e* Stolpitt te losen tot monst *fl* £ —
Eggende *f* *e* *d* *Jacop* . . . . £ 3 — —
fl eert *e* 2 gemeldingh met *d* volck *d* corpens *d* by water te gaen . . . . £ 1 4 —
Betaelt a *d* schip *e* Claus Leewt *d* uit t'heyt tot losen *f* van syn schip
van 14 *d* *e* *f* geent *f* etc *e* quart *f* van *d* *Jacop* a *f* *fl* *fl* 1 . . . . £ 4 — 6
voor my *f* premie a *fl* *fl* . . . . £ 12 17 — | £ 271 1 6

Door *d* gesonden over *d* boeck gesloet adij 19 april A° 1667.
                                       £ 371 11 —

Sans *deo* in london adij 15 *e* april 1667
Reckeningh van den party van 230 *e* *f* Balckhen van *d* kleyne Beleonen *e* *e* opt schip *f* Charliss schip *f* Claer Tynke geladen in te noerweg voor R *e* van my hey broer Thun van Prohelsten tot *d* *f* *f* van Brohuor een *f* *f* en Rente *e* *e* aen phaletze *e* Compt all volght 229 Tonnen Balckh *e* *e* voechnt *e* tot in Mon a 47 *fl* *fl* *f* tot 502: 12: 9 *fl*
230 kleyne Beleonen a *fl* *e* 1 Rijcke . Gespedower daerop . . . . £ 91 9 4 | £ 594 7 4
Betaelt om lichters voor het kleyne goet helcht daermed *d* herte dagen *f* legende *e* den *Jacop* . . . £ 3 14 —
f *f* advert gemaetragen met *d* *f* *f* *f* coolens voor het *Jacop* en t'f broeken legen . . . . . . £ 1 15 —
Betaelt aen schip *e* Claus Tyn tot *f* kesen freyght *e* syn Schip . . . . . . £ 180 — —
f voor my *f* provisie a *f* M *e* *fl* . . . . £ 15 12 — | £ 201 1 —
voor bys gereecken *e* *f* *f* *f* *f* £ *e* 265: 2 a *f* van mon *f* provisie a *fl* M *e* £ *e* *e* 17: 8 *d* . . . . . . £ 393 6 4

Door *d* *f* boeck gesloet adij 26 april 1667 *e* gesonden des selfs daechs

Ick ondergeschreven, bekenn ontfangen te hebben
ady 20? 9ber A1668. in volle satisfactie voor vraght
pilotage primgelt etc. de somma van twentich
vyft ponden dryschellingen & vier penningen
in London ady als boven   Andries Blok   £ 25 3 4

Ick ondergeschreven bekenn ontfangen te hebben
ady 20. 9ber A1668. in volle satisfactie voor vraght
primgelt pilotage etc. de somma van negentich
negen ponden negen schellingen & ses pennings
Ick segge ontfangen   Jacob Christiaensen   £ 99 19 6

Recd the 21. Novemb 1668 in part Two hundred & fifty
pounds for the use of mr Thomas Pomell. I say recd
                         Herbert Pelham   £ 250,, —

Received this 21. November 1668 in full satisfaction to this day
for Lightredge the summe of Six pound Seaventeen shillings
6d I say Recd ——   John Shrewsbury   £ 6 17 6

Received this 21. 9ber 1668 in full to this day for worke &
to this day the summe of three pound and thirteen 8d I say   £ 3 13 8
                         Joseph Garrod

Ick ondergeschreven bekenn ontfangen te
hebben ady 26. 9ber A1668. in volle satisfac
tie voor vraght etc. van 6625 vranges per de
somma van een hondert viertien ponden &
negen schellingen, ende twentich ponden des   14:"
desse date voor quitantie hebbe gegeven is   13 4 9"
Ick segge ontfangen in in volle satisfactie   £ 114 9 —

                         Elias Salzers

Ick onderges bekenne ontfangen te hebben ady
20. 9ber 1668. in volle satisfactie voor vraght
primgelt & pilotage van schip De 449 & per de
somma van sostich een ponden, vyfthien
schellingen Ick segge ontf. van H. Manfors   £ 61 15 —

                         Jürgen Bartels de Jonge

Recd ye 30 of Novemr 1668 of Mr Charles Marescoe
the Some of three hundred pounds upon acct of furrs
consigned to the sayd Mr Marescoe & James Burkin &
Jeudt Evertsen in anno 1665: Itt ys Recd on acct of
furrs then Consigned as aforesayd by Mr Abraham
Van Eyck. & Sent by sayd Mr Charles Marescoe: for
my selfe James Burkin & my selfe   Jt Evertsen   £ 300 — 1

Recevd this 30 of November 1668 of Mr Charles Braneskie
in full for Bringing of Goods out of the Hope
from aboard the ships Beave Hope & St Annd .

Theo T. Charter	fromaboard the Bear 13 thons	. . . .	£	2	17	6
Hovenburg N	fromaboard the St Annd & Bear 56 tons	. .	£	7	12	—
	fromaboard the Beare 13 tons	. . . .	£	1	12	6
Hugh HB Pasley	fromaboard the Hope 13 tons	. . . .	£	1	12	6
Hugh Pasley HB	fromaboard the Hope 19 tons	. . . .	£	2	7	6
Edward Baly	fromaboard the & Bear 2 tons Hope 3 tons	£	1	15	6
Cyriell Bale	fromaboard the Hope 12 tons	. . .	£	1	17	6
John Thomesin			£	19	15	0

167   Ick ondergeschreeven bekenn ontfangen te
hebben ady 2. ober 1668. in volle satisfactie
van vragtt org. Vienik vos ponden seventhie
schellingen vaad Ick oggy   £ 46 17 —
              Willem j: 448 K muller.

Ick ondergeschreven bekenn ontfangen te hebben ady 2 ober
1668 offc. van myn vracht de somma van een   £ 100 —
Hondert ponden ster & jk seggo . . . —
                     Jollo Fjordts

Memorandum dat Ick ondergeschreven hebben in handen
gelaten van Charles Baresoe de somma van beghties
ponden vss Dwelck Ick ordonneere aen Sr Peter Lyson over
te maecken voor rect van myn Reeders d'Heren Directeurs
van de Noorteryckse Maets Comp London dese 2. d bre
              Eliass Jehanssen

1668
8   29 ontfangen van hendrick Jans,   £ 60
    29 ontfangen van Jacob luce voor vraght van 3e thont vleys   £ 84
9be 27 voor netto provenu van 96 t 1/2 ahr groenen met Jacob geus   £ 271   1
Jan 7 voor t netto provenu vey 6621 t 1/2 ahr groenen met Elias denes   £ 1455 5
8   14 voor hautvys a 10f/c van £ 200 opt lande van schoonen   £ 20
    10 voor t netto provenu van 3036 t 1/2 groenen met obet Ericksen   £ 618   6
Marty 4 voor t netto provenu van 5597 stangen yser   £ 1491 16 3
       voor t netto provenu van 4 vaten blick groenen met hendrick Jansen   £ 16   5   8
       voor netto provenu van een vat blick lacoen groenen met hendrick
       bendir   £ 40   13
    19 my gecrediteert door w.m Shinnir door ordre van hendrick Jansen   £ 85   18
    24 voor t provenu van 2413 stangen ijle groenen met compte gulden & in gout £ 409 13
1669 26 op reke groenen a 35 f/d uts te betaling w.m & Jan giles   £ 23   14 4
                                                                                 £4376 6   9

Laus Deo in London ady 30.en April A:1669.

Reeckeninge van den swoep van 1800. Aan ... (in groote party) met schip: Enick Enicksen opt schip Coninck David geladen ... te voorcoopen door mijn hede Jacob memma, onde ...

1669 feb. 11 Aan Nathan Humphreys   £200 weeght £48:2:2 t/t tot £ 5.6 f/d 1669 in 2 maant 257 2 8
           16 Aan Edward Nourse   £200 weeght £48:1:27 t/t tot £ 5.6 f/d 1669 in 1 maart 254 11 6
           26 Aan John Slauter   £200 weeght £48:2:14 t/t tot £ 5.6 f/d 1669 in 1 maart 257 1   10
maart   10 Aan Richard Thorowgood   £ 75 weeght £18:-:21 t/t tot £ 5.8 f/d 1669 in 4 mael   98 4   3
           10 Aan Edward Nourse   £125 weeght £30:1:6 t/t tot £ 5.8 f/d 1669 in 4 mael   163 12 4
           18 Aan Richard Woodfield   £150 weeght £36:1:14 t/t tot £ 5.9 f/d 1669 in 6 mael 198 4   10
           24 Aan Charles Phelps   £140 weeght £33:3:28 t/t tot £ 5.9 f/d 1669 in 6 mael 185 3   2
1669   31 Aan Edward Nourse   £100 weeght £24:1:2 t/t tot £ 5.9 f/d 1669 in 6 mael   132 5
April   2 Aan Bower Spike   £200 weeght £48:2:2 t/t tot £ 5.6 f/d 1669 in 1 maant 258 3
            8 Aan Edward Nourse   £200 weeght £48:2:3 t/t tot £ 5.6 f/d 1669 in 1 maant 257 3   4
              Aan Richard Woodfield   £ 95 weeght £23:-:5 t/t tot £ 5.8 f/d 1669 in 2 mael   125 11 10
           22 Aan William Scott   £115 weeght £27:3:16 t/t tot £ 5.7 f/d 1669 in 2 mael 149 4   6

in alles   £1800 weeght £436:2:12 t/t ... voor   £2336 12 8

Volgen d'Oncosten daarop

Betaalt op de Costuym huys voor tol ... stads reght & paspoort £181:17:4
Lichtergelt om t'goet van boort ... te Keys te brengen, Kays ...   £ 8:17:-
Kruen goet & arbeytsloon om ... te vueren
Carregelt om things te brengen, Aab dijsleven onse carrts te Cuddy
t'af te London; ende t'goet int packings te brengen & vome   £ 4:10:-
Voor vraght betaelt aen schip Enick Enicksen, holle t gehele op
VL Rs warrant gofeet daer om volle hide mets
Nachter ende om t'goet wt wonde schade te brengen betaelt   £ 5:9:6
Packhuys huer voor 48 weeken wt 5 N st weeke   £ 12:-:-
Courtage gowers penningen & quaed goet t/t f/c   £ 19:12:-
Alzo Jck op Rs warrant int forthort boom, ende om 2 Rs van Jaerden
niet te londen, we vinuatoort Jck de navolgende partyen
... wonder mijn profentis tot dat allegoeden sullen ontfangen
zyn, wesende voor £261:17:- vwa 4 maend bogen 6 f/c ons afguds   £ 5:3:1
    ende ... £641:4:10 voor 6 maenden als boven   £ 18:13:5
Voor mijn Provisie van den zwoep a 2 f/c hoom   £ 46:14:8   297 17 -
Deere Rs welweet gofeet adys 30 April 1669 & gesonden 23 30 Ditto   £2038 15 8

Laus Deo in London 30 Aprill 1669

Factura van twen booten pottes olie geladen op hamborgh in schip &
Neptune schipper willem obf van door ordre & door Rekening & risco van ..
Cleve Rulandt & hom geen signert wegen & zeken als volght

No.   1 – 236
      2 – 206
      3 – 268
      4 – 202
PR   5 – 218
      6 – 218
      7 – 242
   1590 gallons a 236 gallons p ton is 6 tonne 174 gallons a
      ... pr tonne   £ 183 12 10
voor Extraordinary Rs uytteren ... daerin de is gesonden met dat
om het out out het Indies boten, ho wt keul daerin de is gesonden met dat £ 3 15 7
Voor mijn provisie a 2 f/c   £ ..
Deere Rs welweet gofeet & gesonden ady 30 April 1669.   £192 15 5

London 15 of May 1669
Invoyce of the cost & charges of 250 pigs of lead had Laden in the Thomas & frances Cap.t Lt. Barn...
bound for venice & consigned there to my Lt Credue van bey gingen, and consyn the one half for acct
of m.r John & Theodore p the other half for acct of me Cleve marscual
250 pigs weighing £296:3:2 .. an 13 1/2 p foddes of 19 3/4 is   190 4   8
Laid for Custom of 14 foddes Crogue or tonne £ ..: 3 f/d poctridge Rayes .. nothing
w.t Lighters £1:19: .. 53 exchrbat 7 f/2 d   £ 16 0   2
The one half there of for m.r John & Theodore   £103:6:11   206 5 10
& the other half of p the ... marscual   £103:6:11
Deere Rs welweet gofeet ady 15 may 1669   106 13 5

(d)

Ady 17. Augusty 1669. Saykt aen
John Stace 32 4/13 carsen Loda & 25.
carsy pick (tot £9 3/4 & £12 3/4 p carsy)
in de windthont schip S wedn Lit-
derdn die voor Vraykt madt tot
Boz. Caplacks IN p carst is 55 fl goirnd
van Stockh naede Plymn en hebbe
hem t' voynemen gend geordelns
in Louain by Texel ale 2 Dentz aden 26. 8br 1669

Ady 20. Augt. 1669. is Godt loft goar
Jacob Giers op de groote Christoffel
1776 . ... baet't van eeven schip ... 397:11:10
567 . quant van eeven schip 70: 4:
1502 . ordinary vendt carden 195: 4:
2066 . ordt. gmill 8 . 8 . ☐ . 311:7:10
106. bundly vandt yson . . 57:9:10
6017 . ... aende J M R woegt 1031:16:10

Ady 23. Augt 1669. is Godt loft goar
Hans michivlus, op de s. Jak Baptist
van Gott ond met 1860 . stan. yson woeg
schip 300 . gel ... doer Kinerich Elcking
doer Osdn van J P & H J.

Ady 26. Augt. 1669. is Godt loft goar
Tho Clancke op de Vrindschap van Stockh
met 27 4/13 carsy Loda ond 15 carsen
Pick, wort gevenn 't wordy wedn loodige —

Ady 31. Augt. 1669. is Godt loft goar
Cars meltu op de ... van
Stockh met 3013 . ... ond o ysen schip 454:13
ond 4283 van voyage ysen schip 478:1
is t'sum 7296 . doer J B woer GDy 937:14
noch 1114 . vandt yson eeven . 256:7
ond 2818 ... ond yson van eeven 380:10
is t' fum 3932 . A M R schip 636:17:

Ady 3. 7br 1669. is Godt loft goar
Abth Roockhead op de Rorpet van Not-
euppen met 568. By dradt schip 51:12 4/...
ond 8. vandy Korvels gemt J R . 13:19 4/...
't summy gel doer J en R schip 65:12:

Ady 6. 7br 1669. is Godt loft goa
Mattys Bonysen op de s. Jacob van
Stockh Koemt met 20. carsy Pick &
57 4/13 carsen Loda gelaedendoork
loodige C. en koofs goedr. s. woeg Loda
loodige & 3. woeg Loda mede ale
half loodige wart wegemberten op g Sckt

Ady 6. 7br 1669. is Godt loft goar
Jacob Grys op de s. Peure van Stockh
met 1660 . vaed ond 20 . ysen schip 218:4
ond 3150 . ... ond. gimo . 422:16
is t' fum 4816 . ... doer J B . van GDy . 691:—
noch 600 . ... gemt 88 . ☐ . J M R schip 152:14
ond 900 . ... tal J P & H Tp . 160:13
3843 . vand voyage ysen schip 382:14:
399 . bovet yson . . 72. 6:
is t 4239 . ... doer DV R schip 455:9:

Ady 10. 7br 1669. gen. ond R eum
V D Lonn C we moeby R goden voer
40. carsy Loda] gvoendr yede Beiwel
30. carsy pick] met Symon Ravun (on
27 4/13 carsy Loda] ger. met Tho Clancke
15. carsy pick]
57 4/13 carsy Loda] ger. met Mattys Bonysn
20 . carsy pick]
is t' oa 124 4/13 carsy Loda & 65. carsy pick

Ady 13. 7br 1669. is Godt loft goar
Eilik Andouen op de forseyn met
35 4/13 carsy Loda & ysoer de Loda Tomp
8. carsy pick]
2 hony esoodye & 3. carsts 1 ton pick waer

Ady 20. 7br 1669. is Godt loft goar
Iuagen Iouroon op de s. Spragen met
51. carsy Loda a 13 woeg pt carr ond
16. carsy pick , a 12. woeg pt. carralls
vlaendr doer de J L koofs geor: 1 ton
esoodye quants: 1 ton pick 4/2 loodige

Ady 20. 8br 1669. is Godt loft goar
Antois Rohlinge op de s. Tackerine
van Gott woeg met
3856 4/12 stan broot schampelwn yson
doer n. P woer J P & H Th schip 642:5
noch 44 carsy pick] doer Ivn Enhorn
ond Eilun Loda]

Ady 30. 8br 1669. is Godt loft goar
Swln Bonysen op de s. nicholal met
2390 . stan yson J V S van Gottenbory
woeyende schip 250.

Ady 30. 8br 1669. is vandea smooke
schip Jacob Mattysn gevomen van
Calmen in 7br carr die my koft
gelvvdr woer R van Dr Born goar
in Diederyk Muyttenbaugh &19
doer loen 68 4/12 carsen Loda ond 8
lonnen pick

Credit voor transport van d'ander zyde — — — — —	£1004. 11. -
voor ẛ scheyds oncosten tot Reeden — — — — —	„ 783. 10. 8
geldo dese blyft in Casse — — — — —	„ 1054. 6. -
	£11879. 7. 8

Credit aen S. Eliab harvey in voll voor ẛ baelen ardassen — —	£ 284. 8. 2
— aen Maria Beeke voor traua willem momma — — —	„ 100. -
— aen Louis & Joseph du Pleuix voor 4 wissbelbev op amsterd. —	„ 240. 14. 11
2. aen James Buckin voor syn briev op amsterdam — —	„ 100. -
— aen arnoudt bartoloni vanden heuvel — — —	„ 71. 15
— aen willem watking hem geleent — — —	„ 100. -
3. aen Thomas Cook voor traua stoven & geer — —	„ 200. -
— aen ditto voor traua Stoven & geer — — —	„ 200. -
— aen ditto Joseph Cox voor traua Stoven & geer — —	„ 96. 8. 9
— aen Jan Lorimer voor traua willem momma — —	„ 300. -

Leonora Marenore
Jacob David

7 genomen tot huys costen — — — — —	£ 50. 12. 9
ditto genomen tot huys costen — — — — —	£ 74. 3. -
— aen Thomas Buckle door orde van nathaniel Pocket	£ 20. -
— aen Rodolf Lee voor traua van Seyling in Hemp̄	£ 162. 5. 3
10 aen Thomas Cook voor traua Stoven & geer — —	£ 200. -
— aen Thomas Cook voor traua Stoven & geer — —	£ 200. -
— aen Jan Langley voor traua willem momma — —	£ 200. -
— aen John Right op rek̄ van ginber van hemgeoghi	£ 140. 0. 00
13 aen Jan lethuullier voor myn ⅕ in 331 Sa: gember	£ 71. 14. 5
— genomen tot huys costen — — — — —	£ 38. 15. -
— aen Jan Cambyn voll — — — — —	£ 47. 18. -
— aen nathaniel Pocket tot behoeft van syn schip	£ 100. -
— aen Jan Lamb door orde van nathaniel Pocket	£ 71. -
14 aen Richard Jenkinsen voor premio — — —	£ 13. 10
16 aen nathaniel Laurence voor 24 st Colchester baȳn	£ 106. 8. 6
— aen arnaud Bartoloni vanden heuvel — — —	£ 32. 15
17 aen Eliab harvey in voll voor byd — — —	£ 128. 18. 8
— aen mary brand ḡ handen mathyas good fellow	£ 30. 12
— aen Daniel nozton voor Lym — — —	£ 26. 12. 4
— aen Sr John lawrence voor traua willem momma	£ 100. -
— aen Sr John laurence voor traua willem momma	£ 150. -
19 aen Daniel andeeve voor premio — — —	£ 9. -
— aen atr lethicullier in voll voor premio — —	£ 28. 10
— aen Jan & Chr. lethicullier voor interest & vallen	£ 50. -
21 aen nathaniel Pocket in voll — — —	£ 105. 6. 2
22 aen Jan wright op rek̄ van gin̄ber — — —	£ 200. -
	£3961. 7. 11

(f)

TABLE 1. The Marescoe-David Books.

Ref. No.	Book	From–To	Business	Language	Width × Height (cm)	Pages	Chancery Ref. No.
A.1(a)	Journal	27 June 1664–31 December 1668	C. Marescoe	Dutch	28 × 43	400	'8'
(b)	Ledger 'F'	27 June 1664–31 December 1668			28 × 43	550	'9'
A.2(a)	Journal	2 April 1668–10 September 1670	C. Marescoe & P. Joye	Dutch	28 × 43	400	'5'
(b)	Ledger 'G'	2 April 1668–10 September 1670			28 × 43	550	'6'
A.3(a)	Journal	1 January 1669–7 June 1677	C. Marescoe & Executors	Dutch	28 × 43	300	'2'
(b)	Ledger 'M'	—missing—			—	—	—
A.4(a)	Journal	—missing—	L. Marescoe & P. Joye		—	—	—
(b)	Ledger 'A'	10 September 1670–20 May 1674		Dutch	33 × 46	500	'19'
A.5(a)	Journal	1 October 1670–24 October 1673	L. Marescoe	French	33 × 46	300	'10'
(b)	Ledger 'B'	1 October 1670–24 October 1673			33 × 46	300	'11'
A.6(a)	Journal	—missing—	L. Marescoe & J. David	Dutch	—	—	—
(b)	Journal	28 August 1677–4 August 1679			33 × 44	260	'13'
(c)	Ledger 'No. 1'	April 1673–4 August 1679			33 × 43	570	'14'
B.1	Invoice Book	1 March 1667–February 1674	C. Marescoe & P. Joye	Various	28 × 43	300	'21'
C.1	Cash Book	January 1669–August 1678	C. Marescoe & Executors	Dutch	16 × 40	90	'3'
C.2	Cash Book	July 1669–November 1670	C. Marescoe & P. Joye		19 × 35	200	'25'
C.3	Cash Book	September 1670–January 1675	L. Marescoe & P. Joye		19 × 35	170	'7'
C.4	Cash Book	April 1673–October 1680	L. Marescoe & J. David		24 × 36	170	?
D.1(a)	Expense Journal	March 1661–April 1674	C. Marescoe & Executors	Dutch	16 × 40	300	'22'
(b)	Expense Ledger	April 1668–December 1672			16 × 37	300	'23'
E.1	Receipt Book	October 1662–September 1673	C. Marescoe & Executors	Various	20 × 30	340	'20'
E.2	Receipt Book	July 1673–September 1680	L. Marescoe & J. David		16 × 40	340	'16'
F.1	Memorandum Book		C. Marescoe & Executors	Various	7½ × 18½	120	'1'
G.1	House Costs		C. Marescoe & Executors	English/Dutch	20 × 30	250	'4'

Convenient though it may seem to have before one a ledger-account for 'Capital', 'Profit and Loss', 'Commission Account' and other central themes, their clarity is deceptive. By their customary nature ledger entries are an abbreviated and less informative version of the journal entries.

However, in their structure these books conform to the best standards of double-entry book-keeping. The daily journal entries are meticulously cross-referenced to their appropriate debit and credit headings in the ledger. Careful cross-checking has left its characteristic pricked marks in the journal margins and extensive analyses of these books have revealed very few errors of transcription or arithmetic. Marescoe personally maintained a high standard of clarity and neatness in the 1664–8 journal which was equalled by Peter Joye who penned the matching ledger. Jacob David, who began to keep both ledger and journal after his appointment in 1668 also possessed an elegant italic hand, though some of the clerks later employed under him did not and there is a marked degeneration in the decipherability of the ledger during the employment of Henry de Gols in 1673–4. David, in fact, was a highly competent book-keeper and most of the intelligibility of these volumes is owed to his hand. It is easy to appreciate why the Court of Chancery was reluctant to allow him the opportunity of altering them by returning them to his custody, and why certain crucial sections of the ledgers were sealed up with red wax and string.

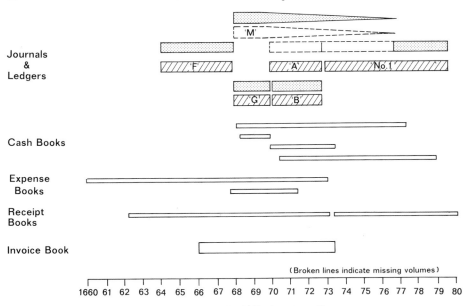

FIGURE I. Marescoe-David Books, 1664–1680.

The journals and ledgers were only the end-products of a process which began elsewhere in the rough working records of the counting-house. For day-to-day purposes the merchant relied on an array of provisional records—waste-books, cash-books, expense-books, receipt-books—whose upkeep was usually the responsibility of an apprentice clerk.

Some remnants of this process survive in the Marescoe-David papers. Two consecutive receipt-books span the period from October 1662 to September 1680. They record the signed acknowledgments of sea-captains, merchants, shopkeepers and workmen for the receipt of money in settlement of freight-charges, bills of exchange, purchases and labour of all kinds. Their value lies less in the holograph entries by a large cross-section of the business community than in the exact information they sometimes provide about the date and purpose of a payment. The same item will appear recorded in the cash-book, will reappear in the journal and finally come to rest in the ledger but in varying degrees of detail and not necessarily under the actual date of payment.

Four cash-books also survive—each linked to a different phase of the Marescoe-David partnerships. One matches Marescoe's personal ledger 'M' and, like that, runs on with scattered entries after his death. Another cash-book reflects the commission transactions of the Marescoe-Joye partnership from July 1669 to November 1670. A third is its sequel, covering Leonora's partnership with Joye until 8 January 1675. The fourth, and most helpful, represents the partnership of Leonora with Jacob David from 28 April 1673 to 28 October 1680. Leonora's large and frequent cash-withdrawals for 'house-keeping' are often boldly entered in her own hand, and the balances struck at irregular intervals bear both partners' signatures. Here again, the value of the cash-books is the slightly greater detail they may sometimes provide about payments also recorded in the journal and ledger.

However, neither the cash-books nor the matching 'Cash' account in the ledgers provide a complete picture of the payments passing into or out of the firm's coffers. For the purpose of analysing its actual cash-flow one needs access to another record—the petty-cash accounts kept separately to cover the multitude of small payments made every day for labour, carriage, packaging, postage, watching and warehousing and gratuities. Fortunately, one such volume survives. Although endorsed 'Charges of Marchandize from '61 to Apr. '74' the book had evidently been inaugurated in the earliest days of the partnership with John Buck for its opening page has entries for January–March 1654. But its continuous use began on page 2 in 1661, with detailed itemization of all the small charges attendant on Marescoe's commission trade and household. Kept initially by Moses Coulon (as were most of the minor records) it continued to serve Leonora until April 1674. Its value is that it specifies payments too petty to appear separately in cash-book or journal. When total disbursements had reached £2,000–£3,000 the sum was transferred to the 'Cash' account of the ledger. Petty though the sums may be in amount, the items recorded here are not insignificant for the historian. They reveal much about the day-to-day affairs of Marescoe and his successors—their comings and goings by boat or coach, their domestic rates, taxes and gifts to the poor, and all the other small circumstances of urban life and business. They reveal, as his other records do not, Marescoe's enforced payments to the Eastland Company as a non-member dealing in 'Eastland' wares, and they also allow one to learn that he was a friend of Josiah Child, for he spent 12s 6d on the latter's pre-nuptial festivities in July 1663.

The most personal of these volumes is a small pocket-book with clasps which Marescoe evidently carried about with him before his death. Only partly used it records (often in English) the agreed terms of sales, the maturity dates of bills of exchange and the cargoes of newly-arrived vessels. It is a useful source for the dating of Marescoe's imports in 1669 and 1670 and makes good the deficiency of the journals, which only reflect the arrival of imports some weeks later, when account is entered of its sale, less freight and customs charges. This incalculable interval between arrival and sale has created a problem for the precise dating of imports, and the difficulty is only partly alleviated by the survival of another important volume, an invoice book covering the period March 1667 to December 1673.

This contains copies of accounts despatched to customers abroad. They are of three main types: either (i) accounts of goods imported, sold in England on commission; (ii) invoices of goods exported, purchased in England on commission; and (iii) accounts of expenses and disbursments (often with accumulations of interest) incurred by Marescoe and Co. on behalf of commission customers. All are of value, but the first two categories are of special importance in providing the clearest, detailed picture of the commission trade in exports and imports. The nature, weight, measure, value and charges attendant upon every parcel are carefully itemized, together with detail about the shipping involved. What is not recorded, of course, is the detail of Marescoe trade on his own account, and from the beginning of his partnership with Peter Joye this has to be elicited from the appropriate journal for 1668–70.

The remaining books are of less significance. A rough 'ledger' itemizes under separate heads the small charges paid out of petty cash between 1668 and 1672, but they are rarely totalled and seem not to have served any useful purpose for they peter out inconclusively. A final, scarcely-used volume is that endorsed 'Charges of yᵉ house in Tower Streat' which fully records in cash-book form every payment made on account of Marescoe's buildings in 1669–70. Down to the watch-dog's collar and ration of liver, every expense is noted and it allows one to discover that while materials accounted for 75.8 per cent and labour 17.7 per cent, the carriage of materials and waste cost 5.2 per cent for the inauguration of Marescoe's great house.

From the inventory numbers endorsed by Chancery officials inside the covers of these volumes it is possible to deduce how many have been lost. Between 'No. 1' and 'No. 25' four appear to be missing and of these the nature of three can be deduced from the organization chart above. The fourth may have been an invoice book to succeed that concluded in 1673— a major loss if it really occurred.

Of one common type of merchant record there is no sign—a letter book in which should have been recorded duplicates of the outgoing correspondence of any well-conducted business. Late-seventeenth century English examples are not uncommon, and Marescoe-David may well have kept them, but if they did Chancery did not require or retain them. What they did not overlook, however, is the second major category of documents—the incoming correspondence.

2. LETTERS occupy, in bulk, nearly half the volume of this collection, filling 19 of 40 large boxes. There are approximately 10,500 of them, distributed across the years 1668 to 1680. Here too there are gaps. The letters received during the first two months of 1668 were not retained, while in 1670 it is only those received in the first two months which survive. In 1671 the letters of January–March have been lost as have those of April–May, August–December 1673. Nothing of 1674's correspondence remains. But from 1675 there is an unbroken sequence, concluding only at the end of March 1680 (Figure 2).

Marescoe's procedure was to endorse each incoming letter with its date of receipt and below that its date of reply—thus:

> 'O' [ntfangen]   12 Sep.
> 'B' [eantworden]   14 Sep.

Folded neatly into a uniform strip about 8 cm wide by 23 cm long the answered letter was placed, endorsed side upwards, upon the growing pile of answered correspondence. At the end of two months the pile, of between 250 and 300 letters, would be tied up with string, endorsed with the months it represented (e.g. 'Brieven van den maent Marty & April 1669') and filed away. The procedure of Marescoe's successors was similar, although they wisely preferred to make smaller bundles at the end of each month. Jacob David also preferred to endorse each letter with its place and date of origin, but in nearly all cases the order which determined its place in the series was the date of reply. The only exceptions are those few bundles marked 'Ongeachte brieven' (i.e. unimportant letters) or 'ontbeantworden brieven' which were not replied to. Perversely, these have often proved to be among the most interesting, and one must be grateful that they were preserved.

No attempt was made to separate the letters from a particular area or a particular correspondent (with the exceptions of a bundle from Benjamin Newland of the Isle of Wight and a bundle from Philip Botte, David's Tar Company patron in 1676–8). As a consequence, these bundles are a polyglot assortment in which letters from Danzig and Dublin, Malmö and Malaga lie side by side with the main streams of letters from Stockholm, Hamburg, Amsterdam and Rouen. As the following chapters will explain, the balance of the correspondence was to shift between centres in the course of these fifteen years. Sweden, Germany and the Netherlands retained their importance to the firm, but in differing degrees, while France not surprisingly became more prominent under Jacob David's management. The distribution of letters received in the years 1669 and 1679, for which the bundles are intact, illustrates their changing geographical distribution (see Table 2).

It is less easy to quantify or analyse the provenance of the third category of documents which I have described merely as 'papers'.

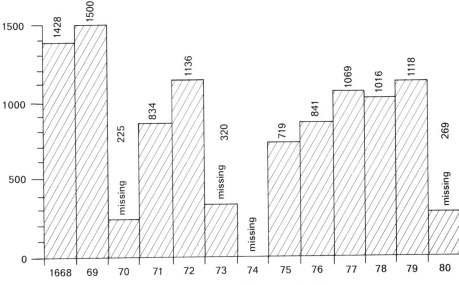

FIGURE 2. Marescoe-David Letters, 1668–1680.

3. PAPERS. This is a residual category embracing a wide variety of documents, ranging from the crumpled remnants of Leonora's housekeeping bills to the legal and business papers of her two husbands.

Four types of document merit special attention. (i) First are those 'Bills of Parcels' in which Marescoe-David's purchases of goods from English wholesalers are itemized by weight and measure. These are invoices of commodities acquired for export, either on commission or own account, and they provide detail of a kind which could find no place even in the invoice book—stating not merely the precise quantity of each cask of sugar, bag of cotton, pig of lead or length of cloth but itemizing also the cost of transport, charges of packaging, and incidentals of shipment. They make possible a more exact assessment of prime costs for the wide range of goods which the firm exported.

TABLE 2. Sources of correspondence, 1669, 1679.

	1669		1679	
British Isles	436	29.2%	160	14.2%
Sweden	237	15.9	134	11.9
North Germany	209	14.0	270	24.1
United Provinces	312	21.0	140	12.5
Spanish Netherlands	43	2.8	6	0.5
France	148	10.0	345	30.7
Spain	24	1.6	40	3.6
Italy	67	4.5	23	2.0
Totals	1,490		1,118	

(ii) From the other end of the process of export come the sale-accounts of Marescoe-David agents abroad—those English or Dutch factors who sold the exported commodities on commission in France, Spain, Italy or the Levant. Itemized again in considerable detail are the freight charges, customs duties, port dues, carriage, weighing fees for each consignment, the precise date and terms of each sale and the final balance of account to be remitted. Like the letters, endorsed with the date of their receipt and the date of their record in the journal, these sale-accounts once formed a series which has survived less well than the letters. Equally patchy are (iii) the documents relating to shipping. Some attempt was evidently made to retain a copy of all bills of lading, for cargoes imported as well as exported, and although the series is incomplete large numbers survive for every year between 1668 and 1679 with the exception of 1670, 1673–4 and 1676. Less numerous are the charter parties and insurance policies but enough survive to give a representative picture which has been drawn upon in Appendix E. (iv) The documents which have survived in some abundance are bills of exchange—duplicates of those remitted abroad or received in London, together with packets of protested bills and their accompanying notarial documents. There is plentiful material here for the student of the international exchanges, with numerous heavily endorsed orginal bills witnessing to an elaborate network of transfers through Venice, Lyon, Lille, Paris, Rouen, Amsterdam and Hamburg. The pattern of exchanges and the rates of exchange are both dealt with in subsequent chapters and in Appendix G.

For the rest, these bundles retain a jumble of personal papers, some of which are possessed of a certain pathos—Marescoe's last will, the catering bills of Leonora Frederick's grand wedding, and the apothecary's bills for her dying sisters. More than one kind of profit and loss is to be glimpsed in this dross.

3. CHARLES MARESCOE'S TRADE, 1664–1667

When Charles Marescoe opened his new Journal and Ledger 'F' on Monday, 27 June 1664, he carried forward from Ledger 'E' liabilities to sundry creditors totalling £12,922 18s 9d. Nearly half this sum represented loans at interest from his family circle—from his sister Elizabeth, his brother Peter, and from his brothers-in-law David Cocqueau and David le Griel. Another £3,003 was accounted for by a single deposit from his late partner's widow, Maria Florentia Buck. This latter sum, however, was almost exactly offset by a group of twelve small loans, all but one at 6 per cent, made on Mrs Buck's behalf. It is clear that Marescoe was simply acting as a trustee for the sum which probably represents John Buck's original legacy, now healthily enlarged by re-investment. The £6,208 lent by his family circle is less easily accounted for and gives rise to a further mystery in May 1668 when Marescoe wrote off the whole liability, now grown to £6,360 in three equal amounts of £2,120, with a formal journal entry declaring it to be 'my own money'.[1] In the absence of any further explanation one can only deduce that these large, uniform sums also represented a family bequest or marriage settlement held in trust for Charles Marescoe until the birth of his first son, which occurred in April or early May 1668.[2] All that is certain is that Marescoe now ceased to pay out interest on this substantial sum which was now fully incorporated in his working capital.

The remainder of Marescoe's liabilities in June 1664 consisted of comparatively small trading debts—balances due on unsettled accounts at home and abroad, premiums due on insurance policies, and a group of 'bad debts' incurred by others for which, as a commission agent, he carried some responsibility. Most of them were to be safely cleared in ensuing months. The overall picture can be concisely tabulated (see Tables 3 and 4).

TABLE 3. CM's liabilities, June 1664.

Liabilities, 27 June 1664

			£	s	d	%
[A]	Loans at interest	5	6,523	18	0	50.5
[B]	Deposits (i) M. F. Buck	1	3,003	0	0	23.2
	(ii) P. Joye	1	480	0	0	3.7
[C]	Goods A/c	2	185	5	2	1.4
[D]	Expense A/c	1	215	18	8	1.7
[E]	Bad debts	7	1,323	3	9	10.2
[F]	Insurance premiums	5	80	10	0	0.6
[G]	Miscellaneous debts	27	1,111	3	2	8.6
	Total accounts	49	12,922	18	9	

[1] The balancing credit and debit entries in Ledger 'F' f. 86 read '*p. diverse schryve aff alsoo de selve myn eygen geldern syn—£6,300*'; '*schryve aff de partye hier over op den 18 deeses, moet op Capitael R⁴- als boven—£6,300*'.

[2] The Swedish Resident, John Barckman, Lord Leyonbergh, to CM (undated, May 1668) congratulated him on the birth of a son. There is no published record of baptism but a 'Charles' heads the list of deceased Marescoe children on the lost memorial in Leyton Church recorded by Strype in his edition of John Stow's *Survey of London* (1720)—A. Hills, 'The Marescoe slab in Leyton Church', *Essex Review* (1942) LI, p. 221.

TABLE 4. CM's assets, June 1664.

Assets, 27 June 1664

			£	s	d	%
[A]	Cash in hand	1	940	1	3	3.6
[B]	East India Co. stock @ 60%	1	450	0	0	1.7
[C]	Loans at interest	1	450	0	0	1.7
[D]	Bottomry loans	6	437	10	0	1.7
[E]	Loans on Mrs Buck's A/c	12	2,962	5	0	11.4
[F]	Goods in stock	4	4,411	3	10	16.9
[G]	Goods sold (i) England	26	7,784	8	10	29.9
[H]	Goods, debts (ii) Abroad	13	3,564	4	4	13.7
[I]	'Voyages' abroad	8	2,332	14	9	8.9
[J]	Bad debts	15	1,902	4	3	7.3
[K]	Miscellaneous debts	13	819	16	3	3.1
	Total accounts	100	26,054	8	6	

The last category, [G], with its minor trading debts distributed round Europe—in Stockholm, Hamburg, Amsterdam, London, Rouen, Seville and Florence—was to be amply offset by the 100 items, brought forward from Ledger 'E', which can be categorized as Marescoe's assets (Table 4 above).

Of these categories, [F], [G], [H], and [I] require some amplification, which will conveniently serve as an introduction to the main objects and areas of Marescoe's trading activities.

[F] Goods in stock, consisted of:

	£	s	d
Iron, 4,811 cwt. 2q. 8lb. valued @ 12s 6d per cwt. =	3,007	4	2
Grograin yarn, 8 bales	315	16	10
Sarsaparilla	819	16	10
Seedlack, 50 cwt. and bezoar, 91 ounces	268	6	0

[G] Goods sold in England, represented short-term debts due to Marescoe for sales on the customary credit-terms, of one to six months 'time'.

They arose from the following commodities:

	£	s	d	
Iron	5,189	19	7	due from 14 customers
Copper and latten	740	8	2	due from 3 customers
Pitch and tar	1,460	11	4	due from 7 customers
Potash	73	9	9	due from 1 customer
Indigo	320	0	0	due from 1 customer

[H] Goods, debts abroad, included debts due upon exports which had been sold but for which payment had not yet been received, and also bills of exchange which had not yet reached maturity. The thirteen items involved arose in the following centres:

		£	s	d	
Stockholm	2 items	1,040	6	3	(loans to Pötter & Thuen)
Hamburg	3 items	339	10	1	(sugar sold; bills of exchange)

Amsterdam	1 item	757	15	8	(a bill of exchange, A. Muyssart & Co.)
Ghent	3 items	456	2	8	(due on linen account)
Lille	2 items	604	19	0	(bills of exchange)
Rouen	1 item	203	3	0	(bill of exchange)
Cadiz	1 item	1623	7	8	(bill of exchange)

Finally, [I] 'Voyages' abroad represented Marescoe's ventures in commodities despatched, but not yet sold. They had been consigned as follows:

		£	s	d	
Hamburg	4 items	1,152	3	4	(cloth, pepper, drugs)
Lille	1 item	309	13	0	(cotton-yarn)
Rouen	1 item	73	2	6	(drugs)
Cadiz	2 items	797	15	11	(cloth)

The geographical range of Marescoe's interests is at once apparent, and they were set in a pattern which was to change comparatively little during his career and that of his successors. Equally clear, when it is appreciated that virtually all the iron, most of the copper and all the pitch and tar was of Swedish origin is the dominant role which Baltic imports played in his business activities. However, where the picture of June 1664 differs interestingly from what was to follow is in the comparatively modest proportion attributable to foreign commissions. All of the iron in stock was held on Marescoe's own account, not on behalf of Swedish principals. The same was true of the other goods in stock and of all those sold, for which payment was still awaited.

This situation was to change markedly over the next few years. Although Marescoe secured an exclusive contract with the Swedish Tar Company to be supplied annually with 1,200 lasts of pitch and tar on his own account, and although he continued to buy in substantial amounts of iron and copper for himself, he came increasingly to handle these and other commodities on behalf of others, as a commission agent. The focus of his attention shifted in consequence, from the direct trading profits to be acquired, speculatively, at home or abroad, towards the fixed percentages which could be gained upon the ventures of others. This shift was, in large part, dictated by the onset of the second Anglo–Dutch war which soon made it extremely convenient, if not essential, to trade at the risk of foreign neutrals. But in the subsequent years of peace, Marescoe and his successors continued to serve both export and import markets primarily as agents, not as principals, and to appreciate why they did so it is necessary to see what they stood to gain.

Upon exports—goods purchased in England and despatched abroad for the account of foreign principals—the London commission agent's normal charge was a simple 2 per cent upon the total cost, 'free on board'. In return for this he was expected to follow his principal's instructions closely, seeking out the quality as well as the quantity of goods designated, arranged their packing and conveyance to port and attending to their clearance through customs. His invoice would probably itemize the prime cost and all the incident charges in some detail, and upon their total his 2 per cent commission would be calculated. Remuneration for his outlay could normally be expected quickly and might often be anticipated by credits made available through bills of exchange before the purchase. It was unusual for Marescoe to be long out of pocket for purchases made on an export commission.

For import commissions, particularly of the large-scale contractual kind which Marescoe was interested in, the financial arrangements might be more complicated and the remuneration more diversified. Although a commission of 2 per cent still formed the basic charge for handling imported goods, there were other responsibilities which yielded other percentages. For, in addition to receiving the goods, defraying their freight, customs and unloading charges, the commission agent was also responsible for finding purchasers, and this entitled him to a brokerage percentage, usually of $\frac{1}{2}$ per cent. Then followed responsibility for procuring payment and remitting the net proceeds abroad. Marescoe demanded, and generally obtained, $\frac{1}{8}$ per cent to set against the risk he ran of being paid in light-weight or false coin—'gecorte penninge en quaet gelt' as his accounts described it. These three heads together made up the standardized rate of $2\frac{5}{8}$ which formed Marescoe's basic commission on imports. However, transfer of the net proceeds abroad created yet more responsibilities from which the agent might profit. Conventionally, he would have sold the goods on credit or 'for time', which could mean payment in up to six (sometimes more) months time.[3] Sales for immediate cash-payment were the exception rather than the rule, and although London's practice did not match Hamburg's, where commodity prices conventionally assumed a 13-months credit term, it was usual to assume an allowance for 'time' in the contractual price. This might then be discounted by the commission agent for early payment at the standard rate of $\frac{1}{2}$ per cent per month. Thus, to take an example from 1664, Marescoe sold some wire on Willem Momma's behalf in October for £177 6s 6d, payable in six months time, but in December, having remitted the proceeds two months after sale, he was able to debit Momma and credit his Profit & Loss account with £3 10s representing four months 'rabat' or discount.

A similar entitlement to interest arose if the commission agent advanced money on goods before they had been sold or, more riskily, before they had even been received. At this latter point it might be easy to confuse the agent's position with that of a purchaser: to all intents and purposes he appears to have bought the consignment, sight unseen. But the vital distinction between his position as an agent, and that of a purchaser on his own account, is that he carried no personal risk for the sale of the goods, which might or might not yield a profitable return. They were merely his security for the certain 6 per cent which he could expect on his cash advance. Interest payments of this kind appear as a regular feature in Marescoe's Profit & Loss account after 1664.

Not all Marescoe's principals were content with the terms he demanded. A Swedish ironmaster commented acidly on a certain inconsistency in having to pay for 'short-change' and 'bad money' when he was also being charged interest for seven months pre-payment on goods sold at six-months time [**45**]. After all, what was a commission agent's 2 per cent for, if not to guard against defective payments? The complaint was echoed by others, and in 1670 Marescoe was driven to an interesting justification of why it cost $1\frac{1}{2}$ or 2 per cent to do in London what could be done for 1 per cent in Hamburg [Appendix A, **6**]. He was not alone in being placed on the defensive. Jacob Lucie, whose firm succeeded for a while to Marescoe's

---

[3] Analysis of Marescoe's iron and copper sales reveals the following terms of payment (by percentage of volume):

	Iron (%)	Copper-wire (%)
For cash	19.7	12.1
1 week's time	2.3	—
1 month's time	8.2	9.3
2 months' time	9.9	12.1
3 months' time	23.9	33.6
4 months' time	9.9	10.7
5 months' time	—	—
6 months' time	9.9	5.7
unspecified	16.2	16.4

copper-contract with Jacob Momma-Reenstierna, argued with some passion for 2 per cent as the prevailing norm. 'I am surprised' he wrote to Reenstierna 'that you should say I have reckoned $\frac{1}{2}$ per cent too much for my commissions. I have never in my life taken less than 2 per cent from anyone, and there is no one who does any business for me but always sets down at least 2 per cent and sometimes $2\frac{1}{2}$ and 3 per cent. I am currently giving 3 per cent to Andries Onkell for the goods he sells for me as well as for the goods he sends in return . . . and I do not know of one merchant on the Exchange who charges less than 2 per cent. If anyone will serve you here for $1\frac{1}{2}$ per cent you are welcome to deal with him. I thank the Lord that I can make a living without doing commissions, and will never serve anyone for less than 2 per cent.'[4]

Despite this fierce disavowal, lower rates were customarily negotiable. Marescoe was probably glad to take only $1\frac{1}{2}$ per cent from two of his largest and most reliable suppliers, Laurens and Gerard de Geer. He was only too eager to offer the same rate in 1670 in a bid for the exclusive London agency for all Swedish copper imports. However, in a detailed analysis of February 1669, [Appendix B] he reviewed critically the terms he was being offered by one of Sweden's most influential copper and iron producers, Abraham Kock Cronström. Through an intermediary, Cronström had offered Marescoe a 2 per cent commission on sales and purchases, which was also to cover Marescoe's commission on any accompanying insurance. For brokerage he would allow the $\frac{1}{2}$ per cent which others enjoyed, and $\frac{1}{3}$ per cent for handling cash payments. For advance payments on goods which had been received already he would offer 5 per cent, and against goods which were still in transit but insured, 6 per cent. For unsecured advances the rate would be negotiable. In return, Marescoe was to pledge himself to deal with no others and to take delivery of such varieties of iron and copper-wire as Cronström believed to be saleable.

Marescoe's carefully considered response was to approve the 2 per cent commission but insist on a minimum of $\frac{1}{3}$ per cent extra for arranging insurance. The $\frac{1}{3}$ per cent for handling cash was satisfactory but he was reluctant to accept only $\frac{1}{2}$ per cent for brokerage on the sale of goods, though on the purchase of goods he would charge no more than $\frac{1}{2}$ per cent provided that he got $\frac{1}{4}$ per cent brokerage for insurance and $\frac{1}{8}$ per cent for securing remittances by bills of exchange. As a gesture of goodwill he would take only 5 per cent on advances remitted against goods in transit, but he wanted to be able to insure them himself upon properly attested bills of lading. Beyond that he held out the bait of an advance of £1,000 to £1,500 over the winter months, repayable in March at 6 per cent and secured against the spring consignments.

The commission agent's profit on imports was thus a cake of several layers. The basic 2 per cent provided its substantial foundation; large cash advances yielded some of the cream. In between there lay some finely sliced percentages which, together, made up an appetizing diet comparing favourably with the sometimes meagre rewards of independent trade.

To these essential services in buying and selling, the commission agent could sometimes add valuable assistance on behalf of his client's shipping. As a matter of course he would be paying import freight charges and port dues on his principal's behalf, but on occasions there were special legal difficulties or financial embarrassments to be relieved. A needy skipper or a shipwrecked crew might require immediate cash assistance. More seriously, an arrested vessel seized on private or public grounds could require lengthy and costly legal protection in the courts. All this the commission agent could be expected to supply—at a price—and with the arrival of the second Anglo-Dutch war both the opportunity and the price were immediately enhanced.

[4] RA, Stockholm, Momma-Reenstierna MSS, E.2512 (Jacob Lucie to Jacob Reenstierna, 20 February 1672).

Thus, in analysing Marescoe's gains over the period of his sole management, between 1664 and the beginning of 1668, one must distinguish between more than a dozen broad categories of profit (Table 5). The primary distinction is between [A], profits earned by trade or investment on his own account, and [B], earnings derived, as a commission agent, from the initiatives of others.

In tabulating these profits I have distinguished under [A] (1) the profits and interest earned on Marescoe's investment in East India Company stock and on loans to bankers, individuals and the City of London. Their nature and significance will be examined more fully later.[5] Secondly, [A] (2), I have isolated the notional profits earned on Marescoe's export voyages (of the kind indicated in his assets under [I], Table 4) financed on his own account, or in partnership with John Lethieullier. Next, [A] (3) are the profits gained on those import commodities which Marescoe purchased for his own account. Unlike the export voyages on his own account, which were largely to different destinations and different clients than those he served on commission, the imports on his own account are not always easily distinguished from those he received on commission. Indeed, Marescoe the commission agent was habitually selling to Marescoe the independent merchant, the left hand pocketing commission and brokerage, the right hand reaping profits on re-sale. It was an operation which the steeply rising prices of 1665 and 1666 made extremely lucrative. However, [A] (4) and (5), profits on exchange dealing and insurance are quite easily distinguished from those transactions he performed on commission.

All these items were posted to the Profit & Loss account in Ledger 'F', and Marescoe's practice was to include with them the interest he earned by discounts and advances made on commission accounts. This has a strict logic: the investment in advances to his principals was made from his own capital and the profits were supplementary to, and not an intrinsic part of,

TABLE 5. CM's gross and net profits, 1664–1667.

	½/1664 £ s d	1665 £ s d	1666 £ s d	1667 £ s d	Totals 1664–1667 £ s d	%
[A] Own Account						
1. Loans, Investments	504 2 6 (26.7%)	270 4 8 (3.8%)	577 12 4 (10.8%)	196 8 1 (4.0%)	1,548 7 7	8.08
2. Exports	102 14 0 (5.4%)	282 15 2 (4.0%)	550 18 4 (10.3%)	581 4 5 (11.8%)	1,517 11 11	7.92
3. Imports	184 8 6 (9.8%)	4,174 1 2 (59.5%)	1,363 8 1 (25.5%)	642 19 2 (13.0%)	6,364 16 11	33.22
4. Exchange A/c	—	192 13 9 (2.7%)	301 10 4 (5.6%)	62 11 7 (1.3%)	556 15 8	2.90
5. Insurance	—	396 0 0 (5.6%)	7 0 0 (0.1%)	—	403 0 0	2.10
6. Miscellaneous	9 9 7 (0.5%)	—	1 12 6 (0.0%)	42 5 8 (0.8%)	53 7 9	0.28
Total Own A/c	800 14 7 (42.5%)	5,315 14 9 (75.8%)	2,802 1 7 (52.4%)	1,525 8 11 (31.0%)	10.443 19 10	54.51
[B] Commission A/c						
1. Exports	167 15 10 (8.9%)	49 3 9 (0.7%)	123 9 5 (2.3%)	233 12 7 (4.7%)	574 1 7	2.99
2. Imports	698 17 5 (37.1%)	328 7 3 (4.7%)	680 19 0 (12.7%)	1,181 13 2 (24.0%)	2,889 16 10	15.08
3. Discounts	38 13 4 (2.0%)	99 5 8 (1.4%)	251 0 0 (4.7%)	484 17 7 (9.8%)	873 16 7	4.56
4. Advances	35 12 10 (1.9%)	25 8 8 (0.4%)	255 11 5 (4.7%)	520 14 4 (10.6%)	837 7 3	4.37
5. Exchange A/c	14 3 9 (0.7%)	87 2 10 (1.2%)	88 16 4 (1.6%)	96 0 3 (1.9%)	286 3 2	1.49
6. Shipping	—	1,062 19 11 (15.2%)	781 8 8 (14.6%)	528 17 4 (10.7%)	2,373 5 11	12.39
7. Insurance	122 19 0 (6.5%)	37 4 0 (0.5%)	349 11 5 (6.5%)	317 2 5 (6.4%)	826 16 10	4.31
8. Miscellaneous	4 12 0 (0.2%)	2 0 0 (0.0%)	18 13 0 (0.3%)	28 12 8 (0.6%)	53 17 8	0.28
Total Commission	1,082 14 2 (57.5%)	1,691 12 1 (24.2%)	2,549 9 3 (47.6%)	3,391 10 4 (69.0%)	8,715 5 10	45.49
Gross Total	1.883 8 9	7,007 6 10	5,351 10 10	4,916 19 3	19,159 5 8	100.00
Net Total	1,424 1 10	6,032 8 6	4,619 18 5	3,656 19 6	15,736 8 3	82.13

[5] See pp. 117–19.

his commission percentages. However, I have chosen to disaggregate these items from the Profit & Loss account and place them under [B], with those items posted in a quite separate Commission account. We thus have [B] (1) from exports, the basic 2 per cent commission; [B] (2) from imports, the customary $2\frac{5}{8}$ per cent (or $2\frac{1}{8}$ from the De Geers); [B] (3), interest on discounts, usually at $\frac{1}{2}$ per cent per month; [B] (4), interest from advances, at the same rate; [B] (5) brokerage on exchange dealings; [B] (6) commission and salvage on shipping cases, and [B] (7) brokerage and premiums on insurance policies. Both [A] and [B] have a small residual category of miscellaneous or unclassifiable items.

However, seventeenth-century book-keeping, though orderly and meticulous, was not based upon the concept of annuality, and there was no conventional accounting period which required a merchant to make regular balances. Marescoe chose to strike balances of his Commission account after 66 weeks, in September 1665; after 111 weeks, in November 1667, and after 30 weeks, in June 1668. After the deduction of certain debit items for losses and charges, the net total of earnings on commission were then divided with his junior partner, Peter Joye, who received one-quarter in 1665 and 1667 and slightly less than one-third in 1668. Marescoe carried over his share to the Profit & Loss account which ran on, without any attempt to strike a balance, until the close of the ledger in December 1668.

Thus it is both difficult and misleading to disaggregate these accounts on a yearly, let alone monthly, basis. Commission earnings and profits on own account were worked out only when it suited Marescoe or his clients. The date of their entry in the Journal bears only an approximate relationship with the date at which they could be said to have been earned or to have reached his coffers. The large profits on goods imported for his own account, for example, which were brought into the Profit & Loss account in October 1665, represent the accumulation of earnings over periods of twelve to eighteen months. Consequently, the accompanying Table of gross profits classified upon an annual basis requires some explanatory commentary to qualify its apparent implications.

For a start, the exceptionally high figure for earnings from loans and investments [A] (1) in 1664 reflects in large part the unusual windfall of East India Company dividends, totalling 60 per cent on his £750 paid-up stock, declared in 1663 and 1664. The same source was to provide the largest items in 1665 (£187 10s), 1666 (£307 10s) and 1668 (£135) as revaluations and a further dividend of 40 per cent pushed up the price of his stock from 60 in 1664 to over par in January 1666. Later that year, as stock prices fell back to 75, Marescoe doubled his holding to £1,500 and also made loans to the Company on its short-term securities which brought in modest interest payments at 5 or 6 per cent. These loans, and others to the goldsmith bankers in 1666 were unusual diversions of capital left idle by war-time constraints on trade. With peace in prospect they were to be quickly recalled.[6]

Meanwhile, in the second half of 1664, Marescoe's risks were unevenly divided. The export 'Voyages' outstanding in June 1664—to Hamburg, Lille, Rouen and Cadiz—were prudently not reinforced on the eve of the pending war. Apart from a one-fifth share in some cloth despatched to Spain and a small consignment of Indian cotton-yarn to Lille, together worth £228 1s 6d (f.o.b) he made no further export ventures on his own account. But he did make substantial shipments on commission, worth £8,755 13s 1d, mainly of West Indian sugar and Aleppo galls sent to Hamburg. Bearing in mind that these figures arise from only a six-month period, the intensity of the effort can be seen to be unmatched by any subsequent year, apart from the post-war boom of 1668. Indeed, this looks like a pre-war boom, hurriedly summoned up by Marescoe's customers before the North Sea was rendered unsafe by winter and war.

6 See pp. 117.

The same motives of prudence and profit-seeking seem to have stimulated Marescoe's heavy stock-piling of iron, copper, pitch and tar during the second half of 1664. With approximately 415 tons of iron sold but not paid for on 27 June and 240 tons in hand, he received shipments of a further 950 tons before the end of the year. Virtually all this he bought in on favourable terms (after charging commission and brokerage) and later re-sold on his own account. As London prices rose steeply, from 13s 9d or 14s per cwt. in mid-1664 to 17s or 18s per cwt. in late 1665, Marescoe was soon making net profits of nearly £3 per ton. In October 1665, when he balanced his iron accounts, he could transfer total gains of £2,453 13s 6d on the sale of 850 tons. Copper imports, in which he took about 45 per cent on his own account, were less immediately lucrative. By December 1664 some 449 cwt. of copper-wire yielded him £156 18s on sales totalling £2,615 5s. Prices had moved relatively slowly from £6 to £6 10s per cwt. But the pitch and tar account more than made up for this. By June 1665 Marescoe could pocket a profit of nearly £1,700 upon 311 lasts of pitch and 865 lasts of tar. It is these accounts which provided the huge profits attributed to imports in 1665, [A] (3), although gained mostly on goods received in the second half of 1664. The same commodities yielded all but a fraction (£681 10s 11d of £698) of the commission earned on imports in 1664, [B] (2).

However, the two categories which do accurately reflect the chronology of Marescoe's earnings are those for shipping and insurance, [A] (5), [B] (6) and [B] (7). Nothing attributable to the former head arose in 1664 but within months of the outbreak of war a stream of business came Marescoe's way in connection with the seizure of Swedish shipping, brought in on suspicion of its possible Dutch identity. Working closely with the Swedish Resident, Leyonbergh, he was soon busy in the Admiralty court and Prize court, piling up impressive expense accounts for legal fees and gratuities and levying a 3 per cent commission on the value of cargoes and ships released by his efforts. At least fifteen cases came his way in 1665, twenty more in 1666 and eighteen in 1667. Some were extremely lucrative. In May 1665, the case of the *St Jan Battista*, brought into Portsmouth on its voyage from Malaga to Stockholm, yielded him £170 in commission, and in October that year he pocketed £505 4s 9d for securing the freedom of the Ostend-bound *St Martin*. The *St Leon* produced £325 in August 1666. These were the exceptional cases, but the majority could still bring in handsome round sums of £20 to £80 from grateful owners. Coupled with these were settlements from insurers and a steady stream of commissions for insurance, mainly on the Stockholm to London run. Altogether, Marescoe negotiated 35 policies in the six months to December 1664, 23 in 1665, 18 in 1666 and 31 in 1667.

These were among the more obvious profits arising directly, or indirectly, out of the war. Losses are less easily calculable. There were certainly no direct trading losses of any significance. Thirty-seven sacks of pepper had to be written off in 1665 at a cost of £183 5s 2d and the great Fire of London destroyed £499-worth of the seedlack Marescoe had had in store since 1664, but these set-backs were in no way attributable to the war. It is clear, however, that while the flow of imports to Marescoe held up well, his exports were reduced to a fraction of their pre-war scale. As his commission earnings under this head indicate, [B] (1), there were few foreign orders, even from neutral Hamburg, and it was only through the short sea-route to Ostend that he was able to fulfil a few commissions for olive-oil and galls placed by merchants of Lille. It was to some of these same merchants that he also despatched in neutral shipping, on his own account, 154 bales of Indian and Barbados cotton and a consignment of lead. The net return, of 8 per cent, scarcely justified the considerable risk and it was from Spain, where he shared in two consignments of English woollens, that he derived profits of 18 and 42 per cent respectively. The lesson of 1665 was well learned. In

1666, all ventures on his own account were directed to Spain and upon five consignments of cloth and one of pepper he reaped an aggregate profit equivalent to 38.5 per cent.

However, the surprising feature of 1666 is the revival of export commissions. In a year of exceptionally adverse conditions for English commerce, Marescoe received some substantial orders, not merely from Lille but from Hamburg. Upon Laurens de Geer's behalf he was even able to arrange a large shipment of lead and coal to La Rochelle. Although commission earnings from these sources were only a fraction of those on his own account, they held some promise of revived demand when the seas were cleared in 1667. Even as the Anglo-Dutch war approached its humiliating climax, Marescoe was despatching large quantities of lead, tin and coal to France on Dutch accounts. And, with the cessation of hostilities he immediately began direct shipments to Holland itself. On his own account he doubled his trade to Spain, and Italy appeared for the first time as the destination for a consignment of tin.

Nonetheless, although exports never entirely ceased to contribute to Marescoe's gains during the war, it was the import account which supplied much the larger share. The stream of Swedish shipping continued unchecked, although molested by seizures and impaired by accidents. At least 630 tons of iron arrived for Marescoe during 1665 which, joined with earlier supplies, allowed Marescoe sales of 530 tons on his own account between October 1665 and August 1666. The profits, recorded in that latter month, totalled £1,204 5s 5d, implying a gain of 11.5 per cent compared with the 18.5 per cent yielded in October 1665. This is hardly surprising: the crest of the London price-rises in iron, copper, pitch and tar, had been reached by late 1665. Thereafter they drifted slowly down, and the sums Marescoe could transfer to his Profit account contracted accordingly. The 1,110 tons of iron which he sold on his own account between October 1666 and October 1668 yielded only 3 per cent, which helps to explain why, as peace approached, he turned increasingly towards the safer rewards of the commission trade. The three staple commodities—iron, copper, pitch-and-tar—produced almost exactly £200 a-piece in commissions during 1666. In 1667, when they yielded £762 11s 9d, they were joined by large consignments of timber, summoned to England by the rebuilding requirements of London, and it was this combination which helped to raise Marescoe's commission earnings to their highest level yet.

Thus, at the close of 1667, Marescoe could look back upon a remarkably prosperous period. In company with Peter Joye the firm had secured, in three and a half years, gross profits of over £19,000 of which about 54.5 per cent had been gained on their own trading account, the rest through commissions. After the deduction of minor losses and expenses and the transfer to Joye of his share in the commissions, Marescoe's net gains amounted to £15,736 8s 3d. He had more than doubled his capital and, hard-faced or not, had unquestionably done well out of the war. One can well understand the expansive mood in which he distributed New Year gifts to his family circle on 1 January 1668—silver to his neice Jane Marescoe, £11 to his sister-in-law Anne Lethieullier, £4 5s to the servants of John Lethieullier and £5 to his clerk, Moses Coulon.

4. MARESCOE & JOYE'S TRADE, 1668–1670

(i) IMPORTS

This brief survey of Marescoe's trading profits between June 1664 and December 1667 has been necessarily superficial, based as it is on the bare evidence of his journal and ledger. But from March 1668 this source is reinforced by the earliest of his surviving correspondence and it thus becomes possible to illustrate in greater detail the dimensions and dynamics of a business which was about to blossom in a remarkable post-war boom.

To depict the complex activities of 1668 it seems appropriate to begin with Marescoe's imports and introduce the central figures in a correspondence which determined so large a share of his family's fortunes. And here one must necessarily begin with the Mommas, who have already been cited as the earliest Swedish contacts of the Buck & Marescoe partnership. In 1911, Per Sondén was confident that every Swedish schoolboy knew about the Momma-Reenstierna brothers,[1] and if that seems not to be true today they still bulk large in the economic history of Sweden's age of greatness.[2] Perhaps it was never quite true of Willem Momma, whose more eminent, younger step-brothers Abraham and Jacob soon eclipsed him. But Willem, born c. 1600, was the pioneer of the family who made his way from Aachen, where the Mommas had been long established in its metal-working industry, via Amsterdam to Sweden where he engaged himself with his fellow-townsman Arnold Topengiesser in the dramatic expansion of Swedish metal-mining.[3] He was part of a remarkable migration of skilled German and Netherlands craftsmen and managers who exploited the opportunities opened up for them by William de Besche, Louis de Geer and Daniel Kock (all natives of Liège).[4] By the 1640s Willem Momma seems to have been well-established in iron- and copper-production around Nyköping and at Färna and Norn in Västmanland. Indeed, by 1647 his diverse interests were sufficiently complicated for him to welcome the assistance of his step-brothers, Abraham and Jacob. Abraham took over the management of Färna and quickly built there, and in the neighbourhood, a complex of some dozen forges and furnaces. He was backed with capital from his brother Jacob, who had been precociously successful in developing a trading-house in Stockholm, and in 1652 their relationship was formalized in an historic partnership.[5]

Within a few years their interests had proliferated. Lured by reports of iron and copper deposits in the far north, Abraham had flung himself into grandiose schemes for the industrial development of Lappland, establishing iron-works at Tornea and copper-works at Svappavara and Kengis. Back at Färna a steel-works was launched under royal patent and Jacob extended his interests into shipping and tar-production. In 1666 he acquired the famous De Geer brass-works at Norrköping. Already, in 1665 and 1666 respectively, Jacob and

---

[1] P. Sondén, 'Broderna Momma-Reenstierna', *Historisk Tidskrift* (1911) p. 146.

[2] E. F. Heckscher, *Sveriges ekonomiska historia från Gustav Vasa* (Stockholm, 1936) 2(i) pp. 370, 372, 446–9, 501, 580, 591, 598; M. Roberts (ed.) *Sweden's Age of Greatness, 1632–1718* (London, 1973) pp. 60, 91, 115.

[3] Sondén, p. 145.

[4] M. Roberts, *Gustavus Adolphus* (London, 1953) 2, pp. 88–120.

[5] Sondén, pp. 152–3. Sons of Willem Momma (Sr) by his 2nd wife, Maria Bau[e]r; Abraham was born in 1623, Jacob c. 1625.

Abraham had received public recognition for their contributions to the Swedish economy by appointment as commissioners in the Swedish Kommerskollegium, and in 1669 they were to be ennobled, as 'Reenstierna', a name drawn from one of their remote, northern developments. Thus in 1668, when their letters to Marescoe begin to survive, they were at the height of their powers, poised to take on still larger (and ultimately disastrous) responsibilities.[6]

The Momma-Reenstiernas were not the only immigrants to make their way to eminence or ennoblement as successful Swedish entrepreneurs. The great Louis de Geer had long preceded them, as had the De Besches, the Van Eycks and the Kock-Cronströms. Others followed close on their heels: Pötter-Lillienhoff, Thuen-Rosenström, Roquette-Hegerstierna.[7] Several of these families were interlinked by partnership or marriage. Henrik Thuen and Joachim Pötter, Dutch-trained and Dutch-speaking sons of immigrants to Nyköping, were cousins as well as partners. Pötter's mother later married a cousin of the Mommas while Jacob Momma in 1652 married a daughter of Elizabeth van Eyck and Marcus Kock. The Kocks controlled the important Avesta copper-works and mint, while Pötter & Thuen, like Jacob Momma, had interests widely dispersed in mining, shipping, pitch and tar.

The interests of these families began to converge more closely in the 1660s when they all became involved in successive government contracts, in which the Swedish crown's copper rights were pledged against large advances of cash and commodities. In Sweden, as in most contemporary states, the necessities of war had set in motion a familiar vicious circle compounded of debt, high interest-charges, anticipation of future revenues and other costly short-term expedients. The commonest of these, as in France and England, was the 'farming' of crown revenues to syndicates of financiers and government officials, and it was in one such contract that Abraham and Jacob Momma, their brother-in-law Isaac Kock, and Pötter & Thuen were joined in partnership in December 1666.[8] The syndicate had been inaugurated in September 1664 by a senior Treasury official, Börje Olofsson Cronberg.[9] Ennobled in 1654, Cronberg was one of the few native-born Swedish financiers to make his mark in seventeenth-century international dealings, but by 1655 he—in conjunction with the Trip family—had acquired the management of Swedish armament sales overseas and he was soon making substantial personal contributions to Charles X's war-effort, secured against future crown copper-revenues. Although he lost the armament contract in 1662 he and Isaac Kock won the copper-contract for 1664–5, against fierce competition, with the prospect of further renewals.[10] In 1665 Cronberg thus extended his partnership to include Pötter & Thuen, and the cashier of the Greater Customs, Olov Starenflycht; in December 1666 they were joined by Abraham and Jacob Momma.[11]

The contractors were not without their critics, and the suspicion rapidly grew in

[6] Sondén, pp. 160–63.

[7] Heckscher, *Sveriges ekonomiska historia*, 2(i) pp. 367, 369, 372, 375, 470, 598, 628; Roberts, *Gustavus Adolphus* 2, pp. 88–102. For brief biographical details see *Svenska män och kvinnor* (Stockholm, 1942–1955) 8 vols.; G. Elgenstierna, *Den introducerade svenska adelns ättartavlor* (Stockholm, 1925–36) 9 vols.; longer biographical essays may be found in the still incomplete *Svenskt biografiskt lexicon* (Stockholm, 1918–in progress). Henrik Thuen, b. 1624, ennobled as 'Rosenström' in 1672, d. 1676; Joachim Pötter, b. 1630, ennobled as 'Lillienhoff' in 1668, d. 1676.

[8] G. Wittrock, *Karl XI:s förmyndares finanspolitik. Gustaf Bondes finansförvaltning och brytningen under bremiska kriget, 1661–1667* [hereafter cited as Wittrock, I] (Uppsala, 1914) pp. 275–6, 421.

[9] Wittrock, I, pp. 239, 244–6.

[10] Wittrock, I., p. 244; J. E. Elias, 'Contract tot oprichting van een Zweedsch Factorie-comptoir te Amsterdam in 1663', *BMHG* (1903) pp. 356–400; P. W. Klein, *De Trippen in de 17ᵉ eeuw* (Assen, 1965) p. 434.

[11] Wittrock, I, pp. 275–7, 421.

government circles that they had done rather too well out of their terms. Against royal copper tribute (which varied between 4471 slb and 3544 slb during the years 1660 to 1666) the partners had offered a price of 53 RD (or 86 dollars 4 öre silver) per shippound, payable in imported silver.[12] In return they enjoyed freedom from customs duties and Stockholm port charges, and with overseas copper prices rising significantly during the Anglo–Dutch war it was clear that they stood to profit handsomely. Feeling against them sharpened further in December 1666 when the contractors made difficulties about underwriting a government issue of bank-notes, except on terms which the government thought intolerable. Negotiations between the Swedish Chancellor, Magnus de la Gardie, and Joachim Pötter ended in mutual recrimination, and the contractors were accused of trying to subvert the state.[13] Yet, a government weakened by the costs of the Bremen war and the death of the reforming Treasurer, Gustav Bonde, was in no position to resist for long, and the Cronberg syndicate secured a further extension until 1667.

However, the contractors also had their grievances. Faced with repeated and excessive demands for advances of cash and goods they could point to the tardiness of Treasury repayments and to the fragility of their overseas credit. As Cronberg pointed out, their resources were not entirely their own: much of their cash advances derived from borrowings abroad and depended, precariously, upon a regular cycle of repayments. Indeed, in October 1667 a tearful Abraham Momma warned the government that his bills of exchange were being returned, protested for non-payment, and an official investigation revealed that of the contractors' 500,000 dollars advances, 300,000 d.s.m. were still owing to them. Not surprisingly, the syndicate remained silent when asked to advance another 800,000 d.s.m. and in September 1668 the Mommas withdrew from the Cronberg syndicate with over 200,000 d.s.m. owing to Abraham alone.[14]

It was not only in government borrowing against copper that Marescoe's correspondents were yoked in a precarious financial relationship. There was also the Swedish Tar Company, in whose management the Mommas, Pötter & Thuen, and Börje Olofsson Cronberg were directly involved. Established in 1648 with a twenty-year charter it had been endowed with a monopoly over only that tar and pitch produced north of Stockholm and Nyen (modern Leningrad), but that was enough to give it control of the main sources of supply in Finland and Sweden and thus of about three-quarters of the whole area's exports.[15] Yet the Company's record was not a happy one. Export levels had first fallen and then been totally undermined by the wars of 1657–60. A steadily mounting campaign of grievance had been levelled against its pricing and marketing policies and in 1658 Charles X had been strongly inclined to make over the whole trade to the Dutch or, perhaps, the English in return for reliable cash-advances.[16] The regency government which succeeded him likewise eyed the advantages of a foreign mortgage, but after intense lobbying the Company was formally reconstructed in July 1661, with an enlarged capital, as 'the New Tar Company'.[17]

Unfortunately, the reconstruction was inept and ill-timed. The new Company found itself encumbered with large, leaking stocks, variously estimated at between 20,000 and 24,000

---

[12] Wittrock, I, pp. 245–6, 275–6; J. Wolontis, *Kopparmyntningen i Sverige, 1624–1714* (Helsingfors, 1936) p. 233.

[13] Wittrock, I, p. 363.

[14] Wittrock, I, pp. 420–3.

[15] A.-G. Hallberg, 'Tjärexport och tjärhandelskompanier under stormaktstiden', *Skrifter utgivna av svenska litterursallskapet i Finland*, 371 (Helsingfors, 1959) p. 114; K. O. Fyhrvall, 'Bidrag till svenska handelstiftningens historia: I. Tjärhandelskompanierna', *Historiskt Bibliotek*, VII (Stockholm, 1880) pp. 289–347.

[16] Hallberg, p. 115.

[17] Hallberg, p. 115; Fyhrvall, pp. 294–304.

lasts, at a time when European prices were falling. Its remaining capital proved inadequate to cope with a steadily rising supply and in April 1663 and May 1665 it secured royal ordinances reducing its liability to purchase tar to 7,000 and then to 5,000 lasts p.a. Exports, which had recovered in quantity to about 6,300 lasts of pitch and tar in 1662, were halved to 3,000 lasts in 1666. The six-year marketing contract settled at Amsterdam with the house of Van Gangelt & Deutz in 1662 was disrupted by the war, and in 1666 the Swedish government granted some of its leading members exemptions to trade independently of the Company's monopoly.[18]

1667 saw the Company enjoying a brief post-war boom. Possibly 9,000 lasts were exported and the Company was able to declare its first and only dividend of 9 per cent. A re-shuffle of the managing directorate replaced Jacob Momma and two others with a new team including Henrik Thuen. The task facing Thuen and his colleagues was still formidable. Unsold stocks in Sweden amounted to nearly 18,000 lasts and total debts approached 600,000 d.s.m.[19] Thus, when the Tar Company's surviving correspondence with Marescoe begins it was in a plight which it could not afford to divulge, although it was clear that considerable importance would attach to the journey which Thuen was about to make to all the Company's major European outlets. The slightly off-hand way in which a Tar Company letter of 4 April 1668 refers merely to the possibility of Thuen visiting London, *en passant*, strikes a false note. He could hardly afford not to do so. The last decade had seen a radical shift in the market for pitch and tar. Where 60 to 80 per cent of the Swedish product had once gone to Holland, by 1660—it has been argued—a good 50 per cent was going to England and Scotland, and only 20 per cent to the United Provinces.[20] In 1664, Marescoe alone had taken about 1,200 lasts (probably 300 of pitch and 900 of tar) solely from the Tar Company. This represents one-fifth of the annual average amount of pitch and tar passing through the Sound in the years 1661–4.[21] In 1665, a year of much reduced Finnish exports, only about 650 lasts reached him, and in 1666 and 1667, with the trade thrown open, Tar Company consignments had been eclipsed by individual suppliers, A. & J. Momma among them. There was thus much to be gained for the Company if a satisfactory agreement could be reached with Marescoe.

Indeed, there are clear indications from Marescoe's ledgers that the large-scale dealers had no monopoly of Swedish production. In iron, as in pitch and tar, there was still room for smaller men to operate outside the orbit of the Stockholm magnates. Gothenburg, generally ice-free, with its advantageous independence of the Sound passage, drew iron down from a different hinterland—from the furnaces and forges of Värmland, where young men like Gustav and Peter Dunt, Sybrandt Valck and Adam Radue, as well as older hands like Jan and Leonardt van Savelant, were opening up production which they offered to Marescoe. In 1666, eleven per cent (by volume) of his iron had come from Gothenburg, and in 1667 the proportion was 26.6 per cent. This should be compared with the tentative figures for Swedish bar-iron exports which suggest that Gothenburg's share of the total averaged about 16.6 per cent in the 1660s.[22]

While four producers had supplied his needs in 1665 (Pötter & Thuen accounting for 45 per cent, Laurens de Geer for over 27 per cent), in 1666 there were eleven different suppliers

[18] Hallberg, pp. 116–18.
[19] Fyhrvall, p. 309.
[20] Hallberg, pp. 108, 114.
[21] Hallberg, p. 175, table II.
[22] K.-G. Hildebrand, *Fagerstabrukens historia: sexton-och sjuttonhundratalen* (Uppsala, 1957) p. 36; S.-E. Åström, *From Cloth to Iron: The Anglo-Baltic Trade in the late Seventeenth Century*, Part I (Helsingfors, 1963) p. 37.

and in 1667, sixteen. Many were light-weight opportunists who never reappeared; others may have been acting on behalf of better-known principals. At the end of the day, only three producers stand out as regular, major suppliers of iron to Marescoe and his successors. The Pötter & Thuen partnership was one, until 1674. Another was Debora van Ruyff, heiress to the Axbergshamer works (near Örebro in Närke) which Jan van Ruyff had acquired for *f*.33,000 in 1649 from his employers Ferdinando and Federico Schuylenburch.[23] The third was the De Geer family, that dynasty of almost imperial dimensions which had partitioned but preserved its great industrial inheritance from Louis de Geer.[24] Of his six sons, Laurens [b. 1614] retained the lordship of Österby, Louis II [b. 1622] held Finspång, Emanuel [b. 1624] managed Lövsta, and Steven [b. 1629] controlled Gimo. Of these, it was Laurens (with his son and heir Gerard [b. 1642]) and Steven de Geer who dealt with Marescoe and, later, David, accounting for never less than one-quarter and sometimes three-quarters of the London firm's supplies.

In the case of copper production the picture is slightly less complicated. With the exception of 1666 there were rarely more than three suppliers and among these the Momma brothers were usually paramount. Laurens de Geer had supplied Marescoe with 50 per cent of his copper in 1664, 27 per cent in 1665, and 21 per cent in 1666, but with the sale of the Norrköping works in the latter year the De Geer family withdrew from the copper market—as far as Marescoe was concerned. Likewise Claude Roquette-Hegerstierna (the ennobled French tailor) had contributed 24 per cent in 1666 and nearly 27 per cent in 1667, but in 1668, with the Momma brothers breathing jealously down his neck, he left the field and the way was clear for the Mommas to dominate copper as they did steel, for which they held a royal patent.

As for pitch and tar, the limited jurisdiction of the Tar Company left room for producers south of Stockholm to despatch shipments, and in 1666 and 1667, with even its partial monopoly suspended, there had been a rush of small producers to fill the vacuum. Six suppliers outside the Tar Company accounted for 92 per cent of Marescoe's pitch and tar in 1666 (by value, c.i.f.) and in 1667 there were eight (of whom six were Gothenburg merchants). Timber demand, in the wake of the Fire of London also created opportunities for some of the smaller dealers to add planks and balks to their modest consignments of pitch and tar. There had been no timber sent to Marescoe in 1664 or 1665, but in late 1666 he received four consignments, worth £1,600, and in 1667 nine more, worth nearly £5,600.

Thus, by 1668 Marescoe had recently experienced a proliferation in the number of his suppliers and at least thirty-five men or firms contributed to the 203 letters he received from Sweden (and preserved) during that year. Yet, letters despatched in Sweden by no means account for the full volume of correspondence dealing with Marescoe's Swedish affairs. The essential characteristic of this trade is that it was multilateral, and heavily dependent on conditions and decisions in Amsterdam and Hamburg as well as London or Stockholm. While the movement of goods was a conspicuously one-way traffic across the North Sea, the movement of credit and cash upon which it depended was a more complex matter of interchange between three or four European centres.

It is at this point that the financial entanglements of the leading Swedish producers acquire their special significance. For, even in normal circumstances, their requirements for credit would have been pressing, especially during the winter months when stocks of iron, copper,

23 J. G. van Dillen, 'Amsterdamsche notarieele acten betreffende den koperhandel en de uitoefning van mijnbouw en metaalindustrie in Zweden', *BMHG* (1937) p. 222.
24 For the De Geer family see E. W. Dahlgren, (ed.) *Ätten de Geer* (Uppsala, 1920) and his 2-volume *Louis de Geer, 1587–1652, hans lif och verk* (Uppsala, 1923).

pitch and tar were being worked, assembled and transported to the coasts for shipment in early summer. But in the special circumstances outlined above, with the Swedish government's copper-contracts coming up for renewal in the late autumn of every year, their need for cash and credit was acute. Pötter, Thuen, Cronberg and the Momma brothers were not bluffing when they warned the government of international repercussions if their resources were overstretched.[25] Behind their advances of silver rixdollars lay a complex and fragile cobweb of credit secured upon merchants in Hamburg, London, Amsterdam and Rouen. To an exceptional degree, the perpetuation of their privileged domestic ascendancy depended upon agents abroad and upon the regularity and reliability with which they could draw funds across the exchanges. Thus it is not surprising to find that one of the principal concerns—sometimes, the central obsession—of their correspondence is their credit rather than their commodities. For all their attention to the design or quality, pricing and marketing of their products there is nothing for which they display greater solicitude than the bill of exchange.

The operation and intricacies of the exchange system will emerge at many points in this study.[26] Here it is enough to confirm that Amsterdam stood at its centre for Marescoe and his associates. A typical instance of its role is the contract arranged by Joachim Pötter in July 1662, and renewed in 1668 by Henrik Thuen, with the Amsterdam firm of Van Gangelt & Deutz on behalf of the reconstructed Tar Company.[27] To supplant the existing agents (Louis and Hendrik Trip) Gangelt & Deutz agreed to advance *f.*250,000 at 5 per cent, partly to buy out existing stocks. In addition they contracted to honour bills of exchange to the annual value of *f.*60,000–*f.*70,000 and to remit payment for cargoes on arrival at a valuation of *f.*70 per last for tar and *f.*120 per last for pitch. Their advances against goods would earn 5 per cent, the unsecured advances 6 per cent. In this and other details the contract offers close comparisons with Marescoe's proposed arrangement with Abraham Cronström, already described, or with the 1663 armaments contract by which Abraham van Eyck superseded Cronberg.[28] While the details and sums might differ, the principles were usually the same. The commission agent was pledged to underwrite the credit of his principals, providing large advances of funds often unsecured against goods.

Thus in Amsterdam (and in Hamburg and Rouen) Marescoe had his counterparts—merchants who handled the local sale of Swedish products in return for substantial obligations to provide cash and credit. The Amsterdam firm of Jean, David and Hendrik van Baerle dealt with the Momma brothers on this basis, and Peter Simons (a young cousin of the Mommas and half-brother to Joachim Pötter) acted not only for the Pötter & Thuen partnership but for the Västervik Ship Company and, on occasion, for the Tar Company, whose principal agents were Van Gangelt & Deutz. The Amsterdam house of Bartolotti & Rihel also played an important part in financing the Swedish 'factorie-comptoir' set up by Abraham van Eyck at the expense of the Trips and Cronberg in 1663.[29] As for the De Geers, they provided an exception. Steven de Geer reversed the normal pattern by living in Amsterdam and managing his Swedish interests through agents such as Claus and Isaac Bex in Stockholm. In Hamburg he had his relative, Peter Juncker, who also acted for the Cronberg syndicate, while the Mommas had their cousin, Jan Jacob Hiebenaer.[30] Indeed, the

[25] G. Wittrock, *Karl XI:s förmyndares finanspolitik. Från blå boken till franska förbundet, 1668–1672* [hereafter cited as Wittrock, II] (Uppsala, 1917) pp. 158–60, 254.

[26] See below, Appendix G.

[27] GA, Amsterdam, Notarieel Archief 2762A (P. van Buytene) pp. 30–6; Klein, *De Trippen*, p. 471.

[28] Elias, 'Contract tot oprichting van een Zweedsch Factorie-comptoir', BMHG (1903) pp. 356–400.

[29] Klein, *De Trippen*, p. 455.

[30] Sondén, pp. 144 n. 1, 147, 151 n. 2.

cosmopolitan merchant community of Hamburg was predominantly Dutch in origin, with family representatives scattered around northern Europe.[31] It is common to find these fraternal partnerships reflected in the Marescoe correspondence, linking Hamburg with Stockholm (Joachim and Hendrik Lutkens, Hendrik and Andreas Muldenaer), Hamburg with Amsterdam (Guillelmo and Louis de la Bistrate, or Pieter and Paul Godin), and Hamburg with Gothenburg (Gerd and Gustaff Dunt, Jurgen and Jan Dominicus Erhorn), to name but a few. Several of Marescoe's consignments from Sweden in 1667 were directed in this way. The widow Putensen and the widow Wolters, Jurgen Erhorn, Henning Helt & Claus Engelke, Johan Behrman and Gerd Dunt had all controlled Gothenburg shipments of iron, timber, pitch and tar from their counting-houses on the Elbe, and in 1668 we find several of them preparing to send more.

However, the Amsterdam correspondence had the greater urgency. Its principal role was to direct the transfer of funds from London, either by despatching drafts or by demanding remittances. Whether the vehicle of the transfer was an Amsterdam bill or a London bill depended on the state of the exchanges and the market for bills, but the net effect was the same—a movement of credit or cash from London to Amsterdam, to answer a similar movement from Amsterdam to Sweden. Marescoe's position at the head of this chain of transfers was determined by no caprice of his principals but by the irreversible currents of European trade. His obligations to Sweden were only a small part of England's general deficits in the north, which were discharged through her credits, either in Hamburg or in the Netherlands. The currents, compounded of goods, credit and cash, thus flowed, anti-clockwise, round their centre in Amsterdam: they could not do otherwise.[32]

What this meant for Marescoe can be seen from an analysis of his ledger accounts with the De Geers, the Mommas, Pötter & Thuen and the Tar Company. By striking a balance at the end of every calendar month one can make a limited but still illuminating assessment of the degree to which their credits, made up of the sale of Swedish goods, were anticipated by debits, arising from the transfer of advances through bills of exchange. For example, over the 48-month period between June 1664 and May 1668, the account of Laurens and Gerard de Geer carried a deficit averaging £1,494 per month for 41 months. The Tar Company account was in deficit for only 17 months of the same period, for an average of £1,296 per month, but Pötter & Thuen's modest deficit of £860 lasted for 40 months. Over a shorter period, of the 24 months between May 1666 and April 1668, during which sales totalling £12,500 passed through their account, A. & J. Momma were 'overdrawn' for 22 months for an average sum of £3,266. Parts of these deficits arose from Marescoe's payments for freight and other trading and shipping costs, but advances remitted by bills of exchange accounted for by far the larger proportion, varying between 71 per cent (for Pötter & Thuen) and 81 per cent (for A. & J. Momma).

The sources and destinations of these bills of exchange differed between individual accounts. Each of Marescoe's customers had his preferred route, or pattern of routes, particularly during the difficult conditions created by the second Anglo–Dutch war. The De Geers, with shipping-agents on the west coast of Ireland, sometimes liked to draw Irish bills at

---

[31] E. K. Newman, 'Anglo-Hamburg trade in the late-seventeenth and early eighteenth centuries' (unpublished doctoral dissertation, University of London, 1979) p. 31; M. Reissmann, *Die hamburgische Kauffmannschaft des 17. Jahrhunderts in sozialgeschichtlicher Sicht* (Hamburg, 1975) pp. 48, 53, 220.

[32] For discussions of this pattern see Åström, *From Cloth to Iron*, pp. 76–121; J. Price, 'Multilateralism and/or Bilateralism: the settlement of British trade balances with "the North" c. 1700', *EcHR* 2nd Series, XIV (1961) pp. 256–9; J. Sperling, 'The international payments mechanism in the seventeenth and eighteenth centuries' *EcHR* 2nd Series, XIV (1962) pp. 450–63.

Limerick (or Dublin) on London. Alternatively, they favoured remittances made in Hamburg. Thirty-five per cent of their bills (by value) were on the former route, 13 per cent on the latter. But the remaining 52 per cent were on the Anglo–Dutch exchange, two thirds of these being Amsterdam drafts on London despatched by Steven de Geer. Fifty-five per cent of A. & J. Momma's transfers were arranged through London bills on Amsterdam (as were virtually all Willem Momma's) but another 30 per cent were Hamburg bills on London, usually drawn by J. J. Hiebenaer. Pötter & Thuen also showed a marginal preference for the Hamburg–London (25 per cent) and London–Hamburg (30 per cent) routes, handled by G. de la Bistrate or Peter Juncker, as against the Amsterdam–London exchange (43.5 per cent) handled by Peter Simons. As for the Tar Company, its drafts were an overwhelming 80 per cent in favour of Hamburg on London, also drawn by G. de la Bistrate, but it is discernible in this, as in the other accounts, that with the return of peace and more normal exchange conditions, transfers between London and Amsterdam recovered their popularity as the most desirable and reliable route.

Thus, Marescoe's commission trade with Sweden generated an important correspondence with Hamburg and Amsterdam which runs parallel with, and is often inseparable from, his correspondence about exports to these centres. The firm of Jean, David and Hendrik van Baerle, for example, was heavily involved in Marescoe's exports of lead, tin and sugar to Amsterdam during 1667, and they were to continue handling them during 1668. But running through their letters, and those of Peter Simons, is a regular preoccupation with the state of the exchanges and a shared concern for satisfying the relentless demands of what they called 'our friends' in Stockholm. Letters of this nature, filled with the routine details of drafts and remittances, do not make for absorbing reading and they are under-represented in the printed selection, although one or two examples will serve to convey their character [**17, 26**].

What was not routine about 1668 was the scale of the opportunities which now seemed open in north European trade. Although Amsterdam correspondents, such as Steven de Geer, remained understandably nervous until the peace of Aachen in May, the Triple Alliances constructed in January and April had created a situation which appeared uniquely favourable to the relations of England, Sweden and the United Provinces.[33] The Swedish correspondence to Marescoe conveys, not surprisingly, a sense of buoyant optimism which, in the case of Jacob Momma, verged on euphoria. He, in March and July 1667, had signed contracts with ex-Queen Christina, leasing the administration and exploitation of her domains on Gotland and Ösel.[34] Underwritten by Willem Momma and Isaac Kock-Cronström, and shared in thirds by Abraham Momma and Daniel Leijonancker, his schemes for the islands' economic development were ambitious and embraced not only tar, lime, potash and timber but also corn, textiles and ship-building.[35] Abraham Momma's letter of 5 February 1668 [**6**] conveys much of this excitement, as does Jacob's own of 14 August [**63**]. Furthermore, with the De Geers and Hegerstierna out of the running, the three Mommas felt confident about the prospects for their copper and brass production. Willem Momma in particular pressed upon Marescoe the diverse artefacts of his brass-workers—kettles, pots and pans of all sizes and designs—and although London copper-wire prices were now dismally low they at least precluded any serious competition from the more expensive Hamburg products. All the Swedish correspondents therefore display a fresh eagerness to know what

---

[33] For the text of the Anglo–Dutch, and Anglo–Dutch–Swedish, treaties of 23 January, 17 February, 5 May and 5 October 1668 see C. Parry (ed.) *The Consolidated Treaty Series, 1648–1918* (New York, 1969–83) X, pp. 397, 409, 441; XI, pp. 33–9.

[34] Sondén, pp. 160–1.

[35] Sondén, pp. 161–2.

England required. 'How much steel will you take?' asks Abraham Momma. 'What kinds of kettles, what types of iron, which quality, what size?'

It is a little surprising to find that the Mommas, who had now been trading with England for nearly twenty years, should still appear uninformed of the vagaries of the English market, particularly as they had been instructed on the preferred 'English assortment' as early as 1656 [Appendix A, **1**]. But market-research of an elementary kind is a consistent feature of this interchange of letters. Both Willem and Jacob asked for, and received, samples of English kettle-designs, as did Pötter & Thuen. Abraham wanted to know the calibre of English cannons and the price of their cannon-balls, as well as the preferred size of hoop-iron.[36]

However, the most serious and searching market inquiry was that launched by Pötter & Thuen on behalf of themselves and the Tar Company. In March they asked Marescoe for an estimate of English pitch and tar consumption in the coming year[37] and in July, as Thuen pursued towards London his tour of the Company's European outlets, Marescoe canvassed his correspondents in the English outports to learn the extent of provincial demand. The response was not encouraging. In August 1668 Newcastle was full of cheap tar, much of it Norwegian, and if an expected cargo arrived the town would hold more than could be sold in one year. 'Please by no means send any hither.'[38] Plymouth, which had been designated the Swedish staple by the commercial treaties of 1665 and 1666, was also awash with two years' supply—'I cannot advise you to send any.'[39] But Hull would take 100 lasts, Yarmouth had a market for 85–100 lasts,[40] and the Isle of Wight put its requirements at 100 lasts. On this kind of basis the slightly disappointing agreement was reached to supply Marescoe with 900 lasts—three-quarters of the pre-war figure—of which 770 lasts would come through London [**32**].

This was not the only disappointment which the English market afforded in 1668. While copper-wire could not be expected to hold its high war-time price of £7 per cwt., which it had reached in the summer of 1666, it was something of a shock that it could fall so steeply from its level of £6 10s in July 1667. Within four months it had fallen to £5 10s and in the spring of 1668, when stocks should have been low, it was having difficulty in fetching £5 2s at 6 months time (Figure 3). These seem to have been the lowest prices for a quarter of a century.[41] Iron was likewise disappointing in most of its varieties. Jan van Savelant complained of a loss of 1 rixdollar per shippound (about 20 per cent) on his 1667 consignments,[42] and Jacob Blome put his loss on iron at 33 per cent.[43] They may have been inefficient producers, but—as Abraham Momma complained—12s 6d per cwt. at 6 months time was a very poor price compared with the 13s or 14s per cwt. which had been obtainable only a few months before.[44]

The obvious remedy was to know exactly which kinds of iron were in demand, and to produce the right quantity in the right quality at the right time. It is the efforts of the Swedish

---

[36] A. Momma to CM, 3 October 1668.
[37] Pötter & Thuen to CM, 21 March 1668.
[38] Robert Ellison to CM, 23 July 1668.
[39] William Jennens to CM, 21 July 1668.
[40] William Skinner to CM, 20 July 1668, Peter Caulier to CM, 20 July 1668. Richard Kingman of Dartmouth put the port's requirement at 300–400 barrels of tar and only 200–250 barrels of pitch (which was in competition with French supplies) [**23**, **24**, **25**].
[41] The statement is based on prices quoted in the Momma-Reenstierna MSS, 1656–80, as well as those in the Marescoe-David MSS, 1664–80.
[42] J. van Savelant to CM, 9 April 1668.
[43] J. Blome to CM, 28 December 1667.
[44] J. Momma to CM, 22 February 1668.

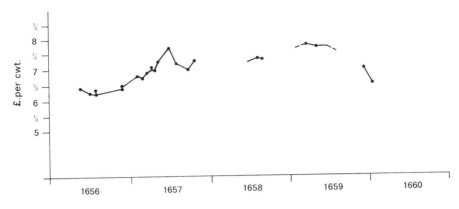

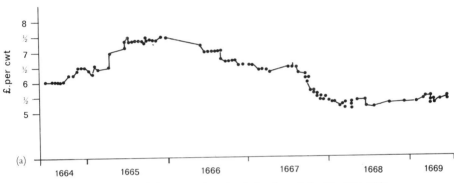

FIGURE 3.(a) Swedish copper-wire prices in London, 1656–1660, 1664–1669.

manufacturers to observe these elementary rules which gives this side of the correspondence its special interest, for most of them seemed eager to adjust within the limits set by their resources of workmen, capital and raw material. Unfortunately, in 1668 a long hard winter had retarded production. Up-country iron had not reached Stockholm as late as 18 April,[45] and a summer drought halted iron- and copper-works for four weeks in September, both in Värmland and Södermanland.[46] When Marescoe started clamouring for more voyage iron in late July it was already too late.[47]

'Voyage iron', which will figure largely in the Marescoe-David imports, was a type destined for re-export, principally to the west coast of Africa. It was sometimes known as 'Guinea' iron, and it was soon to become a staple item in the trade of the Royal African Company of 1672.[48] Produced in bars $2\frac{1}{2}$-inches thick, varying in length, it usually yielded about 50 bars to the ton and fetched about 15–20 per cent more on the London market than ordinary bar-iron. In April 1668 it was eight months since Marescoe had sold his last 250 bars

[45] Pötter & Thuen to CM, 18 April 1668.
[46] W. Momma to CM, 4 October, J. van Savelant to CM, 14 September 1668 [36].
[47] J. van Savelant to CM, 25 August; D. van Ruyff to CM, 29 August 1668.
[48] K. G. Davies, *The Royal African Company*, pp. 170–2.

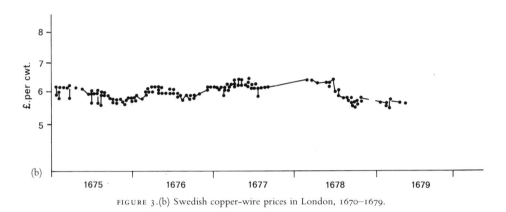

FIGURE 3.(b) Swedish copper-wire prices in London, 1670–1679.

for 15s 10d per cwt., and it was frustrating to be told by ice-free Gothenburg merchants that 'voyage iron cannot be had at present'.[49] Debora van Ruyff was also unable to respond quickly enough and Steven de Geer had to explain why he could send so little [18]. Fortunately, Jan van Savelant, who later claimed to have been making voyage iron for fifty years,[50] was more alert to the European demand. He had done well with it at Hamburg and Amsterdam in 1667 and, in readiness for 1668, had had a large amount expressly made, 'schon ende licht ijser, waer van omtrent 10 staven op het schippont, wil hopen op een goede marckt sal comen'.[51] In England, it certainly did find a good market and was selling on the quayside. Van Savelant found himself besieged in Gothenburg by eager English merchants offering cash or bills on Hamburg, and he was not the only Swedish iron manufacturer to find that the right commodity could be disposed of, at much less expense, on his own doorstep. By July 1668, Pötter & Thuen could cheerfully report that their iron was selling 'like bread from the

[49] G. Dunt to CM, 25 February 1668.
[50] J. van Savelant to LM, 18 October 1670 [137].
[51] Same to CM, 29 June 1668.

baker',[52] and when Marescoe asked Van Savelant for another 1,500 slb before the winter he was offered no more than the last 50 slb still in town.[53]

Thus 1668 produced some instructive paradoxes in the volatility of demand and the quirks of supply. If Marescoe had wanted anchor-flukes, Van Ruyff had them;[54] if he had wanted broad-iron pieces De Geer had them—indeed, he had had them expressly made, but would know better next year [49]. And there were other disappointments. Not all the products measured up to their requisite quality. The Swedes might complain of low prices and excessive commission, but Marescoe could complain of poor design and defective material, particularly in the Momma copper-wares. Willem stoutly defended his kettles and cauldrons—none better were made, and they sold well in Holland and even better in Hamburg, Lübeck and Russia.[55] But he acknowledged the need for better designs, and his brother Jacob was brought to admit the defects of recent wire output by the combined criticisms of Marescoe and the Van Baerles.[56]

Yet these complaints were trivial in comparison with a grievance that struck at the heart of the whole commission system. For if Marescoe's advances were to be adequately secured against prospective sales he needed some assurance of exclusive supplies, and this was what the major producers professed to guarantee. The whole object of Henrik Thuen's tour was to place the Tar Company's supplies in a few selected hands—those of Deutz in Amsterdam, of Thomas Legendre in Rouen, and of Marescoe in London. Steven de Geer assured Marescoe that all the production of Österby and Gimo was reserved for his needs, and the Mommas were professedly channelling all their copper-wares through his hands. It was therefore embarrassing for De Geer to be confronted with proof that supplies of his Österby iron were reaching other dealers in London.[57] Refusing to believe it at first—for he had given strict orders to Claus Bex in Stockholm—he was eventually obliged to admit that a mistake had been made and that 200 slb supposedly destined for Danzig had mysteriously found its way to London.[58] The Tar Company was likewise obliged to explain how 90 lasts of high-value pitch had found their way to London from Stockholm under their noses.[59] Indeed, the Tar Company was greatly exercised by the whole problem of competition from producers outside their monopoly and gave fierce instructions how Marescoe was to deal with 'kladders'[60] from Kalmar and other southern ports, several of whom had approached him. The advice was to beat them at their own game and undersell them—a strategy which made sense in the light of the Company's huge, unsold stocks [50].

It is less easy to understand such a policy when, in the face of low prices and poor demand, it was urged by the Mommas and some of the smaller iron producers. Yet, both in the early spring of 1668—before new supplies could arrive—and in the mid-winter of 1668/9, when shipments had ceased, Marescoe was urged to clear his stocks as quickly as he could. In Jacob Momma's case the intention was ostensibly to prepare the way for new stock, but underlying such a strategy one can detect the perennial compulsion to generate new cash. About this the smaller iron men were frank. Gustav Dunt of Gothenburg urged quick sales for cash down

---

[52] Pötter & Thuen to CM, 17 July 1668.
[53] J. van Savelant to CM, 25 August 1668.
[54] D. van Ruyff to CM, 12 December 1668.
[55] W. Momma to CM, 5 April, 31 May, 29 November 1668.
[56] J. Momma to CM, 28 December 1668; Van Baerles to CM, 21 December 1668.
[57] S. de Geer to CM, 23 March 1668 [8].
[58] Same to same, 3 August, 10 August, 17 August, 4 September 1668.
[59] Tar Company to CM, 24 October, 31 October 1668 [50].
[60] The word 'kladder' is almost untranslateable. The verb 'kladden' simply means to undersell, but the noun has the pejorative undertones of 'huckster', and was frequently employed in this correspondence.

'because I am a young man who needs his money and cannot afford to have it laid out for so long with the people one trades with'.[61] His friend, Heinrich Braun Johan was equally urgent—sell as quickly as possible, but for cash, and remit immediately to Hamburg. He would rather take a lower price than sell for 6 months time.[62] Letters such as these confirm the older men's gibes about necessitous young 'kladders' who spoiled good markets in their hunger for returns.

Yet the older men harboured needs and fears which were no less dangerous for being better concealed. It is possible, however, to read between the lines and detect some of the stresses imposed by their larger capital requirements. Abraham Momma's request in June that he be allowed to draw 9,000–10,000 *RD* through Peter Simons in Amsterdam and another 8,000 *RD* through Hiebenaer in Hamburg was reasonable enough, set against consignments worth considerably more.[63] But his letter of 3 October seeking still further credits is self-consciously and convolutedly apologetic for straining Marescoe's goodwill to the limit. 'Because the winter here is long and the works require great capital, my request is that, if I need it, you will do me the kindness of allowing Peter Simons to draw on you some money for my account at 2 or 3 usances during the winter, with the condition that I shall make good to you the interest and with the first open waters send you goods to set against it which will more than repay you. . . .'

Marescoe, flush with the profits of the Anglo–Dutch war, seems to have been ready to carry these burdens—for the present. His colleagues in Amsterdam were less happy. In December 1666, when the Van Baerle brothers were about to enter into their three-year contract with the Mommas, they were already nervous about Swedish demands. The Mommas' insistence on a 12,000 *RD* advance, if publicly revealed, could harm them on the Amsterdam bourse. 'The mere suspicion would be enough to ruin our credit.'[64] Less than a year later they were yielding to importunities to advance 15,000 *RD* but in general they took a firm line with the Mommas, repulsing supplies of goods in excess of market-demand and insisting on a strict adherence to the contractual terms. They were fully alive to the shift in trading patterns which meant that England and France were now directly supplied from Sweden instead of from Hamburg or Amsterdam, and accepted it philosophically as long as the Mommas did not press their markets too hard.[65] But that, in the Van Baerles' opinion, was precisely what they were doing in 1668. Already in July it was clear to them that London was over-supplied, with the result that copper-wire prices were 4 per cent lower than in Amsterdam.[66] Although they recommended that Marescoe should transfer his unsaleable stocks of kettles and cauldrons to Amsterdam, where they seemed more acceptable, they were far from wishing to recapture his trade. On the contrary, what concerned them was Marescoe's ability to profit, for it was upon his prosperity and the reliability of his bills of exchange that much of their own security depended. It was an immense relief to them when, in July, Marescoe agreed to cover their drafts to a limit of £5,000 at $4\frac{1}{2}$ per cent if need arose.[67]

Their fellow-agent, Peter Simons (described by the Van Baerles as 'a young man of

[61] G. Dunt to CM, 30 June 1668.

[62] H. B. Johan to CM, 21 April, 19 May 1668.

[63] At this date A. & J. Momma's consignments to CM were worth at least £10,000 and by the end of 1668 they had supplied nearly £27,000-worth.

[64] RA, Stockholm, Momma-Reenstierna MSS, E.2498 (7 December 1666).

[65] Ibid. (29 November 1667).

[66] Ibid. (19 June 1668).

[67] Van Baerles to CM, 27 July 1668.

Swedish nationality, who does good business on commission but has otherwise no special capital')[68] was equally affected by Swedish pressures. He confided to Marescoe that he needed to find large sums on behalf of the Tar Company, and welcomed the facility which Marescoe's contract with the Company provided, to draw £5 against each last of tar, £9 against each last of pitch, and £2,000 above that.[69] Yet even this was not enough, and a fortnight later he was seeking further cover for drafts of 6,000 RD due in October.[70] There were clear indications of the pressures Pötter & Thuen had confessed to six months before when, with unusual candour they had told Marescoe of 'the considerable sum we must furnish the King with in the autumn'.[71] This was a rare admission of the underlying difficulties confronting the copper-contract partners.

Thus the 1668 import-correspondence yields the impression of a trading structure rather precariously balanced on credits made available in London and Amsterdam. If handled with discretion and skill, as the Van Baerles devoutly wished, the cycle of credit and commodities could revolve to mutual advantage, although it was vulnerable to unforeseen contingencies and unavoidable constraints. Shipwrecks could be insured against, and potential bankrupts avoided, but the constraint which perhaps most seriously affected the Swedish operation was that cynosure of seventeenth-century commercial policy, the English Navigation Acts. Abraham Momma heartily approved of them—for Sweden's sake. 'The English laws with regard to shipping I regard as very useful for the kingdom of Sweden as they will do a great deal to increase ship-building, all the more as there are plenty of facilities for it at many places.'[72] Yet, like his brothers, he found the application of the Navigation Acts both puzzling and inconvenient. Indeed, to a remarkable degree, some of Marescoe's most important Swedish correspondents of 1668 were still unsure of their exact requirements. Did they mean, asked Pötter & Thuen, that we can send no Swedish-owned ships built in Holland? What is the position regarding ships built in some third country, pressed Debora van Ruyff?[73] 'I understood,' wrote Steven de Geer, 'that all ships that Sweden has acquired up to 1662 were free, as if they were built in Sweden, but not those acquired after',[74] and he also believed, more correctly, that a distinction was made between tar imports (which were enumerated) and iron imports (which were not).[75]

If it seems strange that such experienced traders should have been unsure about principles so clearly laid down in 1651 and confirmed in 1660 and 1662,[76] then one has only to recall the confusion caused by successive suspensions and qualifications of the Navigation Acts during and after the second Anglo–Dutch war, and by the apparent contradictions of Anglo–Swedish treaties. On 22 March 1665 the Navigation Acts had been temporarily suspended so far as they applied to Baltic and Norwegian trade,[77] and partly as a result there had been a

---

[68] Same to same, 13 April 1668.

[69] P. Simons to CM, 14 September 1668.

[70] Same to same, 28 September 1668.

[71] Pötter & Thuen to CM, 21 March 1668.

[72] A. Momma to CM, 12 December 1668.

[73] Pötter & Thuen to CM, 21 March 1668; D. van Ruyff to CM, 2 January 1669.

[74] S. de Geer to CM, 20 November 1668 [51].

[75] Same to same, 16 November 1668 [49].

[76] For the text of the 1651 'Act for Increase of Shipping, and Encouragement of the Navigation of this Nation' see C. H. Firth & R. S. Rait (eds) *Acts and Ordinances of the Interregnum* (London, 1911) 2, pp. 559–62. For the 'Act for the Encouraging and increasing of Shipping and Navigation' (12 Car. II. c. 18) and 'Act for preventing Frauds and regulating Abuses in His Majesties Customs' (14 Car. II. c. 11) see *Statutes of the Realm* (London, 1810–28) V, pp. 246–50, 393–400.

[77] *Bibliotheca Lindesiana*, (vol. 5) *A Bibliography of Royal Proclamations of the Tudor and Stuart Sovereigns and others published under authority, 1485–1714*, ed. R. R. Steele (Oxford, 1910) I, p. 412.

considerable expansion in the Swedish merchant-marine. Numbering about 75 ships, averaging 88 lasts burthen in 1663, it had grown rapidly in 1666 and 1667 and by July 1667 had more than doubled to 194 ships averaging 95 lasts.[78] These were the ships which, as Swedish protests stressed, had kept England supplied with vital commodities during the war. But, answered the English, they were also ships whose truly Dutch identity was only thinly disguised. Like the Hamburgers' notorious flag of convenience, that of Sweden had been no protection against the kind of costly molestation which had made Marescoe rich in 1666–7. In the light of these conflicts it is easier to understand the terms of the Anglo–Swedish treaties signed in Stockholm and London on 1 March 1665 and 16 February 1666.[79] Seeking to appease these misunderstandings in time of war, clause 18 of the former and clause 3 of the latter provided for mutually free commerce of their merchants, *and* their shipping whether built in their respective countries or 'bought from other places with royal consent'.[80] True, the treaty of 1661, signed in London, had already guaranteed such freedom in clauses 4 and 10, but 'provided the laws, ordinances, and particular rights of each nation, concerning trade and commerce, be observed on both sides'.[81] It was this proviso which some English statesmen believed should override the looser terms of the later treaties,[82] and it was inevitable that, sooner or later, the latent contradictions in these clauses would be forced to appear. Although the Order in Council of 18 March 1668 again dispensed timber imports from the operation of the Navigation Acts,[83] their general application to other goods had been reasserted by the proclamations of 23 August and 30 September 1667.[84]

Thus, although Pötter & Thuen knew that they would need special permission to send Dutch ships to England, they had some reason for wondering whether Swedish ships, Dutch-built, might not be free. Like De Geer, they had been confused by the terminal date in October 1662 placed upon foreign-built ships which could be naturalized as English,[85] and its effect on clause 8 of the 1660 Navigation Act, restricting the import of the enumerated goods either to English ships or 'such forraigne ships and vessels as are of the built of that Country or place of which the said Goods are the growth production or Manufacture . . .'.[86] The Swedish Board of Trade had received, apparently, unguarded assurances from the English Resident, the young and inexperienced Thomas Thynne, that imports in Dutch-built Swedish ships would be free,[87] but it is evident that Marescoe had warned Pötter & Thuen that while this might be true for iron and (temporarily) for timber it would not be so for tar.[88]

While this issue hung in doubt there were other threats being levelled in England to

[78] B. Fahlborg, 'Ett blad ur den svenska handelsflottans historia (1660–1675)' *Historisk Tidskrift* (1923) pp. 217, 240.

[79] Parry (ed.) *Consolidated Treaty Series*, VIII, pp. 263–81, IX, pp. 10–20.

[80] The French text reads—'*Qu en temps de Guerre, les Vaisseaux, Marchands de l'un & l'autre des Confederez & de leurs Sujets, soit qu'ils ayents été construits dans le Royaume de la Grand Bretagne ou dans celui de Suede, dans les Provinces & Domaines qui leur sont soumis ou ailleurs, ou achétez en d'autres lieux avec le Consentement, & Permission Royale . . . seront pourvus de tels Passeports & Certificats . . .'* etc.

[81] Parry (ed.) *Consolidated Treaty Series*, VI pp. 469–94.

[82] See Leyonbergh's letter of 14 October 1668 [40] reporting his conversation with the Lord Privy Seal (Lord Robartes). For Leyonbergh's letters to Lord Arlington of 23 and 24 October, appealing to these treaty clauses, see PRO, SP. 95/7 ff. 69, 70.

[83] PRO, PC. 2/60 p. 232; *CSPD, 1667–68*, pp. 285–6.

[84] *Tudor and Stuart Proclamations* (ed. Steele) I, pp. 422, 423.

[85] See clause 5 of the 1662 statute of Frauds (14 Car. II. c. 11).

[86] *Statutes of the Realm*, V, p. 248.

[87] This is alleged by the Tar Company directors in their letters of 24 October [50] and 14 November 1668.

[88] Pötter & Thuen, 18 April 1668.

Sweden's trade in general and to Marescoe's in particular. Long-standing grievances against mounting Swedish iron-imports were brought to a head in February 1668, partly by Eastland Company representations to the Privy Council.[89] After consideration of the arguments, the Council's committee of trade took the view, reported on 7 April, that a fair balance between English and Swedish production (the merits of which were frankly acknowledged) should be struck by some additional imposition on iron imported in foreign shipping.[90] The matter was referred to the House of Commons, just on the eve of adjournments which kept it in abeyance until October 1669, and thus the proposal was not seriously considered until its incorporation in the abortive Foreign Commodities Bill of 1670–1.[91]

1668 was not the first occasion on which proposals for a differential duty on foreign iron imports had been raised. It had been advanced in 1664, and on that occasion it seems the Eastland Company had joined in the successful opposition.[92] Marescoe too had evidently been among those mobilized to lobby about it, and this must be one of the rare occasions on which he and the Company were in accord.[93]

Why Marescoe failed to become a member of the Eastland Company cannot be explained easily. Most of his colleagues and rivals joined—James Burkin and Abraham Wessell in 1662, Benjamin Ayloff in 1663, Adam Lyell in 1666, Samuel Sowton in 1669, George Shuttleworth in 1672, Theodore Jacobsen in 1676, Urban Hall in 1679, Jacob David in 1682, and both Peter Joye and Moses Coulon in 1683.[94] Marescoe, on the contrary, was obliged to pay the Company's impositions on iron and copper at the rate reserved for unfreemen—i.e. 2s per ton for iron, on top of the 7s per ton customs duty required by the Book of Rates. Scribbled entries in his petty-cash accounts are too imprecise about weights to allow an exact deduction of the Eastland Company's tariff, which seems to have varied arbitrarily, but they do reveal that he paid their collector, John Chaplin, at least £40 in 1663 and nearly £90 in 1664. He would doubtless have had to pay more, on pitch and tar, but for a successful skirmish between the Swedish Resident, Leyonbergh, and the Eastland Company in May 1663. On that occasion the King and Council had upheld the Resident's complaint and ordered the Company on May 13th:

> 'not to give any hinderance or molestacon unto any Swedish-built Shipps, Navigated & Manned with the subjects of the King of Sweden, & Laden with Goods of the naturall growth & product of that Kingdome, Trading into any Ports of his Majesty's Dominions, According to the late Act of Navigacon . . . .'.[95]

An undated copy of what must have been Leyonbergh's representation to Charles II is to be found in Swedish diplomatic archives,[96] and it is interesting, not merely for its charge of arbitrary levies and violent seizures by the Eastland Company, but for the fact that it is written in Marescoe's unmistakeable hand. Bearing all the marks of a draft, with certain

---

[89] PRO, SP. 29/238, No. 20—'Report of the Committee of Trade touching an addicionall Impost on Forrain Iron'.

[90] Ibid.; *CSPD, 1667–68*, p. 332. Sir Joseph Williamson's notes on the discussion, 'Iron, 1668', are in PRO, SP. 29/251 No. 183. Other pressure groups included the Blacksmiths Company and Sussex ironmasters—*The Bulstrode Papers, I (1667–1675), The Collection of Autograph Letters and Historical Documents formed by Alfred Morrison*, Second Series, 1882–93 (Privately printed, 1897) pp. 29–30, 33, 35.

[91] *HMC*, 9th Report, Appendix—House of Lords MSS, pp. 8a–9a.

[92] R. W. K. Hinton, *The Eastland Trade and the Common Weal in the Seventeenth Century* (Cambridge, 1959) p. 119.

[93] Marescoe's petty-cash book, 'Charges of Marchandize, 1661–1674' p. 81, records on 4 April 1664 '*om naer Westminster te gaen weegen eenige v[er]hoogingh van de Toll op Iser end st[ael]*—2s 6d.'

[94] Hinton, op. cit. pp. 221–4.

[95] PRO, PC. 2/56 pp. 398, 401, 409; Hinton, op. cit. p. 141.

[96] RA, Stockholm, Diplomatica Anglica, 83 (contained in one of 5 packets of undated drafts).

forceful insertions, its command of English and its fluent legalisms nevertheless suggest that this was a professional production, penned but not composed by Marescoe. Yet, he was intimately involved in the whole operation and certain entries in his petty-cash book suggest that he was acting as paymaster on the Tar Company's behalf. On June 8th, 13th, and 20th he paid £20 to Leyonbergh, 10s to his secretary and £2 to officials for expenses 'aengaende d'Oostlandtse Comp^{a}'.[97]

This resounding success was not the end of the matter: Marescoe was to be embroiled with the Company's representatives at Hull in 1669.[98] But in 1668 Marescoe and Leyonbergh were faced by an even more formidable attempt to levy differential duties on Swedish goods entering London. This was the levy of 'water-bailage' (or 'balliage') by the Mayor and Corporation of London—a charge of allegedly immemorial origin placed upon aliens and foreigners not free of the City of London who brought goods into the river Thames.[99] Currently farmed out for only £27 p.a., it had recently become the object of an attempt by the impoverished City to inflate it into a general tariff on foreign and domestic goods— allegedly designed to yield £8,000–£10,000 p.a.[100] This, its opponents argued, was a flagrant usurpation which challenged the fiscal sovereignty of the King and the Commons in Parliament.

The two men whom the City authorities identified as the 'turbulent' ringleaders in opposition to water-bailage were John Gould and Charles Marescoe.[101] Marescoe had evidently tested and lost the issue in the Lord Mayor's Court during 1664. A note of 8 October that year records payment of 3s 9d 'about giving security to the Mayor's Court concerning water bailage'. John Gould seems to have tried and failed in an action before Chief Justice Keeling in the King's Bench during November 1667.[102] Yet a novel levy on this scale understandably roused the resentment of interests far broader than those Marescoe represented and he was able to assemble impressive support from leading City figures, such as Sir William Hooker, Sir Thomas Alleyn, Sir John Laurence, Sir Andrew Riccard and Sir John Banks.[103] Ultimately, however, it was Marescoe's mobilization of the Swedish Resident which proved decisive.

Marescoe and Joh[a]n Barckman Leyonbergh[104] had been collaborating closely for some years and it was through the latter's representation on behalf of the Tar Company that Marescoe eventually received a kind of official recognition as Swedish 'Royal Factor' by the

[97] 'Charges of Marchandize' pp. 57–8.

[98] W. Skinner to CM, 2 March, 9 March, 11 March, 16 March, [77, 87] 9 April, 20 April, 27 April, 8 June, 1669. In resisting the Hull representatives of the Eastland Company in their demand for impositions on imported pitch and tar Marescoe seems to have invoked the Order in Council of May 1663, but the Company's shrewd final word was 'the goods are yours and you being an Englishman this order will not excuse the goods, tho' brought in a Sweedish ship'—Skinner to CM, 8 June 1668. Marescoe eventually paid the imposition of 1s per last on pitch and 8d per last on tar.

[99] P. E. Jones & R. Smith, *A Guide to the Records in the Corporation of London Records Office and the Guildhall Library Muniments Room* (London, 1951) p. 94; *Analytical Index to the Remembrancia of the City of London, AD 1574– 1664* (London, 1878) p. 322.

[100] Miscellaneous Marescoe papers—undated draft of the prosecution evidence, to be witnessed by Mr Gould, Sir William Hooker, CM and PJ.

[101] PRO, SP. 29/276 f. 204—'The State of the Case of the auntient Tolls of Waterballiage paid to the Cittie of London'.

[102] CLRO, Repertories, vol. 73 f. 11b.

[103] Miscellaneous Marescoe papers—undated. Alleyn, Laurence and Hooker were Lord Mayors of London, respectively in 1659–60, 1664–5 and 1673–4. Riccard was a former Alderman and MP for London (in 1654) and, like Sir John Banks, a director of the East India Company.

[104] For Joh[a]n Barckman, Lord Leyonbergh [Leijonbergh] (b. 1625, d. 1691) see *Svenskt biografiskt lexicon*. He remained in England from 1658 until his death, was made a baronet in 1674 and elected F.R.S. in 1687.

English Privy Council in January 1668.[105] Marescoe, for his part, had acted as banker to Leyonbergh, doling out loans and sharing the proceeds of lucrative deals. Most noteworthy are the profits they managed to cream off from the £10,000 which Charles II had advanced to the Swedish government in 1666.[106] Lent by Edward Backwell, the leading goldsmith-banker, it was shrewdly re-deposited by Marescoe—£6,000 with Backwell at 5 per cent, £4,000 with Francis & Isaac Meynell at 6 per cent. While a needy Swedish government fumed and fretted for its money in the face of Leyonbergh's plausible excuses, the Resident coolly pocketed £174 15s 8d in accrued interest before Marescoe transmitted the sum across the exchanges.[107] They had shared similarly in the fees and gratuities arising from the shipping disputes of the Anglo–Dutch war.

The issue now facing them was to prove less lucrative and more troublesome for it involved deeply vested London interests and touched upon the central commercial policies of the English state. In a memorial, read before the Privy Council on 16 September 1668, Leyonbergh accused the Mayor and Corporation of the City of London, through their agents, of laying novel and illegal duties on goods imported from Sweden.[108] While he acknowledged the validity of certain traditional duties, namely 3d per last on tar and pitch, 6d per ton on iron and 1s 6d per 100 deals, he denounced recent additions, of 12d per last on tar and pitch, 2d per ton on iron and 4d per 100 deals. In response to this challenge the Privy Council called upon the Lord Mayor and the City to explain themselves.

Unhappily, just at this juncture the problem of ship-nationality, which had been troubling De Geer, Van Ruyff, the Tar Company and Pötter & Thuen, was forced to a crisis. Some time in mid-September, the Tar Company ship *Suyderström* was raided by London customs-officers, as it lay half-unloaded at its berth, on the grounds of it being Dutch-built and thus in violation of the Navigation Acts. Its cargo of 100 lasts of tar and 32 lasts of pitch was seized. Two other Dutch-built Tar Company ships, the *Beata* and the *St Anna*, following close behind, were checked in the Thames. By the end of September there were altogether six Swedish Tar Company ships held in suspense as the issue of their freedom to unload was laid before the King and Council.[109]

With these two issues of shipping and water-bailage concurrently in hand, October and November were intensely busy months for Marescoe and Leyonbergh and very lucrative ones for their lawyers. But despite a protracted series of representations and conversations [39–44] the shipping suit did not prosper. Notwithstanding sympathetic murmurs from King Charles, whose overtures to Sweden were at a critical stage,[110] it seems evident that the revived Council of Trade was of Lord Ashley's view[111] and determined to enforce the letter of the Navigation Acts. By 29 October Leyonbergh was conceding defeat, and after

---

[105] PRO, PC. 2/60 p. 133 (17 January 1668).

[106] See p. 117.

[107] For the Swedish government's frustration see B. Fahlborg, *Sveriges yttre politik, 1664–1668* (Stockholm, 1949) I, pp. 452–3; Wittrock, I, pp. 322–3, 406–8. Peter Juncker of Hamburg (see pp. 53, 117) handled these remittances and his correspondence with Leyonbergh survives in RA, Stockholm, Diplomatica Anglica, 108.

[108] PRO, PC. 2/61 p. 12. The draft of what is probably this petition survives in RA, Stockholm, Diplomatica Anglica, 83.

[109] The fate of the six ships was watched closely by the Danish representative in London—see W. Westergaard, *The First Triple Alliance. The Letters of Christopher Lindenov, Danish Envoy to London, 1668–1672* (London, 1947) pp. 39, 47.

[110] This was the eve of the Earl of Carlisle's departure as ambassador-extraordinary to Sweden, bearing the order of the Garter for the young Charles XI as part of the diplomatic consolidation of the Triple Alliance—K. G. Feiling, *British Foreign Policy, 1660–1672* (Oxford, 1930) pp. 276–9, 281; Fahlborg, *Sveriges yttre politik, 1664–1668*, II pp. 522–35.

[111] Leyonbergh to CM, 29 October 1668 [44].

unloading their iron (which was not enumerated) five of the waiting ships slipped away to deliver their pitch and tar cargoes elsewhere.

The water-bailage case was more successful. Pressed again upon the Privy Council on 25 November and 15 January, Leyonbergh's demand for 'Quo Warranto' proceedings against the City of London was granted on 20 January 1669, and after official action by the Attorney General the validity of the levies was condemned in the Court of Exchequer.[112] This was not entirely the end of the matter, and the burden it removed was a modest one when compared with that exacted by the Eastland Company. But the Eastland Company too had suffered a reverse. Its petition of 18 September 1668 for the restatement of its privileges was given little encouragement and it entered now upon the final decline of its effective authority.[113]

Yet the Swedish producers, who had watched the whole business with gloom and irritation, might well have preferred to lose the water-bailage case and win the shipping one. Throughout 1668 their capacity to supply cargoes had not been matched by their ability to freight them [21]. The Mommas, Pötter & Thuen and the Tar Company all complained of a shipping shortage, rendered worse by the ambiguities of English policy. No wonder freight rates were too high to make timber cargoes profitable. Ultimately, the diversion from London of pitch and tar cargoes worth about £3,880 gross (at current market prices) was a troublesome set-back for the Tar Company and a serious blow to Peter Simons' precarious position.

For Marescoe, however, the vexations of October could not spoil a year which was nearly as outstanding for its imports as it was for its exports.[114] His Swedish suppliers had managed to send him forty different ships on a total of forty-two voyages, bearing cargoes for him worth over £49,000 gross (c.i.f.). 5.4 per cent of this sum was accounted for by steel, latten and brass-ware, 21 per cent by pitch and tar and 36 per cent by iron. An unequalled 36.6 per cent was in copper, 158 tons of it—a figure considerably larger than the 1668–9 'Book of Tables' prepares one for,[115] and perhaps less revealing of demand in England than of the needs of the Mommas who had supplied 96 per cent of it. What profit the low prices of 1668 yielded them cannot be established, but for Marescoe the year's imports brought their usual variety of earnings and contributed at least 55 per cent of his total profits.

It also brought prospects of future gains. Joachim Pötter, ennobled as Lillienhoff in September 1668, had been appointed head of the Swedish Mint and he wanted to know if Marescoe could supply Spanish silver from England, and at what price. Jacob Momma had heard the rumours of a planned copper coinage in England and was offering to supply the copper blanks [57]. More helpfully, Willem Momma was trying to put Marescoe in touch with his brother-in-law, Abraham Cronström, the young but very able partner in his family's Avesta copper interests. Abraham was temporarily unavailable, ostensibly touring

[112] PRO, PC. 2/61 pp. 102, 169, 175, 181; CLRO, Repertories, vol. 73 f. 287b; Westergaard, op. cit. p. 74. Samuel Pepys was an interested eye-witness of the hearing on 20 January 1669—*The Diary of Samuel Pepys* (ed. Latham & Matthews) IX p. 421. The City argued that it had mis-pleaded its case and the Chief Baron (Sir Matthew Hale) suspended entry of judgment, but on re-opening the case in 1672 the King in Council ordered it to be recorded against the City—CLRO, Repertories, vol. 75, ff. 2, 16b, 57, 84, 117b; vol. 77, ff. 45b, 79b–80, 81b, 87b, 89, 102, 174, 201; PRO, PC. 2/63 pp. 165, 176, 178, 183, 285.

[113] Hinton, *The Eastland Trade*, pp. 148, 151.

[114] See pp. 577–8. Tables A.1, A.2.

[115] According to the 'Book of Tables'—BL Add. MS, 36, 785—London's copper and latten imports from 'the Eastland' (i.e. the whole Baltic area, including Sweden) totalled $36\frac{1}{4}$ tons between Michaelmas 1668 and Michaelmas 1669. By re-working Marescoe's copper imports to match this accounting period one still reaches a total of $73\frac{3}{4}$ tons—a discrepancy which could be explained if some of Marescoe's copper was recorded as from Germany, which supplied $202\frac{1}{2}$ tons in this period.

German spas but in fact spying on the iron-works of the Rhineland.[116] On his return, however, negotiations with Marescoe were opened which led to the contract already described. If efforts to persuade his brother Isaac Cronström to employ Marescoe had succeeded, the prospects for him would have been dazzling and the Mommas would have achieved their aim to create an effective cartel for the marketing of Swedish copper in London. Finally, to inaugurate the new year of 1669, Steven de Geer put Marescoe in touch with one of the greatest iron dealers of the Netherlands, Louis Trip.[117] Trip's first letter [69] offered only a trial consignment, but it was of the coveted voyage iron variety, and from a man who handled nearly 30 per cent of Amsterdam's iron-imports it made an auspicious beginning to the year.[118]

Not all the promise of 1669 was fulfilled. The Tar Company, denied the use of its Dutch-built shipping, had to struggle to meet its contractual quota, scouring the Baltic ports for a series of small and inadequate vessels, and it was not rewarded for its pains. Marescoe, on 29 January 1669, had sent off a draft schedule for Tar Company shipments:

		Tar	*Pitch*
To: Yarmouth		60 lasts	10 lasts
Plymouth		70	30
London	in June	250	100
Bristol		70	40
Isle of Wight		30	10
Yarmouth		70	20
Hull	in August	60	10
Bristol		70	20
London		220	70
		900	310*

* In Marescoe's draft, this column was mis-totalled as '300'.

He had based this distribution on the sanguine estimates of consumption sent in by his outport correspondents [23–25, 94]. Bristol in particular had held out confident prospects for the sale of 80–120 lasts of pitch and 160–250 lasts of tar [71], and in Yarmouth a normally shrewd and reliable kinsman placed encouraging orders for a whole range of Swedish commodities [72, 113]. Yet the outcome was considerably less satisfactory, and although William Browne of Bristol appears to have done his best, particularly to shift iron, the experience of supplying English outports appears to have left both the Tar Company and Pötter & Thuen thoroughly disillusioned [129]. The lesson they had learned was that no reliance could be placed on small, provincial markets where demand was sluggish and easily spoiled by random, speculative consignments. In several instances, isolated cargoes of Norwegian tar or Dutch iron, on terms and at prices which undercut their own, had deprived them of any prospect of profit, and they sulkily withdrew from the competition.[119] Indeed, several of Marescoe's correspondents of 1668 did not reappear in 1669. Of Hegerstierna there was no further sign, and the Gothenburg dealers made little showing. With two-thirds of their town in ashes after the fire

[116] *Svenskt biografiskt lexikon*, 'Cronström, Abraham' (b. 1640, d. 1696) by B. Boethius, p. 368.
[117] For Louis Trip (b. 1605, d. 1684) see Klein, *De Trippen*, passim.
[118] Klein, op. cit. p. 432.
[119] Tar Company to CM, 18 September 1669.

of 10 May,[120] this is hardly surprising and some, like Nicolas Preus, who had suffered a loss of 19,000 *RD* in two years, turned away from independent trade to supply the larger Stockholm dealers such as Pötter & Thuen.[121] With the expiry of the timber-trade exemption from the Navigation Acts in March 1669,[122] and the defeat on Dutch-built shipping, the Swedish contribution of timber appears to have dried up. Certainly Marescoe received only a negligible amount in 1669, although Jacob Momma-Reenstierna was ready with 20–30 shiploads, if passes could be procured for Dutch-built ships. But they could not, and it was partly to this chronic shortage of shipping that Jacob attributed his inability to send more than a fraction of the copper that he and his brother had sent in 1668. Indeed, had it not been for the appearance of Abraham Cronström as a major copper-supplier Marescoe would have received in 1669 little more than one-tenth of the quantity he had been sent by the Mommas in the preceding year. As it is, his supplies of copper were down by nearly 75 per cent, which is puzzling in a year which, allegedly, saw copper production rise 18 per cent in Sweden.[123] The Mommas' letters talk, rather, of a copper shortage and high prices, and by October 1669 they had sent only 852 shippounds (about 114 tons) to London, Amsterdam and Rouen combined.[124] The truth is, 1669 was another difficult year for the Mommas, both at home and abroad. Jacob's enterprises on Gotland and Ösel were bringing them nothing but trouble; he was quarrelling with the De Geers, and his works faced a series of problems from bad weather, shortages of raw materials and labour-disputes.[125] Abroad, the demand for brass and copper-wares seemed to flag, and although Jacob Momma and the Van Baerles goaded Marescoe with talk of prices in Hamburg and Amsterdam being 1 per cent higher than in London,[126] the truth (revealed in the Van Baerles' letters to Sweden) was that the European market was undergoing some worrying changes. Spanish demand for copper pins had slumped and low grain prices in Poland had stopped sales there. Norwegian copper was undercutting Swedish and—to cap it all—Japanese copper had again appeared in quantity.[127]

For the last decade, the directorate of the Dutch East India Company had been calling for increased shipments—800,000 lb. in 1658, 900,000 lb. in 1663 and 2,000,000 lb. in 1668.[128] They saw no limit to the potential European demand, and it was fortunate for the Swedish producers that actual supplies to Europe fell far short of the Company's targets. In the four war-years, 1664 to 1667, Japanese copper-imports averaged about 380,000 lb. per annum, but in 1668 (according to Professor Glamann) 506,250 lb. arrived, and in 1669, 400,500 lb.[129] The Van Baerle letters to Sweden tend to confirm these proportions, speaking of 400,000 lb.– 500,000 lb. arriving with the thirteen East India Company ships in 1668, and 337,500 lb. in

---

[120] N. Preus to CM, 28 May; J. van Savelant to CM, 29 May; H. Paffraht to CM, 20 June, 1669.

[121] N. Preus to CM, 28 May 1669.

[122] PRO, PC. 2/61 p. 263; Westergaard, *The First Triple Alliance*, p. 76.

[123] Wolontis, *Kopparmyntningen i Sverige, 1624–1714*, p. 221.

[124] RA, Stockholm, E. 2498, Van Baerles to J. Reenstierna, 15 October 1669.

[125] Sondén, pp. 159–61; RA, Stockholm, E.2475 (J. Momma letterbook, 17 December 1667–23 July 1669, pp. 206–9, 226, 230, 233–4, 237, 251–2, 282, 300–1).

[126] J. Reenstierna to CM, 11 January, 5 February, 24 September [**111**], 8 October, [**116**] 22 October, 19 November 1669 [**124**]; Van Baerles to CM, 1 March, 23 April, 24 May, 6 September 1669. In their letter of 6 September the Van Baerles claimed to obtain 4–5 per cent more for their sales of copper-wire than Marescoe.

[127] RA, Stockholm, E.2498, Van Baerles to J. Reenstierna, 2 April, 13 April, 2 July, 24 September, 22 October 1669; 10 June 1670.

[128] K. Glamann, *Dutch-Asiatic Trade, 1620–1740* (Copenhagen/The Hague, 1958) p. 175.

[129] K. Glamann, 'The Dutch East India Company's Trade in Japanese Copper, 1645–1736', *The Scandinavian Economic History Review*, I (1953) p. 52.

the ships of 1669.[130] More significantly, they confirm that the Japanese copper was of a quality which commanded a premium of 2 or 3 per cent above Swedish garcopper, which fell steeply in price on the Amsterdam market, from *f*.61 per 100 lb. in the first fortnight of 1669 to a low of *f*.54 in late May.[131] Although it recovered by August, it settled around the lower figure of *f*.58, whereas in Hamburg, which had experienced a synchronous fall, the recovery was much bolder and more buoyant, partly because of French and Italian demand.[132] J. J. Hiebenaer, who had already taken about 310 slb of copper-wire from Willem and Jacob Momma during 1669, was ready to take another 100 slb as late as mid-December—so brisk were his sales.[133] In England too, copper-wire prices began a sharp rise in late November and December, from their plateau of £5 10s to £6, or even £6 10s per cwt. Yet this was too late to appease Jacob Reenstierna whose dissatisfaction with Marescoe's handling of the London copper market was beginning to become apparent to his other agents in Amsterdam.[134] By the new year of 1670 it is clear that he was considering a transfer of his commissions to some other London correspondent.

However, while copper imports from the Mommas were sharply curtailed in 1669, iron imports reached their highest level so far. At 1,700 tons Marescoe's receipts are equivalent to 53 per cent of the alleged 'Eastland' iron imports of London for the period Michaelmas 1668–Michaelmas 1669, as recorded by the 'Book of Tables'.[135] Although Gothenburg's share fell from its 15 per cent of 1668 to only 9.3 per cent in 1669, the loss of Värmland voyage iron was partly made good by Steven de Geer's strenuous efforts to supply this desirable and profitable commodity.[136] About 40 per cent of his consignments are identifiable as voyage iron, made at the Österby works, although—as he admitted—the quality of the output was coarser and less economical than the usual Gothenburg standard.[137] Debora van Ruyff also had voyage iron produced, although in view of its scarcity she was disappointed that the London price failed to rise much above 15s per cwt.[138] Once again the Swedish suppliers had to warn Marescoe that brisker and more lucrative sales were being made at first hand to English dealers in Sweden, and as the year ended with another autumnal drought, forcing works to a standstill for two or three months,[139] the prospects for future shipments seemed poor. Abraham Reenstierna, who had made particularly large consignments of ordinary iron, was as disappointed as his brother with the London market's behaviour and wrote, unrealistically, of bringing all Swedish iron sales into a few dealers' hands [**109**]. Whether those hands would include Marescoe's was carefully left in doubt.

The threat to Marescoe's agency was deferred until 1670, but 1669 had already brought him its own disasters. One was the death of his infant son, Charles, some time in early May, aged barely one year.[140] The other, which cast a longer shadow over the correspondence, was the bankruptcy of Peter Simons in the middle of March. Although, with hindsight, signs of strain can be discerned in Simons' affairs well before the event, his actual collapse evidently

---

130 RA, Stockholm, E.2498, Van Baerles to J. Reenstierna, 24 July 1668; 2 July 1669.
131 Ibid. 25 September, 9 October 1668; 8 January, 22 January, 22 May 1669.
132 RA, Stockholm, E.2506, J. J. Hiebenaer to J. Reenstierna, 26 June, 24 July, 23 October 1669.
133 Ibid. 11 December 1669.
134 RA, Stockholm, E.2498, Van Baerles to J. Reenstierna, 8 April 1670. They had warned Marescoe of the Reenstiernas' growing dissatisfaction on 23 April 1669.
135 BL, Add. MSS 36, 785.
136 S. de Geer to CM, 21 May, 30 May, 18 October 1669.
137 Same to same, 14 June, 11 October, 18 October 1669.
138 D. van Ruyff to CM, 16 July, 4 September, 25 September, 9 October 1669.
139 S. de Geer to CM, 20 December 1669, 7 January 1670.
140 The Van Baerles offered their condolences on 31 May 1669.

came as a great shock to Marescoe, who stood to lose £800 on bills of exchange drawn for his own account. The loss was all the more bitter since it was, oddly enough, unshared by the other 'friends' who had larger dealings with Simons, such as Pötter & Thuen and the Mommas. Marescoe's resentment of this anomaly probably contributed something to the souring of his relations with his Swedish principals.

However, the ascertainable facts about Simons' bankruptcy have a wider significance than for Marescoe's personal affairs. Simons, it was said, had invested speculatively in Setubal salt which he had expected to sell to the Västervik Ship Company (of which Pötter & Thuen, the Mommas, the Cronströms and Cronberg were major shareholders) and Amsterdam notarial records certainly confirm his involvement in this trade.[141] But he had also extended credits of about *f*.100,000 to various Swedish principals, unsecured against goods, and when faced with *f*.44,000 in bills drawn on him from Frankfurt found himself illiquid and drained of credit. The Van Baerles thought that his assets and liabilities should have balanced at about *f*.200,000. Debts of *f*.60,000 to the Tar Company were partly matched by *f*.41,000 owed by Pötter & Thuen and *f*.8,000 by Abraham Momma-Reenstierna. Other sums were owed to him in Sweden and he was given every facility to collect them by the Swedish authorities.[142] Yet, as the dust settled and a settlement was framed for his creditors it emerged that he could produce for them less than the 50 or 60 per cent that the Van Baerles had initially predicted. With debts totalling *f*.107,000 he offered his creditors only 30 per cent in June. This was pushed up to 35 per cent in August, and in September he wrote to Marescoe, offering 40 per cent,[143] but the Van Baerles began to share Marescoe's dissatisfaction for it was widely known that the Swedish creditors had been paid nearly in full while those in Amsterdam, where the bankruptcy had occurred, were left carrying a substantial loss.[144]

It was a timely warning to the Van Baerles about the risks of their Swedish commissions. At this moment they were already in negotiation with Jacob Reenstierna about a renewal of their three-year contract of 31 May 1667. It was not they but Jacob who was the suitor, offering a six- or even eight-year contract in return for an enlarged, and guaranteed loan-facility. However, the Van Baerles were reluctant to advance more than 16,000 *RD*. They pointed to the example of Peter Simons 'who ruined himself with too great disbursements for his friends' and they demanded that a limit should be set to the amount of drafts which they had to bear on behalf of goods sent to England or to France.[145] As it was, they expressed the opinion that the Mommas were sending too many goods to England; Marescoe's warehouse was bursting and the London market simply could not bear more.[146] Privately, they commiserated with Marescoe. He was not to blame for the sluggish sales and low prices: the fault lay in excessive supplies, and they had told Momma so.[147] Yet at the same time they were aghast at the risks Marescoe was prepared to take with his credit, and thus, indirectly, with their own. They were particularly appalled to hear it rumoured that Marescoe sometimes allowed the Tar Company to draw £4,000–£5,000 above the value of its goods in his hands.[148] With Simons' fate before them this was not an example they

[141] Van Baerles to CM, 29 March, 5 April 1669; GA, Amsterdam, Notarieel Archief, 1543 (J. van Oli) pp. 194, 205, 214; 2797 (P. van Buytene) pp. 81, 93.

[142] Van Baerles to CM, 5 April, 23 April 1669.

[143] Same to same, 14 June, 28 June, 12 July, 9 August, 27 August; P. Simons to CM, 6 September, 1669.

[144] Van Baerles to CM, 13 September 1669.

[145] RA, Stockholm, E.2498, Van Baerles to J. Reenstierna, 9 April, 31 August, 3 September, 8 October, 15 October 1669.

[146] Same to same, 13 April 1669.

[147] Same to CM, 3 May 1669.

[148] Same to same, 29 March, 12 April 1669.

intended to follow. The contract with Jacob Reenstierna, dated 1/10 October 1669 finally committed them to a 10,000 *RD* advance at 6 per cent, plus 5,000 *RD* every winter.[149] In return, Jacob was pledged to despatch them 1,000 shippounds of brass and copper-ware every year for five years, against which he could also draw bills payable at one month's sight. The Van Baerles were to insure the full value of the consignments at Jacob's expense and to receive the normal 2 per cent commission on sales. Under no circumstances was he to reveal publicly the full extent of the Van Baerles' advances, which could embarrass their credit in Amsterdam.[150]

The Van Baerles' caution contrasts interestingly with the inexperienced enthusiasm of two young Hamburg merchants who at this very time were being willingly drawn into the embarrassed affairs of the Cronberg syndicate. Louis and Liebert Wolters, aged 26 and 22 years respectively, were sons of Liebert Wolters, Sr. (1607–63), a nephew of the great Louis de Geer, who had become deeply and dangerously involved in the marketing of Swedish copper during the 1640s.[151] His risks and consequent losses had jeopardized the fortune he had built up by a diversified trade to France, Spain, and Italy, but his widow had stoutly carried on the business and in 1667 she formally ushered her two sons into the business life of their city. Liebert II had immediately turned towards Sweden and established an association with Börje Olofsson Cronberg, promising credits against Cronberg's copper deliveries to Hamburg. The arrangement was renewed in 1668, and by 1669 the brothers were ambitious to monopolize Swedish copper sales in Hamburg at the expense of their two main rivals, Peter Juncker and J. J. Hiebenaer.[152] From the outset, Cronberg fully exploited the credit which the Wolters extended, rapidly drawing 20,000 *RD* on bills which Juncker and others had refused to accept.[153] By 1669 the Wolters were beginning to emit piteous bleats that, as young merchants, it was very damaging for them to have so much money tied up in loans, but as copper deliveries continued to arrive they remained hopefully suspended on the Swedish hook and were reassured by the inevitable rupture between Cronberg and Juncker.[154] It was thus with a jaundiced eye that Juncker reported to London on the dangerous intrigues of the Cronberg–Wolters connection. 'Je vous advertir en confidence si [vous] avez encor affaire avec M. Cronberg a Stockholm d'aller caut [eleusement?]; il semble que les grandes embrassements sont ordinairement plus nuisibles que prouffitables, et les temps nous decouvrera encor beaucoup de chose estant le present temps fort dangereux . . .'.[155]

The ending of Juncker's commission trade with Cronberg has an unsurprising resemblance to the ending, in 1670, of Marescoe's commissions from Jacob Momma. In Juncker's case it was ostensibly caused by a quarrel over an insurance settlement[156] but more probably reflected the exhaustion of Juncker's willingness to extend further credit. In Marescoe's case likewise it was the Reenstiernas' need for fresh and more compliant sources of funds that encouraged Jacob to attempt a furtive transfer of consignments to Marescoe's close rivals, the firm of James Burkin & Joas Evertsen. Writing to them on 28 February 1670 he declared that after supplying Marescoe with commissions for sixteen years a misunderstand-

149 RA, Stockholm, E.2576.
150 RA, Stockholm, E.2498, 31 August, 8 October 1669.
151 R. Lohmann, *Die Familie Wolters in Hamburg während des 17 Jhs. und die Beziehungen von Liebert Wolters Vater und Sohn nach Sweden* (Doctoral dissertation, University of Cologne, 1969) pp. 59–60, 115.
152 Lohmann, pp. 161–171.
153 Ibid. pp. 170–3.
154 Ibid, pp. 171–3.
155 P. Juncker to CM, 23 November 1669.
156 Lohmann, p. 169.

ing had sprung up between them and that he now intended to transfer all his own business and, perhaps, that of his kinsmen.[157] If Burkin & Evertsen would accept drafts against shipments, despatched and insured, he could bring them the monopoly of Momma-Cronström consignments—but they must keep the offer secret: Marescoe would learn of it soon enough as goods began to reach his rivals.

Marescoe's letters to Jacob Reenstierna survive for these months, and they confirm his ignorance of what was afoot.[158] He was certainly puzzled that no further cargoes were reaching him. 'Lack of shipping' replied Momma. Yet Marescoe remained anxious to correspond and, having heard indirectly of the Momma-Cronström plans to send all their future copper-wire shipments to one London agent, he begged to be considered, offering the competitive terms of $1\frac{1}{2}$ per cent commission and 5 per cent interest on advances. Some weeks later, still hopeful, he was moved to write a justification of London's terms of business, which made it impossible for him to accept less than $1\frac{1}{2}$ per cent.[159] As it was, he offered credit terms which he thought so generous that, like the Van Baerles, he dared not allow them to be divulged to his other clients.

Regrettably, the loss of Marescoe's in-letters for all but the first few weeks of 1670 makes it impossible to trace in any detail the course of Swedish imports in the last months of his life. It is clear, however, that the Tar Company was also experiencing dissatisfaction with Marescoe over his refusal to extend full credit upon goods in transit.[160] In early October 1669 it had welcomed his promise to accept Joseph Deutz's drafts for up to £2,000, but at the same time urged him to accept £3,000–£4,000. Deutz, they revealed, had already accepted large drafts from them, totalling 30,000 RD, which would fall due in January and February 1670. It was therefore a matter of urgency that he should be able to cover his position with bills on London. 'A good part of the Company's welfare depends on it.'[161] Marescoe's reluctance to expose his credit beyond the agreed £2,000 forced them to remind him of the 5th article of their contract, under which they were entitled to draw £5 for each last of tar and £8 for each last of pitch. The accompanying schedule of shipments demonstrated their total entitlement to stand at £5,463 by December 1669, but against this Marescoe posed outstanding debts for his sales of pitch and tar, totalling £6,952 17s 10d.[162] His losses through Peter Simons and the fear of further bankrupticies hardened his resolution, and the surviving correspondence with the Company, as with some other Swedish principals, ends on a note of bitterness.

It is therefore not surprising to find Peter Juncker's condolences on Marescoe's death accompanied by a discreet warning to his widow and partner. 'Je vous dis aussi en confidence p[our] gouv[ern]e qu'il y a bien quelques Amis cogneus de vostre ville qui cerchent a vous prejudiquer et de tierer a eux aucunes Commissions, mais j'espere que cela ne leur reuscira pas purveu que vous tachiez de les servir a contentement.'[163]

As will appear, the Widow Marescoe's commission trade in Swedish commodities was never to be quite as lucrative again. From the inception of Marescoe's partnership with Peter Joye in April 1668 they had earned by far the largest portion of their profits from imports and import-related services—82.6 per cent in the first year, 88.5 per cent in 1669 and 56 per cent in the months before Marescoe's death in September 1670. By contrast, the partnership's

[157] RA, Stockholm, E.2483 (fragment of J. Reenstierna's letterbook, January–March 1670) p. 88.
[158] RA, Stockholm, E.2513 (18 letters, March–August 1670).
[159] RA, Stockholm, E.2513, CM to J. Reenstierna, 20 May 1670 [Appendix A, **6**].
[160] Tar Company to CM, 11 December [**130**], 25 December 1669.
[161] Same to same, 15 December 1669.
[162] Same to same, 15 December, 25 December 1669; 20 January, 14 May, 18 June 1670.
[163] P. Juncker to LM & PJ, 27 September 1670.

export commissions had brought in only 17.4 per cent, 8.7 per cent and 6.35 per cent in these respective periods. However, exports on Marescoe's sole account were more important, earning over 37 per cent of his profits on that account in 1668 and nearly 79 per cent in 1669. Altogether, in its diversity and geographical range (see Map 2), the exporting business of the Marescoe firm was far more demanding than the import side, and it is now time to look at the huge correspondence which it generated.

(ii) EXPORT

[a] HAMBURG

Of all the ports to which Marescoe's exports were consigned, Hamburg must rank first in significance both for the total value of the cargoes despatched and for the variety of the correspondence it produced. Indeed, Hamburg ranked in the forefront of destinations for England's export-trade as a whole, for this free Imperial city on the Elbe was the point of entry to a vast north-European hinterland reached by a network of waterways extending deep into Silesia, Saxony, Bohemia, Austria and southern Germany.[164] Overland, through Lübeck, Hamburg reached out to Scandinavia and the Baltic, while annual fleets carried its re-exports (English manufactures and products among them) eastwards to Russia and south to Iberia and the Mediterranean.[165] In the late-seventeenth century England was Hamburg's principal overseas supplier, followed closely by Spain and Holland.[166] The English Merchant Adventurers had had their staple in Hamburg since 1611 and they channelled through this a substantial proportion of England's cloth exports.[167] However, increasingly important for Hamburg and its hinterland were England's re-exports of colonial, Mediterranean and Far Eastern products. After cloth, it is currants and raisins which head the list of Hamburg's imported commodities in the 1670s, with sugar, tobacco, ginger and indigo ranking high behind them.[168] All came from markets where England's competitive position was now strong, if not dominant. She took nearly 85 per cent of Zante's currants[169] and was among the largest purchasers of Malaga raisins.[170] By the 1660s, her West Indian sugar production was believed to have outstripped supplies from Portuguese Brazil,[171] and her tobacco re-exports probably accounted for most of the overseas supplies available on the world market in Amsterdam.[172] Her Far Eastern imports were indeed outmatched by those of the Dutch East India Company, but even with her pepper shipments (four-fifths of which were being

[164] E. K. Newman, 'Anglo–Hamburg Trade in the late seventeenth and early eighteenth centuries' (unpublished doctoral dissertation, University of London, 1979) pp. 7–13.

[165] Newman, pp. 5, 13–16; E. Baasch, *Hamburgs Convoyschiffahrt und Convoywesen* (Hamburg, 1896).

[166] Newman, pp. 2–3. (The surviving Stade Elbe toll figures [for 1678] tend to underestimate England's leading role since they do not reflect the woollen textile imports which formed the largest portion of England's consignments.)

[167] Newman, pp. 231–91.

[168] Newman, p. 2.

[169] PRO, SP. 99/48 f. 148 (John Dodington to Sir Joseph Williamson, 5 December 1670).

[170] R. Davis, *The Rise of the English Shipping Industry in the 17th and 18th Centuries* (Newton Abbot, 1962) pp. 220, 236; R. Gravil, 'Trading to Spain and Portugal, 1670–1700' *Business History*, X, (1968) pp. 81–2.

[171] Josiah Child, *A new discourse of trade* (London, 1669) p. 220.

[172] J. Price, 'The Tobacco Adventure to Russia', *Transactions of the American Philosophical Society*, New Series, 51 (Philadelphia, 1961) pp. 5–6; H. K. Roessingh, *Inlandse Tabak*, A. A. G. Bijdragen 20 (Wageningen, 1976) pp. 238–44.

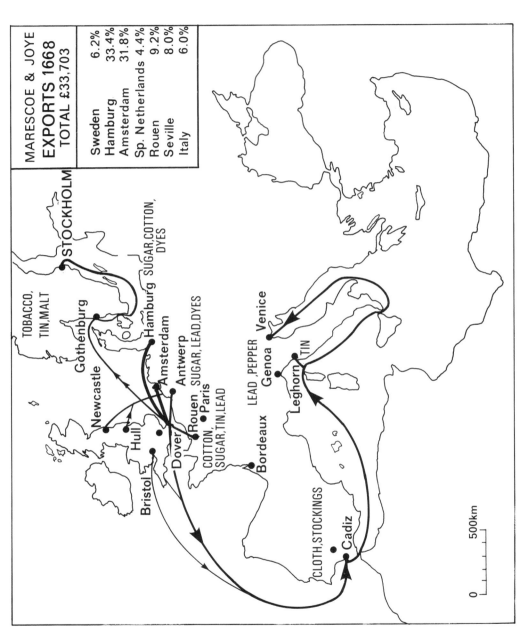

MARESCOE & JOYE
EXPORTS 1668
TOTAL £33,703

Sweden	6.2%
Hamburg	33.4%
Amsterdam	31.8%
Sp. Netherlands	4.4%
Rouen	9.2%
Seville	8.0%
Italy	6.0%

STOCKHOLM
TOBACCO, TIN, MALT
Göthenburg
Newcastle
Hamburg SUGAR, COTTON, DYES
Amsterdam
Antwerp SUGAR, LEAD, DYES
Rouen • Paris SUGAR, TIN, LEAD
Hull
Dover
COTTON, SUGAR, TIN, LEAD
Bristol
Bordeaux
LEAD, PEPPER Venice
Genoa
Leghorn TIN
Cadiz
CLOTH, STOCKINGS

0   500km

Map 2. Marescoe & Joye exports, 1668

re-exported by the 1650s) she was able to hold her own against Dutch imports which were sometimes six times larger.[173]

Thus Hamburg, innocent of colonial possessions and invariably neutral in the maritime conflicts of the century, was an almost perfect setting for the competitive struggle of the great trading powers. Although her population was only one-tenth the size of London's and a quarter that of Amsterdam's,[174] late-seventeenth century Hamburg contained a remarkably cosmopolitan and sophisticated merchant community. Between 50 and 60 per cent of her merchant burghers were immigrants—Dutch, Flemish, Portuguese and English—and many more were resident 'strangers'.[175] Through family or business associations with trading houses elsewhere, in the Baltic, Iberia, the Mediterranean and central Europe, this community was well-placed to act as a clearing-house for information and as a centre for bills of exchange. Indeed, Hamburg was second only to Amsterdam as a centre for international payments and the exchange traffic between the two was greater than their trade in commodities.[176]

Much of this context becomes apparent in the correspondence of Marescoe's Hamburg clients, of whom seven are of importance in 1668. The three Ruland brothers, Arnold, Egidio and Peter—whose family originated in Aachen[177]—traded independently of each other, but Peter was linked by marriage and Egidio by business with another of Marescoe's major clients, the Berenbergs. Originally Dutch, the Berenbergs were (and still are) part of Hamburg's business aristocracy, closely intertwined with other merchant-dynasties.[178] Andreas, Hans and Paul Berenberg had been among Hamburg's large-scale traders to Spain and Portugal in the 1630s[179] and it was the widow of Andreas who carried on the family business with Marescoe, and David, until her death in 1678, aged 74. Until his bankruptcy and flight to Lüneburg in 1669, Paul Berenberg was also dealing with Marescoe, but he is not to be confused with Andreas's son Paul who began to trade independently of his mother and brothers in 1670. The former Paul had a brother, Cornelius, placed in Amsterdam and Egidio, the most adventurous of the Rulands, was using Cornelius and Paul's other connections to carry on trade to the Mediterranean. Further interconnections linked the Berenbergs with Marescoe's special confidant in Hamburg, Peter Juncker. Already introduced above as an agent for the Swedish producers, Juncker was also acting as agent and partner in some of Marescoe's exports on his own account. He was a nephew of the very wealthy Anna van Overbeck, whose daughter was to marry Liebert Wolters II in 1673, and two of her nieces were married to Paul and Andreas Berenberg respectively.[180] It was thus a closely-knit little group which dealt with Marescoe in 1668—the only one for whom no attachments can be found being the seventh, shortlived correspondent, Jacob Jansen.

[173] K. N. Chaudhuri, *The Trading World of Asia and the English East India Company, 1660–1760* (Cambridge, 1978) pp. 313, 600; K. Glamann, *Dutch–Asiatic Trade, 1620–1740*, p. 82.

[174] Newman, p. 1, citing H. Reincke, 'Hamburgs Bevölkerung' *Forschungen und Skizzen zur hamburgischen Geschichte* (Hamburg, 1951) pp. 172–3; H. Kellenbenz, *The Rise of the European Economy: An Economic History of Continental Europe 1500–1700* (London, 1976) p. 204.

[175] M. Reissmann, *Die hamburgische Kauffmannschaft des 17. Jahrhunderts in sozialgeschichtlicher Sicht*, pp. 48, 53, 77, 214–15; Newman, pp. 30–3.

[176] V. Barbour, *Capitalism in Amsterdam in the 17th Century*, p. 127; H. Kellenbenz, *Sephardim an der Unteren Elbe. Ihre wirtschaftliche und politische Bedeutung vom Ende des 16. bis zum Beginn des 18. Jahrhunderts* (Wiesbaden, 1958); Carsten Prange, *Die Zeitungen und Zeitschriften des 17. Jahrhunderts in Hamburg und Altona. Ein Beitrag zur Publizistik der Frühaufklärung* (Hamburg, 1978). [I am indebted to Dr Joachim Whaley for this reference.]

[177] Reissmann, p. 115.

[178] Reissmann, pp. 248–9. 277.

[179] Reissmann, p. 373.

[180] Lohmann, *Die Familie Wolters*, p. 34.

All seven of them were interested in much the same range of commodities—sugar, cotton, ginger, galls, indigo, silk, currants, and campeachy-wood—with occasional inquiries after pepper, salt, coal, cocoa, ox-horns and gum. But within this heterogeneous assemblage there was considerable scope for specialized preferences. Were the galls to be of Aleppo or Smyrna, of Tripoli or Mosul? Was it to be Ardasse, Zerbassi or Tripoli silk? Above all, was it to be the sugar, cotton and indigo of Barbados and the West Indies, or of Brazil, Cyprus or Guatemala? The circumstance which endows this correspondence with special interest is that the products of the English West Indies were only now reaching a point of competitive parity with the staple products of an older world. Running through all the correspondence is thus a cautious, exploratory interest in the changing pattern of world production, as well as an understandable anxiety about relative costs. His Hamburg clients wanted to know two things from Marescoe—not only the price which these goods were commanding on the London market but also the prospects of supply. News of shipping movements was vital to them, and the Hamburg group was insistent on regular reports of arrivals at London or the outports. With just the faintest hint of distrust they took care to let Marescoe know that his was not the only source of information available to them. 'We understand from others,' writes Widow Berenberg, 'that the ship *Virginia* has arrived with a substantial quantity of galls. It is odd that you mentioned nothing of it' [4]. 'You say six or seven ships from Barbados are expected. Other friends tell us that in all ten ships have reached Portsmouth and are expected with the first fair wind.'[181] Against Marescoe's optimistic appraisals of the London market they set their superior information about Amsterdam's. Dutch East India Company arrivals were closely monitored and it is clear that they had swift and reliable information from the Straits and the Levant. Even when Marescoe tried to stampede them towards sugar with news of the Barbados (Michaelstown) fire of April 1668, they responded coolly and knowledgeably. 'Brazilian muscovado supplies were still plentiful and sugar prices would not rise.'[182] And they were right.

Yet it took at least seven days, or as many as fifteen, for a letter to pass between Hamburg and London.[183] A fortnight or a month might thus elapse before Marescoe's output of advice and information could produce a responsive input of commission and purchase, and the correspondence is often a hurried and sometimes irritated exchange, made up of elaborate instructions, last-minute amendments or desperate cancellations as market conditions changed. Marescoe's clients were facing the problems necessarily associated with commodities which endured a lengthy transit by sea, and although some were subject to a predictable season of shipment there could be no certainty about landings. Stray cargoes could come straggling in, weeks after the market had adjusted to the main fleet's arrival, and one or two unexpected ships could transform the price of certain low-bulk, high-value goods. This made it all the more serious that some English ships were evading the requirements of the Navigation Acts and trading directly with Hamburg from the Caribbean and the Levant. On several occasions in 1668 the Hamburg correspondents discreetly refer to English ships arriving 'adroittura' (without revealing any compromising details) and on each occasion it led to the cancellation of orders placed in London [29].[184]

[181] Widow Berenberg to CM, 15 February [4], 6 October 1668.
[182] A. Ruland to CM, 23 June; E. Ruland to CM, 23 June; J. Jansen to CM, 7 July 1668.
[183] Analysis of the 1668–9 letters from Hamburg, and (where known) from London, indicates that 16 per cent took 7 days, 43 per cent took 11 days and 8 per cent took 15 days to reach their destination. They usually went via Amsterdam, but it was necessary to use Antwerp in the autumn of 1668 and summer of 1669. For a contemporary English report on the Hamburg posts see PRO, SP. 29/251, Nos 203, 204.
[184] E.g., Widow Berenberg to CM, 24 July, 18 August 1668; 14 May 1669; A. Ruland to CM, 21 July, 28 July, 14 August 1668; P. Berenberg, 18 May 1669 [84].

Indeed, although 1668 has all the marks of a comparative boom year for Marescoe's commission trade to Hamburg, there are also distinct signs of future difficulties as some Hamburg prices quickly declined to unprofitably low levels. By November 1668 Egidio Ruland had written-off London altogether and was asking for his credit-balances to be transferred to Hamburg or Amsterdam. He had no reciprocal interest in exports to London, nor had most of his colleagues. Only Jacob Jansen was curious to know if Marescoe could handle some linens or timber—and he received no encouragement. There was thus no question of barter between Marescoe and his clients. All commissions to him were accompanied either by bills of remittance to London or by instructions to draw. However, on this point as on others, Egidio Ruland stands out as the most adventurous of his group. Not only did he commission by far the largest share of the 1668 shipments (30.5 per cent of values, f.o.b.) but he showed interest in the widest range of commodities and was the most inventive in contriving remittances to pay for them. Though hardly typical of the group, his correspondence provides the more illuminating introduction to the character of this sector.

Like all his colleagues, Egidio Ruland attentively followed the downward slide of Barbados sugar prices in London, from over 31s per cwt. in January to 28s in March, 26s 6d in August and an alleged 25s 6d in September, but unlike most of the others he also kept his eye on Bristol prices. Hearing of supplies available there at 25s–26s already in March he ordered 20,000 lb., but tried to cancel the order within the month when he calculated that the freight and insurance differential was worth 3s or 4s per cwt. extra on the prime costs at London [**12**]. With Hamburg prices falling from over 8 grooten banco per pound to below 7g he found it wiser to re-sell the Bristol purchase in London and by May was dismissing sugar as a drug on the Hamburg market. Yet he rejoined his competitors in June with an order at 27s and in October was bidding for Barbados sugar at 26s–26s 6d and for Brazilian muscovado at 36s–37s. Like all the Hamburg correspondents, he was puzzled that the arrival of fourteen Barbados ships in early August should have done comparatively little to lower prices and that several more arrivals in October did nothing. London prices actually stiffened in November and December, as was customary before Christmas, and they did the same in Hamburg. But with Hamburg's sugar-refineries fully stocked by the beginning of October and sugars cheap on the Amsterdam market there was little incentive to persevere with this commodity.[185]

Egidio's interest had been more vigorously engaged by other opportunities. He had detected a fleeting prospect of profit in coal shipments to Rouen during early March and had instructed Marescoe to commission his Newcastle correspondent, Robert Ellison. Falling lead prices in France, as Marescoe was to discover, made that article less attractive than it had been in 1667, but he saw a market for 'gum dragant' in Amsterdam and placed a small order at £6 per cwt., half for shipment there and half for Hamburg. He also dallied with Aleppo galls, as did all his competitors, ordering on 3 March at 55s per cwt. but on the 14th, with news of four ships and 3,500 sacks arriving in London from the Levant, revising the price limit to 50s–51s. The same news was enough to make Widow Berenberg cancel her order. Between 1664 and 1667 the London price of galls had ranged between 58s and 67s per cwt. and she had placed an early order which was executed at 58s in February 1668. Her object had been to catch the spring Leipzig fair, whose dealers were buying in Hamburg at the end of February.[186] But her galls, and the accompanying Barbados cotton, turned out to be of poor quality and she was left with ten expensive sacks on her hands. Galls, she lectured Marescoe,

---

185 E. Ruland to CM, 14 November, 18 December 1668.

186 Widow Berenberg to CM, 29 February 1668—'*wensen dat wij se [gallen] alhier hadden, want de Leipziger fieranten syn gecomen, en is nu den rechten tyt van consumo*'.

should be choice, plump and full of colour, not woody or white. The top layer, of acceptable quality, had concealed others which her customers would not touch.

She was not alone in finding galls troublesome. Arnold Ruland started out with orders for Aleppo galls in April, switched to Smyrna galls (15 per cent cheaper) 'as an experiment' in June, and then switched back—in disgust—to Aleppo galls in October. In the middle of this prevarication a rogue English shipment, direct from Scanderoon with 500 sacks, led him and Widow Berenberg to cancel their orders in August, but the Scanderoon galls turned out to be another disappointment. In the event, with Hamburg prices comparatively stable at 38–40 *ML* per 100 lb., it was Egidio Ruland who probably did best of the six purchasers, securing his during May at the lowest price, of 50*s* per cwt. Rumours of 44*s*–45*s* in London led to a flurry of orders in November but Marescoe could only effect them at 51*s* 6*d* and, not surprisingly, Hamburg's interest quickly evaporated. Widow Berenberg reckoned in February 1669 that her city now had two years' supply.[187]

Another choice dyestuff proved more rewarding. Campeachy-wood, or logwood, was a coveted dye which had commanded high prices for much of the century, but the effective establishment of English interlopers on the Bay of Campeach in the 1650s and the legitimating of its import by the legislation of 1662[188] had made it a useful component of England's Caribbean re-exports and a serious rival to Spanish sources. It was Peter Ruland who first raised the subject of campeachy on 28 March 1668. Hearing that it was available at 28*s* per cwt. in London he asked Marescoe to obtain 10,000 lb. at 26*s*–27*s* per cwt. but a month later cancelled the unperformed order because a large quantity from the Canaries had reached Amsterdam where the price had plummeted from *f*.28 to *f*.15½ per 100 lb. However, Egidio reverted to the subject in a postscript on 9 June, and it was he who was to pursue the commodity vigorously through a tantalizing series of price rises to the end of the year. Offering 30*s* per cwt. for 40,000 lb. in June he was delighted when Marescoe effected the order at 28*s* 6*d*.[189] Directing its shipment to Amsterdam he immediately repeated the order on 30 June, which was performed by mid-July at 30*s* 3*d*. Soon after, it evidently became his intention to monopolize supplies for he inquired after London's remaining stocks and by 14 August knew there were only 60 tons remaining—though 200 more might yet come via the Canaries. On the 18th he ordered Marescoe to buy 80,000–100,000 lb. at 31*s* per cwt., plus or minus 6*d*, and obtained 46,000 lb. at 31*s* 6*d*. He then offered 33*s* for another 25,000 lb. on 4 September, knowing that the Canary supplies were no longer a threat, and on the 29th revised his bid to 30,000 lb. at 37*s*–38*s* per cwt. When he heard, on 6 October, that 20 tons had reached the West of England priced at 38*s* he ordered Marescoe to buy it all, and the 40 tons still remaining in London, at 38*s*–40*s* per cwt. 'for I would be glad to have it all in my hands'. After a hesitant cancellation of this ambitious order on 23 October he was back in the market on 10 November at 44*s*–46*s*, but he was too late. Apparently Amsterdam buyers were willing to pay up to 80*s* in London and it was still as high as 65*s* at the end of the year.[190]

Yet he may have done well with his shipments, purchased at an average price of 32*s* per cwt., for the timidity of his brothers and the Berenbergs seems to have left him in sole possession of the field. He had sent 45,000 lb. to Amsterdam and brought 105,000 lb. to

---

[187] Widow Berenberg to CM, 12 February 1669 [**74**].

[188] A. M. Wilson, 'The Logwood Trade in the Seventeenth and Eighteenth Centuries' in D. C. McKay, *Essays in the History of Modern Europe* (New York & London, 1936) pp. 2–13. The prohibition on English imports of logwood was repealed by clause xxvi of the 1662 statute of Frauds (14 Car. II. c. 11).

[189] Although campeachy was ordered by the pound, it was priced by the hundredweight and sold in 'loads' of 1 ton.

[190] E. Ruland, 27 November, 29 December 1668.

Hamburg. The price there had first moved down from 28 *ML* per 100 lb. in March to 21 *ML* in late July, but it had then risen steadily to 30 *ML* in October and reached 36 *ML* in mid-November. In Amsterdam the price had also gradually recovered from its low point in April to *f.*20 in late September and had then jumped sharply from *f.*24 on 2 November to *f.*26 on the 13th, *f.*30 on the 20th and *f.*36 on the 30th. The Van Baerles, writing to Marescoe on 7 December remarked on the rapid oscillation of the price in the preceding week 'being come from *f.*30 to *f.*32, from there to *f.*35 and now again to *f.*30½ and *f.*30.' Clearly, there were opportunities in both centres to profit from the volatility of demand and Ruland presumably did so. At least he made no complaints about the quality of the merchandise nor of Marescoe's performance. Close analysis of the documentation reveals Marescoe to have responded promptly to his instructions. He received the order of 9 June on the 16th and had performed it by the 19th. It was on its way to Amsterdam by the 24th. The order of 18 August was received on the 24th, acknowledged on the 25th and performed by purchases on the 31st and 3 September. Part of the order had reached Hamburg by 7 or 8 September.

Barbados ginger was another New World commodity in which all the Rulands were interested. Ginger was widely used in Europe as a pepper-substitute[191] and competed therefore with the East Indian product. Yet the cultivation of the root in the English West Indies was still on a modest scale and, like Barbados cotton and indigo, it was never to match the success of the island's sugar.[192] But in circumstances such as those of 1668, when no East Indian pepper reached the English Company, and little was sold,[193] the prospects for the West Indian product were good. Certainly the Rulands were optimistic about its future. Arnold prophesied to Marescoe—'I believe that indigo and ginger will come to you in abundance in one or two years'[194]—and Egidio evidently had as high hopes of cornering the market in ginger as he had for campeachy. On 14 March he offered £400 for it at the market price of 27s per cwt. Arnold joined in successfully at 28s on 30 March, and on 4 April bid up to 30s. Egidio matched him on 19 May, but it now eluded them both and proved too dear. Widow Berenberg expressed interest on 4 August but on the 18th she reported the arrival of two ships 'adrittura' from the Caribbean, bringing sugar, ginger and indigo. If this was so— no others refer to it—it did not deter Paul Berenberg from joining in the pursuit. At the end of May he had lectured Marescoe on the high quality ginger he sought—not the thin, small roots which had been coming from Barbados over the last few year but clean, white stuff at 32s or 34s. He was shocked to learn on 27 June that the fine white 'scraped' ginger he sought cost 60s per cwt. in London and that it was the inferior brown or black kind which fetched 32s, but by 8 August he had steeled himself to order 2,000–3,000 lb. of the best at 60s. On 4 September he nervously greeted the news that Marescoe had at last bought some, sight unseen, at 55s, which was despatched on 11 September but did not reach him until 5 October. The same ship brought ginger of both qualities for Egidio Ruland and on 6 October the latter expressed his intention of buying up to 20 tons more of the cheaper quality at 36s–40s per cwt. Paul Berenberg had similar plans. On 25 September he had asked Marescoe for a detailed report on Barbados ginger prospects and confided his belief (which, he said, was shared in Holland) that Barbados ginger was being rooted up and that within two years no more could be expected. If that should really be the case he would know how to plan his sales, for he had much in stock.

[191] Chaudhuri, *The Trading World of Asia and the English East India Company, 1660–1760* p. 322.
[192] C. Bridenbaugh, '*No Peace Beyond the Line': The English in the Caribbean, 1624–1690* (New York, 1972) p. 284; K. G. Davies, *The North Atlantic World in the Seventeenth Century* (Minneapolis, 1974) pp. 147, 188.
[193] Chaudhuri, p. 529; cf. Glamann, *Dutch–Asiatic Trade*, p. 83.
[194] A. Ruland to CM, 21 August 1668.

Such a view, so completely contrary to the expectations of Arnold Ruland, disposes of any idea that Marescoe's Hamburg clients may have pooled their market intelligence, and it may be of some relevance to Paul Berenberg's pending bankruptcy that it was he who was most in error about the long-term prospects. Although no ginger was to come from Marescoe in 1669, it was to figure, sometimes in very large amounts, every year thereafter as Jamaican production flooded in. The Hamburg correspondents are generally reticent about the local market price, which suggests that they were buying and storing for later re-export. Three Hamburg price-currents, for 24 April, 15 May and 26 June, record a static price of 10 or 11 grooten banco per lb., although Peter Juncker, who made an unsuccessful bid for 20,000–25,000 lb. on 19 May, quotes prices as low as 8–10 grooten in mid-June and as high as 11–14 grooten on the 1 and 15 September. It is not clear how far the English re-export was challenged by the Dutch. Though preserved ginger certainly figured on the Amsterdam market, and in May 1668 three East India ships brought 42,000 lb. of it,[195] this was a choicer product, and there is no reference to serious competition from other such supplies in Hamburg.

That was not the case with two other West Indian products—indigo and cotton. Both contended with alternative sources, of differing quality, either from the Levant, the East Indies or from other producers in the Caribbean. Barbados cotton was thus matched with produce from Smyrna and Cyprus, and Arnold Ruland was interested in all three. Indeed, the whole Hamburg group, with the exception of Peter Juncker, had evidently placed orders for Barbados cotton before the surviving correspondence commences, for all six received consignments purchased in February at $8\frac{1}{4}d$ to $8\frac{1}{2}d$ per lb. Jacob Jansen and Widow Berenberg were dissatisfied with theirs and complained of slow sales as Hamburg prices drifted down, from 18–20 schillings per lb. in March to 16s–17s in June and a low of 15s in August and September. The Widow's revealing explanation was that those 'principalities' previously supplied from Hamburg were now receiving their cotton direct from England.[196] Nevertheless, she confessed to a preference for Barbados cotton over the more expensive Smyrna product, for it was of better quality, and this was a judgment which Arnold Ruland came to share.[197] Jacob Jansen disagreed. He ordered Smyrna cotton on 5 May, cancelled on the 26th and turned instead to Turkish cotton-yarn which was purchased for him at $14\frac{3}{4}d$ per lb. But he found that too coarse and affirmed his intention to have only East Indian cotton yarn in future.[198] He ascribed the stagnant autumn market to a glut of supplies from Cyprus and Barbados, and it is apparent that London prices had also dropped 25 per cent by the end of the year.

For Barbados indigo the immediate rival was a higher quality product, from Guatemala, and Hamburg prices reveal a consistent differential of 2–3 schillings per lb., or 20–30 per cent. In clear contrast to the behaviour of cotton, indigo prices rose steadily through the year, both in London and in Hamburg. Regulated as it was by the arrivals of the Spanish fleets from the New World, the European market was affected by their failure to appear. Not a pound would come this year, wrote Peter Ruland, and according to Peter Juncker existing stocks were being held 'in firm hands'.[199] In London, East India Company imports for 1668 were at their lowest for nearly forty years and little was offered for sale.[200] Nevertheless, Arnold

[195] *Particuliere Carga van drie Oost-Indische Retour-Schepen* (printed cargo-list enclosed by C. Berenberg in his letter of 21 May 1668).
[196] Widow Berenberg to CM, 4 August 1668.
[197] A. Ruland to CM, 2 April 1669.
[198] J. Jansen to CM, 2 October 1668.
[199] P. Ruland to CM, 25 February; P. Juncker to CM, 4 August 1668.
[200] Chaudhuri, p. 523.

Ruland pursued London prices, offering 4s 4d–4s 6d per lb. in March and April but like Jacob Jansen, found it too dear at over 5s. Paul Berenberg also chased it vigorously but vainly in September, raising his bid every week, from 5s to 5s 6d and finally to 5s 9d. Then Arnold Ruland resumed his pursuit at 6s in early October but was aghast to find his commission hastily performed at 7s. This led to a major dispute, for Ruland felt himself misinformed and mistreated by Marescoe, whose letters had not prepared him for this shock. For several weeks the preceding correspondence was angrily unravelled as Ruland sought to prove that he had not authorized, nor had Marescoe forewarned of, such an 'extravagant' price, but his letters do reveal, as he finally had to admit, that he gave an order for 600–700 lb. on 9 October without a specific limit on price. It was an elementary lesson in the unwritten rules of this game, but Ruland felt that Marescoe had also broken a more fundamental rule, which was—always to safeguard the interests of one's client. 'Do it, as if for yourself' was the first commandment of the commission trade which Marescoe was never allowed to forget.

No lasting rupture was caused by this quarrel: Arnold Ruland continued to deal with Marescoe and his successors until 1679, as did Egidio. But the latter also had his differences with Marescoe, demanding and eventually receiving a rebate on galls bought above his price limit. Others complained of short-weight or faulty packaging, and there was the serious problem of the 14 per cent tare conventionally deducted on Hamburg sugar-barrels, regardless of bulk. This put a premium on the largest size of English sugar-barrel—the butt—as opposed to the puncheon, or the smaller hogshead. By sending him hogsheads and puncheons, Marescoe had cost him 5 per cent, complained Jacob Jansen; perhaps he kept the butts for his friends?

Yet Marescoe was to learn of these problems for himself, the hard way. His only ventures to Hamburg on his own account in 1668 were two shipments of sugar consigned to Peter Juncker, and through Juncker's informative letters he was to experience personally the special difficulties of the Hamburg market in 1668. Received in February and April his 554 cwt. of sugar (30 butts, 13 puncheons, 12 hogsheads) found falling prices in a market already glutted and stagnant. Hamburg's own sugar-fleet was returning from Lisbon with 1,000 chests of Brazilian sugar,[201] and the large amounts of Barbados sugar already in Hamburg were being sold by the English there at any price, without regard to profit or loss.[202] Unless he was willing to barter, there was little prospect of a sale at more than $6\frac{1}{2}g$. However, Marescoe's confidence in the price rise deferred a decision to sell at the market rate and it was not until August that the thirty barrels sent in April were disposed of for 7g per lb., with the customary 13 months discount for immediate cash payment. Juncker's subsequent sale-account enables one to assess the variety of expenses which had to be set-off against such a sale. Bought in London at 29s 6d per cwt. but invoiced at 30s, Marescoe's 29,148 lb. of sugar had cost him £390 7s 6d free-on-board. Weighed in Hamburg at 30,113 lb. gross they bore the customary 14 per cent tare on the barrels to leave 25,897 lb. net, which at 7g per lb. yielded ML 5,664 15s 6d.[203] From this gross sum no less than thirteen itemized deductions had to be made, but they can be more conveniently grouped under five main heads:

---

201 P. Juncker to CM, 18 April 1668.

202 Same to same, 16 May 1668 [**16**].

203 Hamburg commodity prices were quoted either (i) in reichsthalers (ii) in schillings and grooten flemish, or (iii) in Lübeck marks, schillings and pfennigs. £1 flemish (of 240 grooten) = $7\frac{1}{2}$ ML. Thus, $\frac{25,897 \times 7}{240}$ (= £755.33) × $7\frac{1}{2}$ = 5,664.975. For further details of prices, currency, etc. see below, Appendix I.

		ML	%
[1]	Freight, pilotage, primage	110 00 00	1.95
[2]	Hamburg tolls based on a valuation of Marescoe's sugar at 4,800 ML:		
	(a) 'Heeren & Burgher toll' @ $\frac{3}{4}$% ⎱		
	(b) 'Admiralty & Convoy toll' @ $\frac{1}{2}$% ⎰	60 00 00	1.06
[3]	Wharfage, carriage, weighing, etc.	99 13 00	1.76
[4]	(a) Brokerage @ $\frac{1}{2}$% ⎱		
	(b) Commission @ $1\frac{1}{2}$% ⎰	111 15 00	1.97
[5]	Cash discount @ $8\frac{2}{3}$% for 13 months (approx. 8% p.a.)	451 12 06	7.97
		833 8 6	14.71

Marescoe was thus left with ML 4,831 7s net which Juncker sought to remit to him on the most favourable terms obtainable. Unfortunately, the transfer of considerable sums to England by other English merchants was raising the exchange rate during August and September and five weeks elapsed before he could complete the remittance by the purchase of two suitable bills—one for £200 at 34s flemish, another for £180 at 34s 3g, both at double usance. At 3 Marks Lüb. per schilling flemish the first was worth 2,550 ML, the second ML 2,331 14s, but Marescoe's net receipt of £380 meant a loss on this consignment, and an even larger one was to accrue on the other, earlier consignment which had been invoiced at £440 17s, and sold at $6\frac{1}{2}g$ per lb. with 13 months discount. Yielding a net ML 4,901 13s, remitted in two bills, it produced a return of only £378 17s. Marescoe had thus made a loss of 8.8 per cent on his sugar ventures and, not surprisingly, he expressed his dissatisfaction. Yet Juncker had clearly done his best. 7g per lb. in August and $6\frac{1}{2}g$ in September were fair prices, particularly for the inferior batch of February. What probably irked Marescoe most was Juncker's reluctance to consider a more lucrative form of return—the shipment of specie rixdollars. It is clear from Juncker's letters that Marescoe was pressing him for this favour, but he wisely refused.[204] As he explained repeatedly, specie exports from Hamburg were expressly forbidden by an Imperial prohibition of 20 January 1664 which was, fortuitously, re-issued on 14 August 1668.[205] Juncker admitted that specie-exports were widely practised in remittances to England at an unofficial premium of $2\frac{1}{2}$–3 per cent, but the penalties for being caught were costly, as a mutual friend had recently learned.[206] Although he grudgingly agreed to oblige Marescoe on 30 June—at Marescoe's own risk—the edict of 14 August finally settled the matter: Marescoe would have to take bills.

What Marescoe could not safely reveal was that his appetite for rixdollars had been whetted by Egidio Ruland's example. Between June 1664 and April 1668, when his account was balanced, Ruland had remitted or accepted bills to the value of £1,801 to fund his purchases in England during the Anglo–Dutch war. Nearly 40 per cent of this was sent through his endorsement of five Morlaix bills on various English centres (two on London, one apiece on Bristol, Exeter and St Columb, Cornwall). Another 33 per cent was transmitted by four London drafts on Hamburg and 17 per cent by three Venetian bills on London. One Antwerp–London bill accounted for the residue. However, between April and August 1668 (when another balance was struck) the pattern changed. Goods to the value of

---

[204] P. Juncker to CM, 10 March, 18 April, 30 June, 4 August, 18 August 1668.

[205] Newman, p. 43 n. 1, (citing *Sammlung der von der Stadt Hamburg ausgangenen algemein Mandate* [Hamburg, 1763] I, Nr. 97, pp. 205–6; Nr. 126, pp. 247–8).

[206] P. Juncker to CM, 4 August 1668. (The entire consignment of rixdollars was confiscated.)

£2,411 17s 10d were covered partly by bills and partly by coin. On 2 June Ruland clandestinely shipped, in separate vessels, two sacks of rixdollars containing 1,500 each. He was not pleased to learn that the London valuation of the coin had just fallen from 5s 1d to 4s 10d–10$\frac{1}{2}$d, but by late June Marescoe had sold them to Isaac Meynell, a leading goldsmith-banker, for 4s 11d per piece. Nine hundred ducats followed in July and were sold, by weight, at £4 6s 3d per oz. Five hundred more left Hamburg in September and in November Ruland's correspondent in Amsterdam despatched a further 1,011. But London gold prices had slipped nearly 1$\frac{1}{2}$ per cent between the third and fourth shipment, and thereafter Ruland stuck to bills of exchange. He had realized a total of £1,889 6s 2d sterling on his specie, and while some of this covered Marescoe's purchases of goods he also found it profitable to draw some of it back on the more favourable London–Hamburg or London–Amsterdam exchanges.

It is at this point, in manipulating the exchanges, that the interests of Marescoe's import business overlapped with those of the export trade, for the credit-balances generated by the latter provided useful opportunities to settle debts due on the former. Thus, on Ruland's account between August 1668 and January 1670, over £1,200 (or two-thirds) of Marescoe's drafts on Ruland were made for the benefit of his Swedish suppliers—Jacob Momma, Johan Behrman, Gustaff & Gerdt Dunt. It is a pattern which was to recur throughout the Hamburg commission trade and it exemplifies the general role which England's traffic with Hamburg played in settling her balances in the north.[207]

At the close of 1668 Marescoe could look back on a uniquely strenuous year in his Hamburg dealings. He had despatched fifty-eight separate consignments of goods, weighing over 330 tons in twenty-six distinct shipments worth £11,584 6s 9d (f.o.b.). It was the bulkiest and most valuable sector of his commission trade in this, or any other, year—but in its very bulk it carried the seeds of future disappointments. 1669 and 1670 were to see more modest commissions as the Hamburg market proved incapable or unwilling to absorb the commodities now flooding in from several directions.

Galls were the principal casualty. With two years' supply in stock and more arriving from Marseille, Marescoe's clients showed little further interest. Hamburg prices had edged up to 42 or 43 ML in January 1669 but by April they were falling below 40 ML to hover at 36 or 37 ML from midsummer onwards. London prices seemed to remain stubbornly indifferent to this decline, perhaps because of buoyant domestic demand, but from their high point of 60s per cwt. in January and February, London galls fell to 55s in May and to 50s in June. Rumours of 46s encouraged the Widow Berenberg and Arnold Ruland to inquire after them later in the year, but no commissions were executed for them within their price limit.

Ginger was another absentee, as was campeachy. For the latter, Hamburg prices remained comparatively steady, round an average of 30 ML, but London prices seem to have been consistently too high for Egidio Ruland's bids at 44s–45s per cwt. Arnold Ruland confessed in exasperation that he could not understand the 'misterium' of the campeachy trade and relinquished further interest in it.[208] Yet, other products of Barbados and the Caribbean retained their attraction. Sugar, with the Hamburg refiners holding six-months' supply,[209] seemed an unlikely source of profit early in the year, particularly as London prices of 27s–28s

---

[207] As Sir George Downing asserted in the House of Commons, 28 November 1670—'One of our best trades is from Hamburg, which fully balances its own and that of Sweden', Anchitel Grey, *Debates of the House of Commons from the year 1667 to the year 1697* (London, 1793) I, p. 311.

[208] A. Ruland to CM, 29 September 1669.

[209] P. Ruland to CM, 9 February 1669 [**73**]. Widow Berenberg estimated her own stock at 50,000 lb. (27 April 1669).

per cwt. remained too high for the first three months. Egidio Ruland tried to cancel an indiscreet order for 25,000 lb. at 26s[210] but, to his dismay, received it at a time when Hamburg prices had fallen to 6 or $6\frac{1}{4}$ grooten, with absolutely no market demand. His colleagues held back until the early summer when reports of London price-falls to 23s–24s encouraged a flurry of bids from four of the group. These were all performed between July and August at prices ranging from 23s to 24s 6d—but not without recrimination. The small, yet significant, price differentials in Marescoe's consignments brought to the surface latent jealousies between his clients, although in ways he could not have anticipated. Peter Ruland objected that although the sugar Marescoe had sent to Paul Berenberg cost 6d per cwt. more than his own, its quality was 1s 3d better![211] If so, Berenberg did not agree. 'I see that you provided the others with very good sugar while I am burdened with bad . . . although I expressly commanded only sound, good sugar and would rather have paid more.'[212] Arnold Ruland and Widow Berenberg joined the chorus of complaint: the latter found her sugar 'far worse than we could have imagined'.[213]

With Barbados cotton there was less complaint but more hesitation as the Straits were scanned for news of Levantine supplies. The now negligible price differential between Smyrna cotton and the West Indian product made the question of quality all the more crucial, and it is interesting to find the argument settled in favour of Barbados by at least two of Marescoe's clients.[214] Paul Berenberg preferred to hedge his bets, ordering Smyrna, Cyprus and Barbados varieties, and also bidding for Turkish cotton-yarn.

It is with indigo, however, that the most significant source of competition was made apparent. The market in 1669 was evidently paralysed by uncertainties over the prospects for the Spanish '*flota*' returning to European waters during the course of the year. The role of the *flotas* (from New Spain) and the *galeones* (from Terra Firma) will be discussed more fully below,[215] but here it is necessary to note that Hamburg, directly or indirectly, was deeply interested in their fortunes. Not only did they bring bullion, of which at least one-tenth might be rapidly transferred to Hamburg creditors,[216] but they carried produce which could determine European prices for sugar, cochineal, campeachy and indigo.[217] It was therefore a matter of pressing concern for Marescoe's customers to know when the long-awaited *flota* which had departed in June 1668 would finally return. Widow Berenberg typifies this anxiety. Placing orders for 400–600 lb. of indigo on 10 July 1669 she begged Marescoe to cancel the commission as soon as he heard of the *flota*'s return. In letter after letter he was asked for news of its coming, but even Spanish sources remained unsure of its movements[218] and in this mood of uncertainty the orders placed for Barbados indigo were necessarily tentative, conditional and frequently cancelled. Only Arnold Ruland, who had done so badly with his indigo in 1668, should have been happier in 1669, for his $9\frac{1}{2}$ cwt., purchased at 5s and

---

[210] E. Ruland, to CM, 2 March 1669.

[211] P. Ruland to CM, 27 July 1669.

[212] P. Berenberg to CM, 24 August 1669.

[213] '*vry schlecht buyten onse gissing*'—Widow Berenberg to CM, 10 September 1669.

[214] A. Ruland to CM, 2 April; J. A. Fonck to CM, 7 December 1669. J. Jansen stated his preference for East Indian cotton—31 July, 2 October 1669.

[215] See pp. 94–5.

[216] H. Kamen, *Spain in the Later Seventeenth Century, 1665–1700* (London, 1980) p. 138.

[217] Ibid.; L. Garcia Fuentes, *El comercio español con America, 1650–1700* (Seville, 1980) pp. 509–10, Table 36; J. Everaert, *De internationale en koloniale handel der vlaamse firma's te Cadiz, 1670–1700* (Bruges, 1973) pp. 417–21, 445–6, 458–61, 465–6.

[218] PRO, SP. 94/55 ff. 119; SP. 94/56 f. 7 (Sir William Godolphin to Lord Arlington, 25 August 1669; same to Joseph Williamson 12 January 1670).

4*s* 6*d* per lb., reached a market where prices rose by 25 per cent in the last quarter of the year.

Other commodities were struck by the vagaries of shipping-arrivals, notably from the Levant. Olive-oil from Apulia, a major element in England's returns from the Mediterranean, seemed a tempting prospect in February 1669 with its Hamburg price at a high of 77 RD banco per 820 lb., and Peter Ruland placed an order which Marescoe performed at £28 per 236 gallons, despite its startling leap in one day's trading to £31. Infuriatingly, Ruland found the consignment 'thick, greasy, fiery and old' just at a time when the arrival of three English ships direct from Apulia brought the Hamburg price tumbling down from 72 to 63 RD in a matter of days.[219] Further arrivals direct from the Mediterranean included currants from Zante and cotton from Smyrna, and to make matters worse English factors in Hamburg were still recklessly selling at rock-bottom prices to secure their commission on turnover.[220] Although Widow Berenberg was happy enough to buy her Ardasse silk from them at a price which Marescoe could not match, the Rulands and the Berenbergs generally watched in disgust as the English spoiled an already difficult market.

More predictable were the movements of the great East India Company fleets, both English and Dutch. Sixteen English ships were reported to be coming home in March and thirteen Dutch ones had arrived by June, 1669.[221] The consequences were complacently awaited in Hamburg: there would be significant alterations in many commodity prices, especially of pepper. Yet their expectations were strangely disappointed: pepper remained comparatively dear, despite the substantial quantities received. Both Companies pursued a policy of retaining sufficient stocks to level out prices at the quarterly sales,[222] and Marescoe's correspondents were baffled to hear of pepper fetching 10*d* per lb. in London when they had confidently expected 8*d*, or less. Sales in Amsterdam appear to have been deliberately restrained[223] and although pepper prices had continued to tumble there, from 30*g* in January to 18*g* by the September sales, it quickly steadied at over 19*g* and was thought by P. Ruland to be marginally dearer than its rival's in London. All in all, concluded his brother Arnold, there was no profit to be got from the usual East India goods and ventures into less usual ones, such as cubeben and fustic-wood, proved totally abortive. 'Business here is miserable' wrote Paul Berenberg in the midsummer of 1669, and he spoke for them all.[224]

Nor were the difficulties they complained of entirely parochial ones. Events far away cast their shadow across Hamburg. Rumours of outrages by the English at Cartagena and the French at San Domingo[225] sent tremors of anxiety through the correspondents, and the depredations of Barbary corsairs were gravely noted.[226] Nearer home there was anxiety about Franco–Dutch relations, and Peter Juncker predicted war over the pending Polish succession.[227] 'Nous vivons certes dans un siècle fort dangereux' he warned—more than once. More to the point, however, were the fatalities of their fellow-merchants. Here too Peter Juncker provided a sombre commentary on youthful imprudence and elderly folly.

---

219 P. Ruland to CM, 14 May, 11 June 1669.

220 P. Berenberg to CM, 18 May 1669—'*De Engelse natie cladt alte seer met de goederen*' [**84**].

221 A. Ruland to CM, 16 March; Widow Berenberg to CM, 22 June; E. Ruland to CM, 18 June 1669; *Dutch–Asiatic Shipping in the 17th and 18th Centuries. Vol. III: Homeward-bound voyages* ed. J. R. Bruijn, F. S. Gaastra & I. Schöffer RGP, Grote Serie, 167 (The Hague, 1979) p. 86.

222 Chaudhuri, pp. 319, 529.

223 Pieter van Dam, *Beschryvinge van de Oostindische Compagnie*, ed. F. W. Stapel, *RGP*, Grote Serie, 68 (The Hague, 1929) I, p. 225.

224 '*tis hier miserabele negotie*'—P. Berenberg to CM, 22 June 1669.

225 A. Ruland to CM, 14 May, 4 June 1669.

226 E. Ruland to CM, 26 March 1669.

227 P. Juncker to CM, 6 April 1669.

1668 had seen one or two significant bankruptcies. Vincent Esich, an immigrant from Bremen who had once bought cotton from Marescoe, now brought disgrace on his Hamburg kinsmen when he failed in March.[228] A leading sugar-baker collapsed in late-September, involving many others in his ruin,[229] and in December the bankruptcies of Arnaut & Pierre Passavant in Danzig caused losses in Sweden and Holland, as well as in Hamburg.[230] March 1669 saw the collapse of a young merchant with only two years' experience,[231] while in September the old-established house of Hans & Jurgen Luders ceased trading, owing 120,000 *RD* in Hamburg alone.[232]

So far, Marescoe and his clients had been unscathed, but in August and September 1669 Marescoe began to receive some warning hints from the Van Baerles in Amsterdam, whose solicitude for Marescoe's credit has already been explained. They pointed out to him that a fourth Ruland brother, Jacomo—who traded in Amsterdam—had declared himself bankrupt three or four years ago and had compounded with his creditors for only 20 per cent, a settlement from which he was thought to have done too well.[233] Now he was back in the game, still trading dangerously, and his bills were to be treated with caution. As for the Berenbergs, their black sheep was Paul's brother, Cornelius, who also traded in Amsterdam. Although considered rich, the Van Baerles understood that his estate was largely invested in the East Indies where it was none too well administered.[234] This was all the warning Marescoe had before December 1669 when Peter Juncker informed him, in the polite language reserved for such a calamity, that 'Paul Berenberg has absented himself from the Exchange this week.' His debts were over 100,000 *ML* and he owed Marescoe about £300.

The roots of Paul Berenberg's bankruptcy are not to be found in this correspondence. In piteous letters, drawing attention to his wife and nine children, he attributed it to a series of losses over recent years. This makes it all the more significant that he had become Marescoe's biggest customer in 1669, taking nearly 30 per cent of his Hamburg consignments (by value, f.o.b.). His were the largest commissions for sugar, and he summed up his business-philosophy for 1669, when profit margins were being constricted, as one of rapid turnover.[235] In this he differed from his more cautious, and more solvent, relations whose reactions to the sluggish demand of 1669 was to sit still and wait for better times.

Paul Berenberg's failure was shortly followed by that of his brother, Cornelius. The Van Baerles estimated that he had squandered a fortune of f.38,000, although his marriage three years before had brought him f.12,000 which he might still possess.[236] Perhaps he came to the rescue of his brother, but there is no sign of it. Paul took refuge in the duchy of Lüneburg while his relatives averted their eyes. His name is not mentioned by the Widow Berenberg who was more profitably absorbed in the marriage of her son, another Paul, to the daughter of a rich burgher, Michel Heusch.[237] He was soon to take up trade on his own account, and thus as one Paul Berenberg disappeared from the list of Marescoe's correspondents a new one entered it.

[228] E. Ruland to CM, 31 March 1669; Reissmann, pp. 239, 275.

[229] P. Juncker to CM, 6 October; Widow Berenberg to CM, 9 October 1669.

[230] E. Ruland to CM, 5 December; P. Juncker to CM, 29 December 1669.

[231] P. Ruland to CM, 30 March; P. Juncker to CM, 6 April 1669. The victim was named as 'Reinier Nordenhof'.

[232] P. Ruland to CM, 17 September; P. Juncker to CM, 28 September 1669; Reissmann, pp. 132, 382.

[233] Van Baerles to CM, 17 September 1669.

[234] Same to same, 27 August 1669 [**102**].

[235] *'Soe moet men die met dickquels omtesetten soecken te verdubbelen'*—P. Berenberg to CM, 20 July 1669.

[236] Van Baerles to CM, 17 December 1669.

[237] Widow Berenberg to CM, 26 November 1669; cf. Reissmann, pp. 35, 131, 258, 373, 379.

Other clients were also coming forward to deal with Marescoe. Before his failure, the elder Paul Berenberg had introduced his young partner and brother-in-law, François Bostelman, who began commissioning Marescoe in July 1669.[238] He also recommended Marescoe to a cousin, Johan Baptista de Hertogh, the elder, a man of wealthy family whose experience of trade went back to the 1640s.[239] Yet another of his relatives, his uncle Johan Arnoldt Fonck, introduced himself to Marescoe on the strength of his kinship with Peter and Dominicus Juncker, who were his cousins by marriage, and it was Peter Juncker who discreetly answered Marescoe's inquiry about Fonck's reliability.[240] In the event, all three new correspondents of 1669 were to remain regular clients of Marescoe and his successors until the 1680s.

However, with the loss of the letters received after February 1670 it is impossible to review in any detail the behaviour of the Hamburg market up to Marescoe's death in September. Sugar continued to provide the principal commissions from both Berenbergs and all three Rulands, although its Hamburg price seems to have hovered between 6g and $6\frac{1}{2}g$ per lb., while in London it remained somewhat higher than in 1669. Indigo also continued to attract them, with its Hamburg price apparently holding in the region of 15 schillings per pound. Despite the arrival of substantial amounts of indigo in the long-awaited *flota* of February 1670, the Barbados variety seems to have retained a competitive edge, at 4s 6d or 4s 8d per lb. in London, against 5s for 'Guatemala'. However, in the autumn of 1670 J. A. Fonck evidently turned back to the traditional source of the dye, in India, and bought some 'Lahore' indigo at 7s per lb. He may have shared the belief in its superior quality but the price differential clearly illustrates the severity of the competition which the English East India Company faced in this commodity and of which it gave solemn warning to its Surat factory in 1670.[241] Its pepper also failed to attract Hamburg buyers and instead it was Barbados ginger they bought, at 38s–39s per cwt. Galls also returned to favour with their Hamburg price no lower than in 1669. Finally, they bought silk, about which they had often inquired but for which they had usually found continental suppliers.

Thus, at the end of 1670 Hamburg had received, in all, twenty-seven consignments, worth £3,674 7s 6d—less than one-third of the value consigned in 1668 but as a proportion of the firm's total exports that year almost exactly the average proportion which Hamburg took over the whole period. Indeed, the contraction in Hamburg's commissions was matched elsewhere and seems to reflect a general stagnation in European trade which other sectors of Marescoe's exports evidently shared.

[b] AMSTERDAM

Throughout the period of this study the bulk of the correspondence from Amsterdam was generated, directly or indirectly, by the trade in Swedish exports. It was primarily as a centre for international settlements and only secondarily as a commodity market that Amsterdam mattered to Marescoe and his successors. But a direct trade with the United Provinces sometimes involved a significant proportion of the firm's business and, if it had not been for the interruption of the two Anglo–Dutch wars, the relationship might have been as important and as continuous as that with Hamburg. Indeed, as the Hamburg correspondence

---

238 F. Bostelman to CM, 20 July 1669. He ordered 300 lb. of Barbados indigo at 4s 6d–4s 8d per lb.

239 Reissmann, p. 379.

240 P. Juncker to CM, 28 September 1669—'*J.A.F. est bon et marié depuis un An avec ma cousine . . . P.B[erenberg] est en médiocre estime et F.B.[ostelman] est en son service et le frère de sa femme; ce sont bien des honnêstes gents mais de peu de fond. . .*'

241 Chaudhuri, p. 331.

has already demonstrated, the two markets were in large degree complementary, serving adjoining hinterlands and responding more quickly and sensitively to one another than to any other European centre. An illusion of homogeneity is reinforced not only by the similar price-quotations (often in schellings and grooten flemish) but by the large Dutch component in Hamburg's merchant community, and it is no surprise to find that, while some of Marescoe's exports to Amsterdam were made on Hamburg's account, a similar proportion of his exports to Hamburg were made on Amsterdam's account.

However, his customers in the United Provinces were fewer than those on the Elbe. Before the second Anglo–Dutch war, in the autumn of 1664, he was dealing only with Daniel Planck, to whom he sent three consignments of galls. While he managed to get a small parcel of tobacco to Laurens de Geer at Amsterdam in 1665, there could be no safe exchange of commodities until the second half of 1667. But with peace assured Marescoe made a vigorous bid to enter the Dutch market on his own account, using the Van Baerle brothers as his commission agents. Like Peter Juncker in Hamburg, they were now to perform a dual role, protecting their Swedish principals' interests in Marescoe's imports but at the same time serving Marescoe's interest in his independent exports. The combination of responsibilities and the conscientious way in which they discharged them gives their letters a special importance. Unfortunately, none survive to illuminate their role in 1667 but something can be gleaned from the Journal book and loose accounts. The fate of Marescoe's first venture, a consignment of 200 northern kerseys, can be followed in complete detail, from its purchase in itemized packs by his agent in Hull, to its equally itemized sale by the Van Baerles in Amsterdam. Had Marescoe not panicked at the late arrival of his ship and belatedly insured it at the emergency rate of 10 per cent, he would have made a minute profit. He was more successful with his lead exports, also bought and shipped in northern ports. From Hull, his agent William Skinner despatched $552\frac{1}{2}$ cwt. of lead purchased at £11 10s–£12 10s per fodder, and from Newcastle Robert Ellison sent two ships to Rotterdam with $838\frac{3}{4}$ cwt. Sailing in October, they found a favourable market and yielded Marescoe an aggregate profit of 14 per cent. It must be doubtful whether some later purchases made for Laurens de Geer at £14 18s 9d per fodder (f.o.b.) were quite so successful and Marescoe's own December shipment left a loss, but if he had been able to cast up an end-of-year balance of his account with the Van Baerles, who handled all the sales in Rotterdam as well as Amsterdam, he would have found a net gain of £96 12s 11d on cargoes worth £1,473 6s 2d (f.o.b.).

If Marescoe was encouraged by expectations of such profits he was in good company, for 1668 brought him an unusual number of Amsterdam commissions. Daniel Planck returned, both to buy and to sell, and he was accompanied by Cornelius Berenberg and Egidio Ruland, while from Antwerp Peter Jaspersen directed consignments to his agent at Middelburg, Isaac Fellinger. Of Marescoe's total shipments to the United Provinces in 1668 these four men took, respectively, 24.5%, 7.9%, 6.2% and 5.3% of their value (f.o.b.). The lion's share, of 56%, was on Marescoe's own account, despatched to the Van Baerles at either Amsterdam or Rotterdam.

Heading the list of commodities in 1668, as at Hamburg, was Barbados sugar. This accounted for about 40 per cent of their value and nearly two fifths of it was for Marescoe's own account. Another 40 per cent was accounted for by his personal lead and tin shipments while to his clients went a miscellany of goods which closely resembles that sent to Hamburg—galls, campeachy, currants, gum and ginger. The amounts involved will appear insignificant—thirteen barrels of currants, thirty-one sacks of ginger—but the fortuitous survival of figures for Amsterdam's dutiable imports (and exports) for 1 October 1667 to 30

September 1668 allows one to put them in some perspective.[242] After adjustment to Dutch weights the percentage of Marescoe's Amsterdam consignments never falls below 3 per cent of the total volumes recorded for those twelve months. His lead is equivalent to about 15 per cent and his English tin to nearly 28 per cent, while even his currants account for 3.6 per cent of those received in 1667/68.[243]

The correspondence concerning these shipments is therefore not without relevance to the market as a whole, and—like that from Hamburg—it reflects a well-informed sensitivity to the wider currents of European trade. The Van Baerles were the most reliable commentators, following the Dutch market movements in English lead and tin and advising Marescoe on the prospects for sugar, campeachy, olive-oil, pepper and cloves. Perhaps because they had no direct investment in these commodities their letters lack some of the urgency which characterizes those of the Hamburgers, but this deficiency is amply made up by the bad-tempered letters of Daniel Planck which, with their unrelieved litany of complaints, reveal him as a notably exacting and cantankerous customer. Lacking any informative comments on prices or market conditions, his letters have few compensating virtues and are therefore poorly represented in the printed selection below, although he continued to write intermittently until his death in 1678.

Cornelius Berenberg, on the other hand, has more in common with his Hamburg kinsmen and he brought to his letters a wide-ranging curiosity about an exotic variety of goods—drugs and spices such as asafoetida, camphor, capers, cubeb, cumin, curcuma, fustic and sasafras—as well as sugar, ginger, campeachy, currants, oil, galls, and pepper. He appears to have been feeling his way in an unfamiliar market, bidding for small consignments 'tot een proef'— that is, on trial, or as an experiment. In more familiar commodities, such as currants, he divided his commissions between Amsterdam and Hamburg and (like others) he was not averse to a little smuggling of highly-rated items. He made a long pursuit of ginger, obtaining some early in the year at 29s, and then seeking more as its London price rose beyond his reach, with bids at 30s, 32s, 36s and finally 40s. He also shared the Hamburgers' keen interest in campeachy as its Amsterdam price enticingly doubled in three months, but here too his bids, rising from 30s to 38s and finally to 48s in November, were unsuccessful. The only purchases of campeachy to reach Amsterdam from Marescoe were those made on Egidio Ruland's account in June and July.

Galls attracted rather less attention from the Amsterdam customers than those of Hamburg. Daniel Planck brusquely snubbed Marescoe when he offered prices for Aleppo, Smyrna and 'Moslo' galls. He did not know what Marescoe meant by 'Moslo' galls, unless it was Mosul galls of the kind he had sent before the war, but in any case he was not interested in their names: quality was what mattered, and, having received twenty sacks in June he continued to make intermittent orders for the middle-quality Aleppo variety, and for Zante currants which he designated for re-export to Danzig directly from London. Attention to the

[242] H. Brugmans, 'Statistiek van den in- en uitvoer van Amsterdam, 4 October 1667–30 September 1668', *BMHG* (1898) pp. 125–83. For a critical analysis of these figures see M. Morineau, 'Hommage aux historiens hollandais et contribution à l'histoire économique des Provinces-Unies' in *Dutch capitalism & world capitalism: capitalisme hollandais et capitalisme mondial*, ed. M. Aymard (Cambridge, 1982) pp. 285–304.

[243] These percentages reflect the ratio of the net weight of Marescoe's goods to the recorded Amsterdam totals. However, if (as seems probable) the latter represent the *assessed* net weight and quantities of goods imported on which duties were payable, the percentages must be revised downwards. In those cases where it is known, the *assessed* weight on which the Van Baerles paid duties represented only 84.6 per cent of the actual net weight for Marescoe's sugar, 84.8 per cent for his lead and 83.4 per cent for his galls. E.g. sugar weighing 26,129 lb. in England was weighed in Amsterdam at 26,444 ponds gross, 22,476 ponds net, and assessed for duty at 19,500 ponds.

London market in Mediterranean produce was only lively in the case of Apulian olive-oil which Peter Jaspersen followed closely while its price was between £27 and £28 10s per 236 gallons. By mid-September he was regretting the timidity which had led him to set a price-limit on Marescoe's commission, for its price in Middelburg, as in Amsterdam, rose attractively until mid-November. However, his agent in Middelburg had been consistently sceptical about the profitability of London shipments and had neglected to correspond with Marescoe for the eighteen weeks preceding 10 August: 'den negotie heeft een tijt langh seer slecht gegaen', he explained. Yet even he recognized that the arrival of three or four ships in London could create a favourable price-advantage if quickly acted upon. The speedier communication between London and Amsterdam—usually a matter of three days each way—left Marescoe with less excuse for botched commissions and Planck, in particular, could see no good reason why his order, received in London on a Monday, could not have been performed and reported on by the Tuesday post.[244]

The commission which gave rise to this observation had been for Barbados sugar, and this is the one West Indian product in which the interests of Planck, Berenberg and Jaspersen converged with Marescoe's. The Van Baerles supplied a regular commentary on the Amsterdam price-movements which, like those in Hamburg, show a tendency to fall which became irreversible in 1669. Beginning the year at nearly 8 grooten per pond, Barbados sugar ended it at below 7g despite rallying in midsummer and in mid-October. There were, of course, many varieties of sugar available on the Amsterdam market which were not in competition with each other—refined sugars, muscovadoes and the lower-grade 'paneel' to which Marescoe's purchases belonged—but England's West Indian sugar imports at London alone were probably more than double the annual volume of all Amsterdam's supplies, and their landings and prices could not fail to have some influence on the Dutch market.[245] Conversely, the arrival in the Netherlands of sugar from Surinam (recently lost by the English) did nothing to help Marescoe's sales in 1668, although rumours of 1.1m ponds in transit proved vastly exaggerated. The precarious balance of the market is well-reflected in the Van Baerles' report of 17 August:

'By the arrival of several ships from Barbados at London and also two in Zeeland and another two here there is no safe price in sugar.'

It is not surprising that they sometimes urged Marescoe to dispose of his sugars in London, as did Daniel Planck.

Perhaps Marescoe needed no encouragement to do precisely this. All but the first of his five Amsterdam shipments of sugar in 1668 produced a loss (averaging 3.5 per cent) and he was clearly unhappy with the incidental charges he incurred. Once again, a conventional tare, of 15 per cent on large butts and puncheons and 16 per cent on hogsheads, put a premium on the larger casks. He had sent 44 butts, 35 puncheons and 66 hogsheads, plus 5 small barrels, which was a rather disadvantageous distribution, as the Van Baerles pointed out. Then there was the 1 per cent discount on the price for 'goet gewicht'—an allowance enforced by the sugar refiners to cover wastage and short-weight. Another 1 per cent discount was customary for immediate cash payment. As for the Dutch sugar duties, even the Amsterdam city

[244] D. Planck to CM, 21 September 1668.
[245] For the Dutch sugar-market see J. J. Reesse *De suikerhandel van Amsterdam van het begin der 17ᵉ eeuw tot 1813* (Haarlem, 1908). London sugar imports in the 1660s averaged 19 million lb, according to the 'Book of Tables' (BL, Add. MS. 36, 785) while Dutch East India Co. imports were substantially reduced to *c.* 620,000 ponds p.a. (Glamann, *Dutch–Asiatic Trade, 1620–1740*, pp. 158–9; Reesse, Appendix F) but to these must be added sugars from Brazil and the West Indies which in 1667–8 totalled 7.24 million ponds (Brugmans, p. 175).

authorities thought them excessive. Already in March 1661 they had reviewed the effects of a quarter-century of increasing world production.[246] Not only were Amsterdam's sixty-odd sugar refineries faced by serious competition but price-falls of nearly 70 per cent over the last two or three decades had made nonsense of duties based on the valuations of the 1620s. Indeed, there was growing pressure—which came to a head in 1670–1—to reconsider the whole 'Convoy and Licence' tariff, last revised in 1655, for Colbert's tariffs and the English Navigation Acts required some calculated answer.[247]

In the event, all that happened in August 1668 was the imposition of an additional levy of 1 stuiver per pond on imported syrup[248]—a step which helps to explain Cornelius Berenberg's anxiety to smuggle a consignment disguised as olive-oil [**37**]. The sugar-refiners successfully petitioned for its removal in August 1669 and in the course of their petition they drew attention to the anomalous and inequitable duties borne by sugar in general. They alleged that Hamburg enjoyed a significant tariff advantage which, with the help of huge English supplies, was giving her the command of European markets.[249] A comparison of the duties paid by Marescoe's sugars in 1668 at Hamburg and Amsterdam tends to bear this out although his net returns from the latter were slightly higher as a percentage of the gross sale. Indeed, close analysis of the Van Baerles' sale-accounts does not suggest that they failed Marescoe, although—unknown to him, perhaps—they had a direct interest in the sugar-refining business. David van Baerle had bought a sugar-refinery in 1665 and it is interesting to find him selling some of Marescoe's sugar to the previous owner, a major sugar-refiner called Jan van Veldesteyn.[250] Other purchasers of Marescoe's sugar include notable Amsterdam dealers such as Denis Nuyts and Henrico Matthias.[251]

However, Marescoe's sugars—at barely 4 per cent of Amsterdam's imports—were of much less significance in the market than his lead and tin, which may have represented 14.8 per cent and 27.7 per cent respectively of the volumes imported in 1667/68. In aggregate, both proved profitable to him in 1668, although sales were not always brisk. Two consignments of lead sent from Hull in September 1667 were sold almost at once (the larger part to Samuel Sautin, another notable Amsterdam merchant)[252] but a third batch of 721 pieces, sent from Newcastle in October, moved sluggishly and the last piece was not sold until May 1668. There was, it seems, a dead season lasting from Christmas until the end of March, and although prospects of peace between France and Spain brightened prospects in April, the Van Baerles warned Marescoe that there was little demand for lead in Italy, which was now over-supplied.[253] The Amsterdam price therefore fell, from 30 schellings per 100 lb. in December 1667 to 27s in May 1668. By July it was only 25s and in August—always the quietest month of the year—they thought it had levelled out and could only rise, as indeed it did. The last of his lead (462 pieces weighing 55,840 lb.) was sold to the Dutch East India Company on 14 September at 25s 6d flemish.

[246] Reese, Appendix A, pp. viii–xiii.
[247] H. E. Becht, *Statistische gegevens betreffende de handelsomzet van de Republiek der Vereenigde Nederlanden gedurende de zeventiende eeuw 1579–1715* (The Hague, 1908) p. 92; Reese, pp. 34, 37, Appendix E, p. xcvii.
[248] Reese, pp. 38–9, Appendix E, p.c.
[249] Reese, pp. 37–9.
[250] Reese, pp. 127–32, cxlvii. The building in Zwanenburgerstraat, which possessed living quarters, was called 'de vier suyckerbrooden' and is, I presume, the house in which Rembrandt and Saskia lived in 1638–9—see *Historische Gids van Amsterdam* (Amsterdam, 1974) pp. 206–7.
[251] For Nuyts see J. E. Elias, *De Vroedschap van Amsterdam, 1575–1795* (Haarlem, 1903, 1905) I p. 438, II p. 550; Reese, pp. 115, 117–18. For Hendricus Matthias see Elias, I p. 314; Reese p. 125.
[252] Elias, II p. 575.
[253] Van Baerles to CM, 27 April 1668. See pp. 106–8.

This great Company also had an indirect influence on Marescoe's tin sales, for although the hey-day of Asian tin-imports lay fifty years in the future,[254] modest consignments from Malacca had already earned a reputation for superior quality and malleability and their occasional appearance on the Amsterdam market could be expected to impair the dominance of the English product. Explaining the sluggish sales of Marescoe's tin in late September 1668, the Van Baerles warned him that the Malacca tin which had appeared in the Dutch East India Company's autumn sales was fetching 3–4 per cent more than English because of this superiority. Indeed 'our East India Company is sending for a substantial quantity of Malacca tin, although it is not believed that it will get here before Anno 1670'.[255] Fortunately, none had arrived with the sixteen East India ships of July 1668, but even so the price of English tin remained obstinately static at around $f.50$ per 100 lb., instead of the $f.56\frac{1}{2}$ to $f.53\frac{1}{2}$ it had been fetching between August and December 1667. This is another instance of Marescoe following where others had led, for these higher prices had been obtained by the Van Baerles not on his account but on behalf of his correspondent on the Isle of Wight, Benjamin Newland. Yet with English tin prices comparatively low in 1667 and its production 50 per cent up[256] Marescoe was naturally tempted to follow his friend's example and his first Dutch venture in this commodity, purchased at £3 12s per cwt., was despatched from Plymouth on 31 March 1668. It reached Rotterdam over four weeks later and was not in Amsterdam until the 8/18th of May. It was sold on the 19/29th at $f.50\frac{1}{2}$ with 1 per cent discount for cash, yielding Marescoe a 7 per cent profit. But later consignments, purchased at £3 16s per cwt. found themselves up against a resistant market where they could attract no more than $f.50$ or even, in August, $f.49$. The Amsterdam market was quite unmoved by the failure of any new Malacca tin to arrive in July, or by news of a price-rise in Cornwall.[257] Worse still, a cautious customer who tested one of Marescoe's blocks found it so hard and brittle that the Van Baerles thought it wiser to withdraw the batch from offer lest its poor quality became too widely known.[258] Marescoe obstinately held out for $f.52$ until early November, but even his large share of the 1668 imports could not dictate terms to a market where 'there are few buyers and tin is in several hands'.[259] His reward did not come until February and March 1669 when there was a sudden surge of demand and prices rose to $f.53$ and then $f.56$. Marescoe's response to prospects of a rise was to set higher and higher price-limits, ordering the Van Baerles not to sell below $f.53–f.54$ on 19 January, $f.55–f.56$ on 12 February and $f.58$ on 12 March. Under these conditions he was lucky that the Van Baerles closed on slightly lower offers before the price began to collapse in early May.[260] Although no tin figured in the spring or summer sales of the Dutch East India Company in 1669 the approach of another return fleet in June brought rumours of 170,000 lb. of Asian tin aboard and by 5 July there was no firm price for tin quotable on the Amsterdam exchange. The Company's autumn sales finally pushed prices down to $f.49$ and $f.48$.[261]

Marescoe's profit on his Amsterdam tin therefore seems to have owed much to the good management of the Van Baerles and it is regrettable that ill-feeling should have arisen

[254] F. P. Braudel & F. Spooner 'Prices in Europe from 1450 to 1750' in *The Cambridge Economic History of Europe, IV: The Economy of Expanding Europe in the 16th and 17th Centuries*, eds. E. E. Rich & C. H. Wilson (Cambridge, 1967) p. 424; Chaudhuri, pp. 206, 221.

[255] Van Baerles to CM, 28 September 1668.

[256] J. Whetter, *Cornwall in the 17th Century: an economic survey of Kernow* (Padstow, 1974) pp. 188, 195, 199.

[257] Van Baerles to CM, 20 July, 27 July 1668.

[258] Same to same, 7 September 1668.

[259] Same to same, 24 August 1668.

[260] Same to same, 10 May 1669.

[261] Same to same, 17 September 1669.

between them over the conduct of the Swedish sale-accounts. But the troubles following Peter Simons' bankruptcy, already described, cast their shadow over the whole relationship and Marescoe became increasingly unco-operative over the Van Baerles' drafts on the Mommas' accounts. On 13 December 1669 the Van Baerles observed, reproachfully: 'we are sorry to see from all these settlements that you do not display the same consideration and frankness which we have always shown to you', and by this date Marescoe's despatch to them of exports on his own account had long since come to an end. After October 1669 the Van Baerle letters therefore had nothing to say about the Amsterdam market for English goods, and their careful advice about cotton-yarn produced no response.

Marescoe's exports on commission account also experienced considerable difficulties in the course of 1669, for there was stagnation or decline in commodities from all main sectors. Barbados sugar fell from $7g$ and $6\frac{3}{4}g$ in January to $5\frac{3}{4}g$ and $5\frac{1}{2}g$ between April and July; Aleppo galls drifted down from $f.36$ to $f.30$ and $f.28$ per 100 lb. with no discernible demand during nine months, and East India Company pepper continued its collapse from the $30g$–$25g$ per lb. of 1668 to below $20g$ from July onwards. Although C. Berenberg made a lively show of curiosity about ten different commodities, his purchases of sugar, currants, cubeb and oil may well have been a symptom of poor judgment or desperation. Isaac Fellinger of Middelburg, who seems to have been a shrewd observer, spelled out for Marescoe the calculations which made it impossible for him (and, presumably, others) to continue trading with London in 1669. With Barbados sugar standing at $27s$–$28s$ in London he estimated that a Dutch price of $6\frac{1}{4}g$–$6\frac{3}{8}g$ would mean a loss of $\frac{1}{2}$ per cent on every pond sold.[262] Although he was interested in Apulian olive-oil while its London price was £28 or £27 10s, the fall in its Dutch price from £66 flemish in January to barely £60 flemish in March, £54 in April and £53 in May, left him relieved that Marescoe had not acted on a tentative order placed earlier in the year. Even at £59 or £60 flemish he estimated that oil bought in London at £28 sterling would yield no profit—'and after all, we only undertake something in order to make a profit!'[263] His last letter to Marescoe, on 26 July, after a month's visit to Holland, was a gloomy report on stagnant trade and over-filled warehouses. 'It seems', he wrote, 'as if there is some kind of fatality in business at this time, and whoever is least burdened with stocks is the best off.' Adding the pious hope that times would improve he left Marescoe with the advice that the best thing to do was to sit still.

Cornelius Berenberg might have been well advised to do the same. Instead, his appetite for English exports seems to have been whetted by a visit to London in July and on his return he placed orders for sugar, ginger and cubeb and, later, oil. The ginger eluded him but Marescoe procured him the oil, cubeb and sugar, the latter at the comparatively low price of $23s\ 9d$ per cwt. Yet more than one Amsterdam correspondent felt aggrieved that West Indian sugar had not fallen lower in London with the arrival in late August 1669 of at least eight of the ten ships expected from Barbados, and their letters reinforce the probability that demand elsewhere was putting English sources of sugar beyond Amsterdam's reach. 'As I have said before' wrote Daniel Planck, 'at $24s$ it must not only be good, but very, very good!'[264] He had been infuriated to make a loss on the sugar Marescoe had sent him in late 1668: it had been 3 or 4 per cent below invoice-weight and he insisted on reparation. He thought it a significant comment on the backwardness of English business-methods that he could obtain no publicly-attested record of the original weight in London, and he was therefore extremely reluctant to

---

262 I. Fellinger to CM, 1 March 1668.

263 '. . . *en nochtans is t'om prouffyt te doen dat men yts by der handt neemen*'—I. Fellinger to CM, 12 April 1669.

264 D. Planck to CM, 16 August 1669.

place any future orders. His simmering anger was such as to make his subsequent inquiries about arsenic and gunpowder seem rather menacing.

There was, however, more than a difference of temperament between Planck's conduct and that of Berenberg. There was a difference in business-strategy. Like his brother Paul, Cornelius was desperately seeking to maximize profits by rapid turnover. His orders, revisions, cancellations and reinstatement of orders were sent in rapid sequence—30 July, 2, 6, 9, 21, 22 and 27 August, 6, 10, 13 and 17 September, and so on. It was not until 19 November, after an unusual silence, that a terse letter announced 'I am losing my appetite for trade with London.' His bankruptcy, in the wake of his brother's, was close at hand.

Planck, to whom C. Berenberg had been apprenticed for six years, disowned his former pupil: 'he did not learn to meddle with such business from me';[265] but he offered to assist Marescoe to recover his £300 claim on Berenberg by impounding his latest consignment of currants and cubeb. This proved difficult and was strenuously opposed by other creditors with the result that Marescoe's correspondence with Planck again dissolved in mutual recrimination.

Altogether, 1669 was not a rewarding year in Marescoe's relations with Amsterdam. His own ventures had come to an end with an unprofitable consignment of galls, sent in January but not sold until June. He had been ill-advised to send them at all, for galls were heavily rated in the 'Convoy and Licence' tariff and bore a double percentage of 'lastgeld and veilgeld'.[266] In any event, as his shrewder correspondents appreciated, the market was unfavourable for these or most other commodities. A special combination of plentiful supply and low demand was keeping prices at unacceptably low levels and with an avowedly heavy heart Planck concluded that there was nothing in English trade with which he could profitably speculate. Like his colleagues in Hamburg, he was looking hopefully elsewhere, across the Atlantic, and it was not until 31 January 1670 that he could at last rejoice: 'God grant that the news of the silver fleet may be confirmed. Although I have no stake in it I hope, through the abundance of money, that trade will somewhat revive.'

Yet, despite the arrival of the Spanish *flota* in the first month of 1670 it brought no effective stimulus to Marescoe's trade with the United Provinces that year. His own consignments were limited to some lead, in transit for Italy, and a small quantity of Spanish wool purchased in Bilbao on a joint account with Isaac de la Fortrey. If his Dutch clients placed any commissions in London they were evidently not placed with Marescoe, and the loss of their correspondence for 1670 therefore leaves no grievous gap. Yet, if the trade with Amsterdam had been as important for Marescoe's exchange dealings as that with Hamburg, the picture might have been different. As it is, the modest balances generated there on Marescoe's account were not as crucial to his settlements with Sweden, as can be seen from an analysis of his two main Amsterdam accounts, with Daniel Planck and with the Van Baerles on his own account.

Between July 1664 and December 1669, when the account expires, Planck incurred liabilities to Marescoe totalling £5,164 2s, of which £4,524 18s 8d was for goods received. Against this he could set the proceeds of his own consignments to London (mainly dyestuffs)

---

[265] Same to same, 27 December 1669.
[266] Galls were charged with Convoy duty of 20 stuivers per 100 lb. (compared with 4 stuivers for lead, 8 stuivers for sugar and 16 stuivers for tin). They also bore a 2 per cent (instead of the customary 1 per cent) charge for 'lastgeld' and 'veilgeld' on their assessed weight—Isaac Lelong, *Den Koophandel van Amsterdam* (Amsterdam 1715) pp. 157, 216; Becht, pp. 97, 166, 173–7.

totalling £1,168 14*s* 8*d* net, and bills of exchange to the value of £4,668 17*s* 4*d*. The latter represented thirty-two bills:

	£	s	d
12 Amsterdam remittances to London	2,102	0	0
1 Haarlem remittance to London	100	0	0
1 Konigsberg remittance to Amsterdam	189	3	4
18 London drafts on Amsterdam	2,227	14	0

Seven of the latter, totalling £931 1*s*, were drawn by Marescoe for the benefit of some of his Swedish suppliers.

The remittances of the Van Baerles between December 1667 and December 1668 were bills of more varied origin.

		£	s	d
13 Amsterdam remittances to London		2,956	17	8
4 Venice remittances to Amsterdam		1,351	2	9
3 Amsterdam remittances to Paris		949	9	4
3 Paris		509	2	0
3 Rouen		468	16	11
3 Morlaix	remittances to London	466	13	4
1 Antwerp		200	0	0
1 St Malo		123	19	2
1 Lisbon		81	1	0
1 Amsterdam remittance to Rouen		120	6	8

These were to be set against Marescoe's fourteen consignments of goods, yielding £5,576 18*s* 2*d* net, and sixteen London bills all drawn on Amsterdam, totalling £1,702 11*s*. Not one of them was assigned for the benefit of his Swedish principals, in sharp contrast to the bills drawn in Marescoe's other, much larger account with the Van Baerles where the transactions were almost wholly dedicated to the requirements of the Mommas and their assigns. It would seem, therefore, that Marescoe was able to keep his personal trade-settlements on exports in a separate compartment, immune from the pressures and risks that came from the demands of the north, and this distinctiveness seems to become more pronounced as his interests turned southwards, towards the Spanish Netherlands, France and the Mediterranean.

[c] THE SPANISH NETHERLANDS

Marescoe's correspondence with the land of his birth seems to have owed nothing to sentiment or to family ties. The volume of commission trade he conducted there was never large and it is clear that it served interests more widely spread than those located in Lille, Antwerp or Bruges. Thanks to the neutrality of Spain in the second Anglo–Dutch war, the ports of the Spanish Netherlands proved indispensable to his clients, not only as points of access to France and the United Provinces but also as transit stages for trade with Spain itself. In 1665 Marescoe made use of seven ships bound for Ostend—four with consignments for

Lille and one each with goods destined for Bruges, Rouen and Amsterdam. In 1666 he freighted goods on no less than sixteen ships, destined as follows:

$$\left.\begin{array}{l} 9 \\ 2 \\ 1 \\ 1 \end{array}\right\} \text{via Ostend}$$

9			for Lille
2			for Cadiz
1	via Ostend		for Amsterdam
1			for Rouen, via Lille
2	for Antwerp		
1	via Ypres		for Lille

Of these cargoes, a quarter (by value, f.o.b.) was destined for merchants outside the Spanish Netherlands, and included lead and pepper for Rouen, tobacco and seedlack for Amsterdam, and pepper, stockings and cloth for Cadiz. For the Spanish Netherlands themselves, there was olive-oil for Bruges and sugar for Antwerp, while for Lille there were no less than 185 sacks of Barbados cotton, weighing $17\frac{1}{2}$ tons and amounting to 60 per cent of the value of Marescoe's trade with this area.

Before looking at the clientele and the market for these goods, it is worth noting that Marescoe's exports to the Spanish Netherlands were complemented by a small trade in the import of Ghent linen. This industry was at its zenith in the 1660s and, next to Spain and the Americas, England was its largest customer.[267] To find that Marescoe was taking a half share in the sales of Guillaume Huwe's consignments of bleached linen is therefore interesting but hardly impressive, for at a time when annual production at Ghent is conservatively estimated to have been about 78,000 pieces,[268] Marescoe took 500 pieces in 1664, 300 in 1665 and 300 in 1666. His half-share in the profits on goods worth £2,766 11s 11d (c.i.f.) was only £17 3s 2d.

In 1667, both imports and exports were brought to a halt by the War of Devolution. Marescoe managed to despatch six sacks of cotton to Lille, via Bruges, before Louis XIV's assault on the Spanish Netherlands was launched in May, but that was all. For his linen he had to turn elsewhere, to Morlaix, and take a one-fourth share in imports which must have totalled £10,800 (c.i.f.) in 1667–8.[269] The purchases and the sales were handled by his other partners—Daniel Cognard, Jacques Barré and Christopher Lethieullier—and the final settlement, a profit of £284 1s 3d for Marescoe's share, puts his own management of the Ghent linen sales in a rather poor light. Not surprisingly, he declined to renew his partnership with Huwe in 1668.[270]

By then the situation in the Spanish Netherlands had been radically altered by French military successes which put Louis XIV in possession of large areas of Artois, Flanders and Hainault. Lille had been swiftly taken in August 1667, and by the settlement of Aix-la-Chapelle in May 1668 it was transferred to French sovereignty together with Bergues, Furnes, Armentières, Courtrai, Douai, Tournai, Binche, Ath and Charleroi. The effect of this settlement was to disrupt the economic cohesion of one of Europe's most important industrial areas, for although an article of the treaty implicitly guaranteed freedom of trade

---

[267] J. Bastin, 'De Gentse lijnwaadmarkt en linnenhandel in de XVIIe eeuw', in *Handelingen der Maatschappij voor Geschiedenis en Oudheidkunde te Gent*, Nieuwe Reeks, deel xxi (1967) pp. 133–7.

[268] Bastin, p. 136

[269] According to the 'Book of Tables' BL, Add. MS. 36, 785, London's imports of French 'Lockrams' were worth £129,921 in 1662–3, and £129,695 in 1668–9.

[270] G. Huwe to CM, 18 January 1668.

and transit between French and Spanish territories,[271] the redrawn frontier—with its complex of enclaves—now inhibited the natural flow of raw materials and manufactures to, and from, the sea. Encumbered with Spanish customs posts and discriminatory tariffs, the traditional routes to Ghent, Ypres or Dunkirk were effectively blocked to the textile producers of Lille, Tournai and Courtrai.[272] To counter this, it quickly became a cardinal objective of Colbert's policy to divert this traffic from the Lys and the Scheldt to the Somme or even the Seine. The merchants of Lille were granted free passage across France and plans were laid to improve communications with Amiens, Abbeville and St Valéry-sur-Somme.[273] Not all Lille's traders were to find this reorientation disadvantageous, but serious problems were bound to arise if they lost all means of access to their predominantly Spanish markets or to their suppliers of raw material in the Netherlands.

Lille's well-regulated textile industry was dependent on an eclectic variety of yarns, for while one half of the industry—the *sayetteurs*—specialized in *sayes* and *ostades* of pure combed wool, the other half, the *bourgetteurs*, produced a remarkable range of textiles with mixtures of wool, silk, linen and cotton.[274] And it was an industry which was highly responsive to changing fashions and uniquely fertile in producing new styles. Indeed, the 1660s saw considerable disorder in Lille under the pressures of innovation, such as the introduction of *barracans* (a coarse, untwilled textile of wool and, sometimes, hemp—useful for rainproof garments).[275] There were riots in 1665 and in 1666, and the civic ordinance of 14 August 1666 explicitly acknowledged the stresses arising from the pace of contemporary change.[276] Yet, if this valuable adaptability was not to be lost after 1667, Colbert was quickly made aware that supply routes and markets would have to be preserved. The new *intendant* of Lille, Michel Le Peletier, also reminded him that Lille's excellent dyeing industry attracted textiles and materials from the whole of the Netherlands,[277] while frantic petitions from the *sayetteurs* protested about their markets being lost to Bruges, Ghent and Antwerp, where numbers of their fellow-citizens had already fled.[278]

---

[271] See Nelly Girard d'Albissin, *Genèse de la frontière Franco-Belge: les variations des limites septentrionales de la France de 1659 à 1789* [Bibliothèque de la société d'histoire du droit des pays flamands, picards et wallons, XXVI] (Paris, 1970) p. 115. Although the treaty of 1668 made no reference to freedom of commerce, it confirmed the treaty of the Pyrenees, which did. For the text see *The Consolidated Treaty Series*, vol. XI (1667–8) ed. C. Parry (New York, 1969) pp. 13–32.

[272] The problems of transit and tariffs are discussed in Girard d'Albissin, 114–17; Albert Croquez, *Histoire politique et administrative d'une province française. La Flandre. I. La Flandre wallonne et les pays de l'intendance de Lille sous Louis XIV* (Paris, 1912) pp. 176–7; Maurice Vanhaeck, *Histoire de la Sayetterie à Lille*, Société d'études de la province de Cambrai. Mémoires. Tome XVI. (Lille, 1910) I. pp. 80–1; M. Braure, *Les documents néerlandais relatifs à l'occupation de la Flandre wallonne, 1708–1713* (Lille, 1913) p. 97.

[273] Girard d'Albissin, p. 119; Croquez, *La Flandre wallonne*, pp. 183–6; A. Girard, *Le commerce français à Seville et Cadix au temps des Habsbourg* (Paris, Bordeaux, 1932) p. 475.

[274] For Lille's textile industries in the seventeenth century, see P. Deyon & A. Lottin, 'Évolution de la production textile à Lille aux XVIe et XVIIIe siècles', *Revue du Nord*, xlix (1967) pp. 23–34; A. Lottin, *Vie et mentalité d'un lillois sous Louis XIV* (Lille, 1968) pp. 13–14, 40–54; Tihomir J. Markovitch, *Histoire des industries françaises: Les industries lainières de Colbert à la Révolution* (Geneva, 1976) pp. 171–5; Jan Craeybeckx, 'Les industries d'exportation dans les villes flamandes au XVIIe siècle, particulièrement à Gand et à Bruges' in *Studi in onore di Amintore Fanfani*, vol. 4 (Milan, 1962) pp. 413–68; Jules Houdoy, *La filature de coton dans le nord de la France* (Paris, 1903) pp. 8–28. R. S. DuPlessis & M. C. Howell, 'Reconsidering the early modern urban economy: the cases of Leiden and Lille', *Past & Present* 94 (1982) pp. 63–78.

[275] J. Savary des Bruslons, *Dictionnaire universel de commerce* I. p. 436; Craeybeckx, pp. 422, 429, 434; Lottin, p. 86; Vanhaeck, I. p. 51.

[276] Vanhaeck, II. Document 78, pp. 153–4.

[277] Croquez, *La Flandre wallonne*, pièces justificatives, pp. 7–15.

[278] Lottin, p. 53.

This was the troubled context in which Marescoe's surviving correspondence from the Spanish Netherlands begins, with its largest component coming from a Lille which was on the point of becoming irredeemably French. Yet, economically, its affinities were to remain largely unaltered in the course of 1668 and much of the interest of these letters lies in their tentative assessments and gradual adjustment to the new situation and its potentialities.

The most important of Marescoe's clients in Lille were members of the Libert family— Philippe, Toussaint and, occasionally, Noël. Regrettably they are distinguished not only by their large and regular commissions but also by the illegibility of their letters which are therefore not represented in the printed selection. Yet, between 1664 and 1667, Philippe had been a most reliable customer, purchasing 1,470 gallons of olive-oil, 66 cwt. of Aleppo galls and 19,618 lb. of Barbados cotton. In 1668 he was again Marescoe's largest customer at Lille, ordering both varieties of Barbados cotton (the 'yellow' and the cheaper 'white') and sharing half-and-half with Marescoe in a consignment of choicer Smyrna cotton. His brother Toussaint also ordered cotton, as well as olive-oil. But what is significant about these consignments is that throughout the whole year they were still despatched through their traditional channels, via Bruges or Ypres, and in one case, via Ostend. Indeed, Philippe made it clear that he preferred Bruges, although he also nominated Ostend, Nieuport or Ypres as acceptable alternatives.[279]

This problem of routes was of equal concern to Marescoe's other regular customer in Lille, the partnership of Jean d'Hollandre & Jean du Beron. They too had been customers for cotton and grograin yarn in 1664 and 1665, and it was to these commodities that they returned in 1668. Like the Liberts, they preferred Marescoe to send consignments through Bruges, and this he did until a dramatically terse letter of 6 October cancelled their latest commission. The circumstance to which this note cryptically referred was almost certainly the decree of 12 September 1668 by which the French authorities imposed a retaliatory tariff of 30 per cent on goods entering from the Spanish Netherlands.[280] This effectively put a stop to normal transit and although modified on 24 September the new tariff inaugurated a deliberate French campaign to wean the newly conquered territories from their old dependence on the Netherlands.

Not surprisingly, the usual verdict on the significance of French sovereignty is that it effected a profound reversal for Lille's textile industry and inaugurated its long-term decline.[281] Against such an assumption one may set the apparently unimpaired yield of Lille's textile duties, during and after 1667–8, and the fact that Lille retained its local pre-eminence to the end of the eighteenth century.[282] Marescoe's clientele is too small and too brief in duration to provide convincing evidence for either view, yet one cannot fail to note the resilience and resourcefulness with which Lille correspondents coped with their difficulties. In March 1668, D'Hollandre & Du Beron were confident that—forbidden or not—means could always be found to introduce their goods into Spain or its territories, and on 27 October Philippe Libert displayed none of the pessimism which had paralysed D'Hollandre & Du Beron just three weeks before. He cheerfully hailed news of the safe arrival of more cotton yarn at Bruges: 'je le suis attendant avecq impassince . . . s'il est un peu fin je croy qu'il serat sito vendu a bon proufit, dieu aidant'.

Regrettably, the Lille correspondents reveal little about their customers or the state of their

[279] P. Libert to CM, 5 May, 13 October 1668.

[280] A. Croquez, *Louis XIV en Flandre: les institutions, les hommes et les méthodes dans une province nouvellement annexé, 1667–1708* (Paris, 1920) p. 130; Lottin, p. 47; Girard d'Albissin, p. 117.

[281] Deyon & Lottin, p. 24; Lottin, p. 51.

[282] Deyon & Lottin, p. 33; Vanhaeck, I. p. 80; Markovitch, p. 174.

markets. Few prices are quoted and their inquiries to Marescoe are focussed upon a narrow range of commodities. D'Hollandre & Du Beron remained interested primarily in cottons and grograin yarn, about which they display an exacting, professional judgment. Samples of the required quality were sent to London and samples of the available supplies were returned. Few were found wholly satisfactory in quality or in price. In March 1668 they thought that Barbados cotton-wool at $8\frac{1}{4}d$ per lb. in London was too expensive, but during April—when cotton was selling in Lille at a scarcity price of £46–£48 per 100 lb. they were prepared to go halves with Marescoe in 30 or 40 sacks if he could get them at $7d$ or $7\frac{1}{2}d$ per lb. As for grograin yarn, the arrival of supplies from Smyrna had brought its London price down from $8s$ (for the finest quality) and $6s$ or $7s$ (for middle quality) to $6s$ $6d$ and $5s$ $6d$ respectively by late May. Satisfied with some samples, they ordered two bales of each quality on 9 June, changed their minds on the 30th and finally received one bale of the finest—'assez belle'—and three of middling quality—'assez grosses, et avecq peu de lustre; autrement le fille est assez souple et gras.'[283] It was not a purchase they wished to repeat, for by late September (before news of the French tariffs had reached them) they learned that they could obtain grograin yarn from Holland for 25 per cent less.[284]

Barbados cotton, on the other hand, remained attractive as its price fell towards $5\frac{3}{4}d$ per lb. in London, and they also expressed interest in camel-hair, enclosing samples of the quality required. In return they offered the finished product, *camelots*, a textile for which England hungered but which Marescoe politely declined. Indeed, there was no question of reciprocal trade or barter between the two centres, and the three-cornered exchange they proposed on 3 March is a curious anomaly.

The plan was to barter 5 unsold bales of Marescoe's cotton-yarn against textiles suitable for the Spanish market. First to be considered were *estamines* or *picottes*, light, high-quality textiles sometimes of pure wool or mixed with silks,[285] which were evidently in too much demand to be readily obtained. A second suggestion was *bourats*, another light mixture, semi-twilled, which was said to have a ready market at Bilbao and the Biscay area. Finally, they found an opportunity to barter the cotton for 86 pieces of *polimites* or *nompareilles* (which are sometimes lumped together with *lamparillas*).[286] This is described as a middle-quality product, usually of wool or mixed with flax, used for summer-clothes and cloaks. D'Hollandre & Du Beron proposed to send them to their agents at Amsterdam where they would be given a false certificate as products of Leyden and thus escape the Spanish prohibition of imports from Lille. Marescoe's agents in Spain, the firm of Upton & Bathurst, would procure their sale.

As will be seen [46], Upton & Bathurst gave them a critical reception, finding them of poor quality and in no way comparable to true *lamparillas*.[287] It was partly a matter of presentation: they had been folded and pressed in a manner associated with the cheapest *picottes* to which they bore a suspicious resemblance. To this innuendo D'Hollandre & Du Beron irritably retorted that they had folded them in this fashion on the expert advice of friends at Cadiz. They concluded, crushingly—'Il faut avouer que la nation espagnole a trés peu de cognoissance de la bonté d'une m[ar]chandise de la quelle ils font l'estimation sellon l'extérieur, et non pas de la quallité requise'.[288]

---

283 D'Hollandre & Du Beron to CM, 25 August 1668.
284 Same to same, 22 and 29 September 1668.
285 J. Savary des Bruslons, I. 1900–3.
286 J. Everaert, *De internationale en koloniale handel der vlaamse firma's te Cadiz, 1670–1700*, p. 866.
287 See p. 99.
288 D'Hollandre & Du Beron to CM, 22 September 1668.

The importance of grasping the finer points of textile manufacture was brought home to Marescoe by a correspondent from Bruges, who introduced himself as a former protégé of D'Hollandre & Du Beron. Jacomo van Marissien—'personne de probité, et a qui le capital ne manque'[289]—proposed to open up a mutual exchange of goods in which he would supply *bombazines* or *sayes* suitable for the Spanish market. Later, expressing an interest in Barbados cotton-wool, he asked for a trial consignment and offered in return a sample of yet another textile, so far unnamed, which had been in production for only a few weeks.[290] Marescoe seems to have declined this offer, and one may deduce from this and other episodes that he was ill-at-ease with textiles and preferred to leave their management to his brother-in-law, John Lethieullier.

With sugar, galls and oil he was more at home, and about these commodities he conducted a more lively correspondence with his principal client in Antwerp, Pieter Jaspersen. Already introduced for his consignments to Middelburg, in the care of Fellinger, Jaspersen sat astride the alternative routes into the Netherlands and watched them like a hawk for marginal advantages. No correspondent displays more sensitivity to variations in freight-rates, and no client was more critical of Marescoe's choice of routes. Jaspersen usually preferred his goods to come via Zeeland, or Rotterdam, but after complaining bitterly of Marescoe's freight charges on sugar and olive-oil, calculated that it might be cheaper to get them through Ostend, or Bruges. Friends of his had obtained goods through Bruges for only *f*.16 per last, and from Bruges to Antwerp the charge was only *f*.9, as against the *f*.32 Marescoe was charging or the *f*.27 which Marescoe ought to have obtained for direct shipment to Antwerp.[291] In the event, of the four shipments Jaspersen received in 1668, two went to Middelburg, one to Ostend and only one directly to Antwerp.

The pattern of shipments, for all Marescoe's clients in the Spanish Netherlands, was to become even more complicated in 1669, a year which saw a marked increase in traffic. Fifteen distinct commissions had been performed in 1668 (including the two which Jaspersen diverted to Middelburg) but in 1669 there were thirty-six. The respective distributions, by route, were as follows:

1668	(%) Value (f.o.b.)	1669	(%) Value (f.o.b.)
7 via Bruges	36.0	23 via Bruges	52.5
2 via Middelburg	27.6	3 via Antwerp	13.2
2 via Antwerp	21.0	1 via Nieuport	9.6
2 via Ypres	9.0	5 via Calais	13.9
2 via Ostend	6.4	4 via St Valéry	10.8

The Lille merchants had been the sole patrons of Ostend, Bruges and Ypres in 1668, but in 1669, when they commissioned 21 of the 36 consignments, they received 11 through Bruges, 1 through Nieuport and 9 through the French ports.

This is some measure of Colbert's initial success in diverting Lille's traffic to the south. His correspondence with Le Peletier had concentrated on the encouragement of exports to Spain via Le Havre, but a complementary flow via St Valéry-sur-Somme was also envisaged and

---

[289] Same to same, 22 September 1668.
[290] J. van Marissien to CM, 25 November 1668. He described it merely as '*une nouvelle fabricque, belle et bonne, comme l'incluse eschantillion, des meselanes royez, $\frac{3}{4}$ de large et 2 @ de loinge, valliant le pièche f. 52 de gros*'.
[291] P. Jaspersen to CM, 6 October 1668.

long-term plans were laid for its support.[292] The abandonment of the retaliatory tariff in February 1669 and the exemption of the conquered territories from the tariff of 1667 created a more welcoming climate to which the correspondents of Lille were not unresponsive. Writing on 1 June, D'Hollandre & Du Beron tried to cancel their recent instruction to send a consignment via Bruges:

> 'Sommes mary que ne vous avons ordonné de charger ledit indigo pour St Walleri d'où nous les poudrions tirer sans payer aucune droits d'entre ny de sortie la ou que par Bruges les frais sont assez grands. S'il estoit encor en temps de le faire charger pour les susdit place vous nous obligerez de le faire.'

There were other inducements to change routes. Three months earlier, the passage via Ostend and the canal linking it to Bruges had been interrupted yet again by one in an interminable series of quarrels between the skippers of Ostend and their rivals at Bruges.[293] As recently as April 1667 forty troublemakers had been arrested in an attempt to break the deadlock but in March 1669 it seems that the Ostenders were again obstructing foreign ships in transit to Bruges. However, the dispute was resolved in favour of Bruges by May and it was thereafter open to Van Marissien and the Lillois customers to solicit shipments by this alternative route, which appears to have retained some advantages in speed and safety over the land routes from St Valéry or Calais. 'Il at trop de fres par Caley' complained Philippe Libert in December 1669, and in March 1670 his brother reckoned that scarcely one in ten of his bales of cotton yarn had reached him from Calais undamaged.[294] As for St Valéry, it was a notoriously difficult estuary to navigate, with its shifting sandbanks,[295] and D'Hollandre & Du Beron admitted that a captain would have to be paid a premium to induce him to discharge there. For these reasons alone there could be no complete rupture between Lille and its former routes through the Spanish Netherlands.

As for the commodities ordered from England in 1669, it is no surprise to find the bulk of them related to Lille's textile industry. Cotton (140 cwt.) and indigo (20 cwt.) account for 52 per cent of their value, and Lille's lively interest in a variety of dyestuffs testifies to a year of thriving activity. But here too there were exacting standards to be observed. Marescoe's clients took it for granted that he would be buying only the best Guatemalo indigo: with the Barbados product they were scarcely acquainted. On 6 July D'Hollandre & Du Beron ordered a sample which was duly shown round the dyers but found unsuitable. Indeed, Marescoe's recent purchases of dyestuffs had been so unsatisfactory that he was bluntly advised to give up dealing in them. Cautiously ordering more indigo on 3 August 1669, D'Hollandre & Du Beron warned him:

> 'nous les avons demandé pour les tinturiers de toilles qui ne se servent que de plus exquis quy se rencontre, scavoir du plus bleu et plus léger que s'y en pourrier rencontrer.'

They were also interested in cochineal, but with the price limit set at 21*s*, or 22*s* 6*d* at most, Marescoe was unable to help, and by mid-August of 1669 expectations of the next *flota*'s arrival began to paralyse Lille's will to order either indigo or cochineal.

Demand for cotton-wool and yarn remained buoyant, however. It can be deduced from the Libert letters that they, at least, were supplying not only Lille but customers elsewhere,

[292] Lottin, p. 49; Croquez, *La Flandre wallonne*, p. 186; Girard d'Albissin, p. 119.
[293] J. de Smet, 'De doorvaart voor de binnenscheepvaart te Brugge in de XVIIe eeuw' in *Handelingen van het Genootschap voor Geschiedenis, Société d'Émulation te Brugge*, deel cviii (1971) pp. 192–208.
[294] P. Libert to CM, 7 December 1668; 1 March 1669.
[295] P. Deyon, *Amiens, capitale provinciale* (Paris, 1967) p. 94.

such as Tournai, and the only obstacle to rapid sales was the competing flood of supplies which had put cotton in many hands. Prices were keenly judged and not a penny was willingly conceded, for prices were falling daily.[296] Specific prices are not stated but they were evidently at a level where only the highest quality could command a reasonable profit. The coarser qualities, which Marescoe too often sent, remained a drug on the market and he was urged, again and again, to select only the finest. London prices for best-quality cotton-wool had moved down from 7*d* per lb. between February and June to 6*d* by October 1669, historically low prices at which Marescoe declined to take a half-share with his friends in Lille.

His other, more substantial, commissions were for Apulian olive-oil, for which all his correspondents registered some demand. Of the 10,000 gallons sent, about 60 per cent went to Jaspersen and 28 per cent to D'Hollandre & Du Beron. Toussaint Libert took only a little and regretted even that for it proved a troublesome commodity in the hot summer, much subject to leakage on its long passage to Lille.

Of more significance was Toussaint's order for samples of English textiles in all the most popular colours.[297] Marescoe bought him a range of six high-quality broadcloths (from 5*s* 8*d* to 8*s* 4*d* per yard) and six serges at 56*s* and 58*s* per piece, with which Toussaint was reasonably impressed. But by the time they reached him in late October 1669 the market was displaying the same lethargy of glut which had seized its counterparts elsewhere. There was no sequel to this promising commission.

Other inquiries on the London market proved even more sterile. Pepper and Aleppo galls were found too expensive to compete with Amsterdam's, and nothing came of an isolated inquiry about chocolate, tea and coffee. A request for assistance with coals from Newcastle reflects only a temporary political difficulty created in August 1669 by another stage in the Franco–Spanish tariff war which had made Hainault's coal extremely costly to obtain.[298] The request was not renewed. Only Jacomo van Marissien, with the enthusiasm of youth, plunged into an assortment of experimental commissions, ordering small quantities of sugar, cottons, raisins, currants, galls, tobacco, indigo and oil—all in one breathless letter.[299] But even as he welcomed their safe arrival he acknowledged the common danger which threatened to engulf his country:

'si les Hollandois nous n'assisteront point asseurement que la Flandre se perdrat tout a fait!'[300]

The difficulties of Marescoe's commission trade with the Spanish Netherlands in 1669 may therefore reflect more than one adverse circumstance, but the paramount one here, as elsewhere, was clearly a state of stock repletion and glutted demand. From Bruges, from Antwerp and from Lille, the message was much the same—stagnant markets, low prices and an adverse rate of exchange. With these inevitably came bankruptcies, such as Joseph van den Ast's in Antwerp,[301] and Jacob Aboab's in London.[302] The latter seems to have sent shock-

---

[296] D'Hollandre & Du Beron to CM 26 January 1669.

[297] T. Libert to CM, 29 June 1669.

[298] For this frontier dispute, see Girard d'Albissin, p. 118; *The Despatches of William Perwich, 1669–77* (ed. M. B. Curran) Camden Society, 3rd Series, Vol. 5 (1903) p. 38; PRO, SP. 94/55 f. 89. (Sir William Godolphin to Lord Arlington, 8/18 September 1669.)

[299] J. van Marissien to CM, 25 September 1669.

[300] Same to same, 16 November 1669.

[301] P. Jaspersen to CM, 21 December 1669.

[302] Jacob Aboab (alias Cardoso) appears to have been a member of the Portuguese-Jewish community of London, engaged in import and export trade. See Maurice Woolf, 'Foreign Trade of London Jews in the Seventeenth Century' in *Transactions of the Jewish Historical Society of England*, Sessions 1970–3, vol. xxiv (1974) p. 55; cf. ibid. p. 121 n. 18. For further references to Aboab's failure, see pp. 89, 103.

waves through Lille, Paris, Rouen and Amsterdam and its effects proved damaging in centres as far apart as Hamburg and Leghorn.[303] Marescoe had been warned against the reliability of Aboab's bills by the faithful Van Baerles in November 1669, but news of his failure did not reach D'Hollandre & Du Beron until mid-December, leaving them deeply exposed to the tune of £3,131 11s 2d sterling in bills. They begged Marescoe to provide cover for £750 and offered him security upon consignments of Segovia wool and Bilbao iron already in transit to London. Alternatively, he could draw on their correspondents, Antoine Sadocq, père et fils, of Paris, Paul & Peter Godin of Amsterdam or Jeremias Haskens of Antwerp, but Marescoe declined. There was an element of fraud involved in Aboab's bankruptcy which made it prudent for him to keep clear, and the only comfort that Marescoe could offer them was that Aboab ('le cocquin, ce volleur!') might be caged by his London creditors. 'Cela éstant, on le feroit plustot chanter, et nous espérins d'en tirer quelque satisfaction.'[304] But in fact Aboab was to flutter away, offering composition of only 25 per cent, and it was to take years before D'Hollandre & Du Beron got their satisfaction.

It was also to be some years before Toussaint Libert went bankrupt.[305] In October 1669, D'Hollandre & Du Beron wrote of him as a man 'qui [nous] croions faire doucement ses affaires mais avec peu de fonds'. His bills were probably safe. But in fact Marescoe was to experience occasional difficulties with the exchanges on Lille which may reflect its anomalous position after August 1667. All three Lille firms were to present him with bills which were protested for non-payment, and it seems likely that they had problems in finding suitable drawers from the limited number of Lille merchants with credit in London. In his accounts with Philippe Libert between 1664 and 1670, Marescoe had to draw 19 bills on Lille and one on Ghent. He received only three remittances from Lille. With Toussaint Libert's account his credits were more evenly distributed between five London bills on Lille, totalling £577 3s, and six Lille bills on London, totalling £356 6s, one of which was protested. Settlements with D'Hollandre & Du Beron between 1664 and 1670 were either through London bills on Lille (16, worth £2,190 16s) or Lille bills on London (24, worth £3,726 3s 9d), and clearly this firm had the wider acquaintance among Lille's businessmen, obtaining drafts from some of the leading merchant-houses of the city—Farvaques, LeFebvre, Taviel, Laman. . . .[306] Yet even they presented a £200 bill, protested in October 1666.

Such problems were not apparent in Antwerp, and any lingering doubts about her continuing importance as a European business centre[307] are disposed of by the pattern of bills exchanged between Marescoe and Peter Jaspersen on their respective accounts, between 1665 and 1670. In Marescoe's personal account with Jaspersen—a pure exchange account, unblemished by commodities—he made a profit of £17 on the following bills:

Debits		£	s	d	Credits		£	s	d
14 London on	Antwerp	1,801	3	8	9 Antwerp on	London	1,302	0	0
1 Seville	Antwerp	227	14	8	5 Ghent	London	800	0	0
1 London	Lille	72	0	4	1 Brussels	London	100	0	0
2 London	Ostend	400	0	0	1 Rotterdam	London	50	0	0
		2,500	18	8	1 Lille	London	50	0	0
Profit on the exchange		17	0	0	1 Rouen	London	215	18	8
		2,517	18	8			2,517	18	8

303-307 See p. 82 for footnotes.

His trading account with Jaspersen was, necessarily, more complex but can be summarized thus:

	Debits	£	s	d		Credits		£	s	d
Goods sent		2,752	17	6	23	Antwerp on	London	2,681	19	8
Expenses, etc.		270	17	2	6	Ghent	London	770	0	0
Bills:					1	Courtrai	London	150	0	0
22 London on	Antwerp	2,258	5	6	1	Amsterdam	London	250	0	0
4 London	Middelburg	400	0	0	1	Hamburg	London	190	0	0
2 London	Lille	197	18	0	5	Rouen	London	630	16	10
					5	Morlaix	London	753	14	0
(Total bills £2,856 3s 6d)					2	Bordeaux	London	331	5	0
					2	Venice	London	122	13	8
		5,879	18	2				5,879	18	2

The effect of this contrast is to confirm the impression, derived elsewhere from the correspondence, of the comparative isolation and provincialism of Lille, which had inevitably increased after 1667. Although not immune to conditions elsewhere in the Netherlands, Marescoe's customers in Lille appear more remote from, and less well-informed about, the main currents of European commodity trades. There are few references to prices elsewhere, and no price-currents change hands. There is none of the Hamburgers' well-informed alertness to shipping movements or to wind and weather, and it is significant that when the Lillois correspondents switched their routes to Calais and St Valéry it was to Marescoe's agents that they entrusted their goods, for they had none of their own. Yet, in one important respect they shared to the full the preoccupations of their colleagues in Hamburg and Amsterdam. As 1669 sank into stagnation they too pinned their hopes of revival on the coming of the Spanish *flota*.

In their case the optimism appears to have been justified. 1670 was a year of brisker trade for Marescoe's clients in Lille, and one can deduce from some of its components that it reflected both the consequences of one *flota*'s arrival and the expectation of another's departure.[308] Thus, cochineal, which had been too expensive in 1669 at over 22s 6d, now came within their reach as its London price fell below 20s per lb. to 19s 6d in the autumn.[309] Four consignments of the dye, all to D'Hollandre & Du Beron, account for 45.5 per cent of the year's trade with Lille. Cottons came next, at 23 per cent, followed by Guatemalo and

---

[303] See p. 103.

[304] D'Hollandre & Du Beron to CM, 1 February 1670.

[305] D'Hollandre & Du Beron to JD, 18 January 1679.

[306] For these and other leading Lille merchants see Lottin, p. 52; Croquez, *Louis XIV en Flandre*, p. 109; Louis Trenard, *Histoire d'une métropole: Lille, Roubaix, Tourcoing* (Toulouse, 1977) p. 230.

[307] On this issue, see J. A. Van Houtte, 'Déclin et survivance d'Anvers, (1550–1700)' in Van Houtte, *Essays on Medieval and Early Modern Economy and Society* (Leuven, 1977).

---

[308] See pp. 72, 83 n. 310, 89, 145 n. 130.

[309] Some 2,000 cases of cochineal reached Spain in the *flota* of February 1670—see Henry Kamen, *Spain in the Later Seventeenth-Century, 1665–1700*, p. 138.

Lahore indigoes at 17.4 per cent.[310] Although London prices for cottons had evidently risen above their 1669 levels, there would seem to have been enough buoyancy of demand in the textile industry to justify commissions not only for Barbados cotton wool at 9*d* and 9$\frac{1}{4}$*d* per lb. but also for Turkish yarn at 14*d* and choice Indian at 30*d* per lb. Marescoe's half-share investment in the two latter is sufficient indication that the depression of 1669 had been momentarily lifted, and that Spanish demand was keen.

1670 also brought him new customers in Lille, with new and significant requirements. Charles Angelo's commissions for lead, saltpetre and sulphur have a distinctly war-like complexion which consorts oddly with his order for 50 barrels of preserved sweets, or 'dragees'. Anthoine Wantier and Toussaint Libert also conveyed a demand for lead in Lille which may not be unconnected with the rapid re-fortification programme being undertaken by the military occupation.

But the clearest reflection of a settled French domination is provided by the pattern of routes employed in 1670. Of the 25 separate consignments despatched to Lille by Marescoe this year, all now went through French ports—17 via St Valéry, 5 via Dunkirk, and 3 via Calais. Furthermore, 14 of them were freighted in French ships, a higher proportion than was usual. Colbert's policies were evidently taking effect, in a manner which did Marescoe no particular harm, for they were compatible with a healthy surge in his trade. But the same was not to prove true of his dealings elsewhere, in Rouen and La Rochelle.

[d] FRANCE

Before 1668 Marescoe's relations with France seem to have been less active and rewarding than those with Sweden, Hamburg or the Netherlands. Although letters to France certainly figure in his weekly postal-expenses for 1661–4,[311] the scale of the correspondence seems to have been modest and was almost certainly confined to a trade in bills of exchange. Such is the nature of the two largest of his French accounts in 1664, one with Hermann Wetken,[312] and one with the partnership of Widow Conincq & Robert Oursel.[313] In Wetken's case, Marescoe was simply acting as an intermediary for his correspondent in Newcastle, Robert Ellison.[314] With no direct exchange operating between Rouen and the northern port, Marescoe received Wetken's remittances on Ellison's behalf and honoured Ellison's drafts in return. Between June 1664 and July 1665 over £4,000 passed through the account, on which Marescoe took his usual commission.

[310] The 1670 *flota* also brought 6,500 cases of indigo; 5,500 arrived with the *galeones* in June 1670, together equalling 87 per cent of deliveries in the 1660s and accounting for 46 per cent of arrivals in the 1670s—Kamen, p. 138; Garcia Fuentes, *El comercio español con America, 1650–1700*, pp. 509–10.

[311] Journal, 'Charges of Merchandize, 1661–1674', *passim*.

[312] Herman[n] Wetken came to Rouen from Hamburg, was naturalized and later abjured his Protestant religion; his wife, Anne Dierquens whom he married in 1673, refused to abjure and was imprisoned. See Jean Bianquis, *La révocation de l'édit de Nantes à Rouen*, with *Notes sur les Protestants de Rouen* by Émile Lesens (Rouen, 1885), p. 87; J. Mathorez, *Les étrangers en France sous l'ancien régime* (Paris, 1921) ii, p. 161.

[313] Catherine Coninck (née Crommelin) was born in 1632 into a wealthy manufacturing family with extensive ramifications in the Netherlands. Her first husband, François de Coninck (b. 1621) also came of a notable Flemish commercial family, settled at Rouen in 1650 and died in April 1662. On 15 November 1665 she married her late husband's partner, Robert Oursel. Son of Robert Oursel (1607–86) whose family were long-established merchants of Le Havre, the younger Robert was baptized in January 1634 and died in 1708, predeceased by his wife in 1694. For an account of the Oursel and Coninck families see Philippe Mieg, 'Les de Coninck au Havre et à Rouen' in *Bulletin de l'histoire de Protestantisme Français*, 5th Series (1921) pp. 97–115, 154–74, 252–67; also, Herbert Lüthy, *La Banque protestante en France* (Paris, 1959) i, pp. 70 n. 24, ii, p. 358 n. 17.

[314] See [55].

With Conincq & Oursel the account was larger and more varied, and although bills represent over 75 per cent of the traffic between them there were also commodities— Barbados cotton-wool, East Indian cotton-yarn and Aleppo galls which the Rouen firm purchased on its own account in the late summer of 1664.[315] In 1665 there was lead, 599 pieces weighing 710¾ cwt., in which Marescoe took a half-share. English lead had been the largest and most valuable component in London's export trade to France in 1662–3[316] and although this was probably an abnormal proportion it is no surprise to find Marescoe entering upon a trade for which he had excellent contacts among the lead-dealers of Yorkshire and the Mendips. Yet he was unlucky with this consignment: the ship ran aground off Ostend and it was to take two years before the last block of lead was recovered and sold. Notwithstanding the costs of salvage and reshipment a profit of 13 per cent remained to encourage further ventures of this kind.[317]

Yet, paradoxically, it was to require the second Anglo–Dutch war and the initiative of his Swedish employers to secure the decisive expansion of Marescoe's dealings with France. For despite the declaration of war against France in February 1666 and the subsequent prohibition of French imports it was still open for neutral shipping to traffic between the belligerents in all except certain strategic goods.[318] It was also vital for Sweden to keep open its access to French wines and the salt of the Brouage. Thus, early in 1666 Marescoe was commissioned by Laurens de Geer[319] to handle a complex transaction involving the purchase of salt, brandy and vinegar in La Rochelle and the shipment of Newcastle lead and coal to Rouen. Both cargoes were consigned to Swedish ships, the *Tromslager* and *Koning David* of Stockholm, and the task of Marescoe and Oursel was to settle the consequent bills between them. In 1667 their liaison was reinforced by even larger commissions. Marescoe was called upon to arrange no less than five shipments of lead, coal, butter and vitriol for despatch to La Rochelle from Newcastle and Hull. His total outlay was £5,751 11s (f.o.b.), of which lead accounted for 83.5 per cent and coal 9.5 per cent. Two of the carriers were Swedish and three were Norwegian, seeking return cargoes after their delivery of timber, iron and pitch in northern ports. The proprietors of the goods Marescoe purchased were ostensibly Dutch—for four of the shipments were in the names of Van Gangelt & Deutz or of Frederick Rihel, distinguished Amsterdam houses.[320] The fifth was attributed to Laurens de Geer (recently deceased), but behind these eminent names lay almost certainly the interests of the Västervik Ship Company in which the De Geers were shareholders and for which the two Amsterdam firms often acted as agents.[321]

For Marescoe, the commissions brought not only their due percentage but also a useful

---

[315] Galls at 60s per cwt.; Barbados cotton at 8½d per lb.; East Indian cotton yarn at 2s per lb; the total £668 9s 2d (f.o.b) despatched in four ships.

[316] See BL, Add. MS. 36,785 ('The Book of Tables'). In the period Michaelmas 1662 to Michaelmas 1663, lead exports to France were worth £239,327, i.e. 60 per cent of all London's exports to France. In the period Ms. 1668–Ms. 1669 the proportion had shrunk to 13.4 per cent (£14,608), though there are grounds for thinking that this figure is no less untypical than the first.

[317] Salvage and additional transport costs added 7.4 per cent to the cost (f.o.b.).

[318] R. R. Steele, *A bibliography of royal proclamations of the Tudor and Stuart sovereigns . . . 1485–1714* (Oxford, 1910) i, pp. 416, 420, proclamations of 9 February, 2 March and 10 November, 1666.

[319] The eldest son of the great Louis de Geer, Laurens (b. 1614) died on 1 August 1666. *Ätten de Geer*, ed. E. W. Dahlgren (Uppsala, 1920); E. W. Dahlgren, *Louis de Geer, 1587–1652: hans lif och verk* (Uppsala, 1923) p. 522. He was succeeded in his dealings with Marescoe by his son Gerard (1642–87).

[320] See Elias, *De vroedschap van Amsterdam* I pp. 388–9.

[321] B. Fahlborg, 'Ett blad ur den svenska handelsflottans historia (1660–1675)', *Historisk Tidskrift* (1923) p. 225.

acquaintance with Jean Freyhoff, merchant of La Rochelle,[322] which he was to develop for himself in 1668. He was also introduced to Bordeaux by another of De Geer's commissions to send there 700 cwt. of lead.[323] As for Rouen, he maintained his growing correspondence with Oursel and with the arrival of peace despatched to him a cargo of tin on his own account.[324]

Thus, when the surviving correspondence opens, Marescoe's experience of France and French merchants had been substantially enlarged, although it is clear from Oursel's letters that he still had much to learn. He was ignorant of French weights and measures, unfamiliar with the conventions of sales, and, not least, unaware of the difficulties of navigating the Seine.[325] Oursel's role, like that of the Van Baerles, was to instruct Marescoe and to advise him on the nature of the French market. Like the Van Baerles, he discharged his responsibilities conscientiously, and between the lines of this sober, business-correspondence Oursel seems to emerge as a man of intelligence and integrity. There was also a further ingredient in the relationship which is less evident in others. Oursel was a member of Rouen's large Huguenot community[326] and was clearly a devout Protestant. He cannot have remained for long unaware of Marescoe's own generous attachment to the French Protestant Church in London. It was a point of contact between them which was put to good use when Oursel asked Marescoe for confidential reports on the morals and religion of a young Frenchman working in London with whom a local marriage was to be arranged. Whether Oursel did Marescoe such a good turn by recommending the young Jacob David to his service is debateable, but it was with the eyes of an earnest Protestant businessman that he judged David to be thoroughly competent in the science of book-keeping and a man 'not given to the vices of youthful debauchery'.[327]

However, Oursel found it difficult to resolve the moral dilemma facing him when Marescoe insisted on pressing more consignments upon him than the market would bear. As a commission agent he could not but welcome them, yet as a reputable merchant he feared for the long-term consequences. In March 1668 Rouen was already well-supplied with the principal English commodities. Abundant lead had arrived from London and Hull, and its price—which had reached nearly £170 tournois per mille in 1666—was now at £125 t. and falling. Tin, which had sold at £75 t. in November 1667 was down to £65 t. by May as 'incredible' amounts flooded in from the West of England.[328] After March 1668 there was

---

[322] Freyhoff's brother-in-law was Jean de la Croix (Pierre Chaillet to CM, 31 September 1669) one of a notable Dutch family (originally named Crucius) which had contributed much to the drainage of the marshes surrounding La Rochelle. See Mathorez *Les étrangers en France* ii p. 238.

[323] The recipient was Dirck Budde, with whom Marescoe appears to have had no further dealings. For later correspondence with Bordeaux see pp. 188–9.

[324] 26 pieces, weighing 96 cwt. 3 q. 12 lb. @ £5 per cwt., a price which compares very unfavourably with the purchases of 1668. It yielded a loss of 2 per cent.

[325] Oursel was at pains to warn Marescoe against employing large ships on the Seine. Until the early nineteenth century Rouen remained inaccessible to vessels drawing more than 3 metres [M. Mollat, *Le commerce maritime normand à la fin du moyen âge* (Paris, 1952) p. 364] but on average, *c.* 1683, foreign ships reaching Rouen were 60 per cent larger than French—P. Dardel, *Le trafic maritime de Rouen aux xviiᵉ et xviiiᵉ siècles* (Rouen, 1946) pp. 123–4; Joachim Darsel, 'L'Amirauté en Normandie. VI. L'Amirauté de Rouen (Pt. 1 and 2) *Annales de Normandie* (1973) pp. 39–56, 115–49.

[326] In a population of about 50,000, Rouen's Huguenots are alleged to have numbered some 10,000, but a recent scientific assessment puts their number at less than 4,000—Jean-Pierre Bardet, *Rouen aux XVIIe et XVIIIe siècles* (Paris, 1983) pp. 217–18.

[327] R. Oursel to CM, 11 July 1668.

[328] H. Wetken to CM, 24 March 1668; R. Oursel to CM, 28 April 1668. Yet Marescoe was advised that it was the demand for tin in Rouen which was keeping prices high in Cornwall: Bryan Rogers to CM, 7 December 1668.

little demand for Barbados sugar at £33 *t.* per 100 lb. The duties on it (at £6 *t.* per 100 lb.) Oursel described as 'excessif', while those on cotton-yarn stood at £10 *t.* per 100 lb.[329] Only Aleppo galls offered some prospect of gain at £45 *t.* per 100 lb. and for these Oursel was willing to place an order,[330] but for the rest he was a reluctant participant in Marescoe's successive ventures.

Between January and May 1668 Marescoe freighted nine ships to Rouen (seven English, two Hamburgers) with eleven separate parcels of goods to the value of £3,095 8s 6d. Four of the parcels were of sugar, which accounted for 36 per cent of this sum; three lots of tin, all on Marescoe's account, represented 32 per cent. The rest was made up of Oursel's galls (13 per cent), Marescoe's cotton (11 per cent) and a small consignment of lead (8 per cent). Hermann Wetken had taken a modest share in the sugar, but responsibility for the rest was unevenly shared between Marescoe (57 per cent) and Oursel (38 per cent). Oursel was clearly unhappy about his commitment and concerned about Marescoe's. Like Egidio Ruland in Hamburg, he had heard of the lower sugar prices prevailing in Bristol, and he was politely critical of Marescoe's purchases for two or three shillings more in London. By the end of April he was determined to order no more. Tare, at 13 per cent, and duties and charges exceeding 25 per cent destroyed all chance of a reasonable profit. To crown it all, a rogue shipment direct from Barbados had reached Rouen with 200,000 lb.[331] Marescoe was therefore lucky to snatch a small profit, of about $5\frac{1}{2}$ per cent, from his February sugar shipment when it was sold to Guy Terré, whom Colbert had recently selected to manage the subsidized sugar refineries of Rouen.[332]

Other difficulties prejudiced his cotton-yarn consignments. In addition to the 14 per cent tare, and charges absorbing 11 per cent of the sale, there was a discouraging lack of demand for mediocre quality products of the kind Marescoe had sent. Fine or superfine yarn was another matter: Oursel advised that there was a good market for it provided that it was in small skeins of single threads which enabled the workers to separate it quickly. But Marescoe's East India Company yarn was a little coarse and it had been sold to a particularly difficult customer. Jean Camin (a family friend of the Oursels)[333] had bought it for payment in four months time. This, as Oursel repeatedly advised Marescoe, was standard practice in Rouen. No one ever bought for immediate cash payment: the shortest acceptable term was two or three months, and even then one must allow a little credit:

> 'C'est une maxime usitee entre marchandes qu'on ne paie les cedulles ou promises po' vente de marchandises plustost que une mois et bien souvent 2 & 3 mois appres l'escheance selon les qualites des marchandises & le terme dont on convient.'[334]

Camin declined even to discount his debt at $\frac{1}{2}$ per cent per month and in November had still not paid up.

Marescoe's impatience for his money and Camin's reluctance to pay reflect some special

[329] The 1664 duties on foreign sugar had been raised on 15 September 1665 to £22 10s *t.* per 100 lb. for the best refined, and £4 *t.* for unrefined. Marescoe's sugar qualified only as 'paneel', the coarse, dark, semi-refined quality. For the differential tariffs on West Indian produce see S. L. Mims, *Colbert's West-India Policy* (New Haven, London, Oxford, 1910) pp. 54, 263–6; C. W. Cole, *Colbert and a Century of French Mercantilism* (New York, 1939) ii, pp. 22, 50–1.

[330] R. Oursel to CM, 11 April 1668.

[331] Same to same, 5 May 1668.

[332] Cole, *Colbert*, ii p. 50; Mims, p. 262.

[333] P. Mieg, 'Les de Coninck au Havre et à Rouen', p. 98, n. 3. In 1679 Jean Camin's son married Oursel's step-daughter.

[334] R. Oursel to CM, 14 November; also 5 May, and 1 September 1668 [**28**].

circumstances of 1668. On the one hand, there was an unusually high rate of exchange for Rouen on London. At around 59 pence sterling per French crown it made compelling sense for Marescoe to draw back his proceeds as quickly as possible, for the par was 54*d* and the course rarely rose above 57*d* except in times of war (when it had recently been 62*d*).[335] It was this alluring opportunity which made him press Oursel for early remittances.

Oursel tried to oblige: 'L'achapteur de vos sucres m'ayant offert disconter la partie qu'il doits paier dans 4 mois a raison de $\frac{1}{2}$ pour cent par mois. Je luy ay accorde affin de vous remettre pendant ce haut Change crainte qu'il ne vienne a baisser.'[336] Yet, good bills on London were increasingly hard to find as the market became sluggish, and amid the embarrassing glut of commodities a more embarrassing shortage began to emerge. 'L'argent est icy fort rare & n'y a point ou tres peu de vente en toute sorte des marchandises.'[337]

Shortage of money was in itself no unusual plight in any seventeenth-century economy, and it was accompanied here by the two most familiar scourges of that century—war and plague. The war with Spain, as yet unresolved in the spring of 1668, brought home to the French the cost of Louis XIV's conquests in Flanders, for the Ostenders maintained an alarmingly successful *guerre de course* upon all shipping approaching the French channel ports.[338] Oursel's letters report numerous seizures, and although he regarded English ships as safer than most he was obliged to record that a richly-laden English ship had been taken only two leagues from Le Havre.[339] 'Sy la guerre continuoit & qu'on ne reprime leur insolence tout le commerce sera perdu.' These protracted uncertainties paralysed investment. 'On parle fort de la Guerre icy' wrote Wetken; 'on nous parle tres fort de paix' wrote Oursel. 'Le discours du peuple est sy different qu'on ne scait qu'en croire ou penser, plusieurs apprehendent guerre avecq la hollande quy pouvait engager d'autre nations en la mesme querelle'.[340]

About the plague of 1668 Oursel was less unsure: he believed that its seriousness had been grossly exaggerated. But the authorities had taken no chances with the outbreak which commenced in July and neighbouring towns had soon placed Rouen in quarantine.[341] It was understood to have started with a merchant from Flanders, and its transfer to Dieppe was thought to have been carried in a bag of legal papers.[342] People, goods and even letters were thus restrained in their passage. Oursel attributed some of the shortage of bills of exchange to the prohibition which the Parlement of Rennes had placed on the postal couriers between Rouen and Brittany,[343] and as late as December 13 Paris was decreeing severe penalties for goods moved in breach of the quarantine.[344]

The official Bills of Mortality published weekly in Rouen tend to support Oursel's

---

[335] See J. J. McCusker, *Money and Exchange in Europe and America, 1600–1775: A Handbook* (London, 1978) p. 87. See also Appendix G [c].

[336] R. Oursel to CM, 21 April 1668.

[337] Same to same, 18 August 1668.

[338] R. Baetens, 'The organization and effects of flemish privateering in the seventeenth century', *Acta Historiae Neerlandicae* ix (The Hague, 1976) pp. 48–75.

[339] R. Oursel to CM, 26 May 1668.

[340] H. Wetken to CM, 7 April 1668; R. Oursel to CM, 11 April 1668.

[341] For contemporary documents relating to the plague of 1668, see *Trois opuscules sur la peste de Rouen de 1668*, with an introduction by Dr G. Panel, Société rouennaise de bibliophiles (Rouen, 1911). For a modern assessment, J. Revel 'Autour d'une épidémie ancienne: la peste de 1666–1670', *Revue d'histoire moderne et contemporain* xvii (1970) pp. 953–83.

[342] *Trois opuscules sur la peste*, p. ix.

[343] R. Oursel to CM, 10 October 1668.

[344] *Trois opuscules sur la peste*, p. xviii.

scepticism about the seriousness of the outbreak,[345] but the state of emergency lasted into the New Year of 1669 and had effectively paralysed trade for the second half of 1668. Oursel did not request, nor did Marescoe volunteer, any consignment after May of that year. Yet the fault did not lie solely with the plague. There was an irreducible glut in English goods which was slow to subside. Oursel reckoned that Rouen had received two years' supply of lead by July 1668, and in March 1669 he wrote: 'je crois qu'il y a apresent plus d'estain en france qu'en Angleterre'[346] As a result, Marescoe's consignments of tin remained obstinately unsaleable, not merely in 1668 but throughout 1669 and 1670 as well. His experience must have been shared by other Englishmen trading to Rouen, for the list of goods which he had to offer corresponds almost exactly with the list of English goods most frequently named in the sparse records of Rouen's seventeenth-century trade—lead, tin, galls, cotton, campeachy, pepper. . . .[347]

There was a similar sterility in his relations with La Rochelle. Jean Freyhoff had little to communicate in 1668, and in 1669 he could offer no firm encouragement. Marescoe's one cargo of lead found an uninterested market with prices totally unresponsive to demand elsewhere. Freyhoff acknowledged that the rebuilding of London had advanced English lead prices by 20 per cent in a short time, but La Rochelle and Bordeaux were being adequately supplied from Chester and Liverpool[348] and Marescoe's price-limit of £107 t. was totally unrealistic. By the end of the year he had to be content with £94 t. England's naval operations against Algiers had left the Straits not less but more dangerous than before, and the consequent inhibition of trade in the Mediterranean was pushing lead prices down. He thus gave Freyhoff orders to sell.[349]

The outcome was all the more dispiriting because La Rochelle appeared to have enjoyed a prosperous year, with a good harvest and the promise of a small but choice vintage. 'Nos vignes sont assez belles & ont le temps propre' wrote Freyhoff on 1 July. A month later, 'la vigne a beau temps & nous esperons avoir de bons vins mais pas tant que l'an passé'. A little rain in late August did nothing but good, and he could report a brisk start to the *vendange* in Ré on 16 September, with St Jean and Cognac commencing a week later. His final report was on 10 October: 'Dans les petites & moyennes borderies & Champagne s'y trouve environ la $\frac{1}{2}$ moins de vin que l'an passé; a St Jean y a un peu plus de la $\frac{1}{2}$ & on m'a dit que les vins sont bons; dans les grandes borderies ils attendent encore de la pluye affin d'avoir de meilleur vin & davantage.'

Marescoe made no proffer for wines, and there was nothing he sought for in Rouen. However, it is clear that Oursel, Wetken and Freyhoff had interests of their own in the English and Scottish ports. Wetken, whose relations with Newcastle have been noted already, was anxious to extend his search for cheap coal to Scotland and asked Marescoe to find him a reliable correspondent in Edinburgh or Leith.[350] Oursel also had an interest in Newcastle and Scottish small-coals. His family had acquired a new Dutch *fluyt* of about 300 *thonneaux*—'quy nous a cousté bien de l'argent'—which had so far been engaged in whale-

---

[345] Op. cit. pp. xxiv *et seq.* It is interesting that Oursel judged the death of 41 persons from plague as quite insignificant and unworthy of such draconian measures of control. The bill of mortality for 2 to 9 November 1668, sent to Marescoe by Wetken, recorded only 4 deaths from plague and 42 from other causes. Revel estimates the total plague toll at Rouen as between 300 and 500, in contrast to Amiens and Dieppe where thousands of deaths took 10–20 per cent of their populations.

[346] R. Oursel to CM, 11 July 1668; 9 March 1669.

[347] Dardel, *Le trafic maritime de Rouen*, p. 68.

[348] J. Freyhoff to CM, 14 February, 28 March, 6 May 1669.

[349] Same to same, 5 December 1669.

[350] Marescoe procured for him the services of Charles Linzan of Leith.

fishing under its captain, Nicolas Oursel. Robert Oursel also owned a small barque called *La Nourrice*—'fabrique de ce pays avecq un derriere relevé en fasson de flibot'—which he proposed to despatch from Amsterdam to Hull under the command of Jean Poitevin of Quillebouef. Both vessels were committed to the hunt for those marginal advantages which a timely cargo, swift turn-round and reliable markets could secure. Marescoe's tasks was to secure the first two of these: Oursel hoped to provide the third.

In return, Oursel extended a significant invitation, which reflects the effect of Colbert's bid to establish Marseille as an entrepôt.[351]

'Sy [vous] remarquez que vos marchandises propre po' l'estroit baissent chez vous & que par ce moyen Il y eust quelques choses a faire en les envoyant p. voye de france on pourroit le servir du previlege de l'entrepot que le Roy a accordé aux negotians, c'est-a-dire libre entrée & sortie des marchandises quy seront destiné po' estre porté hors le Royaume sans payer aucune droits. Nous aurons tousjours de bons Navires en charge au havre, po' Cadiz, Alicante & Marseilles.'

Yet, Oursel and Freyhoff recognized as clearly as their contemporaries in Hamburg and Amsterdam the extent of the commercial stagnation affecting western Europe in the late 1660s. Oursel thought it required exceptional courage to venture on any enterprise: 'car il semble qu'aujourdhuy le commerce va tout au contraire de ce qu'on peut juger ou prevoir'.[352] Freyhoff was more accusing. Writing in January 1670, with news of anti-French tariffs pending in the next parliamentary session,[353] he observed: 'si l'on met en vos quartiers de nouveaux droits sur les marchandises de france ce ne sera pas le moyen d'augmenter le commerce'. Both correspondents noted gloomily the wave of bankruptcies that had disturbed centres elsewhere—Jean de Neufville in Amsterdam, Jacob Aboab and Thomas Verbecq in London. The repercussions had reached Paris, where many others had also 'absenté' themselves. Oursel concluded: 'J'estime que le retardement de la flotte d'espaigne y contribuer beaucoup. . . .'[354]

Of all the European economies, the French had by far the largest claim on the profits of the *flota*.[355] For weeks in early 1670 a fleet of twenty-six French ships had been hovering at Cadiz for their shares in the spoils,[356] and when the *flota* of 1670 finally arrived on 31 January there is no mistaking Oursel's excitement. 'On a nouvelle de Madrid p. lettre de 5 courant de l'arrivée de la flotte des Indes au nombre de 17 Navires a Sn Lucar, dont dieu soit loué! C'est une bonne nouvelle quy resjouit fort les negotians de cette ville.'[357] Within a fortnight he predicted the likely effects on the rate of exchange which had stabilized around the normal level of $55\frac{1}{2}$–$56\frac{1}{2}d$. 'J'estimes qu'il hausseroit davantage quand les effets de la flotte d'espaigne commencerent a venir en vos cartier & en hollande; toutefois on en attend aussy bon nombre en ce pays, ce quy pourra tenir les affaires en balance.'[358]

On this more buoyant note the correspondence from France is cut off, but it is evident that

---

[351] The edict of September 1664, accompanying the new tariff of that year, had in fact nominated numerous free ports, including Rouen, La Rochelle, Le Havre, Dieppe and Calais, but the edict of March 1669 placed special emphasis on trade with the Levant via Marseilles—Cole, *Colbert*, i, p. 392; Paul Masson, *Histoire du commerce français dans le Levant aux XVIIe siècle* (Paris, 1897) pp. 160 *et seq.*

[352] R. Oursel to CM, 11 July 1668.

[353] J. Freyhoff to CM, 2 January 1670. He was evidently referring to proposals from the House of Commons' committee on Supply to lay duties yielding £400,000 on French wines, brandy and linen—*CJ* ix, pp. 115, 117, 128 (2, 6 and 9 December 1669).

[354] R. Oursel to CM, 28 January 1670.

[355] Kamen, *Spain in the Later Seventeenth Century*, p. 135.

[356] PRO SP 94/56 f. 25 (Sir William Godolphin to Lord Arlington, 2/12 February 1670).

[357] R. Oursel to CM, 21 February 1670.

[358] Same to same, 4 March 1670 [**135**].

the promise of a rejuvenated trade was not fulfilled as far as Marescoe's trade with Rouen was concerned. Nothing passed between them in 1670 except bills of exchange, and it was to this no less hazardous traffic that they were obliged to turn. Oursel was keen to get bills accepted in London for re-assignment in Rouen and was willing to recompense Marescoe at the rate of $\frac{1}{2}$ per cent per month for the favour.[359] He had a commonsense approach to the vagaries of the rate of exchange and was not prepared to wait for minor improvements: 'en matiere de change il me semble qu'il vaut tousjours mieux suivre le cours, car l'argent restant en caisse 8 ou 15 jours inutile enporte en intherest du moins $\frac{1}{8}$ ou $\frac{1}{4}$ p. Ct & souventes fois on ne le remet pas plus advantageusement'.[360]

For Freyhoff in La Rochelle it was even less easy to pick and choose bills; they were extremely scarce. He assured Marescoe that he would be delighted if they could establish between them a trade in bills, 'mais certes, il est si casuel & il y a si peu de fondement a faire sur les remises d'icy faute de lettres que je n'oze y engager personne, joint que fort souvent on donne autant icy pour les lettres qu'a Paris . . .'.[361]

The great majority of the exchange transactions between Marescoe and his French correspondents was therefore based on Rouen, although an analysis of the Oursel account reveals the auxiliary role played by bills drawn, or payable, elsewhere. On his own account, between July 1664 and December 1668, Marescoe handled twenty bills, worth £2,732 18s 8d, distributed in the following percentages of value:

14	London bills on Rouen	61.28%
1	London bill on Dieppe	8.62
3	London bills on Paris	15.92
1	London bill on La Rochelle	3.38
1	Rouen bill on London	10.80

To set against these, and goods received on Marescoe's account, Oursel remitted twenty-eight bills worth £4,652 6s 11d in the following proportions:

22	Rouen bills on London	68.72%
2	Rochelle bills on London	11.98
2	Rochelle bills on Rouen	13.58
1	Morlaix bill on London	2.18
1	Hamburg bill on London	3.54

Simultaneously, on Oursel's account, Marescoe was engaged in a traffic of similar proportions, debiting his friend with goods and twenty-six bills (worth £3,178 16s) distributed as follows:

11	London bills on Rouen	36.13%
3	London bills on Dieppe	9.43
5	London bills on Paris	28.64
3	London bills on Antwerp	11.64
3	London bills on Amsterdam	12.58
1	London bill on Middelburg	1.57

---

359 Same to same, 23 and 27 March 1669.
360 Same to same, 1 November 1669 [**117**].
361 J. Freyhoff to CM 6 February 1670 [**134**].

This was balanced with Oursel's remittances on a diversity of routes, distributed thus:

24 Rouen bills on London	69.32%	
5 Paris bills on London	13.28	
1 Morlaix bill on London	2.60	
2 Rouen bills on Amsterdam	6.57	
1 Rouen bill on Antwerp	3.03	
1 Rotterdam bill ⎫ on London	3.40	
1 Haarlem bill ⎭		
1 St Malo bill on London	1.78	

But the profits of this strenuous interchange, with all its risks, were never great, and unlike the Hamburg exchange that of Rouen did not serve Marescoe's interests in the settlement of Swedish claims. Despite the appetite of some of Marescoe's Rouen and Paris correspondents to engage in arbitrage the London firm seems to have been reluctant to extend itself too far beyond its liability for goods.

[e] SPAIN

Marescoe's acquaintance with Iberian trade certainly antedated the 1660s. In 1657, while England and Spain were at war, he was sending to Lisbon assortments of textiles which differ little from those he was to despatch to the Spanish market a decade later—Colchester bays, says and serges predominate, and the returns—then as later—were in a judicious mixture of coin and commodities.[362]

John Buck had been the senior partner in these ventures, and after his death in 1661 his place was taken by Marescoe's brother-in-law, John Lethieullier. A shareholder in the East India Company and a leading Merchant Adventurer,[363] Lethieullier was particularly well-placed to assist Marescoe, and it was clearly his knowledge of English and Indian textiles as well as of the Spanish market which accounts for much of the success of this joint operation. It was he who brought their principal shipments from Norfolk and Suffolk, from Devon and Somerset and who saw to their dyeing and finishing, packing and despatch. Marescoe's role was merely to pay his share and, when necessary, buy lead among the dealers of Yorkshire and the Mendips.[364]

Because of Lethieullier's role as principal purchaser, the record of his transactions survives in some detail, for it was his practice to send Marescoe a meticulous invoice of every consignment, specifying the first cost and incidental charges, together with details of sizes, weights and colours. Many of these invoices survive and enable one to construct a patchy but informative picture of certain English textile prices in the 1660s and '70s. They are matched by some equally detailed sale-accounts from the vendors in Spain and this combination of documents allows one to reconstruct the whole course of the export process.

Although Marescoe had minor dealings in Malaga and at Bilbao, the early correspondence from Spain is dominated by one firm, the partnership of Anthony Upton & Benjamin

---

[362] Miscellaneous Accounts: account with Anrique Bröjer of Lisbon, 1657–63. Returns were made in silver *pesos*, Setubal salt and oil.

[363] JL was a member of the Merchant Adventurer's Court of Assistants in 1670 and later became Governor of the Company: House of Lords Record Office, House of Lords Committee Book II (1664–71); K. G. Davies, *The Royal African Company*, pp. 159, 171.

[364] Lethieullier charged his brother-in-law no commission on cloth purchases in return for Marescoe's management of their joint lead and tin consignments to Italy.

Bathurst, a leading English firm located at Seville. Surviving accounts show that they had been acting for Marescoe and his brother-in-law since 1661 at least and in 1668 they announced that they were renewing their partnership for a further term. However, there were other agents in touch with Lethieullier & Marescoe whose value became evident in times of war. The firm of Francisco & Juan van Havre & Christian van Breda at Cadiz[365] provided neutral credentials for the London firm's shipments via Ostend in 1666 and 1667. Linked as they were with D'Hollandre & Du Beron of Lille and Robert Oursel of Rouen they could arrange safe cover, both for English cloths re-shipped in the Spanish Netherlands and for *reals de plata* returned via Lille. Thanks in part to them, Marescoe's exports to Spain were not seriously curtailed by the second Anglo–Dutch war.

At its outbreak in 1664 he had a half-share, worth £697 15s 11d, invested in a typical assortment of Colchester bays, Taunton serges, Exeter perpetuanas, Norwich chenies and East Indian calicoes sent out in June 1663 and March 1664. Sold for *R. Pta* 60,400, he calculated that his half represented a notional profit of £52 14s 1d, based on a rate of approximately 6d sterling per *real plata*. The real profit, however, was to accrue on the returns from Spain which Upton & Bathurst despatched in the form of indigo and silver. The latter, weighing 930 ounces and sold to the goldsmith-banker Edward Backwell for 5s 4d and 5s 3d per oz. helped to push Marescoe's profits up by a further £52 17s 8d, making a total yield of 15 per cent on his outlay.

By the measure of later profits this was a modest one for risks spread over nearly twenty months. The war-years were to prove far more lucrative. Between March 1665 and December 1667 Marescoe shared in twelve consignments to Seville in which his contribution amounted to £3,402 17s. Their sale by Upton & Bathurst promised him £4,184 19s at the notional rate of exchange, but the actual returns did rather better. These were made in silver (64.35 per cent), indigo (16.45 per cent), cochineal (14.09 per cent) and bills of exchange drawn on Antwerp and Amsterdam (5.1 per cent). Worth in total £4,463 12s 9d they added a further third to notional profits averaging 23 per cent.

Within this average there were some striking disparities between the 48.5 per cent gained on shipments sent in October and November 1666 (after a narrow escape in the great Fire of London) and the vestigial 0.2 per cent yielded by a similar assortment sent in May 1667. The failure of the latter can be largely explained by serious damage from water and moth, but there is no explicit correspondence to explain the success of the former. However, the surviving sale-account suggests something of the story. Sold aboard ship on their arrival, in one day, for cash down, the cargoes had evidently found an eager market, which may not be unrelated to the imminent departure of the single *registro* ship licensed to trade to Honduras.[366] This already had on board some of Marescoe's other ventures, handled by the Van Havres and Van Breda. On 100 'paragones' or chenies and 2,200 pairs of stockings

---

[365] For references to this firm see J. Everaert, *De Internationale en koloniale handel der vlaamse firma's te Cadiz, 1670–1700* (Bruges, 1973) pp. 41, 44. A 'Juan van Havre, Fleming' was naturalized in 1692—L. Garcia Fuentes, *El comercio español con America, 1650–1700*, p. 40.

[366] Operating independently of the *flota* and *galeones*, licensed 'navios de registro suelto' were allowed to trade with the more isolated settlements of central America: C. H. Haring, *Trade and Navigation between Spain and the Indies in the time of the Hapsburgs* (Cambridge, Mass., 1918) pp. 87, 88. For the comparative neglect of Honduras as a market in the second half of the seventeenth century, see Murdo J. Macleod, *Spanish Central America: a socioeconomic history, 1520–1720* (Berkeley, Los Angeles, London, 1973) pp. 198–200, 382. The official records (acknowledged to be unreliable) indicate departures of the single ship for Honduras in 1660, 1662, 1664, 1665, and every second year thereafter until 1675. The return ship was more irregular: 1662, 1665, 1666, 1671, 1674, 1675, 1676, 1677, 1678 and two in 1680—L. Garcia Fuentes, *El comercio español*, Appendices, Tables I and II, pp. 417–23; *cf.* Everaert, *Vlaamse firma's te Cadiz*, pp. 209–11.

covertly despatched to Cadiz through the Spanish Netherlands aboard the *Jubon de Plata* (captain Pedro Diaz) the Van Havres exacted a special 1 per cent brokerage and 3 per cent commission for their risk, but Marescoe's one-third share in the proceeds (with Lethieullier and Isaac de la Fortrey) still represented a profit of 37 per cent. This was some compensation for an earlier disappointment when their faulty documentation had forced the *Stadt Brugge* to return to Dunkirk in 1665. Reloaded aboard the *Carlos Quintos* their serges, bays and silk-stockings had missed their American market and sold only slowly in Seville from March to December 1666, yielding a comparatively modest 12 per cent. Misfortune could also threaten the returns: 1,000 *pesos* sent by the Van Havres and Van Breda suffered shipwreck off Zeeland.[367]

These were the unavoidable hazards of trade, but there were other risks which could be offset by timely advice or careful management, and when the surviving correspondence of Upton & Bathurst begins it is clear that they had a good grasp of their responsibilities in these regards. Their advice concentrated on the three basic problems confronting any successful trade with Spain—the analysis of demand, the timing of supply and the procurement of returns.

Of these perhaps the simplest was the nature of Spanish demand. Although Spain was probably England's fourth largest market, taking an apparently long list of commodities, the inventory is in fact strikingly dominated by woollen cloths, for which she was by far London's largest customer in the 1660s.[368] And of these textiles, the particular 'new draperies' in which Lethieullier specialized—Colchester bays, Norwich stuffs, Devonshire serges and perpetuanas alone accounted for 68 per cent of all London's traffic to Spain.[369] Worsted stockings, small parcels of which often accompanied Lethieullier's cloth, accounted for another 8.2 per cent of the London figures. In other words, Marescoe and his brother-in-law were comparatively small and unadventurous participants in the main-stream of Anglo-Spanish trade,[370] in which it might seem difficult to make serious mistakes.

Yet there was scope for advice on the types, qualities and—above all—the colours of textiles suitable for Spain. Upton & Bathurst strained their descriptive vocabulary to its limits to explain the desired mixture of 'sad', 'civil' and 'lively' hues, 'of which we cannot easily express the several colours by name'. The sober tastes of their clients evidently ran to 'haire cullers, light liver, a few bright lead culler' but not to reds. The scarlet 'Bow-dye' serges remained for long unsold, and Colchester bays were desired only if white. Perpetuanas could be black, but not chenies—'which in that comodity is very unpropper'.[371] 'Hounscot' says could be either white or black, but only in Indian calicoes could the full spectrum of greens, blues, reds and orange be tolerated.

Lethieullier had in fact been sending bays and chenies in a range of dyes, and in 1668 he had invested largely in serges, especially 'Bow-dyes'. But Upton & Bathurst found the serges 'somewhat inferior' and by May 1669 were emphatically advising against sending more. The

[367] The silver was eventually salvaged and yielded a good price in Lille through the good offices of D'Hollandre and Du Beron.

[368] 'The Book of Tables, 1662–3; 1668–9'; BL, Add. MS. 36, 785. See also M. Priestley, 'Anglo–French Trade and the "unfavourable balance" controversy, 1660–1685', *EcHR* 2nd Series, IV (1951) p. 47, n. 3.

[369] I have averaged the Book of Tables figures for Michaelmas 1662–3, and 1668–9.

[370] The value of the Lethieullier & Marescoe cloth exports to Spain in 1668 (£2,698 5s 7d) is equivalent to about 0.9 per cent of the averaged total for those textiles in 1662–3 and 1668–9.

[371] Upton & Bathurst to CM, 28 May 1668.

subsequent shift, and decline, in Lethieullier's purchasing is revealed in a simplified table of his shipments (Table 6):

TABLE 6. JL & CM's cloth shipments to Spain,
1667–1670

	1667	1668	1669	1670
Colchester bays	161	44†	56†	207
Chenies	320	100	250	—
Mohairs	94	200	—	—
Says	—	250	—	100
Perpetuanas	1,000	500	100	100
Serges	100	300	—	—
Serges, mixed	200	—	—	—
Serges, Bow-dyes	—	425	110	—
Calicoes	300	597	—	100
Stockings (dozens)	250	—	—	—

† indicates these were mostly wrappers for the packs.

Note: Shipments are classified here by the date of despatch, not by arrival in Spain as in the next Table.

The question of timing for these consignments was a far more critical problem, for Spanish demand was inseparably linked not merely to the cycle of the seasons but to the less predictable and more protracted cycles of the *flota* and the *galeones*. The fundamental importance of these American fleets to the European and Spanish economies has been frequently and massively assessed,[372] but their significance for much of this correspondence is an unavoidable fact which will have to be acknowledged more than once. It has been shown already that in Hamburg, Amsterdam, Lille and Rouen, merchants waited anxiously for the 1668 *flota*'s return. In Seville the anxiety was no less and the fog of uncertainty just as thick, but the focus of concern was perhaps marginally different. While northern Europe was obsessively preoccupied with the huge bullion supplies which would accompany each arrival, traders such as Upton & Bathurst were more keenly alive to the commodity-demand which would precede the next departure. Thus, the *flota* from New Spain and the *galeones* from Terra Firma had scarcely reached Cadiz in late December 1667 before Upton & Bathurst were calculating their next date of sailing.[373] They anticipated these to be June 1668 for the *flota* and the spring of 1669 for the *galeones*. For the next six months, therefore, they could operate in a responsive market, but they warned that once the *flota* had left demand would be virtually dead.

It has been calculated that 88.5 per cent of the foreign trade passing through Andalucia at this time went to the Indies.[374] Marescoe's correspondence seems to confirm this. All their unpopular 'Bow-dyes' and serges had been sold 'to our India chapmen' by June 1668, and in April 1669, when Lethieullier's shipments seemed to be lagging, Upton & Bathurst urged him to hurry to catch the *galeones* by May, for Spain's domestic consumption was likely to be

---

[372] See H. Chaunu & P. Chaunu, *Séville et l'Atlantique de 1601 à 1650* (Paris, 1955–60); C. H. Haring, *Trade and Navigation*; H. Kamen, *Spain in the Later Seventeenth Century, 1665–1700*, pp. 132–3.

[373] Upton & Bathurst to CM, 31 January 1668.

[374] Kamen, *Spain in the Later Seventeenth Century*, p. 117.

TABLE 7. Upton & Bathurst's cloth sales, 1667–1670.

Monthly sales of cloth (single pieces) and stockings (dozen pairs) at Seville by Upton & Bathurst on Lethieullier & Marescoe's account.

		In stock	Arrivals	Sales
1667	December	113	1562	20
1668	January	1655		220
	February	1435	443	285
	March	1593		138
	April	1455		132
	May	1323		311
	June	1012		747
	July	265	1149	228
	August	1186		37
	September	1149	662	116
	October	1695		25
	November	1670		144
	December	1526	463	37
1669	January	1952		16
	February	1936		16
	March	1920		115
	April	1805		850
	May	955	403	564
	June	794		224
	July	570		118
	August	452		23
	September	429		174
	October	255		71
	November	184		30
	December	154		28
1670	January	126		24
	February	102		12
	March	90		5
	April	85		?

'very inconsiderable'. Poor-quality or damaged goods which were unsaleable at home were quickly disposed of on the eve of departures because (they said) the *cargadores* who bought for the fleets, were not 'so curious as our shopkeepers are',[375] and it was even possible to shift some of those doubtful 'lamparillas' from Antwerp.

An analysis of the surviving sale-accounts for 1667–70 (Table 7) shows clearly enough the chronology of demand and its relation to the departures of the *flota* in mid-July 1668 and the *galeones* in June 1669. It incidentally reveals how unlucky Lethieullier and Marescoe were with the late arrival of two shipments in July 1668 and how the poor sales of August 1668 to

[375] Upton & Bathurst to CM, 10 July 1668. Analysis of the sales of 3,060 pieces of cloth and stockings (in dozen pairs) between 1667 and 1668 reveals 61 different purchasers: 17 bought fewer than 25 items; 27 bought between 25 and 50; 12 bought between 51 and 100, and three men bought between 101 and 200. Only two (Francisco Caravallo and Christoforo Alvarez) bought over 200 items. The diversity of this large clientele makes it easier to understand why Upton & Bathurst rejected Marescoe's idea of making forward contracts for deliveries of cloth: 'wee find it is neither convenient for the buyer nor seller to enter into such contracts beforehand'—29 May 1668.

March 1669 were evidently not a reflection of low stocks. On the other hand, it is also apparent that the arrivals of the *flota* in December 1667 and January 1670 were of comparatively small significance for sales, although not for payments on earlier bargains which were often settled 'at the arrival of the New Spain fleet'.

An analysis of prices is less rewarding than one of volumes. Such price variations as occur in these three years seem to reflect variations in the quality or condition of individual pieces of cloth. A sufficient number arrived damaged with water or moth to produce aberrantly low prices when sold off at the end of the season. For cloth in normal condition the standard prices were fairly stable:

	Price per piece
Chenies	$14\frac{1}{2}$–15 *pesos*
Mohairs	13–$13\frac{1}{2}$ *pesos*
Says	17 *pesos*
Perpetuanas, yardbroad	$9\frac{1}{2}$ *pesos*
Perpetuanas, ellbroad	14–15 *pesos*
Serges, small	$9\frac{1}{2}$ *pesos*
Serges, mixed	$15\frac{1}{2}$ *pesos*
Serges, Bow-dyes	23–24 *pesos*

Only Colchester bays experienced a distinct growth in demand and normal prices rose from D.$23\frac{1}{2}$ per piece to D.26 in mid-1669. Indeed, English manufactures in general were reported to have sold better in the Indies during 1666 and 1667 than those of any other nation and Upton & Bathurst were confident that future fleets would take a larger proportion.[376] Yet they also had to admit that supply was outstripping demand and that large amounts had been left unsold. The domestic market could not be ignored, therefore, and should be courted with high-quality products available, preferably, in the early summer or—for the heavier cloths— at the approach of winter.[377] Failing that, it was wiser not to despatch further supplies, and Upton & Bathurst did not hesitate to restrain Lethieullier's eagerness to send more than the market could stand.

However, their third and most serious problem was raised by the question of returns, for it was doubly dependent on the totally unpredictable movement of international shipping. The supplies of silver, gold, cochineal, indigo or campeachy-wood, which were the most favoured vehicles for returns, depended obviously enough on the arrivals of the *flota* and the *galeones*. Their reshipment to England depended, no less obviously, on the departure of friendly shipping from Spain, but this was less regular and reliable than one might assume. Despite the acknowledged predominance of English merchant shipping in the Mediterranean,[378] not all its vessels were suitable for carrying high-value cargoes. The West of England fish-vendors and the Malaga vintage ships were not favoured by Upton & Bathurst, although they might be employed for carrying letters and accounts. Silver needed fast and defensible ships and in the corsair-ridden waters off Spain it is no surprise to find them turning towards the handful of English men-of-war patrolling the Straits. By article 30 of the 'General Instructions to Captains', re-issued in 1663, his Majesty's ships were forbidden to

[376] Upton & Bathurst to CM, 11 September, 18 December 1668.

[377] Same to same, 10 August, 11 September 1668.

[378] R. Davis, 'England and the Mediterranean, 1570–1670' in F. J. Fisher (ed.), *Essays in the Economic & Social History of Tudor & Stuart England* (Cambridge, 1961) pp. 127–32; R. Davis, *The Rise of the English Shipping Industry in the Seventeenth and Eighteenth Centuries*, pp. 228–56.

carry any merchandise except gold, silver and jewels,[379] and this effectively conferred a licence which was widely abused. Naval captains eager to make a clandestine profit were willing to carry anything if the price was right,[380] and in some notorious cases were willing to desert their sailing stations to do so.[381] It was an abuse peculiar to the Spanish trade, which made it plausible for Pepys to record that 'Cadiz is the ruin of all order in the Navy'.[382] Intermittent attempts were made to suppress it, and one such drive may lie behind Marescoe's instructions to Upton & Bathurst that they were not to employ naval frigates for their returns. However, their agents had little choice but to take what conveyance was available, and in most cases this proved to be a man-of-war.[383]

In the course of 1668, Upton & Bathurst despatched returns on Lethieullier's and Marescoe's accounts (see Table 8). Only the first of these shipments (sent to London) and the

TABLE 8. Upton & Bathurst's returns, 1668.

		Goods	Weight	Sale-price		C.M.'s $\frac{1}{2}$ share		
						£	s	d
1.	(a)	Cochineal	756 lb.	@ 24s	per lb.	440	14	6
	(b)	Bar-silver	1,497 oz.	@ 5s 7d	per oz.	1,042	9	6
	(c)	Silver-ware	2,538¾ oz.	@ 5s 0d	per oz.			
2.	(a)	3,000 *pesos*	2,585½ oz.	@ 5s 2¾d	per oz.	693	0	0
	(b)	Silver-ware	2,896 oz.	@ 5s 0d	per oz.			
3.		1,500 *pesos*	1,308 oz.	@ 5s 3¹/₈d	per oz.	680	0	0
4.		1,500 *pesos*	1,306 oz.	@ 5s 3¹/₈d	per oz.			
5.		1,500 *pesos*	—?—	@ —?—		333	0	0

fifth (sent to Leghorn) were despatched in merchant ships. The remainder, all sent to London, came in naval frigates—one of which (the *Greenwich*) was carrying home the English ambassador, the earl of Sandwich. The freight-rate appears to have been one per cent.

Exports of Spanish silver and gold were, of course, strictly illegal and the letters of Upton & Bathurst pay lip-service to this in the coy language they use to disguise their real identity. 'Backwell's lemons', or 'Backwell's wrought-ware' refer, transparently enough, to the silver coin and silver-wares which were usually sold to this, or some other, leading goldsmith-

[379] A. W. Tedder, *The Navy of the Restoration* (Cambridge, 1916) p. 68.

[380] It was estimated that some captains could gain over £2,000 on a single voyage—*The Tangier Papers of Samuel Pepys*, ed. E. Chappel (Navy Records Society Publications, Vol. LXXIII, 1935) p. 166.

[381] A. Bryant, *Samuel Pepys: The Years of Peril* (London, 1935, reprinted 1952) 102–4.

[382] *The Tangier Papers*, 227. Pepys was understandably obsessed with this abuse and references to it occur throughout his Tangier journals, including a specific allusion to JL's use of the King's ships—p. 185. See also pp. xxxiii, 144, 166–9, 176, 181–5, 196, 200–2, 205–6, 211–12, 240–1.

[383] Upton & Bathurst to CM, 11 September 1668; 26 February 1669. An Order in Council of 23 April 1669 re-stated the rule against conveying goods, but still excepted gold and silver. Marescoe's warning not to use naval ships may reflect foreknowledge of Sir Thomas Allin's pending campaign against Algiers which could be expected to dislocate normal passages. See *The Journal of Sir Thomas Allin, 1660–1678*, ed. R. C. Anderson (Navy Records Society Publications, Vol. LXXX, 1940) II p. 233.

banker.[384] Other euphemisms employed over the years were 'powdered sugars' and 'rusty iron' and it is possible to be momentarily deceived by invoices for 'indigo' and 'wool' which turn out only on closer inspection to be precious metals. However, such difficulties as Upton & Bathurst experienced in their transfer of returns were rarely made by the Spanish authorities. In the wake of the Anglo–Spanish commercial treaty of 1667[385] the liberties of English merchants were supposed to be more secure, and the 'dispute with the judge of contrabando in Cadiz who withstandes the priviledges we have by our late Articles' seems to have been exceptional. The only major inconvenience for them had been created by the decrees of May 1664 and August 1666 which sought to restore Seville's trading primacy against the attractions of Cadiz.[386] This policy was to be abandoned in 1680, but it was operative throughout this correspondence and obliged Upton & Bathurst to conduct their business at a distance from the roadstead and quays of Cadiz. This could make all the difference between selling a last-minute bale of cloth to a departing *flota* or having it rot in the warehouse for months.[387] The demonstrable gap between shipping arrivals and the commencement of sales likewise suggests that it could take at least two, and often three, weeks for a consignment from England to pass through Cadiz and the customs at Seville.

Communication with England was also slow and imposed some additional burdens on the agent's initiative. Ordinarily, a fortnightly post from Madrid carried letters by 106 stages through Paris to Brussels, whence they could pass across the Channel by the Ostend packet. Alternatively, they could turn aside at Paris and take the route via Calais.[388] Both were used by Upton & Bathurst, who thought the Flanders post more secure in May 1669 but had changed their minds by December that year.[389] Duplicate letters always followed by the next post and second copies of invoices also came by sea, but few letters arrived within less than four weeks and most took five.

Perhaps the most important decisions to be transmitted by these routes were such as that of 9 April 1669 to switch the despatch of silver and other returns away from England, where prices were falling, to Italy, where the exchanges were more favourable. As Upton & Bathurst explain, the premium on silver had risen steadily since the arrival of the last *flota* in December 1667. At 3 per cent in June 1668, it was at 6 or $6\frac{1}{2}$ per cent by August and had reached 8 or 9 per cent by October. The severe shortage of American silver is revealed clearly enough by the way Upton & Bathurst had to pick up miscellaneous parcels of wrought-silver dishes and ornaments before turning to what they cautiously called 'the yellow sort'—i.e. gold. However, by September 1669 such substantial quantities of gold had been transmitted to northern Europe that its London price had fallen. Hence the decision to send returns to

[384] In the correspondence of William Atwood (Josiah Child's father-in-law) silver is referred to as 'Lumbar-street ware'—PRO, C. 109/23 (15 August 1669).

[385] For the negotiation of this treaty, see F. R. Harris, *The Life of Edward Mountagu, First Earl of Sandwich* (London, 1912) II, pp. 98–108, and for its significance, J. O. MacLachlan, *Trade and peace with old Spain, 1667–1750* (Cambridge, 1940) pp. 10–12.

[386] Haring, *Trade and Navigation*, p. 14; Kamen, *Spain in the Later Seventeenth Century*, p. 131; A. Girard, *La rivalité commerciale et maritime entre Séville et Cadix jusqu'à la fin du xviiiᵉ siècle* (Paris, Bordeaux, 1932) pp. 27, 57.

[387] Upton & Bathurst to CM, 14 May 1669.

[388] Everaert, *Vlaamse firma's te Cadiz*, pp. 155–67; Kamen, *Spain in the Later Seventeenth Century*, pp. 127–8. Unsatisfactory communications led Sir William Godolphin (the English representative in Spain) to urge the revival of Cromwell's packet-boat service between Cadiz, Lisbon, Bilbao and Plymouth—PRO, SP. 94/55 ff. 89, 172–3 (Godolphin to Arlington, 8/18 September, 17/27 November 1669). See also *Calendar of State Papers Venetian, 1669–70* (London, 1937) p. 107.

[389] Upton & Bathurst to CM, 14 May, 10 December 1669.

Italy where bills of exchange drawn on Amsterdam or London could be more profitably negotiated.[390]

In this increasingly competitive context, with only intermittent Spanish–American demand to set against an excessive English supply,[391] the notional profits on sales fell from the high levels of 1665–7. Of the goods despatched in 1668, the says, chenies and *derebands* which just missed the *flota* did well to produce a profit of 20.8 per cent over twelve months, but the Antwerp *lamparillas* which arrived at the same time yielded only 4 per cent. The yield on the whole year's consignments was barely 11.6 per cent, and on those of 1669 only 7.3 per cent. Did charges in transit also contribute to this narrowing in margins? Apparently not. Although no freight-*rates* are quoted in the sale-accounts one can deduce an approximation from the total freight-*costs*, and these actually suggest a considerable cheapening, from over *R. pta.* 100 per pack in early 1667 to about *R. pta.* 50 in 1668 and about *R. pta* 30 in the spring of 1669.[392] Charges at Cadiz, where Upton & Bathurst now employed the firm of John Mathews to superintend their interests,[393] remained steady and negligible at *R. pta.* 4 commission per pack. Carriage to Seville was comparatively costly at *R. pta.* 12 per pack and there were further harbour charges, tolls and carriage costs totalling 13 *reals vellon* per pack. Spanish customs duties, which were being firmly administered at this date,[394] appear at first sight horrifying in their size and complexity. Twenty successive calculations produced a total levy which amounted to 29.104 per cent on the rated value of the cloths, but in fact this rarely exceeded 10 per cent of their gross sale. Finally, Upton & Bathurst exacted an unvarying $2\frac{1}{2}$ per cent commission, plus $\frac{1}{2}$ per cent brokerage and $\frac{1}{2}$ per cent warehousing charge. The total of these expenses at Cadiz and Seville averaged 14.54 per cent on the gross yields and shows no tendency to increase during these three years.

It would seem, therefore, that the apparent deterioration in profits originated in a slight stiffening of cloth prices in England, where Colchester bays in particular gained 2*d* per ell in Lethieullier's invoices between 1666 and 1669. His chenies of 1669, at 42 shillings per piece, were also more expensive than those of 1667 and, unlike the bays, they did not command rising prices in Spain. Upton & Bathurst warned of this inflexibility in prices when they noticed that mohairs were being invoiced at 12 to 20 per cent more than in former years. Disappointing sales in America during 1669 must have further aggravated the glut and depressed the prices obtained in 1670.[395] As for returns, there can be even less certainty about an apparent deterioration in their profitability. In June 1670 Marescoe put his gains on about £3,650-worth of silver, received from Upton & Bathurst since the beginning of 1669, at £37 9*s*—little more than 1 per cent. A posthumous account added a further £19 18*s* 6*d*, but

---

[390] See pp. 105, 112.

[391] Upton & Bathhurst accompanied their sale-accounts for 1667–8 with a note of explanation: 'here hath beene these 2 or 3 years past such quantity of English goods that have glutted the market and brought them down exceedingly'—(10 December 1669). In numerous Spanish analyses of the trade depression of the 1660s a high proportion attributed it to the saturation of the American market—L. Garcia Fuentes, *La comercio español*, pp. 75–6.

[392] For contemporary French policies to secure cheaper freights to Spain (particularly for the benefit of Lille) see A. Girard, *Le commerce français à Seville et Cadix au temps des Habsbourg* (Paris, Bordeaux, 1932) p. 488.

[393] This was a leading English firm at Cadiz, frequently referred to in Sir Thomas Allin's *Journal* (op. cit. I, pp. 155, 190, 194, 197, 213; II, 39–41, 97, 99, 144, 193, 238). Until 1666 they had employed the firm of Thomas Pridham & Daniel Mercer.

[394] Under the administration of F. Baez Eminente, who acquired a new lease of the Seville customs in 1668, there was an intelligent attack on frauds, partly by the lowering of duties—Everaert, *Vlaamse firma's te Cadiz*, p. 224; Girard, *Le commerce français à Seville et Cadix*, pp. 30, 50, 196.

[395] Upton & Bathurst to CM, 18 December 1668, 22 January 1669.

these were only estimates, based upon the invoiced costs in Spain. Unlike those of 1668, the returns of 1669 and 1670 were not in the main sent to London but to Amsterdam or Leghorn where their final yield tended to be absorbed in other transactions. It is not easy, therefore, to extract the real profit arising on Marescoe's Spanish ventures after 1668, and to assess the significance of the transfers to Italy it is necessary to look at Marescoe dealings in Leghorn as a whole.

[f] ITALY

(I) **Leghorn**

As for Spain, so for Italy, John Lethieullier was Marescoe's indispensable guide to a market which he seems to have ignored before 1667. Lethieullier, in addition to his interests in the Merchant Adventurers and the East India Company, was a member of the Levant Company, and Leghorn was for him, as for the company, a vital staging-post in communications with the Middle East. Through the firm of Thomas Death & Ephraim Skinner[396] he sent on letters and commissions to Benjamin Lannoy, the English consul and Levant Company representative at Aleppo.[397] In 1670 Marescoe tried to join his brother-in-law in this lucrative market by seeking admission to the Company but his application was referred and remained still unresolved at his death in September.[398]

Yet Leghorn itself was a substantial market—since 1593 a free port in which the English had soon established a formidable presence. Much of their commercial and naval power in the Mediterranean hinged upon this centre which, by the mid-seventeenth century, had outstripped its rivals to become Italy's chief port.[399] Nine-tenths of England's Italian imports now came through Leghorn and, as the Venetian authorities were only too well-aware, a large proportion of her exports to Italy could pass more cheaply overland from Leghorn than make the longer sea-route through the Adriatic.[400]

These exports consisted mainly of woollen textiles, lead, tin, pepper and fish, and of these it was in lead, tin and pepper that Lethieullier and Marescoe chose to deal on an initially modest scale. In 1667 their venture in 300 cwt. of tin is perhaps less noteworthy for their profit of 10.67 per cent than for its carriage by a future Admiral of the Fleet, Richard Haddock of the *Bantam*.[401] Their only other transaction was in cochineal, transferred to Death & Skinner by Upton & Bathurst, and it is with the safe arrival of this that the surviving Leghorn correspondence begins in December 1667.

[396] Ephraim Skinner had been trading in Leghorn since at least 1655 and was evidently a close friend of [Sir] John Frederick—BL, Add. MS. 34, 015, f. 38. He was later English consul at Leghorn, 1671–7—Peter Fraser, *The Intelligence of the Secretaries of State and their monopoly of licensed news, 1660–1688* (Cambridge, 1956) Appendix vii, p. 157. When Thomas Death retired to London early in 1669 the partnership was joined by Robert Ball—Death & Skinner to CM, 25 January 1669.

[397] Fraser, op. cit. p. 157; A. C. Wood, *A History of the Levant Company* (London, 1936) pp. 64–6; G. Ambrose, 'English Traders at Aleppo, 1656–1756', *EcHR* (1931) p. 261.

[398] Minutes of the Levant Company, Court of Assistants, 1 July 1670: 'Mr Charles Morisco desired to be admitted into the freedom of this Society by redemption upon fine of £250, but is referred to a General Court.'—PRO, SP. 105/153 p. 56. I am indebted to Professor Henry Horwitz for this reference.

[399] Ralph Davis, 'England and the Mediterranean, 1570–1670', pp. 132–5; Ralph Davis, 'Influences de l'Angleterre sur le déclin de Venise au xviieme siècle' in *Aspetti e cause della decadenza economica veneziana nel secolo xvii* (Venice-Rome, 1961) pp. 222–6.

[400] Davis, 'England and the Mediterranean' p. 135; Davis, 'Influences de l'Angleterre', p. 225; *Calendar of State Papers Venetian, 1669–1670*, pp. 30, 83—Piero Mocenigo to the Doge and Senate, 22 March, 2 August, 1669.

[401] *Dictionary of National Biography*, 'Haddock, Sir Richard (1629–1715)'.

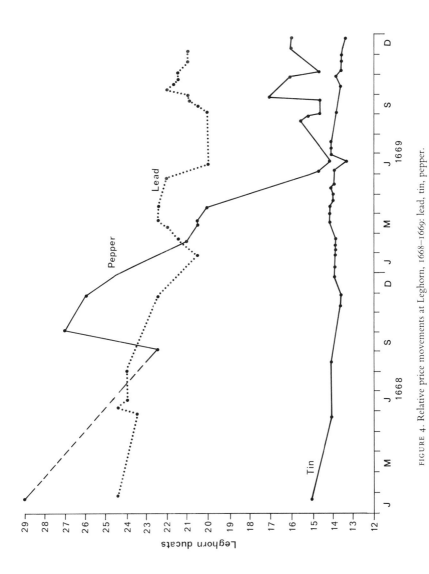

FIGURE 4. Relative price movements at Leghorn, 1668–1669: lead, tin, pepper.

Death & Skinner immediately register the key-note of their later letters, one of pessimism or—at best—caution about the prospects of English trade in Italy. Times were bad, the market was glutted, prices were 'vile'.[402] The year, thus begun, was to end on a note of deepest gloom: 'of woollen manufacturie not any sells, never worsse times or lesse probabillity of there mending' [52]. A chart (Figure 4) based on their price-quotations, amply bears out their message, with lead and tin drifting unsteadily down and pepper enduring a quite striking collapse.

Yet Marescoe and his partner persevered and made modest notional profits on their trade. Two consignments of tin in 1668 yielded 17.5 per cent; eight shipments with lead, pepper and tin in 1669 averaged 8.2 per cent and in 1670 three more consignments of these commodities produced a notional gain of 10.76 per cent. Prices in England gave little or no help to these margins for they generally rose. The tin of 1668 had cost £3 13s per cwt. in Falmouth and £3 18s at London. That of 1669 cost £4 6s in London and £4 11s in Falmouth, though dropping there to £3 17s 6d in 1670. Lead, which had fallen 13 per cent at Hull between March and July 1668 had returned to its higher level of £13 16s per fodder in January 1669 and the consignment of 1670 was invoiced at £13 3s. Only the pepper had eased, from $10\frac{5}{8}d$ per lb. in 1669 to 10d in 1670. Lower freight charges must have made some contribution, as they did at Seville, but there is insufficient evidence to demonstrate this conclusively.[403] Commission and brokerage charges at Leghorn remained consistent at $2\frac{1}{2}$ per cent.

It is possible to illustrate the relative importance of these components from one surviving example. The Cornish tin of 1668, purchased from Bryan Rogers at Falmouth,[404] was invoiced at £422 (f.o.b.). Of this gross total the first cost, at £3 13s per cwt., accounted for 85.574 per cent. Casting the tin into bars added 2.399 per cent; carriage, packing and handling charges totalled 1.112 per cent and customs duties and clearance documents were 6.945 per cent. The 2 per cent commission made up the balance. Sold in Leghorn for $2,350 7 2 freight absorbed 2.872 per cent, carriage, storage and minor dues a mere 0.783 per cent and commission and brokerage the usual 2.5 per cent, leaving net $2,205 14. Marescoe's half share, calculated at the standardized rate of 56 pence sterling per dollar, produced £257 5s, representing a notional profit of 21.9 per cent on his outlay.

Close examination of the individual sales in Leghorn suggests that Death & Skinner handled their marketing of tin with some skill. Between December 1668 and May 1669, when tin prices wavered unreliably between $D13\frac{1}{2}$, $D13\frac{2}{3}$, $D13\frac{3}{4}$ and $D14$ per 100 lb., they sold 42 per cent of their stock at $D13\frac{3}{4}$ and 33 per cent at $D14$. They maintained this high level with another cargo sold in June and July 1669, but it is evident that they were dismayed by Lethieullier & Marescoe's insistence on pressing still more upon a glutted market [30]. Their clear preference was to hold back stocks and it was with unconcealed displeasure that they sold another batch at current prices, lowered to $D13\frac{1}{2}$ by Dutch competition and the arrival of the fish fleet.[405] They wanted pepper, despite its steeply plummeting price. It was, they wrote, 'a comoditie we could wish you would be rather doing in then Tin, being more vendible and on which with little patience are commonly great hitts'.[406] Yet Lethieullier &

---

[402] Death & Skinner to CM, 25 May, 15 June, 3 August 1668.

[403] Sale accounts for tin indicate that the freight rate was $2\frac{1}{2}$ dollars per barrel in July 1668 and 2 dollars in May 1669.

[404] Rogers was a leading Cornish merchant, one of the wealthiest in the West of England—J. Whetter, *Cornwall in the 17th Century*, pp. 153–4, 160, 166; also J. Whetter, 'Bryan Rogers of Falmouth, Merchant (1632–92)' in *Old Cornwall* vi, No. 8 (1965) pp. 347–52.

[405] Death & Skinner to CM, 13 December 1668; also 25 October and 23 November 1668 [52].

[406] Death, Skinner & Ball to CM, 6 September 1669.

Marescoe were evidently not patient men, as their agents noted. 'Tis short accounts and quick returnes pleases you',[407] and there was often some discord between the advice from Leghorn and the orders from London.

Yet communications with Leghorn were generally rather faster than with Seville. Despatched alternately by the imperial posts via Mantua and the French posts via Lyon over 54 per cent of their letters reached Marescoe in twenty-four days (30 per cent in under 21 days). One, of 24 December 1668, took fifty-six days, which Death & Skinner attributed to 'the disorderly goeing of our letters via Mant[u]a, of which others too have lately complained and we know not who to charge therewith'.[408] Generally, however, the Leghorn firm seems to have been quickly and reliably informed of the behaviour of European markets. They knew of Dutch East India Company shipping arrivals very early,[409] and local prices tended to respond quickly to the Amsterdam sales. Indeed, the shipping crowding into their port gave them access to a world much wider than the Mediterranean. From Archangel and Newfoundland, from Ireland, England and Holland, vessels passed through on their way to Venice, Zante, Constantinople, Aleppo, Tunis, Tripoli and Messina. Many were English, sometimes convoyed by naval frigates, and nearly every letter records their movements:

'Four days ago the *Experiment* left for London, *Unity* for Amsterdam with the *Constant Warwick* man of war. The *Speedwell* for Scanderoone, *Robert & Hester* for Smirna, *African* for Constantinople and the *Bantam* and *Industry* for Gallipoly goe hence tomorow. Yesterday arrived the *Golden Fleece* from Scanderoone, and 5 days ago 3 Portugal men of war with their Ambassador for Rome.'[410]

Late in 1669 this tranquil commerce seemed, in London, to be threatened by Sir Thomas Allin's punitive campaign and its repercussions. The Algerians had increased, not diminished, their depredations, and by December Marescoe was alarmed. The new partnership of Death, Skinner & Ball was less perturbed. 'We see the great apprehension you have of the Algeerines, here they are not feared soe much, or the risico thought soe great as you esteeme of it.'[411] Little real harm had been done.

Of much greater concern was the precariousness of Italian credit. Sales were invariably on terms of six or more months 'time' and Marescoe had already suffered one bad debt from the failure of the house of Brandani which finally settled with its creditors for a mere 15 per cent.[412] An even more serious tremor had reached Leghorn from the bankruptcy of Aboab.[413] Two local merchants collapsed within one week,[414] and Aboab's failure seemed to threaten that vital form of communication which found its place at the foot of every letter—the rate of exchange. Death, Skinner & Co usually recorded the rates on London, Amsterdam and Venice, and although Leghorn had its place in a much larger network of exchange which reached north into Germany and France,[415] these three centres were enough for the London partners' purposes. At this stage in Lethieullier's dealings, Leghorn was still a terminus for his Iberian trade through which profits could be returned in bills of exchange.

[407] Same to same, 14 October 1669.
[408] Same to same, 5 April 1669.
[409] Same to same, 15 June, 28 June 1669.
[410] Same to same, 13 September 1669.
[411] Same to same, 17 January 1670.
[412] Same to same, 30 August, 25 October 1669.
[413] See pp. 80–1, and Death, Skinner & Ball to CM, 6 January 1670: 'Aboab's retirement is here publicly knowne, nor did we expect better by him before, though some will have it a cheat in him.'
[414] Death, Skinner & Ball to CM, 17 January 1670.
[415] See Giulio Mandich, *Le pacte de ricorsa et le marché italien des changes au xviiᵉ siècle* (Paris, 1953), and Luigi de Rosa, *I cambi esteri del regno di Napoli dal 1591 al 1707* (Naples, 1955) pp. 21–2.

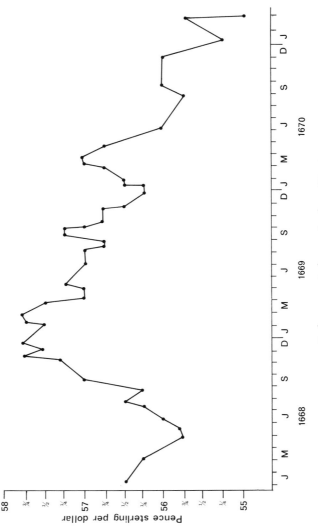

FIGURE 5. Exchange rate: Leghorn on London, 1668–1670.

Later it was to become a staging post for re-investment in east Mediterranean products, such as the currants of Zante and the oil of Apulia.[416]

Thus all Marescoe's gains at Leghorn, and a growing proportion of his gains in Seville, found their way back to London via the bill of exchange at a rate which became unusually attractive in the second half of 1668 (Figure 5). Death & Skinner, with their numerous London clients—Aboab among them—had little difficulty in drawing bills, and all thirty-eight of their bills for Marescoe were drafts on London, 60 per cent of them drawn in their own name. Between May 1668 and February 1671 over £5,300 passed this way on Marescoe's account. It brought him a further real profit of £78 10s 3d to add to the notional gain of £382 4s 4d which he had already credited to his 'Voyages to Livorno' account. This supplement represents the margin by which the actual rate on his bills exceeded the notional rate of 56d per dollar, and within this margin it is impossible to distinguish with certainty any profit yielded by the Spanish silver although an analysis of the returns reveals that 29 per cent of them represented the fruits of trade to Seville (Table 9).

TABLE 9. CM's shipments to Leghorn, profits and returns, 1668–1671.

No.	Goods	Value (f.o.b.)			Profit (%)	Net yields			Share (%)
		£	s	d		£	s	d	
7	Tin	2,103	19	8	11.7	2,349	6	11	44.0
4	Lead	688	19	1	6.9	736	10	4	13.8
2	Pepper	635	11	11	11.3	707	9	8	13.2
6	Silver†	—?—			—?—	1,351	4	3	25.3
1	Cochineal†	188	5	6	4.8	197	6	4	3.7
20	† from Spain					£5,341	17	6	100.0

Leghorn was thus a useful adjunct to the Spanish market, as well as a market in its own right. It was evidently not such an easy one in which to profit with the lavish certainties offered by Seville, but with a degree of good timing and thrifty management staple English products could be made to pay. Marescoe and Lethieullier were, perhaps, at some disadvantage because they were not yet involved in the fish trade. It was, as Death, Skinner & Ball often reminded them, the herring fish-fleet which decided the market in lead and tin, for these were ideal ballast to carry to the Lenten markets of the south.[417] It was for their arrival in January and February that Marescoe's potential customers waited, and until their deliveries had come and gone there would be little movement in other goods. A similar lesson was to be learned in Venice.

(II) **Venice**

While Marescoe's trade to Leghorn was almost entirely an English concern—English commodities carried to an English agent in predominantly English shipping—that to Venice was in some measure Dutch. The commodities were still mainly English in provenance—Cornish tin, Yorkshire lead and some English (as well as Dutch) East India Company pepper—but they were sometimes re-shipped at Amsterdam in Dutch vessels and were all

---

[416] See pp. 147–50.

[417] Davis, *Rise of the English Shipping Industry*, pp. 245–7; Death & Skinner to CM, 23 November 1668 [**52**]; Death, Skinner & Ball to CM, 25 October, 22 November 1669.

superintended by a liaison of Dutch merchants, Henrico Coninck and Anthoine des Bordes at Amsterdam and Pietro van Teylingen in Venice. The Venetian correspondence of Marescoe which begins in June 1668 is thus in Dutch and in its businesslike thoroughness and completely reliable frequency exhibits qualities which one likes to think are also characteristically Dutch. Where Death, Skinner & Ball wrote only intermittently to Marescoe during 1669, sending him some thirty letters and leaving the rest to Lethieullier to pass on, Van Teylingen wrote tirelessly every week, missing only four in the quieter seasons of the year. His only shortcoming is that where Death, Skinner & Ball commented broadly and sometimes critically on the conduct of trade Van Teylingen generally confined himself to a sober record of arrivals and departures, prices and sales—which does not make for stimulating reading. Yet, in aggregate, his letters provide a clear and instructive picture of the market over a period of eighteen months, which a chart can partially illustrate (Figure 6). It reveals the sluggish movement of prices for English lead, contrasting strongly with the plunging price of pepper. Tin prices confirm, by their virtual absence, the almost complete lack of Italian interest in this commodity, and like his colleagues in Leghorn Van Teylingen strongly advised his London principals against sending more. Like Death & Skinner, he wanted pepper, and he wanted it quickly. The high prices of the autumn of 1668 reflected a situation where the small amount of pepper in Venice was held in one hand,[418] and substantial rewards awaited the earliest new shipments.

In response, Marescoe and his partners freighted six ships to Venice in the summer and autumn of 1668, five carrying some 186 tons of lead and two carrying pepper. Four of these ships, *de Lantsman, Europa, Vreede,* and *Gratia* were Dutch ships loaded in Amsterdam, and the pepper they brought was of the Dutch East India Company, 8,371 *ponds* purchased at $25\frac{7}{8}$ grooten per pond. Their progress to Venice was painfully slow. Leaving Amsterdam in June, the *Lantsman* with lead had reached Genoa before the end of August but was still at Leghorn at the beginning of November, leaving eventually in the company of the Dutch convoy to Smyrna. It reached Messina on 18 November, and by 12 December was at Ancona, where it unloaded. Its lead cargo reached Venice in mid-January and had long since been sold at 55 ducats per thousand pounds. Indeed, Van Teylingen had shrewdly disposed of some of the other lead cargoes well in advance of their arrival at a price which, he correctly foresaw, could not be sustained, let alone raised, throughout the coming year. It is evident from his surviving sale-accounts that the Venetian market for lead was a small one, with perhaps less than a score of dealers,[419] and dominated by one or two men, such as Bortolo Marinoni (who bought-up 38 per cent of the known quantities) and Vicenzo Fusi (who took over 17 per cent).

It was a different matter with the pepper market, despite its control by one (unnamed) merchant until the end of 1668. When the two pepper cargoes which had left Amsterdam together in October 1668 eventually reached Venice on 7 February and 19 April 1669, they found the price beginning to slide, although some thirty or forty purchasers bargained for individual bales of 60–70 lb. apiece. The 66 bales which came with the *Gratia* sold slowly between 14 February and 4 July, starting at D.140 per 100 lb. (with a 6 months discount) and ending at D.75 for cash. Other Dutch shipments had arrived in March and early April, glutting a market which Van Teylingen described as dead by early June. The sale-accounts for the six shipments were not completed until October 1669.

Marescoe and his colleagues had to make their end-of-year assessment on the basis of only

[418] P. van Teylingen to CM, 30 November 1668. He estimated the number of bales of pepper remaining in Venice at approximately 20.
[419] From the surviving sale accounts for lead it is possible to identify 14 different purchasers.

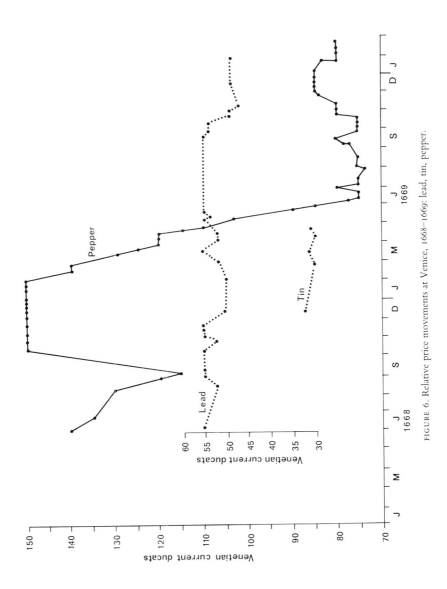

FIGURE 6. Relative price movements at Venice, 1668–1669: lead, tin, pepper.

one lead sale-account, received in mid-November 1668. Showing a notional profit of 19 per cent, it was enough to encourage them to even greater ventures in 1669. By the end of that year they had freighted goods on ten ships (2 Dutch, 8 English), only one of which was common to the ten also despatched for Leghorn. Distributed aboard them were three consignments of tin, three of pepper, nine of lead and one of herring. The invoice value of the goods sent in 1668 had been about £5,500 (of which Marescoe's share was £1,363 9s 9d). The goods sent in 1669 totalled about £9,570, in which Marescoe's investment was £2,783 0s 11d.

How significant were such consignments in the general context of Anglo–Venetian trade? There are no objective measures of volume or value available, but a succession of English diplomats at Venice in the 1670s made very similar estimates, putting the volume of English shipping at 17 to 20 ships per annum, and the value of English exports at about £25,000–£30,000.[420] Five or six fish-ships, arriving in time for Lent with Yarmouth herrings and Cornish pilchards, accounted for over half of the value. The rest, worth some £12,000, was made up of lead, sugar, pepper, woollen cloth and stockings.[421] By this measure, therefore, Marescoe alone was contributing nearly one-quarter of the non-fish imports in 1669, and the consortium to which he belonged must have been the dominant force in Anglo–Venetian trade.

This expansion of the Lethieullier–Marescoe partnership seems to have begun with the purchase of a one-third share in the 200-ton *Providence* in January 1668.[422] Their partners, each with one-sixth, were William Skinner of Hull, James Burkin, Edward Bouverie and George Torriano—all notable merchants with widespread interests. Under its captain, Henry Amyas, the *Providence* made its first venture to Guinea in 1668, securing a profit of 28 per cent. Its second mission, in October 1669, was to carry lead, pepper and salted herring (together costing £4,936 15s, f.o.b.), sell them at Venice and lade a return cargo of currants at Zante and oil at Gallipoli.

The outcome of this venture did not become clear until well after Marescoe's death,[423] but while he lived it emerged that he was doing well with his other Venetian sales in 1669 and 1670. Despite Van Teylingen's pessimistic assessments, he had sold most of the tin quickly and profitably. The lead he had been able to sell in large batches or even in entire consignments to a handful of clients. During one sluggish period, when three competitors were holding 1,000 pieces of lead against his own stock of 1,200, he contemplated selling to the great Arsenale itself. But he judged that the Republic, bowed under the huge debts of the Cretan war,[424] was in no position to pay quickly enough, and he had turned away from the idea.[425] He also did his best to avert disappointments in Venice by procuring sales elsewhere, at Genoa, Leghorn or Ancona, as yet more shiploads made their way to the Adriatic. By late

---

[420] See PRO, SP. 99/49 ff. 38, 68, 152 (John Dodington to Lord Arlington, 7, 27 February, [?] March, 1671); SP. 99/50 f. 186 (same to same, 11 December 1671); SP. 99/52 f. 128 ('A Scheme of Trade with Venice', 30 July 1673); SP. 99/53 ff. 9, 112 (George Hayles to Secretary of State, 2 February 1675; Sir Thomas Higgons to the same, 25 October 1675). But cf. Wood, *Levant Company*, pp. 64–6.

[421] PRO, SP. 99/52 f. 128.

[422] Miscellaneous Accounts, Bill of Sale 13 January 1668. The *Providence*, referred to occasionally in the letters of the English Resident at Venice, was estimated at 180 tons on its arrival in November 1670—SP. 99/48 f. 138 (J. Dodington to Lord Arlington, 28 November 1670); cf. 99/51 f. 80.

[423] See pp. 147–8.

[424] For some of the economic consequences of the war (1645–69) see Richard T. Rapp, *Industry and Economic Decline in Seventeenth Century Venice* (Cambridge, Mass, and London, 1976) pp. 149–53; and Domenico Sella, *Commerci e industrie a Venezia nel secolo xvii* (Venice-Rome, 1961) pp. 50, 54, 56, 64, 107.

[425] P. van Teylingen to CM, 27 September 1669.

November 1669 he had expeditiously closed his account on three consignments, in the face of competitors holding 3,000 pieces,[426] but just as he did so more of Marescoe's ships began to arrive—on 22 November, 14 December and 3 February—bringing 1,770 pieces of small, and 150 pieces of great, lead. He managed to sell 240 pieces of the small lead on 6 December, just before the deadest season of the year for this commodity intervened. There would be no more demand before the herring ships in the spring, and only then if their supplies were small.[427]

Such was the disappointing position when Marescoe's surviving correspondence is cut off in February 1670. In few other centres is this break more regrettable for in no other was there a more purposeful and promising commitment. The value of Marescoe's consignments to Italy in 1669 outstripped those to Hamburg and, unlike those to Germany and the Netherlands, they were all on his own account. His application to enter the Levant Company therefore makes sense as one step in a calculated reorientation of his trading efforts, away from the small gains of northern export-commissions towards the larger rewards of independent voyages in the south.

The survival of his book-keeping and some of the miscellaneous accounts allows an analysis of his investments and gains in Venice. When the books were closed on the 1668 ventures it became apparent that the Dutch pepper had done poorly, arriving too late to catch the top of the market.

TABLE 10. CM's shipments to Venice, 1668.

Goods	Cost (f.o.b.) £	s	d	Sale (net) £	s	d	Profit (%)
Lead	824	15	3	1,053	11	1	+27.7
Pepper	538	14	6	529	7	2	− 1.6
	1,363	9	9	1,582	18	3	+15.6

For the year 1669, the outcome of his consignments was moderately satisfactory, despite the loss of one of the two Yarmouth herring ships despatched by Peter Caulier with lead.[428]

In 1670, with so many of the 1669 shipments still outstanding, the effort was less vigorous, but the rewards were more substantial. Van Teylingen's predictions, that the conflict with Algiers would inhibit imports and raise prices to Marescoe's advantage,[429] seems to have been over-optimistic. His lead sales in 1670 were at D.48 per *mille*, rising to D.50 and D.52 only in the summer of 1671. The pepper of 1670 sold slowly until February 1671 at D.70 per 100 lb. with large discounts. Nevertheless the final profits looked healthy.

What proportion did freight and charges at Venice take of gross sales? Throughout the 1670s, the correspondence of England's official representatives was filled with complaints against the exaction of high port charges and heavy duties on fish (which only the English supplied). These were coupled with accusations of corrupt and extortionate levies in Zante,

[426] Same to same, 8 November 1669.
[427] Same to same, 27 December 1669, 3 January 1670.
[428] An exceptional number of vessels—forty—left Yarmouth for the Mediterranean in the autumn of 1669, laden with herrings, lead and tar—*CSPD, 1668–9*, p. 75 (R. Bower to Joseph Williamson, 25 November 1669). Of the 400 pieces of lead lost in the wreck of the *Hopewell*, 204 were later salvaged and sold.
[429] P. van Teylingen to CM, 10 and 17 January 1670.

TABLE 11. CM's shipments to Venice, 1669.

Goods	Cost (f.o.b.) £	s	d	Sale (net) £	s	d	Profit (%)
Lead	1,586	16	2	1,801	17	8	+13.5
Tin	262	12	2	313	5	6	+19.3
Pepper	828	13	6	910	15	2	+9.9
Fish	55	19	0	80	11	10	+44.0
	2,783	0	11	3,106	10	2	+13.6

TABLE 12. CM's shipments to Venice, 1670.

Goods	Cost (f.o.b.) £	s	d	Sale (net) £	s	d	Profit (%)
Lead	814	12	11	974	4	0	+19.6
Pepper	612	12	1	706	3	0	+15.3
Sugar	45	15	4	60	11	7	+32.3
	1,473	0	4	1,740	18	7	+18.2

where the English took seven-eighths of the currants.[430] This marked discrimination against English commerce may indeed reflect the natural resentment of Venice against the nation which had eclipsed their shipping, their textiles and their mastery of the Levant. It led to a situation where commerce was inhibited and few English merchants cared to remain.[431]

This may shed some light on the Marescoe–Lethieullier liaison with Coninck and Van Teylingen, although it does not emerge anywhere from Van Teylingen's letters that he was deliberately disguising the identity of these shipments. Yet that is precisely the charge which was made to the Secretary of State, Lord Arlington, by John Dodington in March 1671.[432] He cited Lethieullier and Sir John Frederick (among others) as members of a small Anglo–Dutch consortium which 'coloured' English goods through a well-known Dutch firm in Venice 'where they manage a considerable trade, in Lead, Pepper, Fish, Sugar'. He interpreted this as a conspiracy to defraud the English Crown of the aliens' duty on foreign-owned exports. But the real objective may have been to avoid the full rigours of Venetian duties.

---

[430] See, for example, PRO, SP. 99/47 f. 120; 99/48 ff. 14, 21, 32, 157–9; 99/50 ff. 35, 97; 99/51 ff. 9, 85, 96, 97, 115, 117; 99/52 ff. 70, 72; 99/53 ff. 132, 133; CO. 388/1 (Part 1) ff. 75–6. However, some of these complaints were directed against the 'consulage' charges levied for the support of the English resident, see *The Diary of John Evelyn* for 13 November 1672.

[431] PRO, SP. 99/47 f. 107 (J. Dodington to J. Williamson, 25 July 1670); f. 188 (Lord Fauconberg to Lord Arlington, 2 August 1670) 99/48 f. 14 (Decree of the Venetian senate, 20 September 1670); *Calendar of State Papers Venetian, 1668–69* p. 304 (P. Mocenigo to the Doge and Senate, 26 October 1668); *Calendar of State Papers Venetian, 1669–70* pp. 83–4 (same to same, 2 August 1669).

[432] PRO, SP. 99/49 f. 170 (J. Dodington to Lord Arlington, 20 March 1671). See also 99/51 ff. 18, 180, 206 for similar criticism of Aldermen Sir John Frederick and Thomas Lewis for cheating the English customs on behalf of Dutch merchants.

As it is, the charges levied on Marescoe's lead sales seem moderate. The total rarely exceeded 12 per cent and on average was 11.6 per cent. Of this, 3 per cent was accounted for by Van Teylingen's charge for commission and brokerage. The freight component varied considerably, being as low as 5 or 6 per cent on the Dutch ships or as high as 9 to 11 per cent on the English. The evidence is again inadequate to establish the actual freight-rates.[433] The remaining levies in Venice seem negligible. Unloading lead at Malamocco cost 1 or $1\frac{1}{2}$ *grossi* per piece. Charges and fees at the customs were little more than *D*.9 per 100 pieces of great lead. 'Speditie', 'licentie' and 'mandati' added another *D*.2 8 *grossi*, and 'tansa' on the Nation was *D*.2 5 *grossi*.[434] The real sting in the tail of the account was the conversion of these ducats into bank-ducats, on which the premium at this time was 16.66 per cent (usually expressed as an agio of 120).

The rate of exchange, expressed in pence sterling per bank-ducat, also contributed to the narrowing of margins in 1669 and 1670 as it fell from its high level of $55\frac{3}{4}d$ in February 1669 (Figure 7). The rates on Amsterdam followed a similar pattern, and some of Marescoe's

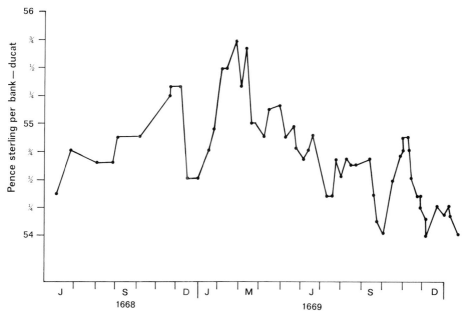

FIGURE 7. Exchange rate: Venice on London, 1668–1670.

[433] Some idea of the range of variation can be gained from the following examples of freight charged on 100 pieces of 'great lead' (about 280 cwt.): from London to Venice:

1669	March	'William & Elizabeth'	*D*.159 06
	November	'Pearl' frigate	*D*.127 10
1670	December	'Smyrna Factor'	*D*.63 17

[434] A Venetian ducat (of 24 *grossi*) was equivalent to 6 *lire* and 4 *soldi* (20 *soldi* to the *lire*). Accounts were kept in current ducats and *grossi*, but certain items, such as freight charges expressed in *reals plata*, were first converted into *lire* at a variable rate which in 1669–70 was 7 *lire* 18 *soldi* or 8 *lire*, per *real plata*. The total was then converted into ducats.

earnings were remitted in bills on Amsterdam. Between the beginning of Van Teylingen's account and February 1670, when it was balanced, he had remitted to Marescoe £1,777 14s 2d, drawn as follows:

		£	s	d
1	Lyon bill on Paris	115	17	3
2	Venice bills on Amsterdam	205	7	2
13	Venice bills on London	1,456	9	9

The Venice bills were drawn in only two cases by members of the small English merchant community, one by the consul, George Hayles, the other by Hayles in partnership with George Ravenscroft. In four cases they were drawn by that notable Dutch–Venetian, Giovanni Druyvestein (whose collusion with London merchants was a specific object of John Dodington's complaints).[435] After February 1670, however, the proceeds of Marescoe's trade were mainly directed towards financing the ladings of the *Providence* and of another vessel, the *John and Thomas*, under captain Samuel Randall. Marescoe had acquired a one-eighth share in this ship. It was sent on to Cephalonia to buy currants which were sold in London during the autumn of 1670, yielding Marescoe's widow a profit of $9\frac{3}{4}$ per cent on an outlay of £409. Future ventures in this trade were to reveal that this had been beginner's luck, of an ultimately expensive kind.

(iii) PROFIT AND LOSS, 1668–1670

It may be no accident that the surviving correspondence begins when it does, in the spring of 1668, for it was at this time that Marescoe's business was acquiring a new structure by its formal partnership with Peter Joye. From April 1668 Marescoe began to transfer to this half of his business the bulk of his commission trade, both import and export, recording it in a separate journal and ledger.[436] He retained for his own account the independent ventures in exports which he was making either alone or in partnership with John Lethieullier. By 1 January 1669 the net assets of this side of his affairs had become clear and they reveal the relative weight of his investment in trade to those centres which have just been reviewed (Table 13).

To the commission trade each partner brought £7,000 but Marescoe also lent further working capital of £10,000, later increased to £13,000. He also brought certain trading assets—debts due to him for sales of pitch and tar, copper-wire, lead and miscellaneous items together totalling £1,515 19s. Set against these, however, were larger liabilities totalling £1,807 10s 6d. Marescoe's net contribution to the partnership was thus, initially, £16,708 8s 6d—a sum remarkably similar to his net assets on his own account. The third and final ingredient in his capital account was cash in hand, totalling £4,513 15s 3d on 1 January 1669. His overall position can thus be summarized:

	£	s	d
capital on his own account	16,681	6	1
capital in partnership with P. Joye	16,708	8	6
cash in hand	4,513	15	3
Total trading capital	37,903	9	10

---

[435] PRO, SP. 99/51 f. 206 (J. Dodington to Lord Arlington, 10 June 1672). Druyvestein was alleged to be working hand-in-glove with Alderman Thomas Lewis, whose son resided with him in Venice—SP. 99/49 f. 170.

[436] See pp. 10–11.

TABLE 13. CM's assets on 'Own Account' 1 January 1669.

			£	s	d	£	s	d	%
A. East India Co. stock: £2,250 80%						1,800	0	0	10.79
B. Shares in ships:	(i) $\frac{6}{16}$ =		1,200	0	0				
	(ii) $\frac{1}{8}$ =		122	0	0	1,534	9	10	9.19
	(iii) $\frac{1}{32}$ =		212	9	10				
C. Loans, mortgage:	(i) =		500	0	0				
	(ii) =		300	0	0	1,101	7	3	6.60
	(iii) =		301	7	3				
D. Goods in stock:	(i) Coffee		167	19	0				
	(ii) Seedlack		224	7	10	779	16	4	4.67
	(iii) Tin		387	9	6				
E. 'Voyages':	2 to France		996	0	1				
	1 to Holland		1,431	6	0				
	6 to Italy		1,780	10	7				
	8 to Spain		2,698	5	7	8,588	7	10	51.48
	1 to Guinea		1,064	15	1				
	1 to Baltic		617	10	6				
F. Debts abroad:	(i) France		752	19	7				
	(ii) Spain		384	19	11	1,486	11	11	8.91
	(iii) Italy		348	12	5				
G. Bills of exchange						665	12	6	3.99
H. Debts at home						725	0	5	4.34
Total assets						16,681	6	1	100.00

This provides an interesting comparison with his position in June 1664 and at his death twenty-one months later.[437] However, the division of the business and the loss of the ledger covering his own account makes the audit of Marescoe's affairs rather difficult and tends to exaggerate the inherent artificiality of applying annuality to his book-keeping. Marescoe & Joye declared their dividends at irregular but logical intervals—on 24 December 1668 (after 9 months), on 1 July 1669 (after 6 months), on 31 March 1670 (after 9 months) and on 10 September 1670, immediately following Marescoe's death. There was no balance struck on his own trading account until his executors had finished their work. However, it is possible to construct an analysis of both his own account and the partnership account, reduced to a common annual basis (Table 14). Columns 4, 5 and 6 record the fruits of the partnership, with the net profits from which each took half. However, Marescoe also drew 6 per cent interest on his loan capital, which had been raised to £13,000 by January 1669 (column 8). These deductions from the partnership's profits account for most of the 'loss' attributed to 1669 in column 5. The much larger loss in 1670 reflects the bad debts of Peter Simons, Cornelius and Paul Berenberg, written off at £2,000.

The profits of the partnership cannot be so minutely analysed as those of 1664–7 for it ceased to be their practice to record separately the commission, interest and discount elements in their gains on imports. But one can attribute to each of the main import commodities the

---

[437] See pp. 17–19, and p. 116.

TABLE 14. CM's total earnings, 1668–1670.

Column	1	2	3	4	5	6	7	8	9
	CM's 'own account'			CM & PJ in partnership			Transfers to CM from partnership		CM's total earnings
	Gross Profit £ s d	Loss £ s d	Net Profit £ s d	Gross Profit £ s d	Loss £ s d	Net Profit £ s d	CM's ½ share £ s d	Interest £ s d	(Columns 3+7+8) £ s d
Jan.–Dec. 1668	3,848 19 10 ⎫ 1,299 19 4 ⎬	1,917 7 0	3,231 12 2	1,959 1 8	49 11 10	1,909 9 10	954 14 11	—	4,186 7 1
Jan.–Dec. 1669	701 12 9	51 9 1	650 3 8	3,849 17 11	1,303 17 7	2,546 0 4	1,273 0 2	1,025 0 0	2,948 3 10
Jan.–Sept. 1670	2,633 16 2	617 19 9	2,015 16 5	2,641 10 8	2,818 12 7	−177 2 1	−88 11 0½	195 0 0	2,122 5 4½
Sept.– 1670 onwards	1,663 6 11	192 7 1	1,470 19 10	—	—	—	—	—	1,470 19 10
Totals	10,147 15 0	2,779 2 11	7,368 12 1	8,450 10 3	4,172 2 0	4,278 8 3	2,139 4 0½	1,220 0 0	10,727 16 1½

TABLE 15. Gross trading profits of CM & PJ, 1668–1670.

	1668				1669				1670			
	£	s	d	%	£	s	d	%	£	s	d	%
A. Imports:	1,461	3	10	74.6	2,770	7	3	72.0	1,483	3	9	56.2
Iron	51.8%				36.7%				57.7%			
Copper	21.8%				26.1%				10.6%			
Steel	0.9%				—				0.6%			
Pitch and tar	19.2%				33.0%				30.6%			
Timber	3.9%				1.1%				0.5%			
Other	2.4%				3.1%				—			
B. Discounts	98	17	9	5.0	405	14	8	10.5	—			—
C. Shipping	9	3	0	0.5	—			—	—			—
D. Insurance	46	3	10	2.4	231	5	1	6.0	47	19	0	1.8
E. Bills of exa.	2	5	3	0.1	—			—	—			—
F. Exports	341	0	10	17.4	334	9	1	8.7	167	17	11	6.4
G. Miscellaneous	—				108	1	10	2.8	942	10	0	35.7
Totals	1,959	1	8		3,849	17	11		2,641	10	8	

contribution which it made to their gains, and also measure the relatively lighter weight of export-commission earnings (Table 15). The very large 'Miscellaneous' item recorded in 1670 is made up mainly of £610 9s 10d transferred from the Expense account—the surplus of petty charges on commissions over the cash actually disbursed; the rest is attributed to possible bad debts by the executors as they closed the account.

Returning to Table 14, columns 1, 2 and 3 reflect Marescoe's independent activities which, as we have seen, were directed mainly towards exports after 1668. These 'Voyages' to Amsterdam, Lille, Rouen, Seville, Leghorn and Venice produced 79 per cent of the 1669 earnings in column 1, and 63 per cent in 1670. The sources and circumstances of these earnings have already been reviewed but there is one large item which generated no correspondence and to which Marescoe made virtually no administrative contribution. Under the auspicious title 'Voyage van *Landt van Schoonen*' he recorded his half-share investment of £617 10s 6d in two ladings of Setubal salt purchased by Gerard de Geer. Despatched to Reval, the proceeds had been reinvested there in rye which De Geer sold in Amsterdam. It yielded a net profit of 110 per cent—a striking demonstration of the large profits which could be made in independent trade. But Marescoe did not live to ponder its significance for after a fever lasting several days he died on 9 September 1670.

The assessment of his estate took some months to complete and the final figures to emerge relate to the position on 28 February 1671. The value of his share in the partnership was quickly established at £21,469 15s 2d, but with the remaining estate differences emerge between the ledger and the inventory presented to the Common Serjeant of the City of London on 23 March 1671.[438] The discrepancies are not necessarily sinister: it was legitimate to classify certain assets as 'doubtful' or 'desperate' debts. Other assets could be justifiably reassessed. But it remains impossible to reconcile exactly the individual items in the ledger with those of the inventory. 'Cash in hand', which had been £4,150 in the former, became

[438] CLRO, Common Serjeant's Book II, f. 240.

£3,341 19s 7d in the latter, and most other items had been adjusted. The clearest statement of Marescoe's capital simply added the accumulated net profits of 1668–70, totalling £5,942 18s 5d, to the capital of 1 January 1669, making £44,008 0s 11d.[439] Another statement added a few more sums, making £44,880 9s 6d, but it seems that the executors took the smaller figure and deducted from it the £5,004 18s 1d which Marescoe was deemed to have spent on his housebuilding since 1 June 1669 to arrive at £39,003 2s 10d as the net capital of the estate. This bears little relation to the £40,424 19s $10\frac{1}{2}d$ net which was later arrived at in the first schedule of assets exhibited at the trial,[440] and since this statement looks more plausible it is worth summarizing (see Table 16).

TABLE 16. CM's estate (excluding real property)
September 1670.

	£	s	d
Partnership with PJ	21,469	15	0
Cash in hand	3,341	19	7
Gold and silver 'medals'*	200	0	0
East India Co. stock, £2,250 valued @ 170%	3,825	0	0
Shares in 5 ships	1,018	4	6
Goods in stock (cochineal, seedlack, oil, lead)	1,275	1	6
'Adventures abroad': Hamburg 4.9% Amsterdam 2.8% Spain 31.8% Leghorn 17.1% Venice 35.9% E. Indies 7.5%	3,154	18	8
Bills of exchange due	2,398	11	3
Debts due on sales	6,096	12	$5\frac{1}{2}$
	42,780	3	$1\frac{1}{2}$
Less liabilities	2,355	3	3
Net estate	40,424	19	$10\frac{1}{2}$

* These consisted of English gold and silver coins from the reign of Elizabeth onwards, together with Imperial, Spanish, French, Portuguese, Dutch and Polish pieces.

Thus the best that can be said is that Marescoe's trading capital was about £40,000 in September 1670—a remarkable accretion of wealth in the five years since 1664. It put him in the upper bracket of mercantile fortunes in Restoration England—less wealthy than many notable magnates who died full of years, but impressive for a man in his late thirties.[441]

The Lethieullier family could claim some credit for this fortune, not merely because John had introduced Marescoe to the profits of southern trade but because he and his brother Christopher lent him some working capital at critical points in his operations. Despite the substantial cash balances already revealed at three points—the £940 of June 1664, the £4,513

[439] Ledger 'M' f. 1 can be reconstructed from the Journal, 1668–76.

[440] PRO, C. 10/138/99.

[441] See Richard Grassby, 'The Personal Wealth of the Business Community in Seventeenth Century England', *EcHR* 2nd series, xxiii (August 1970) pp. 224, 226, 227; also the same author's 'English Merchant Capitalism in the Late Seventeenth Century', *Past & Present*, 46 (1970) pp. 92–3, 94–5.

of January 1669 and the £4,150 of September 1670—Marescoe's liquidity was often strained by the exigencies of his Swedish principals whose demands for large-scale advances were capable of swallowing his reserves twice over. Precisely how he managed to balance the anticipated demands to be made upon him—for discounts, advances, remittances, purchase of goods, etc—against anticipated receipts for goods sold and bills of exchange, remains a mystery, as it does for all seventeenth-century accounting records, which were singularly indifferent to the needs of regular balance-sheets.[442] The meticulous 'Cash' account which runs through 39 folios of the 1664–8 ledger provides an inadequate key to the problem, for— as noted already—there was a separate 'petty cash' account running concurrently with this, the accumulated balance of which was only brought into the main account at irregular intervals.[443] To secure a true picture of Marescoe's cash balance at any one time one must marry the two, which can only be done—short of reworking all the 8,000 entries—by matching up balances at dates which nearly coincide. The gap is rarely greater than 7 days and the discrepancy caused by estimating the petty-cash balance is rarely more than £50. On this basis a picture of Marescoe's cash reserves can be tentatively sketched, starting from the £940 of June 1664 and ending in August 1668, when the division of the business makes the calculations too complex to be safe.

The figures reveal that Marescoe's cash reserve averaged about £1,600 but was capable of violent oscillation plus or minus £3,000–£6,000 in a matter of months. The accumulation of cash in late-1665, as war inhibited the reinvestment of his huge profits, is very striking. It was at this time that Marescoe began to place money out at interest with the East India Company and the goldsmith-bankers. By June 1666 he had £6,300 of his own money invested in various loans, most of them at 6 per cent (Table 17). The addition of £10,000 in July 1666 represents the collusive reinvestment by Marescoe and Leyonbergh of Charles II's advance to the Swedish Crown.[444] This was eventually remitted in a series of bills of exchange, mostly handled by Peter Juncker in Hamburg or paid directly by Marescoe to the Swedish envoys.

These transactions account almost entirely for the deficits which occurred in July and December 1666. Without the transfer of large sums to Lombard Street Marescoe would have been able to meet easily enough the sudden demands placed upon him by the Mommas, the Tar Company and by Leyonbergh. As it is, the deposits with Backwell and Vyner had been at 14 days notice and were therefore sufficiently liquid to cover his immediate requirements in January 1667.[445] The deposits with the Meynells were at 30 days and were more slowly withdrawn. However, by the end of April 1667, with prospects of peace and abundant Hamburg commissions, Marescoe began to purchase export commodities and his need for additional capital led him to borrow £1,000 from the Lethieulliers in early May. This loan, at 5 per cent, was successively renewed in 1668, 1669 and 1670 and was treated as a charge on the partnership with Peter Joye. It was a useful, if not vital, component of the capital-base from which the profits of 1667–70 arose.

Against this background of sometimes precarious liquidity it is not surprising to find that

[442] B. S. Yamey, H. C. Edey & H. W. Thomson (eds.) *Accounting in England and Scotland, 1543–1800* (London, 1963) pp. 186–9.

[443] From June 1664, petty cash balances were transferred to the main cash account, successively, after 73, 101, 38, 14, 31, 23 and 17 weeks.

[444] For this transaction in its Swedish context see Wittrock, I, pp. 322–3, 406–8; Fahlborg, *Sveriges yttre politik, 1664–1668*, I, pp. 452–3. Correspondence relating to these remittances, between Juncker and Leyonbergh, is in RA, Stockholm, Diplomatica Anglica 108, Bundles 2 and 3.

[445] Analysis of Backwell's ledgers reveals that in the period December 1666–March 1667 47% of his customer's deposits were at 10 days notice and 29% at 14 days. See H. G. Roseveare, 'The Advancement of the King's Credit, 1660–1672' (unpublished Cambridge Ph.D. dissertation, 1962) p. 254, Appendix viii, table 2.

Marescoe & Joye's Trade, 1668–1670

TABLE 17. CM's investments, 1664–1668.

		East India Co.		Bankers			City loans	Total loans
		Stock	Loan	Backwell	Vyner	Meynell		
1664	June	£ 750					£100 @ 6%	
	July	,,					,,	
	August	,,					,,	
	September	,,					,,	
	October	,,					,,	
	November	,,					,,	
	December	,,					£200 @ 6%	
1665	January	,,					,,	
	February	,,					,,	
	March	,,					,,	
	April	,,					,,	
	May	,,					,,	
	June	,,					,,	
	July	,,					,,	
	August	,,					,,	
	September	,,					,,	
	October	,,					,,	
	November	,,					,,	
	December	,,	£1,200 @ 6%				£100 @ 6%	£1,300
1666	January	,,	£2,000			,,	,,	£2,100
	February	,,	,,			£1,000	,,	£3,100
	March	,,	,,			,,	,,	,,
	April	,,	,,			,,	,,	,,
	May	,,	,,			,,	,,	,,
	June	£1,500	£1,400	£1,000 @ 6%	£1,000 @ 6%	£2,600	£300 @ 6%	£6,300
	July	,,	£ 600	£7,000 @ 5%	£2,000 @ 6%	£6,600 @ 5%	,,	£16,500
	August	,,	,,	,,	,,	,,	,,	,,
	September	,,	,,	£5,751	,,	,,	,,	£15,201
	October	,,	,,	£4,751	£3,000	,,	,,	,,
	November	,,	,,	£4,000	,,	,,	,,	£14,500
	December	,,	——	,,	,,	,,	,,	£13,900
1667	January	,,		£1,000	£2,000	£2,600	,,	£5,900
	February	,,		,,	——	,,	,,	£3,900
	March	£2,250		,,		£1,600	,,	£2,900
	April	,,		,,		,,	,,	,,
	May	,,		——		,,	,,	£1,900
	June	,,				——	,,	£300
	July	,,					,,	,,
	August	,,				,,	,,	,,
	September	,,				£500 @ 6%	,,	£800
	October	,,				,,	,,	,,
	November	,,				,,	,,	,,
	December	,,				,,	,,	,,
1668	January	,,				,,	,,	,,
	February	,,				,,	,,	,,
	March	,,				,,	,,	,,
	April	,,				,,	,,	,,
	May	,,				,,	,,	,,
	June	,,				,,	,,	,,
	July	,,				,,	£100	£600
	August	,,				,,	,,	,,
	September	,,				,,	,,	,,
	October	,,				,,	,,	,,
	November	,,				,,	,,	,,
	December	,,				,,	——	£500

Marescoe was not greatly attracted by contemporary inducements to lend to the government. Like several hundred other London citizens he participated in the City's loans of £200,000 to Charles II on the credit of the Hearth Tax in July and November 1664,[446] and with 750 others he contributed to the City's war-loan of £75,000 on the credit of the Additional Aid of 1665. This celebrated tax had incorporated Sir George Downing's novel inducements to lend money directly to the Exchequer on the credit of a parliamentary appropriation guaranteeing repayment with 6 per cent interest and the assured transferability of the security.[447] It had been hoped that individuals would gladly purchase these negotiable, interest-bearing 'Treasury Orders' and, indeed, some nine hundred did so.[448] But the City's loan reflected no confidence in Downing's scheme. It was the City treasurer, Sir Thomas Player, who received the 'Treasury Orders', not the individual contributors who had to be content with Player's unnegotiable receipt. It was two years before Marescoe was repaid.

However, Marescoe was attracted by another product of Downing's scheme. The Act of 1665 had also provided for the issue of 'Treasury Orders' in return for goods supplied for the Navy, and although they were not interest-bearing (for they already embodied a substantial premium) they shared the characteristic of loan Orders in being negotiable and registered in sequence. Bought and sold at a discount, pending repayment by the Treasury, they constituted an attractive investment to which even the cautious Pepys succumbed.[449] Marescoe, likewise, was in a good position to exploit the cash-needs of Navy contractors and this he did in the case of Benjamin Newland of the Isle of Wight, buying and selling several of his Orders for discounts which varied from 5 to 24 per cent.

A good deal of contemporary opprobrium attached to this war-time profiteering and it never figured as largely in Marescoe's dealings as in those of much richer merchants, such as Sir John Banks.[450] Marescoe's most substantial and profitable financial investments were made in the entirely respectable form of East India Company shares. In June 1664 he held £750 (paid-up) stock which he valued at £450 (i.e. at 60 per cent.) Dividends totalling 60 per cent were received or declared in 1664 and in September he revalued his shares at 85. By January 1666 he cautiously raised them to par while noting that stock was changing hands at 130 thanks to the safe arrival of three ships from Surat. Dividends totalling 50 per cent were declared soon after, but in April 1666 the stock slipped back to 76 and he now started buying, procuring £500 (paid-up) for £380 and £250 (paid-up) for £190. In February 1667, with stock at 70, he bought £250 from Thomas Papillon and £500 from Christopher Boone for a total of £525.[451] His paid-up stock now totalled £2,250, more than enough to give him voting rights in the Company and privileged access to its sales.[452]

---

[446] For these loans see C. A. F. Meekings, 'The City Loans on the Hearth Tax, 1664–8' in *Studies in London History*, ed. A. E. J. Hollaender & W. Kellaway (London, 1969).

[447] 17 Car. II. c.1—Statutes of the Realm V (London, 1819) pp. 570–4; partially printed in J. P. Kenyon, *The Stuart Constitution* (Cambridge, 1966) pp. 389–91.

[448] Roseveare 'The Advancement of the King's Credit, 1660–1672' pp. 67–71.

[449] D. C. Coleman, 'Sir John Banks, Financier' in F. J. Fisher (ed.) *Essays in the Economic & Social History of Tuder & Stuart England* (Cambridge, 1961) p. 223.

[450] D. C. Coleman, *Sir John Banks, Baronet & Businessman* (Oxford, 1963) pp. 34–9.

[451] Marescoe's ledger entries confirm the registration of share-transfers noted in East India Company records—see E. B. Sainsbury (ed.), *A Calendar of the Court Minutes of the East India Company, 1664–1667* (Oxford, 1925) pp. 429–30—but the dates of declarations and payments of dividends differ slightly from those in W. R. Scott, *The Constitution and Finances of English, Scottish and Irish Joint Stock Companies* II (Cambridge, 1912) pp. 177–9.

[452] Until 1682 only half the subscribed capital was called up. Thus, to obtain £1,000 of nominal stock required payment for £500 'paid-up'. The qualification for a vote in the Company was £500 nominal stock; £1,000 nominal qualified for election to the directorate. Dividends could be taken in kind, and in 1664 Marescoe took 240 bales of cotton yarn in lieu of his 30% dividend.

However, Marescoe's largest investment was in real estate. Early in 1669 he acquired for £900 the site of what had been, until the Fire of London, the house of Peter Vandeput (Sr.), a notable merchant, later knighted. The site was in Tower Street and between May and July 1669 he acquired adjoining sites in Thames Street and Bosse Alley near Billingsgate for £1,250. His plan was to build a mansion house for his family and a group of smaller houses for leasing. By 10 September 1670 he had spent £3,345 1s 11d on building and £83 13s on legal expenses. Three houses were already leased for 21 years at rents of £11, £40 and £30 per annum; three others soon followed.

The mansion house was not ready until mid-August 1671[453] and, although it seems to have been conceived on a handsome scale, much of its elaborate furnishing and refinement was the work of his widow, Leonora. If the widow's inventory of her husband's personal possessions is to be trusted, Charles Marescoe had not been an extravagant man.[454] There were indeed some £500-worth of jewels and silver-plate, Swedish and Hamburg pewter, Dutch chests and Silesian linen, 'a picture of ships' and three other pictures—the whole household equipment, with its beds, chairs, pots and pans valued at some £300. Marescoe's personal wardrobe is eloquent of a decent modesty. It held (as the widow recalled) two black suits, two cloaks, one black 'pourdesay' suit, one camlet coat and one short one, one 'sad-coloured' suit, two satin waistcoats, six or seven plain cambric cravats, six shirts, twelve pocket handkerchieves, six pairs of drawers, and several plain waistcoats, the whole lot valued at £10. Marescoe had been more generous to others than to himself. A regular contributor to the French Church in Threadneedle Street and to the poor of his parish, he left £150 to the Church and £5 a-piece to its ministers. The poor of Low Leyton and St Margaret Pattens received £10 respectively and £50 went to Christ's Hospital. His god-children were remembered, as were his servants Moses Coulon and Jacob David, who received £25 each. He allotted £15 to each of his executors for mourning.[455]

Would he have approved of the £586 2s 3d which was spent on his funeral? It seems unlikely. The elaborate and costly obsequies which accompanied him from London to Low Leyton church were the work of his widow, and they inaugurated a very different style of household management as well as a less prosperous conduct of trade.

[453] E. Ruland congratulated the widow on its completion in a letter of 29 August 1671.
[454] PRO, C. 10/199/30.
[455] PRO, PROB. 11/333 No. 114. A copy of Charles Marescoe's will is also to be found among his miscellaneous papers.

5. LEONORA MARESCOE'S TRADE,
1670–1674

(i) IMPORTS

In the division of property following Marescoe's death his widow initially received nearly £6,000 more than her one-third share of £39,000. This she speedily and shrewdly reinvested in a series of short-term loans—to her brothers, bankers, the East India Company and other merchants. By the end of March 1671 she had £13,000 out at interest (5 per cent for her relations, 6 per cent for the rest), but with the correction of this mistake and the transfer to the City of London Chamber of the children's two-thirds, these loans were retrenched to a total of £6,000 by July 1671.

Despite this promising start as a well-to-do *rentière*, Leonora was not yet ready to abdicate from the trading activities of her late husband. The decision to carry on his commissions in partnership with Peter Joye was quickly taken, and the new company started trading from 16 September 1670. Its capital was to be £10,000, of which Leonora and Joye each supplied two-fifths while Moses Coulon and Jacob David were credited with one-tenth each. However, Jacob David's £1,000 was in fact a loan from Leonora, upon which 5 per cent was payable—although rarely paid. She also lent the Company another £1,000 reduced to £600 in January 1672.

These were slender resources with which to sustain a business previously carried on with over £40,000, and one might reasonably expect some loss of clientele among those Swedish exporters whose credit requirements were so demanding. Indeed, their reactions to Marescoe's death were generally cool and unsentimental—expressing a token regret and passing on quickly to serious matters of business. Only Steven de Geer and the Van Baerles in Amsterdam conveyed a genuine feeling of loss for an old colleague, but the response to the new partnership was generally welcoming and the commissions for imports of iron, copper, timber, pitch and tar seemed likely to continue.

Yet, formal expressions of goodwill could not remove the serious difficulties facing a continuation of the old pattern. Marescoe's position had become increasingly insecure several months before his death and his growing reluctance to extend further credit to the Mommas, to Pötter & Thuen and the Tar Company was founded on a correct appraisal of *their* precariousness. Still smarting from the losses incurred on Peter Simons and the Berenbergs he was evidently making such difficulties about excessive drafts that his relations with Stockholm were approaching a breakdown. By the spring of 1670 it was known both in Hamburg and Amsterdam that Jacob Momma and the Cronströms were looking for a new London agent.[1] On 28 February 1670 Momma had approached the firm of James Burkin & Joas Evertsen, expressing regret that a sixteen-year correspondence with Marescoe was ending and offering them the succession to his, and the Cronströms', commissions in copper, brass and timber.[2] The offer was not taken up: Burkin was Marescoe's kinsman. But in June

---

[1] Van Baerles to Jacob Reenstierna, 8 April 1670; J. J. Hiebenaer to same, 25 December 1669, in RA, Stockholm (Momma-Reenstierna MSS) E.2498, E.2506.
[2] RA, Stockholm, E.2483 p. 88.

1671 Momma welcomed overtures from the London firm of Jacob Lucie & Cornelis van Bommell who were only too eager to step into Marescoe's shoes.[3]

Indeed, there was probably no lack of competition for Marescoe's Swedish commissions. Inside (and outside) the Eastland Company there were other large-scale Baltic merchants who may have had the will and means to supersede him. Benjamin Ayloff, William Blackett, Urban Hall (Sr.), Gilbert Heathcote (Sr.), Theodore Jacobsen, Adam Lyell, Sir William Ryder and Samuel Sowton are but some of the merchants who were making their fortunes in Scandinavian or Baltic trade.[4] The keenness of their competition is indicated by the English East India Company's search for copper supplies between 1668 and 1670. In March 1668 Sir William Ryder (Deputy Governor of the Company) was asked to handle purchases since he was understood to know how to obtain them cheaply in Stockholm.[5] Later, Peter Vandeput (Sr.) was commissioned to buy £10,000-worth of 'Hungary plates' in Hamburg. It was not until 18 June 1669 that Marescoe was approached by the Company to supply Swedish 'rose-copper' (i.e. garcopper), and the surprising answer was recorded five days later 'that Mr Marescoe is no trader in copper'. Instead, the Company turned elsewhere, accepting an offer from Samuel Sowton to supply copper from Stockholm more cheaply than from Hamburg, and also placing an order with Burkin & Evertsen.[6] Although purchases were eventually made from Marescoe in July 1670 Sowton and the others had secured the lion's share of orders worth some £18,000 paid for through J. & C. Banks in Hamburg.[7]

Not surprisingly, therefore, Marescoe's letters to Jacob Momma in the course of 1670 betray a new anxiety to please, offering terms for a new monopoly commision which were so generous that he dared not have them divulged [Appendix A, **6**]. Proposing to accept only $1\frac{1}{2}$ per cent commission and 5 per cent interest on advances secured against goods, he had given a pledge which Jacob was eager to redeem from his widow and partner.[8] It was thus a poor start to the new partnership when Leonora and Joye asked to be excused from these terms and from a promise of £1,200 advanced for the winter. Jacob Momma's resentment probably clinched the decision to commission Lucie & Van Bommell as Marescoe's successors.[9]

Other Swedish correspondents also began to withdraw. There were no more letters or commissions from the Cronströms in 1671. Abraham Momma, who had sent only a little iron in 1670, sent nothing in 1671, preferring to sell to Englishmen in Sweden. Pötter & Thuen, after promising larger trade in October 1670, similarly explained their failure to send anything by September 1671: 'we have for some time not traded to London, finding it better to sell our goods here'.[10] The troubled Tar Company also sent nothing in 1671 and in March 1672 brought its patchy correspondence with Leonora and Joye to a recriminatory close.[11] It was Samuel Sowton who now stepped in to take the agency for London tar shipments for the three years 1673–5.[12]

Behind this loss of clientele lay some profounder changes in the management of Swedish

[3] RA, Stockholm, E.2483 pp. 234–5. For Jacob Lucie (or Luce) see Woodhead, *Rulers of London, 1660–89*, p. 110; Jacob M. Price, 'The Tobacco Adventure to Russia', p. 13 n. 52.

[4] Åström, *From Cloth to Iron*, pp. 122–52; Hinton, *The Eastland Trade*, Appendix C(4), pp. 221–5.

[5] E. B. Sainsbury (ed.) *Calendar of the Court Minutes of the East India Company, 1668–1670* (Oxford, 1929) p. 35.

[6] Ibid. pp. 60, 70, 84, 203, 208, 209, 212, 234, 241, 321, 323–4, 326, 327, 328, 334, 336, 338.

[7] Ibid. pp. 340, 348, 353–4.

[8] Caspar Muyssenhol [Jacob Reenstierna's nephew and bookkeeper, writing during his uncle's illness] to LM & PJ, 10 October 1670.

[9] Muyssenhol to same, 31 October 1670; RA, Stockholm, E.2483, pp. 60–1.

[10] Pötter & Thuen to same, 9 September 1671 [**168**].

[11] Tar Co. to same, 30 March 1672.

[12] Hallberg, 'Tjärexport och tjärhandelskompanier', pp. 122–5.

finance. The copper-loan syndicate built round Cronberg was breaking up as a new man, Joel Ekman (ennobled as Gripenstierna in 1669) pushed his way to the front.[13] While Joachim Pötter clung on, the Reenstiernas withdrew, their credit dangerously over-extended. Although Abraham obtained royal patents for anchor- and steel-manufacture in March 1670 he was facing acute financial pressures which led him to seek government protection in November 1671. On 19 December he made over all his assets to his brother and although he long outlived Jacob it was as a virtually ruined man.[14]

Ruin also faced the Tar Company. Despite tax concessions and other privileges it was unable to shake off the burden of interest-bearing debt and surplus stock.[15] By the spring of 1671 a drastic solution had been agreed to by which the Company wrote off two-thirds of its old capital and sought a large injection of new. The charter for the 'renovated' Tar Company was finally granted in August 1672 but in the interim the weakened state of the Company and the debts of the Swedish government had enabled other interests to intrude on its monopoly. A Scottish-born Stockholm merchant, James Semple, to whom the government and individual ministers were indebted, procured in December 1671 a licence to export 4,000 lasts of pitch and tar per annum for three years—a concession which was to embarrass seriously the fortunes of the 'renovated' Tar Company of 1672.[16]

Thus, 1671 was an inauspicious year in which to re-build a commission trade in Swedish imports and it would have been a dismal one but for the continuing custom of Willem Momma and the De Geers. The elder Momma was not without his problems but he stood clear of the embarrassments of his noble step-brothers and maintained for the moment an independent course. Steven de Geer likewise stood aloof from the worst of the Swedish entanglements and seemed amiably disposed towards the Marescoe house. Furthermore, there was Louis Trip, whose tentative approach of 1669 was now to bear fruit.

These men provided the bulk of the 1671 shipments which in volume and value were 40 per cent down on 1670. Of the £20,000 value (c.i.f.) the largest component was iron (42.1 per cent), followed by copper (39.3 per cent) and accompanied by latten-ware and battery (9.5 per cent). Steven and Gerard de Geer provided 61 per cent of the volume of iron and Louis Trip another 20 per cent. Three smaller producers in Gothenburg supplied the balance. Of the copper, Willem Momma shipped 88.1 per cent and of the latten, etc, 85 per cent compared with his step-brother Jacob's contribution of 2.2 and 15 per cent respectively.

The responsibility for the new partnership's imports was thus in comparatively few hands but, as before, it generated a disproportionately large correspondence shared more widely than ever between Norrköping, Nyköping, Stockholm, Gothenburg, Hamburg and Amsterdam. The Van Baerles continued to perform their dual role, handling drafts on London for the Mommas and advising the widow on prospects in Amsterdam. Their letters to Jacob Reenstierna also provide an invaluable commentary as do those of his Hamburg agent, J. J. Hiebenaer.[17] Bartolotti & Rihel wrote occasionally on behalf of Pötter & Thuen, and even Peter Simons re-emerged, promising redemption of his debt and seeking

---

[13] For Gripenstierna's career see A. Munthe, *Joel Gripenstierna: en storfinansiär från Karl XI's tid* (Stockholm, 1941); also R. Carr 'Two Swedish Financiers: Louis de Geer and Joel Gripenstierna' in *Historical Essays, 1600–1750, presented to David Ogg*, ed. H. E. Bell & R. L. Ollard (London, 1963).

[14] Sondén, 'Bröderna Momma-Reenstierna', pp. 163–4, 167–8.

[15] Hallberg, 'Tjärexport och tjärhandelskompaner', p. 120.

[16] Ibid. pp. 121–2; Fyhrvall, 'Tjärhandelskompanierna' p. 314; Stiernmann, III, p. 950; PRO, SP. 95/8 ff. 147–8.

[17] RA, Stockholm, E.2498, E. 2506.

reinstatement as a correspondent.[18] Perhaps the most interesting series, however, is the collection of 84 letters written to Jacob Reenstierna by Lucie & Van Bommell.[19] Not only do they offer a useful commentary on the London market but they provide the ironic spectacle of this ambitious firm being driven into the same dilemmas which had faced their predecessor as Reenstierna's demands for credit grew more and more burdensome. By the end of 1673 Lucie was aggrieved to detect that he was being betrayed just as he had once betrayed Marescoe, for Reenstierna began to re-open his commissions with Leonora and their correspondence ended on the usual note of acrimony.

In 1671, however, Lucie & Van Bommell were willing conspirators, spying on Leonora's shipments and concealing from her the extent of their own. One may deduce that they received some £6,000–£7,000-worth of iron, copper and timber in this first year, but they were soon reporting a sluggish London market with abundant timber coming from Norway and more than enough iron, some of it from Spain.[20] The situation might have been much worse if the Bill levying additional customs duties on foreign commodities had received the royal assent in April 1671.[21] Debated by both Houses since October 1670 its progress had been anxiously watched by De Geer, the Mommas and the Van Baerles, who were aware that proposed increases of 10s per cwt. on wrought copper (currently selling in London at £5 18s to £6) and 10s per ton on iron (selling at between £15 and £17 according to type) could not be offset by economies in production-costs or by increases in sales-volume. Indeed, for some months the Van Baerles had been impressing on Jacob Reenstierna the changing balance of power in European metal markets. Swedish copper and iron could no longer dictate in Amsterdam, or elsewhere. Norwegian garcopper was arriving in quantity; larger Japanese shipments were expected; Spanish iron could not be ignored, and the metal-working industries at Aachen and Staelburg were finding it profitable to expand at Sweden's expense.[22] It was therefore a matter for intense relief that the English Parliament was prorogued and the Bill lost. A similar threat, of increased export tolls in Sweden, was also postponed.[23]

Against this background it seemed surprising that Swedish copper prices should have risen so suddenly and sharply as they did in the second half of 1671. At 235 copper dollars (about £10 5s per shippound, or £3 16s per cwt.) in June, garcopper rose to 240 in August, 250 in September, 260 in October and briefly reached 280 (or £4 11s per cwt.) in December. By October W. Momma had to insist that his copper-wire, so far selling at £6 or £6 2s, should not be sold for less than £6 10s.[24] Yet prices in London and elsewhere were slow to respond to Sweden's. In Amsterdam, Japanese copper prospects held them down until December, and even in Hamburg it was not until mid-November that garcopper leaped from 65½–66 rixdollars banco per shippound to 85.[25] Initially the Swedish price-rise seemed explicable in terms of a temporary shortage of copper-ore, exacerbated by heavy rains and consequent

[18] P. Simons to LM & PJ, 21 April 1671. By February 1672 Simons had made provision for 40 per cent of his debt and by March, 50 per cent. By late 1671 he appeared regularly on the Amsterdam Exchange, conducting business for the Swedish government (Van Baerles to LM & PJ, 2 October 1671).

[19] RA, Stockholm, E.2512.

[20] Ibid., 3 October 1671; 2 February 1672.

[21] For the draft Bill, with subsequent amendments and counter-petitions, see Historical Manuscripts Commission, *Appendix to the 9th Report*, House of Lords MSS, pp. 8–15; *CJ* IX, pp. 159, 167, 171–4, 234.

[22] RA, Stockholm, E.2498, Van Baerles to Jacob Reenstierna, 30 September 1670; 9 May 1671; 5 January 1672.

[23] W. Momma to LM & PJ, 19 March [**142**], 28 May 1671.

[24] Same to same, 1 October 1671.

[25] Same to same, 26 November, 10 December 1671 [**174, 178**].

transport difficulties.[26] But a more ominous influence became apparent in November when the Dutch embargo on French trade (and hence on brandy) led to an enormous demand for copper distilling-vessels! 'Le cuivre hausse furieusement à cause de quantité des chaudrons qu'on fait pour l'Hollande—celuy en feuilles s'est vendu désjà a 106 *RD* le slb', reported Juncker from Hamburg.[27]

The embargo, which deepened the slump in shipping, was an early portent of the coming war, although few of the firm's correspondents took the prospect seriously. Steven de Geer, the most earnest student of international affairs, refused to believe war a possibility as late as 15 January 1672, although the Van Baerles had reported back in October 'no small mistrust of the [English] King and Court, notwithstanding the Triple Alliance'.[28] Indeed, in July they noted that a prescient Willem Momma, nervous of the ill-feeling between France and Holland, was sending most of his goods to Hamburg.[29] However, there was another reason for this transfer, for there can be little doubt that his goodwill towards Leonora was wearing as thin as his brothers'. Although he agreed to intercede with Jacob for a resumption of commissions so that their sales could by managed as a monopoly[30] he complained that his goods should be fetching 3 or 4 per cent more than they did. He had deliberately narrowed his range of products, abandoning sheet-copper, copper-plate and pots partly as an economy and partly because he lacked skilled workmen, but his expectations of profit from his English-pattern kettles, of which he was inordinately proud, were largely disappointed.[31]

There was thus no pre-war boom in imports. Marescoe & Joye did not seek and probably could not afford the timely purchase of strategic goods on their own account. Deprived of the Tar Company contract, they received only 126 lasts of pitch and tar via Gothenburg from two Hamburg dealers, Reinhold Garlinghoff and Jurgen Erhorn, who were only interested in rapid turnover. As for iron, it remained singularly lifeless both in London and Hamburg, although S. de Geer, remote from his foundries, seems to have been less worried about this than Louis Trip. The latter exercised a much stricter control over the selling price,[32] proudly drawing attention to the special merits of the various types—the 'extraordinarily fine' sheet-iron from which pistols and muskets were made, the 'Guinea-coast' or voyage iron from Liège, the $1\frac{1}{2}$ and $1\frac{1}{4}$-inch square bars marked 'B' or 'H' which were more carefully forged than the others, and the twice-hammered bars—'once on the big hammer, once on the small hammer' which were not to be sold for less than £15 10s per ton.

The Trip ledgers[33] permit a rare glimpse of the profits which were left to one of Marescoe & Joye's clients on sales in London when all charges were met and the exchange rate discounted. For example, 400 bars of Liège voyage iron cost *f*.748 12s (f.o.b.). Weighed in London at 117 cwt. 3 q. 15 lb. and sold at 14s 6d per cwt. to major iron dealers, Westerne & Harvey, payable in 6 months, they rendered £85 9s 2d gross. Customs, at 7s per ton plus other charges totalling £2 17s 6d, lighterage £1 3s, freight £2 14s, labour 10s, brokerage 10s 8d and 2 per cent commission £1 14s 2d left £75 19s 10d net. Converted at 36s 6g flemish per £1 sterling this rendered in bank-money *f*.826 10, and at the prevailing agio of

---

[26] S. de Geer to same, 22 September 1671 [**164**].

[27] P. Juncker to same, 20 November 1671.

[28] Van Baerles to same, 27 October 1671.

[29] Same to same, 28 July 1671.

[30] W. Momma to same, 3 December 1671 [**177**].

[31] Same to same, 6 August 1671.

[32] L. Trip to same, 10 April 1671 [**141**].

[33] G. A. Amsterdam, Koopmansboeken 41–4. Louis Trip's accounts with [a] Marescoe & Joye (1671–3) and [b] Jacob David (1676–81) are to be found in Koopmansboeken 42–4, vizt., Grootboek 1668–76, ff. 112, 114, 202, 209; Grootboek 1677–80, ff. 32, 72, 118; Grootboek 1681–4, ff. 30, 46.

TABLE 18. Louis Trip's iron shipments, 1671.

	Iron pieces	Cost (f.o.b.) Dutch florins	Gross sale £ sterling			Net sale (c.i.f.)			Net return current fl.		Notional profit (%)
1	400	748 12	85	9	2	75	19	10	865	14	15.6
2	675	1,819 7	201	10	1	179	1	3	2,006	6	10.3
3	1,325	2,791 0	290	3	2	258	5	5	2,886	18	3.4
4	2,000	3,924 11	421	12	0	375	15	7	4,244	10	8.1
5	1,550	3,180 8	340	13	3	304	16	1	3,411	3	7.2
6	1,400	2,722 19	293	6	11	261	17	5	2,934	5	7.8
7	150	293 8	31	5	4	27	15	9	293	8	0.0
	7,500	15,480 5	1,664	5	11	1,483	11	4	16,642	4	7.5

$4\frac{3}{4}$ per cent on bank-money this represented *f.*865 14 in current money—a profit on this parcel of $15\frac{1}{2}$ per cent. The figures for Trip's shipments of 1671 are given in Table 18.

Much more iron would have been sent to Marescoe this year but for the perversity of nature which provided that, while torrential rains in Sweden made transport difficult for the De Geers' iron, drought in the Netherlands made the Maas unnavigable for Trip's.[34] He had to hold back another 2,000 bars for 1672.

In the majority of cases Marescoe & Joye obtained sales within the price limits which Trip designated, but they tended to be at the minimum level, and on sales with six months credit Trip felt the price was unsatisfactory. Of the 2,262.4 cwt. sent, all but 300 cwt. fetched 14*s* 6*d* per cwt. and only the choicest batches attained the 16*s* he desired. Long credit also jeopardized his returns, and when the final balance was struck early in 1673 Trip's notional profit of *f.*1,161 19 had been reduced to *f.*870 14 8 (or 5.6%) by losses on the exchange.[35]

Trip's letters betray no serious dissatisfaction with his London sales, but he was fully aware of the position in Sweden where rising costs made his own products seems comparatively cheap. Unable to exploit this competitive advantage by increasing volume (for he himself was a large purchaser of Swedish iron) he saw it as another reason why his London prices should be higher. Indeed, the profits from England compared poorly with the Trip firm's average profits on iron in 1671 of 14.6 per cent.[36] Yet, the break in Louis Trip's dealings with London, which lasted from 1672 to 1679, had less to do with dissatisfaction than with the changing situation in Sweden and the onset of the Franco–Dutch war. The latter was of course decisive but Trip seems to have prepared the ground for a transfer of control which might have happened in any event. In March and April 1672 he advised Marescoe & Joye that he was transferring their iron account to Gerard de Geer and to his nephew Mathias Trip in Stockholm.

1672 iron imports for Marescoe & Joye were thus to come solely from Sweden, and they came in abundance. Volume tripled to 29,160 cwt.: even more had been sent. Gerard de Geer supplied 36 per cent, on his own and Steven's account, and they were rejoined by Pötter & Thuen and by Debora van Ruyff. There was also a promising newcomer, Alexander Waddell, member of that large Scottish community now settled in Stockholm.[37] Like some

[34] L. Trip to LM & PJ, 25 September, 13 November, 24 December 1671.
[35] G. A. Amsterdam, Koopmansboeken 42, f. 114.
[36] P. W. Klein, *De Trippen in de 17e Eeuw*, p. 432.
[37] Åström, *From Cloth to Iron*, pp. 138–40.

other British immigrants—Daniel Young (ennobled as Leijonancker), George Shuttleworth and James Semple—he had large ambitions and confided that he hoped for a controlling interest in the 'renovated' Tar Company. He provided over 29 per cent of the year's iron, Pötter & Thuen (through Gothenburg suppliers) 18.6 per cent, and Van Ruyff 12 per cent.

The latter, now conducting business through her son-in-law Hendrik Cletcher, was always careful to offer an assortment of irons suitable for the English market, with about 44 per cent consisting of 'voyage' iron bars and 15 per cent of 1-inch and $\frac{3}{4}$-inch square bars. Yet, like her rivals, she was surprised at their cool reception in London where a combination of glut, severe competition and unforeseeable contingencies made 1672 a singularly difficult year. First among those contingencies was the 'Stop of the Exchequer' in January which confused mercantile credit and produced an immediate shortage of cash.[38] Second was the raising of export duties in Sweden. Iron tolls were doubled from January, adding £1 per ton to the desired price, and in April copper tolls were raised by between 66 and 45 per cent.[39] London could not absorb such increases and had no need to do so, for—as Jacob Lucie repeatedly advised Jacob Reenstierna—there was too much iron reaching England, with 'daily' arrivals from Bilbao and San Sebastian.[40] 'Kladders' were undercutting Swedish iron and neither he nor Marescoe & Joye could command the kind of prices which their principals expected. Lucie's reiterated message was: 'the town is glutted with Swedish goods—I cannot sell one bar of iron or one coil of brass wire'.[41]

With the outbreak of war, demand for re-exports also dried up temporarily, and only one correspondent was alert to the significance of the re-foundation of the Royal African Company in November 1671.[42] Jan van Savelant, writing from Gothenburg in January 1672, was deeply interested in its implications for 'voyage' iron which was so much desired in West African trade.[43] Future developments justified his expectations: Swedish bar-iron was to prove indispensable to the Company and Peter Joye became one of its major suppliers.[44] In 1672, however, sales were initially sluggish and confined to the circle of some dozen dealers who usually took the firm's iron. Only in August and September 1672 did the demand for iron become exceptionally brisk. In eight weeks the firm cleared its hands of some 34,000 pieces of iron weighing 13,201 cwt. They were subsequently reproached for having done so recklessly and thus contributing to the marked fall in prices,[45] but their orders had been clear enough: to sell existing stocks quickly before the next season's cargoes arrived.[46]

Copper produced similar disappointments, for although it briefly rose higher and more sharply than in the Second Anglo–Dutch war, it failed to sustain these levels and fell quickly from July after three shiploads arrived from Sweden.[47] Dealers were buying only for their

[38] RA, Stockholm, E.2512, J. Lucie to Jacob Reenstierna, 19 January 1672.

[39] Wittrock, II, pp. 343 n. 3, 349 n. 2, 373; Stiernman, III, pp. 896, 901 (decrees of 20 December 1671 and 2 April 1672). Under the previous tariff of 15 December 1671 (Stiernman, III, pp. 605 et seq.) iron incurred a duty of 1 silver dollar per shippound for export in 'free' Swedish shipping, or 1 dollar 16 öre on 'unfree' foreign vessels. The garcopper tariff was 25 dollars $12\frac{5}{6}$ öre on 'free' and 38 dollars $3\frac{1}{4}$ öre on 'unfree'. These were now increased to $42\frac{2}{3}$ and 55 dollars 1 öre respectively. For English diplomatic comment see PRO, SP. 95/8 f. 246.

[40] RA, Stockholm, E.2512, J. Lucie to Jacob Reenstierna, 2 February, 27 February, 8 March 1672.

[41] Ibid. 15 November 1672.

[42] K. G. Davies, *The Royal African Company*, pp. 57–63.

[43] See [**180**].

[44] K. G. Davies, *The Royal African Company*, pp. 171–2.

[45] S. de Geer to LM & PJ, 25 October 1672 [**215**].

[46] E.g., W. Momma to same, 7 July 1671 [**201**].

[47] RA, Stockholm, E.2512, J. Lucie to Jacob Reenstierna, 9 July 1672.

immediate needs, confident of future supplies, and Lucie had to struggle with his sales for Jacob Reenstierna as did Marescoe & Joye for Willem Momma. Their firm received 1,200 cwt. of copper this year (6.5 per cent less than in 1671) with nearly nine-tenths of it coming from Momma, the remainder from Pötter & Thuen. Latten and battery came from the same sources in the same proportions.

It is another of the ironies of the Lucie-Reenstierna letters that, while Lucie was rapidly alienating Jacob with his slow sales and reluctant credits, Marescoe & Joye were breeding similar discontents in Willem for identical reasons. Both firms were receiving similar copper goods, sometimes upon the same ship, and for both firms the crisis in their relations with their principals came at the same time, in October 1672. Despite Momma's demonstration that he was in credit for goods despatched, if not yet received, Marescoe & Joye declined to accept his draft of £800 and drew down a furious response which gradually simmered down to a regretful closing of the account.[48] Waddell's buoyant commissions likewise received a similar rebuff when he tried to draw a total of £3,350 through Hamburg, Amsterdam and Edinburgh. Although he could demonstrate that he had sent goods worth £6,629[49] he was given no choice but to transfer his London stocks to another agent, Edward Nelthorp.[50] For this to happen in September 1672, within two months of the start of their correspondence, is a revealing comment on the inadequacy of the firm's resources, for they had freely admitted that they lacked the means to advance such credits.[51]

The decision to dissolve Leonora's partnership with Peter Joye, taken in late 1672, thus followed closely on the loss of two major clients. Whether the two events were linked and whether one partner carried more responsibility than the other is impossible to say, although it is worth noting that Waddell's reaction to the change was to write—'I am resolved to

TABLE 19. LM & PJ: gross and net profits, dividends, 1670–1674.

	Gross profit			Loss			Net profit			$\frac{2}{5}$ dividend		
	£	s	d	£	s	d	£	s	d	£	s	d
16 September 1670 ⎱ 9 March 1671 ⎰	1,470	9	0	64	7	9	1,406	1	3	562	8	0
10 March 1671 ⎱ 11 September 1671 ⎰	2,200	5	3	14	10	3	2,185	15	0	874	6	0
12 September 1671 ⎱ 9 March 1672 ⎰	1,286	12	0	66	10	4	1,220	1	8	488	0	8
10 March 1672 ⎱ 16 September 1672 ⎰	543	11	5	111	3	1	432	8	4	172	19	$5\frac{1}{2}$
17 September 1672 ⎱ 10 March 1673 ⎰	2,070	6	4	88	7	7	1,981	18	9	792	15	$6\frac{1}{2}$
11 March 1673 ⎱ 20 May 1674 ⎰	1,140	14	9	190	3	4	950	3	4	380	1	8
Totals	8,711	18	9	535	2	4	8,176	8	4	3,720	11	4

[48] W. Momma to LM & PJ, 29 December 1672.
[49] A. Waddell to same, 30 October 1672. His estimate was reasonably accurate: the gross yield of his shipments was £7,398, or £6,129 net.
[50] Same to same, 18 September, 6 November 11 December 1672.
[51] Same to same, 11 December 1672.

TABLE 20. LM & PJ: import contribution to gross profits, 1670–1674.

	September 1670 to March 1671	March 1671 to September 1671	September 1671 to March 1672	March 1672 to September 1672	September 1672 to March 1673	March 1673 to May 1674	Totals
A. GROSS PROFITS *of which*	£1,470 9s 0d	£2,200 5s 3d	£1,286 12s 7d	£543 11s 5d	£2,070 6s 4d	£1,140 14s 9d	£8,711 18s 9d
B. IMPORT PROFITS % share of A.	£1,361 3s 2d	£1,125 16s 0d	£792 7s 6d	£464 3s 4d	£1,362 7s 11d	£857 17s 6d	£5,963 15s 1d
	92.5	51.2	61.6	85.4	65.8	75.2	68.5
% share of B.							
Iron	24.7	51.7	11.8	28.4	59.6	8.8	34.0
Copper	23.8	14.4	14.8	23.0	14.3	8.9	16.5
Pitch and tar	14.4	27.2	31.3	9.3	12.4	3.4	16.6
Timber	4.9	—	1.4	—	0.4	4.3	2.0
Other imports	1.1	0.8	2.4	0.1	1.5	0.2	1.1
Insurance and shipping	—	1.2	6.9	13.4	2.0	55.9	10.7
Interest on advances	31.0	4.7	31.3	25.5	9.8	18.4	19.0
C. EXPENSES gross	—	£3,077 10s 10d	£953 5s 2d	—	£2,630 10s 5d	£473 15s 11d	£7,135 2s 4d
Net profit	—	£849 3s 5d	£278 0s 6d	—	£599 7s 5d	£120 4s 1d	£1,846 15s 5d
Import % share	—	87.8	73.5	—	93.5	97.4	88.6

continue with Madame Marescoe'.[52] There is also a suggestive clue in the marginalia written by Joye upon a letter of Waddell's dated 6 November 1672. Suggesting the gist of an answer (which was sent on 10 December) it instructed Jacob David: 'repeat him the Substance of our last and that too many debts standing out, its most reasonable to bee in some advance & not to disburse the utmost penny; against Xmasse shall send him his account and when has agreed our accounts wee will either remit him or give order to drawe some moneys on us—& soe excuse the matter'.

This casual brush-off did little to appease Waddell and it underlined one of the shortcomings to which most of the Swedish principals objected—the length of credit granted in London and the consequently greater risk of bad debts. Marescoe & Joye had explained (as did Lucie) that English iron-dealers rarely paid cash: they expected six months credit. But given the partnership's limited capital resources there was nothing else that Marescoe & Joye could do but appease their clients with vague assurances and forego the profits from advances upon unsold goods.

The partnership's profits between September 1670 and May 1674, when its accounts were finally wound up, were stated and shared at six-monthly intervals (see Table 19). But what proportion of these earnings were attributable to import commissions? The answer can be given in some detail (Table 20) with the reservation that not too much significance should be attached to variations between one half-year and the next. While the volume of activity, and thus of earnings, *did* vary from month to month the allocation of profits to one period rather than the next was a matter of book-keeping, reflecting the date at which it was convenient to balance a long account. It should also be noted that 'net expenses' were carried over to gross profits at irregular intervals. They represent the balance left when the firm's actual outlay on customs duties, packing, loading and overheads of all kinds were deducted from the charges levied upon customers. Thus, the balance of £849 3s 5d placed to 'profits' in September 1671 is the residue of an account totalling £3,077 10s 10d, of which 88 per cent can be attributed to expenditure on imports. A similar proportion was incurred over the other periods, and it thus follows that imports can be said to have generated not only the 65.5 per cent earnings from commissions and direct sales on the partnership's own account but also 88.6 per cent of the 'net expenses' as well.

The residue, attributable to the firm's export trade, seems in contrast comparatively small, yet the activity it involved was complex and demanding and it produced a valuable correspondence which now requires introduction.

(ii) EXPORTS

[a] HAMBURG

Despite the arrival of the *flota* in February 1670 the expected revitalization of European trade had not made itself felt in Marescoe's export commissions and the total value of his shipments in the last year of his life was down by one-third on that of 1669. The year ended with a continuing depression in the firm's main market at Hamburg.

The partnership nonetheless enjoyed the continuing patronage of Charles Marescoe's clients. The elder Paul Berenberg had fled to comfortable exile in Lüneburg, though relentlessly pursued through the agency of Peter Juncker and the English firm of John,

---

[52] Same to same, 12 April 1673.

Charles & James Banks [or Bancks].[53] In his place, Paul Berenberg (Jr.) son of Andreas, now began active trading, flanked by his mother and younger brother. All three Rulands still corresponded, and Peter Juncker was joined by his brother Dominicus. There were also the three newcomers, François Bostelman, Jan Arnold Fonck and Jan Baptista de Hertogh, whose orders were to be ample compensation for the loss of Jacob Jansen's and Paul Berenberg's. Between them, they were to bombard the widow Marescoe and Peter Joye with an average of six letters per week, combining orders and inquiries with business reports from which some picture of the Hamburg market for English re-exports can be discerned.

Its most significant feature in 1671 is the set-back to some of the new staples and the recovery of some of the old. For Barbados sugar, Josiah Child's exultation at the eclipse of Brazilian muscovadoes looks a little premature in a year which saw the Hamburg sugar-bakers turn their backs on the West-Indian product and buy happily from the large supplies of the South-American which had reached them via Lisbon.[54] There was no demand for Barbados cotton either among dealers, who had decided that, after all, the products of the Middle and Far East were superior. Other Mediterranean products did poorly, however. There was no further demand for Aleppo galls, with two years requirements in stock,[55] and although their price in Hamburg never fell quite as low as in 1669 it remained sluggish and uninviting at about 39–40 *ML*. Apulian oil likewise had never been cheaper, falling to 54 and 52 rixdollars in mid-summer and only recovering its normal level at 66–68 *RD* in the autumn. Finally, English imports of Ardasse silk had become unsaleable thanks to competition from the itinerant Armenians who, every week, brought supplies in from Amsterdam.[56]

These depressing circumstances disposed of most of the firm's usual commissions, but others took their place, thanks in part to the marketing policies of the two great East India Companies with regard to pepper and indigo. The former commodity, which accounted for about 23.5 per cent of the English company's imports between 1669 and 1671,[57] had rarely reached Europe in larger quantities and its price in London and Amsterdam was falling to an historically low level.[58] Nevertheless, both companies seem to have tried to ease the decline by limiting sales, and awareness of this appears to have fostered some resistance to purchases even at the new, lower levels. Certainly some of the Hamburg clients expressed their vexation that the London sales had not produced prices even lower,[59] and this sentiment may help to explain the apparent contradiction that, while 'the combined imports of the two Companies were considerably in excess of current demand' these same years saw ginger emerging as a cheap pepper-substitute in north-European markets.[60] By 1676 it had become a serious threat to the more expensive product.

Thus, 1671 brought Marescoe & Joye a remarkable Hamburg demand for ginger of both

[53] Charles & James Bancks to LM & PJ, 21 May 1672 [**193**].
[54] E. Ruland to same, 16 May, 30 June 1671; P. Ruland to same, 14 August, 12 September 1671 [**166**].
[55] A. Berenberg's widow & Co. to same, 11 April 1671.
[56] Same to same, 5 December 1671; P. Berenberg to same, 12 December 1671. For Armenian traders in seventeenth-century western Europe see F. Braudel, *Civilization and Capitalism: 15th–18th Century*, II. *The Wheels of Commerce* (London, 1982) pp. 122–4, 154–9.
[57] Chaudhuri, *The Trading World of Asia and the English East India Company, 1660–1760*, App. 5, table C.14, p. 529; Glamann, *Dutch-Asiatic Trade, 1620–1740*, p. 83.
[58] Chaudhuri, op. cit. p. 319; Pieter Van Dam, *Beschryvinge van de Oostindische Compagnie* (Eerste Boek, Deel II) ed. F. W. Stapel (*RGP* 68, The Hague, 1929) pp. 221, 223, 224, 225, 227, 228.
[59] A. Berenberg's widow & Co. to LM & PJ, 23 May 1671; E. Ruland to same, 19 September, 21 October 1672; J. B. de Hertogh to same, 19 September 1671.
[60] Chaudhuri, op. cit. pp. 320, 322.

kinds—the inferior 'brown' or 'black', and the cleaned, 'scraped' or 'white' product. Arnold Ruland's prediction of 1668[61] was proved correct as large supplies reached London from the West Indies, and the Hamburg buyers were—as usual—well-informed about arrivals. To Marescoe & Joye's advice that eight or ten ships were expected shortly from the West Indies young Paul Berenberg countered with the *Holland Gazette*'s allegation that one hundred were ready to leave Barbados.[62]

Nevertheless, the Hamburgers failed to keep pace with the price of ginger which, instead of falling with successive arrivals, began to rise from July 1671 onwards. Every week their price-limits had to be revised upwards as brown ginger rose from 38s per cwt. to 42s in July, 46s in August, 48s in September and 50s in October. The rise of the choice white ginger was even more spectacular—from its 50s in April to 60s in August and 75s–76s in September and October. The young Paul Berenberg was foremost in the chase, and his explosive letter of 19 September [166] makes sense in a context of profound frustration as the Hamburg price likewise soared by nearly 50 per cent, from 14 grooten banco per lb. to 20 g in October. Most of the Hamburg correspondents had been deeply interested in its progress and five of them received shipments at prices spread across the whole progression.

The other commodity to interest them was indigo from two of its sources—central America and the Caribbean. There was, of course, a third and older source in Lahore but 'indigo lauro', as it was called, was expensive if superior and was not seriously considered by the Hamburg clients.[63] In marketing this quality product the English East India Company also tried to maintain a controlled level of sales but notwithstanding this policy the price was obliged to halve between 1670 and 1672.[64] In 1671 the choice thus seemed to lie between the Spanish and the English colonial product, and at first sight certain advantages lay with the latter. Spanish American indigo reached Europe infrequently and in 1669 a tax of 10 *pesos* per case had been levied on the Guatemalan output.[65] However, the years 1670–2 saw some of the largest shipments in two decades. According to official Spanish sources 10,920 *arrobas* came from Terra Firma in the *flota* of 1670. Another 2,356 *arrobas* came from Honduras in 1671 and a further 750 arrived from New Spain in 1672.[66]

It was the Honduras shipment which excited Hamburg's interest in March 1671 and all the correspondents alluded to it. Although 'indigo guatimalo', at 6s–5s 6d per lb., was more expensive in London than 'caribse' or Jamaican indigo, at 5s–4s 6d, it was known to be superior and this solitary Honduras ship transformed prices in the German market.[67] From 14½ schillings per lb. in late March it came down to 11s in July and 10s in August, thus confirming all J. A. Fonck's warnings that the indigo trade was 'perilous', particularly as large stocks were still held in Germany and Holland.[68] He withheld any orders but five others placed commissions, among them J. B. de Hertogh who boasted of having traded in indigo for forty years.[69] This amply qualified him to judge and reject the poor quality of some of

[61] See p. 57.
[62] P. Berenberg to LM & PJ, 14 June 1671.
[63] A. Berenberg's widow & Co. to same, 30 September 1671.
[64] Chaudhuri, op. cit. App. 5, table C.10, p. 523.
[65] MacLeod, *Spanish Central America: a socioeconomic history, 1520–1720*, p. 201.
[66] L. Garcia Fuentes, *El comercio español con America, 1650–1700*, pp. 509–10.
[67] F. Bostelman to LM & PJ, 18 April 1671.
[68] J. A. Fonck to same, 28 April, 23 May 1671.
[69] J. B. de Hertogh to same, 23 June 1671.

London's shipments. Indeed, it was indigo more than any other commodity which provoked the most anger and dissatisfaction with the partnership's services.[70]

Yet the commissions from Hamburg were impaired less by bad feelings than by bad weather. Adverse easterly and southerly winds hindered shipping arrivals in mid-October 1671.[71] These could be a problem on the Elbe at the best of times but they were particularly troublesome for the less manoeuverable English vessels. As Widow Berenberg pointed out, English ships were both more expensive and bigger than Dutch and could not easily come up into Hamburg for unloading.[72] It was not uncommon for them to lie three miles down-river at Wittenbergen or Blankeneze. Because of an early winter in 1671 at least one English skipper spent its entire duration there, frozen in. On 10 November the De Hertoghs reported—'winter began three days ago'. The Elbe was soon ice-filled and by the 13th was unnavigable.[73] The Berenbergs decided to leave half their latest consignment where it was, until the spring, and not until 5 March 1672 was the Elbe pronounced clear for shipping.[74]

This early and severe winter curtailed the usual late-autumn arrivals but at the year's end Marescoe & Joye could record a satisfactory increase of nearly 60 per cent in the value of their shipments to Hamburg, with ginger and indigo accounting for most of it, and Paul

TABLE 21. Hamburg purchases, 1671.

Commodity	AB	PB	FB	JdeH	ER	PR	PJ	Value £ s d	%
Barbados sugar	17.6					37.5	44.9	858 15 5	14.75
Indigo:									
(i) Guatemalo	10.2	4.7		18.4	52.6		13.9	948 12 8	16.30
(ii) Caribbean		82.3	8.2	9.5				768 9 8	13.20
Ginger:									
white		22.2	30.1	47.7				837 16 2	14.40
brown	23.7	48.4	8.6	10.7	8.6			1,638 14 5	28.10
Aleppo galls	100.0							145 6 5	2.50
Campeachy			16.5		53.0	30.5		341 6 9	5.86
E.I. Co. pepper					100.0			224 6 0	3.85
English vitriol			100.0					60 9 2	1.04
Total % share	13.4	28.4	9.8	14.1	17.9	7.3	8.9	5,823 16 8	100.00

AB = Widow Berenberg & Co.; PB = Paul Berenberg; FB = F. Bostelman; JdeH = J. de Hertogh; ER = E. Ruland; PR = P. Ruland; PJ = P. Juncker.

[70] P. Berenberg to same, 27 June 1671; J. B. de Hertogh to same, 18 April 1671 (enclosing a notarized declaration by witnesses of the false quantity of two chests). In Lille, at the same date, a correspondent received a chest containing 28 lb. of lead—J. le Camps to same, 18 April.

[71] E. Ruland to same, 24 October, 27 October 1671.

[72] A. Berenberg's widow & Co. to same, 28 August 1671.

[73] E. Ruland to same, 13 November 1671.

[74] A. Berenberg's widow & Co. to same, 5 March 1672.

Berenberg turning out to be their biggest client. There had been orders for sugar and, notwithstanding complaints of its price, for East India Company pepper (Table 21).

Early intimations of the possibility of war may have influenced one or two of these commissions. The astute Peter Juncker had predicted conflict in April 1671 and on 24 November he had written—'puisque il y aura une guerre assuré au printemps il vous plaira veoir ce que pouvons entreprendre a prouffiter quelque chose ensemble'. This invitation to pre-war speculation was evidently declined and none of the other Hamburgers appear to have acted on their fears. As late as 15 March 1672 Egidio Ruland could report that 'many' believed there would be no war, and although most of his colleagues were convinced otherwise they could see no way of predicting the nature of the great changes which would undoubtedly follow.[75] War of the kind they faced did not generate extensive demand—it caused losses, dislocations and diversions of supply, but where these would occur and whether they would cause this or that price to rise or fall could not be safely foreseen. The events of 1672 were to justify the Hamburgers' caution.

The year began with a brief tremor of concern for the English 'Stop of the Exchequer'. Its effects in London on mercantile credit and the security of bills of exchange were noted and then soon forgotten. More serious consequences seemed to flow from the convergence of the thaw (with its consequent surge of shipping) and the outbreak of the Franco–Dutch war shortly after. Both events caused turmoil in the market, from which no clear trend was at first discernible. Most correspondents expected falling prices as the market filled but in fact most of them rose, Paul Berenberg was probably not alone in wishing that he had bought some sugar. Pepper rose from 18 g to 21 g quite rapidly, and at the end of April stood at 26 g thanks to strong demand from France.[76] Apulian oil rose from 68 to 80 RD by mid-March and to 90 RD by early May. Even Aleppo galls began to move, despite large stocks. Barbados sugar recovered levels not experienced since the Second Anglo–Dutch war and stood briefly at $8\frac{1}{2}$ g in early May.

Yet one can deduce that this general movement was only a short-run stockpiling spasm inspired by fears and expectations rather than proven consumer demand. Rising shipping costs suppported the trend for a while: insurance rates between London and Hamburg had reached 10 per cent by 22 March[77] and freights were soon being sought with desperation among the limited number of Swedish ships available. Although the Hamburgers congratulated themselves on their neutrality, experience had taught them that the ambiguous reputation of the Hamburg flag was no protection against English suspicions. The Dutch were also to be feared. Wrote Arnold Ruland on 12 April: 'the risk on Swedish and Hamburg ships differs. The Hamburg ships are subject to Dutch capers; the Swedish ships are let past.'

Once these costs had been absorbed, however, the absence of immediate demand became apparent. By early May stocks of sugar were abundant and the market was 'asleep'. The downturn in prices began in mid-May and continued throughout the year. Barbados sugar was back at $5\frac{3}{4}$ g by late July; Apulian oil completed its trajectory, beginning at 68 RD, rising to 90 and ending at 67. Pepper fell to $16\frac{1}{2}$ g in late September, although relatively high prices in the two East India Companies' sales brought it back to 18 g or more in late October. The early casualties of the war helped to push in the same downward direction. The agonies of Amsterdam, stoically borne by its own inhabitants [**196, 197**], depressed rather than stimulated a city which was more its partner than its rival. At the very least, communications

[75] J. A. Fonck to same, 2 February 1672—'*Met dat men niet weet hoe in deese Conjonturen te gedraegen, en groote abundantie van Koopmanshap ooveral is, is oock qualick te Resolveren*'.

[76] P. Juncker to same, 3 May 1672.

[77] A. Ruland to same; 22 March 1672.

had been broken and posts diverted by the rapid French advance. The exchanges were confused and as the toll of captured shipping began to rise the market was upset by sales of prize-goods. Bostelman, the Berenbergs and E. Ruland [214] all assumed that the Dutch capture of five Barbados ships would raise prices for sugar and ginger. But, as the Berenbergs soon discovered, the actual effect was quite the reverse [216]. Confused and depressed by these uncertainties even the most experienced of the group thought they had never seen worse times.

The effect of the war on credit was no less serious than its impact on commodities. The behaviour of the exchanges gave clear notice of severe difficulties ahead as rates on London and Amsterdam moved abruptly from their customary planes into wildly plunging oscillations. In the last week of March the Hamburg rate on London changed from 34*s* 2–3 *g*, where it had been (plus or minus a few grooten) for some months, to 32*s* 8–9 *g*—a drop of some 4.5 per cent in the value of the pound sterling (Figure 8). The Hamburg–Amsterdam rate deteriorated by some 8.5 per cent in the critical weeks of June.[78] Peter Juncker, who had anticipated something of this, had been eager to play the exchanges back in June 1671. 'Il y auroit a gaigner presentement un bon Interest sur le Change entre icy et Costy mais je ne trouve point des lettres a satisfaction.'[79] He later chose the dramatic last week of March to

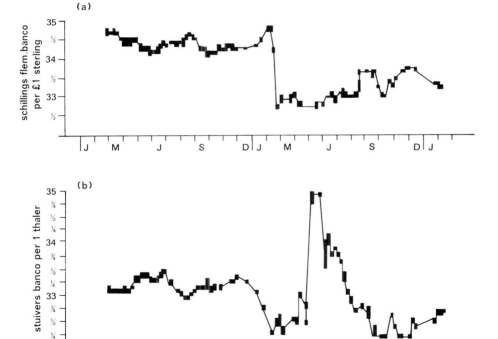

FIGURE 8. Exchange rate: (a) Hamburg on London, 1671–1672; (b) Hamburg on Amsterdam, 1671–1672.

[78] See Appendix G, Table A.11 [a].
[79] P. Juncker to LM & PJ, 23 June 1672.

suggest that Marescoe & Joye might remit £2,000—'if it is convenient for you to advance the money at a reasonable rate of interest'—in the beliefs (i) that the London rate on Hamburg was still 35s and (ii) that the Hamburg rate on London, now at 32s 8–9g, would fall much further.[80] Neither assumption was correct and the Londoners wisely refused. Although Juncker continued to coax—'il y aura a proufiter sur les Changes pendant ces troubles'[81]—he was also the first to record the inevitable casualties. 1671 had been a comparatively safe year. The bankruptcy of Heinrich Julius Duve in June, owing 200,000 *RD*, had seemed quite salutary for he had been a 'kladder', spoiling the market in galls and pepper.[82] The collapse of Dirich Rodenbourg, a Russia-merchant, also left them untouched in December 1671.[83] But in the summer of 1672 their immunity evaporated. There were four or five failures in July, among them Jurgen Erhorn's. He had been one of Marescoe's suppliers, via Gothenburg, and in 1671 he had sent some pitch for which, fortunately, no liabilities remained. More serious was the collapse of Jacomo Ruland in Amsterdam for it brought down his brother Peter. P. Ruland's correspondence, which had been growing sparser, ceased altogether in August 1672.

The worst confusion, however, now reigned in Sweden. Juncker had watched with jealous satisfaction the difficulties facing the Cronströms as copper prices soared in 1671. Like Willem Momma, he was convinced that Isaac Cronström's contract to produce farthing blanks for the English mint would prove a costly disaster. 'Je vous prie de sonder les desseins de M. Cronstrom et prennez bien garde a cequi vous négocierez avec cette Comp[agn]ie' he warned.[84] Fortunately, perhaps, Marescoe & Joye had not been involved in the farthing business although obliged to report on its evolution by the envious queries of the Mommas, Pötter & Thuen and Juncker. In October 1672, however, Juncker's gossip touched on a really sensitive point—their newly-formed relations with Alexander Waddell. Indeed, in a single paragraph, Juncker rang a whole series of alarm-bells:

> 'vous aurez entendu sans doute le mauvais éstat de Abraham Reenstierna aupres duquel dit-on M. Alexander Waddal êstre tout interessé; il y a maintenant grande scarsété d'argent en Suède et l'on ne scais presque plus a qui se fier estant failli aussi icy cette sepmaine Burchard Wortman qui souloit correspondre avec Mr Burkin & Everson—grace a dieu sans mon interest'.[85]

Intentionally or not, Juncker may have made the crucial contribution to the rupture with Waddell which soured the last months of the partnership's import trade.

Among the export-correspondents, however, there was no rupture although vexation was generated by some shoddy consignments. More significant was the Hamburgers' difficulty in discerning any worthwhile commodity which might yield profit and the Londoners' inability to supply it when they did. The Widow Berenberg's letters of 6 September and 1 October [**210, 212**] typify the dissatisfactions and frustrations which attended the usual objects of commissions—galls, sugar, ginger, indigo. Peter Ruland experimented with an order for Virginia tobacco but found it unsatisfactory. Egidio gambled unsuccessfully on campeachy, Andreas Muldenaer, a minor correspondent whose usual preoccupations had been with Swedish imports, ordered cloth. He had been trying since 1669 to open up a commission trade in English textiles, offering German linens in return. This was the

---

[80] Same to same, 29 March 1672.

[81] Same to same, 3 May 1672.

[82] J. J. Hiebenaer to same, 30 June 1671; A. Berenberg's widow & Co. to same, 30 June 1671.

[83] P. Juncker to same, 21 December 1671 ('Dirick Rotenburg' is listed as an Iberian trader in Reissmann, *Die hamburgische Kauffmannschaft des 17. Jahrhunderts*, p. 377.)

[84] P. Juncker to same, 8 August 1671.

[85] Same to same, 18 October 1672.

cornerstone of English trade in Hamburg, under the superintendence of the Merchant Adventurers, but despite his brother-in-law's standing in that Company Marescoe had declined to meddle in it. The tiny consignment despatched by his widow was a furtive and unsatisfactory venture which was not repeated. Only Bostelman appears to have found a lucrative corner in English copperas, or vitriol, which he ordered repeatedly throughout the year (Table 22).

The final tally of commissions in 1672 reveals a contraction of nearly 56 per cent in their value since 1671, and a marked reduction in the range of goods ordered by any one correspondent. Bad weather cannot be blamed for the falling-off in late autumn. Warm south-westerly winds in late December re-opened the frozen Elbe until early January.[86] The main dangers of the sea were now man-made and the risk of seizure by Dutch or Scottish capers tended to narrow the options open to Marescoe & Joye, although the effects were not as serious as one might expect. They had employed nine skippers upon the eighteen voyages to Hamburg in 1671 and four of these were re-employed among the nine who made the eleven voyages of 1672. The significant absentees were the two English skippers of the previous year—Samuel Atkinson of the *Content* and William Green of the *Hamburg Frigate*. In their place one notes a well-known Swedish ship, the *Graeffelyk Huys de la Gardie* under Gerrit Laurens, on its return voyage from delivering copper for Willem Momma, but the remaining newcomers all appear to be Hamburg ships, as the correspondents had specified.

Meanwhile, the arrivals of another *flota* and (allegedly) another Honduras ship, were expected to have a depressing effect on indigo prices.[87] Reportedly bringing only one-tenth as much silver as usual the *flota* of September 1672 certainly did not have the stimulating consequences which accompanied that of 1670 and one can find no trace of speculative

TABLE 22. Hamburg purchases, 1672.

Commodity	AB	PB	FB	LF	PJ	AM	ER	PR	Value £ s d	%
Barbados sugar	23.4			30.6	46.0				861 2 7	33.4
Indigo, Caribbean	100.0								342 13 11	13.3
Ginger:										
white			100.0						87 4 5	3.4
brown	24.0	23.3	52.6						692 4 6	26.8
Campeachy							100.0		105 4 3	4.1
Tobacco								100.0	130 7 6	5.0
Vitriol			100.0						339 9 2	13.2
Cloth						100.0			20 10 11	0.8
Total % share	27.5	6.3	30.6	10.2	15.4	0.8	4.1	5.0	2,578 17 3	100.0

LF = Louis Froment's account; AM = Andreas Muldenaer. (See Table 21 note for other abbreviations.)

[86] F. Bostelman, P. Juncker to same, 20 December 1672; E. Ruland to same, 7 January 1673.
[87] P. Berenberg to same, 18 October 1672 [**216**].

excitement in the Hamburg correspondence. What characterizes the few remaining letters of the spring of 1673 is a cautious probing by the four firms which still wrote, seeking some crumb of comfort in war-news from the Caribbean. Egidio Ruland now acquired a keen interest in tobacco and reported a good demand and rising prices. The arrival of 250 barrels in January and another 217 in February failed to glut this market, and if its London price had fallen below $6\frac{1}{2}d$ per lb. he would have placed an order. But for Barbados sugar, with ample supplies of muscovado from Lisbon, there was little demand and the arrival in London of two East India Company ships from Bantam ruled out all chances of the rise in pepper which was now hoped for (for both Berenbergs had acquired large stocks). The correspondence thus breaks off at a point of depression summed up by Peter Juncker—'la guerre cause mauvais Négoce, estant presque toutes les Marchandises sans debite—Dieu le veuille remedier!'[88]

The shipments which did reach Hamburg in 1673 clearly reflect the restraints of war. Their total value was down 42 per cent on 1672 and was barely 25 per cent of 1671's. An interest in cardamon which the Berenbergs exhibited was gratified by one small parcel and there was a little more ginger for them. Galls returned to favour at the moderate price of 53s 6d per cwt., and Widow Berenberg placed three orders for silk. The main interest of 1673, however, is the arrival of a newcomer, Claus Bene, who joined the surviving trio of the two Berenbergs and Bostelman. Bene was to prove the major Hamburg correspondent in the years ahead and it is regrettable that his introductory letters have not survived.

[b] AMSTERDAM

Marescoe & Joye's consignments to Amsterdam were negligible between 1671 and 1673, but the Van Baerles continued to correspond with great fidelity, partly to serve the interests of the Momma-Reenstiernas but also to instruct the London firm in the state of the Dutch market. Their weekly letters carried a fairly regular report both of exchange rates and commodity prices in those sectors where Marescoe & Joye had interests—Barbados sugar, Guatemalan indigo, Aleppo galls, Apulian oil, East Indian pepper, English tin. The information they convey indicates close harmony between Hamburg and Amsterdam. Pepper prices, unsurprisingly, are very similar in their movements as are those of galls, campeachy, indigo and oil. Quotations for Barbados sugar follow an identical path, dipping in the mid-summer of 1671, rallying in the autumn before a winter trough from which they soared, like almost all other commodities, in the summer of 1672.

Sugar, however, was the only commodity in which the Van Baerles saw some prospect of profit in August 1671. Indigo they had ruled out after the arrival of the Honduras ship, and they held out no encouragement for tin with Malacca tin prices at ƒ.50–ƒ.51½ in Amsterdam. But Barbados sugar, if bought at 23s–24s per cwt., could be rewarding even though its current price in Amsterdam was only $5\frac{3}{4}$ g per pond. News of rising grain prices in early September, attributable to demand in Italy,[89] was offered without response and in October the Van Baerles reported that their brokers were recommending cotton yarn as a promising speculation.[90]

None of these helpful hints were acted upon, but in October 1671 Marescoe & Joye evidently thought of testing the Dutch market with the commodity so eagerly requested in Germany—ginger. In reply, the Van Baerles advised that expensive 'white' ginger was in less

---

[86] P. Juncker to same, 20 January 1673.
[89] J. & H. Van Baerle to LM & PJ, 11 September 1671.
[90] Same to same, 2 October 1671.

demand than the cheaper 'brown', currently selling at *f*.28¾ – *f*.29 per 100 lb.[91] Duties they estimated at about 7 per cent and upon this advice Marescoe & Joye sent 117 sacks of 'brown' and 22 sacks of 'white', together costing £317 11s 7d (f.o.b.). Delayed by contrary winds and somewhat damaged by sea water, they reached Amsterdam in late November, finding a market where 'ginger is held in only two hands, excluding ours'.[92] By 18 December they had been sold at *f*.28½ for the brown and *f*.42½ for the white, but the net yield, at £289 17s, was a discouraging one, and it seems to have disposed of any remaining interest Marescoe & Joye may have had in shipments to Holland.

As in Hamburg, the long, hard winter inhibited trading until early March 1672, and by then the political crisis was almost upon them. The Van Baerles had noted its successive stages—the Stop of the Exchequer [**179**], the precipitate departure of the English envoy, Sir George Downing [**181**], and the attack on the returning Dutch fleet from the Straits.[93] When war came they soberly discounted the rapid rise in prices, correctly judging that it was not an augury of strong demand.[94] They found it difficult to advise how best Marescoe & Joye could employ the £237 16s 5d which they held in the Van Baerles' name on behalf of Louis Froment of Paris. The state of the exchanges between London, Amsterdam or Paris ruled out any question of remittance (Figure 9). Instead they suggested a shipment of sugar, tobacco or

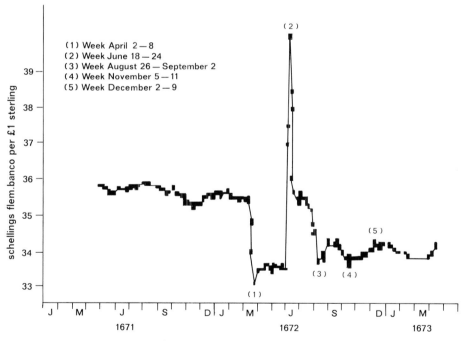

FIGURE 9. Exchange rate: Amsterdam on London, 1671–1672.

[91] Same to same, 20 October 1671.
[92] Same to same, 1 December 1671.
[93] Same to same, 9 February, 1 April 1672.
[94] Same to same, 8 April 1672.

lead, despatched in a Swedish vessel to Amsterdam or Hamburg, and in the end it was sugar sent to Peter Juncker which resolved the problem.[95]

By late June 1672, with the French army a few hours' march away, Amsterdam was in extremities and the Van Baerles' interpretation of the situation, and their response to it, tell their own story.[96] The decision to send silver to England in an English ship at the blackest moment in an Anglo–Dutch war is, however, only one symptom of the continuing commercial interchange which existed between the two states. As the exchanges settled down after the hysteria of June, transfers continued between the two firms, both on their own accounts and on the Mommas'. The check to the French advance, Louis XIV's withdrawal and the safe arrival of the Dutch East India fleet on 3 August[97] restored something like stability, if not normality. The Amsterdam–London exchange remained at an unusually low plateau, near 34s flemish per £ sterling which, with the agio on current money at $5\frac{1}{2}$ to 6 per cent, meant an 11 per cent loss for London, according to the Van Baerles' calculation.[98] Nevertheless remittances continued until November when it was decided that transfers at below 34s 2g were not worthwhile. There was virtually no trading activity to support the exchanges and although the rate on London began to rise in January 1673 the Van Baerles were convinced that, as long as the war continued, there could be no profitable business to be done between them.

[c] FRANCE

(I) Lille

Despite the political reality which now made Lille a French city, the economic reality remained more complex, and continued to bind Lille's merchants to Bruges in the north as well as to Abbeville in the south.[99] This division of loyalties is well reflected in the letters of D'Hollandre & Du Beron who, until June 1671, continued to direct shipments half to Bruges, half to Abbeville.[100] In June, however, prospects of a Franco–Dutch war into which Spain might be drawn obliged the firm to revise its instructions and insist in successive letters that goods should *not* be sent to Bruges but solely to Abbeville.[101] This appears to mark the point of final rupture. Of the goods which Marescoe & Joye sent to Lille merchants between 1671 and 1673 all now went to St Valéry or Abbeville. Very little went to Rouen, however, and although correspondence with Robert Oursel and Hermann Wetken continued it belongs to a sufficiently different context to deserve separate introduction below.

The clientele in Lille remained basically the same as Marescoe's—the two Liberts writing irregularly (and illegibly) but conveying substantial orders for cotton and dyestuffs. Charles Angelo wrote even less regularly but he also placed good commissions and in April 1671 was joined by a new correspondent, Jacques le Camps. In November a former clerk of D'Hollandre & Du Beron, called Jean-Baptiste Cambier of Tournai, decided to set up

---

[95] Same to same, 31 May 1672.

[96] Same to same, 24 June, 28 June 1672 [**196, 197**].

[97] *Dutch-Asiatic Shipping in the 17th and 18th Centuries*, III, *Homeward-bound voyages*, eds. J. R. Bruijn, F. S. Gaastra, J. Schöffer, RGP 167 (The Hague, 1979) pp. 92–5.

[98] J. & H. Van Baerle to LM & PJ, 16 September 1672. See Appendix G, Table A.11 [b], pp. 596, 612.

[99] For the problem of divided loyalties in Lille after 1668 see L. Trenard, *Historie des Pays-Bas français: Les temps modernes* (Toulouse, 1972) pp. 291–4; *Histoire de Lille de Charles Quint à la conquête française (1500–1715)*, ed. L. Trenard (Toulouse, 1981) pp. 286–303.

[100] D'Hollandre & Du Beron to LM & PJ, 23 May, 30 May 1671.

[101] Same to same, 6 June, 27 June [**154**], 18 July 1671.

business on his own, specializing in leather, and in June 1672 Martin Lefebvre, a protégé of Angelo, introduced himself as a dealer interested in lead.

Thus Lille, of all the corresponding centres of 1671–3, gives some impression of buoyancy and expansion which even the war did not entirely extinguish. Yet, her merchants could not ignore the market trends which operated in adjoining communities. For Lille as for Hamburg, Amsterdam and London, the arrival of the Honduras ship transformed the prospects for indigo, which had made up 25 per cent of their commissions to Marescoe in 1670 and was to form 55 per cent in 1671. The expected arrival of another *flota* also complicated their judgment of the best timing and pricing of their commissions. Angelo responded by declining to order any indigo, alleging that there was no demand and that Lille was fully supplied. He and his colleagues had been so unfortunate as to place their orders too early, before the price-falls had taken effect: after June 1671 they ordered none for the rest of the year.

Other commodities had also lost their appeal. D'Hollandre & Du Beron still held Barbados sugar bought from Marescoe in 1668, and at 5d per lb. for yellow Barbados cotton and 8¾d for white, the London prices were thought too high.[102] Oil, they admitted, was cheap enough at £22 16s per pipe, but it was cheap everywhere and Lille had plenty.[103] As for pepper, the prospect of large sales by the English East India Company did not offset the transport- and cost-advantages of buying in Amsterdam, as Le Camps intended to do [**150**].

There were thus limits on the range of commissions which Marescoe & Joye could expect but their Lille clients revealed more eclectic interests than those in Hamburg, enquiring after orpiment, sulphur, saltpetre, silk, cow-hides, cochineal, copperas, campeachy, raisins and lanthorn leaves. About some of these they were evidently ill-informed or inexperienced. Peter Joye felt obliged to instruct J.-B. Cambier that hides were not bought by weight, as he imagined, but by the piece, 'for they can be made to way more or lesse as they have a minde to shave or paire them. They can shave them to be sould for 2s 4d a lb. or they can leave them so thicke to cost but 14d a lb.'[104] He likewise had to ask Charles Angelo to clarify his request for orpiment, for 'or[pi]ment is of severall Coulors, yellow & Red, Ground & ungrownde', adding the warning that 'its not willingly sould to any to transport'.[105]

Yet, about several other commodities it was the merchants of Lille who displayed their exact knowledge of technical requirements. Cochineal, for D'Hollandre & Du Beron, was evidently the cheaper, vegetable dye-stuff known also as 'sylvester' rather than the true, insect-derived product,[106] but it had to be of whole grains 'bien griblé' and not full of powder.[107] Saltpetre, for Angelo, had to be 'd'une sorte dais Indes que lais broches son plus gros comme il s'en trouve en hollande lequel n'est pas si salle'. His lead had to be soft and malleable and his sulphur had to be 'du plus bel rafinage d'italye'.[108] D'Hollandre & Du Beron likewise set out their exact technical requirements for skeins of silk in a manner which confirms their intimate knowledge of textile manufacturing [**149, 154**]. Indeed, most of their commissions were clearly linked to Lille's weaving and dyeing industries, and despite gloomy reports of miserable trade and lack of demand they returned again and again to the same staple needs—indigo, cochineal, campeachy and cotton.

[102] C. Angelo to same, 18 April 1671.
[103] D'Hollandre & Du Beron to same, 18 July 1671.
[104] Marginal note on J.-B. Cambier to same, 19 March 1672.
[105] Marginal note on C. Angelo to same, 23 August 1671.
[106] J. Savary des Bruslons, *Dictionnaire Universel de Commerce*, I, pp. 791–2.
[107] D'Hollandre & Du Beron to LM & PJ, 9 January, 10 October 1672.
[108] C. Angelo to same (undated—? February 1672) and 19 March 1672.

TABLE 23. Lille purchases, 1671

Commodity	CA	H&B	JC	PL	TL	Value £ s d	%
Indigo, guatemalo	—	62.0	14.0	—	24.0	1,152 6 5	68.2
Barbados cotton:							
[a] white	—	—	—	47.3	52.7	426 15 2	25.2
[b] yellow	—	—	—	100.0	—	65 13 10	3.9
Horn leaves	100.0	—	—	—	—	32 18 3	1.9
Sulphur	100.0	—	—	—	—	12 11 9	0.8
Total % share	2.7	42.3	9.5	15.8	29.6	1,690 5 5	100.0

Note: CA = Charles Angelo; H&B = D'Hollandre & Du Beron; JC = J. le Camps; PL = Philippe Libert; TL = Toussaint Libert.

In 1671 the distribution of purchases was as shown in Table 23.

The purchases of 1672 were more varied, although almost trivial in value (Table 24). How far this contraction was due to the onset of war cannot be certain for the attitude of these Lille merchants to the conflict was somewhat ambivalent. They had feared its approach less because of the prospect of a Franco–Dutch conflict than because of the possibility that England and Spain might be drawn in on opposite sides—'& si l'Angleterre se déclare pour la

TABLE 24. Lille purchases, 1672.

Commodities	CA	H&B	J-BC	JC	PL	TL	Value £ s d	%
Lead	74.5					25.5	249 13 11	28.6
Barbados cotton:								
[a] white							211 16 6 ⎫	
[b] yellow				100.0			17 0 9 ⎬	28.1
Turkish yarn							15 19 0 ⎭	
Brazil wood						100.0	17 0 0	1.9
Lahore indigo		100.0					79 12 10	9.1
Hides			100.0				110 4 0	12.6
Raisins			100.0				16 13 6	1.9
Orpiment				100.0			56 12 9	6.5
Sulphur	100.0						18 10 0	2.1
Campeachy						100.0	78 5 1	9.0
Total % share	23.5	9.1	14.5	6.5	28.1	18.2	871 8 4	100.0

J-BC = Jean-Baptiste Cambier. (See Table 23 note for other abbreviations.)

france voila la navigation entièrement empêché'[109]. On the other hand, if England remained neutral, a rosier prospect opened up in which a free English commerce could bring them those fruits of the New World, such as cochineal, which they so desired[110]. For them the war was an enigma carried on by remote, alien powers. It was 'lais francois' who were going to battle—although one cannot fail to observe that when the news of early victories came in they began to glory in the triumphs of '*our* King'![111]

In the main, it was 'business as usual' in 1672, tempered only by the dangers of the Channel crossing and the continuing absence of consumer demand. The intervention of the English East India Company, in buying up cochineal, defeated the efforts of D'Hollandre & Du Beron to obtain it within their price limit at 20s–20s 6d per lb. The Company also thwarted their hopes of acquiring 'indigo lauro' at 4s per lb. Firmly held at 4s 4d in London, it eluded the Lille firm for two months until they finally conceded the full market price.[112] The only other opening for profit created by the war appeared to lie in the exchanges, for the disequilibrium of July 1672 seemed to offer chances of lucrative arbitrage between London, Amsterdam, Venice and Lille.[113] This was not a game which Marescoe & Joye wished to play, but they were under strong pressure to join in, not only from Lille but from Rouen also.

(II) Rouen

The scale of Marescoe & Joye's shipments to Rouen appears insignificant. In 1671 there was a consignment of pepper to Hermann Wetken and a small parcel of Segovia wool transmitted on behalf of a correspondent in Bilbao. In 1672 there was nothing but 266 gallons of cod-oil. These are not materials to afford profound insight into the nature of Anglo–French trade. Nevertheless, the continuing correspondence with Robert Oursel and Wetken possesses interest as much for the opportunities it rejected as for those it embraced.

Oursel was evidently more preoccupied with directing his family's shipping interests than with receiving English commissions. Captain Nicolas Oursel was busy in the whale fishery and Captain Jean Poitevin was bringing home lead from Hull. Marescoe & Joye were able to arrange cargoes for him through William Skinner and in September 1671 Oursel asked them to seek fresh 'sardines' (meaning pilchards) in the ports of the West—Plymouth, Falmouth or Fowey. Correspondents there duly reported on pilchard prices at 10s or 11s per thousand— for it was a summer of good catches[114]—but difficulties were raised about payment. The financing of large-scale purchases for export was a perennial problem in the West of England,[115] for ready cash was scarce and Oursel's preferred method of payment was with a £500 letter of credit. He had evidently forgotten (though William Jennens of Plymouth had not) about a quarrel he had had with the latter in 1670 over a similar transaction when Jennens' commission had seemed excessive. He had called Jennens 'un frippon et un francq cocquin' and had expressed a sentiment to which Anglo–French trade relations have often given rise—'we are not at war with one another—why can't they give up this habit of

---

[109] D'Hollandre & Du Beron to same, 5 March 1672.

[110] Same to same, 12 March 1672.

[111] C. Angelo to same (undated—? February), 13 May, 17 June 1672.

[112] D'Hollandre & Du Beron to same, 13 August, 27 August, 24 September, 1 October, 15 October, 28 October, 19 November, 3 December 1672.

[113] Same to same, 2 July, 16 July [**198**], 10 September 1672.

[114] J. Whetter, *Cornwall in the 17th Century*, p. 204.

[115] Ibid. pp. 101–2.

pillage!'[116] Perhaps it was fortunate that news of poor fish prices in the Canary Islands deflected him from pursuing this commission.[117]

Hermann Wetken, on the other hand, lived to regret his purchase of pepper at $9\frac{1}{2}d$ per lb. Not only was it more than others in Rouen had paid, but its carriage in an English ship had added significantly to its cost. It seems likely that Wetken had been obliged to re-load the consignment at Le Havre in a shallow-draught French vessel, for his parting injunction to Marescoe & Joye was that, in future, they were only to employ French shipping for Rouen.[118] Yet pepper continued to interest Wetken, and he prepared his bid for a further consignment in time for the East India Company's autumn sale. He wanted it at $8\frac{1}{2}$–$8\frac{3}{4}d$ per lb., which he had heard was the intended offer-price, but—like others in Hamburg and elsewhere—was shocked at the final sale-price of $9\frac{1}{4}$ – $9\frac{3}{8}d$ per lb. He refused to buy, but a few weeks later was bitterly regretting the decision for the Rouen price rose steeply in the wake of the Dutch embargo.[119]

Wetken's other interest, in logwood, proved equally fruitless. Desiring only the best he had categorically rejected the Jamaican product which was now generally recognized to be very inferior to the genuine 'campeachy'.[120] He wanted it from Spain via London at $28s$–$29s$ per cwt. and he also looked to London to supply some of the fine 'Indies' cotton yarn which he understood to have arrived in the *flota* of September. As Rouen itself was one of the largest sources of linen exports to the Americas via Spain[121] it is curious that her returns did not keep her exclusively supplied with these products of the Spanish empire. However, it may be that France at this period, as in 1686 (when the French intendant Patoulet reported), took only a small percentage of the colonial imports of Spain—about 15 per cent of the cochineal, 4–6 per cent of the indigo, and 'very little' of the campeachy-wood.[122]

These inconclusive inquiries were soon eclipsed by rising anxieties about the prospect of war. A new correspondent in Rouen, named Benjamin Beuzelin—who was to play an important part in the firm's future trade—discerned the dangers in November 1671. 'On parle fou qu'il va y avoir une Interdite generalle de commerce avecq la hollande, qui no[us] causera d'estranges embarrace, et a la fin en fon a craindre qu'il no[us] s'en ensuire un guerr ouverte.'[123] Oursel, who was equally prescient, judged that a war would stimulate demand for the products of the north and the Mediterranean; Barbados sugar would become dearer, and by April 1672 he could confirm strong demand for native English products—coal and lead among them.[124] Ships from Newcastle were crowding into the mouth of the Seine— but the demand was shortlived. By 19 July, 'le Commerce est icy tout a fait demeuré. On n'a jamais veu sy peu de demande en toute sorte de marchandises ce quy va contre le project de plusieurs quy ont achapté bonne partie au commencement de la guerre sur l'esperance de rehaussé'.[125]

Speculation in English imports was therefore at an end, and speculation on the exchanges was made difficult by a combined shortage of sound bills and ready money. The Rouen

[116] R. Oursel to LM, 28 October 1670.
[117] Same to LM & PJ, 2 October 1671.
[118] H. Wetken to same, 14 July 1671.
[119] Same to same, 1 September, 15 September, 2 October, 20 November 1671.
[120] Same to same, 15 September, 2 October, 1671.
[121] Kamen, *Spain in the Later Seventeenth Century*, p. 119; A. Girard, *Le Commerce Français à Séville et Cadix*, pp. 411–12.
[122] Girard, p. 459.
[123] B. Beuzelin to LM & PJ, 24 November 1671.
[124] R. Oursel to same, 22 April 1672.
[125] Same to same.

exchange on London had behaved less predictably than those of Hamburg or Amsterdam.[126] It had fallen unusually low in the autumn of 1671, probably under the weight of large English exports, and Oursel could find few safe bills. A slight improvement in the Paris–London rate made that route preferable but by early January 1672 rates in both centres had reached such an exceptionally low level (at $53\frac{3}{4}d$ per *W.*) that they could only rise, as they eventually did. But on 1 March Oursel reported a continuing depression: 'les changes demeurent tousjours fort bas, ce quy fait qu'on ne prevoit pas de profit a faire sur les marchandises quy viennent de vos cartiers'. These uncertainties continued throughout the year, and despite the return of the exchange to a more normal level its oscillations still precluded any safe reliance on forward rates. The exigencies of the Anglo–French alliance played their part in depressing the market in early 1673. On 13 January Oursel reported his inability to find any more good bills: 'le change estant un peu diminue a cause de ce qu'on dit que le Roy a envoye 800 mille livres chez un banquier de Paris pour en faire la remise pour Londres. Cela fait que les lettres sont fort couru'.

It was only in Paris, among specialist dealers, that the opportunity to manipulate the exchanges seemed attractive. In July 1671 a former correspondent of Charles Marescoe, Daniel Crommelin,[127] had re-opened his links with the London firm in order to exploit 'le caprice des changes' [**161**], but it was an invitation to which the widow did not respond.

[d] SPAIN

Unlike other sectors of the commission trade which Leonora managed jointly through the partnership with Joye, Coulon and David, exports to Spain and Italy remained largely the concern of the Lethieulliers. Acting on his own and his widowed sister's behalf, John Lethieullier directed more completely than before the shipments to Iberia and the Mediterranean, and it may be principally for this reason that little documentation about it remains in the archive. Only a score of letters survive to record the course of business in Seville or Cadiz and most of these were too preoccupied with old debts to have anything to say about new trade. Of this there was little for the glutted market of 1670[128] seems to have stagnated through 1671. Not until February 1672 did Upton & Bathurst complete the sale of serges sent in October 1668, and a 1669 shipment of bow-dyes only began to sell in June 1671, shortly before the departure of the *flota* of 13–14 July. It was a small fleet, of only four large ships and a patache,[129] and the return of the 1670 *flota* on 23 August 1671 brought but a modest injection of bullion compared with its predecessor.[130] The next departure date, of *flota* and *galeones* together, proved to be 1 March 1672 and it was on this that Upton & Bathurst pinned their hopes of shifting the residue of stock. But they were evidently unsuccessful. On 22 April they admitted: 'we have not been able to sell any of our goods of late that we received of your account in company with Mr Lethieullier, most of what remains being serges dyed in grain which is a comodity that hath but little expense here of late'.

---

[126] See Appendix G, Table A.11 [c].

[127] For the Crommelin family see H. Lüthy, *La Banque Protestante en France*, I, pp. 25, 70 n. 24, 72 n. 32; O. Douen, *La Révocation de l'Édit de Nantes à Paris et dans l'Ile-de-France, d'après des documents inédits* (Paris, 1894) III, p. 81.

[128] 'Here hath beene these 2 or 3 years past such quantity of English goods that have glutted the market and brought them down exceedingly'—Upton & Bathurst to LM, 10 December 1670.

[129] PRO, SP. 94/58 f. 143 (Sir William Godolphin to Lord Arlington, 1 August 1671).

[130] The *flota* of 1671 is credited with bringing about 7 or 8m *pesos*, while the *flota* and *galeones* of February and June 1670 brought over 30m: Kamen, *Spain in the Later Seventeenth Century*, pp. 137–8; PRO, SP. 94/58 ff. 168, 190; but see Everaert, *Vlaamse firma's te Cadiz*, p. 204, for other estimates.

Perhaps the next *galeones* would clear them, but reports from New Spain spoke of disappointing sales for the latest *flota*, which cast a blight upon the domestic market.[131]

Thus, although the reduced consignments of 1670 eventually yielded a reasonable notional profit of 16.8 per cent there can be no surprise at the failure of Marescoe & Lethieullier to send anything in 1671, and when they did resume trade in 1672 it was with new, and perhaps more vigorous, agents. It was the Seville house of John Frederick & John Duncan which took receipt of 34 packs of cloth and 6 barrels of tin with an invoice value of £2,509 6s shared in thirds between Leonora, her brother and Andrew Duncan. No letters or accounts survive to illustrate their reception but Leonora's ledger indicates a steady rate of sales during 1673 which promised a profit of at least 24 per cent when she closed the account in October. A further 28 packs, worth £1,952 (f.o.b.), despatched in the course of 1673, argues for the partners' confidence in their market and satisfaction with its management.

The remaining Spanish ventures of Leonora were on behalf of an old customer of her husband—Simon Campioni of Malaga. Representative of a Venetian firm,[132] Campioni had been seeking a modest exchange of commodities since 1668, offering raisins and wine and requesting cloth in return. His unvarying preference was for Colchester bays, but it was not until April 1671 that he received five packs (of 5 bays a-piece) invoiced at the rather stiff price of $24\frac{1}{2}d$ per ell.[133] Satisfied with their brisk sale he ordered more, which Peter Joye purchased in July 1671 at the even stiffer price of $24\frac{3}{4}d$ and although Campioni grumbled at this it marked the beginning of a correspondence which continued intermittently until 1680.

Campioni sought to finance his London purchases by the despatch of raisins and wine but frequently found his market spoiled by over-eager Englishmen at Malaga whose haste to be first with a new season's produce often pushed up prices by 15–20 per cent. Campioni acknowledged the urgency of timely despatch to catch the pre-Christmas London market[134] but the severity of the competition seems to have left him with a deficit on his sales in England which he had to cover with bills on Amsterdam.

Perhaps it was for this reason that he welcomed the outbreak of war. 'La guerre que nous voyons aprocher nous promet bon negocie'[135] and its effects were soon felt in the reduced price of bays in England—down to $22\frac{1}{4}d$ per ell—and the confused shipping situation in the Straits. With thirty English vessels tied up waiting convoy at Malaga until mid-January 1673, Campioni took his chance with a well-armed Venetian in the Hamburg convoy and confidently looked forward to the 30 per cent gain which raisins had put on since November 1672.[136] But he was disappointed. Seized off Gibraltar by the French on suspicion of being bound for Holland, the well-named *St Antony of Padua and souls in Purgatory* was consigned to the limbo of the Admiralty courts and, with the rupture of the correspondence, its fate remains unknown.

[e] ITALY

(I) Leghorn

The surviving correspondence with Leghorn is even more sparse than Seville's and although

---

[131] PRO, SP. 94/60 ff. 131, 183; SP. 94/61 f. 131.

[132] Campioni's commissions were on behalf of Venerio Venerii of Venice.

[133] Between 1664 and 1670 Lethieullier had never paid more than $22\frac{3}{4}d$ per ell for best-quality Colchester bays.

[134] For the significance of this highly seasonal market see R. Gravil, 'Trading to Spain and Portugal, 1670–1700' in *Business History* vol. X (i) 1968, pp. 81–4.

[135] S. Campioni to LM, 19 February 1672 (writing from Venice during a short visit to his paternal home).

[136] Same to same, 13 December 1671, 10 January, 24 January 1673.

the re-formed partnership of Skinner, Ball and Gosfright[137] politely welcomed the widow Marescoe it was to a lack-lustre market. Local prices for English lead and tin were fairly steady but demand was sluggish and payment for the sales of 1670 slow to come in. Thus, nearly a year elapsed before Leonora participated in a small consignment of lead and pepper handled by her brother. Yet, by the time it arrived, in January 1672, the atmosphere was changing, for prices were moving up and the cargo was quickly sold at a notional profit of 19.5 per cent. Rumours of war provided further stimulus in April and by mid-May, with uncertainties removed, there was a rapid transformation. Lead prices were up nearly 50 per cent by early June and pepper virtually doubled, reaching $D.24\frac{1}{2}$. Leonora's bid to *buy* pepper in Leghorn, odd though it seems, makes sense in the context of high London prices and soaring Venetian ones.[138] She had been informed in a Venice letter of 26 February 1672, received in London on 2 March (Old style), that large arrivals of pepper at Leghorn had lowered prices there, but by the time she acted on 8 April it was too late and her opportunity passed. By 24 June news of English East India Company arrivals in London had a steadying effect and by the autumn of 1672 the whole Leghorn market was back in the doldrums—'so dull a trade we have not known'.[139] Pepper was back at $D.14$, lead at $D.26$ and tin was without demand. Leonora chose this inauspicious time to despatch three shipments—of tin, on her own account, worth £375 14s (f.o.b.), and of pepper and lead in halves with her brother, worth respectively £605 19s 2d and £252 15s 7d (f.o.b.). No letters or accounts remain to narrate their reception and sale but Leonora's ledger records a series of receipts in May and October 1673 which indicated profits averaging 11.7 per cent.[140] This was somewhat more satisfactory than her performance as a whole, for when she closed the account of 'Voyages to Leghorn' (1671–3) she consigned the equivalent of 7.3 per cent to her 'Profit' account on an outlay of nearly £1,700.[141]

(II) **Venice**

Venice proved even less profitable, but in the hands of the industrious Van Teylingen the correspondence was a good deal heavier and the market seemed rather livelier. Lead and pepper were the centre of attention, as at Leghorn, but tin was not. Instead, Van Teylingen addressed himself to the problem of return cargoes of Apulian oil or Zante currants for the benefit of the *Providence* and its syndicate of owners. There was also Captain Samuel Randall and the *John & Thomas* to be provided for. Shortly before his death, Charles Marescoe had taken a one-eighth share, not only in the ship but in its lading of currants at Zante or Cephalonia to be purchased through Van Teylingen's good offices. Posthumous settlement of the account put his profits at just under £40 on an investment of £409. Encouraged, the trustees' investment grew heavier in January 1671, and Van Teylingen was instructed to finance Randall with £500-worth of ducats. Freight charges and local tolls added a further £270. The *Providence* was despatched on a similar errand, seeking for freights at Venice, Gallipoli and Zante.

In both cases the results were disastrous. Winding up the trading account of the *Providence* late in 1672 the trustees registered a loss of £226 15s 10d. As for the *John & Thomas*, its currants fetched a mere 20s per cwt. in London in 1671, compared with the 41s obtained in

---

[137] Skinner & Ball to LM, 23 January 1671. Gosfright joined the firm during the summer of 1671.
[138] Skinner, Ball & Gosfright to LM & PJ, 13 May 1672 [**194**].
[139] Same to same, 28 October 1672.
[140] Ledger (1670–3) f. 17.
[141] Ibid. ff. 4, 24, 38.

1670, and the account was balanced with a stunning loss of £400 10s 3d. This was a severe lesson in the precariousness of Adriatic trade.

The cost was borne by the children's share of the estate, not Leonora's, and it was not until the autumn of 1671 that she was personally at risk with her modest consignments of pepper and lead. She had been amply instructed by Van Teylingen, whose weekly letters carefully traced the fortunes of these commodities on the Venetian market, and the picture he provided was not encouraging. Pepper had drifted slowly down from D.70 in March to only D.64 by October 1671, and an abundance of lead from Chester, selling cheaply, kept its price at a steady low of D.50 per 1,000 lb. Charles Marescoe's posthumous consignments sold quickly enough at this price between May and July, but by September 1671 it was a bad time to despatch more for its price was slipping to D.49 and D.47 [**167, 170**]. Nor was the arrival of the *Providence* particularly well-timed. Prospects of a smaller currant-harvest lifted prices by 60 per cent in early September and it proved impossible to find Captain Peckett a suitable freight. After hanging around expensively in Venice for ten weeks, the *Providence* departed empty for Gallipoli in search of oil, just as its price was lifting to R.pta.$14\frac{1}{2}$ per salme, after months at $12–12\frac{1}{2}$.

The record of mis-timing continued into 1672. Rumours of the pending war had alerted Van Teylingen to the market's possibilities as early as mid-November and he urged Leonora to send more goods in expectation of rising prices. Indeed, lead and pepper were already edging upwards when her October shipments arrived in mid-December, but Van Teylingen's sale of them during January seems regrettably precipitate in the light of the soaring prices of March to June. In justification, he claimed to have obtained better terms than his competitors and he pointed to the rumours of large pepper supplies awaited in London, but these expectations of falling or stable prices were belied by the steady upward climb. Even the arrival of 250 bales of pepper from Amsterdam in late March did nothing to slow the pace, for it was known that Dutch East India Company pepper was fetching $18\frac{3}{8}g$ at home and rising still (Figure 10).

Van Teylingen's interesting assessment of the situation on 13 May [**191**] reveals some of the uncertainties which clouded his judgment, but it still remains difficult to understand his management of Leonora's next consignment of lead. The *Blackamoor* reached Venice on 1 or 2 June 1672 with 900 pigs of lead—50 of which were Leonora's. This was more than the market could absorb for there was plenty in town and there was no pressing demand for it at D.70. Leonora's batch had still not been unloaded by 17 June. But a week later, when others were selling at D.68, Van Teylingen complacently predicted a future rise. Offers of D.64 the following week were therefore refused and he continued to sit tight while prices slipped further and the market stagnated. August passed and by 9 September such lead that remained in town was being held 'in firm hands' at D.63 with every confidence of a rise, for there seemed no prospect of further supplies. Van Teylingen's announcement after a further five weeks silence that he had now sold the lead for D.60 with 3 months discount and 2 months credit therefore comes as a surprise—and something of a blow to one's assessment of his competence.

Yet, the correspondence indicates no dissatisfaction with his performance. Leonora had made a notional $23\frac{3}{4}$ per cent gain on her pepper and the lead sale of January made 22 per cent. That of October represented nearly 33 per cent gain, so there was, perhaps, no great need to lament the opportunities which had been lost in June. More lead was on its way and, although prices steadied, credit-terms lengthened to 8 or even more months by December 1672. Van Teylingen may indeed have exercised a wise discretion in his choice of purchasers, none of

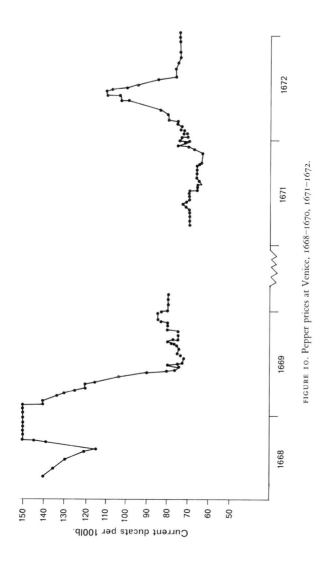

FIGURE 10. Pepper prices at Venice, 1668–1670, 1671–1672.

TABLE 25. LM's lead sales in Venice, 1671–1672.

Date of sale	No. of pieces	Purchaser	Price per 1,000 lb.	Credit terms Discount : Time
1 May 1671	160	Joppo Palazziola	D.52	2 months —
29 May 1671	140	Bortolo Marinoni	D.50	2 months + 2 months
12 June 1671	120	Domenico Ferrari	D.50	3 months —
3 July 1671	90	Bortolo Marinoni	D.50	3 months + 3 months
10 July 1671	788	Bortolo Marinoni	D.50	2 months + 5 months
1 January 1672	50	Antonio Martinelli	D.53	2 months —
14 October 1672	50	Antonio Martinelli	D.60	3 months + 2 months

whom failed to pay up, although his largest customer, Bortolo Marinoni, evidently took his time. The Venetian purchasers of her lead, and their respective shares, are shown in Table 25.

The developments of 1673 are regrettably vague, for only one letter (of 24 February) survives. It depicts pepper beginning to rise again but lead 'asleep' at D.55 with a scarcity of good customers. Zante currants were comparatively cheap at *R.pta* 19 and Gallipoli oil seems so at *R.pta* 12½ per salme. Prospects for the returning *Providence* were therefore mixed but Van Teylingen welcomed news of its cargo of fish, for that—he wrote—was assured of a good market.

In the event, Leonora's 150 pigs of great lead appear to have done only tolerably, selling at D.52, for a notional profit of 11½ per cent. Her one-fifth share in 700 barrels of herrings seems to have been less rewarding at 7½ per cent. Elsewhere, the *Providence* was more fortunate. Loaded with olive-oil at Gallipoli by Sebastian van Dalen of Naples it returned in July to a welcoming London market willing to pay £29 10s per 236 gallons. This was a good price, guaranteeing a handsome profit, and Leonora was thus able to close this account of 'Diverse Marchandises' with a gain of £198 2s 7d.

(iii) PROFIT AND LOSS, 1670–1673

Of what significance were Leonora's profits on her personal trade? The profits on her partnership with Peter Joye, Moses Coulon and Jacob David have been tabulated already, and despite the Company's restricted capital endowment it is not surprising that its half-yearly dividends provided the largest single source of the widow's earnings. She also did well out of her loans, for although her refunds to the children's estate obliged her to cut back from the peak of £13,000 lent by March 1671 she still had £4,000–£5,000 out at interest for most of 1672 and 1673. There was the £1,000 lent to Jacob David and the £600–£1,000 lent to the partnership at 5 per cent; between £500 and £1,500 were advanced on the East India Company's short-term bonds, and from September 1671 she had £1,500 on deposit with the goldsmith-banker, Isaac Meynell, at 6 per cent (Table 26).

Half-yearly receipts of £150 from the Chamber of the City of London also represented interest at 5 per cent on the children's share of the estate, and although this was designated for their maintenance it may be doubted that they received its full benefits. Leonora also extracted £350 from the estate to cover expenses preceding April 1671 'although £700 was spent', and in October 1673 she obtained £291 12s from the estate to cover the funeral expenses of her daughters, Mary and Elizabeth. Meanwhile, the contentious East India

TABLE 26. LM's profit and loss, October 1670–October 1673.

		October 1670–October 1671 £ s d	October 1671–October 1672 £ s d	October 1672–October 1673 £ s d	Totals 1670–1673 £ s d
A.	1. Partnership Dividends	1,436 14 5	661 0 2	792 15 7	2,890 10 2
	2. East India Co. Dividends	225 0 0	900 0 0	—	1,125 0 0
	3. City of London Chamber	150 0 0	450 0 0	150 0 0	750 0 0
	4. Marescoe Estate	350 0 0	—	291 12 0	641 12 0
	5. Interest on loans	592 12 0	550 0 0	226 10 6	1,369 2 11
	6. Trading profits	—	173 11 0	715 19 10	889 10 10
	Gross Profit	2,754 6 5	2,734 11 7	2,176 17 11	7,665 15 11
B.	1. Trading losses	14 11 4	24 2 10	33 7 10	72 2 0
	2. Interest	124 6 0	147 14 10	50 0 0	322 0 10
	3. Jacob David & Moses Coulon	103 10 0	—	35 0 0	138 10 0
	4. Marescoe children	23 14 0	25 4 3	—	44 18 3
	5. Housekeeping expenses	1,126 4 4	2,175 13 6	1,622 4 4	4,924 2 2
	Total losses	1,392 5 8	2,372 15 5	1,740 12 2	5,505 13 3
	Net Profit	1,362 0 9	361 16 2	436 5 9	2,160 2 8
C.	Banker's debt	—	—	−1,500 0 0	−1,500 0 0
	Gain to Capital	1,362 0 9	361 16 2		660 2 8
	Loss to Capital			−1,063 14 3	

Company shares were proving their value with a series of three dividends totalling 50 per cent in 1671 and 1672.

Set amid these gains her profits on 'voyages' seem modest, although as a 10 per cent return on capital employed the record was a respectable one. Of her capital, totalling £13,000, Leonora allocated approximately £3,000 to her ventures under her brother's direction, and although his performance in the Mediterranean was now a good deal less impressive than the partnership's yield of 24 per cent per annum it was one conducted in more uncertain conditions during a singularly unfavourable period.

Yet it has to be said that the really striking feature of Leonora Marescoe's 'Profit & Loss' account is provided not by her earnings but by her spending, cryptically entered in her ledger as 'fraits de mesnage'. Made up of undifferentiated entries, for £30, £40 and £50, the totals attributed to mere 'housekeeping' average over £1,500 p.a.—an extraordinary record of expenditure which contrasts sharply with the thrifty domestic management of the late Charles Marescoe. He had customarily allocated £10–£15 per month to the requirements of his extended household, but his widow clearly made merry. Among the few items which are specifically accounted for are wine, tapestries, Venetian glass, silverware and horses. She bought herself a diamond bracelet in March 1672 and in July spent £210 on a portrait miniature of her late husband surrounded by more diamonds!

Set against these huge totals the sums attributable to her business expenses and trading losses appear negligible. She paid interest to her brother for the loan of some working capital and she specifies some small gratuities to Jacob David and Moses Coulon. The boarding-school fees of the surviving children make intermittent appearances and it may be that more payments of this nature are concealed under 'fraits de mesnage'. But at this rate of expenditure there was little scope for capital growth. The widow had entered business with £13,050 from the estate and £82 14s 10d found in her money-box. Over three years her net gains, transferred to 'Capital' each October, were only £2,160 2s 8d, and even this was jeopardized by a disaster beyond her control. The 'Stop of the Exchequer' of 18 December 1671 and 5 January 1672, by which Charles II deferred repayments and interest on his short-term borrowing, had paralysed the Lombard Street bankers who were his principal creditors. They in return were unable to meet liabilities to their depositors. Threatened by private prosecutions, they received some protection from the King until a final settlement was reached in 1677, but in 1673 no one could be confident that the King would honour his obligations to the bankers or that the bankers would be enabled to meet theirs. It was therefore prudent accounting to regard Leonora's loan to Meynell as a frozen asset which might yet prove a liability. Accordingly, the £1,500 was debited as a 'loss' in the Profit & Loss account—more than wiping out the small net profit of 1673—and this debit was duly transferred to her Capital account. But at the same time the £1,500 deposit was retained as a credit item, and thus as far as Leonora was concerned she was entering upon her 1673 partnership with Jacob David possessed of a capital of £15,292 17s 6d.

6. JACOB DAVID'S TRADE, 1675–1680

(i) IMPORTS

Although the capital with which Leonora and Jacob David entered upon their partnership in 1674 was somewhat larger than Charles Marescoe's in 1664, the context in which they sought to revive his immensely profitable imports commissions was considerably less favourable. The Swedish situation had changed for the worse, with several of the major suppliers in difficulties or on the point of eclipse. Abraham Momma was already bankrupt and Willem Momma seemed likely to be so. Isaac and Abraham Cronström were at loggerheads,[1] and Alexander Waddell had fled from his creditors.[2] Lillienhoff (formerly Joachim Pötter) died in February 1676 and his partner Rosenström (formerly Hendrik Thuen) followed him in October. Jacob Momma-Reenstierna died in March 1678. The Tar Company, of which these men had been major pillars, was tottering on towards its closure in 1682.

Speeding the process of dissolution was a war in which the advantageous conjunctures of 1664–7 were almost exactly reversed. Then, a neutral Sweden had been free to supply an England embattled by Holland and France and her trade and shipping had flourished unhindered. But between 1674 and 1679 it was Sweden which was at bay, besieged in her German provinces by Brandenburg and in her Scanian provinces by the Danes. By July 1675 she was also at war with the Dutch.

For England, which had withdrawn from the Franco–Dutch conflict in February 1674, such a situation offered specious attractions and some very real gains. The unique opportunity to seize a European monopoly from her principal commercial rivals immediately galvanized her shipping, and this is nowhere more apparent than in the Baltic where the Sound Toll tables reveal a dramatic upsurge in English transits.[3] English ships entering the Sound, eastbound, which had averaged about ninety per annum in the best years of the 1660s, rose from 120 in 1674 to 364 in 1675 and 408 in 1676. The proportion of these sailing in ballast declined from the 55 per cent average of 1668–70 to 23 per cent in 1675–80, a clear indication of the extent to which English shipping had captured an unusual share of the carrying trade of western Europe. Lured by Baltic demand for fish, salt, wine and textiles, flocks of English vessels made their way through the Sound upon unaccustomed voyages. Before 1674 only a handful of outports in the British Isles had served the needs of the 'Eastland', but by 1675 over thirty were competing for their share in this unusual bonanza.[4] Freight-rates rose, notwithstanding.

All this is abundantly reflected in the Swedish commerce and correspondence with Jacob David. Where before the partnership's imports had been carried in the *Graffelyk Huys de la Gardie*, or the *Gottlandia* or the *Slott Stockholm*, bills of lading now spoke of the *John* of Yarmouth, the *Providence* of Hull or the *Antelope* of Newcastle. Unmistakeably English skippers—Henry Collins, Thomas Crick, Benjamin King, George Rudstone—supersede the

---

[1] *Svenskt biografiskt lexikon* 'Cronström, Isaac' and 'Cronström, Abraham' by B. Boethius, pp. 356–75.
[2] Coventry MSS, Longleat, Vol. 66 f. 120 (Sir Edward Wood to Sir Henry Coventry, 30 August 1673); *CSPD 1675–76*, pp. 125–6.
[3] N. E. Bang & K. Korst, *Tabeller over Skipsfart og Varetransport gennem Oresund, 1661–1783*, 2nd Part, vol. 1, pp. 83, 99, 114, 125, 136, 150, 163, 175, 186, 197, 209; Hinton, *The Eastland Trade*, pp. 108–12.
[4] Bang & Korst, *Tabeller . . . 1661–1783*, 2nd Part, Vol. 1, p. 215.

Biorssons, Johanssons, Pietersens and Rasmussens of earlier years. From August 1675 a Swedish embargo on their own merchant marine placed them wholly at the mercy of their English friends.[5]

Yet the opportunities were not unflawed. Many of these English vessels proved too small to serve the bulk requirements of the pitch, tar, iron and copper exporters,[6] and others—whose masters displayed an unattractive combination of greed and timidity—were to be used once but never again. Unaccustomed to winter sailings in the North Sea many of the newcomers were reluctant—except at extortionate rates—to undertake those November voyages upon which the Swedish producers' autumnal consignments always relied.[7] Not surprisingly, Stockholm merchants yearned for the return of the cheaper, bolder Dutch. By the autumn of 1675 their hopes were pinned on the completion of a commercial treaty with the United Provinces which would sanction normal seaborne commerce between the two powers even though they and their allies were still locked in conflict.

The treaty, the negotiation of which deeply preoccupied Steven de Geer, was concluded in November 1675 and received the participants' ratification in February and March 1676,[8] but despite Swedish expectations and English fears the returning flood of Dutch vessels did not immediately materialize. In 1676 the English envoy at Stockholm, Sir Edward Wood, observed the speedy arrival of English ships—thirty by 10 May—yet as late as 25 August only one Dutch vessel had appeared.[9] By the close of the year, as the Sound Toll tables reveal, English and Scottish ships still outnumbered the Dutch, with a remarkably high proportion of them entering the Baltic in lading.[10]

This reflected the success with which English and Scottish ships had been mobilized to supply Sweden with fish, grain, wine and—above all—salt. In 1675 it was reported that Leyonbergh had secured twenty English ships to fetch Setubal salt,[11] and in 1676 several more were to be lured into this triangular traffic between Portugal (or France), Sweden and England. Winter dearth, which had been acute in the spring of 1675, compelled Sweden in 1676 to grant English ships the privilege of bringing in all kinds of provisions duty-free,[12] and although the summer produced a remarkably good Swedish harvest the freedom from normal aliens' import duties was renewed in 1677 and concessionary export duties were made reciprocal upon specific imports. Thus, one barrel of salt or six of malt created entitlement for one shippound of iron; six-and-a-half barrels of salt equalled one shippound of copper, and so on.[13]

The official inducements of 1676 and 1677 had been anticipated months before by private bribes. In their anxiety to secure passage for their exports in 1675 contractors, such as Van Cöllen & Uppendorff, had sought out English merchants in Stockholm who would be

---

[5] Fahlborg, 'Ett blad ur den Svenska flottans historia (1660–1715)', *Historisk Tidskrift* (1923) pp. 272–4.

[6] Johannes de Geer to LM & JD, 26 May 1675 [**241**].

[7] RA, Stockholm (Momma-Reenstierna MSS) E.2513, LM to Jacob Reenstierna, 2 February 1675; E.2503, JD to same, 8 September 1675.

[8] R. Hoffstedt, *Sveriges utrikes politik under krigsåren, 1675–1679* (Uppsala, 1943) pp. 95–6; S.-E. Åström, *From Stockholm to St Petersburg* (Helsinki, 1962) p. 33.

[9] PRO, SP. 95/10 ff. 13, 82.

[10] Bang & Korst, *Tabeller . . . 1661–1783*, 2nd Part, vol. 1, pp. 16, 163. In 1675 and 1676 about 54 per cent of Dutch ships entering the Sound eastbound were in ballast; the comparable figures for English and Scottish ships are 23 per cent in 1675, 14 per cent in 1676.

[11] S. de Geer to JD, 28 June 1675; Åström, *From Cloth to Iron*, p. 65.

[12] PRO, SP. 95/9 f. 89; SP. 95/10 ff. 19, 67 (Sir E. Wood to Sir H. Coventry, 31 March 1675; 17 May, 1 August 1676).

[13] PRO, SP. 95/10 ff. 80, 234, 243 (same to same, 12 August 1676, 30 May 1677); Stiernman, IV, pp. 138–9, 161–2, 163; H. Cletcher to JD, 20 June 1677.

willing to 'colour' the goods as their own. Some entered into patently fictitious 'sales' of their ships simply in order to concoct a neutral identity and secure English papers.[14] However, the English envoy, Sir Edward Wood, firmly set his face against these practices which he regarded as fundamentally damaging to the best interests of genuine English shipping. In suspicious cases he refused passports and in 1676 he obtained authority to tender oaths to those English merchants applying for the certificates without which their goods could not pass the Sound.[15] He boasted of dramatic results, but it is worth recording that the clandestine premium which English skippers charged to colour goods dropped from 4 per cent in 1676 to 2 per cent in 1677[16]—a reflection in part of returning Dutch competition but in part of ineffectual control. Judging from Thomas Perman's letter of 12 March 1677 [**340**] it was not thought difficult for David to colour his client's goods simply by writing from London, although—as Willem Momma kept hinting—it would have been easier if he had sent an agent to Sweden to handle matters on the spot [**266**, **305**].

Unfortunately for David, and his English competitors, the success of English shipping was not wholly compatible with success for the goods they brought or for the returns they fetched. The unprecedented influx of laden English vessels produced a series of gluts in Stockholm—first of salt, then of wine and later of rye. At the same time, intense competition for return freights pushed up the price of iron in Sweden and, conversely, depressed it in England. Already in September 1675, on the same day that Jacob David complained of abundant 'ordinary' iron being undersold in London by its needy freighters, Hendrik Cletcher recorded its sale in Stockholm at prices which precluded the need to ship more.[17] By July 1676, Van Cöllen & Uppendorff estimated their probable loss on iron exports to London at between 20 and 30 per cent, and in December Willem Momma concurred, putting the margin of loss on iron at 6 or 7 rixdollars per shippound (i.e. 22 to 25 per cent.) Most of David's suppliers were therefore agreed that it made better sense to sell their production at first hand, in Sweden itself. 'Here are more English ships than are goods to load them with' wrote Cletcher in 1676.[18]

David did not dissent. He had seen Swedish iron lying unwanted on the London quayside and by March 1677 he was advising Jacob Reenstierna to hold on to his stocks and sell in Sweden.[19] His hopes of an improved London market were pinned on successful English re-exports, either of copper-wares to France or of iron to Portugal. He would even have welcomed a recovery of Swedish iron exports to Holland.[20]

However, the skilful exploitation of localized opportunities in the European market for Swedish exports, which even at the best of times required quick and reliable communications, proved quite impossible in the conditions of this particular war. For Denmark's strategic position not merely gave her command of the Sound but of north-west European posts and it was inevitable that from midsummer 1675 she would impose an embargo on Swedish letters.[21] Thus, not the least important consequence of the Scanian war for this

---

[14] Van Cöllen & Uppendorff to LM & JD, 15 May 1675; PRO, SP. 95/9 ff. 131, 173, 324 (16 June, 6 October 1675, 26 April 1676).

[15] PRO, SP. 95/9 f. 325; SP. 95/10 ff. 35, 143–7; D. van Baerle to JD, 23 April 1676 [**289**].

[16] H. Cletcher to JD, 14 March 1677.

[17] Same to same, 8 September 1675; RA, Stockholm, E.2503, JD to Jacob Reenstierna, 8 September 1675.

[18] H. Cletcher to JD, 8 June 1676.

[19] RA, Stockholm, E.2503, JD to Jacob Reenstierna, 16 March, 14 April 1677.

[20] Same to same, 18 May 1677.

[21] Hoffstedt, *Sveriges utrikespolitik under krigsåren, 1675–1679*, pp. 165–6; PRO, SP. 95/9 ff. 158, 161 (28 August, 6 September 1675).

correspondence is its broken, patchy nature. Many letters were evidently written and 90 to 100 per annum were eventually received, but there are frequent references to missing items and the tardy arrival of most communications precluded any quick or flexible collaboration between Stockholm and London.

Yet, the circumstance which perhaps did most to relieve the throttling pressures on Sweden's restricted export channels was the totally unpredictable behaviour of the weather. This displayed a perverse reluctance to strike that fine balance of conditions on which the unhampered production and transport of Sweden's iron and copper necessarily depended. Ideally, well-filled streams would serve the furnaces, forges and mills throughout the summer and autumn, and—if not too severely frozen—would continue to assist production for the late spring shipments. Moderately freezing conditions throughout the winter were indeed essential to provide those hardened sledge-trails across land and water which were by far the speediest and cheapest means of bulk transport.[22] But winters too mild, as in 1671/72 and 1677/78, were as unwelcome as winters too severe, as were those of 1673/74 and 1676/77. Coming in the wake of dry summers, such as that of 1675, the exceptionally heavy snows of April 1672 and March 1676 (with subsequent floods) were as unhelpful as the long, dry winter of 1678/79. If the complaints of David's Swedish correspondents are to be taken at face value (and they are often corroborated by Steven de Geer and the English envoy) then the second half of the 1670s produced scarcely one year favourable for the full or efficient production of iron or copper. In September 1675 Willem Momma predicted as much as a 50 per cent shortfall in copper-wire output, with most of the works lying idle through the winter, and Cletcher confirmed the paralysing effects of the long drought and severe frost on his iron production. In February 1676 Jean Boor estimated the possible loss of iron at one-third, and the standstill continued not only into April but into October and December [**286– 289**]. For three months two-thirds of all iron forges had been unable to work, estimated Laurens Uppendorff in March and April 1677, and in April 1678 he could confirm Jacob Reenstierna's report (in what proved his last letter to David) that the unusually mild winter had rendered sledge trails unusable and prevented supplies and raw materials getting through. The monotonous record of disruption continued into 1679, with half the iron works still immobilized by an autumn water shortage.[23]

Iron

This combination of war, bad weather and broken communications proved most vexatious to Steven de Geer in Amsterdam. Domiciled in a belligerent power, he could expect no compensating support from Holland's ally, Denmark, for (as he ruefully explained to David in September 1675) the name of De Geer was still 'somewhat odious' to the Danes who could not forget his father's role in fitting out the Swedish battle fleet of 1644.[24] It was therefore unwise for him to try to send Swedish goods through the Sound under his own colours or of his nephew, Gerard de Geer. The 3,000–4,000 slb of iron he intended for David in 1675 would therefore have to be despatched by his Stockholm agent, Jean Boor, as if it were David's property, in English ships. It is some measure of De Geer's difficulties in exercising long-range control that David received barely one-tenth of what had been promised by the end of the year, although with the belated arrival of William Maynard's *Constant Friendship* and John Clark's *Samuel* in January 1676 the total was brought up to about 3,800 slb. But by

[22] E. F. Heckscher, *Sveriges ekonomiska historia från Gustav Vasa*, I, pp. 536–46.

[23] A. Wolters to JD, 8 September 1679 [cf. **448**].

[24] See E. W. Dahlgren, *Louis de Geer, 1587–1652*, II, pp. 460–500. He had provided 32 ships equipped with 605 cannon.

then the glut of Swedish iron offered cheaply on the London market by inexperienced dealers had begun to depress prices to unacceptably low levels and Boor was evidently not sorry to predict that bad weather would retard production in 1676.[25] In any event, as De Geer's letter of 14 February indicated, little more would be sent while its London price remained below Stockholm's [**273**]. Instead, De Geer's hopes were pinned on the commercial treaty which, he repeatedly predicted, would displace the extortionate English and restore Dutch carriers. Iron diverted to the wider European market via Amsterdam would then force up London prices, although as matters now stood there were scarcely sufficient stocks in Holland to supply Italian demand.[26]

However, as his expectations of Dutch restoration gradually faded, De Geer turned back reluctantly to English shipping, following closely through his network of intelligence the movements of the English salt fleet and assessing their effect on freight-rates at Stockholm. These remained unconscionably high for the Stockholm–London run, at £4 sterling or even £4 10s per last in 1675 (compared with a pre-war equivalent in current rixdollars of about £2 or £2 10s) but showing a tendency to moderate in 1676 towards £3 10s and £3.[27] For the round trip London–St Ubes–Stockholm–London the 1675 rates of £8 5s and £8 10s per last had declined to £7 in 1676. Dutch freights for the St Ubes–Stockholm–Amsterdam route were, of course, lower still, falling from ƒ.75 in January 1676 to ƒ.64 in April and ƒ.52 in November, where they steadied,[28] but their effect on the London route could only be indirect as long as Swedish exports to England remained an English monopoly. De Geer had to accept this, contenting himself with putting David in touch with Jean van Deurs, his agent at the Sound, and Nicolas Simons, the Swedish consul at Lisbon, to ensure that he would at least be properly informed of the relevant movements in shipping [**334, 342**].

Under these discouragements it is not surprising that De Geer's consignments of iron via Jean Boor were virtually halved in 1676 and dwindled to a mere 45 slb in 1677. His letter of 26 March 1677 had given fair warning of this [**336**], and that of 3 August amply explains why he and David's other iron suppliers contented themselves with domestic sales [**358**]. Frenzied buying in Sweden and incontinent selling in London by inexperienced English dealers made a shambles of the market—and there is no mistaking Louis Trip's contempt for the spectacle [**360**].

Since 1672, when he had prudently transferred this side of his business to his nephew, Matthias, in Stockholm, Trip had despatched nothing to the Marescoe-Joye partnership (although it figures in his ledgers on account of balances due from Charles Marescoe).[29] But in 1675 Matthias had sent 1,657 bars and in 1676 another 1,047 bars, together totalling 401 slb. About one-third of it was the square bar-iron variety, for which David was belatedly asking De Geer, but none of it was of the coveted 'voyage' iron variety. For this Jacob David had to rely upon Hendrik Cletcher, successor to his mother-in-law Debora van Ruyff at Axbergshamer, whose interest in a voyage iron contract with the Royal African Company waxed and waned inversely with Stockholm prices. Demanding £14 15s per ton in December 1674, he was content to get £14 10s in 1675 and early 1676, but by April 1676 it is clear that his enthusiasm was flagging and by 1 January 1677 he firmly declined to re-engage, pleading immobilization by drought [**222, 230, 237, 276, 290**]. This was unfortunate, for according to David's letters to Jacob Reenstierna eleven-foot voyage iron bars were in

[25] J. Boor to JD, 25 March 1676 [**286**].
[26] S. de Geer to JD, 29 May 1676.
[27] Same to same, 19 June 1676.
[28] Same to same, 10 January, 14 February [**273**], 21 April, 27 November 1676 [**320**], 8 November 1677.
[29] GA, Amsterdam, Koopmansboeken 42, ff. 112, 114, 202, 209.

particular demand, even during the glutted months of early 1677. Re-export requirements for Portugal were pushing up prices by June 1677 and by October iron in general, but especially voyage, had become scarce.[30] The 1677 English naval programme for thirty new warships (first mooted in 1675 but only now agreed by Parliament) had quickened demand for square iron, a fact to which De Geer was soon alert but unable to respond.[31] Instead, David's iron in 1677 came from new suppliers—total strangers such as Hendrick Lutkens of Stockholm whose winter shipment to Hamburg in the *Hope* of Yarmouth (captain Benjamin Ames) had to be diverted from the frozen Elbe to its home port on the east coast. Its 5,482 pieces of assorted iron eventually formed 38.5 per cent of David's sales that year, and another of Lutken's shipment added 8.1 per cent in the autumn. A more significant newcomer in 1677 was the partnership of Oloff & Nicolas Törne, important Stockholm merchants whose interests went beyond iron and copper to the import of textiles, in which they were soon to involve David.[32]

The iron imports of 1678 were negligible. Prospects of a European peace remained tantalizingly deferred and England's attempt to coerce Louis XIV to the conference table seemed to threaten a wider conflict [408]. The English embargo of French trade, proclaimed in March 1678, proved more damaging to the prospects for Swedish copper than for iron, but the mild winter which made routes unusable ensured that Swedish home prices were too high to justify export. Thus, despite Robert Clark's tempting talk of 4,000–5,000 slb of fine iron available in return for silver specie [392], Jacob David received little or none from his regular suppliers. In 1679 too the prospects were not good after the long dry winter. 'Alles is onbruyckbaer' wrote Jean Boor of the cross-country routes,[33] and although he alleged that large stocks had been held back from 1678 both Cletcher and De Geer found that demand for domestic sales was more attractive. The former rejected the proffer of a Royal African Company contract in February.[34] The latter, after a convivial stay with Jacob David in London [427], decided to end his frustrating isolation and to take personal charge of his affairs in Sweden. Reaching Stockholm in July 1679 he was at first reluctant to allocate more than 300–350 slb to David,[35] partly because of production difficulties at the Gimo works [467] and partly because he had sub-contracted the Lövsta output to Claes Wilkens [460]. Fortunately, Wilkens was to prove David's largest supplier in 1679, sending a mixture of 'Crowned O' and Ⓛ iron in four autumn shipments in the vain hope that London prices would improve. But David's November sales at barely £12 10s per ton represented a loss for Wilkens, who said he could have sold to English merchants in Sweden for £13 per ton.[36] Evidently Louis Trip—an ironmaster for 54 years—was right to predict that Ⓛ iron would prove less saleable in London than 'O' [469]. Both his letters and those of De Geer reveal considerable willingness to adapt their output to the special requirements of the English market, however unrealistic [476], but it is evident that they faced very sluggish demand. David himself, who had bought in for his own account over 520 tons of iron at a cost of £6,876 6s 8d since 1674, could show a profit no larger than £46 3s 2d after two years.[37]

[30] RA, Stockholm, E.2503, JD to Jacob Reenstierna, 9 February, 16 March, 18 May, 29 June, 5 October, 23 November 1677.

[31] S. de Geer to JD, 4 May 1677.

[32] See p. 169; Åström, *From Cloth to Iron*, pp. 144–5 n. 101, and sources there cited.

[33] J. Boor to JD, 9 April 1679.

[34] H. Cletcher to same, 7 February 1679.

[35] S. de Geer to same, 7/17 July 1679.

[36] C. Wilkens to same, 31 December 1679, 31 January 1680. David's sale of 41 tons averaged £12 10s 7d per ton.

[37] See p. 168.

Copper

The Swedish copper-ware manufacturers were subject to the same vicissitudes of war, bad weather and frustrated communications as the iron producers, but there were some significant differences in their situations, some advantageous, some not. Among the former was copper's higher ratio of value to bulk compared with iron. Pound for pound, copper manufactures were worth eight to ten times more than those of iron, but their export made smaller and less expensive demands on available shipping. While iron freight could absorb 20 per cent of its gross sale, copper cost barely 2 per cent. The sudden shortage of cargo-space in 1675 undoubtedly had severe effects on some of David's major suppliers, such as D. van Baerle, Isaac Cronström, Willem Momma and Thomas Perman, all of whom complained, but their difficulties were more easily overcome than those of De Geer and Cletcher. It is noticeable in the Sound Toll tables that, while iron shipments passed very largely to the English between 1675 and 1680, copper was quickly regained as a substantial segment of westbound Dutch ships' lading in 1676 and beyond.[38] Exports of copper to western Europe were therefore less at the mercy of English novices bearing salt. Indeed, one derives the impression from David's correspondence that the unsatisfactory weather conditions of 1675–80 were a more effectual brake on output, and consequent exports, than the wartime constraints on shipping. Allegedly, copper-ware production was at a standstill in the summer droughts of 1676 and 1679, and in the winters of 1675/76, 1678/79 and 1679/80. Thomas Perman thought that output had been halved in the winter of 1678 and he put the losses in the 1679/80 winter at 20 per cent.[39] Where the war did seriously affect brass-ware production was in checking Sweden's supply of calamine, usually received from Altenburg through the Netherlands or from Limburg via France or north Germany.[40] Cut off from all these by Danish and Brandenburg blockades both Willem Momma and Laurens Uppendorff attributed the reduction of half or two-thirds of brass-ware production in 1675 and 1676 to the shortage of calamine which was not ended until Dutch supplies came through in September 1676 [271, 288, 294, 305].

Such constraints were all the more serious because Sweden's copper faced greater competition than her iron. Norwegian garcopper and Japanese imports were established on the Amsterdam market as alternative sources of raw material,[41] while manufacturers in Hamburg and Aachen were always waiting to take advantage of any reduction in the cost-differential between their excellent but expensive products and those of Sweden. These threatening potentialities were partially realized during the Scanian war. While Swedish exports evidently flagged, Dutch East India Company imports of Japanese copper reached a crescendo between 1672 and 1676 (when they nearly equalled the volume of the preceding ten years).[42] David's correspondence gives patchy but significant confirmation that

---

[38] Bang & Korst, *Tabeller . . . 1661–1783*, 2nd Part, vol. 1, pp. 156, 169, 180, 192, 203, 217.

[39] T. Perman to JD, 13 May 1679 [448], 17 January 1680.

[40] R. A. Peltzer, 'Geschichte der Messingindustrie' in *Zeitschrift des Aachener Geschichtsvereins*, vol. XXX (1908) pp. 334–5.

[41] E. F. Heckscher, 'Den europeiska kopparmarknaden under 1600-talet' *Scandia* vol. XI 2 (1938) pp. 239–43; K. Glamann, 'The Dutch East India Company's Trade in Japanese Copper, 1645–1736', *The Scandinavian Economic History Review* I (1953) pp. 52–3, 56–7; K. Glamann, 'Japanese copper in European markets in the 17th century' in H. Kellenbenz (ed.) *Schwerpunkte der Kupferproduction und des Kupferhandels in Europa, 1500–1650* (Cologne, 1977) p. 287; S. Tveite, 'Die Norwegische Kupfererzeugung vor 1700' in Kellenbenz, *Schwerpunkte der Kupferproduktion*, pp. 275–8; A. Kobata, 'Production and trade in gold, silver and copper in Japan, 1450–1750' in H. Kellenbenz (ed.) *Precious Metals in the Age of Expansion* (Stuttgart, 1981) p. 275; N. W. Posthumus, *Inquiry into the History of Prices in Holland* I (Leiden, 1946) pp. 22, 373–4.

[42] Glamann, *The Scandinavian Economic History Review* I (1953) pp. 52–3.

Amsterdam was adequately supplied without shipments from Sweden until June 1676 when a shortage began to bite and prices of *f*.69–*f*.70 per 100 lb. for copper-wire began to be asked.[43] In 1677, when the autumn return-fleet brought only 1,200–1,300 lb. of Japanese copper, prices again rose and a similar disappointment in 1678 had the same effect. Conversely, the unusually high volume of Japanese copper received in 1679 induced a sharp fall in Amsterdam prices.[44]

The revival of brass-ware manufacture at Aachen was also a matter of some concern, notably to W. Momma, whose simmering resentment about his London sales was not helped by news that his kettles and pans were being undercut by allegedly superior products.[45] The Van Baerles had been the earliest to detect and explain the revival of Aachen, in February 1676, but in the case of Hamburg it was Jacob David himself who was the first to complain, in September 1675, when he attributed the fall of London's copper-wire prices to the arrival of German competition.[46] In Stockholm, David van Baerle's answer to David's complaint was to deny that Hamburg was being supplied from Sweden [**271**], but David was in possession of abundant evidence to the contrary. In April, Lillienhoff & Rosenström had spoken of only 800 coils of copper-wire going to Hamburg, but in May Van Cöllen & Uppendorff wrote that all Swedish brass-wire was being sent there, they themselves having sent 5,000 coils to De la Bistrate & Dufay—a fact which Guillaume de la Bistrate had already revealed.[47] Finally, there was Reinhold Garlinghoff from Hamburg itself, offering all kinds of brass and copper products—'Rolmessingh undt Schwarten undt Blanck Lathun von allerhandt sort Coperslagen von bladt undt schoen stuck'. He later estimated Lübeck's output of copper-wire at 500–600 coils per month and Hamburg's at 1,100–1,200, in which his own share was apparently 25 per cent [**374**].[48]

Garlinghoff's was the first of several overtures which David received from Hamburg, and even as he courted his Swedish principals for exclusive contracts as their London agent he was seeking and accepting offers of supply from north Germany [**267**]. Johan Tomloo, usually an importing correspondent, began to send a series of copper shipments in July 1676, and in 1677 consignments in his name were to account for 47.4 per cent of David's copper sales. It was Tomloo who introduced David to Georg Kohröber of Gozlar [**389**], whose supplies were drawn from the wider hinterland of Hanover and Wolfenbüttel, while it was Garlinghoff who introduced Carl Lubers of Hamburg [**379**]. Lubers in 1678 was to lade seven ships, all English, with some 250 cwt. of sheet, leaf and wire-copper and the three Hamburg dealers between them were to provide 67 per cent of David's supplies in 1677 and an estimated 50 per cent in 1678.

However, Hamburg's exports were not without their difficulties. Denied neutral status by the French, the Hamburgers' shipping was as effectively embargoed as the Swedes', and their customary links with Sweden through Lübeck were seriously impaired by Danish hostility on land and by sea. Figures for Lübeck's trade with Sweden in the 1670s indicate severe contraction in the volume and value of the city's imports, particularly in 1676 and 1677, and

---

[43] De la Bistrate & Dufay to JD, 9 June 1676; Isaac de Gomze to same, 14 July 1676.

[44] Van Baerles to same, 10 September 1677; G. Pincier to same, 21 September 1677, 12 August 1678; A. DuQuesnoy to same, 3 October 1679 [**459**]; A. Wolters to same, 1 November 1679 [**468**].

[45] W. Momma to same, 30 March 1677 [**353**]; D. van Baerle to same, 16 March 1677; RA, Stockholm, E.2503, JD to Jacob Reenstierna, 16 January, 26 January 1677.

[46] RA, Stockholm, E.2503, JD to Jacob Reenstierna, 8 September 1675.

[47] Lillienhoff & Rosenström to JD, 3 April 1675; Van Cöllen & Uppendorff to same, 15 May 1675; G. de la Bistrate to same, 4 May 1675.

[48] Hamburg's production would thus be approximately 3,200–3,500 cwt. p.a. (on the basis of 1 coil = 27 lb.).

Swedish copper and brass was a conspicuous victim.[49] Oloff & Nicolas Törne claimed to have sent all their copper-wire to Lübeck in 1677 (since English shipping had been unavailable)[50] but it cannot be assumed to have reached Hamburg. By August 1678 Hamburg copper prices were exhibiting a 6 per cent rise[51] and throughout the correspondence there are clear signs that the pressure of high domestic costs was making Hamburg's copper-products uncompetitive on the London market. Garlinghoff withdrew after only five months' trial in 1675, returning in 1677 to face renewed disappointment. The repeated insistence of David's Hamburg correspondents on sustaining maximum prices and allowing minimum credit betrays the nature of their difficulties. Even at a time when copper-wire was fetching the unusually high price of £6 15s per cwt. in London Carl Lubers complained that any sale below £7 meant a loss,[52] and Tomloo protested strongly against sales arranged with the customary four months' credit. During 1678 Lubers looked hopefully towards sales of his 'Hungary' sheet-copper to the Royal African Company or the East India Company, and he was particularly pleased when the latter made a purchase for it had a reputation of prompt payment.[53] In general, however, Hamburg's copper products were carrying a premium over foreign wares even in Hamburg itself, and it is not surprising that by November 1678 the Royal African Company was expressing a preference for cheaper and genuine 'Hungary' sheet-copper at 59 *RD* per slb over Hamburg-manufactured sheet at $62\frac{1}{2}$ to 64 *RD*.[54] To make matters worse, there was a suspicion abroad that Hamburg's 'Hungary' plates were embodying inferior material imported from north Africa. Jacob David referred to the rumour in September 1676 and Tomloo incautiously confirmed it in November by inquiring after the availability of 'Barbary' or Angola copper in London.[55] Although Tomloo indignantly repudiated the charge of using 'Barbary' copper Lubers himself sneered at Tomloo's copper-sheets, confiding that they were an inferior product made in Braunschweig.[56]

The Scanian war did not, therefore, uniquely favour Sweden's closest competitor and the Hamburgers had to learn what the Swedes already knew—'dat de messing een coopmanschap is die met menagie moet gehandelt worden'.[57]

This was all the more true now that Willem Momma had virtually collapsed as the strongest independent manufacturer of brass and copper goods. In 1674 he had provided nearly two-thirds of Leonora's copper supplies, which were at a very high level, but the settlement of his debts under royal protection required him to work for his creditors and it was their competing claims which now created some confusion in the Swedish market [**234, 287, 328**]. David van Baerle thought he could contract for all 1,200 slb of Momma's annual output but soon found that he had been out-bid by I. Cronström and Van Cöllen & Uppendorff [**339**]. Uppendorff eventually emerged as the principal victor and by July 1677

[49] A. von Brandt, 'Seehandel zwischen Schweden und Lübeck gegen Ende des 17 Jahrhunderts', *Scandia* (1947) pp. 47–8, 55, 61–3.

[50] O. & N. Törne to JD, 17 January 1678.

[51] C. Lubers to same, 23 August 1678.

[52] Same to same, 8 March, 18 October 1678 [**426**].

[53] Same to same, 25 May, 7 June, 30 July, 23 August, 18 October, 8 November 1678.

[54] Same to same, 8 November 1678.

[55] RA, Stockholm, E.2503, JD to Jacob Reenstierna, 26 September 1676; J. Tomloo to JD, 3 November 1676. North Africa was to become the dominant source of London's copper imports in the 1690s—see Åström, *From Stockholm to St Petersburg*, Appendix I, p. 120.

[56] J. Tomloo to JD, 11 June 1678; C. Lubers to same, 22 July 1678. For an analysis of Braunschweig's copper quality see Peltzer, 'Geschichte der Messingindustrie', p. 254 n. 4.

[57] D. van Baerle, 2 April 1677 [**366**].

he was in a position to offer David a two- or three-year contract for 5,000 coils of brass-wire per annum at a fixed price of £6 per cwt.[58] Nothing actually came of this and Uppendorff provided only $4\frac{1}{2}$ per cent of David's copper in 1677 and less than 2 per cent in 1678. There was in general a large gap between the promises of the Swedish principals and their actual performance. Only Jacob Reenstierna offered little and kept his word, sending copper-wire merely to finance his two sons (Isaac and Jacob) on the Grand Tour with their tutor. A fire in his works in 1677 which destroyed two furnaces and two wire-mills was taken philosophically:[59] he was not greatly interested in competing in the overcrowded London market, although David was urging him to take advantage of rising demand and send more. He claimed to have cornered the market in copper-wire and to be pushing its price slowly towards £6 15s or £7 per cwt.[60] but as Willem Momma had found, such assurances had often proved unreliable and Jacob declined to be impressed.

Analysis of his ledger certainly indicates that David was buying up copper-wire from other London dealers, particularly in the winter of 1675–6 when the price had begun to sag below £6 per cwt. He again bought heavily between March and September 1678 when the price was as high as £6 10s, only to see it slide below £5 18s to £5 15s in October. David's regular clientele for copper-wire numbered eighteen, five of whom took nearly two-thirds of his domestic sales.[61] But when obliged to buy up copper-wire he was able to find at least thirteen different dealers holding stocks. It therefore seems highly improbable that he could achieve the kind of domestic monopoly which he claimed.

Yet although London proved a disappointing and sometimes exasperating market in which to deal it retained certain attractions for even the most cynical Swede, for it was somewhat less susceptible to rival supplies and nearly as responsive to external demand as Hamburg or Amsterdam. Her re-export requirements for Africa or the Far East were not negligible and until 1678 her neutrality gave her privileged access to France. French demand for copper was, indeed, to provide a recurrent lift to London prices between 1676 and 1678 and it was reported in December 1676 that the re-export of a mere 1,000 coils to Rouen had lifted the London price from £6 to £6 4s per cwt in a fortnight.[62] Not surprisingly, copper-ware exports to Rouen were to form the largest sector of Jacob David's traffic with France between 1675 and 1678.[63]

Yet, at first sight, a superficial comparison of the movements in copper-wire prices in Stockholm and London suggests a disparity of demand between the two which could not be adequately bridged by English re-exports. While Swedish prices soared English ones remained sluggish and unresponsive. But the comparison is inappropriate and ignores the fact that, unlike iron, Sweden's copper was both a commodity and a component of currency. Not for the first time in Swedish history the latter role was proving harmful to the former, although throughout the 1660s the minting of copper currency had been deliberately restrained and between 1666 and 1672 averaged less than 11 per cent of total output.[64] But although refined-copper output rose to higher levels between 1673 and 1679 the demands of state finance helped to push up the proportion devoted to coinage from 25 per cent in 1673 to

[58] L. Uppendorff to JD, 28 July 1677.
[59] J. Reenstierna to JD, 22 July 1677.
[60] RA, Stockholm, E.2503, JD to Jacob Reenstierna, 29 June 1677, 29 January, 15 February 1678.
[61] The leading five were William Wathing (25.6 per cent), Richard Woodfield (15.7 per cent), Elizabeth Packer (9.7 per cent), John Bryan (7.7 per cent) all of London, and John Cromwell of Gloucester (7.1 per cent).
[62] Van Baerles to JD, 15 December 1676.
[63] See pp. 184–9.
[64] J. Wolontis, *Kopparmyntningen i Sverige, 1624–1714*, pp. 138–47.

63 per cent in 1674, 83 per cent in 1675 and 79 per cent in 1676.[65] Nearly two-thirds of the mint's supplies came from those private copper-dealers who might otherwise have fed the manufacturing sector. It is to this circumstance that David van Baerle refers in his letters of 4 April and 5 September 1676 [**287, 309**]. Its effect was, as he notes, to make silver (and gold) appreciate in terms of copper and the apparent rise in copper prices (expressed in units of copper-dollars) can be attributed to this for when deflated by the changing ratio of the silver specie rixdollar to the copper dollar it wholly disappears. Between the autumn of 1664 and the spring of 1674 the specie rixdollar:copper dollar ratio had remained stable at 1 RD:$5\frac{1}{4}$ d.c.m. It then began to change with almost every month of war.[66] Hendrik Cletcher can be less easily forgiven for quoting the old rate in January 1676, when it had actually reached 6 d.c.m., than W. Momma for giving it as $6\frac{1}{2}$ d.c.m. in December 1677. It was by then $6\frac{3}{4}$ d.c.m. as Uppendorff correctly reported, and it remained there until March 1681.[67]

Two other monetary burdens weighed heavily on David's copper suppliers. One was the higher rate of duty payable in Sweden on exports in 'unfree' English ships, for even when the flat-rate increase of 16 d.s.m. $29\frac{5}{6}$ öre of April 1672 was removed in January 1673 the disparity between the rate on 'free' Swedish ships and unfree English ones remained 50 per cent.[68] This was a premium which the exporters found hard to bear in the context of falling real prices and an adverse rate of exchange. The latter—the second of their burdens, shared by iron and copper dealers alike—had worsened steadily throughout the war, with the value of the pound sterling rising from its pre-war 21 to 25 d.c.m. in autumn 1676, 26 d.c.m. in 1677, 27 and even 28 d.c.m. in 1679.[69] Actually, few direct Anglo–Swedish exchange transactions were made, as S. van Breda indicates, for 'de wissel wort meest op Hamburg en Amsterdam getrocken'.[70] Some of David's suppliers found it more convenient to take English goods than receive remittances, and others yearned for silver rixdollars or *pesos*,[71] but there is no evidence that David was able to gratify this demand.

Pitch and tar

Ever since Marescoe's death and the subsequent rupture of dealings with the Tar Company, pitch and tar had played a comparatively small role in the partnership's affairs. Supplies from Gothenburg and elsewhere outside the Company's jurisdiction had provided 126 lasts of pitch in 1671, and in 1672 Alexander Waddell's ambitious schemes had helped to provide pitch and tar worth £2,183 gross. But the contract for the Company's English sales for 1672–5 had gone to Samuel Sowton and John Strother and in 1675 and 1676 David was handling virtually no pitch or tar.

In 1677, however, the situation was tranformed and pitch and tar became the most important component of David's trade with Sweden and, perhaps, of his business as a whole.

[65] Wolontis, *Kopparmyntningen*, p. 306; S. Lindroth, *Gruvbrytning och kopparhantering vid Stora Kopparberget intill 1800-början*, II (Uppsala, 1955) p. 390.

[66] Wolontis, *Kopparmyntningen*, Appendix H, pp. 310–11; Appendix N, pp. 320–1.

[67] H. Cletcher to JD, 8 January 1676; W. Momma to same, 3 December 1677; L. Uppendorff to same, 27 November 1677.

[68] Wolontis, *Kopparmyntningen*, Appendix E, p. 245; PRO, SP. 95/9 ff. 116–17, 168.

[69] H. Cletcher to same, 9 November 1675, 9 June 1677, 23 May 1679; Van Cöllen & Uppendorff to same, 11 September 1677; PRO, SP. 95/11 f. 23 (W. Allestree, 'Some reflections upon England's trade with Sweden anno 1677').

[70] S. van Breda to JD, 24 December 1677; cf. Åström, *From Cloth to Iron*, pp. 86, 91, 97–109.

[71] D. van Baerle to JD, 4 November 1675 [**271**]; Van Cöllen & Uppenforff to same, 27 November 1677; H. Bowman to same, 18 May 1677; H. Gerdes to same, 15 July 1679.

It owed this significance not merely to its value or volume, though these were substantial enough, but to the heightened strategic and diplomatic importance which Swedish pitch and tar had acquired since the 1660s. Jacob David's new role, as exclusive agent for the Tar Company's English sales, was now a matter of state concern.

Why this should have been so for David, rather than for Marescoe's similar role in the 1660s, is not easy to explain concisely but among the factors to be taken into account is the development of a more ambitious Anglo–Swedish commercial policy. The agreement between the two powers in April 1672 and the treaty of September 1674 envisaged much closer co-operation between them at the expense of the United Provinces than had been attained in the 1660s, and although a detailed commercial treaty was deferred much thought was given to the feasibility of an English monopoly of Sweden's pitch and tar exports.[72] Sir Henry Coventry, while in Stockholm in 1672, estimated the cost at a mere £20,000, but in a well-informed and detailed paper on the pitch and tar trade William Allestree put the figure more realistically at £35,000.[73] Holland, he estimated, had stocks of some 2,000 lasts (half their usual reserve) but England had only 600 lasts, which was less than half its annual requirement, and there was thus much to be gained, strategically and financially, by cornering the remaining 6,000 lasts in Sweden. A dissenting argument was presented by Joseph Verden on the basis of his purchasing mission to Stockholm in early 1672.[74] He put the cost of engrossing Sweden's annual exports at £39,600 and he shrewdly predicted that the Dutch 'would doggedly look for supplies elsewhere' in Norway or Archangel if shut out from Sweden. Indeed, if England's interests lay in the maintenance of a Swedish pitch and tar industry it would not pay to drive the Dutch to extremities.

In the event, England's requirements for the third Anglo–Dutch war were covered partly by James Semple's privilege and partly by the Tar Company's three-year contract with Sowton and Strother for 1,200 lasts of tar and 200 of pitch annually for 1673–5. It was not until 1677 that problems began to arise with the failure of leading English merchants to take up the challenge of a new 3-year contract. The situation was expressively summarized by Sir Edward Wood in July 1677:

'The pitch & Tarr Company last winter offered the pr'emption of that Comodity to some of our factors here, They not having a sufficient Capital of their own, nor time to advise their principalls (letters being stopt) durst not venture upon it. Then the Company offered it to the Hollanders, who agreed with them, & as our Marchants tell me advanced 5000ˡ. This agreement was basely concealed from us, till some of our shipps were unloaded & then wee asking pitch & Tarr to freight them, were totally refused, so that many will returne only with their Ballast, of this I went & complained to the Treasurer but he favoured the Company. This Company has in London Jacob Davies for their ffactor to whome they p'tend to send as much pitch & Tarr as will serve Engl. Ireland & Scotland And two ffactors in Amsterdam, to whome they assigne the rest, to serve all other parts that want, and there to be their Magazine. I doe not find Mr Davis will freight any of our supply ships here, or whether he will send any of his own, but I hope he gives assurance, that his Ma'ties dominions shall be furnished this yeare with at least 1000 lasts.'

Thus, despite the reassuring anglicization of Jacob David's name, the deal to which he was a party was seen as trebly disadvantageous: it was Dutch-financed, it precluded English shipping and it contained no guarantee of regular strategic supplies. In the context of

[72] The best account of these relations is in Åström, *From Stockholm to St Petersburg*, pp. 30–44.
[73] PRO, SP. 95/8 ff. 73, 147.
[74] Coventry MSS, Longleat, Vol. 64 f. 35; Åström, *From Stockholm to St Petersburg*, pp. 83–4.

England's naval rearmament programme for thirty new ships this was of profoundly serious concern in 1677.[75]

The economic costs were also significant and were cogently discussed by Allestree in another of his reviews—'Some reflections upon England's Trade with Sweden, anno 1677'.[76] The Tar Company 'pretends' to have contracted to supply 'Mr Davis' with sufficient stocks for England's needs in English ships, but they were insisting on offering freight-rates no higher than £2 per last. Most English shippers found this unacceptably low and were returning home in ballast. As a result, there was a loss of 'invisible' earnings, a loss of customs revenue and a pressure of demand for return cargoes of iron which had forced Swedish prices 20 per cent above the level at which English importers could hope to profit. Behind these adverse developments English merchants suspected the malice of the Dutch, for the extent of Dutch influence among the directorate of the Tar Company was notorious.

This was an allegation which Sir Edward Wood could soon confirm, for he found himself strongly opposed by 'the Tarr Company and the Hollanders in conjunction' in his efforts to get an explicit guarantee that England's naval requirements would be met.[77] On this he received oral assurance from the Swedish senate, but a year later he was again forced to protest to the Swedish Chancellor at the Tar Company's deliberate boycott of English vessels. 'It is true wee got some in the Spring when no Hollanders were here, but now that they have 14 or 15 Ships in Port they gett all & wee not a Barrell. He said it was ill done of the Companie, that he would speake about it.'[78]

Disappointingly, there is not the slightest indication in David's surviving correspondence that he or his associates were intent upon an international conspiracy or were even aware of these conflicts of strategic interests. The overtures which led to his acquisition of the agency began innocently enough on the initiative of Steven de Geer. On 1 May 1676 De Geer asked David to help secure settlement of bills due to Sowton in London. The drawer was the Tar Company's representative in Amsterdam, Philip Botte, who introduced himself to David in a covering letter [284]. David duly obliged and by 12 May it is apparent that he had proffered his services to Botte and the Tar Company. Botte reciprocated, asking for a detailed report on the English market for pitch and tar, freight costs, port charges, warehousing rents and conditions of sale. David's subsequent reply was encouraging enough to provide Botte with the basis for an agreement which, he was sure, the Tar Company would accept.[79]

However, nearly a year elapsed before anything came of these overtures, and Botte's formal offer of 13 April 1677 appears to have arrived out of the blue [347]. Its heavy emphasis on complete secrecy seems no more than a natural business discretion, and the detailed terms for David's agency, set out on 10 August, contain nothing out of the ordinary [361]. Earlier, in a letter of 16 July, Botte had put the annual allocation for England at 1,000 lasts of tar and 200 of pitch—the standard amount in this and the preceding decade, based on experience and a realistic assessment of demand. Like Marescoe, Jacob David did some elementary market research and his request for an allocation to Hull of 80 lasts of pitch and 100 of tar was clearly based on William Skinner's report of 19 May. David had received discouraging advice from Ellison in Newcastle; Isaac Tillard at Plymouth put its requirements at no more than 100 barrels of tar and 50 of pitch, and Caulier of Yarmouth saw little scope for competing with cheap supplies from Pillau or Norway.[80] Although David Dorville of Bristol put his city's

[75] Coventry MSS, Longleat, Vol. 66 f. 488; PRO SP. 95/10 f. 257.
[76] PRO, SP. 95/11 ff. 17–31.
[77] Coventry MSS, Longleat, Vol. 66 f. 498 (21 August 1677).
[78] Ibid. f. 585 (20 October 1678).
[79] P. Botte to JD, 19 June 1676.
[80] R. Ellison to same, 19 May; I. Tillard to same, 18 May [348]; P. Caulier to same, 18 May 1677.

annual consumption at 1,200 barrels of pitch and 1,500 of tar [**349**], adequate supplies were expected in a few months time. It was therefore a matter of legitimate concern for David that the Tar Company should exercise the strictest possible control under its charter to restrain any extra-contractual shipments to England, but Botte's reply of 14 September [**367**], which was quite unhelpful, does not suggest that he or the Company's directorate were seriously concerned to impede England's supply of this strategically vital commodity. Indeed, as Botte's marketing strategy evolved over the next few months it became apparent that he was willing to hold large stocks in London warehouses, partly as a reserve in the event of an Anglo–French war and partly as a means of regulating the Amsterdam market. When required, pitch and tar could be sent from London to the United Provinces; they could not be sent from the United Provinces to London. Thanks to the Navigation Acts David was thus assured of a role as entrepôt manager of stocks which totalled 951 lasts of tar and 377 lasts of pitch by December 1678. Far from sacrificing the interests of English consumers to the Dutch, Botte appeared anxious to ensure that both markets were sustained in equilibrium— though, of course, this would be at as high a price level as possible. Responding to David's complaint that Dutch stocks might prejudice English re-export prospects, Botte assured him that he had secured a minimum-price guarantee from the tar-buyers in Holland, to last for one year. No Stockholm tar would be un-shipped for less than ƒ.114 per last and none delivered from a warehouse for less than ƒ.118.[81] By December 1678 the surprising position had been reached where—Botte alleged—there were only 50 to 150 lasts of pitch remaining available in Amsterdam: supplies would now have to be drawn from London.[82]

Botte's solicitude for the English market was in no way altruistic. He wanted large returns, which—given the ceiling on volume sales—meant high prices and low operating costs. His terms of 10 August had set minimum target prices of £15 per last on pitch and £11 on tar. These were soon modified, to £14½–£15 and £10½–£11 on 17 August, and to 10s less on 31 August. David's first sales at £13¾ and £9½ for pitch and tar respectively were rejected as too low and it was not until October that David could obtain the prices Botte had set. Credit terms were also closely watched. Botte had stipulated 3 months credit as the maximum, and he only grudgingly allowed 4 months. When David advised him that only four or five tar-buyers had reliable credit he insisted on knowing their names [**367**], but was aghast to learn later that David was extending credit worth £800–£1,500 to some of these favoured few. No one in Amsterdam extended more than £500 or £600 credit (he claimed) and he insisted that David should stick to such a limit.[83]

However, the crucial component in his operating costs was the freight-rate, which could absorb between 20 and 30 per cent of a cargo's gross sale. It was essential to keep it at the lower limit and on this Botte took a characteristically firm stand. He was looking for a Stockholm–London rate of £2 per last and a Viborg–London rate of £3. In 1677 he had mixed success, procuring ten ships from Stockholm, half of which were at £2 and half at £3 per last. One Viborg ship accepted £2 10s. More would have been employed had enough English vessels been available, but by late October they were not and Botte was left with 22 per cent of his pitch and 23.5 per cent of his tar stuck in the Baltic.[84] In 1678 he therefore sought David's co-operation in finding 600 lasts of shipping-capacity for Stockholm and 450 lasts for Viborg, at an average of £3 per last. His response to the news that no English shipper would accept less than £4 per last was predictable if unrealistic [cf. **386**, **387**], and at the end

[81] P. Botte to same, 19 June 1676.
[82] Same to same, 6 December 1678.
[83] Same to same, 26 July 1678.
[84] Same to same, 24 October 1677.

of the day Botte succeeded in assembling enough vessels which left via Amsterdam in company with 25 others in his employ on 9 May. By the end of 1678 thirteen ships had brought David pitch and tar on Botte's account—nine from Stockholm, three from Viborg (and one of unknown origin). They brought over 1,300 lasts, most of which went straight into the two large warehouses David had rented at Blackwall and Cuckold's Point. The insurance of these valuable stocks was placed partly in Amsterdam and partly in London for neither centre was prepared on its own to cover the £10,000 which was at stake.[85] However, the significant point about these supplies is that, with one Irish exception, all the ships employed in 1677 and 1678 were English, freely chartered at rates which, though below £4, were higher than the £2 alleged in the diplomatic complaints.

The dangers of which Sir Edward Wood and Allestree had warned in 1677 do not appear to have materialized to any extent until 1679, and then for reasons outside David's or Botte's control. The latter's two-year contract with the Tar Company came to an end and the Company itself faced the imminent revocation of its charter.[86] It had been living on borrowed time since its re-foundation in 1672, sustained only by loans to the government and an agreement to pay higher customs duties. Now, under pressure from the Dutch negotiators at Nijmegen and rival domestic interests, Charles XI willingly enough moved towards a cancellation of its privileges which was finally announced in October 1680, to take effect from November 1682.[87] In this intervening period of uncertainty the equilibrium Botte had sought for quickly dissolved. Prices collapsed in London. David professed himself unable to get more than £8 per last for tar or £12 per last for pitch, and Botte threatened to transfer all the stocks to Amsterdam.[88] In Stockholm, meanwhile, there was no pitch or tar left for English shippers by September 1679—too much had gone to Holland, where the price also collapsed. English shippers, desperate for return freights, were now willing to take iron, or anything else, at £2, £1 15s or even £1 10s per last. Observing the scene, Steven de Geer summed up in his idiosyncratic French—'Botte aura fait un movais coup' [**456**].

There were evidently others who were willing to take Botte's place—Laurens Uppendorff and Claes Wilkens among them [**409, 463**]. The former revealed an awareness of England's strategic priorities which is quite lacking in Botte's letters, but it is nonetheless impossible to see the David–Botte alliance in any sinister light, prejudicial to English interests. It was a business gamble which seems to have failed, and David was left fending off Botte's desperate demands for extended credit. He countered by despatching 132 lasts of pitch and 76 of tar to Amsterdam—not to Botte but to the Van Baerles, who were to sell them off and meet Botte's bills with the proceeds. Characteristically, the Van Baerles did a good job, selling the bulk of the pitch and all of the tar to the East India Company chambers of Zeeland and Holland.[89]

David appears to have received no more pitch or tar in 1679, but he had done comparatively well out of his two years as Botte's agent, earning £657 5s 8d in commission, brokerage and interest on goods worth about £19,000. This compares favourably with his earnings from his two largest Swedish customers, W. Momma and S. de Geer. From the former, he and Leonora had gained £1,360 since 1673, of which 55 per cent represented interest on advances. For De Geer the comparable figure was £1,426, of which 47 per cent was interest. Between them, these two seem to have accounted for the largest portion of the

[85] David placed £5,500 at 3 per cent with eleven insurers; Botte secured cover for f. 62,700 at 2¼ per cent.
[86] Hallberg, 'Tjärexport och tjärhandelskompanier', pp. 126–8.
[87] Ibid. p. 128 n. 2.
[88] P. Botte to JD, 3 November, 28 November 1679.
[89] H. van Baerle to same, 18 July, 1 September 1679.

firm's earnings on commission, although it is impossible to establish the exact figure, for unlike his predecessors David did not maintain a separate 'commission' account. However, it is clear that David did less well as an independent dealer in import commodities for although he bought in huge amounts of copper and iron to sell on his own account the profits made between 1675 and 1679 in no way match those of Marescoe in the 1660s. Four separate accounts[90] tell the story:

		Sales			Profit			%
		£	s	d	£	s	d	
[i]	*Diverse goederen* (a joint iron and copper account, September 1673 to October 1674)	9,511	11	7	£158	14	8	1.67
[ii]	*Goederen aen mij aengaende* (a joint iron and copper account, August 1674 to September 1675)	14,826	8	3	£ 51	6	2	0.35
[iii]	*Ijser* (Iron Account, August 1675 to September 1677)	6,922	9	10	£ 46	3	2	0.66
[iv]	*Cooperdraet* (copperwire account, August 1675 to August 1679)	33,488	7	9	£412	11	2	1.23

David had not been lucky enough to experience the conjunctures of 1665 and 1666, when large stocks and soaring prices had brought huge profits to Marescoe's own account, but he cannot be accused of timidity for his ventures in the domestic market were substantial, if ill-judged. It remains to see if his export ventures were better timed.

(ii) EXPORTS

[a] SWEDEN

The successive partnerships' traffic with Sweden had always been a conspicuously one-way affair, and they had rarely participated in the very modest volume of exports or re-exports which England had directed there. Its exact scale cannot be ascertained but the 'Book of Tables' puts the value of London's share of exports to Sweden at a mere £6,213 10s in 1662–3 and at £7,801 in 1668–9, with woollen manufactures acounting for about three-quarters of this.[91] Re-exports, not recorded in the Book of Tables, almost certainly included tobacco and sugar but the English were easily eclipsed by the Dutch as the carriers of Sweden's principal imports—salt and wine.[92]

Such commissions as Marescoe or David received from their Swedish customers were often trivial, personal requests for small luxury items such as watches, tableware, furniture, saddles, waistcoats, stockings, etc. Willem Momma sought pig bristles and yellow ochre for the Swedish Court painter; Jean Boor asked for two English mastiffs.[93] Yet, in every other year there were some more substantial commissions—for sugar and coals in 1666, for tobacco

[90] Ledger, 1673–9 [i] f. 46; [ii] f. 144; [iii] ff. 105, 128; [iv] ff. 143, 183, 194, 246.
[91] BL, Add. MSS, 36, 785.
[92] Åström, *From Cloth to Iron*, pp. 57–8, 67–8.
[93] W. Momma to CM, 31 May, 26 July 1668; J. Boor to JD, 9 April 1679.

and malt in 1668; for sugar again in 1672 and in 1675 a substantial order of gunpowder.[94] The unique circumstances of the Scanian war brought a whole series of commissions for salt, wine and corn, and although most of these proved abortive or disastrous, 1678 saw David dealing in quite large amounts of cloth, partly on his clients' account and partly on his own.[95]

The initiative came from Sweden, for—as Sir Edward Wood and William Allestree reported in November 1676—there was a large unsatisfied demand for English cloth which was expected to produce substantial supplies the following spring.[96] Letters from Thomas Perman and Oloff & Nicolas Törne illustrate that demand [**340**]. Both firms, which were closely associated,[97] were evidently knowledgeable importers and knew exactly where to direct David for his supplies. They named Thomas Wilson of Leeds, an experienced cloth merchant for whose integrity William Skinner was ready to vouch.[98] Skinner's own son, William (Jr.) was resident in Leeds as a factor, and the purchase and shipment of Oloff Törne's consignment to Stockholm via Hull was left in their capable hands. A letter from Wilson of July 1677 indicates that he believed there were certain obstacles in the path of David's direct participation in this traffic, for he was a foreigner and a 'stranger'—i.e. not free of the Eastland Company. In fact, Jacob David's naturalization bill had just received royal assent in April 1677,[99] and—as Wilson admitted—the Eastland Company was now virtually impotent, but the 'jealousies' to which Wilson's letter darkly alludes may well have inhibited David's more active role as a cloth exporter until 1678. Thomas Perman's important order for the Swedish Queen Mother's livery [**393**] was very specific and left David with little discretion, but the extent of his failure to satisfy Perman suggests that he was totally out of his depth in this exacting branch of trade, for all the shoddy goods Perman complained of seem to have been purchased by David himself in London. Between 29 April and 13 June he had made twenty-two small purchases from eighteen separate dealers—a costly, inefficient and perhaps furtive way of proceeding—without reference to his more knowledgeable brother-in-law, Sir John Lethieullier. The result was evidently disastrous and produced one of the most richly abusive letters in the whole collection [**425**].

David could afford to shrug this off for the basis of his agreement with Perman was a peculiarly favourable one, extracted by the exigencies of Swedish needs. It assured him of 12 per cent profit on his London consignment and 14 per cent on those from Hull. Later, he was guaranteed 15 per cent. Oloff Törne was less tractable and objected strongly to the exorbitance of David's charges when his parcel of serges, kerseys, dozens and stockings arrived in November 1678 [**429**]. Comparing David's business conduct unfavourably with that of his Dutch suppliers he was reluctant to continue on this basis and although he did place a further order for shirts and stockings in 1679 his friend, Perman, quietly withdrew. Stockholm fashions changed every three months, explained Perman, and by the time his commissioned goods reached him the whims of demand had moved on. On no account was David to send more.[100]

---

[94] LM & JD supplied 950 barrels of gunpowder to Antony Bruyn of Stockholm in April 1675, valued at £2,612 10s. No letters survive to illustrate this commission but JD received further inquiries from Bruyn for saltpetre and gunpowder—27 October 1676 and 15 February 1677.

[95] At a total value of £2,016 9s (f.o.b.), these textiles would have represented a very large share of Anglo-Swedish trade in normal circumstances, but in 1676 they were part of an estimated five-fold increase in cloth exports—Åström, *From Cloth to Iron*, p. 74.

[96] PRO, SP. 95/10 f. 149 (Sir Edward Wood to Sir H. Coventry, 27 November 1676).

[97] Åström, *From Cloth to Iron*, pp. 144–5 n. 101.

[98] W. Skinner to JD, 26 June 1677.

[99] Historical Manuscripts Commission, 9th Report, Appendix (House of Lords MSS) p. 95a.

[100] T. Perman to JD, 3 November, 11 November, 22 November 1679.

This was a tactful rebuff. Events were less kind to David's other ventures. In 1677, urged on by I. Cronström, W. Momma, F. Krantz and S. de Geer he had finally agreed to share in the latter's plan to freight Setubal salt in English shipping. As a long letter from De Geer of 5 January indicated, he had seen a chance to profit from the interval before the cheap, numerous but more cautious Dutch finally set off in their seasonal convoy for Stockholm. If an English ship could get there first and if return cargoes were ready and waiting the round trip to London should yield a profit, even at a freight-rate of £6 10s per last. In the event, the cheapest rate David could get was £7, offered by his wife's kinsman Peter Caulier as if it were a favour.[101] Admittedly, John Garret's *Concordia* was a new ship, fast and well-found, but its employment seems to have ensured the failure of the venture, for while the purchase of 470 *moys*[102] of Setubal salt cost a mere £289 16s with all charges the freight of these 2,272½ barrels (at 18 per last) amounted to £883 11s. Reaching Stockholm in early June the salt found a depressed, not a hungry, market and H. Cletcher, to whom its sale was entrusted, reported competition from some 14,000 other barrels which were selling at only 10 d.c.m. per barrel.[103] He thought he had done well to sell 2,000 of De Geer's at 10¾ d.c.m., but these were to prove the lowest prices recorded by David's correspondents in the years 1675–8. Although Setubal salt did not again reach the panic prices of October 1675 (when it stood at 18–19 d.c.m.) it regularly exhibited a rise in the late summer when the Finnish tar ships were loading return cargoes, and in early October, when the demand from the Michaelmas fair worked through.[104] Even the arrival of Dutch latecomers did not push the 1677 price again below 12 d.c.m.

Thus, at the high rate of exchange of 27 d.c.m. per £1 sterling, Cletcher's net proceeds at 16,143 d.c.m. left David carrying a loss which he put at £102 12s 2d.[105] It would have been far worse but for Garret's employment with return cargoes of iron and copper worth some £650 in freight, but another of his joint ventures of 1677 offered no such consolation. This was a one-sixth share in wine purchased, under De Geer's direction, at Bordeaux. It reached Stockholm in mid-July 1677 to find the capital glutted with enough wine for two years consumption, and much of it was to remain unsaleable (and undrinkable) on Cletcher's hands. 'The English' he explained, 'have scandalously undersold their wine' and the glut would continue into 1679.[106]

The fact that David found it worth his while to enter the Eastland Company in 1682[107] not only confirms that he continued active trading after the commencement of his suit with Frederick and the impounding of these documents but proves that he chose to continue in this sector of Anglo–Swedish trade. In 1685 he was still among the larger London merchants dealing in Baltic imports and exports.[108] Evidently the disappointments of 1677 and 1678 did not deflect him from renewed ventures of the kind to which he was invited in 1679. Jan Boor suggested that he should send grains and Abraham Wolters repeatedly specified

[101] P. Caulier to JD, 8 January 1677.
[102] The Lisbon *moy* was equivalent to one-quarter of a last—H. Doursther, *Dictionnaire des poids et mesures anciens* (Brussels, 1840) pp. 196, 204.
[103] H. Cletcher to JD, 20 June 1677. According to a contemporary English estimate Sweden required 30,000 lasts of salt p.a.—Åström, *From Cloth to Iron*, p. 65.
[104] J. Boor to JD, 19 May, 6 October 1677.
[105] According to JD's own figures (Ledger, 1673–9 f. 209) the loss should be £112 12s.
[106] H. Cletcher to JD, 15 February 1678.
[107] Hinton, *The Eastland Trade*, p. 224.
[108] Åström, *From Cloth to Iron*, p. 235.

malt.[109] Wolters, who claimed to be holding two-thirds of Stockholm's salt stocks in January 1680, was a persuasive solicitor for this and other English commodities, while at the same time being a sharp critic of English business practices. He was particularly contemptuous of the English community in Stockholm, numbering some thirty.[110] They were inexperienced young idlers who spend 'whole days in wine- and tobacco-houses (which are very expensive here) so that I am not a little surprised that you people do not employ some honourable man who lives here, is temperate and understands business'.[111] In fact, David had just sent a young apprentice, John Gosselin, to watch his interests in Stockholm but he is unlikely to have earned his keep. The boom years of Anglo–Swedish trade were over for the moment. With the peace settlements of 1679 and the Dutch conclusion of a very favourable commercial treaty with Sweden, England's unique opportunities had slipped away. Subsequent diplomatic overtures to consolidate the trading relationship of the war years were ineffectual, and although England's share in Sweden's trade and that of the Baltic never fell back to the meagre levels of the mid-seventeenth century, 1679–80 marks the end of an epoch.[112]

[b] HAMBURG

As the export correspondence from Sweden has indicated, Hamburg was not immune to the wars which raged around her, for her neutrality could not protect her from hostile pressure by land and by sea. Menaced by Denmark, her shipping was molested by Brandenburg and blockaded by the French. In 1679 she faced a serious prospect of siege. But, through all this, the imperial posts continued to run and as a result the Hamburg correspondence for these years seems unflawed by loss or interruption. Leonora and Jacob David received over one thousand letters from Hamburg between January 1675 and March 1680, the bulk of them from a handful of loyal clients.[113]

Claus Bene, who had served the Berenbergs for eight years [**314**], now emerged as David's principal customer, writing nearly one-quarter of the letters and receiving over 36 per cent of the goods sent between 1674 and 1678. His former employers were quite eclipsed, for neither the widow nor her son Paul chose to write to order very much in these years of depression, although their kinsman, François Bostelman, maintained a lively correspondence and commissioned 19 per cent of David's consignments. Egidio Ruland, with 17 per cent of the letters in which bills of exchange figure more largely than goods, also kept up an unbroken dialogue with London. Another veteran of the 1660s was J. A. Fonck, narrowly preoccupied with his linen exports but still holding out the promise of large import commissions (which were never realized) [**244, 268**].

There were losses of old clients, notably of Peter Juncker who, with two unsaleable bales of the London firm's silk on his hands, ceased to correspond after 1675. Arnold Ruland likewise faded away, but several newcomers took their places, notably the firm of Wentzhard

[109] J. Boor to JD, 9 April 1679; A. Wolters to JD, 19 June [**450**], 23 July, 23 August [**461**], 1 November 1679 [**468**], 28 January 1680.
[110] PRO, SP. 95/9 f. 240 (Sir E. Wood to Sir H. Coventry, [?] December 1675); Åström, *From Cloth to Iron*, pp. 122–3, 139–41.
[111] A. Wolters to JD, 27 December 1679 [**473**].
[112] Åström, *From Stockholm to St Petersburg*, pp. 34–44; *From Cloth to Iron*, p. 66.
[113] Of the 1,009 letters received from Hamburg, C. Bene wrote 234, E. Ruland 171, Wentzhard & Ployart 126, F. Bostelman 114, the Berenbergs 64 and J. A. Fonck 46. Their distribution over these years was: 1675 = 186; 1676 = 164; 1677 = 194; 1678 = 209; 1679 = 209; 1680 = 47.

& Ployart, specializing in textiles and clothing. Introducing themselves in November 1675, they commenced an active pursuit of English serges, stockings and gloves which resulted in orders totalling nearly 12 per cent of David's Hamburg consignments up to 1679. Another promising newcomer was young David Geysmer, formerly book-keeper to Egidio Ruland and not yet a burgher, but a shrewd and earnest correspondent who emerged in 1679 [**451**]. His was a more successful entrée to trade than that of five or six others who introduced themselves as willing correspondents, only to be snubbed or discouraged by David's response.

Discouragement, verging on despair, is indeed the keynote of this Hamburg correspondence, for David's clients faced an unfavourable combination of circumstances which seemed to make profitable commerce impossible. The major factor was a lack of domestic German demand which, it was grimly recognized, would last as long as the neighbouring wars continued. Significant portions of the hinterland which Hamburg served were directly or indirectly affected, and its capacity to re-export to more distant markets was seriously impaired. All this seems to have contributed to a stifling of demand for those goods in which David's correspondents had usually specialized, and their letters refer repeatedly to unsold stocks. Aleppo galls, bought two years before, still glutted Hamburg in 1675; Barbados sugar hung on their hands in 1676, and in 1677 there was thought to be enough ginger to last for another three years. Premature hopes of a general peace in 1678 brought a general glut, and in February 1679 Fonck was to complain of pepper, unsaleable for three years.

Such demand as there was—and orders were intermittently placed for cardamon, cottons, galls, ginger, indigo, logwood and silk—ran up against an adverse rate of exchange with her principal supplier. The value of the pound sterling rose from its comparative low of under 32s flem. in early 1675 to a plateau of 34s 8g in 1677—a rise of more than 8 per cent which cut away at already diminished profit margins. London prices showed no inclination to adjust to Hamburg's difficulties, despite the untrammelled supplies which were reaching her from the West and East Indies and the Levant. David's letters did not fail to report every promising arrival, and there were strong temptations as London prices momentarily sagged, but again and again the Hamburgers found themselves baffled by a sudden rebound to higher levels, beyond their reach. Approximately two commissions in every three they placed were either cancelled in alarm or proved unperformable within the limits prescribed.

For all its bulk, this is therefore a correspondence generally marked by much frustration and sterility in which the will to trade was rarely matched by the performance. But there are interesting differences in the responses of David's clients, differences founded as much on temperament and talent as on capital resources and established customer-networks. The Berenbergs, for example, were consistent in their pessimism, regarding an exchange rate of 32s as already unacceptably high and refusing to trade while its rise continued. During 1675 they showed more solicitude for the despatch of young Cornelius Berenberg's sheet-music than for further supplies of goods [**239**]. In 1676 they placed no orders and in 1677 made, and cancelled, only one. Soon after the death of the widow Berenberg in November 1678, aged 74, their letters came to an end.

Bostelman showed more tenacity, but his experiences in 1675 exemplify the frustrations of these years. He ordered ginger three times and tobacco three times and all six orders he cancelled. He ordered galls three times, cancelling only once, and he ordered indigo, raising his price limit three times before cancelling, only to find that the order had been performed. He was left holding some unwanted and unsaleable Jamaican indigo, much inferior (he observed) to the quality supplied by Peter Joye. Bostelman was to remark on more than one occasion that many import commodities seemed comparatively cheaper in Hamburg than in

London, and he was not alone in attributing this to the destructive activities of Hamburg's small community of English factors which was recklessly undercutting prices by selling at a presumed loss. It was the English who undercut Ardasse silk prices (until they themselves were undercut by an enterprising 'Persian' who brought some in, overland). In July 1677 Bostelman complained that 'the English nation' was undercutting *everything*: 'how does one carry on trade under these conditions?' was the despairing question raised not only by Bostelman but by Egidio Ruland.[114]

Ruland, however, had a different solution. Although he took deliveries of silk in 1675, tobacco in 1676 and a large amount of Barbary copper in 1677, his avowed policy was that 'while the war lasts I will not burden myself with goods'. To this extent he shared the Berenbergs' caution, but unlike them he was not intimidated by the adverse rate of exchange. Rather, he rejoiced in it, finding in the relative movements of the London and Amsterdam exchanges an opportunity for profitable adventures in arbitrage. The principal commodity which passed between David and Ruland was thus the bill of exchange—drawn and accepted not primarily as an instrument of debt settlement but as a saleable article to be put on a market where (as most correspondents observed) good bills were in short supply. How profitable this proved for Ruland cannot be known, but Jacob David's two accounts with Ruland suggest something of the margin that could be gained in London. On the one account, directed by Ruland between July 1674 and May 1679, he extracted the usual $\frac{1}{3}$ per cent commission and $\frac{1}{8}$ per cent brokerage charge. On the other, for his own account between August 1676 and February 1678, he gained £77 3s 8d gross on the exchanges, but only £23 17s 1d net after payment of charges, representing a negligible profit on transactions totalling over £8,000 (see Table 27).

The most positive response to the long depression of 1675–80 was Claus Bene's. Unlike the Berenbergs, he did not despair; unlike Ruland, he wanted goods. Bene hung tenaciously upon every rise and fall of the commodity markets, carefully matching up what London and Amsterdam had to offer with the slender opportunities open in Hamburg. His weekly letters brim with queries, instructions and information, and they are generally lacking in the self-doubt and recrimination which sours many others. Orders poured from him and, although skilfully modified or cancelled in many instances, enough were effected upon his terms to make him, by far, David's most reliable and contented customer. His interests differed little from those of his more cautious colleagues. They all discussed and ordered ginger—both the cheaper, 'brown' variety and the cleaned variety commanding double the price. They all considered Aleppo galls, though without the enthusiasm of earlier years for the London price was rising steadily. Certain commodities had completely lost favour. The long-running dispute on the merits of West Indian, as opposed to Levantine, cotton seems to have been resolved in favour of the latter. When Bene and his colleagues ordered 'cotton' they now meant either Smyrna, Cyprus or Acre cotton. All were becoming comparatively cheap in London during 1676 and 1677, falling to $5\frac{1}{2}d$ and even $4\frac{1}{2}d$ per lb., compared with the $6\frac{1}{2}d$ of 1675. By 1679 the disturbed trading conditions of the Mediterranean had helped to raise prices and expose quality differentials, with Smyrna at 6d, Acre at $6\frac{1}{2}$–$6\frac{3}{4}d$ and Cyprus at $6\frac{7}{8}$–7d per lb. By October 1679 Bene was obliged to reconsider the merits of Barbados white cotton at $7\frac{1}{4}$–$7\frac{3}{8}d$ per lb.

The other West Indian product which seems to have temporarily lost their interest was Barbados sugar. There was evidently a great deal of it in stock in Hamburg and its market was described as 'asleep' in 1675.[115] Like Marescoe, David tried to whip up fears of a

[114] E. Ruland to JD, 25 April 1679.
[115] C. Bene to LM & JD, 18 May [**235**], 23 July 1675.

TABLE 27. JD's exchange dealings with E. Ruland, 1674–1679.

	£	s	d	£	s	d
[A] Egidio Ruland 'His account' (1674–1679)				(i) *Debit*		
31 London to Hamburg remittances	4,786	3	7			
9 London to Amsterdam remittances	1,150	0	0			
2 London to Bremen remittances	200	0	0			
Total, 42 bills of exchange remitted				6,136	3	7
Goods despatched to Hamburg on his account				3,438	11	10
Charges—commission, brokerage, etc.				59	12	7
				9,634	8	0
				(ii) *Credit*		
35 Hamburg to London remittances	5,718	12	7			
15 London on Hamburg drafts	2,387	16	6			
1 Amsterdam to London remittance	225	0	0			
2 London on Amsterdam drafts	448	11	8			
3 Venice to London remittances	325	3	6			
4 Rouen to London remittances	605	2	1			
Total, 60 bills of exchange				9,710	6	4
Goods received from Hamburg				130	17	7
				9,841	3	11
[B] Egidio Ruland 'My account'						
23 London to Hamburg remittances	3,963	7	8			
1 London to Lübeck remittance	27	0	0			
Total, 24 Bills of exchange remitted				3,990	7	8
Goods despatched on my account				163	12	6
Profit on the exchanges				77	3	8
				4,231	3	10
24 Hamburg to London remittances	4,177	17	3			
Charges on bills of exchange	53	6	7			
				4,231	3	10

shortage with news of successive Caribbean hurricanes, but the Hamburgers had learned to discount their effects.[116] Instead, Egidio Ruland expressed a deep frustration about this over-abundant product by wishing that, just for one year, no more Barbados sugar would be sent so that other sugars could have their chance![117] He probably had Brazilian muscovado in mind, but there was a good deal of interest in Nevis sugar, apparently on grounds of its better quality, for Bene was prepared to pay 3 or 4 per cent more for it. It was Nevis sugar which he bought in 1675 but his large consignments of 1678 (over 800 cwt.) were from Barbados and he evidently wanted it badly for he pursued it with successively higher bids from 21*s* in June

[116] J. A. Fonck to JD, 14 December 1675 [**264**]; E. Ruland to same, 10 January 1676; Widow Berenberg to same, 10 March 1676; for the hurricanes of 1674 and 1675 see R. B. Sheridan, *Sugar and Slavery* (Barbados, 1974) p. 399.

[117] E. Ruland to JD, 1 July 1675.

to 27s per cwt. in October. This extraordinarily high figure was unjustified by any rise in Hamburg quotations, which generally remained below 6 grooten per lb. throughout these years, but it may reflect Bene's belief in an imminent Anglo–French war, with all that that would mean for West Indian trade. Only the year before, the Comte D'Estrée's expedition against the Dutch West Indies had sent speculative tremors through the Hamburg clientele.

Indigo was another commodity which was at risk if there was trouble in the Caribbean. Its London price had halved quite recently—from 5s–6s per lb. in 1671, and 4s–5s in 1672 to only 2s 3d or 4d by 1675. The quality differential between Guatemalan and West Indian products had almost disappeared in London, although it remained quite distinct in Hamburg. Bene followed its fortunes closely, from month to month, hopeful of significant falls as Guatemalan supplies reached Spain in 1675 and 1677 but disappointed by a simultaneous shortfall from Barbados. While its London price remained steady at the lower level, in Hamburg it drifted even lower to less than 5s flem. during 1678–9, at which point interest in it evaporated.

However, the Hamburgers' attention had switched to another West Indian product for which they had rarely troubled Marescoe. Bermuda tobacco was enjoying a vogue as an inferior but useful commodity, suited for blending and sale in central Europe. Breslau was the immediate destination for much of Hamburg's tobacco, according to E. Ruland, and after the departure of its consignments down the Elbe during October and November there was no real market for it until March following. Bostelman was the first to be tempted to a trial order of 4,000 lb. in June 1675 when its Hamburg price was at $7\frac{1}{2}s$ lüb. and it seemed obtainable in London at 6d. By August his enthusiasm led him to treble the order and remove the price limit, but with Hamburg's price falling to $6\frac{3}{4}s$ or $6\frac{1}{2}s$ in early September he lost his nerve, changed his mind twice, and in the panic caused by the unexpected French blockade cancelled this and all his other commissions. It was Bene who carried through a series of orders in January–February 1676 when he tried to be the first to serve the market with 3,000 lb. of Bermuda roll-tobacco. He was narrowly beaten to it but was among the first to sell at $6\frac{1}{4}s$, which (he estimated) represented 'not much above 9 per cent profit'. Just how fortunate he had been became apparent in future weeks as large supplies came in. Not 50,000 lb., as expected, but 150,000 lb. was on its way and by early June its price was down to $5\frac{1}{2}s$.

This and similar experiences taught Bene, Bostelman and Ruland that tobacco was a tricky commodity to handle. 'Tobacco' wrote the latter sententiously 'is one of those wares with which one can sometimes make a profit, but from time to time it can also produce a great loss.' 'You need good, expert knowledge with tobacco' admitted Bene, 'otherwise one gets encumbered.'[118] Evidently David's knowledge was not expert enough: his half-share in 18,233 lb. (at 6d per lb.) in 1676 and 9,261 lb. in 1678 brought a loss to him and his partner. Some of the quality was poor, a good deal of falsely manufactured tobacco appeared from England in 1677 and in 1678 a broker (whose services were evidently worth his 2 per cent commission) thought that David's Jamaican tobacco would be lucky to fetch $4\frac{1}{2}s$.[119] The Stade Elbe toll figures, which survive only for 1678 in this period, record tobacco worth 636,040 *ML* entering Hamburg by sea on non-burgher accounts—of which about 38 per cent was from England, $23\frac{1}{2}$ per cent from France, and $19\frac{1}{2}$ per cent from Portugal.[120] The

---

[118] Same to same, 25 April 1676; C. Bene to same, 24 December 1678.

[119] Same to same, 7 April 1676 [**281**]; E. Ruland to same, 11 September 1677; C. Bene to same, 22 November 1678.

[120] Cited in E. K. Newman, 'Anglo–Hamburg Trade in the Late-Seventeenth and Early Eighteenth Centuries' (unpublished doctoral dissertation) University of London (1979) p. 172, Table 32.

14 per cent recorded from Holland obviously represents only a fraction of Holland's contribution to the north German entrepôt for the bulk of it must have passed inland. David's tobacco ventures, worth roughly 2,900 *ML* in 1676, 1,800 *ML* in 1677 and 1,300 *ML* in 1678, represented a negligible proportion of English supplies and an infinitesimal element in Hamburg's total imports.

Awareness of rival sources of supply was even more acute in the case of East Indian than West Indian products. David regularly supplied advance notice of the English East India Company's spring and autumn sales, but they were generally received with some indifference. The Hamburgers were resentfully aware of the English Company's policy of price maintenance by rationing the quantities offered—particularly of pepper—and although most of them watched its price movement closely they rarely placed orders. Ruland's reaction in September 1677 [**371**] is quite typical: London's prices were too high— cheaper goods were to be had in Amsterdam, where the Dutch Company's pepper prices had reached their lowest point in the century.[121] There was a slight quickening of interest in 1678 when the prospects of European peace had brightened and its Hamburg price rose from its trough of $10\frac{1}{2}g$ in April 1678 to $14g$ by November. Bene, Bostelman, Ruland and Geysmer all placed orders, and although Ruland was alarmed by its unexpected fall in Holland, early in 1679, Geysmer had the pleasure of catching the pre-Christmas rise to $14\frac{1}{2}g$ in December.

It is clear enough from these letters that it was the Dutch Company and not the English which determined the Hamburg pepper price, for its stocks, and its supplies to north Germany, were much larger. But the London sales were not without significance and discriminating purchase of the cheaper Jambi, rather than Malabar, pepper (which Bene, Bostelman and Geysmer had now learned to insist upon) could be rewarding.[122] Other East India products commanded little interest, however. Inquiries were made about cardamon, preserved ginger and saltpetre, but nothing came of them after 1674. The fault was hardly David's, for he was an assiduous salesman on the English Company's behalf, but in each case the relative prices of London and Amsterdam were against him.

The products of the Levant (into which David was currently trying to make an independent entry)[123] offered a better competitive edge. Here, as in the Baltic, neutrality gave England further advantages to add to her already strong commercial position and the Franco–Dutch struggle in the central Mediterranean put a further premium on secure English shipping. This was partially offset by the menace of north African corsairs, against whom Sir John Narbrough was engaged in vigorous policing between 1674 and 1677, and his war with Algiers saw some far from negligible losses for English commerce.[124] There is some reflection of this in the Hamburgers' correspondence, for they were sensitive to any prospective fluctuations in the supply of galls, cotton, currants, oil and raw silks. They had also developed a new, common interest in 'Barbary' almonds for which they sometimes made concerted inquiry. The north African product usually ranked bottom in the quality-rating which priced Valencia almonds first, at 38 *ML* per 100 lb., Provence second at 36 *ML* and 'Barbary' a poor third at 30 *ML* in 1677,[125] but it was clearly preferred as the re-export commodity best suited for central Germany round about Christmas time. Currants, the other

---

[121] Glamann, *Dutch–Asiatic Trade, 1620–1740*, p. 83; Chaudhuri, *The Trading World of Asia and the English East India Company, 1660–1760*, p. 320.

[122] For pepper price-differentials, see Chaudhuri, op. cit. pp. 320–2.

[123] See p. 201.

[124] Sir Godfrey Fisher, *Barbary Legend: War, Trade and Piracy in North Africa, 1415–1830* (New York, 1957) p. 364.

[125] E. Ruland to JD, 26 June 1677.

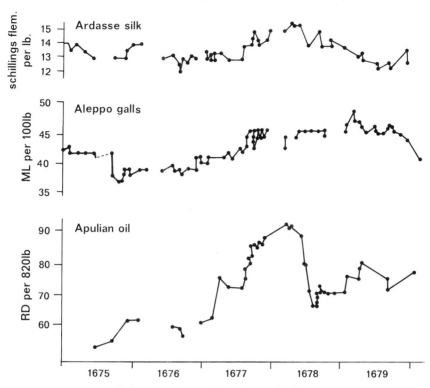

FIGURE 11. Mediterranean commodities: prices at Hamburg: 1675–1680.

seasonal delicacy, no longer interested them as much as before, and they were rarely inquired after. Of all the commodities discussed in this correspondence, currants and galls figured most frequently as the object of illicit shipments arriving directly from Zante or the Levant.[126] The supply of raw silk, particularly Ardasse, was also subject to unpredictable competition overland through Poland. The English community in Hamburg was often criticized for its marketing of silk and one detects that David's clients were not unhappy to see rivals appear. The silk which appeared in this way in 1679 was 1 schilling dearer than the English offering, but it was (wrote the Berenbergs) 'noble' stuff and would yield $1\frac{1}{2}$ schillings more.[127]

The general upward trend of Levant products during the 1670s was unspectacular compared with that of Apulian olive oil, which seems to have been subject to violent fluctuations (Figure 11). One such began early in 1677 when, as E. Ruland reported, no more supplies were expected from Italy.[128] He followed its steep rise, from about 60 *RD* per 820 lb. to 90 *RD* by the end of year, placing an order only in early September when its London price had reached £32 per 236 gallons. However, the shortage from Italy was being made

[126] Widow Berenberg to JD, 24 September 1675, 3 August 1677; F. Bostelman to same, 5 December 1679, 17 February 1680; E. Ruland to same, 17 February 1680; C. Bene to same, 27 January 1680 [**475**].

[127] Widow Berenberg to same, 1 November 1678; [?] Berenberg to same, 26 November 1678 (following the widow's death).

[128] E. Ruland to same, 19 February 1677.

good by exceptionally large English purchases of Seville oil,[129] and with the recovery of Italian supplies in 1678 the Hamburg price dropped more suddenly than it had risen, to 65 *RD*. Ruland had wanted the oil for re-export to Lübeck where there was usually a good demand,[130] but he was probably not sorry that the order was never performed.

This generally lack-lustre performance of the market for English re-exports was probably matched by the record of England's principal domestic export to Hamburg, which was cloth. The indications are that the trade in both old and new draperies was in decline during the 1670s (though destined for a recovery in the eighteenth century) and that the capacity of the Hamburg-based Merchant Adventurers to secure a recovery on their own terms was rapidly diminishing.[131] The Merchant Adventurers Company was in acute difficulties at home, burdened by old debts and beset by new rivals. The suspension of its privileges in 1662–3 and 1666–7 had cast doubt on the legitimacy and utility of their revival, and by 1674 the Company was thoroughly demoralized by attacks at home and abroad. Faced by English interlopers and by German competition it was willing to throw up its charter if its debts could be waived.[132] It is clear from the Company's complaints and its strenuous efforts to reassert control in Hamburg in 1675 that the marketing of English cloth there was no longer solely in its hands. Since 1661, the Hamburg Senate had pressed the right of its own merchant burghers to import English cloth on their own account, and since 1673, when the extra aliens' duty had been abolished by Parliament, they had done so on terms more competitive than the Company's. Indeed, one of the city's most galling complaints against the Company was that its agents sold their cloth more dearly than did native Hamburg merchants.[133]

This is the context in which it was possible for Jacob David to take up the invitation extended to him by Wentzhard & Ployart in 1676 to supply English cloth directly to Hamburg. David was not yet naturalized, let alone a freeman of the Merchant Adventurers, although there is perhaps some significance in the fact that his new brother-in-law, Sir John Lethieullier, was a leading member—later, Governor—of the Company. Wentzhard & Ployart began in February 1676 by ordering 20 dozen pairs of woollen stockings but soon went on to order 2 bales of English serge denims, to be bought direct from the makers in all the most fashionable colours. These parcels arrived by late June and promised a modest profit. More orders followed in July, accompanied by drawings of the desired stocking-designs and samples of the cloth.[134] Their motive in insisting on these being sent to Bremen seems to reflect a brief anxiety about the safety of the Elbe: by February 1677 they were content to specify direct shipment to Hamburg. They also specified purchase in Exeter.[135]

Exeter, at this date, had recovered from the depression of 1658–67 and in 1676 its trade was enjoying a boom which lasted until 1688.[136] In 1676 its cloth exports were almost nine times as large as those of 1666, most of them going to the Low Countries where it successfully defied the Merchant Adventurers' efforts to control the traffic. Exeter's direct contribution to north German sales via Hamburg was mostly channelled through London, sent by carriage overland to Leadenhall market where it paid the 'hallage' duty.[137]

[129] PRO, SP. 94/64 f. 65.

[130] E. Ruland to JD, 18 September 1677.

[131] E. K. Newman, 'Anglo–Hamburg Trade', pp. 105–48, 238–91.

[132] Ibid. pp. 112 n. 4; 239, 249 n. 1, 277.

[133] Ibid. pp. 274–7.

[134] Wentzhard & Ployart to JD, 14 July, 25 August 1676.

[135] Same to same, 13 February 1677.

[136] W. B. Stephens, *Seventeenth-century Exeter, 1625–1688* (Exeter, 1958) p. 85.

[137] Ibid. pp. 99, 104; D. W. Jones 'The "Hallage" Receipts of the London Cloth Markets, 1562–1720', *EcHR*, Second Series, XXV (1972) p. 576.

Jacob David's purchases conform to this pattern. Humphrey Bawden, the Exeter clothier with whom he dealt, could offer regular shipments to Rotterdam, Ostend, Rouen or St Malo, but nothing for Hamburg [**299, 333**]. His packs therefore travelled to London by the Friday carrier, taking six or seven days at a rate of 8s per cwt. The serges which David's clients wanted were at the bottom of the price-range—at 31s per piece (f.o.b.) which meant a first cost at Exeter of about 27s per piece. This, as Bawden frankly pointed out, indicated a type of cloth which was 'very scars and very bad',[138] and he urged David to commission purchases at 1s or 2s more. Wentzhard & Ployart's complaint that they were indeed 'very bad and very coarse' as well as very dear were indignantly received by Bawden who pointed out that 'it was as crass a time for the buying as ever I knew'.[139] Prices had fallen since then and he could now offer better quality. His rival, William Clode, to whom David turned in 1678, also confirmed an improvement in stocks during a slump in the market [**401**].

Wentzhard & Ployart, however, had had enough. They had received in all some 536 pieces of Exeter serge in 1676 and 1677 and although they ordered one or two dozen more in 1678 their interests had now shifted elsewhere, to East India calicoes, for which they placed their first order in March 1677. At a time when the English Company was importing about 250,000 pieces per annum[140] an order for 70 seems insignificant, but it is an interesting portent of the direction in which Anglo–Hamburg trade was going. Over the next sixty years calicoes were to be the major growth element, not merely of English exports to Germany but to Holland as well, for the Dutch East India Company lagged well behind.[141] In the 1670s, however, competition was keener for the Amsterdam chamber of the V.O.C. alone sold an average of 329,000 pieces per annum in the five years 1674–9.[142] Wentzhard & Ployart thought that London's offerings of calico might be cheaper than Amsterdam's but they were wrong and the order was dropped.

Another fruitless initiative, which was even more significant, was the Hamburg firm's suggestion that it should barter German linens for its English serges. Such a convenient exchange was a speciously attractive notion, persistently pressed by the Germans and reluctantly conceded by the English.[143] It was flatly rejected by David. Tied up, as he was, in an elaborate network of bills of exchange he could not afford to forego the cash value of his Hamburg commissions. Furthermore, he had no use for linens. In 1676 London was apparently full of linens and David was still unable to dispose of two cases of 'Marglitzer' linen which had been sent to him by J. A. Fonck in 1672. They were still unsold in 1680! Fonck's growing disappointment did not deflect him from pressing more upon David's unwilling hands. He offered 1,000 pieces per annum and set his heart on contracting with the Royal African Company for 2,000–3,000 pieces per annum. The Company did indeed export 'sletias' (Silesian linens) brought in via Hamburg,[144] but Fonck's were not to be among them. Frustrated of sales, Fonck also suggested barter for cotton, logwood or sugar but received the same rebuff as Wentzhard & Ployart.[145]

David received several more overtures to handle German linens, often from total strangers. From Breslau, Daniel van Reusch, and from Hamburg, Bartholomeus Möll, introduced themselves in 1676, the one recommended by Fonck, the other by Bene [**278**,

---

[138] H. Bawden to JD, 21 February 1677.
[139] Same to same, 23 July 1677.
[140] Chaudhuri, *The Trading World of Asia and the English East India Company, 1660–1760*, p. 282.
[141] E. K. Newman, 'Anglo–Hamburg Trade', p. 162; cf. Glamann *Dutch–Asiatic Trade, 1620–1740*, pp. 143–4.
[142] Glamann, op. cit. p. 143, Table 26.
[143] E. K. Newman, 'Anglo–Hamburg Trade', pp. 146–8.
[144] Davies, *The Royal African Company*, p. 172.
[145] J. A. Fonck to JD, 19 June, 19 September 1676.

291]. Hans Christoph Phantz approached him in 1678, Caspar Anckelman and Jacob de Greve did so in 1680. Phantz had worked seven years for one of the largest German linen-dealing firms, Johan & Herman Luis,[146] and was acquainted with all the major English importers except one—the firm of the Messrs Banks. The names of James Ban[c]ks and his brothers John and Charles frequently figure in this correspondence. Former correspondents of Marescoe, they were a thorn in the flesh of the Merchant Adventurers at whose expense they had obtained a licence to deal directly with Leipzig,[147] and they were evidently formidable dealers whose market share seemed a near-monopoly, much resented by the Hamburgers [**268**, **477**].

The future, however, was to lie with these Hamburgers, not merely in the export of linen but in the import of English cloth. After 1689, when the Merchant Adventurers lost their exclusive privileges, the Company's colony in Hamburg went into a decline, from about forty in 1691 to thirteen in 1728.[148] A new generation of German merchants was more than ready and equipped to replace them in the conduct of Anglo–German trade thanks to developments which can be already discerned here in the 1670s. A minor but interesting feature of David's correspondence is the recurrence of overtures for the training of young Germans as merchant apprentices in good English firms. The widow Berenberg's touching letter [**308**] is only one instance of several. Reinholt Garlinghoff, the leading Hamburg copper-manufacturer, wanted to place his 15-year-old son in London. Wentzhard & Ployart and the De Hertoghs wrote on behalf of Bernhard Schreiber of Lübeck who, at 21 years of age, had already trained in Paris. Jean-Martin Ployart (whose family were merchants of Lyon) sought a place for his younger brother, while Johan Tomloo and François Bostelman wrote on behalf of old family friends—Hendrick Beckhoff's son in one case, Thomas Heger's step-son in the other. David was unable to take on any, let alone all, of these applicants. He had his own full complement of apprentices, one of whom, John Gosselin, he sent to Claus Bene in May 1678 to learn German. Later, convinced that Gosselin would not learn correct pronunciation in polyglot Hamburg, he wanted to send him on to Nürenberg but Bene [**431**] (and Gosselin) stoutly resisted the idea and Gosselin eventually remained for one year, returning home with a good understanding of the language.

These investments in the future of Anglo–German interchange reflect some degree of optimism at a time of deep depression. There had been a high price to pay in Hamburg for the neighbouring wars. A wave of bankruptcies ran through the city between November 1677 and April 1678, linked to similar failures in Amsterdam and London. More than a dozen victims were important enough for David's informants to name, among them Caspar Anckelman, Hermann & Jan van Bostel, the widow & heirs of Heinrich Kalmes, Octavio Buschmann, Albert Schrodering, Jan Andreas Verpoorten and Cornelius van Weede. The latter had the guile to write to David a fortnight before his collapse, seeking credit on a London bill of exchange, and David was lucky to escape for the London acceptant, Bellamy, was to collapse also. Several of the English colony in Hamburg were in difficulties, among them two of the most notable—William Foxley in April 1678 and Francis Townley & Sons in April 1679—men upon whom David had often had bills.

The reasons for Octavio Buschmann's failure, owing 400,000 *ML*, are perhaps the most relevant to this correspondence. He had bought great quantities of pepper, indigo, whale-fins, etc, reported Bene, and he had done so with borrowed money in the hopes of a rise in

---

[146] For this company and its English associations see A. Klima, 'English Merchant Capital in Bohemia in the Eighteenth Century', *EcHR*, Second Series, XII (1959) pp. 39–40.

[147] E. K. Newman, 'Anglo–Hamburg Trade', p. 267.

[148] Ibid. p. 289.

prices—'but the contrary had happened'.[149] Such were the common hazards of international trade at any time, but their pressure upon Hamburg during these difficult years was evidently severe and makes it all the more remarkable that David's commissions were as large as they were.

[c] AMSTERDAM

David's correspondence from Amsterdam continued to be dominated by its preoccupation with affairs in Sweden and, to the extent that Steven de Geer and Philip Botte were its most substantial contributors, has already been introduced. Others who were linked to the London firm's Swedish suppliers were Jeremias van Raey (on behalf of the Cronströms), Pieter van der Mortel (on behalf of Cletcher), Gerard Pincier (on behalf of Perman and the Törnes), Bartolotti & Rihel (on behalf of Lillienhoff and Rosenström) and De la Bistrate & Dufay (who were linked both to Lillienhoff & Rosenström and to the rising star of Laurens Uppendorff). Jean & Hendrik van Baerle, who were by far the London firm's most reliable correspondents, continued their watchful guardianship of the Mommas' affairs, although the emphasis had changed significantly now that their own financial interests were so heavily involved with those of their former principals'. Their disillusion with the Mommas was profound and was deepened by the collapse early in 1675 of both Willem and his Amsterdam-based son, Isaac, whose debts were put at some f.80,000.[150] Fortunately, they remained unscathed but they surveyed with a keenly critical eye Jacob David's handling of their brother David's shipments, setting him more ambitious price targets, urging more vigorous sales, curtailing high commissions and objecting to excessive charges. Sweden preoccupied them to the exclusion of other areas, they wrote in 1677 [329], and they were reluctant to venture on new trades. They had nothing new to offer on their own account and such non-Swedish purchases in which they dealt were on behalf of others. They superintended David's copper shipments to France, they managed his textile purchases for Spain, and in 1679 they helped David settle his accounts with Botte by selling off his surplus of pitch and tar. Comparatively few of their letters now showed any interest in the wider commodity market and although they exchanged East India Company price lists with David the English Company mattered less to them as a potential source of re-exports than as a temporary home for their London balances. In February and April 1678, with the Amsterdam–London exchanges unusually depressed and trade in stagnation, they allowed David to deposit a total of £1,500 at 5 per cent in the East India Company's short-term bonds.[151]

In the three months immediately following the Anglo–Dutch settlement of February 1674 the London firm had re-opened its traffic to Amsterdam with some enthusiasm, sending on its own account four consignments of Ardasse silk and one of Turkish yarn, together with 36 hogsheads of tobacco on Frederick Rihel's behalf, but the initiative was not greatly encouraged by a loss of £16 10s 10d (or 1.3 per cent on the costs, f.o.b.), and there was no sequel in that year or the next. Yet, in 1675, David's Dutch clients had not failed to observe the special opportunities now open to neutral England. Jeremias van Raey was prescient enough to anticipate in January the conjuncture which emerged in June, when the war with Sweden was actually declared. He foresaw the profits which would be available when only the English remained at sea and offered to undertake purchases of shipping and share in the

[149] C. Bene to JD, 18 January 1678.
[150] Van Baerles to LM & JD, 8 January, 7 May 1675 A. van Kuffeler to LM & JD, 24 December 1675 [262].
[151] Van Baerles to JD, 22 February [385], 15 April [395], 20 May 1678.

distribution of any Admiralty passes which David could obtain.[152] Alexander van Kuffeler, though pessimistic about the immediate prospects for European trade, also appreciated England's privileged opportunity.[153]

Yet, little or nothing emerged from this. It was soon apparent that in the fourth year of its war with France Dutch demand was deeply depressed, and 'meest alle coopmanschappen onder de voet leggen'.[154] Price lists were exchanged but, as A. L. Kellerman observed, prices in London and Amsterdam were set at such a parity that he failed to understand why there was any trade between them: it could not be for profit.[155] A year later, in 1676, it was still the same. 'I must inform you that the prices prevailing in the domestic market here are so tight that it is impossible to gain anything by sending things here, unless one enjoys some other advantage which I don't know about.'[156] His pessimism endured into 1677 [**341**] and was evidently widely shared as the war dragged on.

One solution, suggested to David by Robert Hays, was to engage in clandestine traffic, smuggling into England prohibited or highly-rated goods such as brandy, spices or textiles. His brother, Claude Hays, and Jean du Mesnil (who had married John Buck's daughter) could be roped into the conspiracy:

> 'L'envoy et le desbarquement en Angleterre s'en rendroit facile selon mon sens par le moyen de divers bastiments Anglois (dont les Maitres sont a la devotion de mon frere) lesquels venant charge icy ou a Rotterdam s'en retournent le plus souvent avec du ballast dans lequel on pourroit cacher ce que l'on voudroit et le faire descharger au lieu qu'on trouveroit le plus comode . . .'.[157]

There is no evidence that David succumbed to these enticements, but the temptation must have been strong for among these 580 letters from nearly 50 correspondents there were scarcely half a dozen firm commissions.

Alexander van Kuffeler was the most enterprising, sending long lists of current prices for up to 50 different commodities and probing for any marginal advantage which the equivalent London prices might offer. Proffering Dutch linen and copper-ware with one hand he extended invitations for Virginia tobacco, campeachy and brown ginger with the other. But the invitations were conditional, either on price limits (which could never be met) or on David's willingness to share the risk (which he was not). Both these constraints operated in the case of Virginian tobacco leaves, for although the years 1674–7 witnessed some high prices for this produce at Amsterdam the differential between the American and the Dutch-grown tobacco (often 30 to 40 per cent) narrowed discouragingly in 1676,[158] and although good quality Virginia leaf could fetch $f.$30 to $f.$35 per 100 pond in the autumn of 1676 (according to Kuffeler) he was reluctant to pay more for it in London than $4\frac{1}{2}d$ to $5d$ per lb.[159] He may have regretted this in December, for prices rose (as he had half-guessed they would) and a single ship bringing 600 barrels in November found a profitable market.[160] A year later, during which Virginian tobacco averaged $f.$30 per 100 pond, he set an even lower

[152] J. van Raey to LM & JD, undated, January 1675.
[153] A. van Kuffeler to LM & JD, 24 December 1675 [**262**].
[154] Van Baerles to LM & JD, 29 March 1675 [**231**].
[155] A. L. Kellerman to LM & JD, 9 April 1675.
[156] Same to JD, 20 March 1676 [**280**].
[157] R. Hays to JD, 26 May 1676.
[158] J. Price, 'The Tobacco Adventure to Russia', p. 103; H. K. Roessingh, *Inlandse Tabak*, A. A. G. Bijdragen 20, p. 532.
[159] A. van Kuffeler to JD, 4 September, 16 October 1676.
[160] Same to same, 18 December 1676.

London price limit of 4*d* per lb., and in this case he may have been wise for it was on the brink of a downward slide which took it to only *f*.18 in 1679.[161]

David had no better fortune with Van Kuffeler's inquiries for campeachy or brown ginger, and the exchange of East India Company price lists between them only confirmed the marginal advantage of the Dutch prices.[162] Daniel Planck, after a long and angry silence, returned in 1677 with queries about almonds, cardamon and turmeric which likewise proved unperformable.

It was an unfamiliar commodity which provided David with his only substantial commission of these years. This was for English rye and barley which Josias Olmius urged upon him in the wake of the poor harvest of 1675—'Granen syn hier willig, specialyk gerst en Boeckweyts met apparentie van stant tehouden alsoo de oogst daervan dit jahr slecht valt.'[163] News from Danzig that ten or eleven ships destined for Holland had gone to the bottom and that a whole fleet from Konigsberg had been lost with 4,000 lasts of grain heightened the urgency of his letters. Olmius outlined a series of attractive price movements, and he was not unaware of the novel incentive which English grain exports had acquired from the bounties inaugurated in 1673.[164] Handled by his London-based brother, Hermann Olmius, the consignment of 16 lasts of barley and 19 lasts of rye was despatched through King's Lynn and reached Rotterdam in February 1676.[165] But the barley was found to be inferior and the rye was tainted; French supplies from Nantes and others from Douai proved more competitive and by late March prices were beginning to fall in a momentarily glutted market. Only the approach of a new campaigning season with its commissariat demand stimulated sales and by late June the Olmius-David consignment was finally sold, leaving David with a loss of £84 0*s* 8*d*.[166] It was his last serious venture in the Netherlands.

[d] FRANCE

As a native of Rouen and its environs it was natural that Jacob David should seek to enlarge his predecessors' correspondence with that city, and running through many of the letters which came from there after 1674 is a shared concern for David's family circle, his friends and—not least—the Protestant religion. Robert Oursel, his former master, maintained cordial relations and his wife kept a sympathetic eye on the growth of David's young family. The firm of Benjamin Beuzelin, Père et fils, were evidently close friends, eager to entrust

---

[161] Same to same, 18 November, 20 December 1677; Price, 'Tobacco Adventure', p. 103, Table B.

[162] A. van Kuffeler to JD, 16 October 1676, 2 November 1677.

[163] J. Olmius to LM & JD, 3 September 1675.

[164] 'An Act for Raising the Sum of £1,238,750 for Supply of His Majesty's Extraordinary Occasions' (25 Car. II. c. 1) provided in clause xxxi for export bounties of 5*s* per quarter on wheat, 3*s* on rye and 2*s* 6*d* on barley or malt when the prices per quarter did not exceed 40*s* for wheat, 32*s* for rye and 24*s* for barley and malt. For the Act and its context see D. G. Barnes, *A History of the English Corn Laws, 1660–1845* (London, 1930) p. 11; J. Thirsk & J. P. Cooper (eds.) *17th Century Economic Documents*, pp. 162–4. Dutch exploitation of the bounties was complained of by the English representative in Holland, Sir Leoline Jenkins, in December 1675—'for the Dutch sending commissions into England to buy corne, their factors do demand and receive the gratuities of the act, and are accountable for that money to the Dutch, which was intended only for the benefit of the King's subjects . . .'. PRO, SP. 105/239 (Jenkins to Williamson, 24 December/3 January 1675/6).

[165] King's Lynn had established itself as the principal exporting centre (after London) by 1677–8—N. S. B. Gras *The Evolution of the English Corn Market from the Twelfth to the Eighteenth Century*, Harvard Economic Studies 13 (Harvard, Mass./London, 1915) Appendix G, pp. 418–19.

[166] J. Olmius to JD, 21 February, 31 March, 17 April, 24 April, 3 July 1676 [**293**]; Ledger 1673–9, f. 156. David's half-share in 59 lasts of grain from King's Lynn was £355 6*s*. His bounty rebate was £41 19*s* and his share of the net proceeds was £229 7*s* 4*d*.

their younger son and brother, François, to the protection and instruction of David's household and counting-house. It was from a visit to David that Abraham Vrouling returned to Rouen in mid-1676 to take up the family business of his late father and elder brother,[167] while David Gansel—Jacob David's future step-son-in-law—was also an old family friend.

These four correspondents—Oursel, Beuzelin, Vrouling and Gansel—were to provide David with much of his business in Rouen and they put him in a much stronger position to prosper than had been available to Marescoe or Joye. There was also a fifth correspondent, whose intimate friendship eluded David although it would have been the most valuable of all. This was Thomas Legendre (Sr.), probably the most powerful merchant in Rouen, whose son Thomas (Jr.) was later to abjure protestantism, become Inspector General of Commerce and die, ennobled, a multi-millionaire.[168] Both men corresponded amicably with David and were prepared to do business with him, but at a time when Rouen's consumption of pistachio nuts was authoritatively put at three bales per annum[169] it was peculiarly ill-judged of David to encumber the Legendre house with eight. This was not the stuff of *grand commerce* and the Legendres, who were unable to dispose of this embarrassment, generally pursued their wide-ranging commercial interests without much further regard for David's.

Unfortunately, these were likely to clash, for the Legendre firm had for long been the preferred French agents of the Swedish copper manufacturers. They also had intimate ties with the Hamburg copper dealers and in general performed the same role in Rouen which Marescoe, and now David, performed in London.[170] David's ambition to alleviate the sluggishness of the London copper-wire market by shifting surplus stocks to France necessarily made him an intruder on the Legendres' domain and open hostility was only avoided because David had the sanction of their mutual Swedish principals to do so. Nevertheless, one of the most consistent elements in this correspondence—particularly from the Beuzelins—is a deep jealousy of the Legendre family.

Rouen, as Savary des Bruslons noted, was the principal recipient of French copper imports,[171] and her annual intake of copper-wire was obligingly estimated by Legendre himself in 1676 as 10,000–12,000 coils (or roughly a minimum of 125 and a maximum of 160 tons p.a.). Three-quarters of this came from Sweden and between one-quarter and one-fifth from Hamburg.[172] David's despatch of the following quantities must be placed in that context:

	To Rouen	To Bordeaux	Total
1675	1,080 coils	nil	1,080 coils
1676	450 coils	1,020 coils	1,470 coils
1677	1,738 coils	nil	1,738 coils
1678	1,000 coils	300	1,300 coils

[167] In June 1676 Abraham took his younger brother, Simon, into partnership—A. Vrouling to JD, 9 June 1676. The Vroulings originated in Delft—J. Mathorez, *Les étrangers en France sous l'Ancien Régime*, II, p. 289.

[168] G. A. Prevost (ed.) *Notes du Premier Président Pellot sur la Normandie: clergé, gentilshommes et terres principales—officiers de justice (1670–1683)* (Rouen, Paris 1915) p. 130; J. Biancquis, *La révocation de l'èdit de Nantes à Rouen* (Rouen, 1885) p. 53; E. Lesens (ed.) *Histoire de la Persécution faite à l'église de Rouen, par Philippe Legendre* (Rouen, 1874) pp. ix–x; H. Lüthy, *La Banque protestante en France* (Paris, 1959) I, p. 72 n. 31 citing G. Vanier 'Une grande famille de marchandes rouennais aux XVIIe et XVIIIe siècles: les Le Gendre', *Bulletin de la Société Libre d'Émulation de la Seine Inférieure* (1947–8).

[169] E. Willet to LM & JD, 25 May 1675.

[170] Sondén, 'Broderna Momma-Reenstierna', *Historisk Tidskrift* (1911) p. 151 n. 2; B. Beuzelin to JD, 17 November 1676.

[171] J. Savary des Bruslons, *Dictionnaire Universel de Commerce*, I, p. 1629.

[172] T. Legendre (Jr.) to JD, 28 January 1676 [**270**].

Clearly, such amounts placed him in no position to dominate the Rouen market although it was open to him (or his agents) to undersell rivals for the sake of quick returns. That, however, was precisely the charge which the Beuzelins kept making against the Legendres. Again and again they alleged that the market had been spoiled by the Legendres' under-pricing, with generous credit. In this way they also dominated lead and monopolized olive-oil. 'Ces gens-la donnent a touttes mains, et semble qu'ils voudroyent s'il estoit possible mettre tout le negoce en leur pouvoir; de ce que se tirer de Marchandise d'Angleterre, ils en recoivent la $\frac{1}{3}$ ou la $\frac{1}{2}$ et nous savons que la meilleure partie est p. leur Compte. S'ils gaignent sur tout c'est p. faire une fortune extraordinnaire en peu de temps. Dieu les veille benir!'[173] Beuzelin (who had earlier written of the Legendres' Swedish contracts 'nous n'en avons point de Jallouzie') went on to argue, with some inconsistency, that the Legendres did not care whether they made a profit or a loss as long as turnover was brisk.[174]

This sensible business strategy did not make things any easier for David's agents, and if one discounts Beuzelin's personal resentment one can appreciate why Oursel, Vrouling and Gansel had an unhappy time with their friend's commissions. The market for copper-wire at Rouen was not large in volume but it was geographically diffuse and subject to seasonal periods of lassitude. The correspondence sheds little light on the ultimate destination of David's copper-wire and although some was evidently sold to 'out-of-town' merchants a significant proportion appears to have gone to small local craftsmen, such as pinmakers or spectacle-makers, whose own sales were often bound up with the fairs at Caen or Guibray.[175] Gansel, anxious to please, made efforts to find markets in Abbeville or Amiens but was told that 30 coils would satisfy all the needs of the leading pinmakers there. His hopes of big sales at Rugles were also dashed.[176]

Sales of any kind were often subject to considerable risk, for the credit requirements of the clientele were as demanding as they were unsafe. Little copper-wire was sold for cash, explained Oursel. Three or more months time was usually expected and even when payment was due a further three or four weeks grace was customary.[177] To secure these extended payments and cover the heightened risk of bad debts David was obliged to grant his agents a commission of 3 per cent, and even this was a favour from friends who would normally require 4 per cent.[178]

Purchasers, although dilatory in payment, were demanding about quality. They wanted only the best Swedish copper-wire, which they judged to be Laurens de Geer's 'Three Crowns' mark. The 'Crowned N' mark from Isaac Cronström's Norrköping works was also highly esteemed and was worth 2 per cent more than the 'AW' brand. Neither the 'Lion' nor the 'Lily' nor the 'Tulip' brands were desired for domestic consumption but 'Crowned H' wire of Hamburg sold readily from the Legendres' capacious stocks.[179] Copper kettles were preferred to come exclusively from Aachen or Hamburg: Beuzelin and Vrouling agreed that they were better made and David's shipment of some of Jacob Reenstierna's proved their

[173] B. Beuzelin to JD, 20 September 1678.

[174] Same to same, 17 November 1676 [**319**], 14 October 1678.

[175] B. Beuzelin to JD, 16 August 1678 [**417**]; A. & S. Vrouling to JD, 27 April, 4 May, 10 August 1677 [**359**]; D. Gansel to JD, 19 August 1678. For the role of Guibray see P. Dardel, *Commerce, Industrie et Navigation à Rouen et au Havre au XVIIIe Siècle* (Rouen, 1966) pp. 15, 17, 26, 28, 30, 31, 34, 49, 53–5.

[176] D. Gansel to JD, 8 June 1677.

[177] R. Oursel to JD, 6 December 1675; B. Beuzelin to JD, 27 August 1677.

[178] A. & S. Vrouling to JD, 18 August, 21 August, 1676; R. Oursel to JD, 20 December 1675, [?] January 1676; B. Beuzelin to JD, 15 March 1680.

[179] R. Oursel to JD, 22 November, 26 November 1675 [**257**], 12 May 1676, 8 December 1679; D. Gansel to JD, 8 June 1677; B. Beuzelin to JD, 31 August 1677 [**364**], 3 February 1679; T. Legendre (Sr.) to JD, 12 October 1677.

point, for 'ils sont trouer, souder ou pailleux, et d'un cuivre cassant'.[180] Civic inspectors thought they had never seen worse wares and had to be bribed not to report them. As for garcopper, it was said to be used 'daily' but in fact seems to have undergone long periods of neglect. Described (incorrectly) by David's clients as 'rosette'[181] it lay heavily on the Vroulings' hands, although according to Oursel it was finding a new use in the coining of those infamous 4-sols silver coins (authorized in April 1674) which were to cause such havoc in the trade of the Levant.[182]

The fortunes of David's copper ventures were therefore precarious, for of the four major markets for Swedish output—Hamburg, Amsterdam, London and Rouen—the last now offered least prospect of re-export to a wider world. Demand was comparatively small, mainly local and usually seasonal, while the price (thanks to war) was exceptionally vulnerable to a totally unpredictable rate of supply. David enjoyed some small advantage on this point, for neutral London was better served with communications to the north than belligerent France. In September 1676 Beuzelin complained that they had received no Hamburg letters for three months; in August 1677 they had not heard from Sweden for four.[183] The French port depended heavily on English shipping and David was certainly better informed about its movements than even Legendre for whom he had to act as intermediary with the Swedish suppliers. A final handicap, rarely endured by London, was that Rouen could be ice-bound and the Seine unnavigable. Such was the case in the winters of 1676–7 and 1678–9. By mid-December 1676 river traffic was at a standstill and could not resume until mid-January, by which time seventy ships were jockeying for the chance to come up river.[184] In 1679 the dislocation was more prolonged, with the Seine ice-bound in January and February and flooded in March. Over sixty ships were said to be trapped.[185]

Because of these difficulties, greatly exacerbated by the wars in the north, supplies of copper reached Rouen irregularly, creating an alternation of dearth and glut which seriously distorted prices. The effects were particularly marked in the course of 1676 and 1677, and the correspondence traces in some detail the rise and fall of wire prices and stocks. The rise began steeply in the autumn of 1676, preserving the customary 3 or 4 per cent differential between Swedish and the better Hamburg product. Starting from around 80 to 85 livres tournois per 100 lb. in the summer it had reached £94*t* to £96*t* in December, and by January 1677 craftsmen were said to be turning to iron-wire instead.[186] This would have been an ideal moment for David to have shipped some of his stock, but although he had despatched supplies for Rouen on no less than twelve different vessels in the course of 1676 only one, bearing 100 coils, arrived at this opportune moment. A further 1,000 sent on David's account did not arrive until March and April when they were overshadowed by 3,600 coils from

[180] A. & S. Vrouling to JD, 30 October 1676; B. Beuzelin to JD, 8 June 1677.

[181] 'Il vient encore de Suède un espéce de Cuivre rouge, qu'on appelle Rosette, quoi qu'assez improprement'—J. Savary des Bruslons, *Dictionnaire*, I, p. 1630.

[182] R. Oursel to JD, 17 December 1675 [259]; A. & S. Vrouling to JD, 11 April 1679; but cf. B. Beuzelin to JD, 3 December 1677—'*Nous estimons que le cours des méschants pièces de 4s qui s'exportent depuis près de 4 ans ne contribue beaucoup au baissement des changes . . .*'. For the inception and role of these coins see F. Spooner, *The International Economy and Monetary Movements in France, 1493–1725*, Harvard Economic Studies, vol. 138 (Cambridge, Mass., 1972) pp. 191–6. They were devalued in March–April 1679 with consequences described by A. & S. Vrouling to JD, 11 April 1679—'*cela cause une terrible confusion . . . c'est une peine incroyable et toute ruine au négoce*'.

[183] B. Beuzelin to JD, 22 September 1676, 3 August 1677.

[184] Same to same, 18 December 1676, 15 January 1677.

[185] Same to same, 17 January, 7 March 1679; A. & S. Vrouling to JD, 20 January 1679.

[186] B. Beuzelin to JD, 1 January 1677.

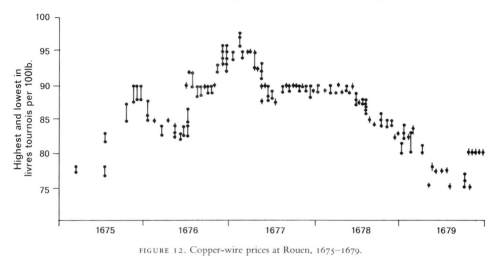

FIGURE 12. Copper-wire prices at Rouen, 1675–1679.

Hamburg.[187] By early May 1677 Gansel put the unsold stocks in Rouen at 3,000, held by ten or twelve different dealers.[188] Prices then began a sharp descent levelling out only during the long empty season of July and August when the artisans were said to have gone to the harvest and the dealers to Guibray fair (Figure 12). September was regarded as the time of maximum demand, but instead of rising in 1677 prices were kept stable by an unusual influx of English ships from Hamburg and Sweden. Two arrived from Sweden bearing 3,000 coils and two more from Hamburg with 1,500. Another 4,000 coils arrived in October, half from Sweden, half from Hamburg. By early November total stocks were put at some 5,500 by Beuzelin (5,000 by T. Legendre, Sr.)[189] and a further 1,600 appeared from Hamburg. 'C'est icy comme une source, il en vient tousjours!' complained Vrouling.[190]

In fact, the spring was about to dry up; there was little autumn demand in 1677 and prices gradually eased. David, who had rashly set a price target of £97*t* on his 1,000 coils, had to accept £85*t* and £83*t* when they were eventually sold in 1678. By then a general depression had made itself felt at the Guibray fair when some of Rouen's regular customers complained of heavy losses on copper.[191] There was none of the usual re-stocking that autumn and the Beuzelin firm, which thought that times had never been worse, was profoundly irritated by the Legendres' profligate dealings below the market price. There were further shocks when 6,000 coils turned up from Sweden in December 1678, with another 2,600 on their way and nearly as much in stock.[192]

By April 1679, with prices drifting ever lower, most of David's agents were ready to resign their interest in this unrewarding commodity and even the Beuzelins could view with some indifference the impressive alliance which Thomas Legendre had struck with Éstienne and Samuel Molié, who were partners in the new Franco–Swedish copper consortium set up

[187] Same to same, 24 April 1677 [**344**].
[188] D. Gansel to JD, 18 May 1677.
[189] B. Beuzelin to JD, 31 August [**364**], 28 September, 19 November 1677; T. Legendre to JD, 2 November 1677.
[190] A. & S. Vrouling to JD, 30 November 1677.
[191] B. Beuzelin to JD, 6 September [**419**], 13 September 1678.
[192] Same to same, 17 January 1679.

by the Du Flon brothers. Jean du Flon (later ennobled in Sweden as Adlercrona) was a French-born Stockholm merchant who had become the financial intermediary for the French subsidies paid to Sweden since 1672.[193] On this powerful basis he had been enabled to succeed to the kind of copper-contracts and privileges once enjoyed by the Mommas, Cronströms and Cronberg, but like them he was to pay a high price. Extremely heavy demands were placed on the Du Flon-Molié consortium in 1678 to finance Sweden's recovery, and a 5-year lease of the 'Crowned N' copper-wire output was part of their reward.[194] But, as Beuzelin smugly observed 'le nouveau Commissaire Molié, qui a traitté des ouvrages de la marque 'N' Couronné ne trouvera pas son compte dans ce rabbais, car il a basty sur le pied de 84 a 85 £t' (and it was now at £78t or below). 'Cet homme entreprend beaucoup—nous doubtons qu'il y reussisses.'[195]

Because of these deep jealousies it is difficult to place complete trust in the accuracy of reports from Rouen, which were quite capable of misrepresenting the prices and quantities of copper-wire available. This tendency grew worse in the course of 1679, when David showed signs of placing greater reliance on the Legendres, and it is a relief to turn to the less highly-charged situation in Bordeaux, where David's copper-ventures pursued a comparatively uneventful course.

They began as a sequel to the disastrous wine shipment sent to Sweden in 1676.[196] The Bordeaux *négoçiant*, Jean Lacam, helpfully advised that considerable amounts of copper-wire usually came from Hamburg and sometimes from Sweden.[197] Leonard Craen, a Dutch merchant resident in Bordeaux, was more specific. He thought he could dispose of 900–1,000 coils per annum and guarantee David a 10 per cent profit.[198] Further, he thought that Bordeaux could absorb some 100,000 lb. of 'rozette' and 50,000 lb of 'Hungary plate'. Kettles were less acceptable: the Périgord region produced great quantities of its own iron-wares which were much cheaper than any imports, and he estimated the annual requirement of sheet-copper at only some 10,000–12,000 lb. He went on to depict a large regional market served from the twice-yearly Bordeaux fairs of 1–15 March and 15–30 October.[199] Its clientele ranged as far as Limoges to the north, and Montpellier and Toulouse to the west. There were important customers to be found in Villefranche, and some of the biggest metal-merchants in the country could be expected to turn up at the fairs.[200]

Upon this encouragement David despatched two shipments of 300 coils a-piece which reached Bordeaux in October and November 1676. As advised, he sent the two most desirable brands—'Three Crowns' and 'Crowned N'—and saw the first sell immediately at £91t half for cash, half payable in three months. As in Rouen, sales at three months time were customary, but 130 coils of the 'Crowned N' were also quickly sold for cash at £91t and 25 more at £92½t. He had been lucky enough to catch the tail-end of the October fair, before the

---

. [193] For the significance of the Molié-Du Flon consortium see A. Munthe *Joel Gripenstierna: en storfinansiär från Karl XI.s tid*, pp. 12, 63, 70–1, 75, 84–5, 87, 112–14, 137–8, 140–1, 149–50, 166; also B. Fredriksson, *Försvarets finansiering: Svensk krigsekonomi under skånska kriget, 1675–79*, Studia Historica Upsaliensia 81 (Uppsala, 1976) pp. 60–5.

[194] B. Beuzelin to JD, 28 March 1679.

[195] Ibid.

[196] See p. 170 and [380]. Lacam was described by Craen as 'a good honest person with good credit'— 24 November 1676.

[197] J. Lacam to JD, 25 January 1676.

[198] L. Craen to JD, 17 October 1676.

[199] Same to same, 26 December, 29 December 1676. For Bordeaux and its fairs see Christian Huetz de Lemps, *Géographie du commerce de Bordeaux à la fin du règne de Louis XIV* (Paris, 1975) pp. 46–8.

[200] L. Craen to JD, 29 December 1676, 19 June 1677, 14 June 1678.

arrival of large amounts of garcopper and wire from London, Amsterdam and Hamburg. Thereafter, the pin-makers were said to be fully supplied and demand slowed down.[201] Brokers were soon offering no more than £88t, considerably less than the £96t David was hoping for. Craen advised waiting for the March fair of 1677 and took delivery in February of 420 coils and 320 pieces of garcopper. The latter, some 5,352 lb., was quickly sold to a Villefranche firm (Alary & Dardene) for £88t per quintal, but few copper-wire dealers appeared at the March fair and Craen was left with a total of 575 coils on his hands. He still had 501 a year later and was not able to close the account until after the March fair of 1679.[202] Over this period copper-wire prices at Bordeaux followed a distinctive course, although its market was clearly aware of the movements elsewhere, at Rouen, Hamburg, Amsterdam and London. It shared in the steep rise of November–December 1676 and the subsequent fall of May–June 1677, but it fell further than in Rouen, only to rise distinctively in the first half of 1678. This appears to have been a local reaction to the English embargo on imports from France, which necessarily struck harder at Bordeaux's prosperity than at Rouen's. Metals such as iron, copper and lead had been the ideal ballast for incoming English wine-ships and their cessation greatly diminished the prospects of supply, for until peace was concluded with the Dutch there could be few alternative sources. Thus, the disappointing October fair of 1678 and the equally bad one of March 1679 were seen as the direct consequence of the English embargo, and Bordeaux's hopes were pinned (vainly) on the new English parliament which assembled in March 1679.[203]

David may have been able to profit from this opportunity, but the evidence that he did is missing. For the period 1675 to 1677 the record is unimpressive. On copper-wire Oursel had secured him a notional 3.9 per cent in 1675 and 2.1 per cent in 1676. The Beuzelins had done better in 1676, with 5.7 per cent, and L. Craen even better, with 5.9 per cent. The best yields were on garcopper, which showed a 1676 profit of 11.4 per cent in Rouen and 10.5 per cent in Bordeaux. But the 1677 performance was much less rewarding, with only 5.4 per cent to show for garcopper at Bordeaux and a mere 1.3 per cent on Beuzelin's large sales of copper-wire worth over £1,500 (f.o.b.). The Vrouling firm secured him 3.75 per cent on half that quantity, but the incompetent Gansel completely wiped out this with an abject loss of 8 per cent.

David had made a vigorous effort to promote these sales in France, partly on his own account, partly for his Swedish principals. Through Craen he had made inquiries in Rochefort,[204] and through Beuzelin he secured contracts in La Rochelle, probing in the ruins of Colbert's Compagnie du Nord [**420, 422**]. As Botte's tar-contract went into dissolution he tried to push unsaleable pitch and tar in the same direction, sending 260 barrels of tar to Craen and 240 barrels to Nicolas Claessen at La Rochelle. Smaller amounts were placed at Dieppe, St Valéry and Rouen, where Beuzelin had already taken delivery of 24 lasts in September 1678. However, France was not a welcoming or very discriminating market for Scandinavian tar. It had its own sources in the hinterland of Bordeaux, from the pine forests of Les Landes. Swedish tar, wrote Beuzelin, was valued less for its intrinsic quality than for the oak barrels in which it came.[205]

---

[201] Same to same, 24 November, 26 December 1676.

[202] Same to same, 1 April 1679.

[203] Same to same, 4 April 1679. Similar hopes of the parliament of 1679 were entertained in Rouen—A. & S. Vrouling to JD, 14 March 1679.

[204] L. Craen to JD, 18 October, 23 October, 6 November 1677.

[205] B. Beuzelin to JD, 29 November 1678. L. Craen also warned against tar—'*tis een zeer lompe coopmanschap'*—8 July 1679.

However, although re-exports of these northern products accounted for the bulk of David's shipments to France, his correspondents drew him into a series of small but significant consignments of goods drawn from the British Isles, from the East and West Indies and from Spain and the Levant. Absorbed in its war, France now stood at a peculiarly unhappy moment in its international trade, with much of Colbert's commercial policy apparently in ruins. The Levant Company of 1670 was in decline after 1672; the Company of the North of 1669 was 'un fiasco total'[206] and virtually defunct by 1677; the French West India Company was suppressed in 1674, and the East India Company of 1664 was to have its privileges soon withdrawn. With Hamburg and the Baltic effectively closed to them, and the Mediterranean in a state of bitter contention with the Dutch, French merchants were unusually dependent on English intermediaries for the products of these areas.

Thus David was approached with numerous inquiries, suggestions and specific commissions concerning goods which might prove profitable in Rouen. The Vrouling firm was especially conscientious in filling its letters with detailed price-data and market analyses, while others occasionally sent the printed Rouen price-currents (none of which, regrettably, have survived). David reciprocated with advance notice of English East India Company sales, but the initiative for trade was usually taken in Rouen despite the general pessimism which pervades so many letters.[207] The list of goods (a) inquired after, and (b) specifically ordered, is a long one and best presented in tabular form (Table 28).

In return, David's friends did not hesitate to press the attractions of French products, notably linens, wine and brandy, but for neither imports nor exports was there any steady or reliable commitment. As in Hamburg, the sluggish markets of 1675–80 offered inadequate security and commerce was now a matter of small-scale opportunism, of seizing some fleeting advantage before others did, for, as Oursel observed, 'en toute sorte de Commerce il n'y a que les premiers quy réussissent'.[208]

TABLE 28. Commodities ordered in Rouen, 1676–1678.

	British Isles	Spain and Mediterranean	America and West Indies	East Indies
(a)	Irish butter	Camel-hair	Cochineal	Cardamon
	Grains	Cotton	Indigo	Cotton
	Hides	Hides	Tobacco	Pepper
	Lead	Soap		
	Pilchards			
	Rabbit-skins			
	Irish tallow			
	Tin			*Atlantic*
(b)	Colchester bays,	Almonds	Brazil-wood	Ambergris
	Kerseys, serges	Barillas	Campeachy	Whalefins
	Coal	Galls		
	Gunpowder	Olive-oil		
	Red lead	Raisins		
		Wool		

[206] J. Meuvret, *Études d'histoire économique* (Paris, 1971) p. 32.

[207] E. g. B. Beuzelin to JD, 8 September 1676—'*Le négoce entre vostre place et la nostre est sy battu que c'est chose rare d'avoir le moindre proffit, les droits son[t] exhorbittant icy a rentrée et la consommation fort petite*'.

[208] R. Oursel to JD, 8 December 1679.

Thus, drought in Provence created an interesting shortage of dried fruits in November 1676; the disastrous olive-oil harvest pushed up prices in August 1677; locusts in the Levant were said to have destroyed the cotton crops, and drought had damaged the soda-plants in 1679.[209] All these natural misfortunes were swooped upon, as were man-made dislocations. The French naval campaign off Messina in 1677–8 had diverted much Marseille shipping, and the Vrouling firm was hopeful of exploiting a consequent soap-shortage by procuring English shipments from Turkey or Alicante.[210] The disastrously poor performance of French textiles in New Spain in 1675 (with losses of 35–40 per cent) depressed domestic markets in 1676 and explains the earnestness with which linens were pressed upon David that year.[211] Despite the arrival of the *flota* and *galeones* in 1676 and 1679, Spanish trade could give little buoyancy to the commercial life of Rouen even after the peace of 1678. As Beuzelin explained in June 1679, 'despuis la paix avec l'espaigne l'on ne ce sert plus de la voye du Havre p[our] les marchandises de Biscaye, mais on envoye tout p[ar] Donquerque, ou il y a assey souvent des navires p[our] Bilbao'.[212] Earlier, in July 1678, anti-French measures in Spain had struck hard at Rouen and its merchants, deepening a depression which was to last some years.[213]

Not surprisingly, David's correspondents were unable to discern the longer term trends, and they frequently mis-read the shorter term fluctuations, misjudging, for example, the supply of olive-oils or the demand for Segovia wool. On grain prices they were thoroughly deceived by the alternation of good and bad harvests, with the Vrouling firm admitting to serious losses on their attempt to profit from the high prices of 1677 and 1679.[214] They had detected shortages in the region of Rouen and of Bordeaux during August 1677 and reported rises in wheat from W.44 to W.50, and rye from W.26 to W.36 per *muid*. By the end of the month best wheat was at W.60–62 and barley at W.28, prices at which they were keen to solicit imports from England.[215] In May 1679 they were quick to observe that good wheat was already at W.70, rye at W.50 and oats at W.48–50 per *muid*. Again and again, they pressed David for advice on English supplies, and brushed aside warnings of abundant shipments and a promising harvest.[216] By January 1680 A. Vrouling was forced to confess that his heavy drafts on David arose from 'une négoce d'extra et de terrible desbours, dont je n'avois pas assez examiné la suitte'.[217] He had 1,200 *muids* (about 1,800 tons) of grain on his hands and his hopes were pinned on selling 400–500 to the hospitals of Paris.

These irregular forays into short-term ventures provide us with few consistent series of

---

[209] A. & S. Vrouling to JD, 6 November 1676 [**318**], 10 August 1677 [**359**], 29 September, 13 October 1679; B. Beuzelin to JD, 24 April 1677 [**344**].

[210] A. & S. Vrouling to JD, 25 January 1678.

[211] Same to same, 16 June, 10 August 1676; R. Oursel to JD, 25 October 1675; B. Beuzelin to JD, 18 December 1676; Abraham Cordier to JD, 22 December 1676.

[212] B. Beuzelin to JD, 2 June 1679 [**446**]. For the diversion of French routes to Spain see Everaert, *Vlaamse firma's te Cadiz*, pp. 89–96.

[213] B. Beuzelin to JD, 19 July 1678; A. & S. Vrouling to JD, 15 July 1678; Kamen, *Spain in the Later Seventeenth Century*, p. 348; Everaert, pp. 342–5, 542–6, 642–3, 696–701.

[214] The seriousness of the grain shortages in 1677 and 1679 is reflected in the prohibitions of exports on 6 October 1677 and 16 May 1679. In 1678, however, free export was permitted on 4 June—A. P. Usher, *The History of the Grain Trade in France, 1400–1710* (Cambridge, Mass., 1913) p. 275. See also J. Meuvret 'Les mouvements des prix de 1661 à 1715 et leur répercussions' in *Études d'histoire économique*, pp. 85–92.

[215] A. & S. Vrouling to JD, 3 September 1677 B. Beuzelin put the rise in grain prices at 50 per cent— 21 September 1677.

[216] A. & S. Vrouling to JD, 26 May, 20 June, 27 June, 4 July, 14 July, 25 July, 8 August, 22 September, 26 September, 17 October, 10 November 1679.

[217] Undated—answered, 26 February 1680.

prices, although the Vroulings were faithful in listing those which they thought might interest David. They depict, patchily, the general upward movement of Aleppo galls and cotton yarn (already observed from Hamburg). They hint at only minor movements in campeachy, cochineal and indigo, for demand was slack. Segovia wool was watched for a while, but an interest in camel-hair quickly waned. The only commodity for which a reasonable series of quotations is recorded is—curiously enough—pepper, for which they professed a deep distrust. 'C'est une marchandise fort ingratte' wrote Oursel (who had 50 unsold sacks on his hands).[218] They shared the Hamburgers' resentment at the East India Company's policy of price maintenance, and frequently blamed the English and Dutch companies' sales for disturbing the international exchanges.[219] David's consignments of pepper in 1676 (to Beuzelin and Lacam) and in 1678 (to A. & S. Vrouling) seem to have been ill-fated, to judge from his 13 per cent loss on his half-share in Beuzelin's and the dismayed comments of the Vroulings.[220]

Only one other commodity received the same kind of attention, and that was brandy in Bordeaux. For wines the information is patchy, although David's friends were quick to inform him of the prospects for the vintage. On 28 August 1676 the Vroulings reported 'on commence la vendage sur notre Rivière qui sera trés belle accause du beautemps & les vins seront merveilleuse'. White wines were particularly excellent, wrote the Beuzelins—'ils passent en bonté ceux de Langon et de Gai[ll]ac ayant une grande liquer et fort agréable'.[221] They predicted for 1677 an abundant Bordeaux vintage, for which nearly 700 English vessels had assembled, but it is safer to record the testimony on the spot, from Craen, that although the vintage was likely to be 25 per cent larger than that of 1676 (which in turn had been 33 per cent smaller than that of 1675) it would produce white wines less sweet.[222] The 1678 vintage also suffered from a dry summer and was reckoned to be 25–33 per cent smaller than in 1677.[223] Such prices that were recorded ignored the *grand crus*—Latour, Lafite, Margaux— and generally concentrated on the sweet white wines of Bordeaux or its hinterland—Barsac, Langon, Preignac, Sauternes, Sainte-Croix-du-Mont. As Jean Lacam's letter of 21 December 1676 indicated, prices for each area could span a considerable range of qualities and such variations that are revealed by these letters are difficult to interpret.

With brandy the picture is clearer and even dramatic, with its steep plunge in the summer of 1677 (Figure 13). 'The English have stopped buying brandy' wrote Craen on 25 May 1677, and in November Henri Chavat predicted that the fall would continue from *W*.50 to *W*.40 'at which price it would not be a bad idea to do something'.[224] English purchases at this lower price seem to have been responsible for the brief re-bound of January 1678 but thereafter the English embargo of March 1678 stifled any further recovery. Even the resumption of Dutch shipments in 1679—not to mention the clandestine exports to England which Craen knew to occur 'every day'—failed to raise brandy to its earlier levels.[225]

Against this somewhat depressing background it is not surprising to find signs of restlessness among David's younger correspondents in France. Religious affiliations also

---

[218] R. Oursel to JD, 7 April 1676.
[219] B. Beuzelin to JD, 31 August 1677 [**364**], 15 March 1680; R. Oursel to JD, 9 October 1676, 23 February 1680; A. & S. Vrouling to JD, 10 November, 17 November 1679.
[220] A. & S. Vrouling to JD, 10 February, 28 February, 25 July, 5 September 1679, 9 February, 15 March 1680.
[221] B. Beuzelin to JD, 8 October [**372**], 5 November, 16 November 1677.
[222] L. Craen to JD, 17 October 1676, 2 October 1677.
[223] Hillaire Reneu to JD, 10 September, 22 October 1678.
[224] Henri Chavat to JD, 6 November 1677.
[225] J. Lacam to JD, 26 August, 25 November 1679.

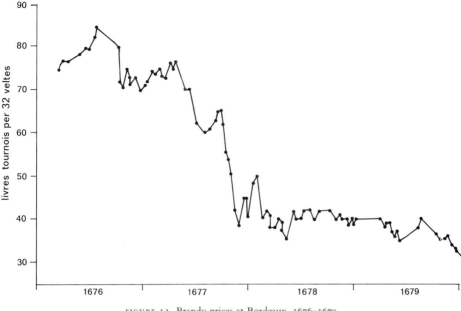

FIGURE 13. Brandy prices at Bordeaux, 1676–1679.

played their part in unsettling several of these predominantly protestant merchants. While Oursel rejoiced in the marriage of the Princess Mary to William of Orange in 1677[226] the Beuzelins and Gansel were uneasy at the course of politics in England and were dismayed by the implications of the 'Popish plot' fury for the protestant minority in France.[227] The arrival of numerous English catholic refugees in Dieppe was widely reported and aggravated the fears of Benjamin Beuzelin for his unemployed son François. As a member of Rouen's Huguenot consistory he had rejoiced in the return of François from a visit to Spain and Italy, unscathed by idolatry[228] and he earnestly promoted his son's desire to settle in London, where he had been warmly received by David and his family. François loved London 'car j'y attends plus de support qu'au aucun autre lieu, j'y suis proche de mes Amis, & l'on y respire un air de liberté quy ne se trouve pas partout ailleurs'.[229] Nevertheless, to his father's dismay, he had decided to go to Spain again and serve his time in some commercial house there.[230] This scheme was evidently linked to those of David's most entertaining correspondent, Pierre Porrée.

Porrée's 25 letters are unrivalled in this collection, not for their grasp of commercial realities or breadth of business intelligence but for their teasing, rabelaisian raillery which is far removed from the plodding sobriety of the Vroulings or Beuzelins. Porrée was evidently one of those fortunate people to whom delightful or preposterous things just seem to

[226] R. Oursel to JD, 9 November 1677.
[227] B. Beuzelin to JD, 21 February, 28 March 1679; D. Gansel to JD, 9 December 1678.
[228] B. Beuzelin to JD, 13 November 1676, 12 February 1677.
[229] François Beuzelin to JD, 4 August 1679.
[230] B. Beuzelin to JD, 5 December 1679, 1 March 1680.

happen—particularly when near water. Porrée could not cross the English channel without being seduced by a charming brunette; he could not visit Hampton Court without falling in the Thames. Frozen on the Loire, he was ambushed near the Elbe and fêted on the Rhine. Bereft, as they are, of much serious content there is sadly little excuse for printing any of these letters and Porrée's significance is confined to the fact that he intended to set up business in Cadiz with Abraham de Sadeler as agent for David.[231] After picaresque adventures in the brothels of Portsmouth and the roadstead of Cowes he set sail in January 1680 while young François Beuzelin followed overland to Bilbao. For all the elder Beuzelin's fears of the Spanish inquisition, Franco–Spanish trade seemed to this younger generation a more hopeful prospect than Anglo–French, and Jacob David's Spanish correspondence helps to explain why.

[e] SPAIN

Sir John Lethieullier dominated Jacob David's dealings with Spain as he had Marescoe's. Of the £7,435 11s 1½d-worth of goods (f.o.b.) sent to Spain by Leonora and Jacob David between 1674 and 1678 only one-third was on their sole account. The remainder represented shares in halves, thirds or eighths with Lethieullier and his associates on goods worth £12,518 12s 10d (f.o.b.). The agents to whom these goods were sent were, almost without exception, Lethieullier's men. The partnership of Upton & Bathurst at Seville had been replaced in 1672 by that of Frederick & Duncan, and Benjamin Bathurst, who had returned to England, was now a frequent participant in the joint ventures of David and Lethieullier. At Bilbao, Lethieullier's former clerk, Robert Hutchings, had been placed in 1671 only to be superseded in 1674 by another of Lethieullier's dependents, George Richards. It was a personal quarrel between Lethieullier and the Fredericks[232] which ruptured David's dealings in Seville after 1676 and diverted his main consignments to Richards at Bilbao.

Nevertheless, these agents corresponded fairly regularly with David and their letters provide some further commentary on the market for English goods in Spain and its American possessions. In December 1674 it is clear that the English propensity to glut Spain (of which Upton & Bathurst had warned in 1669) had not diminished. As a result, the imminent departure of the *galeones* and another *flota* had little or no favourable effect on prices or profits. Even though English textiles had done very well from the last *flota* Frederick & Duncan warned David not to expect great additional demand from the next one.[233] As a consequence, little effort was made to supply goods in 1675 and those that David did send were rather ill-chosen. A consignment of English pins reached Seville too late for the *flota* of July and although highly esteemed in Spain those sent to Bilbao languished unsold for three and a half years in the face of cheaper French competition. David's tentative inquiries for the prospects of copper-wire were not greatly encouraged either. Although its Swedish provenance could be easily disguised 'as if it were from Hamburg'[234] there was apparently little demand for copper-wire in Andalucia, while in Bilbao David's joint consignments with Lethieullier were found to be of the wrong quality.

The Seville agency therefore concentrated on completing the disposal of 1674's large cloth consignments, of over 500 Colchester bays, 300 Bow-dyed serges and 640 perpetuanas. The

---

[231] P. Porrée to JD, Hamburg, undated—June 1679.
[232] There is no evidence in Frederick's letters to David that the quarrel had anything to do with Leonora's rupture with Thomas Frederick.
[233] Frederick & Duncan to JD, 19 February [**229**], 19 March 1675.
[234] G. Richards to JD, 15 November 1675.

problems facing them were not so much ones of sluggish demand and poor prices as of unreliable payment by one or other of the three principal categories of purchaser available in Seville. Firstly, there were the *cargadores* and wholesale dealers who bought for the American fleets. They were generally of sound credit but in the long intervals between departures and arrivals they were only prepared to pay a small proportion of their debts in cash—the remainder being due, according to the contract of sale, 'on the return of the *galeones* (or *flota*)' with up to 12 per cent interest. Lethieullier and David were not very happy with such terms, but Frederick & Co. favoured them in preference to the alternatives, which were either Seville retailers and shop-keepers 'that in 12 m[on]ths do not cleere $\frac{1}{3}$ p[ar]te of any debt they make with us',[235] or out-of-town dealers from provincial centres such as Zafra and Ayamonte. These too bought on credit, nominally of four months duration but always longer in fact. Expensive trips had to be made to these places to collect debts due, but they were evidently an important segment of Frederick & Duncan's clientele for they are frequently mentioned.[236] Indeed, in the long intervals between the departures and returns of the American fleets provincial Spanish demand held out the only real hope of shifting the remaining English textiles. There was a distinct 'winter market' which commenced in September and for which Frederick & Duncan were prepared to wait in July 1675.[237] By October, however, they acknowledged the extreme depression of demand—'the Countrie quite drained of money by all Nations and thiere Goods in as little esteem each as others'.[238] News of a one-third increase in the amount of bullion awaiting the *galeones* in Panama raised spirits later that month and by December 'the Galleons are hourly expected which will supply the Country with moneys and put some life in this Comerce'.[239] When they did arrive, on 17 March 1676, it was confirmed that 'the best sales were to our English Manufactures, Bays, Bowdyd Serges, Long Estamenas, and houndschotts & Semp[iterne]s which at next despatch will make them in request'.[240]

The buoyancy proved only shortlived. Once again, in 1676, Spain was glutted with English goods and by November, when the *flota* returned, it was known that it had 'met with a very bad market and will discourage many that trade with New Spain'.[241] An eighteen-months interval was to elapse before the next departure of *galeones* and *flota*, and Frederick & Co were therefore honest to advise against further consignments. By this date, however, the unexplained quarrel had led Sir John to break off dealings with Frederick and although correspondence with David continued for some months there were no further shipments to Seville after July 1675.

David's ventures were now directed mainly towards Bilbao, where his pins and copper-wire had had a poor reception but where Colchester bays fulfilled all George Richards' promises of a 10 per cent profit. Not surprisingly, Colchester bays were to form 40 per cent of David's shipments to Spain between 1674 and 1678, for while demand for them had not slackened English prices had fallen significantly since 1670–72 when bays had usually been invoiced at 21d–22d per ell. Surviving invoices and bills of sale (although incomplete) reveal a distinct cheapening in first cost among David's purchases between 1676 and 1678 (Table 29). However, the margin this created was not great and Richards discouraged any complacency

---

[235] Frederick & Duncan to JD, 6 August 1675.
[236] Same to same, 30 April, 11 June [**242**], 3 September 1675 [**250**]; 28 April, 23 June 1676 [**295**].
[237] Same to same, 22 July 1675.
[238] Same to same, 1 October 1675.
[239] Same to same, 4 December 1675.
[240] Same to same, 31 March 1676.
[241] Same to same, 8 December 1676.

TABLE 29. JD's Colchester bays purchases, 1676–1678.

Pence per ell	1676	1677	1678	Total	%
16¾	71.0%	50.0%	23.8%	274	43.8
16½	—	7.2%	7.1%	40	6.4
16	20.0%	28.3%	21.4%	157	25.0
15¾	9.0%	4.3%	2.4%	26	4.2
15½	—	9.8%	30.0%	97	15.5
15¼	—	—	—	—	—
15	—	—	15.2%	32	5.1
Total No.	70	346	210	626	100.0

about the prospects if the market was over-supplied. He advised prudent purchasing during the winter months, when English prices eased, and warned that Spanish prices tended to follow the trend of English ones too closely for comfort.[242] He could not secure more than 4¾–5 *reals plata* per *vare* (i.e. 28½d–30d sterling per 33 inches) between 1676 and 1678, and less than one-third of this was for cash down.

In England, however, the fall in Colchester bays prices continued into the spring and autumn of 1679 while in Spain there were signs of a rise. 'Bays keep up here and go selling' wrote Richards in October, 'and I find they render better than anything else at present. The last I received although cost 18½d yealded neare 20 p.Ct advance and whilst they keep up at home I believe there will not be so many sent to overload the market as might be if they fell.'[243] Although English bays prices did climb back to 20d and 22d per ell over Christmas 1679, in Spain they were selling at R. pta. 6–6½ per *vare* and in his last surviving letter Richards was confident he could show a profit on bays bought at 24d.[244] In fact, on four consignments sent between 1676 and 1678 the notional profit to David (at 6d sterling per *real plata*) was 13.6 per cent, a result which compares favourably with Seville, where Frederick & Co. had returned a loss of nearly 6 per cent on their bays of 1674. Some costs at Bilbao were significantly smaller than at Seville. Although exact comparison is unsafe, freight costs to Bilbao were about 16 per cent less than at Seville and the burden of port charges, carriage and duties much lighter. Whereas the 48 Colchester bays sent to Seville in 1671 bore charges totalling 20.4 per cent of their cost (f.o.b.) or 15.4 per cent of their gross sale, the comparable figures at Bilbao in 1676–8 were 9.5 per cent and 7.8 per cent. One cannot discount some degree of customs evasion at Bilbao, for George Richards' total commission of 4½ per cent is the kind of premium rate usually associated with clandestine risk-taking. On his own admission, he had bribed the customs to secure free transit of the prohibited Swedish copper-wire in 1676.[245]

The success of bays at Bilbao would seem to have been at the expense of other English textiles, for Richards reveals no demand for the serges, perpetuanas, chenies and kerseys which had figured so largely in shipments to Spain in the 1660s. However, it was not bays which had taken their place but East Indian calicoes, which account for 47.7 per cent of David's consignments to Bilbao during 1676–8. These were exclusively Lethieullier's

[242] G. Richards to JD, 18 October 1676 [**317**]; 22 July, 28 October, 10 November 1678.
[243] Same to same, 27 October 1679.
[244] Same to same, 15 March 1680.
[245] Same to same, 20 March 1676.

responsibility, purchased by him with the discount appropriate to a director of the East India Company at the Company's sales. By 1677 prices there were generally higher than in 1675, for—despite a brief recession in 1673 and 1676—English East India calicoes were experiencing a twenty-years boom which reached its peak in 1684.[246] Lethieullier's purchases in shares with David for Bilbao consisted of 2,490 'long cloths', 2,960 'narrow baftas', 314 'salampores' and 120 'byrampauts'.[247] Their sale was not brisk, taking about ten months in 1676 and six in 1677 and 1678. Nearly 200 of the 'salampores' proved too coarse and virtually unsaleable, but 'long cloths' sold steadily at between *R. pta.* 80 and *R. pta.* 70 per piece in 1676 and 1677, falling to 75–70 in 1678. 'Baftas' fetched *R. pta.* 20–22 per piece and 'salampores' could fetch *R. pta.* $33\frac{3}{4}$ per piece. Freight and charges at Bilbao were slightly lower than on bays and David was left with notional profits of 12–13 per cent.

Richards has little to say about the customers for these textiles. His sale-accounts indicate a clientele of some 15 different purchasers for bays and perhaps 20 for calicoes, but their identities remain obscure. In 1677 he hoped to dispose of 60 bays to the local convent, but went on to observe an important difference between his market and that of Seville: 'the arrival of the *flota* will have little influence here on the price of goods, only in time to supply us with some money which is at present very scarce'.[248] Missing from these letters, therefore, is much responsiveness to the departure or arrival of the American fleets, and there is also little acknowledgment of the seasonal fluctuations which were recorded at Seville.[249] Nevertheless, Richards was no passive agent for his principals' intitiatives. As his letters of 18 October and 27 November 1676 demonstrate [**317, 321**] he was an observant and well-informed advocate for local requirements. Behind all David's other consignments—of wax, fish, hides and oil in 1676, of shot, stockings and more wax in 1677—lie the promptings of Richards. In 1678 he set David in search of *barragans* from Valenciennes and pepper from Java, and it was he who urged the pepper, cloves and Russian hides which were sent in 1679.

The wheat which was bought in Ireland and received in January 1677 sold only slowly by May, missing the period of acute demand which began in July. The years 1676–8 were ones of poor harvests and high agricultural prices in Spain,[250] so it was quite an achievement (for which Richards blamed David) to have missed the profitable opportunity that existed in the autumn of 1677. Richards was frequently critical of David's management, hinting broadly that he could learn much from his shrewd brother-in-law and pointing out that careless purchasing, finishing and packing of manufactures bought in England ate away at the profits to be made in Spain. The comparative success of the *barragans*, bought in Amsterdam and shipped via Dunkirk by the Van Baerles in 1678 and by Adrian DuQuesnoy in 1679, can be attributed to their careful stewardship.

It can also be attributed to cheaper freights in Dutch or Flemish vessels, for with the Franco–Dutch settlement in 1678 convoys from Holland and Dunkirk were again eagerly awaited in Bilbao. All David's consignments had been sent, so far, in a series of English ships, several of which were employed regularly.[251] Their freight charges averaged 2.2 per cent of the cost (f.o.b.) and 1.8 per cent of the gross sale. Those from the Netherlands appearing in

---

[246] Chaudhuri, *The Trading World of Asia and the English East India Company, 1660–1760*, pp. 285, 540 542, 544.

[247] For the character and provenance of these textiles see Chaudhuri, pp. 500–5. All but the byrampauts and 480 of the baftas were undyed calicoes.

[248] G. Richards to JD, 23 January 1677 [**331**].

[249] But see same to same, 22 December 1679, 16 February 1680 [**478**].

[250] E. J. Hamilton, *War and Prices in Spain, 1651–1800* (Cambridge, Mass., 1932) pp. 125–6; Everaert, *Vlaamse firma's te Cadiz*, pp. 601–3.

[251] Of the 11 English vessels employed 1675–9, one made 6 voyages, one made 4, two made 3 and two were employed twice.

1678 and 1679 averaged 1.2 and 1.06 per cent respectively. It is striking, but not surprising, that of David's eleven shipments in 1679 six should have been in Dutch or Flemish vessels bearing goods—*barragans*, *presillas*, cloves and wax—purchased in the Netherlands by DuQuesnoy of Amsterdam.

This was part of the gradual re-opening of normal European trade which followed the Franco–Dutch and Franco–Spanish settlements of August and September 1678, and this freer climate is also reflected in the enlargement of David's correspondence. From Bilbao Jean de Man & Heinrich Busch (factors for the Hamburg firm of Jacob Eeckhoff & Henning Busch) commenced writing in September 1678. Christopher Lethieullier's servant, Simon Rogers of Cadiz, began to correspond in November [**470**]. In June 1679 David was approached by Abraham de Sadeler of Cadiz, and in November Caspar and Albert Anckelman (late of Hamburg) sought his good offices from Seville. There was a significant community of interest behind these letters, for linking Rogers with the Anckelmans, De Sadeler, Man & Busch and George Richards was a mutual concern to maximize the advantages each possessed for trading, either through Hamburg, London, Amsterdam, Dunkirk or Rouen. Thus, French linens channelled through De Sadeler to Rogers could circumvent the English embargo and could be profitably bartered for cochineal or indigo. Silver bullion, acquired for the Hamburg firm at Cadiz, could be consigned to London in secure English shipping and its proceeds remitted, or drawn on by bills from Hamburg. The Seville–Amsterdam exchange was evidently preferred to the Seville–London route (which is scarcely ever quoted) but English textiles, hotly demanded for the *flota* of 1680, could profit them all. It was to this lively prospect of mutual interchange that the young Beuzelin and Porrée were attracted, although how far their expectations were realized cannot be discerned for as their arrival was awaited the correspondence is broken off.

There is another side of this Anglo–Spanish trade which has to be surveyed—the matter of returns. 'Notional profits', assessed at the standard rate of *6d* sterling per *real plata* continued to be recorded by David, but the true profit can only be assessed from the proceeds in London of silver, gold, commodities or bills. In the 1660s, Marescoe's bullion sales had added 7–8 per cent to his notional profit. What was the reward for David? No complete answer can be given without the missing Journal for 1673–7, which would state the full account of the rates David received on his sales of silver and gold. The invoices are incomplete and even the letters can be confusing with their cryptic references to 'powdered sugars', 'rusty iron', 'wool', 'grain', 'lemons' 'chocolate' and other euphemisms for silver and gold. Now and again, presents of lemons, oranges and chocolate turn out to be quite genuine, but in the main the disguises are transparent enough to allow identification.

Thus, of the returns Frederick & Co made between 1674 and 1676, silver accounted for 91.5 per cent and gold for the rest. The invoiced value of these eleven consignments was *R. pta.* 82,717 (a notional £2,067 18s 6d) but this sum includes not merely small charges incurred at Seville and Cadiz and a $2\frac{1}{2}$ per cent commission but also a variable premium for the purchase of silver *pesos*. This premium had reached 9 per cent in 1669 but was very volatile. It was at 5 per cent in January, and 7 per cent in March 1672. In September 1676 it was only 4 per cent but must have risen higher in Andalucia during the long interval between the return *flota* of November 1676 and the *galeones* of August 1679.

Monetary conditions in Bilbao were evidently quite distinct from those of Seville, and the premium on *pesos* as well as the premium for converting vellon into silver or gold followed a different course from that of New Castile tabulated by Earl J. Hamilton.[252] In George

---

[252] Hamilton, *War and Prices*, pp. 17–35; cf. Everaert, pp. 32–3 n. 3.

TABLE 30. Silver *pesos* premiums, Bilbao, 1677–1679.

1677	1678	1679
March = $4\frac{1}{4}$%	February = $4\frac{1}{2}$%	March = $5\frac{1}{2}$%
May = $4\frac{1}{2}$%	April = $4\frac{3}{4}$%	May = 6%
October = 4%	May = $4\frac{3}{4}$	July = 6%
November = 4%	June = 5%	1680
Decembe**ʀ** = $4\frac{1}{2}$%	September = 5%	March = 6%
	December = 5%	

Richards' accounts for 1677–80 the exchange premium (for the purchase of silver *pesos*) moved as shown in Table 30.

Throughout these Bilbao accounts the silver premium on vellon was calculated at an unchanging 200 per cent until the decree of 10 February 1680,[253] and there was evidently greater difficulty at Bilbao than at Seville in obtaining Spanish silver for returns. Twice Richards included some Italian coins and what he called 'Irish bars' (at a significantly lower exchange premium, of 3 per cent). In default of silver he sent gold; he drew bills on three occasions, and on three occasions he sent goods—iron, whalefins and chocolate. Thus, of returns with a notional value of £5,088 19s sent between 1676 and 1677, silver accounted for 63.5 per cent, gold for 18.6 per cent, goods for 9.1 per cent and bills of exchange for 8.8 per cent. With the help of the Journal commencing in 1677 one can also assess the profitability of the bullion, and the outcome is rather different from the 1660s. In six cases David realized a small profit, totalling £10 0s 7d, but in seven cases he incurred a loss, totalling £16 3s 3½d. In every instance the gold consignments contributed to the loss, a circumstance which may be related to a recent change in the English East India Company's bullion requirements. A collapse in gold prices in India, detected in 1676–7, led to a sharp adjustment in the proportions of gold and silver exported in 1679–80 and there was a downturn in the London gold price from 82s per ounce in 1676 to 80s between 1677 and 1684.[254] This must have affected David's profits, for the goldsmith-banker to whom he sold most of his bullion, John Temple, was among the largest suppliers of treasure to the East India Company throughout the 1670s.[255]

The problem of returns did not entirely spare one sector of Spain with which Marescoe had usually practised a kind of barter. At Malaga, Simon Campioni had always been eager to exchange raisins and wine against Colchester bays. In 1677, after several years of silence, he renewed these offers, suggesting 30,000–40,000 *thonneaux* of raisins against 150 white bays and 50 Norfolk chenies. As an afterthought, 50–60 *quintals* of coperose vitriol (used in dyeing white bays) were suggested as an alternative and this David sent in September. But contrary winds delayed until December the return cargo of raisins which reached England too late to command the high pre-Christmas prices Campioni had relied on. He was the first to acknowledge that this kind of exchange could not work without precise timing, and that raisins had to be procured with ready cash. He proposed that, in future, David should make cash available against drafts at Cadiz, Seville or Antwerp and that he would handle David's

---

[253] G. Richards to JD, 16 February 1680 [**478**]; Hamilton, *War and Prices*, pp. 20, 31.
[254] Chaudhuri, pp. 162, 178.
[255] Chaudhuri, p. 166.

commodity exports at a $4\frac{1}{2}$ per cent commission, bearing all risks with one sinister exception—'bien entendus, hors pour nous le rische du tribunal d'inquisition'!²⁵⁶

Heavy rains ruined the raisin crop in November 1678 but in May 1679 Campioni urged David to seize the golden opportunity for Spanish wines now created by the English embargo on French ones, and when the letters break off in February 1680 it is amid an active exchange of wines for Colchester bays.

[f] ITALY

While all sectors of David's export trade shared in the depressing vicissitudes of the 1670s, none entered such a conspicuous decline as his trade with Italy in general and Leghorn in particular. Where Italy had once taken an average 16 per cent share between 1668 and 1672, it now received barely 3 or 4 per cent of his shipments in 1673 and 1674. Nothing at all was despatched there by David in 1676 and 1677.

In December 1674, when the correspondence resumes, the Leghorn partnership of Skinner, Ball & Gosfright was reporting poor prices for most of the staple English consignments. Lead, after the dizzy rise of 1672–3, had relapsed to the levels of 1669–70 and was to drift below them in 1676. Tin was now at the lowest point recorded since the correspondence began. As for textiles 'all woollen manufactory in very low esteeme, the French outdoing us in cheapnesse, and if [they] gaine farther footing in Sicilly (and wee wish they are not too soone masters of the whole island) wee shall vent no more of our manufactory in that Country'.²⁵⁷

Pepper inevitably shared in the general European decline, although even at 9 or 10 ducats per 100 lb. it offered modest opportunities if skilfully timed. David therefore took a risk on 50 bales for his own account and combined it with some 100 pigs of lead which were received in Leghorn in January 1676. With them he also ventured some Swedish copper-wire but its reception was lukewarm—'wire is a comodity of no great demand here and therefore no great quantity will off'.²⁵⁸ In August 1677 he offered pitch and tar and received an interesting assessment of Leghorn's needs [373] but it was not an encouraging one and the conclusive note of this correspondence was sounded in January 1678—'our trade here consumes as bad as ever so that we cannot give you encouragement to ought'.²⁵⁹

The Venetian correspondence was even more sterile, although the conscientious Van Teylingen continued to fill his now infrequent letters with lengthy lists of commodity prices. He too received David's inquiry about the prospects for pitch and tar and his reply is characteristically detailed, setting out the probable 17 per cent loss which David could expect on a hypothetical shipment of 25 lasts of tar. Nothing could be more expressive of Venice's maritime decline than this depressing assessment of her limited needs.²⁶⁰

Her old enemy, Genoa, offered more lively prospects although the commodity at issue here was the unfamiliar one of whalefins. Jacob David's introduction to this commodity and to Genoa was made by the Amsterdam firm of De la Bistrate & Dufay which commissioned the shipment of six packs in August 1677 [415]. Their chosen agents in Genoa were Van Weert & Stock, but in August 1678 David opened a correspondence with the English firm of Robert Welch & George Styles who soon set in motion an enthusiastic stream of advice and

²⁵⁶ S. Campioni to JD, 7 July 1678.
²⁵⁷ Skinner, Ball & Gosfright to JD, 27 November 1676 [323].
²⁵⁸ Same to same, 22 May 1676.
²⁵⁹ Same to same, 28 January 1678.
²⁶⁰ P. van Teylingen to JD, 24 September 1677 [369].

market intelligence. They confirmed the large demand for whalebone but also urged attention to pepper, lead, tin, sugar, perpetuanas and wheat [**416**]. Even Swedish iron had prospects, and in January 1679 they recommended a shipment of tar.

As for returns, they were ready to remit David's proceeds by bill of exchange but preferred the alternatives of olive-oil, bought from the neighbouring hills of Oneglia, or the lemons of San Remo. Rice, silks or writing paper were other possibilities, much favoured by the Dutch. On this more encouraging basis David directed his efforts in 1679 to eliminating the loss made on his whalebones in 1678. The shortfall of some 18 per cent on his outlay had been attributed to Dutch competition, but by September 1679 the failure of the Dutch convoy to bring any tar with it had created a favourable opportunity for David. Only 30 barrels were said to remain unsold in Genoa in June; by July there were allegedly none at all.[261] It was bitterly disappointing therefore that David's mixed cargo of lead, iron and tar, ready in September, should have been delayed at Plymouth awaiting the company of other Straits-bound shipping. By December the opportunity had passed. Herring ships bound for Leghorn brought with them 200 barrels of tar, enough for the port's immediate needs, and by the time David's vessel, the *Success*, reached Genoa on 30 January 1680 the price advantage had gone. Worse still, the Swedish iron proved too broad; narrow bars were required, and the omission of a deck-cargo of deal boards had wasted a valuable opportunity.[262]

Such were the normal hazards of an unfamiliar market. David, who seems to have begun to act independently of his brother-in-law, clearly had much to learn about Genoa and its requirements. A financial centre, in which some 3 million *pesos* were said to be awaited in October 1679,[263] held attractions which were worth exploring further, and when the correspondence is broken off in March 1680 the dialogue with David was tantalizingly brisk.

[g] THE LEVANT

Jacob David chose an opportune moment to seek entry to the Levant Company. Sir John Lethieullier was exercising a growing influence in this trade and in February 1678 was elected to the Company's Court of Assistants.[264] The Levant trade itself was enjoying a boom and the Company was keenly aware of the opportunity conferred upon it by French and Dutch preoccupation in the western Mediterranean.[265] But its readiness to exploit this was coupled with a determination to exclude interlopers. No concessions were to be made in the Company's impositions on 'strangers', and the regulations governing admission to their society were strictly enforced.[266] Jacob David needed both naturalization as an English subject and recognition as a London merchant-citizen if he was to secure membership of the Company.

The indications are that he began to seek naturalization by private Act of Parliament in 1675,[267] at the time of his marriage with Leonora, but unfortunately for him the autumn

---

[261] Welch & Styles to JD, 12 July 1679 [**452**].

[262] Same to same, 12 July 1679.

[263] Same to same, 4 October 1679. For the proportion of Spanish bullion reaching Genoa in the 1670s see Kamen, *Spain in the Later Seventeenth Century*, pp. 138–9; for seventeenth century Genoese investment see G. Felloni, *Gli investimenti finanziari genovesi in Europa tra il Seicento e la Restaurazione* (Milan, 1971).

[264] PRO, SP. 105/154 f. 76.

[265] A. C. Wood, *A History of the Levant Company*, pp. 99–100; PRO, SP. 105/154 f. 8 (General Court of 14 December 1676).

[266] PRO, SP. 105/153 ff. 417, 428, 430.

[267] He secured Letters of Denization on 6 October 1675—*CSPD*, 1675–76, p. 585.

session of that year was the prelude to an unusually long prorogation which lasted until February 1677. Royal assent to his naturalization bill was not given until April 1677. There is no indication in the Levant Company's records that he now sought admission and he may well have been deterred by the Company's stubborn reluctance to admit a fellow French-born merchant, Humphrey Willet, despite evidence of his naturalization.[268]

David's flirtation with the Levant was therefore comparatively brief and small in scale, although it generated an interesting correspondence with six different firms in Aleppo, Smyrna and Constantinople.[269]

It was inaugurated in 1674–5 by the transfer to Aleppo of 3,000 *pesos* from Seville, despatched aboard the *Providence* by Frederick & Duncan, and by a consignment of ginger in which David had a one-fifth share with his Levant Company partners. The proceeds were exchanged for galls, goat-wool and cotton yarn, and a further 3,000 *pesos* were sent in the *Providence* from Leghorn in 1676. But, here too, David was seeking a new market for his surplus Swedish copper-wire, sending three different samples for Lannoy & Burkin's inspection in June 1675. They put Aleppo's annual demand at between 29 and 36 cwt. per annum[270]—a comparatively trivial amount but enough to encourage David to send 44 coils to another Aleppo correspondent, Charles Goodfellow. He also sent two barrels of brass-ware pans, which were evidently an unwelcome novelty in Aleppo, where plain sheets were preferred. The wire too was not the finely-drawn variety desired by the craftsmen and supplied to them by French and Venetian competitors.[271]

If David's switch of commissions to Goodfellow was based on Lannoy's refusal to 'colour' his goods and perjure himself then he was disappointed, for Goodfellow proved no less conscientious. Both factors felt bound by their obligation not to disguise the identity of 'strangers' goods, which were liable to a 20 per cent 'broke' or surcharge imposed by the Levant Company. Deference to David's friendship with their respective fathers induced Lannoy, Burkin and Goodfellow to continue corresponding with him, but until he became a member of the Company they could procure him no certain profit on his heavily-burdened goods. One-fifth of the copper-wire was seized by the English consul on the Company's behalf.[272]

The correspondents therefore confined themselves to the encouraging advice which factors were expected to provide, depicting the profits which could be hoped for on despatch of cochineal, of weighty Seville or Mexico *pesos* or, best of all, of 'Lyon dollars . . . which make quick returns'.[273] There was no question of David participating in the Company's main exports on the 'General Ships' which in 1676 carried to Scanderoon 1,342 bales of cloth, 1,665 cwt. of tin, 19 fodders of lead and no less than 71,585 dollars.[274] But he could share in the commonest returns, which were principally galls, silks and cottons. The high price of galls in western Europe—already remarked on in Hamburg and Rouen—took its origin from the high level of demand at Aleppo, for although the *racoltas* of 1675 and 1676 were

---

[268] PRO, SP. 105/154 ff. 44–5, 53, 60.

[269] From Aleppo, JD received 13 letters from Timothy Lannoy & John Burkin, 19 from Charles Goodfellow; from Smyrna, 3 from J. & H. van Crayestein, 3 from John Richards; from Constantinople, 2 from Simon Middleton, 4 from Samuel Lannoy. The English communities at these places were possibly 50+ at Aleppo, up to 100 at Smyrna and 25+ at Constantinople—Wood, *Levant Company*, pp. 126–7.

[270] Lannoy & Burkin to LM & JD, 3 September 1675 [**265**].

[271] C. Goodfellow to JD, 12 May 1676.

[272] Same to same, 1 June 1676.

[273] T. Lannoy to JD, 7 March 1677. The Levant Co. treasurer had reported difficulty in obtaining Seville or Mexico *pesos* in June 1676—PRO, SP. 105/153 f. 428.

[274] PRO, SP. 105/167.

good, prices of between \$30 and \$45 per quintal (about $3\frac{1}{2}$ cwt.) were reached where before they had been at \$24 or \$25. Silk thread, such as 'Burma Legi' which arrived from Persia by the Baghdad caravans, was also plentiful in 1677 but rose under pressure of export demand from \$10 per *rottolo* (about 4 English lb.) to \$$11\frac{3}{4}$ by 1678. Destruction of silk-worms by locusts also helped to push up local silk prices.[275]

However, the severest shock to England's trade in the Levant was administered by the more rapacious agency of man. The accession of the Grand Vizier Kara Mustafa in 1676 brought to Constantinople a singularly ruthless administrator whose respect for the Levant Company's privileges was a good deal weaker than his predecessor's. Suspecting the Company's frank declaration of 200,000 lion dollars, imported in 1677, as a cunning disguise for counterfeits he seized the whole amount and, although they were found to be full-weight, retained \$15,000.[276] This sombre news was the main burden of Timothy Lannoy's last letter and it may explain why David made no response to his brother Samuel Lannoy's friendly overtures from Constantinople. Smyrna too remained closed to him until he became a member of the Company, and thus, as the shadow of the Frederick law suit lengthened, his correspondence from the Levant came to a barren and unprofitable close.

(iii) PROFIT AND LOSS, 1673–1679

By the test of profitability, Jacob David's business partnership with Leonora compares poorly with Charles Marescoe's achievement. In mitigation it can be conceded that he was denied the golden opportunity offered to Swedish imports during the second Anglo–Dutch war, but even those opportunities he was given—the Tar Company agency and large-scale supplies from the major iron and copper producers—failed to produce comparable rewards for his own account. Over the whole period from the autumn of 1673 to the summer of 1679 (when the Journal and Ledger were being wound up) David achieved little more than 1 per cent profit on copper, iron and other imported commodities, worth nearly £65,000 in total, bought in for re-sale on his own account. Copper-wire had done relatively well at first, yielding him 3.25 per cent during 1675–6, but his strenuous attempts to corner supplies in England and dispose of stocks in France, Italy and the Levant ended in 1679 with a loss of 1 per cent.

In contrast, the earnings made on import commissions continued to be ample, and nothing better illustrates the attraction of this kind of agency than the fat percentages David extracted from his Swedish principals. Commission, brokerage and discounts brought in the largest portion of the partnership's earnings attributable to imports, and to these must be added the large gains accruing from credit and advances extended to his suppliers.[277] 'Interest on current accounts' in Table 31 represents 6 per cent per annum, cast up at irregular intervals, on loans extended to the Mommas, the De Geers, the Cronströms and other Swedish producers, averaging nearly £5,000 per annum. Their shipping requirements were also responsible for most of the commission earned on the insurance account.

Because Leonora and David chose not to distinguish earnings under a separate

[275] T. Lannoy to JD, 11 December 1676 [**337**]; PRO, SP. 110/14 ff. 32, 44b; C. Goodfellow to JD, 27 February 1677.

[276] Wood, *Levant Company*, p. 101; G. F. Abbott, *Under the Turk in Constantinople: a record of Sir John Finch's Embassy, 1672–81* (London, 1920) Ch. 14; G. Ambrose, 'English Traders at Aleppo, 1658–1756', *EcHR*, 1st Series, 3 (1931) pp. 24–6.

[277] See Table 31, 'Gross Profits' items 2, 3 and 4(a).

'Commission Account' and 'Profit & Loss Account' it is not possible to allocate their profits on import commissions quite so distinctly as in 1664–7 between those earned from their own initiative and those received on behalf of others (Table 31). But on the export side it is easier to differentiate, for export commissions were usually to different destinations and to different clients than those in France, Spain and Italy to whom 'Voyages' were despatched. At first sight it would seem that the latter proved the more profitable, but the distinctive feature of David's trading is that he invested a greater proportion of his resources in exports on his own account than had Marescoe. Whereas 71.75 per cent of Marescoe's exports in the period 1664–70 represented commissioned goods, over 51 per cent of Leonora and David's exports between 1673 and 1678 were on their own account. The proportion rose particularly sharply after David took sole charge in October 1675 and although he relied heavily on his brother-in-law's backing in Spain, Italy and the Levant the enlarged investment in trade to Rouen reflects his personal initiative. Yet here too his profit record was poor. Copper-wire to Rouen earned less than 4 per cent in 1675, about 5 per cent in 1676 and barely 0.7 per cent in 1677. His grain venture to Rotterdam left a loss of £84 and his losses on salt and wine sent to Sweden in 1676–7 were only made good by his guaranteed 14 per cent profit on cloth sent in 1678. These results contrast with those from Spain where his notional gains averaged 6.7 per cent between 1675 and 1678. In 1679 the Bilbao account was closed with a profit of £468 2s 5d, which represents much of the gain attributable to 'Voyages' in that year.

The partnership's trading profits were supplemented by a few other items after the marriage of 1675. The East India Company dividends totalling 40.5 per cent, issued in three declarations of 1677–8, were followed by a further 40 per cent declared in 1679 which does not figure in these accounts. 'Apprentices' represent the down-payments which accompanied the acceptance of John Waite in 1673, Jacob Fahlgren in 1675 and John Gosselin in 1677. Rents of houses and payments by the Orphans' Court of 5 per cent interest on the Marescoe children's estate make up the other earnings attributable to Leonora's fortune.

To set against these there were certain 'losses'—significantly larger than any suffered by Charles Marescoe, who had faced war, plague and fire. Jacob David's 'losses', however, are indicative less of misfortune than of mismanagement, for the largest single source of them is interest paid on borrowed capital.[278] This in itself would not be reprehensible: it might reflect a commendable enterprise. With a trading capital of £15,292 17s 6d in 1673 and of £15,875 10s 11d in 1675, Leonora and Jacob David were not fully-equipped to carry on the same scale of business sustained by Marescoe and Joye, with over £47,000, between 1668 and 1670. It made good sense to borrow sums of £2,000, £700 and £500 from brothers John and Christopher Lethieullier in 1673 and 1674. These family loans, at 5 per cent, rose from £3,200 to £3,500 in 1676–7, to £3,800 in 1677–8 and to £4,200 in 1679. But they were not alone. There were five other creditors in 1674, six in 1675, eight in 1678 and nine in 1679. Among them were John Strype, the incumbent of Low Leyton (with £100, rising to £250, at 6 per cent), the French Church, Threadneedle Street (£90, rising to £150, at 6 per cent) and men like Jan Delmé and Thomas Frampton who drew regular quarterly payments at 5 per cent per annum from fixed deposits of £1,000 and £400 over the whole six-year period (Table 32). This long-term credit must have been crucial to sustaining the large-scale advances which were so unavoidable a feature of the Swedish commission trade. They must also have served to enable participation in the joint ventures of John Lethieullier and his friends. But why were they necessary? Why were Jacob David's growing requirements not being met by the accumulation of profits?

---

[278] On average, 60 per cent of the 'Loss' recorded in Table 33, column 2, represents interest on the Company's borrowings.

TABLE 31. LM & JD, gross profits, 1673–1679.

Gross Profits	1673–4 £ s d	1674–5 £ s d	1675–6 £ s d	1676–7 £ s d	1677–8 £ s d	1678–9 £ s d	Totals £ s d	%
1. Exports:								
(a) 'voyages'	4 1 1	151 16 6	177 8 10	69 8 9	237 17 2	814 6 1	1,454 18 5	10.40
(b) commissions	129 7 10	115 15 9	57 7 4	203 1 4	92 15 0	119 7 2	717 14 5	5.13
2. Imports	575 6 11	994 8 5	365 16 2	1,312 7 4	761 10 7	400 6 8	4,409 16 2	31.57
3. Provision, discount	59 12 03	16 19 6	2 6 7	19 1 7	133 5 4	140 12 01	371 17 4	2.66
4. Interest:								
(a) Current accounts	2 1 03	726 19 7	59 12 9	544 11 6	299 3 11	78 2 2	1,710 11 2	12.24
(b) Loans	151 17 11	105 16 7	73 10 0	91 8 0	158 11 11	421 15 5	1,002 19 10	7.18
5. Bills of Exchange	35 3 04	98 14 6	93 16 9	31 12 7	162 8 9	133 16 7	555 12 6	3.97
6. Insurance A/c	130 11 6	51 14 3	31 17 1	93 4 6	15 6 0	30 19 0	353 12 4	2.53
7. Shipping A/c	3 14 0	—	—	—	60 0 0	294 16 6	358 10 6	2.56
8. Expense A/c	—	199 13 3	—	—	153 15 8	—	353 8 11	2.53
9. Apprentices	150 0 0	150 0 0	—	—	200 0 0	—	500 0 0	3.58
10. E. I. Co. dividends	—	—	—	450 0 0	461 5 0	—	911 5 0	6.52
11. Orphan's Court	—	—	—	200 0 0	200 0 0	200 0 0	600 0 0	4.29
12. Rents	—	—	—	33 6 8	321 9 11	61 9 10	416 6 5	2.98
13. Sundries: Particular A/c	—	—	—	—	117 1 0	135 16 8	252 17 8	1.81
Totals	1,241 16 2	2,611 18 3	861 15 6	3,048 2 3	3,374 10 3	2,831 8 2	13,969 10 7	100.0

TABLE 32. Borrowing by LM & JD, 1674–1679.

At year end	At 5%	At 6%	Total
1674	£4,100	£600	£4,700
1675	£6,500	£660	£7,160
1676	£5,200	£815	£6,015
1677	£5,200	£840	£6,040
1678	£6,500	£940	£7,400
1679	£7,050	£970	£8,020

The answers lie principally in the sparse but appalling figures for Leonora's and Jacob's household expenditure. The extravagance which had already emerged between 1670 and 1673 continued unchecked, and although the details are still veiled by the simple entry 'fraits de mesnage' or 'cassa aen myn vrouw getelt' there are enough itemized luxuries to raise the most uncensorious eyebrows. £40 for a carriage in May 1674 was followed by £347 10s for a collar of pearls and diamonds in June. There were expensive linens, looking-glasses, tapestries and much wine. In November 1675, on his nuptials with Leonora, Jacob charged to 'Loss' £640 for 'a jewel for my wife' and £320 for two diamonds. The same month saw the £1,500 bank deposit with Isaac Meynell written off as a bad debt. But the largest undifferentiated item attributed to 'loss' continued to be mere housekeeping— £1,673 8s 11d gross in September 1677, £1,760 14s 10d in September 1678 and a more modest £776 5s 6d in August 1679 (Table 33).

It is this rate of domestic expenditure which stunted the capital growth of the company and denied David the chance of rising to half the stature achieved by his predecessor. But it seems unlikely that he or Leonora greatly cared. Cushioned by the resources of her wealthy brothers Mme David could aspire to the aldermanic grandeurs of their rank while Jacob, called upon to entertain a De Geer or a Cronström during their visits to London, had to cut a figure comparable with these merchant-princes. Running through their letters, and those of humbler friends like Pierre Porrée, are warm recollections of a bibulous household and a lavish table, and although the path which the Davids trod may have been as crooked as the Fredericks alleged it was clearly a very enjoyable one.

TABLE 33. LM & JD: net profits, 1673–1679.

	Company Earnings			Leonora's dividends (a)	Non-Co. receipts (b)	Total (a) + (b)	Net expenses	Transfer to Capital
	Gross Profits £ s d	Losses £ s d	Net Profit £ s d	£ s d	£ s d	£ s d	£ s d	£ s d
1673–4	1,241 16 2	248 17 8	992 18 6	744 14 0	1,861 6 2	2,606 0 2	1,839 2 4	766 17 10
1674–5	2,611 18 3	578 2 6	2,033 15 9	1,525 6 10	2,756 15 8	4,282 2 6	3,737 7 1	544 15 5
1675–6	861 15 6	447 1 9	414 13 9	414 13 9	407 6 4	822 0 1	*4,795 9 9	–3,973 9 8
1676–7	3,048 2 3	675 3 4	2,372 18 11	—	—	—	1,583 1 11	†789 17 0
1677–8	3,374 10 3	761 17 9	2,612 12 6				1,748 4 10	864 7 8
1678–9	2,831 8 2	1,072 13 5	1,758 14 9				768 5 6	990 9 3

Notes:

* £1,500 of this represents the deposit with Isaac Meynell, written-off as a bad debt.
† On Leonora's marriage with Jacob in November 1675 his assets, of £1,114 16s 7d, were added to make a joint capital of £15,875 10s 11d.

THE MARESCOE-DAVID LETTERS,
1668–1680

'. . . men geen negotie sonder brieven can drijven . . .'
Steven de Geer, 25 September 1676

A NOTE ON (i) THE PRESENTATION, (ii) THE TRANSCRIPTION, (iii) THE TRANSLATION AND (iv) THE DATING OF THE LETTERS.

(i) In preparing these letters for publication priority has been given to presenting their substance rather than their form. Thus, no attempt has been made to preserve the superficial appearance of any letter. The date and place of origin of each is given in modern English; in some cases they have been shorn of their flowery salutations and their equally ornate valedictions. Punctuation, capitalization and italicization (of ships' names notably) have been supplied and paragraphing introduced where it assists to clarify the text. On the other hand, no passages have been suppressed, however trivial, and any indecipherable words have been indicated [– – – –] and any tentative readings followed by [?].

(ii) The rules governing the transcriptions from English and French are as follows. The original spelling remains unaltered, but contractions have been expanded in modern English (or French) form. Punctuation, capitalization and italicization have been supplied but no attempt has been made to intrude modern or even contemporaneous conventions of accenting to the letters in French. The acute accent appears rarely, there is scarcely one grave accent, circumflex or cedilla. Grammatical errors in English or French have been left uncorrected, although on reading the latter aloud the common failure of verbs to agree with the number or gender of the subject tends to disappear, confirming the impression that some of these letters were dictated to a careless or overworked clerk. Lamentably, some of the most incoherent letters are in English and in one or two such cases an explanation has been appended.

(iii) In translating from the Dutch and German some freedom has been taken to ensure that the letters make sense in modern, colloquial English. Occasionally it would have been easier to follow the original sentence construction or literal meaning more closely, producing a somewhat stilted and synthetic 'seventeenth-century English', but the temptation has been resisted, and in view of the availability of the originals in microfiche I have felt freer to replace Dutch idioms with equivalent English ones. Thus, when prices are said to be 'onder de voet' they can be described merely as 'low' or, more forcibly, as 'rock-bottom', if the context justifies it. When goods are reported to be selling 'als broot by den backer' they can be legitimately said to be 'selling like hot cakes', and so on.

However, one usage which is peculiarly difficult to translate is the italianism 'costi' (or 'costy') which is essentially equivalent to the French 'chez vous', though sometimes adopted by French merchants themselves as an alternative. Commonly employed by Swedes and Hamburgers, though slightly less frequently by Dutch writers, in their letters to Marescoe or David (who in turn employed it in their letters to Sweden) it can be taken to mean in the former context either 'London' precisely, or more generally 'England'—but which? Used in the listing of exchange rates at the foot of a letter it clearly means 'London' but in a sentence which might report five ships laden with sugar reaching 'costy', or a shortage of pitch in 'costi' it could be a matter of some importance whether London or England is intended. Sometimes it is easy to deduce the intention, but in many cases it must remain doubtful and although I have had to make my choice I have been careful to bracket my '[England]' or '[London]' wherever it translates 'costi'. Less common but equally ambiguous is the closer Dutch equivalent of 'chez vous' which is 'bij Ue'. Here too I have bracketed it as either '[in England]' or '[at London]'. In other cases where the meaning of the Dutch or German is obscure or my translation is markedly free I have supplied the original in a footnote. The original language of a translated letter is indicated either as [D] Dutch or [G] German, and in all cases except those which are unfit because of fragility or illegibility the original letters have been reproduced on microfiche, indicated by an asterisk in the following list (pp. 211–20).

(iv) The dating of letters is, wherever possible, that given in the original letter, without specific amendment as either New Style or Old Style (which is rarely indicated in the originals). Thus, letters from Italy, Spain, France, the Spanish Netherlands and the United Provinces can be taken to be dated according to the New Style or Gregorian calendar, which at this period meant a difference of 10 extra days from the date in any Old Style country. Sweden, Hamburg and England retained the Julian calendar and are thus in harmony, but it would be possible for a hypothetical letter from Rouen, or Lille or Amsterdam, dated (say) 28 May to reach London on 24 May after a journey evidently taking six days. These discrepancies can be easily detected, for nearly all these letters bear two further dates, both in Old Style, endorsed upon the outer cover. These are (a) the date received, and (b) the date answered, and they are given here in the right-hand margin of the letter heading in the form (e.g.) $\frac{24\ May}{26\ May}1670$. It was the second of these dates which determined the letter's position in the accumulating bundles, but in order to provide a consistent, unambiguous basis for the arrangement of this selection I have used the first date (a) to determine the order in which the letters are printed here. Not all letters bear a distinct endorsement of the date of reply, and in such cases, I have indicated it, either by '[——]' or, where other evidence justifies it, by the probable date, e.g. *[26 May]*.

In many cases letters were accompanied by a second copy of the preceding letter, and where the original is missing, damaged or indecipherable I have sometimes selected the copy for translation or transcription—e.g. Nos **30, 132, 266, 322, 439**. In these cases the date of receipt refers not to the original but to (i) the copy and (ii) the accompanying letter, indicated (e.g.)

$$(i) + (ii)\ \frac{26\ May}{26\ May}.$$

The letters selected fall into three groups:

		Letters
A. Letters to Charles Marescoe	1668	**1–60**
	1669	**61–127**
	1670	**128–135**
B. Letters to Leonora Marescoe & Peter Joye	1670	**136–138**
	1671	**139–177**
	1672	**178–218**
	1673	**219–221**

C. Letters to Leonora Marescoe & Jacob David

$$\begin{cases} 1675 & \textbf{222–266} \\ 1676 & \textbf{267–325} \\ 1677 & \textbf{326–379} \\ 1678 & \textbf{380–430} \\ 1679 & \textbf{431–470} \\ 1680 & \textbf{471–480} \end{cases}$$

A. LETTERS TO CHARLES MARESCOE:

1668

1. Thomas Death, Ephraim Skinner & Co., Leghorn, 16 January.
2. Anthony Upton & Benjamin Bathurst, Seville, 29 November (1667).
3. Richard Crumpe, Bristol, 7 March.
*4. Widow Berenberg & Co., Hamburg, 15 February.
*5. Widow Berenberg & Co., Hamburg, 22 February.
*6. Abraham Momma, Stockholm, 5 February.
7. Deborah van Ruyff, Axbergshamer, 20 February.
*8. Steven de Geer, Amsterdam, 23 March.
9. Robert Oursel, Rouen, 28 March.
*10. Joachim Pötter & Hendrik Thuen, Stockholm, 29 February.
*11. Jean & David van Baerle, Amsterdam, 6 April.
12. Egidio Ruland, Hamburg, 21 April.
13. Thomas Wright, Stokesley, 2 May.
14. R. Oursel, Rouen, 16 May.
15. Widow Berenberg & Co., Hamburg, 16 May.
16. Peter Juncker, Hamburg, 16 May.
17. J. & D. van Baerle, Amsterdam, 1 June.
*18. S. de Geer, Amsterdam, 22 June.
19. Upton & Bathurst, Seville, 19 June.
20. John Papen, Limerick, 3 July.
*21. A. Momma, Stockholm, 24 June.
*22. Arnold Ruland, Hamburg, 11 July.
23. Peter Caulier, Yarmouth, 20 July.
24. William Skinner, Hull, 20 July.
25. Richard Kingman, Dartmouth, 21 July.
*26. J. & D. van Baerle, Amsterdam, 3 August.
27. W. Skinner, Hull, 10 August.
28. R. Oursel, Rouen, 1 September.
29. Paul Berenberg, Hamburg, 8 August.
30. Death, Skinner & Co., Leghorn, 3 August.
*31. S. de Geer, The Hague, 14 September.
*32. Tar Company Directors, Stockholm, 22 August.
*33. Tar Company Directors, Stockholm, 29 August.
34. R. Oursel, Rouen, 6 October.
35. Johan Barckman Leyonbergh, London, 27 September.
*36. Jan van Savelant, Gothenburg, 14 September.
*37. Cornelius Berenberg, Amsterdam, 12 October.
*38. Adam Radue, Stockholm, 19 September.
39. J. B. Leyonbergh, London, 13 October.
40. J. B. Leyonbergh, London, 14 October.
41. J. B. Leyonbergh, London, 21 October.
42. J. B. Leyonbergh, London, (?).
43. J. B. Leyonbergh, London, 24 October.
44. J. B. Leyonbergh, London, 29 October.
*45. J. van Savelant, Gothenburg, 19 October.
*46. Peter Simons, Amsterdam, 13 November.
47. Upton & Bathurst, Seville, 16 October.
*48. Pietro van Teylingen, Venice, 2 November.

*49. S. de Geer, Amsterdam, 16 November.
*50. Tar Company Directors, Stockholm, 24 October.
*51. S. de Geer, Amsterdam, 20 November.
 52. Death, Skinner & Co., Leghorn, 23 November.
 53. W. Skinner, Hull, 4 December.
 54. Bryan Rogers, Falmouth, 7 December.
 55. Robert Ellison, Newcastle, 12 December.
*56. P. van Teylingen, Venice, 7 December.
 57. Jacob Momma, Norrköping, 23 November.
 58. Peter Ruland, Hamburg, 11 December.
 59. T. Wright, [Stokesley], 17 December.
 60. W. Skinner, Hull, 22 December.

1669

 61. J. Pötter & H. Thuen, Stockholm, 5 December.
 62. Abraham Kock-Cronström, Stockholm, (12?) December.
*63. J. Momma, Visby-in-Gotland, 14 August 1668.
 64. Sir Edward Walker, Whitehall, 15 January.
 65. Tar Company Directors, Stockholm, 19 December.
 66. Jean Freyhoff, La Rochelle, 10 January.
*67. P. Berenberg, Hamburg, 8 January.
 68. J. B. Leyonbergh, Covent Garden, 22 January.
*69. Louis Trip, Amsterdam, 1 February.
*70. J. van Savelant, Gothenburg, 24 December.
 71. William Browne, Bristol, 6 February.
 72. P. Caulier, Yarmouth, 8 February.
*73. P. Ruland, Hamburg, 9 February.
*74. Widow Berenberg & Co., Hamburg, 12 February.
 75. Willem Momma, Nyköping, 14 February.
 76. Dominicus van Uffele & Bartholdus Beckman, Hamburg, 9 March.
 77. W. Skinner, Hull, 16 March.
 78. J. & D. van Baerle, Amsterdam, 29 March.
 79. W. Browne, Bristol, 22 March.
*80. W. Momma, Nyköping, 7 March.
 81. D. van Ruyff, Stockholm, 16 March.
*82. J. Momma, Stockholm, 27 March.
*83. A. Ruland, Hamburg, 14 May.
*84. P. Berenberg, Hamburg, 18 May.
*85. Nicholas Preus, Gothenburg, 28 April.
 86. Benjamin Newland, Isle of Wight, 7 June.
 87. W. Skinner, Hull, 8 June.
 88. R. Ellison, Newcastle, 11 June.
*89. J. Pötter & H. Thuen, Stockholm, 12 June.
*90. Tar Company Directors, Stockholm, 19 June.
*91. J. Pötter & H. Thuen, Stockholm, 19 June.
 92. W. Browne, Bristol, 12 July.
*93. A. [Momma] Reenstierna, Stockholm, 30 June.
 94. William Jennens, Plymouth, 20 July.
*95. A. Ruland, Hamburg, 16 July.
*96. Widow Berenberg & Co., Hamburg, 16 July.
*97. Daniel Planck, Amsterdam, 2 August.
*98. A. Reenstierna, Stockholm, 14 July.

*99.   J. Pötter & H. Thuen, Stockholm, 17 July.
*100. A. Cronström, [Stockholm], 21 July.
*101. Tar Company Directors, Stockholm, 24 July.
*102. J. & D. van Baerle, Amsterdam, 27 August.
 103. W. Browne, Bristol, 1 September.
*104. Jan Arnold Fonck, Hamburg, 31 August.
 105. W. Browne, Bristol, 11 September.
*106. A. Reenstierna, Stockholm, 28 August.
*107. D. van Ruyff, Stockholm, 28 August.
 108. B. Newland, Isle of Wight, 22 September.
*109. A. Reenstierna, Stockholm, 15 September.
 110. P. Caulier, Yarmouth, 11 October.
*111. J. [Momma] Reenstierna, Norrköping, 24 September.
*112. J. & D. van Baerle, Amsterdam, 15 October.
 113. P. Caulier, Yarmouth, 18 October.
*114. Tar Company Directors, Stockholm, 25 September.
*115. W. Momma, Nyköping, 26 September.
*116. J. Reenstierna, Norrköping, 8 October.
 117. R. Oursel, Rouen, 1 November.
*118. P. van Teylingen, Venice, 25 October.
*119. P. Ruland, Hamburg, 12 November.
*120. Widow Berenberg & Co., Hamburg, 12 November.
*121. Andreas Muldenaer, Hamburg, 13 November.
*122. Tar Company Directors, Stockholm, 9 October.
*123. P. van Teylingen, Venice, 22 November.
*124. J. Reenstierna, Norrköping, 19 November.
 125. R. Oursel, Rouen, 13 December.
*126. P. Berenberg, Hamburg, 30 November.
 127. T. Wright, [Stokesley], 13 December.

1670

 128. W. Browne, Bristol, 3 January.
*129. J. Pötter & H. Thuen, Stockholm, 11 December.
*130. Tar Company Directors, Stockholm, 11 December.
*131. A. Muldenaer, Hamburg, 14 January.
 132. Death, Skinner & Ball, Leghorn, 10 January.
 133. J. Freyhoff, La Rochelle, 27 January.
 134. J. Freyhoff, La Rochelle, 6 February.
 135. R. Oursel, Rouen, 4 March.

B. LETTERS TO LEONORA MARESCOE & PETER JOYE:

1670

*136. J. van Savelant, Gothenburg, 3 October.
*137. J. van Savelant, Gothenburg, 18 October.
*138. J. van Savelant, Gothenburg, 25 October.

1671

 139. W. Browne, Bristol, 4 March.
*140. S. de Geer, Amsterdam, 10 April.
*141. L. Trip, Amsterdam, 10 April.

*142.   W. Momma, Nyköping, 19 March.
*143.   J. [Pötter] Lillienhoff & H. Thuen, Stockholm, 18 March.
*144.   Tar Company Directors, Stockholm, 1 April.
*145.   W. Momma, Nyköping, 1 April.
*146.   Cornelis de Hertogh, Hamburg, 28 April.
*147.   L. Trip, Amsterdam, 15 May.
*148.   J. Reenstierna, Stockholm, 22 April.
 149.   Jean d'Hollandre & Jean du Beron, Lille, 16 May.
 150.   Jacques le Camps, Lille, 23 May.
*151.   A. Ruland, Hamburg, 9 May.
*152.   W. Momma, Nyköping, 30 April.
*153.   J. van Savelant, Gothenburg, 23 May.
 154.   J. D'Hollandre & J. Du Beron, Lille, 27 June.
*155.   Tar Company Directors, Stockholm, 10 June.
*156.   J. & D. van Baerle, Amsterdam, 7 July.
 157.   W. Skinner, Hull, 7 July.
*158.   J. & D. van Baerle, Amsterdam, 18 July.
*159.   J. van Savelant, Gothenburg, 10 June.
*160.   S. de Geer, Amsterdam, 28 July.
 161.   Daniel Crommelin, Paris, 29 July.
*162.   J. A. Fonck, Hamburg, 27 July.
 163.   Isaac Tillard, Plymouth, 15 September.
*164.   S. de Geer, Amsterdam, 22 September.
*165.   P. Ruland, Hamburg, 12 September.
*166.   Paul Berenberg (Jr.), Hamburg, 19 September.
*167.   P. van Teylingen, Venice, 18 September.
*168.   J. Lillienhoff & H. Thuen, Stockholm, 9 September.
*169.   W. Momma, Nyköping, 10 September.
*170.   P. van Teylingen, Venice, 25 September.
*171.   Widow Berenberg & Co., Hamburg, 20 October.
*172.   S. de Geer, The Hague, 10 November.
*173.   P. Berenberg (Jr.), Hamburg, 14 November.
*174.   W. Momma, Nyköping, 26 November.
*175.   Hermann Paffraht, Danzig, 8 December.
*176.   Widow Berenberg & Co., Hamburg, 12 September.
*177.   W. Momma, Nyköping, 3 December.

1672

*178.   W. Momma, Nyköping, 10 December.
*179.   J., D. & H. van Baerle, Amsterdam, 29 January.
*180.   J. van Savelant, Gothenburg, (9?) January.
*181.   S. de Geer, Amsterdam, 5 February.
*182.   Hendrik Cletcher, Stockholm, 27 January.
*183.   P. Berenberg (Jr.), Hamburg, 15 March.
*184.   L. Trip, Amsterdam, 8 April.
 185.   W. Skinner, Hull, 2 April.
*186.   L. Trip, Amsterdam, 12 April.
*187.   S. de Geer, Amsterdam, 19 April.
*188.   P. Berenberg (Jr.), Hamburg, 5 April.
 189.   J. D'Hollandre & J. Du Beron, Lille, 16 April.
*190.   W. Momma, Nyköping, 7 April.
*191.   P. van Teylingen, Venice, 13 May.

*192. C. de Hertogh's widow, Hamburg, 10 May.
 193. Charles & James Bancks, Hamburg, 21 May.
 194. Skinner, Ball & Gosfright, Leghorn, 13 May.
*195. Isaac & Jacob Momma, Amsterdam, 21 June.
*196. J., D. & H. van Baerle, Amsterdam, 24 June.
*197. J., D. & H. van Baerle, Amsterdam, 28 June.
 198. J. D'Hollandre & J. Du Beron, Lille, 16 July.
*199. Alexander Waddell, Stockholm, 26 June.
*200. E. Ruland, Hamburg, 12 July.
*201. W. Momma, Nyköping, 7 July.
*202. A. Waddell, Stockholm, 24 July.
*203. Widow Berenberg & Co., Hamburg, 2 August.
*204. P. van Teylingen, Venice, 19 August.
 205. Archibald Jossy & Thomas Pawson, Edinburgh, 22 August.
*206. J., D. & H. van Baerle, Amsterdam, 2 September.
*207. P. Berenberg (Jr.), Hamburg, 30 August.
 208. John Kingstone, Deal, 9 September.
 209. A. Jossy & T. Pawson, Edinburgh, 7 September.
*210. Widow Berenberg & Co., Hamburg, 6 September.
*211. J. Lillienhoff & H. Thuen, Stockholm, 14 September.
*212. Widow Berenberg & Co., Hamburg, 1 October.
*213. W. Momma, Nyköping, 29 September.
*214. E. Ruland, Hamburg, 11 October.
*215. S. de Geer, Amsterdam, 25 October.
*216. P. Berenberg (Jr.), Hamburg, 18 October.
*217. S. de Geer, Amsterdam, 9 [December].
 218. Walter Cheislie, Edinburgh, 14 December.

1673

 219. A. Jossy, Middelburg, 29 December.
 220. Simon Orchard, Weymouth, 2 February.
*221. A. Waddell, Elsinore, 3 May.

C. LETTERS TO LEONORA MARESCOE & JACOB DAVID:

1675

*222. H. Cletcher, Stockholm, 12 December.
*223. Claus Bene, Hamburg, 8 January.
*224. S. de Geer, Amsterdam, 25 January.
 225. Skinner, Ball & Gosfright, Leghorn, 4 February.
*226. S. de Geer, Amsterdam, 22 February.
 227. Samuel van Breda, Stockholm, 6 January.
 228. J. Frederick, R. Godschall & J. Duncan, Seville, 11 December.
 229. Frederick, Godschall & Duncan, Seville, 19 February.
*230. H. Cletcher, Axbergshamer, 19 February.
*231. J. & H. van Baerle, Amsterdam, 29 March.
 232. John Hardy, Exeter, 10 April.
*233. S. de Geer, Amsterdam, 17 May.
 234. Isaac Cronström, Stockholm, 1 May.
*235. C. Bene, Hamburg, 18 May.
 236. Timothy Lannoy & John Burkin, Aleppo, 29 March.

*237.   H. Cletcher, Axbergshamer, 22 May.
*238.   J. A. Fonck, Hamburg, 1 June.
*239.   Widow Berenberg & Co., Hamburg, 4 June.
*240.   Reinholt Garlinghoff, Hamburg, 8 June.
*241.   Johannes de Geer, Stockholm, 26 May.
 242.   J. A. Fonck, Hamburg, 25 June.
 243.   C. Bene, Hamburg, 25 June.
*244.   Frederick, Godschall & Duncan, Seville, 11 June.
*245.   Frederick, Godschall & Duncan, Seville, 25 June.
*246.   H. Cletcher, Stockholm, 26 June.
*247.   Jacob Trip, Amsterdam, 30 July.
 248.   Louis de la Bistrate & Frederick Dufay, Amsterdam, 3 September.
 249.   Frederick & Godschall, Seville, 20 August.
 250.   Frederick & Godschall, Seville, 3 September.
*251.   J. & H. van Baerle, Amsterdam, 4 October.
 252.   François Bostelman, Hamburg, 24 September.
 253.   J. A. Fonck, Hamburg, 28 September.
 254.   R. Oursel, Rouen, 12 November.
 255.   Lewis Thompson, Belfast, 6 November.
 256.   P. Caulier, Yarmouth, 15 November.
 257.   R. Oursel, Rouen, 26 November.
 258.   Frederick & Godschall, Seville, 29 October.
 259.   R. Oursel, Rouen, 17 December.
 260.   Van Schoonhoven & Co., Nantes, 17 December.
*261.   Josias Olmius, Rotterdam, 20 December.
*262.   Alexander van Kuffeler, Amsterdam, 24 December.
 263.   C. Bene, Hamburg, 13 December.
*264.   J. A. Fonck, Hamburg, 14 December.
 265.   Lannoy & Burkin, Aleppo, 3 September.
*266.   W. Momma, [Nyköping], 12 September.

1676
 267.   William Foxley, Hamburg, 11 January.
*268.   J. A. Fonck, Hamburg, 14 January.
 269.   S. de Geer, Amsterdam, 28 January.
 270.   Thomas Legendre (Jr.), Rouen, 28 January.
*271.   D. van Baerle, Stockholm, 4 November.
*272.   J. & H. van Baerle, Amsterdam, 11 February.
*273.   S. de Geer, Amsterdam, 14 February.
 274.   P. Caulier, Yarmouth, 1 March.
*275.   P. van Cöllen & Laurens Uppendorff, Stockholm, 3 February.
*276.   H. Cletcher, Axbergshamer, 5 February.
 277.   Skinner, Ball & Gosfright, Leghorn, 16 March.
*278.   Daniel van Reusch, Breslau, 28 March.
*279.   S. de Geer, Amsterdam, 14 April.
 280.   Adam Laurens Kellerman, Amsterdam, 20 March.
*281.   C. Bene, Hamburg, 7 April.
*282.   F. Bostelman, Hamburg, 7 April.
*283.   W. Momma, Nyköping, 14 February.
*284.   Philip Botte, Amsterdam, 1 May.
 285.   George Richards, Bilbao, 1 May.
*286.   Jean Boor, Stockholm, 25 March.

*287.   D. van Baerle, Stockholm, 4 April.
*288.   L. Uppendorff, Stockholm, 15 April.
*289.   D. van Baerle, Stockholm, 23 April.
*290.   H. Cletcher, Axbergshamer, 14 April.
 291.   Bartholomew Möll, Hamburg, 9 June.
 292.   Henning Busch, Hamburg, 10 June.
 293.   J. Olmius, Rotterdam, 3 July.
*294.   W. Momma, Nyköping, 4 June.
 295.   Frederick & Godschall, Seville, 23 June.
 296.   Jacob David, Paris, 22 July.
 297.   T. Lannoy, Aleppo, 26 April.
 298.   Jacob Crommelin, Paris, 12 August.
 299.   Humphrey Bawden, Exeter, 5 August.
 300.   H. Bawden, Exeter, 7 August.
*301.   E. Ruland, Hamburg, 8 August.
 302.   H. Bawden, Exeter, 21 August.
 303.   J. Crommelin, Paris, 12 September.
 304.   Pierre Legendre, Rouen, 15 September.
*305.   W. Momma, Nyköping, 23 July.
*306.   S. de Geer, Amsterdam, 25 September.
*307.   C. Bene, Hamburg, 15 September.
*308.   Widow Berenberg, Hamburg, 15 September.
*309.   D. van Baerle, Stockholm, 5 & 6 September.
 310.   Charles Goodfellow, Aleppo, 3 July.
 311.   C. Goodfellow, Aleppo, 8 August.
 312.   Lannoy & Burkin, Aleppo, 31 May.
 313.   Lannoy & Burkin, Aleppo, 9 August.
 314.   Widow Berenberg, Hamburg, 10 October.
 315.   Widow Berenberg & Co., Hamburg, 10 October.
 316.   A. van Kuffeler, Amsterdam, 27 October.
 317.   G. Richards, Bilbao, 18 October.
 318.   Abraham & Simon Vrouling, Rouen, 6 November.
 319.   Benjamin Beuzelin & Son, Rouen, 17 November.
*320.   S. de Geer, Amsterdam, 27 November.
 321.   G. Richards, Bilbao, 27 November.
 322.   Samuel Lannoy, Constantinople, 29 May.
 323.   Skinner, Ball & Gosfright, Leghorn, 27 November.
*324.   J. Boor, Stockholm, 30 October.
 325.   W. Skinner, Hull, 22 December.

1677

*326.   I. Cronström, Stockholm, 7 September.
 327.   Frederick & Godschall, Seville, 22 December.
*328.   D. van Baerle, Stockholm, 9 December.
*329.   J. & H. van Baerle Amsterdam, 26 January.
 330.   W. Skinner, Hull, 29 January.
 331.   G. Richards, Bilbao, 23 January.
*332.   C. Bene, Hamburg, 23 January.
 333.   H. Bawden, Exeter, 3 February.
*334.   Jan van Deurs, Elsinore, 17 February.
*335.   Widow Berenberg & Co., Hamburg, 23 February.
*336.   S. de Geer, Amsterdam, 26 March.

337. T. Lannoy, Aleppo, 11 December.
338. T. Lannoy, Aleppo, 5 January.
*339. D. van Baerle, Stockholm, 24 February.
*340. Thomas Perman, Stockholm, 12 March.
*341. A. L. Kellerman, Amsterdam, 9 April.
*342. Nicholas Simons, Lisbon, 29 March.
*343. F. Bostelman, Hamburg, 10 April.
344. B. Beuzelin & Son, Rouen, 24 April.
*345. Widow de Hertogh, Hamburg, 27 April.
*346. H. Cletcher, Axbergshamer, 5 April.
*347. P. Botte, Stockholm, 13 April.
348. I. Tillard, Plymouth, 18 May.
349. David Dorville, Bristol, 19 May.
350. G. Richards, Bilbao, 25 June.
351. S. Lannoy, Constantinople, (?).
*352. J. & H. van Baerle, Amsterdam, 23 July.
353. W. Momma, Nyköping, 30 March.
*354. Jacob & Hendrick van Crayesteyn, Smyrna, 1 May.
355. J. & H. van Crayesteyn, Smyrna, 3 June.
356. John Field, Hull, 20 July.
*357. L. Uppendorff, Stockholm, 29 June.
*358. S. de Geer, Amsterdam, 3 August.
359. A. & S. Vrouling, Rouen, 10 August.
*360. L. Trip, Amsterdam, 6 August.
*361. P. Botte, Amsterdam, 10 August.
*362. A. Ruland, Hamburg, 30 July.
*363. Claus Wilkens, Stockholm, 18 July.
364. B. Beuzelin & Son, Rouen, 31 August.
*365. De la Bistrate & Dufay, Amsterdam, 7 September.
*366. D. van Baerle, Stockholm, 2 April.
*367. P. Botte, Amsterdam, 14 September.
368. Jacob Fahlgreen, Stockholm, 26 July.
*369. P. van Teylingen, Venice, 27 September.
*370. A. Ruland, Hamburg, 21 September.
*371. E. Ruland, Hamburg, 25 September.
372. B. Beuzelin & Son, Rouen, 8 October.
373. Ball, Gosfright & Co., Leghorn, 24 September.
*374. R. Garlinghoff, Hamburg, 2 October.
375. G. Richards, Bilbao, 21 October.
*376. P. Botte, Amsterdam, 21 December.
*377. A. van Kuffeler, Amsterdam, 24 December.
*378. C. Bene, Hamburg, 14 December.
*379. Carel Lubers, Hamburg, 18 December.

1678

380. J. Boor, Stockholm, 26 November.
*381. J. A. Fonck, Hamburg, 15 January.
*382. A. Ruland, Hamburg, 15 January.
383. G. Richards, Bilbao, 21 January.
*384. I. Cronström, Skultuna, 12 December.
*385. J. & H. van Baerle, Amsterdam, 22 February.
386. P. Caulier, Yarmouth, 18 February.

*387.   P. Botte, Amsterdam, 8 March.
*388.   Widow de Hertogh, Hamburg, 26 February.
*389.   Georg Kohröber, Gozlar, 21 February.
*390.   E. Ruland, Hamburg, 5 March.
 391.   Robert Clark, Gothenburg, 3 January.
 392.   R. Clark, Gothenburg, 5 March.
*393.   T. Perman, Gothenburg, 2 March.
*394.   S. de Geer, Amsterdam, 12 April.
*395.   J. & H. van Baerle, Amsterdam, 15 April.
 396.   C. Goodfellow, Aleppo, 28 January.
 397.   C. Goodfellow, Aleppo, 8 February.
*398.   C. Bene, Hamburg, 23 April.
*399.   J. & H. van Baerle, Amsterdam, 6 May.
 400.   W. Skinner, Hull, 29 April.
 401.   William Clode, Exeter, 18 May.
*402.   D. van Baerle, Stockholm, 9 April.
 403.   G. Richards, Bilbao, 13 May.
 404.   B. Beuzelin & Son, Rouen, 14 June.
 405.   C. Goodfellow, Aleppo, 24 March.
 406.   W. Clode, Exeter, 6 July.
 407.   T. Lannoy, Aleppo, 20 March.
*408.   Jan Hedenström, Stockholm, 11 May.
*409.   L. Uppendorff, Stockholm, 11 May.
*410.   Widow Berenberg & Co., Hamburg, 16 July.
*411.   C. Bene, Hamburg, 19 July.
*412.   J. & H. van Baerle, Amsterdam, 2 August.
 413.   W. Skinner (Jr.), Leeds, 30 July.
 414.   W. Skinner (Sr.), Hull, 5 August.
*415.   Van Weert & Stock, Genoa, 30 July.
 416.   Robert Welch & George Styles, Genoa, 3 August.
 417.   B. Beuzelin & Son, Rouen, 16 August.
*418.   P. Botte, Amsterdam, 26 August.
 419.   B. Beuzelin & Son, Rouen, 6 September.
 420.   P. Briains & D. Bion, La Rochelle, 4 September.
 421.   Van Schoonhoven & Son, Nantes, 24 September.
 422.   P. Briains & D. Bion, La Rochelle, 2 October.
*423.   J. A. Fonck, Hamburg, 1 October.
*424.   W. Momma, Nyköping, 25 May.
*425.   T. Perman, Stockholm, 8 October.
*426.   C. Lubers, Hamburg, 18 October.
*427.   S. de Geer, Amsterdam, 25 November.
*428.   F. Bostelman, Hamburg, 22 November.
*429.   Oloff & Nicholas Törne, Stockholm, 19 November.
 430.   B. Beuzelin & Son, Rouen, 30 December.

1679

*431.   C. Bene, Hamburg, 14 January.
 432.   B. Beuzelin & Son, Rouen, 14 February.
 433.   W. Momma, Nyköping, 5 August.
*434.   W. Momma, Nyköping, 14 October.
*435.   J. & H. van Baerle, Amsterdam, 21 March.
 436.   Estienne Molié, Paris, 4 April.

437. G. Richards, Bilbao, 31 March.
438. R. Clark, Gothenburg, 7 March.
*__439.__ Georg Christian Fuchs, Amsterdam, 18 April.
*__440.__ Wilhelm de Hertogh, Hamburg, 8 April.
*__441.__ Andreas Ingolstatter, Nuremberg, 11/21 April.
*__442.__ Hans Hendrick Berenberg, Hamburg, 25 April.
443. André Amsincq, Rouen, 9 May.
*__444.__ W. de Hertogh, Hamburg, 29 April.
*__445.__ T. Perman, Stockholm, 2 April.
446. B. Beuzelin & Son, Rouen, 2 June.
447. A. Amsincq, Rouen, 13 June.
*__448.__ T. Perman, Stockholm, 13 May.
449. John Tyler, Riga, 13 June.
*__450.__ Abraham Wolters, Stockholm, 19 June.
*__451.__ David Geysmer, Hamburg, 8 July.
452. Welch & Styles, Genoa, 12 July.
453. C. Bene, Hamburg, 8 August.
*__454.__ L. Trip, Amsterdam, 15 September.
*__455.__ D. Geysmer, Hamburg, 5 September.
*__456.__ S. de Geer, Stockholm, 27 August.
457. G. Richards, Bilbao, 15 September.
*__458.__ D. Geysmer, Hamburg, 19 September.
*__459.__ Adrian Du Quesnoy, Amsterdam, 3 October.
*__460.__ A. Wolters, Stockholm, 23 August.
*__461.__ A. Wolters, Stockholm, 30 August.
462. David Brond, Danzig, 23 September.
463. C. Wilkens, Stockholm, 9 September.
464. C. Bene, Hamburg, 26 September.
465. John Lewknor, West Dean, 17 October.
466. G. Richards, Bilbao, 13 October.
*__467.__ S. de Geer, Stockholm, 31 October.
*__468.__ A. Wolters, Stockholm, 1 November.
*__469.__ L. Trip, Amsterdam, 12 December.
470. Simon Rogers, Cadiz, 4 December.

1680

471. G. Richards, Bilbao, 22 December.
472. Welch & Styles, Genoa, 27 December.
*__473.__ A. Wolters, Stockholm, 27 December.
*__474.__ H. H. Berenberg, Hamburg, 9 January.
*__475.__ C. Bene, Hamburg, 27 January.
*__476.__ S. de Geer, Lövsta, (?) January.
*__477.__ Jacob de Greve, Hamburg, 3 February.
478. G. Richards, Bilbao, 16 February.
*__479.__ A. Du Quesnoy, Amsterdam, 12 March.
*__480.__ A. van Kuffeler, Amsterdam, 8 March.

All the original German and Dutch letters have been reproduced in microfiche. Enquiries should be addressed to The British Academy, 20–21 Cornwall Terrace, London NW1 4QP.

$$\frac{30\ Jan.}{1\ Jun.}1668$$

1 THOMAS DEATH, EPHRAIM SKINNER & CO. to JL & CM

LEGHORN 16 JANUARY 1668

'Wee writt you, Mr Lethieullier, the 6th instant in answer to yours of the 2nd past when advised you have received bill ladeing for your 92 barrels tinn on the *Bantam*, since which is come to hand yours of the 9th past pressing the sale of your cocheneale wherein noe endeavors are omitted, but this—as all other comodities—are soe downe the wind that though we court to sell we cannot, yet hope we t'will not be long err some good effect may come thereof, of which as ought is effected we shall advise you, for now the exchange is rissen to $56\frac{1}{2}$ twilbe good also remitting you its proceed wherein we shall then neither loose noe tyme. Could we have had your cocheneale sooner from Genoa it might long err this have binn sould but thence though there never wants conveyances, yet the bad weather in the winter tyme makes them very tedious, and we waited some time too to see whether the captain would comply with his obligation in bringing it hither, which since they doe but what they please you would doe well in the future give your frends caution if any direct conveyances offer to imbrace them rather then for Genoa, though now we are in tymes of peace we hope we shall have the lesse occasion of them and that our owne navigation wilbe imployed from whome we find fairer dealeing. Lead that hath binn lately sould at D.23 p.mille[1] was againe rissen before the *Mary* imported 3 daies since with 700 pigs to D.$24\frac{1}{2}$. Tinn offerd at D.15 and pepper rissen againe to D.29 with which latter comoditie & a parcell of saltpeter now (upon apprehension of warr in Ittaly) much demarded after. A small vessell to be dispatcht out before any other supplies can come then what the ships already expected bring might, in our judgments, be a good designe, for the Dutch convoy that's daily expected departing 2 daies before the *Mary* from Allicant bring that we hear not any, and the vessell (which in these tymes of peace you may doubtless have cheap) should you not incline to have her returned home with Galipoly oyle at D.14 the salme or currance, there's noe doubt but shee may meete imployment heer to your advantage. The *Red Hirt* for London departed yesterday and the *Supply* following the *Affrican* goes at last for Galipoly, whome the *Mary* will also follow, and is what for present offers, Sirs, at your command &c.

Venice—$103\frac{1}{2}$.[2] Amsterdam—99g.[3]'

---

[1] Leghorn lead prices are quoted in ducats per 1,000 lb.; tin and pepper in ducats per 100 lb. The ducat was equal to 7 livres (of 20 soldi and 240 denari each); the dollar was equal to 6 livres.

[2] The rate represents Leghorn dollars per 100 Venetian bank ducats.

[3] I.e. 99 *grooten* flemish per 1 dollar. The rate on London, when cited, represents pence sterling per 1 dollar.

$$\frac{3\ Feb.}{2\ Mar.}1668$$

2 ANTHONY UPTON & CO. to CM

SEVILLE 29 NOVEMBER 1667

'Since the foregoeing wee have received yours of the 7/17th ultimo and this day wee have receaved the good newes of Capt. Boneal's arrivall at Cadiz, for which God be praised. Wee have ordered the sending upp to this Citty all your goodes that come by him, and when they come to hand wee shall use our best endeavours to dispose of them to your best advantage; and wee should bee glad it had layen in our power to have finished the account of your former cargoe, before the arrival of these, but wee could not possibly putt of 50 pieces of your yard-broades, which wee have still unsould, and some of your stockens. All the rest of your former cargoe is disposed, though a good parte of the money is still oweing amongst our shoppkeepers, but wee hope on the arrivall of the *galleones* shall recover the most part of it. We hourely expect them, and it is thought, being they stay soe long, they have beene forced to repaire theire shippes in the Indyes, which may have detained them some dayes more then was expected. In the meanetime wee find noe comoditie, either of the groath of this countrey or the Indies, that wee dare adventure upon for returnes at the prizes they now rule— Indicoes being worth $7\frac{1}{2}$ to 8 *R. pta.* p. lb. putt aboard, and cuchenille 94 to 96 ducats [per arroba]. The latter may yeild a small advance and besides wee looke upon it as a riseing comoditie since there cann come noe more of it into Europe wee suppose in more than two yeares, and we intend to send two bagges to your selfe and Mr Letheilleire by the first merchant men, haveing excused to lade anything for youre account on the friggatts in regard by your order to the contrary. They now give out will departe in all this weeke, and there is noe merchantman that goes in theire company, bound for London, only a small Hamburger. Wee know not what comodityes to advise you to send to this markett at present, since wee conceive it will be overladen with most sortes of our English manufactoryes. What doth now promise the best expence are cheneyes, mixt serges, some black and white hounscotts which must be fine ware to cost about 50*s* per piece; and when all the *galleones* come wee shall be able to advise you our opinion what may be remitted against the despatch of another fleete for the Indies, and according to the encouragement they have found in those partes wee may guesse at the repute our goodes will have this next summer and what demand there will be to them, as alsoe when another fleet may goe for the Indies, which according to what is at present supposed there will bee one dispatched for New Spaine in June next, and the *galleons* about September or October.

All the comodityes made in Lysle[1] are proclaimed for contrabando and all other that are like them, except they come with testimonyes that they are made in the dominions of those that are in amity with this Crowne. Soe, as such comodityes may be brought from England, and those sortes will undoubtedly have good demand in these partes, wee had some dayes past a few picotes made at Norwich which were here better liked then those made at Lysle, but our friendes advised us they cost in England neare 40*s* per peece, and heere the flemmings use to sell theire picotes, which contain 33 Spanish *vares* (which are 8 per cento lesse then English yards) at 11 pieces of eight per peece, in this citty. Soe if those sortes cannot be made in England to be afforded a little more or lesse as they have been from Flaunders there is noe dealing in them, though indeed they are more substantiall. If you can gett them cheape and finde encouragement to send any you need not question but they will have good expence; and having not else wee crave leave to remain, &c.'

[1] Vizt. Lille, captured by the French in 1667 and soon to be permanently ceded by the settlement at Aix la Chapelle.

$$\frac{9\ Mar.}{14\ Mar.} 1668$$

3   RICHARD CRUMPE[1] TO CM
BRISTOL   7 MARCH 1668

'Sir, Yours of the 3d instant received. In answer, Barbads sugars is now worth in parcell 27*s*. per cwt., much havinge binn bought and shipt of for Hamborow. About tenn dayes since itt was bought from 25 to 26*s* per cwt., att which price I sould a conseiderable parcell. Indegoe little or none to bee had: its worth 4*s* 8*d*. Lead now £13 10*s* per tonn. Cotton woole 8*d* per lb. Vergine tobacco in leafe to shipp of 6*d* per lb. if good. Sir, about two monthes since there was a shipp from Barbads sunke in our river in which was much cotten and under water for sume shortt time of which I have about 30 baggs all dreyed and if you please may see a sample of it in Alderman Ellin's house,[2] he havinge three bags of said cotten sent him since by Mr Ballard, my parttner in the same, and if you please att 6*d* per lb. may have the whole quantyty or part. Yours to command, &c.

[P.S.] Advise how insurance runeth to and from Vergine and Barbads.'

---

[1] Although the signature looks like 'Richard Crumper' it would be in keeping with Marescoe's usual choice of leading figures as his out-port correspondents if this is Crumpe, a substantial Bristol merchant, knighted in 1681 (sheriff of Bristol in 1665–6, Mayor in 1677–8, Member of Parliament 1685–7). See P. McGrath (ed.) *Merchants and Merchandize in Seventeenth Century Bristol*, Bristol Records Society XIX (Bristol, 1955) pp. 219, 220, 263.

[2] The reference is possibly to Alderman Sir Thomas Alleyn of London.

$$(i) + (ii) \quad \frac{10 \; Mar.}{20 \; Mar.} 1668$$

4 ANDREAS BERENBERG'S WIDOW & HEIRS tO CM

HAMBURG   (i)   15 FEBRUARY 1668

] In answer to your letter of the 31st of January, we are still awaiting the account and bill of lading of the 20 sacks of Aleppo galls which you have bought. May God bring them in safety! We understand from others, in a letter of January 24th, that the ship *Virginia* has arrived with a large amount of galls. We are surprised you made no mention of it. We shall be glad to learn that you have bought and shipped the sacks of white Barbados cotton, and will be content if you have not spent more than $8\frac{1}{2}d$ per lb., free on board, for choice quality. If our commission for indigo guatemalo came too late we must be patient. It has risen here from $11\frac{1}{2}$ to 12*s* [per lb.]. Demand for silk is very slack and shows no sign of rising. Barbados sugars are too dear in [London]. They must either fall there or rise here, otherwise there is nothing to be ordered. We shall be glad to hear what else is happening, for guidance in giving these commissions. A dio, &c.

(ii)   22 FEBRUARY 1668

5 We write today, by the grace of God, on the 22nd of February, with yours of the 7th instant. With it we received the account of the 20 sacks of galls purchased and loaded in Marten Jansen Tiel. We have checked the account and agreed it with you. May God bring them in safety. The market is weak here and from others we have learned that these same goods can now be had for 55*s* in [London], so in future they are likely to fall lower here. Meanwhile we hope you have bought and shipped the 20 sacks of Barbados cotton. The greatest speed is essential—also that the goods are clean and soft.

We hope you have procured payment of the £200 sterling which we remitted to you, drawn on William Rivet. With that you can pay for the cotton you have bought.

Sugar is too dear in [London] and one can count on no profit in sending it here, so one must wait for it to fall lower in [London] or rise higher here. One can easily get it here at 8*g* for lack of buyers. Silk is plentiful and cheap—Ardasse can be got for $17\frac{1}{2}s$.

We have accepted the bill of exchange for £170 drawn at 34*s* 10*g*, at double usance, payable to Caspar Bruyn or order, and when it falls due it will be promptly paid. Meanwhile we have debited it to your account.

Would you please find out, discreetly, if one could get 20,000 to 30,000 ox-horns in [London]—and how much per thousand they would cost, with all charges, free on board, and if one may export them wheresoever one wishes? Please give us reliable information about this and we will gladly serve you in return. With cordial regards, &c.

Carsten Steen has arrived here. Nothing is yet heard of Marten Jansen Tiel. Barbados sugar no longer fetches even 8*g* here, choice quality being left without buyers. The highest it will now make would be $7\frac{1}{2}g$, so one would make a loss by sending it from [London].

[London]:   34*s*
Amsterdam: $32\frac{7}{8}st$.

$$\frac{16 \ Mar.}{27 \ [Mar.]} 1668$$

6 ABRAHAM MOMMA to CM
     STOCKHOLM   5 FEBRUARY 1668

[D]   The above, dated 4 January, is a copy of our last letter. We have since received yours of the 13th of December and 3rd of January and fully understand the contents, to which our answer briefly follows.

   Concerning the Tar Company's bill of exchange, the matter will be settled as soon as Mr Hendrick Thuen returns home. He is away at present and has been expected back for some days. We have noted what has been happening in the sale of our goods and will await the account thereof. It is good to see that Dirck Thyssen has delivered to you the 324 bars of iron and the 20 barrels of steel on our account, and we also note the price at which you have sold the steel, but we are not happy to learn that some of the barrels were of such short weight. We will make enquiries here, as they were weighed at the works by our own people who have express orders always to ensure that, including the barrels, they weigh net 120 lb. Danzig-weight. We weigh it in this manner, as in Danzig, so that the barrels together with any excess weight have been paid for. See if they weighed it in this way in [London], or have weighed the steel only without the barrels, and please let me know for my future guidance. And as I have the opportunity to send a good deal of such steel (having that privilege from His Majesty) I beg you to let me know how large an amount you would be able to consume yearly so that I can employ my works accordingly.

   I note that pitch and tar have fallen in price in [London]: I shall be glad to be kept informed of further developments. I have also noted the money you have remitted to Mr Caspar Bruyn, as well as the £20 you have paid to Mr Johan Simons. I shall be grateful if you would help in every way, and if he should need another £20 or £30 please let him have it. Any money which you may have due to us, please make over to Caspar Bruyn as he will need some money on our account. I have already written to Mr Pelt Emanuels that he should place the money which Capt. Fix paid to you to our account. I trust he had done so and will not be writing to you about it any more as we have put his account right.

   We long to hear that Capt. Coomen, who is sailing to [London] from Gotland, has arrived safely and that his timber has found a good market. Our agent in Gotland tells us that it is very fine timber, and doubtless with the rebuilding of London a great deal of wood will be required. Please find out for us if some ships' lading of such balks and deals would sell on delivery and if one could get a good price for them, as we would gladly oblige. No one is in a better position to do so as we can have all the timber which Gotland produces in our hands. So please make inquiries and let us know what you think. We can have it cut to such lengths and breadths as people want, and the deals also, but you must write to us with the measurements—and please find out if we are free to send them in Dutch ships.

The 6 tuns of potash, which will be sent to you with the first available ship, are only an experiment, and if we perceive any profit in it we will send a larger amount. It is the same with the Gotland tar, which always costs more than Swedish tar. Do your best in all this as if it were for yourself, and let us have your detailed comments so that we can act accordingly. We have noted what you wrote about the kinds of iron which sell, and it is most instructive. With God's help we will provide you with a large amount in the spring.

As my brother Jacob will not be living here regularly but will be spending most of his time at his brass-foundry in Norrköping, we have divided our trading, and what hitherto came from here please regard as mine only, unless it is expressly stated to belong to someone else's account. You will likewise get directions from me about what has, and will, come from Gotland, so from now on I will be writing to you in my own name and you can reply to me likewise so we can settle matters with one another. However, what you have just remitted to Amsterdam and have in your hands from here and Gotland is still in both our names. Farewell, &c.

$$\frac{16\ Mar.}{1\ May}1668$$

7 DEBORAH VAN RUYFF to CM
   AXBERGSHAMER   20 FEBRUARY 1668

•] I have received your letter of the 10th past with the sale-account of the iron which was sent with Erick Peerson. I have looked it over and recorded my agreement.

I am now having a quantity of the same sort of iron forged, and also have other kinds in stock, of which—God willing—I shall send you a quantity next summer. Every year I have some $\frac{3}{4}$-inch square iron forged, though it is not much, but I could send you what I have if you would first tell me for how much more it can be sold than the other sorts. Here it always fetches more than the other sorts.

Since you say that in [England] one usually sells for 6 months time I suppose I must put up with it and rely on you to see that you always sell to good, reliable people.

As for the £310 which you have remitted to Pieter van der Mortel on account of the iron from Erick Peerson, I have credited you. With heartiest regards, &c.

$$\frac{16\ Mar.}{20\ Mar.}1668$$

8 STEVEN DE GEER to CM
   AMSTERDAM   23 MARCH 1668

•] My last to you was about a week ago; since then I have received yours of the 6th instant.

As I wrote to you in my last letter, I shall not be sending any salt. I have made a note of the £110 which you have paid to Mr Sleuyn, tutor to the young Count Wrangel.[1] If they send to you, you could let them have another one or two hundred pounds.

They write to me from Sweden that all the Orgrons iron has been bought up, so all of it will come here, and you can also expect all the 'O' and 'G' iron,[2] which means that it can be held at a suitable price; for that reason I have expressly not wanted to sell it for delivery in Sweden, in order that it can be kept in one hand and not undercut.

One should be able to insure from London to Guinea and back again for 14 to 15 per cent, independently of any Dutchmen, because since most of that coast is now occupied by them the insurers would raise difficulties about a ship trading to a place where it is not permitted to go. It would run the risk of being seized, and if one made difficulties about putting in a proviso they would guess what the intention was and insist on more than a doubled premium.

Please let me know how things stand with the salvaged cannon-balls, for I have heard nothing about them.

As the insurance to Guinea is not a normal one and as my usual insurance-broker is not very suitable, he has not categorically agreed to it, it being his opinion that the objections mentioned above will be insisted upon.

Please charge my account with £200 drawn at 2 usances and set it against your special account. I will let you know the rate of exchange by my letter as I forgot to find out today.

[1] Carl Philip, son of Carl Gustaf Wrangel, Count Sylfnitzburg (1613–76), a famous Swedish soldier and diplomatist, and his wife Anna Margreta von Haugwitz. The youth, 'being for many years sickly and indisposed' died on his visit to London during early April 1668—*The Bulstrode Papers, I, 1667–1675* (Privately printed, 1897) p. 35.
[2] I.e., iron from the De Geer works at Österby and Gimo, shipped through Öregrund (hence 'Orgrons').

$$\frac{24\ Mar.}{26\ Mar.}1668$$

9   ROBERT OURSEL to CM
       ROUEN   28 MARCH 1668

'Ma derniere a voz graces estoit le 21 courant, dudepuis j'ay receu la vostre agreable du 12 ditto. Veu par icelle que pretendez m'envoyer quelque cottons filez. Vous en aurez veu le prix par mes precedentes quy me semble estre tres bas, la demande estant petite en cette marchandise. Les droits d'entrée sont 10 livres p.cent et viron 14 p.cent de perte sur le poix. Sy resolvez d'en envoyer vostre advantage sera procuré comme sy c'estoit pour moy mesme.

Guerre advenant contre les Estats ou autre nations on tasche de mettre les amis a couvert le mieux possible. Je ne puis croire neangmoints que nous ayons rupture avecq les Estats d'Hollande, quoyque le bruit en soit grand dans le commun, toutefois on ne scait pas les choses a venir. Pour prevenir le mal, il me semble qu'il seroit a propos de consigner les marchandises qu'envoyerez comme pour le compte d'un amy de Hambourgh avecq lequel je tiendray correspondance soulz vostre couverte affin d'eviter que mes lettres ne fussent transferez. Dieu vueille nous donner une bonne paix; guerre advenant ne seroit que la ruine des pauvres marchandts.

Plusieurs navires sont arrivés au bas de nostre riviere entre lesquels sont Thomas Frost et William Atkinson, mais n'ay peu apprendre sy Pierre Dickson est du nombre—Dieu les amené tous a bon port. On attend grand nombre de sucres dans cette flotte ce quy en fait diminuer le prix. J'ay vendu ceux quy estoient chargé dans Batten a 33 livres le cent a 6 mois auquel prix il n'y a point de profit car les droits sont excessif. Je ne croy pas pouvoir tant obtenir pour les autres sy ce n'est qu'ils se trouvent plus belles. Le plomb diminuera aussy de prix selon les aparances, car on en attend plus de 6 a 7000 pieces. Se vend presentement a 125 livres le millier et peu de demande. Estain 70 livres le cent, galles 42 livres. Sy en quelque chose je vous suis utile disposez librement de moy, car je suis, monsieur, &c.'

[London]:   59*d* ⎫
Amsterdam: 103   ⎬ 2 usances.
Anvers: 101   ⎭

$$\frac{30\ Mar.}{3\ Apr.}1668$$

JOACHIM PÖTTER & HENDRIK THUEN to CM
STOCKHOLM   29 FEBRUARY 1668

Our last letter to you was on the 26th of February. Since then we have heard nothing from you, hence the brevity of this.

We are now daily expecting captains Hans Focken and Claus Simensen Schult from Hull with their cargoes of malt—may the Lord bring them in safety. We also await the invoices and the accounts of the timber cargo.

We would be very glad if you could obtain from your King freedom for two or three Dutch ships to be allowed to come to [London] from Åbo and Viborg with tar, for we are unable to obtain other ships. We would then be able to provide you with a good quantity of pitch and tar. Meanwhile, please let us know for how much these wares are selling so that we can regulate ourselves accordingly. Whatever you may have to spend on obtaining this freedom we will gladly make good, and look forward to your answer as soon as possible.

For the rest, we long to hear that the remainder of our iron and copper-wire has been sold and that the account can now be closed. With cordial regards, &c.

$$\frac{30\ Mar.}{3\ Apr.}1668$$

JEAN & DAVID VAN BAERLE to CM
AMSTERDAM   6 APRIL 1668

Our last letter was about a week ago, with which we remitted to you a bill of exchange for £166 9*s* 2*d* sterling for your account. Herewith goes the second copy in case the first is lost. Since then we have received your letter of the 20th past with the following remittances for the account of Mr Willem Momma at Nyköping, vizt.

£240 at 34*s* 4*g*, 2 usances, in your own bill on Nicholas Korf;
£80 as above, on Anselmus Hartsen;
£100 as above, in a bill of Jean Dorville on Frederick Dorville;
£74 13*s* 4*d* at 34*s* 7*g*, 2⅓ usances, in a bill of Daniel Porten on Joseph van Ast at Antwerp.

We have secured acceptance of the first and also the last, and have informed Momma. The remittances were for the proceeds of the copper-wire out of Pieter Hartman and William Greene, of which we have made a note. We look forward to learning what else has occured in the sale of the remaining copper-wire and brass, though while the exchange is so very low please do not remit the proceeds. We must hope that the exchange improves; meanwhile, sell for the shortest time possible.

As regards Nicholas Korf, he is a man of little credit and small business, who is not much to be relied on; we understand he is going to live in Rotterdam next month, for your information.

We have received the bill of lading for the sugar shipped in John Goldsborough, but the invoice and the list of weights is not with it, so please let us have it. Concerning the freight, we will see if they will be satisfied with 4,000 lb. net per last; if not, we must pay for the gross weight as is customary here.

We see that you have recorded your agreement with the account of the sugar from Mackrel, but that the tare, short-weight and allowance for prompt payment takes away most of the profit. The tare of 15 per cent on big barrels and 16 on small is a customary condition here which it is useless to dispute; the 1 per cent for making good short weight has also been claimed by the sugar-refiners for some time and without it they will not offer a penny; and the 1 per cent for prompt payment is advantageous to the vendor if he otherwise has to wait three months for payment.

The price of Barbados sugar remains still between $7\frac{3}{8}g$ to $7\frac{7}{8}g$ according to quality. We have had no news of James Hatton or of John Goldsborough, although as the wind is favourable we expect to have news of their arrival any day.

Of the lead, we have only sold 50 pigs of the great lead from Anthony Winter to Jacob Charles at 28s 6g flem. with 1 per cent discount for payment within 3 weeks. There is no demand for small lead at the moment. We have written to our friend in Rotterdam to sell the 100 pigs of lead from Bywater as best he can but have had no answer. English tin is selling at $f.50\frac{1}{2}$ but it is believed it will shortly fall to $f.50$ since, according to the latest letters which came from France three days ago, it seems there is again some hope of agreement being made with Spain. What foundation there is for this we shall see.

We herewith forward Mr Hanson's answer to your letter. With heartiest regards, &c.

London: 34s 7–6g
Paris: $100\frac{5}{8}$ } at 2 usances
Rouen: $100\frac{1}{2}$

Hamburg: $32\frac{7}{8}$
Antwerp: $2\frac{1}{8}$ } at sight.

$\dfrac{6\ May}{8\ May}1668$

12 EGIDIO RULAND to CM
HAMBURG   21 APRIL 1668

[D] I find I have your very welcome letter of the 10th instant. You have received the first and second copies of the bill of exchange for D.713, endorsed to you, together with the first for D.800 from Mr Chamberlain, of which the second endorsed copy has also been sent. You will know how to procure payment of the one and of the other.

You have heard nothing of Capt. Carsten Pietersen—may the Lord protect him! He should be leaving some money with you: how much, I shall expect to hear, so that I can know how much to debit you.

I see that the Levant ships and some Straits ships, together with one richly laden from Cadiz, have arrived with currants, which will make trade flourish. I look forward to hearing what you have done about my order to buy galls, as well as currants, for which you can lay out 43 to 44s for really sound goods. I can well believe that, before these voyages, the Levant trade was making very little profit.

You received my order to lay out £300 to £400 on Barbados sugar and have bought 24 butts of very good quality at 28s, to be laden in [Capt.] Andries Rump. I look forward to hearing that it has been successfully completed, and to receiving the account and invoice. I wish very much that I had not given you my order to buy 2,000 lb. at Bristol for 26*s* now that you have bought for me in [London] at 28*s*, since the expense and risk between Bristol and [London] amounts to more than 2*s* per cwt. It would have been best if the price differed not less than 3*s* or 4*s*; so please revoke my order for that amount since no profit can be made by it, seeing that that commodity has also fallen here from 8*g* to $7\frac{1}{2}$, $7\frac{1}{4}$ or 7*g* according to quality. I see little prospect of it improving unless it rises in price in [London] and less comes from Barbados, as you believe.

40*s* per week for a big warehouse rental is too much money and too burdensome. [. . . . . .].[1] If the ships bring any tamarind to [London], I shall be glad to hear, and with cordial regards I commend you to God's protection, &c.

London:	33*s* 10–11*g* 2 usances
Venice:	$91\frac{1}{2}$
Amsterdam:	$32\frac{1}{4}$

[1] Holes obscure several words here.

$$\frac{6\ May}{[\text{———}]}1668$$

3 THOMAS WRIGHT to CM
STOKESLEY[1]   2 MAY 1668

'I wrote to you the 14th of March last but neaver did receave any answer. I thought good to write you a few lines to advise you that now the seasone is come on for buyinge of new butter which att present is sold for 15*s* per firkine. What it may bee when the cheesemongers doe all beginn to buy is uncertaine, and whether it wilbe dearer or cheaper depends on the marketts abroade. If you thinke good to have any bought ether to send for Holland or for France uppon your advise I will do you the best servis I cann. If you wold send for Holland heere is shipping often to bee had. If for France ether you must send a vessell or else one must be hired on purpose which may bee done. Sume doe goe every yeare in May or June from this porte to Burdeux or some other ports in France, but then the marchant which sends them lodes them. While for leade, it continues about £13 10*s* and £13 5*s* some at Newcastle and £14 5*s* att our porte, 22 cwt. to the fodder.

These thinges I thought good and convenient to advise you of, beinge my parte soe to doe, and you may make what use of it as you think convenient for your own behoofe, only I wold gladly receave a line or two from you thatt soe I might the better know how to order my owne affairs for this yeare. I have not else to add but shall pray for your health and prosperity, &c.

[P.S.] Sir, If you think good to send any coles a vessell may go on to Newcastle and take in what coles you think convenient and soe call heere at the Tees and take in what butter you have very conveniently.'

[1] 8 miles from Stockton-on-Tees, Yorkshire.

$$\frac{13\ May}{18\ May}1668$$

4 R. OURSEL to CM
ROUEN   16 MAY 1668

'Ma derniere a voz graces estoit le 12 courant a laquelle je me refere; dudepuis la vostre agreable du 30 passé V. Stile m'est bien parvenue, pour reponce a laquelle vous diray qu'il est ainsy que j'ay passé pour droit de romaine de 3487½lb. de cotton filé, encor qu'ils n'ayent pesé a la vicont net que 3019½ lb.[1] C'est que sur toutes marchandises on fait paier les droits d'entrée sur le poix de Paris quy est 4 p.cent plus leger que celuy ou on pese les marchandises vendue, et sur quelques marchandises qu'on a mis au rang des espisseries on donne quelque tare pour les futailles ou emballages, et cela selon le caprice ou fantasie des commis des fermiers sy bien que quand ils sont de bonne humeur vous obtenez quelque fois un peu davantage de tare que les futailles ou emballages ne pesent mais cela arrive rarement. Il est vray qu'en autres lieux le marchand a quelque faveur mais icy il n'est pas de mesme. Les fermiers sont horriblement rigoureux; sy on fait la moindre faute demande aussy tost a faire tout confisquer.

Les sucres ont pesé ordinaire a la romaine 14300 lb. et ont diminué 1850 lb. pour la tare sy bien qu'il reste net 12450 lb. comme je vous ay passé en compte. Le frait a esté paié aussy sur le pied de cequ'il ont pesé ordinaire, le maitre de navire n'estant subject a donner tare. Lors qu'aurez visité les comptes desdits cottons et sucres sy n'y trouvez aucune erreur je vous plaira les linnotter daccord, m'en donnant sy vous plaist advis a vostre commodité.

Advant la reception de la votre j'ay vendu vos 17 pieces d'estain par Luckett au Sr Humphrey Wilkings a 64 livres le cent a payer en lettres sur Paris a 5 usances. Je souhaittes avoir receu vostre ordre en peu plustost puisque dittes y avoir a perdre les vendant a moins de 70 livres. Sy desirez j'en achepteray d'autres pour remplacer cette partie, ne doutant ou l'obtiendray au mesme prix ou peut-estre a moins, car on en attend encor grosse partie de West England, quy le fera encor diminuer n'y ayant point ou peu de consomption en cette marchandise.

Diricq Roys est, graces a Dieu, bien arrivé devant cette ville. Je tacheray de faire decharger vos 18 pieces d'estain et ne les vendray jusqu'a autre ordre sy ce n'est que j'en puisse obtenir 70 livres, mais je croy qu'il faudra garder longtemps advant qu'on en puisse obtenir ce prix y ayant comme je vous ay dit cy-dessus plus d'aparence de rabais que d'augmentation au prix. Je seray bien aise que les galles soient charge dans un navire anglois, les Ostendois les respectent plus qu'aucune autre nation. Est a craindre que William Olofson que j'estime hambourguois venant a en faire recontre ils ne l'ameinent a Ostende cela estant il cousteroit de grands fraits pour retire les marchandises.

Le change commence un peu a roidir: par le prochain aurez remise de vostre avance je trouve estre viron *W*.250, les fraits sur les cottons et estain estant diminue. Je n'ay peu encor parler a l'achepteur de les cottons pour scavoir s'il veut disconter; ce sera le plustost qu'il ce pourra, et vous donneray advis de succes. Voila ce quy s'offre a vous dire, et que je suis, &c.'

[London]:　　　　59¼*d* ⎫
　　　　　　　　　　　　　⎬ 2 usances.
Amsterdam:　　102½*d* ⎭

---

[1] Commodities imported at Rouen were twice weighed and assessed for duties—firstly *à la romaine* (the commonly-used balance, described and illustrated by Jacques Savary in *Le Parfait Negociant* II, Ch. X.) on which weight the royal customs tariff was levied; secondly *à la vicomté*, for the local duty payable to the ancient jurisdiction of 'le Vicomte de l'Eau'. Thus the cotton consignment referred to here paid (on the tariff of £10*t* per 100 lb) £348*t* 15*s à la romaine* and £1*t* 15*s à la vicomté*. For tariffs and jurisdictions at Rouen see Joachim Darsel, 'L'Amirauté en Normandie. VI—L'Amirauté de Rouen' in *Annales de Normandie*, XXIII (1973) pp. 39–56, 115–149.

$$\frac{23\ May}{29\ May}1668$$

15　A. BERENBERG'S WIDOW & HEIRS TO CM
HAMBURG　　　　　　　　　　　　　　　　　　　　16 MAY 1668

[D]　The above is a copy of our last letter. Since then we have heard nothing from you, which causes us some surprise as we would gladly have had news of what is happening in [London] to various commodities, for our guidance in case it was advisable to commission something further. Please give us punctual information concerning sugar, indigo, cotton, Ardasse and galls, together with your views, which will be gratefully received.

Everything here is selling badly—

Ardasse	16 to 17s [per lb.]
Barbados sugar	$6\frac{1}{2}$, $6\frac{3}{4}$ to 7g [per lb.]
Barbados cotton	18 to $18\frac{1}{2}$ g [per lb.]
Aleppo galls	$38\frac{1}{2}$ to 39 *ML* per 100 lb.
Indigo guatemalo	$12\frac{1}{2}$ to $13\frac{1}{2}s$ [per lb.]

—all with small sales.

We have received our 10 butts of sugar. Five are good and five turn out to be bad: they are not entirely the choice goods we ordered but we must be patient. With cordial regards, &c.

[London]:	33s 8–9g
Amsterdam:	$33\frac{1}{16}st$
Antwerp:	$32\frac{3}{4}st$
Venice:	91d at usance.

$$\frac{23\ May}{29\ May}1668$$

5   PETER JUNCKER to CM
HAMBURG   16 MAY 1668

'Je suis estonné d'apprendre par deux cheres vostres du 24 Avril et le premier courant que mes precedentes du 18 Avril et 2me May ne vous estoient pas encore parvenues. J'espere pourtant qu'en apres elles seront comparues et vous aurez veu par icelles que j'ay bien receu vos sucres de maitre Eppe Gerbrants mais que cette marchandises (estant venus icy en si grandes quantite et cela en mains des Anglois qui ne laissent pas de vendre a tout prix sans regarder perte ou prouffit) est baissé et presque sans demande puisqu'il n'y a point de consumption. C'est la cause qu'a mon regret jusqu'a cette heure je n'ay peu rien de debiter des vostres. Les Anglois les presentent desja a moins de 7d pour avoir de l'argent et gaigner la provision mais je n'ose pas les suivre si il n'est que vous m'ordonniez expressement de vendre a prix courant. Asseurez-vous pourtant que j'auray tousjours a mon coeur votre interest comme propre, attendant la dessus votre responce pour mon gouverne. Cependant je vous renvoye enclos la premiere de change de £200 accepte par Maccabeus Hollis qui est icy commissionaire comme la plus part des autres qui dependent de leur maistres en Angleterre. C'est pourquoy l'on ne scait que juger d'eux, je vous diray seulement en confidence que les Anglois ont icy generalement peu de credit excepte trois ou quatre.

Par la premiere occasion je vous bonifigneray les £12 sterling qu'il vous a pleu y fournir a mon frere, demeurant oblige pour vos faveurs. Si vous y pouvez aschepte de bon gingembre ongevleekt en wel gevuld[1] que la livre ne vienne a couster icy que $6\frac{1}{2}$ a 7 deniers de gros contant il vous plaira m'en envoyer 20 a 25,000 lb et sitost que j'auray votre advis de l'effect je vous en remettray la provision a veue pour advancer au change. Il vous sera aussi libre d'y prendre $\frac{1}{4}$ ou $\frac{1}{3}$ s'il vous plait et alors pouvez faire la partie tant plus grande—et si trouvez a desseigner sur quelque autre chose je m'intresseray avec vous de moitie. Mais des huiles il y en a encor assez ici et les galles se presentent maintenant a 39s, poivre a $26\frac{1}{2}d$, indigo guatimalo 12

a $12\frac{1}{2}s$, plomb 27s. Fer de Suede est beaucoup recherché de 19 jusqu'a 20s suivant la qualité—
p. advis.

    Puisque la Triple Alliance s'est faite entre l'Angleterre, Hollande et Suede l'on croit que l'argent promis aux derniers ne manquera plus a venir. Si vous en apprendre quelque chose par dela je vous prie de me le communiquer et d'estre persuade que je suis de tout mon coeur.'
                        &c.

[London]: $33s$ $9–10g$
Paris: $48\frac{3}{4}$
Anvers: $32\frac{1}{4}st$
Amsterdam: $33\frac{1}{16}st$
Venice: $91d$

    ¹ Unblemished and plump.

$$\frac{25\ May}{29\ May}{}_{1668}$$

17   J. & D. VAN BAERLE to CM

AMSTERDAM   1 JUNE 1668

[D]   Dear Sir, We last wrote about a week ago; since then we have received yours of the 15th past to which the following is our answer.

    We have sold the 26 hogsheads of Barbados sugar, which came with [Capt.] Adrian Goossen, to Paulus Kalckberner at $7\frac{1}{2}g$ with 1 per cent discount for immediate payment, and the 42 blocks of tin from [Capt.] Philip Cockran to Matthys Booden at $f.50\frac{1}{2}$ per 100 lb. on the same terms. Herewith we send the account of both, together with an account of the 693 pieces of small lead from [Capt.] George Fowler. The net proceeds of the sugar amount to $f.2676$ $17st$; of the tin, to $f.4674$; and of the lead, to $f.5753$ $1st$ $8g$, all in bank money. Please check them, and, if you find no mistakes, make a record of them.

    The amount of sugar which has come to Zeeland from Surinam is not nearly as great as we had first been told, and seems to be about 400,000 lb., as a result of which Barbados sugar is being maintained at $7g$ to $7\frac{1}{8}g$, but as the demand for refined sugar is small there is little prospect of it rising and we cannot guess what future prices can be obtained, so we wish you would consider it preferable to sell it in London.

    Great lead was selling in Rotterdam for $27s$ $6g$ flem. and it cannot be sold here for more than 28s at three months time. Since you have complained about the low price we have kept unsold what there is here and at Rotterdam. As for the small lead out of Henry Kirckhouse we have sold 100 pieces to Marten Van Lidt at $27s$ $3g$ with 1 per cent discount for immediate payment. Since then, we have been offered only 27s at three months. We shall be glad to learn if the tin account answered your expectations. Various amounts have been sold at $f.50\frac{1}{2}$, and if the expected East India ships bring no tin the price could well improve. You will have heard by now what the three East India ships which arrived here brought with them: we forgot to tell you in our last letter.

    We still cannot send you the sale-account of the 18 barrels of sugar in [Capt.] Mackrel since we have not settled with the captain yet. We find that some of the barrels in Mackrel, as well as in Goossen, do not weigh as much as they should according to the invoice. We suspect they have been tampered with by the sailors though we do not know any means of getting restitution as the barrels seem, to all appearances, intact. The captains will not admit to any knowledge of the reduced weight.

We intended to remit you herewith all your proceeds, but have been unable to find satisfactory bills as so much money has been remitted to London today that the exchange has risen, as you can see below, so we remit you only:

£700 sterling in a bill of Bartolotti & Rihel, to be received at 2 usances from Laurence Dibusty @ 34*s* 11½*d*;

£168 12*s* 4*g*, which is W.745 23*s* @ 54½*d*, dated 6 April, drawn on Rudolf Lee, endorsed by us and reckoned at 34*s* 11*g*. Please procure their acceptance and credit us. As for the £100 sterling @ 35*s* 6*g* which you have remitted us on Dirck van Huisbergen due on the 4th instant, we shall procure payment and make you a return. We understand that Nicholas Korf has left for London. Your two drafts on him have been registered in the bank for us by his brother-in-law Barthout Ockers. This first is due in six days and the other before the departure of the post.

We regret to see the poor price of copper-wire and do not know how to advise you except to follow the orders of our friends in Sweden. The copper-wire from Norrköping is nearly as good as Hamburg wire and is now selling at *f*.55 per 100 lb. The 'Crowned N' variety is selling at *f*.54 so it is no use bringing it from here or from Hamburg at the price it is fetching with you. Although the amount which our Swedish friends have sent is too large, the kettles, pans, latten and other brassware ought to fetch a good price, seeing that the French have wrecked the brass-works round Aachen and chased away the workers.

Jacob Momma advises us that a ship called *St Jan Battista*, Captain Claes Symons Schult, is being loaded for London in which he intends to send a good quantity of brass and iron. We were also glad to see that the amount coming here has not made the price weaken. In due course you will please make good the proceeds as Momma doubtless will instruct you. Herewith is one of his letters for you, with which our hearty regards, &c.

London:	34*s* 11*g*–35*s*	} 2 usances.
Paris:	101¼	
Antwerp:	2⅜%	} at sight.
Hamburg:	32$\frac{15}{16}$	

$\frac{16 \, Jun.}{19 \, Jun.}$ 1668

8 S. DE GEER to CM
AMSTERDAM   22 JUNE 1668

Your letters of the 29th of May and the 5th of this month have been safely received. It is not the case that I wrote that the cannon-balls should come to London, nor was it ever my intention, and if it seems to say so in my letter of the 8th instant then it was badly copied, for the intention is that if a good opportunity should arise at the place where the cannon-balls are lying to send them to Lisbon then it should not be neglected but taken at once.

I am glad to see that you have sold a quantity of iron. I shall not be able to send so much voyage iron this year, for it was only made at one forge and I ordered all of it to be sent to you, and as the forge was making other sorts of iron last winter there will probably not be so much. They write from Stockholm that iron is coming in rather slowly, so it may be rather late before the ships depart, and if there is a demand for what you already have, try to regulate consumption by concealing $\frac{1}{8}$ or $\frac{1}{9}$ of the quantity.

I have been approached here about selling my share of the iron which was in the *Stockholm*, wrecked on the English coast.[1] They think to get it for 4 or 5 per cent, but I have disposed of it for one-third. If I decide otherwise I shall send someone from here to fish it up. Time will tell what further developments may follow.

News has reached here from St Kitts that more than 2,000,000 lb. of sugar has been destroyed by fire on Barbados and that few houses have been damaged. I hope it is not really so bad: may the Lord grant consolation for such a heavy affliction.

Herewith I remit you £221 5s @ 34s 10g for your account. I have not yet had the account from Reval, but that can do no harm since the man must have money. I wish it was the same with that from Copenhagen, where I am lacking both the account and my money. I am thinking of sending someone there shortly in order to know exactly how things stand.

If Clignet draws £120 or £130 sterling, please pay it, mais ne luy donnez pas avis que vous en avez ordre unless it is drawn.

The remittance is in a bill of Froment in Paris drawn on Guill^e Carbonnel, negotiated with Pardicques—*W*.900 at 59d are £221 5s and f.2312 1st for which I have debited you. I remain, &c.

[1] This loss was one of three suffered by Swedish ship owners in the winter of 1664–5.

$$\frac{6\ Jul.}{20\ Jul.}1668$$

19 UPTON & BATHURST to CM

SEVILLE   19 JUNE 1668

'Wee have since the foregoing [of 29 May] received yours of the 27th Aprill, and by the last Paris post of the 5th current wee wrote Mr John Letheiuleir whatt offered and in particular advised him of our haveing loaden on board the frygotts advised in copy the quantetys of Backwell's ware therein specifyed to himselfe and you, and wee then remitted under a blank covert to you both the bills of ladeing by which you will perceive there went for your account fifteene hundred pieces of Alderman Backwell's ware upon the *Mary Rose* frygott, Capt. Thomas Darcy, and other fifteene hundred upon the *Antelope*, Capt. Francis Wilshaw, for which wee debitt your account R. pta. 25,692 being, besides the principall, 3 per cent exchange, $\frac{1}{2}$ per cent commission in Cadiz and 1 per cent conveyance and $2\frac{1}{2}$ per cent our commission with R. pta. 12 for proportional part of small charges, as boat-hire on board to take the bills of ladeing, portage, etc., which you may please to note accordingly. Wee are now to advise you thatt five dayes since arrived in the bay of Cadiz the *Merchant's Delight*, Capt. Daniell Browne, by whome wee have received invoyce and bill of ladeing for one case and six bales you have consigned to us for account in halves betwixt your selfe and Mr John Letheuillier, which goods wee have ordered up to this Citty and shall do you the best service wee are able in their disposall; and wee have also by this day's post received advice from Mr Paul and Peeter Godin of Amsterdam to have consigned us for your account 86 pieces of palomettes per the *Seaven Provinces* which wee thinke is arived in company of the Dutch convoy that came into Cadiz the last weeke, and have given order to our freinds there to remitt us the same heither as supposeing itt to be the best markett for their disposall, and our next shall give you advise of what they may yeild.

As for your goods heitherto received wee have very few of them remaining unsould, haveing these days putt off some quantety for the shipps designed for New Spaine who will be ready to goe on their voyage in 14 days, and then, God willing, wee shall draw out your account of all former parcells and hope may fully cleare them. All your Bow-ayed serges are sould and the mixt serges. We shall very gladly forward Capt. John Randall in his fraight for Venice if itt lyes in our power, butt wee feare hee will find little or nothing, for wee have lately endeavoured to secure some woolls or other comoditys for the *Merchant's Delight*, butt find none in these parts, and at Alicant those few that there are will be carryed per said *Merchant's Delight*. After the departure of this New Spaine fleet wee shall have little expence for English goods untill the entrance of winter for the country's expence, and also provissions will be then needed for the galleons whome wee thinke will be dispatched about the next Spring and will carry very considerable quantetys of our English goods. Wee shall in due time advise you the certainty, and what wee aprehend most fitt for them.

Wee take notice of your order to have us send returnes for Livorne or for Amsterdam in want of conveyance for England, which shall be observed, and haveing nott else wee crave leave to remaine,' &c.

$$\frac{13\ Jul.}{8\ Aug.}1668$$

0   JOHN PAPEN to CM
LIMERICK   3 JULY 1668

'Sir, I have receaved butt yesterday your letter dated 30 Mey with an enclosed to Mr John Clignett and according your desire I have delieverd the same to his owne hand. About deale bordes, they are for the present att a great rate, good bords are worth £9 to £10 sterling the 120 and it iss like that detto comodite may continue to a good rate, raisin those townes wich were lett formerly from yeare to yeare, and by thatt meanes the houses much dekayett, are let now by leasses for 21 yeares. Now be pleased to onderstand that heare iss no selling by whole ships-loading; in so doying itt would bee to a prejudiciall price; but it most bee by retaille of quarters, half or whole honders, wich make a pretti long, but I doe not doubte, a good account. Most commenly the price iss £6 the hondert. Ass for iron, there is a good quantitey in towne. The price iss 16 a 17s and 18s according quantite comes from Holland, butt these commodite iss sould to marchant, and it iss 6 moneth before the seller may reakon for his monies, wich is the inconveniencies of itt, yett itt iss no dekaying comodite and allways worth his monies.

Ass for tarr, there is butt little vent for, the most use that they have for itt heere iss for sheepe. Twoo a 3 last would bee enough—the price you may reakon upon 24 a 25s. They have nott taken notis hithertoe in what vessell detto comdite is brought hither. They suffer the Hollanders ass well ass other nations to bring detto comodite to avance the treade.

If ani thing presents to your servis you may freely command. My wyf hath send in my absents a cargo to Mr Freehoof, your correspondent at Rochell, and whereas I have notis of a other frend that detto goods iss sould att least 2 moneth ago yeatt I doe nott heare of him. If you write to him pray minde him of itt.' &c.

$$\frac{13\ Jul.}{17\ Jul.}1668$$

1   A. MOMMA to CM
STOCKHOLM   24 JUNE 1668

]   I find myself owing an answer to your letters of the 27th of March, 3rd, 10th of April and 8th of May, which herewith follows.

I have looked over the accounts you have sent and have adjusted them as you will have
seen in the enclosed note. If you find them correct please make a record of it. The 65 *RD* from
Baron Sparr[1] have not yet been received but they will be shortly and will then be placed to
your credit. The £30 you have paid to Mr Jan Simons has also been noted, and if he should
want another £30 or £40 please let him have it and place it on my account.

The *schuit*[2] which I am thinking of using for salvage work is now ready to sail. It is called
the *St Peter* and the captain is Matthys Meyer. I have consigned her lading to you for my
account as you will see from the enclosed bill of lading. May God protect her and bring her in
safety! I rely on you to do your best to sell the goods. Among them are two bundles of band-
iron, hammered not drawn, and I shall be glad to learn how well they sell. In Holland band-
iron has sold at $2\frac{1}{2}$ to 3 per cent higher than fine bar-iron, and if it fetches a good price in
[London] I am in a good position to have it made. I await your comments.

I have read the detailed report which you have written to me about timber, which is
instructive, but to charter as many ships as you suggest is hardly advisable as freight-rates are
too high. However, I shall see what I can do. We are expecting two salt-ships at Gotland
(may God bring them safely) and they will then be sent to [London] with timber.
Meanwhile, keep me informed about what is happening to this commodity in [London].

I see that you have sold the 16 lasts of Gotland tar at £10 10s per last, which is a poor price.
It may well be that it is not as highly esteemed in [London] as Stockholm tar, but in other
places they give a good deal more for it than for what comes from here. To charter ships from
[London] to here is not opportune as by now as many as 14 Setubal salt-ships are passing
through the Sound from here and they all have consignments in them.

Jan Juyst has paid me the £67 10s for Jan Simons' bill of exchange, and I have credited
your account.

I see you have been unable to get any buyers yet for the 6 tuns of potash. They were only
sent as an experiment: please do your best with them and see how much they can fetch, for
our future guidance. If it proves worthwhile we may send a further quantity.

I note you to say that at least 6,000 houses are being built in [London], which must
consume a great deal of timber. You also say that you think at least 1,000 to 1,500 lengths of
Gotland beams at 40s per length and 20,000 to 25,000 deals at £6 10s per hundred could be
sold—to which you await our decision. In answer I can only say that I cannot supply such a
quantity while freight-rates are so high. However, we will see what we can do. My brother
Jacob is in Gotland at present and has a ship-builder with him as we are thinking of having
some fluyt-ships built there—so with wood and timber-ware may God grant us fortune and
His blessing!

Meanwhile, keep me always informed about what is happening in [London] concerning
timber-ware. I am glad to see that small-iron is now sought after in [London], because what I
send is mostly of that sort. Keep me informed how each type is selling. That you have been
able to get 15s [per cwt.] for our 'voyage' iron is good news. If I were certain that it could
always sell like that I would have a large amount forged, so I shall await your opinion on this.
Please also let me know how Setubal salt is selling in [London].

I see that you have consulted with Jan Simons about the surety for the goods which are still
in the wreck of the *Stockholm* and I note your opinion on the matter, which is helpful. I have
written to Jan Simons at greater length in the enclosed letter. Please hand it to him and help
him in every way, for which we will be most grateful.

I have not been able to get the *schuit* ready for use sooner, otherwise it would have left for
[England] by now. God protect him and bring him in safety—and then I hope something
may be achieved this summer, as time will tell.

I have loaded for my account in the *Deensche Pheenix*, which will be ready in a few days:

Slb. 884.12   various sorts of fine bar-iron;
Slb. 263.6   rod-iron;
106 casks of steel in tall casks;
52 ditto in flat casks;
$83\frac{1}{2}$ dozen long deals, to complete the cargo,

all of which is consigned to you. The bill of lading will be sent with my next letter, and when the ship arrives in [London] I beg you to unload it as soon as possible and speed it on its way to St Ubes in ballast as it has also been chartered by Mr Pötter as usual so that it can complete its journey before the winter. Please help the captain, who is Claus Willman, in every way, and we will be most grateful.

I have ordered these goods, as well as those in the *schuit*, *St Peter* to be insured by Peter Simons in Amsterdam. I hope to God the premium will be justified. Since I have charged him with some bills of exchange which are going to fall due soon, I have written to tell him to correspond with you and to draw on you for my account; and if some misfortune should overtake the goods (which God forbid!) you could draw on him in return as he will have had them insured. And I would like you to allow Mr Simons to draw on you nine or ten thousand rixdollars. Please accommodate him. The interest on what you advance will be made good, and I shall shortly be sending you more goods of which you will be advised.

Your letters of the 15th and 22nd of May to my brother Jacob have been received in his absence, and—following his instructions—I have opened them and read their contents. I am delighted to see that Capt. Erick Erickson has arrived. God be thanked for his blessings! As to the money you have advanced on his goods—he will gladly make it good, regarding $\frac{1}{2}$ per cent per month interest as cheap. It is good that you have told Mr Hiebenaer that he may draw on you up to 8,000 *RD*, and if it does not inconvenience you, you could, according to your offer, remit the remainder to Messrs Van Baerle as it is more profitable for my brother. He will make good the interest on what you advance.

However, I am not happy to see that the price of copper-wire is so low, and I hope it will improve. Here copper prices are rising as the copper mine is producing little because of some roof-falls which have occurred. I shall inform my brother of what you write about the various sorts of wire, and I shall be glad to learn to whom the 1,650 coils of wire from Cock[3] have come. As for my brother's affairs, I hope he will have returned home in a month or six weeks time. Your enclosure to Mr Hegerstiern[4] came to me under the cover of Mr Caspar Bruyn's and was accidentally opened in the presence of two good friends. Nothing in it was read, but it was sealed up again and sent to his house where he opened it and then sealed it again and returns it to you again. In future, please do not send him any letters under cover to me or Mr Bruyn. Wherewith, regards, &c.

---

[1] Axel Carlsson Sparre (b. 3 August 1620, d. 16 April 1679), a Swedish privy councillor.

[2] A sailing-barge or lighter, usually limited to inland waters.

[3] Possibly a reference to one or other of the Kock-Cronström brothers.

[4] Claude Roquette, a French immigrant to Sweden and former tailor, ennobled as Hegerstierna, whose share of Marescoe's copper imports was 24 per cent in 1666 and nearly 27 per cent in 1667.

$$\frac{20\ Jul.}{24\ Jul.}1668$$

22 ARNOLD RULAND to CM
HAMBURG   11 JULY 1668

[D] My last letter to you was on the 7th instant. Since then yours of the 26th of June and the 3rd instant arrived together.

As long as sugar remains at 27 to 28s in [London] I see no chance to making any profit with it, but if it should fall to 26s please perform my commission. A large amount has arrived in Holland with the East India ships; in Portugal the Brazil fleet is also expected to bring a great quantity, and although in the last two months not much sugar has come from the Barbadoes we still have enough in stock, so it must fall further. Galls must do likewise since I understand that a ship with 3,000 sacks is expected shortly in [London]. If you can thus get some fine Aleppo goods at 50 to 51s please buy some 2,500 to 3,000 lb. for me, but if you have to pay 52s please get only 1,200 to 1,500 lb. I am waiting to hear if you have bought me 6 to 8 sacks of Smyrna [cotton] yet; if not, please leave them until that ship arrives. I am still waiting to hear if any ginger and indigo have come from the Barbadoes, and what is happening to these commodities; also how much sugar is selling for in Bristol.

I am glad to see that payment for the aniseed has at last come in, and I hope to hear soon about the rest of the organzine. Enclosed is a bill of exchange for £200 drawn on Edmund Soames. Please get it accepted and return it to me together with the other one I sent you in my last letter. Meanwhile, with cordial regards, &c.

London: 33s 10–11g 2 usances.
Amsterdam: $33\frac{1}{8}$ at sight.

[P.S] Regarding the Barbados sugar—if it is really good I will not tie you narrowly to the price and you may buy me 1,200 to 1,300 lb. at 26s 6d and 2,000 to 2,500 lb. at 26s, sending it here at the earliest opportunity.

$$\frac{22\ Jul.}{6\ Aug.}1668$$

23 PETER CAULIER[1] to CM
YARMOUTH   20 JULY 1668

'Sir, In answer to yours of the 15th and 18th currant I see the recept you send me. I shal make us of it. I have not any farther occasion of it at present but as occation present I shal advis you.

As to your proposition of pitch and tar, I thinck this towne vends some 70 or 80 last tar and 15 or 20 last pitch. The commodity is most brought in by Daines from Norway, as latly there was 2 with some 30 or 40 last sould it for £8 10s and £9 per last. There is one expected in Yarmouth with 30 last has contracted to deliver it heare at £9 per last. If at this price you can doe any good and that the once time with a quantity to suply all occasions I beleave thos other traders wil be discouraged for some tymes. Its worth £9 and sometymes £10, £11 and £12 per last to sell in smal peice. A great warhouse to hould the quantity of 7 or 800 barills may cost some 5s per week, 20s per month. If in anything I can serve you or your frinds heare you may dispose of me. I am, &c.'

---

[1] Caulier was a leading merchant and shipowner in Great Yarmouth, Norfolk, becoming a freeman in 1667 and serving as joint Bailiff for the burgh in 1669 and 1678 [H. Swinden, *The History and Antiquities of the Ancient Burgh of Great Yarmouth* (Norwich, 1772) pp. 951, 952; *A Calendar of the Freemen of Great Yarmouth, 1429–1800* (Norwich, 1910) p. 99]. He could evidently claim kinship with Marescoe (and later David) through the Lethieulliers [**256**].

$$\frac{22\,Jul.}{6\,Aug.}1668$$

4 WILLIAM SKINNER[1] to CM

HULL   20 JULY 1668

'Sir, I have yours of the 15th instant. For answer, our port doth yearely vend a farre greater quantity of pitch and tarre then 100 lasts of all sorts, but I conceave 40 lasts of tarre and 60 last of pitch of the Stockholme sortes may easily finde sale here in a yeare, and if you thinke good to make the tryall I shalbe willinge to serve you in it. The first yeare's expence will show you what future tymes may doe.

Lead is at £11 17s per fodder, and soe, &c.'

[1] A regular correspondent of Marescoe and David, William Skinner was from 1662 an Alderman, and in 1664 Mayor, of Kingston-upon-Hull. He was among the richest inhabitants of Hull in 1673 and a large benefactor to charity at his death in 1680. See K. J. Allison (ed.) *A History of the County of York East Riding, I. The City of Kingston upon Hull*, The Victoria County History (Oxford, 1969) pp. 118, 123, 161, 303, 337.

$$\frac{24\,Jul.}{6\,Aug.}1668$$

5 RICHARD KINGMAN to CM

DARTMOUTH   21 JULY 1668

'Sir, I have yours of the 16th instant. In answer to your desire have indeavoured to bee informed touching the quantitye off piche and tarr may bee yearrly spent in this place which cannott bee iudged off. Tar less then betwixt 3 and 400 barills, butt off piche les in regard wee youse alltogether French rosen piche for grauffinge our shippes under so thatt I conseave 200 or 250 barills off that commodety would supply the place unles our trad and shipping bee increased which is verey licklley to bee by the good nuise wee have from the Newfoundland.[1] Sir, I have once more mad bould to guiffe you a littell troble with the inclosed bills on Mr Isaac Demariado att Amsterdam for 411 guilders 12 stuivers payable to your order. The £80 shall draw on you when find opportunity, wharin I may sarvffe you pray command him who is, &c.'

[1] News had reached the West of England of large catches of fish in Newfoundland, and the season later proved exceptionally good. *CSPD, 1667–68*, p. 484; *CSPD, 1668–69*, pp. 17, 23, 54.

$$\frac{27\,Jul.}{31\,Jul.}1668$$

6 J. & D. VAN BAERLE to CM

AMSTERDAM   3 AUGUST 1668

] Our last letter was about a week ago with the account of 200 pieces of great lead in [Capt.] James Hatton and a remittance of W.2500 at $102\frac{1}{4}$ on Paris, of which the second copy is enclosed. We have since received your letter of the 17th past, from which we see that Mr Jacob Momma has asked you to remit us some money and that he will agree the interest with you—about which you await our opinion. To which we answer that we find it more profitable for Momma and more convenient for us to draw on you at double usance, as we wrote previously, and therefore beg you to make no remittances unless something is rebated and paid down by the purchasers or unless the exchange rises higher in the near future. You will charge Momma 6 per cent per annum interest on the money you advance on account of his goods (as is provided in our contract with him) making good our share. We trust you do not find it strange that we enjoy some profit thereby, because after all we advance the full value of the goods without having them in our hands. Nevertheless, if you think $4\frac{1}{2}$ per cent to be too little interest, you can deduct 5 per cent and leave us to enjoy 1 per cent. Please do not betray this to Momma, so that he is given no grounds for allowing us less than the 6 per cent stipulated.

About six weeks ago, 20 chests of small copper bars were sent to Isbrant van Holten at Elsinore, to be consigned to you from there. The proceeds of this are also to be at our disposal and we will be glad to learn of its arrival. We have procured acceptance of the £100 at 35s 7g double usance on Peter Dorville. We shall retain the bill of exchange here in case you place it to Momma's account and endorse the second copy to us. We have today drawn on you, for the same account, £600, namely:

£200 ⎱ at 2 usances, payable to Joos and Jan Debats
£100 ⎰ or order, value of themselves;
£200 ⎱ at 2 usances, payable to Michael Block or
£100 ⎰ order, the value of himself.

We entrust to you the honour of our bills. We find we have not remitted to you the full amount of your proceeds, so we herewith remit you our first bill of W.500 in a bill of Jean des Planches to receive at 2 usances from Thomas Legendre the younger at Rouen negotiated at 102g per W. for which you will please credit us. The exchange on France remains firm, as money is scarce there, so we believe you would do well to remit your money there. Of your lead we have just sold 100 pieces of small lead to Jacob Charles at 25s payable in 3 months. Great lead is selling at 25s 8–6g. Sugar is weakening, good Barbados selling at $6\frac{1}{2}$g. From [Capt.] John Clarke and Marten Bilke we have heard nothing because of contrary winds. We are now in the deadest season of the year and believe it would be better to hold back the sugar, on which we will be glad to have your opinion. We will be glad to see that you have sold the campeachy wood, following our advice, since it has weakened here to about *f*.17. For English tin blocks one cannot get more than *f*.50; Apulian oil £60 to £61 flems.; Swedish garcopper has risen from *f*.$55\frac{1}{2}$ to *f*.56; large plates *f*.58; sheet copper *f*.$63\frac{1}{2}$ to *f*.64; copper bars *f*.64; otherwise little change in Swedish commodities. Wherewith our hearty greetings, &c.

London:	35s 2–1g ⎱		Hamburg:	$33\frac{1}{8}$ ⎱	
Paris:	$102\frac{1}{4}$ ⎰ 2 usances.		Antwerp:	$1\frac{3}{4}-\frac{5}{8}$ ⎰ at sight.	
Rouen:	102 ⎰				

$$\frac{12\ Aug.}{8\ Oct.}1668$$

27   W. SKINNER tO CM
      HULL   10 AUGUST 1668

'Sir, I have yours of the 6th instant, adviseinge you have ordered your freind at Stockholm to send mee 40 last of Tarre and 30 last of Pitch for your account, which you suppose may come to arrive here about 2 months hence, if shipping can be gott, and therefore you advise it a good way to informe such as deale in saide goods of the expectation of those parcells.

For answer, I shall make the best preparation I can for the speedy sale of the said goods against their arrivall, but my feare is they'l come to land in a dead tyme for sale, as winter allwayes is, onely they'l be ready for the Spring market, when wee have oft tymes good sale for these goods before any shipps can arrive out of the East, and my hopes are also that before said parcels arrive our towne may be well emptied of those sortes which have bene lately imported in diverse considerable parcels, and some of Yorke, whoe had pitch and tarre consigned to them from Stockholm, have sold it here at such lowe prices as none here have before knowne, Stockholm tarre at £8 8s and pitch at £10 10s per last.

Lead was lately to be bought at £11 16s to 17s per fodder. Tis at present somethinge started. They ask £12 5s and are unwilling to sell. Here is noe want in the country and forraigne marketts full. After Michaelmas that the occasion for the shipps be supplyed it must againe fall as I am opinioned,' &c.

$$\frac{2[?]\,Aug.}{[\text{——}]}\,^{1}\,1668$$

28 R. OURSEL tO CM
ROUEN   1 SEPTEMBER 1668

'J'ay receu la vostre agreable du 13/23 passe. Comme vous dittes le change a diminué la semaine passée quoy que a mon advis c'est sans beaucoup de fondement, car le peu qu'il y a de contagion en cette ville fait grand peur a tous noz voisins quy ont interdit nostre commerce, et les seigneurs des villages ne veulent pas souffrir qu'aucun de Rouen se retire en leurs maisons a la campagne, non pas mesme que les paysans nous viennent rien aporter—sy bien que cela continuant il ny a point d'esperance de vendre aucune sorte de marchandise de longtemps. Dieu vueille nous en delivrer par sa grace. Le mal n'est pas considerable mais le bruit en est grand, d'autant que noz magistrats par leur exactitude ont pensé couper pied au mal, mais les inventions des hommes ne sont rien sans la benediction de dieu. C'est luy quy est le grand medecin auquel faut avoir recours et le prier de nous pardonner noz peches quy en sont cause. Tant que nous serons afflige de contagion il ne sera point a propos d'envoyer icy des cottons de quelle qualite qu'ils soient, car on n'en voudra point achapter a aucun prix pour les raison susdites, outre que les cottons de Smirne sont desja a grand marché en cette ville, partant ne puis vous conseiller d'en achapter chez vous sy ce n'est pour envoyer ailleurs. Les sucres de Barboudes sont aussy sans demande, les sucriers en sont fournis pour longtemps et n'auront point de vent, non plus que d'autre marchandises advant que noz voisins ayent perdu un peu de leur severité a quoy on espere que nostre parlement apportera remede lors qu'il sera rassemblé.

J'estime le debiteur de vostre plomb homme assuré, et ne ferois difficulté de luy confier sommes bien plus considerable, mais les meilleurs ne payent d'ordinaire qu'un mois apprez l'escheance de leur promesses pour marchandises.

Cy joint remise pour mon compte de *W*.800 a $59\frac{1}{2}d$ escheant le 4 courant sur Perrin Girard de quoy il vous plaira faire procurer le requis et m'en faire remise de bonne lettres sur cette ville ou Paris ainsy que trouverez mettre le plus advantageux. Je ne vous serois donner aucun conseil pour les changes. L'advenir est trop incertain, lors qu'on pense bien faire on se trouve souvent trompé. Une chose scay-je bien, c'est que l'argent est generallement rare et qu'on a grand peine a le retirer de ceux quy doibvent, que rien ne se vend contant ny a longtemps et qu'il faut paier de grands droits quand il arrive des marchandises, tout cela espuise les bourses quy doibt faire maintenir les changes. Neangmoins tout va souventes fois a rebours de noz

pensées. N'ayant aucun je vous salue et demeureray, Monsieur, vostre tres affectione
serviteur.'

Costy: $58\frac{1}{4}d$ ⎫
Amsterdam: $102\frac{1}{4}g$ ⎭ 2 usances.

¹ 27 or 29 August.

$$\frac{17\ Aug.}{21\ Aug.}1668$$

29 PAUL BERENBERG to CM

HAMBURG   8 AUGUST 1668

[D] I find myself with your welcome letter of the 20th past in which I see that you will be sending
me one sack of scraped ginger at the earliest opportunity. Since then two merchantmen¹
from [London] have arrived but I could learn nothing of it from them, which I could have
wished for in order to be better able to judge of its quality. Meanwhile I have seen a sample of
it, thanks to another friend. If you can now get some that is plump and with large roots at 60s
please buy for me 2,000 to 3,000 lb. and send it with the first ship available.

Sugar has fallen again to 27s in [London] but I find there is little to be done with it since it is
selling daily here at 7g and is being undercut, but if you can get some thoroughly sound stuff
at 26s you may buy me 12,000 to 15,000 lb. and send it here. Not long ago an English ship
arrived here from Scanderoon *a drittura* with 400 to 500 sacks of galls, some of which have
sold at 34–36 *ML* [per 100 lb.], a price at which one can get nothing from England. There is a
large amount here from [London] which will yield no profit, and it is the same with oil, for
thanks to the arrival of two or three English ships that have come *a drittura* out of the Straits
this summer it has been brought down to rock-bottom. If that nation continues to bring
goods here in this way there will be little to be done between here and London. Meanwhile,
however, I shall be glad to learn what is happening in [London] with one thing or another. Of
your myrrh I sold 1 barrel yesterday for 10s per lb.² I shall try to dispose of the rest also, but
the stuff turns out to be very bad. God bless you, &c.

¹ '. . . *2 boyers van costi* . . .'.
² This consignment must antedate June 1664.

$$(i) + (ii)\quad\frac{31\ Aug.}{[\text{——}]}1668$$

30 DEATH, SKINNER & CO to JL & CM

LEGHORN   (i)   3 AUGUST 1668

'This weeke is come to our hands your joynt letter of the 29th June by which we note
acceptance to the severall remisses made you distinctly, soe of their due discharge we have
noe doubt, since your account is cleared as particularly you have been advised, whereto referr
you. Now we see 'tis your intentions to be doeing againe, particularly in another parcell of
tinne, in the disposall of which we can onely promise you to doe our best endeavours, but
encouragement we can give you little it goeing very heavily off at D.14, nor anything else
sells, the markett never being more overlaid with all sorts of goods nor lesse demand thereto;
lead finding not now buyers at D.24 and vast quantities in towne, our woollen manufactorie
selling also to losse, Italians and others that gaine by their silkes hence underselling us and

will we fear in time beat us by these means out of all trade, which were worth the considderation. Pepper keeps still up at D.$22\frac{1}{2}$ but now the East India fleete are arrived in Holland 'twill fall we believe allsoe fast. To be sure, 'twill doe so on any fresh supplyes thence. Russia hydes at 26 soldi to $27\frac{1}{2}$ the lb. as in goodnesse, calve skinns 14 soldi the lb. The *Fame* for Zante and *Margerett and Elizabeth* for Gallipoly went hence this weeke, the *Phenix* on departure for Tunis and the *Guinny* frigate and *George* bound for Smerna. Gallipoly oyle at about D.83 per salm aboard at Gallipoly, and is the present needfull, &c.'

London—$56\frac{1}{4}$.　　Venice—$103\frac{3}{4}$.　　Amsterdam—$98\frac{3}{4}$.

(ii)　17 AUGUST 1668
(not selected)

$\dfrac{7\ Sep.}{8\ Sep.}$ 1668

31　S. DE GEER to CM
THE HAGUE　　　　　　　　　　　　　　　　　　　　14 SEPTEMBER 1668

D]　I wrote to you by the preceding post and since then I have received your letter of the 28th past.

　　Concerning the square iron—£13 in cash is a low price and is not very satisfactory. It would be better next time to sell it at £13 10s for time, and my idea was to dispose of only a little in the hope that square iron would soon be in demand since so little has been sent. You should know best whether there is much square iron around in your area, and if so, you should be able to judge how much to withhold. I rely on you in this to do as you think advisable. I do not quite understand your intention—that is, whether you meant to sell it for cash or to barter it for tin and account for it as if the tin had been paid for in cash. If it should be paid for in tin you can send it over here straight away, but please make sure that it is smelted cleanly and not with coal, as it is presently at a rather low price and people are rather choosy[1]—and if it is pure one immediately has an advantage in selling it.

　　You must do this for the square iron but not for the flat iron, unless there is only a little flat iron remaining, for if one should reckon 80 tons of square and 20 tons of flat at an average of £13 per ton then the square iron would work out at scarcely £$12\frac{1}{2}$ per ton, since flat iron is worth so much more than £13 per ton. According to my best recollection there must be still about 3,000 bars of flat iron, though I may be mistaken as I am in no position here to check it. Please reflect on this and do what you judge suitable. You should also take into consideration that, by all appearances, not more than 2,000 slb of 'O' and 'G' flat iron can be expected, apart from the voyage iron—that is, if Bex despatched in one ship the rest of the iron he was ordered to send here.

　　If I gave £6 per ton for what is to come from Barbados I would be obliged to load the whole ship, or else he would have to look around for the rest of his lading and I would have to make up for what falls short, or else be responsible for a share of his cargo. It is strange that Abeels has not written to advise us how things stand over there, for our guidance.

　　Since it is rather late for the *Pyper* to go to Sweden, it is best that he goes to La Rochelle or Bordeaux for the *vendange*, for unless some other good opportunity arises I am confident he will get a good return at Bordeaux. Please advise him of this. He reached the Sound on the 3rd of this month but since then has had contrary winds.

　　　　With which, I remain, &c.

---

[1] '. . . *de luyden wat keurig syn* . . .'.

$$\frac{14\ Sep.}{25\ Sep.}1668$$

32   TAR COMPANY DIRECTORS TO CM
STOCKHOLM   22 AUGUST 1668

[D]   We are now at the 22nd of August: the foregoing on the other side is a copy of our last letter,
about a week ago, to which we refer you, and as the ordinary post has not yet arrived we have
so far received nothing from you. So this will serve merely to confirm the preceding. We sent
with it the bill of lading for Capt. Andries Johansen's and Capt. Andries Jacobsen's cargoes of
pitch and tar consigned to you. Their ships are still lying here off-shore but will depart with
the first good wind. May the Lord protect them! Herein we send the bills of lading for Jolle
T'Jerdts and Jacob Jacobsen Grys, also consigned to you, the first of which having 52 lasts
8 tuns of tar and 17 lasts of pitch, the other having 73 lasts 11 tuns of tar and 20 lasts of pitch.
May the Lord guide them also! Captains Elias Johansen and Hans Johansen have also been
chartered: the first is now loading and the other will begin shortly.

We had written this far when we got your letter of the 31st of July with which came a
copy of the contract which you and Mr Thuen have made together concerning our
Company's business. Through a lack of time we cannot read it over, and we will let you
know what we think of it by our next. You say that you want us to send 550 lasts of tar and
120 lasts of pitch to [London], and the rest of the 700 lasts of tar and 200 of pitch to Hull,
Yarmouth and the Isle of Wight. You will see from the bills of lading how much we have so
far sent to [London], being in all 432 lasts 1 tun of tar and 144 lasts of pitch. In addition, as we
have just said, Elias Johansen is loading and Hans Johansen has been chartered, so you can
expect to get the requested amount of tar at [London] and a good deal more than the
requested amount of pitch. But as regards the amounts requested for other places such as
Hull, Yarmouth and the Isle of Wight, we fear we will find no shipping going there, but we
will do our best and let you know what we arrange. Concerning insurance and cash advances,
we refer you to our previous letter, not doubting that whenever our goods arrive you will,
according to contract, advance the money, and we request you to correspond with Mr
Simons about this as we said in the copy above. Meanwhile we are very glad to hear of the
arrival of Capt. Hans Tennissen: may the Lord God be thanked who with His gracious help
may have since brought the others in safety, as they followed him shortly after. We expect to
hear soon. If we are going to insure the ships still lying here off-shore we will advise you,
closing this with cordial regards, &c.

$$\frac{21\ Sep.}{25\ Sep.}1668$$

33   TAR COMPANY DIRECTORS TO CM
STOCKHOLM   29 AUGUST 1668

[D]   The above is a copy of our last letter, to which we refer. We have since received yours of the
7th instant. We have now looked over the contract made by you and Mr Thuen and find it
very advantageous for you. Nevertheless, we will agree to it and get further clarification on
Mr Thuen's arrival here. We have credited you with the £150 sterling which you paid him.

It is a good thing that you have chartered Capt. Heinrich Meyer of Norrköping to go
from here to either Hull or Yarmouth. We have done our utmost to find shipping from here
to any of the places you requested but until now without success. We are now in negotiation

with someone but it seems he has little desire to go. We will advise you of our success by our next letter. Meanwhile, we shall get this Capt. Meyer unloaded on his arrival here and notify you of his return journey. The amount of tar and pitch despatched to [London] is stated in the copy above. The amount of pitch is not reduced this time. Please let us know with whom the 90 lasts of pitch from here came and who has received them. With cordial regards, &c.

$$\frac{30\ Sep.}{1\ Oct.}1668$$

4   R. OURSEL to CM
ROUEN   6 OCTOBER 1668

'Ma derniere a voz graces estoit le 3 courant, du depuis le poste n'estant venu je n'ay receu aucune des vostres quy causera cette plus courte et servira seullement pour accompagner l'incluze lettre de change de $W.500$ a $58\frac{1}{2}d$ du 4 courant 2 usances, que je vous remets pour vostre compte sur Thomas Waring en lettre de George Burrish. Il vous plaira en faire procurer le necessaire et m'en faire crediteur. J'esperois vous remettre le reste de vostre avance par cet ordinaire mais les lettres pour costy demeurent rarre je ppens que cela ne durera pas longtemps pour les raisons advisez par ma precedente. Je vous prie me dire sy pourriez faire fournir au Neufchastel au Sr. Nichollas Oursel deux ou trois cent livres sterlings peu plus ou moins a sa premiere demand et a quy il se pourroit addresser audit lieu pour cet effet. Il a achapté un vaisseau en Hollande l'hiver passé quy nous a cousté bien de l'argent avecq lequel il a esté a la pesche de la baleine et est de retour depuis un mois avecq 400 barils d'huile et 15 a 16 milliers de fanons. Presentement avons dessein de luy faire entreprendre quelque voyage. Ne scay sy au Neufchastel on luy fairoit tenir la quarantine, ayant attestation des magistrats du Havre qu'il ny a point de mal contagieux audit lieu. Attendant sur ce subject un mot de reponce je demeureray, vostre tres affectione serviteur.'

Costy: $58\frac{1}{2}$ a $\frac{1}{4}d$ ⎫
Amsterdam: $103g$ ⎬ 2 usances.

$$\frac{30\ Sep.}{[\text{——}]}1668$$

5   JOHAN BARCKMAN LEYONBERGH to CM
[LONDON]   27 SEPTEMBER 1668

'La memoire que j'ay presenté au Roy touchant les 3 vaisseaux a eté lue au Conseil, sans avoir pu obtenir autre resolution dessus, si non que les Loix doivent estre observés. Mais j'espere d'y réussir ayant quelques patience. C'est pourquoy il est fort necessaire que vous laissez les susdits vaisseaux dans Hoope jusques a ce que j'y puisse avoir employé d'autres voies.

Par le depart de la Cour j'ay beaucoup a faire a la Cour, que je ne puisse encore a un ou deux jours vous voir chez vous ou sur l'echange. Je ne mancqueray pourtant pas a vous témoigner bien tot, que je suis,' &c.

$$\frac{2\ Oct.}{2\ Oct.}1668$$

36   JAN VAN SAVELANT to CM

    GOTHENBURG   14 SEPTEMBER 1668

[D]   My last letter to you was on the 25th, to which I refer you. As I have not heard from you this serves only to say that Captain Anders Beursen arrived here some days ago and tells me that the 450 slb of voyage iron which I last consigned to you aboard him was sold as soon as it landed, which is good.

    Since then, we have had so little water inland that we could not get any voyage iron, but we have now had so much rain that water is very abundant and we have now got over 300 slb from up-country. Anders Beursen only has 100 slb aboard him, but the rest will go together in his ship which you can expect in due course. I have seen some Englishmen here who would gladly buy this consignment from me, but we could not agree. Someone called David Matson bought a quantity from me some time ago and shipped it to England.

    Samuel Rutter writes to me that in addition to the £85, he has paid out to you £154 8s 6d for my account, which I hope you will have remitted to Mr Bex before receiving this, as well as anything which arises from the sale of my iron.

[P.S.] Monsieur Marescoe, before closing this I received yours of the 21st and 25th past by which I learn that you had only sold $\frac{2}{3}$ of the iron received from Anders. I have no doubt that you will have sold the rest since then. From the English here I have had many requests for voyage iron, but to prevent it coming into too many hands I shall not sell. I am glad to see that you have remitted £350 to Mr Bex for my account at 35s 6g, double usance. I have also made a note on the account concerning Samuel Rutter. Rutter has sent me, via Anders Beursen, an account of the ship's sale and other matters between us. He is an experienced and good seaman to whom one may safely entrust a ship. It is a good thing he is now free from Cuttler, who must be an unscrupulous person. May God protect me from the like! Once more, greetings, God's blessing, &c.

$$\frac{6\ Oct.}{9\ Oct.}1668$$

37   CORNELIUS BERENBERG to CM

    AMSTERDAM   12 OCTOBER 1668

[D]   In answer to yours of the 12th and 15th September, I see you have at last bought 6 barrels of fine currants at 44s. If they are choice, I shall be glad, and hope to learn by your next in whom they have been shipped. You were unable to achieve anything regarding sugar. If, with the arrival of future shipments, it should faller lower and you judge the price to be at its lowest, then buy me 12,000 to 15,000 lb., but it is no use to me if it costs more than 26s, and it must be choice stuff, because there is plenty here and I must have only the very choicest, choice quality. Always bear that in mind when buying for me. The ships from Scanderoon have arrived and in your opinion galls are at their lowest. If you can get 20 barrels for less than 50s make sure the galls are big, heavy and blue. Aleppo galls are also welcome here. Camphor is regarded as a drug; it comes in little tubs, looks like snow but when refined is like crystal and at present fetches here 40 stuivers unrefined and 50 stuivers refined. If what they call camphor in [England] can be had for 6 to 10s it must be something else, so if possible send me a sample of the raw commodity for my guidance. If it can be brought here for less than 40 stuivers I would buy 500 lb. It is also used for perfume.

Sir, I would like to have 2,000 to 3,000 lb. of syrup from [London], but syrup is not allowed to be imported here unless it pays 1 stuiver per lb. To avoid that, I should like to ask you to get 2 empty pipes of oil that have been boiled clean and firmly reinforced with hoops so that they do not leak. Fill them up with syrup and firmly close up the tops with nails so they cannot be opened. They should get in safely, and I would then give you a good commission, but they must be kept steady and above all the casks must be thick so that they do not discover by leakage that it is not oil inside. Also, in shipping them you must not give the captain to understand that there is anything but oil inside, and on the bill of lading put down that they are to deliver these pipes to Hay t'Yercks marking them HTY in case of any unexpected hitch, although do not make any difficulty about the manner in which it is done.

If there is any new English saffron in [London] please send me a sample and the price, and please mention how much the enclosed sample of indigo would fetch in [England]. If there is anything in which I can be of service, please command me—with God's blessing, &c.

[P.S.] This sample is refined camphor, only I have ground it up in order to enclose it: otherwise it comes in lumps, for your information.

$$\frac{13\ Oct.}{16\ Oct.}1668$$

38 ADAM RADUE to CM
STOCKHOLM   19 SEPTEMBER 1668

D] Sir, I have received your very welcome letter of the 14th of August, from which I am glad to learn of your good health. As for me, I thank God I am well. I see that you and Mr Hendrick Thuen drank my health in a glass of wine: thank you for your kind remembrance of me, and as soon as Hendrick Thuen comes home again we shall drink your health in return.

I see that Mr Thuen has been establishing a secure business for the Tar Company in [England], in which he will use you—which I am very happy to learn. It would be a good thing if our company could at last be put on a firm footing so that we could for once be allowed to enjoy some profits, which could be achieved with good management. I hope that Mr Thuen has put things in good order in [England], as well as in Holland and other places.

Thank you for your kind offer to serve me whenever I have any goods to send, which I will accept. I cannot overlook you since you have served me so well in the past, which encourages me to employ you further—and I would have done so already if it were not that iron has been at so low a price in [England] that I and others have been frightened off from sending any iron to [England]. For at £12½ and £13 per ton there is nothing to be done: it must fetch £14 to £15, and then I might have something to send. I see that broad iron is fetching the highest price. It is important that I should know which kinds of iron are in most demand and fetch the most money, so that I can have them made at my works. If I knew what price anchors were at in [England] I could yearly send you 100 to 200 slb. Here they cost 30 to 32 copper dollars per shippound. I have about 80 slb of large anchor-flukes lying here, which I cannot easily sell. If I could sell them in [England] I would send them to you—to which I await your reply.

I and some other friends have decided to carry on an iron-works located in Värmland which can produce 2,000 to 3,000 slb of iron yearly and likewise 100 to 200 slb of copper at the least. If the mine were extended it could well produce 300 to 500 slb of copper, but I cannot guarantee so large an amount until we see how the mine turns out, which one can do better when it is working. We will send the iron and copper to Gothenburg. When the works are in operation I shall probably have need of 3,000 to 5,000 *RD* at a low rate of interest. If you were willing to accommodate me I could ensure that you receive large commissions. Please send me your views on this as soon as possible, as well as the price of anchors and bar-iron. If I see any profit in them I shall send you some in the Spring. I look forward to your answer on all this, with cordial greetings, &c.

[unendorsed]

39   J. B. LEYONBERGH to CM
LONDON   13 OCTOBER 1668

'Je croy que vous pouvez fort bien donner ordre aux Maistres de Suede qu'ils monter la riviere et qu'ils dechargent leur marchandises, car il nous est permis en nostre Traitte d'achepter des vaisseaux et de nous en servir moyenant que les Maistres soyent Suedois. Et je tacheray bien a les defendre. C'est tout que peut dire.

[P.S.] Je seray a la Bourse ci devant Midi en esperance de diner avec vouse.
En cas des troubles je ne mancqueray pas de soustenir nostre priviledge.'

[unendorsed]

40   J. B. LEYONBERGH to CM
[LONDON]   14 OCTOBER 1668

'Honored friend, I was this morning at Court with my Memorial and when I was recommending it to My Lord Privy Seal,[1] he immediately told me that it was to no purpose to deliver it over to the Lords Commissioners to expect their resolution on it, for they could not [move?] absolutely in it, after that the King and Councell had given once his resolution to the contrary. And whereas I grounded my Memoriall upon the 10th Article of the Treaty of London and the 19th of the Treaty of Stockholm,[2] he immediately told me that he would tell me as a friend, that he knew those articles grounded upon some provisoes and therefore advised me as his friend to apply me directly to the King, assuring me that for all he was my friend he would be against me if I had it once more for the Councill. I send you the treaty that you may see the proviso of the [18th] Article[3] as also an extract of the other, but I have left out all words which ware between here and there to our prejudice, as that word *tempore belli* and the like.[4] So that I think it the best to stay a day or 2 rather then to spoile the whole business by too great an importunity. I will be with you tomorrow upon the Exchange and speake further with you.

Adieu.

[P.S.] I intreat you to send me the remnant of your promise. My man hath a generall quittance under my owne hand.'

---

[1] Lord John Robartes (1606–85).

[2] The treaties of 1661 and 1665 respectively—Parry, *Consolidated Treaty Series* VI, pp. 469–94; VIII, pp. 263–81.

[3] Leyonbergh mistakenly writes '13th'.

[4] In a postscript to his letter of 15 October, Leyonbergh adds the text of the inconvenient proviso in article 18 of the Stockholm treaty of 1665, vizt. '*Quod tempore belli naves utriusque Foederatorum eorumque subditorum mercatoriae, sive fuerint in Regnis Magnae Britanniae Sueciaeve illisque subjectis Provinciis et Ditionibis vel alibi extructae, sive consensu vel permissione Regia aliunde emptae. . . . [to] . . . nihil praeterea ab illa exigatur . . .*'. For the text see Parry, VIII, p. 272.

[*unendorsed*]

41 J. B. LEYONBERGH to CM
LONDON   21 OCTOBER 1668

'Honored friend, I did really believe that I should have had an answer from the King about
our ships. But as I had been at least three hours waiting for an opportunity to speak with His
Majesty he was pleased himself to come out of his cabinett and to tell me that [he] was in great
haste, and would be taken up all forenoon in a business of importance. So I must forbear till
this night or tomorrow. I have some appearance of a good success, therefore lett us have
patience rather then to bring us self inconveniencies by too much importunity.

You may rest assured that I am watchful in it and that I will hope to give you a good
account.

[P.S.] Nous scaurons quelque chose d'importance aujourdhuy ou demain.'

[*unendorsed*]

42 J. B. LEYONBERGH to CM
COVENT GARDEN PIAZZA, LONDON   [undated]

'Je viendray demain sur la bourse pour vous parler touchant le Memorial, et si vous voulez
avoir pret l'autre concernant les vaissaux Hollandois vous m'obligeray, car le Roy va partir.
L'Attorney General estoit present quand ma Memoire fut lue, et fut commande de s'informer
de l'affaire. Il en parla au attornois de la Ville, qui presse pour avoir le Memoriall. C'est
pourquoy qu'il me faut tirer cet order de Conseil, le quy je feray aujourdhuy ou demain au
matin. Mr Robinson, le Gouverneur de la Tour, m'en a parle aujourdhuy et a voulu soutenir
que c'estoit vous qui m'avez instigue pour cela, disant que l'affaire a este debattu devant le
King's Bench. J'ay soutenu que ce n'estoit pas vous, mais que Sa Majeste de Suede m'avoit
envoyé un Memoriall dresse par le sujets de Suede par lequell ils se plaignent que Mons.
Marescoe mettre plus de frais en ses comptes depuis 12 mois qu'il n'ay fait les annees
auparavant, et que le Roy, mon maistre, m'a donne en charge particuliere de m'en plaindre
devant le Roy. Il m'a repondu la dessus que ce n'eut pas ete necessaire, et que j'eusse mieux fait
si je m'eusse adresse a luy ou a Lord Mayor, et encore dis je que Mons. Marescoe m'en a prie
d'en parler premierement au Lord Mayor, je n'ay pas pu faire, par ce que les ordres de mon
Maistre estoit pour en parler au Roy. Il me dit la dessus que si je vouloir luy en parler en ces
jours il m'en donneroit toutte la satisfaction et que l'affaire pouvoit bien etre vuidee entre
nous deux. Mais je vois bien que l'affaire n'est pas si franche comme on croit, et qu'en voudra
bien me caresser pour ne pas le pousser plus au Conseil, en douttant fort de leur advantage,
puis que je m'y mesle. Je vous en parleray plus des dumain, me recommandant cependant a
vostre bon grace, Je suis &c.'

[*unendorsed*]

43 J. B. LEYONBERGH to CM
COVENT GARDEN PIAZZA, LONDON   24 OCTOBER 1668

'My bussiness concerning those Swedish ships was the last and the only privat bussines
whaich was taken in consideracon and would not have been done this day, it being almost 8 a
clok before Lord Maire and the Aldermen went from Whitehall, had I not delivered the King
himself my Memoriall at his going into the Councill Chamber. And although it had for this

night no other success then that it was ordered that the Comite of Trade should upon Monday next consider the contents of the Treaty and the priviledges granted to the Suedes therein, and that they should make a report thereof to the Councell upon next Wednesday. Yett deare I assure myself of a good issue, because all my friends of the Councell at their coming out told me that His Majesty himself was my best advocate, and that he had said he was inclined to shew to the subjects of Sweden all the favor that might in reason be demanded. I shall watch them Monday morning and about noone you shall know what is past. In the meane while pray send me those other five and twinty pounds and you will highly oblidge, &c.'

---

44   J. B. LEYONBERGH to CM   *[unendorsed]*

LONDON   29 OCTOBER 1668

'I am heartely sorry that against all my hoops and expectations I shall not be able to gett these 3 ships free to unloade. It is impossibel, and I can not write what a great deal of troubles I have taken therein. The King had a dessin to favorise us therein but my Lord Ashly[1] and others of his humor remonstrated the King all the inconveniencies that would proceed from it that the King was forced to yield to them. In case the saison did not presse them, I would trie as yett what may be done, but the King is gone and will not be back again before Tuesday night, so that I see no likelyhood to doe any thing before the King's return for the discharge of the *Söderström*. In the other business there was nothing spoken. I believe that could not be amiss if the Commissioner of the navy which Mr Joye spoke of spoke with the Duke about it or used any other meanes for to make the Court sensibel of its wants. I shall as yet doe what I can, but deare no more assure me of a good issue, Adieu. &c.'

[1] Anthony Ashley Cooper (1621–83) later 1st Earl of Shaftesbury.

                                                                         $\frac{6\ Nov.}{6\ Nov.}$1668

45   J. VAN SAVELANT to CM

GOTHENBURG   19 OCTOBER 1668

[D]   My last letter to you was on the 5th inst., to which I refer you. Captain Anders Beursen went to sea on the 6th and I hope he will have arrived before this reaches you. Try to get the highest price you can and sell only to good, reliable people so that there is no risk of bad debts.

I have looked over your sale-account of the 4,344 bars of iron. Your expenses are extraordinarily high. You bring into the account £5 12s 1d for brokerage, short-change and false money. I suppose I must put up with the brokerage, but I do not think short-change and false money ought to be charged to me, for selling my iron. I think it is up to me to look out for good money and avoid short-change. Likewise, you bring into the account £30 6s 4d for 7 months' interest at 6 per cent per annum, and have sold my iron for 6 months time. It should be possible, on the safe arrival of Anders Beursen, to sell my iron for cash or at a rebate of 6 months, and so run no risk of bad debts. Concerning the £350 due from you, please remit it at the first opportunity to Mr Abraham Bex.

[P.S.] Before closing this I received your letter of the 2nd inst. from which I see you have remitted £210 to Bex at double usance for 35s 8g drawn on Cornelius Berenberg. Bex informs me that he has got it accepted and I trust that due payment will follow and be recorded on the account. I shall let him read what you say about Beckman and send an answer in due course. Please remit to Bex anything you have in cash on my account. Once more, God's blessing.

$$\frac{6\ Nov.}{[6\ Nov.]}1668$$

6 PETER SIMONS to CM

AMSTERDAM   13 NOVEMBER 1668

[)] I have safely received your letters of the 23rd and 30th of October, and have noted the serious situation of the ships *Suyderström, Beata* and *St Anna*, about which I have written today to the Tar Company and the Västervik Ship Company. And as the two latter ships have received no permission to unload in [London] please have them sail to La Rochelle and address themselves to Mr Theodore van Sevenhooven, who will benefit from their cargoes. We have no room for their tar here; in Portugal it is not in demand, and it is only in France that it may be sold best. I have written to the Sound today, about the *Beer*, telling them that, in case it has not yet passed through, it should be sent here—although I fear we shall have difficulty in finding room for its cargo, as everything is full. However, if he should come to Gravesend please order him to go to Mr Sevenhooven at La Rochelle like the two others. As for the cargo of the *Suyderström*, do your best to obtain its release, which I do not doubt you will. Please continue to give surety for the ship and I will supply a collateral guarantee, not doubting that the company will save us harmless. Just make sure that the ship is not rated at its full value, and I will remain your security.

Your letters for Stockholm have been duly forwarded, and I request you to hand on these enclosures to the captains.

For some days I have been lying in a fever so I have been unable to write myself. However, with God's help I hope to be well soon, although I am still very weak. Wherewith, &c.

[P.S.] Herewith is the bill of lading of Slb. 174.13.10 of iron which Mr Abraham Momma has consigned to you in the ship *Halve Maen*, the proceeds of which you are to consign to me.

$$\frac{9\ Nov.}{14\ Dec.}1668$$

7 UPTON & BATHURST to CM

SEVILLE   16 OCTOBER 1668

'Since the foregoing wee have received yours of the 31st August and to Mr Letheuileir wee have given advise of the remitting for your account in halves the three thousand of Alderman Backwell's ware mentioned in coppy per the *Greenwich* frygott. Besides the trunke of wrought ware and bill of ladeing for the same hath beene sent you, wee hope it is well come to your hands, which shall be glad to heare. The last post we remitted under a blanke covert a bill of lading for three thousand pieces of Alderman Backwell's ware, remitted for account in halves betwixt your self and Mr John Letheuillier per the *Ann & Judith*, Capt. Stafford consigned to Mr Thomas Death and Mr Ephraim Skinner of this citty sort[1] with order to remitt the same in good bills to each of you the halfe. Wee hope said Capt. Stafford is a good way toward that port ere this. Wee make you debtor in your new account for the amount of this parcel 13,320 *R. pta.*, being, beside the principall 7 per cent exchange, 1 per cent conveyance, $\frac{1}{2}$ per cent commission in Cadiz and $2\frac{1}{2}$ per cent our commission. That sort is now worth in Cadiz 8 to 9 per cent exchange, soe for the future wee must rather chuse to send of the yellow sort. Your account current wee send you herewith, wherein are included all parcells wee can perfect as yett, only in the debtor wee have not charged this parcell per Stafford but in the new account, being Mr Letheuilleir's account was not charged with itt, which wee remitted him two posts since, and we have made you good the ballance of this account in your new account, being three thousand five hundred and one *R. pta.*, which finding right you may please to note accordingly. Wee have charged you therein the money oweing per Laureano di Vrietta for your account formerly, but wee are nott without hopes to recover some part of it hereafter which whenever it is shall be made you good.

As for your *lamparillas*, we have advised those gentlemen that bought them, Mons. de Hollandre & Company, their qualletty as well in the coursenesse and ill sortment of cullers, and to take off their lookeing like *picots* wee have got them doubled like *lamparillas*, that may the better putt them off when time serves, which for the *Galleons* wee hope to doe and wee think their voyage will be in the spring if the last orders from the Counsell be observed, butt if soe will be without any *flota* ships. Wee have advised Mr Letheuilleir the arrivall of Capt. Stafford and the receipt of your goods by him. At present wee have a very dull markett and very few of our English goods sell; the vintage ships at Malaga somewhat glutt the marketts; bayes have now the best expense and rissen here to 24 ducats.

Your accounts merchandize wee keepe to send by sea, which shall goe per a small vessell that may be goeing home in 10 or 12 dayes. Logwood is here worth seaven pieces of eight per quintall and therefore wee doe not adventure to send you any. Here is very little in the country and like to come none till towards the end of the next summer. Indico worth 11 *R. pta.* per lb. first penny and cucheneil 98 ducats per *arroba* att which rates little hopes of advance and of all sorts little in the country. Exchange for Antwerp att 116 grosse per ducat.

Our trade being soe dull for the sale of goods wee cannot tell what sorts to advise for till can make some further progresse in the sale of whatt wee have, wherein you may be confident noe endeavours are wanting on our parts, and haveing nott else wee rest.'

  ¹ I.e. Seville-minted *pesos*.

$$\frac{\textit{10 Nov.}}{\textit{12 Nov.}}\textit{1668}$$

48 PIETRO VAN TEYLINGEN & CO to CM
      VENICE   2 NOVEMBER 1668

[D] Since our last letter, of the 19th October, we have heard nothing from you. By the foregoing letter you will have learned from your brother-in-law, Mr John Lethieullier, of the sale of the 448 pieces of small-lead on the *Europa* to Bortolo Marinoni at 55 ducats, less 1 per cent tare and 6 months discount, to pay in three months time. We decided on this as we see little prospect of it doing better, as there are at present over 1,000 pieces in town unsold, and there will shortly be a quantity coming with the fish-ships, probably before the *Europa* reaches Leghorn. So we were of the opinion it was more likely to fall than otherwise.

  Concerning the 467 pieces of small-lead on the *Lantsman* (which was on the point of leaving Leghorn) we are in negotiation and, if we cannot do so at the foot of this letter we will advise you of our success by our next, and we do not doubt that you will be grateful for what we decide.

300 pieces have been unloaded from the *John & Thomas* and delivered to Lorenzo Bettoni. The rest is to follow next week, and we hope to be able to send the account by our next letter. Pepper was selling at 150 ducats at 2 months time and is still being held at that price. Good quality cinnamon is at 108 dollars (poor quality is unsaleable), cloves at 65 dollars, sappan-wood at 70 ducats with 4 months time. Otherwise no changes of any importance.

$$\frac{10 \; Nov.}{13 \; Nov.} 1668$$

9 S. DE GEER to CM
AMSTERDAM   16 NOVEMBER 1668

)] Since my last letter of the 9th of this month, in which I drew £830, I have received your letters of the 23rd and 30th October.

I have come to an agreement with Rosheuysen concerning the £80 in view of the fact that he has not settled with me for the expenses.

I hope you have been able to procure freedom for Capt. Grys as well for the *Beer*, in the event of them having to be newly-built, for the fine iron should be more serviceable to you. Please let me know if it is only ships with iron which can come in freely, because I understand that previously a distinction was made between iron and tar. I had always thought that broad iron was in demand [in England] and consequently had it expressly made. I shall now give orders to make no more, but only flat iron of various breadths like that which, I trust, you have now received and which you can count on in the future.

I had not expected any letter from Clignet, although he is sometimes rather hasty. I shall give some thought to it at once. The best of it is that he does not have much left on his hands. I wrote to him at length three weeks ago about what he claims and sent him an account, allowing him what is due for his trouble. You can always open his letters to me, as well as mine to him, if you want to: they were only sealed in order to spare you any trouble, and if they were left open you would be able to judge the facts for yourself, inasmuch as the letters are sometimes lengthy over small points of trade-accounts.

I am glad that you are writing at once to Londonderry via Dublin, for I cannot understand what is hindering me from getting letters from there.

I do not know if I sent you the invoice of the iron in the *Beer*, or a note accompanying that for the *Halve Maen*, saying that it is an old Swedish ship. Bex writes me that he has so far loaded 550 slb of iron in the ship *Fortuyn* and that he is expecting about 3,000 bars which I suppose the *Pyper* will take aboard, if it is going to London. How much voyage iron there is in these two last-named ships I do not know yet. The *Halve Maen* as well as the *Fortuyn* are ships built in Sweden. The *Beer* was built here but has been a Swedish ship for 8 or 9 years, so I hope these three ships will encounter no difficulty.

I remain, &c.

$$\frac{23 \; Nov.}{27 \; Nov.} 1668$$

0 TAR COMPANY DIRECTORS to CM
STOCKHOLM   24 OCTOBER 1668

)] The above is a copy of our last letter [of the 3rd of October], to which we refer you. Since then we have received your letters of the 11th and 25th past and the 2nd instant, wherein we see that you have settled the suit with the insurers to pay 70 per cent, payable by the 26th of November. That is good news, and we shall expect from you a brief account of the settlement.

God be praised for the safe arrival of Alexander Davidson, though it is to be feared that none of the others has yet come to shelter. However, we hope they have appeared by the time you receive this.

You say that you see no chance of ships bought in Holland being granted freedom, since the Resident, Lord Leyonbergh, put in a memorial to the King's Council about it and got the answer that the laws of the land had to be obeyed. Nevertheless it is to be hoped that, with the help of the recent letter from the General College of Commerce, the Resident will obtain it. Had the English Resident here[1] not so firmly assured the College of Commerce of it we would not have despatched the ships thither.

You also say that other people have been loading substantial quantities of pitch and tar which have arrived in England, and you tell us you would have been obliged if we had forewarned you about the amounts we had sold to other people for despatch thither—to which we say that not a single last has been sold for despatch. We cannot find that any tar has been sent from here, but pitch certainly has, of which we have previously advised you. We would be glad if you would tell us the captains' names and to whom the goods were sent.

Herein we send the bill of lading of Capt. Hendrick Hoyer of the ship *De Groene Jager*, destined for Hull and consigned to Mr William Skinner with 57 lasts and 4 tuns of tar and 30 lasts of pitch. Please give further orders to Mr Skinner, and herein is a letter for Mr Skinner which you will please give him.

Mr Thuen has written to you that you should undercut your rivals' low prices, which is our view also, because if these people are allowed to undermine us they will finally get on top and domineer, so we think it is best to anticipate them and deprive them of the opportunity. Please handle it carefully.

Capt. Oloff Ericksen of the ship *Halve Maen*, which we have mentioned before, is now ready and has on board 12 lasts of pitch and 31 lasts 5 tuns of tar. Please procure insurance on him and on Hendrick Hoyer, according to contract.

Mr Simons has written to you that he must pay *RD* 6,000 for us and that he has to draw that amount on you, but there is still some time to run so we have written to him to delay a little. For those amounts which he has already drawn on you and which you have accepted, please honour them, but we had not intended to burden you before the arrival of the ships.

You will have learned from our previous letters that we have been unable to find the Lord Treasurer[2] at home in order to present him with your bill of exchange. By our next we hope to be able to tell you if he will accept it, though we fear payment will follow only slowly, but we will earnestly press it and on receiving it place it on your account. But you have valued the rixdollar too high—it ought to be only 4s 6d as the exchange with Hamburg does not yield any more. Remaining, &c.

---

[1] Sir Thomas Thynne, b. 1640, d. 1714, later 1st Viscount Weymouth. He served in Sweden from 1667–9.
[2] . . . 'd'Heer Rentemeister' . . .

$$\frac{23\ Nov.}{24\ Nov.}1668$$

51 S. DE GEER TO CM
AMSTERDAM   20 NOVEMBER 1668

[D] Since my last letter, of the 16th instant, I have received yours of the 6th from which I see that Capt. Grys's iron has been unloaded. I am delighted, because I was as afraid for him as for the iron in the *Beer* since I had been informed that his ship was also Dutch-built. I understood that any ships which had been acquired by Sweden by 1662 or thereabouts were regarded as free, as if they had been built in Sweden, but that any bought subsequently were not. I shall be glad to learn what the facts are.

Capt. Pyper has arrived at Stockholm. Enclosed with this is the invoice of the iron shipped in the *Fortuyn*. The ship is Swedish, as well as the *Halve Maen*—both were built in Sweden. I remain, &c.

$$\frac{7\ Dec.}{14\ Dec.}1668$$

52 DEATH, SKINNER & CO to CM
LEGHORN   23 NOVEMBER 1668

'This weeke is come to our hands yours of the 19th past, ordering what you would have done in the sale of your tinn, which we have made note of, though there's little or noe likelyhood we should effect ought, there beeing now offerers of that comoditie at D.13½ without buyers, and oyles at present not to be had at any rate, beeing as it is said noe more old oyle left in the cuntry, though if against new which may be had in January and leave us at liberty to doe as well as we can you incline, we shall use our best endeavours in your service, though 'tis of late our mishapp to have the freedome to act when we are noe more in time to doe itt, since might we have done at first what now we have liberty 'tis possible your goods had err this binn despatcht, but as our comodities have declined there's, you see, have gained favour, the last oyles haveing binn bought up at D.14⅓ the salme, *p. aviso*, Lead offerd also at D.22½ without buyers, it beeing the opinion of these people that when the herring fleete arrive 'twill yet be had cheaper; pepper also declined to D.26, selling slowly, and of woollen manufactorie not any sells, never worsse times or lesse probabillity of there mending. The *Experiment* this day imported from London and a catch with pilcherds is said to be now comeing in, which beeing the present needfull, with due respects, remaine, &c.'

$$\frac{7\ Dec.}{12\ Dec.}1668$$

53 W. SKINNER to CM
HULL   4 DECEMBER 1668

'Sir, I have both yours of the 22th past and primo instant. I have not bene unmindefull of your commission for buyinge lead, but if I could have met with any parcels to sell at or about £12 per fodder I should have beene buyinge for you untill your parcel had bene compleated; but for 10 dayes at least together here hath not bene any great lead to sell in towne except 80 piggs which were limitted to sell at £12 5s per fodder. Here are great parcels lyinge in towne and yet every mans hands' are restrained, whether by combination amongst the lead men or a general expectation of a rise, is not yet discoverable. I cannot at present buy 20 piggs of lead in all this towne, the like whereof I have seldome knowne, and I doe the more wonder at it in regards this time of yeare is a dead season, and now the great parcels for the Streights are bought and gone. I can say no more, but as you have told mee your occasion and left it to mee to effect after the best manner I can, I shall watch all opportunitys to fulfill your orders both for the first and last in ordered parcel, if the tyme shall give mee leave to serve you in it.

Schipper Hoyer would not hearken to your proposition of £30 freight and £5 piloatage to goe for Plimouth soe wee are now againe unloadinge and layinge up pitch and tarre, our market being at present soe overlaide that I am bidden but £10 per last for pitch and £7 per last for tarre to take the whole parcel, which are priced soe farre under the rates you sell at there that I doe not lissen to them but hope for better afterward, and in the interim, as opportunity offereth soe shalbe sending you some to London, and soe at present remaine,
Yours att command, W.S.'

$$\frac{11\ Dec.}{12\ Dec.}1668$$

54 BRYAN ROGERS[1] TO CM
FALMOUTH   7 DECEMBER 1668

'Sir, I have your of the primo currant, observeing thereby your intentions if tinne would come resonable, which as yet, contrary to expectation, it houlds up at £3 16s per cwt., occasioned by the greate demand for Roan, here being now two or three smalle vessells in loadeing for ditto place. What it may be at when the coinage is, which will be about the primo January, is uncertayne, but surely if menn had been but patient and not soe exceeding hasty it might have been bought on much easier termes. If you please to have aney money invested in ditto comodety you must allowe some time for getting your money in place, exchange being exceeding scarce and usually at 1 per cent. los. I shall not omitt to advise you from time to time how the price rules, for your government, and as you have occation gladly receive your commands which shall faithfully be descharged.
I remayne, your affectionate friend & servant,'

¹ Rogers, a leading Cornish merchant and tin-dealer, who frequently acted on behalf of London interests, was later reputed 'the most opulent figure of any merchant in the West'. See J. A. Whetter, *Cornwall in the 17th Century: an economic survey of Kernow* (Padstow, 1974) pp. 153–5, 160–6; and Whetter, 'Bryan Rogers of Falmouth, Merchant (1632–92)' in *Old Cornwall*, VI No. 8 (1965) pp. 347–52.

$$\frac{16\ Dec.}{17\ Dec.}1668$$

55 ROBERT ELLISON[1] TO CM
NEWCASTLE   12 DECEMBER 1668

'Loveinge friend, I have yours of the 8th present and before it com had usd my indeavors to accomplish your order to buy lead and indeed did thinke to have found it fall in price, but contrary to my expektations I found the market much alter so as I was affeared I should not have got your lead for £11 15s. It's well I had this last letter or else I am confident I had missed my best tyme, for many commissions are in towne to buy and strangers' ships expeckted, and that which was worse, severall small parcells bought to send to Holland though at this time a-yeare, but this and the other makes it hyer then I expeckted. I tryed all the lead men in towne. Some would not sell under £12, others £11 17s, but I did at last with very much ado buy of Mr Ralph Gray and Mrs Briggs 100 fothers at £11 14s per fother. I shall get it weighed up and charge the mony as opertunity offers. I wish it may please you and be to your proffit. Pray let me have your approbation, for I have really saved you £5 which they said they would not abayt to any but that I should have it to myself, but I do not desire it. I have writt into the country but I see such inquiry into the commodity that I durst not deffer it.

I am, Sir, your loveing friend.'

¹ Until his death in January 1678, Ellison corresponded regularly with Marescoe & David and was succeeded by his son John. A leading merchant since the 1640s, member of the Newcastle Merchant Adventurers Company and the Company of Hostmen, Ellison served the city as sheriff and as Member of Parliament, 1647–8 and 1660. He played a leading part in resisting the claims of the London and Hamburg Merchant Adventurers for jurisdiction over Newcastle. See R. Howell, *Newcastle upon Tyne and the Puritan Revolution* (Oxford, 1967) pp. 12, 168, 183; *Extracts from the Records of the Merchant Adventurers of Newcastle-upon-Tyne* [ed. F. W. Dendy] Publications of the Surtees Society, XCIII, CI (Newcastle, 1895, 1899) passim.

$$\frac{18\ Dec.}{[18\ Dec.]}1668$$

6 P. VAN TEYLINGEN & CO to CM
VENICE   7 DECEMBER 1668

)] We find ourselves with your very welcome letter of the 6th past, in answer to which we herewith enclose the second bill of exchange for D.500, in case the first is lost. We hope to remit you the remainder by our next. We have made a note of the 20 sacks of pepper laden for your account in the ships *Gratia* and *Vrede*, departing from Amsterdam, and of the 100 pieces of lead on the *William & Elizabeth*, half for your account and half for your brother-in-law, Mr John Lethieullier, from whom we have received the bill of lading. May the Lord bring them in safety. We shall not fail to press for the highest price possible. Lead is now offered at D.50 on delivery and for prompt delivery at D.50¾, but falling, for there are daily more enticements to buy so that I fear there will be a further decline as this is also the deadest season of the year for sales. Pepper is still being held at D.150, because there is not much in town. If the *Gratia* arrives early I still hope to find a good market, but with one thing and another I may not be able to do such good business. The *Lantsman*, according to the latest letters, has not yet arrived at Leghorn—I mean, Ancona. Indeed, he delays too long and [- - - -] must be taken. May the Lord protect him from mishap. Likewise with the *Europa*, whose departure from Leghorn you will have seen in my last letter. As for the sale of lead, I cannot say if it has been well done so far because, as yet, there is no better prospect to be hoped for. If it should increase further in England it may well go the same way here: one must hope so. As for that which has just been laden in Amsterdam, and which will have to fetch a better price if it is not to produce a loss, I assure you that it will be dealt with as if it were my own.

English tin still remains here at the price of D.32 per hundred-weight (corresponding to that of lead). If not too much more arrives we are of the opinion that it will remain at that price. Zante currants were being held at R. pta. 40, Cephalonian at R. pta. 35 to the first buyer, with the likelihood of not falling as there are still two or three ships to go there to load. It will be possible to lade the new Apulian oil next month at D.13½ per salm, for casks on board. The *John & Thomas* departed last Monday. The *Merchant's Delight* has been prevented from following by contrary winds.

London: 55*d.*
Amsterdam: 97.

57   JACOB MOMMA to CM
NORRKÖPING   23 NOVEMBER 1668

[D]   I last wrote to you on the 9th of October, from Hamburg. Since then I have arrived here in good health and have found all my people likewise well, praise be to God who protects us.

I now find myself owing you an answer to your letters of the 9th, 23rd and 30th of October—but that of the 16th, in which you sent the account of the 1,064 coils of wire, 76 chests of copper bars and 349 Hungary plates, has not yet come to my hand, so I shall await a copy as well as a sale-account of the above-mentioned goods. I have received the account of the 50 cases of steel: I shall check it and debit you accordingly. It is very welcome news that Petersen Muller has arrived safely. I hope the other two ships from Gotland will also arrive soon and that their timber will find a good market.

I see that Jacob Grys is not permitted to unload his pitch and tar in [London]: for what reason, I would very gladly learn. I saw also that you were offered £5 16s for the remaining latten and that you sold it for £5 18s. I urge you to you to do your best for my brass and copper as if it were your own and that, if possible, you get it sold before the winter, because I can send a new lot in the spring. With the remaining bars you should bide your time and take care only to dispose of the small parcel of copper-wire rods. It is good garcopper of a kind which you can no longer get and without it one cannot make bars. I hope it will sell well. As all the ships are going to [Guinea?] it is not advisable to sell the bars at £5 15s or even £6. It is better to bide your time. I have noted what is happening to iron.

You have now paid all the drafts from the Messrs Van Baerle. I would like a clear statement of how much you think you will have at your disposal on my account from now on, for my information.

The sample of kettles which you sent with Matthys Meyer has not yet appeared in Stockholm. As soon as they arrive I shall let you know whether or not I can get them made, though I think I can, and you will have my thanks. I want to know how much they cost and I will place it to your credit. At 7s per cwt. the calamine is no use to me.

You can expect two more ships from Gotland laden with beams and planks. They will also have a quantity of sandstone of the kind we use in this country to ornament our houses as chimney-pieces or fireplaces. I have ordered the captains to take it aboard as ballast beneath the timber. If there is anything to be done with it I could deliver a great quantity. It was selling in Holland by the foot at 18, 19 and 20 stuivers per square foot, but while freight-rates are so high one cannot get as much for it as one ought, for it should cost at least 25 to 26 stuivers per foot. I shall be glad to learn what happens. If there should be any major buildings, such as churches or mansions, being constructed in [London] and if one could make a contract for a large quantity I would agree to it even if it were for as much as 30 or 40 ship-loads, provided that they unload it. I could supply it, free-on-board, at 12 *RD* per 100 square feet and at [London] sell the best at 52 *RD*, provided that the buyer paid for the importing and expenses in [London]. You could look into it with this trial offer and let me know your views.

I hear that large amounts of sheet-iron are being forged in Hamburg this year and sent to [London]. I beg you to let me know how much it may be selling for, what size and weight it is, and if further amounts are being demanded, for I could deliver a good quantity if there were some profit to be made by it. And I want you also to inquire if it has been decided in [England] to have a copper coinage made, and if so, whether one could not deliver a quantity of copper blanks. Please find out, in secret, and let me know about it. One could earn a substantial commission on a commodity like that. Wherewith, my heartiest regards, &c.

$$\frac{21\ Dec.}{24\ Dec.}1668$$

8 PETER RULAND to CM
HAMBURG   11 DECEMBER 1668

)] My last letter to you was on the 10th past. Since then I have received yours of the 27th in reply. I see that you were unable to do anything about my order for new currants since they were not to be had for less than 45s. Old stuff is of no use to me at any price, so I want you to leave it until a better opportunity arises. 27s for sugar is also too expensive for it to be brought here as it is likely to be cheaper in a couple of months, and if I have news of it I shall send an order for some. Every shop and corner is full-up here and none sold, so for the moment there is no lack of it. Once the season for galls is over they should become cheaper. There is little to be said about other goods. £32 10s for oil is still too dear: it will have to be cheaper before I order any. If changes occur in any commodities please inform me with a note.

You have seen that I was expecting a quantity of chests of lemons in a ship from Genoa, for which I cannot obtain permission to bring them into [England] as it is against your Navigation Acts. However, if it is obliged by ice to over-winter in one of your harbours I think you might spend something on getting it freed. I hope it will not happen, but if it should I herewith give you orders to spend something on procuring its freedom to be imported and unloaded, so that they can be sold. It must not be risked with a severe freeze-up; just wait long enough until something is decided, in case it does not freeze at all. There are 250 chests altogether, with the accompanying mark, loaded aboard the ship *St Jean Battista*, master Joost Claesens, a Hamburger. In each case there are about 400 to 500, according to their size, and they are of a size which one usually sells here at *RD* 9–10 per case, for your guidance. If by any chance you can get a good price for them you can have them unloaded and sold (as above) to my best advantage.

Herewith is an order to the master, and if that is not enough you can write to Jacomo Ruland at Amsterdam for the bill of lading, who will do it himself and send it on.

With hearty regards, &c.

$$\frac{21\ Dec.}{22\ Dec.}1668$$

9 T. WRIGHT to CM
[STOKESLEY?]   17 DECEMBER 1668

'Sir, I have both your letters of the 5th and 8th currant by which I perceave mine of the 3rd came to your hands. I wish I had this your last comission when I wrote those lines: that might have beene don then which cannot bee done now, for, Sir, the next day after I received your letters I went about your businesse but I found an alteration in things and although I were at all or most of the lead owners yet they had all inteligence that leade was on the riseinge hand beyond seas in many places and alsoe had advise that seaverall lead mines were drowned in Darbyshire soe that on theese newes seaverall wold sell none at all for present and those that wold sell hold it hard at £12 per fodder, and indeede I saw that price given by one that is an agent to a marchant of noe meane trade, and heere is very many comissions come downe to buy leade, so that, Sir, had I not met with 2 men that stood in greate need of mony I had not bought a fodder of leade under £12 per fodder. However, because I wold not alwayes ride and goe about business and doe nothinge I adventured to buy some, though I give you my wages—which I refer to you. I bought 10 fodder to bee delivered att Newcastle and 23 fodder to bee delivered at Stockton, and it cost mee £11 15s per fodder and £3 over in the whole, which £3 I refer to yourself, and, Sir, I will waite all opertunityes to buy the remainder of what you gave mee comission for. Sir, the leade wilbee all redy downe (if bad weather hinder not) at the saide ports within a month. Sir, beinge the persons were in want of mony I was forced to draw uppon you sooner then I did intend, but I hope you will excuse mee in that I have drawne 3 bills on you, one of £200 payable 20 dayes after sight to one Mr John Bell, the value received of Mr George Hodgson; the other 2 bills are of £60 a-peece payable 20 dayes after date to Mr Lancelot Westgarth or his order, the value received of himself. The bill is dated the 16th instantt. Sir, I desire to heare from you and in any thinge you order mee I will doe the best I can, and in the spring I cann send you your leade from Stockton either to London or to Holland, as you thinke good. Soe with my prayers to God for you and yours, with my servis presented to you, I remain, Sir, your servant to comand.'

$$\frac{25\ Dec.}{29\ Dec.}1668$$

60 W. SKINNER to CM
HULL   22 DECEMBER 1668

'Sir, I have yours of the 19th instant. For answer, here is yet noe lead in towne to sell, and I feare the price of £12 15s at London will confirme our lead men in their expectations of an advance, for that is the market they are most governed by. I am most sorry that your commision is with mee in a tyme of soe great difficultye, it being clearly against my opinion to buy at great prices without a considerable advance at forraigne markets. And yet, if there be soe little lead left at London, and soe much weekely expended on the Citty buildings as is said, in all probabillity they'l strive to keep it up and to sell deare what they soe buy. 'Tis said they buy at £12 16s in the country, and aske £13 a £13 10s per fodder for furder parcels. If you order mee still I shall get your parcel bought per first after any orders come to towne for sale.

   I have not sold any parte of your pitch and tarre and have noe hopes to obtaine your limitted prices. I shalbe therfore lookinge out for shipps to send you some by, and soe, presentinge my respects, I remaine,

                        Yours at command, W.S.'

$$\frac{4\ Jan.}{5\ Jan.}1669$$

61 J. PÖTTER & H. THUEN to CM
STOCKHOLM   5 DECEMBER 1668

[D]   As I have been unexpectedly occupied all day today with some good friends, I shall postpone writing at length until the next extra-ordinary post. Meanwhile this is necessary to advise you that we have today drawn a large sum on Simons in Amsterdam, with orders for him to draw to the value of 9,000 *RD* on you at double usance, which we beg you to honour. To set against that you can expect a good quantity of iron as soon as we have open water here. You can be especially assured that you may expect at least 2,500 slb of voyage iron, 2,000 slb of broad schampeleon,[1] and a further 2,000 slb of ordinary fine iron, flat and square, either from Gothenburg or from here, though mostly from Gothenburg. And if the price holds up, more will follow. Advise us what orgrons[2] iron sells for, and if it is worth sending much. Will write more fully per next.

[P.S.] Once more, we urge you to do what is required for Peter Simons, and we await our current account.

[H. Pötter].

---

[1] In Swedish 'schamplun', an archaic term for certain kinds of pattern, model or design; in this context, bar-iron forged according to special instructions as to its length, breadth or thickness. See *Ordbok över svenska språket* (Lund, 1965) cols. 1355–9.
[2] I.e. from Öregrund in Uppland, the major export harbour for iron from Lövsta, Gimo and Österby (see Map 3, p. 566).

$\frac{4\ Jan.}{8\ Jan.}$1669

ABRAHAM KOCK–CRONSTRÖM to CM
STOCKHOLM   [12?] DECEMBER 1668

Fourteen days ago, on the 28th of November, was my last letter to you, which was brief and mainly to accompany the bill of lading of Slb. 160.19.11 of wire and Slb. 31.5.13 of Hungary plates consigned to you aboard Gerret Laurens, which I hope you have received. Since then the ship has departed and as it had a following wind I hope, with God's help, it has arrived in [England]. Furthermore, Mr Hansen has returned from England, assuring me that you have shown yourself very favourably inclined to administer my affairs over there, and as I should be very glad to see all the Swedish commissions together in one hand I have asked him to send you my views and the conditions on which I want to correspond.[1] I trust he has done so and that you have accepted them, for none of my friends in Holland, Hamburg and France refuse them. And although I have addressed a consignment to you before I can receive your answer, I trust that I shall nonetheless be treated generously by you, which will give me grounds for continuing with even bigger commissions.

You yourself know that at these miserable prices for wire there are losses, but that if it all came into one person's hands it could be held in better esteem. I beg you to do this, and not to let it go for less than £5 12s or £5 10s. As for [copper] plate, since it usually fetches a good price, please sell it at the current price because I do not doubt it will be fixed at £6 10s. Let the captain keep the bill of lading if he has it, but the other, endorsed by me, is to be handed over; and have the empty casks of steel delivered to Messrs Burkin & Evertsen.

It would be friendly service to me if one could, quietly and securely, conclude an agreement with the East India Company for a considerable quantity of copper. Tell me what you think, in confidence, and also what you have heard from the Resident, Leyonbergh, about my case concerning the plundered galliot called *de Paerel*—whether anything is coming of it or not. You could easily inquire and assure yourself that it is being handled as it should be. I await your advice concerning the prices of our Swedish commodities and your counsel concerning next Spring's cargoes, and send herewith, cordial greetings, &c.

[P.S.] In my last letter I ordered you to insure the goods aboard Gerret Laurens for 8,000 *RD*. I hope that has been done; if not, please have it done without delay.

---

[1] For these see Appendix B.

$$\frac{11\ Jan.}{15\ Jan.}1668$$

63   J. MOMMA to CM
VISBY-IN-GOTLAND   14 AUGUST 1668

[D]   Since I last wrote to you, on the 16th of May, I have nearly completed my visits to Ösel and Gotland and have put everything in order on both islands, so I only need a favourable wind to complete my journey back to Sweden—God grant me a speedy voyage!

This letter serves mainly to say that I have, lying here in Slite harbour, two Dutch ships which came from Portugal with salt. The ships are called *De Hartogh* (of which Claes Jacobs is captain) and the *St Margreta* (captain, Cornelis Jacobsen) and I am having them loaded with timber, such as large and small beams, planks and firewood. I am also putting some limestone in as ballast, just as an experiment. Very fine lime can be burned. You could enquire if there is any chance of selling it: for your information, one can get three tons of lime from one ton of limestone. You will be hearing from Mr Jacob Kroes how much it costs. As for the timber which is coming in the above-mentioned ships, you will find it much better timber than any from the Baltic or Norway. Indeed, an English builder assured me that it was as good as any northern or Dutch oak. You will find it to be mostly of large beams, over one foot thick in diameter, so I am hopeful it will sell for much more than it did last year. I am relying on you to do your utmost with them.

I am also expecting at Klintehamn two large ships from Holland which will also be loaded for [London] with extremely fine timber. They will be consigned to you and I do not doubt that you will seek my profit. Please pay the freight charges to the aforesaid captains according to the account which Jacob Kroes will send you if he writes to you. If the timber-ware should fall short of the balance due on the freight (which I hope it will not) I shall make provision for you from Sweden. I am relying on you, and if the timber sells well and if Dutch ships can freely come to [England] with such goods next year I am thinking of sending 10 to 12 ships-lading of timber. May the Lord God grant you good health, &c.

[P.S.] I should like to know how much corn sells for in [London], what the expenses are and how the measures compare with Dutch measures, as I am expecting 800 to 900 lasts of grain on Ösel this autumn. If there is anything to be done with it through you or elsewhere I could deliver a substantial amount.

[unendorsed]

64   SIR EDWARD WALKER[1] to CM
WHITEHALL   15 JANUARY 1669

'Whereas the matter in difference between the Resident of Sweden and the Lord Mayor and Aldermen of the City of London concerning the duty of waterbaylage is appointed to be heard at this board on Wednesday the 20th of this instant January; And it being represented to the said Resident that there are divers persons who are conceived essentiall wittnesses in the said Cause, who may refuse to come voluntarily; It was thereupon ordered (His Majestie present in Councell) that all and every the persons hereunder named doe, and thei and every of them are hereby required to make their personall appearance at this board on the said 20th day of this instant at nine in the morning, to testifye their knowledge in the cause afore-said, whereof thei nor any of them may faile at their perill.
                        Eduard Walker.

Sir,

The Resident hath disned today at my Lord Carlisle's and is not yet come in, and (as I heare) overladen with liquor, soe that this night I cannot return to you, nor bring either bill nor acquittance. In the mean time here is a copy of the order.

I am, &c.'

[1] Clerk of the Privy Council.

$\dfrac{\text{12 Jan.}}{\text{15 Jan.}}$1669

TAR COMPANY DIRECTORS to CM

STOCKHOLM   19 DECEMBER 1668

Since our latest letter of the 28th past we have received yours of the 13th ditto, which we ought to have had eight days earlier. This week's ordinary post has also not arrived.

We have noted that Resident Leyonbergh has been unable to achieve anything, although he has done his duty in trying to procure freedom for the ships, and that captain Johanson was ready to depart for Rochelle although the Resident still had hopes of obtaining his freedom, which would be very welcome to us as we would rather not send the goods to Rochelle where there is already so much that they will not be sold for a long while. It is a good thing that you are summoning the *St Pieter* from Yarmouth, because our friends from Hull and Yarmouth have written that so much tar and pitch from others has arrived that it will not be sold in a year. We beg you to seize every opportunity to dispose of our goods at whatever price they will fetch so that foreign competitors are thwarted and not allowed to dominate the market.[1] We shall now wait to hear of further developments.

From the accompanying extract you will be able to see how much Mr Simons has accepted for us and when the amounts fall due. We have made out a short account showing how much we can draw on you according to contract against the goods we have sent you, being in total 404 lasts and 6 barrels of tar and 170 lasts and 8 barrels of pitch (besides the three consignments which have to go to Rochelle and with which you can now no longer be of any service to us) rated according to contract at £5 per last for the tar and £8 per last for the pitch, making a total of £3,384 from which is deducted the £1,300 which Simons has already drawn. That leaves £2,084 to be made good, followed by the £2,000 which you have promised to furnish in the spring, altogether totalling £4,084 which we have ordered Mr Simons to draw on you in the month of February next or whenever the said bills fall due at 2 or 4 usances. We beg you to be so kind as to accept his drafts for that amount and we trust that the goods will easily yield that much and more—but in case they do not we shall save you from any loss by sending you at the first opportunity in the new year a sufficient quantity from which you can reimburse yourself. We await your favourable response to this, never doubting in the least that you will assist us, and request that you correspond with Mr Simons about it. In the meanwhile may God bless and protect you.

[P.S.] The moment we finished this we immediately received your letter of the 20th past with the sale account of goods from Hans Teunissen and Alexander Davidson which we will have checked over, let you know our findings and then record our agreement. We were sorry to see that Lord Leyonbergh was unable to procure freedom for the ships and that the *Beata* and *St Anna* have also departed for Rochelle. We greatly regret that. We had always had high hopes that their freedom would be obtained. These hopes are now dashed. We had also hoped to have the benefit of the proceeds, but that also cannot be done, so we beg you to honour our drafts of £4,084 according to plan. You said you had to guarantee security of £2,000 for the *Suyderström* and asked us not to draw anything against it. We hope—and recently we have had assurance—that its freedom will be obtained, and the captain also writes that ship and goods could be freed on payment of £150. Nevertheless, we shall guarantee you against any loss and provide your collateral security. The Salt Company will do likewise for their share of the ship and goods. It is good that the cargo from Jolle Tiersen has been mostly sold and that you can see your way to disposing of the remainder from the *Suyderström*. Please sell it for whatever it will fetch. God willing, we shall send you a consignment as soon as the waters are open again and in order to do so have already chartered all the necessary ships. With regard to the matter of the court-judgement we shall see what happens. We shall also see to it that the Resident gets another letter to spur him on which we hope to send with the next post, remaining meanwhile, &c.

[Enclosure:]

		Tar (Lasts: barrels)	Pitch (Lasts: barrels)
Shipped to London from Stockholm:			
11 June with	Hans Tenissen	38: 4	11: 0
14 July	Jacob Christiers	24: 12	14: 0
29 ditto	Alexander Davidson	36: 0	10: 0
15 August	And. Jacobsen	103: 0	32: 0
20 ditto	Jolle T'jersen	52: 8	17: 0
to Yarmouth:			
1 October	Pieter Cornel[issen]	60: 12	20: 0
to Hull:			
23 ditto	Hindr. Hoyer	57: 4	30: 1
to London:			
29 ditto	Oloff Ericksen	31: 5	12: 0
13 November	Jurgen Kohne	—	24: 7
		404: 6	170: 8

According to contract, 1 Last of Tar @ £5   £2,020
Pitch @ £8   £1,364

£3,384
From which Mr Simons has drawn   £1,300

remains   £2,084
In the new year Marescoe will accept   £2,000

£4,084

[Enclosure verso]

A note of the amounts drawn on Mr Simons and when the same will fall due:

Falling due Anno 1668	1 December	RD 2,077.45	ƒ.5,194.15
,, ,, ,, 1669	1 January	2,515.00	6,287.10
,, ,, ,,	1 February	17,000.00	42,500.00
,, ,, ,,	1 March	5,000.00	12,500.00
,, ,, ,,	17 April	1,500.00	3,750.00
,, ,, ,,	24 May	1,100.00	2,750.00

RD 29,192.45   ƒ.72,982.05
Premium on ƒ.23,000 for Rochelle: 808.10

ƒ.73,790.15

[1] 'Wij v'soecken Ue gelieft allemael onse goet aftesetten wat gelden will om de vreemde Cladders in de weer te coomen op datse niet moogen meester speelen.'

6 JEAN FREYHOFF TO CM
LA ROCHELLE   10 JANUARY 1669

'J'ay par ce dernier ordinaire a la fois les deux vostres agreables du 14 et 21 du passe, vostre stile, et dans celle-cy ay trouve le cognochement des 511 saumons ou pieces de plomb que vous avez fait charger pour vostre conte a Bristoll par Mons. Wm Browne a bord de Capitaine Thomas Cooke a moi addresse. Dieu ayant amene ledit vaisseau a sauvete je feray tout devoir pour en procurer une vente avantageuse, mais a vous dire ce que j'en croy je doute fort que j'en puisse faire sitost £110t du millier comme vous me marques, s'en estant donne depuis peu a £95t. Il y en a d'assez bonnes parties de vieille main en cette ville; mais puisque cette marchandise aussi enchery en Angleterre de 8 a 10 pour-cent il se peut que cela suivra icy de mesme, ce quy fera que je ne me presseray point en la vent a moins d'en tire approchant de £110t. Il y a icy de droits d'entree £6t 16s par millier—je dis £7t—et il y a environ 20s par millier de frais pour apporter du bord et mettre en magazin. Le quintal ou cent de Bristock fait icy 102 lb., peu plus ou moins, mais vous notterez s'il vous plaist que l'on donne icy 4 pour-cent de bon poids, tant pour plomb qu'estain et plusieurs autres marchandises de sorte qu'au lieu de beneficier sur le poids d'Angleterre il y aura 2 pour-cent de perte ou environ, et si l'on pezoit a nostre poids du Roy des fardeaux de 100 lb. ou environ on perdroit plus de 12 a 15, voire 16 a 17 pour-cent, mais d'ordinaire on n'y peze que des fardeaux de 3 a 400 lb. et audessus, allons le poids du Roy s'accorde a peu pres avecq celuy des marchands, c'est a dire ajoutant a ce dernier les 4 pour-cent de bon poids. Il y a pourtant les beurres quy se pezent touts au poids du Roy quelqu' petits que soyent les barrils et ainsi du suif, pour gouverno. L'estain vaut £62t a £63t le cent, les droits d'entree sont de £3t 15s a £4t par cent. J'auray l'oeil en vendant vostre plomb d'avoir a faire a gens que je jugeray asseures—et si vous trouves quelqu' encouragement a en envoyer davantage vous ne deves douter que le mesme soin pour la conservation de vos intherests ne soit apporte. Parfois on trouve occasion d'en vendre en Cherante plus avantageusement qu'icy ou les droits sont a peu pres esgaux, mais pour cela il faut que le navire entre en la ditte riviere ce que Capitaine Cooke apparemment ne fera pas, et d'envoyer le plomb d'icy en Cherante par des batteaux les frais emporteroyent le benefice outre qu'il y auroit quelque risque a courir de la part de notre douane quy n'est pas de la mesme dependance que cette de Charente. Ainsi je prevoy qu'il faudra descharger vos 511 saumons en cette ville, du success je vous donneray avis en son temps. L'eau-de-vie en Cherante est a £54t a £53t les $\frac{27}{v}$ quitte; vins de petite borderie £90t a £92t—ditto de St Jean £68t a £70t le tonneau quitte a bord, avecq tres peu de demande. Jusques icy il n'y a eu que 2 petits vaisseaux de 40 thonneaux chacun quy ayent pris des vins nouveaux en Cherante pour Londres. Comme ils se porteront bien au frelattage selon toute apparence il se pourra que la traitte en sera plus grande. Sel d'Olleron £250t—de Seudres £240t—de Re £235t a £240t le cent, quitte abord; vinaigre de Re £48t, ditto de Cherante £60t quitte. Beurres de Youghall £23t a £24t; ditto de Limerick et la autour £12t a £15t le cent. Il y en a nombre en ville de cette derniere sorte. Harangs d'Escosse £8t a £10t le barril et quantite d'arrives, pareillement harangs sort de Yarmuy[1] £14t le barril.

Je vous baize tres humblement les mains et apres vous avoir souhaitte toute sorte de bonheur dans cette nouvelle annee suivie de plusieurs autres je demeure, vostre tres humble serviteur.

Paris: au par a usance.
Londres: 25 pour-cent. ⎫
Amsterdam: 17 pour-cent. ⎭ 2 usances.

[P.S.] Un fodder vaut a La Rochelle 1960 lb @ £12 16s @ 56d —   £164t: 10s
      Fret et avarie   £10t : —
      Asseurance a 2 p.ct & 2 p.ct d'provision   £8t : —
      Droits d'entree en France, &c   £16t : —
      Menus fraits   £1t : 10s

      1960 lb. @ £110t le millier vallent £215t—   £200 : —

      Un fodder vaut 1960 lb. a £110t le millier   £215 : —
      Fraits   £35 : —

                                                              £180 : —

      Reste £180t qui font *W*.60 a 56d font £14 [sterling]'

¹ Yarmouth.

$\frac{18\ Jan.}{22\ Jan.}$ 1669

67 P. BERENBERG to CM

HAMBURG   8 JANUARY 1669

[D] My latest letter to you was on the 29th past and since then I have heard nothing from you. This serves to inform you that in September last I loaded in the *Phoenix* (Capt. Robert Clark, an Englishman) bound from here to Venice, 10 bales of pepper, bearing the mark adjoining, and 512 pieces of campeachy wood which weighed here 15,733 lb., as well as a quantity of iron cannon-balls. I now learn that the said captain struck on the Goodwins and, having suffered some damage, ran into Dover where he unloaded the whole ship and wrote to the interested parties here asking for remittance of his expenses, which it is said will run high. So my request to you as a friend is, that you will immediately write to your friend at Dover to discover what costs he has incurred and to urge him to have some regard for my goods. As for paying the costs of unloading and reloading, that can hardly be done unless a proper division is made, and I would judge it best that the captain tries to borrow the money and leaves the division of costs until he has delivered in Venice. Meanwhile, since it will be undoubtedly a long voyage and I understand that pepper is fetching high prices in England I would be glad to see you receive the 10 bales of pepper and also the campeachy wood lying at Dover, agreeing with the captain for half the freight or, failing that, paying the whole freight and keeping the expenses as low as possible. And if you can sell the pepper for 23d or 24d [p. lb.] and the campeachy wood at about 50s [p. cwt.] please do it, and also find out how much that type of cannon-ball fetches in England. I am sending you herewith the bill of lading, the endorsement left blank, as well as a letter to a passenger and friend of the captain and owners who is now on the ship, called Henrig de Valet, who I am urging to persuade the captain to follow your advice in all matters, as I trust he will do. There was also loaded here in the said ship a small barrel of cardamon marked 'P.B.' which the captain said, on signing the bill of lading, he had not found. Please inquire if it has now been found in the process of unloading; if so, it can be sent on to Venice. I beg you to forgive me for giving you this trouble, and please do your best to serve me, urging your trusted friend at Dover neither to lose the bill of lading nor to fill it in before it is known what the captain will allow to be done with the goods. I am also sending herewith the bill of lading for the cannon-balls in case you need it and it seems a good idea not to reload them. I know very well that such goods as pepper and [campeachy] wood are not allowed to be imported into England from here; however, I hope that in this regard no notice will be taken and that you will know just how far one can go.

Sir, as I found the cotton you sent reasonably good, excepting one bag which was very dirty inside, I herewith request you that if there is no prospect of further decline in that sort you will, at your convenience, look for similarly good cotton and if you can encounter a quantity which is clean and white to be had for $6d$ to $6\frac{1}{4}d$ then get me another 15 to 20 sacks of Smyrna, as well as 10 of Cyprus, cotton—and if such clean and white stuff is to be had at $6\frac{1}{2}d$ or $6\frac{3}{4}d$ please buy it and send it at the first opportunity in the spring. Above all, you must procure good quality, which can be done very conveniently since there is no prospect of a price rise. I can see no opportunity here for poor quality, for your information.

[unendorsed]

68 J. B. LEYONBERGH to CM
THE PIAZZA, COVENT GARDEN, LONDON   22 JANUARY 1669

'Monsieur, L'ordre du Roy ou de Conseil sera prêtt cet aprésdiner a 5 ou 6 heures. Je vous les envoyéray ce soir. Elle est couché pour un Quo Waranto dans la Cour Royalle d'exchequer, et le mot de 'forthwith' y est insere, mais je n'ay pas pu arester les autres trialls comme j'ay essayé selon le desir de Mr Thomas.[1] S'il y a quelque autre chose a faire, vous n'avez qu'a m'en advertir. Je n'oublié pas l'affaire de *Suderstroom*, et j'en tacheray d'en venir a bout du main. Adieu.

Votre tres humble serviteur,

[P.S.] Monsieur, voicy une lettre pour le père de ce gentilhomme qui m'a baillé la lettre de change. Je vous supplie de l'envoyer. J'espère que le sieur Bertelt Festingh, demeurant a Åbo en Finlande (ce qu'est 50 lieu de Stockholm) la payera.'

[1] Marescoe's attorney.

$$\frac{26\ Jan.}{[\quad]}1669$$

69 LOUIS TRIP to CM
AMSTERDAM   1 FEBRUARY 1669

D] Your letter of the 1st of this month[1] has been safely received and this serves as an answer. Although it is still hard winter here as soon as the waters open you will be sent from Dordrecht 720 rods of entirely smooth and soundly forged iron which comes from Luxemburg and was loaded at Liège—that is to say, iron for the Guinea coast weighing 21,560 lb. Amsterdam-weight. They are made according to the measurements which the blacks there demand.[2] I have sold large quantities of the same iron, or similar, to the West India Company at $f.7.5$ stuivers and $f.7\frac{1}{8}$, but as iron prices are now rather quiet[3] I have sold 10,000 rods at $f.6\frac{7}{8}$—which is what you wanted to know in your letter. This small batch is going just as a sample. If you want some certificate, besides what the captain brings with him, that it was loaded at Liège, please let me know. Please do your duty and sell it, and then inform me for my guidance if it can be serviceable in [London].

      &c.

1 '*Vanden pr. deser*'—presumably a confusion with the date received and/or the date of this reply.
2 '. . . *gelyck aldaer de swaarten begeeren.*'
3 '. . . *t'yser nu wat slapper in prys is.*'

$$\frac{4\ Feb.}{5\ Feb.}1669$$

70 J. VAN SAVELANT to CM
   GOTHENBURG   24 DECEMBER 1668

[D] Yours of the 6th past and 4th instant have reached me safely, by which I have been glad to learn of Capt. Anders Beursen's arrival with my iron, which doubtless has been correctly delivered.

 When I mentioned increased costs in my letters I was not referring to ordinary expenses such as brokerage and suchlike, but was thinking that I shall have to carry the costs of selling goods to reliable people and bear the discount on good money—that is to say, *quaet gelt*.[1] I will gladly bear any loss, whether it arises in [England] or here, and I understand perfectly well the difference between exchange and current money. If my goods were sold on such terms I must be satisfied with them. Regarding the sale of my iron with a rebate of 8 per cent—I will gladly grant that, if you will stand liable for bad debts, but I think it is too risky for me to bear bad debts in return for 6 per cent rebate on goods sold at 6 months time. God knows, I have had my share of bad debts in [London] and the effects of the great Fire of [London] begin to emerge now as in cases such as Scherley[2] and may yet be revealed more fully with time. Consequently, one must be careful to whom one sells.

 The £150 @ 35*s* 10*g* on Amsterdam remitted to Mr Bex for my account on 2 October at double usance drawn on John Lodge & Co has been accepted. I trust payment will follow, for which I have credited your account.

 I urge you to sell my iron which has come with Beursen to reliable people. As there is no fitting-out taking place in [England][3] demand is very small, so one must wait and see. I have had a lot of inquiries after Beursen's iron from the English here but I did not want to let it get into other hands. Please let me know in due course how things turn out with Scherley. Our Company is owed quite a lot, as you well know, which the partners find strange.

 I am thinking of travelling up-country at the earliest opportunity and expect to stay there for some time. Meanwhile, my regards, &c.

1 Savelant is referring to the customary charge of $\frac{1}{8}$ per cent to cover the risk of being short-changed with false coin—'gecorte penninge en quaet gelt'. See p. 20 and [**45**].
2 The firm of Thomas Sherley & Peter Blackburrow owed £1,446 4*s* in 1668 for deals sold to them by Marescoe on behalf of three sets of principals. The company of Rokes, Savelant & Hartzen of Gothenburg was owed £584 15*s*.
3 '*Is Costy gheen Equpering soo is den aftreck dewelken wel clein . . .*'.

$$\frac{8\ Feb.}{11\ Feb.}1669$$

71 WILLIAM BROWNE[1] to CM
   BRISTOL   6 FEBRUARY 1669

'Sir, I have yours of 2nd February and have treated to have your lead shipt of at your lymited price but cannot get any thing abated of £3 per tun, and at that price the Captain ses can have as much as he is willing to carry in her of that comodity. Lead is now at £11 5s. p. tun. Whither it may rise higher I know not. If it comes up to your price shall sell it if noe order to the contrary. In the meanetyme heere is hardly an oppertunity of shipping for Plymouth or Falmouth but in the season for pilchards. I hardly know now how to informe myselfe what freight is worth. There are severall vessells goe about land from Wales with coales which I suppose would take it in but will be a great charge to ship it here and there re-ship it againe.

Stockholme pitch is heere worth at present 28s p. barrell and ditto tarr 20s p. barrell. This city spends of the first about 600 barrells and 1,500 barrells of tarr in the yeare. I understand they are most sarved from London. If you plese to send any I suppose can vend some up Severne as at Gloucester, Worcester, Tuexbury, Upton, Bewdly, Shrowsbury, etc.

I am glad the *Armes of Bristoll* is arived. Sir, heere is a considerable trade in this city for deale boards which are now worth £6 p. cent or upwards, boards of about 10 foote longe and about 10 inches over, soe if you could without much difficulty procure a ship of about 200 tuns betweene your selfe, my father-in-law and my selfe we would hould for her in thirds between us, but it must be a cheape vessell at freight and if a strainger be sure it be one of the same country. Pray a word what you thinke of it and about what rate you judge the freight will come at. Soe I rest,

[P.S.] Sir, I have this night given my bill on you for £20 at 4 dayes sight payable to Mr Robert Perry vallew of Mr Richard Higgins, which place to the account of lead bought for you. I have noe more mony yett from Mr Smalridge although I heere he hath ordered me £10 more.'

[1] William Browne was the firm's regular Bristol correspondent in 1668–70 (see Nos. **79, 92, 103, 105, 128, 139**) and an active Bristol merchant—P. McGrath (ed.) *Merchants and Merchandize in Seventeenth Century Bristol*, Bristol Record Society Publications XIX (Bristol, 1955) pp. 68, 69, 71. P. McGrath (ed.) *Records relating to the Society of Merchant Venturers of the City of Bristol in the Seventeenth Century*, Bristol Record Society Publications XVII (Bristol, 1952) pp. 31, 37, 61, 195.

$$\frac{\text{10 Feb.}}{\text{11 Feb.}}\text{1669}$$

2 P. CAULIER to CM
YARMOUTH   8 FEBRUARY 1669

'Loving Cozen, I have yours of the 6th courant to which I answer sinths my coming home I have agried the remainder of the tar, being 10 last 12 barrels at £9, 13 barrels per last, as it rysses at six months, and 2 last pitch at £12, the same time, soo there remaines some 13 last pitch yet to sel which I hope this somer may put of. You may if yo thinck fitting order some 60 last of tar and 40 or 60 tuns of iron to come in May or June next. Pray recomend them that the tar be of the best new barrels and the strongest they have for its most for exportation, and the iron let it be $\frac{1}{3}$ broad, $\frac{1}{3}$ square and $\frac{1}{3}$ ordinary breth iron. If they have 2 sorts of square iron pray let half that $\frac{1}{3}$ be of one sort and the other half of the other. Such a sortiment wil sel wel.

I see Joseph Gother was aryved by you. I know when I was come up they made him pay the Dover peire dutys which I thincq was some 16s. It is an unconsconabel duty.[1] The ships going for London should pay it yet Mr Dawson here requirs it and as men pay it he reseves it heare for Sir Edmond Turner by you. If yo think fitting yo may speake to him to see if you can get it excused. The duty cesses in June next. It has byn a more cheat to the nation.

This is all at present. I rest, your loving kinsman and servant,

[P.S.] If it be not to mutch trobel to yo pray order your frinds at Stockholme to send me 10 or 12 fadom of fyer wood in the ship they stow it between and upon the casks.'

¹ The Act for repairing Dover Harbour, of 1662 (14 Car. II. c. 27), revived Elizabethan and Jacobean legislation and provided for a 7-year levy of 3*d* per ton on English-owned vessels of 20 to 250 tons passing to or from London or from, to or by Dover.

$$\frac{18\ Feb.}{19\ Feb.}1669$$

73   P. RULAND to CM
HAMBURG   9 FEBRUARY 1669

[D]   My last letter to you was on 11 December past. Because no special occasion has presented itself I have not written to you since then but I have meanwhile received yours of 24 December and of 22 [January], in answer to which the ship *St Jan Battista*, of which you wrote, has since arrived in the Texel with this favourable wind and the cargo has come to a profitable market at Amsterdam, for which God must be thanked, for I was not a little afraid that it would be frozen in. For the last 14 days the ice has been melting so that the Elbe is nearly entirely free of it, and yesterday the mussel-fishers started coming up again.

I have been glad to see what Barbados sugar has been doing [in London]. The price of 27*s* is still too high for me and since it seems likely to rise in [England] there is nothing to be done with it here in the near future because there are too large amounts in too many hands of people who would be glad to sell at $6\frac{5}{8}$ to $6\frac{3}{48}g$. But little is disposed of because our leading sugar-refiners provided themselves before the winter with such large stocks that for 6 months or more there will be no shortage. Consequently, unless its price weakens in [London] there will be few orders from Amsterdam or from here. However, if it should show signs of falling to 24*s* or 24*s* 6*d* please buy 15,000 to 20,000 lb. and send it to me. If you draw on me for the requisite funds at once, due honour will be done to your bills, but above all see to it that it is dry and white or else leave it alone, for dirty, clammy stuff is of no use to me. Despite cotton being so cheap with you it would not be advisable for it to come here as there is no demand for it. Oil was falling to £29 with you: if you can get some clear, sweet Apulian oil which has freshly arrived you can buy me 6 or 7 barrels, but take good care that there is no dirt in it and that there has been nothing strong or bitter-tasting in the casks before. I would prefer you to buy the best barrels, of 140 to 150 gallons, and send them here as above at the first opportunity. Galls here are at 42 to 43 *ML* @ 13 months time. 60*s* for them in [London] is too high. Large quantities have reached Marseille and they are cheap there so I consider that those in London are as high as they will be. Wherewith I commend you to God's protection, &c.

$$\frac{22\ Feb.}{24\ Feb.}1669$$

74   A. BERENBERG'S WIDOW & HEIRS to CM
HAMBURG   12 FEBRUARY 1669

[D]   We have not written to you for several posts because it has been deep winter and the waters have been closed. Meanwhile, we find ourselves owing you replies for several of your letters, the last of which was on the 15th past, to which we will briefly answer.

We cordially thank you for your advice about various commodities and will be glad to learn how things continue as the waters open and we begin to make some investments for the spring. There are no certain prices for many of the goods here, since none of them are selling, but we must hope for better. There is a large quantity of galls in town, more than can be disposed of in two years, and as people are expecting a ship from Marseille here with yet more London can expect no commissions for this commodity while the price remains so high. Sugars have fallen to $6\frac{3}{4}g$ and $6\frac{1}{2}g$ which is a low price and it cannot be brought from [England] for less. We still have the two small consignments which you provided us with last year, and we wish it would rise somewhat in [England] so that we could recover our capital and perhaps make a little profit. We shall be glad to hear what further developments there are, as well in Ardasse, indigo, ginger, oil and cotton. Other friends in [London] have reported to us that white Barbados cotton is at $6d$. If you can obtain fine, clean, white goods you may buy us 20 sacks and send them at the first opportunity, for the speediest despatch is required if it is to be sold at the Easter Leipzig fair.[1] Apulian oil fetches 72 *RD* per 820 lb., for cash; campeachy wood *ML* 30 per 100 lb.; white ginger $16g$; black ditto, $12g$; wherewith, we remain, with friendliest regards, &c.

London: $34s$ $8g$.
Amsterdam: $32\frac{11}{16}$.

[P.S.] You can draw on us for the cotton and it will be duly honoured.

[1] Leipzig's three major fairs were held in January, after Easter and at Michaelmas.

$$\frac{11 \text{ Mar.}}{12 \text{ Mar.}} 1669$$

WILLEM MOMMA tO CM
NYKÖPING   14 FEBRUARY 1669

Since my last, of the 10th past, I have received yours of December 24th and January 15th. From the first I understand that you have remitted to Messrs Van Baerle £300 sterling for my account in three bills at $35s$ $8g$ at 2 or 3 days sight. I have also had news of their payment and have therefore credited you. You will have forwarded by now the kettles and other unsaleable brass-ware to Messrs Van Baerle, and I shall expect the expense-account as well as the sale-account for the rest of the pots and pans. I am happy to learn of the *Halve Maen*'s arrival, and that you have unloaded the goods. Although I gave you order to follow others in setting the price I hope the delay in their sale will turn to my advantage and that they will rise a good deal higher. I am also pleased that Cronström has despatched about 150 slb to you, laden in Gerrit Laurens, though it will be some time yet before that ship can depart because of the freezing conditions which still continue here. But the frost is not strong and I hope we shall soon have open waters. I think that Cronström will continue to send his goods to you. Some days ago my brother came back from the mining district[1] where he had also spoken with his brother-in-law, Isaac Cronström, about sending his goods to you, so that they would all be in one hand, but he—on the contrary—pressed that we should send our goods to his man. That will not be done, and the amounts he makes are not so big, so each of us will have his own way.

   My brother, Jacob is at Norrköping, seeing if a galliot can be chartered for [London] in which I am thinking of loading a batch of wire, latten and pots as soon as the waters open and it can be reached. Meanwhile, I hope you will dispose of what you have by you at a good price and remit the proceeds to Messrs Van Baerle who are accustomed to settling my accounts on the last day of May. Closing herewith, I commend you to God's protection, with hearty greetings, &c.

¹ '. . . *de bergslagen* . . .'.

$$\frac{16\ Mar.}{19\ Mar.}1669$$

76 DOMINICUS VAN UFFELE & BARTHOLDUS BECKMAN to CM

HAMBURG   9 MARCH 1669

[D]   For lack of matter, we have not written to you for a long time. Since only one galleon is being prepared at Lisbon to leave for Goa in April, this serves to inquire whether you can tell us if any ships are being prepared in [London] for Surat or other places in the Indies, for we would be glad to send some letters to Goa. We have had some letters, of February 1667, via Lisbon, from Sr. de Prado of Goa, in which he advises us that he was consigning to you, for our account, a Bisalt diamond with the first English ships from Surat. According to common rumour, the English East India Company ships are expected in the month of May—may the Lord bring them in safety!—and we hope to hear in due course that you have safely received what is coming for us. We shall be glad to receive news of the ships.

   As you still have the two diamond pendants deposited with you, please inquire on receipt of this what is the highest price they can fetch for ready money, and let us know what it is. If anything can be obtained for them we might bear a loss, or else have them brought back here, since the risks at sea are not so considerable now. We await your reply. Adio, &c.

$$\frac{19\ Mar.}{20\ Mar.}1669$$

77 W. SKINNER to CM

HULL   16 MARCH 1669

'Sir, My last to you was the 12th instant, since which I have yours of the 13th. For answer, the pitch and tarre shipt in Henry Dickinson is reckoned at 12 barrels per last as our custome is alwayes here to doe. I have now shipt in the *Virgine* of Scharbro', John Potter master, 10 last of tarre and 9 last of pitch at 16s per last freight, and I shall shipp you further parcels untill your whole quantity be dispatched as I meete with opportunity of shippinge. The coppy of the order which you have sent mee I shall shew and advise you what reception it finds and whether it will excuse your goods from payment of the Eastland Company's impositions. They write from London that you doe there frequently pay double impositions, the truth whereof be pleased in your next to advise mee.

   Jean Poitevin is not yet dispatcht, but now in few dayes I shall send him away haveing bought 100 piggs lead more for his loadinge at £12 15s per fodder which is 2 a 3s under price courant. The [thing?] shalbe mannaged as much as may be to your advantage but Poittevin will meete with some difficulty to cleare the vessell as a Dutch vessell which he intended and to that end put that Dutchman in as master but the Custome officers are suspitious of the designe and will not passe my bills till the vessel be made out to belong to Holland or that the dutys for a French vessell be paide, and this is the reason she is in noe greater forwardness in her loadinge. The master wants some mony for his ship's use which I fournish him on your account and hope you'l approve. The bill of loadinge shalbe made for delivery of the lead to your selfe or assignes at Rowen.

W m. Rawden with your 100 piggs lead intended for Rowen hath bene long detayned here by contrary windes and put to see but this day sennight. I hope you may speedily heare of his arrivall, and soe, presentinge my respects, I remaine, &c.'

$$\frac{23\ Mar.}{26\ Mar.}1669$$

8 J. & D. VAN BAERLE to CM

AMSTERDAM   29 MARCH 1669

'] Our last letter was about a week ago; since then we have received yours of the 12th instant with sundry enclosures for Sweden which have been forwarded. We have noted that the proceeds of the 4 casks of pans and kettles which came with Claes Scholts amounted to £251 14s, and that the 3 chests of latten, 4 casks of pans and kettles and one cask of pots which came with Willem Muller yielded £440 4s 8d. As for the remaining copper rods and sheet-copper from J[acob] M[omma] as well as the copper-wire from W[illem] M[omma] please dispose of as much as possible if the price recovers. We wait to learn if the 4 casks of W.M.'s pots which came with Andries Jornson have been sold. We shall postpone drawing on you for J.M.'s account until next month and then not more than £500 to £600 sterling in all, and if we can manage it we shall entirely forego drawing and expect you at your convenience to make remittances for our friends in good bills. However, it is very awkward for us to be out of pocket for so long on account of the money we have advanced upon these goods since the amount is so large.

Herewith goes the account of the 40 barrels of tin received with Simon van Houten, of which the net proceeds amount to f.6,196.12s bank-money. We have placed it to your current account. Please check it over and if you find no errors please approve it. We will not sell your remaining tin for less than f.58 until further order. So far no buyers have come forward for the galls although we have several times commissioned brokers. We shall continue to do so whenever we see the opportunity.

We have made inquiry with Peter Simons' book-keeper as well as in the Bank to learn if the £250 sterling bill of exchange of 1/11 January at 36s with double usance drawn by you for the benefit of Jacob Cornelisen and endorsed to Widow Forkenbeck had been enrolled as he said it had been when he wrote to you on the 12th inst., but from both we received the answer that it had not been done. So, according to your request, we have today paid the sum to the aforesaid Widow Forkenbeck by declaration before a notary that it had been done for the honour of the drawer, as appears in the deed accompanying the bill of exchange and protest sent herewith, amounting with interest and expenses (according to the enclosed account from Forckenbeck) to: f.2,708.16.00

for a copy of the protest and deed for the honour of the drawer: 2.03.00

for our commission on the re-draft and brokerage: 10.03.08

                                                                        f.2,721.01.08

We have today drawn on you £256 2s 6d sterling, payable at 2 usances to Gerard Weymans, the value of Michiel Gerard junior, which you will please honour and set against the aforesaid amount. We have also told Abraham Bex and Jan Aries Snoeck that we will pay the £110 @ 36s 3g and the £44 4s 4d @ 36s on the date due, for which amount with expenses we will also draw on you. The above-mentioned Simons has left for Sweden and has written to someone that he will be back within two months and will give everyone satisfaction. We too were of the opinion that he did no business on his own account but we now find it was otherwise and that he carried on a trade with Portugal, as well as with Sweden, in salt. In addition, during the war, he had taken shares in various Swedish ships with all of which he made no profit. Yet he has advanced about *f*.100,000 to various people in Sweden, for which he expected goods in the spring, and as he had no means of his own he had to use other people's money; and a broker whom he was accustomed to use failing not long ago several amounts were called in and seeing that he could get no credit to make good the amounts which were drawn by him on Frankfort (being about *f*.44,000) he decided to depart. His outstanding loans and assets nearly balance his liabilities, being about *f*.200,000, but in the latest letters from Sweden it is said he has had orders from the Tar Company to draw £2,000 sterling on you. We do not doubt that you enter into Swedish obligations carefully enough, but we have been asked to believe that you yourself sometimes stand burdened with £4,000 to £5,000 on account of the Tar Company over and above the value of the effects you have in your hands, which we cannot credit.

Herewith we return the bills of exchange for £200 and £100 accepted by Daniel Planck. The £100 on Van Raey remains still without acceptance for the reasons we explained in our last. As the time is too short for it to be endorsed he has promised not to plead exception to the endorsement so we shall protest if it is not settled at the due date.

With warm regards, &c.

London:	35*s* 4*g* ⎱ 2 usances.	
Paris:	99¾ ⎰	

Hamburg:	32½ ⎱ at sight.	
Antwerp:	1½% ⎰	

$$\frac{24\ Mar.}{29\ Apr.}1669$$

79   w. browne to cm

BRISTOL   22 MARCH 1669

'Sir, I have yors of the 20th instant being glad you have received the Balance of your account, and to the Pitch & Tarr I have this day informed my selfe as fully as I can & finde that 1,000 to 1,500 barrells of Pitch may sell in a yeare worth now 11£ p. ct[1] but will alwaise sell from 28 to 30*s* p. barrell, of Tarr 2 to 3,000 barrells in a yeare worth now 20*s* p. barrell but will alwaise be sould from 18 to 20*s* according as here is a greater or a lesse quantity; I find I may sell 1,000, or 1,500 barrells together, & as they spend them soe may take soe many more, if it may be afforded heere at about 12*d* p.Ct more then what it is sould with you in London for, I finde you may drive the whole trade of this Citty for said Commodity, you know the ould saying light gaines makes a heavy purse, & it will be selling at small profitt will make the greater quantityes vent, this being the largest account I can give you at present to your desyres, is all for present from,

Sir, your assured friend.'

[1] This must mean £11 per last (of 12 barrels).

0 W. MOMMA to CM

NYKÖPING   7 MARCH 1669

)] My last letter to you was on the 14th past. I have since received yours of the 29th of January and 12th of February. With the latter you sent the account of those remaining pots which were sold in October with the expenses deducted, together with the account of the other 15 barrels and brass-ware which were sent, from which you have rebated £3 10s for 6 months discount which you claim to have paid, but as you have not stated at what date the goods were sold and have sometimes allowed four or five months to pass before sending the account and yet have still claimed rebates, I have decided to send you the account, indicating from your letters the dates at which the goods have been sold.[1] You will please examine it and have your servants remedy it accordingly. As for what remains, and the 1,043 coils of wire, I trust they will have been sold by the time you receive this and the proceeds remitted to the Van Baerles. I should also like a summary of what debts still remain outstanding. I do not think it is advisable any more to sell on such long-term credit unless with a rebate or a reduction of the price for cash, because I cannot buy any copper here except for cash and none is sold in Hamburg except for cash and likewise in Holland it is sold for immediate cash-payment, rebating 1 per cent. And unless your prices rise higher I shall not find it convenient to send any more. Others can do what they like, but they too will get weary in time.

    Winter still continues, but the sun is beginning to melt the snows. With warmest regards, &c.

[1] Mr Charles Marescoe   Debit

From the end of 1668, balance of preceding account: £4 0 0

In November you sent an account of what was sold: vizt:

  on 12 June, 80 pieces of latten, $\frac{1}{2}$ @ 6, $\frac{1}{2}$ @ 12 months   £238 10 0

  on 26 ditto, pots, $\frac{1}{2}$ @ 6, $\frac{1}{2}$ @ 12 months   £98 12 10

  on 25 September brewing-plates and pots @ 6 months £148 17 0

  on 23 October pots @ 8 months   £62 11 2

                  £548 11 0

From this you deduct a discount for 8 months £21 6 0

and for expenses   £41 19 10

                  £63 1 4

                 net proceeds: £485 9 8

These items fell due:

  1668—end of December £168 11 5

  1669—end of March   £148 17 0

      —end of June   £231 2 7

             £548 11 0

In December you sent an account of what had been sold, vizt.

  on 6 June, 210 coils of wire @ 4 months time   £298 12 3

  on 23 July, 234 coils of wire @ 6 months £332 15 6

on which you discounted for 6 months   £9 14 0   £323 1 6

                      £621 13 9

  From this are deducted expenses: £77 16 5

             net proceeds: £543 17 4

These items fell due:
    end of July   £323   1   6
    end of October   £298 12   3

                      £621 13   9

On the same date, another account, vizt.
    on 18 December, 411 coils of wire @ 6 months which you did not rebate in the
    preceding account so as to bring it all into one account, falling due at the
    end of June 1669:   £519 18   6

On 1669 12 February you sent an account of pots sold
    on 23 October @ 8 months   £120   0   0
    from which you rebated ⎱   £3 10   0
    6 months   ⎰
Due at the end of December £116 10   0; deducted for the sale of
previous goods sent   £61 12   8   £54 17   4

                  totalling according to your account   £1,608 2 10

                                              Credit

In 1668, on 28 November fell due 3 bills from the Van Baerles   £700 0   0
    on 24 December, for 3 bills remitted by you   £500 0   0
    on 26 ditto, for 2 bills drawn by the Van Baerles   £300 0   0

                                    £1,500 0   0

1669 7 March there should be due to me according to
    your accounts to balance this   £108 2 10

                                    £1,608 2 10

$$\frac{2\ Apr.}{6\ Apr.}1669$$

81 D. VAN RUYFF to CM
    STOCKHOLM   16 MARCH 1669

[D]   My last letter to you was on the 26th past, in which I ordered you to pay Mons. Paulo Ferin £60–£70 sterling if he asked you for it. I herewith confirm that, and request you to let him have the enclosed.

    I have now received yours of the 29th January and 19th past, from which I see that you have sold the consignment of iron from the *St Jan* at 15*s* per cwt., which is good. I hope the load from the *Halve Maen* will also be sold, and will await the account by your next and also expect to hear that you have remitted the proceeds. If God permits, I intend to send you a good quantity with the first ships in the spring. I shall first send you a batch of voyage and broad iron. I trust the *Fortuyn* will have arrived before the receipt of this, and will expect to hear whether that sort of iron is in demand in [England]—it is 2 inches broad. I want you to remit the proceeds of that iron to Philip Pelt Emanuels, but of that from Jolle Tiards and the *Halve Maen* you can remit to Pieter van der Mortel, if it has not been done already.

    It is good that one can send iron to [England] in Swedish ships even if they have been built elsewhere, for it would otherwise be difficult and inconvenient as most of the ships one hears of here were built abroad. With cordial regards, God protect you, &c.

$$\frac{16\ Apr.}{[\text{———}]}1669$$

82 J. MOMMA to CM
STOCKHOLM   27 MARCH 1669

[G] From your letters of the 12th and 26th past, safely received, I have seen what you recommend concerning the ships *Margarita*, *den Herzog*, and *die Hoffnung*. My brother Abraham Momma will have already answered, and I refer myself to that. I have also seen that you have sold some quantities of copper-wire. We cannot congratulate you on the price, so we beg you with this—as we already have before—to let no good opportunity pass by, but dispose of the whole amount, doing your best for me as if it were your own, for I depend upon you.

Regarding what I wrote to you about coals from Newcastle, I hope to learn what success you have had in arranging it. Weights work out as follows: a *muid* of Spanish salt amounts of 5 tuns here, and 18 tuns amount to 1 last. Otherwise, Mr Cutler, or Mr Sowton, or Mr Blackett can furnish you with further information, and for the rest I refer you to my earlier letters.

[O] As I have seven ship-loads of beams and planks lying ready on Gotland, I beg you to let me know if Dutch ships are allowed to bring such a commodity to England. If not, I beg you, please persevere in obtaining permission for twenty or thirty ships to bring Gotland timber over to you, since Gotland timber is much better than that which comes from other places. If you can do it I shall freight the ships to you. Otherwise, if English ships can fetch timber from Gotland themselves I can sell them large amounts.

$$\frac{21\ May}{[\text{———}]}1669$$

83 A. RULAND to CM
HAMBURG   14 MAY 1669

[O] Your welcome letters of the 16th and 30th last and 7th of May have been safely received, in which I have seen what ships have arrived as well as what is happening in trade. Goods continue to have poor sales here and buyers still want things cheaper than they can be offered from [England], so for the present I have decided to wait and see. I have heard from others that one will be able to get new Barbados sugar for 23s, which I could well pay, but for the moment they want it cheaper here and it is believed that still larger amounts are daily expected from there, as well as other wares such as cottons, ginger, indigo, etc. The latter commodity remains quiet here, but with the latest Spanish letters they write they have had news that the English—I mean to say, the French—have taken over St Domingo,[1] which I can hardly believe, although it seems that that nation, as well as the English, have been set on one scheme or another against the Spanish, and as a consequence there could be some change coming in indigo. If you can get earlier information of any such I shall be glad to share it. I shall also be glad to learn what kinds of commodities the ships from Jamaica bring and also if campeachy-wood comes with them. Straits wares are also in as bad repute here as those of Barbados, likewise East Indian which, when the expected ships arrive in [England] as well as Holland, are likely to fall much further. If any commissions come with the ships that have arrived from Livorno I shall be glad to learn what they fetch. Galls are not required from [England] unless they come for less than 50s.

The collection of what remains owing to me is most earnestly recommended to you, with cordial regards, &c.

London: 34s 8–9g   @ 2 usances.
Amsterdam: 32½   at sight.

[P.S.] I shall also be glad to learn if these ships from Barbados brought much indigo.

¹ The French had been established in San Domingo since the 1630s: this must refer to the restoration of the French West India Company's authority, and the exclusion of the Dutch, by De Treillebois' expedition in 1668. See S. L. Mims, *Colbert's West India Policy* (1912) pp. 150–3.

$$\frac{24\ May}{29\ May}1669$$

84 P. BERENBERG to CM
HAMBURG   18 MAY 1669

[D] Since my last of the 9th past I have received yours of the 9th and 23rd past and 7th instant. In answer: about the goods from the ship *Phoenix* there is no need to reply as you now correspond about it with Egidio Ruland himself, and it is right that you have placed the expenses and postage of letters exchanged about it on his account.

I have received the 30 sacks of cotton out of Harmen Vilter and found them good. It is lamentable that all goods, lacking vent, are at low prices and nothing can be sold at a profit. The English nation undersells goods too much.¹ Here is a quantity of Smyrna cotton selling at 12g, though rather bad; Apulian oil—as 3 English ships have come *adrittura*—is selling at RD 63; so there is no profit to be got by ordering these commodities from England. I myself have bought 40 rixdollars-worth of it here in order to keep it.

I warmly thank you for news about the sale of pepper in [England] and about the arrival of one ship or another. If something turns up by which we can hope for some profit I will try to maintain our correspondence. Meanwhile I shall be glad to learn from you now and then what is happening in [England] with regard to one commodity or another. Barbados sugars have been sold here by the English at 6g. I have all mine still standing here and cannot bring myself to sell at a loss. I shall be glad to learn what price that commodity fetches in [England] if the remaining ships from Barbados arrive safely. Meanwhile, friendly regards, &c.

¹ '*D'Engelse natie cladt al te seer met de goeder[e]n.*'

$$\frac{7\ Jun.}{11\ Jun.}1669$$

85 NICHOLAS PREUS to CM
GOTHENBURG   28 APRIL 1669

[D] Yours of the 29th past has been safely received. In reply, Mr Simons departed from here for Amsterdam by way of Hamburg on the 23rd instant. I trust he will give everyone satisfaction. He was with me at an unfortunate moment as on the 20th from about 4.00 o'clock in the afternoon until the following morning, about three-quarters of the town was laid in ashes by a raging fire, by which God knows I suffered great loss. May the good

God richly give back what he has taken away! I am now living in the country about three-quarters of a mile from the town which I visit 2 or 3 times a week to see to my affairs.

The iron has not yet come down. If Messrs Pötter & Thuen order me to send something to England you will be advised of its shipment in good time. I am sorry that I cannot send any iron on my own account though at a price of £15 [p. ton] something could be done. Since the confiscation of my ships in Amsterdam one misfortune has followed another, so that in two years I have suffered about *RD* 19,000 loss, although God be thanked I can and will give each his due, but unless I can obtain a little credit through the help of good friends here and abroad I shall have to quit the iron trade in the coming year. If during the autumn or winter I could wholly depend on being able to draw on you £100–£200 one could provide you with goods and repay you with interest, and be assured that I would honourably support you in everything. I began my business with nothing and in a few years God blessed me. I hope He never takes from me His generous hand. With heartiest regards, &c.

$$\frac{11 \; Jun.}{12 \; Jun.} 1669$$

86 BENJAMIN NEWLAND[1] TO CM
      ISLE OF WIGHT   7 JUNE 1669

'Sir, Since my last I have beene at Portsmouth 2 daies that hindered my wrighting the last post. I have yours 5 inst. The inclosed bill for £50 18s 4d drawne p. Mr Claessen at Rochell I doe returne you inclosed and accepted and shall God willing provide the money in your hands by the time it falls due of which please to acquaint the concerned.

As touching pitch and tarr for which you sende me the bill loading I was at Portsmouth wherre was landed 12 lasts and as much more in severall parcells have come into this country all within this 14 daies, and yet noe newes of yours soe that it is prejudice to the sale much when it comes. However I shall give you 9£ p. last for the tarr 13 barrells and 11£ 10s for the pitch and pay you at 3 or 4 monthes at most for it, sooner if my money comes in on the Eleaven monthes tax as I believe it will, and more I cannot resolve to give till I know when it will arrive and what the pitch may way. Shipps that come now out of France tell me doe buy theare tarr a single barrell at 13.*ll* [livres?] and I finde it plenty in other places, soe that such goods being cheape your parcell will be longe goeing off coming late and I hope you would have me noe looser, not to benefitt yourself. When it arrives I shall give you notice. The *Frances*, one which you insured for me and for my father Salesbury,[2] is arrived. Noe newes worth your notice, so I rest. I shall pay the freight of the pitch and tarr and the custome. Adieu.'

   [1] A regular Navy supplier, Benjamin Newland (1633–99) was member of the Levant Company and the Royal African Company (of which he later became sub-governor). Influential both in Cowes and London he served frequently as Member of Parliament for Southampton between 1678 and 1699, was knighted in 1679 and was a City of London Alderman 1683–7. See B. D. Henning (ed.) *The House of Commons, 1660–1690* III (London, 1983) pp. 135–6; J. R. Woodhead, *The Rulers of London, 1660–1689* (London, 1965) p. 120.
   [2] Hugh Salisbury, Navy Board official (Clerk of the Survey) at Portsmouth.

$$\frac{11 \; Jun.}{12 \; Jun.} 1669$$

87 W. SKINNER TO CM
      HULL   8 JUNE 1669

'Sir, I have yours of the 5th instant. For answer, I have not yet shipt you any further parcel of pitch or tarre, nor can I this day advise you of the sale of any more but one way or other it shalbe dispatched now presently. If I cannot sell it att your limitt it shalbe forthwith shipt on the best tearmes I can. The next parcel you send I hope shall finde better successe. As to my advise of fillinge up the tarre, if I be in any error therein I am sorry for it but I wonder you should imagine that it should be shipped without fillinge up, for by that means people might wrong the goods what they please and not be discovered and the charges would be paide out on the goods you had not.

Here with you have now the Coppy of the order of the Councel returned you. The officer of the Eastland Company hath perused it but will give noe result to the release of your last of pitch untill he hath direction therein from the Eastland Company at London. His name is Richard Gleadowe.

Lead is at 13£ p. fodder and many buyers. Thus presentinge my respects I remaine, &c.

[P.S.] The Eastland Company say the goods are yours and you being an Englishman this order will not excuse the goods though brought in in a Sweedish shipp.'

$$\frac{14\ Jun.}{19\ Jun.}1669$$

88   R. ELLISON to CM
NEWCASTLE   11 JUNE 1669

'Loveing friend, I have yours of the 5th present and cannot buy lead under 12£ 10s. As for fraght for Yarmouth I doubt not but it may be gott but it will be as dear in a manner as to London. For Mrs Packer's bill we shall advise how it is in the next letter haveinge not time. My brother being in the country now I dare not advise you for ani adventure of iron, pitch and tarr from Stockholme. There are now 3 ships at Stockholme which load for this place and they wer so fully furnished is as it would I feare be loss to you to have any unless sould very much to your disadvantadge. Would lye at least till the springe and then is a hazard whether it would prove to profit and for pitch is not considerable and that sort of tarr sells only for ships and not much vented but Bargene tarr and Warberren[1] sell more ofte by much but seldom to proffit to the importer. When I know the charge of the *Fortune*'s iron I shall order you your money. I have not else but, Sir, loveing friend, &c.'

   [1] I.e. Bergen (Norway) and perhaps Viborg (Finland), or Varberg, (W. Sweden).

$$\frac{2\ Jul.}{9\ Jul.}1669$$

89   J. PÖTTER & H. THUEN to CM
STOCKHOLM   12 JUNE 1669

[D]   Since our last of the 15th past, of which we confirm the contents, we find ourselves honoured with yours of the 23rd and 30th April and 14th May. Mr Peter Simons will have undoubtedly reached Amsterdam now. Capt. Swen Rassmussen has taken in all his cargo, namely:

1,135 bars	Slb. 138.16½	light voyage iron, 2½ inches broad;
684 ,,	Slb. 116.14½	ordinary bar-iron, well-forged;
370 ,,	Slb. 49.9	square iron—altogether totalling
2,199 bars	Slb. 305.—	

of which the bill of lading will be sent to you in our next. We have ordered the said ship to sail to Bristol and you can commend the iron to your friend there. Next week he will take in the rest of his burthen of pitch and tar and then, in the name of God, depart. We have also loaded in Pieter Klunder's ship 661 bars, Slb. 122.11½ of the same kind of ordinary, 2-inch broad bar iron sent to Bristol. That ship will go to [London] as will likewise Capt. Jean Clopstock who will take aboard 500 slb of all kinds of iron, and there is so far laden in him—576 bars   Slb. 104.6 of 3-inch schampeleon;

        and   255   ,,   Slb. 80.1 of 3½-inch flat iron.

He will take in the remainder next week. We shall advise you of completion by our next and send the bill of lading. We shall then load in the *St Anna*, Capt. Jacob Gries, 600 bars of all kinds of iron, and from Gothenburg you can expect per next to get 1,500 bars. We have put everything in good order and will explain more fully by our next. Please have Swen Rassmussen's iron insured for *RD* 1,500—that is to say, fifteen hundred rixdollars—and in our next letter we shall inform you how the rest should be insured, requesting that you will have it done by good insurers, with our cordial regards, &c.

[P.S.] The little chest which Jan Simons handed over to you please have forwarded to us at the first opportunity.

$$\frac{\textit{10 Jul.}}{\textit{16 Jul.}}\textit{1669}$$

90   TAR COMPANY DIRECTORS to CM
    STOCKHOLM   19 JUNE 1669

D]   Since our last, about a week ago, we have received yours of the 21st of May together with an account of the 60 lasts and 12 barrels of tar and 20 lasts of pitch sent to Yarmouth with Pieter Cornelissen, the proceeds of which amount to £527 1s 6d. We have checked the account, found it correct and recorded our agreement.

    We see that the case of the *Suyderström* was settled by a composition, and you say that if it had not been done it would have been condemned to pay the whole amount, and that the letter of His Majesty [the King] of Sweden, delivered by Resident Leyonbergh, had little or no effect. We will expect the account by your next to see how the case was settled.

    Mr Simons has arrived safely at Amsterdam. We shall learn in due course how he settles his affairs, meanwhile we are glad that the drafts made for us have all been honoured. You should have received the bill of lading of Capt. Nils Anderson consigned to [London] by our preceding letter; herewith goes that of Swen Rasmussen, consigned to Bristol, having with him 40 lasts of tar and 30 lasts of pitch. May God bring him and the rest in safety. We shall advise you about the insurance hereafter. We have seen to it that the barrels of tar and pitch are in good order, wherewith our cordial regards, &c.

[P.S.] Capt. Anders Jacobsen has also been chartered for [London] and we are now daily arranging further charters. Regarding the proceeds, please follow no other orders but ours, of which we shall say more when the goods arrive.

$$\frac{\textit{10 Jul.}}{\textit{16 Jul.}}\textit{1669}$$

91   J. PÖTTER & H. THUEN to CM
    STOCKHOLM   19 JUNE 1669

[D]   Our last was about a week ago, of which we confirm the contents. We have since received yours of the 21st past. We see that Claes Simonsen Scholdt was at Foy[1] and from there took a freight to Bergen for £100 sterling. We would be glad to hear that the captain did not part with any of the freight he earned.

Here inclosed goes the bill of lading concerning the iron loaded for our account, vizt.—in the ship called *d'Vergoute Steeren*, Capt. Pieter Klunder:

661 bars—Slb. 122.11½	schampeleon iron,	3½ inches broad;
306 bars—Slb. 56.2½	ditto	3 inches broad;

| 967 bars—Slb. 178.14 | altogether. | Please have it insured |

These two go for [London]

for *RD* 800—we say, eight hundred rixdollars, by good insurers.
—in the ship called *Fortuna*, Capt. Teunies Clopstock,

1,287 bars—Slb. 242.18	schampeleon iron,	3 inches broad;
565 bars—Slb. 178.7	ditto	4 inches broad;
687 bars—Slb. 85.16½	fine bar iron;	altogether,

2,534 bars—Slb. 507.1½.   Please have it insured by good insurers for two thousand five hundred rixdollars.

In the ship called *St Jean*, Capt. Swen Rassmussen

444 bars—Slb. 81.17	3-inch broad schampeleon iron;
240 bars—Slb. 34.17½	fine bar iron;
379 bars—Slb. 49.9	square iron;
1,135 bars—Slb. 138.16½	very light voyage iron; altogether

2,198 bars—Slb. 305.0   We herewith confirm our previous order to insure it for fifteen hundred rixdollars. The said ship is to go to Bristol—the Lord protect him—and the other two are coming to [London]. The ships are lying ready and will depart by next week. In the *St Anna* there will also be loaded next week 600 bars and we hope to send you the invoice by our next, as well as of what has been loaded at Gothenburg. May God grant that these wares maintain their repute. You are urged to see that the varieties of iron specified above are each kept to their appropriate place as the iron is all made of good materials, very accurately and well-forged. You will also urge your friends in Bristol to see to it that they seek our maximum advantage in the sale of it. There has been much iron loaded here for [London] and England so we fear that it will come to a standstill on arrival, but we must trust you to handle it as if it were your own.

We long to hear how Peter Simons, who has now arrived at Amsterdam, has satisfied everyone—we hope everyone will be content. Wherewith our cordial greetings, God protect you, &c.

[1] Fowey, in Cornwall. William Jennens (Marescoe's correspondent at Plymouth) arranged for Scholt an experimental consignment of 30,000 'holling stones'—valued as ballast and trades goods.

$\frac{14\,Jul.}{27\,Jul.}$ 1669

92   W. BROWNE to CM

BRISTOL   12 JULY 1669

'Sir, I have yours of the 10 instant taking notis of its contence and finde that our ropemakers are at present pretty well suppleyed with tar, a Scotchman about a month since having sould them 600 barrells of tar he brought from Dublin but however I suppose yours may goe of at 18s p. barrell the tar, and 26s p. barrell the pitch or thereabouts, it may be some what more. Your Sweedish iron I have enquired about of three severall persons whoe all conclude it may yeald about 13£ p. tun but heere is one whoe saith if it be good and the squares soe small that they will make window barrs or there abouts, and the flatts handsome iron for use hee cares not if he buyes 40 or 50 tuns himselfe and if it well likes him and that you plese to give him a little tyme with it he will give you 14£ p. tun for it—the person I judge to be very responsable.

Sir, on Thursday last your brother in law Joye gave his brother of Waterford in Ireland a letter of creditt on me for ten or tewenty pounds, the which being presented me I paid the younge man what he desyred which was ten pounds and tooke his bill at sight backe on your brotherlaw for the said sum payable to Mr Richard Tylor junior, which question not will be compleyed with all. I shall mind Mr Smallridge when he comes heere at our faire and what I receive of him shall remitt you in the best bills I can procure, and this being all for present I rest.

[P.S.] For the pitch and tarr, if I may have liberty that others may not undersell me I am confident in a little tyme might have all that trade in my owne hands. Tobacoe of Virginia is now sould in parcell for $4\frac{1}{2}d$ p. lb and the buyer to have the benefitt of the additionall duty; shugars of Barbados at about 20s p. cwt and Nevis at about 23 and 24s; lead at 11£ 8s p. tun. If I can sarve you in any of these, or aughtelse, pray command me.'

$$\frac{19\ Jul.}{30\ Jul.}1669$$

93 A. [MOMMA] REENSTIERNA[1] to CM

STOCKHOLM   30 JUNE 1669

[C] The foregoing, of the 5th inst. is a copy of my last letter to which I refer you; I have since received yours of the 28th past and have noted the contents, to which an answer briefly follows.

I note what you write about the iron in the *Fortuna* and will be very glad to learn that you have sold it at a good price. You say that the iron-buyers are holding back because of the prospect of more ships coming shortly from here with iron. That may well be, and every year large amounts do come from here, and if only the shipments were held by you the iron would not weaken so much, especially if it mostly came into strong hands. I wish it could be arranged.

I have chartered for [London] Capt. Jacob Giese of the ship *Den Grooten Christoffel* which now lies ready to sail, and have loaded therein—according to the four bills of lading enclosed:

Slb.	662.19.10 of 'Crown' iron, small, thin and square;
	57. 9.10 of band iron, ditto, forged somewhat thinner;
	311. 7.10 broad and flat small iron—altogether totalling
	1,031.16.10

1,031.16.10 with various marks, all well-forged and all good English commodities,[2] so I hope it will find a good market. I have ordered Jean & David van Baerle to see to the insurance and have also given them order to draw *RD* 5,000 on you for my account at 1 or 2 usances, which bills you will please to honour and place to my account. With my next I shall send you the bill of lading of what further is shipped and provide everything for you. &c.

---

[1] A. & J. Momma announced their new title to CM in a letter of 15 May 1669.

[2] '. . . *all goede engelsche goedingh.*' I.e. all designed for the English market.

$$\frac{23 \text{ Jul.}}{31 \text{ Jul.}} 1669$$

94 WILLIAM JENNENS[1] TO CM

PLYMOUTH   20 JULY 1669

'Sir, I have yours of the 15th instant. For answeare, 30 a 40 tonns of Sweeds iron to bee sold for ready mony would not sell heare butt att a verry low rate, I suppose about 10£ per tonn. As to pitch and tarr tis uncertaine what quantities would sell here yearly because most ships from Norway or Sweeden bring more or less that a man cannot make any accompt. At present the twone is full and some quantities exspected in ships of this twone from Norrowey. I doe belive good tarr and large band would not yeeld above 14s if that, soe that I cannot give you any incouragement. The currant commoditie from Sweeden is deales, and that is of late much fallen in price. Deales of 11 a 12 foot that weare sould about 2 month since at 6£ are now under 5£. If in any thing I can serve you please to command, your servant, &c.'

  [1] Mayor of Plymouth in 1662, Jennens later became engaged in a protracted suit with the city over rights to 'Jennen's Quay' and was rejected when he stood for Parliament in 1676. See L. Jewett, *A History of Plymouth* (London & Plymouth, 1873) pp. 223, 224; R. N. Worth (ed.) *Calendar of Plymouth Municipal Records* (Plymouth, 1893); Crispin Gill, *Plymouth. A New History (II) 1603 to the present day* (Newton Abbot, 1979) pp. 39–40. In 1677, claiming ill health and poverty at 70 years of age, he petitioned against his appointment as sheriff of Cornwall—*CSPD, 1677–78*, p. 480.

$$\frac{26 \text{ Jul.}}{30 \text{ Jul.}} 1669$$

95 A. RULAND TO CM

HAMBURG   16 JULY 1669

[D] My last letter to you was about a week ago, since which I have received yours of the 9th instant by which I see you have bought for me at 4s 6d p. lb rather more Barbados indigo than I ordered because your friend did not want to break up the consignment. I expect you to send it at the earliest opportunity since in the meantime yet more may arrive from Barbados, and if you can then get good quality stuff for 4s 3d or 4s 4d you may buy me another 600 to 700 lb. and send it here at once. Regarding the sugar, if it does not fall to about 21s there is nothing to be done, but if it should come to that price you may buy me 12,000 to 15,000 lb. and send it here at the earliest opportunity, making sure that it is good stuff. I shall not tie you down to 6d more or less, except that at 22s buy only 12,000 lb.

  Since galls at present fetch only 50s [flem.] here they can hardly be brought from [England], and as those which were expected from the Levant do not seem likely to come to 50s there are a large quantity standing here unsold. I have no news of what prices oil is fetching in Apulia but from Marseille they write me that they daily expect it to be cheaper. In Spain that commodity is also good.

  For your information, there is an English ship here from Venice and Zante with currants and other goods—and for all wares there is poor consumption. As now and then some opportunity turns up at Bristol to do something in one commodity or another I wonder if in such case I may take the liberty of drawing £200 or £300 on you from there so that you can draw back on me, because there is no direct exchange from here on that place. With cordial regards, &c.

Amsterdam: $32\frac{5}{8}$ at sight.
London: 34s 6g   2 usances.

$$\frac{30\ Jul.}{30\ Jul.}1669$$

96   A. BERENBERG'S WIDOW & HEIRS to CM

HAMBURG   16 JULY 1669

[0]   We wrote to you by the last post, in which we enlarged our limit for the indigo so that if you could not do better you might lay out 4*s* 8*d* for 600 lb. of fine Barbados indigo, provided that there was no news that the *flota* had arrived in Spain with indigo and that a ship was on the point of sailing here. We cancelled the commission for Ardasse; this we now confirm. We have since received your letter of the 9th inst., together with the account of the 10 butts of sugar sent with Capt. Willem Oloffsen and now received. We shall look it over and, finding no errors, will record our agreement. We have examined the weight in the casks and we find it turns out reasonably well, but we shall lose 800 lb. by the tare of the butts. The sugar suits us well except that 2 butts turn out to be not so white as the other 8; that is our opinion. If we write to you for white and fine stuff you may get us something similar to the 8 butts in this consignment which have turned out to be white without any brown or rusty stuff amongst it. Please do not hesitate to pay 6*d* more, but for 1*s* more it must be extra-choice. Do your best for us. Another friend writes us with this post that great quantities of sugar are expected from Barbados, and the more it declines in price the better you will be able to obtain it. Do your best, because the profits between here and [England] are very meagre. Thus, if you can find an entirely fine batch you may buy us 10 or 12 butts and send it here. We shall see if we can remit you a sum at short sight by the next post; if not, you may draw the amount on us and your bills will be duly honoured as has been the £150 sterling which you drew on us at 2 usances for the sugar, to pay to the order of Marselis van der Hulst.

We shall be glad to hear what further happens to this commodity as well as your opinion about pepper. We are glad that you have bought us 24 sacks of Barbados cotton, big and small, at 4¾*d* [p. lb.]. We shall expect the account and your drafts. There is nothing to be done with it here at present and if more comes from [England] it must decline further, for there is no consumption. We hope that you have not bought us any Ardasse for it has fallen greatly here from 19*s* to 17*s* within 3 weeks. Therefore, please do not buy us any for we could make no profit with it.

If you buy Barbados indigo please see to it that it is saleable and of high quality, because weak, blue stuff is not required—for your information. As long as galls are unobtainable in [London] for 46*s* or 47*s* it is no use thinking about them for the quantity here is too great and they are very cheap. If any changes occur in [London] please communicate with us. Wherewith we send our friendliest regards, and remain, &c.

London:	34*s* 6*g*
Amsterdam:	32 $\frac{9}{16}$
Antwerp:	32 $\frac{1}{8}$

$$\frac{30\ Jul.}{[30\ Jul.]}1669$$

97   DANIEL PLANCK to CM

AMSTERDAM   2 AUGUST 1669

[0]   My last letter to you was about a week ago with which I sent you the bill of lading for 10 barrels of fine blue-dye. Since then I have received yours of the 16th past together with the sale-account concerning the 20 barrels of ordinary, and 8 of fine, blue-dye, which I have examined and found correct. You put down commission at 2 per cent but I hope in future you will be satisfied with $1\frac{1}{2}$ per cent, as on purchases, because the profit we make on this is rather meagre.

I see you are unloading the 3 barrels of *arsenicum*, though you do not expect to sell it for more than 20*s* since it is a very poor commodity in [England]. I know perfectly well that a large quantity will not sell. I frequently sell quantities to Englishmen here who send it themselves to [London], paying here for the purchase *f*.$10\frac{1}{2}$ or *f*.11; they must then pay here for an export licence and in [England] for its import, so if they can only sell for 20*s* they must be very foolish. You must try to get the most you can.

According to what you write sugar must now be at its lowest, and I would be favourably inclined to buy some, partly in order to dispose of the last lot I got from you—which is still unsold—at a somewhat lower price, and partly in order to mix that with somewhat better quality to make it appear more respectable for sale. But because of the way you served me last time I am very apprehensive, fearing to get bad quality instead of good. If you can do better and obtain extra-good quality at 24*s*, then buy 30,000 to 40,000 lb., but get nothing other than the very choicest for as I have already said it is only to serve to improve the appearance of the other lot.[1] If you cannot get it to your satisfaction you must let it wait as it does not necessarily have to be done today. You can distribute it in 2 or 3 ships and lade them here at the earliest opportunity. I urge you most strongly to procure only the best quality, and see that in weighing it my prescribed weights are observed.

You indicated ginger to be at 48*s*. If you can obtain good quality at that price, free on board, please buy 8,000 to 10,000 lb. and send it here also. Cubeb, I understand, are selling at £6 10*s* in [London]. If they can still be had for that you may also undertake the purchase of 1,000 or 1,200 lb. Six ships have returned safely to this country from the Indies, namely four from Ceylon (of whose cargoes you have heard already) and two from Batavia of which the cargo is not yet known. With best regards, &c.

London: 35*s* $4\frac{1}{2}g$
Hamburg: $32\frac{1}{2} - \frac{9}{16}$

---

1 '. . . *alsoo glyck geseght alleen dienen sall om d'andere partey een oogh te geeven.*'

$\frac{31\,Jul.}{6\,Aug.}$1669

98   A. REENSTIERNA to CM
STOCKHOLM   14 JULY 1669

[D]   The foregoing, dated 30th past, is a copy of my last, to which I refer you. Since then I have received yours of the 11th ditto and noted the contents, to which my answer briefly follows.

I have seen what you write about timber and I shall be happy to participate in whatever may develop. I would be glad to learn if something could be done to procure passes, for we have rather a lot of timber lying on Gotland which cannot be got to [England] for lack of shipping space but which otherwise could come this year if one could get passes.

The price at which you have sold the iron from the *Fortuna* I have noted, as well as the price at which you say the English are selling the iron which has come this year. They will get little profit by it as I believe it will begin to cost more here. It is lamentable that such an imperishable commodity should be undersold, and if they continue to conduct themselves in this way in [England] while large amounts are still coming things will go badly this year, for I see that much has been shipped from here, but I trust that it comes into firm hands and remains there at a good price.

You will have learned from my previous letter what I have sent to you, and I hope the ship is now well out to sea—God bring him soon in safety. I have also noted the price of copper-wire, copper-sheets and rods, and it will serve for my guidance. Swedish-built ships to carry timberware from Gotland are not to be had here, and are also too expensive to charter. I shall expect the account of the iron from the *Fortuna* at the earliest opportunity. I am sorry to hear from Amsterdam that Peter Simons' affairs turn out quite differently from what he told me here. He wrote to me on the 25th past and has begged me to beg you to sign the agreement with him as he will always try to satisfy you. I ask you to oblige him as far as you can, not doubting that he will be grateful.

I have consigned to you in the following ships iron as follows:

779 bars—Slb. 103.11 } flat, ordinary 'Crown' iron with Capt. Claes Holtz of the
866 bars—Slb. 118.10 } ship *De Gecroonde Parel* according to the enclosed bill of lading; and also, 999 bars—Slb. 152.14 flat iron, with Capt. Jacob Grys of the *St Anna*, of which the bill of lading will be sent by my next. I have ordered the Messrs Van Baerle to see to the insurance. I hope to send you the bill of lading of another cargo by my next. Please make the proceeds over to the Messrs Van Baerle. Herewith farewell, &c.

$$\frac{14 \text{ Aug.}}{20 \text{ Aug.}} 1669$$

99 J. PÖTTER & H. THUEN to CM
STOCKHOLM   17 JULY 1669

D] Our last letter to you was three weeks ago, to which we refer; since then we have received yours of the 11th and 18th past, to which this serves as a reply. You will do us a kindness if you will show my lord Helmfeldt's son[1] all courtesy if he calls, for we do not doubt that before the receipt of this Teunis Clopstock and Pieter Klunder will have arrived safely at [London] as well as Swen Rassmussen at Bristol—God willing! We commend to you the sale of our iron as if it were your own. Enclosed herewith is the bill of lading of further iron laden in the ship *St Anna*, captain Jacob Gries, vizt.:

486 bars—Slb. 69.9 ordinary fine iron } together 160 Slb 13 lispound.
424 bars—Slb. 91.4 flat iron   }

You will please insure it for *RD* 800—that is to say, eight hundred rix-dollars—with good insurers, and kindly send us a little account of this as well as previous insurances made on Clopstock, Klunder and Swen Rassmussen. We would have loaded more iron in the *St Anna* but because of contrary winds it has not arrived. By our next letter we will advise what other batches you can expect from here and from Gothenburg.

Concerning the delivery of copper of which you were thinking, we are not much inclined to it and cannot make up our minds as copper is very dear here and at the price you mentioned it would render a poor account. It is rising daily so that one can make no firm estimate. We can probably do better by selling our wares here.

We were very surprised to learn of the serious situation of Mr Simons' affairs in

Amsterdam. He had informed us otherwise when he was here, and we have learned nothing else from him than that he had reached agreement with Mr Abraham Momma about how you were to be reimbursed. We now hear the contrary. Since he had so many claims on the Tar Company here he should have been able to obtain the necessary means, and we are heartily sorry that you are so deeply involved. God knows, we would have watched out better for you if we had known. You can expect a good quantity of iron from Gothenburg, although it is taking so long that one gets weary. Cordial regards, &c.

[P.S.] Please give the enclosed open letter to captain Nils Anderson, skipper of the ship *De Witte Duyve*, freighted to you by the [Tar] Company and demand of him the freight money he has earned and hold it until further disposition, and whatever the captain may need for the ship's requirements you can let him have back.

¹ Unidentified son of Baron Simon Grundel-Helmfelt (1617–77), soldier and privy councillor, twice-married, and a veteran of Swedish embassies to England.

$$\frac{14 \; Aug.}{24 \; Aug.} 1669$$

100   A. CRONSTRÖM to CM
[STOCKHOLM?]¹
                                                                    21 JULY 1669

[D] My last letter to you was on the 14th inst. to which I refer you. I have since received your very welcome letter dated the 18th past, most of which is answered by my last letter and for the rest this will serve.

Regarding what you proposed concerning a person who approached you about a consignment of garcopper and 'Hungary plates', without specifying the quantity, and for which you quoted him the price of £5 14s for the garcopper and £6 for the Hungary plates—in reply to which, I could not easily deliver it to [London] for less if I am to gain anything by it. Coppers have risen here because those abroad, as in Holland and Hamburg, are also somewhat raised in price. As a result, I cannot afford to take less, and that for cash down or within 1 month of delivery, and you should please be prepared to allow me to draw on you at double usance for at least three-quarters of the value of the cargo as soon as the bill of lading has been sent. If your friend can agree to these terms he can order as much as he pleases—but he must answer at once, otherwise the copper-market here will be over and it will be too late in the year to send anything out, for winter is nearly upon us. We shall therefore await your, or your friend's, decision, but if we wait much longer nothing can be done before the winter.

Concerning my remaining wire, I urge you most strongly to dispose of it at the first opportunity, but I cannot agree to let it go for less than £5 8s or £5 9s.

Coppers rise here daily and look likely to rise still higher, so I shall have very little profit on the above-written conditions. If the market does not alter and I am to make a start I must quickly get moving.² Please let me know in reply to this the quantity of rods which [England] can consume yearly and at what times they are most in demand.

Messrs Pels complain that you had their £200 bill of exchange protested on the grounds that they had drawn £30 or more than I had given order for. I am greatly astonished for I never imagined that they had gone over the limit, and even if they had you might well have considered that it would not happen again and that I would have acknowledged the amount for my account. I trust that for the present there will be enough time to procure payment of the amount. I urge you most strongly not to treat those gentlemen's bills with disrespect. I remain, &c.

[1] In error, Cronström addressed the letter as if from London.

[2] '. . . *moet ick dit-mael daer over-heen stappen.*'

$$\frac{21 \ Aug.}{27 \ Aug.} 1669$$

1 TAR COMPANY DIRECTORS tO CM

STOCKHOLM   24 JULY 1669

] Our last was about a week ago. We sent with it the bills of lading for captain Matthys Boriesen, destined for [London] with $57\frac{3}{13}$ lasts of tar and 20 lasts of pitch; also of captain Swen Pieters destined for Plymouth with $32\frac{4}{13}$ lasts of tar and 25 lasts of pitch, to which we refer you. Your letters of 25th past and 2nd inst. have now come to hand, in which we see that you have given up the two warehouses at Deptford and two others at Blackwall, debiting us with £24 for their rent, and have leased two others at Blackwall for 3 years at £50 per annum, of which we have made a note. It is a good thing that you have only hired two for the moment. Whenever one needs more one can easily find the opportunity.

With the Company ships being unfree exports are going rather poorly, for the little *schuits* can take in so little. We sent you a note a week ago about how much had so far been sent to all places, but a mistake was made about captain Thomas Klerck where he is noted as having 60 lasts of tar and 20 lasts of pitch whereas according to the accompanying bill of lading he had taken in $27\frac{9}{13}$ lasts of tar and 15 lasts of pitch. Since then we have chartered two others for [England], that is—captain Erick Anderson Brandt, of the *schuit Fortuna*, and captain [blank]. The former will have his cargo aboard within three days and the other, God willing, will be cleared within eight days, so we hope to send the bills of lading by our next letter. We are doing our best to obtain further ships and think it not inexpedient to send another 1,000 lasts of pitch and tar as soon as we find shipping for it, wherein we are doing our best and missing no opportunity.

We are unhappy to see that none of our ships have yet arrived. We hope the Lord will have brought them in safety by now as the wind has been favourable for some time.

We have credited your account with the freight paid to captain Jurgen Kohne as well as with the gross avarage. We also note that the cargo is sold. When it has been delivered we shall expect an account as well as our current account at your convenience. For the rest, we repeat our request of a week ago that you will write to Mr Deutz at Amsterdam that you will accept for us £2,000 stg. which we will draw on him at 6 months sight and he can draw on you. Meanwhile, before it falls due, nearly all the goods will have been sent out. We await your answer hereon and commend you to the protection of the Lord, &c.

$$\frac{21 \ Aug.}{24 \ Aug.} 1669$$

2 J. & D. VAN BAERLE tO CM

AMSTERDAM   27 AUGUST 1669

] Our last letter was about a week ago; we have since received yours of the 10th and 13th inst. with 5 bills of exchange, vizt.:

£190 sterling on Jean Gilles & Albertus Pieters;
£200   "   on Dirck & Jan Willinck;
£100   "   on Gerrit & Jan Huycken;
£100   "   on Francois Sellier;
£230   "   on Cornelio Berenberch.

We shall procure acceptance of all these and send them back by our next. Concerning the last-named, people tell us that he is reputed a man of means who can boast of some capital of his own, but we now understand that for the most part he has nothing in hand but investments in the East Indies which are only moderately well-administered by his trustee, and as he cannot draw on it he is obliged to use his credit on the Exchange rather too much.

Herewith goes the second bill of exchange of £114 5s 8d on John Skepper as well as the receipt for the £85 0s 3d stg. paid to Cornelis Claes [senior] and Cornelis Claes, junior, @ 35s 5g per £ sterling with the deed of guarantee under surety passed before the notary. We have debited your current account with f.903 5st bank-money for it, in addition to the second bill of exchange of £250 on Jean Corsellis. Lacking the second bill of exchange of £200 of 6th August on Cornelio Berenberch, whereof the first copy—handed to him for his acceptance—was lost by him, we beg you to have the second copy sent to us.

Your inclosures for Sweden have been forwarded, and accompanying this are two letters for you received from there.

Yesterday Peter Simons agreed with his creditors for 40 per cent—vizt. 35 per cent to pay under bond, half in cash and the other half in 6 months time; the other 5 per cent to pay on his credit within a year. Wherewith our hearty regards, &c.

London—35s 4g 2 usances.

$$\frac{3 \ Sep.}{4 \ Sep.} 1669$$

103   W. BROWNE tO CM
         BRISTOL   I SEPTEMBER 1669

'Sir, I have yours of the 28th past thankeing you for the payment of my 10£ bill to Mrs Joanes. Your inclosed I have given to skipper Swen Rasmussen as alsoe the bill and letter of advise on Mr Jean Freyhoff and have received of Mr Anthony Gay on account of his said freight £129 3s and said Mr Gay hath promised me the other £100 the next weeke which I suppose he will comply with—he is very responsable. I have all the iron a shore but have as yett delivered but 1 tun of sqares and that at £14 10s which mony I am to receive tomorrow. I feare I shall not be able to attaine neere the price you write me for the iron, and besides those which now deale in that trade cannot pay ready mony for such a parcell being trusted by the Forrest masters[1] of iron from 6 months to 6 months. He that deales most in said commodity and the most responsable man is out of towne and will not be home tell next weeke, and then shall see what they will doe, but as farr as I can guesse yett they will not come to above £13 10s or £14 at most for the whole parcell together and for the Ginny iron heere will be noe vent for it but to the iron mongers, wee from hence having noe trade that way. Be sure what I can advance it in price for you shall be performed by, Sir, your loving freinde, &c.

[P.S.] I thinke the skipper sailes tomorrow morning, and the skipper hath given me up your Charter party writt in parchment which you may have sent if you please.'

---

[1] I.e. the Forest of Dean iron-masters.

$$\frac{8\ Sep.}{10\ Sep.}1669$$

04 JAN ARNOLD FONCK to CM
HAMBURG   31 AUGUST 1669

)] As far as I know I have never had the honour of writing to you before. This shall therefore serve to assure you of my keenness to correspond with you. My brother had the honour of saluting you in [London] about one-and-a-half years ago with my cousin, Dominicus Juncker, and to inquire if we could establish a regular correspondence between us. I have been greatly inclined to get a good quantity of Barbados sugar, but only of the finest and best quality of the sort you provided for my nephew Paul Berenberg. In procuring the purchase make sure it is at a reasonable price and in the right condition—especially if it reaches 22s or, at most, 23s. Also Barbados cotton at 4-pence and good Aleppo gall-nuts at 45–46s, as a friend of mine says he has had, which are likely to be 46s. Please also tell me how much nice, dry English leather is fetching. Here it is at a very low price and I am sure it can only be at 6d in [England].

For some time I have been selling a good deal of linen *alamodes* to the English here, which is apparently sent to Barbados and the colonies. Please find out in [London] how much a piece of 70 ells, $\frac{7}{4}$ broad, would fetch, a sample of which is here enclosed and which I can have made in all kinds of fashions. If you also had the opportunity to dispose of about 100 barrels of tin, of the mark of the Horse, which is the best sort, I could provide it. If you cannot reach agreement in [London] you could take the tin barrels, which are RD 21 (I say, one and twenty) free on board, and set against them a delivery of sugars and Barbados cotton (which must be entirely good) and I shall set against it as much money as the tin is worth and you could take the commission on both the tin and the sugars. I have arranged to do so with a friend here and it has worked out well. I would at once send you the 100 barrels of tin and remit you RD 2,000 which would at least provide for the above-said sugars.

[P.S.] You must expect, since most of my business is with Germany, that I must try to dispose of commodities coming from there, and on this basis we could co-operate and do important business together every year. I await your answer and remain, with friendly regards,
&c.

[P.P.S.] If pepper should come down to 8–$8\frac{1}{2}d$ in [London], free on board, then buy me 20 sacks and send them here with the first ship. I shall remit to you at sight, and if it should fall lower you will know how to look out for my interests, I relying upon you to provide the [East India] Company's freshly received goods.

$$\frac{13\ Sep.}{18\ Sep.}1669$$

105 W. BROWNE to CM
BRISTOL   11 SEPTEMBER 1669

'Sir, I have yours of the 9th instant. I hope you have myne by last post in which I sent you up two bills of Exchange for £150 more, which I hope you will have punctuall comployance in and that Mr John Gibbs before this hath accepted the first bill for £100 and alsoe the second for the like sum. I'le assure you I take all the care I can to gett you punctuall and good bills and shall allwaise use my best endeavours for you but if a losse (which God forbid) should come I hope you doe not expect that I should make it good. Yesterday last I sould all your iron to Mr Taylor & Gunter at £13 10s p. tun together, except the 240 barrs which you rated to me at £15 p. tun and that the same persons have bought att £12 10s p. tun, and to pay for it ½ at the end of 3 monthes and the other moiety at the end of the three months after the first pay-ment, and on Munday they begin to way it which as soone as wayed and the accompts ajusted they will give me notes of theyr hands for each man for his part alone, but one will not be oblidged for the other though I thinke they are both very responsable. Now My Taylor sayth if I please he will pay me the ½ of his share presantly provided I will stay 9 monthes for the other pay-ment to which plese to give your answere. Heere is 20 tuns of Dutch iron more come in this weeke and 30 tuns more expected by Mr Charles Williams daily. Mr Anthony Gay sould his parcell as I am credably informed at £12 p. tun and for tyme too. I cannot tell how you may like this sale but I have tryed to the utmost of my skill would give me leave and could not advance it. Your squares were much more vendible then the rest especialy had they beene a little smaller. Sir, if you finde good to be done about this price and that you will order for such sortes as I shall give you orders for I may dispose for you a considerable quantity in the yeare. Pray advise if you deale in iron rods and how much they may be afforded heere p. tun; alsoe iron potts, frying pans, white platts and steele, and this being all for the present, I rest, your humble sarvant, &c.'

$$\frac{17 \text{ Sep.}}{24 \text{ Sep.}} 1669$$

106   A. REENSTIERNA to CM

STOCKHOLM   28 AUGUST 1669

[D]   The foregoing, dated the 21st past, is a copy of my last letter, to which I refer you. I have since received yours of the 25th and 29th of June, and 9th and 30th of July, the contents of which are fully understood and to which the answer shortly follows herewith.

I have received the account of the iron sold from the *Fortuyn* and found it correct. I have debited you with the proceeds, £325 11s 6d and credited you with the RD 140 from my lord Pistolhielm at 4s 9d each, being £33 5s. The idea that I should be paid here at the rate of 5s 6d is a mistake, for they can be got for no more than $5\frac{10}{32}$. [d.c.m.]

I have seen what you write about the price of iron and other things, and it is annoying that some dealers should undersell by offering it at £14 per ton on delivery. They achieve nothing but loss by doing so as they have bought it dearly here. I hope it remains at a good price so that one will continue to want to send it. I expect to hear in due course.

With regard to what you write about charges on the iron I send to you, you are to understand it as we have done formerly, namely that for whatever expenditure you incur you can take interest, and if any losses should occur—which God forbid! it is well-insured and you will recover your outlay from those gentlemen who have drawn on you for my account, so you run no risk and there is no need for you to make difficulties. It seems to me rather strange, what you say you have written to Messrs Van Baerle, that they should not draw on you before the ship has reached [London]. If they are to fulfil my drafts on them they must be able to draw RD 2,500 on you. My request is that you will allow them to draw as much on you as the proceeds approximately come to, though deducting what you may have advanced for me already according to the accompanying account. And as regards what has happened, I have looked into it and find that when the 158 barrels of steel were estimated to be worth £160[1] you were already about £340 out of pocket. Please let Messrs Van Baerle have any proceeds arising in excess of that amount. I depend on that as I have charged them with my drafts and will draw accordingly on future deliveries.

Hereinclosed I send 3 bills of lading of iron laden for my account in the ship *Mars*, captain Hans Johanson, together amounting to Slb. 872.10, including various sorts of 'English-style'[2] bar-iron and Slb. 117.15.10 of forged band-iron. NB that in future it must be sold at higher prices, as I have written to you before and to which I refer you. Herewith also is a bill of lading from Capt. Hendrick Claessen Boender for Slb. 305.15.10 of 'English-style' bar iron, all of which I am consigning to you, and I have another batch which will follow. In selling it I urge you to have as much regard for my profit as if it were your own: I depend upon it.

I have read what you tell me about Peter Simons and am surprised that you did not write to me at once about what you let him draw on you. I never thought his affairs would turn out so badly, and as for me being indebted to him for *f*.8,000—I can prove the contrary as he owes me for Portuguese drafts, so I do not know how I can help you. I do not doubt that he will try to satisfy you in full, as he has written to me, only you must enter into the agreement with him. God protect each and all from misfortune, &c.

[1] The steel actually sold for £161 gross, £119 18s 9d net.
[2] 'Engelse goedingh stangh iser'.

$$\frac{20\ Sep.}{24\ Sep.}1669$$

7 D. VAN RUYFF to CM
STOCKHOLM   28 AUGUST 1669

] My last letter to you was on the 31st past, with the bill of lading for 4,239 bars of iron, weighing Slb. 455.5 on Capt. Jacob Grys, which I hope will have arrived before the receipt of this. I have now got yours of the 23rd and 30th past and of the 3rd inst. in which I am delighted to see the safe arrival of Capt. Pieter Klunder. I hope to learn by your next that the said iron has found a good market, as well as the iron in the *St Anna*. You will do well to sell it as soon as possible as there are large amounts being loaded here now for [England].

Regarding the insurance, I find that one can get it cheaper in [London] than in Amsterdam, but against that one must lose 14 per cent in London in the event of a misfortune. Mr Van de Mortel informs me that the insurers will only make good *f*.130 for avarage on the *Fortuyn*, though it should very nearly recompense the loss. I have credited you with £592 18s 4d stg. which you have remitted to Mr Philip Pelt Emanuels. Thank you for the accommodation, with my regards, &c.

$$\frac{27\ Sep.}{30\ Sep.}1669$$

8 B. NEWLAND to CM
ISLE OF WIGHT   22 SEPTEMBER 1669

'Sir, I have yours 18 present and ordered severall sumes to be remitted you out of the country on my account. What comes with that £50 pray receive. I did much admire my £1,177 2s 9d on the Eleaven monthes tax[1] was not come in, and did feare you might not order your man to call, soe it is that I am advised by a friende which had occasion to search about some money of his owne that the 1216 and 1217 order assigned to you by Wade through my order have beene readie to be paid more then this two monthes. He tells me exactly £1,177 2s 9d uppon those two orders are in banck and have beene soe rede since the 10 July last, and that you may fetch the money when you please, and in truth hath beene much dammage to me its not received depending it would have beene readie before that time. I pray omitt noe time but on receipt of this sende your man for the money and place it to my credit giveing me due notice thereof, and now I will loock over your accounts and wright the needefull in answer to them and keepe busnesse exact. I drew uppon you £25 12s 8d payable to Mr Thomas Papillon or order: pray discharge the same. I sallut you and rest.

[P.S.] Pray loose not an houres time in receiving those £1,177 2s 9d. It hath been exceeding great dammage and prejudice was not done all this time. The prejudice to me is greate. Pray loose noe time more for your servant, &c.

[Margin.] About the bill of Pollea, it was Mr Rogers advised me he was at Dover. I hope I shall not loose that 10£. If you do occasion to wright Mr Rogers put two lines in my behalf.

[Verso.] Pray give me your advice what I may doe about the bill of bottomry for £50 at 30s p. month of Richard Butler which is in your hands. The shipp was putt into Barbados in her voidge to Virginia, fitted thence and trades twixt Virginia and New England. Now when is the money due one the bill, and what may I doe about recovering it. Mr Butler wrights me gave you Copie of a wrighting about some gunes for which having met with base factors I must content my selfe with 15£. Pray sende me the wrighting.'

¹ 18 & 19 Car. II. c. 13 granted Charles II £1,256,347 13s in eleven monthly levies of £114,213. The Act included provisions for borrowing at interest on the credit of parliamentary guarantees and for the registration 'in course' of other government liabilities, notably to Naval suppliers such as Newland who were owed considerable arrears. Under this arrangement Newland held Treasury Orders Nos. 1216 and 1217, assignable instruments which entitled him (or his assigns) to repayment when sufficient funds had reached the Exchequer. The Treasury gave notice in *The London Gazette* when Orders had reached maturity and were ready for settlement.

$\frac{4\ Oct.}{8\ Oct.}$1669

109   A. REENSTIERNA to CM
STOCKHOLM   15 SEPTEMBER 1669

[D]   We are, God be praised, at the 15th of September; the above, of the [2]8th past is a copy of my latest letter to you, to which I refer. Since then I have received yours of the 6th [past] the contents of which I have seen and to which in answer say it is very bad news that iron is beginning to fall, especially as such large amounts have been sent to [London]. I had hoped that the undercutters would not have moved in so suddenly.¹ It is much to be wished that this trade could be brought into a few hands and by that means preserve its reputation. You will know how to seek the most advantage for my consignments, which remain commended to your care.

As the prospect of bringing some timber to [England] in foreign-built ships and getting passes for them has faded for the moment, we must let it pass until a better opportunity arises. I have still about 800 to 1,000 shippounds of iron standing ready which I intend to send in the ship *Jupiter* unless some other shipping turns up so that I can divide the consignment, but I very much hope that it will obtain a better price. At the present price I think it advisable to be careful with my consignment and wait for some improvement. Then, I beg you, let the

Messrs Van Baerle have what they need for my account. I am of the opinion that iron will not remain at such a low price, and would also be glad to know your views.

Herewith goes the bill of lading of Hendrick Claessen Boender which I forgot to insert in the foregoing.

Let the Messrs Van Baerle have as much as the iron proceeds amount to, and I will make good the interest on what you advance. The ship *Mars* is lying in harbour here and will sail out with the first good wind—may God protect him.

I have seen what you say about Mr Peter Simons and I am very sorry that it is so. There is little to be done with a procuration as, so far as I know, he has scarcely any effects here, and to set against those I must have my protested Portuguese bills of exchange so they will amount to very little. I wish you had sent to me in April or May—I would have been able to do something but it is too late now and I must hope that he, Simons, will take good care to satisfy you. I wish that from my heart and commend you to God's protection, &c.

¹ '*Ick en hadde niet gehoopt datter soo subitelyck de claedde ingekoomen syn soude . . .*'

$$\frac{15\ Oct.}{16\ Oct.}1669$$

P. CAULIER to CM
YARMOUTH   11 OCTOBER 1669

'Sir, I have yours of the 7th ditto, to which I repley. Mr Muns was dissatisfied in the tayle of the lead soe I caused my porter to tel it over in his presents and there is but 355 pieces soe he is inclinable to alow me for the 2 pieces, but pray tel me at what price—I supose about £12 per tun. I shal doe there in as for my self. I see the price you offer [?] of iron, flat and broad £13 10s and square £14 10s, to which I say our smiths wil not come to thos prisses. They have it from Holland more resonnabel and 6 months tyme with it. I should nead some 30 tuns for my owne occation if the ship come in tyme, if you could let me have it at £13 5s or £13 10s at most, 6 months, as the last was. I canot aford to give more, the comodity is soe abroad. Its chiefly for ballast; or if you thinke fitt to propos me a price in generall for all iron, pitch and tar you send me yearly, free me from al charges to you, I shal see if we can agree. That is to say, I to pay al custome, wharfage, warhouse roum, coopers, porters, town dutys, a broker [?] and provision also included. It may be as wel for you and as wel for me. I may save something in the towne dutys, being a freeman of this place. Pray consider of it and [resolve to goe neare the wind with me as possible you can]¹ for accomodation I supose you wil give me 6 to 8 months tyme, and soe you shal be sure to maik noe bad debpts, for I find that if I continu this trade I must be fayne to buyld me a storhouse aporpos, for the tar spoyles all the houses it comes into and except your frinds send me good cask, better than the last, I had rather be without that commodity than have it. My warhous in which the last tar lys is all afloot of the tar. This is all at present. In haest I rest.'

¹ Marginal insertion.

$$\frac{19\ Oct.}{22\ Oct.}1669$$

J. [MOMMA] REENSTIERNA to CM
NORRKÖPING   24 SEPTEMBER 1669

My last letter to you was on the 27th of August with which I informed you that I would make good interest on the £200 stg. which you advanced for my account to Mr Burckin on bottomry. For the rest, I refer you to my letter. I have since received your very welcome letters of the 20th and 27th past as well as of the 3rd inst., of which the last two were received together about two days ago. The answer briefly follows. I shall take them one with the other and after looking over the current account let you know my findings by next—God willing. I have noted what goods of mine still remain with you unsold and hope they will also quickly find buyers like the rest.

It is possible that if shipping-space turns up this autumn I shall send you an assortment of thicker wire, but since the departure of Capt. Abraham Richart no opportunity of freighting to [London] has occurred.

I was very glad to learn of Richart's safe arrival—God be praised! I have further seen what you say concerning your friend who wants to do business about a consignment of copper, and that he has offered to take 600 'Hungary plates' and has at last gone so far as to offer £5 18s payable on delivery be the end of November. You should have learned from previous letters that I really cannot oblige by sending any quantity of copper to [England] this year—partly for lack of shipping and partly (and principally) because copper has recently become so tight and scarce here that it can hardly be got for money. But if your friend will wait for a consignment to be sent with the first available ships going to [London] from here in the new year, and if you could persuade your friend to pay you the money now, I would agree to the price of £5 18s—for your guidance.

My friend, because I have bought these large copper-works I must necessarily take care to keep my people fully employed, but I have no resources to enable me to supply the ['Hungary'] plates unless I can command money at Hamburg. If you will accommodate me with some money at 6 per cent interest I would probably be able to send you more supplies. Whether the business of the plates goes forward or not, and as you now have all the Swedish copper-wire under your hand, I hope you will fix the price rather higher than it has been—I depend on it. I urge you to sell the thick copper-wire rods; wherewith my regards, &c.

$$\frac{19\ Oct.}{22\ Oct.}1669$$

112 J. & D. VAN BAERLE to CM

AMSTERDAM   15 OCTOBER 1669

[D] We have received your letters of the 24th and 28th September and 1st instant. In reply, we will tell you in our next how much the remittance of *RD* 500 current-money amounts to in bank-money. We have been paid the £100 stg. at 35s 11g drawn on John Lodge, and have credited your account.

We are sorry to see that you are in dispute with the Västervik Ship Company. Our friend at Rotterdam wrote us on the 11th instant that he has sold another four 8-pounder cannon at [*f*]8: 15¹ on the same terms as the last, and as the guns are old and inferior we consider he has done well. However, we have since then written to him to hold back from selling for a while.

We have taken expert advice about the sample of cotton but find that it is too coarse for East Indian yarn and most resembles yarn from the Straits, of which there is at present a reasonable amount in town. The yarn sold by our East India Company is fine, like the accompanying sample, and sells at 28 to 27 s[tuivers] per lb. That which was sold at 16½st was badly made up and as a result it fetched less than others just as fine. But we judge that cotton yarn which is no coarser than your sample should sell for 16 *st* per lb., and you will please note that the finest are the most sought after. Such yarn is mostly used at Haarlem for textiles and other stuffs,[2] and because little has arrived here this year from the East Indies we believe it would not do badly if you could find something finer—or certainly not coarser—than the sample you sent.

We see that the price of copper-wire has risen somewhat and is likely to continue to do so as little has been sent to London. We have noted how much of J. R[eenstierna]'s wire has been sold, and we hope you will soon be able to close the account of W.M[omma]'s copper-wire. We have procured the necessary acceptance of the £935 12s 2d stg which you remitted to us in ten bills of exchange for my Lord Jacob Reenstierna's account and he has been informed of it.

You wrote to us about remittances being made against A. Reenstierna's iron on its arrival or earlier: as against the iron in Jacob Giese you have remitted £1,000, since which have arrived Jacob Jacobsen Grys with Slb. 152.14 and Claes Molt with Slb. 636.17, against which nothing has been remitted. Your next letters will possibly inform us further.

Peter Simons is lying sick in bed. As his settlement has not yet been signed by as many creditors as are required for it to take effect we suggest that you demand his guarantee in case the remaining creditors refuse to sign and he is released from his obligations. What happens next only time will tell.

As you ordered us not to hurry with remittances we shall return your accepted bills of exchange of £100 on Jean de Roy and £200 on Roelandt Cockey with our next—wherewith our heartiest regards, &c.

London: 35s 2½g 2 usances.
Hamburg: 32$\frac{5}{16}$ at sight.

[1] This reading is tentative.
[2] 'tot manufacturen en andre stoffen . . .'

$\frac{\text{20 Oct.}}{\text{28 Oct.}}$ 1669

3 P. CAULIER TO CM
YARMOUTH   18 OCTOBER 1669

'Sir, For answer to yours of the 16th courant I say that Mr Muns has not since my last byn with me to adjust his bisnes, but I purpos to preserve your interest in the lead as my one and shal doe with him when he comes the best I can. And as to the bisnes of the ship *St Gorge* from Colmer, if she comes heare I shal arrest her and the master and purser as you order.

As to the proposition I made you consirning pitch and tar and iron, I say that as to the quantity I say 150 last tar and 20 or 30 last pitch wil be enof, and 60 tun iron, the first ship to be heare in May and the last in September, and as to the price I leave that to you to propos. I conseave its proper for you to make your demands. You may essely see the charge by the accounts I sent you and thereby maek an estimate. Now if you plese to consider that I profit to become your debptor for the hole that you send and that you wil for future run noe risks but be ponctially complied with at the tyme we agree for I thinck it wil be to your intrest to be at asurtainty. If therefore you plese to consider the hole and to pitch me aprice resonnabel both that it may be worth my trobel and paynes and cost, you shal soune have my answer. This is al at present. I rest, Sir, your assured frind and servant.

[P.S.] The reson that I maek you this proposition to be at a sertainty is because that I have often occation myself to fil up my ships that goe to the southward with thos goods for ballast and being in my own hands I can then dispos of it as I please. It is not for the great profit it turnes to but for the acomodation of my conveniency, and if I did not vent great part of it my self it is not the $\frac{1}{2}$ the quantity could be disposed of here by any man but my self. I leave it to your consideration and rest.'

$$\frac{26 \text{ Oct.}}{29 \text{ Oct.}} 1669$$

114 TAR COMPANY DIRECTORS to CM
       STOCKHOLM   25 SEPTEMBER 1669

[D] Our last letter was about a week ago, to which we refer you. Since then we have received yours of the 27th past and 3rd instant, by which we are delighted to hear of the arrival of Thomas Klerck. We hope the Lord will have brought the others in safety. By our last you should have had the bill of lading of Capt. Erick Fix, his cargo being $32\frac{4}{13}$ lasts of tar and 18 lasts of pitch. We have given orders for the insurance thereon, as well as on Hans Johanson and Anders Krock, and wait to learn the result. Please also take care of the insurance, according to contract, of Jacob Pieters Potteut's cargo, being 74 small lasts of tar and 39 lasts of pitch. Capt. Olof Erickson's ship will be ready for loading soon, and Nathaniel Fabrius's ship is expected from Calmar every hour. We have also chartered the ship *Jupiter*, Capt. Jacob Fix, which will be coming in for loading next week. Hans Reyser's ship was built in an unfree place so we have not dared to load it.

Meanwhile, Mr Jacob Sempel has procured a recommendation from his Excellency the English Ambassador for the free export of 150 lasts of pitch, since he has paid the Company for permission, and the goods are all consigned to you. We have loaded 85 lasts of pitch for that voyage, for your information.

We have examined the four sale-accounts of tar and pitch and found them correct and debited you for the proceeds. We shall try our best to send 70 lasts of tar and 10 lasts of pitch to Yarmouth and 40 lasts of tar and 15 lasts of pitch to the Isle of Wight, but we see no chance of doing so as there are few native-built ships here and they have all been freighted for [England] by others; and as long as there is a shortage of goods in London we think it inadvisable to send them to the small places.

We note that you have been approached by two friends who want to buy 600 lasts of tar and 200 lasts of pitch to be delivered to them between now and March next, for which they have offered £$8\frac{1}{2}$ and £$11\frac{1}{2}$ respectively, payable in 6 months, with nothing for warehouse rent—to which you await our answer. We will tell you, then, that we would sooner have the highest possible price as the warehouses are already hired, and we also hope that the goods will be in demand in the spring if all the necessary ships can be obtained. But if your friends want to be reasonable and pay the money on delivery we would not quibble about ten shillings.

We see you were obliged to pay £152 concerning the verdict in the water-balliage case, and you say you would be glad to know if you should spend something more to prevent the case coming to a halt. If you believe it would help and see that something can be gained thereby we shall be glad to spend something more, but we could not agree to making our expenses still bigger and then lose the whole sum. For the rest we leave it to you to do as you judge best and as you find matters stand.

Concerning the case of Mr Peter Simons, we can truly say that nothing would please us more than to assist you but there is not a penny to be got from him here, and we swear on our conscience that we are owed three times as much as you are, of which we see no chance of getting a stuiver. He has given us his guarantee, but that is not money, and we do not see how that can help us, or you, in this business. We must break off here and commend you to God's protection, &c.

$$\frac{26 \ Oct.}{29 \ Oct.} 1669$$

15 W. MOMMA to CM
NYKÖPING   26 SEPTEMBER 1669

)] Since my last letter I have received yours of the 27th past, from which I understand that 200 coils of my wire have been sold to Ch[arles] Phelps at £5 9s payable in 6 months. With regard to the price it is, as you say, far too low now that there is no wire in any other hands, and I shall have little inclination to send more to [England]. There is none to be had from Holland; at Hamburg they give 62 *ML* cash-down, with the prospect of going higher, so there will be little desire to send it from here. The wire you have just sold you have had in your hands since it was shipped from here in March 1668, and to sell it now for 6 months time means that one has been waiting for one's money for more than two years, which is something this commodity cannot support. You must improve on this long delay. Wherewith my heartiest regards, &c.

$$\frac{26 \ Oct.}{29 \ Oct.} 1669$$

6 J. REENSTIERNA to CM
NORRKÖPING   8 OCTOBER 1669

)] I last wrote to you at length on the 24th past, to which I refer you. I have since received simultaneously both your letters of the 10th and 17th past, to which the answer follows forthwith.

Concerning the £200 advance on bottomry for the Calmar ship, I understood that this had been drawn on and that Mr Pels had disbursed the money while you have not paid out the £200 to Messrs Burkin & Evertsen, so please hold it back until the next post. I shall firstly correspond with Mr Anthony Bruyn the elder about it and then give you further advice.

The kettle-designs[1] have reached Gotland, from whence I am now awaiting them. I hope at last you will get it right for once.

As for your friend who is asking for a consignment of copper, I cannot accommodate him this autumn as I have already told you, and since he is in such a hurry for a delivery I must allow him to be supplied by others. I cannot yet be sure whether I can send anything to [England] this year, but as for next year—God willing—if you agree with my previous proposal, to supply me with money this winter at 6 per cent interest, you could count on receiving a substantial quantity in the spring and I would be able to make a big saving by keeping these large works with all their people in full employment all through the winter— to which I await your decision.

I again commend to you the sale of my goods, especially the thick copper rods. Please sell them for the best you can get—they are good for making small bars from and are quite as good as garcopper.

I have now examined your current account and credited you with £2,316 16s upon a new account dated 6 August—that is to say, for two thousand three hundred and sixteen pounds sterling and 16s.

While brass-ware is now coming solely into your hands I hope you will drive the price up rather higher than it has been so far, particularly as garcopper is steadily getting more expensive. Wherewith, my regards, &c.

¹ '. . . *de Modellen van de keetels.* . .'

$$\frac{27\ Oct.}{28\ Oct.}1669$$

117   R. OURSEL to CM
       ROUEN   1 NOVEMBER 1669

'Le 18 courant estoit a voz graces ma derniere avecq 3 lettres de change accepte par Robert de Pardé le jeune, Pierre Satrin, et Jean Camin, dudepuis j'ay receu les vostres agreables du 4 et 11 passé. Pour responce, j'ay fait payer suivant vostre ordre au Sr Caspersen dans Paris les *W*.300 qu'avez tiré sur moy en sa faveur dont estes debite a vostre compte. Voicy voz 2 lettres de change sur Wildigos et Messrs Le Couteux de retour acceptes et remise pour vostre compte de *W*.1,013 23s 6d en une lettre de *W*.1,000 a 56¾d negotiée a 56d avecq le Sr Jean Musnier quy vous la endossée sur Thomas Rowe a Londres. Il vous plaira en faire procurer le requis et m'en donner credit. Je suis desplaisant de ce que m'avez cy devant ordonné de ne me presser a vous faire remise sur l'esperance que le change auroit augmenté car sytost que voz deniers ont esté receus j'aurois peu vous remettre a 56½d ou tout au moins a 56¼d, au lieu que a present j'ay eub grand peine a obtenir 56d p. *W*. En matiere de change il me semble qu'il vaut tousjours mieux suivre le cours, car l'argent restant en caisse 8 ou 15 jours inutile enporte en intherest du moins ⅛ ou ¼ pour-cent et souventes fois on ne le remet pas plus advantageusement; neangmoins on ne peut mal faire en suivant l'ordre des amis. J'ay eub depuis peu plusieurs marchands pour vostre estain mais nul ne veut venir a £70t du cent. On n'offre que £64t auquel prix il n'y peut avoir de profit, ains grosse perte. Le mal est qu'il y en a grande quantité en ce pays et peu de consommation, non plus qu'en d'autre marchandises.

Cy joint 2 lettres de change, une de *W*.703⅔ a 56½d sur Richard Marsh a Bristoll, et l'autre de *W*.357 a 56½d sur John Hollister aussy a Bristol, toutes deux payables dans Londres desquelles je vous prie faire procurer acceptation et les garder a l'ordre du Sr Jean de Conincq d'Anvers, vous m'obligerez.

Je vous prie me dire sy avez quelque correspondance a Edenborgh en Escosse pour lequel on pourroit donner une lettre de recommandation au Capitaine Oursel quy en cas qu'on prinst resolution de l'envoyer a limkiel¹ charger de cherbon pour revenir en cette ville, que je suis d'advis de proposer aux autres intheresses en son navire a quoy sans doute ils inclineront. Ainsy je vous prie en tout cas en reponce de cette sy y avez quelque cognoissance de m'envoyer une petite lettre de credit affin qu'il puisse tirer sur vous ce quy conviendra pour la charge et nécessité de son navire affin qu'il la puisse porter avecq luy. J'espere par le prochain vous dire ce quy aura esté finallement resolu affin que puissiez en advertir par terre vostre amy. Voilla ce quy s'offre, et vous baizant les mains je demeureray, Monsieur, vostre tres affectionné serviteur.'

Costy: 55⅞ a 56d ⎫
Amsterdam: 99¾g   ⎬ 2 usances.
                      ⎭

¹ Unidentified.

$$\frac{18 \; Nov.}{19 \; Nov.} 1669$$

8 P. VAN TEYLINGEN & CO to CM
VENICE   25 OCTOBER 1669

)] Since our last letter of about a week ago we find ourselves with yours of the 24th past.

In reply, we have sold the remaining small lead received with the *St Justina* at D.50 with 3 months time to Vincenzo Fieri. Accompanying this is the account of the proceeds, your one-third share amounting to D.906 5*g* bank-money. Please credit us, without prejudice, as if the money had come in, and if you check over the account and find it correct please make a note of your concurrence. We are doing everything possible to dispose of the remaining 250 pieces of small lead from the *Thomas and Francis*, and although there are no buyers now at D.49 with 3 months credit we shall let no good opportunity pass.

As you will see at the foot of this letter† we have also sold the remaining 6 bales of pepper from the same ship, together with 21 from the *Pearl* which, God be praised! arrived here this week with the *Frederick*. They took in a passenger at Zante who had been taken there from Candia, and as result they have been unable to obtain *practica*.[1] All the cargo has been sent to the Lazaretto and the pepper as well must be re-packed in other sacks. This will cause further expense, but as there is no other remedy we must be patient. If good purchasers make offers for the remaining 4 sacks we shall take good care of it. We have been made offers for the first to arrive, which we believe will fetch a reasonable price. We understand it ought to be selling in [England] somewhat cheaper but we fear the quantity will pull the price down and we hope that that which your brother[-in-law] John LeTheullier and his friends intend to send will be the first to come to market.

The best Stockholm tar in thin casks was lately sold here at D.42 per 1,000 lb. with 30 per cent tare for the casks. There is not so much demand from buyers for it in thick casks and it sells at D.4 per 1,000 lb. less with 33 per cent tare—all gross weight. Any ship which comes fully laden with these goods, among others, enjoys freedom from the new impost on currants loaded at Zante.

Some salted Irish salmon came with the *Pearl* for which no price has been established but we imagine it will fetch about D.28 to D.30 per barrel. Barbados sugar is at D.6 per hundred-weight with 12 months discount. Spanish muscovadoes are at D.8 with 6 months discount. Gallipoly oil is D.15$\frac{1}{4}$ free on board, and Zante currants have been bought at about *R. pta.* 29.

Be assured that anything further you may be pleased to order will be dealt with as if your, and your friends', interests were as close to our hearts as our own. We remit you herewith another D.1,200 as indicated at the foot of this letter.§ Please do the necessary and credit us accordingly. Herewith goes the second copy of the bill of exchange for D.100 remitted you by our previous letter.

† 1 bale to Rocco Sansonio; 1 to Iseppo Sansonio; 4 to Iseppo Tasso, all at D.75 with 2 months credit.   4 to Gio. Gueringo; 3 to Antonio Michielli at D.75 with 3 months credit.   4 to Gio. Maria Laghi at D.78 with 3 months credit.   10 to Pietro Gerrardi at D.77 with 2 months credit.

§ D.1,200 at 54$\frac{3}{4}$*d* sterling [per ducat] in a bill of Gio. Druveysteyn on Gio. Davis.

We have sold the 100 pieces of lead from the *Pearl* at D.50 with 4 months discount to Bortolo Massalini and it is now being unloaded and delivered to the buyer. This saves the expense of bringing it in. At the moment we see no prospect of improvement to judge by the demand of buyers so far.

[1] I.e. clearance from quarantine.

$$\frac{20\ Nov.}{26\ Nov.}1669$$

119   P. RULAND to CM
HAMBURG   12 NOVEMBER 1669

[D]   My last letter to you was on the 29th past. Since then I have received yours of the 22nd and
29th past, in answer to which I see that you have not been able to fulfil my order for sugar
within my limits because of a price-rise occasioned by the hurricane in Barbados, which
undoubtedly caused much damage, so there is no hope of expecting any this year, particularly
as I revoked my order in my last letter. I perceive it has made great changes in [London] but it
is given little credence here and there is absolutely no change, with reasonable goods still
selling at $6\frac{1}{8}$ to $6\frac{1}{4}g$ @ 13 months discount. I do not believe it will cause any price rise for the
moment as there are good stocks here and our sugar bakers are well provided so that there
will be no lack of it for six months. Consequently there will be no commissions sent to
[England] for a while and the price of sugar in [London] may well fall, particularly as it is
believed that the damage in Barbados was not very great. In addition, it is believed that
satisfactory amounts will be obtainable in the spring and, besides that, the present freight-
rates and the dangers of the sea give one good reason for leaving it alone now.

   Jan Heere coming from England is—God help us—stranded down the Elbe, although the
dry goods have been mostly salvaged. Thank God I have nothing in her.

   Thank you for news of changes—please continue to let me know what is happening
in trade for my guidance. Pepper is quiet here at 19 to $19\frac{1}{8}g$; Aleppo galls 38 *ML*; currants
30–31 *ML* @ 13 months; campeachy-wood $30\frac{1}{2}$ *ML* for cash; oil *RD* 68 to 70. I find nothing
worth doing there.

[P.S.] Whale-fins have risen from 620s. Raisins at 19 to 20 *ML*, or 11 to 12 *ML* per basket,
according to weight.

London: 34s 8g   2 usances.
Amsterdam: $32\frac{1}{3}$ at sight.

$$\frac{20\ Nov.}{16\ Nov.}1669$$

120   A. BERENBERG'S WIDOW & HEIRS to CM
HAMBURG   12 NOVEMBER 1669

[D]   Our last was on the 29th past. We have since received your welcome letter of the 22nd past
from which we have learned the price of various goods, for which we thank you. We shall be
glad if you will continue to inform us sometimes of the price of Ardasse, cotton and sugar,
together with your opinion of these commodities. It is too dangerous to order anything now,
just before the waters close. The weather is so bad that *De Soon* of Hamburg, coming from
[England], has been stranded on Heligoland. One must now wait until the spring, all the
more as there seems to be nothing one can make a profit with to judge from the prices. Sugar
will not rise because of the hurricane in Barbados; the only good it will do is stop it falling
lower. It is now selling for $6\frac{1}{8}$ to $6\frac{1}{4}$ and $6\frac{1}{2}g$ according to quality. The last batch which was
sent still stands unsold—the three butts which were so rusty and bad spoil the whole lot.

   The £240 stg. drawn to pay to the order of Peter Joye @ 35s 7g, 2 usances, has been accepted and will be promptly honoured. We now await from you our current account to see if everything is in order. Wherewith our very best wishes, &c.

London: 34s 10g.
Amsterdam: $32\frac{3}{8}$.

$$\frac{20\ Nov.}{23\ Nov.}1669$$

1 ANDREAS MULDENAER to CM

HAMBURG   13 NOVEMBER 1669

I have safely received yours of the 22nd past and read all its contents. I am surprised that Capt. Hans Johansen, who is carrying 14 lasts and 11 barrels of pitch for my account, had not yet arrived. I hope to God he will have arrived by the time you get this: I long to hear. As regards its sale, please do your best, and if not much is to be got for it I shall have to be satisfied for it was sold for cash. May our dear Lord grant us only good news of it!

As for what you say concerning Mr Maricie[1] having told you that he is in negotiation with me about cloth—I can tell you that I have not been much away from home for seven years, but my father-in-law has frequently contracted with him for large quantities and I have often sent the same people large amounts of iron from Sweden. We have been dealing with one another for $2\frac{1}{2}$ years, but we do not do so anymore and find it is best to take only ready cash. And when one has had no money to buy goods of which one has had need this man has treated us very well but since he has been in the cloth court[2] our trade with one another has come to an end. Since then we have yearly bought large amounts of crown rashes and other sorts of English manufactures. Now we have our goods brought from [England] and every year we make two voyages—one early in spring and the other just before winter. So, please inform me if you have any knowledge of cloth and other manufactures and whether or not you are involved in the Court and whether you can supply me at first hand in return for a yearly commission? If so, we can under God do big business with one another and in return you will be promptly sent other goods such as that in the accompanying bill of lading for a case of linen of the kind which I have sold great amounts of every year to Mr Moricie's factor here. If you can dispose of it a large amount could be sent, and in the accompanying invoice we have stated the price which Mr Moricie's factor always paid us so you can see whether it is reasonable to continue with selling the same.

Please also advise us if steel bars are a good commodity and at what price per ton or per pound they are selling. May God bring the case of linen in safety, with our regards, &c.

[P.S.] Before now I have been sending to [England] iron-bound chests which come from Nürnberg. I do not know if it is convenient for you to deal in them; if not, could you please recommend them to someone who buys such [chests] and let me know what price they fetch. I await your advice on all this and also, if one buys cloth, crown rashes, serges, at what rate they pay duty and whether or not they are burdened with heavy taxes. I understand that if one is a member of the Court one has a great advantage in the duty. If you cannot send the goods here they could well be unloaded at Glückstadt or Stade, as long as they only pay a moderate toll.

---

[1] This may possibly be John Morice who was on the Court of the Merchant Adventurers Company by the 1670s—PRO, C. 8/270/50.

[2] '. . . *maer dardien hee in dee Lacken coort is so woort onse negotie met melcander eyndigen . . .*'. Subsequent references here to 'de Cort' suggest that Muldenaer is referring to the governing body of the Merchant Adventurers in London, of which Marescoe's brother-in-law, John Lethieullier was soon to be head.

$$\frac{29 \; Nov.}{3 \; Dec.} 1669$$

122   TAR COMPANY DIRECTORS to CM

STOCKHOLM   9 OCTOBER 1669

[D]   Our last letter was a week ago, to which we refer you. We have now received together yours of the 10th and 17th past. We looked over the sale account and reported our findings to you in our foregoing letter. We have now received the current account and will have it examined next week before telling you our findings.

We will be mindful of sending the requested 10 lasts of pitch and 70 of tar to Yarmouth as well as the 15 lasts of pitch and 40 of tar to the Isle of Wight if only we can find suitable shipping. We shall use our utmost endeavours. The 4 ships mentioned in our last letter are now all lying together being loaded and by our next we hope to send you all their bills of lading. We are at the moment in negotiation with another to go to [England]: with what success we will tell you later.

The Lord God be praised for the arrival of Matthys Boriesen and Erick Anderson—may He bring the others in safety! It is good that you have been able to sell all the cargoes of the above mentioned and we hope the rest will be similarly disposed of.

Concerning the proposition of your two friends about buying 600 lasts of tar and 200 lasts of pitch, we refer you to our previous letter and would prefer to look for the highest possible price, though if your friends would move a little further and go up to £9 and £12 we would agree to it. The offer of £8½ and £11½ is too little. [We are doing our best to bring it to the highest price.][1]

Concerning the case of the water balliage on which you seek our approval for spending more. We urge you to do as you would for yourself, and if you see something to be gained by it we shall gladly spend more, but if it is a matter of spending yet more on an uncertainty and then losing the case we would rather lose now than later, so we suggest that you do as you would for yourself. The directors of the Västervik Ship Company have probably forgotten to advise you about placing £177 15s 2d expenses on their account, but they entered in to it voluntarily and in fairness they must do so because it is their case as much as ours. We shall speak to them about it so that you can get instructions from them.

By our previous letter we asked you about giving Mr Deutz another £2,000 stg. on top of the first £2,000 because we would be sending you as much or more in goods, and now you say you have written to Mr Deutz that he could draw £200–£300—by which you doubtless mean 'thousands'. If that is the case, and if you will remit to him as we requested, we most cordially thank you. He will not have done so yet, but we are very pleased that you have written to him and that you will duly honour his bills when he draws on you, though most of the drafts we have made on him fall due in January and February. We hope you have taken care of the insurance on all those ships as we ordered.

As we have said to you before, though with much regret, there is nothing here to be hoped for from Peter Simons. It is very annoying that one must suffer loss for one's good will, but what can one do? We too think it is hard. We remain, &c.

---

[1] This is a marginal insertion, in German, probably by the director Jacob Porteous.

23 P. VAN TEYLINGEN & CO to CM

VENICE   22 NOVEMBER 1669

D] We find ourselves with your welcome letter of the 22nd past. In reply, we await your convenience to know if, having received the accounts of the 901 pieces of small lead and the 100 pieces of great lead sold at Genoa, you have found them satisfactory. We send you herewith the account of the 250 pieces received from the *Thomas & Francis*, of which half the proceeds amounts to D.528 16g bank-money. Please credit us accordingly, without prejudice, while the money comes in, and after you have checked the account and found it correct please record your agreement. That commodity remains here still at D.48 because there is plenty in town and the buyers are for the moment well-provided since—God be praised—the *John & Thomas* arrived here yesterday bringing another good quantity. But as the price remains stable in England and apparently little more will be sent we hope it may improve in price, particularly in the spring.

The 462 bars as well as the 17 casks of tin are being offered at the highest price possible, but we regret that the 9 casks which we received earlier must be kept in the warehouse as the quantity does not suit the buyers. We hope the batch in the casks will do better and find a quicker sale. We will let you know how we fare in our next.

We see that you have loaded in the *Providence*, for your account, 50 bales of pepper and 75 pieces of great lead, and that Mr Lethieullier and other friends will load yet more, amounting to 300 bales of pepper and 450 pieces of lead. We thank you for your kindness in recommending us to others and we shall not fail to do our duty, seeking at all times to sell quickly and at the highest price possible and making speedy returns to your friends. We hope to hear by your next that the ship has departed. May the Lord protect him from mishap and give him a speedy arrival so that the pepper gets here before the candle-days.[1] Otherwise, the season will be over. Many say that whoever arrives here before the others can expect to profit, for undoubtedly the first to arrive will get the best prices.

We understand that *The Brothers* has also been consigned here with a large amount, and was lying in the Downs on the point of departure, but as he must go and load the rest of his cargo with furs we hope the *Providence* will get here before him. We see that your friends then plan to procure returns in oil. The latter is selling at D.15½ per *salm*, free on board, at Gallipoly where it is better value than elsewhere in Apuglia and where most of it is loaded for [England] and other regions. At Bari it is fetching D.15¾ free on board, the measure there being about 6 per cent larger than at Gallipoly but the oil is of worse quality. One can get reasonably good oil at Taranto but we understand there are no good barrels to be obtained there and the price of the oil is about the same as at Gallipoly, so in our opinion it would be best to be provided there. The new oil should be clear by the end of January. It was ordered here that a quarter of last year's oil should not be put on sale and the remainder kept at a high price, but nevertheless it is the opinion of our friends that it may initially fall rather lower as long as no large commissions are obtained. I believe the said ships will be able to lade the new oil and think it might not be inadvisable to lade 20 lasts of heavy oil as ballast, as was tried last with the *Gratia*. The oil was well-stowed and arrived with little leakage, and since the last of oil is small we should be able to count on loading at least 700 *salm* or more, at 10 *salms* per last, as it is a ship of 160 tons. You and your friends can best decide what you judge to be advisable and order us to act accordingly.

There have been no further letters from Zante. The general opinion is that currants there will cost more than *R. pta.* 32; on Cephalonia they are paying *R. pta.* 26 and 27. The *John & Thomas* is also going there to fetch its lading and will need a pretty large amount.

Barbados muscovado sugar—D.6 with 12 months time; ditto from Lisbon—D.6 with 6 months. Pepper, since there is little or none left in town, sells at the second hand for D.84. Veronese rice D.18, with freight for Amsterdam *f.*65 per last. No change in other commodities.

We remit you herewith D.400 as detailed at the foot of this letter, for which please procure the needful and credit us accordingly. Wherewith our cordial regards, &c.

London—54⅓d.   Amsterdam—95⅝.

[P.S.] D.400 at 54⅜d sterling drawn on Henry Mudd by Hailes & Ravenscroft. In the pepper account there is a mistake: your ⅓ amounts to D.1,002 13g. Please alter it.

¹ '. . . *voor de ka[a]rs daghen* . . .'.

$$\frac{4\ Dec.}{17\ Dec.}1669$$

124   J. REENSTIERNA tO CM
         NORRKÖPING   19 NOVEMBER 1669

[D]   My last letter to you was on the 5th instant, to which I refer. I have now got both yours of the 15th and 22nd October together, to which the answer now follows.

I have seen how much of my goods you have sold and that you think you could dispose of the rest quite shortly and are therefore expecting what further I should have despatched to you, especially in the ship you are awaiting from here—but you will have learned from my last letter that I have heard nothing more of that ship, in which I would otherwise have sent a consignment, and since no other opportunity of shipping has turned up you must wait until the spring. Meanwhile you would not do badly to sell all my remaining goods in your hands at the highest possible price so that we can close the account, and in the spring—God willing—I can supply you with new goods. As for having more small rods made I shall take note of what you wrote.

I have credited you with 7s too little which you entered by mistake for the freight you paid to Jacob Grys. You will have learned already that I have assigned on you the £200 stg., which you should have paid to Messrs Burckin & Evertsen, to pay to the order of Mr Anthony Bruyn the elder, who will have sent the assignment to Mr Philip Pelt Emanuel—which I beg you to fulfil. As for the £296 stg. which you remitted to the Messrs Van Baerle for my account on the 8th of October, I have already credited you with it on the advice of the Van Baerles—as I informed you in my last letter.

I have seen your reply about advancing money to help keep my copper-works going and I am grateful to you for being willing to pay the value of any goods of mine you have in my hands.

Mr Marescoe, I cannot neglect to advise you that I have been approached by others from whom you have goods on commission that I should agree to join them in placing our [English] commissions in other hands. The reason is that you do not manage the expenses very well and tend to make them rather too large. How much truth there is in that you can best judge for yourself but I can only give you this friendly advice to serve as far as possible as a warning of what to expect, for without it you could easily lose their commissions, especially the principal commission for copper-ware and rods as well as of iron. I have delayed any such change, and but for that it would have happened. Wherewith, regards, &c.

$$\frac{9\ Dec.}{13\ Dec.}1669$$

25 R. OURSEL to CM
ROUEN   13 DECEMBER 1669

'Le 3 courant estoit a voz graces ma derniere avecq remise pour vostre compte de *W*.1,011 en 2 lettres dont voicy une seconde de *W*.300 n'ayant peu encor avoir l'autre de l'endosseur; dudepuis la vostre agreable du 22 passe Vieil stile m'est bien parvenue avecq remise pour vostre compte de *W*.1,188 en 2 lettres sur cette ville et Paris. On procurera le payement de l'une et negotieray l'autre au pair, pour vous en faire crediteur. Voicy de retour vostre lettre de *W*.300 acceptée par Salomon Faulcon de Dieppe et remise pour vostre compte *W*.2,000 a $55\frac{1}{2}d$ $2\frac{1}{2}$ usances sur Humphrey Grave a Londres en lettre Humphrey Wilkings dont il vous plaira faire procurer le requis et m'en faire crediteur. Les changes se tiennent bas j'avois esperé vous remettre ce-jourdhuy le reste de vostre avance mais n'ay peu rencontrer de lettres d'entiere satisfaction, ce sera Dieu aydant par le prochain n'estoit qu'il y eust entretemps apparence de rehausse ce que j'observeray comme sy c'estoit pour moy mesme.

Au commerce peu de changement. Il y avoit quelque chose a faire aux fanons de balaine. Il y a 8 jours que j'en ay vendu bonne partie a £80*t* le cent quy en auroit a present pourroit obtenir £100*t*. L'estain demeure a £65*t*; plomb £115*t* le millier sans demande. Sy remarquez que voz marchandises propres pour le d'Estroit baissent chez vous et que par ce moyen il y eust quelque chose a faire en les envoyant par voye de France on pourroit se servir du previlege de l'entrepost que le Roy a accordé aux negotians, c'est a dire libre entrée et sortie des marchandises quy seront destines pour estre portes hors le royaume sans payer aucuns droitz. Nous aurons tousjours de bons navires en charge au Havre, pour Cadiz, Allicante et Marseille, ce quy vous sert d'advis, et n'ayant autre je vous salue demeurant, Monsieur, vostre tres affectione serviteur.

Costy:	$55\frac{3}{8}d$
Amsterdam:	$98\frac{1}{4}g$ $\}$ 2 usances.
Anvers:	$97\frac{1}{4}g$

Sy joint avez une seconde lettre de change de *W*.700 sur Thomas Rowe a Londre.'

13 Dec. 1669
4 Jan. 1670

26 P. BERENBERG to CM
HAMBURG   30 NOVEMBER 1669

Since you will have learned from others that your drafts relating to the last batch of sugar cannot be met, I find myself obliged to reveal to you that it has not been done out of ill-will or design but simply because I have gone out of business.[1] All last year I suffered great losses here, as a result of which I have not only lost my capital but have fallen into debt. I had hoped with time and God's blessing to recover myself and have done all that was possible but, as credit has been very scarce in these troubled times and has finally deserted me, it has been necessary to acquaint my creditors with my lack of means and as a demonstration of my honesty I have decided neither to run away nor to trouble people further but have proffered my books with all their debts to reveal my whole condition and to contribute all that still remains to me in the world to re-payment. Each and everyone feels compassion for me since they see what misfortunes have overtaken me. I hope that no further injuries will be inflicted upon me, and I herewith beg you with much boldness to be pleased to give such orders about your claim that the business may be settled all the easier. Its furtherance in such circumstances is to your advantage and that of all the creditors, while holding up the business will inflict great prejudice on all the interested parties. If the Lord is pleased to bless me again I shall discharge myself to you and all the others so that everyone will be able to see my good character clearly. This business has not been contrived to distress anyone or to benefit me by one stuiver, but great losses have forced me to beg for compassion from each and everyone. I shall also call upon the Lord my God, that he may richly recompense the interested parties for their loss, and will also do my best to deserve it so that I can satisfy my friends to the best of my ability, seeking from God his his grace and blessing, to whose protection I commend you, remaining, &c.

¹ '. . . dat het mij aen de markt heeft ontbroeken.'

$\frac{17\ Dec.}{18\ Dec.}1669$

127 T. WRIGHT to CM
[STOKESLEY]   13 DECEMBER 1669

'Sir, I have not had one line from you since those of the 31th of July: I hope mine of the 21th of August came safe to you and I hope you received the salmon I sentt but feare not in soe good condition as I cold have wished it, but the weather was hott. The schipp master told mee hee tooke as greate a care of it as hee cold.

Sir, the tyme of the yeare beinge come that you did use to provide leade ocations mee to give you the best advise I cann. This drie sumer hath much hindrd the makeinge of leade haveinge wanted water both to theire mills and alsoe to wash theire ore, soe that leade is somethinge scarcer and for price none to bee bought under £13 p. fother, 21 cwt. to the fother, soe if you please to have any bought I will doe you the best servis I cann. Butter is now with us to bee hadd for 17*s* p. firkine the best. Sir, haveinge given you theese advises I have noe more to add but shall pray for your prosperity, wishinge you a merry Christmas, a new happie blessed and comfortable new year, soe with my servis to you selfe and Mrs Marescoe I remaine, Sir, &c.

[P.S.] My servis to Mr Joy.'

$\frac{5\ Jan.}{8\ Jan.}1670$

128 W. BROWNE to CM
BRISTOL   3 JANUARY 1670

'Sir, I have yours of the 1st instant in due tyme and am sorry to see how high the premio on insurance runs in the Streights. I cannot beleive the dainger to be soe great as they make beleive by theyr high demands, soe unlesse you can gett it effected for me on the *Robert &*

Hester for 2 p.cent p.mens. if for 6 monthes certaine and soo only for £250, the rest being willing to run the adventure, off my selfe and 150£ on my $\frac{1}{16}$ part of the cargo of the *Resolution* from Zante if to be done at 10 p.cent for Bristoll. More I am not willing to give because I am confident they will have convoy downe from Legorne. I see how you have vallewed my interest upon both ships which is, I know, lesse then what I am concerned but that matters nothing to the busynes. If it cannot be effected at the above prises I shall desyre you to keepe by you the policyes yett a little longer. I have not received any more mony for you yett when have shall advise you. I hope the last bill of 100£ on Mr Gibbs will be well paid you and soe I rest, your loving freinde, &c.

[P.S.] The ironmongers begin to want iron soe if you can fitt such a parcell as I gave you a memory off to be heere in the spring I suppose will goe off to content and by that tyme the pitch and tarr in the citty will be well consumed.'

$$\frac{8\ Jan.}{11\ Jan.}1670$$

129 J. PÖTTER & H. THUEN to CM
STOCKHOLM   11 DECEMBER 1669

[D] Our last letter was a fortnight ago, to which we refer. We have since received yours of the 19th November with the sale account of the iron sent with the *St Anna*. We have looked it over, found it correct and noted our agreement with you.

We see you have paid £100 sterling to Capt. Jacob Gries for which he has signed a bottomry bill and you request our approval—to which we answer that the bottomry bill is valueless as our colleagues will not approve it. He shall repay the £100 here and it will then be remitted to you. The captain did it without instructions and had no reason to imagine that he needed the money as our colleagues had taken care that he could get credit at Lisbon if he found himself short for his salt cargo.

We see you have sold 238 bars of iron from Gothenburg at 13s 6d p. cwt. That is good and we urge you to keep our interests at heart with the remainder as the consignments sold this summer have turned to poor account.

The Messrs Louis de la Bistrate & Jacob Frederick Dufay at Amsterdam advise us that they have drawn £330 sterling on you, not doubting that you will have honoured these drafts as you have previous orders and noted them on our account.

Trade has finished here for the year and the sea and all rivers can only be traversed with horse and sledge, and there is a great shortage of water at the works so there will not be much iron ready for the spring. We suggest therefore that you hold on to our remaining iron, for the market must rise.

As for the £100 which you gave to the captain of the *St Anna* on the credit of his salt cargo we shall, as we said above, make you a remittance as soon as it arrives. The captain had no need to trouble you. The price at which the iron has been sold in Bristol is disgraceful—it would have been better to sell it here. As for the samples of materials[1] you sent, they are not in demand here—we can get them cheaper in Holland, wherewith our cordial regards, &c.

---

[1] '... *de gesondene modellen van stoffen* ...'—presumably textiles.

$$\frac{8\ Jan.}{11\ Jan.}1670$$

130 TAR COMPANY DIRECTORS to CM
STOCKHOLM   11 DECEMBER 1669

[D] Our last letter was about a week ago, to which we refer, and since then we have received nothing from you. In our foregoing letter we said of Capt. Jan Pietersen that he had run into Boswyck in order to repair his ship, but the leak was nothing serious and was soon mended and he has since gone to sea again, so we hope to hear of his arrival soon. Meanwhile, a week ago, we made a note of the insurance you made upon him and have credited your account with £22 6s 7d for the premium and expenses. We long to hear that you have also taken care of the insurance on the ships following, and with regard to that we refer you to our preceding letter.

Concerning the advance of money on our goods according to contract, we send herein a detailed account[1] specifying how much they amount to. As we have repeatedly told you, we have to make good that total to Mr Joseph Deutz on whom we have drawn *RD* 30,000, but Mr Deutz says that he has not yet had full agreement from you as to the sum which you will accept, and that you will only accept as much as the goods in your hands amount to. But that was not the intention of the contract which clearly states, in the words of the 5th article, that whenever the Company sends the bill of lading for any pitch or tar and gives orders for it to be insured, then the Company may draw or have drawn on you for each last of tar £5 and for each last of pitch £8, which you promised to accept and pay. So we again request you to make good and pay Deutz the sums specified in the above-mentioned statement when he draws on you, because the time is approaching when our bills on him fall due. We shall let Deutz know that he can proceed with assurance, for we would lose his respect if we gave any orders contrary to the terms of our contract. Our credit would plunge steeply and you can be sure that he would not be so ready to take our bills in future. Therefore we must show him that he can get his reimbursement from you, or anyone else. We await your reply with quiet confidence, breaking off here with our best wishes, &c.

 [1] The detailed account is in fact enclosed with the Company's next letter of 15 December. It put Marescoe's liabilities for 635$\frac{2}{13}$ lasts of tar and 286 lasts of pitch, despatched but not sold, at £5,463; for quantities already sold, £1,064 3s. Against this it credited him with £895 3s 1d, but Marescoe's note of sums owing to him for pitch and tar sold to 14 clients by 20 January 1670 puts the total outstanding at £6,952 17s 10d.

$$\frac{25\ Jan.}{[25\ Jan.]}1670$$

131 A. MULDENAER to CM
HAMBURG   14 JANUARY 1670

[D] I last wrote to you on the 17th of December, to which I refer. Since then I have safely received yours of the 31st [December] and am surprised to see that you had not received my latest. I have received all your letters and am delighted to learn of Hans Heeren's safe arrival—the good Lord be praised!

To your news, that the pitch and the linen are safe in the warehouse awaiting buyers, that you have sold some pitch at £12 per last payable in 8 months time, and that you hope to get a still higher price I say in reply that I heartily wish you had not sold it at such long time, for a lot of mishaps can occur during 8 months. I beg you as a friend not to sell at such long time if possible, and I do not doubt that it will suit you to do so seeing that you are content to do without double commission. Besides, it will breed more business. I long to know what is happening and I wish with all my heart to hear from you regarding the linen and to know what we can do with it. If the price yields something I shall send you 1,000 pieces or more every year, as long as consumption is that large, and I shall not seek any exceptional profit as long as I can cover my costs, because between here and Nürnberg we are making a loss. My brother-in-law is on the point of departure for places like Linz where the linen comes from and where he will obtain another consignment. We wait to hear what you think about sending another batch as soon as the rivers unfreeze. As regards the wool, it still remains unsold but we have had offers from an Englishman here who will make a deal for it, half in cash and half in goods. As wool remains at 15s per lb. I am not sure what to do. If, at your convenience, you could inform me at what prices silk stockings and all kinds of men's and women's stockings are selling I shall see if I shall have some bought.

Some days ago Joris Schrodering, a member of one of our great houses,[1] went out of business and two days ago killed himself in depression, causing the failure of George Mattzen as a result of many great suspicions. He had served many important merchants on commission, but I am involved only to the extent of 1 barrel of Nürnberg-ware, a remnant of eight years' dealings. Things are very bad here.

You were perhaps corresponding with the Swedish Treasurer, Borgh Oloffson Cronenberg, in Stockholm? He has been dismissed and so have Generals Wilhelm Drakenhielm and Starrenflicht. Hinrich Thuen is now the Royal Treasurer and people are now making great efforts to find ways of serving him.[2]

Since times are so bad here I shall make use of your offer of help and may well draw £125 or £150 on you in my next letter, as long as you will advance the money at $\frac{1}{2}$ per cent per month until my goods are sold to that amount. I beg you to accept my bills and wish you a prosperous New Year,

&c.

[1] For the Schröttering family see Reissmann *Die hamburgische Kaufmannschaft des 17. Jahrhunderts*, pp. 79, 82, 85, 97, 192, 269 n. 313, 372, 379, 381.

[2] These dismissals and appointments were part of an important shake-up in De La Gardie's administration, for which see Wittrock II, p. 254. Olof Starenflycht was one of the copper-contractors of 1667 in Cronberg's syndicate; Wilhelm Drakenhielm was Administrator-General of Customs (or 'generaltullförvalteren')— Wittrock, II, pp. xvi, 133, 180, 188, 191, 192, 254 n. 1.

(i) + (ii) $\frac{31\ Jan.}{21\ Feb.}$1670

32   DEATH, SKINNER & BALL to JL

LEGHORN   (i)   10 JANUARY 1670

'Sir, Haveing none of yours unanswered these are cheifely to tell you that many parcells of lead haveing binn this weeke bought up at D.21 the 1,000 lb. we have soe also cleared the accompt of your small lead soe soone as consigned which hope may be next week you shall have the accompt sale thereof. 3 or 4 barrels more of your tinn we have also sould at D.13$\frac{1}{2}$ and soe we intend to refuse noe good buyers that may present. Severall bags of pepper hath also binn bought up to consigne at D.14$\frac{7}{8}$ soe that the Itallians being now themselves ingaiged therein and a rumour too of difference twixt France and Holland in which its thought we must also necessarily be ingaged, there's noe appearance in our opinion it should fall. Pore jack goes selling at 41 *giulio* the quintall,[1] pilcherds 21 [dollars] the hogshead. The *Jersey* and

Centurion men of war, with the *Bantam, George, Industry, Phenix, Falmouth* and *Pellican*, togeather with a Hollander under there convoy, went hence the 7th current; the *Concord, Ingram, Dorothy* and *Welcome* for Apuglia, *Martin* for Venetia and *Merchant's Delight* for Zante waite onely a faire wind. The *Faulcon* and *Speedwell* men of warr, being to victual here, may be yet some daies in porte. About 1,500 salme of oyle hath binn this weeke bought up for contant at *D*.15 the salme, monies of Naples and measure of Galipoly.

London—56¾*d* riseing.   Venetia—105¼.   Amsterdam—100.   Naples—93.   Genoa—1½ per cent losse to the drawers.'

(ii)   17 JANUARY 1670
(not selected)

¹ There were 10½ *giulios* (or Julios) to the ducat, 9 to the dollar and 1½ to the livre, and thus at the current rate of exchange on London 1 *giulio* = 6.3 pence sterling. The 'poor jack' quintal was 150 lb.

(i) + (ii) $\dfrac{14\ Feb.}{[\quad\ ]}$1670

133   J. FREYHOFF to CM
         LA ROCHELLE   (i)   27 JANUARY 1670

'Monsieur, Le 23 du courant j'ay respondu a la vostre agreable du 23 du passe et vous dit le necessaire, depuis m'est parvenue celle du 3 de ce mois et voy que ma remise de £120 sterling sur Mons. Batailhe vous estoit bien parvenue et que mesme vous en avies eu acceptation, ce quy est bien. Pour les regard des autres remises sur Paris Mons. Cadelan me mande qu'il les avoit bien receues, qu'il en procureroit acceptation et vous les envoyeroit ce que je veux croire qu'il aura fait depuis. Il est vray qu'il y a quelque douceurs a present sur le change a remettre d'icy pour Londres mais les lettres sont le plus souvent si rares que dans un mois ou 6 semaines on n'en trouvera pas pour *W*.1,000 quy fait que l'on est oblige faute de lettres de garder l'argeant des amis en caisse et de plus nous avons icy tant de gens quy recherchent des lettres estrangeres quy font ordinairement la banque que moins que de donner quelque chose audela du cours. Il n'est pas facile d'en trouver si bien que c'est un negoce en cette ville quy est fort casuel, neantmoins si vous desirez y faire quelque chose de bon coeur je vous y serviray et menageray vos intherests comme propres. On a d'ordinaire ½ pour-cent de commission et l'on ne paye point de courtage. Les lettres pour Paris se negotient le plus souvent au par a uso a present perdent ¼ a ½ pour cent pour avis. Je vous suis oblige de vos souhaits en cette nouvelle annee et reitaire les miens a ce quelle et plusieurs autres vous soit heureuse, demeurant toujours, &c.

Londres—28 a 28½ pour cent, 2 usances, et tres peu de lettres.'

(ii)   6 FEBRUARY 1670

134   'Monsieur, Nous sommes au 6 Fevrier, ce que de l'autre part estant copie de ma derniere du 27 du passe a lequelle me refere. Depuis j'ay la vostre agreable du 13 dudit a laquelle j'ay peu a dire y satisfaisant par ma ditte derniere, vous priant de croire que j'aurois bien de la joye que nous puissions establir ce negoce de change et que je vous y servirois de bon coeur mais certes il est si casuel et il y a si peu de fondement a faire sur les remises d'icy faute de lettres que je n'oze y engager personne joint que fort souvent on donne autant icy pour les lettres qu'a Paris et plus. Quant a mes remises provenant de votre plomb je ne doute point qu'elles ne vous soyent parvenues depuis quoy que je n'aye receu aucune lettre de Mons. Cadelan depuis ma derniere.

Je suis bien aize que ne soyez intheresse dans la faillette du Sr Thomas Verbecq; je n'y suis pas nonplus, Dieu mercy. Voila un miserable temps!—Dieu nous en donne un meilleur, s'il luy plaist.

Le plomb a este vendu en Cherante £94*t* le cent. Il ne reste plus de bon vin de petite borderie a vendre, seulement quelqu' 150 tonneaux de grand borderie et des vins de St Jean. L'eau-de-vie est a £58*t* les $\frac{27}{v}$ quitte, avecq plus d'apparence de hausser que de baisser, pour avis.

Je vous baize les mains et vous prie d'estre persuade qu'en quoy que ce soit ou il songera de vous rendre service, je m'y employeray avecq plaisir ayant pour vostre personne toute la veneration que je doibs avoir—je suis vostre tres humble serviteur.

Paris: au par a uso.
Londres: 28 pour cent.   ⎫
Amsterdam: $21\frac{1}{2}$ a 22 pour-cent. ⎬ 2 usances.
                             ⎭

$$\frac{28\ Feb.}{[\text{———}]}1670$$

35 R. OURSEL to CM
    ROUEN   4 MARCH 1670

'Monsieur, Le 28 courant est a voz graces ma derniere avecq remise pour vostre compte de *W*.650 a $56\frac{1}{2}d$ 2 usances sur Richard Bogan du depuis n'ay receu aucune vostre cequy causera moins dire et sera seullement pour vous remettre encor cy joint pour vostre dit compte *W*.380 4*s* a $56\frac{3}{8}d$ p. *W*. en une lettre de *W*.380 55*s* a $56\frac{1}{4}d$ du 12 Febvrier 2 usances sur Thomas Littman a Bristoll payable dans Londres au logis de John Martins.[1] Il vous plaira retirer la premiere lettre acceptee en vertu de la presente seconde que je vous envoye et m'en faire crediteur. Les changes ont peine a rehausser et a esté fait ce jourdhuy comme au piedt de cette. J'estimes qu'ils hausserent davantage quand les effects de la flotte d'Espaigne commenceront a venir en voz cartiers et en Hollande; toutefois on en attend aussy bon nombre en ce pays ce quy pourra tenir les affaires en balance. Depuis ma derniere n'ay eub aucun marchand pour vostre estain. Je ne laisseray perdre bonne occasion quand il s'en presentera, vous donnant advis du succez, et n'ayant autre je vous salue, demeurant Monsieur vostre tres affectione serviteur.'

Costy: $56\frac{1}{2}d$ ⎫
Amsterdam: $98\frac{1}{2}g$ ⎬ 2 usances.

---

[1] The foot of this letter carries Marescoe's scribbled calculations that 380 crowns, 4 sous, at $56\frac{3}{8}d$ sterling per crown were equivalent (as nearly as could be, at £89 5*s* $6\frac{1}{2}d$) to 380 crowns, 55 sous at $56\frac{1}{4}d$.

B. LETTERS TO LEONORA MARESCOE & PETER JOYE

(i) + (ii) + (iii) $\frac{14\ Nov.}{18\ Nov.}$1670

136   J. VAN SAVELANT to LM
GOTHENBURG   (i)   3 OCTOBER 1670

[D]   In his last letter, of 30 August, the late Mr Marescoe also enclosed the sale account of the iron which was sent with Hans Stoltervoet. I have looked it over and agreed the account for net proceeds of £476 19s 3d. According to our agreement with the late Marescoe please remit the money either to the widow of Liebert Wolters at Hamburg or to Mr Abraham Bex at Amsterdam, wherever the profit for me seems likely to be the greater.

I have now received Mr Peter Joye's letter of 9 September, informing me of Mr Marescoe's death—may the Lord grant him a blessed resurrection and us also when the time comes. Your sorrow touches me to the heart, but we must bear patiently with the will of the Lord, against which there is nothing we can do.

I have been delighted to learn of the arrival of Capt. Anders Beursen with my Slb. 238.12 of iron—God be praised! I hope it has come to a good market. There are some voyages to Guinea fitting out in [England] so I have no doubt that this consignment of voyage iron will be found useful, particularly as I have had all the defective bars picked out during the weighing. God be with you.

(ii)   18 OCTOBER 1670

137   The above, of 3 October, is a copy of my last, to which I refer you. I have now received a letter from you and Mr Peter Joye dated the 9th past—I mean to say, the 23rd past. As I mentioned before, I await my current account so I can record my concurrence.

I am unhappy to see that you have found the iron which I sent with Beursen to be not as good as I described it to be, and that you suppose it to be the remnants of iron which I was unable to sell here. To reply, I have never in my life had to pick and choose any iron but have always sold and delivered each lot as it comes. I have now been dealing in voyage iron for over 50 years and before I came to Sweden I supplied large amounts in Holland, at 34 bars per 1,000 lb.—Holland-weight and have had it done so here without any complaints. Six weeks ago the West India Company of Groningen bought 200 slb of voyage iron without any complaint and they were satisfied with 34 bars per 1,000 lb. as above.

I beg you to do your best to see that the owners of the ship *De Vergulden Valck* can obtain their payment as well as the owners of *Den Witte Swaen*. I urge this upon you most strongly if you intend to continue in business. You undoubtedly know well the agreement which existed between me and your late husband—that I should allow him 3 per cent for provision in return for which he would bear all bad debts and the cost of remittances through the exchanges, and advance money at 6 per cent. I shall be glad to hear if you are willing to continue on the same terms. With regards, &c.

(iii)   25 OCTOBER 1670

138   The above, of the 3rd and 18th of October, are copies of my previous letters despatched with Capt. Peter Carelsen who, because of contrary winds, is lying here still. He has mostly pitch on board, with which there is little to be done. This is going by the ordinary post, to be sent on to you under Abraham Bex's cover in case Peter Carelsen is a long time on his way. With regards, &c.

[P.S.] Remit the money to Hamburg to Widow Wolters or to Abraham Bex at Amsterdam, wherever the exchange is most profitable.

$$\frac{6\ Mar.}{18\ Apr.}1671$$

39 W. BROWNE to PJ & CO
BRISTOL   4 MARCH 1671

'Sir, I have yours of the 2nd instant by which I see you cannot make an absolute bargaine for 100 tuns of Swedish iron tell you heere from thence, soe what my freinde would be willing to give he will not say but I veryly believe if I had 100 tuns heere such as your Brother Marescoe consigned me in August 1669 anno and assorted as that was I might have from 16 to 17£ p. tun for it, for iron is at present very scarce in towne and our Forest iron mungers keepe them but from hand to mouth.

When any parcell of Jamaica indigo arives that may be worth your buying I shall give you notis of it and in what else I may be sarvisable to you plese to command, your assured frende, W.B.'

$$\frac{3\ Apr.}{4\ Apr.}1671$$

40 S. DE GEER to LM & PJ
AMSTERDAM   10 APRIL 1671

I wrote in haste by the last post and have since received yours of the 21st and 24th of March by which I see that you have sold the remaining iron at £16 10s [p. ton] for cash, which is very good. I hope to see the account soon.

I have also noted what has been happening with that person concerning the 60 tons to be delivered at Stockholm, free on board. The proposal will certainly not suit me. I would not want to deliver it to an English ship for only £12 because the customs liability on each shippound would amount to about a quarter of that, quite apart from the Sound Toll which will be at least 150 RD. And as for going to France to fetch salt and bringing it to Stockholm, that will not do because there is no demand for French salt in Sweden and there would be no return from the investment. It is better to drop the whole idea until May when the amount of iron coming in will increase. No ships can leave Sweden before then because I doubt that there have been more than four days of thaw so far.

If your friend tries to go looking for a cargo for his ship in the manner you describe his ship would be at least half-pawned[1] before it came home again. I would not advise him to go to Sweden with an English ship: the difference in duties is too great.

The bill of lading for the remaining pan iron which we have here was sent to you by the last letter. The captain is quite ready to go but the low water prevents him from leaving, with which I remain, &c.

---

[1] '. . . *syn schip well halft af-boort eer weder te heuys quam.*'

$$\frac{3\ Apr.}{7\ Apr.}1671$$

141 L. TRIP TO LM & PJ
AMSTERDAM   10 APRIL 1671

[D] I have received your letter of the 24th of March. If you had sent me the account of your sales of the 400 bars of iron I would have been able to decide whether or not to send a further quantity. I shall only decide to do it if I receive the account and can reckon on some profit. I must say that to sell at 6 months time is too long, and for the money to be discounted without prejudice to you is really too much of a risk. As soon as the money comes in I shall expect its remittance.

I have sent you 400 bars of square iron in Jacob Hendrixsen's ship *De Schol*. As Liège iron, one-inch thick, this iron must be sold for at least 15s 6d [p. cwt] or else it cannot be sent. I hope it will go higher. I am paid here £7¾ [flem.] per 100 lb. in cash for the kind I send to England. As a sample I have sent with the captain 25 bars of light, flat-iron weighing (in our weight) 600 lb. It is marked with an 'S' and is extraordinarily fine, tough iron as you will be able to see, and it is the sort of iron from which pistols and muskets are made. Find out what price per hundred-pounds you can sell it for and if I consider there is some profit to be made I shall send you a quantity. The square iron is marked 'B' and is of much better material than the flat-iron I have sent. God protect you, &c.

[P.S.] I have just received your letter of the 28th and must say that if you had sent the account I would have been able to make an estimate. The iron I sent you which you have sold is carefully forged and is purer than Swedish. And as for what you say about somewhat thinner iron, I cannot deliver you any although I could pick out some of the longer bars from the kind marked with the Lute, but then you would only get 32 or 33 bars instead of 34 in every 1,000 lb. The ship in which the square iron is loaded sailed for the Texel this evening and will go to sea with the first favourable wind.

$$\frac{8\ Apr.}{11\ Apr.}1671$$

142 W. MOMMA TO LM & PJ
NYKÖPING   19 MARCH 1671

[D] My last letter to you was on the 19th past, to which I refer you. Since then I have received yours of the 10th and 17th ditto.

Regarding the copper farthings, I have made a further calculation and if the Master of the Mint can get them for £6 15s he had better buy them and leave the sellers no profit.[1] Unless I can get £7 5s there is no point in my starting, for it involves much expense and great wastage and they cannot be delivered profitably for only £6 15s.

I see that you have sold more of my wire to Smith & Bryan at £6 5s for 50 coils payable in 6 months; another 30 coils to William Schevin[2] at £6 and 15 at £6 5s, payable in 1 month; and to Elizabeth Packer 20 coils at £6 5s payable in 6 months. So there remain only 197 coils to sell, since I have had news of another 163 being sold. You will continue to do your best to sell the remainder and I shall await the account. I have a quantity of wire lying at Stockholm ready to load into the first ship going for [London] but it will not be leaving very soon because we cannot expect open water for another month. Iron is dear here at 30 to 32 d.c.m.

per shippound and it appears that the duties on iron and brass will increase, so I see no prospect of a fall in prices. Time will tell, wherewith my regards, &c.

¹ Momma is referring to the Mint's offer of 14½d per lb. (i.e. £6 15s per cwt.) for Swedish copper blanks, the terms which Pötter & Thuen found acceptable [143] and which Cronström finally contracted for. See *CTB, 1669–1672* (ii) pp. 819, 1094–5; C. Wilson Peck, *English Copper, Tin and Bronze Coins in the British Museum, 1558–1958* (London, 1960) pp. 601–3.

² I.e. William Sherwin, ironmonger and a regular customer of the firm.

$$\frac{8\ Apr.}{14\ Apr.}1671$$

3   J. [PÖTTER] LILLIENHOFF & H. THUEN to LM & PJ
   STOCKHOLM   18 MARCH 1671

] Our last letter was on the 18th past, to which we refer. We now find ourselves with yours of the 10th and 17th past and have seen what is happening in [England] regarding trade in our Swedish wares, which is instructive.

We understand that you write about the farthings which [England] wants made, and we think we could make them as well as anyone at our own works if we could reach agreement with the Master of the Mint about the price, and provided that he would specifically order a fixed quantity. But if he ordered £5,000-worth we would have to have £2,000 in advance, for which we would give adequate surety in Amsterdam or Hamburg. We would be able to deliver at least one English pound for 14½ pence, free of duties and expenses here, so that the buyer only has to pay freight and customs in England. That is just about the best we can do, and we would be delighted if you could bring it about.

As regards what you are forwarding by the Resident, we cannot dissuade you from taking his assignment on Sweden but do so on condition that you have his guarantee in case of non-payment, and we shall then see what service we can do you, just as we always do in managing expenditure. Please let us know everything that happens in the iron trade. Wherewith our cordial regards, &c.

[P.S.] If you would like to send two ships here with Setubal salt for your own account but in our name we shall ensure that you enjoy the same duties on import and export as free Swedish ships, which is quite a penny-worth.

$$\frac{22\ Apr.}{28\ Apr.}1671$$

4   TAR COMPANY DIRECTORS to LM & PJ
   STOCKHOLM   1 APRIL 1671

] Since our last letter we have received yours of the 17th of February, with which you informed us of the sale of some pitch and tar and also that you hoped to tell us of another sale by your next, of which we shall be happy to learn. We await the sale account and are glad to tell you, in short, that everything must be disposed of and a good purchaser found.

You say that a friend at Yarmouth has offered to buy 40 lasts of tar and 10 lasts of pitch at £8½ and £11½ per last respectively, the purchaser to pay all expenses as well as the freight, to which you wish to know in answer whether we want to send any. For the moment we are unable to decide, because our Company is about to undergo a change and until it is settled on a firmer basis we can decide about nothing, but we hope with God's help to be able to let you know shortly what can be done.

You think that the late Mr Marescoe's promise of $1\frac{1}{2}$ per cent for commission and 5 per cent for interest applied only to the goods that might be sent afterwards or by Mr Deutz, but you will not find that in his letters which speak much more in general about the goods which were then still unsold. When you look through his letters you will find it to be so. Wherewith we commend you to the Lord's protection, &c.

$$\frac{27\ Apr.}{5\ May}1671$$

145 W. MOMMA to LM & PJ
NYKÖPING   1 APRIL 1671

[D] On the 19th past was my last letter to you and since then I have received yours of the 28th of February and 3rd of March.

In reply, I confirm what I said in the foregoing, that as regards making farthings at £6 15s there is nothing to be done, and the contractors cannot know what they are doing. I would say the same about delivering a quantity of copper-sheets to the East India Company at £5 13s per cwt., because the sheets will cost quite as much as that by the time they are free on board ship and I am not including freight, expenses, commission, risk and the interest on money. Mr Mitford is the contractor and his partner is Mr Sowton who is at present in Stockholm and whom I know well. They must be wishing they were free of it because if they hold to their contract they will not escape without loss. Furthermore, they will not be able to get them made unless by the Cronströms, my brother or me—and none of us will want to do it without profit since we are all hard-headed businessmen,[1] and for me to be involved with them I do not consider advisable.

I see that as a result of some quantities of wire coming from Hamburg the price has been brought down again to £6 3s at 4 to 6 months time. I have had various amounts of wire bought at Hamburg and sent to [England] and its cost amounts to at least *RD* 62 to 63 free on board ship, so you can work out what profit can be made on it. In order to close the account I want mine sold as well as others. I have ordered 100 shippound at Stockholm to be loaded into a ship for [England] but the ship has now been entirely freighted by the Cronströms or Wolters who will not suffer any others to load anything in her. However, some time will elapse before the ship will be ready and I hope meanwhile some other opportunity will offer, which you will learn of in due course, wherewith my regards, &c.

1 '. . . *sodat dit al resolute coopluyden syn* . . .'.

$$\frac{8\ May}{12\ May}1671$$

146 CORNELIS DE HERTOGH to LM & PJ
HAMBURG   28 APRIL 1671

[D] Our last letter was on the 25th instant, in which we informed you that in order to accompany the King of France the Count Otto Wilhelm Königsmarck[1] has undertaken a journey to Dunkirk and may possibly come to [London] for some money or else send his steward. So we have ordered you to pay his Excellency or whomsoever he may send three thousand (we repeat, 3,000) rixdollars against a receipt—which we herewith confirm and request that on his Excellency's arrival you pay over as much as you possibly can in cash. You will oblige us greatly by doing so, and to avoid any error we are sending herewith an example of his Excellency's signature which will serve for your guidance in paying out.[2] Forgive us for giving you so much trouble. As for your reimbursement, we have explained that in our foregoing letter to which we refer you.

We shall now answer your letter of the 18th instant which has come safely to hand and in which we are delighted to see the happy arrival of Capt. Borchert Reincke from whom you have received a sealed bag with 500 ducats. While it is very welcome to learn that, we are— on the contrary—very surprised to hear that the 500 ducats are very light-weight and will scarcely amount to 9s 2¼d [each], on top of which the exchange has also fallen by 2d, so that the outcome differs considerably from our estimate of 9s 5d and 35s 7g [per £1 sterling]. Seeing that there is no prospect of anything but loss (with which we must have patience) it is better that no more ducats are sent. Please do the best you can with them, and if you should make no remittance you can set them against the moneys which his Excellency may have need of.

We look forward to being informed by your next letter about what has happened in both these matters, and we further thank you for the news of what is happening in trade. As regards indigo guatemalo, it would be wise to reflect carefully about it, for the *flota* is expected within three months with which large quantities are likely to come and it cannot fail to fall in price significantly. In the meanwhile general consumption is very small. Wherewith our regards, &c.

London: 34s 6g.
Amsterdam: 33 1/16.

[1] Field Marshal Otto Wilhelm von Königsmarck (1639–88), later victor of the battle of Rügen in 1678, had formerly been Ambassador Extraordinary to England in 1661.
[2] Königsmarck's signature on a small slip of paper is enclosed with this letter.

$$\frac{8\ May}{12\ May}1671$$

47 L. TRIP TO LM & PJ
AMSTERDAM   15 MAY 1671

[D] I have been away for a while and on returning home I found your three letters from which I understand that the square-iron has arrived and been sold so I shall expect the account, and while the new duty remains undecided I have loaded in Cornelis Olfersen (who is thinking of leaving at the first opportunity):

1,075 bars of Namur flat-iron marked '⊕' which is iron designed for the African coast, weighing 32,504 lb. It is a type which is not as tough as the Swedish but is forged to the same dimensions, yielding 34 bars to the 1,000 lb. There is no other kind of iron sent from here to the coast of Africa so that the other traders have to buy it for as much as they will give, and it must be sold for as high a price as possible and for not less than 14s 6d because it cannot be sent from here for less.

I have also loaded 250 bars of square iron weighing 8,844 lb. which has been even more carefully forged than the foregoing. It is marked 'H' and must be sold for as much as possible and at least for 16s because that also cannot be sent for less, and since I find that you sell everything on credit I beg you to sell it to reliable purchasers.

I must thank you for the trouble you have taken to speak to Mr Webb. In the morning I will write to the widow of my brother, Mr Samuel Trip,[1] who is now married to the burgomaster of Brill [and receiver of customs?]. When an assignment is sent to me it will be forwarded to you by the next post, meanwhile I commend you to God's protection.

[1] For Samuel Trip and his widow, see P. W. Klein, *De Trippen in de 17ᵉ eeuw*, p. 103.

$$\frac{13\ May}{16\ May}1671$$

148 J. REENSTIERNA to LM & PJ
STOCKHOLM   22 APRIL 1671

[D] On the 8th past was my last to you: since then I have got your welcome letter of the 24th past from which I understand that you had sold 40 coils of wire at £6 1s and 7,000 lb. of copper-bars at £6 10s, half payable in one month, the other half in four months. I urge you to sell the remainder of my goods, and the pans as well, so that I can at last close the old account.

I hear that the new duties have now been fixed and that copper sheets and brewing vessels as well as copper-bars were raised.[1] If any other commodities should be increased please keep me informed. There is no trade being done here at present. Ships are beginning to arrive from abroad but goods are still lying inland so none can be taken off yet. As regards the farthings, I have not heard that any are being made here yet, so that I rather doubt that anything will come of it. Please share with me anything you may learn about it. Wherewith my regards, &c.

[1] A reference to parliamentary supply proposals (which proved abortive) to raise additional duties on foreign commodities—5s per cent on copper plate, 10s per cent on wrought copper.

$$\frac{13\ May}{19\ May}1671$$

149 JEAN D'HOLLANDRE & JEAN DU BERON to LM
LILLE   16 MAY 1671

'Madmoiselle, Nous voyons vollontiers par l'agreable vostre du 28ᵉ passé qu'avez pris la peine d'aller trouver Aboab pour avoir payement de son obligation de £75 sterling mais qu'il vous a prie de voulloir quelque peu attendre, en suitte de la promesse que vous luy aviez fait, que ne regarderiez a un mois ou 6 sepmaines apres l'escheance. Il est juste de tenir sa parolle, et vous prions lors de le solliciter a la satisfaction, et scaurons vollontiers s'il est presentement libre et d'accord avecq tous ses crediteurs.

Nous remarquons que l'indigo guatimalo se tient a 5s 4d la lb. a en achapter 3 a 6 caisses; autres amis nous marquent le prix a 5s 1d a 2d de sorte qu'en achaptant 18 a 20 caisses a la foix vous les devriez obtenir a 4s 10d au plus, le tant plus que sommes d'opinion qu'il viendra au dessoubs le dit prix cy-tost que les navires d'Espagne arriveront et comme l'on asseurre que la flotte doit arriver au mois d'aoust et que elle en rapportera grande quantitte, n'ozons y entrer pour grande partie, pour en estre encore chargé, et de plus que doubtons qu'en achaptant a une seule personne 18 a 20 caisses nous tomberions a en rancontrer diverses d'inferieure qualitté, aymants mieux de donner un denier ou 2 davantage et que chosisiez quelque chose de fin, que s'y en pourrez obtenir 8 a 10 caisses d'entiere perfection a 4s 10d a 5s pourrez les achapter et en envoyerez 6 caisses a Bruges au Sr. Jacques Neyts et les autres 4 caisses les envoyerez a Abbeville au Sr. Foucque, nous en donnant compte et avis de succes. Icy joinct trouverez une lettre d'eschange de £100 sterling que vous remettons pour notre compte sur Laurens Bretland de la quelle plaira en procurer le requis, nous dizants votre sentiment du dit Bretland.

Voyons que de nos laines l'on vous offre seullement 22*d* de la plus fine, a cause que l'on dit qu'elles sont grosses et neanmoings nos amis de Bilbao nous asseurrent que ce sont les plus fines quy se rancontrent, et qu'ils en ont envoyé de la mesme qualitté a Mr Mathias Dasselaer de chez vous et qu'il s'en loue et que le dit amis trouveroit a nous faire vendre les dittes laines, vous prions de luy parler et de sortir des dittes laines au plus hault prix qu'il sera possible, nous confiants en tout en votre diligence, demeurons, &c.'

$$\frac{16\ May}{26\ May}1671$$

150 JACQUES LE CAMPS to LM
LILLE   23 MAY 1671

'Madamoiselle, J'ay deux agreables votres du 14 passez et 5 courant par lesquelles me mandez attestation que la caisse d'indigo No. 3 ne fust ouverte en chemin pour mettre l'affaire en arbitrage contre le Sr. Browning que l'at vendu, lequel vous dittes ne vous donner autres satisfaction que ce qu'il aurat d'Espagne, ce qui ne me peut suffir veu que cela ne me rend pas satisfait, outre ce que son action d'Espagne ne me regarde en rien et ce seroit chose bien iniuste de me vendre du plomb pour de l'indigo.[1] Mettez doncq l'affaire en arbitrage et fait que puissiez tirer d'autres raisons de cest homme et de ce que le passerat m'en donnerer du succes advis.

Je voy que la Compagnie des Indes de chez vous doibt faire la vente le 16 de ce mois et qu'il se vendra grande partie de poivre et que croiez que le prix se gouvernera au tour de 9*d* la lb. La vente que l'on at fait en Hollande l'at donné a un prix aussy bien avantageux a 17⅛*g* ou que j'en ay acheter assez grand partie et comme l'on proffit de 14 pour-cent de poidx et de l'avance sur les remises je trouve qu'il est plus avantageux de l'ordonner a Amsterdam que chez vous et pour de l'indigo je ne voy aparence de vous en ordonner veu qu'il n'y at icy aucune demande, la ville en estant trop furny. C'est ce qui s'offre pour le present, et suis, Madamoiselle, votre affectione serviteur.'

[1] On receipt in April of chest No. 3, purporting to contain 527½ lb. of indigo, Le Camps had found it to include 25 lb. of lead.

$$\frac{17\ May}{23\ May}1671$$

151 A. RULAND to LM & PJ
HAMBURG   9 MAY 1671

[D] Your welcome letters of the 11th, 21st and 28th past have been safely received. Regarding the purchase of a quantity of indigo, I have been unable to make up my mind since that commodity is in declining demand, and I also understand that great deceits have been found inside the sealed boxes which have come from [England] and some batches have been found to be extremely oily. Sugar also will do no wonders here notwithstanding the fact that there is little obtainable in [England]. Large amounts are coming from Portugal and just now 5 ships, mostly laden with it, have arrived from Oporto. The ships which are expected daily from Spain will also not fail to provide good quantities of indigo, so I can see no advantage in bringing these two commodities from [England] unless they should come to very moderate prices on the arrival of the Caribbean ships. If there should be some change, especially in sugar, I shall be glad to participate. Ginger has been in some demand here but since substantial amounts have arrived in [England] and more are expected it should soon fall in price. Cottons will do no wonders here for the moment, though little may come this year; pepper seems not yet to be at its lowest level, and galls—as I have said before—will not rise for the present. I would be glad to know how much *semencina*[1] or *semensaet* costs in [England] and whether there is much in stock, and I look forward to more fruitful opportunities arising from our correspondence. I remain, with cordial regards, &c.

London: 34*s* 4*g*   @ 2 usances.
Amsterdam: 33$\frac{1}{16}$ @ sight.

[P.S.] I shall be glad to know if the ships from Barbados must serve quarantine in [England].

Endorsed] Semencina @ 2*s* 6*d* a lb.

   [1] A vermifuge, imported from the Levant.

$\frac{20 \, May}{26 \, May} 1671$

152   W. MOMMA to LM & PJ
NYKÖPING   30 APRIL 1671

[D]   I last wrote to you on the 1st of this month and since then have received yours of the 14th and 31st of March. In reply, you will have learned from my last letter that I certainly do not find it advisable to participate in the contract for making farthings. How the contractors will fare, time will tell. I can also foresee no profit in sending copper-plate or sheet copper, especially since the duties have been raised. I wish you would send me an exact list of the duties on all imported Swedish wares for my guidance. As for the rest of my wire, I hope you will soon dispose of it so that I can close the account. As for the wire I had at Stockholm, since I could not load it in the ship freighted by Cronström and as no other opportunity arose, I let it go to Hamburg.

The inland waters are just beginning to thaw and so the goods from up-country can now begin to come down. I hope we shall soon have the convenience of some shipping. I have noted that I can draw on you when the bills of lading for goods are sent and orders given for their insurance. I shall be glad if you would send me some samples of pans and kettles aboard a ship coming from [London] to Stockholm. I have tried to obtain them before but have not been able to. And please write and tell me whether or not latten is used by your copper-smiths, so that I can act accordingly. At Amsterdam they consume at least 200 to 300 slb and I am sure you could use as much.

Because of floodwater we have not been able to work for the last two or three weeks, but it is now beginning to fall. The brewing-plates[1] are now in hand, and please write and tell me if you could not use some round pots of 20, 30, 40, 50 and 60 lb. a-piece and whether large amounts of brewing plates and pots could be disposed of. If so I shall have them made. Wherewith, my heartiest regards, &c.

   [1] '*De brouplatten . . .*'.

$$\frac{12 \text{ Jun.}}{16 \text{ Jun.}} 1671$$

3   J. VAN SAVELANT to LM & PJ
    GOTHENBURG   23 MAY 1671

·] Your letters of the 14th, 21st and 25th last have reached me safely, from which I have learned that you have sold and delivered the 997 bars of voyage-iron which I sent with Hans Michelsen. I have received the sale account, examined it, found it correct and debited you with the net proceeds of £188 8s 3d stg. which you mentioned in your letter, without prejudice. As you know perfectly well, the 3 per cent which you charge me relates to the sale of iron and to the remittance of bills of exchange as well, as was agreed with the late Mr Marescoe. You have undertaken to continue on the same conditions which you have confirmed in several letters, though I can quite believe that you did so precipitately. You will have debited the £4 11s 0d for the 20 bars which Anders Beursen delivered short, although since I have received some information from the *Crown* galley I expect to be able to make good some of it.

I have credited you with 30s for the blue waistcoat. I have received 150 slb of iron out of Värmland, but as it is of only ordinary quality I have not wanted to send it but thought of using it as ballast in our ships and sending it to Portugal where it can make *RD* 8 per slb. Pitch has fallen into diverse hands here and is exported to [England] by various people and then undersold. I have spoken to several and told them that a friend of mine wanted to lay out some money, but what can I say, seeing that there are various 'cladders' here who also want to do so. The same thing is beginning to happen with iron. There are some who, for cash down, are selling at 8 or even 12s lüb. per slb below the ordinary price. It is also falling in price in Hamburg. If I can get it to Portugal before these others there might be no great loss—time will tell.

It is a good thing that the new duties in [England] on iron and other wares will not commence this year. The King here has also been thinking of raising the duty by 16 stuivers per slb, though so far it has not been done, but some small ships have had their exemption taken away and must now pay 8 stuivers more per slb, though the King has been petitioned about it. If any changes should occur we shall learn in due course.

I have obtained acceptance of the £100 remitted to Bex at Rotterdam at 36s 1g and today I got news from the widow of Libert Wolters that you had remitted her £188 for my account in two bills at 35s 3g, for which acceptance has been procured. I shall be glad to learn soon from Mr Bex what remains to be remitted to Amsterdam.

Anders Beursen arrived here over three weeks ago without delivering to me the basket with 24 bottles of Spanish Canary. Before your letter of the 21st of April came the basket was delivered to someone else who thought that Jan Kreuger had sent it to him, and the customs official and some others have enjoyed some of the bottles. Nevertheless you have my thanks, seeing that there is no other way of demonstrating my gratitude from this country-town. Wherewith, my regards, &c.

$$\frac{22 \text{ Jun.}}{27 \text{ Jun.}} 1671$$

54 J. D'HOLLANDRE & J. DU BERON to LM
    LILLE   27 JUNE 1671

'Madmoiselle, Nous avons bien receu l'agreable vostre du 9ᵉ courant avecq le compte de 4 caisses d'indigo que faittes monter a £191 6s 10d sterling. Nous les visiterons et n'y trouvant erreur le notterons en votre credit de conformitté et procurerons les dittes 4 caisses du Sr. Foucque d'Abbeville pour ou voyons qu'elles sont party dans le navire de Jean d'Aussy, esperant que par les premieres lettres aurons avis de son arrivée, estant bien que deviez charger les 4 autres caisses pour St Valery de quoy attenderons l'effect avecq le compte d'icelles.

Voyons que nous avez tire £200 sterling a 35s 7g payable a 2 usances moins 8 jours a Robert Frand de Surmont qu'avons accepte pour votre honneur, veu qu'en vous donnant la susditte comission vous avons tres expressement ordonne de ne nous tirer, mais de nous mander qu'en cas qu'estiez pour effectuer notre ditte comission que vous en ferions cy-tost la remise comme nous faisons par cette comme verrez cy-bas, et s'il s'agist pour le peu de temps que ferez en desbours de vous bonifier ⅓ pour-cent. Pourrez nous en debitter mais avecq nos amis ne sommes sy stricts et il nous semble que faisant semblables achapts vous pouvez demander un mois de terme pour attendre les remises, a fin de n'estre en desbours et veu que trouvez la susditte traitte sy avantageuse pourrez nous faire remise de semblable partie escheante au mesme temps, que pourrons contreposer a votre ditte traitte, ou en deffaut nous nous prevalerons sur vous, estant juste que vous observiez nos ordres, car a moings que cherchions le dernier avantage et vous aussy, il ne pourroit nous tourner a compte de vous continuer nos comissions.

Avons fait refletion sur les corrons de soye cy-devant nous envoyé, que vous renvoyons cy-joinct, a fin que nous voudriez pourvoir nous de chasque sorte environ 150 lb. esperant que l'obtiendrez a moings du prix que denotez, mais il faut, sy vous plaist, que la ditte soye soit retorte et presse a tindre, comme la monstre cy-joincte, ce que ferez faire au meilleur marche que pourrez, ce que serons bien aises d'apprendre, parceque s'il cousteroit chez vous trop nous nous resoudrions de la faire venir icy, pour y la faire tondre. Il faut bien recommander aux ouvriers de tondre le premier fillet avant d'y joindre le second, a fin que la soye soit tant mieux perlee et de meilleur usage. De coustume ils ne le font pas chez vous, ce pourquoy leur en ferez particuliere recommandation; cy tost que le tout sera prest en ferez une balle que nous envoyerez par la voye d'Abbeville. Sy pouviez rancontrer un autre sorte de soye plus grossiere et de moindre prix, en pourrez nous envoyer 20 a 30 lb. pour monstre, sur quoy attendant votre responce nous nous dirons, Madmoiselle, vos tres affectionnes serviteurs.

[P.S.] Ainsi, avant de faire quelque achapt de soye plaira nous dire combien coustera chasque lb. de 24 onces pour tondre.'

$$\frac{3\,Jul.}{14\,Jul.}1671$$

155 TAR COMPANY DIRECTORS tO LM & PJ
STOCKHOLM   10 JUNE 1671

[D]   Our last letter was on the 3rd instant, since which we have had nothing from you to answer, so this will be all the briefer and is only to say that we hope you have sent the 40 lasts of tar and 10 lasts of pitch from [London] to your friend at Yarmouth as we cannot do it from here. This is because we have sold about a hundred lasts of tar and pitch to some friends here and in return pledged that nothing will be exported by us to England or any other places. You seem to believe that when these commodities get into other people's hands we shall get a poor price and spoil our market, but we can assure you that our friends will do no harm with their goods because they have paid us so well for them that if they want to sell them without loss they must keep up the price. We hope that all of ours are now sold and disposed of. If not, please let us know what remains unsold. There are some here who offer to buy them from us and deliver them. We will probably agree to do so in order to close the account quickly, so that next year—God willing—we can begin trade afresh. Meanwhile we hope you will continue to maintain a correspondence with us and that you will notify us at once if you desire to contract with us for a quantity of pitch or tar next year on certain conditions, as the contract we made with these friends ends next October. We shall await your answer to this and your conditions for serving us, wherewith we commend you to the Lord's protection, &c.

$$\frac{3 \, Jul.}{14 \, Jul.} 1671$$

6 J. & D. VAN BAERLE to LM & PJ

AMSTERDAM   7 JULY 1671

[Your welcome letters of the 16th, 20th and 23rd past have been safely received and the enclosures forwarded to Sweden. Herewith we return the bill of exchange for D.1,050 accepted by Juan Tayspil. The acceptor is a person of great undertakings and small credit. The usance from Spain on Amsterdam is two months.

We have informed ourselves about the prices of pitch and tar which are namely, for pitch of 12 barrels per last and tar of 13 barrels per last—Stockholm pitch fetches about £16 [flem.] and tar £14½ [flem.]; Calmar pitch £15½ and ditto tar £13½; Gothenburg pitch £14 and ditto tar £9½ per last. And since there is little consumption at the moment there is more prospect of a decline than a rise in prices. For the freight from here to London one should be able to get it at *f*.12 or 22*s* sterling per last of 12 barrels. If the Stockholm tar is in oak barrels one might possibly get served for a little less but not much.

For export duties one pays for a last of pitch of 12 barrels:

for Convoy duty	*f*.1	13	8
for *directie*, rated at *f*.75 @ ½ per cent	–	7	8
	f.2	1	0

For a last of tar of [13] barrels, for Convoy	*f*.2	–	–
for *directie*, rated at *f*.45 @ ½ per cent		4	8
	f.2	4	8

We did not neglect to urge the brokers to bring forward the cotton-yarn buyers and they promised to do their best but nothing further has happened so we must be patient, as with other commodities. Today news arrived that 5 ships returning from the East Indies were off the coast, but we have had no list of their cargoes. Copper has risen to *f*.60 and *f*.60½; Hungary plates, *f*.63 to *f*.64; campeachy wood *f*.17½ to *f*.18; Aleppo galls, *f*.33 to *f*.34; cochineal, 40*s*; indigo guatimalo 11 to 10½*s*; pepper 16⅞*g*; Apulian oil, £49 to £50.

You will please inform us, for our guidance, what moneys are still outstanding on the account of Abraham Reenstierna's iron, and also if the debt due from the widow of Thomas Birkenhead has been paid promptly. Wherewith our heartiest regards, &c.

London: 35*s* 9½–10*g*   @ 2 usances.
Hamburg: 33¼ @ sight.

$$\frac{10\ Jul.}{12\ Jul.}1671$$

157 W. SKINNER to LM & PJ
HULL   7 JULY 1671

'My last to you was the 4th instant, adviseinge the needfull, unto which I referre you. I have now yours of the same date and according to your order have bought and schipt 20 piggs great lead more aboard Jean Poittevin, who is now wholy dispatched and intends hence the next tyde. You have herewith bill of loadinge, signed by the captain. I also send you inclosed invoice of the cost and charges of the lead, amounting to £637 1s 8d and his receipt for £50 paid him, the duplicate whereof I keepe by me. You have likewise the account of the vessel's cost. Charges amount to £14 18s 4d which I have bene as good a husband in as the time would give me leave. Please to give me credit in account for all these summes.

Here are two other French vessels loadinge for Rowen, but their lead not beinge provided before their arrivall they'l not finde speedy dispatch and wilbe necessitated to give higher prices for lead, which doth at present advance by means of them. I have not else at present. I remain.

[P.S.] I have drawne upon you £102 11s payable to Mr Isaac Meynell or order @ 20 days sight. Since makeinge up your account the officer for the crown per tun[1] demands that duty upon the 20 piggs of lead shipt since clearinge. What I pay him I shall in my next advise.'

[1] The duty of 5s per ton on French shipping loading, or unloading, in English ports imposed, in retaliation for the French duty of 50 sous per ton, by the 1660 Navigation Act (12 Car. II. c. 18, §.17).

$$\frac{12\ Jul.}{12\ Jul.}1671$$

158 J. & D. VAN BAERLE to LM & PJ
AMSTERDAM   18 JULY 1671

[D] We received your letter of the 14th instant with the enclosure for Sweden which we have forwarded.

Regarding the information you ask for concerning the goods of Jacob Reenstierna, we can tell you that the late Mr Marescoe, being asked by us to advance money on the goods which the said Reenstierna had sent him at our disposal, desired that we would permit him (in case of bad debts or being otherwise unable to recover his outlay) to re-draw on us, which we agreed to; but now that the said Reenstierna has asked us if he can reckon upon and dispose of the value of the goods which have just gone to you in London we seek to be freed from the liability of such debts, since they only concern Reenstierna, not us, and we could have justly refused Mr Marescoe's request because we were only obliged to cover his commission, not his debts. And although you say that no bad debts need be expected to arise from the sale of these goods, we trust that the debt due from the widow Birckhead[1] will be collected and that you will confirm that we run no risk concerning any debt arising from the said Reenstierna's goods and that we need expect no retrospective demands or re-drafts. In that case we can allow the remaining advance to be credited to Reenstierna and paid according to his order.

Mr Willem Momma wrote to us some time ago, that he was disinclined to send goods to London because of the poor prices and the length of time it took to recover debts; and Lord Reenstierna no longer sends any goods at our disposal to other places, in order (we believe) to save the commission-charges. And because of the hostility between this country and France he is sending much of his output to Hamburg where there is better business than here.

We understand that the Lord Cronström was here for only a few days before returning; Mr Louis Wolters is still here but is returning to Hamburg shortly, and it is believed that Mr Libert Wolters will then be coming back here. These are people with big ideas and many worries.[2] We remain, &c.

London: 35s 11–10½g   @ 2 usances.
Hamburg: 33 3/16–33¼ at sight.

[1] The widow Birkenhead.
[2] '*Sy syn luyden van grote concepten en veel omslach.*'

$$\frac{13\ Jul.}{21\ Jul.}1671$$

9 J. VAN SAVELANT to LM & PJ
GOTHENBURG   10 JUNE 1671

] On the 30th past was my last letter to you, in which I mentioned that I had had news from the widow of Mr Wolters that she had procured acceptance of the £188 you remitted in two bills of exchange, and so I have credited you.

To my great loss I did not go up-country last winter and consequently I have got a quantity of iron which was badly forged and most unsuitable which I have sold to the Hamburgers here since it would not do to send it to [England]. And as my cousin, Volrath Tahm, has obtained a quantity of voyage, as well as square, iron I have recommended you to him and he intends to send you 200 slb which you can expect from the bringer of this letter, Capt. Swen Beursen, who is fully loaded with it.

I am now on the point of departure for a journey inland where I shall travel to pick up a quantity of voyage iron from one place or another, such as the 100 slb which has come to Wemersborg.[1] But, for lack of freight, it cannot be shipped at the moment. And as the ships are thinking of leaving [England] for Guinea in July I shall be glad to learn if anything can be done with voyage iron before their departure.

I have debited you with the £10 received from Marck Laurens, wherewith I commend you to the protection of the Almighty, &c.

[1] I.e. Vänersborg, about 75 km north of Gothenburg, at the foot of lake Vänern.

$$\frac{21\ Jul.}{[21\ Jul.]}1671$$

0 S. DE GEER to LM & PJ
AMSTERDAM   28 JULY 1671

] I find myself indebted for your letter of the 30th of June and the 4th and 14th of July. I have made a note of the £110 drawn by I. van Hoegarden.

The Messrs Cronström and Wolters have been here and have left for Spa, so it seems likely to be a month before they go to London, and as far as I can tell Cronström will then see how matters stand with regard to some great plan which I cannot penetrate but which seems to be some speculation about copper pieces[1] which is now secret. Indeed, neither I nor others can be sure, so one can only guess at what is intended. Certainly neither I nor anyone else is in a position to judge.

They write to me from Stockholm that a quantity of iron was expected very soon which would then be shipped off to London. You can expect further news at the earliest opportunity. Wherewith I remain, &c.

Garcopper: *f.*62
Iron: *f.*$6\frac{3}{4}$ to 7.
Orgronds: *f.*$8\frac{1}{2}$ to $8\frac{1}{4}$.

---

[1] '. . . *speculatie . . . int stuck vant cooper . . .*'. 'Stuk' can mean a gun, as well as many other 'pieces' but in this context almost certainly refers to copper coins, and the pending contract to supply the English Mint with blank farthings.

$$\frac{24\ Jul.}{[\text{——}]}1671$$

161   DANIEL CROMMELIN to LM & PJ
          PARIS
                                                         29 JULY 1671

'Monsieur,
Depuis assez longtemps je n'ais point eu l'honneur de recevoir de vos lettres ny de vous avoir escript manque de sujet. Comme parfois il se rencontre occasion de pouvoir lier quelques affaires ensemble par le caprice des changes, je souhaitterois scavoir sy faisant tirer sur vous un millier ou deux d'escus vous l'auriez agreable soit d'Anvers ou d'Amsterdam, mais je crois que les rencontres pourront plustost naistre de cette premier place, on suitte de quoi la provission suivra tousjours en tres bonnes lettres sur Londres, 3 sepmaines ou un mois avant l'escheance des traittes. Sy je vous remettois a long jours vous m'esconteriez sur le pied de $\frac{1}{2}$ pour–cent par mois, en attendant responce je demeure, vostre tres affectione serviteur.'

Londres: 56d
Amsterdam: 100g   } 2 usances.
Anvers: $99\frac{1}{4}$ a $\frac{1}{2}$)

$$\frac{9\ Aug.}{11\ Aug.}1671$$

162   J. A. FONCK to LM & PJ
          HAMBURG
                                                         27 JULY 1671

[D]   I have got your letters of the 14th and 21st instant with the sale account of the blue-dye, which has turned out very miserably. There ought to be more discrimination between goods, for there have been others that have been bought for 8 or 10 rixdollars per 100 lb. which differ greatly, and as a result I lose $\frac{1}{3}$ of my investment. If I should have the same luck with my linen it would be better if I gave up trade with [London]. Regarding this I have said all that was necessary in my last letter, to which I refer you.

I am waiting to hear what has happened regarding the return of my £150 in good and secure bills. I also confirm the order I gave about *olibanum*,[1] and since a substantial amount arrived with the latest ships I have no doubt that you will be able to obtain it within my limits. There is no hurry. Barbados sugar will have to fall lower if it is to be ordered for I doubt whether you can imagine in [England] just how bad business is here now, with all goods in decline without demand and indigo guatemalo much cheaper than in [England].

I am glad to know that my brother[-in-law] Juncker has arrived safely in [London] and I am greatly obliged to you for the honour that you do him. Please give him my regards and tell him that the last letter to him was sent to Paris addressed to our cousin D'Hertog. Wherewith my regards, &c.

London: 34*s* 3*g*.
Paris: 47$\frac{1}{2}$.
Amsterdam: 33$\frac{3}{8}$.

[P.S.] If the [East India] Company in [England] holds its sale earlier than [the Dutch] in Holland I presume it is still expected in Holland that pepper will fall lower in price.

   [1] I.e. frankincense, the aromatic gum-resin.

$$\frac{18\ Sep.}{19\ Sep.}1671$$

ISAAC TILLARD[1] to PJ & CO

PLYMOUTH   15 SEPTEMBER 1671

'Sir, Yours of the 12th current I have receeved and there by observe your desier for the furnishinge a Master of yours with 500 to 600£ that is soodainely to bee heare or in Cornewall on my good frend Mr Nath. Herne recomendation who could have aquanted you how much I am straightned for the payment of fish bought for there accounts and what course I take for the supply of our occassions, little mony offeringe heare by exchange and for that one and 2 per cent is given for the exchange and I gave my selfe in Exon the last weeke I per cent soo that if your occassions bee urgent I know no other way to supply your need but from thence and as for my provition wee shall not differ, if it bee done by my hands. If it bee for the payment off fish or tine or any other debts I shall stand for your master untell monye cane bee procured which may bee done in a weeks time—haveinge sufficient testemonie from my said freind the post of your punktuall complyance; I say procured in Exon or heare in a weeks time, and if it bee to 600 pounde heare or in Cornewall, you need not question but the busnesse will bee done on my promise for soe short a time or if it bee longer it will not bee questioned but will cost I per cent the Exchange att least, there beinge great want of mony for to pay off the pilcherd owners. In any thinge else I can serve you bee pleased freely to dispose off, your humble servant, I.T.'

   [1] Described as a 'staunch Royalist and Churchman' [R. N. Worth, *History of Plymouth* (Plymouth, 1890) p. 397] Tillard was later nominated as an Alderman in the re-modelled Charter for Plymouth of 1683—L. Jewitt, *A History of Plymouth* (London & Plymouth, 1873) p. 246 (mistakenly transcribed as 'Eillard').

$$\frac{19\ Sep.}{22\ Sep.}1671$$

S. DE GEER to LM & PJ

AMSTERDAM   22 SEPTEMBER 1671

I find myself with your letters of the 1st and 8th of this month, from which I have seen that Pottuyt had not yet arrived, which I hope he has since done as various ships have recently arrived here from the Baltic.

I see that the 'O' iron would fetch a reasonable price but it is now too late in the year to have it made, and there is none that has been made because iron has been in too much demand and little was made in previous years.

The latest letters tell me that a *schuyt* with about 600 slb of 'O' and 'G' iron was under way to Stockholm on which there was also a quantity of pan iron and that it would be quickly unloaded. It will then be loaded all together in the *Graf Wrangels Palais* as agreement has been reached with the skipper about the freight. I estimate that about 1,000 slb will be shipped in him, of which the bill of lading will be sent to you in due course. I have no doubt that iron will hold its price with you, as it does here, and sell just as easily as it has been, ordinary iron being sold at $f.7\frac{1}{4}$ and $f.7\frac{3}{8}$ and 'O' and 'G' at $f.8\frac{1}{2}$ to $f.8\frac{3}{4}$. They have had so much rain in Sweden that the roads could hardly be used, and so not quite as much iron will be despatched as was intended, for it is now too late in the season. Au reste Mademoiselle je ne puis finir celle si qu'avec un souhait particulier a vous et toute vos famille dans vos maison neuve parachevee, qu'il plaise a l'eternell (auquel vous en avez sans doute fait la dedicace) Deuderorome Cha. —[1] vous y combler de ses saintes benedictions tant spirituele que temporele et qu'insi vous puissiez en partant de cele si entrer en celuy qui nous a prepare de toute esternite, c'est la le veu, &c.

I have no time to write to Samuel Omelicius. Please give him £4 or £5 commission.

[1] Deuteronomy, Chapter 26?

$$\frac{\textit{19 Sep.}}{\textit{29 Sep.}}\textit{1671}$$

165   P. RULAND to LM & PJ
HAMBURG   12 SEPTEMBER 1671

[D]   I last wrote to you on the 1st of last month. Since then I have received yours of the 28th of July, 4th and 22nd of August and 1st instant, which for lack of occasion I have not answered earlier. Thanks to your letters I fully understand what has been happening to trade [in London]. Business here is poor in general and as a result I have not had the courage to order anything and I am all the more reluctant because goods are so cheap that a good deal of cheating is going on by mixing bad stuff with the good. I have had proof of that by several consignments from you, the latest being with the campeachy wood which was not packed as it should have been. Every day I have to hear much complaint about it and there are many people in this city who will certainly never buy any more from me. It lacks any colour, as if it had been ground and boiled out completely, just as one finds it when it has been baked in some great fire. In short, you have badly encumbered me, which makes me reluctant to order anything more. Today the East India Company are selling their goods in [London]. There is nothing to be done with pepper as it is so abundant that it is being undersold and will only yield a loss. Barbados sugar is definitely not required now that muscovadoes are so cheap that one can buy them for 8g in current money with 13 months to pay. One can get reasonably good [Barbados sugar] for $5\frac{1}{2}g$ at 13 months in current money which differs by $4\frac{3}{4}$ per cent from bank-money. I see that it is now down to 20s in [London] and that is for good quality. In short, I have no relish for any just now. However, I shall meanwhile expect a note now and again saying what is happening to that and other commodities. Oil has risen again here, but because I have been badly served by you on two occasions I am afraid to acquire any. It has soared from *RD* 52 to 62. Black ginger is at 12g with 13 months time; galls 41 to 42 *ML* at 13 months. The price-list states that there is a two-fold price for campeachy wood: please explain what that means. I have made a note of the way in which your bills of exchange will be signed. May God grant that something will turn up which will produce some profit, so that we can have something satisfactory to exchange bills about! Meanwhile may you remain in God's keeping, &c.

London: 34s 6g   2 usances.
Amsterdam: $32\frac{15}{16}$ at sight.

$\frac{26 \; Sep.}{29 \; Sep.}$1671

66   PAUL BERENBERG (JR.) TO LM & PJ

HAMBURG   19 SEPTEMBER 1671

D]   I last wrote to you on the 12th of the month and since then have received yours of the 8th and 12th instant, by which I see that instead of 34 sacks of white ginger you have only loaded 24 in Hendrick Roys' ship. The invoice has been received and noted, but I have further observed that you have only bought 6 sacks of white at 70s, the rest being of another kind, at which I am extremely astonished and upset because I emphatically ordered you long ago to buy 5,000 lb. at the lowest possible price and to lay out any credit balance on my account on white ginger, and only if none was to be had to get black ginger. You repeated my orders in your letters of the 18th and 25th of August, the 1st, 8th and 12th of September. In your letter of August 25th you wrote that the best price at which you could get 4,000 to 5,000 lb. of white was 68s; in the letter of September 1st you were still doing your best; in the letter of September 8th you wrote that, on the day before, white ginger was fetching 70s 6d on the Exchange, and in your letter of the 12th you say that there are not 100 sacks left in the whole city and that the last batch went for 72s 6d. Notwithstanding the fact that I gave you a free hand, and although the price in [London] has been 68s, 71s 6d and 72s 6d according to what you write, you failed to buy me any. I certainly never restricted you to any price so you ought to have been able to get hold of it as you promised. I have every reason to complain about you in this way. What is the point of writing to me with every letter that you had made a note about buying for me at the current price and in the meantime doing nothing about it? You can judge for yourself whether you have done well for me or badly. If you had complied with my order and bought white ginger it would have turned out very well because this sort of ginger is very scarce here and dear, so I am extremely vexed that you wasted this excellent opportunity and instead of white bought me black. However, I suppose I must have patience and credit you with the 20 sacks of brown ginger at 47s, 5 butts and 6 puncheons at 48s, and about 110 sacks at 50s. I have made a note of them and trust that this batch will turn out to be exceptionally fine since you have paid such an exceptionally high price for it. Brown ginger is at a standstill here; there is plenty in stock and no demand. I shall expect an invoice and a bill of lading as soon as all my ginger is shipped, and I hope you have divided it between two ships. As for indigo and campeachy wood, you had better leave them alone. I must break off in haste, and cordially commend you to God's protection, &c.

[P.S.] If you can get choice white ginger for 72s, or for 75s at the most, please buy me about 3,000 lb. and send them here as soon as you can. I shall remit you the money and make good your outlay. As the East [India] Company has had its sale I think the exchange will fall considerably. Wherewith again, adieu.

London—34s 8g   2 usances.

$$\frac{26\ Sep.}{6\ Oct.}1671$$

167 P. VAN TEYLINGEN to LM & PJ
VENICE   18 SEPTEMBER 1671

[D] Not having heard from you we confirm that the above is a copy of our last letter.[1] You will
have seen from it that the *Providence* has arrived. The ship is now entirely unloaded and is
lying ready to depart, only it lacks a good cargo and nothing has appeared so far except
40 tons of currants to be shipped to England from Zante, but as that is too little we have not
undertaken it. We see little prospect of getting any freight at present as the *St George* is short
of half its cargo and is looking for freight, and that is a capital ship in which one would rather
load than in the *Providence* if there was anything. We expect a friend's letter shortly from
Zante about another 20 to 30 tons of currants to be laden in the same way as the
abovementioned 40 tons. If we could have them both together we would not wait for
anything more in order to get the ship on its way, because we firmly believe that our friend
would want more that *R. pta.* 20 per ton if the ship were to lie here a long time, costing
money, just in order to supplement its cargo. We would send the cash and the barrels to
Zante and urge our friend to obtain the best goods at the least possible price. We hope this
will turn out to the satisfaction of your friends and that good business can be done with the
currants, which have turned out to be very fine and dry this year. The price has not yet been
settled. The proceeds of your goods, which will be coming in shortly, will serve for payment
of your share of the currants. We will let you know what happens, and remain meanwhile,
with cordial regards, &c.

[P.S.] Since the earlier orders of the owners have been confirmed, to obtain at least 100 tons of
freight, we dare not decide to take less for fear of incurring displeasure. We await further
orders about what we are to do and meanwhile will do our duty in looking for some other
good cargo. The new sacks of currants are selling here at *D*.8$\frac{1}{2}$. Pepper *D*.66 with 4 months
discount. Lead *D*.49 with 5 months discount.

London—52$\frac{1}{2}$*d*.   Amsterdam—94$\frac{2}{5}$.

¹ 11 September 1671.

$$\frac{30\ Sep.}{20\ Oct.}1671$$

168 J. LILLIENHOFF & H. THUEN to LM & PJ
STOCKHOLM   9 SEPTEMBER 1671

[D] For lack of material we have not written to you for several posts. Meanwhile, we find
ourselves with several of yours, the latest being of the 18th past, by which we see what is
happening to Swedish commodities in [England]. We thank you for the information, but for
some time we have been reducing our business with England as we have found it better to sell
our wares here than to export them.
     Concerning your claim on the Resident, Leyonbergh, we have had the matter continually
in mind but have been unable to obtain anything. The Resident's secretary has also been
unable to get to the bottom of his affairs but all his claims have now come to maturity and he
will get an assignment of his claim on his master's principal and has promised to pay what is
owing to you. But he has asked that you should send us power of attorney so that he can get a

receipt from us in return for the money. We think it would be best if you obtained a bill of exchange from the Resident, drawn on his secretary, payable to us and then we will do our best to obtain the money, if it is possible to cash it, and handle it to your best advantage. Meanwhile we shall expect to hear what is passing in trade. God preserve you, &c.

$$\frac{30\ Sep.}{6\ Oct.}1671$$

9 W. MOMMA to LM & PJ
NYKÖPING   10 SEPTEMBER 1671

)] My last letter was about a week ago, to which I refer. I have since received yours of the 18th of August. I am glad that you have accepted my bills of exchange for Mr Hiebenaer, and I do not doubt you will do likewise with those to follow. I hope to learn by your next letter of Claes Molt's arrival.

As regards what is happening to copper-wire and other brass ware, there can be no fall in prices for copper is rising more and more in Stockholm and is now held at 250 d.c.m.

Herewith is a bill of lading for 4 barrels of pots and 2 barrels of black kettles, loaded for my account at Stockholm in the ship *St Anna*, captain Jacob Grys, and although it is stated there to be only Slb. 18.15 in weight it correctly weighs as follows:

2 barrels of pots. Nos. 32, 33, marked WM 'M'} weighing net Slb.		9.00.00
2 barrels of pots, Nos. 34, 35, marked WM 'H'}		8.14.16
2 barrels of black kettles, Nos. 36, 37, marked WM, weighing net		4.07.10
	net Slb.	22.02.06

Please get them insured for £300. The pots have been accurately made according to your design and ought to sell for £7, although I am not binding you to a price. They are 14 to 15 inches large, or less. That two barrels are marked 'M' and two marked 'H' is because they contain pots made by two different master-craftsmen, so they can be distinguished, but I trust they are both equally good.

This week there will be despatched to Norrköping for loading in the ship *Graeflyck Huys de la Gardie*, captain Gerrit Laurens, about 1,000 coils of wire and about 15 to 18 slb of pans, from the largest to the smallest, made according to your design, and if I hear that they are in demand I shall work on them diligently throughout the winter so that, God willing, I can provide you with a lot more in the spring.

It may well be that Messrs Luce & Van Bommell are expecting a large amount of copper-wire, and I think it will be in Gerrit Laurens's ship. I understand that my brother is offended that you allowed his bills of exchange to be protested. What reason you had for doing that I do not know. The English are buying up iron in Stockholm at 31 d.c.m. per slb so that I perceive more profit in selling it here than by risking it across the seas.

I shall be glad to know if latten is selling [in London] and I trust that the business of the farthings is not going ahead. If it does it will be to the great loss of the contractors. The brewing-plates ought not to sell for less than the wire, and as they are glutted with pitch and tar everywhere there will be little profit to be made in that trade. Wherewith my heartiest regards, &c.

$$\frac{30 \; Sep.}{6 \; Oct.} 1671$$

170   P. VAN TEYLINGEN & CO to LM & PJ

VENICE   25 SEPTEMBER 1671

[D]   We find ourselves with your letter of the 25th past by which we are glad to see that you have obtained acceptance of our remittance and credited us accordingly, and that you have received the sale account of the lead in the *Coninck David* and recorded your agreement with us. There is no further reply needed about that. The money still outstanding on your account is being collected with all diligence and as soon as all the proceeds are in we shall remit them to London in reliable bills and get your account balanced up as soon as possible. And if you should be pleased to favour us with your commands we shall prove to you how affectionately we take your interests to heart and how desirous we are to serve you well.

You will have seen by the foregoing letter our news about the *Providence* and that we cannot obtain 100 tons of freight for him. The 40 tons we mentioned in our copy [of 18 September] has been taken by the *St George*, which departs next week. We are doing all that is possible as we would be happy to help the ship on its way. If we could get only 80 tons in the next few days we would take it. Meanwhile we await further orders from your friends about how we are to conduct ourselves if freight is lacking. Currants at Zante have been scarcely obtainable at *R. pta.* 30 since three ships are loading up there. At Cephalonia the opinion is they will cost about [*R. pta.*] 26. According to letters the harvest this year has turned out to be about $2\frac{1}{2}$ millions smaller than last year but the goods are completely perfect.

Pepper—D.65 with 3 months discount. For substantial amounts, one can scarcely get D.64. Lead—D.49 with 5 months discount. Indigo guatemalo—D.125; indigo lauro—D.120. Campeachy wood D.90 with 4 months discount. Sappon wood—D.70 with 3 months discount, Gallipoli oil—D.13. In other goods no change.

God be praised for the safe arrival in [London] of the *George & Thomas*. We are glad that you have found the *shenaca*[1] which we sent with it to your satisfaction. We remain, &c.

[P.S.] We remit herewith for your account D.632.22 at the rate set out below. Please obtain the necessary acceptance and credit us. We shall not neglect to remit more as soon as further proceeds come in, and if you should be pleased to favour us with new employment you will see how your interests will be taken to heart. With pepper selling at $15\frac{7}{8}g$ in Amsterdam we hope it will soon be in demand here also, and begin to influence its low price with you. Lead D.47, the quantity in town beginning to decline.

London: $52\frac{1}{3}$ to $\frac{2}{5}d.$
Amsterdam: 94.

D.632.22 @ $52\frac{3}{8}d$ amounts to £138 2s 6d on Gio. Harvey's bill from Leghorn dated 18th inst. exchanged with Emanuel Leni dal Banco.

   [1] Senega?

$$\frac{30\ Oct.}{31\ Oct.}1671$$

A. BERENBERG'S WIDOW & HEIRS to LM & PJ
HAMBURG   20 OCTOBER 1671

We wrote to you by the last post informing you about the first copy of a bill of exchange for £250 sterling payable by Abraham Momma at 8 days after sight but assigned to Philip Collin for value received, which we hereby confirm. Having heard nothing from you this letter will be brief and serves mainly to accompany the second copy of the bill for £250, in case you have lost the first. We hope you will have got it accepted and promptly paid when due—but if not, you will know how to get it protested in [London]. Enclosed herewith goes a letter to the said Momma which you will please have passed on to him and procure an answer. Our friends, Paulus and David van Stetten of Augsburg, correspond with this Momma and remitted him some money towards the purchase of some goods (which we think were furs) and for some posts they have had no letter from him. In his last letter he wrote that he was going into the country because he was unwell but that as soon as he was better, the following week, he would be coming back to town. So they are afraid that he may have died or that his business is in a bad way, and have asked us to write to our correspondents about it to inform them about his condition and to draw on him £250 sterling as he still owes them £300 stg.— all which we have done in our previous letter, sending you the bill of exchange and enjoining you to do what was necessary. The Messrs Van Stetten, who are such great friends of ours that we cannot refuse them, now further request us to warn our friends in [England] in case this Abraham Momma, with his business in a bad way, does not accept the bill of exchange though the goods which they ordered have not been sent. In that event, they have sent us the enclosed power of attorney written in Latin, wherein they give us complete authority to act on their behalf and settle matters with him, together with a clause allowing us to substitute whoever we want where they have left our name blank, in case it should be necessary. So we have substituted your name, to demand an account from the estate of the said Momma on behalf of the Messrs Van Stetten. You must forgive us for taking this liberty but since we have no other correspondents in [London] we could not call upon anyone else. We shall be greatly obliged to you and will wait for you to send your expenses and other charges regarding this business. It may be that the man is perfectly well and there is nothing to worry about, in which case it will not be necessary to the use the power of attorney, but please hold it in [London] until further order. Meanwhile, keep us informed how matters stand, forgiving us for the trouble. Keep a separate note of the postage of these letters so that we can recover it from our friends.

As regards trade, we know of little to say. If war should break out between France and the Dutch we believe there will be changes in the prices of many goods. Ginger is at a standstill. We have checked the account of the 41 sacks of black ginger, found it correct and recorded our agreement. We now await the bill of lading. The wind continues steadily east so no ships can come and Jacob Giese will also be driven back should God allow him to continue his journey. This commodity is too high in price, one should keep one's hands clear of it. As we said in our last letter, we want no more ginger or indigo. The price of sugar has increased a little and if you can obtain a good batch you may spend 22 to $22\frac{1}{2}s$. We shall now wait to hear what you advise. Fine Barbados cotton is no use to us at more than $4\frac{1}{2}d$. We shall be glad to hear whenever the ships arrive from the Levant at what price galls are offered, as well as Ardasse, fine camel yarn, Smyrna or Acre cotton and also what further developments there are with indigo and ginger. With our most friendly regards, &c.

London—34s 3g.

$$\frac{3\ Nov.}{[3\ Nov.]}1671$$

172   S. DE GEER to LM & PJ
THE HAGUE   10 NOVEMBER 1671

[D] My last letter was about a week ago, by which I sent you the bill of lading for the iron loaded in Harman Backer, which I hope you have received. I also hope that the ship will arrive soon as the captain said he was ready to sail in his last letter. I have been at The Hague for some days and may have to stay rather longer than I thought. Yesterday I sent my book-keeper, Westhuysen, an order to draw £300–£400 on you. If he has done so I commend the honour of my bills to you. I would not have drawn them if I did not have these [bills?][1] to pay concerning Cronström and Wolters, but I have taken this liberty not doubting that, if Capt. Backer soon appears, you will be able to recover your money from him and do all that is required when their payment falls due.

Since the prohibition of wine imports[2] the exchange on France has fallen heavily here, so I can see from your letters that one can draw from London more advantageously. I shall probably send you some bills on Rouen which you can draw in, and I shall then draw back on you from here.

The way things stand at present it looks as if it will be the spring before we know how matters will develop. Cologne has taken the protection of the Emperor and of this state and will probably seek that of more princes, so it may well become the *sedum bellum*. May the Lord grant that everything turns out for the best, to whose protection I commend you, &c.

[P.S.] Please see to the enclosed as soon as possible.

[1] A hole in the letter occurs at this point.
[2] The Dutch embargo on imports from France of October 1671.

$$\frac{27\ Nov.}{28\ Nov.}1671$$

173   P. BERENBERG (JR.) to LM & PJ
HAMBURG   14 NOVEMBER 1671

[D] I last wrote to you on the 11th of this month and informed you that the 11 items of 'blue' ginger and the 30 sacks of white had been received but that some of them were damaged, which the captain said had been received in this bad condition when loaded on board his ship. I also informed you that I have got into a dispute with Capt. Jacob Gries over the freight of the 11 barrels[1] of ginger, which I now confirm. He claims that there are 4 butts to a last and that 6 puncheons were also reckoned to equal one last, just as sugar butts and puncheons always are. But I understand that one last is reckoned to weigh 4,000 lb.,[2] while a butt of ginger only weighs 600 to 700 lb. and a puncheon about 400 lb. As against that a butt of sugar amounts to at least 1,100 or even 1,500 lb. and a puncheon of sugar between 700 and 1,000 lb. But he insists that he had expressly stipulated and agreed with you and that you had accordingly instructed him that he might take them on such conditions. Whatever the truth is, please inform me in answer to this, for he will not concede one stuiver, which I consider unreasonable since in this way I shall have to pay nearly 3 or 4 times as much freight as I should. In future, I beg you not to send any more ginger in casks. Here we are always accustomed to have it in sacks, for which we must buy linen and have it sewn, which causes great inconvenience and expense.

There is no consumption of ginger here. I shall be most grateful if you will tell me what is happening in [England] with regard to silk, and beg you to find out as much as you can and as carefully as you dare what quantities are coming to Smyrna of Ardasse and Legee [silks] and also what the prices are likely to be. Please do not bother to send a price-current unless there are from time to time some alterations—the letter-post is too expensive. Wherewith my cordial regards, &c.

[P.S.] With my last letter I remitted £37 2s 5d on my account to balance the current account with one of our bills drawn on you. A note of it will be made and therewith my account will be balanced. I remain, &c.

London—34s 2g   2 usances.

[P.S.] As regards our firm, I confirm that you are not to buy any pepper, but to draw up our current account and to remit any balance that remains as advantageously as you can in an absolutely trustworthy bill of exchange. It is thawing here quickly now and the frost has gone.

---

¹ The eleven barrels consisted of 5 butts and 6 puncheons.
² This was correct—see Doursther, *Dictionnaire des poids et mesures anciens*, p. 203; and below, Appendix I.

$$\frac{18 \ Dec.}{22 \ Dec.} 1671$$

74 W. MOMMA TO LM & PJ
NYKÖPING   26 NOVEMBER 1671

[D] My last letter, to which I refer you, was on the 12th instant. Since then I have received yours of the 17th and 27th past. From the last I understand that the insurance on the ship *Het Graefelyck Huys de la Gardie* has been completed for £900 at 4 per cent, £250 at 5 per cent and £350 at 6 per cent, amounting with expenses and commission to £79 18s, for which I have credited you. In view of the high premium I trust the ship will have arrived in safety with the others. I could not order any insurance from you before the cargo was loaded and I also believe that nobody else has insured except my brother Jacob. I trust the goods will sell as they ought. Copper has risen to RD.76 at Hamburg, and brass ought to fetch proportionately. It is true, as you say, that while goods are coming in such abundance the retailers ought not to see the extent to which they come. Even more, this ought to be kept in mind by the wholesalers who ought not to sell for less than it costs to make. Otherwise it would be better for the works to close down, just as those at Lübeck and Hamburg must now do, for while they get only 6 to 8 rixdollars per slb more than the present price of brass they cannot keep on going. So it is only you who can alter things, and I repeat what I have said before—I would rather that you leave goods unsold for 6 months than sell them for 6 months credit.

I have no doubt that you will do your best for me. As for the farthings, I have said before that it is a most damaging contract for the Cronströms, as well as for all others who have contracted to deliver copper or plates. I would not have sent the last lot of latten unless it had been convenient to send with the other goods, and as the amount is not large it will be easily used up by the copper-smiths.

Herewith I have drawn on you 6 bills to pay £750 to my sons Isaac and Jacob Momma or order at the end of February—one of £200, one of £150 and four each of £100—which you will please accept and return to them so they can use them whenever they need them. Nothing remains but to send you heartiest regards, &c.

$$\frac{18\ Dec.}{22\ Dec.}1671$$

175 HERMANN PAFFRAHT[1] TO LM & PJ

DANZIG   8 DECEMBER 1671

[D] Lacking matter, I have not written to you for a long time and I am only doing so now because it is believed here that a war between France and Holland can be expected in the new year and that England will be involved in it. If that should happen I would be glad to be informed of the certainty of it at the earliest moment. And I should like to know if tar, pitch, iron, 24-foot planks of 2-inches thick, firewood and ordinary Västervik and Kalmar deals of 12 or 13 feet can be sold at a good price; and also fine potash, and whether it is safer for Dutchmen to sail in Swedish, German or Danzig ships; and also what changes can be expected in flax and hemp. I shall do something if I can count on some profit.

Regarding the cargo sent with Cornelis Jansen in 1660, I would like to see how the account stands and beg you to send me a copy out here because I have much to do here and must spend the winter between here and Konigsberg. I gave up my account with chief commissioner Struve[2] in February 1661 and avoided dealing with him any further because he is a very variable and changeable fellow and his commissions have done me more harm than good, as the Lord God and other decent people know to be true. I shall now do business on my own account, so I beg you as a friend to keep me informed about what I have written above at the earliest opportunity. If there is anything in which I can serve you, you have only to ask. Send my letters under cover of Carlos [?] or simply by the post. It has been very stormy here for some days and many voyagers have come to harm and the high seas have also done much damage—for your information; wherewith, my cordial regards, &c.

[P.S.] English tin is selling here at 13 guilders per centner. Fresh Martinique tobacco for 12, 13 or 15 *gros* per lb., according to quality.[3] If 10,000 lb. could be brought here at once I could sell it at Konigsberg to the Russians and Poles for a good price and get flax and hemp to return with the ship that brings it. Weights here are 12 per cent heavier than at Konigsberg, so one has a 12 or 13 per cent profit on the weights at Konigsberg. The licence is $1\frac{1}{2}$ *gros*. 3-band flax costs 4 guilders 10 *gros*; Paternoster or Littauisch flax 5 or $5\frac{1}{4}$ guilders per stone of 40 lb., Konigsberg-weight. The flax is well prepared and properly washed. This year linseed is 9 to $7\frac{1}{2}$ guilders per ton.

---

[1] For some account of Paffraht (described as a young merchant in 1667, from Kristianopel) see Oscar Bjurling, *Skånes utrikessjöfart, 1660–1720* (Lund, 1945) p. 118.

[2] Balthazar Struve (see Bjurling, pp. 118–9).

[3] At Danzig the Polish *guilder* (rated at 3 per rixdollar) consisted of 30 *gros*, and the *gros* of 18 *penins* or *deniers*. At 4*s* 6*d* sterling per rixdollar, David Brond's figure of 18*d* [sterling] per guilder [**426**] is accurate enough.

$$\frac{19\ Dec.}{22\ Dec.}1671$$

176 A. BERENBERG'S WIDOW & HEIRS TO LM & PJ

HAMBURG   12 SEPTEMBER 1671

[D] Our most recent letter was by the last post, in which we told you not only to buy us 4,000 to 5,000 lb. of good, white scraped ginger at the best price possible but that the black ginger had better be left alone since the price was running so high, and that if you bought Barbados indigo it must be absolutely choice and saleable stuff.

In this letter we only want to say that there have been no letters from London today so we do not know if any changes are occurring in commodities. We want to know in your next letter what you have been able to do for us regarding the white, scraped ginger. As for the black, we shall think about it for a while since the price is too high and the sale of it begins to diminish, so the price will fall again as it is already beginning to do. With regard to galls, everything is very quiet; as for cotton and Ardasse, there is no demand. Of indigo we hope you have bought us nothing since you must have also heard in [England] of the arrival of the *flota* in Spain, very richly laden with great quantities of indigo and campeachy wood. For people well know that when great amounts of some merchandize arrive the price always falls. Doubtless you have considered that, and we shall be glad to hear that before you saw this letter you had not bought us any. Please leave it alone since there is no profit to be got from it.

We find that the most recent letters mention Barbados sugars as being at $21\frac{1}{2}s$ to $21s$, by which they think they must be at their lowest; but we doubt that, because there is so little consumption of refined sugar and unrefined is in such poor demand that there is a rebate of $8\frac{2}{3}$ per cent on $5\frac{1}{4}g$ in current or common money (which differs by $4\frac{1}{2}$ per cent from bank money) which is a miserable price. We do not think it has ever been as low as $5\frac{1}{2}g$ banco before, except for a short while before leaping strongly upwards. And we recall that it was once at $20s$ and $19\frac{1}{2}s$ in [London] and the exchange was more favourable than it is now, so it may well fall back to $20s$ or below, which would not be strange in view of the high rate of exchange and poor sales through lack of consumption. Seeing in the latest letters that 5 or 6 ships from Barbados were unloading, take the risk of finding for us a nice little consignment of really choice stuff, which must not be dirty, and if you can get it for $21s$ $6d$ at the highest, free on board, you may buy us 10 butts and send it here under our usual mark. Once before we had a batch which was in small barrels of about 300 lb. per barrel, which was very white and completely dry: we would be glad to have similar, or even better, goods. Ordinary coarse stuff is no use to us, even for $20s$ or below; we have fixed the price rather high in order to have good quality. You may watch out for us to see if you can obtain such a fine consignment of 10,000 to 11,000 lb. but if it is not obtainable, let it go.

We remit with this, for our account, £200 stg. at 2 usances and [blank] days in a bill of Samuel Free payable by Mr William Robinson. Please procure the necessary and let it serve towards the purchase of our goods. Wherewith we send you our most cordial regards, &c.

London: $34s$ $6g$.
Amsterdam: $32\frac{15}{16}$.

22 Dec. 1671
5 Jan. 1672

7 W. MOMMA to LM & PJ
NYKÖPING   3 DECEMBER 1671

I wrote to you about a week ago drawing on you £750 in six bills payable at the end of February to my sons Isaac and Jacob Momma or order. I have since received yours of November 3rd in which—God be praised!—I see that Capt. Jacob Grys has arrived safely. I hope that Capt. Gerret Laurens has followed him and that Steffen Steenoort has also turned up.

A considerable rise in brass-ware can be expected as copper is at *RD* 80 per slb in Hamburg, at *f*.65 per 100 lb. in Holland, and still rising, and not to be got here for less than 265 d.c.m. with every prospect of rising higher. I would much rather see my goods lying around for a while than selling at so low a price, because it must change. At Hamburg and Lübeck all the brass-works are lying idle, so that nothing can be expected from there, for your information.

The contractors for the farthings, who I understand are to deliver 5,000 slb in the coming year, will suffer a great blow since copper has risen so much that no ordinary merchant could handle it.

I shall speak to my brother Jacob at your request as he is travelling here from Stockholm—probably in time for the holidays. I shall see if I can persuade him to return to you, because it is better to have all the goods in one hand than in many, but I am afraid it may be difficult as he is in possession of the advance payment for the winter, which has also been offered to me. As there is nothing else, I remain, &c.

$$\frac{1\ Jan.}{5\ Jan.}1672$$

178   W. MOMMA to LM & PJ
NYKÖPING   10 DECEMBER 1671

[D]   My last letter to you was about a week ago, to which I refer. Since then I have received yours of the 17th of November from which I understand that of my brass you have sold to John Wise, at 3 months time, 28 sheets of latten, 5 cwt. of 'Scottish' pans[1] and 34 brewing-plates at £6 7s 6d, which you judged to be a high price and a risky one. But in my opinion it ought to have fetched much more, and will shortly rise to £7 since it cannot at present be made here for the price at which it is selling. Copper is now selling at 280 d.c.m. in Stockholm and in future you ought to keep yourself in line with other places. Copper-wire has risen at Hamburg from 66 *ML* to 70 *ML* per 100 lb. in eight days and at Rouen from 80 to 85 £*t.* with every prospect of rising higher. And if I had sent the brewing plates to Amsterdam they would be fetching *RD* 8–*RD* 10 per slb more than you are selling them for. Therefore, do not be in a hurry to sell, even though others undersell you, because what is now being made here must fetch more in the spring. At Lübeck and Hamburg no brass is being worked and in view of the dearth of copper it is selling at Hamburg for *RD* 80 per slb and at Amsterdam has risen from *f.*62 to *f.*69 for your information.

I hope the *Graffelyck Huys de la Gardie* as well as Steven Steenoort have arrived safely and that you will arrange things as I advised, wherewith my heartiest regards, &c.

    ¹ 'Schotse pannen'.

$$\frac{23\ Jan.}{2\ Feb.}1672$$

179   J., D. & H. VAN BAERLE to LM & PJ
AMSTERDAM   29 JANUARY 1672

[D]   We have received yours of the 5th instant and have been glad to see that you acquired acceptance of the bills we remitted for your company's account and for Madame Marescoe's private account.

We are astonished to learn of the disorders following the closure of the Treasury,[1] which is a matter of very evil consequence and we fear that bankruptcies are likely to follow.

We cannot foresee any great changes in commodities as a result of the war with France, except with salt, which has already risen from £40 to £60 flem. [per last], and saltpetre, which has risen from *f.*32 to *f.*33 [per 100 lb.]. But if England should also go to war most of the goods from the Mediterranean must cost more. As against that, it is worth bearing in mind that we will not be able to sell anything as the war will make it dangerous in such troubled times to encumber the Rhine and Munsterland with too many goods.

Barbados sugar $5\frac{1}{4}$ to $5\frac{1}{2}g$; pepper $17\frac{1}{4}g$; brown ginger *f.*29; campeachy wood *f.*18; Apulian oil £59–£60; garcopper *f.*58; copper-wire *f.*64 to *f.*$64\frac{1}{2}$; sheet-copper fallen from *f.*72 to *f.*70; wherewith our heartiest regards, &c.

London:	$35s\ 8$–$8\frac{1}{2}g$	} 2 usances.
Paris:	$95\frac{1}{2}$	
Hamburg:	33 to $33\frac{1}{16}$	} at sight.
Antwerp:	$\frac{5}{8}$ premium	

¹ The 'Stop of the Exchequer', by which Charles II postponed payment of interest and principal on government debts, was inaugurated in a temporary form on 18 December 1671 and implemented fully by an Order in Council of 17 January 1672. C. D. Chandaman, *The English Public Revenue 1660–1688* (Oxford, 1975) pp. 227–8.

$$\frac{29\ Jan.}{2\ Feb.}1672$$

180   J. VAN SAVELANT to LM & PJ
GOTHENBURG   [9?] JANUARY 1672

[D]   My last letter was on the 5th past, to which I refer. I have now received yours of December 1st from which I understand that a Guinea Company has been set up in [England] to which many people have subscribed a substantial sum,¹ as a result of which you believe that voyage iron will be in greater demand than before. If the Company goes ahead please write so I shall know better what to do.

The fact is that I used to have a quantity of voyage iron made every year at an iron-works up-country but as it lies a rather long way away from me and since I was accustomed to visit it only once a year I have been obliged, by unfaithful smiths and unreliable servants, to sell my iron-works on my latest visit to see it. However, I am thinking of travelling up-country in a week's time and I shall do my best to order a quantity, though I must say that last year a great deal of ordinary iron was taken from up-country and bought up dearly. Note that voyage iron is also rather more troublesome to make and that not so many places can make it nor get it. Nevertheless, I shall do my best up there as far as possible to order a quantity, wherewith my regards, &c.

¹ £110,600 was subscribed by two hundred investors in the new Royal African Company between 10 November and 11 December 1671—K. G. Davies, *The Royal African Company*, p. 59.

$$\frac{29\ Jan.}{2\ Feb.}1672$$

181   S. DE GEER to LM & PJ
AMSTERDAM   5 FEBRUARY 1672

[D]   I wrote to you by the last post and since then have heard nothing from you. It looks as if this country is going to be at war with England, Ambassador Dow[n]ing having taken his departure very suddenly and unexpectedly,[1] so it looks as if England must be rather deeply involved with France.

Sweden will evidently remain neutral and will apparently enjoy free passage. Nevertheless, although I shall be completely free in Sweden, in order to avoid all disputes please place all the goods which you have under the name of Gerard de Geer, and likewise write all letters to him to avoid any risk of suspicion, treating everything as if for the account of him and our friends in Sweden. Otherwise, as regards business here, nothing is happening so I shall close, remaining, &c.

[1] Sir George Downing's precipitate departure was in breach of his instructions and Charles II ordered his imprisonment in the Tower where he remained for six weeks—J. Beresford, *The Godfather of Downing Sreet* (London, 1925) pp. 263–5, 268.

$$\frac{19\ Feb.}{23\ Feb.}1672$$

182   HENDRIK CLETCHER[1] to LM & PJ
STOCKHOLM   27 JANUARY 1672

[D]   Your letter of the 22nd of December has been safely received, and I have checked the current account and found it correct.

It is definitely settled here that the duty on iron will be raised by 30 s[tuivers] per shippound.[2] I shall wait to hear if this raises the price in [England]. It is a severe winter here which means that not so much iron will be made as last year since the works cannot be provided with what they require. With regards, &c.

[1] A frequent correspondent with the London firm on behalf of Deborah van Ruyff (his mother-in-law?) Henry Cletcher successfully petitioned the English crown for his right to bear the arms of his family by right of his descent from his English grandfather, Thomas Cletcher. *CSPD, 1673*, pp. 339, 393.

[2] Iron duties had been raised for one year by 1 d.s.m. (or 32 öre) per slb on 20 December 1671; large increases on copper were imposed on 2 April 1672—Stiernman, III, pp. 896, 901; Wittrock, II, p. 343, n. 3.

$$\frac{23\ Mar.}{26\ Mar.}1672$$

183   P. BERENBERG (JR.) to LM & PJ
HAMBURG   15 MARCH 1672

[D]   I last wrote to you on the 8th inst. and remitted £100 for my account in a bill of Jean Jacob Hiebenaer at 2 usances on Jacob Lucie. Enclosed herewith is a second copy to serve in case the first is lost.

Let me know in your next what you have done regarding the purchase of choice Caribbean indigo. Above all, please be very careful to ensure that it is saleable or high quality stuff, and get it as advantageously below my price-limit as possible. And, as I also said, do not buy it unless there is no war with Holland and prompt opportunity to send it here in free ships. All the merchantmen[1] from [England] are here in the Elbe bringing great quantities of all kinds of goods—much sugar, ginger and indigo, which will undoubtedly be sold cheaply, so that one ought to reduce things to more reasonable prices when buying in England if one is to hope for any profit. I am glad that galls are rising in price in England. I have 20 sacks, which you provided two years ago, lying here unsold and waiting for a rise. Wherewith, my cordial regards, &c.

London—34s 8–9g @ 2 usances.

[1] '*Hier syn all de boiers de Costi op d'Elve . . .*'.

84   L. TRIP to LM & JD
     AMSTERDAM   8 APRIL 1672

D]   I wrote to you more fully on the 29th of March, and I have no doubt that you will have acted upon it, of which I am awaiting news.

Regarding the balance which is due to me from you, I have made a deal with Gerard de Geer that the amount which is owing by you should be made good by his debtors in Sweden to my nephew Matthias Trip in Stockholm by the delivery of so much iron, for which orders have been given in Sweden. So, please credit the said De Geer with as much as is due to me and follow his orders accordingly, and close my account, commending you to God's protection, &c.

85   W. SKINNER to LM & PJ
     HULL   2 APRIL 1672

'Since my last of the 26th past I have yours of the 28 ditto, adviseinge receipt of the invoice of the lead shipt in Capt. Poitevine, and that you have given mee credit in account for the amount thereof and will take care duely to discharge my bills, for which I thanke you.

The dread of this unexpected warre hath made lead here to fall to 11£ 12 to 10s per fodder. Howe it governes I shall, as you desire, be sometimes adviseinge you, but I beleeve it will not fall much more at present, except all exportation be stopt, and in future it will rise or fall accordinge as our fleete meets with successe against the enemy. I am glad Peter Thompson is arrived, and soe presentinge my respects I remaine, Sir, att command, &c.'

86   L. TRIP to LM & PJ
     AMSTERDAM   12 APRIL 1672

D]   I have received your despatch of the 26th of March together with the bills of exchange, as below—vizt.,

£150 at 35s on Eduart Vandervoort;

£100 at 34s 10g on Roelant Cockey;

£123 0s 8d on Louis & Josep du Lume at 34s 9g;

£200 at 35s 1g on Philip Pym in Rotterdam—on all of which I have procured acceptance as well as on the bill you sent earlier, drawn on Towse & Manning in Hamburg. I have credited you with them all.

I wrote to you on the 8th that I have arranged with commissioner Gerard de Geer that you are to pay over to him what is due to me on account of those goods of mine which you have sold, unless you have already remitted the proceeds. Please credit his account and let me have a statement so that I can write to Sweden and tell my nephew Matthias Trip how much iron he is to order. I also asked you to keep me informed if any of my creditors[1] should not pay up promptly for the iron which has been delivered to them. In such case I would reimburse you for any such money you may have advanced to me. Meanwhile, I trust that the amount which was due on the 1st of April has been received and beg you to tell me who is still owing money and how much the sum amounts to.

I have written today to my nephew Matthias Trip at Stockholm to find out if one can profitably trade to London. According to the latest letters the Swedes are raising the duty on iron by 2 or 3 dollars to 31 d.c.m., but I think that when they get news from here about the war the price of iron will return to its old level. Iron prices are weak here since none can be exported and Sweden must follow suit unless all the English come and buy a lot and thus inflate the price. Other commodities, on the contrary, have risen very considerably. Let me know from time to time the price of iron in England for my guidance.

[P.S.] I have received your letter of 29 March together with 2 bills of exchange, each of £100, for which I shall obtain acceptance.

¹ *Sic.*—'*crediteuren*'—in error for '*debiteuren*'?

$$\frac{16\ Apr.}{[16\ Apr.]}1672$$

187   S. DE GEER to LM & PJ
AMSTERDAM   19 APRIL 1672

[D]   Since my last letter of the 5th/15th instant I have received yours of the same date.

Mr Trip tells me he has demanded acceptance for the remittances which you sent him for the £190.

The ship *Coninq David* will probably be the first to leave Stockholm for [England]. I expect to get further news about it in the next letters from Sweden as in the last they said the waters were still not open. You will be receiving a good quantity of iron when she comes.

Sweden will be remaining neutral this summer. If a ship can be found going to Stockholm, and if time does not allow you to wait for my further orders, please procure just 20 pipes of the best Barbados sugar you can buy and ship it off for the account of the Directors of the [Swedish] Sugar Refining Company, sending me the bill of lading and the account and drawing on me at double usance. Only please make sure it is the best.

Please let me know what one has to give for insurance in London from there to Stockholm.

Copper-wire is selling here for *f*.63, garcopper at *f*.67 to *f*.68; Gothenburg iron for *f*.7, Stockholm iron for *f*.7½ to 7¾, Orgronds *f*.9 to *f*.9½, since the 'O', 'G' and 'L' marks, as well as some others, are in firm hands.

Lead, 12s; Barbados sugar, 7g to 8g, Muscovadoes, 11g—few buyers. Wherewith I remain, &c.

[P.S.] So far no ships have been brought in here and all Swedish ships will be allowed to go free, without being brought in, whether they are going for England or France, provided that they have no contraband goods aboard. Consequently, if in future a Swedish ship has English goods it will go freely for 'a free ship makes free goods', provided that the same is also permitted by England and France, so that Swedish ships may come here. But if they do otherwise and hold up ships destined for here and not allow them free passage we shall do likewise.

$\frac{17\ Apr.}{19\ Apr.}$*1672*

8 P. BERENBERG (JR.) to LM & PJ
   HAMBURG   5 APRIL 1672

)] Your two letters of the 19th and 26th of March have reached me safely, by which I am glad to
see that my remittance of £200 on Jacob Lucie has been accepted, but I regret that I remitted
it for the exchange has since fallen to 33s and 32s 10g. But what is done cannot be undone.

Since the war has been proclaimed many commodities have risen in price here, especially
sugars. I wish I had bought some in time, but I could not conceive that there would be a war.
The sea will now be very unsafe and scarcely to be used. We now pay a 10 per cent premium
to send goods here from [England] on free ships, and if we once get news that any ships have
been seized by the Dutch or other capers I certainly believe we shall not find insurers at any
price. I do not know what to order: the time for making profits has passed by and been lost,
and whatever one tries to get now must be snatched out of the fire, as time will tell.

When the £200 I remitted is received please hold the money at my disposal. I may see
what to do with it if the fleet from Barbados arrives next month, or if I see some other
opportunity arising meanwhile and hear how things stand at sea, wherewith cordial regards,
&c.

$\frac{17\ Apr.}{3\ May}$*1672*

9 J. D'HOLLANDRE & J. DU BERON to LM
   LILLE   16 APRIL 1672

'Madamoiselle, Pour responce aux agreables votres du 8 et 29 passé, nous avons prins
consideration sur le prix des marchandises que nous marquez, mais n'y trouvons riens a faire
qui auroit prevu. Cest guerre auroist bien gaignie aux huilles veu qu'elles sont monté a £40 et
veu que la recolte des cottons est manquer en Barbados il debvra icy aussi hausser. Nous avons
encor celuy que nous avez pourveu passé quatre ans n'ayant sceu nous resoudre de vendre a
perte. Voyons que la cocchenille continue a 20s 6d a 21s, a moins qu'il se reduire a 19s et
d'avoir quelque chose de beau et nette ne trouvions compte a en faire venir, et comme la
consomption en est partout petit et qu'il s'en rencontre bonnes parties sommes de sentiment
qu'ils baisserat, venant a notre sudite limite et que puissions vous faire la remise pour jouir du
change serions content que nous en pourvoiriez une caisse de 200 lb. de rougette et point de
grisset. Veu qu'Aboab avoit promis de payer voulons croire l'aurat effectire, de quoy
attenderons le success. Si notre sudite comission de coccheníl prennoit son effect plaira nous
dire s'il ne seroit pas bon de l'envoyer a Douvre pour estre charge pour Calais ou la tragette
est fort petit et a combien l'on trouveroit a assurer, que si il venoit aussi ruptur entre l'Espagne
et la France vous ne nous pourvoirez rien, car l'on ne scauroit coment avoir icy la
marchandise; sur ce nous vous baissons les mains, Madamoiselle, &c.'

$\frac{26\ Apr.}{30\ Apr.}$*1672*

0 W. MOMMA to LM & PJ
   NYKÖPING   7 APRIL 1672

)] My last letter to you was on the 24th past. I have since received yours of the 8th ditto and seen
that you have sold 60 coils of my wire to Smith & Bryan for £6 10s at 3 months which is

quite a good price but not what it ought to fetch in future in view of the price of copper here, on which the duty has been raised to $42\frac{1}{3}$ d.s.m. money per slb. On brass it has been raised from $9\frac{3}{4}$ to 15 d.s.m. per slb and so in future these goods ought to cost more in [England].

So far I have not been able to arrange any shipping at Stockholm for [London] because the inland waters are still frozen and we have also learned that there is open war between England and Holland as a result of the unexpected but ineffective attack on the Smyrna fleet and the others which were joined with it. We are assured here that our ships will be allowed to sail unmolested by the French and English and we hope that they will not be refused by the Dutch.

I am sorry to see that you have had a misunderstanding with my brother Jacob. I do not know what to say, but if only you had written to him in good time about what debts were still outstanding and which were doubtful. At the close of every account one ought to specify whether debts are still outstanding or not, and I beg you not to omit this when you send me my account as I also think one ought to be quite precise. Meanwhile, thank you for the offer you have made to my sons, to accept up to £300 if they should draw on you: I think you have about that much in hand on my account. They write to me that they do not have any need of it for the present, but in future please accept their bills up to the value of £400–£500 on my account, for with this war-time situation it could well happen that, through one change or another, they may stand in need of it.

I have sent a quantity of wire to Stockholm to be despatched to [England] in the first departing ship. May God himself preserve you in safety, &c.

$$\frac{17\ May}{17\ May}1672$$

191   P. VAN TEYLINGEN & CO to LM & PJ
VENICE   13 MAY 1672

[D]   We find ourselves with your welcome letter of the 9th past. In reply, your brother John Lethieullier has revoked the purchase of pepper for his account and we shall do the same for yours. Indeed, it really must be done because that commodity is daily held at D.100 to D.103 without any prospect of abatement. These wars endanger shipping to such an extent that nothing can be brought from [England] or Holland without great risk. If France fails to obtain the pepper which is known to have just arrived at Lisbon in the ship from the East Indies it is likely to come to Italy which may well cause some fall in prices since this country is well-supplied with it and it is only these troubles which stiffen the price. But if the war continues for long and the only pepper coming to Italy comes out of France the price may rise higher, which God forbid!

There is no change in the price of lead apart from the last purchases we informed you of. Since then it has been at D.70 but there are no buyers and there is a large amount in town. Therefore, on the arrival of the *Blackmore* (which God grant may arrive soon in safety) we think it advisable to dispose of your 50 pieces at the highest possible price. We do not see any prospect of any great alteration in the immediate future. At Leghorn it fetches D.$31\frac{1}{2}$, which is much less than here. We will be glad to hear from you about this, if you think it worthwhile. Large quantities of lead are being brought from Germany now and are selling at D.70.

Since you have procured acceptance of the D.235 which we remitted to you we do not doubt that you will be duly paid. As soon as the rest of what is due on your account is received we shall remit it immediately. Bortolo Marinoni owes for lead which came from the *Coninck David*. We have presssed him diligently and will let you know when we succeed. The *Sommission* which came from Lisbon with sugar is loading oil here. Muscovado sugar fetches D.8$\frac{3}{4}$ with 4 months time; powdered sugars D.12 to D.14, according to quality. There is very little left in town in the wholesalers' hands since it has been mostly bought up by engrossers. Barbados sugar, D.6; pepper-powder, D.11 with 10 per cent tare; oil at Gallipoli is D.13$\frac{1}{3}$ free on board. In other commodities there is no change and from overseas we have heard nothing of importance, so we shall break off here, remaining, &c.

[P.S.] We see no prospect of doing anything in your commission for pepper. The *Blackmore* had left Leghorn, bringing a good quantity. If it can now be sent from England we shall see little more change.

London:　　52d.
Amsterdam:　89.

$\frac{17\ May}{21\ May}$1672

92　　C. DE HERTOGH'S WIDOW TO LM & PJ
HAMBURG　　　　　　　　　　　　　　　　　　　　　10 MAY 1672

[⊃]　We find ourselves with three of your letters of the 12th and 19th of April and 3rd of May. In reply, we are greatly obliged to you for news of what is happening in trade. As you must know, pepper was released by the [Dutch East India] Company at a fine price and quickly rose there in Holland and here also, but it did not last long and is now at 23$\frac{1}{2}$g without buyers. How it will fare after this time will tell. Various other kinds of goods have also risen in price here but there is a lack of demand and they are only being sold and marketed by a few people. White sugars, 16g; Muscovadoes, 11$\frac{1}{2}$g; Barbados [sugar] 8$\frac{1}{2}$g; black ginger, 15g; white ditto 19$\frac{1}{2}$ to 20g; indigo 13s; cochineal, 48s; oil, RD 90, with which we provided ourselves when it was cheap, so that is all right. We cannot make up our minds to buy anything while they are so dear because they are equally liable to many changes, but meanwhile we thank you for your kindness and your offer to serve us. We remain obliged to you and beg to know how much 100 marks of fine silver from Spain renders in [London] and for how much the mark fine has been selling; likewise, what price pieces of eight can fetch. We might well decide to arrange for you to have some returns from Spain.

Herewith we take the liberty of sending you 3 bills of exchange—of £85 sterling on Adrian Beyer, and £75 sterling on Cornelis van Deurs, and 1,000 [piasters?] @ 115g on Daniel Mercer, payable in Antwerp. Please procure their acceptance and send them back, and also see that the latter puts down the address in Antwerp, for which we shall be obliged. We remain, with regards, &c.

London:　　33s
Amsterdam:　32$\frac{7}{8}$.

$\frac{31\ May}{4\ Jun.}$1672

93　　CHARLES & JAMES BANCKES TO LM
HAMBURG　　　　　　　　　　　　　　　　　　　　　21 MAY 1672

'Madam Marescoe, Wee owe answer to your acceptable lines of the 23 past, and your remittance for £200 stg. being yesterday paid us doe herewith returne you the same in our owne bill, viz.,

£100 stg. @ 32s 9g 2 usances on Thomas Kent;

£116 stg. @ 32s 9g 2 usances on Charles Shorter, unto which please to procure the needfull and credit us with the same. At my being in Lunenbourg did discourse with your debtor Paulo Berenbergh who finde there well seated with his family, and in good employment; but notwithstanding hee pretends great poverty and incapacity of satisfying his debts I urged him with all the perswasione I could not to let mee returne unsatisfyed but finding nothing but fine words and excuses from him told him must seeke to obtaine your right the best way wee could. Soe the best way which can pitch upon to force him is to get our Resident Sir William Swann to write the duke of Lunenbourg such arguments as to perswade him not to grante protection to any that soe fraudulently wrong you but to recall ought in that nature, unless hee gives you satisfaction, which shall see that hee presseth closely home, as also this other business of Hans Christ. Helme; Sir William having beene yesterday with our burghermaster about it; soe shall have him to morrowe cited; and when appeares finde some way or other to secure your debt on his person. Sir William doth promise us to doe his uttmost in both these businesses which question not but will be performed, having for his encouradgment assured him of your thankfullness and a handsome piece of plate if can recover you these two debts. Bee assured that nothing shall bee wanting on our side to bring all to a speedy conclusion, and as ought farther passeth therein worth your notice you shall be duely advised thereof by, Madam, your most humble servant, &c.'

Amsterdam:	$32\frac{3}{4}$	sight.
Antwerp:	$32\frac{5}{8}$	at usance.
Paris:	$46\frac{3}{4}$	} 2 usances.
Rouen:	$46\frac{1}{2}$	
Venice:	$86\frac{1}{4}$	at usance.

$\dfrac{3 \text{ Jun.}}{20 \text{ Sep.}} 1672$

194 SKINNER, BALL & GOSFRIGHT to LM
LEGHORN   13 MAY 1672

'Madam, Wee have this weeke binn favard with your of the 8th past ordering us to buy up 50 bags of pepper for your accompt if at most it might be had at $D.16\frac{1}{2}$ where in unhappily we cannot serve you, the same beeing not now to be had under D.18 soe we must wait some other good occasion of your command, which we are very ambissious of. The exchange for London also risse to $54\frac{1}{2}d$ and noe monies neither to be had soe, all occasiond by its rise in France. Commission come lately for Ardasse upon its rise in England risse also here to *giu.* $12\frac{1}{2}$ the lb., and oyles which may however be had at D.14 the salme, new measure, at Galipoly, Therewith lades home the *Affrican* and *Raynebow* in porte, the furst bound for Messina, the other with the *Vine* for Palermo laden all with corne. The *Hamburg Merchant* bound home alone and the *Expectation* that imported 5 daies since from Palermo and *Tunis Merchant* 3 daies since from Tunis yet unresolved, and are all the English we have now in porte. The French gallies, 10 in all, imported yesterday and are bound as its said for Tunis to make peace, which beeing the present needfull with due respects remaine, &c.'

Venice: 104.
Amsterdam: 92.

$$\frac{18\ Jun.}{21\ Jun.}1672$$

5   ISAAC & JACOB MOMMA[1] to LM & PJ
AMSTERDAM   21 JUNE 1672

>]   Yours of the 24th past and 4th instant (old style) have come safely to hand and therewith the bills of exchange which you have accepted and sent back. They will be useful in due course. Your letters to Sweden were forwarded and we enclose some from there which we have received on your behalf, together with 8 bills of exchange drawn on you to a total of £1,200 sterling which we request you to accept and send back. It is a good thing that we agreed some time ago that you would honour our bills up to £500 in case of need. If it arises we shall let you know in due course.

We are experiencing very distressing times here and it seems likely that the King of France (if the Lord God does not intervene) will make himself master of this country. He has approached within 4 hours march of this city, but we hope he will not come any further for the moment, since the country has been flooded. It is to be lamented that the King of England has also been instrumental in the ruin of the Protestant religion;[2] we hope this dreadful news will open his eyes and that he, and other powers, will come to the help of this city. May he be moved to do so by the Lord God, to whose protection we commend you, remaining, &c.

London: 37s 0g ⎫
Rouen: 102d   ⎬ @ 2 usances.
Hamburg: 38s @ sight.

[1] The sons of Willem Momma, and not to be confused with Isaac and Jacob Momma-Reenstierna whose Grand Tour Jacob David helped finance on behalf of their father, Jacob Reenstierna, in 1678.
[2] '*het is te beclagen dat den Coningh van Engelandt tot de Ruin van de gereformeerde Religie mede een Instrument geweest is . . .'.*

$$\frac{20\ Jun.}{21\ Jun.}1672$$

6   J., D. & H. VAN BAERLE to LM & PJ
AMSTERDAM   24 JUNE 1672

•]   Our last letter was on the 21st, and since we have received nothing from you this serves to advise you that, for the reasons given in our last letter, the exchange rate on London has risen still higher. As a result, the money from your company and that of Madame Marescoe remains undisposed of. Various towns and places are surrendering without resistance and one can clearly discern that it has been done in collusion with some great ones who seek to change the government and possibly the religion of this state. Forsaken by everyone, we do not believe this city will hold out long.

Because of this high rate of exchange we thought it advisable to draw on you £407 10s payable at 2 usances to the order of Robert Styles for value received of the same, vizt.,

£95 sterling for the account of Louis Froment;

£200 } for our account, to set against our half share in the

£112 10s. } proceeds of the 400 coils of copper-wire.

Please honour these bills and place them to the said accounts. If the money for the copper-wire does not come in when it is due we shall make you some other provision. We cannot believe that this high exchange will last long. Wherewith, heartiest regards, &c.

London: 40s }
Paris: 101 to 100 } 2 usances.
Hamburg: 37s at sight.

$\frac{22\,Jun.}{25\,Jun.}$1672

197 J., D. & H. VAN BAERLE to LM & PJ

AMSTERDAM   28 JUNE 1672

[D] Our latest was on the 24th instant, whereby we advised you that we had drawn on you £95 sterling at 2 usances for the account of Louis Froment and £312 10s for our own account. Since then we have received yours of the 7th, 11th and 14th instant with the following remittances on behalf of your company, vizt.;

£150 @ 34s 2g } on Ott[avi]o Franc[is]co & Nic[ol]o And. Tousinc, due on the 27th instant;

£100 @ 34s 1g } on Roeland Cockey, falling due on the 30th instant; and for the account of Madame Marescoe £750 @ 33s 11g, namely:

£300 on Phil, de Surmont
£200 on Eduart Vandervoort
£150 on Joan Hervey Muysken,
& £100 on Jacob Derson
} falling due on 3 July.

For all these payment has been procured but only through the bank because payment cannot be demanded outside the bank (as you ordered). Many people have removed their funds from the bank and are daily doing so, and as one cannot be altogether sure that there is enough some of them are buying their bank-money at 2½ and 3 per cent loss. However, we cannot discover that there is any danger of the bank running short of money unless by plundering, against which we believe the civic authorities will take good care. We would have much preferred that you had drawn back these remittances in view of the loss which you will suffer by returns at the present high rate of exchange. However, it is beginning to weaken a little since our last letter.

The Messrs Momma have presented us with their bill of exchange for the £300 which still remains due to them but we found it inadvisable to take it at such a high price. Gold is being exchanged at a 10 per cent premium. Yesterday we gave Capt. Peter Hunt of the *Boston Merchant* two sacks of pieces of eight for the account of Mrs Marescoe—vizt. one sack of Mexican *reals* weighing 65 marks 5 ounces, and one sack of Seville *reals* weighing 45 marks, which we have lumped together in the bill of lading as 1,000 pieces although, through lack of time, we were unable to check them. With our next letter we hope to send the bill of lading and advise you of the amount. We are informed that no rixdollars or pieces of eight are obtainable in Rotterdam and we do not think it advisable to send any that way for the time being. We have looked for goods to send in London-bound ships but have not been able to obtain any yet. As soon as we are given permission we shall arrange some goods to consign to you and with every opportunity of English shipping will send you some bank-rixdollars.

Herewith we return the bill of exchange for £100 sterling on Coymans & Voet with the protest for lack of acceptance which we forgot to send by the last post because of these present troubles. We also remit to you for the account of Charles Godyn £600 sterling in 4 bills, of £200, £150, £150, and £100, drawn by Willem Momma on May 12th to be received from yourself on July 31st. Please credit Godyn's account and reserve the money until further order.

Pepper was selling lately at 19*g*; nutmegs at 45 to 47 stuivers; wherewith our heartiest regards, &c.

London: 38*s* 6*g* to 38*s* @ 2 usances.
Hamburg: 36*s* 6*g* to 37*s* @ sight.

[P.S.] We thank you for your friendly offer of help in these misfortunes. We intend to wait and see what outcome the Lord God will grant.

$$\frac{\textit{10 Jul.}}{\textit{12 Jul.}}\textit{1672}$$

J. D'HOLLANDRE & J. DU BERON to LM & PJ
LILLE   16 JULY 1672

'Madamoiselle, Pour responce a l'agreable votre du 28 passé, nous avons pris consideration sur les prix que vaillent chez vous; les merchandises nous marques mais le tout icy telement abondant, que ne voyons sur rien a proficter, seulement quelque peu sur l'eschanges, s'ils continuent comme nous les marques, scavoir sur icy a 2 usances a 34*s* 3*g* et sur Amsterdam a 36*s* 6*g*, poudres nous tirer £400 sterling comme dessus et nous remettre la mesme partie sur Amsterdam a 36*s* 6*g* et ne manquerons de faire tout honneur a vos traittes, cependant nous vous baissons les mains et demeurons, vos tres humbles serviteurs.'

$$\frac{\textit{19 Jul.}}{\textit{19 Jul.}}\textit{1672}$$

ALEXANDER WADDELL to LM & PJ
STOCKHOLM   26 JUNE 1672

For lack of occasion I have never before had the honour of corresponding with you, but I do so now at the persuasion of the Lord Lillienhoff who, according to his enclosed letter, recommends me to you and assures me that when I transfer all my London business to your hands you will do me all the good offices possible. Thereupon I have decided to consign to you my own ship, called *De Hoop*, which sailed for London from here only a few days ago. The captain is Simon Leysten, with whom I have loaded a quantity of iron and deals for my own account, as you can see from the enclosed invoice. At first I had addressed them to Mr William Strang of London but have now come to a different decision and herewith direct them to you, requesting you to arrange their reception and to sell them to my greatest advantage. I have given orders to Mr Strang that, if the ship arrives before the letter and is unloaded, he should transfer all my goods to you for my account, but if not the captain has orders to deliver to you. Mr Strang will hand over all the papers regarding this, for there are some parcels of iron which belong to other friends at London who are to shoulder the freight charges according to the signed bills of lading, whereof a detailed specification goes herewith. And as the captain is a bit dimwitted[1] please give him some help in case he makes a mistake about the freights, which you will be so kind as to receive and credit to my account, holding it for my further disposal. Lord Lillienhoff has also assured me that whenever I send you goods, even up to £2,000-worth, I shall be able to draw up to three-quarters of the value in return for reasonable interest. I trust that you will allow me to enjoy such accommodation, about which I await your answer. I shall thereupon send you further ships' cargoes such as iron, pitch and tar, as well as of hemp, so that you will have quite enough goods of mine in your hands.

If Captain Lysten is already with you Mr William Strang has orders to send him on to Scotland, and as he began this correspondence he may as well finish it, and on this occasion you need not incommode yourself. I hope that Mr Strang will not refuse you the goods in the ship *De Hoop* if it has already arrived and been unloaded before my countermanding orders. I shall send you a letter of attorney by the next post so that if he will not do it willingly he must deliver to you by the force of such a letter; wherewith, awaiting any relevant news, I remain, &c.

¹ '. . . ende alzoo den Schipper wat eenvoudig is . . .'.

$$\frac{20\ Jul.}{26\ Jul.}1672$$

200   E. RULAND to LM & PJ
         HAMBURG   12 JULY 1672

[D]   My last letter to you was on the 8th in which I advised you that I have procured the acceptance of the £160 drawn on Conrad de Schmit and that I would get it paid when due, together with the bill for £136 at 34s 2g which was already accepted. I can now confirm this. I have since received yours of the 5th by which you have remitted me another £90 at 34s 3g on Alexander Gilbert, for which I have also obtained acceptance and will procure payment in due course, crediting you meanwhile.

Because the situation in Holland remains so serious people here are not thinking much about trade or buying goods, of which we already have more than enough. Many, who are in need of ready cash, are disposing of their goods for what they can get, so this is no time to order more, even though commodity prices in [England] have fallen greatly. I shall be glad to know if yet more sugar is expected from Barbados this year. It is a commodity which is very cheap here now and virtually unsaleable. Meanwhile I must thank you for news about what is happening in [London] in one commodity, or another. I am glad to see what speculative opportunities there are, and I would welcome it if you would continue. With cordial regards, &c.

[P.S.] Please get accepted the enclosed bill for 172 ducats @ 53d and keep it until the second copy is shown to you.

London: 32s 9g 2 usances.
Amsterdam: 34 @ sight.
Antwerp: 33 @ sight.
Paris: 46 @ 2 usances.

$$\frac{7 \text{ Aug.}}{9 \text{ Aug.}} 1672$$

01 W. MOMMA to LM & PJ
NYKÖPING   7 JULY 1672

] My last letter to you was about a week ago. Since then I have received yours of the 7th and
14th past from which I see that you have insured Jacob Fix for £2,400, of which £1,900 is at
5 per cent and £500 at 6 per cent—the cost of the policy, brokerage and commission
amounting to £141 12s, for which I have credited you. I hope the said ship has arrived safely
and that you have likewise insured for £1,500 the *St Anna* of Capt. Jacob Grys, for whom I
have already sent you the bill of lading. In two days time I am hoping to send to Norrköping
100 slb of 5-band wire and possibly some iron pots for loading aboard Gerret Laurens's ship. I
shall let you know by my next for how much you are to insure them.

I am not happy to see that my wire and brass, remaining from last year, is still unsold, and I
hope it will be disposed of before the new lot arrives. Furthermore (as I have mentioned to
you before) please sell my goods as soon as possible after their arrival. I would prefer that you
determine the market price for others rather than let others determine it for you. What I need
most are sales:[1] then I can send you even more.

With my last letter I drew on you for £800, payable at the end of September, and £700
due in the middle of October payable to the orders of my sons Isaac and Jacob Momma.

The melancholy state of affaires in Holland has considerably altered business here, but God
will see that everything turns out for the best, with heartiest regards, &c.

[1] 'De consumbsie is my best . . .'.

$$\frac{10 \text{ Aug.}}{13 \text{ Aug.}} 1672$$

02 A. WADDELL to LM & PJ
STOCKHOLM   24 JULY 1672

] My last letter was on the 13th instant in which I drew £1,000 on you against the goods
aboard the ship *De Hoop* which I earlier ordered you to insure for £1,200. In case you have
had no news of its arrival I now confirm this. I expect to have news soon from the Sound
about the ship *Halven Maendt*, against whose cargo I have today drawn on you £800 payable
at 10 weeks from sight to Timotheus van der Boom or order at Amsterdam. I beg you, as a
friend, to honour this, although I have also ordered Nathaniel Watson of Hamburg to draw
RD 1,000 against the same cargo. I hope you will accept his bills as well, debiting my account
accordingly. If, by the time you have received my drafts, the ship *Halve Maend* has not yet
arrived but you have had something from him—that is to say, you have heard from him—
please have it insured for £1,500 stg. by reliable friends as security for acceptance of my
drafts. I am relying heavily on you to honour my drafts promptly, especially the £800 from
Timotheus van der Boom which, together with others, I have drawn on you in view of the
promises which Lillienhoff has made to me and still makes. Consequently I do not doubt that
you will accept and honour my bills.

I send enclosed herewith a bill of lading from Gothenburg regarding 200 slb of iron
consigned to you from there in the ship *Konig David*. Please take receipt of it and, after paying
for the freight according to the bill of lading, procure its sale to my maximum advantage and
let me have word of your success.

The above-mentioned ship, the *Halven Maend*, is definitely a well-known Swedish ship and is wholly Swedish-owned and for your information there are no other goods but mine loaded aboard.

I expect you are already well aware that the old Tar Company intends to re-form and reinforce itself, as a result of which I may get some employment, and if a directorship should be conferred on me I shall solicit vigorously for the exclusive commission to be diverted to you again—all the more so when you have satisfactorily accommodated me; wherewith my cordial regards, &c.

[P.S.] Mr Nathaniel Watson is not drawing on you, but today I have sent him a bill of exchange for £250 sterling, payable 10 weeks from sight, drawn on you and payable to him or order for my account.

$$\frac{10 \ Aug.}{16 \ Aug.} 1672$$

203 A. BERENBERG'S WIDOW & HEIRS TO LM & PJ
HAMBURG   2 AUGUST 1672

[D] Our last letter was on the 26th past, which we sent by way of Amsterdam. This one is going through Antwerp because it seems quicker, and we have today safely received yours of the 26th past by the same route. We have seen therein the prices of various commodities, for which we thank you, and we would be glad if you would continue to send them. Although prices are low we cannot decide to order anything because nothing is selling here and there are large quantities of goods in town. Some people, who are in need of ready cash, are spoiling the market so one must just sit still and wait. Campeachy wood has fallen here to 17 *ML*, current money; pepper is at 18¼*g*; Barbados sugar, 5¾ to 6*g*; Aleppo galls 41 to 42 *ML* per 100 lb; new currants *ML* 28; indigo Guatemalo is at 10*s* flem. and Barbados indigo at 8½*s* flem. We are glad to hear that Ardasse has risen, because we are already supplied with some.

You were advised that if you could get fine brown ginger for 40*s* or below, free on board, you could buy 6,000 lb. for us, but we are relieved to see that there is little or no prospect of it for we immediately had letters saying that it would be ordered for us if it could be obtained. Because of the number of capers which will be putting to sea from Holland nothing will be getting through.

It is a good thing that Farrington and Claypool have paid their bill. We hope the rest has also come in. We will let you know soon what we want done with our proceeds. Friendliest regards, &c.

London: 32*s* 11*g*.
Amsterdam: 33¾.

$$\frac{27 \ Aug.}{20 \ Sep.} 1672$$

204 P. VAN TEYLINGEN & CO TO LM
VENICE   19 AUGUST 1672

[D] We find ourselves with your letter of the 19th past, by which we were glad to see that Bulivant had paid the *D*.331 13*g* we remitted, and since you have credited us with it there remains nothing further to be said. When, at your convenience, you have looked at and approved the current account we sent and credited us with the balance all outstanding debts are settled.

Regarding the sale of your lead, nothing has happened through lack of buyers who are being very cautious, and for nearly two months nothing has been sold. Henceforth we hope there will be some further demand, and if any good opportunity presents itself we shall not fail to push forward your 50 pieces as best we can: of this you may be fully assured, and we shall keep you informed of what we are able to achieve.

As a result of the news, that 14 ships have arrived in Holland from the East Indies, pepper is quite dead and is valued by some at only D.76, but we will not sell the batch we have being of opinion that it will improve since it can scarcely be brought from England or Holland, and the selling-season is nearly here. We shall adjust our prices here according to the prices the Company sets in England. If you decide to send us some supplies at the first opportunity, as with the lead, we do not doubt that we will do some good business. Cloves, D.60; cinnamon, D.100–120, according to quality; sappon wood, D.80; campeachy wood, D.80 at 4 months; indigo guatemalo, D.116 at 6 months; cuminiglio, D.4½; quicksilver per *vel* of 260 lb. at D.110 banco; Gallipoli oil, D.13 free on board. How the new currants turn out and what price the 3 English ships have paid for them we shall soon hear and let you know. Muscovado sugar from Lisbon D.6–7; ditto white, D.10–12 according to quality. Breaking off now, we remain, with cordial regards, &c.

London: 53½d.
Amsterdam: 93½.

$$\frac{28 \ Aug.}{3 \ Sep.}1672$$

5 ARCHIBALD JOSSY & THOMAS PAWSON to LM & PJ
EDINBURGH   22 AUGUST 1672

'Our last was of the 10th instant and since one of yours of the 10th detti giving us leave to draw upon you if need reqwier the somme of a 1,000£ sterling. As for our own proceeds they ar as yett but littell effected being com to leat boeth as to salt and iron, and buying of schip and salt, the best schips and most of the salt being bought away befor owr arival be several factors from Norway, Denmark, England and Irland and other lands who heath bein hier leing since for said desing. The vice Admiral heath yet 3 Dutch flaybots loaden with salt which we have survayed and have profered him for the best of them (being a neu schip of burthen about 430 *moyers* of salt which is a 140 last) with her loading £850 sterling, but most of her chieffe rigging is missing being plundered away be the capers that took her soe that it will cost at least 200£ sterling to rigge her owt to sea yet he demands £1,000 sterling for her and loading as she lyes but we hop that heel condeschend if we doe proffer him the other £50 sterling mor. The other 2 schips he intends to send to the east contry for his own accompt. What salt yet remeaneth is all in the citicens hands, who finding soe many factors from all pearts to bay it causeth them keep up the priece which is for present 6s 8d and 7s per barrel. As yet we have bawght non of them hearing that those 2 foresaid veschels that the vice admiral intended for the east he is now discouradged to adventur them owt to sea being advised of soe many Dutch capers at sea soe that hope to geat salt of him at ane easier reat. Please give us your advice citto and what you intend with schip *Hop* and your absolut order whether wee shall buy a leading of salt for her or not. The priece of iron is verry low and noe ready money to be had for it be reason of a Gottenburg veschel be name *Dove* loaden with 1,200 schippounds iron that is braught up hier and adjudged prayse and the said iron sold as be report to 20d per ston, which is all from your humble servants, &c.'

$$\frac{30 \ Aug.}{6 \ Sep.} 1672$$

206   J., D & H. VAN BAERLE to LM & PJ
AMSTERDAM   2 SEPTEMBER 1672

[D]   Our last letter was on the 23rd past, in which we remitted for your account £21 12s and £138 sterling. A second copy of the latter bill accompanies this. We have since received yours of the 9th and 16th past, with the accepted bill for £150 sterling, and we thank you for your trouble.

Huyberts van Vlissingen has not yet written to us about your money so we trust he has found the opportunity of remitting it to you since the disorders in Zeeland have mostly quietened down.

Herewith we send your current account, by which you owe us a balance of f.87.18.8. Please check it and, if you find no mistakes, make a note of it. The protest for non-acceptance against Coymans & Voet, costing f.1.16, has not yet been reimbursed by them and they tell us we must demand it from Hugh Forth.

The exchange has also fallen greatly here, apparently because our East India Company will soon be holding its sales and also because a great deal of money remitted overseas in panic is now returning.

We still have no news of the ships the *Coninck David* and *St Jansborg* which left Stockholm and Norrköping for Rouen. If they have fallen into the hands of the capers our Swedish friends will not escape without loss, even though they are free Swedish ships.

Many bills of exchange on Abraham Reenstierna, and also some on Jacob Reenstierna, have been returned protested from here and Hamburg. We fear that the former is about f.4,000 in our debt and if you have any proceeds of his in your hands please let us know, so in case anything should happen to him we can recover our guarantees from it. And please keep all this secret.

Business remains at a standstill. Pepper is about 17g; lead, 28 to 29s; tin, f.54; Barbados sugar, 5½g.   With our heartiest regards, &c.

London:	33s 9–8g	⎫
Paris:	98	⎬ @ 2 usances.
Rouen:	97⅛	⎭
Hamburg:	33 1/16	⎫ @ sight.
Antwerp:	2½ per cent	⎭

$$\frac{11 \ Sep.}{13 \ Sep.} 1672$$

207   P. BERENBERG (JR.) to LM & PJ
HAMBURG   30 AUGUST 1672

[D]   I last wrote to you on the 16th and since then have received yours of the same date by which I see that a fleet of ships from Barbados has been expected every day. If and when you perform my commission regarding brown ginger I shall expect to hear in your next letter. So far we have not heard of any Hamburg ships being seized by Zeeland capers and if you do not hear anything to the contrary in [London] and find the opportunity of a good Hamburg ship in [London] which (as far you can learn) only belongs to free people, I shall be content if you will load in it about half of any ginger you may buy and send it here, retaining the other half until further order. It would be best if the shipment were delayed until the captain is nearly ready to depart so that one can act according to the latest news one receives from sea.

Things are in a very bad way here for all commodities. Pepper, 17g; indigo is at rock-bottom prices and galls also; I still have the 20 sacks of galls lying unsold which you bought for me two years ago, as well as Caribbean indigo. Though I suffer loss by keeping it for so long one must be patient. May God bring better times!

With cordial regards, &c.

London:—33*s* @ 2 usances.

$\frac{11\ Sep.}{12\ Sep.}$ 1672

208   JOHN KINGSTONE to LM & PJ
      DEAL   9 SEPTEMBER 1672

'Sirs, I have yours. In answer the officers of the Admarlty here will not deliver the iron till it is mad appear in the court that you are the proprieters. What you have done at London they will take no notice or nor of any warrant from thence, it being landed here. I have pleaded soe much about it that I am sommoned to appeare at the court to morrow at Dover and I shall there doe what I can to serve you there. If I can satesfie them the goods is yours will determine the salvedge which I feare will be above a 3rd part and the court charges will be great. I shall use my utmost endeavor to bring it as low as may be. They have entred it in court as the Lord Warden's goods which is his Royall Highness the Duke of Yorke. I must fee an atturney which is my freind, to assist in it. The men will looke after noe more unless they can have the one moiety for salvedge as they tell me.

I am, Sir, your servant at command, &c.

[P.S.] God willing you shall have a first account when have bine at the court to hear what they say.'

$\frac{14\ Sep.}{17\ Sep.}$ 1672

209   A. JOSSY & T. PAWSON to LM & PJ
      EDINBURGH   7 SEPTEMBER 1672

'Our last was the 27th past, shewing that had bought a ship with her loading of Spanish salt, and had drawn upon you at 1 month's sight payable to Mr Charles Bickerstaffe or order £400—since none from you. We hope shall have noe further occasion of drawing upon you since have sold the greatest part of our iron at 29*d* per stone payable in 14 dayes and are indeavoring to dispose of the rest as soon as possible. We expect every post your advice of ship the *Hope* her coming hither, being about buying a loading of Spanish salt for her, but would willingly hear the certainty of her coming before we close. The most of the Sweedish and Danish ships brought up here are declared free. Here's dayly expected a frigate from England to conduct all ships bound from hence to London. Here lye severall prized ships bought by factors and bound for the East but dare not venture out to sea for fear of being retaken by the Dutch, who have many capers out [as are informed][1] the certainty of which please advise us. No more at present from, A.J.   T.P.'

[1] Marginal insertion.

$$\frac{17 \; Sep.}{23 \; Sep.} 1672$$

210   A. BERENBERG'S WIDOW & HEIRS to LM & PJ
HAMBURG   6 SEPTEMBER 1672

[D]   We have not written for a few posts and our last letter was on the 16th past in which we
ordered that, if you could obtain fine brown ginger for 40s, free on board, you might buy to
the value of £200 sterling and store it in a good [London] warehouse until our further order.
This we confirm.

   Since then we have heard nothing from you but have seen what is happening in [London]
in your letters to our brother Paul, for which we thank you. Things continue so desperately
bad here that one lacks the courage to order any goods, for nothing is selling and prices are so
low that there is rather more prospect of losing than of profiting. It really is dreadful, and
since one daily hears of the many prizes which the Dutch capers are bringing in prices will be
undercut even more for their goods are so cheap that one simply cannot compete. However,
since our money is lying idle in [England] please take note that if you can get fine Aleppo galls
for 50s or below you can buy 20 sacks for us—that is, free on board, but keep them in a safe
place for us. But they must be of good quality, plump and blue and not mixed with gall-
wood otherwise they will be like the last 17 sacks you provided, still lying here, which turned
out to be very dull, small and coarse. We had many prospective purchasers for them but no
one wanted them. The 30 sacks which you provided before that were much better, while
these last 17 sacks seem to be damaged goods, so we have been very badly served. We trust
you will not miss any opportunity now to provide us with ginger or galls, all the more as a
large quantity of the latter have come and are finding no sales. You know how to do it most
advantageously and to let us know what success you have. It would be very good if sugar
prices would rise because we still have both consignments on our hands, with friendly
regards, &c.

London: 33s at 2 usances.
Amsterdam: $32\frac{11}{16}$ at sight.

$$\frac{9 \; Oct.}{11 \; Oct.} 1672$$

211   J. LILLIENHOFF & H. THUEN to LM & PJ
STOCKHOLM   14 SEPTEMBER 1672

[D]   Our last letter was on the 11th instant, to which we refer. Since then we have received your
communication of the 23rd past, from which we see that 700 bars of our iron have been
salvaged from Anders Biorsen. We hope that still more has been salvaged since then because
the captain was supplied with 1,700 bars when he arrived at Gothenburg. We beg you kindly
to continue to take care of our interests, and we urge this most strongly.

   Thank you for accepting our drafts of £480 sterling and we do not doubt that you have
accepted our last of £500 at 1 month and £500 at 2 months after sight, as well as the £200 at
2 months drawn 3 days ago payable to the order of Mr Teixera.

   We have been happy to learn of the safe arrivals of captains Hans Meyer, Hans Michielsen
and Johan Kruse with our iron—for which God be thanked! But we are sorry to hear that
iron prices are falling in [England]. We urge you to continue to protect our interests and we
rely on you to waste no time in selling our iron.

We have also received a bill of lading of 20 hogsheads of Barbados sugar loaded aboard Jacob Erick's ship. May God protect him and bring him in safety. On his arrival we shall unload the sugar and do our best to benefit your account, which we believe was your intention, for we cannot take it on our account. It will be a very long time in yielding any payments as the Sugar Company is glutted with too much stock, and it will scarcely sell or be paid for in less than 10 or 12 months. However, as we have interests in the above-mentioned company we shall do the best we can to help.

We are reasonably well-supplied with iron, which we are thinking of sending to you if only the duty were removed, as every one hopes it will be if God grants peace. Please let Messrs Bartholotti & Rihel of Amsterdam have *RD* 5,000 out of the proceeds for our goods, which they are insuring, if and when they are sold. And as our iron- and wire-works are very burdensome and we are overloaded with iron and wire which we cannot turn into money in these difficult times, we request that you give us sympathetic support in these circumstances and accommodate us as far as you can without prejudicing yourselves—i.e. by allowing us to draw on you for 8 or 10 months the balance to which our goods amounts to, payable to the order of Manoel Teixera. He can oblige us, and we have formed a special friendship with him.

We calculate that the amount of iron, including what is in the ship *De Patientia* (which, God permitting, will have arrived before this)

totals	2,250 slb	from which must be deducted		
	250 slb	in the wrecked Anders Beursen,		
	2,000 slb	which should be able to render about		
RD	14,000.			
RD	7,800	for the wire in Hans Meyer, totals		
RD	21,800;	from which about £1,680 sterling has been drawn is	*RD*	7,000
		To Messrs Bartholotti & Rihel:	*RD*	5,000
RD	12,000		*RD*	12,000

RD 9,800 approximately should remain. If we could now draw *RD* 7,000 as we have before it would be an act of great friendship, and as for the remainder we would reckon it as the *RD* 2,500 due from the Lord Leyonbergh. Next week the following will be cleared, namely: an obligation dated 27 July from Abraham Wolters to pay at 6 months for *RD* 397.25; also an assignment on the bank to pay on 29 November 2,400 dollars copper money, and 3,409 dollars copper money to be paid in cash. The rest will be paid next week with an obligation from Caspar Robbert though without prejudice to us. Of these, the obligation from Abraham Wolters has come in and the others from Caspar Robbert and the bank.

We have seen with nothing but great astonishment what you say about our wire, which is nevertheless in as great demand here and in Holland, Hamburg and France as any other. We beg you to take the proceeds, for the difference is quite considerable, and they must be wicked people who refer to it in this way. We urge you to take care of our interests.

As regards the seizure of the ship *De Dolphin*, Mr Caspar Robbert will write to you more fully, and the King has got the Admiralty to write to the envoy Leyonbergh about the goods.[1] I again commend to you the reclamation of my small consignment, since it is hardly important enough for the envoy to do it. If the Lord permits you may easily procure my half, for it is only some varnish which I need for my house, wherewith our cordial regards, &c.

[P.S.] We have spent about *RD*.50, and we hope that it will be acceptable to you to rely on your discretion in our difficulties.

¹ The capture of this vessel roused considerable English hopes that it would prove a legitimate Dutch prize— *CSPD, 1672*, pp. 446, 461, 622; *CSPD, 1672–73*, p. 37; *CSPD, 1673–75*, pp. 278, 369, 504.

$$\frac{11\ Oct.}{11\ Oct.}1672$$

212 A. BERENBERG'S WIDOW & CO to LM & PJ
HAMBURG   I OCTOBER 1672

[D] We find ourselves with your two letters of the 10th and 23rd past, from which we have noted what you say about one commodity and another, and that you wish that there was some opportunity to invest our money in something profitable. We wish so too, but we really cannot believe there is any chance of gaining anything, for the times are becoming too dangerous and everywhere there is fear of war, as a result of which very little is being bought and one can no longer recommend any firm price for commodities. We have never before witnessed such bad times, and because so many Barbados ships have been captured at sea there is much undercutting of Barbados goods, so one simply cannot compete with them to make it worth paying out any money.

It is a good thing that you made a note to buy for us £200 stg.-worth of good black ginger (if it can be had at 40s or below, free on board) as well as 20 sacks of fine Aleppo galls, if they can be had for 50s per cwt. However, as galls are standing at 53 to 54s it is no use thinking that anything can be done with them. However, some other friends of ours hold out the hope that brown ginger may well fall to 38s. You will know how to procure them advantageously for us, and when you have done so divide them between two Hamburger or other free ships and send them here, giving us due notice by which captain they are sent—but please do not send them in English ships.

Since indigo seems likely to be at reasonable prices please also buy for us about £130 stg.-worth of fine Jamaican or Caribbean indigo which looks saleable and of high quality, if you can get it for 3s 1d or 3s 2d at most, free on board. And please make sure that it is not of small, dirty pieces to which people strongly object: a weak blue is of no use to us. You can send it to us here under our customary mark. Pepper still fetches $16\frac{3}{4}g$ here but vendors are happy to deliver it for 16g at 6 months time and good quantities are sold. The world is full of pepper and demand is very small. We shall have to wait and see; we believe it may perhaps be sold more cheaply by some individuals, or it may stay at the same price—time will tell.

20 to 21s for sugar is certainly not dear although there is nothing to be done with it here. Nevertheless, if we had room in our own houses we would order some but they are full up with goods and unless we hire a warehouse, which is very expensive here, we can not have any. We are also well-supplied with Ardasse and it is cheaper here than in [England]. Meanwhile we shall be glad to learn more about what is happening with one thing or another so that we can act accordingly. Friendly regards, &c.

London: 33s 8g   2 usances.
Amsterdam: $32\frac{1}{3}$ to $\frac{3}{8}$.
Antwerp: $32\frac{1}{4}$.

W. MOMMA to LM & PJ

NYKÖPING   29 SEPTEMBER 1672

My last letter was on the 8th instant. Since then I have received yours of the 13th and 23rd past from which I see that you have procured insurance on Gerret Laurens's ship of £400 at $4\frac{1}{2}$ per cent and £950 at 5 per cent. I hope you have since been able to procure the remainder. I have also received the current account which you closed on the 13th of August by which there is due to you £5,237 15s 8d. I agree with that, but find that you have brought together into the outstanding debts due on recent sales old debts amounting to £1,594 16s 2d. New debts cannot be mixed up with old debts. I also find that Anthony Hatch, Skepper, Slutter[1] and Sampson delay somewhat. I hope they have paid up since then, and please ensure that no new debts are put down with the old ones. Also, specify how much each person owes without lumping together two or three persons unless they are in partnership and the one is liable for the other. Prices are bad and insurance costly so it does not help to make bad debts. Please take care therefore, as you have until now. You seem to believe that my goods have been fully drawn against so I must calculate according to your own account what brass has been sent to you,

vizt.— remaining of the old   Slb 20.02.02
            with the *Jupiter*, Jacob Fix   152.16.00
            with the *St Anna*, Jacob Grys   101.15.00
            with Gerret Laurens   111.01.16
                                            _____
                                            Slb 385.14.18

which I calculate to yield about 1,022 cwt. at £5 15s over and above expenses:

	£	s	d
	5,876	10	0
For the 159 slb of iron in Jacob Grys, about	263	10	9
	6,140	0	0

It is true that the iron ought not to be included in the calculation because it is not insured, but without the same it would not differ by more than £100–£200, if you have accepted the £800 which has just been drawn on Gerret Laurens. The great decline in prices goes beyond what I had expected, and I had hoped to have £400–£500 more in proceeds in hand. I do not doubt that you will accept this £800 as well as what I have drawn against the goods in Erick Anderson Boy. You can expect no more this year. My view is that your prices are now at their lowest point and that with winter coming they will begin to fetch more.

I have noted that you sold, in addition to the 250 coils of wire on 2 August to Wathing & Woodfield, another 350 coils to the same, all at £6 10s with 4 months time; to John Skepper 20 brewing-plates, cwt. 10.1.8 lb. of pots at £6 10s and 12 cwt. of latten at £6 with 6 months time; and to Grice the remaining pots from the *Jupiter* as well as 23 cwt. of latten at £6 10s in 6 months, and this account you have put with the outstanding debts due on the old account.

I have now received by the last post in my sons' letters news that Capt. Jacob Grys was intercepted and brought in to Rotterdam by capers, although I hope he will soon be released as petitioned for. If not, it would be advisable if you sent over the policy on the brass, which is insured only against the risks of the sea, with a simple attestation that the iron is not insured. My sons will probably have written to you about it. I hope to have better news about Gerret Laurens and Erick Anderson Boy, God willing. Regards, &c.

[1] John Slaughter.

$$\frac{19\ Oct.}{25\ Oct.}1672$$

214   E. RULAND to LM & PJ
HAMBURG   11 OCTOBER 1672

[D]   In answer to yours of the 23rd of September, tobacco leaf begins to be in demand and at 5s 6g one should easily find buyers. If I can get 6s current money for what I buy from you I do not believe I should lose much. I shall be glad to take my brother P[eter]'s advice if you ask him for it, but it cannot be of much help to me.

I shall be glad to learn how the [English] East India Company are selling their goods. Someone wrote from Rouen recently that the *flota* had reached Spain from the Indies and I foresee that indigo will fall still further.

Many Barbados ships have been captured and brought into Zeeland which should cause a rise in sugar prices, and I see that sundry Straits goods are likely to rise also. Please inform me if it is true, as they write, that ships are going to Italy from England.

Pepper here is at $16\frac{3}{4}g$; ginger at 12g with 12 months time. It is said this evening that a ship from England is in the Elbe which will have a good quantity of tobacco-leaf aboard. Whether it is from [London] or from Bristol I do not know. With cordial regards, &c.

London: 33s 8g   2 usances.
Amsterdam: $32\frac{1}{4}$.
Antwerp: 32.
Paris: 47 at 2 usances.

$$\frac{19\ Oct.}{25\ Oct.}1672$$

215   S. DE GEER to LM & PJ
AMSTERDAM   25 OCTOBER 1672

[D]   Since my last letter of the 19th instant I have received yours of the 4th and 8th, from which I see that the ship *Zon*[?] had arrived in the river—for which the Lord God be thanked—and I trust it has now safely reached the city.

Captain Jacob Grys also is now entirely free so he is ready to take his departure for London at the first opportunity.

It is very good to see that you have sold more iron, but I am not glad to see that the price is falling so much for it is not at all adequate, and as for what you were offered for the remainder, the time allowed for payment is also much too long. If one sells a batch in that way, even if it is a lot, the price is bound to decline. Nevertheless, as I really see no present prospect of much improvement I am forced to think that one must go along with it. I trust that with these low prices the said iron will now sell rather better and in the coming year fetch rather more once it is better known.

Regarding the accounts of these ships: I cannot see that much iron of importance will be shipped out of Sweden to London. It is not merely because of these low prices, heavy freight-charges and expenses but also because there are no more ships to lade, all the large ships having been already despatched. It looks as if the increase in the toll will be set aside. I have received news from the Sound that Capt. Hendrick Mattson has arrived safely there—for which the Lord be thanked. Let me know at once for how much you can sell timber and deals.

A letter from Stockholm dated the 28th tells me that they will know shortly whether the duty will be reduced or remain the same.

There are still two large ships lying at London[1] which should soon be ready to depart, loaded mainly with iron, as I believe. I long to have the account of the iron cargo sold at Hull.

I have obtained acceptance for your remittances and have also drawn on you for approximately what you say the iron amounts to. I shall wait for the rest, not doubting that you will allow me the remainder also, which I will take with Mr Suasso at 3 or 4 usances, granting somewhat more time than usual because I am rather in need of more cash.

Captain Erick Ericksen of the ship *Konig David*, going from Hull to Norrköping, has also arrived in the Sound.

I have no further news so I shall conclude this and remain, &c.

[P.S.] I shall write to my brother Jan[2] in Stockholm that he should tell you the amount of iron being despatched, which should be made good to me or Gerard de Geer.

[1] *Sic*. Presumably a slip of the pen for Stockholm.
[2] Johan de Geer, fifteenth child and fifth surviving son of Louis de Geer, b. 1632, d. 1696.

$$\frac{29 \ Oct.}{1 \ Nov.} 1672$$

16   P. BERENBERG (JR.) to LM & PJ

HAMBURG   18 OCTOBER 1672

)]   Your two letters of the 27th of September and the 4th instant have reached me safely. By the latter, which I received first, I see that you have bought for me 50 sacks of brown Barbados ginger at 40s, free on board, and that you intend to load it on D[irick] Roys. I am waiting to hear that you have succeeded and to receive the bill of lading and invoice. I hope you have obtained good quality because I hear that a great deal of bad stuff has been coming from [England]. Please do not buy any of it for me or mix it with what is destined for our firm, because it inconveniences me here—for your information.

I also wait to hear how you have employed the remainder of my money in buying brown Barbados ginger and sending it here. The capers have been capturing ginger at sea and taking it to Holland where it sells at a low price, so the prospects are that it will begin to be undercut here as well.

Everything is going so unspeakably badly with commodities here that one simply cannot describe it—great abundance of everything and tiny consumption, as a result of which everything must be sold at a considerable loss. It is believed that among the fleet which has arrived in Spain from the Indies is also a ship from Honduras, so doubtless there will be a great deal of indigo and consequently a considerable decline in price. With cordial regards, &c.

London—33s 6–7g 2 usances.

$$\frac{3 \ Dec.}{6 \ Dec.} 1672$$

17   S. DE GEER to LM & PJ

AMSTERDAM   [9 DECEMBER][1] 1672

)]   Accompanying this is a copy of my last letter, and since then I have received yours of 22 November.

As I wrote, I have ordered the making of the pan iron in Sweden, but it will all be of the 'O' and 'G' variety, for I cannot be absolutely sure that I can make the other sort (of which I once sent a sample from here) and decided it was better to prefer the certain for the uncertain. What is more, I know that it is good.

At Bordeaux there is lying a ship lading for London, belonging to His Excellency Gustaff Soop,[2] named *De Pasientia* and about 70 lasts in burthen. On board is [the body of] the captain who was drowned at [the Isle of] Wight, so it is being conveyed by the mate, and as he is unknown to me please be helpful to him and do what he may want you to do and receive the freight money. Furthermore, handle his account as if you were the captain and consider where it would be most advisable to send him, where there might be some serviceable freight. I am writing to him herewith to follow your orders in every particular. Please let me know at once how much it costs to export from Bordeaux. He wrote to me from Bordeaux that he was well and had agreed upon 42s per vat.

People are trying to persuade me (although I simply cannot understand it) that Swedish ships must state in their passes where they are going to and what they are carrying. That may well be true if they are coming from Stockholm, but if they are sailing for other places it is quite impossible, because they cannot know what country they are going to before they have acquired a cargo, and by then it is too late to write for a pass. Please let me know how you understand it, and whether or not a captain, sailing from Stockholm to London with a pass saying he is coming with pitch and tar from Stockholm to London, may then sail with the same pass from London to Bordeaux and from there back to London or Hamburg?

Herewith comes a note from Johannes de Geer about the iron he has sent you this year. The ship *Drie Salmen*, captain Jan Cornelis, is likely to come here from Stockholm, being loaded there with iron and 528 coils of copper-wire by Johannes de Geer and Abraham Wouters and consigned to Steven de Geer. All in all, it has 2,732 slb of iron and 49 slb of wire. Please have it registered in London as well as in Scotland if you judge it likely to journey there. The ship *De Coninq David*, captain Hendrick Matson, with its cargo of timber taken aboard in Norway for the ship's account, is to sail to either Bordeaux or Lisbon, as the captain thinks advisable. The captain has orders to enquire if there are any letters from you waiting for him if he should be driven into the Downs by contrary winds, so that if by chance timber—that is, deals—are expensive with you and likely to fetch much more than at Bordeaux, then he might as well go to London. So please write to your agent to keep an eye open for the said captain, and decide whether you consider it a good idea for the cargo to be unloaded in London, or in Portsmouth or [the Isle of] Wight, where it might sell readily and a return freight of bottles[3] for Bordeaux might present itself. Please deliberate with the captain about what might be best to do. Furthermore, I strongly urge upon you the reclamation of my goods in the Muscovite ship,[4] of which I send the invoice for your fuller information. I trust that everything is in hand and that you, through your agents, will be able to recover them. The expenditure which I mentioned previously you will know best how to manage and bestow as time and opportunity permits.

Herewith also goes a note to Lord Leyonberg which will likewise be useful, as occasion serves.

Our Ambassadors have arrived safely at Rotterdam. I am thinking of going to The Hague shortly and if anything of importance turns up I shall let you know. May the Lord give us a good peace, to whose protection I commend you, &c.

---

[1] Mis-dated 9 November.

[2] Gustaff Soop (1624–79) Swedish privy councillor, President of Reduktionskollegiet 1660–3, and Governor-General of the Queen Mother's estates.

³ '. . . *een vracht mett Pulse naer bordaux mocht presenteren* . . .'. 'Pul', a nautical term for a jug, tankard or stone bottle—of which the latter seems most appropriate for Bordeaux.

⁴ De Geer had sent 600 roubles to Moscow via Archangel in a Swedish ship under Captain Lars Oloffson. On its return journey to Amsterdam it had been seized by Scottish capers and, as [218] indicates, after trial in the Admiralty Court its alleged Dutch identity was held to be proved. De Geer's goods on board included 40 vats of tallow.

$$\frac{23\ Dec.}{24\ Dec.}1672$$

18 WALTER CHEISLIE to PJ
EDINBURGH   14 DECEMBER 1672

'Sir, Yours 3 instant being long a coming to hand I could not answer sooner. As to entring of thos vessells mentioned in yours of our Admiralls court since it is your desyr I schall doe it, but the last you caused me enter from Moscovia being brocht up by our privatiers to this place and proven so quyt contrarie to my entring him a Swed as you ordered hath dashed all to peaces the credit of anie such entries. As to giving you anie incouradgment in poynt of reclamacion I cannot exept I abused you if ther be not much mor to be said than what hath hitherto apeared in the whole process, which is all at present from your humble servant, &c.'

$$\frac{13\ Jan.}{17\ Jan.}1673$$

19 A. JOSSY to LM & PJ
MIDDELBURG   19/29 DECEMBER 1672

'These ar to give you notice how misfortunately we encontered with a Hollands caper named Jan Schlumer, captain of a galliot named the *Schlues* and that under the Jewtlands cost, 9 a 10 liegs from the Skaa,¹ wher he manned owr measter's schip the *Diemant* and send us up a costi, wher he arrived on the 17/27th December and mead present inqwisition for our schip and soe ar informed that she is in salvo att Campfier.² Alsoe the same Schlumer heath teaken and send up the schip the *Hoop*. Schiper Lichten is hier with us but as yet noe newes of his schip. This day boeth the schipper and I have consulted the bussinesse with one advocat and one procorator hew gieveth us good cowradge since that they ar boeth Swedisch schips and teacken in a free river and that within seight of land. They have not only teacken owr schips but plundered us to the verry smock, which the Lords of the Admiralitie teaketh in verry wel peart. I have written to my measter this post but knoweth not hew is his factor in Ambsterdame therfor coweld not draw any money ther, but shall intreat you in favers of my measter and according to his order given me to pay to Mr Mark Fletzer or order the somme of £25 sterling and please that to his accompt. Pray yew faill not to honor this bill or then its a hundereth to one if we doe not loose owr reight in boeth the schips for as ye know yowr selfs we can not be heard hier without money and we have noe acqwentence hier into such tyme we shall have ane answear of my letter from my measter and then I doe expect order to draw upon his factors in Amsterdam, and what shall be further doen in recleaming of boeth the schips shall freqwently advice yew, soe this be vertew of my measter's order is all for present from him who is, your humble servant.'

¹ I.e. the Skaw, the northenmost tip of Denmark.
² Veere, the port 4 miles north of Middelburg.

$$\frac{5\ Feb.}{11\ Feb.}1673$$

220 SIMON ORCHARD tó LM & PJ
WEYMOUTH   2 FEBRUARY 1673

'I wrot you the 24th ultimo, sence which have not herd from you. I then gaive you aconmpt
of the preis of tobacco and shewmeck and desiered you to receve of Mr Nicolas Gould one
hundred pounds and sent you a smale bill on Mr William Pitte. I understand that the
Cottenborge fleat is arived so that I supose pich and tar is fallen. I have disposed of mine so
that if it bee fallen I am willing to bey halfe shuch a parsel as I last bought of you. If you had a
smale ship of aboute a hundered tunes with pich and tar, iron and deale boards that you
would send here I would bey the cargo of you. Pray, Sir, let mee here from you by the first
post and send mee a prented corrant adviseng mee if you deale in Reaise hemp[1] and whether
you could get a free ship to go for Crosique for salt and to com hether and att what rate. Oure
desine for Bordix is laid aseaid so that if I deale with you for ani comodateis if you doe not
send it mee by the ship that bringes it I most have it donne by the vesles that carris stone from
hence to London, which is all at present. Doe rest, Sir, yours att comand.

[P.S.] Bee plesed to inquier if ani vesles with you bound for Weymouth. They comonli land
there stones a Fishereiche[2] side nere the bridge. Youre liter man knoes where they unload.'

[1] Riga hemp.
[2] *Sic.*—presumably Fish Street, near London Bridge.

$$\frac{12\ May}{[\quad]}1673$$

221 A. WADDELL to LM & PJ
ELSINORE   3 MAY 1673

[D] Since my departure from Stockholm about a fortnight ago I have found here several of your
letters, some written in partnership as well as individually. However, I have seen, not without
great shock and astonishment, that you have neither honoured my drafts nor Mr Beck's,
which is in direct contradiction of your own letter in which you wrote that you would not
satisfy the £1,700 to Mr Neltorp[1] but that I could expect to draw £1,000 on you at 2, 4 and
6 months time. I have now followed your instructions and given orders to Mr Beck in
Hamburg to draw that much on you. Now comes your latest letter, refusing payment! As I
wrote to you, with my resources otherwise disposed I really do not know how I am to
interpret this, and I cannot guess what you intend by it. I certainly intend to have control over
things myself, so I must ask you, in the friendliest way, to let me know at once how much of
my resources are disposed of and to whom, so that I can have a balanced account. I must tell
you, truthfully, I do not know where I am, standing here between two fires. I proceeded on
the basis of your letters and arranged my plans accordingly, but—God help me—find myself
mistaken, so that I am thrown off my bearings.[2] You have truly done me a great wrong by
this, for which I must appeal to God. I beg you, just let me know how my assets have been
disposed of and whether they can be recovered. Whether or not you have paid others without
orders you will know best; I do not know, because I employed you as my agent. When, for
the first time, you would not pay the money to Mr Neltorp it was much the same as
protesting the bill of exchange, and after that you gave me instructions to draw up to £1,000
on you, which I did, and gave you no other orders except to satisfy Mr Beck. If you have paid

money to anyone else it is without any instructions from me and is no concern of mine. It is quite unreasonable that a Christian man should let down another in such a way, and it is not the way that merchants behave. You have not the least right in the world to control my money as you think fit, without my orders. Be assured, this has struck me so hard that I and my whole house could be ruined by it, for which you will have to answer severely before God. My servant in Scotland informs me that he too will remit to you for my account, if you give order to draw upon him, £300 and afterwards more. I request you then to send me an account of how much is owing to me and how much I can draw on you, for I cannot now continue my journey before I have your answer. Patience! I have no doubt that you will show some Christian kindness and consider how I am dealt with since I rely so much on your letter; and now, since it is so entirely out of my hands, I must leave off. I shall look forward to your answer at the earliest, and remain, with regards, &c.

[P.S.] I beg you, on the receipt of this letter to give Mr Beck order that he may draw on you, or that you will immediately remit as much money as is due to him, for before that is done I cannot set out on my journey or pursue my plans. This is now of great importance to me, so I beg you to bear that in mind, and I shall await your reply forwarded from Mr Beck. For God's sake, deal with me as a Christian so that I shall not be further obliged to appeal to God and to molest you with my letters of lamentation, specifically awaiting your answer and the net sum due to me so that I can govern myself accordingly.

[1] Mr Edward Nelthorp.
[2] '. . . *mij hele compass verdraeyt is.*'

C. LETTERS TO LEONORA MARESCOE & JACOB DAVID

$$\frac{11 \text{ Jan.}}{15 \text{ Jan.}} 1675$$

2 H. CLETCHER to LM
STOCKHOLM   12 DECEMBER 1674

[Your letters of the 30th of October, 6th and 13th past have been safely received, and from them I see that some person has offered to deliver my voyage iron to the Guinea Company for £14, which seems to me very strange because no one other than you has written to me about it, and, much less, has any proposal been made by me. I am, furthermore, not intending to trade with any one other than you, since it is with you that my first proposal was arranged. However, about 3 or 4 days ago an English merchant questioned me whether I would contract with him for all my voyage iron in the coming year, but I do not want to do so while I am doing business with you. Therefore I shall wait to hear what you have achieved with the company and if they have no great desire to reach agreement you ought not to press them as I have no intention of giving my iron for less than £14 15s. Now I shall wait to hear your answer whether my proposal to deliver iron for the Company account will be able to go ahead.

I hope to hear by your next of the arrival of Capt. Pyper. Since his departure from the Sound I have heard nothing from him, so I hope he has sailed in to Norway. *De Vliegende Wolff* has passed the Sound—may the Lord God guide both of them in safety. My maximum advantage is commended to you, as always, and I hope you will obtain £15 for the voyage iron and £14 for the other. Greetings, &c.

$$\frac{25 \text{ Jan.}}{26 \text{ Jan.}} 1675$$

223   CLAUS BENE to LM

HAMBURG   8 JANUARY 1675

[D]   As by the grace of God the old year is ending and a new year beginning, so I must wish you
much happiness, well-being and success, as well as all the prosperity and contentment you
may wish for in everything you may undertake in this and many coming years, beseeching
God to grant you above all everything that can make for salvation.

My last letter to you was on the 29th of December, 1674, with which I sent you the second
copy of a bill of exchange for £120 sterling endorsed to you so that you can procure payment
in time. I have since received yours of the 18th and 29th of December, by which I see that you
have bought for my account 1 bale of Ardasse at 10s 6d on condition that I can receive the
drawback of half the customs duty, which—according to you—means that it will cost me
about 10s 4d net. But that is quite expensive enough, and I fail to see that you have looked out
for my interests in making this purchase, for others tell me that they can get good Smyrna
Ardasse at 10s, and Aleppo at 9s 9d, which differs considerably from your purchase. This is
not the way to go about things. You say that it is worth 4d more than usual: time will tell—
particularly if it were re-sold in England and you were able to make 4d above the current
price which you paid for it! But you say in your last letter that, in the event of re-export, I can
recover half the customs-duty, so it must follow that if it remains over there I can recover
nothing, and so I cannot discover what advantage you have obtained. I also cannot see what
reason you had to make this purchase so hastily, since you yourself say that the ships were not
yet unloaded. With your next letter I shall expect the account so that I can make a record of
it—for there is no remedy for what is done, and one must be patient.

God be praised, Capt. Boys Ipsen arrived here some days ago, as you will have heard from
others. I shall procure the delivery of the bales[1] which you sent and let you know how I find
them in my next. Since you loaded nothing more in him there is nothing else of yours for
which he needs to sign. You did well not to buy anything more of this kind since it is being
maintained at a quite indecently high price, and if one makes a purchase disadvantageously
one cannot expect any great profit. But I do not understand why you say that you want to
buy 2 further bales of Begbesar, because I have given no new order for Begbesar since the
2 bales sent with Ipsen were bought, so please buy nothing. But, if the 2 bales of superfine
Angora have not been obtained yet, please buy them as best you can though not for more
than 5s or 5s 6d, or in their place get 2 of the ordinary fineness of the kind sent with Hendrick
Weever, for although it is not entirely white it is good and very similar and I used to prefer to
use it. However, as you say there is no lack of it, it is best that I leave you to use your own
judgement. It is not freezing here yet, so—God permitting—W. Oloffsen can still get here,
and I should be glad to have my 2 bales of Angora.

Enclosed herewith goes the second copy of the bill of exchange for £100, payable by
Caspar Kaus on the last day of this month and endorsed for payment to you. Please procure
payment in due course and place it to my account. As for what is to be done with it—I mean
to say, with regard to other things—it is good that the whale-fins are still unsold. They
should fetch more next spring since this week (God help us) four train-oil refineries were
caught in the fire and, together with much equipment and train-oil, 100,000 lb. of whale-fins
were destroyed, the damage being estimated at about *RD* 50,000. May God comfort the
afflicted. This misfortune will not make that commodity any cheaper in [England]. Please let
me know how much duty you were able to recover on the first consignment of whale-fins

and add to it what you agreed on for warehouse rent, so that I can make a note of it, for I would rather not confuse it with the other consignment. Since indigo is likely to fall it is good that you are not in a hurry to buy any. As for the proceeds of the whale-fins, I shall let you know in a later letter what I have decided to do with them. I hope you have also been cautious in going about to procure a parcel of white, scraped ginger for it seems likely to fall further in price. You can see that sooner than I can and will surely have acted accordingly.

Thank you for the news about the [doicapi?] of Naples—it will be most useful.

I hope you have sent my current account. If not, let it be done. Thank you for your New Year wishes and may God confirm them in return. With hearty regards, &c.

[P.S.] The £150 drawn by you payable to the brothers Du Pré falls due on the 3rd instant, but since the Bank is closed as usual from the end of December to the 14th instant it cannot be paid any earlier but it will then be promptly done, unless you hear otherwise. I am obliged to you for the safe receipt of the letters from Barbados. C.B.

¹ I.e. 2 bales of Angora yarn (weight unrecorded) costing £100 3s 9d f.o.b.

$$\frac{25 \text{ Jan.}}{2 \text{ Feb.}} 1675$$

4 S. DE GEER TO LM

AMSTERDAM 25 JANUARY 1675

My last letter to you was on the 15th instant. Since then I have heard nothing from you. The ship *Gottlandia*, which must have left the Sound at about the same time as various other Swedish ships bound for London, is now here—God be praised! Apparently it has been lying in Norway, so Claus Wiens and the others should be with you now, or be likely to arrive at any hour.

The Baltic situation is beginning to look rather darker, Holland having declared that if Sweden does not withdraw itself from Brandenburg territory it will be regarded as grounds for a rupture, and as Sweden is also considered as an enemy by the Allies, I fear this situation will deteriorate further. Then all seagoing commerce from this country to the Baltic will come to a standstill and it will only remain open for England, so one ought to give some thought to how one is going to arrange things for the salt ships which are going to Portugal. Therefore, let me know at once what sort of expenses would arise if I should trans-ship salt — for example, I am expecting a Dutch ship from St Ubes, and if I should get it to run into one or other of the English harbours (the Downs would be best, or the river Thames) and transfer it to English ships, what sort of expenses would arise, so that I can make a few calculations? I remain &c.

$$\frac{19 \text{ Feb.}}{26 \text{ Mar.}} 1675$$

5 SKINNER, BALL & GOSFRIGHT TO LM

LEGHORN 4 FEBRUARY 1675

'Madame, The present is only to advise you the arrival of Capt. Peckett two daies since, by whom you have consigned us a hundred piggs of lead which wee shall receive and endeavour to dispose of to your most advantage and remitt you its proceed when in cash. Said commodity is now worth D.21½ p. 1,000 lb. but a few buyers. Pepper D.11½, tynn 12⅞, miserable prices, Ruskia hydes 26s p. lb. now being imported two Holland shipps from Ruskia with said commodity and caviera.[1] Capt. Peckett will be dispatcht in a day or two for Scanderoon, and for London is on departure the *Martin* and *Morning Star*. The *Industry*, imported this weeke from Lisbon and bound for Venice, may saile in 3 or 4 daies time, which is what att present occurs worth your notice, so with due respects wee remaine Madame att your command, &c.

Exchange for London—57½d p. dollar.'

    [1] *Sic.*—caviar.

$$\frac{\textit{19 Feb.}}{\textit{19 Feb.}}\textit{1675}$$

226   S. DE GEER tO LM
           AMSTERDAM   22 FEBRUARY 1675

[D]   I find myself with your welcome letter of the 2nd instant. They write to me from Stockholm that the ships which are lying in Elsenap[1] will over-winter there as the wind has not helped them. So your iron prices should remain good. It has been freezing hard there for 4 or 5 days but if they had the sort of weather we have been having they should soon be in open-water again, and from the Sound they write that the winter is already past.

I very much doubt that it will come to open war between Sweden and this country. We shall soon see which way things will turn. According to some, Brandenburg has come to an agreement with Sweden—but time will soon tell.

If all the 20 ships[1] have been chartered to go to St Ubes for salt there should be no lack of space for freight. Please let me know at once what freights have been agreed upon and whether the ships have been long gone. If you can learn the net number, within 2 or 3, I am anxious to know. Should it come to war between Sweden and this country it would be best that most goods should go to London though some proportion should come here even though with English ships. But what I do believe is that iron will keep its price for the moment, because it will be some while before one will be able to get iron at Stockholm. Through lack of sledge-trails this winter little iron will have been brought to the water-side, though I shall have further information within a fortnight. I trust that ours will have reached the coast, but from the principal mining-areas there will be little, for they must first make up their stores, if they can be obtained while the winter continues.

I hope Claus Wiens has arrived safely with you and that, regarding Momma, you are not out of pocket in salvaging the consignment from the *St Jean*. If you think it necessary to get an injunction to prevent others do it only if it can be done without any difficulty, and not unless you have received enough by that post to be satisfied. According to what they write from Sweden it was only a rather poor lot and suspected of no good purpose.

His Highness has courteously declined the offer of the Dukedom of Gelder,[2] which is a good thing because the community was very much against it.

If the money from the *RD* 2,000 bills of exchange from Momma to my brother Jan can be found by you, please let me know for either I or Wollters at Hamburg must have it. If it amounts to so much write to me only and I shall then get you the necessary order,
                                        remaining, &c.

[P.S.] People are talking much of general peace or, at least, of a cessation of arms at sea, which is all the more to be believed as there is no talk of fitting-out [a fleet]. The latter possibility I can believe, but the former I doubt very much.

¹ I.e. Elsnap, or Elsnabben on contemporary maps (today Älvsnabben on Muskö) on the southern approaches to Stockholm via 'the Daalders' (off Dalarö).

² The Sound Toll Tables confirm that 20 English ships did leave Portugal for Sweden in 1675.

³ The unanimous offer to William of Orange by the States of Gelderland on 29 January 1675 of the titles of Duke of Gelderland and Count of Zutphen caused deep concern in Holland and a run on the Bank. See S. B. Baxter, *William III* (London, 1966) p. 123.

$$\frac{29 \; Feb.}{5 \; Mar.} 1675$$

27 SAMUEL VAN BREDA to LM
    STOCKHOLM   6 JANUARY 1675

D] May God Almighty grant a prosperous and successful New Year, with all the good fortune you desire for yourself.

In answer to yours of 29 November and 4 December which have just arrived together, I would have been glad to see that my order had arrived rather earlier and been followed by the sale of my iron, but it cannot be remedied now and the consequences must be faced with patience. In view of what you say I shall expect to see soon the account of my iron as well as remittances, and if they have not fallen due yet please advance it at interest.

I am astonished that you should say that that sort of iron is not in much demand in [England]. Please explain the reason to me, for it was well forged of good materials. I have contracted to deliver some consignments in the spring so if there is something which can be done with them in [England] I shall send an assortment of such kinds as you may be kind enough to inform me of.

Regarding the drafts from France on [London] and from [London] on Hamburg or Amsterdam as mentioned in my letter of 4 November, I know that double provision and brokerage was promised, but against that it ought to be observed that from here to Hamburg and Amsterdam the course of exchange is usually 3, 4, 5 and 6 per cent higher than in the spring. We have found this over many years of dealing with one another, and if we then get them to purchase in France during the winter and then draw at 2 usances, as is customary, on Hamburg or Amsterdam, this way we can provide very speedy remittances from here. If it is done through [London] then the time is prolonged for 2 months and in the spring it is immediately remitted from here by the advantageous exchange, by which means the provision and brokerage are abundantly gained. Last year the course of exchange at short sight was 21 *ML* on Hamburg, payable in banco, and at $19\frac{5}{8}$ on Amsterdam, payable in cash. We have now drawn good sums at $22\frac{1}{4}$ *ML* on Hamburg and at $20\frac{3}{8}$ on Amsterdam. I am thinking of getting a quantity of miscellaneous goods bought in France this winter, for cash. If I decide to allow them to draw on [London] I shall inform you in good time who it is you are to collect their reimbursement from, and I firmly rely on you for a punctual performance.

[P.S.] Please address the letter for me here to Mr Hendrick van Felde at Hamburg so they can quickly get to me at Amsterdam. If God permits, I am intending to travel there and to Amsterdam at the end of this month, and Van Felde always knows where I shall be.

$(i) + (ii) \quad \dfrac{9\ Mar.}{2\ Apr.}1675$

228 J. FREDERICK, R. GODSCHALL & J. DUNCAN to LM
SEVILLE   (i)   11 DECEMBER 1674

'Madam, Wee have not rescavd any fresh lines from you since our last of 2nd October, since which from time to time as have wrote the worshipful John Lethieullier, Sheriff, have desired him to imparte to you what hath offered in your concernes and this poast have sent you the usuall way under said covert the particulers of the powder sugars sent for your account in the *Providence* according to your order, beeinge 17,400 *R. pta.* which may please to note accordingly. Said vessell arrived at Cadiz the [?]19th past[1] and will not gett soe quick a dispatch from Cadiz as expected, the Contraband office puttinge such hinderance by new wilds contrary to our articles to gett money and though wee nationally complaine to our Embassador wee find noe redress. In a small chest of ex'lent haspiada cucheneele grape p. the *Morninge Starr* you are $\frac{1}{3}$ parte interist beeinge consignd Mr Andrew Duncan that will give you coppy of the invoyce which cost $73\frac{1}{2}$ ducats p. *arroba*. Your parte doth amount to $2,846\frac{1}{3}$ *R. pta.* which please to note in the same nature. Wee find at present all strangers hands soe full of English goods and sell soe cheap that wee dare not accept of the rates and to trust good menn with halfe money and the other at trust to pay 12 p. cent interist at the returne of *Galleons* wee have not liberty to doe itt soe must waite and see if ready money sailes will offer though at less profitt. In case your markett gave any encouragement to have some of your goods trucked for grayne or indicoe itt may help them the better and sooner off, soe may please as occacon offers to lett us know your pleasure in the case. Per the *Providence* and *Jerusalem* bayes have been sould aboard at 18 ducats per piece, 2 months payment and small goods pro rato. God send us better times and keep you in health and prosperity are the desires of, &c.'

   [1] The date may be '29th'.

                                                             (ii)   19 FEBRUARY 1675

229 'Madam, The foregoeing is coppy of our last which confirm. Since have not received any lines from you, the usuall way this day do send you the particulers of the powder sugars sent per the *Bristoll* frigate, being 8,742 *R. pta.* for which your account hath debitt and hope before these some time will bee safe in your hands, and debited your account 8,700 *R. pta.* by Sir John Lethieullier's order for the cost and charges of 10 ducats more sent per the *Providence* for Aleppo for your account haveing formerly charged you with but 20 ducats and the charges which should have been three thousand, and will now sett that affaire to rights so pleas note it there in the same nature. Wee now send Mr A. Duncan the account sale of the 21 packs bayes per the *Katharin*, your $\frac{1}{3}$ parte beeing—15,076. With the 8 barrills of tinn p. the *New Affrican* your $\frac{1}{3}$ —*R. pta.* $1,853\frac{1}{2}$ is past to the creditt of your account which may pleas finding right to note accordingly. Wee cannot cleere the sales of any others so against the next poast shall if possible send your account current that you may the cleerer see how your affaires rest in our hands. Your goods now com, wee say bayes per the *Vyner* and *Aleppin* are comeing up hither, though our f [actor?] at Cadiz used all meanes possible could not find any buyer for them such dead times wee have and all the strangers wee have on the place hath theire hands full as well as our nation of woollen goods, which have brought the prices soe loe. What the dispatch of *flotta* for the New Spaine may produce time must tell us, though wee feare few will engage deep in English goods by them. The 14th current *Galleons* departed Cadiz. God send them well out and home that this comerce may bee revived and goods beare a better price, which is all at present offers from, Madam, your most humble servants, &c.'

$$\frac{29 \text{ Mar.}}{2 \text{ Apr.}} 1675$$

30 H. CLETCHER to LM

AXBERGSHAMER   19 FEBRUARY 1675

D] I have safely received yours of the 15th and 22nd past, together with the sale account of the iron in Hendrick Janssen Pyper, which I have checked and found correct and debited you for the proceeds of £220 1s 9d. I hope too *De Vliegende Wolff* has now arrived safely, because the news from Hamburg must have been a mistake, for while they were reporting about the ship from Hamburg it was still lying at Marstrand. So I hope to hear by your next letter of its happy arrival and that its iron has sold at a good price, and when that is done, please close the current account and send it over.

Regarding the amount of iron which the Guinea Company wants to contract for, I shall be fully content to deliver to them all the voyage iron which I can get made in a year in addition to anything I can obtain of other types. As you know from what I have told you, in future years I shall be able to deliver about 200 tons per annum of this sort, but this year it will not be so much, as not all my forges are suitable. If the Company will give £14½ for what I can deliver this coming summer then I shall send it over at that price, but not for less—to which I shall now await your answer. Meanwhile,

Greetings &c.

[P.S.] Capt Hendrick Matson will have to over-winter here, as you will have heard. I hope that you will not agree on the voyage iron for less than £15 because I insist that I cannot count on such a quantity in the coming year, and that to all appearances there is none of that variety in stock.

Please send me some pins by the first returning ships. And please also send two smooth, white, knitted woollen waistcoats. They must be rather large, for a man to wear; also a white knitted petticoat for a woman.

$$\frac{29 \text{ Mar.}}{2 \text{ Apr.}} 1675$$

231 J. & H. VAN BAERLE to LM

AMSTERDAM   29 MARCH 1675

[D] We find ourselves with yours of the 2nd past, by which we were glad to see that you had agreed with and recorded the current statement of your account, as well as that for you and Mr Peter Joye in partnership. The balance due on the latter we have made good to Mr Joye in full according to his order, since he writes to us that he has satisfied you for your half share and we do not doubt that he has done so.

Since the collapse of Isaac Momma his father Willem has also fallen short, unable to meet his bills of exchange and other debts, but the King of Sweden has protected him so that no-one can molest him, as you have apparently heard. And as we have significant sums tied up with him we ask you as a friend to let us know if you have any money or effects of his by you on which we could lay our hands, which would oblige us greatly.

There is very little business being done here, most commodity prices remaining at rock-bottom. The East India Company has begun to sell its Molucca wares, which are fetching as follows—cloves, about 84 stuivers; nutmegs, 51 to 52 stuivers; mace, 18½ to 19 stuivers per lb. Pepper fetches 15½g, Barbados sugar 5¾ to 6g, Ardasse silk 17 to 17½ schellings p. lb. with

13 months discount. English lead is at $25\frac{1}{2}$ to 26 schellings p. 100 lb.; block tin at *f*.52; Swedish copper-wire *f*.58 to 59 per 100 lb. As our brother David has become a burgher of Stockholm, and because we fear that this country will go to war with the Crown of Sweden, we have decided to make a separation of our company, so henceforth his name is not to be used, for your information. With heartiest regards, &c.

London: $34s\ 6\frac{1}{2}-6g$ ⎫
Paris: $101\frac{1}{4}$ ⎬ 2 usances.
Hamburg: $34\frac{3}{8}$ stuivers per dollar ⎫
Antwerp: $1\frac{1}{4}$% premium for bills ⎬ at sight.

$\dfrac{12\ Apr.}{[12\ Apr.]}$1675

232 JOHN HARDY to LM
EXETER   10 APRIL 1675

'Madam, I received lately a letter from Mr Alexander van Kuffeler of Amsterdam marchantt, wheare in was an order to draw some monies on you, thearefore have now to advice that have drawn on you for thurty one pound fifteen shillings. The bill is payable at three days sight to Mr James Crop or order. Madam, allthough I am unknown unto you, yett I hope you will pardon mee if I enlarg in a line or two and acquaint you my trade is alltogather in buying serges and that I can furnish you with any sortts. If you deale in my way and will please to give your order to buy I shall bee very forward to serve you. No more at presant butt my humble service presented, I rest, your servantt to command, &c.'

$\dfrac{11\ May}{14\ May}$1675

233 S. DE GEER to LM
AMSTERDAM   17 MAY 1675

[D]   My last letter was on the 3rd instant. Since then I have received your of the 23rd of April.
     As regards Hoegarden,[1] we shall have to wait for an answer to learn for what reason Burkin & Townley make difficulties about delivering the proceeds of the iron.
     The ships which are lying at Elsenap dare not depart as they have had news that capers are entering the Baltic with Brandenburg commissions. One has passed through the Sound. It should be declared that if he is captured he is likely to be treated as a pirate. They are now getting the Stockholm convoy ready to escort the ships through the Sound, but that will further delay their arrival so the iron which you have will, I hope, be sold before any new comes, and this delay will make the price rise. I am intending to send some 3,000 slb of iron to [England] this year, if it can be conveniently done. Indeed, I may possibly send rather more if your iron prices are maintained. But, as against that, it may not be easy to get ships for [England] if the salt ships are going to be at Stockholm, which I presume are now lying ready to sail at St Ubes. Their number is not as great as you said it was, being only thirteen in all, whereof twelve are going to Stockholm and one to Gothenburg. The ships at Elsenap will not depart except with a convoy but we are negotiating with the Elector of Brandenburg today. People have also complained against the sale in Zeeland of six Swedish ships with Brandenburg commissions which does not sound too well here on the Exchange where the goods are bought. . . . [?]

[P.S.] It would be a good thing to keep up the price of iron, if you see any opportunity for selling, because it will be late before anything of importance comes out of Sweden, even if everything turns out for the best.

¹ Isaac van Hoegarden, De Geer's agent stationed at Querrin on the Shannon estuary, Ireland.

$\dfrac{17\ May}{18\ May}1675$

234   ISAAC CRONSTRÖM to LM
STOCKHOLM   1 MAY 1675

D]   Since my last, of the 3rd of April, I have received yours of the 19th of March and 2nd of April. You will have been relieved to see from my previous letter that in giving orders regarding the funds which are entrusted to you I never meant M. de la Bistrate to dispose of more than the £1,250, or RD 5,000 which were also ordered for Mr Becceler, and as for what the wire sent in the *Swarte Beer* might yield, that is to be all sent for M. Van Raey and he, and no one else, may draw upon it. You will have also found that M. de la Bistrate is in agreement with me. Meanwhile M. Van Raey has been informed and says in his letter of 16 April:

'I am sorry that you have to tell me that Widow Marescoe, in answer to your order to place the £700 draft to your account, does not want to accept it and says that she is not expecting any more drafts from me; also that she says she has written to M. de la Bistrate about it and can do nothing before she gets an answer from him.'

He is disgusted with that, but I do not doubt that you have subsequently given him satisfaction as you promised. Doubtless wire manufactures will sell more readily soon, if that which has been lying here all winter and is now all shipped meets with no further hindrance. But as they cannot leave before we have found convoyers and are certain how things stand with Holland and Denmark, nothing will be going from here, and so far we have heard little of English shipping. I also consider that the consignments of '74 should be disposed of before you receive these of '75. I have decided to unload what I have lying here in 2 ships and to send it to Hamburg in order to gain time. I shall then urge M. de la Bistrate to do everything possible as diligently as he can to get it into your hands.

As you say, the confusion in Mr Willem Momma's affairs is working to the disadvantage of the brass-trade and is quite unhelpful, but he will never again be as strong as he was. I have sold my iron to a reliable friend here and so I do not export it anymore, but I could do so for the copper bars if the Guinea Company will make up its mind. However, as it cannot be sent in that name or with any security for shipping this summer, unless in English ships, I shall have to arrange things so that either it is sold and paid for here or else my trustworthy friend in Hamburg will have to accept drafts against the credit of the bills of lading—provided that I run no further risk once it is loaded free on board ship. And I should have to demand RD 60 for each Swedish shippound which would work out at about £ [blank]¹, and then there is no need for 5 per cent for advance of money, etc. I wait to hear what the Company will offer and remain, &c.

¹ Valuing the rixdollar at 4s 6d sterling and the shippound at 2.67 cwt. it would work out at £5 1s per cwt.

$$\frac{27\ May}{28\ May}1675$$

235 C. BENE to LM
       HAMBURG   18 MAY 1675

[D] My last letter was on the 7th instant, in which I said that you should not give more than 2*s* 4*d*
     at most for fine Jamaican indigo, and that I would rather have some good scraped ginger at
     29–30*s*—vizt. for 50 or 60 sacks. I also ordered you to buy whale fins at £120 and 2 bales of
     extra-ordinary fine Angora yarn, if it can be had at 5*s* 4–6*d*. This I now confirm. Since then I
     find myself with your three letters of the 26th of April, 4th and 7th instant, by which I see that
     the ships from Scanderoon have at last arrived at Zante and that some ships from Barbados
     have arrived in the Downs—for which news I thank you, as I shall find it helpful. You should
     by now have found opportunity to procure about 50 or 60 sacks of white scraped ginger at a
     reasonable price and I wait to hear news of your success. If you perform my commission for
     the yarn please do not buy the indigo, because all my credit balance will have gone, and as for
     the bale of Ardasse silk—as I said in my earlier letter—please sell it, because it will not
     perform any miracles here. You have urged me so much to make this purchase although
     knowing perfectly well that there was much of it in stock and more expected. I have been out
     of pocket for so long now that I shall be lucky to make any profit, so I expect you to put an
     end to the matter.
         I have ordered you to sell the whale-fins at £120: this I not only confirm but order you to
     dispose of them at £116, since there is no prospect of an improvement. As you know best,
     when one has bitten into a sour apple the sooner one gets rid of it the better!
         I shall be glad to hear when the £100 on W. Robinson has been received, and it is right that
     you should demand the settlement of the £75 when it is due. Accompanying this I remit you
     another £100 at 2 usances, drawn on Jacques Crop and negotiated here with Samuel zum
     von Brock. Please demand its acceptance, though not sooner than the next letter because the
     drawer gave notice to the acceptant only three days ago.
         It is not surprising that sugar is falling in price in [England] because it is very quiet here.
     Business is almost at a standstill. Everyone feels alarmed at the rupture of Brandenburg with
     Sweden and is reluctant to buy goods. Brown ginger can be had for $4\frac{1}{2}g$, and if it should fall to
     16*d* in [London] one might be able to consider ordering some. If you are unable to effect the
     foregoing order for 2 bales of super-fine Angora, please buy in its place 2 bales of ordinary
     Begbesar, if it can be had for 3*s* 3–4*d*, of the same quality as the bales Nos. 5 and 6 which you
     last provided and sent with Boys Ipsen. They were quite satisfactory. And as for any credit-
     balance which remains, please lay it out on Barbados indigo at 2*s* 4*d*—though do not include
     the £100 which I remit herewith. With regards, &c.

     London: 32*s* 4*g*   2 usances.
     Amsterdam: $34\frac{3}{4}$.

$$\frac{1\ Jun.}{24\ Jun.}1675$$

236 TIMOTHY LANNOY & JOHN BURKIN to LM
       ALEPPO   29 MARCH 1675

'Your obligeing lines of the 24th October by the ship *Providence* have received. She arrived
Scanderoone the 24th past; these are by returne of said ship. Your 3,000 pieces of eight have

received. They wanted of due waight dollers 27½, the remainder—2,972½—we have changed into Lyon dollers at 5 p. cent advantage and have given you credit for Lyon dollers 3,121,10 aspers.[1] We send you by this ship 80 sackes gaules amounting to *LD*. 2,136 27 @ cost *LD* 30 34 @ per kintall, and three bales of goats wool amounting to *LD*. 321 9 @ at *LD*. 134 per kintall. We have also sent by said ship 130 sackes of ashes, in which you are concerned a fift part, which comes to *LD*. 212 72 @. Your whole adventure, which God preserve, is *LD*. 2,670 28 @. The ginger, in which you are concerned a fift part, as yet we have not bin able to dispose of any, it being at present here a very bad comodity. When we sell it shall give you credit for your part. Here is severall good ships in lesse then a month expected, by one of them shall send the remainder of your money invested in gaules and goats wooll, if find them to be procured for reason. We were not able to comply with our orders to buy for each owners' part 100 sacks of gaules, they rizeing from 28 *LD* to 34 *LD* per kintall, which made us judge it most for the interest of the concerned to let the ship take in goods for Legorne, the fraight for said place being greater then for England, and we have hopes shee may there fill up againe. We returne you our humble thenkes for honoring us with your comand. We promise as farr as lies in our power to advance your interest, hopeing to have your approvall of what we have already acted, which is all at present. We remain, your most obliged and faithfull servants, &c.

[P.S.] The invoice of your gaules and goats wooll inclosed. Mr Loe the factor mareen will send the bill of lading.'

[1] There were 80 aspers to the Lion dollar at Aleppo and Scanderoon.

$$\frac{11\ Jun.}{18\ Jun.}1675$$

237 H. CLETCHER to LM
AXBERGSHAMER   22 MAY 1675

D] Your welcome letters of the 2nd, 13th and 16th past have been safely received, in which I see that you have agreed with the Royal African Company to supply 100 tons of my voyage iron at £14 10s per ton, with which agreement I am well content, having given you adequate instruction to that effect in my previous letters. Indeed you have done well to make this agreement because I am confident that a substantial amount of that variety will be forged this winter. As regards the other condition, you can rest assured that I shall deliver just as good voyage iron as before and it will be others who will suffer the most loss for bringing my iron into disrepute. This year I shall deliver 200 tons and perhaps even more, including the consignment in the *Coninck David*, and I will certainly deliver the whole amount this year, but I cannot bind myself so precisely to the delivery-date—namely, the end of August, especially because there is at present a general stoppage of all shipping. Ships are not allowed to depart, which is why the *Coninck David* is still lying here. I have about 200 tons lying ready at present, and when the quantity in the *Coninck David* arrives you can include it in the account for the contracted 100 tons. I shall load the rest in the first ship for [London] and for the future I propose that when I signify by bill of lading that I have loaded the iron in due time I shall have fulfilled my obligation because I cannot be answerable if ships are held up by embargoes, long detours or otherwise. Please have that put into the agreement.

By your next I hope to hear that the iron in Claus Wiens has been sold.

Regarding Mr Perman's bond, I find that it is in the requisite form. It is customary in this country to use no other ceremony in making a bond than to authenticate it with the person's signature and seal without using any witnesses. If there is an error in the pledge regarding the name of Mr Leyel it cannot prejudice it, since the bond is essentially sound. I shall therefore not speak to Mr Perman unless he again asks you that I should do so. If there is anything further in which I can serve you I shall be happy to do so, since I am your servant, &c.

$\frac{11\ Jun.}{11\ Jun.}$1675

238   J. A. FONCK to LM
        HAMBURG   1 JUNE 1675

[D]   Yours of the 23rd of April was duly received and from it I have seen how business is going in London and how much one commodity or another is fetching. I warmly thank you for communicating this and wish that something could be arranged in one thing or another, but at present I can find nothing profitable to undertake. We must let these times run their course until they improve. However, I take this opportunity to urge the sale of my 2 chests of Marglitzer linen and that you will please do your best to dispose of them. As soon as I receive the account of their sale I shall provide some new cases which are standing here ready. The said linen is sought after here because, as a result of the war, the folk in Germany are unable to make it. I hope it is also sought after in [England] and, awaiting to hear what is happening, I remain, with cordial regards, &c.

[P.S.] I do not know if you do much business in this linen, which has been lying around for so long, but if you could find a market for it I could send you considerable amounts yearly and employ the proceeds on goods from [England]. So little is happening at the moment that it is painful to think about buying goods, so we must patiently bear what pleases God Almighty. I remain, &c.

$\frac{11\ Jun.}{11\ Jun.}$1675

239   A. BERENBERG'S WIDOW & CO to LM
        HAMBURG   4 JUNE 1675

[D]   We have not written to you for several posts, for lack of material. Since then we find ourselves with your letters of the 7th and 11th past, together with three bills of exchange, vizt.:

£300 sterling ⎱ in bills on Jacobsen & Leemkuell, at 2 usances, payable
£200 sterling ⎰ by the Directors of the Chamber.
£100 sterling—in a bill of John Mertens, at 2 usances and 8 days, to be satisfied by Jean Bernhardt Giese. Enclosed herewith we return them, duly accepted, as you requested. If we can serve you further in this, just command us.

We also find that the account of your drafts which we made concerning the Stockholm drafts was very badly done. At the time we had a great deal of correspondence, so it was checked in haste. Please forgive the error, and we thank you for pointing it out. In its place we are sending another, and please credit us for the £5 flem. on your account.[F]

We thank you for the prices of sundry goods. With prices so very low we do not know how to make any profit, for nothing is selling here with all goods at rock-bottom prices. We wish we could be rid of our ginger and sugar without loss, for brown ginger sells at $4\frac{1}{2}g$ and Barbados sugar at 5 to $5\frac{1}{4}g$. There is nothing to be done with Ardasse and we still have our 2 bales lying here. Too many goods are coming from all countries and the war daily gets worse everywhere; one sees many fleeing people and goods coming in here, for the country is full of dread and no one here has any pleasure in taking any risks but is glad if they have nothing outstanding to lose. May the good Lord grant that we may be blessed and profitable!

Our brother Cornelius returns Mr Davidson's[1] friendly greetings and is sorry that he has had so much trouble concerning the pieces of music he requested, but he is very glad that some of them have been promised to him by another friend. The outcome, and their despatch, will be very welcome to him.

The exchange here also begins to fall, as you can see at the foot of this. With very cordial regards, &c.

London: $32s$ 2 usances.
Amsterdam: $34\frac{13}{16}$.
Antwerp: $34\frac{5}{8}$.
Paris: $46\frac{3}{4}-\frac{7}{8}$ 2 usances.

Pepper, $15\frac{1}{8}g$. No demand for Turkish yarn. Aleppo galls at 41 to 42 *ML* per centner.

(F)—hoping that something may yet occur to you in which we can deal with one another.

[1] I.e., Jacob David.

$$\frac{14\ Jun.}{18\ Jun.}1675$$

0   REINHOLT GARLINGHOFF to LM

HAMBURG   8 JUNE 1675

;]   I have safely received your very welcome letter of the 28th past. I see from it that business is going very badly in [England], especially in copper-wire, which rather dampens my courage. Every week I have at least 100 coils delivered to me at home, which until now I have had good opportunity to dispose of, partly here and partly to other places. But now demand begins to become rather slack, yet if I am to keep my people employed I cannot afford to slow down and I shall be delighted if you can help me in disposing of some quantity. You need not worry whether it is good stuff, for my wares are well known. At my mill I also make brass, and black and white latten of all varieties, which is in demand everywhere. Similarly, I also make all kinds of beaten copper, sheet-copper and fine pieces. If, as you write, you can sell for me a quantity of copper-sheets at £7, I shall undertake to deliver it and if you can undertake to sell a good pennyworth I can deliver 10 slb every 8 days. But you must give me accurate information about how large and how heavy it is expected to be. Let me know everything that happens. I have goods lying at Gothenburg which I wish could be sent to [England] but I see no prospect of it. With friendly greetings, &c

$$\frac{22\ Jun.}{2\ Jul.}1675$$

1   JOHANNES DE GEER to LM

STOCKHOLM   26 MAY 1675

•]   Some weeks ago I sent you an open letter about releasing Willem Momma from his arrest since he had promised to put up good security and to pay promptly all bills of exchange as they fall due. I thought this the best means for all sides concerned to settle the business amicably without causing resentments. But, nonetheless, a letter of attorney would be useful to you if you suspected that insufficient guarantees had been pledged. I therefore trust that you have received everything and that matters will be brought to a satisfactory conclusion.

I have now received your letter of the 7th of May, from which I see that nothing is happening in trade. It is deplorable that one can get no passage out of here, and even if one could one would not dare as long as the situation is so uncertain and nothing is settled with Denmark. However, in a few days we shall know how things stand.

Please let me know at once if there is anything to be done in England with cannon, and whether one could dispose of, sell, or—best of all—contract for them; and also how much per Swedish shippound or 100 lb. Dutch-weight they are likely to fetch? I could send a good quantity if I knew what calibre was most sought after and required. They are among the best cannons made in this country.

De Koning David lies here still and cannot leave. There are some English and Scottish ships arriving here but they are small vessels and will not be able to carry much.

I remain, &c.

$\dfrac{2\ Jul.}{2\ Jul.}$ 1675

242 J. A. FONCK to LM
HAMBURG   25 JUNE 1675

[D]   To reply to your kind letter of the 28th past, I thank you for the trouble you are taking in selling my linen. I am surprised that you do not have more opportunity to do so as it has always been a very acceptable sort for the Guinea Company. I have sold 15–20 cases here and have just as many standing here which I could send you if there was only some demand. Please take the trouble to find out some fundamental information—whether such a quantity could be sold in [England] and at what price—as soon as you can learn it from your friends who trade to Guinea. I should then order an equal amount of ginger, sugar, gall-nuts and other things which suit me. I await your decision, and remain favourably disposed if something of significance can be done which will repay the trouble. Meanwhile, friendly regards, &c.

London: 32s.
Amsterdam: 34¾.
Paris: 47.

[P.S.] On closing this I received one of the 18th instant, from which I see that you are keeping my linen in mind. I shall await your success, and if you do succeed with this commodity we shall be able to do good business together. I am much inclined to it and hope to achieve something of importance.

$\dfrac{2\ Jul.}{2\ Jul.}$ 1675

243 C. BENE to LM
HAMBURG   25 JUNE 1675

[D]   I wrote to you by the last post, in which I said that I would be expecting the protest for lack of acceptance of the £50 bill of exchange, together with a draft for the amount and the expenses. This I confirm. Since then I have received yours of the 18th inst. together with the bill of lading for the bale of Ardasse and 2 bales of Turkish yarn loaded in Sybrant Claesen's ship. May God bring him in safety. The account of the 2 bales of yarn, Nos. 'B' and 'C', I shall check, and finding them correct will record my agreement and let you know. As for the whale-fins, I expect the account by your next letter so that I can see how much I shall have lost. I really believe the purchaser must be well-satisfied, for they were of good quality.

Regarding the Swedish copper-wire of the brands you named, as far as I can learn there should be about 3,000 coils in town, and the said brands fetch 61 to 62 *ML* per 100 lb, for cash. If any change should occur I shall not neglect to let you know. For freight charges from Lübeck one pays 3 to $3\frac{1}{2}$ *ML* per 300 lb., less or rather more, according to the total weight. What charges there are at Lübeck I shall write at once to find out and let you know in my next letter. Meanwhile, I believe they are inconsiderable though I cannot say how much more the route via Lübeck costs compared with that by sea. But it is certain that, of copper-wares, copper-wire seldom comes here from Sweden by way of sea but rather by way of Lübeck and Wismar. It may be useful for you to know that Wismar is further from here than Lübeck and that people believe it will be besieged by the Elector of Brandenburg since he has totally routed the Swedish army, capturing much artillery and all its baggage.[1] In sum, the army is totally destroyed and, according to what they write, the general, some other great men and the French minister, the Duc de Vitri,[2] only narrowly escaped. This will change people's ideas: the suspicion which I mentioned before has vanished away, God be praised.

If I can be of any service in expediting the purchase of wire or other goods, please just ask me to gratify your commands, assuring you that it will be done as advantageously as possible.

Thank you for news of the prices of sundry goods. As regards sugar, I shall tell you in my next letter whether I am inclined to purchase any. I estimate that you should have about £60 in hand if all my remittances are received together, which you will please employ on fine white scraped ginger. Please see to it that it is extra-fine. That which you last sent is plump and good but lacks lustre and it does not look white. Get if for me at the most advantageous price.

The exchange on [London] continues to be high, so I have remitted nothing to you. I hope it will fall. Wherewith, cordial regards, &c.

London: 32s 1g   2 usances.
Amsterdam: $34\frac{3}{4} - \frac{13}{16}$.

[P.S.] As the bill of exchange for £50 was not accepted I expect the protest concerning it and a draft at short sight. A dio.

[1] This was the battle of Fehrbellin, of 18 June.
[2] François-Marie de l'Hopital, duc de Vitry (1620–79).

$$\text{(i)} + \text{(ii)} \quad \frac{12 \, Jul.}{9 \, Nov.} 1675$$

4   FREDERICK, GODSCHALL & DUNCAN to LM

SEVILLE   (i)   11 JUNE 1675

'Madam, The foregoinge is coppy of our last which confirme. Since is com to hand your wellcome lines of the 2nd Aprill which some dayes since received, beeinge chiefly to advise you that wee have sould 150 pieces of your Bow-dyed serges to Gaspar de la Plata at 23 *pesos* per piece to pay $\frac{1}{3}$ ready money and $\frac{2}{3}$ by a sure mann on the place to bee paid at the arrivall of

Gallones which wee chosed rather to do then by slow sales at long runn to sell them to the Safra people[1] or shopps which would require a farr longer timé to get in the money. To those of Safra goe sellinge your perpetuanas from 15 to 16 *pesos* per piece and some bayes at 20 ducats per piece to pay in 4 months, though double the time will not cleere a debt, but havinge no other way to spend your goods dare not slipp the present markett least stay longer and fare worse, the markett beeinge so glutted by all menn's hands and largly. Some have trusted for the W[est] I[ndies] so that a gainst the winter season may goe providinge a fresch sortment while they may bee had cheap as now they will bee at home. By the late discouragement that goeth of what sould in Spaine they will fall considerably their, and the best parte of the proffitt consisteth in the cheap buyinge up of goods their and those that have deep ingagements for the Ind[ie]s will not bee to forward to send goods againe for the winter which may please to consider and put in execucion as best think fitt. With all due respects take leave as beeinge, &c.'

(ii)   25 JUNE 1675

245   'Madam, Foregoinge is coppy of our last. Since have yours of 10th past. You will have heard the arrivall of the *Olive Branch* and since the *London Merchant* is arrived though doe nott find you are concerned in either. As to the Swedish latten wire, vendible here they are the sortts followeing, and are knowne in Hamborgh by said names, vizt.

Passa perla fina	which is a sortment for this place and you
Passa perla basta	may please to governe yourself as please in
Tercio perlero fin	the quantity. Here good store spends all the
Tercio perlero basto	year. It comes in bundles of 10 lb. weight
Corchettes	and is worth at present 1 *R. pta.* p. lb.
Clavar del paer de 32 vueltas	

The duties are moderate. Its rated in the Customehouse at 40 *mvs* p. lb. and pays 15 per cent the Almo [jarifazgo][2] and the rest of the duties as in the account of other goods by which you may easily calculate the charges. Wee cannot advise you to send any pinns for this markett. The expence is not considerable nor will anything in businesse considerable pass in this place until God send home *Galleones*, to whose protection comitt you and rest, Madam, your most humble servants.'

  [1] Zafra, about 110 km north of Seville.
  [2] Duty payable on goods imported into America from Europe.

$\dfrac{21\ Jul.}{23\ Jul.}$ 1675

246   H. CLETCHER tO LM
STOCKHOLM   26 JUNE 1675

[D]   I have safely received your agreeable letter of the 28th past. For a reply I refer you to my last. This will serve to tell you in addition that I have arranged to load 530 slb in two English ships. I would have gladly loaded a further quantity, but I could not get more space. Thus I shall not be able to load the rest of the contracted 100 tons earlier than the return of the salt ships which are now daily expected as they have all passed the Sound. All the iron in the *Coninck David* must now be unloaded and placed in the salt ships because, with this war, no Swedish ships can depart. I hope to be able to deliver the iron before the end of August, but if it does not arrive precisely on time I trust the Royal African Company will not take such a narrow view of it in these times.

God protect you, &c.

$\dfrac{26 \; Jul.}{30 \; Jul.}$ 1675

7 JACOB TRIP[1] to LM
  AMSTERDAM   30 JULY 1675

•] Several of your letters have been received from time to time (for which communications I thank you) but have remained unanswered, for lack of opportunity. This letter will serve only to enquire what chance there is of obtaining shipping-space in [London] and if two ships could be found which, at 4,000 lb. to the last, will sail to Stockholm and return here loaded with iron, and also what difference it would make between sailing from Stockholm to here or to [London]? Both ships should be of 90 or 100 lasts, or else one of 180–190 lasts as long as it is obtainable at a reasonable rate. The English are asking 34 to 35s per last here, which is a very great deal. I await your reply at the earliest.

I have been negotiating today with Steven de Geer about supplying a ship which he has lying here, of 110 lasts burthen. If you could find a suitable man in an English ship who could sail as captain we could easily find the rest of the crew here because there are plenty of Englishmen to be had. If this can be done please give De Geer orders to buy for you a ship of identical size and, at the first opportunity, send over the captain for a voyage to Stockholm. Concerning the money for the purchase of the ship, you will give it on bottomry. If you need the name of the ship in order to put it in the pass, it is called the *St Jacob*. De Geer also has a big galliot which he will transfer on the same basis, to which your speediest answer is awaited as well as your opinion concerning the business of Pym. Breaking off, I remain, &c.

[1] Jacob Trip [1650–95], son of Hendrick Trip [1607–66] and nephew of Louis Trip [1605–84].

$\dfrac{30 \; Aug.}{3 \; Sep.}$ 1675

8 LOUIS DE LA BISTRATE & FREDERICK DUFAY to LM
  AMSTERDAM   3 SEPTEMBER 1675

•] We find ourselves with your kind letter of 23 July from which we understand that the ships which were loaded at Stockholm for England and spent the winter in Elsenap have all been unloaded again without any of them completing their journey. Consequently our iron remains on shore, which we did not know about. It is lucky that we did not have it insured: our friends must have forgotten to inform us about it and, because of the rupture between that kingdom and this state, dare not write fully because of the penalties on Dutch property there. However, we wrote to Mr Uppendorff at Hamburg who informed us that you had a commission from our friends in Stockholm for chartering a ship or ships to go and fetch away the goods at Stockholm, and that consequently we must learn from you how things stand. If you can give us some further information concerning this please communicate with us and, because of the present conjuncture, arrange with our friends in Stockholm to take our iron in your own name and correspond with them as if it were on your own account. From the bills of lading already sent to you you will be able to see what it amounts to, and when you receive our iron please do your utmost to procure its sale, as if it were your own.

Furthermore, we thank you very much for your good and exact information about what has been happening to commodities. We could wish that times were better so that we could take pleasure in speculating profitably in something. We hear that on the 9th of this month the sale of East India goods by your Company was postponed until 4 o'clock on the 21st instant. Here too our [East India Company] directors write that the day of the sale of a quantity of East India goods has been definitely fixed. You will undoubtedly have received a list of the cargoes of the ships which have arrived. Goods are pouring in, pell-mell, whatever the demand. Pepper ought to sell cheaply from the Company: it now fetches $14\frac{3}{8}g$; cloves, 86*st.*, nutmegs, 58*st.*, fine cinnamon, 80*st.*, indigo guatemalo in boxes, $6\frac{1}{2}st.$, fine cochineal, 30*s*, campeachy wood, $f.8\frac{1}{2}$, and Aleppo galls $f.33$.

Nothing much is happening in Swedish goods—copper-wire $f.57\frac{1}{2}$, garcopper, $f.57$, for cash; Swedish fine iron $f.6\frac{1}{4} - \frac{3}{8}$, ditto Orgrond $f.6\frac{3}{4}$ to $f.7$; coarse or anchor iron fetches $f.6\frac{1}{8} - \frac{1}{4}$. Clean Riga hemp is $f.41$ per slb.

We wish we had the opportunity of being of service to you. Enclosed herein are two letters for you from Hamburg received from Sweden. The Lord Hendrick Thuen-Rosenström writes us to send with his enclosed letter the bill of lading for 42 slb of wire consigned to you, on which he says we may draw up to *RD* 2,200 which he has to furnish us with by the 12th and 19th of October. And he says we should correspond with you about what measures to take to ensure for him the cheapest remittances from [London] or drafts from here on [London]. Regarding this we shall wait to see your answer to know what we may do.

The first convoy from Greenland has arrived here and in their company eleven ships bring with them $127\frac{1}{2}$ whales, which is a good catch considering there are not more than eleven ships in the convoy. And in Hamburg the latest letters say that two ships have arrived which only had 5 whales each, so many people conjecture that in general their catch is not large— time will tell. Meanwhile it is believed that in September, October and November the new train-oil will be available at $f.27\frac{1}{2}$, and fins at $f.38-38\frac{1}{2}$. We remain, &c.

$$(\text{i}) + (\text{ii}) \quad \frac{25 \ Sep.}{9 \ Nov.} 1675$$

249 FREDERICK & GODSCHALL to LM

SEVILLE   (i)   20 AUGUST 1675

'Madam, The foregoeinge is coppy of our last, confirme. Since is com to hand yours of the 12th July which served only for covert to Mr John Woliston of [Tanger?] letter which shall bee forwarded to him per the first good conveyance that presents that way. The 3 small cases of pinns wee have sould one with another at 28 *R. pta.* per dozen to Isidro de los Santos, beeinge 72 dozen to pay in 4 months, each moneth the quarter parte, which doubt not but will render you a pleasinge account. For the future you may please to take notice that Nos. 6 and 7, beeinge the biggest sort of pinns, is what pleaseth the Spanish ladys of which you may please cause send two hundred dozen. We shall indeavour to sell them for 4 *pesos* per dozen, the charges to the best of our calculate will not exceed 5 *R. pta.* per dozen with commission and by which you may take your measure. The Dutch sort are sould at 24 *R. pta.* which are much bigger, though not so white nor well made. English will allwayes bee preferred in sales before the others. Per the next post shall send you the account sale of what sould that you may bee at the more certainety in what may provide for the future for this markett. Som few bayes wee have sould this week at 18 ducats per piece to bee paid at the arrivall of *Gallones* to the shopps, those that may bee trusted. Some few have sould at the same rate to pay weekly. As fast as wee can gett in money shall goe makeinge you returnes as good convoyance offers. The next shippinge hope the goods you intend for this markett will com that they may partake of the winter markett our Safra people will give us, which shall indeavour to make better then the present times, or in any thing else that lyeth in our way to compleate your commands.'

(ii) 3 SEPTEMBER 1675

0   'Madam, This week wee have not received any lines from you. The account sale of the pinns promised in coppy you have here inclosed and accordingly the nett proceed past to the creditt of your account, being 1,612 *R. pta.*, which finding right may pleas to passe in the same nature, and as find encouragement send the quantity desired in coppy, and wee shall do our best to make them render you a pleasing account. Nos. 6 and 7 are the sortment that this markett will best sell, per avizo, to our Safra and Ayamonte[1] customers with som of this place of the best paymasters. Wee have sould bayes from 18 to $18\frac{1}{2}$ and 19 ducats per piece whites, that give some parte money and the rest at 3, and som at 4, months time, which are the best termes wee cann meet with these misserable dead times, that wee canot recover bills of the goldsmithes save at a tedious runn, all menn now putting off untill the arrivall of *Galleones*, which God grant may gett home safe in a short time, when hope shall see better times, that may send you a large supply of sugars. Wee hope per the next shipping you will send us the desired sortment of goods for the winter expence that wee may keep feeding our customers as fast as they goe supplying us in payment, and if bayes goe faling there you may enlarge as thinck fitting. This markett spendeth them apace and of the large parcells that was on the place to sell the best parte of them is allready consumed and the winter will require a considerable quantity, per avizo. Wee hope speedily shall be able to cleere all accounts of your resting goods, and as effects com in goe making you returnes, so wishing you all health and hapiness wee rest, your most humble servants, &c.'

  [1] Ayamonte, 60 km west of Seville, on the Portuguese border.

$$\frac{28\ Sep.}{26\ Oct.} 1675$$

1 J. & H. VAN BAERLE tO LM
AMSTERDAM   4 OCTOBER 1675

]   We have your letter of the 10th past to which this serves as a reply. It is good that you have obtained acceptance of the £85 sterling bill remitted to you on John Langley (of which the second copy goes herewith) and credited us accordingly, as well as for the money for William Wathing to draw on.

By reason of the bad state of trade at present we can find little opportunity to apprentice the said Wathing to any good merchant. We have approached several of our acquaintances but they have no opening for one. Furthermore, we have consulted a broker who is accustomed to arranging the apprenticeship of boys, but he told us that for him to be accepted in a good firm he would have to find at least *f.*300 to *f.*400 per year for his keep for four years and give security for his fidelity to the sum of *f.*4,000 to *f.*5,000, and as Mr Wathing is not inclined to bind himself for so long there is nothing we can do in the matter, remaining, &c.

London: $35^s\ 3\frac{1}{2}g$ } 2 usances.
Paris: $101\frac{1}{4}$ }
Hamburg: $34\frac{3}{8}$.
Antwerp: 1 per cent premium on bills.

$$\frac{4\ Oct.}{5\ Oct.}1675$$

252 FRANÇOIS BOSTELMAN to LM
HAMBURG   24 SEPTEMBER 1675

[D]   My most recent letter was on the 21st. This one only serves to say that you should hold back from the goods I requested—ginger, indigo, tobacco and galls—and buy nothing until further order. And if by any chance you have already bought something and loaded it aboard some of our Hamburg ships please unload it again, *coûte que coûte*. Even though one may have to pay the captain some conditional freight, I beg you not to load in Hamburg or Bremen ships since we have today received bad news from France that the King has declared war against us and given orders in all his ports that our ships are to be seized and confiscated wherever they may be found. We learned of this all too directly since a Bremen ship coming from [London] laden with goods was taken in the Elbe by a Dunkirk caper. Thank God I am not involved, and may the Lord protect us from further attacks!

Consequently I want you not to load anything you may have bought into Hamburg shipping. If by any chance you have bought the galls you can send them here in an English ship, but not any other goods. And in the bill of lading state that it is for your account and not for mine, which could be useful if it is intercepted. But, God knows, how easy it is to be innocently caught up in all-too painful losses! I have no doubt that you will help me, if it can be done without loss to yourself. Wherewith, regards, &c.

[P.S.] If you have bought some tobacco and indigo do not send it here but keep it in London until further order. This goes by way of Amsterdam and I have also sent you the same contents by way of Antwerp so that at least one of them may not be lost. Again, adieu.

$$\frac{4\ Oct.}{15\ Oct.}1675$$

253 J. A. FONCK to LM
HAMBURG   28 SEPTEMBER 1675

[D]   I have received your letters of the 20th of August and 12th instant, and will expect to hear in your next what has happened in the sale of the Marglitzer linen, and whether you think it advisable for me to send you a further quantity. For I am sure that all English shipping will now be fully employed and become the sole masters of the sea. If you could enquire about an English ship of 30 to 40 lasts, which you could charter to come here for a reasonable price and load train-oil to take from here to Rouen, it would not pay badly for I have worked it out that train-oil bought here at 30–31 *ML* per quarteel[1] (which is what it is costing at present) with all expenses, commission and freight at 17 crowns per last (of 10 quarteels) should cost 54–55

£*t* on delivery at Rouen where, according to the latest letters, it could fetch 65–66 £*t*, which is a decent profit. And I am sure you could procure the freight for 8 French crowns per last of 10 quarteels (which are contained in 20 barrels) since you say that £5–£4 10*s* was being asked from [London] to Stockholm and back from there to [London], which is more than twice as far as from here to France. You have only to take up this venture, for which little capital is required, to make a decent profit. My brother at Amsterdam would take one-third and you two-thirds, for I would rather sit quietly and do without commission than trade without enthusiasm. If you decide to do something about it, hurry up, for winter draws near. At Rouen I use Mons. Anthoine van de Hulst, a good and zealous man who has served me well with this commodity. The voyage is a short one, the goods are not far from your country, so you have only to make up your mind and despatch a ship.

Goods from [England] remain lying here at rock-bottom prices, so there is little enthusiasm for getting any more. If cotton prices fell somewhat lower, as well as Caribbean indigo, I might well decide on some. Pepper has been extremely under-sold at 14*g* and below, which is a poor price and gives no encouragement to order more, with which I remain, &c.

London: 32*s* 6*g*.
Paris: 47.

[P.S.] Have you got a good friend to whom you will consign the cargo, or will you leave it to me? And if you are inclined to insure something there are good insurers to be found here at 4 per cent.

  [1] While olive oil was sold by the 820 lb. unit, train oil was sold by the quarteel of 448 lb.

$$\frac{9\ Nov.}{11\ Nov.}1675$$

54 R. OURSEL to JD
        ROUEN   12 NOVEMBER 1675

'Ma derniere a vos grace estoit le 5ᵉ courant, depuis laquelle j'ay receu la vostre agreable du 25 passe (V.S.). Pour reponce je vous diray jusques a present que vos deux thonneaux de fil de latton venus par le navire *Le Prospereur*[1] n'ont peu estre deschargez a terre nonobstant toutes les sollicitations que j'ay faites au maitre pour les avoir. Cela n'a pas empesche que je ne les aye venduz au Sʳ Jean le Page a £88*t* le cent a payer a 4 mois, estant livres le compte vous en sera aussytost envoyé.

Jean Hacker, dans lequel sont chargez les autres dix boucaux est, graces a Dieu, bien arrivé aubas de nostre riviere.[2] Estant monté devant cette ville j'en procureray la vente, vous donnant advis en son temps du succes.

Le cuivre en planche vaut £95*t* le cent; dito en rosette £77*t* 10*s*. Chaudrons rouge, £98*t* a £100*t* selon qu'ilz sont bien faitz. Les petits ont de plus prompte vente a present que les plus grands. Les cuivres en planches et les chaudrons payent pour droitz d'entrée a la romaine £5*t* du cent, et le cuivre en rosette £2*t* 10*s*. Vous pouvez faire vostre compte, pour les autres menuz fraits ne sont pas de consequence.

J'esperois vous faire remise la semaine passée et ceste ordinaire du reste de vostre advance, mais je ne scay par quel capprice le change a baissé tout subitement de 58*d* a 57½*d* et encor je n'ay peu rencontrer de lettres de satisfaction, ce quy me donne desplaisir. Je tascheray neangmoins de vous remettre sy je rencontre des lettres a un prix un peu raisonnable, car je tiens pour maxime (l'ayant experimenté en quantite de rencontres) qu'il vaut mieux en matiere de change suivre aveuglement le courant que de garder l'argent en caisse inutile sur l'esperance d'augmentation du prix dont on se trouve bien souvent trompé.

Je suis attendant un mot de reponce sur ce que je vous ay proposé touchant la navire quy est a Geluckstadt pour me servir de gouverne.

Je vous prie de me dire ce que vaut chez vous l'indigo guatimalo, quels droits d'entrée ils payent et sy on peut esperer d'en trouver chez vous prompte vente. J'en attends partie de Cadix que je vous pourrois envoyer sy je prevois qu'il y aye quelque chose a faire. Je vous prie aussy me dire s'il ne se pourroit pas vendre chez vous quelque partie de noz thoilles propres pour Espaigne, scavoir des *blancarts* et *florettes*. Elles sont icy a grand marché. Estant ce quy s'offre je vous sallue, demeurant, Monsieur, vostre tres affectionne serviteur.'

[London]: $57\frac{1}{4}d.$
Amsterdam: $102\frac{3}{4}.$

[1] *The Prosperous*, Captain Joseph Hudson, bringing 180 coils of copper-wire.
[2] John Hacker, captain of the *Elizabeth*, brought 500 coils of wire.

17 Nov. 1675
14 Feb. 1676

255 LEWIS THOMPSON to JD
BELFAST   6 NOVEMBER 1675

'Yours bering date the 26 of Ocktober came to my hand and by the first opertunitey will draw on you for what money I have yours for within six hundred pound for the account of Mr Jacob Vandepoth of Hamborgh and as for John Clugston[1] of whome you inquire he hath lived in this plase from a childe but trewley at present his estate and reputation are both verey low in esteme with the most that know him for he hath bene out of credit, stok and trade this four years and if you be cler of him keepe soe and if he owe you money I canot se aney prowbilitey how it will be had for he hath ben on his defens from his crediters this gret while and wher he is at present I know not but he hath a wife and five small children in this plase who are verey por and as for this plase it is a contrey that doth preduce a bundans of goodes by the which severell both in London, Holand and Flanders and maney other parts doe consern them selves and make a great profit but the season of the year [hole] the great prowbilitey of profit for in money onley when I drew my last bill on you I could have drawen a thousent pound at six pound the hundred and nou noe money to be had though at even handes and soe most yeares the exchange doth fall and rise with the sesen and as for goodes our contrey afordes great store of taned lether of all sorts and befe and buter and talow and green hides and salt samon and woll and much linin cloth, which is most yoused for sheets and shertin for men and women and of a resonable prise generaley a bout three qwarters and haulf a qwarter in bredth and from eyght pens the yard to eyghtten pens the yard but it is loked on to be the best comaditey that goes to Verginey or New Ingland. Tand lether is generaley sould at five pens the pound and shiped to Frans or Spayne and that is to be had at all times in the yeare but buter, befe and talow is most redey [and salt hides] betwixt the first of Agust and the furst of Jenewer which is shiped most to Frans, Ostend and som times into Holand and verey often talow is shiped from hens to London, Bristow and other parts in Ingland and is sould for [— — — — — — — — — — (1 line lost in the frayed crease of the letter) — — — — — — — —] butter is sould this yer generely from 24 to 26 shilling the hundred, talow from 26 to 28 pond the tun. We have 120 to the hundred of buter besides the cask wayght and but a hundred and twelve of talow. Befe is this yer worth twentey shillins the barill; salt hides of the largest sort worth twentey two to 23 the hundred. Samon is genereley sould in June and shiped of to Spayn and is sould at 16 to 17 pound per ton. Small hides salted is worth 16 to 17 the hundred; candles the pound by sale generelay three pens half peney. Salt herins which doe com out of Skotland by great cuantitays are sould hear for 15 to 16 per barill. We have our returns to this plase often in wines both Frans and Spanish and in brandey but money is the best comoditey that we have. As for our harvest it hath ben verey great and all sortes of grayn verey cheape as wheat from ten to twelve the Bristou barill; barley from 5 to 6 the Bristoll barill; oten meall, which is a greate comoditey in Norway, about five pounds the ton, soe perues all this and if you have ocation to be informed in aneything as to the trayd of forin good let me have your minde by your leter and in what I can be servisable to you may asure yourselfe that I will be both redey and willing to be to my pour your frend and reall servant whilst I am, L.T.

[P.S.] Pray faver me with a line or two when your time give way and excus my playnes.'

¹ Probably John Clignet of Limerick, indebted to Steven de Geer. See [**20**, **49**].

$$\frac{17\ Nov.}{[\text{——}]}1675$$

6 P. CAULIER to JD
YARMOUTH   15 NOVEMBER 1675

'Sir & Honoured Cosin, I am with yours of the 11 and 13th to which I answer, I see your desire of being concerned in herrings for Marseille provided it bee in the first ship, to which I say your order comes too late this yeare to be effected. There is a ship or 2 gone and one more to goe—besides one in the river to whom herrings are sent. The second is a ship of mine, the *Olive Branch*, Capt. Richard Lewis commander, of 10 guns, which I hope may gett her port as soon as the first. Had you wrote in time you should have bin accomodated in what you pleased, the common freight wee have is $1\frac{3}{4}$ dollars per barrell and $\frac{1}{2}$ [dollar?] per pigg of lead. Said ship I purpose shall returne for London. She is consigned to Mr Hill & Jago of Marseille. If you desire to have any [summa?] on her home she is at your service.

I take notice by yours of the 11th that you were espoused to my cosin Marescoe and soe become our kinsman. My wife and self congratulate you both and wish you all happiness and felicity and that you may be a comfort to each other. Wee understand by sister Gosslyn that you have bin pleased to send gloves for us there which was more than wee expected, being at so great a distance, but since it was your kindness wee most kindly accept of them and returne you our hearty thankes. Shall weare them for your sakes, so praying God to accumulate you with his blessings we kindly salute you and rest, honooured Cosin your most oblidged servant and kinsman, &c.'

$$\frac{27\ Nov.}{29\ Nov.}1675$$

7 R. OURSEL to JD
ROUEN   26 NOVEMBER 1675

'Ma derniere a vos graces estoit le 22 courant, par laquelle je vous ay remis *W*.850.50*s* a 57*d* de 2 lettres que j'espere vous seront parvenues, dudepuis j'ay receu la vostre agreable du 11/21 ditto et vollontiers veu par icelle qu'avez trouvé le compte de la vente des 100 torches fil de latton en son debvoir et annotté de conformite, ce quy est bien. J'estime le sieur Le Page fort a son aize. Il est icy en bonne reputation, luy ayant encor vendu 200 torches de la derniere partie receue par Hacker au mesme prix et conditions que la precedente, ainsy que je vous l'ay advisé par ma derniere. J'estime aussy les autres ausquels le reste de la dite partie a esté vendue tres bons. Sy desirez je vous repondray des debtes moyennant double provision, c'est a dire 4 pour-cent au lieu de 2, et vous feray bon le provenu un mois apprez l'escheance des debtes soit qu'elles soient receues ou non, surquoy seray attendant vostre reponce. Affin que les choses que nous arresterons demeurent constantes, tant pour ce quy est desja vendu que pour l'advenir, que sy ne desirez agreer cette proposition soyez assure que cela n'empeschera pas que je n'aye tousjours un soin particulier de ne faire mauvaise debtes et que je ne procure vos intherests comme sy l'estoit pour moy mesme. Vous vous pleignez que le terme de 4 mois est un peu trop long: vous pouvez croire que sy j'avois peu obtenir plus court terme je l'aurois fait mais je n'ay pas creu quand on a affaire a des debiteurs qu'on estime bons qu'on doibve rompre un marche pour un mois de temps plus ou moins. On ne scauroit garder les marchandises en magazin qu'un mois ou deux se treuve insensiblement escoulé et quand il se presente marchand il faut encor accorder autant de temps pour le payement comme on a demande au commencement. Le principal est de prendre garde aux debiteurs quy soient d'entiere satisfaction.

Je m'informeray de la diference qu'en fait icy entre les marques de la tulippe, de l' $\frac{www}{AW}$ marque, de la [——?]M, et de l' N̈ pour vous l'adviser s'il ce peut encore au pied de cette. Les chaudrons de cuivre jaune ont esté icy autre fois bonne marchandises, mais sont a present fort demeurez et ne se vend que a des chaudronniers dont la plus part sont tres mauvais payeurs, ainsy je ne serois vous conseiller de n'envoyer de grande parties, seullement un thonneau ou deux pour essay, et sy vous y voyez de profit allons on pourra continuer d'en envoyer plus grande parties. Je vous ay dit que les droits de romaine pour l'entrée sont £5t du cent pesant; les autres frais sont comme sur toute autre choses, pour le frait, portages, visitation, droits du poix, courtages et seullage, que vous pouvez a peu pres calculer sur les comptes de fil de latton, dont je voy que desirez encore m'envoyer 300 torches, scavoir 200 torches de la mesme sorte de celuy que m'avez envoye et 100 torches de la mesme marque mais beaucoup plus gros. Cette derniere sorte ne sera pas bien propre icy, ainsy sy'l n'est chargé advant la reception de la presente j'estime que ferez bien de n'en point envoyer plus de 50 torches pour un essay, mais ne pouvez manquer d'en envoyer de l'autre sorte ou en treuvera bien le debit. La marque de la tulippe n'est pas estimee icy. Ce sera pour garder longtemps le magazin.

Celle de la marque $\frac{www}{AW}$ se vendroit mieux; on l'estime 40s pour cent moins que N̈, mais les trois couronnes de Laurens de Gier sont icy en estime pardessus toutes les autres marques, selon quoy pouvez vous regler. Je ne croy pas que cette marchandise soit pour baisser de prix sytost a cause de l'hiver et de la guerre contre ceux de Hamborgh a moins qu'il n'en vienne de trop grande parties de chez vous a la fois. C'est a quoy vous debvez prendre garde et sur cela prendre vos mesures.

Je seroy ravy de vous pouvoir proposer quelques choses au negosse ou il y aye apparence de profit et d'y prendre part avecq vous, mais la guerre m'a sy fort rebutte que je n'oze rien entreprendre. Sy je remarque cy apprez qu'il y aye quelque chose a faire je vous le proposeray vollontiers. Je voy le subit rabais des changes pour France. Cela a esté contre le sentiment de plusieurs et m'a empesché en partie de vous remettre le reste de vostre advance sur l'esperance de mieux faire comme il c'est fait icy ce jourdhuy au dessus de $56\frac{1}{2}d$ et que selon les apparences cela ne peut continuer longtemps; sy me croyez il me semble qu'il seroit mieux de remettre pour Paris a 2 ou 3 usances, moyennant $\frac{1}{2}$ pour-cent pour mois rencontrant de bonne lettres ou le bailler sur la place a intherest pour 6 mois a raison de 5 ou 6 pour-cent pour an, selon que l'occasion se rencontrera, surquoy seray attendant vostre advis. Je voy le peril qu'il y a en la proposition que je vous ay faitte. Je ne croy pas qu'on y tienne sy fort la rigueur y ayant assez de personnes quy ne font pas tant de difficulte mais toutes personnes ne me sont pas propres. Ce sont choses desquelles la fidelité et le secret sont fort requises, quy ne sont a confier que a des gens qu'on cognoist parfaittement bien. Je feray reflection sur ce que m'escrivez et vous diray mon sentiment par le prochain. Je vous remercie de l'advis du prix de l'indigo. J'en ay icy 18 caissons que je souhaitte chez vous; je ne scay sy on ne pourroit pas les y envoyer par navires anglois.

Le Sieur de Banquemare a promis accepter vostre lettre de $W.364.29\frac{1}{2}s$ par laquelle vous sera renvoyée par le prochain; estant ce quy s'offre je vous sallue, demeurant, Monsieur, vostre tres affectionne serviteur.

[London]: $56\frac{3}{8}d$ $\Big\}$ 2 usances.'
Amsterdam: point de prix reglé

29 Nov. 1675
3 Feb. 1676

8 FREDERICK & GODSCHALL to LM
      SEVILLE   29 OCTOBER 1675

'Madam, We have not of late received any lines from you which will occation brevity at present beeinge chiefly to acquaint you that of some sugars wee have sent hence for Cadiz wee have ordered the value of £100 sterling to bee sent you per the *Mary Rose* friggate that may departe thence in a few dayes time. The letters are now com. Per the *Avizo* of the 15th May from Cartagena the plate was not come downe to Panama which may tard the returne of *Gallones* 3 months and upwards, there beeinge one-third parte *plata* more expected down then former yeares and *Gallones* carryinge one-third less goods will cause them to make a pleasinge markett and make ammens for their stayinge for the plate. God send them safe home that we may see better times when doubtless English goods will bee in better esteem, especially bayes, seeinge sould so well in the West Indies by all. December or January at furthest *Gallones* may bee at Cadiz when all sorts of sugars do not question but will be had resonable and goods find ready money sales, especially bayes if cann be given resonable aboard, &c.'

$\frac{20\ Dec.}{23\ Dec.}1675$

9 R. OURSEL to JD
      ROUEN   17 DECEMBER 1675

'J'ay receu la vostre agreable du 29 passe/9 courant; vollontiers veu par icelle qu'avez obtenu acceptation de toutes les remises que vous ay faittes pour vostre compte, ce quy est bien, et qu'avez receu le compte de la vente de vos 500 torches de fil de latton. Je ne doutes ou l'aurez treuve en son debvoir, ce que j'aprendray vollontiers a vostre commodité.

Je ne croy pas que les 4 pour-cent que je vous ay demandé pour provision et repondre des debtes soit trop, particulierement en m'obligeant de vous faire bon les debtes un mois apprez l'escheance d'icelles, soit qu'elles soient rentrez ou non, car encor qu'on aye bonne estime des debiteurs on peut estre trompé, outre que bien souvent les meilleurs sont bien 2 mois et quelque fois 3 mois apprez l'escheance advant qu'ayent entierement satisfait, ainsy j'ayme mieux me contenter de 2 pour-cent pour la provision ordinaire et n'estre respondant des debtes que d'en repondre et avoir 3 pour-cent pour provision et assurance.

Je voy qu'avez fait charger dans le vaisseau le *Hopefull Mary*, dont est maitre Phelippe Pucket, 400 torches fil de latton de la mesme sorte du precedent comprins 50 torches de 3-bandes—Dieu vieilles l'amener a bon port. Estant arrive j'en procureray la vente au mieux possible, vous donnant en son temps advis du succez. Comme on en attend 2,500 torches de Hambourg par un navire quy est tout prest a partir et qu'on doibt esperer du premier vent propre, cela fait un peu diminuer de prix y en ayant eub depuis peu partie de la marque des 3 Couronnes, L.D.G., de vendre a £87*t* 10*s* le cent a 4 usances. Cependant au prix que me marquez qu'il vaut chez vous je ne voy pas qu'il puisse beaucoup diminuer sy ce n'est qu'il en viene plusieurs petites parties en diverse mains quy voudrent s'empresser de vendre a l'envy les uns des autres, sans considerer la perte que leurs amis en soufrent. Depuis ma derniere il n'y a pas de changement au prix des cuivres en rosette et chaudrons de Suède, quy demeurant tousjours sans demande, je dit les chaudrons. Le cuivres en rosette treuveroit plus aisement le debit a cause qu'on en employe a faire des pieces de 4*s* d'une nouvelle fabrique dont l'argent est beaucoup moindre que celuy des escus blancqs, ce quy vous sert d'advis.

Je voy que la cochenille mesticque vaut chez vous 17*s* la lb., il n'y a rien d'en faire achepter chez vous au dit prix pour estre revendue icy £13*t* a £13½*t* la ib. Voicy une notte des frais quy se payent ordinairement sur icelle, surquoy pouvez vous regler. Je voy qu'avez ordonné a Messrs Schoonhoven, pere et fils de Nantes, de tirer sur moy pour vostre compte *W*.1,000 peu plus ou peu moins, a quoy je feray honneur et cy joint je vous remets *W*.600 a 56*d* p. *W*., 2 usances sur Gawen Laury a Londres en lettre de Jean Scoulter de laquelle il vous plaira faire procurer le requis et m'en faire crediter. C'est viron le reste de vostre avance avecq les *W*.1,000 cy-dessus que je garderay a l'ordre de les Sr. Schoonhoven, et estant ce quy s'offre je vous sallue, demeurant, Monsieur, vostre tres humble serviteur.'

[London:]　　56*d*–56¼*d* ⎫
Amsterdam:　101½ 　 ⎬ 2 usances.
　　　　　　　　　　 ⎭

$$\frac{21\ Dec.}{3\ Feb.}1675$$

260　VAN SCHOONHOVEN & SON to JD
NANTES　　　　　　　　　　　　　　　　　17 DECEMBER 1675

'Nous avons ce jour receu la vostre du 29me Novembre, vieu stille, avec celle de Mons. Herman Olmius qui a tarde une ordinnaire, touchant l'ordre que nous donnez d'achepter pour vos deux comptes a moitie 70 a 80 thonneaux de seigle et les charger pour Rotterdam a l'adresse de Mons. Josias Olmius, les pouvant avoir a £72*t* le thonneaux, mesure de Vannes, et de ne regarder pas a petite chose; tacherons a l'effectuer au plus vostre advantage, dont aurez au prochain advis. Nous prendrons un moix pour la reception des bleds. a nos bons points pour attendre l'occasion de quelque bons vaisseaux qui se presente icy fort souvent, mais auriez aussi bien fait d'en avoir frette un chez vous. Les derniers frette pour Hollande a este a £40*t* par lest et vingt sols par lest pour le chappeau du maistre, mais doibt aller charger en Bas Bretagne. Quand ils chargent icy en riviere ils font bien 30 a 40 sols par lest de meilleur marché, ainsi nous tacherons a achepter les bleds icy et donnerons plustost vingt sols par thonneaux davantage, aussi sont ils meilleurs. Les derniers seigle ont este vendu icy £66*t* et £67*t* le thonneaux; a Vannes £72*t* et £73*t*; a Hennebon £86*t* le thonneaux, mais ne sont pas si bons. Les froment icy £88*t* a £90*t* le thonneaux; ditto orges £64 a £66*t* le thonneaux, mesure au comble, qui est 20 pourcent plus grande que l'autre.

Les eaux de vie tienne icy prix vallent £79*t* les 29 veltes,[1] mais selon toute apparance viendront entre sesy et un moix au tour de £74*t* a £75*t* les 29 veltes et a plus bas prix. Le sel a la Baye £23*t* la charge; Poulquyn et Croisicq £19*t* a £20*t* le muydt; miel de Bretagne £11*t* le cent. Le harang d'Yrlande vault icy £15*t* a £16*t* le baril; ditto beure £18*t* a £20*t* le cent. Beure d'Angleterre £20*t* a £22*t* le cent; ditto estain £55*t* a £60*t* le cent; ditto plom £80*t* le millier. Vous nous ordonnez de tirer vostre part des bleds sur Mons. Robert Oursel a Rouan, ce qui nous ferons, mais les lettres perdent beaucoup icy, l'argent estant tres rare et a este fait comme sy desoubs. Nous sommes vos tres humble serviteurs.

Londen: $57\frac{3}{4}d$ 2 usances.

Paris: }		$1\frac{1}{2}$ a $1\frac{3}{4}\%$ }	
Rouan: }	perdent	2 a $2\frac{1}{2}\%$ }	a 20 jours de date.'

[1] The *velte* or *verge* is a measure of capacity, estimated at 7.258 litres, commonly used for brandies. At La Rochelle and Cognac the barrel of brandy usually held 27 veltes; at Bordeaux 32, and at Nantes 29 veltes, expressed $\frac{29}{v}$.

22 Dec. 1675
28 Jan. 1676

JOSIAS OLMIUS to JD

ROTTERDAM   20 DECEMBER 1675

Your letter of the 30th past has reached me and this serves as a reply.

My brother, H[ermann] Olmius, tells me that two small ships have already been chartered at Wells[1] to bring grain to me here on your joint account. May the Lord bring them safely. I hope they are still over there at the moment as the weather has been very terrible on our coasts with these daily north-west winds.

Grains are just as quiet as they were before, especially barley, of which the best that comes from England is selling at £23 flem. Rye is at 136, 140 and 145 [gold guilders], wheat at 155 to 160 and 170 [gold guilders], malt at £18–£21 flem., but if exports from England come to an end in February, as people tell me, grains will undoubtedly rise for Brabant promises to double its demand, and so it would not be unwise to store up what is coming from you.

I am extremely grateful for the kindness you have demonstrated in wanting to continue our correspondence through a profitable business. On my side I shall keep you informed whenever I spot anything profitable. Barbados sugar is very scarce and since the bad news from Barbados no one who has any will sell it, and the manufactured sugars have been sold before they are ready so it must rise considerably, in my judgement. The last were sold at $5\frac{3}{4}g$ but now there is no price quoted.

The exchange on France has risen to $103\frac{1}{2}$, with all the signs of rising higher, and it has been pointed out to me that with the exchange from [London] on Paris at $54\frac{1}{2}d$, to give that price there and send the bills to be negotiated here and send you returns at 36s 8–9g (as it is today) is a way of earning a rather nice interest.

If there is anything in which I can serve you or your friends, freely command, yours &c.

[1] Probably Wells-juxta-mare, Norfolk.

262   ALEXANDER VAN KUFFELER to JD

AMSTERDAM   24 DECEMBER 1675

[D]   Yours of the 19th past has reached me safely, from which I was happy to learn that you have married Mrs Marescoe. I hope the Lord will bless you with mutual happiness and allow you to live long together to salvation, in all the prosperity you could wish for.

Meanwhile, because the business is now in your hands, we shall continue our correspondence. I wish we had the opportunity to make it rather larger but things are in such a bad way here that nowhere is there anything to be done. Thank you for informing me of the prices of goods. I have carefully considered each one but could not find anything likely to be profitable. Indeed, several commodities which you mention and which must necessarily come from [England] have been sold here at a loss. May the Lord soon give us better times and a general peace and then trade, which is disrupted in nearly all parts of Europe, should revive again. People are expecting that the ambassadors of all the countries involved will soon be meeting for peace negotiations at Nimwegen. May God grant that this long-wished-for work may proceed so that in the coming year (in which I wish you all success and prosperity, as above) we may be cheered by news of peace.

The two kind letters of your wife, of the 24th of September and 1st of October, reached me in due course. I am glad to see that you sent the sample dishes to Rouen. Mons. Schockfeuer writes me that they were safely received and I must thank you for taking such trouble with them. It is also good to see that you obtained acceptance of the £80 drawn on Caspar Kaus—payment will undoubtedly follow. For the £57 11s which Mr Brodridge has drawn on I have credited your account.

I have just assigned on you a small bill of £3 3s payable to Mr John Elwill of Exeter, being the balance due on an account. Please pay it on presentation and place it to my account, forgiving the pettiness of it.

Now, concerning trade—as you say, thanks to the conjuncture of war England has become the general warehouse and has nothing to complain about. Here, on the contrary, little or nothing is happening, nearly all commodities being at very poor prices and little or no demand for them. Regarding prices, I refer you to the enclosed price-current.[1] Corn has been very high in price here and for some time large amounts have been coming from England. Something might well be done with that. I understand it has fallen in price at the moment but, even so, it fetches good prices, vizt.:

English	wheat fetches	from 168 to 178 *ggl.*	
	rye	from 130 to 140 *ggl.*	per last, according
	barley	from 95 to 100 *ggl.*	to quality, each gold
	malt	from 94 to 98 *ggl.*	guilder is 28 stuivers.
	oats	from 54 to 58 *ggl.*	
	buckwheat	from £24 to £30 *flem.*	
	rape-seed	from £36 to £42 *flem.*	per last.
	linseed	from £29 to £31 *flem.*	

It is rumoured here that the King may abolish the customs or duty which is given on its export from England, or perhaps prohibit its export altogether. If that were done it would cause a striking increase in price here. But otherwise I can see little signs of any change in the immediate future, and large amounts would have to come from England before it caused any decline—for your information.

So, if I can be of any service to you, you have only to command me, and with cordial regards I commend you and Madame, your wife, to the protection of God, and remain, &c.

London:	$35s$ $8g$	} 2 usances.
Paris:	$99\frac{1}{2}$	
Hamburg:	$34\frac{1}{8}$	} at sight.
Antwerp:	$\frac{1}{8}$ p. cent loss	

[1] Missing.

$$\frac{27\ Dec.}{31\ Dec.}1675$$

63 C. BENE to JD

HAMBURG   13 DECEMBER 1675

[D] I last wrote to you on the 10th inst. I have since received, last Saturday, your three letters of the 26th and 30th of November and 3rd of this month. By these I have seen your commission to buy 600 coils of Swedish 5-band brass-wire for 62 *ML* at the most, of which I have made a note. But I am sorry to say that there is nothing to be done, as you will have seen quickly enough[1] from my previous letter, for the price of wire is rising daily here and now no Swedish wire can be had for less than 66 *ML*. This type is nearly all in the hands of one man who is maintaining the price as he pleases, and the stock which he has is believed to be not much more than 1,000 coils. None can come from Sweden for the next year, and elsewhere not much will be worked for lack of money and credit. One should be able to obtain Hamburg wire at 66 *ML*, but I fear it will rise higher.

From Rouen has just arrived, fully-loaded, Thomas Frost sailing Hendrick Weever's ship called *De Perell*, in which I do not dare to load anything although I suppose it is as safe as if it were built in England. He last came here with it from [London] and is now, as I understand, chartered by a friend but before that will take in some wire for Rouen—I mean, for [London]. There have been some English ships in lading here which, for a fortnight, have not dared to take in anything except from Englishmen. But others have taken in goods for anyone, and they are not especially obliged to go to other places, so on that point there is no difficulty—for your information. The Holstein ships are also passing freely. One from Tonningen was brought in to Fryck[?] but by orders of the King was freed and his costs repaid. People also have great hopes that our ships will again be allowed to sail freely. Philip Muncker, in whom your wire is loaded, is completely ready and only waits for a good wind. His ship is a galliot and has no other name. May God help him arrive in safety.

Enclosed herewith is going the account of the 150 coils of wire loaded aboard him, amounting to £382 9s 2d, for which I debit you. Please check it, and if you find you agree with it make a record of it. To all appearances you should do well with it. Besides Muncker there are two other small ships laden for Rouen, which are also lying in the Elbe because of contrary winds. Altogether I think these three ships are carrying away about 4,000 coils and nothing of other copper wares such as sheet-copper or brass, etc, as far as I can learn. To know the exact details one must spend something on the customs lads, which I shall do and then inform you in my next. If you continue to want reports about this please let me know so that it can be arranged.

The friend who has about 1,000 coils has told me that he had decided to send them to

Bordeaux, and then another 200 coils of the 'Lily' brand, which can still be had for 65 *ML*, and to receive them without regard to the quality. For as soon as our manufacturers discover that so little Swedish wire remains they will push up the price of their other brands. These types [of wire] have been usually paid for immediately, and it could well be impossible— especially in these times of rising prices—to stipulate payment by waiting for remittances from London. And even if prices were not rising one would have to pay more if one sought to defer it. So, if you want this commission to be performed, please enlarge your price-limit and also give me permission to load in Thomas Frost, who will be ready in a few days. At the present there is no other alternative. If I had performed the commission already I would have drawn on you for my outlay, as you ordered, and consigned it to you as instructed.

The weather here is still mild, without any cold but plenty of rain and storm.

The bill of lading for the 103 sacks of ginger has been received and will be useful. I hope the purchase of 10 sacks of cotton at $5\frac{1}{2}d$ has also gone ahead because, since they have been bought outright, the buyer ought to keep them. And I would judge that the hurricane in Barbados can make little difference because, apart from this lot, nothing much from there has arrived for a long time. If one can still get such good quality for $5\frac{1}{2}d$ I would be content to go shares with you in 30 sacks for which I think the price is so low that one can hardly go wrong with them. If you are favourably disposed towards the idea please obtain such a quantity and send it here, on the understanding that not more than 10 sacks are bought for me. If you think it advisable you can delay this purchase until the ships expected from Smyrna arrive. It sells here for $13g$ and $13\frac{1}{2}g$ in lots of 1 or 2 bales. Our ships from Spain have not yet arrived but are expected every hour. With regards, &c.

London—33*s* 1*g*.

[P.S.] Thank you for the news about the hurricane. As a result, Barbados sugar and ginger are selling rather better and if it continues it will cause further changes.

> [1] '. . . als Ue uyt myne voorgaende a'bastanza *sal gesien hebben* . . .'.

$$\frac{27\ Dec.}{31\ Dec.}1675$$

264   J. A. FONCK TO JD
         HAMBURG   14 DECEMBER 1675

[D]   I have received your welcome letter of the 19th past and wish you all good fortune and God's blessings in your marriage with Madame Marescoe, so that you may enjoy all the prosperity you could desire. And I hope we shall have abundant opportunities to cultivate our correspondence, for which we need an early peace. If you could contrive to get the Guinea Company to buy from you 2,000 to 3,000 pieces of Marglitzer as well as other sorts of the cloth which the English buy in Germany, we could establish an important business together. I am eager to know if one can do anything with 'aurum' pigment in [England] and whether a decent amount could be disposed of? Sugar remains at a low price here, although people will talk about a hurricane in Barbados, but this news has already come too often and there is a good quantity of sugar chests here. There is also such a quantity of blue indigo that it is likely to fall to $4g$. Our ships will bring a substantial amount of indigo from Spain; all silks are lying unsold and very cheap, and the silk-weavers cannot recover their debts outstanding in Sweden and Denmark. I understand that good quality Smyrna cotton is available at $5\frac{1}{4}d$, and I would buy a parcel of it if the Marglitzer linen were sold, so I ask you to do your duty about this. If we allowed such a current commodity as linen to lie unsold for such a long time we would lose all our commissions. We have to sell what arrives from Germany as quickly as possible and make returns in cash or goods, so we have to accept most of the goods on our own account and pay for them. If you grasped this maxim you would dispose of more goods, so please give some thought to it immediately. I shall not be able to dispose of any great quantity of sugar, cotton, ginger, indigo, oil or galls for you this year, remaining, with friendly regards, &c.

London: 33*s* 1*g*.
Paris: 46.
Amsterdam: $34\frac{5}{16}$.

$\frac{|\quad\quad|}{3 \ Feb. \ 1676}$

55   T. LANNOY & J. BURKIN to LM
        ALEPPO   3 SEPTEMBER 1675

'Your letter of the 24th June sent by way of Legorne we received the 2[?]th past by which take notice to what date you had received of ours. The ginger which we received by the *Providence* in which you are concerned we have at last bartered against cotten yarne, giveing 2 [quintalls] of ginger @ *LD*.19 in money per q[uinta]ll yarne. We were the more willing to dispose of it the worme being gott and no money buyer appearing. We should have sent you full returnes by these ships but they refused taking in any goods but silke, except those who had taken tunnage in England. We shall not faile doeing it by the return of our General ships, and send you your accounts.

    The samples of Swedish wyer you sent in your letter all three sorts are verry propper for this place and sells by the R[ottol]o of 600 drames which is some small matter under 4 pound English and sells for here, as we are informed, when at lowest *LD*.$1\frac{3}{4}$ per said Rottolo of 600 drames, at present *LD*.$2\frac{1}{4}$. We never sold any but the best we can learne the charges may come to aspers 20 per Rottolo with our fraight and Consolage, the latter if shipped from England there is no thing due. This place consumes a bout hundred to a thousand Rottolos per annum, which is all we know worth your notice. We remaine your most faithfull and obliged servants, &c.'

(i) + (ii) $\frac{|\quad\quad|}{5 \ Feb.}$ 1676

66   W. MOMMA to LM
        [———————]   (i)   12 SEPTEMBER 1675

D]   The above is a copy of my last, which I fear may not have reached you yet since letters are being held up by these grievous wars, and I have likewise received no letters from you nor any German letters so that I have no idea of what is happening abroad. As a result, this will be brief, and I refer you to the foregoing copy.

    The English ships are at present still lying near Stockholm without anyone knowing when they will depart, and according to my son's letters thay have bought about 600 slb [of copper-wire] but to whom it is going I do not know. It will cost about 57 to 58 *RD* per shippound, free on board, and I am of the opinion that it will be selling for over £7 with you before the spring. For this year not one half as much—indeed, not much above a third—will be made as last year, and as the works are mostly lying idle at present very little will be worked up this winter, for your information.

I shall wait to hear what is happening with you. If these wars continue and England keeps its shipping free I would advise you to send two or three ships to St Ubes to load salt this autumn and send them on to Stockholm with an agent early next year.

I remain, &c.

(ii) 7 NOVEMBER 1675
[not selected]

$$\frac{24\ Jan.}{[\text{———}]}1676$$

267 WILLIAM FOXLEY[1] to JD
HAMBURG   11 JANUARY 1676

'Sir, In answer to yours of the 24 pasto, my forwarding your packets doath not by farr deserve that acknowledgement yow are pleased to make, but be assured where in can serve them shall doe it to the utmost of my power. Now Sir William Swan tells me if I have anye letters, will putt them under his covert direct to Sir Edward Wood of Stockholm,[2] soe if you have anye further occasion I shall take due care of them. Please to lett the letters be as small as maye be; if a bigg packett he presseth whether there be not Dutch letters in.

I have inquired after Sweedish and Hamburg weyer: the Swedish is worth hier 65 a 66 *ML* per 100 lb., Hamburg 66 a 67 *ML* per 100 lb. contant in Banco. The 100 lb. hier makes with yow about 107 lb.[3] Of the Hamburg weyer hier is great quantities in towne, but of Swedish but little. The most is 500 rings each 26 a 27 lb. I heare not of much weyer gonne for Italy but of the Swedish weyer there is a prety quanti gonne of late. There is alsoe much of these two sorts sent for London, and trowly if you resolve one anye thing I doe count this the best time for the buyinge in for the following reason—being now in the dead tyme of the yeare and frozen upp soe noe trade and I beleave might be able to procure each sorte 1 *ML* a 1½ *ML* per cent cheaper than what have a boved coated[4] and I beleave after open water they will yeald full as much as have above rated them to you at; as alsoe this exchange is now high and beleave maye fall considerably. Please to be confident where in can serve you shall doe it with all diligence.

Barbados sugar, the best 5½ *g* per lb. 13 months discount; ginger 7½ *g* per lb. 13 months discount; Cadiz soult 62 a 63 *ML* per last; ditto Lisxbarry[5] 70 *ML* per last; ditto St Hubes 103 a 104 *ML* per last of 18 tunns. Please to note the last hier is 10 per cent better than with you. Further as to the price of comodities referr yow to the inclosed; is the needfull from your most humble servant.'

London:	33s 2g	2 usos, falling.
Amsterdam:	34⅜	usa.
Antwerp:	34½	usa.
Parris:	46	usa.

[1] The Foxley family were Merchant Adventurers resident in Hamburg, who were to go bankrupt in 1678. William Foxley was introduced to JD by JL in November 1675 as an intermediary capable of getting JD's letters round the Danish blockade into Sweden.

[2] Sir Wiliam Swann was English representative to the Hanse Towns and Resident at Hamburg, 1663–78. Sir Edward Wood was the English representative in Sweden, 1672–9.

³ Beawes *Lex Mercatoria Rediviva*, p. 897 put the 100 lb. of Hamburg (which is not be confused with the centner of 112 lb.) as equivalent to 107 lb. 5 oz. avoirdupois. I have thus transcribed Foxley's 'Ct' not as 'cent.' let alone 'centner' but as '100 lb.'.
⁴ *Sic.*—'above quoted'.
⁵ I.e. Lisbon.

$$\frac{24\ Jan.}{28\ Jan.}1676$$

68 J. A. FONCK to JD
HAMBURG   14 JANUARY 1676

[D] I have received yours of the 31st past. I wish with all my heart that God will grant that this new year may begin and end in such a way that will honour Him and bring us to salvation.

Concerning the Marglitzer linen—you are incorrectly informed that Banques[1] has contracted to deliver it to the Guinea Company in England. It is true that there are three or four Englishmen here such as the two Townleys and others that buy it and send it to England and I am sure that Banques has a share in it, but the idea that any monopoly should arise from that is odious and accursed of God. No one could imagine that a monopolist has emerged, particularly when everyone over here is so anxious lest the Company should bind itself to buy from only one person. Mine could only be sold for a 10 per cent loss at 15s, and for some time it has been selling at 18s. If you could obtain a price of 17s I might at last decide to strike a bargain—or I could sell it here for delivery to England, for there is a demand.

I am eager to hear further news about how things are going with Barbados goods and, if you think I should keep or sell some Barbados goods which I have bought, I beg you to participate. Brown ginger can be had for $4\frac{1}{4}g$ so it can hardly be brought from [England]. Smyrna cotton is definitely not to be despatched (though other sorts could be) otherwise I might have contemplated having a good quantity from you. Pepper is at $13\frac{1}{2}g$ and I am sure it will soon be at $13\frac{1}{4}g$. To sum up, goods are so plentiful here that sales cannot make any impression on them. May God grant an improvement and allow us to deal freely with one another, remaining, with cordial regards, &c.

London: 33s 2g.
Paris: 46.
Amsterdam: $34\frac{9}{16}$.

[P.S.] Finally, I give you a free hand to do the best you can with the linen.

¹ John and James Banckes were among the major suppliers to the Royal African Company—K. G. Davies, *The Royal African Company*, p. 171n.

$$\frac{24\ Jan.}{28\ Jan.}1676$$

69 S. DE GEER to JD
AMSTERDAM   28 JANUARY 1676

[D] My last was about a week ago, and since then I have received yours of the 19th inst. which I shall answer more fully by my next. The maritime treaty with Sweden is now here and we shall hear shortly if it has been ratified, though there is little doubt that it will be. It is all right if Swedish ships cannot sail freely as long as those of Denmark are also at a standstill, but many are of my opinion, that Dutch ships will be able to come and go to Sweden bringing and fetching everything, and that Denmark cannot stop them according to the treaty with this state, by which 'free ship makes free goods'.

Regarding what is due to you of the RD 2,000 from Momma, please draw the balance on Mr Wouters of Hamburg, payable to my order—and please write a note to Jan de Geer about it, advising him that you have drawn so much on Wouters concerning the balance of £[blank] which was due to you, and that you have made it good to me, having no more of Momma's in your hands than £[blank]. Besides that, send me those bills of exchange of Momma's, together with the protest, and also give Jan de Geer full details about it, sending a note to Momma as well that no more objections will be made in Sweden, and send it all to me so that I can forward it to Wouters who will then honour your drafts.

I received the enclosed from Sweden on your behalf,

remaining, &c.

$$\frac{24 \ Jan.}{[24 \ Jan.]}1676$$

270   THOMAS LEGENDRE (LE JEUNE) to JD
ROUEN   28 JANUARY 1676

'J'ay l'honneur de la vostre de 10ᵉ courant, dont je vous rends mes tres humbles graces de vos obligantes expresions et civilites qu'en touttes occasions je feray mon possible pour recognoitre.

Il ne m'a pas encor esté posible de vendre les pistaches que Mr Goodfellow m'a consignée pour y parvenir. J'en ay envoye 4 balles a Paris mes on n'y en ofre encor rien non plus que de celles qui j'ay icy, cela ayant a present peu de consommation a joindre qu'elles sont veilles. Je les ay abandonee a £50t le cent mes je n'en ay encor aucunes ofres. Vous assure que je continueray tout mes soings et du succes je vous en donneray advis.

Il est vray que nostre negoce est a present fort ingrat et c'est un mal a les general—dieu veuille nous donner mieux!

Il ce consomme ordinairement icy par an 10 a 12,000 torques de fil de laton, tant de suede que de Hambourg, les ¾ ordinairement de suede et ¼ ou ⅕ de Hambourg. Presentement je n'en scay dans Rouen que 90 torques quy me reste. Dens la disette que nous en avons j'en ay receu 1,000 torques de chez vous que j'ay vendu £90t, £87t 10s et le derniere £85t. J'aprens que s'en atend encor de chez vous viron 1,000 torques et nous avons deux navires arives au Havre de Hambourg quy en aporte viron 3,000 a 3,500 torques; ce quy la fait baiser a £85t et je crains qu'il ne tombe a £82t 10s a cause q'y en a sur cest 2 navires de Hambourg pour plusieurs et il se rencontre toujours dens un sy grand nombre quelqu'uns empresse de vendre, ce quy fait tomber le prix.

Le plomb en egard a ce bas prix de chez vous donne a present quelque petit profit car le vaut icy £103t; l'estain se vent £61t et estant a bas prix a Falmouth suivant les advis qu'en ay se donne aussy un profit honneste.

Les belles peaux de lapin sont fort demendée, valle a present les 104 peaux £28t et n'y a de droits que 40s du cent pesant et ainsy cela donne aussy avantage p. les prix que j'ay advis qu'elles valle chez vous.

Je seroit ravy de pouvoir vous donner quelques bons advis quy vous fus avantageux, estant parfaitement, vostre tres humble serviteur.'

Londres: 56⅜d.
Amsterdam: 101.

71   DAVID VAN BAERLE to LM

STOCKHOLM   4 NOVEMBER 1675

)]   In due course I received yours of the 18th of May, 8th of September and 8th past, from which
I have learned what is happening with Swedish goods in [England] for which I thank you.

I would have answered your letters before now and sent a quantity of brass to [London] if I
had not encountered numerous obstacles due to the outbreak of war, but I have been
hindered from doing so and until recently I have been unable to obtain a complete disposition
of my goods. And since the season is now well advanced I shall have to wait until the spring
before I shall be able to ship anything. Meanwhile, I see that the prices of brass as well as of
iron are very bad in [England]. However, there is very little brass being sent from here so
whatever is being sent to [England] must be from old stocks that have been lying at Hamburg
and worked up there. It looks as if very little brass-ware will be made here this winter, partly
because of the poor prices abroad and partly because they will be short of calamine.
Consequently, these wares ought to be able to fetch a better price in the coming year if not
too much is worked up at Aachen and Hamburg.

However, the price of iron in [London] seems unlikely to improve for the present as the
greatest proportion of our exports has to be shipped to England, and the ships which have
been held up nearly all year are about to arrive with substantial amounts of iron—bringing
more than can be consumed in a whole year. For some weeks the price here has been standing
at about 24 to 25 copper dollars, excluding expenses, but seems likely to fall lower. Garcopper
is at 217 to 218 dollars per shippound, and 'Crown' copper-wire will cost about $57\frac{1}{2}$ to 58 *RD*
per shippound on board a free ship with all expenses paid (each *RD* being worth 5 copper
dollars). Pitch is at *RD* 40 and tar at *RD* 20 to 21 per last, free on board, though it cannot be
shipped from here except through the Tar Company, and someone called John Strother[1] has
contracted with them for everything which goes to England. St Ubes salt is at $16\frac{1}{2}$ to 17
dollars per ton.

The war is making business very bad here and people see very little prospect of peace,
which we pray God may grant. But I understand that there are negotiations for the freeing of
trade between this kingdom and Holland and if they succeed it must soon be made public.

If there should be any changes in the price of brass-ware I beg you to let me know, and also
tell me how much the pieces of eight called 'pillar'[2] are bought for in London and whether
they are allowed to be exported.

If there is anything here I can serve you in, please ask freely. I remain, with heartiest
regards, &c.

---

[1] John Strother, originally of Newcastle and a member of the Eastland Company, was Sir William Blackett's
factor in Stockholm and had been associated with Samuel Sowton's contract for England's pitch and tar imports
from the Tar Company, 1673–5. The contract referred to here proved abortive and in 1677 Strother was
petitioning the English government for assistance in recovering large debts owed to him by the Swedish Tar
Company and Tobacco Company—Coventry MSS, Longleat, Vol. 66, f. 197; Åström, *From Stockholm to St
Petersburg*, p. 84; *CSPD, 1677–78*, p. 108.

[2] The distinctive silver piece-of-eight produced at the Mexico mint, with twin crowned pillars on the reverse.

$$\frac{8\ Feb.}{11\ Feb.}1676$$

272   J. & H. VAN BAERLE to JD

AMSTERDAM   11 FEBRUARY 1676

[D]   We find ourselves with yours of the 18th and 28th past, to which this will serve as a reply. First we must thank you warmly for your New Year wishes and likewise wish you all good fortune and prosperity.

Regarding your proposal that you join with us and our brother David to contract for all the copper-wire that is presently being made in Sweden up to the month of November next: although you are of the opinion that a good profit could be made for the various reasons which you allege, we think that while it is true that little copper-wire is being made in Sweden and that this country and Hamburg have few stocks of this commodity and there is also little of it in London or Rouen, nevertheless they are beginning to make copper-wire in Aachen and in Hamburg itself and are likely to continue doing so as long as it will sell well. Furthermore, as long as this ruinous war continues consumption will never be as great as it was and therefore we see no future prospect of any great rise in prices and (for that reason) the market for it will be postponed. Above all, we are faring so badly with the Reenstiernas and Momma that we have no more desire to make any contracts with them, so there is not the slightest chance of one being made. Also we would not dare to trust our goods in Sweden, particularly as the treaty of commerce between that Crown and this state has not been ratified because of some hitches. We are also not keen to engage in any other business as long as the war continues.

Meanwhile we are grateful to you for your kindness in offering to involve us in this and other undertakings, and likewise for your news of the price of various commodities. Swedish copper-wire is selling here for about *f*.64 per 100 lb. The prices of other wares you can see from the enclosed price-current,[1] to which we refer. Mr William Wathing has asked us to draw for him *f*.150 (that is to say, one hundred and fifty gulden) but as Madame, your wife, has ordered us not to pay him more than *f*.40 or *f*.50 and as he has previously told us that he has no need of money we have not dared to do so without your further order. Your bill of exchange on Messrs Bartolotti & Rihel is returned herewith, accepted, and we remain, with cordial regards, &c.

London:	35*s* 7*g*	} 2 usances.
Paris:	$98\frac{1}{2}$ to $\frac{1}{4}$	
Hamburg:	$34\frac{3}{8}$ stuyvers per dollar	} at sight.
Antwerp:	at par	

[1] Missing.

$$\frac{10\ Feb.}{18\ Feb.}1676$$

273   S. DE GEER to JD

AMSTERDAM   14 FEBRUARY 1676

[D]   My last was on the 4th inst., and since then I have received yours of the 28th of January.

About the 'O' and 'G' iron, your reasoning is very good and I can well understand your argument, but since the prices of iron are at present so low it would turn out to be rather too expensive, and as your iron is now selling for less than it costs in Stockholm it is my opinion that very much less will be shipped this year, particularly as the commercial treaty between Sweden and this state is likely to come into effect. We shall learn the outcome in a few days. The estates of Holland are assembling within six days and if it goes ahead there are plenty of salt ships here ready to depart, and as a result there will be no need to have anything to do with English ships. As the salt ships can go nowhere but here with their return cargoes freight rates will fall and as prices are much better here the iron will also be shipped hither. However, you must meanwhile continue to organize your sales as you have so far and as you find most convenient, only give some thought to what I have said above.

As soon as we have the outcome of the treaty of commerce I shall let you know in case there is anything worth thinking about with regard to salt. About 30 ships from St Ubes are expected here any day and there are about 60 lying here in lading, several of which, if trade is freed, will set off for Stockholm in June for ƒ.64 to ƒ.63 per last, so there is no need to have anything to do with English ships. However, if one could charter one for £6 or £6 5s then one might risk sending it to St Ubes and then on to Stockholm. If you can acquire such a one I would be content for you to charter it for us provided that it sets sail at the earliest opportunity and so can arrive in time to join this fleet. Meanwhile, please find out if there is anything of value over there which could be freighted for Portugal and Stockholm. There is someone [in London] who has obtained six or seven ship-loads of salt for delivery in Stockholm at a fixed price and who has given orders to charter ships here—indeed, if he can obtain the right price he will buy salt here and send it on to Stockholm. I am expecting six or seven ships in the first fleet to arrive, but whether they will be going on to the Baltic I cannot say yet. If you were inclined to take a one-fourth or one-third share in one or two, assuming that I can arrange for them to go there, I would give you preference before others. I seldom take others as partners but between us it could be arranged.

I am also considering chartering one or two for St Ubes–Stockholm–Amsterdam, and if you want to participate please let me know. I would guess that the ships which are now being chartered will be leaving about the 5th or 10th of April, and they could be in the Baltic by September or October, provided that there is a convoy at St Ubes. I estimate freight at about ƒ.64 to ƒ.65 per English last, and ƒ.3 or ƒ.4 more if they are not to wait for the convoy, but one must be careful to state in one's orders for the Sound whether the voyage is to Stockholm, Reval or Riga. Reval lasts cost ƒ.2 or ƒ.3 more; Stockholm and Riga lasts are the same as here.

As for the insurance, find out how it should be arranged over there and let me know— with my thanks for informing me.

I shall write about the pan-iron and see that they reckon up the numbers better.

I am delighted that the suit with Mr Townley has now been settled.

I have heard nothing more from the Baltic, and from Italy the news is rather conflicting, though all speak of a hard and skilful fight by the French, and no ships taken, though some speak of one and others of two left behind.[1] People are also talking of a second battle, or the beginning of one, but there is as much guess-work as certainty about the business, so we must wait for another post—wherewith I remain, &c.

---

[1] A fiercely-fought but inconclusive engagement between the fleets of Admirals DuQuesne and De Ruyter occurred off the Lipari islands on January 8 1676.

$\lfloor\overline{\qquad}\rfloor_{1676}$
11 Apr.

274 P. CAULIER to JD
YARMOUTH   1 MARCH 1676

'Sir and Honoured Cosin, I hope this will find you and my cosin your lady in good health
with all the family which pray God continue. You know when I was in London I discoursed
you about the trade of Zant and told you what my cosin Houblons had lately done that way
which doubtless will turne to their great advantage this yeare, therefore to lay the better
foundation for the next season I have wrote as I promised you I would both to Mr Thomas
Cordell of Zant, who was recomended me for a very honest man as also to Signor Gio.
Druyvestein of Venice, my old correspondent. Last post I received Mr Cordell's answer at
large which I send you here inclosed that you may see his discourse. In a post or 2 I expect
Signor Druyvesteyn's answer at large which shall lett you see also and then wee may consider
before winter whither he doe anything or no. Probably I may be in London about midsomer
or presently after so may have time enough to discourse it. If you bee enclined to be
concerned I shall seek no other partners but Druyvesteyn or Cordell, one of the 2, that may
manage it abroade. The capitall outward will not bee great, £1,000 or £2,000 for 3 or 4 of us
will be easily borne and that I hope will purchase her loading back as you may judge by this
letter. As to the freight of the ship out and home you shall be sure to be dealt withall on civill
termes and as a good friend for shall be glad of any opportunity since you are now so near
allyed to us to find some good rencounter of augmenting our friendship.

I had in my cosin Marescoe's life time 2 or 3 ships sent me directly by his order from
Stockholme with pitch and tar which sold currantly to his content. Pray advise me whither
you could not order a ship of 60, 80 or 100 last of tar and pitch (I say Stockholme) to be sent to
me for friends' account. I beleive I should dispose of it here to their content, the comodity
being wanted and comes in but scarce and especially Stockholme tarr which is most desired
by reason of the goodness of the cask which must particularly be recomended for that is most
for exportation. If wee proceed on that designe for Venetia next season 2 or 300 barrels tar in
good cask would doe well, therefore pray write me what may be done therein to procure
them if cannot be sent for friends' account. If I should send a small ship from hence what you
judge it may be procured for a last there, p. governo. This being the needfull at present I
kindly salute you with your good lady my cosin, to whom I wish much prosperity, and rest,
from your reall friend and kinsman, P.C.

[P.S.] Please to returne the inclosed.'

$\lfloor\overline{\qquad}\rfloor_{1676}$
7 Apr.

275 P. VAN CÖLLEN & LAURENS UPPENDORFF[1] to LM
STOCKHOLM   3 FEBRUARY 1676

[D]   Madame, for lack of material we have not written to you for some time and had also heard
nothing from you, but we have now received your letters of the 22nd of December last year
and the 13th of January, and have seen your proposal to bring all copper-wire under one
hand. It would be a good thing to achieve, if only one could insist on the performance of
what is promised and agreed, for in order to do it one must be absolutely sure that, in the
event of one drawing any bills, neither we nor our friends in Hamburg or Amsterdam would
run the sort of risk which has befallen us formerly and which has happened to Rosenström

over the wire which was loaded in [Capt.] Kool—i.e., the bills of exchange which he drew against it have been left unpaid in Amsterdam. In such a case it is better to promise nothing so that one relies on nothing, than to allow matters to turn out adversely. It greatly weakens credit, which in these times and especially in these parts is quite tight enough already. You can understand that better than we can explain it.

If you would be satisfied with these conditions—vizt. to advance us £3 15s or £4 sterling on each shippound of wire as soon as the bill of lading is despatched, and then the remaining £12 10s or £13[2] as soon as we have news that the shipload of wire has passed the Sound, we will be able to deliver into your hands all the wire which Cronström and Rosenstrom produce (with the exception of those factories which are now little worked) provided that you make known these conditions to all those friends in Hamburg or Holland on whom we shall have to draw. Please draw up a written agreement to these conditions with Mr Uppendorff. We shall also be well satisfied if you would carry the risk of the goods being seized by some enemy action, for it will be cheaper for you to arrange their reclamation.

Our Mr Uppendorff will settle with you about that. We have noted that you have remitted 66⅔ crowns to him at Paris, and we have credited you with £16 2s 3d accordingly. The woollen stockings have been mostly sold for about 5d—truly a wonderful commodity with which in future we shall want to have nothing to do!

We await your answer and to know in what manner the bills of lading are to be signed and forwarded.

With cordial greetings, &c.

[P.S.] Please hand the enclosed to Mr Uppendorff, and if he has already left you upon his journey here return it to us, with apologies for troubling you.

[1] Uppendorff, whose partnership with Van Cöllen broke up in 1677 [**357**], later secured English naturalization, with David's assistance, by private act of Parliament—29 Car. II. c. 22. W. A. Shaw, *Letters of Denization and Acts of Naturalization, 1603–1700* (1911) p. 118.

[2] This seems to assume a London price of about £6 8s per cwt.

7 Mar.
———1676
7 Apr.

76 H. CLETCHER to JD
AXBERGSHAMER   5 FEBRUARY 1676

[D] I have safely received your letter of the 13th past and from the accompanying power of attorney I have been delighted to learn from you for the first time that you have entered the bonds of matrimony with Madame Marescoe. I had only heard about it last week from Mr Urban Hall who came to visit me here, because your letters—which would have informed me—have not yet come to hand, and consequently I have not been able to discharge my obligation to wish you happiness together. This will therefore serve principally to wish you all good fortune, praying the Lord God to bless you and grant you many years of joy and prosperity together.

I have noted with pleasure the safe arrival of Captain Goldstone and I have no doubt that the Company[1] has taken the iron at the same price as before, as was intended, according to your previous letter, for it is not my fault that the iron has arrived rather late. I expect to hear by the first post whether you have agreed with the Company to deliver my voyage iron this summer for the price of £14 5s, as you wrote in your last so that I can organize myself accordingly. For unless that is done I doubt whether I can arrange things so advantageously since little iron has been forged here this winter and large amounts have been bought up for pretty high prices.

With regard to the proceeds of your salt, I have written to you at length that it would be to your best advantage if I settled it against your current account, because the iron was dearly bought and it was not advisable to store the salt since it could not be sold for so high a price in the spring. I am now being offered a ship-load of salt by English merchants for 15 dollars per ton and I see that you are thinking of consigning me another quantity of salt in the new year. If you do so I shall dispose of it to your best advantage.

Regarding the bill of exchange on Johan Fahlgreen: it is not yet paid. I have sent your letter to him, and I do not doubt that payment will soon follow as I have had news from Westras,[2] where the money is to delivered, that it is daily expected there, so I hope your letter of attorney will be unnecessary. Johan Trotzig has not yet paid up and I can get no answer from him, though I have been told by his brother-in-law in Stockholm that he would pay shortly. In future you would do well not to extend such credit, as you can be sure of a heap of trouble and a long wait. I have sent the *RD* 100 bill of exchange on Johan Staelhaus to Stockholm for acceptance and will give you news of it by my next. I see that Captain Guttery has arrived at Gothenburg and I have written there to know how things stand with the goods. It is dreadful that the posts are so unreliable and that we are mutually lacking so many letters. I cannot tell what remittances you have made for me to Mr Van de Mortel and, since the 20th of August, I have received no letters from him. However, I hope you have withheld the proceeds of the iron in the last two ships in order to offset the proceeds of your salt and the sum of the bills of exchange which, I think, altogether should just about balance each other.

I have advised you before this that Mr Perman has given orders to Mr David Leyel [in London] to pay you the £150 relating to Jacob Fahlgreen;[3] and with regard to your claims on Willem Momma I have not until now (with the power of attorney) received the necessary information, but as the goods have been sold to Mr Perman (as I wrote to you before) there is nothing which can be done now. Also, Momma says that he is no longer in debt to you, as you perfectly well know. You would do well to obtain your claims on him amicably, like a sensible chap.[4]

Because the money in your account has now been offset there is nothing to be said about the purchase of brass, but if you send a consignment of salt in the spring please write fully to order what you want done with the proceeds. I commend you to the protection of God, together with Madame, your dearly beloved;

&c.

[P.S.] Regarding the exportation of iron, I shall inform you further.

---

¹ The Royal African Company.
² I.e. Västerås, 111 km west of Stockholm.
³ Jacob David's Swedish-born clerk-apprentice, taken on for £150, and later sent to Sweden to sort out his, and David's, affairs. [See **368**.]
⁴ '*T' gene Ue van hem te vorderen hebt sal Ue wel doen van met goetheyt sien te krygen alsoo een persoon is die met pratyken om gaet.*'

$$\frac{28 \text{ } Mar.}{6 \text{ } Apr.} 1676$$

277   SKINNER, BALL & GOSFRIGHT to JD
LEGHORN   16 MARCH 1676

'Sir, Since the above is come to hands yours of the 3rd past recomending to us the sale of your goods, part of which you have seene is allready effected and this weeke have we concluded the sale of one caske wyer mentioned in coppy to Sr. Comaccio at $D.20\frac{1}{2}$ per 100 lb. and of your 100 piggs lead to Sr. Gio. Zeffi at $D.20\frac{3}{4}$ per 1,000 lb., but on this wilbe an additionall charge of 3 *cratches* per pigg,[1] the G[rand] Duke haveing for the benefitt and increase of trade taken off all his customes and in leiu thereof all goods that are at present here and what comes hereafter are to pay soe much more stallage at entrance and afterwards bought and sent abroad without any duty as our E[phraim] S[kinner], if you desire it, will more particulerly informe you. Your pepper is not yet all consigned soe cannot send you the account but may per next as also of the lead which we fear at these low prizes will produce little incouragement. However, they are allways vendible, for your government, and rise or fall according to the quantitie arrives and the prizes they sell for at home. Mr Goodfellow was lately here and is now at Lucca improveing his Ittalian tongue, as we suppose he may have fully advised his relations ere this. Your inclosed for Aleppo shalbe carefully forwarded. Of shipping is this weeke only imported the *Henrietta* frigate from Malta bound home, confirming that Sir John Narborough had burnt 4 Tripolines in port, and was on departure from Malta again for Tripoly and with him *Providence, Martin, Guiny* and *Ormond* bound for Scanderoone who if Sir John makes peace will proceed alone else hee'l affoard them convoy, and being what occurs with due respects we remaine, at your service, &c.

London — $54\frac{1}{3}d.$'

[1] There were 12 *craches* to the livre (thus 72 to the dollar and 84 to the ducat) and at the current rate of exchange 3 *craches* = $2\frac{1}{4}$ pence sterling.

$$\frac{3\ Apr.}{4\ Apr.}1676$$

'8 DANIEL VON REUSCH to JD
    BRESLAU   28 MARCH 1676

;] For lack of introduction and of matter I have not written to you before, but I have been encouraged to send these few lines by Johan Arnold Funck in Hamburg, from whom I understand that you are of service to your friends in handling bills of exchange as well as goods.

At present, when (as occasionally happens) I am in debt on account, I send off my money and, as I understand, it is often drawn away to other places. If, Sir, you would care to serve me and in return for the customary rate of commission stand surety and honour my drafts up to a total of 2,000 to 3,000,[1] and likewise draw on other places as I order, and if you had the opportunity to sell our linen of such varieties as are best desired and can keep me well-informed of the prices of crown rasches and perpetuanas, I would see whether or not we could not establish and build up a useful business relationship between us. In return I beg to serve you in all your requirements, and in expectation of your answer remain, &c.

[P.S.] I would be grateful if you would also inform me reliably what sort of man Gabriel de la Porto is, and if one can really trade with him or ought to avoid him. I shall keep your advice secret and, if the opportunity arises, do the same for you. Wherewith again, adieu.

Hamburg: 110.
Amsterdam: $107\frac{1}{4}$.
Nürnberg: 100.

[1] Probably rixdollars were intended, though not indicated.

$$\frac{8\ Apr.}{18\ Apr.}1676$$

279 S. DE GEER to JD
AMSTERDAM   14 APRIL 1676

[D]   I find I have your letters of the 10th and 24th of March, from which I have seen the manner in
which English shipping is going to proceed. But it seems to have been overlooked that that is
all right as long as they are chartered by Englishmen; but if they are chartered by others who
are also friends of Denmark, how are they going to manage? If they lade in English ships they
are going to need other certificates, and in my opinion that is not very advantageous for the
English ships and not many are going to be chartered by foreigners. However, as some people
were of a different opinion a few have recently passed the Sound which were loaded here, so
everything is continuing on the old basis.[1]

I have written to Sweden to inform them along the lines which you advised and all the iron
which has been kept back will be shipped for your account. I shall sell it solely to you and you
can be the guarantor or insurer against all risks and take it over on its arrival in return for a
gain of $1\frac{1}{2}$ per cent.

Winter is now ending over there and they will soon have open waters. There are also
about 300 slb of pan iron lying at Stockholm which I would send to you with the first
available English ships if any were lying there and if the freight charges were reasonably
cheap. But at the moment there are still about 600 slb of ordinary iron over and above that,
which I must consider first. Furthermore, I have given orders for improvements in the future
manufacture of pan iron so that the bars are more even, for they seem not to have been
turning out smooth. I have no doubt that those which are coming will be entirely
satisfactory.

As I have to pay rather a lot of Swedish bills of exchange during the month of May I now
have to ask you if I can draw on you £500 at two or three usances. I would be greatly obliged
if you could accommodate me. And please let me know at once how much premium is at
present being demanded [for insurance] from Stockholm to London and to Amsterdam in
English shipping.

At present there is little news. Il est vray qu'il es fort difficile de dire qui aura l'avantage,
neanmoin je suis persuadé par les predictions qu'on m'en fait tenir qu'elle tomberont du coste
de la france et qu'avant le mois de Novemb. nous pouvions bien voir grand Changemt. et qui
sait si ce ne sera pas en Septemb. qu'au temp on ne se peut pas tant arreter mais avec le temp le
tout reussira pour le bien de l'eglise de Dieu nonobstant qu'on ne fait que cultiver tout le
contraire et que des Grande miseres la doivent preseder.

The letters from France speak of a heavy incursion of the French into the Walloon
country against the defences there which are all in fire and flame.[2] The soldiers are suffering
great misery in a place where they have been repulsed by a Dutch regiment which lay there,
but it was hard fought and according to another letter which has since arrived three regiments
(two Dutch and one Spanish) have fallen, and it is said that 12,000 to 15,000 men are dead.
I remain, &c.

[1] At Stockholm, Sir Edward Wood noted on 26 April 1676 that 'we have several English ships come hither
lately from Holland, where they have taken in their lading' which though he knew might be real English goods
yet appeared suspicious. PRO, SP. 95/9 f. 324.
   [2] The French campaign of 1676 began with the siege of Condé on the Scheldt in Walloon-Flanders—see
Hollandtze Mercurius (April 1676) p. 62; F. J. G. ten Raa, *Het Staatsche Leger*, VI (The Hague, 1940) p. 54.

$$\frac{13 \ Apr.}{30 \ Apr.} 1676$$

280   ADAM LAURENS KELLERMAN to JD
AMSTERDAM   20 MARCH 1676

[D]   I find myself with three of your welcome letters of the 23rd of November last year, the 3rd of January and the 3rd of March, which I ought to have answered much earlier but since there has been little business to be done this winter I have been out of town for most of the last three months, settling matters with my debtors in other places and thus they have been left behind, so I beg you to excuse the delay.

From the first letter I have learned with joy of the marriage which you have made with the widow of the late Charles Marescoe, for which I heartily wish you much happiness, blessings and prosperity as well as long life and lasting contentment.

Further, you have been pleased to share with me in that, as well as the two following letters, the news of what is happening in trade at [London] for which I am obliged but I must confess to you that current market prices here are so restricted that it is impossible to gain anything by sending things here, unless one has some other advantage (which is unknown to me) or has the good luck of a favourable change in prices while the goods are on the way. For the last nine months we have done nothing in Swedish trade because no Dutch ships have been able to sail there, and this year will be still worse because the King of Denmark is beginning to detain English ships and to check whether they carry Swedish goods. People have been talking for a long while about a treaty of commerce between the Swedish crown and this state and saying that Dutch ships going there will be allowed to pass the Sound unmolested, but we have seen little result from all this and not much reliance is to be placed upon it.

Finally, I must thank you most humbly for your kind offer, whereof I shall take advantage if opportunity occurs, and in return offer my unworthy person to share in the honour of your commissions: you can assure yourself of good and punctual service. The prices of all sorts of goods you may see in the enclosed[1]—wherewith my hearty regards, remaining, &c.

London: 35s 9g   2 usances.
Hamburg: $34\frac{1}{4} - \frac{5}{16}$ at sight.

   [1] Missing.

$$\frac{14 \ Apr.}{14 \ Apr.} 1676$$

281   C. BENE to JD
HAMBURG   7 APRIL 1676

[D]   I last wrote to you on the 4th instant and since then have heard nothing from you so this will be short and serve only to inform you that I sold our joint consignment of tobacco[1] to Mr Cornelio Berenberg for $6\frac{1}{2}s$ [lübs.] but on closer inspection he found that the contents of the casks were very dry and of much worse quality than the samples he had seen, so he rejected them and did not want them except for 6s. At last he offered $6\frac{1}{4}s$, at which price I sold them to him. I could scarcely bring myself to agree, seeing that the price is miserable and does not leave much above 9 per cent profit, but your urging to sell at the earliest opportunity and the fact that others are selling moved me to do so. And in my opinion I did well, for various people have it for sale and much more is expected. We would have done better if ours had arrived earlier, for a friend of mine has had 22 casks which he received with an earlier captain and he sold them at $6\frac{5}{8}s$. There is also news from England that another ship from the Bermudas is expected this year which will bring a good quantity and I believe this must be the reason why good quality stuff is already being offered today at $6s$ which puts that which was bought for $6\frac{1}{2}$ [d] in London in a bad position. I wish you had not also bought this last lot, though if it is thoroughly good we must see if it cannot be sold perhaps for a rather higher price. Among those which I sold were various rolls which were so rotten and completely dry that they could be crumbled into powder, and the purchaser consequently claimed a 30 lb. deduction. How far we should agree with him let me know in your next. As soon as the captain completes his loading the account will be sent with him.

If the campeachy wood which I asked for has not yet been bought please forget it for I fear that much has arrived with the *galleons* in Spain and it may perhaps fall lower in price. If the fleet from Virginia has arrived I would be favourably inclined to go halves with you in a trial quantity of Virginian leaf. If you decide to do so, please buy 6,000 to 8,000 lb. for our account at a price of about $4\frac{1}{4}d$, making quite sure that it is good quality and undamaged. You must also see that it is bought advantageously at the best time, for unless one makes an advantageous purchase there is no chance of making a profit these days. I shall be glad to learn now and again what is happening with regard to ginger.

Enclosed herewith is the second copy of the £100 sterling bill of exchange on John Banks, endorsed to you. Please procure the needful and place it to my account. With cordial regards, &c.

London: $33s$ $3-2g$ 2 usances.
Amsterdam: $34\frac{5}{16}$ at short sight.
Venice: 85.

¹ 12 hogsheads, in which JD's half-share cost £57 19s f.o.b. and yielded net proceeds of £61 14s 4d, a profit of about $6\frac{1}{2}$ per cent.

$$\frac{14\ Apr.}{14\ Apr.}1676$$

282   F. BOSTELMAN to JD

HAMBURG   7 APRIL 1676

[D]   I have received your letter of the 24th of March from which I have seen that Bermuda tobacco has risen and is unobtainable below $6\frac{1}{2}d$, and if none can be had one must simply be patient. The other day a quantity of nice stuff was bought for $6s$ lübs. so you can work out whether any profit can be obtained for $6d$ since tobacco bears more than 2 per cent brokerage as well as some other expenses.

I have sold your barrel of indigo as well as I possibly could and the account is going herewith.¹ If you should be inclined to dispose of the proceeds here I would be glad to give you some suggestions, if only there was something or other on which one could rely, but all goods such as those which come from [England] are selling more cheaply here than they cost in [England] with interest and expenses into the bargain. I can hardly understand how foreign trade can be carried on. If anything of interest turns up please share it with me, as a grateful friend, with regards, &c.

¹ One barrel of Jamaican indigo, of 219 lb., costing £25 19s, f.o.b., yielded £27 2s net.

$$\frac{24\ Apr.}{16\ Jun.}1676$$

283 W. MOMMA to LM
NYKÖPING   14 FEBRUARY 1676

[D] The above is a copy of my last. We are now, God be praised, at the 14th of February, 1676. This is in answer to your undated letter, though from the account accompanying it I find it to be of the 13th of January. I am now still lacking your letters of the 3rd of September, and of the '16th instant', which I think must mean December. I have safely received the account of the wire sold from [captains] Marten Olofsen, Roelof Anders and John Wilmot, together amounting to RD 1,720. I have checked it and recorded it, but I am extremely astonished that you allowed the wire to lie around when you could have made between £6 3s and £6 5s for it yet did not sell a single coil for eight months. Now you are selling it for the scandalous price of £5 16s to £5 18s, and that for 4, 5 or 6 months time! I had much rather that you had left it lying, because in these difficult times it cannot be delivered and the ships which left here last autumn did not have very much aboard. This year even less will come as very little was manufactured—about 25,000 coils less per annum than are made in time of peace, for your information.

You have also not sent me any account of what was sold between October 1674 and January 1675, being about 2,000 coils, which I shall await, as well as the account of the coils sold in Rouen which you have not sent me. I expect the loss to be settled, for the longer one delays the worse it is, and I am surprised that the insurers of the *Caritas* lay claim to the full insurance. It is quite true that they ran the risks while the ship was lying in the Daalders and were liable, and also for the risks of going to London when, because of the war, the goods might have been lost. I am not liable to pay for the insurance to London, and I ask for nothing more than what is just and fair. You can judge it impartially yourself.

You say, regarding the said goods, that you have sent a power of attorney because someone has assured you that Hiebenaer is making some claim on them. Whoever wrote that to you has deceived you with lies and it is quite unnecessary for you to meddle with it and send powers of attorney, for I myself shall answer for it here.

Regarding the latten, black kettles and basins, please make an end of them and do not haggle about the price. I was influenced by the advice I got from [England] on April 11th, 1671, when someone else stated that 400 shippounds of black or yellow kettles could be disposed of every year, and perhaps even more, but I see now that one cannot rely on such advice.

I am also not a little surprised that you remind me to take care that I reimburse you for your outlay, yet I have not received any account and do not know what your claims are. I shall therefore await an account first, and with regards, remain, &c.

$$\frac{24\ Apr.}{25\ Apr.}1676$$

284 PHILIP BOTTE to JD
AMSTERDAM   1 MAY 1676

[D] Sir, Until now I have not had the honour of writing to you, and I do so now on the recommendation of my Lord De Geer.

£400 sterling falls due on the 3rd instant, payable by Mr Samuel Sowton to Gerard

Weymans for my account, and although I have been careful to provide for its payment in these distrustful times I beg you to accept my bill of exchange and to pay it if Mr Sowton is unable to do so, in return for which I enclose remittances drawn on Jan Kroeger,

vizt.— £200 at ½ usance }
        £200 at 1 usance }   drawn by Lucas Hidden.

I shall make it up to you, together with interest for the time-difference, and it looks as if I shall have further occasion in these times to correspond with you. When my bills of exchange come from Sweden, which are one month overdue, would you please take them instead of Mr Sowton, who may fail to observe my orders about these bills which are also for Weymans, who should have protested against Mr Sowton though I hope he will not. And if Mr Sowton has paid I shall give other orders for your guidance, wherewith I remain, &c.

$$\frac{6\ May}{24\ Aug.}1676$$

285   GEORGE RICHARDS to JD
         BILBAO   1 MAY 1676

'Sir, I have receaved yours of the 6 past, for answer whereto the pinns I shall endeavour to putt of the best I can by the first occasion may offer. I know there's nothing to be got thereby at the pryse you charge them at, they know here that ditto Inglish pinns are neater worke then come from elcewhere but of late quantitee comes from France and those which are weightier than yours are sould at 27 and 28 R. pta. I note you had passed the account of the wyer in conformity. Here is quantitee of that comodity come from Hamburg and although it may be deare there, and in Holland, it cannot be sould here as your former parcell was whylst it is so plenty, so I thinck best to let it ly a whyle. I shall assoone I see any thinge of incouragement be most ready to informe you and to mayntayne a corresponency with you. If Colchester bays are to be bought at 16d to 16½d you may adventure on 30 or 40 pieces and send them in blackes, for though they have been here verry lowe yet they seeme now to stiffen and if to many come not I am apt to thinck they will gaine esteeme, here beeing not so many in towne as some imagine. What I have now sould at ready money render 10 per cent but you must have a particuler respect that the charges there be managed to all advantages. 2 pieces cutts drawne and 3 crowns a bale and 8s per piece dying as Sir John pays (between us); others pay 10s [which] is 2 per cent differance, and more I have not so add but my dew respects and that I am your assured servant, G.R.'

$$\frac{24\ May}{16\ Jun.}1676$$

286   JEAN BOOR to JD
         STOCKHOLM   25 MARCH 1676

[D]   Sir, Your letters of the 4th and 17th of February have been safely received, as well as that to Mr Trip, to which the answers follow.
       I am glad to see that the ships have arrived but I fear that Joris Yard[1] has been wrecked for we have received no news of him.
       I am delighted that John Clark arrived and I shall be glad to hear how you find his cargo. It

must be removed first, for the bars had to be weighed more than once before they were loaded into the ship and although the man is honest his mate is rather unreliable at counting.[2]

I have always feared that whenever so many goods arrive in [England] all of a heap they would fall in price, but I hope they will do rather better if the whole lot is bought up. Iron prices should stay steady this year as there will be much less made than last year because many forges have been unable to work for lack of water. And the iron will be late in arriving since there have been hardly any sledge-trails for it up-country.

I have taken note of the prices which commodities are fetching [in England] and I am grateful to you for the news, which will be helpful. However, I am astonished that you have not yet received the bill of lading or invoice; the letters must have been held up on the way. It is distressing that the posts are working so badly—it is because of the Danes. I hope that different arrangements will be made. May the good God grant that peace may soon come so that trade may soon return to a better condition.

With regard to the iron sent to you last year, please follow the orders of the Lord De Geer at Amsterdam. I made this request in one of my earlier letters sent to you under his cover, which I do not doubt you have received.

Two English ships have arrived here with salt for which they are asking 16 dollars. If the Dutch could come here we would see salt being sold for 12 dollars.

I commend you to the protection of God Almighty,
&c.

[P.S.] If the vessel should come directly from [London] I beg you to be kind enough to send me a dozen of your bottles of sack, of the best sort. Ask the Captain to see that they are well-packed. Also half a dozen table-knives. Place the cost to the account of my Lord De Geer at Amsterdam and give me news of it—forgiving the trouble.

[1] I.e. Captain George Yard.
[2] '. . . *zyn stirman ginck watt los int tellen voort.*'

$$\frac{24\ May}{16\ Jun.}1676$$

37 D. VAN BAERLE to JD
STOCKHOLM   4 APRIL 1676

)] Sir, I find myself with your letters of the 16th of November, 22nd of December, 13th of January and 5th of February, with information about what has been happening with regard to Swedish trade, for which I thank you.

Your considered opinion concerning copper-wire I judge to be well-founded, and by buying it up you will make your intentions clear and be able to control the market according to your desires. But as for your proposition that all the copper-wire which may be made up to November next year should be placed in one person's hands and not be allowed to cost more than £5–£5 5s in London, there is not the slightest prospect of it for the simple reason that the creditors of the 'Three Crowns' and 'Crowned N' works have to contribute payments to help the works get going, and as a result the owners are not free to dispose of the brass which is produced at their works. Secondly, all the brass which has been made here for the last year has cost not less than 245 to 250 dollars per shippound, because the high price of copper has been supported by the launching of the copper coinage, and it could not cost less than £5 14s in London, with all expenses included, even if it could be bought here for 250 dollars. Indeed, that price has been offered in vain and it looks as if it will rise higher still as soon as the ships come to be loaded because little has been produced—the 'Three Crowns' works having been at a standstill for a whole year, and the 'Crowned N' works going slow and at a standstill for the last two months. For the last fifteen months I have had about 470 slb from the 'Three Crowns' works lying at Norrköping which I was prevented from exporting by last year's troubles. It consists of about 313 slb of copper-wire, 50 slb of latten, 50 slb of black kettles, 30 slb of 'English' kettles, 10 slb of 'Scottish' pans and 5 slb of pots. Mine was part of a consignment which should have gone to London but which cannot be sent now as I understand there is a restrictive order in force requiring one to declare that the goods loaded in English ships are for English accounts. It is good of you to offer to take on all the risks and to reclaim the goods as if they were your own, being consigned in your name, in return for a reasonable consideration, but you have not stated how much and these wares can only bear a little. If it could be done for 1 per cent above the ordinary insurance rate I might well agree to it; at 2 per cent there are plenty here who could do it but I would find that too much. If you would charge only 1½ per cent on top of the sales-commission and order my brothers at Amsterdam to arrange the insurance and manage the expenses so as to avoid the deduction which London insurers make in case of loss[1] I shall be interested to hear your opinion and await your decision at the earliest opportunity. If by any chance some shipping-space should turn up and permit the despatch of some goods on these conditions the insurance should be calculated on the basis of £13½ sterling per shippound and the sale made in as short a time as possible so that no bad debts can arise.

Notwithstanding the fact that iron is fetching little abroad the price here is being maintained at 24 and 25 dollars per shippound.

I wish you and Madame Marescoe all happiness and prosperity in your marriage, with heartiest greetings, &c, I remain, &c.

[1] See Appendix E for the customary rebate of 10–15 per cent which London insurers imposed on claims.

$$\frac{24\ May}{16\ Jun.} 1676$$

288   L. UPPENDORFF to JD
STOCKHOLM   15 APRIL 1676

[D]   I am under a deep obligation to thank you for your manifold favours and entertainment, and I hope I shall have the good fortune to be able to recompense you, which would make me very happy. God be praised, I arrived here on the 24th past but found that Lord Lillienhoff was no more, having died on the 27th of February. The beloved [wife] of Lord Rosenström has also been taken away—may the Lord grant them both a joyful resurrection.

The times are bad here at present but as the waters are now open I hope things will soon change. Meanwhile we shall preserve the good repute of our Swedish wares, so that I am sure it will be better to sell them here than to send them abroad in these present times unless, of course, they rise in price in [England], of which possibility I shall be glad to learn. There has not been one half as much wire made this last winter as in previous years through lack of calamine and other materials, so you will do well to uphold the reputation of what you have remaining unsold. Also, not so much iron has been made here through lack of water, so if the commercial treaty with Holland goes ahead, as it is believed it certainly will, the said commodities will make a leap—one must hope so.

Last Sunday a warship of 40 guns was burnt out in front of the town and today the Admiralty's rope-yard was also destroyed by fire. God be merciful to us and protect us from further misfortunes, to whose merciful protection I heartily commend you, Madame your dear wife and her daughters, remaining, &c.

[P.S.] To all the friends at Tottenham, Mr & Mrs May, Miss B. Buck, Mr Du Mesnil, Mons. Vroulingh and all others, very cordial greetings! More by my next—adieu.

$$\frac{24 \ May}{16 \ Jun.} 1676$$

89 D. VAN BAERLE to JD
STOCKHOLM   23 APRIL 1676

[D] Sir, My last letter was on the 4th instant, and since then I have received yours of the 17th of February from which I see that my brothers were not favourably inclined towards the plan concerning brass-wire and that for the reasons I outlined in my last letter it can hardly be arranged, so we had better put it out of our minds. I also proposed in my last letter that you should take a cargo of brass in your own name and at your own risk, but this also cannot be proceeded with as the English ships will load no goods unless they are shipped by Englishmen or unless they have a certificate from the English Envoy that they are for an English account. So I see no means of shipping them to England, but will negotiate with an Englishman to buy them on condition that they are consigned to you and bought from him on delivery in London. Please do not place any charges on the goods which will be sent you by him on my recommendation.

English ships are arriving here daily and when the ratification of the commercial treaty comes from Holland, as is expected every hour, there will be plenty of Dutch ships also so that freight-rates will be cheaper than last year.

There is a shortage of water here so that many works are at a standstill and as a result the price of iron remains at 24 to 25 dollars. Copper-wire is at 258 to 260 dollars per shippound and St Ubes salt at 13 dollars per ton, with signs of falling lower.

With heartiest regards, and God's blessing, &c.

London:	23 dollars per £ sterling, @ 2 usances.
Amsterdam:	$20\frac{1}{2}$ ⎫ Marks ⎫
Hamburg:	$22\frac{1}{4}$ ⎭ per *RD* ⎭ 1 month's sight.

$$\frac{12 \ Jun.}{17 \ Jun.} 1676$$

290 H. CLETCHER to JD
AXBERGSHAMER   14 APRIL 1676

[D] My last letter to you was on the 31st past by way of Gothenburg. Since then I have heard nothing from you so this will serve to inform you that I have received the balance due from Mr Fahlgreen, being 1,260 dollars, less 1 per cent for the cost of transport, which you will please make a note of. Lord Axel Oxenstierna has now arrived here and I will pay his bill of exchange at the rate of only 21 marks lübs per rixdollar. The *RD* 15 bill of exchange drawn on Mr Tibou he has refused to pay saying that he has already given the money to someone called Mr Mollié,[1] but if in fact it has not been paid he will honour the bill.

By my next I shall let you know what can be done about brass-wire and whether or not I can employ the proceeds of your bills of exchange on it, as you ordered. As for iron, I can see no advantages for you at present as it is dear, so if I cannot achieve anything according to your instructions I shall remit you the remainder of the money. I do not believe I shall be sending much iron on my own account this year as it can be sold here at good prices. Furthermore, the English merchants here will no longer allow any Swedish property to pass under their names, and the poor prices in [England] rob one of any desire to send any. The [Royal African] Company ought to take the consignment in the *Coninck David* at the previous price, as was agreed, for the fact that the iron arrived rather late was not my fault. As a result I have not much desire any more to contract with them.

From the accompanying letter you can see what Mr Perman has written to me about the £150. Regarding Antony Pingar, I have found out that there is little or nothing good to say since he has married a woman of ill repute. I have sent the documents on to Stockholm to see if anyone will take on the case, but it cannot be done without money, and for that I have no orders. It is also to be feared that one is throwing good money after bad. With regards, &c.

¹ Étienne or Samuel Molié, agents for the French subsidies to Sweden.

$$\frac{17\ Jun.}{27\ Jun.}1676$$

291   BARTHOLOMEW MÖLL to JD
HAMBURG   9 JUNE 1676

[D]   On the recommendation of my good friend Mr Bene (who may have also mentioned me to you) I take the liberty of troubling you with a letter. My object in seeking the honour of your correspondence is to find a good friend on whom I can rely when opportunities arise, for I like to enjoy peace of mind and my previous friend in [England] has given me reason to distrust him.

A good friend in Zittau with a profound knowledge of linen has today sent me some samples which I am sending herewith. The first two, of 51 and 54 Zittauer ells, have been additionally bleached and many are now going to [England]. If you, or a good friend, trade in them you can be readily served directly from the producer and from the same friend that serves Mr Stübbing¹ at Dresden and others.

I have been much accustomed to send Sleswig serviettes and table-linen to [England] but as a result of this latest war they have not been selling. Please let me know at once if table-linen is in demand and how much it fetches. You can also send me the prices of calf-skins and shoe-leather, indigo, &c. If there is any profit to be counted upon I am favourably disposed to spending something, to make a start. Trade and turn-over in wares are completely awful here, though God may improve matters, to whose protection I commend you, with cordial regards, &c.

¹ John Stubbing, an English merchant who came to Dresden in 1662 and established himself as a major linen-dealer in central Europe. See A. Klima, 'English Merchant Capital in Bohemia in the Eighteenth Century' in *EcHR* 2nd Series XII (Aug. 1959) p. 39.

$$\frac{21\ Jun.}{27\ Jun.}1676$$

292   HENNING BUSCH to JD
HAMBURG   10 JUNE 1676

[D]   From your welcome letter of the 12th past I have seen that my draft has been accepted, which is very good news.

Poor trade cannot do other than cause miserable prices, and if one buys something on one day one finds it is cheaper on the next! May God give us a good peace so that we can continue our correspondence more fruitfully. The prices of [English] wares are so low here that one cannot order anything at a profit.

The proceeds for the iron should soon be coming up for payment and if they have please remit them in good bills during this favourable rate of exchange.

Barbados sugars, $4\frac{1}{4}$ to $4\frac{1}{8}g$; brown ginger $4\frac{1}{8}g$; Virginia leaf, $5-5\frac{1}{2}s$. Nothing more at present. Cordial regards, &c.

London:	$33s$ $5-6g$.
Amsterdam:	$34\frac{1}{8}$.
Paris:	47.

$$\frac{28\,Jun.}{30\,Jun.}1676$$

93 J. OLMIUS to JD
ROTTERDAM   3 JULY 1676

'Sir, Since a while I have been silent, however I make no doubt but you have heard from my brother that I have made an end of the saile of your rie from Linn[1] for the prix of 104 gold florins with much adoe for it was over heat and did smell musty. It is a hazard for then they was a little of request and now the price is fallen. Hereinclosed the account of the said rie and also of your barley and for the neat proceed comes the summe of [blank].[2] The French rie gives now 112 and $114£$, French barley 21 a $22£$, English wheat 135, 140, 145 a 150 *ggl.*, English rie, 100, 110, 120 a 125 *ggl.*, English barley, 19, 20, 21 a $22£$. As your said rie hath been sold for time it can not furnish to supply your draught of £300 which will fall due the 12th instant, so bee please to supply me what I shal want for the performance of the payment of it. The madders of this yeare will not proofe so good as the last, which makes that the old crapt maders holds their price from 21 to $24f.$, the uncrapt from 16 to $18f.$ Caribes indigo 27s; indigo lauro $7\frac{1}{2}s$; Aleppo galles $34\frac{1}{2}f.$, Smyrna galle 31. If you bee pleased to honour me with your commands I shall bee ready to follow your orders. In the meane time I am, your most humble servant, &c.'

[1] King's Lynn, Norfolk.
[2] The net yield on the consignment, which had cost £355 6s, f.o.b., was £237 2s 10d, a loss of 33 per cent.

$$\frac{1\,Jul.}{18\,Jul.}1676$$

94 W. MOMMA to LM
NYKÖPING   4 JUNE 1676

My latest letters to you were on the 16th of February by way of Stockholm, on the 1st of April by way of Gothenburg and on the 4th instant through Stockholm. I have sent copies with each one and refer you to them. I have since received your welcome letter of the 10th of April, from which I more fully understand your discourse about the free passage of ships and what arrangements you have organized and, above all, that I should speak with our friends here about bringing all the wire into your hands to prevent undercutting. And since your competitors have now all been bought out and all the wire is only in your hands the price has risen to £6 5s and could well be held at £6 10s, and before the end of the year you will have no difficulty in getting £7—which makes it all the more surprising to me that you have not been able to sell my wire for more than £6 and have left if lying for eight months and have been selling it quite disgracefully although you knew that this change could be achieved and in spite of my warnings that it could well have been kept another two or three months!

I also find that I have no relevant answer to my letters, for in those of September 1675 (which you have received) I wrote about the account of the wire sold by you at Rouen and making good the loss, but to that I have had no answer and there still remains due to me the account of more than 2,000 coils which were sold in 1674. I shall expect both accounts so that I can see how to organize myself. You crave only that all these goods should come into your hands but do not consider the risks which the owners would have to run, for even if one had them fully insured it would still be unsafe because one cannot be certain nowadays that bills of exchange[1] would arrive on time. If you want to get all the wire into your hands you must do it differently and send a servant here who can acquire it and also pay out the money and declare them to be English goods. Otherwise all this writing is in vain, as I have said to you before.

There are now a good many ships from England arriving at Stockholm, but I doubt that they will make any great profit, selling salt at 11 to 12 dollars per ton, and even if they gain handsomely on the incoming cargoes I suspect they will have to sit still and wait for the outgoing ones, for they cannot load their ships with anything but tar, pitch and iron, of which there is plenty and which will be so abundant in England that it will be unsaleable. But not as much wire will be coming as is wanted because little is being manufactured here, and without some unforeseen events there is likely to be a lack of calamine and clay which this country does not produce and without which the works cannot go on. It was only a little while ago that you said that the clay, which I asked for and you sent, was of small importance—but to me it is extremely important,[2] and having nothing more to say I remain, &c.

[1] The word 'brieven' can mean either letters, or bills of exchange, but in this context the latter seems more appropriate.
[2] Writing to Thomas Legendre of Rouen in May 1669 Jacob Momma-Reenstierna had asked for '*kroose aerde— segge fransse aerde . . . daarde de kroosen van gemaacht soo het messingh in gesmolten woordt*' [ie. clay for the crucibles in which brass could be smelted]. RA, Stockholm, E.2475 (Jacob Momma's letter-book, Dec. 1667–July 1669) pp. 446–9. However, it is not clear from this reference or the next [**305**] what kind of clay W. Momma required.

$$\frac{10\ Jul.}{24\ Aug.}1676$$

295   FREDERICK & GODSCHALL to JD
SEVILLE   23 JUNE 1676

'Worthy Sir, The foregoeing is coppy of our last, which confirm. Since is com to hand your wellcom lines of 18th May which wee received yesterday and from others of a fresher date. The *Advance* frigatt that arrived from Plimouth saw the *Rose* frigatt goeing in there. Wee do hope the sugars will produce a good account seeing there is such a want of them. The accustomed way you will receave the particulers of your said powder sugars per the *Henrietta* frigatt beeing 4,352 *R. pta.* which God send safe to your hands. Shee departed som days since with severall merchant shipps in her company. In a few days departs an *avizo* for Terra Firma with the King's packetts and to advise the arrival of *Galleons*, for whose dispatch English goods will bee in good demand and bayes neere a thousand pieces have been bought up of late at 17 ducats per piece, at Cadiz $14\frac{1}{2}$ ducats aboard, a misserable rate for such a redy money comodity. Wee goe selling at 19 ducats white, part money and the rest 4 months time, to our Safra customers; colours 2 ducats per piece more; Tanton mixt serges, 25 *pesos*; perpetuanas $15\frac{1}{2}$ and 16 *pesos* per piece; yard broads 10 *pesos* per piece; callicoes at 2 *R. pta.* per *vare*; Bow-dyed serges 24 and 25 *pesos* per piece; cloath [?] in fine and woosted hose, good silk stockings of 4 ounces and 3 lists at the end, well sorted of light and sad coleurs, a few with some stripes may here reach 22 *R. pta.* each pare. Pepper at 2 *R. pta.* and 4 *mvs*; cinamon 16 *R. pta.*; cloves 20 *R. pta.* per lb. is the rates wee sell at.

Sir John Leathieullier's leaving our house without any cause but all due service given to his affaires and comands with anticipations, to find them dashed at the insistance of a stranger to give to his servant that will not in haste know well how to turne himself in these times, forced us to resent it, but since it is his pleasure wee have no more to say to it, but leave time to shew the advantage it may produce. Wee esteem your friendly expressions and when wee cann serve you in anything desire you not to spare us, seeing you shall really find us, Sir, your humble servants'.

$$\frac{15\ Jul.}{[\qquad]}1676$$

96 JACOB DAVID to JAN REUDER[1]
PARIS   22 JULY 1676

'Monsieur Reuder, J'ay receu la vostre du 3e courant; pour responce ne vendez que peu de fil de laton sans pourtant faire paroistre que este une marchandise que doive hausse, mais plus tost conseiller les de n'en achete dans l'esperance qu'il baissera a l'arrivée des vaisseaux.

Vous pouvez vendre les 500 pieces de 8 a Temple[2] pourveu qu'il vous en donne autant que l'on en donne a Sr John Lethieullier et a d'autres, au rest il les fault vendre le mieux que vous pourrez.

Payer a Mons. Christopher Goodfellow l'interest qui luy est deu[3] et faittes endosser cela et l'argent que je luy ay payé sur l'obligation.

Je n'ay pas chez moy de chaudrons et cuivre rouge et pour ceux que j'ay je ne veux point en envoyer a Mons. Vrouling qu'il n'ay vendu le boucault qu'il a comme vous dittes. Mons. Oursel a mal fait d'avoir vendu mon fil de latton.

Il est bien que les bayettes sont chargées pour Bilbao. J'espere que l'on aura aussy pris un certificat ou attestation de la coustume comme est marchandise Anglois et que vous l'aurez envoyé a Mons. Richards. Je vous recommande de charger tout l'ordre pour Amsterdam sans perte de tems.

Sy vous voyez que la lettre de change a este veritablement receu par Cletcher outre cella que Cletcher mande avoir receu vous en pouvez paye le montant au jeune homme Funk mais prener y de pres garde.

Je me recommande a vous et a Jacob[4] et demeure a tous deux, vostre amy.

[1] Jacob David's clerk.
[2] The goldsmith-banker, John Temple, one of the largest purchasers of silver for East India Company re-exports in the 1670s. See above p. 199.
[3] Goodfellow, one of David's creditors since 1674, had £300 on deposit with him in July 1676 at 5 per cent.
[4] Jacob Fahlgren (or Fahlgreen), David's other clerk.

$$\frac{22\ Jul.}{3\ Aug.}1676$$

297   T. LANNOY to JD
ALEPPO   26 APRIL 1676

'Mr Jacob David and ever honoured Sir, your letter of the 20th and 22nd October have received and much rejoyce to understand of your being married to soe worthy a lady. I wish you both all the contentment this wourld affords, with long life and etarnall happinesse in the wourld to come. Your letters came to my hands but the 11th present by which I understood of your sending me 3,000 pieces of eight and your order to receive the fifth part of the fraight the *Providence* hath made from England, and to send you returnes by the same ship if possible. As yet none of the money come up but expect it in 3 or four daies. They will sell for the best cambio any pieces of eight hath sold for these ma[n]y years. I not knowing of your sending of any before the ships arrived hath hindered me from providing returnes, which now is impossible being no goods in towne, nor hath their bin any gaules this yeare bought for reason being exceeding scarce, though have made a shift to gitt 300 sacks against the *Providence* arrived that shee might not loose any time. They are for account of Sir John Lethieullier, Mr Burkin and Mr Torriano and were sent for Scanderoon before the ship arrived. The Company haveing made an Order that all unfreemen that traid a broake of 20 per cent (on what goods soever are sent from hence) should be paid, soe that I presumed it might have altered your intention of sending downe any money. It remaineing behind will be no prejudeice to you, for we expect no ships here tell our Generall Ships arrive, and in 3 months will be new gaules and silke, which are alwaies procured at first very cheipe, and I hope by that time to understand your being free of our Turky Company. It lies not in my power to culler your goods in my name, the whole factory being sworne to give in a true entry to our consul of what goods we send, though not for money we receive.

    Your ship *Providence* may be ready to depart in 20 daies, your 100 sacks of gaules being not laden will be no prejudeice to her for shee will make an extraordinary fraight to Legorne, thrice as much as the voyadge before. The *Assistance* and *Dartmouth* frigatts may depart in company with her as alsoe the *Martin*. I am sorry to let you losse soe brave a convayance but cannot be helped. As I act in your concernes shall advise you. I would send you a sortment for cloth but its to late for next ships nor should we give you any great incurradgement to send any but ready money, pieces of eight or lyon dollars from Holland with which can procure what goods you desire and send quick returnes, which is all at present, we remaine Sir, your most faithfull and obliged servant, T.L.'

$$\frac{5\ Aug.}{16\ Aug.}1676$$

298   JACOB CROMMELIN to JD
PARIS   12 AUGUST 1676

'Si je ne vous croyois homme sincere et de bonne amitie je prendrois les remerciemens que vous me faites par la vostre du 27ᵉ passe (votre stile) pour un reproche legitime du peu d'accueil que je vous ay fait car comme je me sens coupable envers vous de ce manquement de debvoir que l'on doit aux amys de dehors et particulierement a une personne de votre merite je vous confesse ma faute ingenument, mais je vois que vostre bonté supplée a tout en m'honnorans outre ce de vostre bienveillance qui m'est chere et advantageuse; faites moy la grace de me la conserver long temps et d'estre toujours persuadé de ma recognaissance. Il ne se presentera pas d'occasion que je ne vous la fasse parestre ny d'amys auxquils je ne vous recommande. Je le feray non seulement pour reciproquer vos faveurs mais par une inclination particuliere de vous servir, et lors qu'il se presentera quelque chose a faire dans les changes, soit en tirans ou en faisans tirer, je prendray la liberté de le faire sur vous. Uzer en de mesme, je vous prie, et pour telle somme qu'il vous plaira j'y feray honneur, et si a l'escheance me remetter a longs jours je trouveray a esconter a $\frac{1}{2}$ pourcent par mois, ou bien je retireray sur vous. Je vois ce que me mandez de la marchandise arrivée par un navire et de celle qu' attendez encore par quatre autres. Il sera bon d'attendre a parler d'affaire qu'ils soient arrives. Mon sentiment est qu'encore que le poivre se pourra donner a 7*d* et au dessous; neanmoins il n'y a rien a faire pour la raison qu'il n'y a point de consommation et qu'il pourra demeurer a ce prix un fort long temps, car il en viendra toujours assez pour le besoing et j'aimerois mieux sauf vostre meilleur advis donner sur d'autres marchandises sujettes a une rehaussé plus prompte et desquelles on pourra a plustost manquer que de poivre. Je suis bien de sentiment de hazarder quelque chose avec vous lors que verrez lieu de entreprendre; vos premiers advis me diront ce qu'il y aura a faire quand vos 4 navires seront arrives. Souvenez-vous qu'il y en a nombre arriver en Hollande et que les marchandises s'y donneront aussy a grand marché, car d'achepter et ne rien gaigner est chose facheuse. Je vous salue et demeure, vostre tres humble serviteur.

Londres—5 5$\frac{7}{8}$*d*.'

$\frac{7 \text{ } Aug.}{8 \text{ } Aug.}$1676

99 HUMPHREY BAWDEN to JD
    EXETER   5 AUGUST 1676

'Kind Sir and my very loveing frind, yours of the first corant I received with the inclosed paterns and I have bought part of the goods and I shall this day and Monday I hope complet the buying of them. I wish you had advissed me if yow would have them milld thick as many of thes sorts ar. Som are mild to 18 yards and 18$\frac{1}{2}$ yards and som mild to hold 22 yards or ther about whearfor I shall pray you to adviss me by the very first post and your order shall be observed. Allsoe I observ that your order is to have them sent up to London which I shall observ if you plees soe to have it, but the carig is 8*s* per cwt. besaids halleg and other small chargs which will be saved if you ship them ofe hear and wee have vessalls goe out of our harber for Roterdam every 3 weeks or a month at most and likwis for Ostent or Bridges but non for Hamborow, soe haveing noe mor att present with my harty love to your self and our good frient I take leve to remain Sir your truly affectionatt frind and servant to command.'

$\frac{9 \text{ } Aug.}{17 \text{ } Aug.}$1676

00 H. BAWDEN to JD
    EXETER   7 AUGUST 1676

'Ser, I writt you the 5th currant to which I refer, only I omited to advise you conserning the searge denims which are very scars to be had hear and thare are but two men in our toune that cane make them any way good and the[y] have promised all that they cane make for sume time but yet I have proviled with one of them to make five peses for me in a munths time or thar about but I beleve I cane gett sume made in a plas distant from this city if you cane stay the time which will be 2 months after advise given, so disiring your answar per first post I rest, Ser, yours to command.

[P.S.] My letter to you of the 5th currant was misdireckted, that is Jeams, wharas it should have bine Jacobe but I hope itt came saef not withstanding that.'

$\frac{16\ Aug.}{18\ Aug.}$ 1676

301   E. RULAND to JD

HAMBURG   8 AUGUST 1676

[D]   I find I have your letters of the 30th of June and 11th of July. Concerning your Bermuda tobacco, I have now got a buyer for it but he will not offer more than $5\frac{1}{2}s$ since he says that he can get quite enough from others. I cannot make up my mind about it. I hope that things will soon improve and go better in the autumn—time will tell. Business otherwise is still miserable here and I see that the price of goods is still falling in England. Ardasse silk can be had at 9s for the best. When I bought mine I thought it was at the lowest price and could not fall lower but it seems that one can never rely on that. Commodities are arriving in too great abundance and consumption is small. May the Lord grant some improvement.

Last Friday we had a fierce fire here which laid 25 to 26 houses in ashes. The damage is estimated at over *RD* 300,000—may the Lord comfort the losers. God be praised, I am not among those involved.

With friendly regards, &c.

[P.S.] On closing this I received your letter of the 28th of July, to which there is little to be said. I see that the [East India] Company has decided to sell its goods on the 5th of September when one thing or another ought to be quite cheap, but for myself I cannot decide to encumber myself with further goods, for however cheaply one buys there is always something cheaper around. It is best to sit quietly for a while, hoping that these bad times will at last change and get better. I thank you for the news about various commodities—I have been glad to see their prices and they will be useful for me to think about, wherewith I remain, &c.

London:	34s 4g 2 usances.
Amsterdam:	$33\frac{3}{4}$ at sight.
Paris:	$47\frac{1}{4}$
Venice:	87 at usance.

$\frac{23\ Aug.}{9\ Sep.}$ 1676

302   H. BAWDEN to JD

EXETER   21 AUGUST 1676

'Kind Sir and loveing frind, my last was of the 19th corant; sinc I have yours of the 17th dito and your orders for one ball of 30 pieces which I shall provid and send you with all speed. The 3 paks you formerly orderd I did pake last Saterday and sent them by Mr Bryant & Minchen and wagon and the will be in Londen the 26th instant. The pris is 8s per cwt. carig [holes] for soe is my agrement with them for the wholl your, I think you will doe well if you see them wightend for I have heard of some complaynts. As for serg denims a twelf month sins ther weur prety many made hear but Norwigh did goe beyond use for spring, soe that trad went there and sins ther are but to makers in this plas which maks any which I have againe this day spocken with and one of them tells me as formerly that he is soe ingag that he can not spar one piece being ingaged as a forsaid for all that he maks and the other maker will spar me two pieces a week and begine the next week if I have your order. The prisse he sells is £4 5*s* per piece and he will as I belev abat to me 1*s* or 2*s* per piece what he sels to others for I buy much other goods of himme. Pray give me your mind by first. Inclosed is the invoys and paterns of said goods. I have markt them by the said of the pake and namd them according to the invoys soe you m[a]y set the same or any other mark or nam in the head if as you think fit. I have noe more at present but take leve and remain, Sir, yours to comand, H.B.

The invoys of three packs of searges contining ninty peses being markt and nombred as p. margant and sent to London by Mr Gundry p. wagon Agust the 19th 1676.

	£	*s*	*d*
162 contining 30 peses of mixt searges which cost	44	9	6
163 contining 30 peses of mixt searges which cost	50	10	0
164 contining 30 peses of mixt which cost	57	15	6
3 balls ninty peses which cost	152	15	0
Dresing and finishin at 2*s* per piece	9	0	0
the charges of packing is as folows: for each pack £0 3 9, bords 1*s* 6*d*, courd 1*s* paper and twine 1*s*, canvas 4*s* 2*d*, per pack; so all the charges of one pack is 11*s* 5*d*	1	14	3
	163	9	3'

$$\frac{6\ Sep.}{2\ Oct.}1676$$

3 J. CROMMELIN to JD
PARIS   12 SEPTEMBER 1676

'J'ay la vostre du 16ᵉ passé, votre stile, avec le notte des marchandises que votre Compagnie des Indes doit vendre vers le mois prochain. Cela n'est pas bien de mon fait veu que je ne puis vendre a Paris, n'estans pas marchand, et ne me meslans que de la banque et negoce des changes. Ce que je pourrois faire seroit de m'interesser avec vous, ou pour mon compte particulier, dans l'achapt de quelque marchandise a bon marche pour la laisser sur les lieux et attendre le rencher. Le poivre est une marchandise sur laquelle il y a peu de dechet mais le mal est qu'il n'y a point de demande, et qu'il en vient tous les ans grand nombre que le fait baisser; mais en attendant quelque bonne rencontre et affin de faire quelque chose ensemble j'ay ordonne hyer a Mons. Jean de Coninck d'Anvers qu'en cas le change pour votre ville soit a 35*s* 11*g* a 36*s* de vous tirer pour mon compte a 3 usances £300 sterling; s'il effectue l'honneur de ses lettres vous demeure recommande, ne doutans ou vous aurez provision devant l'escheance. Vous voyez bien que c'est pour gaigner quelque chose sur ce change que j'espere haussera considerablement dans un mois par les fortes carguaisons que l'on fera a Bordeaux,

Rochelle et Nantes, pour lesquels lieux l'on affrette nombre de vaisseaux a Amsterdam, Rotterdam et Londres. Quand vous plaira faire la mesme chose lors que vos changes seront hauts chez vous uzer en avec toute liberte et pour telle somme qu'il vous plaira, car je suis asseurement, Monsieur, votre tres humble serviteur.'

$$\frac{9 \ Sep.}{18 \ Sep.} 1676$$

304 PIERRE LEGENDRE to JD

ROUEN							15 SEPTEMBER 1676

'Mon pere s'est resolu d'envoyer mon frere aprendre la langue avant que de le mettre dans votre contoir. Je vous seray tousjours oblige des soins que vous avez prit et je voudrois bien les pouvoir recognoistre par quelque bonne occasion. Il s'en presente me si vous vouliez y entendre qui est de faire venir des poudres a canon en France, mais sur tout il faut garder le secret de ce que je vous escrit jusques a ce que les choses reussissent, alors il n'a pas tant de precautions a prendre. Il me semble que les bonnes poudres a canon se font a au Neufchastel, et qu'elle se donnent a tres bon marche. C'est ce qu'il faudroit que vous secussiez exactement, et les frais qu'il y auroit a faire pour les mettre abord, les droits et ce que couteroit le fret pour les a porter a Dunkerque, Callais ou St Vallery, et le nombre que l'on en pourroit tirer a la fois, si on pourroit pas aussy y charger des meches, comme aussy le prix de plomb, ou si vous scavis quelqu' autre port ou on en puisse avoir et a bonne composition—escrire pour en avoir des avis tres exacts. La sortie n'en sera pas difficile, puis qu'il ne s'agit que d'une simple permission de les enlever que l'on obtient fort facilement. Messieurs Dulivier en ont chargé a Londres pour icy et St Vallery; vous pourriez tacitement vous informer quels biais ils ont pris pour l'obtenir. Si vous vouliez m'en fournir pour votre compte, c'est a dire que vous en couresus les risques jusques a ce qu'elles fussent arrives dans un des ports pour lequel elles seroient destinees pour un prix dont nous conviendrions outre le premier achapt et les frais ordinaires qu'il convient faire jusques abord et pour le prix du fret, c'est a dire que je vous donnerois tant pour-cent pour votre provision, celle de votre amy et pour les risques de la mer, sur quoy je vous prie de me donner reponce positive et le plus promptement que vous pourrez. Ne vous addressez qu'a des gens secrets et de grande ponctuellité. C'est une affaire qui pourra vous en aporter d'autres avec bon proffit, puisque cela ce pourroit monter a des sommes considerables. Je vous diray qu'il n'y auroit point de risques a courir du coste des armateurs de France car j'auray des passe-ports du Roy, ainsy chargeant dans un anglois et faisant les conoissements commes pour l'Isle de Wigt ou outre lieu et ayant aussy passeport du Roy d'Angleterre il n'auroit que les risques de la mer, que l'on pourroit faire assurer, soit a Londres ou Paris ou icy. C'est ce qui s'offre et que je suis, Monsieur, votre tres humble serviteur.

Costy—$55\frac{1}{4}$ a $\frac{3}{8}d$.'

$$\frac{12 \ Sep.}{12 \ Sep.} 1676$$

305 W. MOMMA to LM

NYKÖPING							23 JULY 1676

[D]	On the 4th of June I wrote letters to you by way of Stockholm and on the same date by way of Gothenburg, which I hope have come to your hands and to which I refer. I have since received, by way of Gothenburg, your welcome letter of June 16th in which there is much that requires an answer.

I have grasped what you relate at length about the sale of the 1,720 coils of wire which you included as sold in three accounts of 1675 (in September, October and November) and on the 5th and 13th of January 1676, but I have plenty of reason to complain about it for since the 15th of January 1675 you have scarcely written to me about what has been sold except to say, in the account dated 13 January 1676, that since 15 January 1675 (when I last had news) my copper-wire has remained lying unsold while others have been selling at £6 and £6 2s for 2 months time, at £6 4s and £6 3s for 4 months time, and £6 5s at 6 months time. And according to your recent letter of June it has continued selling since then at £6 4s and 5s and £6 3s and £6. I can hardly accept your excuse that there were such large amounts of wire from others and that theirs was preferred before mine, for in several letters you have said that most of it has been bought up, that very little was out of your hands and that you soon expected to have your 'turn' and intended to sell at higher prices. Take a look at your letters from the beginning of 1675 up to June—I have had little news since then that it has been my 'turn'! It is as if you had no wire of mine in your hands. And now I have unexpectedly got the account of the 1,720 coils sold as above, so you must not find it strange that I complain excessively. I shall not clear your account of the debt but make a note that you have administered such an amount. And as for the wire which was sold in 1674, you say the account was sent at the proper time but I cannot find it in any of your letters, much less find any mention of it. Now I have got the copy of three accounts, but in none of the three is the time stated from which you have credited my account. In the one concerning 900 coils I have nothing to say except that you have made an error of 7s 3d in the parcel sold to Elizabeth Packer on the 27th of November—in place of the £158 1s 11d which you put it ought to be £158 9s 2d. In the other account, of 700 coils, I find the weight is rather less than it ought to be and the time for some parcels should be altered from 1 month to 6 or 7 weeks.

But the third account, of 870 coils, I cannot find acceptable at all, since you state them to have been sold without putting any date or time, and also without naming any person but simply 'to sundry'—which is not a style that ought to be used. And, above all, these 870 coils are over 10 centner short of their weight—which you will please have checked and then give me some pertinent explanation.

I have now also received the account of the 360 coils of wire sold in Rouen, and in that it is stated that you have to make good £7,728t 7s 11d for the proceeds and that you have made good to me alone £7,575t 10s 6d. How that comes about you will know best, and about the compensation for the damage on the ship *Samson* (where there is also 7 centner short on the weight of the kettles) there is nothing mentioned—which is all taking too long.

I intend to do nothing about Townley's claim, for it is an unjustifiable claim, as all upright and impartial persons can judge. It is the same with the insurance on the *Caritas*, on which the insurers will hand over no more than the premium, while the insurers in Holland in a similar case raised no questions.

The reason why you have had the *RD* 2,000 bill of exchange returned is—you say—because you have little or nothing for me on account, alleging further that there is a bad debt owing by someone called Harrison for goods sold in the time of your partnership with Mr Joye. But I find that that item was made good to me over four years ago in my current account and as no mention of it was ever made it does not convince me. It is no wonder that you have nothing for me if you handle things in such a manner!

I quite understand that it is not permitted to export earth[1] on pain of death—one cannot afford to run such a risk. It is abundant in our area around Aachen and also in the Liège country and in France but the war prevents us from being able to get any here.

People have been saying for a long while that the trade treaty with Holland would be concluded, ratified and exchanged, but since then it has remained quiet. Meanwhile the English alone have the trade of Stockholm, though I believe it will be of little profit for they dispose of their goods at Stockholm reasonably cheaply and on their return cargoes (and especially iron) they will lose a great deal. They behave in the way you described—as soon as they have acquired their cargoes they are forced to sell in order to pay for the freight and expenses, but it is not for someone like me to object—one must know how to make a profit until this squall is over, for like the last I do not think it will endure for long and as soon as the shipping returns I believe things will go for me as they did before. I can send nothing as long as these wars last, nor would I advise you to send anything to my son unless you also send a servant who could declare them to be English goods. I remain, herewith, yours &c.

[1] '*Dat de aerde op lyff straff v'boden is niet uyt to vooren v'staen.*' The export of fullers' earth and other scouring clays had been long prohibited in England, most recently by Acts of 1660 and 1662 (12 Car. II. c. 32 and 14 Car. II. c. 18) but the penalties fell well short of death!

$$\frac{19 \text{ Sep.}}{6 \text{ Oct.}} 1676$$

306 S. DE GEER to JD

AMSTERDAM   25 SEPTEMBER 1676

[D] I arrived back here about two days ago, and before my departure from Middelburg yours of the 1st instant came safely to my hands together with an account of the iron received from Willem Mynart,[1] with which I have recorded my agreement.

I was not happy to see that a quantity of 'OO' iron has come to London despite the fact that I was afraid it might arrive by mistake. My nephew, Trip, bought a quantity at Stockholm for delivery here, as was agreed, but later it slipped his memory so that when he heard that iron was much dearer in Stockholm than here he gave orders for it to be sold, forgetting to write that it was not to go London, and that is how the mistake occurred. I would have gladly remedied it, but it was too late. You can judge if the people will make anything with it, having paid $26\frac{1}{2}$ to 27 dollars per shippound in Stockholm.

Before my departure from Middelburg I wrote to tell you to insure the iron in the *Zebulon*, captain Joseph Pyll,[2] for £1,000 sterling which I trust has been completed. The said captain had rather severe weather in the Baltic and lost his mast and came to the roadstead off Danzig to refit, according to my nephew Trip there who left from Stockholm in his company. I hope he has now got fine weather so that we can soon expect him. Boor writes to me that he sent the letter containing the bill of lading by way of Gothenburg so it may soon arrive here or reach you. There was also some pan-iron expected which would also be sent to you with the first available ship. No other iron will be sent to you for the present, so what you have should hold its price. Iron is scarce in Sweden and all that has appeared is now being shipped here.

We are trying to do something about getting the posts going and have sent orders to the Resident Lemere[3] to speak with the King of Denmark about it, but he could not comprehend why it was not taken too well here, knowing that one can drive no trade without letters. We have decided that if Denmark does not show any understanding we shall pay them no subsidies until the posts are going freely again, and I believe the Danes will soon change their minds.

I have today received letters from Stockholm dated 14/24 August which mention that

Captain Pyll lay ready to depart, so if nephew Trip had not written that he had come to Danzig I would assume that it must be another ship—unless there are more captains with the same name.

Herewith goes the bill of lading, which is the fifth. The others have to date not yet arrived. Some more iron will be loaded with the first available ship.

I suppose it will not inconvenience you if I drew against this cargo while the present rate of exchange is rather high, for cash is quite scarce now that the ships from Sweden are about to arrive.

By the next I shall write to the Lord Douglas in case he comes to speak with you. Please tell him that I have today drawn on you £651 17s 3d according to the details below,[4] which are recommended to your care:

£200		to Ab. Gerard's order;
£100	at 2 usances	to Jacob van Ghesel's order;
£150		to Seger Corselis's order;
£151 17s 3d		to Stephen Boarcroft's order in London.

Concerning the wine cargo which I mentioned before, I shall now only say briefly—that the freight must cost no more than 5s or 10s more (or less) than others; that one must look for a captain who is known to be an enterprising seaman, a man who can judge a situation well; the ship must not be too big and its bills of lading must be correct for the Baltic. Let the insurers take care of the cargo, worth 5,000–6,000 £t. I suppose the premium from here will be 9 or 10 per cent, or rather less. Lacam at Bordeaux is good.

There is little good wine to be sent from here, but from France nonetheless the expenses are just as large. I shall enlarge on all this by my next. If you think it is a good idea give such orders as you think fit. I cannot tell whether it will turn out well, without any mishap. If the ship is rather bigger load it also with such new goods as are in demand from there, but make sure they are good things which are loaded. My time has run out so I must break off until the next post. Meanwhile, I remain, &c.

[1] William Maynard, captain of the *Constant Friendship*.
[2] Captain Joseph Pyle, of the *Zebulon*.
[3] Jakob Le Maire.
[4] De Geer has omitted £50 in one of these bills.

$$\frac{25 \text{ Sep.}}{26 \text{ Sep.}} 1676$$

307   C. BENE to JD
HAMBURG   15 SEPTEMBER 1676

[D]   I last wrote to you about three days ago. Since then I have received yours of the 8th instant, from which I have seen that Smyrna cotton is not to be had below $5\frac{1}{2}d$ and that consequently there was nothing that could be done about my commission. So one must be patient and let it rest for the moment. I have recorded my agreement with your account of the indigo and likewise with that for two bales of Ardasse, so there is nothing to say arising from these. Your cask of Jamaican indigo has turned out well, which its purchasers cannot deny, but they will not agree to give a higher price for it. However, I shall do my best with it and if there is anything to report I will let you know.

William Cutler has arrived here, God be praised! I shall now procure the receipt of the two bales of silk and try to sell them as soon as possible to our maximum advantage. I see you have no great inclination to sell it for time, but it may not be possible to avoid and if I decide to do so I shall stand surety for you, not doubting that you will allow me 1 per cent for it, for it is customary here for people to deduct 4 per cent for selling and standing surety for Italian silks. However, to encourage our relationship I shall answer to you for $2\frac{1}{2}$ per cent.

The campeachy wood went for *ML* 7 8*s*, which is a poor price. A friend of mine received a quantity with Cutler's ship which cost him 10*s* in [London], so I hope yours will not cost more, otherwise I could not support you. Swedish garcopper can be bought for *RD* 58 and is selling in Rouen for 74£*t* which does not leave much margin in my opinion, so I may not perform your commission. The expenses here are about the same as on the wire, so you can best work it out. Of Swedish wire there is none to be had and, as I said in my previous letter, there is also none arriving at Lübeck. If it was here it could be fetching 68 *ML* and Hamburg wire fetches 70 *ML* per centner, so in that commission there is also nothing to be done. About 250–300 coils of Hamburg wire have been shipped to Bordeaux. For Rouen I have not been able to learn quickly what has been shipped. The expenses on wire, here and at Lübeck, are about $7\frac{1}{2}$ *ML*, not counting the freight from Sweden to Lübeck, per shippound of 320 lb. Most of it is brought by way of Lübeck—it seldom comes directly, for your information. A great quantity of iron has arrived at Lübeck which may weaken the market rather, but of copper and wire people think little will come out of Sweden this year because of the large duty and the unfreedom of their ships.

If my 4 barrels of blue-dye are still unsold, please look after them, for one hopes this commodity will rise in price because henceforth only a limited quantity will be made. If you have achieved anything for me with regard to the [East India] Company I expect to hear. Please buy another 4 cases of indigo guatemalo at 2*s* 8*d* or below and, if it is possible, pour out some so that you are not deceived, or otherwise check one barrel thoroughly to see if it is a high-quality blue. If it is fine, without anything false or mixed with powder, please take it and inform me of it. Your draft of *RD* 50 in specie will be promptly paid and debited to you. Concerning the information about the position of Sirps, I am grateful to you. A friend here has also had letters from him, but the letters in which he gave orders for his reimbursement failed him. However, he does not doubt that he will give him complete satisfaction, wherewith cordial regards, &c.

London: 34*s* 4*g* 2 usances.
Rouen: $46\frac{7}{8}$.
Amsterdam: $34\frac{1}{8}$.
Venice: $88\frac{1}{4}$.

[P.S.] Regarding what I said above, at least 1,000 coils of wire are going to Rouen with a Holstein ship provided with a French pass, but according to letters received today from Amsterdam the same ship has been seized at Dunkirk. Enclosed herewith is a price-current[1] for your inspection. About white scraped ginger, please wait for the arrival of the Barbados ships.

    [1] Missing.

$$\frac{25\ Sep.}{29\ Sep.}1676$$

308   A. BERENBERG'S WIDOW to JD
HAMBURG   15 SEPTEMBER 1676

[D]   I have never written to you privately before, and with this I take the liberty of telling you that my life has been very blessed with four sons and two daughers, and since the time approaches when they ought to be employed in learning something and as I cannot find work for them all in my counting-house (although my eldest has been employed there for three years) I would be very glad if, by next summer, I could place my second son (who has been studying Latin so far) in some good firm where he could learn something. And since you and your dear wife have been so highly praised by my brother Cornelis I would esteem myself fortunate if you could take him into your business to serve for five years. He is seventeen years old, writes German, Dutch and Latin letters (as the enclosed will show).[1] He is also under instruction in accounts and I shall use him in the counting-house this winter to perfect him. I shall have him learn as much English as he can here by next April or May, for he has the opportunity to get some acquaintance with the language by practising with my brother Cornelis as well as with my eldest son, who speaks English and writes it. I therefore await, at your convenience, a few words in reply and a favourable decision. For as he has always been a dutiful son, quiet and modest, so I would rejoice if he could find a good counting-house to serve out his time, do some travelling[2] and then return to his country. Wherewith my friendliest regards, remaining, &c.

[1] Enclosed are four samples of Paul Berenberg's writing, in German, Dutch, Latin and English.
[2] '. . . *een reissten te doen* . . .'. This reading is doubtful.

$$\frac{6 \text{ Oct.}}{10 \text{ Oct.}} 1676$$

)9 D. VAN BAERLE to JD

STOCKHOLM 5 & 6 SEPTEMBER 1676

)] I received in due course your letters of the 3rd of March, 10th and 24th of April, 16th of June and of the 18th past, from which I have seen what is happening to trade [in England]. At Norrköping this year there has been absolutely no shipping-space available for any destination and because of the dispute between the Crown and Queen Christina over the customs duty no goods have been able to come here from Norrköping. I have been waiting in vain for some opportunity to ship out something. There is now going there a small English ship called the *John & Edward*, captain John Stabler, from Bridlington, which is chartered for the account of Francis Townley and going from there to the river Thames where it will receive orders from Townley whether it is to travel to Rouen or unload at London. But I am quite sure that it will sail off before you can load any goods in her. There is a quantity of brass loaded in the said ship, ordered by Mr John Greene, who wants it insured in [London], and on my recommendation it is addressed to you. Please serve him to the best of your ability. You will receive orders from him about the amount of the premium to recover from my brothers in Amsterdam.

I understand that another English ship, with salt, is expected shortly at Norrköping. If it is returning to London you can expect a quantity of brass with it. It is a troublesome business that one can hardly succeed in loading anything. If it were not so late in the year I would make up my mind about getting a small vessel to come from England, and I would have done so already if I had not been given hope that the dispute over the customs duty would have been settled by now.

The coarse cloths called 'dozens' have been selling at a good profit this year, likewise the calicoes, such as bleached 'moorees', 'hummums' and 'addaties' and all kinds of French haberdashery.[1]

Because of the quantity of copper coins which have been minted, silver and gold have risen so one might easily make 10 or 12 per cent on pieces of eight or silver ware.

Fine iron remains still at 25 to 27 copper dollars, copper at 220 dollars, brass-wire at 260 dollars, and little to be had. Setubal salt is again at 12 dollars per ton, French salt at 7 to 8 dollars, wherewith my heartiest regards, &c.

[P.S.] Today, being the 6th of September, I have received news from Norrköping that an English ship of about 170 lasts has arrived with salt. If it is returning to London I shall obtain room aboard it for a consignment of goods.

¹ '. . . & alle fransch kramwaaren . . .'.

$$(i) + (ii) \quad \frac{16 \ Oct.}{20 \ Oct.} 1676$$

310 CHARLES GOODFELLOW to JD
ALEPPO   (i)   3 JULY 1676

'Sir, The above is coppy of my former which I confirme, since which none from you which will cause brevity. I am now advised by my father that the Parlementt being latly ajourned you could not then be made free till next sitting, contrary to your desyn, so please to looke to your business least should be forced to pay 20 per cent broaks which the times cannott bare. The bills laeding runn in your deare Laydys name or otherwise mightt be free as being a stranger: all that I can doe in this is only to give timely notice so you may account as thinke convenient. I have nott yett disposed them in hopes to have a better price, which shall ly a little longer and iff doth nott answer my expectations shall take the price current that you may have speedy returnes. This sort of comodities ar nott for this place, for poore people buying them cannott gett mony enough to buy a good parcell butt by degres with a greate deale of trouble, yett doubtt not but my actions therin may procure your aproval and a futur correspondence another way. Trade here att presentt being the hott season but dull so have nothing more to add having given you the nessisary advises. Our ships departed Cipres in company of 2 men warr the 14 past, vizt. *Providence*, M[- - holes along crease - - -] *Guinny* frigatt [- holes -] any way concerned should have given you the cargazoones being allwayes ready with a double dilligence to serve my frends in anything.'

(ii)   8 AUGUST 1676

311 'Sir, The above written is coppy of my lastt since which hath little happned worth your knowledge. I have now begun and sold some smal parcels of your wire and wish all the remaine could procure the same price but for that doubt nott the saile off only the brass pannes, having tryed severall wayes to putt them off but cannott, being no comoditie for this place as I have formerly advised. Your orders was to returne them iff could nott find saile to benefitt, which I endeavered to follow as you will perceve by my former letters, as also by Capt. Peckett, having left both them and the wire att Scanderoone till understood whatt price they bore here, and sent for up 3 or 4 of ditto to shew the people here, which was accordingly done, and upon ther offering a good price here att that time did send for upp the remainer which when arived here the same men that bid me mony before then would give no price thinking to have them for little or nothing, as I suppose ther designe was, which to frustraite I have till now kept them and tryed other men, butt as yett cannott dispose of them having bin severall times in great hopes. I shall use my earnest endeavors to procure itt and doubt nott yett butt may meete with a chapman, for the markett will nott be supplied with this sort of goods so have it all to my selfe. The wire is a comoditie here butt for small parcels, the French, &c, bringing itt and much can nott be consumed, p. aviso. However, I doe nott in the least feare butt to give you a good accountt at last being nothing wanting on my parte to hasten the returnes—which refer you to the aproval of my actions, which doubt nott butt will procure a future correspondence, everything considdred in the true staite I here representt you, this being what this season of the yeare will permitt me att presentt to advise you, the towne being empty of all goods, reffering you to the per contra coppy of my last to your concernes there, expecting your speedy answer, nott doubting but you may find such favor or some way wherby to save your broaks till you have leave, and most respectfully remain, Sir, your most humble servantt.

[P.S.] My brother being laetely arived here presents his humble service to your good selfe and dear Lady as also your humble sarvant.'

$$(i) + (ii) + (iii) \quad \frac{16 \; Oct.}{20 \; Oct.} 1676$$

12 T. LANNOY & J. BURKIN to JD
ALEPPO

(i)   31 MAY 1676

'Sir, my last was the 15th, its copy forwarded the 16th. The 25th present sailed the *Providence* and *Martin* from Scanderoon, the *Assistance* for their convoy. Pray God send tham a good voyadge. The *Providence* will doe well, and I hope will incurradge you to send her againe. You pieces of eight remaine yet undisposed of. What received for other friends have changed at 11 per cent. I doe not question, giveing a little time, but to sell yours for $14\frac{1}{4}$, soe that returnes being omitted sending by these convayances will rather be your advantadge then otherwise, for all goods will be plentifull and cheep now the ships are out of port, and I hope your next will informe me of your being free of the Turky Company and that my brother Samuel will have the honour of your comands at Constantinople, and from thence as goods are sold the money remitted hence or to Smirna as finding incurradgement, which often turnes better to account than sending of pieces of eight or lyondollers. By the last ships my selfe and partner received 8 large bags of cocheneile from Cadiz which have disposed of at LD 15 per oake against Ardasse silke which will be under 6 LD per Rotolo, no bad account the charges on cocheneile being but small. Few daies since arrived some Borma Legee which was bought at LD 10 per Rotolo. There is good quantity of more to follow which hope will be bought cheepe. I know not anything more worth your notice at present, I remaine, &c.'

(ii)   9 AUGUST 1676

3 'Sir, The above copy of my last, since have received yours of the 5th February by way of Legorne, by which you advise me of goods and money sent me by the ship *Providence*. Your 3,000 pieces of eight sent by Mr Skynner & Co. of Legorn have advised you in my former letters to have received, but have not received any goods soe presume were not laden according to your order. If you had sent cocheneile would have made you a good account, for when the *Providence* arrived was in demand and could have sold a larger quantity than we had at above price, though at present its fallen under 12 LD per oake occasioned by the French who have had some and expect a great deale more soe will goe off but slowly for the futer. Your 3,000 pieces of eight have disposed of, the cambio comes to LD 13 to 12 per cent, there arriveing quantity, or else had got you $14\frac{1}{4}$; at present worth 9 per cent. Few daies since arrived some new gaules; its reported to be plenty this year soe if find them cheepe shall invest your money in said comodity, and shall ly ready for the first good convayance provided you are free of the Company or else shall not send them, for the Company are so strickt that they will make you pay 20 per cent, they haveing made new orders of late, that with out breach of oath cannot be cullered by a factor, being sworne to give a true entry to the Company Treasurer here. If gaules be not cheepe shall see to gitt you some interest which is usually here at 9 to 10 per cent per annum, which is all at present. I remaine, &c.'

(iii)   9 AUGUST 1676

[A postscript].

'Sir, Your letter of the 6 Aprill we have received and we are sorry to find the cotton yarne we sent you to be soe bad a comodity. We took it in barter of your ginger or else should not have sent you any. He that took the ginger is not able to sell it and if we had not disposed of it as we did could not have sold it for it was much perished by wormes. It remaines yet in our warehouse but weighed of. Sir, we returne you thankes for your promises to inlarge your traid to us. We shall use our utmost indeavours to advance your interest and hope you will find incurradgement by the returnes of your 3,000 pieces of eight by the *Providence*, for which we have given you credit LD 3,394 @ 40 [aspers]. By this convayance we send an account of what fraight she made to Scanderoon and have carryed the $\frac{1}{5}$ part, being LD 145, 75 [aspers] to your credit. We refer you to the letter and account sent under Sir John Lethieullier's cover, which is all we know worth your notice at present. We remaine, &c.'

$\frac{18\ Oct.}{20\ Oct.}$1676

314   A. BERENBERG'S WIDOW TO JD
HAMBURG   10 OCTOBER 1676

[D]   Your letter of the 29th past has come to me safely, from which I see what you have to say about the request I made, in offering my son to be taken into your counting-house. I must confess that I did not know the conditions which prevail in England as well as I now understand them from you. Things are arranged quite differently here. It is true that in some cases money is given by those who are widows, who wish to continue living with their sons. For they have little knowledge of places abroad and are unwilling to send their children away, and since they are people of means they are quite happy to give a sum of money so that they can be accommodated and keep their children at home. Some are taken on for nothing—or, at least, without money—as we did with our servant Claes Bene who, as we know, corresponds with you about the purchase of his goods. For six years he served us for nothing, and for the other two years that he was with us we gave him *RD* 100 per annum.

Meanwhile, I see that you are very willing to take my son and prefer him before others who have been offered to you if I will engage him for seven years, give surety for his honesty in the sum of £2,000 sterling and pay £300 sterling for seven years. Regarding the first two points I could well consent, namely that he should serve seven years and I could give security of £2,000 for fidelity for of that I am entirely confident. But to pay £300 sterling in addition I think is rather too much, seeing that there is no trade and very little going on, so that our lives are very constricted. When some improvement is expected I would be very willing to give £200 flem. or *RD* 500 in order to have my son in your firm, but since you say you have offered to do his pleasure for the former condition of £300 sterling but not for £200 flem. or

RD 500 I must thank you for your kindness. In passing I have since discovered that, while young men in [England] do give money, there are other conditions which you did not mention—that those who have served out their apprenticeship and carried themselves well and want to remain with the firm can enjoy a half-share of the commissions and several other conditions, which you know better than I do. It means that they can soon earn back the money they have paid for their service. What you decide about this I hope to learn in due course. With very friendly regards, I remain, &c.

$$\frac{\textit{18 Oct.}}{\textit{22 Oct.}}\textit{1676}$$

15   A. BERENBERG'S WIDOW & HEIRS to JD

  HAMBURG   10 OCTOBER 1676

D]   We find ourselves with yours of the 15th and 29th past, from which we have seen in full the prices at which the East India Company goods were sold, as also the prices which other goods are fetching in [London]. We thank you for all your trouble but, as we have often said, we can see nothing profitable among the one or the other, for there is no demand and the exchange rate on [London] remains high. Prices are being much undercut here by the English, as well as others, so if one wants to invest one's money one can do it here more advantageously than in [England]. We still have the last 265 sacks of ginger which we bought, lying here unsold with other lots, and are negotiating to buy another 400 sacks here which we are being offered at 4g per lb. with $8\frac{2}{3}$ per cent discount. Among them are many sacks of white ginger and we are offering $3\frac{3}{4}g$ on the above conditions. Whether we can obtain them for that a few days will reveal. As for what else trade has to offer, pepper is going very cheaply in Holland. We are expecting a quantity for ourselves. Campeachy wood is cheap and we have been considering speculating in it for some time but cannot as yet make up our minds. It fetches only $7\frac{3}{4}$ *ML* per 100 lb and the old was $8\frac{3}{4}$. Grains are continuing to sell, such as rye at *RD* 57 to 58 and fine wheat at *RD* 61 to 62 per last. The wheat is likely to be cheaper than the rye in future. Insurance on English ships has jumped because with every post one hears of them being intercepted and held, and the Germans will hesitate to be as liberal about lading in them as they have been. To sum up, things are daily getting worse for trade, and we must have patience and wait for the amendment of our lives. With friendliest regards, we remain, &c.

London:	34s 3g	2 usances.
Amsterdam:	$33\frac{11}{16}$·	
Venice:	$88\frac{1}{4}$	at usance.

$$\frac{\textit{20 Oct.}}{\textit{28 Nov.}}\textit{1676}$$

6   A. VAN KUFFELER to JD

  AMSTERDAM   27 OCTOBER 1676

)]   In answer to yours of the 13th instant, I am grateful that you will be of assistance to the Lord G[?] on his arrival. In a similar case I would be likewise at your service.

  I further see that you have not been able to achieve anything in the purchase of tobacco, since nothing good was obtainable below 6d. It is true that I see no prospect of it falling here for the moment, but I do not think it would be advisable to spend more than 5*d* per lb. for there would be nothing we could do with it when the expected ships arrive in [London] and good quality stuff is obtainable at 5*d*. I refer you to my foregoing letter.

You report campeachy wood at 10*s*, at which price there is nothing to be done, I find. However, I am told that it is being sold for 9*s* in [London] so if you could buy it at that price, free on board, and will take a half share, I would gladly take the other half of 25,000 lb. on trust. It sells here for *f*.6¾ per 100 lb., but with such a quantity one might have to settle for *f*.6½. English copperas fetches *f*.6¼ to *f*.6½ per 100 lb. and I would be glad to learn what it costs in [London], for there seems to be something to be done with that as well.

Thank you for news of ships arriving in [London] as well as of what is happening in trade. Little is happening here. Bermuda tobacco comes here seldom and at present there is none in town. If any should come it would not fetch above 4 or 5 stuivers per lb. Brazil tobacco in varieties are from 9 to 10 stuivers per lb. to 12½ and 13 stuivers for the best. Indigo guatemalo is at 28 to 30 stuivers per lb., Pernambuco wood at *f*.34 per 100 lb. Roman alum 47*s* per 100 lb and English 33*s*. Cochineal is mostly at 30½*s* per lb. Aleppo galls are *f*.34 per 100 lb., Smyrna ditto, *f*.27½. Senegalese gum is at [blank], White Brazilian sugar, 10 to 11*g* per lb., and muscovadoes 8½ to 8¾*g* per lb.; Barbados sugar 6½ to 6¾*g* per lb. and Nevis 6¾ to 7*g* per lb. Lead is 24*s* [per 100 lb.], tin *f*.45 [per 100 lb.]. Brown ginger *f*.11½ per 100 lb.; white ditto *f*.13. Apulian oil £57 flem. per tun; Seville ditto, £56; Port Oporto and Lisbon £53 to £55. Zante currants *f*.16 per 100 lb. Milanese rice 47*s* per 100 lb. Cardamon 44½ stuivers per lb.; cubebs 8½ stuivers. Ardasse silk, 16 to 16½*s* per lb. Because of the great differences in Turkish yarn there is little I can say about them. Ordinary Angora is at 3½ to 5*s* per lb.; better sorts at 6 to 10*s* per lb., and the best from 12, 13 to 15*s* per lb. Begbesar from [hole], Camel hair is in reasonable demand here. Aleppo fetches from [hole] to 33 and 34 stuivers per lb.; Smyrna from 28 to 29 and 30 stuivers. Smyrna cottons are 10 to 12½*g* per lb.; Cyprus cottons 12 to 13*g* per lb.; Barbados yellow [cotton] 15 to 16½*g* and white ditto 14 to 15½*g* per lb. The best nutmegs now sell for 55 stuivers per lb.; poorer quality fetch 50 stuivers; cloves are 80½ stuivers and mace 16½ to 18*s* per lb.; cinnamon from [hole] to 60 and 70 stuivers. Madder, *f*.25 to *f*.26; unprocessed ditto from *f*.18 to *f*.19. Cut whalebones are *f*.45, iron pots *f*.7½ and copper kettles *f*.62½ per 100 lb. The best Danzig steel in small barrels now fetches only *f*.11¾ per 100 lb. Since I sent you the notice of our [East India] Company prices other wares are selling as in the enclosed notice and in Zeeland they began their sale yesterday.

The English draperies trade is absolutely at rock-bottom here since there is no demand for the goods and they are selling at very low prices. The smallest white pack-cloths of 28 yards length have been sold for from £11 to £11 flem.[1] per piece, according to quality, and I notice that white northern kerseys are now reasonably current, fetching from *f*.18 to *f*.22 per piece. Mixed grey kerseys are from *f*.20 to *f*.22 per piece, for your guidance. If you see any service I can do for you, you have only to command, wherewith I remain, &c.

[1] *Sic.* for £11½[?].

$$\frac{25\ Oct.}{20\ Nov.}\,1676$$

317　G. RICHARDS to JD
BILBAO　　　　　　　　　　　　　　　　　　　　　　18 OCTOBER 1676

'Esteeemed Sir, I have now before mee yours of the 24th August. For answer, my former carried you account of the bays which weare sould for the most that comodity will yeald as yet. If you finde any account thereby you may governe your selfe accordingly in sending more but I am apt to thinck they will fall consederably with you now in the winter when you may procure them on better tearms. You had also by the same convayance 500 barrs rusty iron, and assoone the remaynder of the proceed of the goods comes in it shall be also made you home in the same manner, which is the best way of returns as the times now are. Hambro wax when cheape bought in may sell here to advantage and although the proffit be but moderate its a stable comoditye and goes of to good men. I thanck the recommendation (of the ship of corne intended hither) to mee. I have this yeare had 8 or 10 thousand bushells of that comodity which sold at losse, it coming after the fayre. Many shipps arriving therewith before and a promiseing harvest approaching lowered the pryse above 30 per cent although whats good sells now somewhat better. This is no market for that corne but that for 2 years past was a scarcity in Castill made it here extreame deare, but licence beeing granted for its coming freely from France brought a supply. However, if yours bee good it may sell for about 8*s* sterling per *hanegas*, whereof 2 bushells inglish make one, and 6 per cent losse more. In Ireland I am informed its verry cheape. If you have any friends there which are concerned this way pray afford mee your recommendation to them. From thence are brought hither quantities of tanned hyds, salmon and hake. The wyre, unlesse I can meet an occasion to putt it off according to your order, shall remayne. For the other part of the letters good advyse and kind inclination I render you my dew acknowledgments but I am sorry to finde my selfe without the other part of your good opinion. I will assure you, I so much esteeme the honour of your service that weare there any designe I would incourage you to ingage in with such successe that I might appeare without shame I should be always at yours, but as trade now goes I am almost afrayde to mention almost any comodity haveing soe often miscarryed in my expectation, and for Sir John I will affirme and desire you to believe mee, that I never discovered but his prosecuting this trade is more for my advantage then his own intrest, always ordering mee to incourage any friend to what I can and he will send what they will not, whereby you may be sensible you are in your thoughts under a misteke. I know you are able to send one hither fitter for the imployment but not more cordiele to you, nor can I see how another will now as the times goe bring to passe what I have donne. It was my shallow experience made mee singly undertake what I did, but I thanck God I am now securely planted for those difficultyes I formerly encountred and [if] in any thing I may be serviceable to you, you will assuredly find mee in all sincerity and affection as well your faithfull as obliged servant.

Sir John hath consigned mee 11 bales calicos wherein you are $\frac{1}{2}$ concerned and 18 bales wherein you are $\frac{1}{3}$ which God sending safe I shall take care to remain and in forme you in dew time of there sale.'

$$\frac{2\ Nov.}{2\ Nov.}1676$$

318 ABRAHAM & SIMON VROULING to JD
ROUEN   6 NOVEMBER 1676

'Le 3ᵉ fust a vos graces notre derniere a la quelle nous referons. La poste de chez vous ne doibt venir que demain, ainsi en aurons moins a dire. De vos chaudrons ne pouvons encore vous dire aucun succes; nous n'y espargnons ny soing ny peine; aprez quelque demarche que nous avons faitte il faut attendre ce que nos marchans diront, et aussytost qu'il se passera quelque chose en aurez advys. Le vent continue du nord depuis quelques jours, ainsi esperons que

Th.Hun[1] avec nos 100 torqs fil de latton comparoistra et que John Gay[2] dans qui debviez charger nos 20 balles de laine ne tardera pas aussy. Nous attendons le connoissement de ce dernier et prions Dieu qu'il conduise et l'un et l'autre. Du fil de latton nous envoyerez une petite facture avec votre provision pour vous en crediter. Cette denree ne veut point icy aller a l'advenant quelle le debvroit; il y en a peu ou point, et ce neantmoins demeure en un estat. Il c'est vendu hier encore du Suede a £93*t*. Nous n'esperons pas grand avance avec nos 100 torqs; ce que nous en fesons est pour essay pour prendre mieux mesures et si prevoyons quelque avance raisonnable vous en commettrons plus grand partye. Ce negoce debvroit faire miracle: faittes nous le grace de nous aviser ce que s'y passera chez vous pour nous gouverne. A Hambourg il n'y en a point du tout, mais comme il y en a plus chez vous qu'en tous autres lieux on ne manquera pas d'en envoyer icy. Faut se gouverner suivant le temps et verrons si aprez ce qu'il y aura a faire et s'l y a lieu de vous y servir vos interes seront assurement preferes a tout autres. Votre rozette ne vendrons point a moins de £85*t* suivant la note qu'avons faitte de votre ordre.

Toutes les laines se maintiennent, le debit n'estant que mediocre demeurent en un estat. Nous verrons avec nos 20 balles Sigovie si ce sera un negoce pour y retourner; du prix ne vous en peux dire, on se gouverne sur la veue de la marchandise. Il s'en est vendu jusqu'a 36*s*; comme les notres ont esté choisies par Monsieur, votre pere, ne doubtons ou sera marchandise dont ferons aussy un bon prix. Le temps nous le dira; en attendant envoyez nous en la facture. Castille vallent 23, 24*s*, Sorie 24, 25*s* la lb.; agnelins de Pologne tres fin, 27, 28*s* la lb. Une de vos traittes avons accepte, celle du *W*.1,000. L'autre de *W*.500 recevera tout honneur aussy a 54½*d* comme denotez. Vous en debitons en £340 12*s* 6*d* sur notre conte et creditons de £3 3*s* 4*d* pour vos frais envers Mr Jean Pelt. Notez-le si vous plaist de mesme afin que nous allions en tout d'accord et s'il y a quelque chose sur le conte de Ab.V[rouling] le passerez sur celuy de notre compagnie et nous en donnerez advys.

Comme vous avons dit, fer blancq vaut a prezant couramment £80*t* le baril et paye 15 p. baril d'entree. C'est une marchandise ordinairement ingrate ou il n'y a pas grande avance, neantmoins a 20*s* chez vous y auroit encore du proffyt et respond presque aussy bien qu'a le faire venir adroitture de Hambourg ou il vaut 36 a 36½ *ML* les 300 feuil. Voyez si vous en voulez essayer, pour le prix de £80*t* pouvez faire estat. C'est une marchandise qui change peu mais il faut qu'il soit assorti d'un ⅓ a la croix, et nous vous managerons les frais autant que nous pourrons. L'acier de Suede se consomme aussy icy, mais non pas en tres grande quantite; celuy en botte de Hongarie est le mieux requis, vaut presentement £28*t*, £29*t* la botte et les petits barils de Suede £16*t* 10*s* a £17*t* le baril; d'autre qu'on appele 'Egel stael', icy 'acier a la rose', de 140 a 150 lb. le baril, £36*t*, £37*t* le baril. Toutes ces sortes payent d'entree 28*s* du cent et s'en consomme assez bon nombre, mais vers le printemps est le plus grand debit et se vendt mieux d'advys. Autre negoce sans changement. Le poivre vaut 12*s* 3*d*; poil de chameau 30 a 32*s* la lb.; galles d'Aleppe £42½ a £43*t* le cent; garence nonrobée, £27½*t* le cent; grappe £37½*t* a £38*t* le cent; campesche £10*t* 10*s* a £11*t* selon l'occasion; cotton filé d'Aleppe, 16*s*, 17*s* la lb.; cotton de Smirne £42*t* 10*s* le cent; fanons Grand Baye, £70*t* il cent; Hollande et Hamburg vallent 8 a 10 pour-cent mieux. Les huilles icy sont toutes en une main; de Portugal il n'y en a point du tout. Pour 10 bottes arrivees de Port a Port j'en eu vu offrir £29*t* du cent. La recolte en Provence a beaucoup paty accause de la secheresse, et apparemment qu'il en viendra peu de la; au printemps alors que c'est le veritable temps du debit cette marchandise pourra bien faire miracle. Les soudes vallent £16*t* le cent; en Guatino le saffron baisse. Il s'en est beaucoup achepte a £14*t* 10*s* et plus haut, presentement a £13*t* 10*s* la lb. on en auroit. Les grains continuent a bon marche, ble le muid *W*.40, seigle *W*.24, orge *W*.26 le muid.

Nous vous sommes obliges de l'honneur que ferez a notre lettre de recommandation; en aucune occasion ne nous espargnez, qui aprez nos baisemains a Madame et toute la famille demeurons, vostre humble serviteurs.'

Amsterdam:　　$101\frac{1}{2}d.$
Anvers:　　　$100\frac{1}{4}d.$
Costy:　　　　$55\frac{1}{2}d.$
Hamburg:　　au pair.'

　[1] Captain Thomas Hunn.
　[2] Captain John Gay of the *Jonas*.

$\dfrac{13\ Nov.}{13\ Nov.}$1676

319　BENJAMIN BEUZELIN & SON to JD
　　ROUEN　　　　　　　　　　　　　　　　　17 NOVEMBER 1676

'Nous recepvons prezantemant vostre lettre du 2/12 de ce mois; en responce le navire de Francois Sely est Dieu mercy bien arrivé et avons fait decharger les 20 balles de poivre de votre envoy, que nous ferons garbeller au premier jour et en procurerons la vanthe sans aulcune perte de temps. Elle n'est pas trop eschauffee a cauze du nombre qui en vient. Puis que nous y avons y intherest vous pouvez croire que nous negligerons rien. L'on n'a encore aulcune nouvelle de la navire qui a les 20 balles restante. Par le calcul que nous fezons il n'y a rien a faire sur les dittes poivres; c'est une marchandise ingratte. Nous aurons soing aussy des 100 torches de fil de latton que vous nous avez addressees pour votre compte particullier. Le vaisseau ne peult tarder car le vent a esté bon despuis 4 jours.

　Nous avons cognoissance particulliere des Srs. Van Ceulen & Uppendorf et avons esté en traitte de leurs affaires, mais nous n'avons peu tomber d'accord des conditions qui nous sembloyent trop dures. C'est M. Legendre et Henry Amsincq qui les feront, ayant esté plus hardis que nous. Nous n'en avons point de jallouzie—Dieu benie les ungs et les autres. Voilla tout ce que nous en dirons. On nous a escrit de Jacob Reenstierna, beau-frere de Abraham Cronstrom, comme d'un homme tres mal en ses affaires. Nous avons heu sy peu de satisfaction de la pluspart de correspondants de Suede, que nous nous en sommes tires. Il nous y en pourtant d'heub encore des parties que l'on a paine a recouvrir et voudrions y avoir perdu pour n'y plus songer.

　Il est arrivé ung petit navire d'Hambourgh qui a 400 a 500 torches de fil de latton. Avecq ce que Mr Midfort pretend envoyer icy, et ce qui s'en attend adroitture qui est environs 1,000 torches, nous craignons que le prix ne vienne a mollir. Nous vous donnerons advis de ce qui se passera. Vous savez que l'on a optenu la main levee d'un autre vaisseau d'Hambourg mene a Donquerque qui debvoit icy. Il a encore autour de 1,000 torches, ainsy cette marchandize ne nous manquera pas.

　Nous n'avons rien a vous dire au regard de bois de Campesche, le pouvant avoir a 10s sterling le thonneau nous vous confirmons nos ordre. Sy vous n'y voullez point intherest, achetez en pour nous 40 thonneaux, Dieu vous emmene les vaisseaux que vous attendez de la Jamaicque.

　Nous sommes bien aise que vous ayez receu les 2 demi-ponsons de vin, et plus encore qu'ils soyent a vostre goust. Il est trop tart pour le vin blanc, car la foire est passe; nous y advizerons pour la prochaine, ce qu'attendant nous vous baizons les maines et vous prions de voulloir faire l'acceptation de les 8 lettres de change, nous les renvoyer par vos premieres. S'il y mancque a quelques une vous observeres le necessaire et nous tiendrez pour a faire accepter.

W.   700 a 56¼ en lettre Reau et Dupuy sur Michel Chesham.
W.   800 a 56¼ en lettre desdites sur Thomas Ball.
W.   726 a 56¼ en lettre desdites sur Joseph Seward.
W.   600 a 56   en lettre Lostau sur Samuel Swinock.
*W.*1,500 a 56   en lettre Reau et Dupuiy sur Thomas Dade.
W.   400 a 56   en lettre Lostau sur Joseph et Leon Dulivier.
*W.*1,000 a 56   en lettre Thomas Arundel sur James Brace.
W.   800 a 56   en lettre Thomas Lewis sur Henry Strode.
‾‾‾‾‾‾‾‾‾‾
*W.*6,526

Amsterdam: $100\frac{3}{4}g$.
Anvers: $99\frac{3}{4}g$.
Londre: $55\frac{1}{4}d$.

Je vous prie nous dire le prix du resin de Malgues.'

$$\frac{24\ Nov.}{27\ Nov.}1676$$

320   S. DE GEER to JD

AMSTERDAM   27 NOVEMBER 1676

[D]   My last letter was on the [blank]. Since then I have received yours of the 10th instant.

Our people in Sweden have no need to sell our iron without orders. What came last year was due to a misunderstanding, as I explained to you.

As for the 1,500 slb, it is neither 'O' nor 'G' iron. My brother Emanuel,[1] who also has works in Sweden, always sells his iron in Stockholm. It may well be that your friend has bought some of that iron, but I believe he will have paid dearly enough for it. It is an iron which always come here as a rule. It is also an Orgronts iron, but he will first have to make people familiar with it. The smiths always mark it [D] and there is none in England. Everything that was made last year came wholly here, and next year's production has not yet been sold. He is accustumed to sell all his iron to one man in one place, and this year nephew Trip has had it. He makes about 6,000 to 7,000 slb per annum, so this 1,500 slb must be old stuff. If the purchaser is wise he will have that iron sent here. It would yield him more than the 19*s* [per cwt.] in London for it is familiar here.

About the time that the ships were coming out of the Sound they passed the *Nachtegael* which had been forced by contrary winds to run into Norway. Since Mr Lacam[2] cannot achieve anything about chartering a ship we shall have to let it lie. It would not have been a bad voyage, arriving before the winter, but in the spring it would not be advisable for there will be quite enough provided from here.

I trust the price of wine will change considerably for it is low here but rising, and is doing so in Sweden, so I believe the English will not be fetching so much in the coming year. Those who were there with salt ships this year will lose their appetites for going again, and because Dutch ships now have free passage there will be no English ships which can sail there at that price. One can freight from here to St Ubes to Stockholm and back again for less than *f*.52 per last of 18 tuns, if delivery is at Stockholm. I would judge that freight-rates at Stockholm will be low next summer and one can already reasonably foresee that the price of salt will not be very high.

About this commodity, I have been speculating that because it is forbidden in Portugal to come to St Ubes in ballast there are few ships here which want to go there, and if that remains the case while winter comes on I might find that not many ships have been chartered to go there, and then it might be worthwhile chartering one or two English ships, if they can be got for less than £6 sterling, in view of the fact that with few English ships coming to Stockholm freight rates at London may be quite cheap. I shall thus be glad to learn from you at what price one should be able to obtain them. If one could succeed in getting them for £5 it would be tolerable, even allowing for the fact that because of the high rate of exchange the money would be worth more and amount to at least *f.*57. But the return freight would be paid for in heavy money and another advantage to set against it is that, with the English sailing without convoy, they should be able to get to Stockholm rather earlier if the Dutch ships are not called for in time.

I am not at all of the opinion that the English will want to go to St Ubes at that price, but they might be willing to when the winter is nearly over, and to take away their fear of lying waiting a long time we could stipulate two months for the total loading time at St Ubes and Stockholm. If the ship going to St Ubes is clear to load up we must write to my correspondent, N. Simons, who can ensure that he is loaded within 14 days.

The freight-rate between here and St Ubes is less than *f.*28. I shall now wait to hear from you at approximately what price it can be expected to be [in England] for my guidance in case the St Ubes fleet has departed from here.

If you have any inclination to have a Dutch ship fetch a load of salt and go to Stockholm, please let me know. I am thinking of chartering one for myself. Please be quick. I shall leave it to you to inform me; otherwise I shall keep it to myself for time does not allow one to wait for an answer.

The answer about the premium on the *Coninck David* will have to be awaited at leisure, but please tell them to hurry up the business. I do not think that I ought to bear the interest whilst the consignment is not credited to me. It is due to you, but it must be found from that item for I have already paid for it here and so far I have had nothing out of it but trouble. I long to know what the item will yield.

If the business of Townley is not settled yet, please let me know. I shall then write to Mr T. so that he can persuade those good people to make an end of it.

My correspondent at Lisbon is Nicholas Simons, consul of His Majesty [the King] of Sweden. I am sure it will be more advantageous for him to draw bills on us here than on London, though I do not know what the exchange rate on London is. You should be able to calculate what the rate was on drafts in the spring. For the English salt ships the exchange on us here was at 61*g* [per cruzado].

The insurance rate here on Stockholm is 10 per cent. Our ships, which are due to come from Stockholm, are taking rather longer than I had expected so I am running a little short. Thus I trust you will permit me to draw £500–£600 on you against drafts falling due. If the effects of mine which you have do not cover it when it falls due I shall make it up some other way.

Please let Negrinus[3] have another £20 and help him sort things out so that he can be certain of getting his papers over before the spring.

The letters from Denmark have arrived but bring no further news with them. The Swedish army draws further off and those at Hamburg write for certain that Malmo has been relieved and that the Danes are afraid that Sweden might well enter Bleking and besiege Carelstadt.
                    Wherewith I remain, &c.

[P.S.] I have today revoked a bill of exchange for £100 from Exeter so it must not be accepted. I beg you to guarantee that amount and send the bill and the protest to Isaac van

Hoegarden at Limerick so he can put things in order. If acceptance is lacking the holder of the bill will speak to you.

¹ Steven de Geer's elder brother (1624–92), ninth child and third son of Louis de Geer and heir to the Lövsta works.

² Jean Lacam, of Bordeaux.

³ In the tradition of his father, patron of Comenius, Steven de Geer seems to have financed young scholars on visits to Oxford. Nigrinus had drawn £40 on David by 12 October 1676.

$$\frac{28 \ Nov.}{18 \ Dec.} 1676$$

321   G. RICHARDS to JD

BILBAO   27 NOVEMBER 1676

'Estemed Sir, I have now before mee yours of the 13 past, noting the receipt of the account of the bays and that you had past it accordingly, which is well, but you make no mencon of the 500 barrs remitted you by Roch¹ who was some times before the date of yours there arrived. I trust your next will doe it, I am glad you find that profitt by the bays which I calculated, and shall indeavour by the returns to add theretoe. That comodity continues about the same pryse and if it falls in London as I believe it will it may be brought against the spring to advantage. I know iron² is not so good for returns as hard lemmons, unlesse it can be taken in truck to advance the pryse of the comditye given for it when it is worth more in the west of England than in London. Woalls for some goods (as barre tinne from the west country at £3 10s per cwt. abord) may be taken to advantage, also pepper, bays and sempiterns, good and cheap, will buy the best woolls. For wax I referre you to my last advyse, whereby you will be incouraged to send some. What you are concerned with Sir John Lethiellier he hath advysed mee in the same conformity with you and I hope speedily to send you account of the 11 bales of callicoes which may render reasonable well. For wheat I have given you my opinion. Its here worth about 4s per English bushell and under I doe not thinck it will be these 8 months but I am informed its in some partes of England at 2s and 2½s per bushell. The properest sort for this market is the large, white grayne—from Bristoll are propper here tannd hyds, shot and stockings worsted. Tanned hyds at 5 to 5½d per lb. aboard, shott and stockings are there cheap where of my friend and Sir John's, Mr David Dorvile, thence hath sent mee a quantitie. From Ireland tanned hyds of 16 to 18 lb. each at 4 to 5d per lb.; under leather which are cheapest in Corke and Drogeda, salmon from Londonderry, Belfast and Colraine when at £13 to £14 per cwt. Last yeare Sir John lost mony by it; this yeare I believe it will sell for more here, litle arriving as yet; and from Hambourough blew paper Slesias, wax, lattine plates, Sloyers or Slesia lawns fine, (and Russia hyds which are here worth 2¾ R. pta.); from London most manufacturys. In any thing I can serve you I shall esteeme it a happinesse. I am obliged to you for your good opinion and you may beleeve that the Spanish ayr is not of that ill consequence but that you will always find mee with all diligence and punctuallity as I am, your most assured servant, &c.

[P.S.] Sempiternas must be from Colchester:

    3 blacks
    2 blews
    2 scharlets
    1 green
    3 hayre coullour
    1 violets

12 pieces in a bale neatly pressed with a guelt seale to each piece—and 24 yards on the other scale of 48s per piece aboard. Others send mee good waxe.

If you ingage in corne in a vessell freighted out and home let her be for England, Holland or Rouen whither some freight or other may offer.'

¹ Captain Luke Roach, of the *Biscay Merchant*, carrying 500 *pesos* invoiced as 'rusty iron' bars (referred to in [**317**]).

² In this instance Richards really means iron, as opposed to silver 'hard lemmons'.

(i) + (ii) $\dfrac{—\ Dec.\ 1676}{25\ Jun.\ 1677}$

322   SAMUEL LANNOY to JD

CONSTANTINOPLE   (i)   29 MAY 1676

'Honoured Sir, I must acknowledge that by promise I am obliged to trouble you with a letter, but be pleased to be assured the respects I have so justly for you would not have permitted the losse of any longer time to expresse themselves had there been no such like engagement. First, Sir, I begg your acceptance of my harty congratulation of your happy marriage (the which have been advised from England) wishing you all imaginable joy and prosperity. Secondly, beleiving you are become a naturall subject of the King of England (knowing it was your intentions so to be) I hope that all things desired and designed thereby may be effected to your full content, and under the protection of so noble a prince may you see many happy days.

Sir, I call to mind now your most obligeing promise to honour me with your comands if at any time you thought of trading to this place, in answer to which I doe assure you of all faithfullnesse and greatest dilligence to manage your affaires (when comanded) for your most advantage. I must confess the trade of Constantinople, as alsoe all Turky over, is I believe (I may say almost all the world over) is much deficient from its former life and vigour, but the hopes wee have to see our marketts much amended (and with good reason) doth much rejoyce us. This city being the imperiall city and usuall seat of the Emperours did allways, through the presence of the Court, enjoy a briske and lively trade, which since the raigne of this present G[rand] Sig[no]r¹ has much decayed, haveing ever since he was crowned much delighted in pleasures of country and lived continually at Adrianople; but thankes be to God wee are now in expectation to enjoy him here, he having some time lay encampt not farr from hence, comanding all his seraglioes in this city to be new furnished and repaired, which makes us thinke he may continue with us, and it is a thing that all ways hath been observed, that never any city obtained a greater benefitt through the presence of theire prince, and the contrary by his absence, than Constantinople, but more particularly to his owne subjects. Sir, as for goods proper for this markett, are as follows: tin in barrs, leade in piggs, etc; detto white, detto, redd; Brazeile-wood; ordinary Brazeile sugars; ordinary loafe sugar; pepper and ginger, but this last and first at present in very low esteeme. Tinn, once the best comodity England exported, through that vast quantity which hath be sent into all parts of Turky, is become a drugge, but the consumption of it here is so considerable that it cannot long remaine so. The rest of the aforesaid comodity have mett with indifferent good marketts, the price current of which at the foot here of shall advise you. Sir, I have here with presumed to trouble you with directions for sortments of cloths, intreating if you thinke fitt to try this markett to keep as neare to the directions as tis possible, for the trade of this place being cheifly a mony trade and now trusting is forbiden by the Company, customers are forced to come into our warehouses with their baggs in theire hands, so are very nice and curious in theire choice of cloths, but am confident if you keep to any of these sortments need not doubt theire likeing. Sir, my small experience in the affaires of this place as yett will not permitt my giveing you a more ample account, so for what is wanting shall make bold to referr you to my master (Mr Wm Hedges) whose knowledge in the affaires of Constantinople I am confident equalles any man's, and of whome, if you will please to enquire, I doubt not but will assist you to the utmost of his power, having not else at present.

Tin, *LD* 26 in 27 per kintall, which equals English 118 pound-weight.
Lead piggs, *LD* 6 per kintall; detto redd *LD* 8 per kintall; detto white *LD* 11 per kintall.
Ordinary Lisbon sugar, *LD* 18 per kintall.
Ordinary loafe sugar, *LD* 20 per kintall.
Brazeile wood, *LD* 19 in 20 per kintall.
Pepper, *LD* $\frac{2}{3}$ per oke, which equals English 2 lb. 11 ounces.
Ginger, *LD* 1 per 6 okes.'

    [1] Sultan Mehmed IV, deposed 1687.

                                                                    (ii)   13 JUNE 1676
                                                                          (not selected)

                                                                       $\dfrac{13\ Dec.}{[\quad]}1676$

323   SKINNER, BALL & GOSFRIGHT to JD
          LEGHORN   27 NOVEMBER 1676

'Sir, Wee received two lines from you, being only a covert to your letters for Turky (the 14th October) which were only forwarded and now wee have received yours of the 20 October, approoving of our accompt currant except that wee had creditted you $734.19.6 in lieu of $727.12.3 for proceed of the wyer, which wee find to bee as you say, so that wee shall debt you for the errour in a new accompt in $7.7.3. Inclosed you have an exact price courant will enforme you how all commodities governe here,[1] which certainly never were so low, nor our trade worse, lead sould dayly att *D*.18½ p. mille and yet wee cannot compute any gaine made theron though very cheape in England. Tinne *D*.11½, pepper at *D*.10, about which prices its judged these commodities may govern and if pepper doe not fall lower wee judge money is got therby. Such another parcell of wyer as you sent us may also find vent att same price, all woollen manufactory in very low esteeme, the French outdoing us in cheapnesse and if gaine farther footing in Sicilly (and wee wish they are not too soone masters of the whole island) wee shall vent no more of our manufactory in that country. The *Richard & William* and *Freind* for Naples and *Madera Merchant* for Palermo are this weeke departed and none being imported wee have not to enlarge but with due respect remaine, Sir, att your command.'

    [1] Missing.

$$\frac{25\ Dec.}{29\ Dec.}1676$$

24 J. BOOR TO JD
STOCKHOLM   30 OCTOBER 1676

D] Your kind letter of the 17th of August has reached me safely, and also that for Matthias Trip in his absence as he is on a journey to Holland.

I have seen what you report in both the one and the other about what is happening to commodities. I am grateful. It is much to be feared that iron-wares will achieve no great miracles this year. Because of the great numbers of your ships which have sailed from here, with more to follow, I can envisage a serious decline in prices. Since you say that the consignment of iron from Mr Trip is still lying unsold you can correspond with him about it in Holland. May God soon give us better times by a good peace settlement for the commonwealth of Christendom, as I said at length in my last.

The twelve bottles and half-dozen knives have reached me but you have forgotten to add in your letter how much they cost. Meanwhile I thank you once again for your trouble and would be happy to serve you in return.

Herewith goes a copy of my last-written letter, together with a note about the shipments. I hope you received long ago the bills of lading which were sent via Amsterdam from Gothenburg and by other routes. No fleet has been neglected. God grant that the ships may arrive safely! I cannot imagine where my letters have been lost. I sent some from here to Elsinore and I long for your reply.

Much salt has now arrived here with the Dutch ships, so it has fallen from 13 dollars to $11\frac{1}{2}$ and 12 and may well fall lower. Since most of it which was sent on account is now gone it may well improve in the spring. French wine at 150 to 160 dollars per hogshead will also be a good commodity in the spring for whoever comes first to market. Iron prices have been pushed from 25 to 26 dollars per shippound though there is little demand now. Coarse iron is from 20 to 21 dollars.

Herewith I remain, &c.

[Enclosed] A note of iron for the year 1676 so far shipped to London with the following captains:

19 July: with Capt. Joseph Pyle in the ship *Zebulon*, shipped for London:

	Pieces	Shippounds
Gymmo pan iron	2,500	$489.4\frac{1}{2}$
ditto pan iron	636	123.7
Broad schampeleon	985	$202.9\frac{1}{2}$
	4,121	815.1

30 August: with Capt. Henry Sutton in the ship *The Swan*, shipped to London:

	Pieces	Shippounds
Gymmo pan iron	1,423	295.17
Broad schampeleon	630	$129.16\frac{1}{2}$
	2,053	$425.13\frac{1}{2}$

7 September: with Capt. Bartholomew Harley, shipped to London in the ship called
                The Nightingale:

Österby ordinary iron	1,985	300.00
ditto, square	761	100.00
Gymmo pan iron	112	21.12
	2,857	421.12

These copies have been sent several times.

$$\frac{25\ Dec.}{26\ Dec.}1676$$

325   W. SKINNER to JD
          HULL   22 DECEMBER 1676

'Sir, I have yours of the 18th instant. For answer, I have bought 300 piggs of lead in parte of
the parcell I am to buy for the *Providence* at £10 8s per fodder. The rest I shall also buy on the
most moderate tearmes I can, and with the first open waters shall dispatch it away, and then
you may expect invoice of your 100 piggs.

     Your commission for buyinge some Swedish latin wyer I have bene actinge in and find
some quantities here of the marke ')(' and crowne, which is one of those sortes which you
advise for, and all that is in towne is of that marke. Some of it came in a ship that was stranded
and 'tis wett with saltwater, which I presume doth somewhat damage it as I conceive and soe
shalbe cautious of buyinge that. For the other I have bene in treaty for about 200 ringes but
can have noe lower price set then £6 per cwt., which is above your order. The ½ duty payable
to the exporter beinge but 3s 4d if I can get it within your limitt I shall buy and ship it for
Havre, here beinge a vessell now in loadinge thither. But if I cannot buy under £6 per cwt.,
which I feare I shall not, I shall expect then your further order about it. I finde here is about
400 ringes of wyer in all in towne of the marke ')(' and crowne and noe other, and now noe
more can be expected this winter. A vessell yesterday arrived from Stockholme in his
comeinge through the Sound 8 days since understood the Danish army in Schonen had
suffered a great over-throw and lost 5,000 men,[1] the confirmation whereof you'l have in few
dayes. Presentinge my respects, I remaine, Sir, yours at command.'

[1] A reference to the battle of Lund of 3–4 December, notable for its heavy losses of 5,000 Danes and 3,000
Swedes.

$$\frac{4\ Jan.}{16\ Jan.}1677$$

326   I. CRONSTRÖM to JD
          STOCKHOLM   7 SEPTEMBER 1676

[D]   I find myself honoured with several of your letters of various dates, to which this will serve as
      a reply.
          Concerning trade, as I see from your letters that it is completely awful in England, and in
      view of the present situation and the great risks at sea, I have decided to have all my wire, iron
      and steel sold on the market here this year—all the more so as it is selling well at a good price.
      If the Lord God grants us peace and times improve I shall see what more can be done.

Meanwhile I have learned (not from you, but from another) that you have decided to enter into matrimony with Madame Marescoe—from which I wish you much happiness, God's blessing and all prosperity. May you enjoy the fruits of that state.

Here enclosed goes a certificate from the Royal College of Commerce concerning the settlement of the insurance on the previously arrested ships. It is intended to help you obtain something from the insurers, and if this does not suffice you can also obtain a certificate from Hamburg through Mons. Guillelmo de la Bistrate, testifying to the value of the goods he loaded in these ships. He has settled with his insurers there, but it is irritating that one has to deal with such difficult people who will not believe the truth of what one tells them.

Also accompanying this is a copy of the account from which you will see that you have reckoned the duty on me much higher than others have,[1] and as I have no doubt that you will want us to continue dealing with one another I hope you will do so for the same costs as others. Please pay over the balance which is due to me to Mr Uppendorff against a receipt, for which I shall be most grateful. And as Mr Uppendorff has instructions to settle accounts with Mr Burkin about a consignment of blank farthings sent to him in 1674 and needs advice on various matters, especially with regard to what has happened at the Mint about these farthings, please be helpful to him with advice and information, though discreetly, for which I shall be especially grateful and indebted to you. Please give my regards to Madam, your wife. &c.

[1] The enclosed account demonstrated that on 645 cwt. of copper-wire, Leonora Marescoe had charged Cronström for customs, and port charges, £269 15s 8d, while on similar amounts others would charge £217 9s.

$$\frac{15 \text{ Jan.}}{22 \text{ Jan.}} 1677$$

327 FREDERICK & GODSCHALL to JD
SEVILLE   22 DECEMBER 1676

'Worthy Sir, The foregoeing is coppy of our last, which confirm. Since have not received any lines from you the accustomed way you will receave the particulers of your powder sugars[1] by the *Swallow* frigate, Captain Thomas Fowler, that ten days since departed Cadiz with severall merchant shipps under his convoye. God send them all safe home. We have given your account debitt 6,898 *R. pta.*, which finding right may pleas to note it in the same nature. These dead times money cometh in so slowly that it is a shame to trust goods. The best paymasters pay as they pleas, not a piece of goods to bee sould for ready money but to considerable losse, and the markett glutted with all sorts of goods from the north. The countrie canot consume them, and before the dispatch of *galleones* appeareth shall have such a glutt that wee dare not encourage you to send any. Wee wish you a healthfull and prosperous new yeare, as beeing, Sir, your humble servants.'

[1] I.e. 500 silver *pesos* from the Seville and Mexico mints.

$$\frac{19 \text{ Jan.}}{26 \text{ Jan.}} 1677$$

328 D. VAN BAERLE to JD
STOCKHOLM   9 DECEMBER 1676

[D]   Above is a copy of my last letter. Since then I have had nothing from you, although I have heard that several others have had letters from you.

This serves mainly to say that I have the opportunity to make a contract with Willem Momma about getting a quantity of brass manufactured at his works, for 600 slb or more, up to a total of 1,200 slb per annum, which is as much as his works can produce as long as he is running them. The works are managed in the name of his brother-in-law,[1] who is regarded as an honourable man and who holds a privilege from the King that the products manufactured at the works cannot be seized because of Momma's debts but remain at the disposal of the owners. The conditions of the contract are that one must deliver copper at Nyköping and three months later one will receive back the same amount of brass-wire, paying 25 dollars per slb for the cost of manufacture. So far others have had things made on similar conditions and have been successful, so I am thinking about undertaking it too, even though it means negotiating with Jacob Reenstierna on the same basis. It will give both me and my brothers considerable worry to be involved in both works at the same time.

I thought it might be a good idea to suggest to you that you might like to take a half share in the quantity contracted with Momma's brother-in-law for one year or longer, if you thought it advisable. We could then keep it in our hands, for it is a good brand and, according to the present price of copper, the copper-wire should cost us only about 250 dollars, which means we ought to be able to have it free on board for 282 or 283 dollars, which should yield a good pennyworth of profit in view of the advantageous rate of exchange. Please give it careful consideration and if you should decide to take part I will serve you for a reasonable commission and the goods belonging to your share will be loaded just as you order. I have not yet written to my brothers about making this proposal, so you could discuss it with them and convey your decision to me through them, wherewith I remain, &c.

London: 25 dollars per £1 sterling ⎫
Amsterdam: 23 Marks per *RD*   ⎬ at 1 months' sight.
Hamburg: $24\frac{1}{4}$ Marks per *RD*   ⎭

  [1] Jacob Momma had married Elizabeth Koch, sister of Isaac and Abraham Cronström.

$$\frac{20\ Jan.}{26\ Jan.}1677$$

329 J. & H. VAN BAERLE TO JD
AMSTERDAM   26 JANUARY 1677

[D] We have received your letters of the 5th and 9th instant, and with the latter have got back the three duplicate bills of exchange in question. Mr Bar has since corrected the mistake in the endorsement. Your letter to our brother David van Baerle at Stockholm was forwarded at the earliest opportunity, and trust that he will have the opportunity to get 500 rings of 4-band wire made, but there will be no copper-wire of other brands such as 'Three Crowns' for the reasons we told you about.

Since your rate of exchange has fallen to 36s 8–7g it is a very good thing that you do not remit us any more bills, unless it begins to rise again. We are delighted that the ship *Paradise* has at last arrived and that the cargo is unloaded.

Since copper-wire is no longer selling as well as it was and now fetches no more than £6 5s sterling we must simply be patient and hope that things will improve in the spring. We cannot grant your request for unrestricted freedom to sell ours since we cannot agree to have it sold for less than £6 5s sterling. And we have no inclination to accept your proposition to join in chartering ships to go from [England] to St Ubes and from there with a salt cargo to

Stockholm and back again to London at £7 sterling per last. We are so preoccupied with our old Swedish problems that we have no desire to acquire any new ones. We also consider that there will not be much profit in it, believing that quite enough salt will be brought there and that the freights from there to [London] will be very cheap.

We cannot omit to mention to you that our brother David has learned that Francis Townley obtained insurance on the *John & Edward* for a premium of only 4 per cent, while you gave 7 per cent. That is too great a difference, and we would be glad to know how it came about, remaining, &c.

London:	36s 4–5g	} 2 usances.
Paris:	99¼	
Hamburg:	33⅜ stuivers per dollar	} at sight.
Antwerp:	1½ per cent premium on bills	

$\frac{31\ Jan.}{8\ Feb.}$1677

30 W. SKINNER to JD
HULL   29 JANUARY 1677

'Sir, I have yours of the 25th instant with the inclosed packett for Gottenburgh which I intende this day to deliver into Anthony Woodhouse's owne hands and to recommende to him the carefull conveyance thereof. I note your order not to exceede the price allready for Stockholme wyer, at which price I have not bene yet able to buy above 190 ringes and doubt I shall buy noe more. I am seeking shippinge for, but as yet here is noe vessell loadinge for Havre or Rowen. I hope though some may.

Your orders for buyinge in of Northerne manufactures I shalbe willinge to receive and can accomodate you with such as are Leeds affoards as well as other places. My son is at present there resident for buyinge in goods of that nature and you may transmitt your orders to him there, or mee here, as you thinke best, but pray give as much time for their provideinge as you can for at present wee have many buyers of all sortes of woolen manufactures. The prises of dosins drest, ordinary, are 3s to 3s 6d a 8d per yeard; fine dosins 4s to 5s 6d per yeard as in goodness; soe likewise white kersayes differ in price according to their goodness from 26 to 34 a 36s per piece of 22 yeards long. The charges to aboard are common, but to reckon every portion from the country to aboard I have not time at present, the post being on departure. I am, Sir, yours at command, W.S.'

$\frac{5\ Feb.}{8\ Feb.}$1677

331 G. RICHARDS to JD
BILBAO   23 JANUARY 1677

'I have now before mee yours of the 18 past. For answer, my former will have acquanted you of the arrivall of Mr Burton[1] in safety and I have now to add that I have received of him exactly 1,000 *hanegas* of wheat, whereof I have sould about ½ at 48 and 50 *R. vn* per *haneck*, which is about 9s sterling. Had not the freight have been so extravagant there might have been some proffyt, but that will eat out all I feare. I could have freighted a ship hence to France thether and back much cheaper, for your government. I shall dispose of the remaynder the best and soonest I can and send you the account with the returns in dew time a part according to your order. I have serveyed the pryses of the comoditys thence according to Mr Cossart's[2] advyses but cannot discover any thing of incouragement thereby, they are so deare. For wax I have sould Mr Christopher's[3] on good tearms and to there content I hope and at £7 per cwt. aboard, and what its now worth here it might render about 12 per cent and its no quantitie from Edi[nbur]gh[?] can prejudice this market, unlesse a whole cargoe almost from Hamb[urgh] as it usually coms, and I doubt may be here ere you can send any from England after recept hereof. If that from Barbary be good cleare and yellow it may sell well but without care thereto a cheat may be met with. Mr Christopher's was Danzigh which is rather better than English, and I beleeve Sir John will intrest you in what he hath bought. I have receaved your 60 bays and shall be able to putt them off to your content. The arrivall of the *flota* will have litle influence here on the pryse of goods, only in time to supply us with some mony which is at present verry scarce, and I beleeve notwithstanding bays seeme to keep up. They have had such a bad fayre in New Spayne that you will be soone sensible of it in England, it beeing reported the *flota* will not out againe this yeare would make manufacturys decline. I have sould almost all the Long Cloths in company with you and Sir John but there remayne 200 pieces of course sallempoores which assoone I can dispatch you shall have the account and by my next that of the grayne and the rest assoone its possibel to cleere them and returns my best manner in dew time. In the spring I shall be able to comply better in that nature when the friends come to visit us with pieces of eight. About the salle,[4] you shall have notice if I can find any thing thence may promise advantage, and in any thing else I may demonstrate my respects in you will find mee most assuredly, kind Sir, your most faithfull servant.

[P.S.] Sir John it seems had great cause of offence from my brother Jam[e]s his foolish proceeding and resolvs against his readmittance in his service there, although I perceave he inclins to have him here although with a proviso of submision, which he cannot but doe, and I write my brother with such an order by this post, although, upon Sir John['s] excuse I say I dare not undertake to persuade him contrary to his inclination. I never can understand of any unfaithfull action, more than folly, or that he hath been guilty of any defrauding in his accounts, so pray, a day or two after receept hereof, favour mee with your good word in his behalfe and move somewhat of his coming to Bilbao, which I am apt to thinck will take effect. I am yours, G.R.'

[1] Capt. William Burton, of the *Oak* of Whitehaven, coming from Dublin with 516 tons of wheat and 40 hides in which David had a ⅓ share.

[2] I.e. David Cossart, of Dublin, the shipper of the above cargo.

[3] Christopher Lethieullier, Sir John's brother.

[4] *Sic.*—sallempores.

332 C. BENE to JD

HAMBURG

5 Feb. / 9 Feb. 1677

23 JANUARY 1677

[D] My last letter to you was four days ago; since then I have received yours of the 5th, in reply to which I thank you most warmly for your kind wishes for the forthcoming year and pray to God that He will allow them and grant everything that may make for salvation.

As far as I can learn about Swedish wire, there are about 900 to 1,000 coils which have arrived here by way of Lübeck. They are of various brands such as 'the Crown', 'the Rose', 'the Lily', 'the Three Crowns' and also some of the 'Crowned N' mark, but how much of each and what varieties I cannot quite discover, though as far as I can understand they are mostly 4- and 5-band. Few of the Swedish wire-sizes have been awaited here but those which someone has taken sold for 69 *ML* per 100 lb. and one will hardly get them for less. Swedish garcopper is at *RD* 61 per slb, Hamburg wire is at 70 *ML* per 100 lb., copper kettles at *RD* 70 and sheet-copper *RD* 67½ per slb. Barbary copper is not sold for cash here but is usually bartered against sheet-copper and the like, with about *RD* 20 per slb thrown in according to how good it is and how well refined. But if you want to know about the sale and demand for sheet-copper, I think it should not do badly. Please give it careful consideration.

A ship was ready to depart for Bilbao before the winter but has been prevented by the ice. I believe it will have another opportunity to go as soon as the waters re-open. Yellow Danzig wax sells for $24\frac{1}{4} - \frac{1}{2}g$ and seems to be in good demand. If you want some of this commodity please feel free to command me. God knows, I have a thorough knowledge of it and will endeavour to serve you in this or any other commodity to your greatest advantage.

Thomas Whayman is loading up for Rouen and will hurry off as soon as the waters here are clear, which will take at least three weeks although it is thawing quickly. William Cutler is lying here at Dockenhooven[1] on the Elbe and is all right.

Concerning the Swedish wire: if you would like some I think it would be best if you gave the order sooner rather than later as it will soon be bought up.

I am glad you found that you agreed with the account I sent and have made a record of it. I have checked your account of the 10 sacks of cotton and my current account, found them correct and have noted my agreement.

I shall wait to hear by your next letter if you have obtained the little parcel of Barbary almonds within my price limits. As you said, plenty are expected and I doubt whether those who own them will be in a good position. If you cannot obtain them at 37*s* I do not want them, and if you have no success with them you would do well to have obtained a good bale of Ardasse below 9*s*. Let me know for certain in your next. For your news of what is happening in one trade or another I am most grateful and beg you to keep me informed of any pending changes, and also of the departure hither of Barker and Lawson, for my guidance.

Enclosed herewith is the first copy of a bill of exchange for £150 sterling at 2 usances and 8 days, payable by Jacques Crop, assigned here by Samuel Zum Vorbrock. Please procure its acceptance and keep it by you until further order. I intend that B. Sirps shall make good the letter-postage for Debora van der Eckholt. He is expected here so I shall have it put in order then. Meanwhile please put it to one side. With cordial regards, I remain, &c.

London: 34*s* 6*g* 2 usances.
Amsterdam: $33\frac{11}{16}$.

[1] Dockenhuden, then a small village near Pinnenberg on the north bank of the Elbe, between Hamburg and Glückstadt.

$$\boxed{}_{27\ Feb.}1677$$

333 H. BAWDEN to JD
EXETER   3 FEBRUARY 1677

'Kind Sir, Yours of the 30th past I received and in said letter your orders for 200 sergs and I am very sorry that your frind complains of the former goods. I doe ashore you that the wear all very good and cheap in the prises and if your self and frinds had bine hear present could not doe beter or buy cheaper for I know its the very life of trad to have goods weell bought and weell drest which is and shall be my gret car and indever, and all ways I have and I hope ever shall hatt one just gaine.[1] I know that I am all ways in the presens of God who doth knoweth and taks notis of all things. I doe hat to wrong yow or any other person and I question not but that your frinds upon a 2nd veu ar of another mind. The[y] m[a]y much govern them selfs and ther judgment by the wight of the goods and that is noe good way for the fine goods is much in ther good woalls and notting of springs in and well seet together and a cours serg m[a]y be soe hevy as a fine serg and I think you have often heard it as a comon saying that holland is not soe thick as doulis[2] yet much beter. In a word I have and shall with all faithfullnis car and diligent performe my trust which you and others doe or shall comit to me. [—Torn—] land carige would be saved which is much, I doe believe that ther is noe opertunity as yet for to sent them away and it will be for your advantig to forbear buying yet for a fortnights time before the vessall be home which are now in loaden for Roterdam for ther hath bine for 3 weeks past and yet is much buying for said vessells and for Ostend in soe much that thes lower sorts ar rissen 6d and 1s per piece. I shall wayt and take the best opertunities for buying and if yow have ocassion for any goods for Rowen or St Mallos wee have vessalls goe henc pretty often for said plasses. I take leve and remain, Sir, your truly affectionatt frint and servant to comand.

[P.S.] I shall looss noe good opertunity for the buing and effecting your bussinis.'

[1] The obscurity of parts of this seems to demand translation—vizt: 'I do assure you that they were all very good and cheap in the prices, and if yourself and friends had been present [you] could not do better or buy cheaper, for I know it is the very life of trade to have goods well bought and well dressed, which is and shall be my great care and endeavour, and always I have and I hope ever shall hate unjust gain.'
[2] Evidently a reference to the superior quality of 'hollands' linen over French 'Dowlas'.

$$\frac{1\ Mar.}{27\ Apr.}1677$$

334   JEAN VAN DEURS to JD

ELSINORE   17 FEBRUARY 1677

[D]   Your letter of the 26th of January only reached me yesterday. I am delighted that Steven de Geer, whom I have long served, has recommended me to you.

I have noted that Captain John Chapman, sailing the ship *Tomazine* laden with wine from Bordeaux, has already left Bordeaux and also that Captain John Garret of the ship *Concordia*, coming from St Ubes with salt, was ready to depart so that, God willing, they might arrive here soon and that I should accommodate them with money—to which I say that as soon as they arrive I shall not only supply them with the required toll-money as well as the ships' expenses but give them counsel and do as much as possible to assist them. And, if God permits, I shall at once inform you of their arrival and, in accordance with your request, keep separate accounts of what I have to pay for the cargo and for the ships' expenses.

But all English, Scottish or Irish captains who pass the Sound have the liberty (as long as they are in credit) to pay the un-free Sound toll on their return journey from the Baltic, with the condition that the merchant to whom they are recommended here must enter into a pledge to the English Resident that, in the event of the captain not returning (which God forbid), they will immediately pay the Sound toll themselves. But since you say that I should pay it, and make no mention of using this English custom [so that nothing need be given here if the English style is used][1] I shall follow your instructions unless you manage to order me to use the English right or style before the captains arrive to pass the Sound.

An Englishman has to pay here for his ship's expenses:

1.	To the English Resident, Sir Paul Coryate	*RD* 2.1.8
2.	*Viergelt* (in ballast, *RD* 2) a loaded ship, specie	4.1.0
3.	*Schoyss gelt*, to the clerks, current	1.0.0
4.	Sealed paper 4*s*; to the pass-writer 12*s*,	0.2.0
5.	The seal-presser, or stamp-presser,	0.1.8
6.	For the poor,	0.1.8
		8.8.0 [*sic*.]

A Dutchman, or whoever he may be, pays altogether as above, with the exception of the payment to the English Resident. And if any captain arriving at the toll-post to pay for his licence has no specie rixdollars he has to pay a premium on Danish crowns or cross-rixdollars of 3*s* per rixdollar. Before, he used to pay 4*s* but I have never had to charge my friends' accounts with more than 4*s*—that is, 2*s* per rixdollar. If it should happen that a large fleet of ships all arrive together and bank-money is in demand, then it could cost $2\frac{1}{2}s$ per rixdollar, though that happens rarely. However, the exchange rate at Copenhagen and here usually differs by 1, or $1\frac{1}{2}$ or 2 per cent, because there are few 'givers' here but mostly 'takers', and as soon as the captains arrive the money must be immediately ready, and that causes the difference. Thus one always has to dance to the toll-officers' pipe, as they well know, and the captains dare not blink an eye or they will be held up. However, come what may, I shall make your payments and you may be assured that none of your ships, on safe arrival, will be neglected for one quarter hour but everything required of me will be done properly. I hope to conduct myself in such a way that I shall earn your desire not merely to continue using me here but to recommend me to others of your friends.

If you also desire me to send you every post-day, or every 8 or 14 days, a notice of the out-going or in-coming ships, of whatever nationality they may be, and where they may be going as well as what their cargo consists of, I shall gladly do it. As soon as I know your mind I will agree with one of the Sound-toll officials about how much I should give him for the notification of what I request; and since the toll-officials are not allowed to do it, except in secret, it would be well if it were kept quiet—for your information.

God be praised! We have had open waters here for the last eight or ten days, and five days ago a Bremen ship, which lay at Copenhagen all winter, came out of the Baltic and passed the Sound on its way to Bremen. And now, four days ago, two Copenhagen ships which trade to Spain arrived in the road-stead. They are Jacob Maertens Cloodt of the ship *Charlotte Amalie*, mounting 28 guns, as well as Pieter de Verver of Copenhagen, sailing the ship *Christiaen Quintus* with 30 guns, both destined for St Ubes and from there to Lisbon.† As soon as the wind is favourable they are thinking of setting off, in God's name. This for your information, &c.

† In my opinion, first to Lisbon, then to St Ubes.

[1] Marginal addition.

$\dfrac{\textit{1 Mar.}}{\textit{9 Mar.}}$ 1677

335 A. BERENBERG'S WIDOW & HEIRS TO JD

HAMBURG   23 FEBRUARY 1677

[D] For lack of anything to say we have not written to you for a long time, but we find ourselves
with two of your welcome letters of the 5th and 16th past from which we see that you spoke
to Adam Groenen about the pack which was left lying at the water-side and that he has had it
fetched away so that it can be sent to our brother-in-law Jean Meinss by a well-known
captain as soon as the waters open. We shall look forward to that, thanking you meanwhile
for all the trouble you have taken and also for the information about that well-known person,
and furthermore for all the news and advice about prices and various wares.

At the moment we can find nothing profitable to do because of a lack of sales and because
the rate of exchange remains obstinately high. If it had fallen to about 33s we would have
remitted something for our account so that when it came up for payment we could consider
how best to employ it, but because the exchange has been for some time at 34s 9–10g, and
today is still at 34s 7g at double usance, we have not found it advisable to remit at such a high
price, all the more so as we do not know how to use the money. You advised us to dispose of
our Barbados commodities since their ships are expected by May with an abundance of
goods. We have partly done so, and have sold the sugar, which we had been keeping for so
long, at 6g per lb. Yet it seems we were not wise to do so for it looks as if sugar is going to rise
since it is beginning to be scarce here and in Holland. The stocks in Portugal are also not large,
and those of black ginger have also been bought up. Ten or twelve sacks at a time could
hardly be had for $4\frac{1}{2}g$ but are now selling for $4\frac{3}{4}g$, and how it will develop only time will tell.
Campeachy wood remains at $7\frac{3}{4}$ ML per 100 lb.; indigo guatemalo at $6\frac{3}{4}$–7s flem.; fine
caribbean indigo is at 5s flem., and Aleppo galls are at 40 to 41 ML per 100 lb.; pepper is
selling in batches of 10 to 20 sacks at $11\frac{3}{4}g$ per lb., and in batches of 3 to 4 sacks is not to be had
for less than 12g. It is a low price. We have a reasonable amount of it by us as we have been
buying it at one time or another while the price got lower and lower in order to offset the
higher-priced stuff, but it has all been at a loss and we dare not order any more. Fine dry wax
sells here at $23\frac{1}{2}g$ flem. and fine Turkish Angora yarn is sold by the English here at $7\frac{1}{2}s$ flem.
Currants are at 19 to 20 ML per 100 lb. and oil is rather more keenly priced as it is all in strong
hands. Seville and Portuguese oil sells at RD 60 to 62 while Apulian oil is at RD 65 per 820 lb.
Grains are very dull and choice rye can be had for RD 52 per last. A quantity is expected from
Hull and other places, and it is likely to fall to RD 50, if not below, for there seems to be big
supplies. 400 lasts are expected from Magdeburg in three or four days, so some people are
going to lose a lot of money. Buying up almonds is not going to make any great profit.
Ardasse at 9s per lb. of 24 ounces is not too dear. When the exchange was not so adverse we
still had one bale of it lying unsold which you had supplied us with some time ago, but
because it was so coarse people would not have it, which is very annoying. The price here is at
13 to $13\frac{1}{4}s$ flem. with $10\frac{2}{3}$ per cent discount, which is very low.

Because of this burdensome war, trade is falling away in Germany and everywhere else,
and at the moment we see little prospect of a peace. The river is now open again, however,
and we see that one or two ships from France have arrived off the city, so we must hope that
this will put some life into trade. Please let us know if there is any change at [London] in the
prices of sugars, pepper, ginger, indigo, galls, Ardasse and the like, for which we shall be most

grateful. If we perceive anything profitable and if the exchange begins to be more moderate we shall not neglect to give you some commissions, wherewith our friendliest regards, &c.

London: 34s 7g   2 usances.
Amsterdam: $33\frac{1}{2} - \frac{7}{16}$.

$$\frac{20\ Mar.}{23\ Mar.}1677$$

36 S. DE GEER to JD
AMSTERDAM   26 MARCH 1677

D] I find I have your welcome letter of the 9th instant. With regard to iron I am also of the opinion that its price will remain steady in Sweden, partly because many works have had to remain at a standstill through lack of water and have made only a half of what they are accustomed to produce; and partly because so many English ships have been chartered to go to St Ubes that there will be a shortage of return ladings.

I have contracted for about 1,500 slb of 'O' iron, which I shall keep to myself, so you cannot expect any to come this summer unless I have about 400–500 slb of the 1,500, which is lying ready, despatched in the chartered salt ships. The rest will come straight here, and if your iron prices improve somewhat I can have some 'G' iron shipped to you, which the wholesalers are also familiar with. So, of the two brands, none will get into other hands than yours, and it will take some time this summer before you are able to sell what you have.

Now, as regards the Ⓛ iron which, as I mentioned previously, had not yet been contracted for—I shall not be doing so this time because that brand is not so very well-known [in England] and because the raw material is not available. It used to be made from one ore, but as the old mine is now finished and the new one is not so good at first, it may well be a year before the ore begins to be as good as it was. There is no more of the old ore near the Ⓛ works. There is some round about the 'O' works which is being mixed with the new ore, and at the 'G' works there is mostly old ore, so that is now turning out best—voila! on nous enformes pour vos gouverno.

Everyone says that the number of ships going to Stockholm is 18 or 20, and I am sure that many will not find it worthwhile, particularly if they all arrive at Stockholm together and have to leave together. We must first see how things go in the spring. Apart from two or three ships which are now about to arrive from St Ubes, there are so many others that it may well be September or October before the Dutch ships will be able to arrive, for in April they first have to go to St Ubes, and I calculate the number going either to the Baltic or here is at least 50 vessels, which will result in very slow loading.

If Mr Scheurman comes here I shall be able to learn from him how it will affect the freedom of the ships if they bring wine as well as other goods which are expected every hour. But of your ships I shall make no mention.

Je vous remercie pour vos nouvelles. It will be an extraordinary summer if it continues as it has begun with Valenciennes[1]—such a strong and substantial city taken at the first assault, so unexpectedly for besiegers and besieged! And now it is the turn of Cambrai. Who knows what may follow, for this year of '77 may bring forth some strange things. I remain, &c.

---

[1] Valenciennes had been taken by the French in a surprise assault on 17 March.

$(i) + (ii) \quad \dfrac{2 \ Apr.}{25 \ Jun.} 1677$

337   T. LANNOY to JD

     ALEPPO   (i)   11 DECEMBER 1676

'Sir, I have already writt you in Company,[1] to which humbly refer you. This is in answer to yours of the 11th September by which take notice of what letters you had received of mine and am very sorry our not sending the returnes should occasion your anguer. If possible could have bin don I would not have omitted the conveyance, but the Company is soe strict that all factors are sworne to give a true entry of what goods they send and for whose account to the best of their knowledge, but when my father incurradged you to send us the money the pennalty was only to pay a double imposs[iss]ion at home which was very inconcederable. Sir, I am very cencable their wants not those that coarts you for your imployment and offers you considerable advantages to procure it for their sonn or friend abroad, but I hope as I have had the honour of your comands already you will not make a change tell you have cause. I will asshure you I have not bin wanting to serve you to the utmost of my power and if I had as much money in friends hands in England should order the ballance of your account to be paid you by this convayance, but I presume a few months more or lesse will be no prejudeice to you, and by the Generall ships shall send Sir John Lethieullier a far greater some for my owne account then yours amounts to, with order to give you full content, and if you take your freedome of the Company and that we have your imployment I promise your concernes shall be mannaged to the utmost of my power and on the same termes as our other friends. Concerning what you proposed in your letter to consigne your goods to a friend of mine and afterwards to be delivered you by a letter of further date is not possible to be don, for I knowing for whose account the goods are for, my entry which I give in to the Company treasurer must be false, which is contrary to oath and soo hope you will excuse me.

    Gauls are plentifull but deare this yeare, being no other goods in towne, soe that every one runns upon them. The price of those we have already bought cost LD $33\frac{1}{4}$ per quintall which are as cheepe as any that hath bin bought this yeare for that sort. We expect in 10 daies a carravan with Borma Legee in which shall lay out what remaines of yours, but if galls come in before shall buy them if to be gott with reason, which is all I know worth your notice at present. I remaine, &c.'

    [1] I.e. with John Burkin, his partner, on 5 December 1676.

(ii)   5 JANUARY 1677

338   'Ever honoured Sir, The other side copy of my last which sent via Constantinople. These are by the returne of our Generall ships with order to be sent you overland from Legorne and serves cheifely to acquaint you that I have sent Sir John Lethieullier by the *Scipio* and *Thomas & William* 75 sacks of gauls, 20 bales of goats' wool and 3 bales of silke, out of the proceed of which have desired to pay the ballance of your account, being LD 3,686 67 aspers, as you will see by the inclosed account currant. I have left it to yourselfe and Sir John to vallue the Lyon dollers as you judge it may be worth here, but if you have taken your freedome of the Company and desire the same some to be sent you in gauls or any thing else shall be duly complyed with, without our chargeing you with provission; or if you judge it more for your advantadge to sell your Lyon dollers to be paid in Aleppo your bills shall by duly paid. We had formerly oppertunity to put money out at interest at one per cent per month, but for neere two years past hath bin no interest money to be gott, trading not giveing incurradgement to take any up, though severall of our factory would let it out at $\frac{1}{2}$ per cent, which I have thought it convenient to advize you, that you might not thinke we have kept your money to take the interest our selves, which if we had made any should have bin made you good and I have hopes you will look upon what have acted in your concernes hath bin intended for the best and the cambio your pieces of eight found is better then if we had let your pieces of eight goe back by the ship, which is all shall give you trouble at present. I remaine, Sir, your most obliged and faithfull servant, T.L.'

$$\frac{3\ Apr.}{4\ Apr.}1677$$

39 D. VAN BAERLE to JD
STOCKHOLM   24 FEBRUARY 1677

D] My last letter was on the 9th of December last year. Since then I have received your welcome letters of the 9th of September and 23rd of November, from which I see that several of your letters are missing. Likewise Mr Green has had no letters from you so far and has no idea what has happened regarding the goods in John Stabler and their insurance, nor what has happened about those loaded in William Evelyn since you mentioned little about them in your latest letters. I hope that Evelyn has since arrived and that the goods have found a good market, so that I can be encouraged to continue trading to England in future.

So far I have got little in stock, because my debtors have not kept their word. The reason is that, with the present demand for copper-wire, they have obtained from others better conditions than those they agreed to with me, as a result of which the proposal to have it manufactured by Willem Momma cannot go ahead since it has been necessary to take the said Momma to court. In addition, copper has risen to 228 and 238 dollars per slb. Undoubtedly this will continue as little has been worked. At Norrköping production has only just begun and at Nyköping only seven forges are working. But the Cronström and Rosenström works are being driven hard, though most of it is being made by Cronström who has contracted with Van Cöllen & Uppendorff. And because copper is at a high price abroad the copper-wire made at Hamburg can hardly be sold for any trifling price.

Because of the continual frost and lack of water that we had in the new year most iron-works have been at a standstill, so little iron will be produced this spring and iron of ordinary quality is selling here at 27 to 28 dollars per slb. Setubal salt remains at a low price of $11\frac{1}{2}$ to 12 dollars per last, but as less came in the new year than had been expected its price may get better, wherewith I remain, &c.

$$\frac{3\ Apr.}{4\ Apr.}1677$$

40 THOMAS PERMAN to JD
STOCKHOLM   12 MARCH 1677

G] My last letter to you was on the 27th of November, to which I refer. Since then I have been away from home, up-country. I have also been with Jacob Fahlgreen at the Kopperberg and have tried to be as helpful to him as possible. Mr Fahlgreen is still at the Kopperberg, putting his affairs in order, but I hope that within a fortnight he will be here again. I will forward your letter to him by today's post, without fail, and here inclosed is the letter which Mr Fahlgreen has written to you. As soon as Mr Fahlgreen returns here he will take the first opportunity of returning to London.

Since my last letter I have safely received from London your welcome letters of November 10th and 23rd, December 29th and January 16th, to which this will serve as a reply. I see that trade in iron has been going badly. Iron prices here are high at 28 to 29 dollars. During the winter I bought about 3,000 slb of 3-inch iron and 1-inch square iron which I am expecting here from the works as soon as the rivers are open. May God bring them safely. I shall sell it all here. But I have also bought 300 slb of garcopper during the winter which I am having made mostly into wire, but—God willing—I shall send you a quantity and I shall send it in your name. But the English Resident here has to give the captains a note or certificate that the ship and the goods are English and that the merchant is truly English, so everyone must declare on demand that the goods in the ship are strictly English. If you could write to the Resident to give me a certificate that the goods I have loaded are for your account, as is everything I have loaded, then the Resident is likely to help me. As you are getting 2 per cent you could well declare them to be your own and answer for them. Besides, I shall also be ordering all kinds of English merchandise, such as all sorts of cloth serges and bays, and as soon as I know that you have got me free to leave Stockholm waters I shall be wanting something from you. However, I intend to pay freight and duties here myself at the rate of 12 per cent though, as you know, I could put it under our Swedish names if I have to make use of other friends. I await your answer to this.

I see that Capt. Nicolas Payton has arrived safely at Harwich, God be praised! I hope he will soon reach London and deliver the 350 coils of brass-wire which he has for you. I trust you will do your best for me. I am in no great hurry for the money and only want you to seek the highest possible price. I also expect at the earliest opportunity an account of the 1,280 coils whose proceeds, I see, amount to £1,666. I had expected £100 more. I hope that the RD 6,751 23s Dutch current-money has been remitted to our friends in Amsterdam, although I dearly wish it had been remitted net, as I ordered, for I have ascribed it to our friend that way in my books. This is all by way of reply; may God bless you, &c.

[P.S.] The letters I have just received will be immediately forwarded, each to its appropriate place.

[*Verso*. Notes by Jacob David.]

Yardbroad

	Kersies 30 to 38s all Colours.
	half Yorks. kersies ¾-yard 16 to 2[0]s.
Double	Northern Dozens, 3 to 5s 6d.
36 yards	Serges, 35 to 40s.
	Fyne laekens 6½ tot 12s the yard.
	Narrow Manchester bayes witte 35s to 40 a piece 44 yards.
	Dying & dressing about 12s a piece.
	Penistones ¾-yard-broad van 40 tot 50s, 43 a 44 yards.
	Dying & dressing 12s a piece.

$\frac{9\ Apr.}{4\ Sep.}$ 1677

341   A. L. KELLERMAN to JD

AMSTERDAM   9 APRIL 1677

[D]   I find I have several of your letters (of which the latest is of the 16th of March) with which you have been pleased to honour me and to communicate what is happening with regard to trade in [England]. I must admit that I have been somewhat negligent about answering them in good time, but I would have been prompter if I had been fortunate enough to find any advantage which we could extract from our correspondence. However, the scarcity of opportunities and the fact that prices are falling nearly every day and also that those in [England] are closely related to those here means that one can hardly earn any profit. Even if one imports something carefully, without extra-ordinary costs, one can easily suffer loss if the least thing happens. So I have been unable to make any ventures in getting anything bought in [England] and trade with Sweden is at present so depressed that our friends cannot export anything, and there is nothing specially worth doing in that area because the high freights which one must pay to English skippers eats up the profit, and as a result commissions from those regions are declining greatly.

However I am extremely grateful to you for your good advice and your willingness to be of service, to which you will always find me equally willing to perform anything you may care to command.

In the last eight days grains have risen at least 20 to 25 per cent because of strong demand from Brabant. Such large amounts are no longer coming from England, and if the imports from [England] should cease there is likely to be a major rise, but most people are of the opinion that the high market price will bring plenty from [England]. The exchange on Hamburg has fallen to $33\frac{3}{16}$ but this increase in grain prices will raise it again.

The East India Company has sold its Molucca wares and they have all been very dear— cloves at 74 to 76 stuivers [per lb.], nutmegs 44 to 50 stuivers [per lb.] mace 16s to 18s [per lb.] and cinnamon according to its quality between 54, 64 and 74 stuivers per lb.

With heartiest regards, &c.

London:	36s 2–3g.
Paris:	99g.
Antwerp:	$1\frac{1}{4}$ per cent.
Hamburg:	$33\frac{3}{16}$ to $\frac{1}{8}$.
Danzig:	$238\frac{1}{2}$ groschen [per £ flem.].

$\frac{15\ Apr.}{7\ May}$1677

42   NICOLAS SIMONS to JD

LISBON   29 MARCH 1677

[   ]] I received your letter of the 29th of February from Captain Jan Garret of the ship *Concordia* when he arrived at Setubal (God be praised) together with six others from [England] four or five days ago. The order to let him have a suitable cargo of Setubal salt was also received and will be performed according to instructions. As regards the good measure and quality of the salt, together with the promptness of its despatch, you may rest assured that no one will be more advantageously dealt with, but the fourteen days allowed for loading are too short for any satisfactory despatch, for it must necessarily take a month, and even if one could get it clear in less than a month one would have to wait for his accompanying ships, which will need to have at least four or five weeks. Please bear in mind in future that it is no use limiting the captain to twelve or fourteen days, more or less, if it states in the charter-party that he is to leave in company with others. Furthermore, I am quite sure that I can give better despatch and as much speed as anyone if he is loaded in a more leisurely way, which also permits one further advantage in the measurement of the salt.

The price of the salt and the accompanying costs are always agreed at Setubal and there has been no change in them for the last fourteen or fifteen years. However, during times when there are 50 or 60 ships together loading, they sometimes have to remain lying there for eight or ten weeks; and it sometimes happens that when the opportunity arises to join suitable, good company which would allow some of the ships to depart, or they decide to join a foreign convoy, they will spend £50 or £60 for the benefit of speedy despatch. But the same haste often occasions great prejudice in the measure and quality of the salt. Otherwise, as I said above, the charges and the price of the salt are always agreed. Here at Lisbon the price follows the market, though it is usually cheaper than at Setubal where the measure and quality of the salt is more advantageous and better than that here—for your advice.

I had news from Mons. Steven de Geer at least three or four weeks ago that you had chartered the above-mentioned ship, and probably yet more. On their arrival your orders will be punctually followed, but there seldom occurs any opportunity to draw bills on [London] which has to be done on Amsterdam where the rate of exchange is also more favourable. At present it is at 62 to $62\frac{1}{2}g$ [flem. per cruzado]. Whether the total costs of the above-mentioned ship are drawn on De Geer (as he instructed) though by way of [London] or Amsterdam, it will always be by the most favourable rate, the success of which you will learn in due course.

Since Swedish shipping has been prevented from coming here by this dreadful war there is a great shortage here of all Swedish wares. Iron could at present fetch between 3,000 and 3,200 *reis* per quintal of 128 lb. A Swedish shippound counts for about 294 lb. here, and on each quintal falls about 450 *reis* duty and charges. Deals, according to size and quality, are 30 to 40 to 45 crowns[1] per 122 pieces; beams are likewise (according to quality) 500 to 1,500 and 2,000 *reis* per piece. Masts of 15 to 24 palms are, one with another, 70,000 *reis* per piece. Tar, 3,000 *reis* per tun—free on duty and charges since the purchaser usually pays these. Only with iron is it customary for the owner to pay the duty and expenses—for your guidance.

I take the liberty of troubling you further with a bill of exchange for £88 12s sterling at 8 days sight drawn on Johan Crogher, value of myself though stated *pro forma* from Pieter Meyer, arising from an assignment which the said Crogher received from Sam. Sowton drawn on one, Thomas Thussen, iron dealer in [London] in payment of a bill of exchange passed for my account on the said Sowton. Now a year and a day has passed during which the said Crogher has kept me waiting, notwithstanding that I have written to him several times and exhorted him through a friend in Amsterdam but he never answered a single letter, only writing occasionally a note to the friend in Amsterdam and putting him off with fair promises. At last he wrote to my friend on the 12th/22nd of December last year, informing him that he had received the proceeds of the assignment from Thussen and that he would remit the total to me through his brother, Captain William Crogher, at a rate of exchange of 6s 7–8d per *mil reis*, together with other small details, for which I have been waiting. Now his brother has arrived at Setubal with these latest ships from [England], but with no letter, no news, much less any remittance from Crogher, which is very un-mannerly. I beg you to obtain friendly satisfaction for the aforesaid bill of exchange and after deducting something for commission and similar small expenses remit the remainder to me here so that I can at least get something. The enclosed letter to him is going open, which you may close at pleasure, forgiving me for troubling you with such small matters. I remain, always ready and willing to serve you in anything you may be pleased to command as De Geer is so close a friend, yours &c.

[P.S.] Mr. Steven de Geer has also ordered me to load three boxes of china apples, marked 'I.D.', which are loaded with the other three you ordered.

---

[1] 1 silver crown or *cruzado* = 400 reis. 1,000 *reis* = 1 *mil reis*.

$$\frac{17\ Apr.}{[17\ Apr.]}1677$$

43 F. BOSTELMAN to JD

HAMBURG   10 APRIL 1677

D] I have received your letter of the 3rd instant, from which I see that you have bought 40 hogsheads of vitriol at 9*s* 3*d*, with 1 per cent discount for prompt payment, and are sending them here with Capt. Richard Scrutton. May the Lord bring them in safety! I had hoped that it would be different since you wrote to me that there would be 2 per cent deducted for prompt payment, and now only 1 per cent has been allowed. Since it has now been done I shall have to put up with it. Even with the exchange rate running so high I would have remitted you the money had I know that you were completing the purchase. Patience!

Meanwhile, I would be glad to learn for how much the Rohe-glatzer linen sells for in [England] which is sold here in lengths of 72 ells. I notice that a great deal of it, as well as other kinds of linen, is sent to England by others. Only I understand that large duties are paid on what belongs to foreigners, which English nationals do not pay themselves but are exempted from. I should be glad to know if anything could be done with it, and whether one could hope for some profit by it. If you were favourably inclined to enter them as your own goods and stand surety for their sale let me know what commission you would want.

For the report on what the Smyrna and Scanderoon ships have brought I am most heartily grateful. I await to hear about their quality and price. Wherewith, my regards, &c.

$$\frac{18\ Apr.}{23\ Apr.}1677$$

44 B. BEUZELIN & SON to JD

ROUEN   24 APRIL 1677

'En responce de la vostre du 5/15 de ce mois nous vous dirons estre bien aize que vous soyes satisfait de la vanthe des 500 thorches fil de latton que nous avons faitte. Le rettardemant des aultres 500 per Hakar[1] vous sera prejudiciable parce qu'il en est arrivé par 2 navires d'Hambourg qui ont heu ung bref passage pres de 2,500 thorches, dans ce nombre bien 1,500 pour les Legendre et Vroulingh, ce qui a fait non seullement calmer la vanthe mais aussy baissé le prix, s'en estant desja donné a £92*t*, ce qui nous fasche pour l'esperance que nous avions de nous pouvoir deffaire de votre partie au mesme prix que nous avions optenu de l'aultre. A prezent il n'y a pas de remede estimant que le plus seur sera de suivre le course, car il fault notter que quand il n'en viendroit de Suede de plus de 2 mois ce qu'il y'en a prezantemant icy suffiroit pour la consommation, mais avecq cella c'est qu'il s'en attend encore bon partie de Hambourgh ou ces haultes prix a fait resveiller le travail des ouvrages et sur ce que cette marchandise a haussé chez vous et baissé icy. Il est a croire qu'il vous en sera beaucoup envoyé, de sorte que nostre santiment seroit de vandre pour n'estre prevenu d'un plus grand raval que l'on verra apparamment; pour ce qui vous touche de deca nous y ferons comme pour nous et du succes aurez advis. Nous acquitterons vos traittes et en attendrons le rembours sur le provenu de vostre fil de latton, car en effect nous considerons bien que les retraitte vous seroyent dezadvantageuze. Nous vous remercions de la cargue de ses 4 navires qui s'attendent de Turquie; sy les galles d'Allep a les pinne qui sont les plus estimees ne se donnent a 52*s* [sterling] ou 53*s* il n'y a du tout rien a faire, ny au cours des aultre marchandizes que vous nous costez et ce qui fait nostre estonnanant est non obstant cella il ne laisse pas d'y avoir nombre de personnes qui en font venir. On nous mande de Marseille du 13 de ce mois que l'on avoit advis par ung navire arrivé de Sayde[2] que les saulterelles avoyent fait ung grand desgast en ce pays-la et broullé touttes les plantes de cottons jusques a la racinnes, ce qui apparament les feroit monter de prix, ce qui pourroit bien estre sy le mal estoit universal, mais c'est ce que l'on ne dit pas, et pour s'engager a l'achapt il faudroit encore avoir des advis plus certaines.

Les sucres baissent icy continuellement par la grand nombre qui en vient des Isles. C'est ung negoce qui donne a prezant plus de perte que de proffit. Les huilles de Gennes les meilleures se maintennant a £37t a £38t; celles de Maillorq et Seville a £32t a £33t. Voilla les seulles marchandizes qui ayant donné du benefice cette annee a ceux qui en ont receu. Nos changes sont comme vous voyez cy bas, et nous sommes tousjours, Monsieur, vos tres humbles serviteurs.'

Amsterdam: $101\frac{1}{4}$
Londres: $55\frac{3}{8}$ } 2 usances.
Anvers: 100

[1] John Hacker, captain of the *Rouen Factor*. His bill of lading is dated 10 February (O.S.) but his arrival was delayed by bad weather until mid-April (N.S.).
[2] I.e. Seyde (Sidon).

$\frac{5\ May}{25\ May}$1677

345   C. DE HERTOGH'S WIDOW & HEIRS to JD

HAMBURG   27 APRIL 1677

[D]   Our last letter was on the 20th instant, with the bill of lading for 900 *pesos* laden at Cadiz in the ship *The Swan*, captain Richard Carter, of whose safe arrival we long to hear. Meanwhile, having heard nothing from you, this will serve only to advise that the English captains sailing from here to Spain are glad to have English names put into the bills of lading to safeguard them from the capers. So this is to request that you will please allow us to use your name for the few things which we may lade or return in English ships. We are not asking you to be bound under oath to reclaim the goods as your own but only to do a kindness in case it should happen that one or other of the ships is held up by the French and you are written to about it by the caper, when you simply have to affirm that they are yours. In this confidence we shall always keep you informed of what has been laden, as we do herewith. Please note that Cornelius de Hertogh's Widow & Heirs have laden for Bilbao in the ship *The Eagle*, captain Thomas Haselwood, 11 tuns of yellow wax, Nos. 68 to 78, ⊕ consigned to SS. Jean Battista de Bacquer & Estevan de Lane; for Cadiz, in the ship *Margarita*, captain Joseph Keble, 1 chest with 160 *schock*[1] of Friestad linen, No. 2, ⊕ consigned to SS. Balthazar Coymans & Pedro van Belle by Johan Battista de Hertogh the younger; for Cadiz in the ship *Margarita*, captain Joseph Keble, 1 case (No. 1) with $154\frac{1}{2}$ *schock* of Friestad, 1 pack (No. 2) with two cases of Jaurisch linen, 1 case (No. 3) with 132 *schock* of Friestad, BR, consigned to SS. Hendrick & Jacobus Rolle; another pack (No. 33) with 20 rolls of leather, and 1 pack (No. 34) with unbleached linen, ⋈ consigned to S. Juan T'Hermollen; another pack with unbleached linen (No. 43) ⊕ consigned to S. Pedro de Licht.

The captains are downstairs now and hope to be going to sea with this favourable wind— may God Almighty preserve them from all evil encounters so that these precautions prove unnecessary. Meanwhile we promise ourselves this kindness from you and if we have the opportunity we shall not fail to reward you with some acceptable service. With regards, &c.

[1] The *schock* = 60 pieces.

$$\frac{12\ May}{18\ May}1677$$

46   H. CLETCHER to JD
AXBERGSHAMER   5 APRIL 1677

D]   Your letters of the 26th of September, 25th of January and 9th of February have just been
received all together. As for that of the 26th of September, there is nothing which needs to be
said except that Mr Boor has given me the answer that he remitted the 1,755 d[ollars] 16 [öre]
to Rouen more than three months ago and has also had news that it was accepted, so there is
nothing to be done about that bill of exchange though it will be retained until further order
because letters are going so unreliably now. It is strange that until now you have received
nothing from either of the bills of exchange which I remitted to you on the 18th of October,
namely £140 and £100 on William Benson, whereof I sent the first and the second copies.
When I come to Stockholm I shall send the third copy if I receive no further news from you
meanwhile.
   So far I have been able to learn nothing from your agent. My servant writes me that he has
travelled to Fahlund[1] so I wrote to learn what his intentions were. I have now written to him
again that he should find out through Thomas Perman and Oloff Hansson if he wants to load
any wire for your account in the *Thomazine* so that there is room for it. Regarding these
persons, I know nothing other than that they are good, especially Oloff Hansson whom I
know to handle good and great affairs with promptness. The other I do not know so well,
though I do not doubt his reliability. I shall keep a wakeful eye open to watch your interests,
notwithstanding that these folk are adequate enough.
   Regarding the ship with wine, as soon as it arrives I shall do my best to take care of it and
follow all your orders and communicate with your agent. I had thought that one would be
able to get this cargo in as Swedish, duty-free, but I have now received news that this cannot
be, because this year no goods or ships will enjoy Swedish duty-freedom. If this should be the
case for the ships bringing salt it will fall very heavily on the goods coming in and going out
on the *Thomazine*, as it makes a difference of one-third in the duty. I now hope that a further
order will come as a decision about it has been deferred by the King. It is to be feared that the
ship will arrive at just the moment when there will be an embargo on all shipping since it
appears that our war-fleet will be in the Daalders[2] at about that time. If such is the case, and if
one cannot enjoy the full freedom from duties, I do not think it will be advisable to load this
ship for your account, because even if the first eventuality does not occur it will be burdened
with the high duty, and it would be better if your returns were loaded in the salt-ship as long
as the increase in the toll is in prospect. However, I shall always act for your greatest
advantage as circumstances offer and as soon as the *Concordia* has arrived I shall take good care
that it is fully laden by others. Mr Boor will also have a consignment to load. I shall do my
best to sell the wine for cash as far as possible, but so far as I can learn from others these goods
are not often sold wholesale for cash. Now that the returns need not be held up I shall be able
to go to Stockholm immediately at the end of the month, so your agent can meanwhile
prepare everything. Wherewith regards, &c.

   [1] Falun, the major copper-mining centre, 240 km north-west of Stockholm.
   [2] Dalarö, at the entrance to the Stockholm sea-ways.

$$\frac{12\ May}{18\ May}1677$$

347   P. BOTTE to JD
STOCKHOLM   13 APRIL 1677

[D]   Whereas I have contracted with the Directors of the re-formed Tar Company here about the consignment of pitch and tar to England, Scotland and Ireland during the current year, 1677, and the coming year, 1678 (as Mr Samuel Sowton formerly did) I am favourably inclined to enter into an agreement with you for the performance of this commission, and as soon as I arrive safely in Amsterdam where, God willing, I shall remove myself in a fortnight's or three weeks' time, I shall correspond more fully with you. Meanwhile it is my friendly request that you would please inquire what stocks of pitch and tar are lying throughout the kingdom and in what ways you consider the business can best be managed, and also at what price they now are—all which you will please convey to my brother-in-law, Claes Wilckens, for which I shall be obliged. Also give him order concerning the loading of the ships. And for the rest I beg you, if anyone should come and ask you if you are getting these commodities on commission or for your own account, do not reveal to anyone the real circumstances, on which I rely, remaining, &c.

[P.S.] Please forward the enclosed to Danzig by way of Amsterdam for me.

$$\frac{21\ May}{[\text{——}]}1677$$

348   I. TILLARD to JD
PLYMOUTH   18 MAY 1677

'Sir, Yours of the 15th current I have received. The iron still remains by me.[1] To gratefie the desier of you and Sir John Lethieullier I have by his consent taken it to my account at £13 [per] tune and sent the account of sale the other post and presume Sir John hath given you coppie thereof; if not, upon the notice shalbee sent you from hence. The proceeds shalbee invested in tyne and the part consigned to yourselfe according to order. The Sweds tarr and pitch is in best esteeme. If you have a minde to send any heather lett not exceed 200 barrells, if lesse the better. For present sale the large band tarr is the best. If you intend a vessell direct may order 100 barrells of tarr, 50 pitch, 10 to 20 tune iron and soe to fill up with the best deals, of which this place vants great quantetee every yeare, but if you intend the tarr and pitch from London you may send the lesse att a time and when I knowe your minde you shall have my opinion how to send it me on the cheapest termes, and give you and your lady our humble service and remane, your humble servant, I.T.'

  [1] This was 1,227 pieces of genuine Spanish iron (unlike the 'rusty iron' or silver, sent on other occasions, as in [**317**]) weighing 300 quintals 31 lb. and despatched by George Richards from Bilbao on *The Swan* in December 1676.

$$\frac{23\ May}{[\text{——}]}1677$$

349   DAVID DORVILLE to JD
BRISTOL   19 MAY 1677

'Sir, In answer to yours of the 15 present, the Stockholm pitch and tarre are generally best in demande here. At present here is very little of either sorte in towne unsoulde but in 6 weeks a

2 months time some quantiteys are expected. The last pitch was soulde at 24*s*, tarre at 21*s* per barrill, and at present its soulde at same price, but when any quantity comes in suppose it may fall to 23*s* and 19*s* per barrill but not under. If you finde any incorridgment to sende any here and please to consigne it to mee I shall doe my utmost to sell it to the most advantidg. Riga reyn hempe 28*s*, ditto paste hempe 23*s* per cwt.; Barbados suger 21*s*, blew ginger 17½ a 18*s*, logwood 9½*s*, fustick 5¼*s* per cwt. cleare aboard, Barbados and Nevis indigo 1*s* 10*d*, ditto Jamaica 2*s* per lb. So after my due respects to your selfe and my cosen, your ladie, I remain, your loving cosen at comand.

[P.S.] This cittie vends in a yeare
     about 1,200 barrills of pitch
          1,500 barrills of tarre.'

$$\frac{3\ Jul.}{19\ Jul.}1677$$

0   G. RICHARDS to JD
BILBAO   25 JUNE 1677

'Sir, I have received none of yours since my former so I have the lesse to in large. Of the arrivall of the Bristol vessell you have been acquainted and of Roch.[1] Of the callicos by him I have sould the 12 bales of Long Cloth at a bout 70 *R. pta.* per piece and so there's about 15 a 16 per cent proffit. The narrow bafts I hope will also yeald the like. They shall be putt of by all good occasions and the other goods where in you are concerned, and as the accounts can be cleered they shall be forwarded. That of the wyre Sir John will deliver you. I find no incouragment for more thereof. This carrys you bill of loading and invoyce of a barrell of fyne waxe consigned you by Roch for your account, amount *R. pta.* 11,682, which finding right please to give me credit for. The wrought plate I beleeve will render better than pieces of eight. Sir John Let[hieullier] sells it at 4*s* 11*d* per onze. It's mixed with branne so you must have care there be none lost in partinge it. Sir John Lethieullier will deliver you the coppy or let you have the perusale of the account of Hunter's cargoe of fish, etc. For your ⅛ I credit you *R. pta.* 4,979¾ and by Roch shall goe also account of the corne. That comodity is here risen extreamely within 6 days time, but it will assoone fall I doubt, large quantities beeing expected, which is all at present, with my respects, I remayne your verry humble servant.'

 [1] Luke Roach, captain of the *Biscay Merchant*.

$$\frac{11\ Jul.}{[\qquad]}1677$$

1   S. LANNOY to JD
CONSTANTINOPLE   [UNDATED]

'Honoured Sir, Since my arrivall here have presumed to trouble you with 2 letters, the former bearing date the 29 May last, which heare had the misfortune not to arrive your hands, the French vessle by whome t'was sent being taken by the Tripoleens in its way to Marseille. However, doubt not but its coppy accompanyed with my last, of the 13 June past, sent per our Generall Shipp, the *Mary and Martha*, had better luck though mett a long and tedious passage, and hope you were pleased to receive therby those harty wishes for your health and prosperity as from a person that really desires the same, being obliged thereto by the undeserved kindness you were pleased to to doe me by your curteous promise to trust the management to me of what concernes you should finde encouragement to send this way. Sir, I once againe begg leave to enclose directions for sortments and colours of cloth, but to my sorrow (through the badnesse of our trade at present) have but little hopes you should concerne your self therein and dare not engage for more then my owne endeavours, with all imaginable dilligence to promote your interest (if possible) when ere receive a command from you. This trade was very sencible of the presence of the Court last summer, and equally as sencible of the contrary when the same againe departed, but the satisfaction the G[rand] Sig[no]r received in being here last sumer hath, God be thanked, invited him back againe, the fore-runners of his court being arrived already, and what adds more to our comfort shall certainly enjoye him here for alltogether, which will not only cause a double consumption of all sorts of goods but alsoe much advance theire prices, of which, God knowes, as yett was never more need. Tin, *LD* 26 per kintall, but trough the small quantity brought per last Generall Shipps beleive may rise; Lead worth *LD* 6 per kintall; detto white, *LD* $9\frac{1}{2}$; detto redd, *LD* 7 per kintall; Brazil wood *LD* 20 per kintall; pepper, *LD* $\frac{63}{120}$ per oke; cinomon, *LD* 5 per oke; cloves, *LD* $5\frac{1}{2}$ per oke; nuttmeggs, *LD* $3\frac{3}{4}$.

Sugars for sometime like to be very cheape through the unknowne quantity that is lately arrived here. The bearer hereof (Mr Thomas Cook) is Cancellier here for the Levant Company, who hath been pleased to promise to deliver this letter to you with his owne hands, not haveing else, save all respect and service where justly due, crave leave and rest, Sir, your most humble servant at command.

[P.S.] Sir, I request you would be pleased to give my humble service to Esq. Fredirick, who please to assure may always finde an humble servant here upon all occasions.'

$\frac{17\ Jul.}{20\ Jul.}$1677

352   J. & H. VAN BAERLE to JD

AMSTERDAM   23 JULY 1677

[D]   Your letters of the 29th past and 6th instant have reached us safely, together with the account of the 1,650 coils of copper-wire received by you from the ship *John & Edward*, captain John Stabler, of which you state the net proceeds to amount to £2,203 sterling. We have checked it and find that the customs, scavage, passport and town duties amount to a great deal and are much above our estimate. Madame your wife and Mr Peter Joye, in the year 1672, when we sent them 400 coils from here, only brought £32 16s into the account for customs, scavage, passport and town duties, but for these 1,650 coils you put down £167 5s, which differs considerably. Please check it again and if you find a mistake please correct it, as well as deducting the extra $\frac{1}{2}$ per cent commission which you have incorrectly put down. Our brother David wrote to us that he had agreed with you that you would only charge $1\frac{1}{2}$ per cent in the account for the brass consigned to you by John Green. Otherwise we have found no error in the account, which we are returning herewith so that you can correct it and interline what has been omitted.

We see that, instead of having any money for us in cash, you are actually out of pocket. The exchange is now too low for discounting any bill. However, we thank you for your offer to continue serving us in the disposal of our remaining copper-wire before the arrival of new wire from Sweden. It is welcome, but if it cannot be arranged and other people begin to undercut our prices for that commodity you will please not follow them too closely as we are not willing to have ours sold for less than £6 5s, for your guidance.

We are glad that you have sent the remaining kettles to Rouen in accordance with our order, and have credited us with the ƒ.192.15.8 bank-money paid to Vincent Maillant, remaining herewith, &c.

London: 36s 1g ⎱
Paris: 99g ⎰ 2 usances.

$\dfrac{19\ Jul.}{3\ Aug.}$1677

53 W. MOMMA TO JD
NYKÖPING
30 MARCH 1677

The copy of your letter dated the 26th of September I answered on the 11th of December. Since then I have received the original, and that of the 10th and 23rd of November as well as those of the 22nd of December and 16th of January, most of them all at the same time. I have also the account which you sent with them, and the letter of the 23rd of November which you said was sent via your servant. It was delivered by Mr Klitzert,[1] and from your servant I have heard nothing. And I understand from your letters that none of mine have come to your hands which I wrote on the 24th of August, the 5th of October, the 16th of October (under cover of Mr Klitzert) and the last of 11th of December under cover of Mr Perman (as I supposed). I am astonished that you should have received none of them.

Coming now to reply, I must say that I have partly checked your account and find that you have left out *RD* 2,000, which you paid long ago to Mr De Geer, which was properly entered into my books in conformity with your letters, and entered it shall remain. If you find yourself falling short on other items they ought not to have been sold in that manner. I can also not approve of the bad debts, for you wrote nothing to me about them between 1672 and 1675, although the account was settled annually. The last time you sold anything to John Skepper[2] was in 1672 and it was over a year before anything was paid, when you credited him with £53 7s 4d in 1673. Now I happen to know that others sold to him in 1674 and have been paid, and it was not until 1675 that he absconded, in which time one could have easily demanded the debt. I corresponded for a long time with your predecessors, Jan de Buck and Marescoe, and before that with their employer, Mr Jacques Bove, but I have never encountered anything like this in these unseasonable times. You have also reckoned all the interest on the debts at 6 per cent though you know it should be only 5 per cent. I know perfectly well that you should not have to carry bad debts, but I know even better that one ought not to be kept in suspense but be informed in a business-like style, annually on the closing of accounts, of any outstanding debts—of which, during four years, I was told nothing. So please understand that I shall not close this account until everything is sold and the final total agreed. Then we can reckon the interest as it ought to be, so please make an end of the sale as soon as possible.

I was greatly misled when I was told in writing that one could sell 400 slb per annum of black kettles, or the like, and thus to send so many pots to England which you were to sell to the Guinea Company or to Spanish or Muscovy merchants. It is a good product, and what I have had manufactured recently I have been selling at Stockholm to the Russians and get more for them than I would abroad. You will please make an end of them and not quibble too much about the price, but do not sell to people who are unreliable about paying, as

Skeppart was. I would not be insisting on this if you had kept your fine words to have a watchful eye, as you could and ought to have had over the last three or four years.

It is unnecessary to write any more, as you can be better informed from your correspondents at Stockholm about the way trade is. At this place there is nothing to be done, and I commend you, with regards, &c.

[P.S.] If you participated last year in sending calamine here from Amsterdam, please inform me as I have previously requested.

¹ H. Cletcher?
² John Sheppard.

(i) + (ii) $\dfrac{21\,Jul.}{[\text{———}]}$1677

354   JACOB & HENDRICK VAN CRAYESTEYN to JD

SMYRNA   (i)   1 MAY 1677

[D]   On the 9th of March and the 27th past we received our Hendrico's letters from [England], saying that he had arrived there safely on the 25th of November last year. And as he has had the honour of being consulted by you regarding trade he has requested us to give you advice about what is happening to it here. Thus we take this opportunity of free postage by the departure of six French ships (two for Leghorn and four for Marseille) to trouble you with our notes about the goods which are called for here from [England], as well as about those which are sent from here to [England]. In addition we describe some assortments of Dutch linens, perpetuanas and calculations about linens with 28 stuiver coins and also Dutch steel. From these you will be able to see what you may profitably turn to account. If you should be inclined to make a trial of one thing or another we beg that we may be favoured. You may be assured that you will be so well satisfied that you will want to continue.

Firstly, the principal goods brought here from [England] are 'Londons'—of three sorts, each selling according to its quality, which are called perpetuanas—lead, and iron wire as well as other goods which you can see from the enclosed note. The goods which [England] most demands from here are silks (Ardasse, Legis or Serbassi) Angora or Beybesar yarn, cotton wool and cotton yarn, gall-nuts, testick-wax,¹ or *hoeden wol*, aniseed and [—blank—].

Secondly, the goods from Holland on which a good penny-worth can be gained are the smallest cloths, Danzig-steel, brown gum-lack, stockings of grey '*bont-werk*',² and (above all) most preferred are Dutch textiles which one must exchange against Turkish yarn from Angora or Beybesar and against cotton-wool, gall-nuts, aniseed, testick, mastic, palm-wood and wax; also against silk (Ardasse, Legi and Serbassi). In bartering for [silk] one must always provide half the value in money, and for all other goods one-third in cash, so that the costs of freight, consular charges and other sorts of outgoing and incoming goods can be paid for. The most useful and profitable specie are Lion dollars which are currently being struck in [England] and sent here in large quantities, together with 22-, 26- and 28-stuiver coins out of Holland, which are packed in between the cloths. One can make a good profit on these coins, as well as on Danzig-steel which can be got in Holland for *f.*10 or *f.*11 per hundred pounds, free on board. The latter is presently selling here for *LD* 8¼ per *cantar*³ and is sometimes at *LD* 10 or *LD* 11 according to the amount in town. Gum-lack is *LD* 1¼ per *oque*,⁴ grey *bont-werk* stockings are *LD* 6½ to 7 per hundred, first-quality cotton-wool *LD* 7 and second-quality *LD* 5¾ per *cantar*.

For further news of what is happening in the course of trade please look at the accompanying price-current, and—as we have said—if you are disposed to see some advantage in making a trial we beg that we may have the honour. You will have satisfaction and enjoy quick returns, as time will tell.

Six days ago we received letters from a friend saying that the great Sultan had publicly entered Constantinople in unusual pomp together with his mother and the Grand Vizier.[5] Nobody here had believed it would happen. And as the great man is now trying to keep his head he has demanded the head of his brother, but since his mother is very protective of him no one knows how it will turn out. Two days after the said great lord entered Constantinople he forbade any women to be seen on the streets any more and one afternoon, sitting in his seraglio by the sea-side he saw sailing by some vessels with women, which ran aground. He had the poor women drowned. If things go on like this one must wonder what is coming next.

For the last five days there has been seen here, for three hours every midnight, a comet-star rising in the north-east among the stars on high. It is about an ell long and hovers a little towards the due-north. What this may signify the good Lord alone knows, to whom I pray that He may keep you in good health, and closing, remain, &c.

(ii)   3 JUNE 1677

55 The above is a copy of our last, with which we took the liberty of offering you our services, an offer which we have the opportunity of renewing by the departure of a French ship for Leghorn. We again beg you to favour us if you see any advantage in making a trial of one thing or another mentioned in the copy. You will be fully satisfied and receive quick returns.

On the 24th last the ship *Providence* arrived here from [England] after 62 days, bringing with it nothing else but 900 'loaves' of lead and brazil-wood, as a result of which the first has fallen to *LD* $4\frac{7}{8}$ per *cantar*. Three [Levant] Company ships are in lading for England and are to leave in three of four weeks. In their company there will also be another English ship, the *Europa* (which lately arrived) going *addritura* to Holland. It has a good freight and you will get a note of its cargo, as well as that of the three Company ships when they depart. On the 29th past two English ships, the *Son Joseph* and *Catiador*, arrived from Leghorn after 30 days, without any cargoes, and on the 1st instant two French ships arrived from Marseille after 50 days, together with a Venetian ship, the *Servio* from Venice. On the 2nd an English ship, the *Benjamin & Elizabeth*, arrived from Genoa and Leghorn, loaded with goods from Holland consisting of about 600 cloths, besides other goods. There was also a *ragoute*[6] from Venice. With all these ships we have had no special news exept that a convoy of four merchant ships were on the point of departing to come here from Holland under the protection of 30 warships as far as Sicily, from where they will be convoyed here with a considerable fleet. May the Lord bring them in safety. Otherwise there is nothing here and we refer you to the enclosed price-current. If you see any advantage, command us freely.

[P.S.] The comet-star has not been seen since the 2nd of May.

---

[1] Testic.
[2] While 'bont-werk' means fur or peltry the sense here seems to indicate a style of variegated, knitted stocking.
[3] The *cantar* or quintal, equivalent to 100 *rottolo* or approximately $3\frac{1}{2}$ cwt.
[4] 45 *oques* = 1 *cantar*.
[5] Kara Mustafa Pasha, Grand Vizier, 1676–83.
[6] *Sic.*—a Ragusan vessel?

[Enclosed]

A. (i) Goods brought to England from Smyrna:[1]
      Silk, Ardasse.
         Legi.
         Serbassi.
      Yarn from Angora.
      ditto, Bybasar.
      Currants.
      Testicq.
      Galls.
      Palm-wood.
      Cotton yarn.
      Cotton wool.
      Aniseed from Gallipoli.
      Corduane.
      Ditto, yellow.
      Carpets, of the dearest sort.

(ii) Goods from England traded at Smyrna:
      Indigo of all sorts.
      Pepper.
      Cloves.
      Cinnamon.
      Nutmegs.
      Ginger.
      Walrus teeth.
      Storax in boxes.
      Iron wire.
      Steel.
      Lead.
      Tin.
      Brazil-wood.
      Tin-plate in cases of 450 sheets.
      Varieties of 'Londons'.
      Perpetuanas from London,
      and from Ancona.
      C[– – ? – –]

[1] For a similar Dutch list of goods traded in the Levant see K. Heeringa (ed.) *Bronnen tot de geschiedenis van den Levantschen Handel* (Deel 2) *RGP* 34 (The Hague, 1917) pp. 215–17.

J. & H. VAN CRAYESTEYN *contd.*]

B. (i) The assortment of colours for perpetuanas currently
in demand at Smyrna.

Crimson red	10 pieces	Dark green	20 pieces
Scarlet	10	Violet	10
Light blue	15	Yellow	20
Dark blue	20	Purple	10
Light green	15		
			60
	70		70

Together,   130 pieces.

Assortment of Dutch cloths presently in demand at Smyrna:

1 light green	2 purple
2 rather darker	1 scarlet
1 dark green	1 hair-colour, darkish
1 cinnamon colour	3 green (1 light, the other
1 violet	grass, 1 darker)
2 purple	1 violet
2 crimson red	1 blue
2 scarlets	2 crimson red
12	12

[Marginal note] Among two or three packs there can always be a
black piece included, being black cotton.

These cloths must all have small calico-lists, with the arms of Leyden on
the fringe. Above all, they must not be stained, should be well-pressed and not
obviously stretched, of 55 to 60 ells length, as one pays freight and consulage duty
per piece, for your guidance.

Calculation on cloths and 28-stuiver coins:

1,000 ells of Dutch cloth bought at *f*.4 5*st*. (f.o.b.)	*f*.4,250
Costs in Smyrna *RD* 280 @ 50 stuivers [per *RD*]	700
	4,950
2,000 28-stuiver pieces packed between the cloths or boards	2,800
Capital	*f*.7,750

(ii) 1,000 ells of cloth render in Smyrna 1,030 *piecques*
on which the exchange sought is 3 *RD* per *piecque* to
receive in Holland on goods that one sent from Smyrna   [RD] 3,090

2,000 28-stuivers, at 3 for 2 Lyon dollars $1,333\frac{1}{3}$

These $1,333\frac{1}{3}$ *RD* given with the cloth yield a premium
on the exchange for Holland at 24 per cent: 320

                                            [RD] $4,743\frac{1}{3}$

@ 50 stuivers [per *RD*] are: *f.*11,858
　　　　　Deduct capital   *f.* 7,750
　　　　　　　　　　　　　　　　 ─────────
　　　　　　　　　　　[Profit]   *f.* 4,108

Calculation on steel and 28-stuiver coins:
　　500 casks of Danzig steel bought in Holland at
　　*f.*12 per cask, free on board,　　　　　　　　　　　　　　　　*f.* 6,000
　　Expenses at Smyrna:　　　　　　　　　　　　　　　　　　　　　1,200
　　　　　　　　　　　　　　　　　　　　　　　　　　　　　　 ─────────
　　　　　　　　　　　　　　　　　　　　　　　　　　　　　　f. 7,200
　　3,000 28-stuiver coins:　　　　　　　　　　　　　　　　　　　　4,200
　　　　　　　　　　　　　　　　　　　　　　　　　　　　　　 ─────────
　　　　　　　　　　　　　　　　　　　　　　　　　[Capital]   *f.*11,400

　　500 casks of Danzig steel sell at Smyrna (weighing
　　about 430 *cantar* @ *LD* 9 per *cantar*)　　　　　　　*LD* 3,870
　　3,000 28-stuiver coins, 3 per 2 *LD*　　　　　　　　　　　　2,000
　　　　　　　　　　　　　　　　　　　　　　　　　　　　　　 ─────────
　　　　　　　　　　　　　　　　　　　　　　　　　5,870 at exchange

　　for Turkish yarn or other goods sent for Holland at 24 per cent
　　is [*RD*] 1,408 40 stuivers @ 50 stuivers [per *RD*]:　　　　　*f.*18,197
　　　　　　　　　　　　　　　　　　　　Deduct capital   *f.*11,400
　　　　　　　　　　　　　　　　　　　　　　　　　　　　 ─────────
　　　　　　　　　　　　　　　　　　　　　　Profit   *f.* 6,797

$$\frac{23\ Jul.}{24\ Jul.}1677$$

356　JOHN FIELD to JD
　　　　HULL　　　　　　　　　　　　　　　　　　　　　　　20 JULY 1677

'Sir, I have yours of the 17th and for anser the 8 bayles of drapery receved from Mr Thomas
Wilson of Leedes are this day shipped aboard of the *Merchants Goodwill* of Hull, Edward
Hodgson maister, for Stockholme and consigned to Mr Gilbert Heathcote.[1] The shipp is
English bult, burthen sixty last, belongs to this place and is he a new shipp and the maister a
knoweing, sober man. Supose he will sayle in 6 or 8 dayes. Heare is a bill of ladeing. The
charges in shipping is to [£]12 8*s* 4*d* which I shall draw on said Wilson if hear I may serve
your command. Sir, your friend, J.F.'

　[1] 1652–1733; later one of the most successful merchants of his generation and reputed 'the richest commoner in
England'; Director of the East India Company 1698, Director and Governor of the Bank of England, Member of
Parliament, Knight and Baronet. For the scale of Heathcote's Swedish trade in the 1670s see Åström, *From Cloth to
Iron*, p. 142 (cf. p. 234).

$$\frac{24\ Jul.}{3\ Aug.}1677$$

357　L. UPPENDORFF to JD
　　　　STOCKHOLM　　　　　　　　　　　　　　　　　　　29 JUNE 1677

[D]　My last letter, to which I refer you, was sent from Gothenburg. Since then I have only just
　　received, yesterday, yours of the 12th of April from which I see what you have to say about

the copper coins. As it is now forbidden to export them I can send no great quantity. Nevertheless I have ordered them to send you some from Gothenburg and will write in the morning (God willing) that they are not to send you more than 4 or 5 tuns. However, I remain of the opinion that this commodity must rise and hold its price since no garcopper of any importance can be sent from here as long as one has to pay the un-free duty—which means that not one shippound of garcopper can go from here for less than 450 dollars—which, reckoning the £1 sterling at 25 dollars, means £18. Now, as soon as you receive it from Gothenburg I shall be glad to learn at once what can be done with it. At present wire costs 290 dollars per shippound; iron is at 30 to 32 dollars, which are good prices, and voyage iron is 33 dollars, so I do not think that one can send any iron to [England] if one wants to recover the money invested. Things are very bad here with regard to freedom from duties. Whoever brings in no salt, ammunition or ordinary woven cloth must pay the un-free duty, which makes a difference of at least 3 *RD* on a shippound of wire. Consequently business is quite extraordinary here at present.

Your 2,000 coils of wire will have been sold long ago. If not, you should sell them at once as 3,000 coils are going from here to [England]. So far, little has gone for Lübeck, Hamburg, France or Holland, but I shall be sending some to these places in order not to spoil the market in [England]. It will be explained to you more fully in our next letters that Mr Van Cöllen and I have separated and that from now on you are to accept nothing for our partnership unless it is signed by us both in our own writing. Please bear this in mind.

With regard to anything I may send you (which could be considered as sold, free-on-board, when it is delivered) I shall draw nothing on you before the ship leaves the Daalders.

I am delighted that the business is going forward in Parliament[1] and look forward to hearing the outcome at your convenience, wherewith—besides offering my unqualified services—I send warm regards to you, your wife and whole family, remaining, &c.

[1] A reference to his bill of naturalization, now passing through Parliament (see [275] n. 1).

$$\frac{30\ Jul.}{3\ Aug.}1677$$

358 S. DE GEER to JD
AMSTERDAM   3 AUGUST 1677

[D]   I find I have your letter of the 17th past. It is astonishing how things are going in Sweden with regard to the purchase of iron, the English buying everything that appears for 30 dollars per shippound. My brother has sold 3,000 to 4,000 slb of his 'Ⓛ' on commission for that much and Boor has also sold some of my 'O' and others besides similarly. There were so many ships there that they did not know how to get any London-bound cargoes for £2 or £2½. I would guess that when these ships arrive in London there will be not a little undercutting in iron prices, so I think it would be most advisable if you sold what you have of mine before the ships arrive and iron gets into too many hands. As for pan-iron we must look into it. There will be little or nothing coming this year so it should eventually find its buyers, but we must let it lie for a while and be patient.

It is now too late to have 1¼- and 1½-inch iron made. If only I had had your letter earlier, there were 300 slb lying at Stockholm which have now been shipped to [blank].

I shall now be getting some letters from Sweden which I am sure will yield a bad account unless Cletcher has bought tar for you in good time, for I am afraid there has been too much in the country.

Mr Botte tells me that he has acquired for himself all the tar that goes to London, and that he has consigned it all to you so that it remains in few hands.

Let me know if you have anything concerning the wine lading. I see from Boor's letters that Cletcher has sold the salt for less than $10\frac{1}{2}$ dollars. That is too low. Boor has also sold some for me but I think he would have done well to leave it. There is plenty there but nevertheless the price is too low, wherewith I remain, &c.

[P.S.] Voyla bien, mechante nouvelle pour le danois encore,[1] qu'on le balence aise et toutefois il n'en sera pas encore quite a ce pris, comme nous aussi du nostre—so it must still go on, et puis une paix avec la france separee, voyla encore mon opinion.

[1] De Geer is probably referring to Sweden's victory over the Danes near Landskrona on 14 July 1677, but Danish naval success that month left honours even and ensured a prolongation of the war.

$$\frac{4\ Aug.}{16\ Aug.}1677$$

359 A. & S. VROULING to JD

ROUEN   10 AUGUST 1677

'Depuis notre derniere avons l'honneur de la votre du 12ᵉ passe. Il est bien que nous crediterez de la remise pour votre conte de *W*.506.44s a $55\frac{1}{2}d$ et *W*.500 a $56\frac{1}{4}$. Nous ne doubtons ou elle entrera ponctuellement quoy que vos debiteurs soient assez tardifs et que quelques uns remettent apres la foire de Guybray sommes assez empesches a vous faire valoir le reste de votre avance. Le change non seulement pour chez vous mais pour tous autres lieux comme pouvez voir au pied aussy steriles qu'ils sont ostent le courage de faire la moindre avance. Neantmoins comme quelques ordinaires se font passer fort froidement dizette de lettres de Bretagne et ce dernier ordinaire le change baissé chez vous nous fait resoudre a vous faire encore quelque remise pour le mesme conte, ne prevoyant pas qu'en deux ou trois postes il puisse varier sauff aucun inconvenient, ainsi vous remettons encore a conte *W*.300 a $55\frac{1}{4}d$, 2 usances moins 8 jours, sur Jean Longuet, *W*.400 de mesme sur Alexander Mercall, lettre Herman Wetken. Vous en ferez procurer le requis et nous en crediterez £2,100t. Les lettres et l'argent se font obstinees, ainsi qu'il ne c'est presque rien fait pour chez vous et tout ce que nous avons pu est d'optenir 8 jours. Soyez en persuadé que ce que nous ferons sera tousjours pour votre avantage.

A notre plus grand chagrin et desplaisir votre rosette demeure la; nous esperons pourtant en faire bientost fin, prevoyant quelque demande en cette denree; en ce qui dependera de nous aurez assurement, Monsieur, tousjours la derniere satisfaction. Au fill de latton aucun changement considerable, seulement un peu plus roide, le debit neantmoins tousjours assez mediocre comme nous ne prevoyons pas qu'il en vienne partye considerable de Suede. Notre opinion est qu'en breff il doibt remonter et prendre faveur. A Lubeck il en estoit arrivé deux navires que n'en aportoient pas plus de 200 torques et restant a 69 *ML* a Hambourg on n'en peut aporter icy avec profffyt au prix de £90t le cent. La misere du temps et la quantité de mains auxquelles il vient icy en petites partyes fait qu'il ne se maintient pas comme ailleurs; venant changement en serez informe et vous prions nous donner vos bons avys. Quand a nos laines, nous esperons que dans l'automne pourra venir quelque petit changement. Il en est venu hier encore un navire de Bilbao avec plusieurs laines[?] Il suffit que demeuriez avec nous d'accord de patianter encore un peu que puissions trouver quelque petit profffyt au nostres. Il est fascheux et au reste si commun a prezent de negotier a rebours que l'un ne doibt point s'estonner. La patience seule nous doibt gouverner. Nous souhaitterions avec patience vous pouvoir proposer quelque negoce avantageux pour pouvoir courir la fortune avec vous mais nous trouvons tout si limite et particulierement le negoce de chez vous que nous nous ferons peur d'animer le moindre de nos amys en aucun negoce. Si nous voyons quelque autre chose d'ailleurs vous en ferons part et vous prions, mon cher Monsieur, de la mesme faveur. Les huilles generalement baissees, il en est ce neantmoins par divers navires de chez vous arrivé plusieurs partyes. Les especieries tres debiles, le poivre £52½t le cent; le girofle a esté un peu recherche depuis 8 jours sur un avys de Hollande et quelq'uns en ont achepté partie a £5t 12½s la lb. et s'en estoit donné devant a £5t 10s; ne penetrons point avec quel fondement en estant arrivé si grand quantité a la compte de ce pays et croyons qu'il y en a assez en mains de particuliers pour demeurer en estatt jusqu'a la vente de la Compagnie. Indigo 43 a 45s; le beaux cochenille £11t 10s la lb.; nos thoilles a grand marché accause que la flotte ne part pas cett'annee pour Nuova Spagne pourroient peutestre bien encore decliner et l'indigo et la cochenille principalement cette derniere dont il n'y a pas tres grand nombre venir. De mall en mieux le temps nous l'apprendra. Les grains un peu hausses en ces quartiers, de mesme vers Bordeaux ou il en faudra porter par mer et en ces cantons la recolte ayant souffert en plusieurs endroits a Paris et icy le blé a la halle est haussé de *W.*44 a *W.*56, le seigle de *W.*26 a *W.*36, pourtant rien de bien regle, la recolte n'estant partout finie, selon les apparences neantmoins doibt un peu prendre faveur. La suitte vous sera avisee; icy rien de nouveau. A[braham] V[rouling] vous a bien de l'obligation de vos bons souhaits, le sera pour l'advenir; ce que l'on vous a dit n'est qu'une fausse alarme; il n'est pas encore delibere a changer la condition, mais surtout il ne changera jamais la qualite de vos trés humble et obligé serviteurs.'

Amsterdam:	100¼*g*.	Londres:	55¼*d*.
Anvers:	99*g*	Hamburg:	1 p. cent.
Lille:	97½*g*.		

$$\frac{6\ Aug.}{7\ Aug.}1677$$

360   L. TRIP to JD
AMSTERDAM   6 AUGUST 1677

[D]   From your letter of the 20th of July I understand that the iron which my nephew Matthias Trip sent you has not yet been sold, so I am again requesting you, please sell it at the current price, as I have written before. Please comply with this friendly request so that this long drawn-out account can be closed. It is true, as you write, that it cannot be brought out of Sweden for less than £12 without loss, but it seems that it is the humour of the English nation to sell immediately, cost what it may. It is beyond reason but in these latest letters I have been informed that the English are now buying iron for 30 dollars which was last year selling at 25 dollars, while the salt which was sold last year at 12 dollars is now selling at 10½. You can well conceive what a difference that makes. One should be able to say that, because it was bought up at such a high cost, the price of iron must rise. In other places they would hold on to it, but not the English! They must sell, cost what it may, so once again I beg you and order you to sell my iron at the market price, for large amounts will be coming from Sweden.

$$\frac{6\ Aug.}{7\ Aug.}1677$$

361   P. BOTTE to JD
         AMSTERDAM   10 AUGUST 1677

[D]   On my arrival home, which was at the end of last month (God be thanked) I found your
      letters of the 18th and 25th of May as well as of the 19th and 3rd of July, and yesterday I
      received yours of the 27th of July in which I find the answer to mine of the 16th/26th past
      from Hamburg.
         I perfectly understand your feelings about the consignment of pitch and tar, as well as your
      argument about selling and marketing.[1] I am also grateful for the conditions you have
      offered. I have already let you have my views about these matters and if you are willing to
      undertake the business for me in [England] on the following terms we can try each other out
      for this year, and if I am satisfied (which I do not doubt) I shall be glad to continue with you,
      vizt.:
      1. In accordance with your request, the goods will be sent to [London] with the exception of
      80 lasts of pitch and 100 lasts of tar, which will be ordered for Hull as you asked.
      2. On their arrival you will do your best to sell them from the ships according to the prices
      which I shall, from time to time, recommend and if these prices cannot be obtained the goods
      are to be stored in a good and convenient warehouse until such time as an opportunity offers,
      for which one ought not to be in too great a hurry as these quantities are not large.
      Furthermore, it means I can sell as I choose, and as the prices here are $£22–£22\frac{1}{2}$ flem. for tar
      (which, with discount and rebate amounts to $f.120$ net) my present advice would be that the
      consignment sent aboard Robert Young and due to arrive soon should not be sold below $£11$
      sterling for the tar and $£15$ sterling for the pitch. It should be sold at 3 months time precisely,
      so that the bills of exchange can be paid; and in order that I may sleep all the sounder I would
      ask you to stand liable for debts, which you are better able to settle than anyone, having
      knowledge enough about your customers not to give credit to anyone other than reliable
      people.
         If you do so I shall:
      3. allow you 2 per cent commission, and for interest (according to your demand) $\frac{1}{2}$ per cent
      per month for your outlay on freight charges and bills of exchange. Further:
      4. I have agreed not to draw on you more than $£5$ per last on the tar and $£7$ per last on the
      pitch from the time the goods arrive until the time when they are sold, when you will always
      allow me to dispose of the balance in such a way that what remains unsold from time to time
      is only charged with $£5$ per last of tar and $£7$ per last of pitch, including all expenses.
         I have no doubt that these conditions will please you and that you will consent to them,
      handling the costs as if they were your own, on which I shall rely and await your decision by
      your next letter. Wherewith I remain, &c.

      London: 36s $1–1\frac{1}{2}g$ 2 usances.
      Hamburg: $33\frac{3}{16}–\frac{1}{4}$ at sight.

      ¹ '... *neffens Ue sustenu wegens t'vercoop & vertier* ...' which one might translate alternatively as 'sale and
      distribution'.

$$\frac{10 \ Aug.}{31 \ Aug.}1677$$

362 A. RULAND to JD

HAMBURG   30 JULY 1677

[D] I have received yours of the 6th of April and 19th of June. I note what you write concerning Van Deurs. With friends in Amsterdam I have been well treated this way, but no satisfaction can be had in the way you describe. You could find the opportunity to reprove him somewhat and show him in that way that you are not inclined to abandon entirely my interests in [England] so that I am not properly served there.

Thank you for news of what is happening to trade in [England]. I see more prospect of a decline than a rise in indigo prices at present since large amounts have arrived with the East India ships. I understand that in Spain and Portugal corn is scarcely satisfactory. Some say it is also so in the region of Nantes in France, but that it is abundant in England and that large amounts have been contracted for in Spain. I shall be glad to know what truth there is in this, and how much a last of wheat will cost in [England], free on board. Fish and grain from [England] are probably in some demand in Spain. Exactly what demand there is I do not know, though with the great shortage they will have to do the best they can. Here, God be praised, we have had a reasonable year, although how large [our crops are] one does not know yet. With cordial regards, &c.

$$\frac{16 \ Aug.}{17 \ Aug.}1677$$

363 CLAES WILKENS to JD

STOCKHOLM   18 JULY 1677

[G] Your letter of the 18th of May, together with a copy of the same, reached me only four days ago, and I also have one of the 19th past which arrived safely today. From these I have seen your news of what is happening with regard to the pitch and tar trade in England. Thank you for the information, and since Mr Botte has contracted to undertake the business and has instructed me to arrange the shipments to you, I have consigned to you the following (which will be followed quickly by the bills of lading)—in Captain Robert Young, 62 lasts of tar at 13 barrels per last (consisting of $47\frac{1}{6}$ lasts of Stockholm tar and 20 lasts of Viborg tar at 12 barrels per last) and 20 lasts of pitch at 12 barrels per last; likewise with John Chapman $23\frac{1}{13}$ lasts of tar and $5\frac{10}{13}$ lasts of pitch at 13 barrels per last; likewise in Henry Sutton $28\frac{8}{13}$ lasts of tar and $6\frac{6}{13}$ lasts of pitch. John Garret and Francis Benson are still lying in lading and when they have their full cargoes I shall send you news of it. More will follow shortly so I hope you will be able to have the required amount. Since Mr Botte already set sail a fortnight ago on his journey to Amsterdam by way of Lübeck I hope he has arrived long before you see this and has corresponded with you about what is necessary for this business.

It is true that in Kalmar and Västervik one can obtain no more tar for any money, and from Gothenburg, Halmstad and Viborg no more is expected.

Thank you for offering your services to me. I shall bear that prospect in mind when the dear Lord grants us peace. Because of these troubled times we citizens have had all our business taken away and have had to leave it all to foreigners while we patiently wait for better times, which the dear Lord may soon grant.

Because there is little iron in stock here the price is high, and the recent severe winter and great thaw have restricted many works, which are remaining at a standstill, to which the floods of the spring and the subsequent great drought have contributed not a little. So far this year Holland has not ordered much iron and most of it has been sold to Englishmen resident here.

With cordial regards, &c.

$$\frac{27\ Aug.}{[27\ Aug.]}1677$$

364   B. BEUZELIN & SON to JD
ROUEN   31 AUGUST 1677

'Nous venons de recepvoir vostre agreable du 16/26 courant qui nous dit le debvoir des 2 remises que nous vous avons faittes de W.1,500 et W.245$\frac{2}{3}$, ce qui est bien. Nous procurerons le necessaire des 6 vostres, W.2,000, 500, 500, 1,000, 250 et 250 et vous en rendrons creditteur. Il nous fasche que le change pour chez vous soit cy bas, car nous y avons fait a 55d. S'il est plus hault a Paris, nous vous fairons faire des retours dudit lieu, et comme nous vous avons cy-devant escrit en quelque maniere que se soit, il ne vous en coustera qu'un provision et ung courtage. Sy nous trouvons icy quelque lettres de satisfaction et a prix raisonnable, nous ne laissons pas de vous remettre sans attendre l'escheance des vostres. Vous saurez par le prochain ceque nous aurons peu effectuer. Nous vous creditterons de ce que vous avez heu la bonte de payer a mon filz.

Au regard des 100 torches de fil de latton qui nous reste a vous, puisque vous ne dezirez pas que nous les vandions a moins de £97t, nous observerons vos ordres, mais il fault qu'il y arrive bien de la demande avant que de parvenir a ce prix la. Il est vray que d'Hambourg on nous escrit qu'il doibt attendre peu, parcequ'il leur mancque de mattiere pour le travail, mais d'ung aultre costé il s'attend 2 navires de Suede, l'un pour le Sr Thomas Legendre qui aura 2,000 torches et ung petit bastimant avecq 1,000, tout cella remplist. Ledit Sr Legendre la sepmaine passé en vandist autour de 400 torches a £89t de la marque de 'H' couronnee qui estoit venu d'Hambourg. Il est indubittable que sy l'on y voulloit tenir ung peu la main l'on en optiendroit aussy bien £92t que £89t mais chacun fait comme il l'entend. Nous advertirons Mons. Gansel de ce que vous nous mandez et qu'il ne vande point votre partie a moins de £97t. Nous souhaittons fort que luy et nous y puissions parvenir et que le vaisseau venant de Stockholm qui avoit touche a Harwich dans lequel vous avez 560 torches de fil de latton et partie de bré et goudron puisse heureusement arriver icy. Nous vous sommes beaucoup obligez de la continuation de votre bonne volonte en ce rancontre—assurez-vous que nous en aurons toutte la recognoissance possible, et que vos intherets nous seront tousiours en la mesme recommandation que les notres. Nous nous tiendrons fort exactemant dans les limittes de vos ordres pour cette partie, et nous esperons que le bré et goudron dont la consignation e[s]t faittes a Mons. Louis Hays se vandra fort bien parce qu'il est tres peu de l'un et de l'autre icy.

Nostre homme e[s]t allé chez la veuve Hacquet pour luy presanter la lettre de £400 sterling; vous saurez au bas de celluy sy elle l'aura accepte ou non.

C'est ung grand bien pour votre Compagnie d'Orient que l'arrivée de ces 4 navires—Dieu veille avoir conservé le 5e duquel on estoit en paine. On nous mande d'Amsterdam que les poivres y avoyent hausse a 11$\frac{5}{8}$$g$ non obstant le grand nombre que en estoit arrivée. Ces messieurs ont des addresses merveilleuzes pour faire hausser leurs marchandises. Ilz ont fait achepter icy tous les geroffles et lus plus advizes sont ceux qui ont vendu, car d'enchere il ne fault pas esperer, veu le peu de consommation qu'il-y-a a touttes sortes de marchandises. Les huiles baissent a cauze des apparences d'une grande recolte, tant en France qu'en Espagne et Itallie; les dernieres se sont vandues a £30t le 100—c'est encore ung bon prix. La courier va partir, ainsy nous nous hastons de finir, &c.

[P.S.] La lettre de £400 sterling est acceptée par la veuve Haquet et nous la gardons suivant votre ordre. Nous n'avons peu rien trouver a la bourse audessus de 55d. Il est resté beaucoup d'argent et peu de lettres.'

Amsterdam: $100\frac{1}{4}g.$
Hamburg: $1\%.$
Lille: $97\frac{1}{2}g.$

$$\frac{1\ Sep.}{4\ Sep.}1677$$

65   L. DE LA BISTRATE & F. DUFAY to JD
AMSTERDAM   7 SEPTEMBER 1677

D]   We last wrote to you on the 13th past, and since then we have had nothing from you.

If the last two ships carrying our 10 packs of whale-fins have departed for Genoa we shall be glad to hear and await the expense account. Concerning our remaining whale-fins, we had hoped that the ravages of the French in Greenland would have caused some considerable alteration,[1] but since we have heard nothing about it from you and since the price here is weakening again because the ships have returned home with very good catches, we have decided to dispose of ours cheaply and likewise request you to sell at £105 sterling [per ton]. And if you cannot obtain that please, without delay and by the first opportunity of a good ship, send them also to Genoa for our account but in your own name. Consign them to SS. Carlo Dominico Cichi & Co. and inform us promptly when it is done.

Concerning the pending sale by your East India Company, we had expected further information from you. We are now advised that it will happen soon and that large amounts of pepper are likely to be sold, so we have no doubt that it will be going cheaply. If you can obtain it at $6\frac{1}{2}d$ [per lb.] please buy 20 or 30 bales for us, and if you have to pay $6\frac{3}{4}d$ get no more than 10 to 15 bales. We will promptly arrange your reimbursement. Enclosed here are the cargo lists of another 6 East India ships which have arrived. The Company are expecting that all their pepper will have to go cheaply. We remain, always ready to be of service, &c.

[P.S.] Enclosed herewith we send a calculation on the basis of pepper being (as it was before with you) at $9\frac{1}{2}d$, but allowing for rebate and 2 per cent discount for prompt payment and restitution of half the duty, for your guidance.

---

[1] The Dutch whale-fishery catch for 1677 was some 25 per cent smaller than the average for the 1670s—see A. R. Michell 'The European Fisheries in Early Modern History', *The Cambridge Economic History of Europe*, V, p. 169.

$$(i) + (ii) \quad \frac{5\ Sep.}{28\ Sep.}1677$$

366   D. VAN BAERLE to JD
STOCKHOLM   (i)   2 APRIL 1677

[D]   My last letter was of the 16th past and went by way of Gothenburg. Since then I have received yours of the 26th of January and 9th of February.

In reply, you will have seen by my previous letter that because I am engaged in a suit with Willem Momma the proposal I made to you cannot be put into effect. I now see that you are introducing difficulties by suggesting that the business was hindered because I could not make up my mind to participate on grounds that are no concern of mine. With regard to the insurance on John Stabler, the reasons you give for the high premium do not satisfy me since the difference between the 4 per cent given by Francis Townley and the 7 per cent given by you on the same ship and at about the same time is too great. It would be a big enough difference if one granted an extra 1 per cent for the reliability of the insurers but in addition you put down another 1 per cent for the clause that, in the event of loss, payment would be made without deduction, and on checking through your earlier letters I find that in one of the 16th of June 1676 you wrote that such a clause made a difference of only $\frac{1}{4}$ per cent; and that still leaves another 1 per cent which you cannot explain.

I beg you to believe that brass-ware is a commodity which needs to be handled with skill. I cannot commend anyone who is neglectful about arranging insurance but to give it away in haste and to have no regard to what an insurer puts is also not commendable and takes away a large part of the profit.

I hope you have done your duty in selling and have made some recompense by selling at a good price. Brass-wire remains at about 270 dollars per shippound, garcopper at 226 to 227 dollars, ordinary fine iron at 28 to 29 dollars and St Ubes salt at 12 dollars per ton. With which I remain, &c.

(ii)   18 JULY 1677
[not selected]

$\frac{7\ Sep.}{11\ Sep.}$1677

367   P. BOTTE to JD

AMSTERDAM   14 SEPTEMBER 1677

[D]   I refer myself to my last letter of the 31st past. Since then I have been at The Hague for a while concerning business affairs and on coming home found your letters of the 24th, 28th and 31st ditto, in answer to which I cannot agree to sell any tar for less than £10 10s sterling, be it at Harwich or at London, and if our friends will not agree to that please store what belongs to me. They can sulk,[1] and they can receive what is due to them if they need it and thus be able to pay up all the more promptly. And I am not obliged to follow them because of any disputed points about which they make claims, as set out in your last letter of the 31st of August. For although I have been assured by the Directors in the contract settled on the 3rd of April this year that for a period of two years they would not sell tar for England to anyone but me, our friends cannot guarantee that no Viborg or Stockholm tar besides mine will arrive, firstly because it could be stolen and secondly because malicious people here or at Lübeck could buy up assortments and have them sent to [England] in order to make claims, for which I have no desire. So, as I have said before, it is best to sell, which I urge you to do.

If you cannot arrange any freight charters for Stockholm at £3 sterling per last you do not need to go to any further trouble. I shall wait until next year, and it is much better that one does not get too much this year in view of the quantities which have arrived from Västervik and are yet expected.

Thank you for mentioning the idea of chartering salt ships for St Ubes next year. I shall think about it and may well decide to charter a consignment if it can be obtained at £5 sterling—i.e. from St Ubes to Stockholm and from there to [London] at eighteen tuns of salt per last and a similar lading in return. Let me know more in due course.

In your letter of the 28th of August I have found the account for the cargo in Captain Robert Young, consisting of 62 lasts of tar and 20 lasts of pitch, which you have forgotten to sign. Please get it right in future. I have checked it and find that you have charged me £5 8s for brokerage, short-change and false money at $\frac{5}{8}$ per cent, which according to my contention ought not to be charged to me as it is not the practice here and is covered by your commission. For if one has regular tar customers one does not need to deal with brokers, and if a cashier receives false money he ought to pay for it, for what he does not see with his eyes he ought to feel in his purse. So I expect you to reimburse me for this item. Secondly, while you have rebated two months from the total proceeds (so that the goods have only yielded 1 per cent) you have additionally charged me four months interest on expenses totalling £216 9s, which is also a mistake. For if you have reckoned the full rate of interest on this £216 9s so much the less ought you to rebate for two months. There is also a mistake of £2 3s 3d which you will please credit to me. Apart from this I find your account correct.

You were pleased to tell me that you have written to Mr Cletcher at Stockholm that the tar and pitch loaded in the *Thomasina* were absolutely for your account. Now you may remember that you have promised me before to tell no one for whose account these goods were going, so I have said nothing to Mr Cletcher nor anyone else at [Stockholm]. I beg you always to keep it secret, for one does not need to give anyone unnecessary information.

Regarding the hire of a warehouse, I rely on you to arrange it as carefully as possible.

I am glad that, following my instructions, you will not sell the tar for less than £10 10s. I shall rely on that, and am in agreement with you on all the conditions so far as concerns debts. Since you write that there are only four or five [customers] that one can trust I beg you to let me know their names so that I can inform myself about them. I am very apprehensive about this because I have had my fingers burnt before and if you could remove my uneasiness on this score I cannot see anything to sever our correspondence provided that you follow my instructions in selling. I beg you to give it further thought and let me know your good ideas. I can assure you that if we once get our relationship settled on a firm foundation you will be able to earn with me a handsome commission.

Please do not forget to send the Canary sack to Stockholm at the earliest opportunity, addressing it to Claes Wilkens, and if you are able to charter some ships, as you said, please address them to Wilkens and to Burghermaster Hans Smitt at Viborg.

I shall not neglect to recommend you to my friends, but it will not be necessary to do so for Breda[2] because if I had not had his previous recommendation I would not be corresponding with you now.

When the opportunity occurs I beg you to send me sixty bottles of good Canary sack, and make a note of it on my account.

With regards, I remain, &c.

London—35s 11g 2 usances.

---

1 ' . . . *so konnen sij montjes maek* . . . '.
2 Samuel van Breda, of Stockholm and Amsterdam.

368   JACOB FAHLGREEN to JD

STOCKHOLM   26 JULY 1677

'Sir, My last to you was the 18 instant with Mr Chapman, whereby advised you that his loading was only 546 slb 17 lispound 7 lb. of '♛ N' weyer, 25 last tarr and $6\frac{1}{4}$ last pitch at 12 barrels per last. Also that I had received your welcome lines from the 18 May, whereby I did see that you had not received any from mee since the 10th of March. However, I have written to you these following letters, the 24 March, 21 Aprill, 16 and 21 May, 9, 13, 16, 23 and 26 of June and 10 of July, and that all were gone per via Gottenborgh under covert of Robert Clarck except the last which went with a frind per Sound under Van Deurs' covert. I also advised you what difficulty my contra party yett makes about Mr Perman's and my father's bale, for they will not lett mee have a farthing but put it all in security for the bale, and that you could help mee to bee master of my own if you did send me the bale back againe, then I would put all what I gett in your hands—this is about the contents of my last. I have received sinc your wellcome lines of the 22 June, where of I doe see that you have not received a word of answer on all your letters to mee about your bussinese here, and because your affaires doe not require to keep mee here you give me order to come back by way of Gottenborgh before September. For answer, your 3 letters of the 29 December, 16 and 25 January I did not recive before the 28 of March and sick on my bed occasioned thorrow an onlucky faal I had on my right side upon a iron plate which keept mee 3 weeks to bed, and that is the reason I did not answer your letters before the 21 Aprill. Yours of the 26 January with copie of the 25 ditto, 16 February with copies of the 9 and 13 ditto, 21th March, 2 and 4 Aprill I all received the 12th May when I came to Stockholm, all which I did answer the 16 ditto per via Gottenborgh at large. The 21 May I advised you about William Momma's bussines, and if you did send Spanisch silver for this plase that it would turne to a good account, and 9 June advised you the arrival of the *Concord*; 13 ditto the arrivall of *Thomasine*; 16 ditto the sale of your loading salt; 23 ditto the contract which I had made with two merchants here, Mr Oloff Root and Thomas Cupp for a parcell of English manufactuars for about £1,500 sterling att 16 per cent profitt to bee delivered eigther here or att Gottenborgh, they paying all charges whatsoever except assurance money. I also did send you there's memorandum for to buy the goods affter. The 26 July and 10 July sent you also the copie of the 23 June. Sir, this is my declaration both for the time when I received your letters, also when I have answered them, and thought it dos not, may bee, answeer to your expectation yet I doe hope that you will not in the least deminidge your good will you have for mee. Whatsoever I have done amise I pray for it, and what is to bee mended I will loose noe time to imploy my outmost power for to doe it. It may bee that some frinds have seen mee here that went for England, but truly I did not know so much, for I did write per Gottenborgh which I thought was the securest way and recomended my letters to Mr Robert Clarck that hee should send them away with the very first opportunity of frinds and ships. If Mr Clarck have not observed my orders but letten the letters ly hee is much to bee blamed, for hee aught att least let mee know so much that I might have governe mee there after. Yesterday I did write to him for to know what he has done with my letters.

Toward the beginning of September, please God, shall I live in Gottenborgh for to goe for England if I don't get contrary orders from you before, and about that time doe I expect those goods I have written for. As soon as the ship *Concord* is departed this port I doe intend for to goe up in the country for 2 weekes for to settel my affairs in as good a order as I can before I returne for England. By this inclosed letter of Mr Cletcher you shall understand what her loading is. You will also have the account of the salt, the neet amounting to 16,143 dollars 6 ore copper mony. Mr Cletcher is gone from hence to his workes at Axberghhammer and did give mee order for to make up the account with the master, which I also have done, and has given mee a recept for 1,595 dollars copper monys, where of hee has payd all the port charges. The recept I am orderd to send to Mr Cletcher with the first post. The master has in for your account 40 tillts of deals, which cost with the toll and all 195 dollars 4 ore; 4 fadomes wood to stow the tarr cascks cost 28 dollars, the port charges amounting to 481 dollars 18 ore. I should have bought you some good birtch wood but here is non to bee had for mony. However, I have given order to the master thatt in case hee meets any boats with good wood that hee shall buy you 4 or 6 fadoms and stow it up from the tarr. The wind has been very good this 8 days for Mr Chapman. I hope hee shall have a short voyage. Having noe more to inlarge but wisching the ship *Concord* a good voyage and after my humble service presented to my mistress and the rest of the house I rest, your faithfull servant.'

$$\frac{1 \text{ Oct.}}{6 \text{ Oct.}} 1677$$

369 P. VAN TEYLINGEN & CO to JD
VENICE   27 SEPTEMBER 1677

[D]   In answer to your letter of the 27th past, we must say that pitch is certainly not required here and is even less valued than tar, so it would not be advisable to send any here. There are about 500 barrels of tar lying unsold in town, and the demand is not very great because of the small amount of sea-borne traffic here at present. Two months ago we sold some for D.32 with 6 months discount and 30 per cent tare for the oaken casks (which are those most in demand). Below I have set out some calculations for your guidance. No other tar comes here except some from Muscovy: most is from Sweden. Pitch is indeed made in Dalmatia but we have never seen tar from that area. Between now and June next year about 400 casks could be sold. Lead is at D.41, pepper at D.51 and both are likely to rise higher. Currants at Zante are at 35 R. pta. since the crop is meagre. Russian leather, D.52 per lb., with 8 per cent tare. Coppers are at D.260 per mille, more or less according to the quality, and that from Hungary is at D.280.

   If there is anything else in which we can be of service, please command us, remaining, with cordial regards, &c.

London: $52\frac{1}{2}d$
Amsterdam: $94\frac{1}{2}$.
Hamburg: 92.

[verso]

300 barrels, or 25 lasts[1] of tar @ £9 per last, free on board—£225

Total weight at Venice	lb. 82,610 great weight	
30 per cent tare for the barrels	lb. 24,783	
	lb. 57,827	
	at D.32 per mille	D.1,850
	6 months discount	83
		D.1,767

Freight at *l.*8 on 375 [barrels]² is   *l.*3,000 ⎱ *l.*3,150 is   *D.*508.2³
Primage   150 ⎰

Workmen's wages, speeding weighers, etc.	33.0
Import duty	109.0
Expenses of the *dogana*	19.0
Brokerage at 2 per cent.	37.0
Commission at 2 per cent	37.0

D. 743

D.1,024

Deduct 20%   171

in bank money   D. 853

at 52½*d* per ducat makes £186 12*s* sterling. You can see by this that you would lose a great deal.⁴

¹ Here he has calculated the last at 12 barrels per last.
² Here the last is calculated at 15 barrels per last.
³ The ducat is valued here at 6⅛ livres.
⁴ The loss is 17 per cent.

2 *Oct.*
––––– 1677
6 *Oct.*

370   A. RULAND to JD

HAMBURG   21 SEPTEMBER 1677

[D]   I find I have your letters of the 31st past and the 11th instant. From the latter I note what is happening in [England] with regard to grains, about which I asked on July 30th. I would be glad to know how much one last would cost with all expenses, free on board, and how many quarters one reckons for a Dutch or Hamburg last?¹ Also if there are any ships to be had which will go to Cadiz and Leghorn, and about how much freight one should pay if one wants to unload at Cadiz, and how much if one wants to have goods at Leghorn? If one wants to embrace this trade one must have options in both places. I reckon that ships leaving [England] will not do bad business for I understand that wheat is being bought at very reasonable prices. If the price began to fall again I would be very interested in participating though only on the condition above, that one could get the goods either to Italy or to Spain as one wants. I shall await further enlightenment from you, and also news of what is happening concerning wheat and rye. I am told here that corn is at such a reasonable price that one can enjoy a certainty in exporting it, about which I would gladly be further informed.

    I see that you have no correspondence with Johan Schryner of Lübeck. I should be glad to know who it was from here that recommended his son to you and where he has been acquainted with Van Deurs, for reasons of some importance.

    What you write about other trades is most useful to me. With cordial regards, &c.

London:	34*s* 7–8*g* 2 usances.
Amsterdam:	33⅓ at sight.
Venice:	90½ to ⅓ at usance.

¹ The English last, of 10 quarters, is reckoned the equivalent of 29.08 hectolitres; the last of Amsterdam 29.18 hectolitres, and the last of Hamburg 31.65 (Doursther, pp. 194, 196.)

$$\frac{2\ Oct.}{3\ Oct.}1677$$

371 E. RULAND to JD
HAMBURG   25 SEPTEMBER 1677

D] I have received your letter of the 18th instant together with the second copy of the bill of exchange remitting £150 at 35s 3g on N. Henriques, which will be useful. I have also received the bill of £75 on R. Thanes returned protested, for which I shall procure what is necessary. It is good that you have obtained acceptance of the other £710 remitted in three bills for your account and have credited me accordingly. It is also good that you have paid out on presentation of the second copy of the £100 bill of exchange on C. V. Beselar.

I see that nothing is to be done with oil from [London] so we must leave it be. Thank you, however, for news of the prices at which the [East India] Company has sold its commodities in [London]. Things are all very dear; pepper is to be had in Holland for $10\frac{1}{2}$ g. Regarding copper wares—there is little garcopper coming here from Sweden and it is all in the hands of one person who wants to push up its price again, though no one wants it. Some copper is coming from Hungary. If no English ships bring any copper out of Sweden I believe that the prices of one sort and another will have to rise higher. I shall be glad to learn what prices garcopper, sheet copper, wire and Hungarian plate-copper fetch in London, as well as the price of currants.

For the cost of the protested bill you sent I have credited you 5s. In my preceding letter I remitted you £180 on Thomas Shepherd for your account; £198 on John Croger, and £100 on the same for my account. Herewith are going second copies of each to serve if the first are lost. The exchange on us here was rising—please remit my balance and if you can do it for 1s 5g or 1s 6g better on Amsterdam I would rather you sent it there. With friendly regards, &c.

[P.S.] Please send my two bales of Ardasse silk as ordered to the friend in Lisbon. Even though the first ship would not take it another will do so, for Mr Joye used to send various quantities for me to Lisbon. I wait to hear that you have succeeded. With cordial regards, I remain, &c.

London:	34s 7g 2 usances.
Amsterdam:	$33\frac{3}{8}$ at sight.
Paris:	$46-46\frac{1}{4}$ 2 usances.

$$\frac{3\ Oct.}{8\ Oct.}1677$$

372 B. BEUZELIN & SON to JD
ROUEN   8 OCTOBER 1677

'Despuis notre derniere nous avons receu la vostre du 20/30 passé; en responce il est bien que vous nous ayez credittez de touttes les remises que nous vous avons faittes pour notre compe. Nouse sommes marris du peu de profit que vous trouvez sur ces parties; c'est une malheur que le change a tousjours esté en baissant, comme il fait encore touts les ordinaires, n'y ayant presque point de lettres a $54\frac{1}{2}$d icy, et a Paris il ne ce fait qu'a $\frac{3}{8}$d. Il ne peut pas demeurer encore long temps a ces bas prix, puisqu'il y aura grand vendange a Bourdeaux et a La Rochelle ou les frais ne seront pas chere veu le prodigieux nombre de navires anglois quy y sont aller chercher employ. L'on nous a dit qu'il y en estoit allé pres de 700.

Nous avons fait mettre a terre les 560 torches de fil de latton hors de la *Thomasine*, mais il s'en manque une, dont le maitre Chapman est bien adverty, les ayant luy mesme fait recompter chez nous. Quant a la venthe nous observerons ce que vous nous avez ordonne, mais pour pouvoir atteindre au prix limitté il faudra ce donner encore patience, car le prix n'est encore qu'a £89*t* et £90*t* au quel prix ceux quy en ont receu par ces derniers navires venus d'Hambourg vendent avecq empressement. Le navire que Mons. Legendre attend de Stockholme a passe le Zondt. Il a abord 2,000 torches, et le reste bray et goudron quy vaut icy *W*.80 a *W*.81 le last et le goudron *W*.58 en par laste. Il est arrivé du bré de chez vous que l'on dit qu'on peut establir icy a *W*.75 le last, ce quy nous fait croire qu'il n'est pas pour hausser davantage du prix qu'il est a present. Pour le goudron le temps de la consummation n'est qu'au printemps, et il y en a assez en ville pour ce qu'il en faut. Nous vous remercions de l'advis que vous nous donnez de la vanthe des marchandises de la Compagnie d'Oriant quy vent tousjours plus advantageusement que ne font les particuliers et rarement il-y-a a gaigner ausquelle. Les huilles sont touttes acheptees icy en une main, de sorte que celles de Siville vaudroyent a present £32½*t* la 100; le savon d'Allicant est fort demande a £45*t* le 100; ris de Milan vaudroit £20 le 100. Il n'y en a d'autres tous point en ville. Nous vous baisons les mains et somme tousjours, Monsieur, vos trés humbles serviteurs.

Amsterdam:	99¼	⎫
Londres:	55½	⎬ 2 usances.
Lille:	97½	⎭
Hambourg:	¼%	

$\frac{6\ Oct.}{22\ Oct.}$1677

373   BALL, GOSFRIGHT & CO to JD

LEGHORN   24 SEPTEMBER 1677

'Sir, Wee have now received yours of the 16th past. In answer, pitch and tarre are commodities of small consume here, not 100 barrells of tarre sold here in a yeare unless since the French and Spaniard have been with theire fleetes in these parts when neare 2,000 barrells may have been consumed. In Legorne at present wee compute there may bee about 1,200 barrells most whereof in the consumers' hands, who since this commodity hath been very cheape have provided themselves. About 400 barrells that is in first hands wee may believe may bee had for 6 [dollars] or under but is esteemed every day a rising commodity. Pitch held at $7 and about 100 barrells arriving first may yeeld $6½ or thereabouts and two in three hundred barrells will suffitianly supply our markett this commodity being of farre lesse consume then the other. This is the best enformation wee cann give you concerning these commodities.

Pepper now risen to *D*.10 and by the continiall discouragements the Italians have had by engrossing this commodity wee find they have att present but little remaining on their hands, and none or very little in first hands to sell, so thatt in few daies in all probabilitie this commodity must come higher so that if our [East India] Company in England sell cheape good wil bee done thereby. Lead continues at *D*.18¼ but with little demand att presant, there being a good quantity in towne. Tinne at *D*.11 and what is good goes of very corrently but of late much hath been inported of an ordinary quallity, supposed with some aloy of lead, which will ly by some time for sailes, and since this commodity cheape in England good may bee done therby, but care ought to bee taken it bee of its true allay and marked with the antient marke, the Rose and Crowne, for our change of markes (some of late having been imported marked with a Lion) gives a disrepute. Russia hides 24 soldi per lb., logwood *D*.26 per 100 lb.; calve-skins 15*s* per lb.; all woollen goods a very greate drug.

In port, of English wee have only the *Benjamin & Elizabeth* as yet void of employment. Two ships are now entring, if knowne ere closure shall bee denoted hereunder, and being the presant needfull with due respects and remaine, &c.

London: 54⅓ per [dollar].
Venice: 104⅞.
Amsterdam: 98¼

Just now is arrived the *Teneriffe Merchant* from Allexandria, *Mercury* from Tunis, *John & Joseph* from Tunis, and *Riga Merchant* from Genova.'

$$\frac{9 \; Oct. \; 1677}{1 \; Jan. \; 1678}$$

374 R. GARLINGHOFF to JD
HAMBURG   2 OCTOBER 1677

[G] I safely received your letter of the 31st of August, and the reason why I have not answered it earlier is that I have been away in the country for these last three weeks. This must serve as an answer to your questions concerning the copper trade. There is little garcopper in stock and, what there is—about 200 or 300 slb—is under firm control and maintained at a high price. One would not be able to buy it for less than *RD*.70 bank-money per shippound. Of copper-wire made in Hamburg there are scarcely 400 coils ready in stock, and that is in demand at 72 *ML* bank-money per 100 lb., and if the garcopper were brought at the price mentioned above the wire would have to cost more, or else we would have to let our works come to a standstill. As I said, there is little or nothing in stock, but our Hamburg works can produce 1,100 to 1,200 coils every month, and at Lübeck, 500 to 600 coils. That is all that the works in this country can produce in any month.[1]

If there is any way I can be of service in one thing or another you may freely command, and I must also thank you for the manifold efforts you have made on behalf of my son, which I beg you to excuse. We shall try to make them good, and for the rest remain, &c.

    1 ' . . . *dass is all dass werk dat hier in lande da von alle monat kan gemachet werden* . . . '.

$$\frac{31 \; Oct.}{26 \; Nov.} 1677$$

375 G. RICHARDS to JD
BILBAO   21 OCTOBER 1677

'Sir, I have now before mee yours of the 24 past, whereby I perceave you had received the account sent you and noted them accordingly. I am sorry the wheat rendred no better. Its now here worth 2¾ and 3 pieces of eight per *fanega*, and at Cadize and Mallaga neare 4 pieces of eight, so that had you made use of my former advyses it been advantagious. It cannot be had any wheare cheape enough at present unlesse in Ireland, and in France the exportation of the comodity is prohibited. The monye standing out on yours shall be recovered and made you home with all speed. I note how the returns made you rendred. Of the yellow sort I shall send you no more; that in the barrell cost 1 per cent lesse than Sir John's, and no more is at present to be met with so by Foreland[1] I sent you some barrs which I hope by this time are come to your hand. That sort will ryse. Assoone these fears are over I shall make it my only businesse to cleere all the accounts which can bee finished. What calli[c]os you are concerned in with Sir John will, I hope, yeald proffit, although they cost deare. I cannot incourage you to any thinge particulerly at present. Bayes are now cheaper at home and coming against the springe will render advantage. Hambro wax when the exchange from London is high, and lattine plates is that you understand. The 'XX' and thickest are dearest in England, and the thinnest are most esteemed here. They may be had at about 18s per cwt. aboard. For the government thereof you may send 30 barriles. I thank your advyse of Mr Let[hieullier] and with my respects remayne, Sir, your humble servant.

[P.S.] The chocolate is gonne, I hope it will prove good.'

[1] Captain Jacob Foreland, of the *Biscay Arms*. He carried 1,500 'bars' (i.e. *pesos*) invoiced as 'rusty iron', and sold to goldsmith John Temple at 5s $2\frac{5}{8}d$ per oz.

$$\frac{15\ Dec.}{21\ Dec.}1677$$

376   P. BOTTE to JD

AMSTERDAM   21 DECEMBER 1677

[D]   On the 10th instant was my latest; since then I have received yours of the 4th/14th instant, to which in answer I have made a note of my agreement with the three last sale-accounts, as well as the one preceding, vizt.

	£	s	d
the cargo of Robert Young	616	18	7
of Nicholas Reymers	246	17	2
John Chapman	223	18	6
John Garrett	488	11	1
Henry Sutton.	280	16	6
Thomas Webber	603	17	11
together rendering	2,458	19	9[1]

for which I have debited your current account.

In addition the following have arrived and, according to your reports, are unloaded, namely:

	Pitch	Tar
Francis Branson	15	$34\frac{2}{13}$
William Roberts	12	$96\frac{4}{13}$
Thomas Richards, at Hull	8	$62\frac{6}{13}$
Joseph Wadlow	12	78
Samuel Cooper	$19\frac{10}{12}$	$95\frac{6}{13}$
John Croger	$30\frac{1}{12}$	$132\frac{1}{13}$
Total lasts	$96\frac{1}{12}$	$498\frac{6}{13}$

On these you have promised to accept £7 sterling per last of pitch, which is £672, and £5 sterling per last of tar, which is £2,492; which, together with what has been sold, is a total of £5,622 19s 9d.

Against that I have drawn on you to pay the following:

28 August	to Dor. Wilhelms	£250
31 August	to Davit Rutger's order.	£400
24 September	to Conrad Block's order	£200
5 October	to Abram Gerard's order	£1,000
9 October	to David Rutger's order	£400
19 November	to Joseph Deutz's order	£1,500
10 December	to Gerard Weyman	£600
	to Davit Rutger's order.	£600
	For Canary sack	£91 11s.

Total   £5,041 11s.

Thus, according to our agreement, I can still draw £600 on you, at interest, until the goods are sold. It therefore seems rather strange to me that you should forbid me to draw any more without your consent. If I had been able to get out from Stockholm all the goods for which I have paid, you would find that I should not have to draw to the utter limit, but now—for lack of more than 300 lasts still lying in Sweden, for which I have paid—I have to make those goods which have arrived as serviceable as I can. I hope you will be kind enough not to insist too strictly on what was promised and not object to an extra £400, for no business of any importance would be done if one were so narrowly watched that one was always afraid of running short. I hope that, in view of what you still have in your hands, and other things, you will not feel uneasy about me. Thus, I have drawn two more bills of exchange, sent herewith, payable at double usance to the orders of Joseph Deutz,

vizt. £600 at 2 usances

£400 at 2 usances, which I beg you to return accepted by the next post. If, by the time they fall due, you are unable to sell enough of what remains still unsold to cover the balance in excess of the £5 and £7 plus expenses, I give you my permission to draw on me what is lacking and I shall accept your drafts.

The quantity which remains unsold is not of much consequence, and if the customers will not buy it directly from the ships, so that one has to incur expenses, please hold the price of tar at £11 and the pitch at £15 sterling.

I should be glad to see you arrange the charter for St Ubes at the price, and on the conditions, you previously described, but if not one must let it rest, for it is better to let it go than to do it at a loss.

I shall send the letter of attorney concerning Sowton in my next, and meanwhile I beg you to try and content him. You will find it difficult to understand what he has to say about my accounts. With regards, I remain, &c.

¹ Jacob David's own notes on this letter correct this and other alleged mistakes in Botte's arithmetic. The total here should be £2,460 19s 9d.

² The total for pitch should be $96\frac{11}{12}$ lasts, i.e. nearly 97 lasts, and David reckons this as worth £672 pounds but the $498\frac{1}{2}$ lasts at only £2,490.

$\dfrac{17\ Dec.}{18\ Dec.}$1677

377   A. VAN KUFFELER to JD

AMSTERDAM   24 DECEMBER 1677

[D]   Although I have nothing of yours to answer, nor any special reason for writing to you, I cannot neglect to inform you that Jeremias van Raey, a substantial merchant here, has gone bankrupt. I hope you are not implicated, which I shall be relieved to hear. Let this serve as a warning against any further involvement. I am not involved, but more through good luck than judgement. It is indeed lamentable that such a pillar should come to fall, but what can one say? We live in very miserable times. There have been two or three other small bankruptcies not long ago and as a result one does not know whom one can trust. On the Exchange credit is entirely dead and one may shortly hear of further failures, so if the Lord is not merciful to us in granting a good peace many honourable folk will be ruined by this lengthy and disastrous war. One hears of nothing but losses, and business is so bad that one has to run great risks at sea from capers and other dangers. Instead of profits, commodities are frequently yielding losses, for in general business has been ruined and most kinds of merchandize are at such low prices that it is astonishing. Nothing is selling because demand is very poor. The whole of Christendom is troubled and the war has impoverished so many people that wares simply do not sell. There are many folk who, inspired by the low price of various goods, sent large amounts here in recent years in hopes of a peace and a rise in prices, but they have been greatly deceived in their expectations. The older the goods the more they are slighted. Capital is in confusion[1] and we can see no sign of any improvement—*enfin*, it is better to sit tight than to invest, and that is the reason why I dare undertake little, for if one balances the risk against the small prospect of profit neither the one nor the other is encouraging. May the Lord drive away these dark clouds and give us a long and durable peace!

The burghermasters have allowed Van Raey a free pass so that no one can molest him for a given time, on the grounds that his business is not in such a bad way but has been overtaken by bills of exchange and some goods have been delayed here and there. The Lord will settle everything for the best, to whose protection I commend you and, offering my services, remain, &c.

London: 35s 8g ⎫
Paris: 95¾ ⎬ 2 usances.
                 ⎭

[1] *'Capitaelen over stuyr . . .'*.

$$\frac{25\ Dec.}{28\ Dec.}1677$$

378 C. BENE to JD

HAMBURG   14 DECEMBER 1677

[D] My last letter was on the 7th instant. Since then I have received yours of the 7th, by which I see that you have not yet bought the 10 sacks of Smyrna cotton which I ordered because of a lack of ships coming this way. The Elbe here has been full of ice but is now navigable again and there are two ships which have arrived here from [England], and since you said that you were arranging for a ship to come here I assume you have performed my commission and await the account and the bill of lading.

I shall maintain the price of your remaining cotton at 14g, for it ought to fetch as much as it costs in [England], but because it is now an unfavourable time of year one ought to take that into consideration a little and wait until there is further demand. I have sold nothing of our Ardasse yet. I am holding it at 15s and it would have sold readily if a Persian had not arrived here who brought a good quantity overland through Poland and ruined the market. One must have patience. As I told you, ours are too coarse and stringy. In future, obtain something better, I shall regulate myself according to the way things go in [England] and if I discover anything good or likely to succeed will let you know.

I am glad that Mr Martens Ecking has taken the £20 remitted and placed it to my account. It can serve towards the commissioned cotton. With this letter I am remitting you for that account £50 at double usance on John Banks negotiated here with Jan & Herman Luys at 34s 4g. Please procure what is necessary for the enclosed first copy of the bill of exchange and credit my account with £85 16s 8d.

I was glad to hear that you are not involved in the recent bankruptcy here and hope you are likewise free of those which have since followed, as I am, God be thanked! May He protect us from wicked men. I shall be glad to hear more of what is to be hoped for from [England] regarding peace and war, and also if there are any changes in commodities taking place. There is little worth mentioning here, partly because of the many bankruptcies and scarcity of money. Apulian oil costs *RD* 92 per 820 lb. for cash; currants are 30 to 31 *ML* per 100 lb. with $8\frac{2}{3}$ per cent rebate, since a quantity has arrived here from [England]. Barbary almonds are at 32 *ML* per 100 lb., Aleppo galls at 45 to 48 *ML*, brown ginger $4\frac{1}{4}$ to $4\frac{3}{8}$ g per lb., and scraped ginger at 9 or $9\frac{1}{4}$ g with $8\frac{2}{3}$ per cent rebate. Of Swedish copper-wire there are only about 250 coils here. Most of it is 'Great Crown' and the residue 'Crowned N' and it cannot be had for less than 70 to $69\frac{1}{2}$ *ML* per 100 lb. Hamburg copper-wire is at 71 to 72 *ML*, while copper kettles are at *RD* 70, sheet copper at *RD* 68 to 69, Swedish garcopper *RD* $64\frac{1}{2}$ to 65 and Hungarian plates *RD* 60 to 61 per shippound. If there is anything in which I can be of service please inform me and command.

B. Sirps has been here and as far as I understand has not yet returned to [England]. If he arrives in [London] you will know how to demand the letter-postage from him, as already requested. I shall expect my current account and hope to hear how much I am to get for the rebate of duty on our Ardasse, so that I can make a record of it all. Meanwhile, with cordial regards, &c.

25 Dec. 1677
1 Jan. 1678

79 CAREL LUBERS to JD

HAMBURG   18 DECEMBER 1677

G] Dear Sir and unknown, yet dearly valued, friend—greetings! For lack of material I have never before had the honour of writing to you, but I am doing so now on the recommendation of my good friend, Mr Reinholt Garlinghoff, principally to let you know that I am sending to you at [London] for my account Simon Morris[1] with 50 large pieces of copper-sheet manufactured here, weighing Slb. 10.9.1, and 50 coils of Hamburg brass-wire, weighing 1,411 lb., as you may see from the enclosed bill of lading. The captain is ready to depart and is now waiting for a good wind. May God bring him in safety. On his arrival will you please receive the goods and do your best for me in selling them at the highest possible price, preferably for cash but if for time only to good and reliable people. This is only a trial, and if I find it advantageous and you do not reject my correspondence I shall continue to send you further consignments—but do be careful always to sell to reliable people. I have the opportunity provided by another ship of sending another 50 coils which are standing ready. Since it is at my own risk I do not want to venture too much in one ship. There is a consignment here of 200 coils of Swedish wire with the mark of the 'Great Crown' and the 'Crowned N'. I would be glad to learn what price it fetches in London and whether there is much in stock. Please also mention the prices for sheet-copper, pots and brass-ware and of all kinds of iron, such as ordinary iron sheets, square iron, schampeleon and voyage iron.

There is a special reason why the [copper] sheets are not marked with my mark. With friendly regards, May God protect you, &c.

¹ Captain of the *Mary* of Topsham.

$$\frac{26 \text{ Jan.}}{29 \text{ Jan.}} 1678$$

380 J. BOOR to JD
STOCKHOOLM   26 NOVEMBER 1677

[D] Your welcome letter of the 5th past reached me on the 21st instant. The following will serve as a reply.

It is true that, because of the great quantities, wine will not sell here in the least. There is enough lying here to last for two years, and it is in so many hands that one cannot undercut prices without selling at a great loss. To tell you the truth, there is never any profit which an isolated individual can make here for there are too many old-established wine merchants who obtain the wine on their own account and drive no other trade. These people have all the tap-houses under their thumbs so it is quite impossible for anyone to compete against them except with loss to his colleagues. Also there is no truth in the idea that one can send it for an immediate sale, much less procure remittances, because this is a commodity which is sold on long-term credit. Thus, I could not give your friends full satisfaction, but if I can be of service to you or your friends with any other commodity you may freely command me. I would be grateful for your recommendation, and you may be assured that your friends will be completely satisfied, for I shall take care of their interests as if they were my own.

The brandy will all be sold, some for 300 and some for 280 dollars per hogshead, according to what Mr Cletcher tells me about that which he has taken back since his return from the country. But of the other, little or none is sold, and according to what Mr Cletcher tells me he is on the point of selling to one of the wine dealers. I cannot see him getting more than 140 dollars per hogshead on average, for there is much bad stuff among them. Your friends have been very badly served by those in France. I can obtain 160 and 180 dollars per hogshead for the best sort, and the longer the time it takes the more loss by leakage occurs, so that from two bad barrels the best one must be chosen.

I am very relieved that you will be suffering no loss by the cargo since you are not involved, but I wish that those who are involved might get as much profit as possible.

The un-free toll and expenses are too great. May God transfer their loss to someone else! You will be further informed about what happens regarding the sale. For your report about what is happening in trade I thank you—it may come in useful. It is very obvious that our goods this year in England will cost [—missing—]. Ordinary iron is selling for 26 and 27 dollars; fine iron at 28, 29 and 30 dollars of the sort which was previously selling for 33 dollars, but this decline has come about because there is no shipping-freight available for [England] or Holland, and many goods are lying about. Garcopper costs 244 dollars, and wire 336 to 340 dollars per shippound. Salt is now put out of the market and the first [to arrive] has been sold by me for $13\frac{1}{2}$ dollars per ton, and that is for two ships' lading, for your information. Just how things will develop in the spring time will tell, and you will be informed.

You complain about the Österby and Gimo iron, that it is not as good as it used to be, yet that ought not to be so for I can think of no change which has taken place. Please let me know at once, exactly, what it is about which you are complaining. Winter is now close on our heels, so the waters are beginning to freeze. Wherewith I remain, &c.

Amsterdam: $24\frac{1}{4}$ }
Hamburg: $25\frac{1}{2}$ } Marks at 1 month's sight.

$$\frac{26\,Jan.}{1\,Feb.}\,1678$$

381 J. A. FONCK to JD
HAMBURG   15 JANUARY 1678

[D] You have my thanks for the happy New Year wishes you sent me in your letter of the 1st of January. I reciprocate them, wishing you all the prosperity and good health you could desire for yourself.

It seems that I must remain patient about my Marglitzer linens since they are of the good old-fashioned sort and not of the kind currently being made. I believe they were once without demand for six years but were then much sought after and their price leaped up. That time could come again for they are no longer being made.

We have so many bankruptcies daily here that business is at a standstill and all the goods which had been sold on credit are now at rock-bottom prices, so that the commitments I have made for myself and others (to whom the Lord God may teach a lesson) have become hateful.

However, could you procure some indigo guatemalo which could be delivered here for $5\frac{1}{2}$ schellings flemish, with $8\frac{2}{3}$ per cent discount? Also some 300 or 400 barrels of figs of middling quality—that is to say, well-conditioned and dry (only they must be well-sugared). I bought similar good parcels from some Englishmen for $7\frac{1}{2}$ *ML* and 8 *ML* per 100 lb., cash, on which those fellows made a good profit as is known to me from participation in one such parcel. I would gladly take a share with you in a consignment, but please work out whether it can be delivered profitably at the above-mentioned prices and before your country becomes involved in a war. I trust that the ships arriving will not be full of it and moreover that you will obtain the quality I described. Take very good care to see that it is not damp, or so black that it is unsaleable. I await your answer, and also your feelings about grains, pepper and oil. If Provence almonds, newly-pickled, can be delivered here at 30 *ML* per 100 lb. (with $8\frac{2}{3}$ per cent discount) please see about it at once. I remain, with friendly regards, &c.

[P.S.] I hope you have no interests involved in Octavius Buschman who has gone bankrupt as (God knows) others may, I fear. One is in a state of continual apprehension. If you will stand surety for money at my disposal in return for $\frac{1}{2}$ per cent per month commission, please let me know for my guidance.

London: 34*s* 2*g*.
Amsterdam: $33\frac{1}{3}$.
Paris: 46.

$$\frac{26\ Jan.}{5\ Feb.}\ 1678$$

382 A. RULAND to JD

HAMBURG   15 JANUARY 1678

[D] I find I have still to answer your letter of the 23rd of October, concerning the trade in grains
from [England]. If ships are now under way, either for Italy or Spain, they will do excellent
business. There is now plenty ready to go, principally from Holland, and although it is much
cheaper—especially the wheat—it will be left standing if, because of this freeze which seems
about to descend, it is not allowed to leave. In such case it would be well to send some from
[England]. Therefore please tell me in answer to this, how expensive would it be per quarter,
free of duty, for wheat, rye and buck-wheat? The last two are useful for Italy but not for
Spain; the wheat for both places. I have often before sent buck-wheat to Guinea[1] which one
first dries and then it is very durable. Otherwise this commodity very easily heats up,
especially if it goes during the summer.

  People here hope that the marriage of his Highness the Prince of Orange will lead to a
stronger understanding with the Dutch and the promotion of a general peace. The Swedes
have totally routed the Danes on the island of Rugen, wherewith cordial regards, &c.

----

  [1] *Sic.*—in error for *Genua* (Genoa)?

$$\frac{29\ Jan.}{15\ Apr.}\ 1678$$

383 G. RICHARDS to JD

BILBAO   21 JANUARY 1678

'Sir, I have now before me yours of the 24th past, with bill of loading of 80 pieces Colchester
bayes you had consigned me for your account by the *Biskey Armes* which I pray God send
safe, as also those you intend by Pooke. I shall use all dilligence in there sale and make use of
all occassions to procure ready mony for them as also for your other goods to accomodate yo
with the quicker returns. By Roach you will have received some fine ware, and against the
next conveyance I shall provide some more of the same. Of your narrow bafts, now received,
I have sold one trunk at 21¾ *R. pta.* per piece. The rest will also reach that price and they with
your long cloth render reasonable good advantage, and if a warr should succeed between
France and England all goods will be here in more esteeme. I cannot indeed mencon any
commodity to yo at present which promises more then ordinary advantage. Sempeternos I
all wayes goe selling more or lesse. Sir John hath good experience therein and I finde sends
them cheapest. He will lett you have what share you desire at any time with him. For lattin
plates it will be now to late to ingage any for the next vessell from Hambourgh I doubt will
bring to many. What Sir John hath coming I hope will render well. I have formerly written
you about Hambourgh waxx, wherein I finde Mr Boverie is frequently concerned. The
exchange falling soe from France for England, I suppose it is rissen for Holland and
Hambourgh, when what goods you order thence will come out to you soe much the cheaper
from Holland. What's here vendible are cloves and cinamont. By the latter Sir John made a
good account last year and hath 30 quintalls more coming. Also Russia hydes have also here
considerable expense, the best are now worth 2¾ a 3 *R. pta.* per lb. The error in the account of
your callicoes Sir John hath advised me of, being about 10 *R. pta.* which shall be charged in

the next account I send you. Your wheat was not all sold for ready mony, neither indeed have I recovered much more then I have remitted you thereon. I shall nevertheless verry speedily send you the remainder, which pray acquaint Mr Hayes with my service. Wheat is now worth here 3 pieces of eight per *hanega* and more at St Sebastian, and I believe it will still rise. I have not to add at present but my respects, and remaine, your humble servant, &c.'

$$\frac{\text{11 Feb.}}{\text{12 Apr.}} 1678$$

84 I. CRONSTRÖM to JD
SKULTUNA[1]   12 DECEMBER 1677

D]   I am most gratefully obliged to you for the various letters I have received from you in the course of the year, with useful information about trade and what has been happening with Swedish goods. As I have been selling my products here at home there has been no material on which to keep up our correspondence. However, this letter is occasioned by the fact that Commerce Councillor Nicholas Preus is going to London from Gothenburg with a certain royal commission, and I have asked him as a friend to settle the account concerning the blank farthings which was in Mr Burkin's hands. I understand he has died and I want to recover the remaining effects, which I transferred some time ago to Jeremias van Raey in Amsterdam. Since I understand that Van Raey has employed you before in his affairs I am sure that you are well-informed about the matter, so I am asking you as a friend to supply Mr Preus with all the information you may have and give him good advice about how this task may be handled with the greatest circumspection.

For this, it is necessary to know:
1. Who is now managing the estate of the late Mr Burkin and what do you know about such person?
2. In what relationship does the family of Burkin stand with the Controller of the Mint, Sir James Hoare?
3. If the copper farthings are still in use, and if new farthings were minted for 1675, '76 and '77?
4. If the remaining 182 barrels of farthings are still in the hands of the Burkin family, or whether they have been delivered to the Mint?
5. Whether, of the whole consigment of 326 barrels,[2] only 144 were paid out of the Mint, or whether perhaps Mr Burkin retained them all in his hands and kept a running account with the Mint?

About this and anything more which may serve to illuminate the task of Mr Preus, please inquire closely and let him know. I shall be most greatly obliged to re-pay you with gratitude, friendship and service for any assistance you may be able to give me.

The reason why I began to get involved in this trade was to help my brother Abraham Cronström, in so far that the deliveries might be completed according to contract, and it was my intention to give the commission to your dear wife, Madame Marescoe. But my brother warned me off, saying that the firm was not reliable but on the contrary suffered from great internal jealousies and that nothing but quarrels would ensue since Burkin had been promised by the contract that he would have an exclusive commission; and if it came into other hands it would be regarded as raw copper yet pay duty as if it were manufactured copper—as it mostly did afterwards.

I shall expect a regular report about what happens in this and other aspects of Swedish trade, especially in what ways one can get coal to Stockholm at the best possible price. I should also be glad to know the price of malt and hops in England, for my guidance, with information about how English malt compares with that of Danzig or Riga.

        With regards, I remain, &c.

   [1] Isaac and Abraham Cronström acquired the Skultuna works (about 125 km. from Stockholm, N.N.W. of Västerås) in September 1670.

   [2] Of some 2,225 barrels of copper-farthing blanks delivered to England by the Cronströms between 1672 and 1675, the 326 were the last consignment, received in February 1675—*CTB, 1672–75*, p. 478.

$$\frac{18\ Feb.}{19\ Feb.}1678$$

385 J. & H. VAN BAERLE to JD

    AMSTERDAM   22 FEBRUARY 1678

[D] Our last letter was on the 15th instant, by which we ordered you not to remit our money until further order (as we understand that the exchange in [London] has fallen to 35*s* 5*g*–4*g*). This we now confirm. Since then, we have received yours of the 1st, 5th and 8th instant (Old Style) with remittance for our account of £100 at 35*s* 4*g* to receive at 2 usances from Israel Hayes. We have obtained promise of its acceptance and have credited you for it in our account. You should since then have received our letter of the 15th instant, so we shall expect no more remittances during this low exchange. It is good that you have deposited £500 sterling with the East India Company at 5 per cent interest per annum until the 25th of March in the hope the exchange will meanwhile improve. We would be well content if you placed amounts with the Company on the same terms, as the money comes in, since according to your promise there will be no commission charged on it. It would oblige us greatly.

    We see that the prospect of war with France has diminished [in England]. There are many here who hope that Parliament's firm resolution may well dispose the King of France to peace, which should shortly be proclaimed. We remain, with cordial regards, &c.

London: 34*s* 5*g* ⎫
Paris: $95\frac{1}{2}$ ⎬ 2 usances.
Hamburg: $33\frac{7}{16}$ stuivers per schelling ⎫
Antwerp: $\frac{1}{4}$ per cent premium on bills ⎬ at sight.

$$\frac{20\ Feb.}{21\ Feb.}1678$$

386 P. CAULIER to JD

    YARMOUTH   18 FEBRUARY 1678

'Sir and Honnored Kinsman, For Answer to yours of the 16 instant. Yo say yo want ships for Stockholm and Wyborow to England to London to which I say yo say not wether the ships shal goe in the ballast hens or must come to London to load thens. We should be glad to serve you if it might sute with our conveniency and safty but as things loock lyke a war yo must expect we shal demand more then formerly. We have John Garret our *Concourd* now come from Rochel to this port. I have my ship *Bar* of 220 tun or 120 last. If yo plese to propos the most yo give others if possibel can shal serve yo but the voyage cannot be imagened to be done so soone as yo propos and it canot be imagined if this feared war goes on with France that it must come to a ruptur before we can returne. Therfor pray be plaine in yor proposition, wither we shal have convoy out and home or only home; if outward, when redy to sayle; if homwards only, wher the convoy shal meat us, or wether you propos said ships must goe and come without convoy. Pray mention what we must load thins. If pitch and tar, what iron eatch ship shal have or none at al and wether we must be bound to goe to boeth ports to load or load up at one part. Be plesed to explaine yourself as fully as yo can and when you have agreed with any Londoners if you plese to prefer us upon your admishun returne you our answer. In the meane tyme I salut you and our cosin your lady and family and rest, &c.

[P.S.] Cosen, since the above I have consulted with Mr Garret and he is willing to serve yo and he proposes if yo plese to accept his ship from hens to Stocqholme and bacq to London. We wil serve yo at £5 per last home to London provided yo put in 50 last of iron and the rest pitch and tar or what you plese.

St Ubes salt none in towne but Spanish salt to be had at £4 5s or ther abouts. If you incline to buy any the sooner the better. It is arissen comodity—for French salt is advanced from 46s to £3 and £3 5s per way and Spanish salt is always 20s per way better. Heare is some quantity of Spanish in towne. If yo resolve ought yo must not slep one it.'

2 Mar.
8 Mar. 1678

87 P. BOTTE to JD
AMSTERDAM 8 MARCH 1678

[D] My last letter was on the 4th of March in which I sent you a bill of exchange for £200 sterling drawn on John Croger so that you could get it accepted and return it, which I am accordingly waiting for. Since then I have received both your letters of the 19th and 22nd of February, to which I must say that I am very sorry you have refused to accept my drafts. This is the first time that has been done to me. It might be the case that they were drawn payable to a good friend of mine and were only done *pro forma*, but while the first is true the second is quite the contrary. You should know perfectly well that when I draw a bill of exchange which affects the honour of a merchant I am careful that I do not over-draw, for I am aware that any one who accepts bills without the security of effects is giving me credit, and if he is not inclined to do it he will not pass them. Therefore I have to know that he has sufficient effects, which on this occasion I have done. But, from the beginning, I have noticed that you have had no inclination to accept anything unless it was covered by effects which you have not sold so I have not asked, thinking that with God's help I might avoid having to do so. But with my effects sold at a fixed price to reliable customers, as you have done, no one can claim that I have been served in conformity with the original proposal on which I began to correspond with you. I am more astonished that you have not been willing to honour my drafts than you are astonished that I drew them! After all, to accept drafts and pay them as money comes in from the sale of goods does not require one to venture any capital. And one is getting a handsome commission. People without capital can easily do that. If one wants more, one must stipulate better conditions. I must declare that I am heartily annoyed that you have done such dishonour to my drafts, all the more as I know you were not lacking sufficient means to fulfil them. It never occurred to me, with regard to you personally, that you would not be sufficiently confident about the reliability of your customers to give me credit for my effects and that I would thus come to suffer some loss. So far, God be praised, I have found no reason to complain about my correspondents and it would depress me to find the first grounds with you—God forbid! Now patience.

I shall expect a sale account and current account from you, which you will please send by the next post so that I can see how we stand with one another. I can make calculations about it myself since nothing is forthcoming on my latest drafts. If the consignment which went to Bristol has been paid for please remit me the proceeds in good bills payable at sight, for you have already deducted your commission.

Since I see that the English are demanding £4 sterling for freight on a last of tar from Stockholm, and will not sail for less, please do no more about it. I shall arrange for everything to come here first, which I can have done for *f*.18 per last at the most; and I can get it carried from here to [London] for 18 or 20 schellings per last, so my freight will not amount to more than £3. And by that means I hope to demonstrate to you that you will have no reason to complain about having to advance money on my behalf, and I shall no longer have to live in fear of insults to my drafts.

May God give us a peace, to whose protection I commend you and remain, &c.

$$\frac{7\ Mar.}{8\ Mar.}1678$$

388   C. DE HERTOGH'S WIDOW & HEIRS to JD

HAMBURG   26 FEBRUARY 1678

[D]   Your letters of the 15th and 19th instant have been safely received, by which we see more fully that the exchange has fallen greatly through fear of a war, which does not surprise us greatly since it has done so here even more and already no money can be got below 32*s*. However, it now seems that there is a change approaching and a lot of money is arriving without bills of exchange, whereby we hope that the exchange will rise again. We are glad that you have lent our money to the East India Company at interest, but since we have no knowledge of the security we are well satisfied that you should enjoy the profit from it, and if the exchange rises again we expect you to remit in reliable bills and trust that you will manage it without loss.

Everything is going contrary to expectations, and one can place no reliance on any price since the consumption of all goods is extremely poor. Pepper can be had for $11\frac{1}{4}g$, galls at 43 to 45 *ML*, Ardasse silk at 15*s* flem., Cyprus cotton at 15*g*, and Smyrna cotton at 13*g*. Long raisins from Malaga are at 21 *ML* and in baskets they are 11 *ML*. Indigo is at $6\frac{1}{2}g$.

We must hope for peace, so that trade may revive again and provide us with further opportunity to augment our business, to which we are very favourably disposed. So we beg you to call upon us freely at every opportunity.

Just today an Englishman, Mr De Clercq, has gone bankrupt. God be thanked we are not involved and likewise hope you are not.

With hearty regards, may God protect you, we remain, &c.

London: 32*s*–32*s* 2*g*.
Amsterdam: $33\frac{1}{2}$.
Paris: $45\frac{1}{2}$ [?].

$$\frac{\textit{10 Mar.}}{\textit{19 Mar.}}\textit{1678}$$

389 GEORG KOHRÖBER to JD
GOZLAR 21 FEBRUARY 1678

[G] Although it is true that I have never before had the honour of writing to you for lack of a suitable occasion, I cannot neglect this God-given opportunity of making a beginning. Johannes Tomloo of Hamburg mentioned in a letter which he wrote on the 6th of this month that you had written to him on the 29th past, saying that all the copper bars which were sent for my account had been sold and would be delivered at the first opportunity. I have ordered him to draw on you £600 sterling at double usance, which should be long enough for their delivery and the money to come in. The honour of my bills is most earnestly commended to your care.

And because I am now so much more relieved that none of the copper has been left unsold I have ordered Tomloo to consign 100 Hungarian plates to you for my account, which you will do your best to sell on their arrival at the highest possible price to good and reliable customers. I urge you to see to this because of the bankruptcies which are happening everywhere. And when I see the results and find them satisfactory I shall not only continue to send even bigger consignments which I have lying ready at Hamburg, with Tomloo and other friends, as well as here (for I have a 6-year contract, not only with His Highness the Prince of Hanover and Wolfenbüttel for all the garcopper belonging to him, but also to manage the copper mines for others in this country, for whom I make all their brass and brass- or copper-wire) but also bigger quantities of copper and wire. And when I am assured of your diligence in seeking my profit, as if it were your own, I shall continue—and may God grant it, remaining, &c.

$$\frac{\textit{15 Mar.}}{\textit{29 Mar.}}\textit{1678}$$

390 E. RULAND to JD
HAMBURG 5 MARCH 1678

[D] I have received your letter of the 26th of February. In reply, since Messrs Cortezia & Benzoni have accepted the *W.*400 drawn by Westcombe there is nothing more to worry about. Meanwhile, I see that Westcombe has refused to see reason and has stopped all the bills that have been accepted, which must be an astonishing blow.

I see that you have lent £230 on my account to the East India Company at 5 per cent per annum until the 25th of March. But, as I mentioned in my previous letter, it does not suit me to have my money lying tied up. Therefore you will please recover it when it falls due and find some suitable opportunity to remit it. The exchange can quickly change and, as you can see below, it is already beginning to rise.

Thank you for news of what is happening to trade in [England]. There is very little happening here at present. Our convoy with the Spanish ships has arrived here safely (God be praised!). As for public affairs, they seem to be at a standstill. Meanwhile France continues its progress. How things will turn out finally only time will tell. God grant a good peace, to whose protection I commend you, with friendly regards, &c.

London: 32s 5–6g, 2 usances.
Amsterdam: $33\frac{7}{16}$ at sight.
Paris: $45\frac{3}{4}$–46, 2 usances.
Meanwhile France continues its progress.

$$(i) + (ii) \quad \frac{28 \ Mar.}{12 \ Mar.} 1678$$

391   ROBERT CLARK to JD

GOTHENBURG   (i)   3 JANUARY 1678

'Sir, The inclossed is from your servant Mr Fallgreen, caling to mind yours Sir, off the 17
Agust last, wherin you are inclined to ane trad hier, the which I have offten considered butt
unto I had som incuradgement could not wryt as to purpos, but noue haveing prevealed with
my friende Roluff Lambertson Shult and France Kock, wee haveing ane asignation togither
from the lordes of the King of Sweedens Exchaker to Mr John Aldercron for 25,000 dollars
silver money to be paid out off thee French subsidie moneys second tearme, that the same
asignation might be indorsed to you, the which is performed and cometh under HCr Schultz
covert. Sir I doubt not off acceptance neather off your knoueing the value off the money to be
$1\frac{1}{2}$ dollar silver money for a Rixdollar. In this asignation I have near 8,000 dollars silver
money to my clear. If it stand with your convenience to send me the effter specified goods,
the $\frac{1}{2}$ upon your own acompt and the other $\frac{1}{2}$ upon my accompt, then I doubt not to mack
profiet to content and mack the returns in subside bills or iron, pitch, prys weshells[?] or
wooden goods as you shall advyss. The parlament is to sit hier the nixt monthe. Ther is one
Capt. Hendrie Martin a coming hier from your place. I have ordred him to speak with you
with whom iff consent to send thos goods it will be a fit ocation for I intend to have him
wholl free beffor he can aryve which is all at present so kynd respects from, Sir, your assured
freind, &c.

1,000 yairds gray dossins betwixt 3s 6d and 4s per yaird.
2,000 yairds ditto at $2\frac{1}{2}$s to 3s per yaird.
1,000 yairds ditto bleu ⎫
1,000 yairds ditto red   ⎬ $2\frac{1}{2}$s to 3s per yaird.
                          ⎭
  100 yairds black some 4s and 6s per yaird.
                              Cottons
2,000 yairds yellou ⎫
1,000 yairds reed   ⎪
1,000 yairds bleu   ⎬ at 8d per yaird.
1,000 yairds gray   ⎭

20 pece plains reed
20 pece $\frac{1}{2}$ thicks off severall collours (as newe cloak collours, reds, bleu, green and yellow).
                    All mad up 2 in one.
Iff this com weell to hand you shall see ane incouradgement by God's grace.'

                                                    (ii)   5 MARCH 1678

392   'Sir, The above written is copie off my last the 3 January to which I reffere and confirme, not
doubting but the above mentioned bill is before this presented and acceptance promised
against the falling tearme. The bearer heeroff, Petter DeFlon, brother to H^r Adlercron harth
promised me to procure acceptance iff not done alreadie, for he wilbe cautjus and not reffeuse
to accept to pay what is for a frontire garrisson. Those goods above mentioned wilbe
acceptabl heere at present and you shall see, Sir, that you shalbe furder incuraged in a trade
heere. I am leyke to agree with a gentellman heere for 4 to 5,000 slb iron off a fyne, midling

sort. Iff money can be brought in by sea in specie banco rixdollars for his payment then he is to rebeat upon the currant pryce one halff rixdollar upon each slb. Iff you have a mynde to interess ther in lett me knowe in tyme. Also please advise me what 1s weight silver can stand the lb., and what Spanish peeces off eight giveth by you and then posabl can move that gentellman to tack lb. silver or peeces off eight in payment for his iron. If this goe one it may last some years but seeing I am not abl to doe it off my selff I shall waitte your advice. He hath promised iff the present modell off iron be not for the markett allone he will lett beat out what sorts I shall advise him off. That iron nowe beat out her I have sent muche off it to London and Edinburgh and founde alwyes a good market. It is about 14 foott longe, thin struct and markt '℗' iff I be right remembrit. To all which please lett me have your answer and en indevour for proffeit shalbe made by, Sir, your assured freind to serve, &c.

[P.S.] This inclosed is from Mr Pearman who returned from this to Stockholme the 3 instant. His reason he saith writte you him selff.'

$$\frac{28 \ Mar.}{12 \ Apr.} 1678$$

393 T. PERMAN to JD

GOTHENBURG   2 MARCH 1678

[G] I have been away from home for the last eight weeks attending the Riksdag on behalf of the Stockholm burghers. The Riksdag was held recently in Helmstadt and because I learned that there was an English ship lying at Gothenburg whose captain was thinking of returning to England I decided that I would go over to England aboard this ship. But then I got news from Stockholm that my wife is very unwell and thus I have to cancel my journey and travel from here to Stockholm, which is the cause of this letter and my request that, as a friend, you will buy me the goods set out in the memorandum below and send them to me in the first available ship on the same conditions on which I sent you goods last summer through Mr Piltarff and subsequently wrote to you about—namely, that you will buy the goods and ship them in your own name and deliver them to me in the river or waters of Stockholm. Mr Piltarff has already informed you, as you may remember, of the same conditions on which you sent goods to Oloff & Nicholas Törne last summer.

I am sending you enclosed herewith four first bills of exchange drawn on Samuel van Breda, to pay *RD* 1,400 in Amsterdam and *RD* 600 bank-money in Amsterdam, which *RD* 2,000 you will get paid, place to account and employ as instructed. The goods which I am likewise shipping with this Captain Hiel are 300 pieces of copper money plates, which are going under the name of John Harwitz[1] who serves James Leyell and Callender. He has been here and is sending the plates to his father and has written to inform him that I shall be receiving these 300 pieces of plate from him. But since I cannot come over I beg you to receive the 300 plates from Harwy, pay his expenses and then sell them. Place the proceeds to my account and employ them as instructed. In themselves the proceeds will be too little for the proposed purchases, but with the first ships leaving Stockholm this spring you will receive 60 slb of copper-wire, which are already lying ready at Stockholm. I had thought of sending them last autumn but had no opportunity. In addition I have another 50 slb at the works in Norrköping which I shall get as soon as the waters are open, all of which I shall send to you. I shall make good anything more you disburse on my behalf at the rate of $\frac{1}{2}$ per cent per month interest until you have the payment for my goods in your hands, in accordance with the terms of the contract which I sent over last summer through Mr Piltarff. I also hope that the remainder of the money due has now come in. As I said in the last letter I sent over—another time you must not sell to people who do not pay up promptly. Furthermore, I beg you on receipt of this to serve me well with good quality wares at reasonable prices. You will buy the dozens and kerseys in Hull and the others in London, and let them all go in the first available ship under your name for delivery to me in the river before Stockholm. I know no other way of doing this except according to the contract, by which you will pay the customs or duties in England, insurance on everything and the Sound tolls at Helsingor. In return your profit will be reckoned at 12 to 15 per cent. I know no other way except on these conditions, which I must insist upon. All the kerseys and serges and [—?] are to be laid with three pieces inside one, and all the bays and cottons are to be packed two together, and the silk camisoles and stockings you may have packed with the six packs of yellow bays, some in each pack.

Herewith, may you remain in God's protection, &c.

[Enclosure:

Memorandum. From Hull:

	50 pieces black.
	20 pieces red—they must be blood red.
[sample]	60 pieces ice grey.
	30 pieces dark, nutmeg-brown.
[sample]	40 pieces, brown or new colour.

200 pieces fine and good dozens, from 3s to 4s 6d per yard.

45 pieces red.
18 pieces yellow.
12 pieces May green.
60 pieces new colour or brown.
24 pieces fine red cloth kersies

} 135 pieces good pressed kersies.
N.B. 3 pieces lying inside one.

Memorandum. From London:

[sample]	2 pieces ice grey, like the sample of fine cloth at 7s per yard.
	2 pieces ditto of finer cloth at about 8s.
	2 pieces ditto still finer at about 9s.
	2 pieces of new colour at about 7s.
[sample]	2 pieces ditto still finer at 8s.
	2 pieces ditto at 9s.

18 pieces May green.
9 pieces black.
9 pieces new colour.

36 pieces of good material, 3 pieces packed inside 1.
6 pieces yellow.
6 pieces red.
6 pieces ice-green.

The silk camisoles and stockings to be placed with the yellow bays.

18 pieces of fine bays.

  3 dozen black silk large men's stockings.

24 pieces light nutmeg or new colour.

12 pieces May green.

36 silk ladies' camisoles.

24 pieces fine dark brown or new colour serges of the first fineness.

  4 pieces or 200 yards black.

  4 pieces or 200 yards red.

  8 pieces or 400 yards May green.

  4 pieces or 200 yards ice-grey.

  4 pieces or 200 yards new colour but light.

  2 pieces or 100 yards yellow.

  2 pieces or 100 yards blue.

  2 pieces or 100 yards white.

       1,500 yards, good thick cottons.

N.B. 2 pieces, or 120 to 130 yards in each piece.

200 bottles best Canary wine.

  5 pieces of best cheese.

                       Gothenburg   *2 March 1678*

¹ I.e. Harvey.

                                      $\frac{6\ Apr.}{9\ Apr.}$*1678*

394 S. DE GEER to JD

AMSTERDAM   12 APRIL 1678

[D] I find myself with your letters of the 8th and 29th of March, and must thank you for your report concering the salt ships which are coming from St Ubes. I shall be glad if you would share with me anything more you may learn about them. In my opinion, Sweden will be adequately supplied from here this year, and if more comes from England matters will be worse than they were last year. But if there is a war, England will be needing the salt itself.

Your iron prices will have to be higher if one is going to bring it from Stockholm. And the freight charges will have to be lower, which is likely to be the case if all the salt ships arrive there and push down the rates. According to my calculations £16 will scarcely be enough with these freight and exchange rates.

I shall expect an account of the iron, and with it a report on how much pan-iron from that works you are going to keep in your hands.

The wine ought not to be going straight to Stockholm where it is now so cheap that it would be better if it came directly here. However, it is best that you sell it and close the account, and if these damaging exchange rates continue for a while I would prefer to have my money received there, unless arrangements can be made for investing it in something else. Let me know at once how things stand so that I can write and tell you to whom the money should be given at Stockholm.

I shall expect to get an account of the 56 slb of wire which still remains unsold, together with an account of the wine.

In Sweden they have had a bad winter, so many works have been poorly supplied and although they believed that iron would easily maintain its price there is at the moment not much demand here. I shall be glad to learn your opinion about it in [England].

Some French goods are still not prohibited here. We still hope for a peace, but if it should be delayed it might well happen that England will go to war with France and then we might decide on a general prohibition also. But that would be to embargo oneself, since no ships would be able to sail and no one would be free, and one would know all too easily if anything came from France. Je suis de vos avis touchant la gerre. Si vous en pouvez apprend quelque chose par M. Leyonberg en avance vous m'obiligerez. The Riksdag in Sweden has ended well, with money and men supplied from all sides. Si je ne me trompe cette année encore gerre par tout et peut estre revolutions assé étrange. Then one will have to begin to make peace, commencent de l'un ou de l'autre bout, car le generale cannot.

I remain, &c.

[P.S.] I hope this week to clear up the business with Clignet and am sending over to you an express so that it can go from you to Dublin. The two packets of old letters have been received today. I see that if the packets are thick the postage is higher. Many letters go from here for the Sound by way of Lübeck and then by sea.

$$\frac{10\ Apr.}{12\ Apr.}1678$$

395 J. & H. VAN BAERLE TO JD
AMSTERDAM   15 APRIL 1678

[D] We have your letters of the 26th and 29th past (Old Style), to which this serves as a reply.

We are very pleased that, by the favour of one of your brothers-in-law, a director of the East India Company, you have been able to arrange for the £1,000 which we lent to the said Company at interest until the 25th of March (Old Style) to be continued for another six months at 5 per cent per annum, together with another £500 at interest on our account. Please keep the bond for it by you.

We must also thank you for offering to advance us money if we should have need of it. We shall probably not have to do so unless the exchange rises significantly. It would be welcome to us if you would bear in mind the need to sell our remaining brass and handle it as if it were your own.

We have obtained acceptance of the three bills of exchange drawn for your account, together amounting to RD 1,400 current money, drawn in Stockholm by the directors of the Tar Company on Samuel van Breda here, dated the 12th of January last (Old Style) and payable three months after date. When they fall due we shall procure payment and, after deducting our commission and brokerage, make you returns in good bills. Van Breda makes some difficulties about paying us on these bills since they were endorsed to you by Thomas Perman without instruction to follow his order. And he also forgot to put his name under the endorsement of one of them. As we understand he is in [London] we shall expect as soon as possible a second copy duly endorsed.

Of the two bills of exchange, each of RD 300 drawn on the above-said Van Breda and payable in Hamburg, we have also obtained acceptance and, according to your instructions, sent them there to Claus Bene.

We see that a war between England and France is firmly expected by you. Here we consider peace to be not entirely beyond hope. May the Lord grant us some salvation. We commend you to his protection and remain, &c.

[P.S.] P.B.[1] is dilatory in his payments and is of little credit.

London: 33*s* 10*g* } at 2 usances.
Paris: 96   }

[1] Probably Philip Botte.

(i) + (ii) $\frac{30\ Apr.}{[\quad]}1678$

396 C. GOODFELLOW to JD
ALEPPO   (I)   28 JANUARY 1678

'Sir, My last to you was of the 16th November, since which have had nothing of importance to advise butt now being happy in the news of your naturalisation and hope next to be more happy in your freedome of the Levant Company. I presume to tender myselfe as your humble sarvant in whatever you may please to thinke me capiable of, being imboldnded therto by your owne good promises, so here inclosed I send you a sortment for cloth, both for collors and quality, which if you shall please to deme me worthy to serve you therin please to follow as neare as possible, and I doubt nott butt cloth will doe better the insuing year than now, supposing there will nott come such quantitys. Lyon dollars also will doe very well, if pass current here as formerly, which we expect hourly to here of from Stamboll, all the mony that come by the General ships being now under our Basshaw's seale and *LD* 1,000 sent thether to be tryed before the Grand Signor, they pretending them to be bad though they were tryed here and proved very good, so doubt not butt will doe the same there, of which shall advise you per first, for mony hath the choice of all goods and may doe very well if cheape bought in Holland and good, otherwise they may be confiscated. Silke, all sorts very deare, Tripole *LD* 12; Burme Lege *LD* 11¾ and 11½ per rottolo, butt a carravan of ditto silke dayly expected with *in circa* 270 bales galls, *LD* 38 to 40 per quintal. I intended the sortment of cloth per this opportunity but understanding itt will be very tedious, being to stay att severall ports and another opportunity ofering per via M[arseille] in 7 dayes by which shall forward itt, but if this should chance to arive you first you may send ⅔ redds and the rest good cullors, but substantiall cloth from £9 to £10. We have now received answer from Stambole that the mony proved good though itt will cost *LD* 18,000. Not else, I rest, &c.'

(ii)   8 FEBRUARY 1678

397 'Sir, The per contra I confirme coppy of my last, this serving cheifly to cover the inclosed sortment for cloth which if you shall thinke convenient please to follow as neare as possible. For redds ½ I suppose may be enough, for having bin wonted this yeare most people may send the next and so be to many, and for Lyon dollars till see a little better how things will passe itt may be better, for feare of the worst, for ther is now seized 10 per cent for the charges of passing them here. Pieces of eight now worth 14¼ per cent, per avizo, and wonted. This being what I can advise you att present as to your government, goods being all deare with greate prices being given for all goods will undoubtedly cause plenty the insuing year, when hope shall be so happy to injoying the honnor to serve so good a frend and patrone to my desire and your content. Burma Lege now bought att *LD* 11¾ mony and Tripole *LD* 12½ per rottolo; galls *LD* 38 to 40 per quintal and other goods pro rato, which being all I shall presume to trouble you with att present, being alwayes in readyness to imbrace your commands, so crave leave and most respectfully remaine, your most humble servant. &c.'

$$\frac{30 \ Apr.}{30 \ Apr.} 1678$$

398   C. BENE to JD
HAMBURG   23 APRIL 1678

[D]   On the 16th instant was my last letter to you, by which I remitted you for his account
£145 18s 7g [flem.] at 18 days sight drawn on Sir John Banks and exchanged at 32s 9g with
Jan & Harmen Luys, making £238 19s 2d [sterling] being the proceeds of the RD 600. I also
informed you that I had sold your three sacks of cotton at 14⅛g, which I now confirm.

Since then I have received your welcome letter of the 12th instant, together with the
protest of the £219 bill accepted by Burkin & Watt, which will be useful to me. You will also
please return to me the bill of exchange. The endorser will doubtless know how to claim the
payment. That the drawer has been deceived by the acceptor cannot be blamed on the
endorser, and from whom could he learn that no value had been paid for it? Here such excuses
are not valid, for the acceptor must pay without any evasion. For that reason every one
should know from whom he accepts bills of exchange.

Enclosed herewith goes the second bill of exchange for £145 18s 7g remitted you
previously, which you will know how to use if the first is lost.

That you have made a note about my commission for ginger is good; and I shall wait to
hear what can be done about it on the arrival of the Barbados ships.

It is vexing that the negotiations for peace or war have been so protracted, for as long as
there is uncertainty about the one or the other one does not know what to undertake in trade,
which is nearly at a standstill. God grant us peace, for that will be best for the whole of
Christendom.

We are glad to hear that you are not involved in the bankruptcy of Bellamy in [London].
His correspondent here, Cornelis van Weed, has also failed—without any involvement of
mine, thank God! I am likewise free of those who have failed in Amsterdam. These are
dangerous times, so one has good cause to look carefully at those one trusts.

Our Ardasse is still unsold, for one cannot get more than 15½s for it and I am unwilling to
sell it for so little. I shall be glad to learn what is happening in England to this commodity and
to Jamaican indigo. With cordial regards, &c.

London: 32s 6g.
Amsterdam: 33⅛ − 1/16.
Venice: 88½.
[P.S.] Please tell me what the protest costs.

$$\frac{30 \ Apr.}{3 \ May} 1678$$

399   J. & H. VAN BAERLE to JD
AMSTERDAM   6 MAY 1678

[D]   On the 3rd instant was our last letter, with which we remitted you £15 16s 9d sterling, the
residue of the net proceeds of the RD 1,400 current money.

Since then we have received your letter of the 19th past (Old Style) to which this serves as
an answer. We have informed ourselves about the *polomites* and *baracans* of which you write
and understand that they are two special kinds of material. There are no *polomites* made at
Valenciennes but plenty of *baracans*. The *polomites* are made at Ryssel and there are also plenty

made in this country. *Baracans* from Valenciennes are about 40 brabant ells long and $1\frac{1}{4}$ wide.[1] They cost here from *f*.36 to *f*.60 per piece according to quality. The Ryssel *polomites* are 40 to 45 ells long and $1\frac{1}{16}$ ells broad, costing here 13 stuivers per ell. Here inclosed[2] you have some samples with the prices set down beside. At present there are no English ships loading for Bilbao or Cadiz for your information. With cordial regards, &c.

London—34*s* $4\frac{1}{2}$ *g* at 2 usances.

---

[1] The Brabant ell was about $27\frac{1}{2}$ inches, English measure.
[2] Four cloth samples remain enclosed with this letter, marked as follows:

    1. Barcane de Valencienne de 55 florins la piece. [Mid grey-green]
    2. Barcane de Valencienne de 48 a 55 florins la piece. [Light grey]
    3. Polomite de Lille de 13 sous l'aune. [Khaki-green]
    4. Polomite de Lille de 13 sous l'aune. [Brown, with light fleck]

$\dfrac{1\ May}{4\ Jun.}1678$

400 W. SKINNER to JD
HULL   29 APRIL 1678

'Sir, I have yours of the 25th instant, adviseinge you are upon sale of your pitch and tarre in my hands and may shortly give me order for its delivery, which I shalbe expectinge.

Your order for buyinge 40 dosens and 30 prest kerseys of colours mentiond in your letter I shall forthwith transmitt to my son, William Skinner junior at Leeds, and you may be assured it wilbe speedily effected with all due care and I doubt not to your freinds satisfaction and advantage. My son resides at Leedes and is versed in buyinge in all the manufactures of these parts and when you have occasion will readily embrace your comands. Your letter directed to him at Leeds will come well to hand. Please to accept his bills for the rest of these goods.

The embargo upon all ships bound for the Balticque sea is taken of, and the winde beinge faire severall shipps bound for Stockholme and other places in the East are this morninge goeinge downe. Pray God conduct them. To his keepeinge I comend you and am, Sir, yours att command.'

$\dfrac{20\ May}{[\text{——}]}1678$

401 WILLIAM CLODE to JD
EXETER   18 MAY 1678

'Sir, Upon my wife's late selling you goodes doe presume to geive you this trouble, which hope will bee pleased to excuse. Wee have heare very flatt markets and all sorts of goods are generally cheape, and if you have any farther occasion for that sort of goods or any other and will be pleased to imploye mee thearin, doubt not but may geive you such incouradgment as may enduce you to a future trade and upon your tryall I hope will finde itt to be a cheaper way to have goods from this, then to buy them in London. Could yesterday buy hear a very good sort of long els for 31 and 33*s* per piece, the very best for 34 or thear about. Ottery[1] long ells for 44*s* will contain drest full 28 yards and all other sorts of goods answerable in cheapness, both mixt collors and whaites, but of the two sorts mixt collors are the cheaper att present. If in this or any other can serve you bee pleased to command him who is, your most humble servant.'

---

[1] I.e. Ottery St Mary, Devon.

$$\frac{23\ May}{6\ Aug.}1678$$

402   D. VAN BAERLE to JD
STOCKHOLM   9 APRIL 1678

[D]   I answered your letter on the 24th of December past and sent a copy on the 5th of January,
but by your letter of the 26th of February, received today, I understand that neither of them
has arrived.

I had informed you by them that there was no prospect of buying any 'Guinea' or
'Scottish' pans within your limits of 270 to 290 dollars per shippound, free on board. They
would eventually cost at least 308 to 310 dollars per shippound, without the duty, and the
duty is now about 23 to 24 dollars per shippound. The Russians are buying here many such
'Guinea' pans and are paying 330 to 340 dollars for them without the duty. The person who
was accustomed to make the best sort was involved in a law-suit with me and let his works
fall idle and ten or twelve days ago he finally died,[1] so of the kind you ordered there are none
to be had even if you had not restricted the price.

There is now no garcopper in town but some is expected shortly and will be selling at
about 240 dollars. Brass-wire is at 295 dollars; ordinary fine iron, 30 dollars; St Ubes salt, 12
dollars per ton. If there is anything in which I can be of service I would be delighted,
wherewith I remain, with friendly regards, &c.

---

[1]   This was Jacob Momma-Reenstierna, who died on the 27th of March, 1678, in Norrköping, and was buried
there in the German church.

$$\frac{23\ May}{23\ May}1678$$

403   G. RICHARDS to JD
BILBAO   13 MAY 1678

'Sir, I have now before me yours of the 15th April noteing you had received your proportion
of what I remited Sir John by Wood. I have since sent you 1,000 barrs more by Pooke and
Foreland, who I hope are by this time neer home. Of Helman and Roaches arryval I have
acquainted you. Your callicoes by them shal be disposed of for your most advantage as also
those Sir John hath now loaden in Martin and Wood, God sending them safe. The account of
your former narrow bafts and long cloth I hope to send you speedily, which wil render
reasonable wel. Of your bayes I have as yet sold only 4 bales. The rest shal be disposed of
against the next ships arryve, for I perceive that commodity goes falling at home. What I can
principlely recommend to you from Holland are *barraganen* from Valentia[1] which wil cost
there about 38 a 40 florins per piece. There wil be shipping from Holland comeing hether
about 2 month hence or something more. Sir John wil get wel by his cinamont but when
t'was bought in the exchange went at 36s 6g or higher: now I hear its fallen to 34s—is a great
difference. In case of warr shipping from Hambourgh hether wil runn great danger unless
they come for the Downes and thence with English or Dutch convoy. Hetherto our English
shipping have bin inployed in that trade but if a breach follow with France it wil meet with a
great obstruction. Then waxx may rise here and I beleive fall at Hambourgh. It must be that
with 3 seales, whereof I observe Mr Boverie sends considerable parcels from London. The
freight from Hambourgh to London is but little and from London hether very reasonable.
What comes directly from Hambro wil cost more freight and if the custome in England be

but little that may henceforward be the best way to bring it hether. I shall endeavour speedily to cleer Mr Hayes' account, and is all at present from, Sir, your humble servant.

[P.S.] I have lately bought at San Sebastian about 350 quintals of whal fins for Sir John, whereof all but 100 are gonne and these 100 are loaden there which I expect [hole] first good weather about. If you thinck good to accept thereof I have writt Sir John offer them to you. They will stand in about £90 per ton landed in England, and they are since risen 15 per cent at San Sebastian. They cost all ready money.'

¹ I.e. Valenciennes. See [**412**].

$$\frac{8 \text{ Jun.}}{13 \text{ Jun.}}1678$$

404 B. BEUZELIN & SON to JD
ROUEN

14 JUNE 1678

'Nostre derniere a esté du 7 de ce mois, vous advizant du necessaire, dudespuis la vostre du 27 passe, vieil stile, nous est parvenue, accompagnee des 2 secondes de *W*.1,000 et *W*.800 dont les premieres acceptees estoyent desja a nostre disposition. Il nous fasche de ne vous en pouvoir procurer le retour aussy promptemant et advantageuzemant comme nous le voudrions, mais la difficultée des lettres et le bas change nous en empeschent nous avons prié nos amis de Paris de la faire a 56¼d comme ilz nous costoyent le change, mais par leur derniere du 13ᵉ receu de ce mattin ils nous mandent que les mesme difficultez se prezantent chez eulx et qu'il est baissé jusques a 55¾d et point du tout de lettres. Nous les avions pourveus pour ce subject mais nostre fonds est demeuré inutile; il est donc de toutte nécessité d'attendre, et comme il est sans doubte qu'il le fera en bref des chargemants a Bordeaux, La Rochelle et en Bretagne les lettres seront plus frequentes pour Londres et le change pourra monter. Sy vous voullez entre temps que nous faisons quelque choze a longz jours affinque vostre argent ne demeure inutile nous en cercherons les occasions. Nous avons bonne esperance que la paix avecq la Hollande sera ung fort acheminnemant a nous la donner generalle, et c'est en cette consideration que sa Majesté a fait ung rabbais de 6 millions sur les tailles l'annee prochaine, prevoyant qu'il n'aura plus besoing d'un sy grand fonds pour la subsistance de ses armees et que d'hier aussy la publication fust faitte pour l'ouverture des ports en France; ainsy le negoce ouvert qui jusques a prezant avoit esté en quelque sorte fermé. Tout cella veult dire que nous demeurerons bons amis, et que le commerce pourra reprandre vigeur, Dieu la veille.

Nous eussions fort souhaitté que vous eussiez donné dans nos sentimans pour la vanthe de vostre fil de latton, car oultre le peu de demande qu'il y a prezantemant c'est que nous y craignons du rabbais, et ne pouvons plus parvenir a £90t. Nous y ferons du mieux possible. Le navire qu'on attendoit d'Hambourg a passé en 8 jours et en apporté pres de 1,500 torches, ce qui ne nous fera pas de bien. Il est a croire qu'il se viendra aussy a-droitture.

Les fanons de ballaine n'ont point de vanthe. Il y en a grand nombre icy, les dernieres vandus n'ont passé £55t, encore auroit on peine a trouver marchand; les debts sont cazuelles, plusieurs de nos balleniers se sont atterroyes de sort que l'on est fort empesché a qui fier. Nous estimons qu'il est mieux de faire passer vostre partie a Londres.

Pour vos droguets nous n'avons peu les faire prandre a celluy qui nous en avoit offert 24s mais comme nous en avons souvant bezoing pour revestir nos pauvres voyez sy en nous en accommodant vous voudriez bien nous en faire quelque petit rabbais; c'est une charitté que vous ferez en faveur de nos dites pauvres dont nostre compagne vous aura de l'obligation, surquoy attendant de vos nouvelles nous continuerons a demeurer, vos trés humbles serviteurs.[1]

Amsterdam: $96\frac{1}{2}$ *g* 2 usances.
Londres: pas de lettres.

$\dfrac{29\ Jun.}{[\quad\quad]}1678$

405   C. GOODFELLOW to JD
          ALEPPO   23 APRIL 1678

'Sir, Thes are to conferme the above coppy, since which hath little more happned worth your knowledge, only an empty town for goods (att presant being all bought up att the above prices[1]—so that suppose must bare a good price in England, we being here jealous of a French warr and long to here the certainty for better government in trade. Nott having received any from you long since will cause brevity, waiting your further comands (and orders for the balance of your account). The same men I sold your wire to have bin demanding more of me, so that such small parcels as you sent before, or more, may sell, for the Venetians have butt little trade now. This is all I can saifly advise you, for I am not of the humor of some of our factory to write for great quantitys of severale goods and when they arive will not answer expectations. If a French warr happens cloth here must rise as well as goods in England, though at present those that sent mony have had the advantage and raised the prices of goods upon those that bartered with cloth above $\frac{1}{2}$ *LD* per rottolo silkes (mony allways comanding choice of goods, so that both togeather will helpe each other). This being what I shall trouble you with att presant crave leave and most respectfully remaine, your humble sarvant, &c.'

  [1] In his letter of 8 February, a copy of which accompanies this, the following prices are given: 'Burma Legee' *LD* 11, 3 aspers for cash; Tripoli silk, *LD* 12; galls *LD* 38 per quintal; pieces of eight $14\frac{1}{4}$ per cent premium.

$\dfrac{8\ Jul.}{[\quad\quad]}1678$

406   W. CLODE to JD
          EXETER   6 JULY 1678

'Sir, I did of late geive you the trouble of a line or two advising of the government of our markets and my readiness to serve you in that way or any other to the utmost of my power, since which sarges are something fallen and stil doe continue lowe, and although are but few made yet att preseant less bought. If have now any occasion for any sort of long ells or any other sorts, either of white sarges or mixt collars and will please to make a tryall of mee thearin I question not but make geive you such incouridgment as may enduce you to a future trade. I have omitted the geiving you the exact prices of every sort because hear are many sorts made and are att divers prises, for wee can buy from 14*s* per piece to £4, so that if will please to geive mee a line or two what sorts doe generally deale in I shall by the next returne of the post geive you an exact account how shuch sorts are heare to be bought, by which I hope may find out a cheaper way then to buy goods in London. Thus expecting the honour of your commands doe crave leave and rest, your humble servant to command, &c.'

$$\frac{10\ Jul.}{[\ \ \ \ ]}1678$$

7 T. LANNOY to JD
ALEPPO   2 MARCH 1678

'These are by returne of our Generall Ships, and in answer of yours of the 25th June. Concerning the ballance of your account Sir John Lethieullier advised me to have paid you some time since. As for the intrest of 6 per cent which you are pleased to leave to me, I made you good parte of it in the cambio of your pieces of eight, which findeing I could not send you returnes I sold at time by which you got upwards of 3 per cent more than any other of my frinds. After I received your money in possestion if could have got you any more intrest had been faithfully allowed, but being sorry you lost the benifitt of the investment of your money I charged you with no provision for receiveing, all which I hope will satisfye, and if take your freedome of the Turky Company that you will be pleased to honour me with your imployment, which I promise shall be done to as much advantage as any of my other frinds. I shall not trouble you with a sortement of cloth, nor doe I desyre you, if you incline to trade this way, to send any but peeces of eight, lyon dollers and cocheniele, by which you will have quick returnes and in those goods you desyre. We have had this yeare a great deale of trouble and charge, the old Vizier being dead,[1] he that is present in his place is so pore or covitious that from all Christian imbassidors hath exacted great somes of money and from those that are not willing to parte with it he makes one pretence or other and so takes it per force, as he hath don to our imbasador, pretending our new Lion Dollars which were brought by the last Generall Ships were falce, but parte of them being tryed were found to be good, not withstanding he would have his demands, being *LD* 15,000 or elce would have melted the whole sume which was *LD* 200,000, there being no remedy but patience, but our imbassadore wrights that no further trouble will be given for the future, which hope will take care to prevent or elce our trade in these partes are lost. Sir, by the *Prosperous*, Capt. Henry Clarke, I have sent a sayet of

I pistaches, which beg your acceptance, being marked and nombred as per margin, which is all I know worth your notice at present. I remaine, Sir, your most humble servant at comand.'

[1] Köprülü Fazil Ahmed Pasha, Grand Vizier 1661–76.

$$\frac{15\ Jul.}{6\ Aug.}1678$$

8 JAN HEDENSTRÖM to JD
STOCKHOLM   11 MAY 1678

Your very welcome letters of the 15th of February and 12th of April came to me safely, from which I have seen what prices Swedish goods are fetching in [England]. I am most grateful to you, but because of the pending war between France and England and other sad circumstances that one sees developing more and more, every day, one dares not risk sending anything from here. One is living here almost as if one were bound hand and foot, and the iron, garcopper and copper-wire which comes to market here is mostly sold to strangers. There can only be one person in a hundred who is currently exporting on his own account, and when anything does get done it is in the name of someone overseas, which still carries its dangers. Apart from that, we are living in great ignorance about what is happening abroad since our correspondence has been taken away and it can easily be three months before one can get any answer from Holland and [England]. This creates uncertainty, so that it is nearly impossible to get anything insured, and when correspondence is removed in such a way the insurers are not happy to venture without taking a high premium, which is enough to smother any profits which the owner should have enjoyed. And if the ship should on its way suffer any mishap in these circumstances the insurers are very evasive, so that one has to write off half one's capital. But for you in [England], who have a punctual correspondence from all places, it is much easier to arrange anything for your own account.

Garcopper is presently very cheap here, at 235 to 236 dollars, and it may well fall to 230 dollars. Fine iron, serviceable for London, is at 30 or 32 dollars, medium quality at 27 to 28 and coarse anchor iron at 25 to 26 dollars. Copper-wire is at 270 to 280 dollars.

So, if you want to arrange for something to come on your account, please keep me in mind and be assured that you will be as well served by me as by any others in Stockholm. Meanwhile, people are in good hopes of peace and trust that it will not come to a rupture between England and France. This would be the best for the whole of Christendom, and I trust also that all the princes who are engaged in this war will feel it too and already have their share of weariness.

Wherewith I commend you to the loving protection of God, and remain, &c.

$$\frac{15\ Jul.}{6\ Aug.}1678$$

409   L. UPPENDORFF to JD
STOCKHOLM   11 MAY 1678

[D]   I have safely received yours of the 12th of April, from which I have seen what is happening to trade [in England]. I am most obliged to you, and beg you to continue as opportunity arises.

In my opinion it would be best now to see which way, and how, matters develop between England and France.

Iron is now readily fetching 32 dollars for fine quality. Wire is 290 and garcopper 236 to 240 copper dollars per shippound. May God grant peace! There ought to be something to be done with copper, especially when the East India Company in London wants to make its yearly contract, about which you could do a lot through Mr Lethieullier who I beg you to greet heartily with my dutiful respects. Likewise, something could be done with voyage iron but in these troubled times it is best that it remains at home. I shall set them to work on it.

Similarly, one ought to be able to agree with the Tar Company for 1,200 to 1,500 lasts of tar and 300 to 400 lasts of pitch yearly, as you mentioned, but during this war I do not believe the English here will allow it, unless it could be arranged in [London] under the pretext that His Majesty the King of Great Britain wants to be assured of having such a yearly quantity in the country and, accordingly, His Majesty has agreed with you (or someone else) to procure such a quantity and consequently forbidden (or, at least, will not permit) anyone else to bring in such commodities unless you (or whoever it is in whose name it is done) shall permit it and unless he charters it or orders it through you. That could turn out well, and if you would like to take a half share I would do my best here and you could arrange your half in [London]. And with the ships that fetch the goods we could send other commodities of one kind or another on which something could be gained in [England], and now is the right time to be thinking about it, for when we have peace there will be many standing ready to do so. Thus, if you have any inclination to take part, I beg you to let me know at once and I will see what is possible to arrange here.

Lacking the account of the plates which you have sold I shall be glad to learn how much they rendered, for my guidance.

At the earliest opportunity please send me six good watches and chains that work correctly, of the kind which you bought for Mr Hedenström, since I have been asked for them by good friends.

Bless you, and with heartiest regards I remain, &c.

$$\frac{24\ Jul.}{30\ Jul.}1678$$

10 A. BERENBERG'S WIDOW & HEIRS to JD

HAMBURG   16 JULY 1678

[D] We find ourselves with several of your letters this year, of which the latest are of the 21st and 28th past, and from these we have seen in full what you have to say on the subject of trade, with your opinions about it and news of what ships have recently arrived from one place or another. For all this we are very grateful

We are sorry that the times are so miserable that one can find nothing about which to correspond, for so far we have seen no commodities from which we could profit—there is no consumption. The ginger which came in these latest ships—nice, plump, clean, brown ginger—was allowed to sell for $3\frac{1}{4}g$ with $8\frac{2}{3}$ per cent rebate, prices never heard of before, with fine, white scraped ginger at $8\frac{1}{4}g$, but there is no demand. At $15s$ in [London] it is very low; other friends have it for $14s$, but their letters are more recent, for your last, of the 28th, has only just reached us today.

Oil has fallen considerably here, fetching *RD* 90 for the last three or four weeks, and now Malaga oil can be had for *RD* 68 and Seville at *RD* 70. Two ships are expected direct from Gallipoli, and if they arrive safely we believe it will decline even more. Good cardamon is at $3\frac{1}{4}g$. Ardasse will have to fall lower in [London] as a good quantity of silk from the East Indies has arrived in Holland and none is selling here or elsewhere. For the war has totally ruined trade and it seems that instead of the anticipated peace we can expect a harder and fiercer war. May God avert the latter and grant the former! As long as these troubles continue we expect nothing good.

However, we would be interested to know about the cost of good English calf-skins, smooth and white, prepared in [London], and the worser quality prepared in Hull, and if the customs duty on them is high. We shall be glad to learn, at your convenience, whether there is any change or decline in prices, and if pepper can be had for $12d$.

With very cordial regards, we remain, &c.

London:	$33s$ 6–$7g$. @ 2 usances.
Amsterdam:	33 to $32\frac{15}{16}$.
Paris:	46.
Venice:	$87\frac{1}{2}$ at usance.

$$\frac{27\ Jul.}{30\ Jul.}1678$$

411 C. BENE to JD

HAMBURG   19 JULY 1678

[D] My last letter to you was on the 12th instant. I have since just received yours of the 28th of June and cannot understand why it has been held up for so long. As I told you in my last,

Captain John Bate arrived here safely, and I have been diligently trying to sell our ginger as quickly as it can be received from the ship in order to reduce expenses, but it will not succeed because I have been obliged to bring it in to the warehouse. Although I have been superintending for the last two nights the captain has only delivered 193 sacks and I shall not pay him his freight until all the rest are received.

Since then I have sold 150 sacks, namely 100 to Mr De Heusch and 50 to Adrian Justus at $3\frac{3}{4}g$ with $8\frac{2}{3}$ per cent rebate for payment in bank money. They will collect them in the morning and I shall try to sell the rest so that I can send you the account. In my last letter I ordered another 100 sacks of brown ginger to be bought at 15s or below, and if you are interested in going halves let us take 200 sacks. This I now confirm. You know what sort of quality to obtain. What I have here is good, and the freight is very reasonable, which will make it easier to have a coarser quality. It will be useful for your guidance to know that if the sacks are rather bigger the expenses here can be better managed, for one has to pay just as much tare, brokerage and other expenses if the sack is of 100, 120, or 80 lb., so if the quality is good the bigger sacks are to be preferred.

I hope you have performed my commission for white, scraped ginger. Regarding Bermuda tobacco, as I said before, please do not pay more than $5\frac{1}{2}d$, and for good Barbados sugar do not give more than 21s 6d to 22s, buying 10 butts for my account or 20 butts for us in partnership. And it may be useful for your guidance to know that one makes the most loss by the tare on the heaviest butts, for here the tare is 14 per cent while in [England] it is as much for a heavy as for a light butt. Such Barbados sugar as has arrived here is selling for $5\frac{3}{4} - \frac{7}{8}g$ on average, with $8\frac{2}{3}$ per cent rebate. Because a rupture is still foreseen please take care that what you send to me is loaded in ships which are going with convoy. It would be very unwise to load it in German ships sailing with French passes for I fear the English will not suffer it. I hope you know how to guard against that.

I have been told today that Nath. Mathew has absented himself from the Exchange and as a result I fear his father in London may follow him. I long to know that the £100 drawn on him, falling due on the 24th instant and remitted to you on the 5th, has been settled. Meanwhile, with cordial regards, I remain, &c.

London: 33s 6g.
Amsterdam: 33–32 $\frac{15}{16}$.

$\frac{27\ Jul.}{2\ Aug.}$1678

412   J. & H. VAN BAERLE to JD
AMSTERDAM   2 AUGUST 1678

[D]   In answer to your letter of the 19th past, this is to tell you that, according to your order, we have bought for you 40 pieces of *baracans* from Valenciennes and 12 pieces of *polomites* from Ryssel, of which some samples are sent herewith. The *baracans*, coarse and fine together, cost on average *f*.46 per piece, and the *polomites f*.17 per piece, with 1 per cent discount for immediate payment. These we shall consign to George Richards at Bilbao. Please let us know if we should load them in one ship or two, for it will be a fortnight before they depart. As soon as the above-mentioned goods are loaded we shall send you the invoice and bill of lading. Meanwhile we are thinking of drawing £200 sterling on you next Friday for our payment.

The above-mentioned *baracans* are mostly dark-grey and the *polomites* are mostly dark

nutmeg colour, since we are informed that these are the colours most in demand at Bilbao.
People here are full of uncertainty whether or not the peace will come about.
With our hearty regards, &c.

London—34*s* 8–9*g* @ 2 usances.

$$\frac{3\ Aug.}{17\ Aug.}1678$$

13 WILLIAM SKINNER (JUNIOR) to JD
LEEDS   30 JULY 1678

'Sir, Yours of the 25th instant this post come to hand ordering the buying double the quantity
of goods I provided for you the last Stockholme shipping and of the same sorts, which shall
accordingly be done; and my endeavours noe ways awanting in the procuring you
substantiall goods and good pennyworths, I have all ready made a considerable beginning,
our markett this day being well provided, thought great quantitys are bout, many now
buying against the next Hambro shipping; and in a while little cloth wilbe made, harvest
drawing near when the makers wilbe employ'd therwith; soe I thinke the more hast is made
the better and when the goods are ready they shalbe dispatcht to Hull with directions to be
shipt for Stockholm consigned to Mr Thomas Perman as formerly. Sir, I give you a thousand
thanks for your great respects to me, and shall as much as in my lys strive to deserve them
better then T.W.[1] and desire you wilbe assured what ever commands you laye on mee shalbe
done as for my selfe. I humbly kiss your hands and remaine, your humble servant, &c.'

   [1] Thomas Wright, of Stokesely?

$$\frac{7\ Aug.}{17\ Aug.}1678$$

14 WILLIAM SKINNER (SENIOR) to JD
HULL   5 AUGUST 1678

'Sir, I have yours of the primo instant, and am glad your tarre is arrived. I am shippinge you a
smal parcel tarr to cleare a seller and prevent that further charge and I should be very glad to
advise you the sale of your remainder, but as I have advised you, this sorte is not suitable to
the use of this country, which requires thick tarre and hath had supplyes thereof all a long,
being principally used for sheep. Your sort is very well knowne, but the country people
esteme it not for their purpose and though I have formerly sold good quantityes it hath bene
for exportation, which doth not now offer. Here are severall ships arrived in 5 or 6 dayes, that
come from Stockholm cheifly iron loaden but have quantityes of pitch and tarre also on
board, and I finde the tarre is designed to be reshipt for London and other places, and I thinke
you will doe best to order yours for some other market. Since receipt of your letter I cannot
meet with any of our masters that are willinge to goe for Rouen, but probably I might get it
carryed for Havre at 20*s* per last.

   Here is sone wyer arrived of the marke ')(' and Crowne. They aske £6 5*s* per cwt. but
will sel it cheaper. I am, Sir, yours att command.'

$$\frac{12 \; Aug.}{[\text{——}]} 1678$$

415   VAN WEERT & STOCK to JD
        GENOA   30 JULY 1678

[D]   With today's post we safely received your very welcome letter of the 27th past, whereby we
      have seen what you asked to know about the trade in whale-fins.
          In reply, we can tell you that we seldom receive fins from Biscay, for our friends in
      Holland send us as many as we can sell here. Those most wanted here are the blackest or the
      biggest kind, but no small ones. Furthermore, we see that you say that those from Biscay
      weigh from 4, $4\frac{1}{2}$ to 5 lb., per piece, so they must be nearly all of the same size, and they
      would sell for 16s*[oldi]* per lb., more or less, according to quality. The white ones should be
      thrown out, otherwise they cause offence here. The black and dried ones will all sell as there
      are none in town apart from those in our hands, for your information. Dutch fins are also
      from 3, $3\frac{1}{4}$ to $3\frac{1}{2}$ lb., and 100 lb. Dutch-weight amounts to 150 lb. here for wares which do not
      perish, such as lead, iron, pepper, or the like, and whale-fins of one type always spoil more
      than the other since they are shipped moist.
          A piece-of-eight is worth £5, or 100 s*[oldi]*. Charges on fins, pepper, lead as well as many
      other goods are few since they are mostly sought after duty-free and only have to be stored.
      Concerning warehouse rent, it is ordinarily (though contrariwise for all cloths, bays, says,
      linens) a duty charged on the seller of 1 per cent on a valuation of the goods, though the prices
      have been once again raised. Pepper sells at present for $10\frac{1}{8}$ *soldi* per lb., great lead at £$16\frac{1}{2}$ per
      cantar which is the same as 100 lb. Dutch or 150 lb. of theirs. If there is anything in which we
      can be of service you may with all freedom command, with heartiest regards, &c.

$$\frac{12 \; Aug.}{28 \; Aug.} 1678$$

416   ROBERT WELCH & GEORGE STYLES to JD
        GENOA   3 AUGUST 1678

'Sir, Wee have now the honnour of your most oblidging lynes the 27 June and shall not be
unmindfull to give Capt. Peckett maney thanks for the undeserved character he hath been
pleased to give yow of us and proceed more from his owne good disposition then our deserts.
However, pleasing to command us ought in these parts shall make it our businesse to give you
all sattisfaction and continue as, God be praised, it hath been our fortune to doe and still
continue in businesse of consequence from Alderman Dashwood, Mr Denews and maney
others our good freind there, from whome may soone take cognisence of our method and
respect to freinds and there interest.
    Heere is great consume of whalebone in fins, which the more they way the better, and at
present our markett is bare of that comoddity soe the sending a quantity our broker tells us
might arrive to *D*.25 in 26 per quintall this quintall of 106 lb. English. As to costome thers
non paid thereon on the seller and all other charges besid portadge ashore, weighing, brokage
and provision is very inconsiderable; but must be shure it be well dried—from Holland it
constantly wants of its weight in bill of loading, per avisa. Other comodities proper for this
consume are pepper, lead, tynn in small barrs, white substantial good Elbroad of 32 yards
extent and Berbados sugers, all would doe well. Wheate worth *D*.7 per meane of $13\frac{1}{3}$ English
bushells[1] and tis thought that aboute 6 may continue all the insueing yeare, soe if would doe

might adventure on a parcell. Swead iron worth $D.3\frac{1}{2}$ to $3\frac{1}{4}$ this quintall, which beeing all the present affords most respectfully salluting you wee remayne. Exchange for London 54*d* per Ducat.'

¹ This is a slip of the pen for '$3\frac{1}{3}$'—corrected in the following letter of 10 August. The *mine* of Genoa was estimated at $\frac{1}{25}$th of the last of Amsterdam (of 80 bushells English).

$$\frac{12\ Aug.}{19\ Aug.}1678$$

17 B. BEUZELIN & SON to JD
ROUEN   16 AUGUST 1678

'Nous recepvons prezantemant la vostre du 1/11 de ce mois; en responce il est bien que vous nous ayez donné credit de nos remizes de *W*.600 et *W*.1,000. Pour cette derniere sy nous avions peu la reduire comme lettre de change nous l'aurions fait. Il nous semble pourtant qu'estant a vostre ordre vous en pouvez dispozer car elle sera acquittee a l'escheance ponctuellemant. Nos changes baissent et ne se trouve pas une seulle lettre pour chez vous. Nous n'avons jusques a cette heure aulcuns nouvelles du navire ou sont vos 477 torches de fil de latton. Nous croyons neangmoins que du vent qu'il a heu il doibt estre en riviere, de quoy nous prandrons a la place information. Nous avons ung sensible desplezir du peu de demande qu'il y a a cette marchandize et ce qui l'augmente davantage est que nous prevoyons vizibilemant qu'il y aura encore du rabbais, tant par le nombre qui en est desja venu que de ce qui s'en attend encore. Nous savons bien aussy qu'il en est arrivé bonne partie a Lubeck par 3 a 4 navires de Suede et qu'il s'en espere encore qui fait que nous fezons tout qui est en notre pouvoir pour n'estre prevenuz d'un plus grand rabbais. C'est icy la plus morte saizon de l'annee pour la vanthe, qui ne se resveillera qu'au retour de la foire de Guibray ou tous nos marchands sont prezentamant. Au fin, nous continuerons nos soings, c'est surquoy vous pouvez tousjours faire fonds.

Nous nous refferons a ce que nous vous avons mande touchant les cuirs et serons bien aize de savoir sy vous y aurez fait quelque choze. Pendant qu'il y a sy peu de bré et goudron icy il nous semble que vous feriez bien d'ordonner en dilligence l'affrettemant a Hull d'ung moyen vaisseau, car ceux qui priment ont d'ordinnaire l'advantage. Le sieur Louis Hays a heu beau moyen de s'estre deffait de ce qui luy en restoit car il n'y avoit que luy seul pardeca que en avoit.

C'est une bonne nouvelle pour le pays que l'arrivee de ces navires d'orient; ung amy nous en a envoye la charge qui est riche. Sur les nouvelles de la paix qui l'on escrit avoir este signee a Nimegue le 11 de ce mois sur les 11 heurs de soir les espiceries ont haussé en Hollande et icy. Il faudra non obstant cella bien du temps pour restablir le negoce car la Compagne qui fait la principalle consommation des denrees est fort mizerable et chetive par la longeur des guerres.

Il nous vient tousjours grand nombre de sucres des habittations francoise en la Mexicque, et nous en avons vandu y a peu de jours a £22*t* mais fort moyens; ainsy il n'y a rien a faire a ceux de Barbades a 22*sd* 6*d* ny moins encore au gingembre qui n'a aulcune demande en France. Il faut panser a des marchandises plus liquides. Les huilles ne vallent plus que £30*t*. Il nous en reste encore autour de 100 pipe dont nous esperons nous deffaire en bref, car il y a tousjours raizonnable demande. Ung amy de della nous en avoit envoyé un partie de 40 pipes que nous avons aussytost vandue a £30*t*, £31*t* et £32*t*. C'estoit alors le cours; beaucoup de marchandises pourront recepvoir du changemant sur ces nouvelles de la paix.

Nous vous remettons £300*t* en ung recipiree de Mons. Dumoutier, dont vous nous donnerez s'il vous plaist credit a votre compte. Nous luy avons fourny ung credit de *W*.500 a *W*.600 a Paris pour les y prandre s'il en a bezoing.

  Nous vous baizons les mains et continuerons a estre, vos trés humbles serviteurs.'

Amsterdam: 97 ⎫
Anvers: 97 ⎬ 2 usances.
Londres: $55\frac{5}{8}$ ⎭

$$\frac{21\ Aug.}{23\ Aug.}1678$$

418   P. BOTTE to JD

AMSTERDAM   26 AUGUST 1678

[D]   My latest letter to you was on the 16th instant, to which I refer, and as I did not have the time to answer your letter of the 9th of August—I mean to say, the 30th of July—I shall do so here.

  My friends at Stockholm have been unable to hinder the consignments which are reaching [England], or those which are yet to arrive, but from the 15th/25th of July you can be assured that there will be no more goods to be had from Englishmen or others at Stockholm, except from me, because there are some Dutch ships there which are taking away all there is to be had. For your instruction, it is not advisable that we should sell anything at present but rather let the others undercut each other. Our time will come. As already mentioned, I shall not be arranging for any more ships to go to [England] this year. In 1676, over 3,000 lasts of tar and 600 lasts of pitch were sent to England, which were altogether consumed before any of mine arrived, but this year, besides my total, less than a quarter as much will be shipped.

  Concerning what you propose about the conditions on which I can draw £4 per last on tar and £6 per last on pitch at the arrival of the ships: for the reasons you allege I shall draw no more than £4 per last on the tar until it is sold, but once sold I may (if I need to) always draw the surplus on each ship's lading without waiting for the money to come in. And on the pitch, since each last of pitch costs me twice as much as the tar, I would gladly see you allow me to draw £8 per last, which is not unreasonable. As for bad debts, I shall guarantee you, and likewise against the risk of fire (which God forbid!) but I cannot agree to allow you to sell to others than the previously specified tar-buyers, since you judge the danger of bad debts to be so great.

  You request that I should reimburse your outlay if you need it: I am always quite willing to reimburse you within two months of being informed by delivering over to you such effects as will suffice but on the condition that you only charge $\frac{1}{2}$ per cent commission on their account. On these conditions, and provided that you always follow my orders about selling, we can again continue to deal with one another.

  On these conditions I have today drawn, payable to Joseph Deutz's order:

£400 ⎫
£300 ⎬ at 3 usances   ⎫
£300 ⎭   ⎬ together £1,500,
£500   at $2\frac{1}{2}$ usances. ⎭

which bills of exchange I send herewith for acceptance. Please return them with your next so that I can use them. Captain Henry Robinson has passed the Sound as well as James Boulton from Viborg. May God bring them in safety. With regards, I remain, &c.

$$\frac{31 \text{ Aug.}}{5 \text{ Sep.}} 1678$$

19 B. BEUZELIN & SON to JD
ROUEN 6 SEPTEMBER 1678

Nous avons receu vostre lettre du 19/29 passe. En responce il nous est extrememant fascheux de voir le fil de latton baisser a veue d'oeil, s'en estant donné despuis l'arrivee du dernier navire d'Hambourg qui en avoit 1,300 torches a £82½t a £83t, de sorte que vostre ordre estant de suivre le cours nous nous sommes laissez aller au courant, et en avons vandu 250 torches a £83t et £83½t, dont il y a 100 a livrer, ce qui se fera demain. Appres le hault prix qui cette marchandise a vallu nous vous advouons que de long temps nous n'avons fait affaire plus a regret, d'aultant plus que nous avions tousjours este dans la santiment de vandre, a choze faitte le conseil est pris. Nous tascherons de vider du reste du mieux que nous pourrons, ne voyent pas esperance de mieux puis qu'il s'en charge encore a Hambourg a ce que nous apprenons, et que les ouvriers se plaignent qu'ils ont heu fort petite demande de leurs espingles a Guibray voire a perte en ayant qui nous doibvent y a tantost ung an dont nous avons extrememant de la paine a estre paye. Cella soit dit en passant pour vous faire voir que la mizere est grande, et qu'en mattiere de marchandise nous sommes dans ung temps ou le plus seur est tousjours de suivre le cours.

Le petit navire dont vous nous parlez est arrivé de Hull au Havre avecq 24 lests de goudron que nous avons ordonne d'y descharger et de vendre ce que l'on pourra, en nous envoyant icy le reste, car ce n'est pas une marchandise que requiere la garde. Nous y ferons comme pour nous; sy vous eussiez assorty la partie de quelque bre il n'en auroit este que mieux.

Il n'y a pas heu de la perte sur les cuirs que ont este acheptees par della et aurions vollontiers souhaitte que vous y eussiez fait quelque chose.

L'on a affiche icy un declaration par laquelle le Roy entend que les hollandois ne payent a l'advenir des marchandises qu'ils apporteront en France sur le pied qu'elles estoyent taxees par le tarif de 1664, que sera ung grand accroissement de commerce pour eulx, et fort prejudiciable au vostre, car par exemple le charbon qu'apportent vos navires taxe a £120t du 100 de barilz, ils n'en payeront que £40t, l'estain 50s du 100 qui est a £12t 10s, ainsy consequamment de plusieurs denrees, comme fanons, huiles de ballaine, drapperies et autres que l'on reduit a l'antien droit, de manier qu'ilz attireront ainsi la navigation pandant que vos vaisseaux demeureront sans employ au regard de la France. Avec tout cella, la paix n'a pas este encore ratiffie par les Estats, mais on la tient pourtant imancable, voire mesme qu'elle sera generalle, non obstant les grands apprets que vostre estat continue de faire pour la Flandre. Dieu nous donne ce qu'il voit mieux que nous nous estre necessaire en achevant. A prezante nous venons de vandre encore 200 torches de fil de latton a ung de nos ouvriers de dehors a £85t. Nous avons ung peu plus que le cours de ces gens-la, parcequ'il fault aussy attendre davantage pour le payemant. Nous ferons valloir ce prix la pour d'autre que en pourroyent encore avoir bezoing affin de voir sy nous ne pourrions pas remonter. Il n'y a que ce qui s'attend encore que nous embarrasse car cette marchandize tombant d'ordinaire en plusieurs mains le prix est fort difficille a se maintenir. Nous y ferons comme nous vous dizons du mieux qu'il nous sera possible.

M. Dumoutier nous a randu avant que partir *W*.50, ainsy son billet ne vaudra que pour £150t, par advis.

Nous vous baisons les mains, &c.

Amsterdam: $97\frac{1}{4}$ a $97\frac{1}{2}d$
London: $54\frac{7}{8}$ a $55d$ $\Big\}$ 2 usances.
Hamburg: $1\frac{1}{2}\%$

[P.S.] Despuis la presente escripte le Roy a donné une autre declaration due 3ᵉ courand parlaquelle il deffend sur peine de la vie a touts armateurs de molester en rien les vaisseaux hollandois, mais de leur prester tout aide et secours comme aux amis et alies de la Couronne, ce quy leur sert de passeport general pour venir en nos ports.'

$$\frac{4\ Sep.}{5\ Sep.}1678$$

420 P. BRIAINS & D. BION to JD
LA ROCHELLE   4 SEPTEMBER 1678

'Nous avons recue la lettre que vous nous avez fait l'honneur de nous escrire en datte du 8ᵉ du mois passe que doit estre vieille stille, et nous sommes obliges a Messrs Buzelins de ce qu'ils nous ont fait la grace de vous parler de nous. Nous voudrions bien en leur consideration et en la vostre pouvoir vous rendre quelque service qui vous fust agreable. Pour satisfaire a ce que vous nous demandez nous vous dirons, qu'il est vray que Mons. Hersemitte comme l'un des directeurs en cette ville de la Compagnie du Nort recevoit les marchandises que en venoient pour le compte de la ditte Compagnie, laquelle avoit des previlesges qui consistoient en ce qu'ils payoient moins de drois que les particuliers, mais cette Compagnie est a present comme estinte. Nous ne scavons sy a present que la paix sera faitte ils reprendrons en quelque facon ce commerce, mais nous voyons qu'il y a desja long temps qu'on travaille a la liquidation. Ils ont vandus tous leurs navires et tout ce qu'ils avoient de matteriaux et chose propre pour la construction, ainsy nous croyons qu'il ne viendra plus de marchandises pour ce compte-la. La principale consommation du bre, gouildron et chanvre est ce qu'il en faut pour les magazins de Rochefort, dont les achapts ce font publiquement pour toutes les choses dont l'on a besoing pour les magazins, et presentment ils sont assignes pour la douze et quinze de ce mois. On achepte la a livrer de celuy quy fait le meilleur marche, et mesme le Roy fournit a l'advance une partie du payement. Les marchandises que l'on y livre ne payent points de droits d'entrees. Aux vantes qu'ils se firent l'annee derniere le bre du nord cy vand £16t le baril, le gouildron mesme pris, le chanvre de Riga £15t le quintal, le cuivre en feuille ou platte 20s la livre, la rosette £80t le cent, cuivre de Barbarie que se tire aussy d'Angleterre £88t le cent,[1] mais il pourra cette annee y avoir du changement acause de la facillite que la paix donnera pour le transport, et qu'aussy les risques seront moindres, ainsy l'on ne peut encore dire ce que ce pourra estre ny quel pris tiendrons les dittes marchandises; ce sera selon qu'il viendra du nord. Quand a ce qui est de la consommation qui s'en fait dans cette ville, on nous dit que deux ou trois cens barils sufisent, a cause que l'on ce sert du brais sec d'Arcanson[2] que est a beaucoup meilleur marche. Il faut toujours du gouildron, comme aussy des cuivres en platte; cela vient ordinairement d'Hollande mais nous estimons qu'on les peut tirer a meilleur marché d'Angleterre. Le chanvre seroit de longue vante, a cause de la grande quantité que s'en recueille en France et qu'il est a bas prix. Vous avez cy-joint un estat des droits que les dites marchandises payent icy d'entrees. Il faut faire estat que c'est a peu pres mesme chose du pris de ses marchandises que ce qu'il est a Rochefort. La paix a fait hausser les eau-de-vies; elles sont a present icy a £40t et en Xaintonge a £32½t et 33t; les froment vallent £100t a £105t au grenier—voilà ce que nous pouvons vous dire et vous baisant tres humblement les mains nous demeurerons, Monsieur, vos trés humbles serviteurs.

[P.S.] Excusez la mauvaise escriture de notre homme—nous n'avons pas de temps a faire recopier ses lettres.

[Enclosed]

Droits d'entree sur quelques marchandises:

Bré le lest de 12 barrilz ordinaires	£9t 5s
Gouildron mesme chose	
Chanvre le cent pesant	11s
Cuivre et rosette	£3t 2s le cent.
Estain aveq le nouveau droit	£15t 10s le cent.
Plomb, 10s le cent pesant.	

Eaux-de-vie a la Rochelle pour tous droits et frais de sortie environ £7t par barique de $\frac{27}{v}$.

Eaux-de-vie de Charente pour tous droits et frais environ £19t par barique de $\frac{27}{v}$.'

[1] An error for £68t, corrected in their next letter.

[2] '*Brai sec . . . galipot liquéfié dans des chaudières, filtré et coulé dans des moules creusés au milieu du sable pour lui donner la forme de pains*'—C. Huetz de Lemps, *Géographie du commerce de Bordeaux à la fin du règne de Louis XIV*, p. 647.

$$\frac{23\ Sep.}{[\quad]}1678$$

21 VAN SCHOONHOVEN & SON to JD

NANTES 24 SEPTEMBER 1678

'Despuis quatre jours je suis de retour de mon voyage et vous suis infiniment oblige de tous les bien faits et civilitez que j'ay receu de vous, estant a Londres. Je souhaitterois pouvoir trouver occasion de m'en revanger, je seroit de grand coeur, c'est pourquoy nous vous prions de vouloir disposer de nous en ce que nous jugerez cappable de recevoir vos commandement. On commense a vandanger tout le long de nostre riviere cette annee. Nous aurons des vins exquis et on les croy a pris raisonnable, quoy qu'il y en aura ¼ moins que l'annee passe. Les eaux de vie a £49t $\frac{29}{v}$ avec assez bonne demande. Nos froments ont cette annee mencque et sont charbonne vallent £90t a £100t le thonneau. Nos seigle ont este beaux, vallent £65t a £70t le thonneau. Le sel a la Bay de Bourneuf £16t a £17t la charge. Poulquyn et Croisicq le muyt, miel de Bretagne £9½t le cent; plon d'Angleterre £90t le millier; estin £48t a £50t le cent. Nous n'avons point eu ou peu de fruyt cette annee et oultre cela beaucoup de secheresse si bien que selon toute apparance les beurre d'Yrlande et Engleterre vaulderont de l'argent, et nous croyons celuy d'Irlande autour de £22t a £23t le cent, celuy d'Engleterre autour de £25t le cent. Le fret pour Hollande £16t a £17t par thonneau. Estant ce qui s'offre pour le present, nous sommes apres vous avoir salue, vos trés humbles serviteurs.

Londres:	55½d.	} 2 usances.
Amsterdam:	22	
Paris:	1% de perte aux lettres a usance.	

[P.S.] par vostre permision je salue madamoiselle David et tout vostre aimable famillie. Je vous prie d'avoir la bonte de faire donner addresse a l'incluse, pour vostre amy, Mons. Caulier.'

$$\frac{4\ Oct.}{[\underline{\qquad}]}^{1678}$$

422   P. BRIAINS & D. BION to JD
         LA ROCHELLE   2 OCTOBER 1678

'Nous avons receu vostre lettre du 5ᵉ du mois dernier qui accuse la reception de le nostre du 4ᵉ
de nostre stile. Nous ne voyons pas que les meprises y soyent cy grandes comme vous y
penses; il y a veritablement quelque chose a dire sur le pris du cuivre de Barbarie, qu'on a mis a
£88*t* au lieu de £68*t*. C'est une erreur de plume. On nous a encore redit que l'an passe le bre
noir et goutrant furent vandus a £16*t* l'un portant l'autre, et aux vantes qui ce sont faites
depuis quinze jours le goutrant de Stokolm a este vandu £13*t* 5*s* le baril. On a laissé le bré
noir a £15*t* 10*s* mais il n'a pas esté accepté et la vanthe n'en est pas faite. On a livrée du cuivre
de Barbarie a £60*t* et on a laisse celuy en rosette a £80*t* que l'on n'a pas accepté disant qu'il y a
des marchands de Paris qui offre de le livrer amoins. On n'a point parlé du cuivre en placque
ny en feuille, l'estain d'Angleterre a este vandu a £53*t* le cent et le plomb a £86*t* le millier. Le
chanvre £13*t* 17*s*. Voila ce qui conserne les vantes pour les magazins du Roy. Pour ce qui est
de la consomation qui ce fait en cette ville de les marchandises on nous dit qu'il ne faut pas
deux cens barils de bré noir pour un an, acause que l'on ce sert de celuy d'Arcanson qui est a
beaucoup meilleur marche. Les marchands nous disent qu'ils l'achepte d'ordinaire £13*t*, mais
nous ne doutons pas qu'il ne se vande davantage. Ils mettent le goutrant a £12*t* et £12*t* 10*s*.
La consomation en est beaucoup plus grande que de bré mais aussy comme il viendra
souvent des navires de Suede et de Norvegue ils en aporteront directement. Ils ce fait icy
grande consomation de planche de sap de Noergue. Le cuivre en feuille l'est vandu jusque a
present £100*t*. Il vaudra autour de £95*t* hors les livraisons qui ce sont pour Rochefort, il n'en
faut point en Rosette. Le fil de laton n'est pas de grand debit icy; ceux qui en ont besoing s'en
pour avoient par autre voye a cause des droits d'entree qui sont de quatre livres du cent et
entrant par Charente pour aller dans les provinces de Saintonge, Angoulois, Limousin et
Auvergne ils paye moins. Il vaut icy nonante livres. Toutes les marchandises se vandent
presque au comptant. Vous avez cy-joint un mesmoire des droits et frais. Vous notterez que
ce qui ce livre au magazin de Rochefort ne paye point de droits d'entree. Les cuivres de
Barbarie sont pour Rochefort. Nous ne voyons pas d'autres gens qui en achepte. Voila ce que
nous pouvons vous dire sur le sujet de vostre ditte lettre et vous baisant tres humblement les
mains nous demeurons, Monsieur, vos trés humbles serviteurs.'

[Enclosed]

'*Drois quy se payent icy sur les marchandises suivantes:*
Bré noir: 15*s* 4*d* le barril.
Gouildron: 15*s* 4*d* le barril.
Cuivre en plaque ⎫
Rosette   ⎭   £3*t* 2*s* le cent.
Fil de latton: £4*t* 12*s* le cent.
Estain: £15*t* 12*s* le cent.
Plomb: 10*s* le cent d'une part et 16*s* du millier d'autre.
Chanvre: 11*s* le cent.

Les menus frais venu a peu de chose.'

$$\frac{14\ Oct.}{18\ Oct.}1678$$

23 J. A. FONCK to JD
HAMBURG   1 OCTOBER 1678

)] In answer to yours of the 10th past, I have already learned from others of the arrival of the tin-plate, sent as an experiment, and am now waiting to hear what happened regarding its sale. Those here who work for the Germans on commission selling this commodity, most of which is sold for two or three months credit, stand liable to their employers in return for a commission of 2 per cent in total, while others only enjoy a $1\frac{1}{2}$ per cent commission. There may not be much of this type. I wish you could dispose of plenty. I would then send you a good quantity every year. I await your report, together with advice. If the Marglitzer [linen] is not in better demand let us make an end of it. I shall send you enough of 'X'[1] but it is dearer, as you should know. I would like to hear what difference is made between the one and the other in [England].

Everyone is waiting now for the general peace, and as long as we do not have it I see no further demand for goods. One ought to give some thought to those countries which produce them, such as Germany, Poland and Hungary. The great abundance of goods which come from there keep their prices very low, despite every artifice to raise them. People no longer have such fat purses.

I am sure that individuals can obtain pepper in [England] for $6\frac{1}{2}d$, free on board. Please tell me if any more ships are expected from the East Indies. I remain, with regards, &c.

London—34s.   Amsterdam—$33\frac{1}{3}$ at usance.   Paris—46.   Venice—87.

[P.S.] The captain has delivered over the tin-plate to Mr Elking so I am surprised you have not sent over the money. Please do so.

[1] Tin-plate.

$$\frac{14\ Oct.}{12\ Nov.}1678$$

24 W. MOMMA to JD
NYKÖPING   25 MAY 1678

D] My last letter to you was on the 3rd of December, 1677. Since then I have received your letters of the 29th of January, 15th of February and 12th of April, and as you make no mention of mine I suppose you have not received them. I understand from you what is happening with you as regards trade, and also concerning rumours of war. We here live in hopes of peace, but what pertains to trade—which is now mostly carried on by the English—is bad. Some ships have arrived at Stockholm, and two ships loaded with coals from Newcastle have reached here. Iron is sold at 31 to 32 dollars per shippound; brass-wire is at 290 to 295 dollars per shippound (which is what was at £6 10s with you) and as there are only 4,000 coils in stock I trust that you will do your best with what you last had, for there will be no great quantities coming. Because of the bad winter the works could get no supplies and thus both the brass works and the iron works were at a standstill most of the time. As far as I am concerned, I am thinking of not exporting anything as long as the war lasts, and am not a little surprised that the pots and kettles have remained unsold for so long and that people attribute this to their bad quality. But I know otherwise, for the pots are not to be bettered and the kettles are no worse than those I have always sent to [England] or Holland. If they were in Holland they would not remain unsold one month, but it seems to be contrived that they simply eat up expenses in interest and warehouse rental. I shall await an account from Hiebenaer of such expenses as you may incur through the law-suit[1] and have them paid, and I shall make good such expenses as you may have incurred for me concerning Townley. Having nothing more to say I remain, with hearty regards to your wife, &c.

> [1] '. . . *door de vervolginge*'—indicating a prosecution, probably for debt.

$$\frac{18\ Oct.}{20\ Oct.}1678$$

425   T. PERMAN to JD
STOCKHOLM   8 OCTOBER 1678

[G]   My most recent letter was on the 1st instant, to which I refer, and enclosed herewith follows a copy of it. I am writing this only because I find I have not replied about the two invoices for the 3 packs from Hull and the 14 packs from London, which I would have answered long ago if I had not been prevented by my serious illness. So this will serve as a friendly comment on the 3 packs of goods from Hull, which I received as per invoice. I was well-satisfied with the goods, but I do not know where the £5 6s 4d comes from since W. Skinner brings £16 12s 3d into his account for expenses at Hull.

But, my dear Mr David, I have something to say about the 14 packs from London! Some of the wares are good, and some of them are bad, though I found the total number correct according to the invoice. The pack No. 1 with 30 pieces of northern kerseys was so bad that I cannot describe it. You put them down at 17d to 18d and 19d, but if you offered me such tattered goods for 10d I would not have them! They are not half as good as cottons, and are nothing else but trash. So, likewise, are most of the dozens. I have never seen such wretched goods. You must have bought the dozens and kerseys from a Quaker[?].[1] He has put two pieces together, but he must have been a scoundrel who sold you the 30 pieces of kersey and 40 dozens. He has deceived you like a fool. You know that I ordered you to buy the dozens and kerseys in Hull and not in London, and to have three kersey pieces wrapped in one but not two dozens in one. In London one can get no good dozens, only old, wretched things which seem at first like boards and full of worms, and the inside piece is so awful that I am ashamed to look at it. You have charged me for them at 3s 8d, 4s and 4s 6d and so on, but they are not worth 2s on average. They are nothing but rubbish.

However, the cottons and the bays and silk camisoles are good. I note that you put 3 pieces of bays wrapped up in one, but that is not what I ordered. I wanted each piece on its own, and the camisoles among the yellow bays, some in each piece. I was soon able to dispose of them. The three pieces of bays were very heavy and not very well sewn together with strong thread or sail-yarn. In packs 9, 10 and 11 were serges, with which I was also well satisfied, as much with the goods as the packing with three pieces wrapped in one. In pack 12 I was also well pleased with the coloured cloths, and in packs Nos. 13 and 14 I was content with the pieces, although the colours do not match well with each other. All in all, I am well satisfied with them except with the wretched 40 dozens and 30 pieces of kerseys. You must not buy such commodities in London another time. This is friendly advice to you, with which I commend you to God's protection.

[P.S.] The 30 pieces of kersey from Hull were not laid, three pieces in one, according to my orders, instead of each piece on its own. Another time, strict attention must be given to following orders.

N.B. On closing this letter I received yours of the 6th of August under Mr Pincier's cover, from which I see that you have ordered some goods from Hull. In reply, I must say that I would rather not have had them because I will not receive them at the right time. I have already supplied myself with as many dozens and kerseys as I can sell over the winter. I have just seen that the captain has arrived from Hull, but he has no account with him, only the bill of lading and a small freight bill. Farewell.

¹ '. . . *muss der gekauff haben von ein qucker . . .*'.

$$\frac{25 \text{ Oct.}}{25 \text{ Oct.}} 1678$$

426 C. LUBERS to JD
HAMBURG   18 OCTOBER 1678

[G] Your letter of the 8th instant has reached me safely, from which I see that the copper plates I sent aboard Captain Blauwers have been sold to two people who will pay in two and four months time. I had hoped you would sell to the Guinea Company, or to someone else, for cash payment as you always assured me you would in your letters. I would have been much happier to see you had done so, but since you have done otherwise there is no point in changing it. I hope these people are doubly reliable, otherwise I wish you had rather left my goods unsold and waited for a cash-customer. I must content myself with the thought that the transaction will have been a good one if the people turn out to be good.

You write of '£5 4s at 4 months' and '£5 2s at 2 months'. This must be an error, and should be £6, otherwise I would be doing badly and could not approve of the sale. I have seen in other letters from [London] that such plates can fetch £6 4s for cash. Furthermore, I hope you will be satisfied in both cases with 2 per cent commission so that I can enjoy some profit thereby. This will give me some motive for continuing, otherwise I shall have to suspend the trade. Sheet copper at £6 10s is a bad price—with that one can expect no profit but only loss. When, at the existing rate of exchange, one can make £7 sterling I shall send some more. Because I have my own mill I can provide you with a quantity of sheet-copper plates and pots at a fixed price, when I know what assortment sells. Only I would rather trade for payment in cash and would only grant two to three months credit when I can stipulate a good price from reliable people.

Likewise, I shall also send black latten and white when you can give me a fixed price which you will stand by. It is a commodity which is in demand in [London].

I thank you for honouring my draft of £150 sterling, because the rate of exchange was such that it might have been refused. In order to enjoy this rate again I am taking the liberty of drawing another £100 sterling, not doubting that you will honour it with due acceptance.

I have loaded 50 pieces of plate in Leonard Bushell for my account, marked **Ł**. He will be ready to sail in a few days time. With my next letter a bill of lading will follow. I cannot agree with Captain Meerwich, who has already departed, about the freight. I rely on you to treat me like a friend in the matter, and commend you to God's protection, &c.

$$\frac{20\ Nov.}{6\ Dec.}1678$$

427   s. de geer to jd
        amsterdam   25 november 1678

[D] & [F]   Monsieur, Apres vous avoir remersie tres humblement de toute vos grande sivilites et tres
bon acceuil et tretement, je vous diray bien tout franchement pour couper court que j'en
conserveray la memoire perpetuelement.

   Our journey was extremely successful and no less comfortable since we were only at sea
for two days which passed very quietly. It can happen that one is not at all comfortable at sea,
but if it does not last long one can endure it.

   I probably learned more English on the way than during my stay at London as it was my
turn to do all the talking. The two other gentlemen did not know enough to order a shoulder
of mutton, so I got us a piece of roast beef and besides that enjoyed very fine company.

   I have spoken to Mr Botte. I think it will be all right; I shall speak with him further.

   From Sweden I shall order 400 to 500 slb of pan-iron to be made for the coming year.
None has been made this year as the summer has been rather dry. I shall get them to make
some in the spring so that we can have some early.

   Enfin le Brandenb[ourg] occupe toute la Pomeranie. Gripswold, Stettin rendu. Ainsi les
Swedois hors de calemay apparemment pour quelques peu de temps. De la paix generale ou
avec l'empereur [ou] l'espaigne one still cannot rely upon. Tout se doit faire en peu ou tout se
doit rompre avec ces messieurs et la France.

   Tous les pais de Julier, Cleve, Liege et Cologne se vont ruiner. In short, some changes, or at
least a serious state of affairs which should also affect England, I remain &c.

   [P.S.] Mes respects a Madame, vos bien aimée, Mademoiselle la future Epouse, sans oublier le
vieu Pattron avec tous ces decendens et Mademoiselle du Piquet—and so a cup of strong tea
for us all![1] God speed Porrée.

   Vous aurez apris la mort de M. Jean van Baerle; le frere Davit estoit en chemin mais il rapelle.
On dit que les maladies diminuent; elles n'ont pas tant este dan la comune que bien entre les
plus releves. The dead also diminish—270 last week.

   M. Beuzelin trouvera s'il luy plaist mes besemains; adieu tous les Camers [camarades?] car ma
foy elles estoit bonnes met hock—demande le a Mons. Po[rree?] J'ay peur d'ecrire sans
oublier le vieu Deodati . . . [??].

   [1] Throughout this increasingly incoherent but engaging letter De Geer gives the impression of having
consumed something stronger than tea. The last lines are almost unintelligible.

$$\frac{30\ Nov.}{6\ Dec.}1678$$

428   f. bostelman to jd
        hamburg   22 november 1678

[D]   My last letter was about a week ago. Since then I have received yours of the 8th instant.

   I have received the galls from Cutler, but I have to tell you (although to my regret, for I
greatly dislike complaining) that I am astonished you should send me such goods. Ten or
twelve of the sacks are passable, although I had hoped for better, but the rest are so extremely

bad that I have never had the like in twenty years of trading. It is bad, uncultivated stuff, mostly of bush-galls. If one takes them out of the sack with a ladle[?] or dish[1] there are no blue galls to be seen underneath but only wild galls. What can I say? It is annoying to be served in such a way. One pays over good money for it yet is obeyed in nothing even though I gave such explicit orders and asked you to send only good, plump, blue galls or else nothing at all, and not to quibble about 6*d* or 1*s* more. I do not know how to sell such terrible stuff here, much less can I send it to my friends. I would lose their commissions. I would like to know, what am I to do with these awful galls? If you do not believe me you can tell Mr Ruland or Mr Lethieullier so that they can see them and give you better advice. As I do not seek your harm, I would rather that you did not desire mine. I am heartily sorry that I have to press this. I still need 6 or 8 sacks of choice quality galls, and to my great annoyance I must buy them from others, which is very painful. God preserve you, &c.

[P.S.] If the galls were tolerably good, and if among the remaining 12 or 14 sacks of bad ones there were still some blue ones to be found or seen, I would not be so annoyed, but there are enough such galls here and one dare not procure them from [England] without great expense and risk. The above-mentioned 10 or 12 sacks are good, although we have had better from the English here. However, there is nothing more to be said: finally one must let it pass—but the remainder are too bad!

[1] '. . . *met een malge oft schoetelle* . . .'.

$$\frac{17\ Dec.}{20\ Dec.}1678$$

29 OLOFF & NICOLAS TÖRNE[1] TO JD

STOCKHOLM   19 NOVEMBER 1678

Your various letters, together with the goods aboard Captain Joseph Newcombe, have been safely received. We have found the goods to be correct but are not so well satisfied with the 15 per cent which you have charged on top of the expenses, which in these times we regard as very inappropriate. All the goods which we order from Holland—not only those wares which are sent on credit, but also those which our factor buys for us for cash—are sent directly to us and we are aware of no other expenses apart from those which are customary in Holland. We trust that all goods will be as free in English ships as they are in Dutch, and if they are to be burdened with such large costs we would do better to despatch our returns to Holland and order English goods from there. They would not cost as much as they do on such conditions as you have stipulated for us in the account. Things are very different now from what they were before, with Mr Darbey. Then the English were sole masters and we had to allow them to do as they liked, but now things are different. If you will not treat us reasonably it will oblige us to do business with someone else. Last year Mr William Cooper sent us some goods but was aware of nothing more than ordinary charges. You can take it from this that we will not stand for it, or pay for it. We recently sent you wire, which reached you unhindered; why then cannot our goods come unmolested?

If you will serve us as a factor and provide us with good insurers every time we will do further business together and order larger amounts than ever before. But if not, we shall have to find another who will serve us in return for his commission.

You will send us our account by way of Livland and compile a proper expense account so that we can settle this consignment with one another. Awaiting your answer we commend you to God, and remain, &c.

[1] Oloff Hansson Törne, a mayor of Stockholm and raised to the nobility as Törnflycht. For the family's significance see Åström, *From Cloth to Iron*, pp. 144–5 n. 101.

430 B. BEUZELIN & SON to JD

ROUEN 30 DECEMBER 1678

'Nostre derniere a esté du 23e de ce mois, vous donnant advis du necessaire; dudespuis nous avons receu la vostre du 9/19 dudit qui ne nous oblige pas a grande responce. Nous avons fait honneur a la traitte de *W*.500 que vous nous avez faitte pour nostre compte, sur lequel ayant jetté les yeux nous ne trouvons pas vous debvoir plus de £41 1*s* 5*d* sterling que nous sommes bien marris de ne vous avoir remis. Pour eviter la perte de ce bas change nous ne savons pas ce que mon filz a peu prandre de vous aujust affin de vous en creditter, ce qu'il vous plaira nous faire savoir. Ceppandant nous vous debitterons pour vostre ditte traitte de £110 8*s* 4*d* [sterling]. Le change commance a hausser et nous n'avons pas voullu remettre a 54$\frac{1}{2}$*d* cet ordinaire soulz esperance qu'il montera davantage veu la paix publiee a Paris avecq l'Espagne, et celle de l'Allemagne bien advance et immancable; ce qui resveillera ung peu le negoce.

Nous avons heu des lettres de Stockholm par Lubecq du 20/30 passe qui nous advisent qu'il estoit party 2 vaisseaux pour icy, l'un desquels nous est addresse avecq environ 1,000 torches de fil de latton et quelque peu de bre. Ung autre vient au sieur Thomas Legendre le jeune qui en aura dumoins mesmes quantité—oultre encore 730 arrivees par ce dernier vaisseau d'Hambourg. Ainsy nous tenons pour assuré que cette marchandise ne haussera point. Ung ouvrier auquel nous avons cydevant vandu quelque partie de fil de latton des 3 Couronnes nous a faite plainte qu'il ne trouve pas bon, qu'il est cassant, aigre et difficile au travail, cependant c'estoit aultre fois la meilleure marque, cella nous fasches a cauze de ce que nous en avons a vous. Ce que nous attendons est de la Couronne, des ouvrages de Mons. Isaac Cronström, qui nous mande qu'il va recommancer le travail. Nous prevoyons que l'este prochain ces marchandises abonderont. Vous ne debves pas ce nous semble tenir sy fort la main a ce que vous en avez veu ce que nous vous dizons, vous en uzeres touttefois comme vous le trouveres a propos.

Il n'est arrivé aulcune fruits d'Espaigne cette annee, qui vaudroyent bien de l'argent.

Nous ne pouvons rien descouvrir de ce nomme Pierre le Roy. Il est arrivé au havre en 6 jours ung navire de Gottemborgh qui a seullement 8 lasts de bré, 400 schippon de fer et quelque planches et mats. Le commis nous est recommande. Nous nous refferons a nos precedantes pour le regard du bré que nous ne vandrons point. Jusques a aultre advis, nous sommes entierement, Monsieur, &c.'

Amsterdam:	97*d*.
Londres:	54$\frac{1}{2}$*d*.
Hambourg:	2%.

431 C. BENE to JD

HAMBURG 14 JANUARY 1679

[D] My last letter to you was on the 24th of December. Since then I find myself with your welcome letters of the 6th, 13th, 20th of December and 3rd instant, and have seen thereby that you had not yet received the Barbary almonds which you bought for me, and that you were of the opinion that you ought to delay their receipt for as long as possible. I am glad of that since we will not be having open water very soon and in the meantime the almonds would suffer rather from the rats, like those on a ship from Barbary which delivered its cargo somewhat damaged. And I note that in this way we may get them cheaper, but I beg you please make sure that you receive nothing but good quality, for bad quality goods are no use to me at any price. Please keep yourself informed if newly arrived goods are sold at lower prices.

I am glad that the £85 remitted for your account was accepted. I have received the protest concerning the £100 on B. Sirps and will know what to do with it. Concerning the £100 which you have paid for the honour of Lubers, I have debited you for £100 18s 4d. I could have wished that you had returned the bill of exchange together with the second protest, but as you have not done so by now it should not be necessary for us to correspond about it again, and I believe that in future this Lubers will behave himself with more discretion than he has shown towards me.

I have sold your Jamaican tobacco to Hans. P. Dimpfel at $4\frac{3}{8}s$ per lb., for cash, payable in bank money. Please make a note of it. With my next letter I shall send you an account. I could not push the price up any higher, and I would rather have taken $\frac{1}{8}s$ less in bank money than sell it for current money, for the agio on it is $3\frac{1}{2}$ per cent and there is uncertainty whether it might not go higher. I have also sold 48 sacks of our scraped ginger which came with Hendrick Weever and delivered them yesterday to Hermann Harvart for $7\frac{1}{8}g$ with $8\frac{2}{3}$ rebate payable in bank money. The price is rather poor and we shall not gain much by it, but as there is so little demand for it now I did not want to let the opportunity pass. The account of this also will be sent by my next, and if the money has come in a remittance will be made to you. Meanwhile I think we shall also get in the money for our last bale of Ardasse because the debtor has promised it. As for our Bermuda tobacco, with the waters closed I can still find no buyers, but if any opportunity offers itself it will not be neglected. I wait to hear if any nice Virginia-leaf can be had in [England] and at what price and when the ships are expected. I shall inquire how the purchaser fares with your tobacco and keep you informed. As far as I can discover he sends it into Germany in place of another variety.

I see that you have been persuaded to believe that one cannot learn any good German here and as a result have requested your servant[1] to be sent to some place in Germany where he can better perfect the language. I would gladly see to that if I did not believe that it would not be profitable either for you or your servant, for you ought to consider the fact that he will not learn to pronounce the language like a born-German within five years and will be little use to you unless he can write the language correctly, which is what you want him mostly to do, and he can just as well learn to write here as in Germany, for there is no difference; and he is already so far advanced that he can read and understand any book in High German just as well, if not better, than Dutch and also speaks High German, so it only remains for him to learn the style of German letters, which cannot be easily done except in a counting-house. I hope to help him find one, and expect to hear from houses in Nüremberg. If, in answer to this, you persist in your plan I shall arrange it but I consider it unnecessary, for your information. Enclosed herewith is a letter from him which may be useful to you.

Regarding your good wishes for the newly-commenced year, I most heartily thank you and pray to God to preserve you, your wife and children in good health and prosper you in every way he can in this and many coming years, which I trust the Lord will do and keep you in his protection, remaining, &c.

London: 34s 0g 2 usances.
Amsterdam: $33\frac{3}{16}$ short sight.
Venice: $87\frac{1}{2}$ at usance.

[P.S.] It freezes here unusually hard.

¹ John Gosselin, who spent the period May 1678–April 1679 with Bene at Hamburg before returning to England with a reasonably fluent command of German.

$\dfrac{\textit{10 Feb.}}{\textit{13 Feb.}}$1679

432   B. BEUZELIN & SON to JD
          ROUEN   14 [FEBRUARY]¹ 1679

'Nous avons receu la vostre du 23 Janvier vieil stille, qui nous fait seullemant savoir ce qui se passe au cours du negoce. Nous trouvons qu'en acheptant les poivres de la Compagnie a $6\frac{1}{2}d$ randus a bord, comme Messrs. Frederick & Herne nous mandent que l'on pourra avoir, ils reviendront encore icy a 57 ou $57\frac{1}{2}d$ et ne les vandant que £60t le 100, nous ne trouvons pas que le proffit vaille la paine de s'en mesler; ainsy il faut laisser aller les plus presses et cercher quelques meilleures occasions d'ailleurs. Ce n'est pas nostre pense qu'il vienne de grand ordre de France pour achepter et la Compagnie d'Orient en ayant sy grand nombre sera peultestre obligee d'en cercher le debit ailleurs. Cette marchandise abonde tant que quand il n'en viendroit de 2 ou 3 ans il y auroit encore asses pour la consommation qu'il y a. Nous estimons que touttes ces mauvaises affaires de della porteront beaucoup de prejudice a vostre negoce. Dieu veille mettre la main et vous conserve, et tous nos bons amis en des temps sy fascheux.²

La rehausse des galles par della n'a pas produit grand changemant et ne vallent encore que £47t a £47$\frac{1}{2}$t les 100. Nous trouvons que les marchandises se maintiennent mieux en prix que par de ca ou l'on ne demande que le plus necessaire. Il y avoit cette annee beaucoup a gaigner sur les vins et raizins parcequ'il ne n'est du tout point venu, et l'on auroit vandu la pipe du vin £400t estant bons. Commes nous entrons dans le caresme il est presantement trop tart pour y penser. Le plomb vaud £95t et £96t le millier et les huiles £31t a £32t.

Le 11ᵉ il est arrive en cour en expres qui porte les nouvelles de la paix conclue avecq l'Empire et on escrit que celle du nord est indubittable. L'envoye de Brandebourgh a desia heu 2 audiances du Roy et l'on tient l'accommodemant bien advance avecq la Suede, a laquelle on restituera bonne partie de conquestes qui avoyent este faittes sur elles. Les princes du nord ont heu crainte de l'armemant qui se fait a Brest et dans les costes de la Rochelle, qui sera prezantement pour quelque aultre dessoing. La navigation estant libre dans le nord il ne nous manquera pas de marchandizes, c'est pourquoy nous cerchons l'occasion de nous deffaire de vostre reste de fil de latton et par preference a ce que nous en avons. Le prix est prezantement a £83t ayant baisse despuis ce qui en est venu de Hambourg. Nos amis qui avoyent tenu sy ferme nous mandent de vandre sans limitation, mais pour cella il fault trouver marchand, et comme la riviere demeure tousjours fermee et les chemins tres mauvaises; par le carroy rien ne s'en leve.

Nous vous remercions au surplus des nouvelles que vous nous donnes de mon filz. Il nous a aussy escrit ung mot de Donquerque pour nous adviser de son arrivée. Nous souhaittons fort qu'il puisse reussir en l'affaire pour laquelle vous l'avez envoyée. Le temps est tres difficille et fascheux en touttes mannieres et peultestre aultant icy que chez vous. Il fault remettre le soing de nos affaires a la providence de Dieu qui n'abandonnera pas les siens, nous le prions qu'il vous aye en sa sainte garde, et sommes tousjours, &c.'

Amsterdam: $96\frac{1}{2}$.
Costy: $54\frac{7}{8}$.

[P.S.] 'Nous vous prions de nous faire la faveur de faire accepter cette lettre de $W.333\frac{1}{3}$ a $54\frac{1}{2}d$ sur Pierre Paravicin et nous la renvoyer. Nostre frere Benjamin nous escript de Dunquerque qu'il ne scait pas s'il sera assez a temps a Londre pour aquitte une traitte de $W.800$ a $54\frac{1}{2}d$ que nous avons faitte sur luy payable au Sr. Thomas Goddard, nous vous prions en faire le payement et pour votre rembours tirer sur Mons. Gillot de Paris, parceque le change est tousjours chez vous en peu plus haut sur cette place-la que sur celle-cy. Il debvoit oultre cella tirer encore $W.500$ a $W.600$ de sorte que ce seroit $W.1300$ a $W.1400$, nous croyons que dans quelques ordinaire le change pourra estre chez vous a $54d$, nous avons mis bon ordre pour l'acceptation de vos lettres.'

¹ Mis-dated '14 January'.
² These and subsequent references to difficult times are guarded allusions to the 'Popish Plot' hysteria now reaching its peak in London.

$$(i) + (ii) \quad \frac{15 \; Feb.}{28 \; Feb.} 1679$$

433   W. MOMMA TO JD
NYKÖPING   (i)   5 AUGUST 1678

[D]   The above is a copy of my last letter. Three days ago I received yours of the 8th of June with a copy of that of the 7th ditto, of which the original has not yet arrived. I am surprised that none of my letters have come to your hands, and it means that there is little to reply to, although I have seen what is happening to trade in [England]. Here, iron remains at 31 to 32 d.c.m. per slb and wire at 285 d.c.m. per slb. I can well believe that my wire is now in demand as the best, and in order to ensure it have had all the short pieces thrown out.¹ But I am not a little surprised that the pots and kettles are not wanted. If they are of no use there it would be best if you sent them to Messrs Van Baerle at Amsterdam and let them sell them, making good the proceeds to you. It is inexcusable to leave such saleable goods² lying around for four years. I am considering not allowing you any interest or warehouse-rent on them because I sent them at your request and they were a further consignment which I sent in accordance with your memorandum, for your information. With regards, &c.

(ii)   14 OCTOBER 1678

434   The above is a copy of my last letter, to which I refer. I have since received yours of the 9th of July and 6th of August. There is little to reply to either, although I have seen that you have sent a barrel of kettles to Ireland, with which I am not satisfied. I confirm what I said in my last, that you ought to send them all to Messrs Van Baerle at Amsterdam and let them make good the proceeds, so that I shall get one account of everything and be able to see how many hundred pounds are due to you. For, to tell you the truth, I am not at all satisfied with the way you have handled my goods in these troubled times, and if it goes on any longer it will only add more and more to your claims. Therefore, I must request you to make an end of the business. Otherwise, there is no change in trade here but we have certain news that peace has now been settled with France by Spain as well as Holland, and we hope a general peace will follow, which God grant, to whom I commend you, with hearty regards, &c.

¹ '... & om het daertoe tebrengen so late alle de korte eynden daaruyt smyten'.
² '... sulke liquide goederen ...'.

$$\frac{15\ Mar.}{25\ Mar.}1679$$

435 J. & H. VAN BAERLE to JD
AMSTERDAM   21 MARCH 1679

[D] Our last letter was on the 14th of this month, and since then we have received yours of the 28th past, to which this serves as a reply.

We have now been busy for some years, employing all means to obtain our payment from Mr Willem Momma, in which we have so far made little or no progress, and there seems to be little chance of us escaping without a serious loss. The best that we have been able to contrive is to arrange for him to go on managing his works and to supply him with a quantity of copper which, in exchange, he returns back again as manufactured brass. The wages for it are deducted from his debt and although this will take a very long time (and also cannot be done without employing a good deal of money) we have decided it is better to deal with it on this basis than to let the debt run on still longer. But we believe there is still nothing that can be done for you as long as you have not settled accounts with Momma and got him to acknowledge the debt, which will only be obtained with difficulty, for according to our observation he will stir up some dispute. In his letter of January the 3rd, which we received yesterday, he complains much that his goods remain for so long unsold in London, being astonished that his kettles and pots have not been sent to us to sell in accordance with the orders which he gave to you last summer, since the proceeds would be made good to you. Having got no answer about this he asks us to write to you to find what reason there is for delay, to which we await your decision. And in case you feel some difficulty, for fear that we shall make our claims on it, we hope it will not inhibit you, assuring you that if they can be sold here the proceeds will be sent to you. With regard to our kettles and pots, we have hitherto not restricted you to any price limit and once again we beg you to make an end of the matter the sooner the better so that the account can be closed. With heartiest regards, we commend you to God and remain, &c.

London: 35*s* 5–6*g* ⎫
Paris: 95¾   ⎬ 2 usances.
Hamburg: 33 stuivers, at sight.

$$\frac{1\ Apr.}{3\ Apr.}1679$$

436 ESTIENNE MOLIÉ to JD
PARIS   4 APRIL 1679

'Je me trouve avecq vostre lettre du 17 Mars dernier; par mesme j'ay receu les copies des recommendations pour vos parties sur les subsides. Depuis ma derniere il ne s'y est rien passe en cette affaire; vous en aures au premier jour des nouvelles.

Il est bien vray que la brouillonerie des marchans Englois gâste entierement le negoce de Suede. Ils ont eu leur reigne pendent quelques annees; assure que la Hollande recommence a prendre la navigation et que les marchandizes que les Englois portoit a Stockholm y seront portees par d'autres nations avecq grande esconomie, cella faire que beaucoup de vos messieurs abandonneront ce negoce.

Je fais travailler bon nombre de fil de latton, chauderons et autres ouvrages, j'en voudrois avoir journellement a Londres ou la consumption en est grande, mais quent je considere le pris je n'y vois pas seullement un honeste intherest, cella m'en fait perdre l'envie. Faudra voir comme les affaires ce disposeront. Vous pouvez estre assure qu'en tout ce qu'il sy presentera de mes affaires ou de mes amis sur vostre ville passeront par vos mains. Sy en cette ville je puis vous estre utille ou a vos amis, disposes librement de mon service.

Il me semble que le bruit a couru a Stockholm que le bré n'estoit plus tout entre vos mains mais q'un chacun en pouvoit envoyer. Sy l'on pourroit faire que le fil de latton tombast tout dans une main il seroit une bonne affaire, mais je ne vois par quelles mesures l'on pouroit prendre pour cella.

J'ay envoye aujourdhuy a Mons. Axel Fleming une lettre de credit sur vous de 587 escus. Je vous prie de les lui faire conter suivent le cours du change a 2 usances que vous tireres sur moy pour vostre rembours. Je vous baise les mains et suis, Monsieur, vostre tres humble serviteur.

[P.S.] Je vous prie de faire rendre l'incluse lettre a Mr Karlstrom, gentilhomme Suedois. Il est de la suitte de Mons. le Wachtmeester[1] qui est venu de Suede vers vostre Roy.

Sy la vaisselle d'argent que j'ay fait retirer de l'orfebvre n'est pas encore partie je vous prie de l'envoyer par quelque bon navire a Rouen a l'addresse de Mons. Thomas Legendre le Jeune.'

[1] Axel Wachtmeister, Swedish major-general, sent to England in February 1679 to negotiate for Franco-Swedish interests—R. Hoffstedt *Sveriges utrikespolitik under krigsåren 1675–1679* (Uppsala, 1943) pp. 317–18.

$$\frac{9\ Apr.}{14\ Apr.}1679$$

437 G. RICHARDS to JD
BILBAO   31 MARCH 1679

'Sir, I have none of yours since my last, so is this to accompany your account current, by ballance whereof is dew to you R. *pta.* 40,548 in silver, which I gave you credit for in anew account, and pray (finding it right) passe it away accordingly, the contratation house haveing thought good that all goods be sould in that specie to prevent the inconvenience of reduction.[1] What you have to noate is that silver is in vallew $9\frac{1}{4}$ per cent more than gold, as formerly reduced.[2] You have also herewith invoyce and bill of loading of one parcell of fyne ware consigned you by Pooke, for the cost whereof please to give mee credit R. *pta.* 7,897 also in silver. The remainder I shall goe remitting you with all diligence. Of the tarre about $\frac{1}{3}$ part is sold at 6 to 7 *pesos* per barrell and the rest may sell this sommer. Your *baragaenns* are neare sould but that other sort are to deare and not so propper. *Baragaenns*, if they are cheape bought in cannot doe amisse, beeinge a staple comodity and always expence theretoe. Colchester bayes I beleeve will ryse here, for your government. If they can be had resonable in England, dying $6\frac{1}{2}s$ per piece and other chargs accordingly, they will always sell and make short accounts. Hunter, I understand, is againe bound hether. I knowe not what he will doe here, three shipps beeing already without any loading or hopes of it, which is all at present. With my respects, I remayne, Sir, your humble servant.'

[1] Until March 1679, Richards' sale-accounts had been complicated by a double process of converting prices (quoted in silver *reals plata*) first into vellon, at a premium of 200 per cent (thus 8 R. *pta.* = 24 R. *vn*) and then into a gold *pesos* valued at 22 R. *vn* (a premium of 175 per cent).

[2] Thus, in the account accompanying this letter, the net balance of 44,235 *reals* in gold yielded 40,548 in silver, a 9.25 per cent premium.

$$\text{(i) + (ii)} \quad \frac{\text{12 Apr.}}{\text{25 Apr.}} 1679$$

438 R. CLARK to JD
GOTHENBURG   (i)   7 MARCH 1679

'Sir, To myn of the 15 January, 24 ditto, 10 February and 24 ditto, I refer you, not doubting but all ore some are com to your hands, but haveing non from you in answer could not omit to give you the contents of all, vizt. that the 25,000 dollars silver money is to be devyded betwixt Mr Shult, Mr Cook and my selfe as hier under specified and ordered that my pairt of the same should be perussed as hier affter folueth, to 500£ starling theroff, ore 2,000 *RD*, from Paris should be remited to Amon Andersson in Hamburg ore your own correspondent, adwyssing me ther of for my regulation; allso to let 4 a 5,000£t stand at Nantz, for which you are to send me 100 moys Frensh salt from Crossick in one ore two wessells two tonns Angue wyne, some of it reed wyne, at least 2 oxheads, 7 or eight tonns brandie, 2 tonns viniger, 2 smal casks of Nantz prouns, one baskit or chist of earthen pots that falleth at Crossik, 100 rime wryting peaper, 20 rim ditto for prenting, tray our merkite with some walnuts and chestnuts. Tack your own conveniencie to fraught eather Inglish or Scots ships at Nantz that seeketh fraught ther, ore to fraught them from the west off Ingland. I doubt not but you will seik to mack the fraught eassie and let the ships com hier per first for the getting of the merket, which I hope you will doe. Alsso I ordred to pay Androu Allexander in Rotchel 86 French crouns, and to Mr Patrik Layel in Helshingor £48 7s 6d starling, all which pray accomplish and what more in cash for me keep unto furder order, which is all at present save kynd respects from, R.C.

Mr Cooke 1,762½ ⎫
Mr Shult 14,035¾ ⎬ 25,000 Dollars silfer money.'
My selfe 9,201¾ ⎭

(ii)   22 MARCH 1679
[not selected]

$$\frac{\text{12 Apr.}}{\text{18 Apr.}} 1679$$

439 GEORG CHRISTIAN FUCHS to JD
AMSTERDAM   18 APRIL 1679

[D]   Until now I have not had the honour of being known to you, although you have long been known to me through your correspondence since I was living with the Messrs De La Bistrate & Dufay, from whom I have recently parted with all due honour and cordiality. And as I had observed in what good esteem you were held by the aforementioned gentlemen and that you were practical and precise in all kinds of trade, I found no difficulty in recommending Mr Andreas Ingolstetter of Nüremberg to address himself to you,[1] who had requested me to find him a reputable and reliable correspondent who would be willing to serve him in the purchase of English tin. He initially wanted to know the varieties and prices of it, and at what cost it could be delivered to him at Bremen, so that he could see if he would find it profitable, and in future wants to send for any other English products suitable for Germany. If you are now inclined to favour him with the *raguagly*[2] of tin and other wares I have no doubt that in due course a mutually satisfactory correspondence can be established, especially if the good God grants us a general peace. You can be assured that he is a man of complete reliability, precise and accurate in his affairs, of which I can give you certain testimony as I know him intimately, having lived with him for many years. But in case you do not take my word for it, since you do not know me, he will be able to inform you of enough reliable people who will be able to assure you about his condition. In any case, if you join together in a correspondence his own conduct will give you adequate testimony to his promptitude and reliability. It is a matter of indifference to him whether you correspond with him in Italian, French or Low German, though the Low German will be the best for him as you are not accustomed to writing High German.

Besides Mr Ingolstetter, I have recommended your person and condition to Mr Willem Grassel at Nüremberg,[3] who will perhaps write to you about a trial purchase of tin, in which case you would do well to serve him as he is also reputed reliable and is one of the principal persons in the city, though he is not so intimately known to me as Mr Ingolstetter, who makes no fuss about himself but goes about his business quietly and confidently. You can, if you wish, write to them directly in reply when they write to you or, if you judge it necessary, write to me, giving the letters to the ordinary post to be forwarded by Mr Christian Meschman. As it suits him that I should come at once to London I shall seek to have the honour of waiting upon you. Meanwhile, with friendly regards, I commend you to God's protection, &c.

¹ See [**441**].

² I.e. report, or account.

³ Grasel concurrently wrote as 'Guillaume Grasel' on 4 April 1679—'*C'est dans l'estaing fin d'Angleterre que je desire faire une petite emplette pour un essay, en suitte si le compte tourne augmenter la commission.*' He asked for consignments to be sent via Bremen to Mons. Marcus de Medoch and authorized David to draw his bills on Giovanni Christoforo Pommer at Venice. Having seen the price of English tin as £3 4s per cwt. for blocks and £3 9s for bars according to the Price Currents he was displeased in June to be charged £3 13s by David for his consignment of 10 blocks, and the correspondence ceased.

$$\frac{14\ Apr.}{27\ May}1679$$

440   WILHELM DE HERTOGH to JD

HAMBURG   8 APRIL 1679

[D]   I find myself honoured with your letter of the 21st of March. Likewise, I owe you an answer for yours of the 30th of November past, for which I humbly thank you. I am grateful for your remembrance and your offer of service. I can have no greater satisfaction than the honour of your correspondence and therewith the maintenance of our good friendship. But the times have for so long been so miserable and also so dangerous that one has had enough to do to preserve oneself, without going to all the trouble of trade. But it may be that we shall soon have a general peace (unless it is again transferred to another place, which the Almighty prevent!) by which everyone may recover themselves and trade may begin to improve. May God grant it and allow me the chance of being able to gain and enjoy your correspondence. There is occasionally something to be done with goods from [England], if only consumption were rather better. It has been extremely bad because of the misery throughout Germany, but undoubtedly it will now improve. Meanwhile I shall attend to your advice and make my speculations accordingly, wherever there is a chance of profit.

Herewith you will receive one of our price-currents, and from it the news that there is little oil in town, as a result of which it has risen to 75 and 78 *RD* per pipe of 820 lb. net. A great many almonds have arrived here and are selling at 30 to 32 *ML*. Ardasse silk has sold at $14\frac{1}{2}$ to 15*s* but is now going for $13\frac{1}{2}s$.

If you perceive the least chance of profit in one commodity or another, and are willing to do something about it in partnership, half and half, I shall on news from you make you a remittance, or you can draw on me. I await your decison and must say further that my brother, Jan Battista, is going through Brabant to Paris without visiting [England] but it could easily happen that he will do so on his return journey. So he could have the pleasure of being assured by you of our mutual inclination, which I feel in particular, humbly commending myself to your dear wife, with all my heart, &c.

$$\frac{28 \ Apr.}{9 \ May} 1679$$

441 ANDREAS INGOLSTATTER

NÜREMBERG   11/21 APRIL 1679

[D] Until now I have not had the honour of writing to you, but one of my friends at Amsterdam has acquainted me with your name and circumstances.

Although there is still very little going on in trade with England I nevertheless wish to ask you to write at once and tell me on what conditions you could supply me with genuine English tin for delivery at Bremen. There is an Englishman here, called Merry, who deals in it and other wares, but I would gladly have it at first hand so that I can enjoy all possible advantage. And if we can do business together I shall give you addresses in Amsterdam where you can inform yourself about me, but I can assure you that you can deal with me without risk or suspicion.

With other English manufactures there is nothing particular to be done here, except with stockings, but I supply myself from Hamburg as the English Court[1] will not suffer us to supply ourselves from London. I once had a bale taken away from me which I only recovered with great trouble and expense. I was also advised that my stockings would be better made at Hamburg than my English white woven stockings, since those of their style have better sales.

If you can do something with German wares over there please just commission them. My business is principally with friends in the Netherlands, Italy and France, supplying them with Nüremberg and other German manufactures. Your answer would reach me best by way of Antwerp, either through the post or through Denys Potteau, merchant-factor, who was recommended by my principal correspondent there. I remain always, &c.

[P.S.] Jean Daniel van Braech, who has been established at Amsterdam for about one year now, served me here for four whole years, and George Christian Fuchs for eight years, who has since come to Messrs De la Bistrate & Dufay, though he is shortly leaving their service. I think it would be quicker to contact him since he is shortly visiting friends in London.

---

[1] The Court of the Merchant Adventurers at Hamburg.

$$\frac{3 \ May}{27 \ May} 1679$$

442 HANS HENDRICK BERENBERG to JD

HAMBURG   25 APRIL 1679

[D] I did not write to you by the last post—I should say, for several posts—and I find myself meanwhile with your letter of the 11th instant, from which I have seen the prices of sundry goods as well as your opinion about one sort or another, for all of which I thank you. Sales are so small that prices are stifled and are as likely to produce losses as profits, as is the case with those in [London] who have bought pepper from the East India Company, for it cannot be sold here at $12\frac{1}{2}g$. It is said that a quantity was sold at $12g$, and that is how things are with other goods, as far as one can see, so that one is forced to sit tight. The higher rate of exchange, as you can see at the foot of this letter, also harms commodity prices. Black ginger can be had at $3\frac{1}{2}$ to $3\frac{5}{8}g$; scraped ditto, $7g$; Caribbean indigo of extremely choice quality, $4\frac{3}{4}s$ with 13 months rebate; Aleppo galls, 47 *ML* per 100 lb., as before. Whether Turkish or Levant wares will increase in price through the danger from the Turks, time will tell. The bale of Ardasse which you last provided is still lying here unsold. The English have got a quantity, with which they are heavily undercutting the price at $13s$, with $10\frac{2}{3}$ per cent discount, which is reckoned to have been bought in [London] at $9s$. The exchange is at $34s$ $5g$ and the net charge for insurance is 2 per cent. Although, as you truly say, the price is low, nonetheless there is no profit to be made, which is a miserable state of affairs. Of Zerbassi, Legi and other varieties one can buy here as cheaply as you can offer it in [London]. It is the most delicate stuff that one could ever see, so wonderfully has that trade been driven. If there should be any changes in silk, galls or ginger, please let me know.

Please hand the enclosed, undamaged, to Mr Samuel la Motte and procure an answer. I have been asked to obtain it by my friends in Germany and beg you to forgive the trouble. With very friendly regards, may the Lord protect you, &c.

London: $34s$ $5g$ 2 usances.
Amsterdam: $32\frac{15}{16} - \frac{7}{8}$.

$$\frac{3\ May}{8\ May}1679$$

443 ANDRÉ AMSINCQ to JD
ROUEN   9 MAY 1679

'Le 5 du courant fust ma derniere, dudepuis nulle vostre, ne servira la presente que pour vous confirmer ma derniere pour l'achapt des 2 balles de creseauz[1] quy doibvent contenir 20 pieces et pour y adjouster:

4 demy-pieces de bonnes et fortes frizes a la godde blanches frizees, une verge de large; un demy piece est de 44 @ a 54 @ ou de 34 a 44 godde, quy se vandent les bonnes, tous frais abord comprises, de 27*d* a 30*d* la godde.[2]

4 demy-pieces ditto, moyennes de 23 a 26*d* la godde.

2 ditto vertes mais qu'elles soyent fortes bien frizees et d'un vert gay, c'est a dire d'un vert qui soit un peu tirant sur le vert jaune. Je veux dire quy ne soit pas un vert brun ou terne.

2 ditto rouges de couleur vifve, mais il faut absolument qu'elles soyent bien fortes, bien couvertes et bien frizees.

2 ditto bleues turquin, c'est a dire un bleu quy soit bien brun et non terne et surtout qu'elles soyent tres fortes et bien frizees et toutes lesdits frizes d'une verge de large.

6 pieces de beaux et bons creseaux gris bien meslez, un peu differents en couleur et qu'ils soyent gais a l'oeil.

Tout cela sera pour voir comme vous reussirez bien a l'achapt dont dependt entierement le proffit desdits drapperies, c'est pourquoy Monsieur je vous prie en cas que vous n'ayez une plaine connoissance desdites marchandises de faire employer quelqu'un quy s'y connoisse bien. Ledit achapt doibt estre faict pour les frizes de couleurs suivant la bonte depuis 32 jusques a 35*d* la godde rendus a bordt, c'est a dire tous les frais, provision jusques au bordt du navire comprises, mais audit prix il faut qu'elles soyent tres tres bonnes, bien fortes et bien couvertes et bien frisez. Les droits de sortie doibvent estre payer comme Anglois et non comm'estranger et lesdits marchandises doibvent estre emballes en 2 ballots soulz ma marque 'AA' et chergez pour Dieppe a mon ordre chez Mons. Nicolas Neel, marchand a Dieppe, par navire francois ou Hollandois parcequ'il n'y a que ces 2 nations quand a present quy ont l'advantage de payer les droits sur le tarif de 1664, les Anglois et autres nation payent encore l'augmentation de 1667. Dieu veille quy le parlement revocque la deffanse des manufactures et crus de Franse affin que le negose puisse reprendre son premier cours et que les Anglois puissent jouir des mesmes privileges que les Hollandois ont a present.

Les saigles, blees et toute sorte d'autres grains sont icy augmentez parceque on se deffie des grains sur terre pour n'avoir pas eu le temps convenable, c'est pourquoy dittes moy le prix des saigles jusques abordt du navire et ce qu'il faudroit payer du tonneau ou du lest ou du muy comme ausy dublee. J'estime que 60 boisseaux font le muy de ceste ville. Les graines ne payent pas des droits d'entree en Franse et s'il me soubvient bien les grains sortants d'Angleterre on paye quelque chose a celuy quy en enlesve ou on rendt les droits a ceux quy en ont faict venir et quy sortent dans l'an. Dittes moy ausy Monsieur l'apparanse des grains sur terre parce que nous en avons affaire icy puisqu'il ne se treuve plus guerre de grains du pays, la derniere recolte n'ayant pas este bien forte. Comme Paris n'a encore rien tire d'icy cela faict qu'on n'a pas encore faict grand estate de la manque des grains, mais je crains que le temps froid ne soit contrair aux grains quy sont en terre, c'est pourquoy il faut s'instruire ou on prandra des grains sy les choses empiroient. Je vous baise tres humblement les mains et suis, &c.

[P.S.] Monsieur, le saigle de Champagne se vandt icy *W*.50 le muy; les blees de Magdeburg venus d'Hambourg ont monte de *W*.60 a *W*.62 qu'ils valoient jusques a *W*.74 estants propres a faire du pain blanc. On attend encore diverses navires d'Hambourg cherges de blée.

Monsieur, je vous prie de me notter tousjours le cours des changes pour icy, Paris, Hambourg et Hollande lorsque vous m'escrivez.'

¹ Kerseys.
² The English goad (of 54 inches) seems intended; the verge, English measure, was synonymous with the yard—Doursther; Savary; R. E. Zupko *A Dictionary of English Weights and Measures* (Madison, Milwaukee & London, 1968).

$$\frac{8\ May}{27\ May}1679$$

444   W. DE HERTOGH to JD

HAMBURG   29 APRIL 1679

[D]   My last letter to you was on the 8th instant. Since then I have received your welcome letter of the 11th ditto, with news of what is going on in trade over there, for which I warmly thank you and refer you to what I said in my previous letter. I firmly believe that there could be something to be done with goods from [England] if only sales were somewhat greater than they have been because of all the miserable unrest in Germany. To all appearances things may soon improve because the peace has been largely settled and there is good hope that God will grant the remainder. We may then look about for something profitable to invest in. Ardasse, if it is choice quality, can fetch 14 to 14½*s*; poor quality can be had for 13 to 13½*s*. Oil remains at the same price still and is selling for *RD* 80 per pipe, since there is little in town. Indigo guatemalo is at 6s. There are few raisins to be obtained, and I refer you for the rest to the enclosed price-current.[1]

I should be glad to know when a convoy is going from [England] to Spain. One of my good friends want to make a journey there and is minded to go by sea from [England]. You will oblige me greatly if you would have the goodness to inform me when there is a chance of a convoy, in time for him to get there from here. He would be glad to see if there was one about the middle of June. I await to hear what there is.

Further, I must ask you, as a friend, to send me with the earliest ship 400 glass bottles and 500 or 600 cork plugs to close them with as I understand that they are very much cheaper and better than here. I have had some Champagne wine sent to me from France and it can be better preserved therein than in the casks. This may be troublesome for you, but I hope you will not take my sudden requests too badly. I shall gladly serve you in return at any opportunity, and remain, with friendly regards, always, &c.

[1] Missing.

$$\frac{21\ May}{30\ May}1679$$

445 T. PERMAN TO JD
STOCKHOLM   2 APRIL 1679

[G] My last letter to you was on the 21st of October 1678, sent by way of Lübeck together with a copy of my letter of the 19th ditto, despatched aboard Captain Joseph Newcombe. Accompanying both was a copy of a memorandum about various wares, to which I refer you and which I hope you received safely and obeyed before the arrival of this. Your welcome letters from London of the 13th and 20th of December were received, to which this serves as an answer. Concerning the 844 coils of copper-wire, I will let the matter drop until another time. I trust that Mr Hall will pay me what he owes. As regards your 2 per cent commission for the purchase of the manufactures and other wares—if you will buy them for me and insure them for risks from enemies and the sea, I will take them on trial, but I beg you to buy them according to my memorandum and for the least possible expense. I hope you will always do your best for me, and since you can credit yourself with $1\frac{1}{2}$ per cent commission I trust that you will do everything possible on my behalf. You will be getting a large amount of commission from me this summer since, at the earliest opportunity, I shall be despatching you returns, shipping everything in your name as if it were going for your account and risk. I shall write to you beforehand so that you can have everything insured. I have 200 slb of copper at Reenstierna's works at Norrköping. 74 slb are already made into wire and the rest will follow shortly, all of which I will send to you. I have bought iron from H.F., 1,700 slb, which I shall be getting with the first *schuit*. But I shall be selling it here, since I hear from [London] as well as Amsterdam that prices are very bad.

I await your account of the 844 coils of wire at the earliest opportunity, and thank you for crediting me with the Slb. 26.8.10 lb. In cordial reply, I commend you to God's protection, &c.

$$\frac{27\ May}{29\ May}1679$$

446   B. BEUZELIN & SON to JD
         ROUEN   2 JUNE 1679

'Nostre derniere a esté du 26 passé, dudespuis nous avons receu la vostre du 15/25 ditto. Nous vous mandions par nostre ditte precedante de nous debitter £3,694*t* 16*s* 2*d* pour le retour de la lettre de *W*.1,200 sur Sartillon, mais il y a une petite erreur parce que nous n'avons pas pris garde que la ditte lettre n'estoit payable qu'au 24 passé, et comme nous avions compté le retour du change sur le pied qu'il alloit chez vous le 1er May, comme il vous estoit plus aventageux, il n'auroit pas esté raisonnable de n'allouer au tireur d'icy qu'un pour 100 pour le temps que la ratraitte auroit en a courir, veu que du 1er que nous comptions le change a 52$\frac{3}{4}$*d* jusques au 24, que votre lettre escheoit que le change estoit rehaussé a 53$\frac{1}{4}$*d*. Il y auroit encore pres d'un mois ce qu'il nous a fait remarquer en payant, ainsy il a fallu encore luy allouer $\frac{1}{2}$ pour 100, ce quy vous est encore plus avantageux que d'avoir compté le change sur le dit pied de 53$\frac{1}{4}$*d* comme il alloit quand vostre dit lettre de change a escheu. C'est doncq £3,676*t* 16*s* dont vous aurez a nous debitter pour le dit article comme il est porté dans votre compte courand que nous vous envoyons cy-incluse soldé a ce jour par le quel y compris la remise que nous vous faisons avecq presente de *W*.800 a 54$\frac{1}{2}$*d* comme cy dessoubs elle est specifiée. Nous vous trouvons que vous nous restes debitteur de £1,705*t* 13*s* 5*d*. Il vous plaira l'examiner et le trouvant d'accord le notter en conformitté, nous en donnant advis. Sur cette somme porté par la solde il nous entré quelque argent de vos marchandises mesmes au della, ainsy nous vous ferons quelque remise par nos present. Les lettres sont icy sy rares que l'on a paine a en trouver de bonne, a cause qu'il ne ce fait aucune chargemants, de sorte que nous avons esté obliges d'avoir recours a Paris, et nous vous endossons la dite lettre de *W*.800 sans notre prejudice. L'on ne nous a point encore renvoyee de Paris la lettre de *W*.770 que vous nous avez envoyee pour faire accepter; vous l'aurez Dieu aydant par nos premieres.

Nous coullons tousjours la vanthe de vostre fil de latton a £78*t*, cella va fort doucement. Nous ne perdrons aucune occasion, car nous souhaittons pasionnement que ce compte-la peust estre soldé et nous ferons comme pour nous mesme.

Nous nous servons a Vallanciennes du Sr. Nicollas George Serret dont on nous a rendu toutte sort de bon tesmoignage. Il nous paroit aussy fort entendu aux achapts des ces baracans dont nous luy avons commis il ya a quelque temps une paques. Ils sont a present encheris a ce qu'il nous mandoit par sa derniere et valloit £38*t* a £39*t* ceux propre pour Bilbao. Depuis la paix aveq l'Espaigne l'on ne se sert plus de la voye du Havre pour les marchandises de Biscaye, mais on envoye toute par Donquerque ou il y a assez souvent des navires pour Bilbao. Les fraix de Vallantienne la sont tres petits, n'y ayant point de droits a payer.

Les grains rehaussent tous les jours icy et il y a apparence d'une mauvaise recolte. Le bon froment va estre a *W*.80 le muyd, le moindre *W*.72; seigle *W*.50 et avoine *W*.50 qui est ung prix excessif, mais elle est partout le nord fort chere. Il en est venu autre fois d'Irlande quy ce trouvoit tres bonne, et apparament que sur ce prix la il en viendra encore. Les huilles sont venues en grande quantité de Siville et vallent £30*t* et £31*t* avecq assez bonne demande. Sur ce nous vous baisons les mains, et sommes, &c.'

[P.S.] 'Remize pour votre compte *W*.800 a 54$\frac{1}{2}$, 2 usances en lettre Catillon sur Charles Trinquan.'

Amsterdam: 98$\frac{1}{3}$*d* $\Big\}$ 2 usances.
Londres: 54$\frac{1}{4}$*d*

447   A. AMSINCQ TO JD
         ROUEN   13 JUNE 1679

'En responce de la vostre du 26 de May j'ay receu la facture des marchandises que vous avez cherge dans le bord de Rene le Duc pour Diepe. Dieu le veille ammener a bon port, quy soit loué de l'arrivement de Thomas Quarante devant ceste ville. Je retireray les 2 balles de Kiersey que vous y avez cherge pour mon conte et je vous manderay le trouver. Il est certain que d'Exon on tire les serges et autres draperies a meilleur marché que de Londres. Dans le navire de Lenard Guillaume quy est icy bien arrivé d'Exon j'ay 17 ballots de serges et 2 de kersey et comme il y a bon nombre desdit drapperie pour d'autres nous voila honestement pourveu pour longtemps. Il faudroit m'advertir lors que les drapperies sont a meilleur marché chez vous affin d'en faire provision en temps parceque je pretens continuer ledit negoce des drapperies tant que j'y trouveray un interest honest, prefferant ce negoce plustost que de donner mon argeant en depost en un temps sy dangereux qu'on a dela paine de connoistre le monde, c'est pourquoy a mesure que j'en vends a mesure j'en remplace—voila pourquoy je vous ay prie de m'achapter 6 ou 8 pieces de draps de couleur suivant les eschantillons que je vous ay envoyé du prix de 8½, 9 jusques a 10s sterling, mais non plus cheres car sur les draps fines que Mons. Porrée m'a envoyé j'ay perdu plus de 10%. Je vous prie de prendre guarde qu'elles soyent fines et d'une belle couleur et en cas qu'il s'en rencontre de couleurs meilleurs que lesdits eschantillons de m'envoyer des eschantillons affin que je vous dise mon sentiment.

Quand vous me tirerez le montant des marchandises tout honneur sera faict a vos lettres. Il est cependant facheux d'achapter argeant contant les drapperies qu'il faut prester icy un et tout et qu'on paye quand ils ont de l'argeant. A tout le moins on debveroit beneficier du disconte et menager les frais autant que vous pourez pour me les envoyer par navire francois ou hollandois et non par d'autres adroitture pour cette ville, surtout que les draps soyent fines et bonnes pour leur prix et que j'aye bon aulnage parcequ'icy il faut donner 21¼ @ pour 20 @ payable.

Je vous remersie du prix de sucres et je vous prie de continuer quand on aurez occasion de m'escrire, cela sert a me gouverner. Dittes moy s'il vous plaist les prix des huisles de balaines quy ont este faittes en mer ou a terre a Groening et s'il en reste encore beaucoup chez vous. Icy il ne reste que viron 600 bariques des huisles basques que j'achapté au mois d'octobre en plus grand nombre a £44t la barique contant et que je vands a present a £55t la barique parceque Paris ne veult pas des huisles d'Hollande a cause de la puanteur la ou les huisles basques faittes ou brusles en mer n'ont point d'odeur.

Lors que la Compagnie vandra des thoilles de cotton je me pouray resouldre d'achapter quelque partie: dittes-moy sy vous y avez bonne connoissanse. Je tacheray a practiquer quelque personnes a Paris pour la revante parceque moins de cela il ne s'en faut pas mesler puisque ceux quy se meslent dudit commerse sont liguez et font fouler le foin a ceux quy en font venir.

J'apprendray volontiers les prix des cottons en laines et cottons fillez, noix de galle et autre marchandises de Levant. Pour Calandre il faut attendre le retour dusdit Porrée parce que mon cousin le Sr. Henry Amsincq pretend qu'il a satisfait au procureur et qu'il luy a tiré le montant. Ledit Sr. Porrée est a present a Hambourg ou il ne tardera pas longtemps. Je vous baise les mains et suis, &c.'

$$\frac{28\;Jun.}{7\;Jul.}1679$$

448   T. PERMAN to JD
          STOCKHOLM   13 MAY 1679

[G]   My last letter to you was on the 21st past, to which I refer you. Since then I have received
      from London yours of the 12th of November, 13th of December, 28th of February and 15th
      of March, from which I have seen what is happening in trade. I see that copper-wire prices are
      very bad. May God forgive Urban Hall if he is the cause of it. I hope that before long he will
      at last pay me what he owes.

      I see also that you have sold 300 copper blanks, for which I am glad. I have set the proceeds
      of £81 3s 4d down to your account. Business in this country is still very bad, particularly
      because we have had a long, dry winter, which still continues. This spring we have had hardly
      any rain and the sea has been frozen from the continued cold, which means that all iron and
      copper works have been at a standstill for lack of water. I am sure that not half as much iron
      has been worked this year as at other times in the past. I have been waiting all spring for
      1,000–1,200 slb of iron to come down with the first barge, but so far have had no more than
      600 slb, and that is on account of the shortage of water. Although I would wish you to have
      2,000 slb it will be rather slow to go now. Likewise, I also have 100 slb of copper at Nyköping
      and 200 slb at Norrköping, which I have ordered to be made into copper-wire, but because of
      the lack of water it is also delayed for a long time. Meanwhile, there is an English ship lying at
      Norrköping which will be leaving soon and I shall load on it, consigned to you, as much as is
      now ready. Otherwise there is nothing special to report and I refer you to my previous letters,
      commending you to God's protection, &c.

      [P.S.] My dear Mr David, I hope that your servant, Jacob Fahlgren, will soon be back with
      you, and that he has done you true and honourable service. I must ask you to be so very kind
      as to return me my obligation or surety, as a matter of life or death.

      Here inclosed follows the bill of lading for 393 coils of copper-wire sent with Captain
      Leonard Bushell. May God bring him in safety.

$$\frac{5\;Jul.}{[\rule{1cm}{0.4pt}]}1679$$

449   JOHN TYLER to JD
          RIGA   13 JUNE 1679

      'Sir, Yours of the 9th of May I reseived the 2th instant, and I should have readdyly followed
      your order had it bin in my power, but wheate heare is very bad and no quantytys to be had,
      it not being orderney to ship much from this place—and that which is worse then the rest, I
      have not half mony enough to loade our pinke with wheate. Before I reseived your letter I
      had livered out salt and taken in part of our loading of rye to goe for Stockholme upon fraite,
      but you adviseing me not to medle with pitch or tarr (with which I designed to loade at
      Stockholme) I thought it best to cleare my self of the voyge and take the loadeing of rye upon
      our owne account, which accordingly I have don, with which I designe to goe for
      Gottenburg or som other place in Sweaden wheare I think I maye gett the best prise, from
      whenc I designe for Dantzick, which is the best place in the Baltick for the loadeing of wheate
      (wheare I may lay out what mony I have and take the rest of our loadeing upon fraite). If you

think fitt pray lett me have a line or two from you to Dantzick, and if you think fitt to have me lay out our mony in wheate pray let me know for what place you wil advise me, that I may know the better how to take the remainder our loadeing upon fraite. I sould our salt at 25 specie dolers per last, and I made out a boute 60 last which amounts to a boute 1,250 dolers, alcharges paid, and I have loaded heare betweene 60 and 70 last of rye at 24 dolers per last, which coms to a boute 1,600 dolers which I suppose wil be a boute 300 dolers more then I have, which I intend to take upon bottomere to the place that I shal goe for. I hoope to be ready to sayle in 3 or 4 days. This being al at present I remaine, Sir, your most humble servant, &c.'

$$\frac{7\,Jul.}{11\,Jul.}1679$$

450 ABRAHAM WOLTERS to JD
STOCKHOLM   19 JUNE 1679

[D] I have never had the honour of writing to you before. I am doing so now because Mr Hendrick Cletcher handed over to me on the 13th instant a letter of yours, dated the 16th of May, together with a bill of exchange for *RD* 2,100 drawn on His Excellency Erick Fleming, with orders about what to do if it were not paid. Mr Cletcher gave me the letter because he was about to set off on his journey to his works, as you can see from the accompanying letter from him, to which I refer you. You can be assured that I shall serve you promptly and reasonably. Concerning the bill of exchange, I tried to show it to the acceptant but as he died some weeks ago in the country and as his wife is still there I have had to let the widow know about the bill by letter and, if she is willing to accept the same, have asked her to let one of her friends write to me and assure me that the bill would be promptly paid. If the acceptant asks me to send the bill of exchange I cannot decide whether or not to send the original into the country, but I am keeping to the letter he wrote to me and as long as it is accepted there should be no difficulty. These people want to make it good and I do not doubt that it will be promptly honoured as the widow wants her son to maintain his credit, of which they stand in need. Herewith goes a letter to him which I beg you to forward as soon as possible. He writes that he will pay me in cash. If so I shall await your orders, being at your command at any hour, for at the present there is no chance of remitting to London or Hamburg or Amsterdam at a rate of 24 dollars per £1 sterling, as no one wants to do it on London for less than 27 dollars, nor Hamburg for 26 marks and Amsterdam for 25 marks, so there is nothing to be done, and I can see no prospect of improvement.

Iron is at 29 or 30 dollars, according to quality, and one can get good iron for 30 dollars and very fine iron for 31 dollars. There is little sign of any change. Wire is at 280 to 282 dollars and it is thought that it might perhaps rise higher since not so much is being made as last year. There is no pitch or tar for sale as the Company itself has none here to load its own ships with, though things may be better in the summer when more is likely to come in. If you could send a ship with malt, which now fetches 16 dollars per ton and looks very likely to fetch more by August, and take a return cargo of tar and some wire and iron, you would not do badly.

Whatever your order, you can rest assured that it will be promptly attended to as soon as it comes. If there are any other matters in which I can be of service you have only to command. I handle the affairs of Steven de Geer and David van Baerle, who assure me that they are well satisfied, and I am sure you will likewise find it so. For the present there is nothing more except friendly regards, &c.

$$\frac{15\,Jul.}{28\,Jul.}1679$$

451   DAVID GEYSMER to JD
         HAMBURG   8 JULY 1679

[D]   My last letter was on the 1st instant, to which I refer. Since then I have had yours of the 27th of June, with which you sent me the invoice and bill of lading for 25 sacks of Aleppo galls which you have consigned to me in the ship *De Perle*, Captain Charles Seyers. If the Lord brings him in safety I shall take possession of the same and put them in a good place in the warehouse and meanwhile await your orders, for you will have seen from my foregoing letter that I have left the proffered galls for your account, and there they can remain. My intention, when I gave the order, was to have some if there was any considerable rise in prices being maintained. You will by now have cancelled my order, and I am meanwhile waiting to hear what you want to have done with them, and whether you wish them to be bought by me. You can rest assured that your interests will be safeguarded as if they were my own, and that you will find me punctual and prompt in everything, in order to encourage you to entrust me with further commands, I trust that the opportunity will present itself so that we can have more dealings with one another. May God only grant that business will improve! At present there is little demand for galls and things are rather quiet, but I hope that before long things will go better. Meanwhile, the Leipzigers have come, who usually buy a good quantity. I have been now and again offered 47 *ML* per 100 lb., with 13 months rebate, for a quantity of mine, but I have not wanted to sell them since you persuaded me that they would not decline in price. Now, others are selling good quality stuff at $46\frac{1}{2}$ *ML* per 100 lb., but I hope that they will pick up again as soon as there is more demand. This will be governed by the quantity coming from [England], which will be known to you, and if the price is reasonably firm I shall either keep them or dispose of them.

     I see that pepper has risen in price in [London]. It remains here at $12\frac{3}{4}\,g$ per lb., but may well be influenced by that. I still have mine all together in hand, which at first were selling at a loss for 12*g*. Raisins have been greatly sought after. Please learn what can be expected from [England]. Good quality should sell in handfuls for 30 to 31 *ML* per 100 lb. If you can send any please do so freely, vizt. choice quality, if you can haggle for it at 12*s* per lb. Oil and many other Marseille goods are falling; only capers have newly arrived and are selling in handfuls at 52 *ML* per 100 lb., with 13 months rebate and a 30 per cent tare.

     Friendly regards, the Lord protect you, &c.

$$\frac{21\,Jul.}{28\,Jul.}1679$$

452   WELCH & STYLES to JD
         GENOA   12 JULY 1679

'Sir, Confirming what above have since your courtious lynes the 26 May, gladly observeing thereby the safe arriveall of the *Providence*, for which God bee praysed, hopeing the oyle consigned you by her arrived to noe unpleaseing markett, as shall in due tyme attend you oblidge us with notice of. Wee should be glad to understand you had shipt of some tarr heere, beeing non in Ittaly, or any expected, to our notice. You weare in tyme for to attempt the businesse by Capt. Paxton from whome have a letter this post, and that might bee dispatched in 20 daies with the convoy. Soe hope by him or others you slipped not soe good an oppertunity as shall with devotion attend to understand. Some Swead flatt bard iron would alsoe doe well, with some Gynnea small barrs, leade and pepper. Mean while, assure your selfe wee remayne, with all cordiallity, your most oblidged servants, &c.

Exchange for London, 53*d* per dollar.'

$\frac{16\ Aug.}{22\ Aug.}$ 1679

453 C. BENE to JD

HAMBURG   8 AUGUST 1679

D] My last letter to you was on the 29th of July. Since then I have received yours of the 29th of July, and by way of answer I can tell you that Captain John Johnson has not yet arrived. May God bring him and also Thomas Master in safety as he has with Charles Siers. I have received the ginger which he brought and found the quality reasonably good, so there is no further need to discuss it.

I am surprised that many goods are dearer in [England] than here. It seems the English do not want to sell in [London] at a reasonable price but would rather send them here and take less for them than they can get in [England]. This is bad business, but as it seems irremediable one must simply be patient.

I would have very gladly had some cotton, and I regret that you have been so slow about purchasing it. It is now too dear and the exchange too high for it to come. Enclosed I send a second bill of exchange for £100 at double usance on Mr William Gore, payable to my order. Please procure its acceptance and keep it by you until further order.

You have bought for my account about 4,000 lb. of Bermuda tobacco at 5*d* [per lb.] on the condition that you paid for the barrels and the costs of packing. Put that down to me, although I fear that the expenses will be very great and may easily amount to $\frac{1}{8}d$ [per lb.], as the subsequent account will probably show. If you cannot achieve anything with regard to the commission for Barbados indigo please buy about 50 sacks of white, scraped ginger at 30*s* [per cwt.], but the quality must be as fine as the last lot, otherwise it is no use to me. Please despatch it as quickly as possible, and let me know if you succeed. And if you can obtain good Barbados sugar at $21\frac{1}{2}$ –$21\frac{3}{4}$ shillings, free on board, please buy me 10 or 12 butts and send them here. You can draw on me for the cost at double usance, as advantageously as possible, and your bills of exchange will be duly honoured.

The English earth[1] about which I have written to you before is a kind which is used by the silk-weavers if they want to weave the silk in a hard colour—that is to say, not liable to wash off—which, by the action of the earth becomes suppler, since it contains a secret which is unknown to most people, and those that know it will not reveal it to others. I would like you to ask for such an earth from a weaver, but do not let it appear that it is to be used for weaving for then he could see what kind it is and learn its use. If you can get it you would do me a friendly service, and if there is anything in which I can serve you please command me freely, and I shall prove my friendship. I remain, &c.

London: 34*s* 9–10*g* 2 usances.
Amsterdam: 33 stuivers short sight.
Venice: 88*g* at usance.

---

[1] Presumably he means fullers' earth, the export of which was forbidden in England. See [**305**] n. 1.

$$\frac{9\ Sep.}{12\ Sep.}1679$$

454 L. TRIP to JD
AMSTERDAM   15 SEPTEMBER 1679

[D] From your letter of the 29th of August I understand that Robert Tisdall has arrived, and I
trust that since then Steven Garret has arrived with 717 bars, weighing Slb. 100.2.0 lb. I do
not doubt that another 300 slb have been loaded in accordance with my orders. I urge you to
sell them as if they were your own so that we can continue to send them in return for some
profit.

    The total amount of 'O' iron sold in the spring was 300 slb. Whether it has gone to London
or other parts is unknown to me, though nephew Steven de Geer has sent you a quantity of
fine iron marked '**Ç**' which will not be undercut, and I would say that 'O' is now better
than '**Ç**' for now that the fine iron is mined it is better than it was before, as you will find.

    I shall be glad to learn how sales go, and remain, &c.

$$\frac{12\ Sep.}{12\ Sep.}1679$$

455 D. GEYSMER to JD
HAMBURG   5 SEPTEMBER 1679

[D] My last was about a week ago, to which I refer. Since then I have had nothing from you,
which surprises me. I long to hear that the £50 bill of exchange has been accepted as the
drawer assured me it would be, and upon which I gave him the value.

    I confirm my order about buying for me 25 bales of pepper, and I must now wait to hear at
what price you have obtained them. You will have seen from my preceding letter that I have
punctually honoured your bill of exchange for £200 and set against it a bill for £200 at
34s 11g for which you have been credited with 2,618.12 ML. The said amount is remitted for
my account and can serve for the pepper.

    I have just now seen in a letter to Mr Ruland the prices which have been set by the [English
East India] Company on one commodity and another. I greatly wish I might have known
this eight days earlier so that I could have rushed off an order, since not much cardamon was
sold. I had imagined that the price would have been higher, but 3s per lb.[1] is quite reasonable.
I wish I had commissioned it together with my preceding order, but if the Company has not
raised it much higher than it is now, and if you can obtain it in one way or another so that it
will yield a little profit, I would gladly have 500 to 600 lb. I should also be glad to have 10 or
15 pots of preserved ginger, as a trial, at the least price obtainable. But please buy nothing
other than good quality and look after my interests as if they were your own. For your
reimbursement please draw the total on me for payment at the beginning of next month and
your bills will be punctually honoured. I could have remitted to you today for 35s, at sight,
but I find that I have already disposed of my balance and can only take in bills at the
beginning of next month at the earliest, on which you may rely.

    If you cannot obtain fine quality ginger at 14s I shall be glad to hear by return of post since I
shall then given an alternative order and make a remittance. I shall also be glad to learn, in
reply to this, what prospect you see concerning the cardamon.

    Yesterday I had a buyer for two sacks of galls [that with][2] the same took one sack of mine,
which satisfied him well, so one must let him have his way. One of your sacks of galls was also

sold to Hans Ellers for $46\frac{1}{2}$ *ML* per 100 lb. at 13 months discount, and this morning a weaver has promised to come and fetch a sack. I shall dispose of them as best I can, but I wish I could find just one buyer for your galls. If he would take the whole batch I would be glad to lower the price. One must wait for an opportunity, and I shall allow no chance to slip by. You can be assured that I shall do my duty, but one cannot always sell as one wants to here, and I notice that others are unable to sell anything, or have sold anything since the Leipzigers went away. Friendly regards, God protect you, &c.

¹ This is an error for 33s per lb.
² Conjectural: a hole in the text obliterates two words.

$$\frac{17\ Sep.}{26\ Sep.}1679$$

456 S. DE GEER to JD
STOCKHOLM   27 AUGUST 1679

& [F] I wrote to you some while ago and mentioned my arrival here, and also indicated how much pan iron you could expect this year, since in total there has been shipped Slb. 333.19.0 lb. You have likewise been informed in time by my agents about what ships it has been loaded in. I shall now wait and see how much there will be for the coming year and take care that the lengths of the thick bars are not uneven but trimmed off, as some have been.

I now have before me your letter of July the 11th. Cletscher is not here but is expected soon and we shall then discuss your affairs. Young Momma is here, telling everyone of the wrong you do them. The only thing I had to say is that the objections to paying were quite ordinary ones et que j'en estois autrement informé, and that Mr Cletscher had since got orders to see what could be done, mais je vous diray bien mon sentiment, the gentleman is so much behindhand that there is nothing to be got from him. J'auray soin de vostre interest, mais vous ne ferez pas mall de donner vos ordres un peu amplement a Mr Cletscher if you want to reach a settlement.

The exchange on Amsterdam is high here, at about 26 dollars, et fort peu de bonne lettres.

There is not much iron in stock: all the works are at a standstill for lack of water and abroad there are no sales. The English come here with salt to lade tar. There is little pitch and now little tar also, but more is likely to come. Botte aura fait un movais coup. Without the pitch we would have difficulty in finding the running capital, in my opinion. Mr Wouters¹ has bought for you a quantity of 'O' iron at 31 dollars and given 32 for '℺'. This is to make up for the exchange rate. There are now four English ships here which will have difficulty in obtaining any freight or cargo if no tar arrives, because there is not as much iron in town as they need for their lading.

Voyla la pais conclus entre les Rois du Nort! I hope that matters will now go rather better.

La sell se vent a $13\frac{1}{2}$ dollars now, and if an English ship had not arrived with some it would have risen. There is still one more expected, et puis les vesseaux holandois are somewhat delayed, it may well rise again.

There is little copper in stock. It has all been coined and stands at 290 dollars. Wire can be got at 270 to 272 dollars.

Abraham Cronström is expected in town any day. I shall then obtain his power of attorney and send it, but he behaves as if evite de rencontrer Momma, for he will then be perplexed and not know what to say. Enfin, un monde plin de trouble et tromperie et que faire hett lyter all.² There is nothing more to mention, so I remain, with my usual compliments, &c.

¹ Abraham Wolters.
² De Geer's alternation between French and Dutch is frequently incomprehensible, as in this case.

$$\frac{23 \ Sep.}{29 \ Sep.} 1679$$

457   G. RICHARDS to JD
          BILBAO   15 SEPTEMBER 1679

'Sir, I have this post receeved yours of the 18th August, noteing you has past away the
accounts of your tarr and *barraganen* accordingly with me and given me credit for the iron by
Steele.[1] By the next conveyance I shall remitt you farther returnes. Of the arryval of the
vessel from Dunkerk I have acquainted you, and pray God send those safe from Holland.
Your goods by them I shal dispose of by all good oppertunityes and take the best care I can
possible to prevent bad debts. The account of your bayes is sent you, and I shal make you the
returnes of there proceed exactly as you order, although I have seen noe such order before.
That commodity I hear is now fallen againe at home and wil doubtlesse yet considerably
more. If you would be concerned in any wools, some Colchester bayes, *barraganen*, cloves
and cinamont would buy the best and accompts might be soone cleered and yeald as much
profitt as otherwyse. In Rouen they sel best at present. Here are also good quantetyes of
Russia hides sold and its a staple commodity, but the benefitt might be by haveing them
cheape bought in. The exchange for Holland, etc, is now verry advantagious to have any
goods provided there. Your pepper cost dear and therefore rendred the worse. Mr
Christopher sent me some Bellepatam which cost 8 per cent cheaper. If you send halfe of that
and halfe Jambe, the one may help off the other and both yeald as much as the best alone. I
shall pay Mr Anckeman the 200 pieces of eight you order and serve him in what else I can,
which is all at present, but I remaine, Sir, your humble servant, &c.'

[1] Capt. John Steele of the *Dorothy* who carried back silver and gold under the usual fictitious bill of lading as
'iron'.

$$\frac{27 \ Sep.}{29 \ Sep.} 1679$$

458   D. GEYSMER to JD
          HAMBURG   19 SEPTEMBER 1679

[D] I have received your welcome letter of the 12th instant. I am glad that you have accepted my
     bill for £200 and made a note of it. I also see that you have, according to my order, bought 25
     sacks of pepper at $7\frac{1}{8}d$ [per lb.] and I have noted how you have loaded it. In order to enjoy the
     full discount you had better receive it and pay for it, for which I thank you warmly. I shall
     gladly make good to you interest for the time during which you must have been out of
     pocket, which you have only to inform me of, and I shall nonetheless remain obliged for your
     kindness.
         I see that all the cardamon has been bought up and that no more is to be expected. I must
     therefore wait and see what kind of preserved ginger you have bought for me; and I will learn
     in due course whether you have been able to perform my order concering white ginger.
     Meanwhile, thank you for news of what prices are being fetched by one thing or another.
         Concerning your galls, you will have seen how much of them has been sold. Since then I
     have achieved nothing more, but I continue to do my best, hoping that as the Leipziger fair
     approaches they may be more sought after. If any good opportunity arises I shall not let it
     slip, and you will share in anything I achieve. You can expect to receive promptly any profits
     that are obtained.

People here are getting rather suspicious about the Danes, as it is said that their King is coming this way with many men and that ten Danish warships are coming to the Elbe. I hope it is not so. If this arrives in time and the captain is still at [London] with my 25 sacks of pepper, please put down in the bill of lading that they are for the account and at the risk of Mr Adrian Ruland of Amsterdam, so that they can go in peace. However, I do not believe that they will dare to inspect English ships in any event. May God grant us peace, in whose holy protection I commend you, with friendly regards.

[P.S.] If, on receipt of this the white, and also the preserved, ginger are not yet bought, please do not buy any for me but let it rest until further order. I shall meanwhile see how things develop between the Danes and this city. If you have got my balance in hand you can remit it here in reliable bills as advantageously as possible at double usance.

Here enclosed is the second copy of the £150 bill of exchange, recently endorsed. Please make use of it. Adieu.

Thank you for the enclosed price-current, but it is not necessary to send it to me. Mr Ruland obtains plenty of them and he can supply me adequately.

$$\frac{27\ Sep.}{10\ Oct.}1679$$

459   ADRIAN DU QUESNOY to JD
         AMSTERDAM   3 OCTOBER 1679

[D]   Your welcome letter of the 19th/29th past was safely received and the enclosed letters for Stockholm and Gothenburg have been forwarded today, since—for your information—the post always leaves here on Tuesday and Saturday.[1]

You now order that £200 sterling should be laid out on *presillas*, instead of £100. The amount which was to be had for £100 has already been ordered. I have never despatched any Brabant goods by way of Dunkirk before but if the costs are more reasonable than they are from here I shall see to it. This is a free port for the export of Brabant goods, so the duty only has to be paid on export from Brabant and on import here. There is going to be a convoy departing from here for Bilbao between the 20th and 25th of this month, and I believe in Middelburg I shall have the best opportunity of handling things for you as if for myself.

I have procured acceptance of your four bills of exchange and I shall keep them by me as you ordered, awaiting your commands for our East India Company sale. No one knows when it will be but one of our returning ships is now in harbour and the enclosed will tell you more fully about the cargo, for your consideration. An unusually large amount of copper is coming from Japan, as a result of which copper has fallen considerably here.[2] There is also a great quantity of silk.

I confirm again that you, or others, would do very well to remit now any money that is needed over here, now your Company has had its sale, for the frenzy of drafts will lower the exchange rate. Money will be needed when we have our sale and there is likely to be plenty of money coming to [London] from Cadiz, which should also find its way here. I have no doubt that anyone who understands your trade will know how to extract some profit from this.

There is much going to Sweden. If there is anything here which might be useful to you, or any goods which can be brought from there, any purchase of cloths or otherwise, be pleased to command, I intend you to take satisfaction in my management, and you can easily experiment with a small trial-order. But as regards salt, a great deal has been sent from these parts. The ships are chartered for St Ubes and from there go direct to Sweden.

While writing this I have received letters from Ghent saying that linen has risen but in three or four weeks will fall again. Meanwhile my friend will risk finding out what can be done.

With greetings from, A.D.

[P.S.] Our ships departing for Bilbao call in at your [Isle of] Wight. The bills of exchange are all accepted.
Exchange: 36s 1g at 2 usances.

¹ 3 October (New Style) was a Tuesday.
² After two years without any arrivals of Japanese copper, 1679 saw the import by the Dutch East India Company of some 7,919 cwt.

$$(i)+(ii)\quad \frac{29\ Sep.}{14\ Oct.}1679$$

460 A. WOLTERS TO JD
STOCKHOLM   (i)   23 AUGUST 1679

[D]   My last letter to you was on the 16th instant, to which I refer. Since then I have received your letter of the 11th of July which reached me yesterday together with various enclosures which have all been duly forwarded. I gave De Geer his personally.

You will have learned from my previous letter that I have received the *RD* 2,100. I now see your order about how you want it employed. No one knows how the exchange goes, according to Mr Jacob Fahlgreen, or whether it will continue. It is just not possible to remit good bills of exchange for [London] at the moment for 25 dollars, or to Hamburg, or to Amsterdam. The reason is that bills on London can fetch 28 dollars, on Hamburg $26\frac{1}{4}$ to $\frac{1}{2}$, and on Amsterdam $25\frac{1}{2}$ to 26 marks, so there is nothing to be done.

It is difficult to spend anything on pitch or tar. There is scarcely any pitch and little tar in stock, so that whoever takes it gets bad stuff for 130 dollars. I hear that it scarcely fetches £7 in [London], so that also must be passed over. As for orgronts iron, such as 'OO' or 'Ꮐ', the latter is not obtainable but I have ordered as much of the 'OO' as your funds here with me extend to for 31 dollars, which the other English here would have gladly taken but I obtained the preference. 'G' is to be had, but not for less than 32 dollars. It is in Claes Wilkens's hands and he has sold it to various Englishmen at 32 dollars, so I hope you will be content with this amount. About 200 slb will be shipped tomorrow morning with Captain William Norham, an Englishman, for [London]. I have agreed the freight at £2, or forty shillings, per last. I shall consign it to you and give orders to Jan van Deurs at the Sound that he draws the Sound toll on you. This serves to inform you in case you find it necessary to order some insurance.

The rest of the iron is expected from the works in eight days. I shall then ship it as quickly as possible and let you know when it is done. There is no square iron nor yet broad iron, but some voyage iron. As soon as the bill of lading is signed it will be sent to you.

You would do well if you could send some English malt. There is none in stock here, little is expected and a great demand is approaching. But, above all, the malt must be choice, which I believe could easily fetch 19 or 20 dollars. You cannot fail to make a profit.

(ii)   30 AUGUST 1679

461   The above, of August 23rd, is a copy of my previous letter sent by way of Lübeck, to which I refer you in full, and as I am still without anything from you this will be all the shorter and serve only to accompany the bill of lading for Slb. 235.0.13 of three varieties [of iron]. The captain left the city this morning—God grant him a safe journey. As soon as the rest of the iron arrives it also will be quickly shipped and advice of it given to you, together with an account of everything. In trade, as I said above, there is a great demand for malt. It is true there is a ship here from [England], but it has brought bad malt, though as there is none in stock it fetches 16–17 dollars. Once again, if you have anything in which I can be of service you have only to command. I remain, &c.

29 [Sep.][1] *1679*
6 Jan. 1680

462 DAVID BROND to JD
DANZIG   23 SEPTEMBER 1679

'Worthy freind, I made bold some weekes past to trouble you with a line or two according to my promise when was in England, and for feare that it should misscarry I presume the second time to write unto you and give you a small account of our present trade here which lyes at present onlie in grosserys wares, as ginger browne, worth here at present 3 florins 24 *grosse* per stone, which is here 24 poundes—about 22¾ English pounds. 30 *grosse* makes a florin and a florin is 18*d* [sterling] which I suppose is well knowne unto you. Sugars as in goodnesse; white powder sugar in chestes, 10 to 11 florins per stone; browne, 5 to 7 florins per stone; currants *f.*8½ to 9½ per stone; pepper *f.*11¾ to 12 per stone; tobacco in small twine, 13 *grosse* per pounde. You may buy it with you at 5*d* per lb. Indigo quatuamalo *f.*2, 12 *grosse* per lb.; Carebs indigo *f.*1, 26 *grosse* per lb. Tinn worth *f.*72 per *centner*, but great quantitys expected from London. If can buy it for £3 5*s* or ther abouts ther will be good proffitt gott buy it. Spanish clothes fine of about 12*s* [from 9*s* to 14*s* per yard]² per yard sell well. All theese abovementioned commodityes sell here for ready mony, onlie Spanish clothes which we sell here at 6 months time but then wee gett a price accordingly and take care they be sould to good men. Serges as in goodnesse *f.*36 to 39 per piece. Now as for the commoditys from hence I imagine they are not unknowne unto you, and every thing cheap here except our linnens. Pieces are scarce but reasons the waters above are so low that they cannot bring them downe, but quantities expected every day, so if you will be pleased to make a small tryall this way in any of the above mentioned commodities I shall see to give you farther incouradgement, and wherein so ever you are pleased to intrust mee you may relye I shall be faithfull and punctuall in all my dealings and desire more my freinds interest then my owne. So if can serve you or any freinds of yours pray please to lay your commands upon him who is so desireable to serve, assuring your selfe I am, your true freind and servant.

[P.S.] My humble service to your good lady and tell her I have sent her a barrell of small spice cucumbers which I would desire her to accept of. My mother will deliver it, to whom pray remember my duty when see her.'

¹ The twice-weekly London–Danzig posts took 14 days, and it is therefore possible that the letter-cover is correctly endorsed by David as written on '23 7ber' (New Style) and received on '29 dto' (Old Style).

² Marginal insertion.

$\dfrac{3 \text{ Oct.}}{7 \text{ Oct.}}$1679

463 C. WILKENS to JD
STOCKHOLM   9 SEPTEMBER 1679

[G] I have not had any of your letters for a long while, which occasions the brevity of this.

Because of the cheap freight-rates to [England] in free English shipping I have decided to send you a quantity of iron for my own account, as a trial. It will consist of orgronts iron, up to 800 slb of ordinary plate ' $\mathbb{C}$ ' iron, and about 450 slb of schampeleon and other sorts of ' 👑 ' iron. It has been distributed and loaded in the following three ships, each with about the same amount—in the ship called the *Providence* of London, of which Ralph Johnson is captain; in the ship *Industry* of London, captain Henry Collins, and also in the ship named *John* of Yarmouth, captain John Allen. And because they will be sailing in the autumn I dare not take any risks, so I must ask you to be so kind as to have them insured against all risks by good and reliable insurers, each of them for RD 2,200, which for all three ships amounts to RD 6,600. You need have no doubts about the shipment being made, God willing, and you have only to ask Mr Urban Hall and other friends who used to live here about me to be satisfactorily informed. The freight rate has been agreed at 30 shillings per last of 15 shippounds, and in the bill of lading it has been stated that it has been shipped by me for your account and risk, so will you please write accordingly to Jean van Deurs at Elsinore in order that he can lay out the toll-money for you and draw it on you. If the dear Lord will give us a secure peace I will send you a good quantity each year, provided that I find it worth my while. For I must be served by you on reasonable terms, in controlling the expenses and taking care to whom you sell, though I cannot tie you down to any fixed price. I also hope you will be satisfied with a $1\frac{1}{2}$ per cent commission and an allowance of 4 per cent on any advance of money you may make on receipt of the bills of lading. In your reply I shall expect to learn how much you will permit me to draw on you from Hamburg, and please mention in it what your friend is called and commend to him the honour of my bills of exchange. If you insist on asking for a higher rate of interest I shall have to submit to it patiently until the goods are sold, although the bad prices which I am advised there are in [England] will not bear any high interest charges.

If there is still a lot of pitch and tar for Mr Botte's account lying on your hands unsold, please keep me informed about it, because I also have some interest in it. But do not mention it to him or let him know that I have sent you any goods on my account. He has no share in it.

The news is that there is no tar nor pitch here in town, and the English ships lying here are unable to get any, which is the reason why they have to take the iron for such a cheap freight. One cannot expect any tar before the month of October, but iron is fetching reasonably good prices here. With friendly regards, &c.

[P.S.] If, in the coming year, you would like to contract for the pitch and tar coming to England so that it can all be held in one hand I shall be glad to help you in preference to others, but it is necessary that you have a capable man of English nationality living here who can defend the contract for you against the resident English, and when you have a ship here he can run along to the authorities and obtain permission for it to export something in one way or another. A last of tar, of 13 barrels, is 130 copper dollars free on board, which according to the current rate of exchange is about 20 to 21 rixdollars; and a last of pitch, of 12 barrels per last, can be had for 212 dollars, or 33 to 34 rixdollars, according to the rate of exchange, which may serve to inform you. Adieu.

$$\frac{3 \text{ Oct.}}{7 \text{ Oct.}} 1679$$

464 C. BENE to JD
HAMBURG   26 SEPTEMBER 1679

D]   My last letter to you was on the 19th instant, in which I informed you that I had sold about
$7\frac{1}{2}$ barrels of our tobacco for 5s, payable in cash, to Jean Cordes. This I now confirm.

Since then I have heard nothing from you although I long to do so, so that I can see the
account of what was loaded in Thomas Hill in order to know what it involves. Now and
again, instead of receiving your letters by way of Amsterdam, I occasionally get them by way
of Antwerp and they sometimes arrive one post late, which is inconvenient. Please always
send them by way of Amsterdam.

In my preceding letter I ordered you not to buy anything more for my account. This I
now confirm. Although I am not greatly afraid of any trouble we may get from the King of
Denmark, it has nonetheless caused business to worsen here, and apart from that the exchange
is so extravagant that I am not willing to have any drafts. You will oblige me if you can
recover what you have disbursed for me from the remittances and I will provide you with an
appropriate rate of interest as long as this damaging rate of exchange continues.

I have been unable to achieve anything in the sale of our remaining bale of Ardasse, nor
likewise with our Bermuda tobacco. Since I fear that things will go badly for this commodity
I am going to barter it for Jawers linen, if any opportunity offers, and send it to [England],
which I hope you will not oppose. I shall inform you if I have any success.

I await news of Hill's departure. John Bates arrived here in a very few days from England.
May God also guide him in safety.

Concerning the present troubles, I have written to your servant at greater length in High
German to give him some practice. Apart from that, the King of Denmark has requested
some members of this city to be deputed to meet him at Pinnenberg. They have gone today,
and consist of one Burgermeister, one Syndic, two senators and one of the secretaries to the
city. It is thought that His Majesty will outline his demands. Meanwhile, the city is provided
with soldiers and troopers and is in a state of defence, but I hope it will soon all blow over—
which God grant!

If you have already bought some of the sun-dried sugar please ship it over here, but if not,
let it rest. With cordial regards, &c.

London: $35s$–$34s$ $11g$ at 2 usances.
Amsterdam: 33–$32\frac{15}{16}$ at short sight.
Venice: $88\frac{3}{4}$ at usance.

$$[\underline{\qquad}] 1679$$
$$24 \text{ Oct.}$$

465 JOHN LEWKNOR to JD
WEST DEAN[1]   17 OCTOBER 1679

'Sir, It was no litle sattisfaction to understand by the coachman that you and Mr Du Menel
were safely arrived in London, when the badness of the wayes and weather might justly give
me occasion to fear your miscarriage. My mother and Jenny are your humble servants and
hope to see you [and] our good mother here when your occasions will permit you to let us
have the happynes of your company longer. I am not likewise a little rejoyced to find you

have hopes of those new remedies which are applied to my litle French sister. Mr High Sheriff having occasion to retourne moneys for London, he got me to signe a bill for eight hundred pounds so that, Sir, I thought fit to give you this information least the greatnes of the sume might make any delay in your payment to the High Sheriff. The money I have already received here, so that you need not scruple the payment of it, and will be within these three days payed out to the respective creditors. The Borrough of Midhurst have done me the honour to depute me their Burgesse for the ensuing parliament, where of fifty two that were present and did vote but two voted against mee. I find I am not French man good enough to understand your letters without the helpe of one to explain, and how inconvenient that may be I leave you to judge. There-fore I beg you to write to me in English. I rest, Sir, your humble servant, &c.'

¹ West Sussex.

$$\frac{28\ Oct.}{24\ Nov.}1679$$

466   G. RICHARDS to JD
BILBAO   13 OCTOBER 1679

'Sir, I have received yours of the 15 past, advysing of the receept of the account of the bays and peper, and that you had past them accordingly, which is well. Your tarre and peper you intended by Hunter, God sending it safe, shall be disposed of for the most, as also cloves and cinament, if you order any from Holland. I have sould 2 parcells of cinamon which have produced well, and cloves, but cloves are the currentest comodity if they can be had reasonable, as I believe they may, the Dutch East India ships beeing, I heare, arrived at Holland. Of the *barragans* I have sould 26 pieces and shall put off the rest by all occasions. The Dutch ships from Holland beeing, as its said, arrived at San Antono, may bringe your others. My last carryed you invoy[c]es and bills of loading of what consigned you by Steele and Roch, who sayled with the convoy and I hope are now at home. I shall hasten more returns also. Your San Sebastian bill my friend hath about 8,000 *R. pta.*-worth of goods on for security and is provyding to prosecute the carryer's estate if he will not comply. I hope nothing will be lost there, nor shall I sell any of your good[s] without dew consideracon to whome it is. To ask any consideracon for security of all debtes I am unwillinge because the proffits are so small now adays that it will not admitt of any extraordinary charge. I shall however have the same care as the goods weare my owne. I knowe not of any such losse you have as yet, your wheat beeing sould to poore people is the reason its so tediously paid for. However I shall endeavour to putt an end thereto speedily, or prosecute the partys. Colchester bays are at present the best comodity from London. I have sould neare 50 balles by these ships and they yeald no badd account, As they are deare at home they keep up here. White bays are also in demand. I kisse your hands and remayne, Sir, your humble servant.'

$$\frac{20\ Nov.}{25\ Nov.}1679$$

467   S. DE GEER to JD
STOCKHOLM   31 OCTOBER 1679

[D] & [F]   My last letter was on the [blank], since which I have heard nothing from you. Nevertheless, I am writing to tell you how things stand with the Mommas. The old man is at Nyköping and the young man is here, but there is nothing to be done with them. They are stiff-necked and refuse to listen to reason. The one living here is usually drunk everyday from the morning onwards. Enfin, in my opinion, if one proceeds against them one will be only throwing good money after bad.

I shall see if something can be arranged with Mr Cletscher about the interested parties, but it will not be easy. Also a salt licence will first have to be obtained. This gentleman is no commission-agent and he concerns himself only with his own affairs, au reste, honnete homme.

I long to get your letters and my wine, which is taking a long time. Otherwise it will be too late, for we shall be in the depths of winter before the two voyages can reach the inland sea. At the earliest opportunity please let me know your opinion about the pan iron and how much one might have made for the coming year. I shall give orders for the rough ends to be cut off and, to make it lighter, I shall make use of the old pig-iron which is very good. Send me a note about it, because they have asked to know how much they should make of each sort.

There is also some '$\mathbb{G}$' iron available which turns out a little harder than the other sort, and as it comes from good iron we use it here for hooping heavy wheels as we find it stronger and more durable than the other kind. If I knew the breadth which is most often required in England for binding wagon-wheels I would have one or two sorts made as an experiment. Please send me a note about it, but leave the memorandum open so that Westhuysen[1] can send me a duplicate.

Overseas iron prices are low, and over here most works have made only two-thirds of the amount they made last year because of the lack of water. As a result, I cannot send you any ordinary 'G' sheet-iron, though I hope it will be possible to do so next year. Let me also know about 'OO' iron and how suitable it is, as well as the '$\mathbb{L}$', of which Mr Wilkens has sent you a quantity this year. Also, let me know if the 'OO' square-iron should be of 1 inch, $1\frac{1}{8}$ inch and $1\frac{1}{4}$ inch as well as $1\frac{1}{2}$ inches, and how much of each sort would be best.

As I am afraid that the ships which are now lying here loading up may not get away in time, and as I have to make some payments at Amsterdam in December, I shall have to ask you to accommodate me with three or four hundred pounds which Westhuysen could draw upon you for me, or else you could remit it to him. I shall be glad if it can be done, but please let Amsterdam know how it would suit you best. It will only be for a little while and Westhuysen will let you know whether he will need it in December or February.

I had written as far as this when your letter of the 26th of September arrived. I see that the ships have come and note the amount of pan iron that is required for next year. I shall have it made, in the same assortment as before, and will make sure that it is done properly in order to encourage the customers, though in your last letter you wrote that I was not to make the thickest sort or, at least, not as they were now made because the ends were not even, but I should now be able to supply them.

If I pass through Nyköping I shall see if I can speak with the elder Momma. The dispute is making no progress, et doit plus qu'il n'a de bien.

Iron seems to be very dear here, but the exchange on Amsterdam is reckoned at 26 marks per dollar, and as the return freight-rates to London are not dear this year it has been possible to send it.

Concerning copper-wire, I have told Mr Wouters to inform you how things stand as he is best acquanited with it. I cannot judge whether one can deal safely with him. Pour moy je na fay difficulte de lesser de mes effaits entre ces mains et je le trouve vigilent et qu'il pren bien garde a ces affaires. Je souhaite toute sorte de prosperite aux nouveaux maries[2] comme aussi a

Madame leur mere, et vous aussi Monsieur son pere (alias step-father). Quand vos vesseau sera venu, qui sans doute sera bien tost, nous aurons soin de nous resouvenir de leur sante, le saison en estant fort propre, car on se pourmene bravement sur les glaces! This is all that is necessary for the moment, so I remain, &c.

¹ S. de Geer's clerk book-keeper, remaining in Amsterdam.
² A reference to Jane Marescoe and John Lewknor.

$$\frac{20\ Nov.}{2\ Dec.}1679$$

468 A. WOLTERS to JD
STOCKHOLM   1 NOVEMBER 1679

[D]   Today is the 1st of November and the above, of the 8th of September, is a copy of my last letter. I am sure that it has reached you safely as well as the despatched 235 slb [of iron] since the ship passed through the Sound a long while ago. For the rest, I refer you to my letter.

Since then I have received your letters of the 5th and 19th of September, which I should have answered earlier but I have been hoping every day that the iron would arrive and that I would be able to send you the bill of lading. I am extremely annoyed that it is taking so long and my Lord De Geer can be my witness that it is no fault of mine, as the wind has always been so contrary that nothing has been able to come from the works. For six weeks [the iron] has been lying in the barge, somewhere between the works and this city. Secondly, letters have been held up. We have been hoping every week that the posts would go again since peace was concluded, but they have been held back until now, so that it is only with this post that one can make a start with the correspondence, since the normal post is leaving.

In my last letter I wrote to you that I had debited you 8,293 dollars and 15 öre for the 235 slb of iron, but in making a record of it I find that I have made an error amounting to 1 dollar 16 öre copper money. In reckoning the Slb. 235.13 of iron @ 31 dollars I had put it down as 7,303 dollars 20 öre, but the total ought really to be 7,305 and 4 öre, so that your net debit on the account of iron stands at 8,294 dollars and 31 öre, which you will please note and forgive the mistake.

Herewith is the bill of lading for the remaining quantity of Slb. 162.4.10 lb. of iron despatched to you aboard Captain Hans Kroger. I have procured a somewhat lower freight-rate, but it will have to pay rather more toll since the ship is entirely without a free pass. It can be bought for half a dollar or something, so your iron is not too heavily burdened, and I will take care of it as if it were for myself. The last one, in which the 235 slb was shipped, had partial freedom and I paid for the rest so that it got total freedom, but this ship has absolutely no freedom so something must be paid which we recover through the freight-rate, as we have cheaper freight than before. When the duty is paid an account will be sent to you. The shipment will be ready to depart in a few days. He is mostly loaded with tar for the owner's account.

Hendrick Cletcher has transferred to me your power of attorney and other documents concerning Willem Momma at Nyköping and asked me to pursue the matter so that it can be brought to a conclusion. He further says that you gave him instructions to make me such a request. In fact, you have written nothing to me about it, and it is also a very troublesome commission which looks like being a thankless task, but out of regard for you and at the persuasion of Mr Cletcher and also of De Geer I have undertaken it and had your power of attorney translated into German and have served it on him, requiring him to answer to me about the account. The son, Isaac Momma, who is here, has answered me in place of his father, who is in Nyköping. He says he will send the copy of the power of attorney to his father and let me know the answer. He was sure that his father would not allow him to come to any agreement or compromise until, or before, you debited him in his father's account with the *RD* 2,000 which you once wrote (to the said Momma) that you had paid to De Geer, but he would let me know his father's answer. Steven de Geer has refuted all this to him, but it seems that there is little happening, so it is now necessary to learn from you what you want ordered to be done about it if he will not agree to reason, and how much you will allow me to deduct from the account, or what else you will concede. I beg you to let me know a little about your views of the matter. I shall know how to manage things properly and will try to do the best that is possible for you. The sooner the case is settled the better, for at the moment there is something to be hoped for but later there may not perhaps be so much. I look forward to learning what you have ordered and will govern myself accordingly.

I see that the ships will be ready to depart at the earliest in mid-October, so we shall begin to get ready for them. It is to be wished that they come soon, with salt selling at 17 dollars. I was selling all mine at 18 dollars, but since the arrival of two Dutch ships and one English it has been running at 17 dollars and as we are selling it daily we hope the price will continue so, since nothing more is expected from Holland, where it is very dear and selling at £64 [flem.]. Malt, if it is good, will also fetch a lot of money since there is little English malt in stock here. If God grants its arrival I shall take care of your interests as if they were my own, on that you can rely.

I see that in [England] our Swedish wares are very cheap, while here they remain dear. As I wrote previously, iron is at 31 to 32 dollars, according to its quality, and there is not much in stock. Pitch and tar are as before. There is little tar here, though one can obtain something at the previous price. The Company is sending nothing to Holland as there are sufficient stocks there. Letters from Holland say that the commercial treaty between this Crown and Holland has been concluded.[1] We have not been able to learn the main points yet, but it is not doubted that the Company will come to an end, of which you in [England] will have earlier news than us.

Although copper prices have dropped so much in Holland, with plenty coming from the East Indies, it still remains dear here and is still selling at 245 dollars. On the exchange it is 260 dollars and it is the same with copper-wire which is still at 275 dollars, and none selling for less. But the demand is also very bad and there is none to sell. Here in town there are about 200 slb in stock. A similar amount is expected but there is no one to buy it. The English have absolutely no desire for it, and in the last two months not more than 80 slb have been sent to [England], vizt. 70 slb in the month of September and 10 slb in the month of October, which is very little, and one hears nothing so far that any of it has been sold. If I intend to do anything I shall let you know. Now that we have got water all the works are in full production, but little will come of it this year. Most of the wire is sent to Holland and France, and most of it to the latter. With this I must close, with regards, &c.

---

[1] The treaty is dated 2/12 October 1679—C. Parry (ed.) *Consolidated Treaty Series*, XV, pp. 351–4.

$$\frac{6\ Dec.}{[6\ Dec.]}1679$$

469 L. TRIP to JD
AMSTERDAM   12 DECEMBER 1679

[D] I have received your letter of the 25th of November and from it I understand that you have
sold another 30 tons of my iron, which is good. I wish the rest was sold. Although the price is
very low one must sell as one can, following the market. However, concerning what you
wrote previously about a quantity of the 'Ⓛ' [iron] reaching you, I think you will find, as has
been found here, that the 'O' iron sells for 4 or 5 per cent more than the 'Ⓛ'.

I wrote to you previously to say that 500 slb of 'O' iron was selling at Stockholm and that I
presumed it would be sent to London, but I am now informed in letters of the 8th of
November that the English only bought 200 slb and the rest is being sent to Hamburg.

You will please deal with my iron as if it were for yourself. I have ordered the square 'O'
iron to be made so that it can be sent to you in the spring, as it was before, but as for the sheet
iron of $3\frac{1}{4}$ and $3\frac{1}{2}$ inches thick I have not ordered it because it would be too thick, and thus
unsaleable. Instead I have ordered them to make the sheets of the usual breadths but as light as
possible. However, in reply please send me a paper showing the thickness and breadth [you
require] so that I can judge whether it can be made, for I have been an iron-master for over 54
years.

Regarding the voyage iron for Genoa[1]—we get it made inland, from Luxemburg and
Germany and could easily deliver it here to the agent for 76 and 78 guilders per ton, in a large
quantity. I have before now delivered 20,000 to 25,000 bars in one year, but I must get £15$\frac{1}{2}$
to £16 [sterling] for it. Farewell.

¹ *Sic.* for Guinea?

$$\frac{27\ Dec.\ 1679}{4\ Jan.\ 1680}$$

470 SIMON ROGERS to JD
CADIZ   4 DECEMBER 1679

'Sir, I have none of yours to answer. These are to advise you that with the second letter that I
carried to Mr Sadeler he delivered me the 9 double bales of Roan linnens, being 7 *florettes* and
2 *blancarts*. The price is low at present, they not being worth above 2 *reals* 12 *maravedis*, but I
hope they may rise against the goeing of *flotta*, for though there are great quantitys in towne
yet the *flotta* likewise must carry great quantitys, when I hope may find to sell them to
advantage. Shall not barter them, seeing you are against it, though against cocheneele might
not doe amisse, being a very staple commodity worth at present 50 ducats per *arroba*. Indigoe
5 *R. pta.* per lb., free of dispatch. Colchester bays, 24 ducats; long mixt Taunton serges 18
pieces of eight per piece, both which commoditys are now in great demand, so that a parcell
of each per first ships you may promise to your selfe quick sales. Of long ells of $1\frac{1}{4}$, 14 pieces of
eight; silke hose, *R. pta.* 14$\frac{1}{2}$ to 15; black says, 12$\frac{1}{2}$ to 13 pieces of eight; callicoes, *R. pta.* 2 per
vare; yardwide perpetuanos of 22 yards are also much demanded to come in 100 pieces 50
redds, 32 grass greens and 18 light blews. A parcell of the above goods if you thinke
convenient may send per first oppertunity, and please to remarke that good goods find
allways the quickest sale. Vinor's ware has been of late cheap ever since the West India fleet
arrived, so that if you remit monys hither by exchange to be returned therein you would not

mislike the account. I should be very glad to have you and Mr Christopher Lethieullier come in shares togather; neverthelesse if that cannot be yet my dilligence shall not be wanting in your concerns, both as to sales and quicknesse of returnes, and I find that the trade seems to revive for most of the goods that came per last ships were immediately bought up and now this year the *flotta* is to goe and we expect likewise the *gallioons* may goe in October next. Goods must of necessity be in demand all the year long, so you may the more boldly venture upon goods. We have advice from Tangier that the moors attackt that place with a numerous army and blew up 5 small forts that the English diserted. The vice-admiral being then there he landed near 400 men for their assistance with whom they sallied out and beat the Moores from their trenches. They are retreated from the towne at present. Likewise from Gibraltar we have advice that the *Hampshire* friggat had retaken an English Newfoundlandman with 10 Moors in her. Here is nothing elce of novelty at present, so with salutefull respects I crave leave to remaine, Sir, your most humble servant.'

Exchange: Amsterdam 123*g* per ducat.
         Antwerp 122$\frac{1}{2}$ *g*.
         London 4*s* 2*d* per pesos.'

$\frac{5\ Jan.}{5\ Jan.}$*1680*

471 G. RICHARDS to JD
BILBAO   22 DECEMBER 1679

'Sir, I have this post yours of the 24 past, with bill of loading and contents of 2 balles of *prissilla* linnings for your account by the *St Henry*, which I pray God send safe with what was more loadinge when I shall dispose thereof for your most advantage. Cinnamon, as you say, sould to deare in Holland to turne to account here, but by the clovs I hope you will make a better businesse. Wax beeing so cheape in London, here's a good quantitie come. I suppose you finde it comes cheaper thence then it can be had in England. Of the *barragans* I have sould about $\frac{1}{2}$ and shall putt of the rest by all occasions. Mr Duquesnoy writes me they are fallen at Vallencia, but I observe the exchange is also lower for London which may make them as deare to you. If you find it otherwyse and that the pryse is considerably lower that they may be sent with more conveniency, they are a sound comodity, but pray order him to keep to their goodnesse for others send better goods. All goods there as well as in England are generally provyded on better tearmes in the winter, and the spring here I find the best time for sale. Hose of Tournoy are here a current comodity and many sell. I cannot tell what account they may produce, haveing never sould any. He is acquanted with the sort propper, and I have sent Sir John a muster of picotes, which he hath sent Duquesnoy. Is a comodity hath good vent here, if they can be had at about 12 *reals* per piece, as they might lately; also *pelos de camelo*, the broader sort, which are worth here 4$\frac{1}{2}$ to 5 R. *pta.* per *vare* as in goodnesse, but these goods must be bought in when cheape and the exchange favourable to turne to account. Of the pepper I had sould 12 baggs at 44 R. *vn* ere till had any news'twas risen in England and Holland. The rest I hope to putt of at a better rate, but your tarre I feare will yeald but a slender account, here beeinge a good parcell more arrived and the consumption of that comodity here is but litle. I shall make the most of it I can. Sir John advyseth mee of 12 balls of Russia hydes he hath loaden in Roch, $\frac{1}{2}$ for your account. I shall sell them for the most they will yeald and hope there may be reasonable advantage thereby. Bays, I observe, weare risen at home to 22*d* per ell. Its not impossible but they may keepe up, the *flota* goeing for the

Indies in June and the *Galleons* in September or October next. It would be amisse to buy them deare if they should fall and be brought cheaper, but if they fall not at home I am perswaded they will ryse proportionable here, as they have donne for some monethes and seaverall accounts I have lately sent home of them have yealded well. Here are moreover few in towne, and if they fall not at home I beleeve verry few will be sent, for your government. In the spring and summer that's a comodity goes presently offe and lesse proffit may satisfie then by other goods which ly by long and sell to worse paymasters, as *pressillias* whereof I have some of Sir John's I cannot sell. I never writt for them. If you order any more *baragans* or any other Flaunders good let them come by way of Dunckerke. Ther's lesse charge on them and they come free of the danger of Turkes. I observe Mr Duquesnoy's intention was to have some of the goods consigned to another. I thinck he hath litle reason, for yours weare I suppose provyded by him by my meanes. I thanck your friendship, as I have more than a treble obligation in what soever I can serve you I will with a particuler sense and reallity. I wish you a merry Christmas with all health and many more and remayn, Sir, your most humble servant.'

$\frac{5 \, Jan.}{5 \, Jan.}$*1680*

472   WELCH & STYLES to JD
         GENOA   27 DECEMBER 1679

'Sir, Confirming the above lynes[1] have last post your gratefull letter the 24 past, observeing thereby the departure from Plymouth of the pink. God send her in safety, hartily wishing yew had incerted the day of her sayling from thence, the convoy's force, and how farr designed, things very consequentiall. We note that, notwithstanding your former advice, much tarr was shipping off for these parts, which newes wee understand alsoo from other penns, which comeing to the Ittallians notice, as undoubtedly must, will keepe them from buying any, though ours should gitt the startt. This is the worse, and if soe must be landed rather then goe at loss. In fine, yew may rest assured our utmost studies shalbe imployed to advantadge your intrist all lay in our powers, giveing yew due advice of what further passeth. What our $\frac{1}{4}$ proportion of charges amounts to in the man's dispatch to Plymouth may please to note in our debts. Certaine it tis that the pincke retarding will afford us an accommodation in capturing new oile, which hope may be late enough to procure for her, though till March non wilbe made. Be confident, noething with in the earth of our capacities of advantadge shalbe omitted in promotting that intrist to the utmost posabillity. Your bill exchange on us was duely sattisfied some daies since and booked accordingly. There is a French ship now on departure for Haver di Grace with aboute 150 tunns ould oyle, cost £39 per barrel, and 400 chests lemons cost 2 *piastres* per chest, which undoubtedly will doe well, soe that the notion yew make for the pinck are affraid wilbe too late seeing others are before us. Pray oblidge us in wrighting your freind there 2 lynes in our favour that in all there commands heere wee should be most willing to serve them. French Newfoundland poore jack hath a great consume heere and farr esteemed above English, soe that in case yow had meanes to procure a loading for this port against next yeare may take a share with them of $\frac{1}{4}$ there in or $\frac{1}{3}$ and wee'le accept $\frac{1}{2}$ of yours of your hands to returne the proceed of that fish hence in oyle, or the fish may adventure to take our proportion at arriveall heer to consigne us on this point at £29 in 30 this quintall, as yearely is heare to Ittallians contracted 3 in 4 ships loadings, all French. Pray oblidge us in seeing what may be done. There alsoe comes hither from Bourdox or close by a greate quantity of rowle tobacco of that groath which currently sold heere in ships loadings of 100 to 140 tunn, at about 6 *piastres* this quintall of 106 lb. English, by which greate gaines are made soo may deserve your information and putting in execution for a small French ship to this port and to returne back with oyle, some Roome allum, which have certaine advice may doe well. Our proceed in the *Providence*'s oyle may please, if can gitt incurradge and any secure convayance, ready to send in soe much lead with some alsoe for your owne account, or another parcell of Swead iron, but must see to gitt the freight cheape, otherwise please to keepe it by you at the disposeall of them that most assuredly are, your verry humble servants.'

¹ Copy of 13 December.

$$\frac{19\ Jan.}{27\ Jan.}1680$$

473   A. WOLTERS to JOHN GOSSELIN
STOCKHOLM   27 DECEMBER 1679

[D]   I found myself honoured three days ago with your very welcome letter of the 5th instant, together with three bills of exchange totalling £400 drawn on Mr William Smitt, of which I have procured acceptance, and with God's help I do not doubt I shall get due payment.

You have now ordered that, if the money has been paid, I should lay it out this winter on some good sorts of iron from reliable people. In reply, I must say in a friendly way that I cannot exactly follow your order for the reason that the money only falls due at the end of January and February, and then there is no iron to be obtained; and if there is any to be obtained now it must be by means of money—but that is not due yet. Now, for the space of a week or a fortnight, is a rest-period when those with money travel up-country to provide the works with everything they need, such as coal and ore which is used in the making of iron. However, as it is up to me to take care of your interests so that your money is not lying idle, and in order that you should profit from the low price of iron, I sent to a person two days ago, who was on the point of selling to another but gave me preference, and agreed with him for 400 slb of iron, of which 200 slb will be ordinary sheet-iron, 100 slb broad, schampelion iron and 100 slb square iron, to deliver here in Stockholm with the first open water at 27 dollars [per slb]. He takes over the bills of exchange and will discount them or negotiate them as best he can, though I remain liable for any failure of payment.

The iron is of good material which has been always sent, year after year, to one Mr Strodder¹ in England. The works once belonged to Utterclo² and its mark is 'XX' but the works have now been sold to another and it is with him that I have contracted, and I am assured that we will be well treated. Mr Strodder, the English merchant, gave 30 dollars for iron last year. There are 200 slb lying ready at the works which I can have immediately. But it is a pity that you did not write how broad the schampelion should be. It has been ordered in various breadths. Please let me know at once in answer to this so it can reach me in time.

I have no doubt that you will be well satisfied with this business, but orgronds iron was not to be obtained. For the 400 slb at 27 dollars you owe me 10,800 dollars, against which we can set the bills of exchange unless their payment fails, which I trust it will not. If it should please you to place this order as it suits you (for this consignment will not be disadvantageous for you) I shall be able to help you with further amounts. You can be assured of my promptitude and reliability and that I will take care of your interests as if they were my own. God protect you, &c.

Hamburg: $27\frac{1}{2}$ to 28.
Amsterdam: $26\frac{1}{2}$ to 27.

¹ John Strother.
² Johan Utterclo, 'assessor' in the Swedish Kommerskollegium and an important figure in the direction of the Tar Company.

$\dfrac{19\ Jan.}{20\ Jan.}$*1680*

474   H. H. BERENBERG to JD
HAMBURG   9 JANUARY 1680

[D] I have not written to you for a long time and meanwhile find myself with your letters of the 12th of September and of the 4th and 25th of November last year. Until now I have deferred my answer because this city has been troubled by war concerning some differences between the Elector of Brandenburg and the King of Denmark, but they were all settled some weeks ago. After that, winter descended and although we have had little frost and the waters remain navigable the damaging west wind has lasted for three weeks and has gathered a great number of ships here. There are at least 350, large vessels as well as small, among which are 100 laden with oats destined for France, but the west wind keeps them all in, which is very vexing. However, since they will be going in the spring we must hope for an improvement in our lives and that trade will go rather more briskly. Meanwhile, thank you for the prices of sundry goods as well as your opinions on one thing or another. I beg you to continue sending them occasionally as well as news if any changes occur in the following commodities, such as silk, pepper, ginger and gall-nuts. I might well ask for some of the latter if fine quality can be obtained and the price is not too high. I await your opinion on the matter.

The ship of which you were thinking, which came here '*adritura*' with 200 sacks, brought only poor, small stuff which will not sell. Two or four sacks were sold for about 43 *ML* [per 100 lb.] but good quality can fetch as much as 46 or 47 *ML*. Ardasse silk sells for 13*s* with the customary rebate; pepper, $13\frac{3}{4}$ *g*; white, scraped ginger, 7*g*; ditto, black or brown ginger, $4\frac{1}{2}$ to $4\frac{5}{8}$ or $4\frac{3}{4}$ *g*, and so far there is for all commodities very poor sales.

It is a good thing that you received from Mr James Banks the £134 11*s* 10*d* I remitted and made good the proceeds to Mr John Wigget. I have so far had no letter of news from him, but since it concerns him or his friend Edmont Waaff I suppose it is not necessary. With very friendly regards, the Lord protect you, I remain, &c.

Amsterdam: $33\frac{5}{16}$.
Venice: $88\frac{1}{2}$.
London: 34*s* 7*g* at 2 usances.

$\dfrac{9\ Feb.}{10\ Feb.}$*1680*

475   C. BENE to JD
HAMBURG   27 JANUARY 1680

[D] I last wrote to you four days ago and remitted therewith for your account £113 6*s* 8*d* sterling at 34*s* 5*g* in a bill of exchange for 500 ducats drawn at Leghorn on the 8th of January at $54\frac{2}{5}$*g* on Antonio Gomez Serra and negotiated here with Philip Verporten.

Since then I have received your welcome letter of the 20th instant, and with it your extensive news of what has been happening to one commodity or another in [London]. Since goods there are nearly all dearer than here it seems that the trade between here and there must perish, for over there they are maintained at high prices and are sent over here by the owners but as soon as they arrive they are sold for what they will fetch, which is ruining trade. Barbary almonds are sold here thus, which because they can be freely brought to [London] can be profitably sent here at 40s. Silk is also sold here for poor prices, so that I cannot make up my mind to invest 9s [per lb.] for them in [London]. It will have to wait until next May, when probably quite enough will arrive. I do not believe that the currants which have been sent here will do very well, for a good quantity are expected to come here *addrittura*.

That the East India Company is holding a sale on the 9th of March I have noted, and when I receive the details I shall at once consider them and if I decide on any purchases I shall let you know. Sugars have little demand here at present and I cannot decide on enlarging my price limit. I have also seen letters from others in which they advise that good quality [sugar] could be had for 20s or 20s 6d, free on board. Please see if you could not obtain some for less from someone in need of cash, though it must be of good quality, otherwise my balance may as well as lie in London.

Enclosed herewith I am sending a note about the weights of the 10 hogsheads of Jamaican sugar. Please show it to the man who sold them to you so that he can see what is lacking. The weights are only of the casks, from which ¾ per cent was deducted here, and a hundred-weight in [England] must yield 104 lb. here. Captain Lomax brought all his crew ashore in order to take oath, but I did not want that since I would then have had to pay all the expenses here, and I did not know if I could obtain anything in [London]. Now Lomax is no longer here and it is too late for his people to swear. Since you still have the seller in hand he will have to be satisfied with the note, though if he will not believe honourable people I shall send him a notarial deed, provided that he pays the expenses. If, in addition, I could send you the testimony of the crew it would already have been sent to you. I urge you to take care of my interests as if they were your own.

Enclosed I send you the account of the remaining Bermuda tobacco, of which your promised half is £69 8s 0g, for which I shall give you credit if the money is paid in. Please check the account, and if you find no mistakes, please make a record of it. I also remit you herewith, for your account, £100 at double usance in a bill of Jan & H. Louis drawn on Pickering & Robinson. Please procure the necessary and credit me with £171 13s 4g at 34s 4g [per £1 sterling]. The second copy of the bill for 500 ducats is not yet here; it will be sent to you later. Please send my current account as soon as possible. With cordial regards, &c.

[P.S.] If you cannot effect my commission for sugar but can obtain good campeachy-wood at 9s, free on board, please buy me another 200 cwt. and send with another captain for the least possible freight, though if the sugar has been bought buy no campeachy-wood. Adieu.

$$\frac{\textit{16 Feb.}}{[\text{——}]}\textit{1680}$$

476 S. DE GEER to JD
LÖVSTA[1]   [——][2] JANUARY 1680

[D] I have been unavoidably detained here for a long while by an accident which happened about five weeks ago to my leg, which was broken clean through just above the ankle, though now—God be thanked—it has improved so much that I am beginning to get up and I hope within a fortnight to be completely recovered, without any impediment.

This has prevented the journey which I was planning to take to Nyköping, so I have been unable to do anything about your suit with Momma. With Mr Cletscher things stand as before, for he will not waive any of the interest since the debt is too great, though about the salt-licence he is not doing much good. There too there is some good reason for it, but it has been caused by his own fault. I have told him it is cheap, and as soon as the repayment comes in from others I shall settle it in order to close the account.

I am glad that the pan-iron was found to be so good. That which is now being made will be done in the same way, and the coarseness removed from it.

It is not feasible to make the 3-inch sheet-iron only $\frac{1}{4}$-inch thick. It would bend about, for even the smallest iron cannot be made $\frac{1}{4}$-inch thick, but I shall have it forged as thin as possible. Let me know at once if more will be paid for it than for the 'OO' or the 'Ⓛ', for it must sell for more, otherwise it will have to be sent to Amsterdam, though as an experiment I shall send you some.

It must have slipped my memory, but according to my calculations I should still have a balance of about £300 with you if the proceeds of the last lot of pan-iron and the total on the *Thomazine* have been paid up, unless I have made a mistake. You can expect more pan-iron and other iron as soon as we have open waters.

Let me know at once what ships you have chartered to go to St Ubes and then come here, and at what price, and when you estimate they can arrive here. Also, whether many grain ships are going to the Straits this autumn from your area. In these regions we are having a pretty tolerable winter, not very severe, and all the rivers are flowing so supplies are readily obtainable. I shall be glad to know if iron has been enjoying some sales with you and what you think about it. The high rate of exchange will remain as it was last year and all the principal iron-works have made contracts accordingly.

It would have been a good thing if I had known that you were favourably inclined towards one or other of the works apart from the 'Ⓛ'. There were about 4,000 to 5,000 slb made this year and they were mostly shared, one half to London and the other half to Amsterdam. It is now much too late, but otherwise I should certainly have despatched some. One now draws on Amsterdam at $26\frac{1}{2}$ to 27 marks per *RD*. I could have obtained that iron for 31 dollars but I would guess that others now have to give 32. It stands at about [illegible].

This mishap will rather delay me in all my affairs and I shall have to remain rather longer in the country than I intended. Wishing you all happiness and success in this new year and many others to come, I remain, &c.

[P.S.] Your letter of the 25th of November has arrived at last.

¹ Endorsed by De Geer (in Dutch) 'from Leufsta, where the 'Ⓛ' is made'. Lövstabruk lies some 70 km north of Uppsala, within 30 km of the Österby and Gimo iron works.
² Possible reading 'Jan. p[rimo] 1680'.

$$\frac{16\ Feb.}{27\ Feb.}1680$$

477 JACOB DE GREVE to JD
HAMBURG   3 FEBRUARY 1680

[D] This serves only to say that for some time I have had one case of Jauwers linen and one case of Sloyers in the hands of Mr James Bancks in [London] which he says he cannot sell. I think that is strange, seeing that linen is daily rising in price here. From time to time I sell plenty of the same sort to the English here who send it to [England] themselves and do well with it. So I suspect that, because the said James Bancks and his brother John Bancks especially trade actively in linen themselves and because they know that I have as good an opportunity to do so as they, they do not want to serve me with regard to linen and by not being able to sell any hope to make me decide not to send any more to England so that I will no longer be any obstacle to them. I wrote to him to this effect, since I saw that he could not sell any, and said that I had the opportunity to sell them to a friend here over a year ago, to which he replied that he would be delighted to transfer them to whomsoever I might order.

Thus (in order not to invite any jealousy that the transfer might occasion, since James Bancks in [London] and Charles Bancks over here are my good friends) I have today drawn up a deed of assignment that the said two cases are to be transferred at the order of my brother [-in-law] Jean Baptista d'Hertogh, and this has been endorsed by him to you *pro forma*. It comes herewith. So I ask you to send this assignment to Mr James Bancks and demand the aforesaid two cases to be transferred on presentation of my assignment, mentioning nothing more than that you are doing this on the orders of my brother [-in-law] Jean Baptista, and that it is for his account. By doing this you will oblige me greatly, and if you will sell the said Jauwers and Sloyers to my greatest advantage, either for cash or to people without liabilities, and if the experiment succeeds I shall keep you always supplied with these and other sorts of linen suitable for [England].

You do not have to pay Mr Bancks any charges or anything else for them since I have written to him that I will make it good to his brother Charles here. In order to know that they really are my cases they should, in addition to my usual mark in black on the lid, be marked with a red mark thus, . The case of linen [Jauwers] is also marked 'No. 5' and the case of Sloyers *ℱ*. Perhaps, through standing around so long, the paper wrapping on the Jauwers and Sloyers have become rather unsightly and soiled, so please take off some layers and put fresh pieces on top which you can let the buyers see first, and then let me know what they can sell for.

The dry weather continues and we may well have a short winter and be able to commence the sailing season somewhat earlier. Your advice to my sister Mahuis about prices will be useful for my consideration so that if the peace holds and the clouds of war pass by we can make a trial of something or other. May the Almighty protect you. With cordial regards, I remain, &c.

$$\frac{25\ Feb.}{8\ Mar.}1680$$

478 G. RICHARDS to JD

BILBAO   16 FEBRUARY 1680

'Sir, I have this post receved yours of the 19th January adviseing the arryval of Hunter, for which God be praysed. That you had given me credit for what I sent you by him is wel. I have since desired you to drawe 1,500 pieces of eight for your account to Cadize or Sivil, and I shall goe remitting you other returnes as fast as I can directly, which shall be in white mony as you desire, but I hope shortly we shal meet with some better way for returneing your effects. Vellon, which hath bin the distrucktion of all trade here for many yeares, is lowered to ¼ part of what it past for, and the piece of eight is expected dayly to fal to its former rate by a second order from the King and Counsel, which wil undoubtedly alter trade much. The account of your pepper and *barraganen* I shal soone send you, and you may adventure upon more of both. The major part of your cloves I have contracted for at 18 *R. pta.* per lb. (on arryval) in Madrid, which wil be about 17¼ silver neat, and at that rate as your returnes goe home and the goods cost you, you wil get 20 per cent. This is a staple commodity. Here are but few woollen goods in towne and for Colchester bayes I have binn offerd 6 *R. pta.* per *vare*, and if to many come not, which we can't expect if they keep up at home, they will answer there cost here. For our wax and *presillias* I have binn in treaty to dispose of them for wools. If I doe it, it shal be on such tearmes that you shall receive sattisfactory proffitt thereby, but I am not yet resolved thereon. *Picottillias*, Mr Duquesnoy writes me, are rysen in Holland. To buy many dear there would not be prudence because I am of the oppinion they wil fal againe as soone as the *flotta* is provided, but I am perswaded in regarde soe many of those woollen goods and of our English manufacturyes are carryed now together for New Spaine they wil ryse here considerably, as bays have donn and we may expect wil yet doe. I have not to add, but that I am, Sir, your humble servant.'

$$\frac{10 \; Mar.}{16 \; Mar.} 1680$$

479   A. DUQUESNOY to JD
         AMSTERDAM   12 MARCH 1680

[D]   I received your letter of the 27th past, Old Style, as you will have seen from the note sent to you.

      As one can always obtain cloves from the East India Company for 75 stuivers per lb. or less throughout the whole year there is nothing to be done with them.

      There is a ship lying here loading which is leaving for Bilbao at the end of the month, with or without convoy, mounted with 12 guns—a brave man.

      Your balance will be laid out on cinnamon from the East India Company, as ordered.

      The *baracans* are at about the same price in Valenciennes as they were the last time I procured some for you. I do not believe they will fall lower. I enclose a sample of the colour which is in demand at Bilbao.[1]

      I forgot to enclose the paid-up bill of exchange to Mr Pencier of which a notarial copy goes herewith. You said you would be returning the *f.*400 received from Steenhoven. I do not understand, but if you want me to pay it back to the said Steenhoven I shall do it and inquire about him. As I said before, he seems a knowledgeable man.

      I cannot advise you about other trades to Bilbao. Many people sell *baracans* and it is a steady trade. This sample is lighter than those usually taken there, but they are all of this mixture.

      If I can do anything of service, please command me. With regards, God protect you, &c.

[P.S.] *Baracans* are not usually as good as this sample.

   [1] The attached sample is a mid-grey.

$$\frac{11 \; Mar.}{16 \; Mar.} 1680$$

480   A. VAN KUFFELER to JD
         AMSTERDAM   8 MARCH 1680

[D]   Both your welcome letters of the 20th of January and the 13th past reached me safely. In reply, I have found my current account to be correct and have credited you with £12 10s 8d sterling on a new account.

I am glad that you would have accepted Mr Th. Heath's draft of £50 or £60 on my account, though he has had no opportunity to use it, having had no need of it. However, if he draws it, I shall remain liable as before, and should you meanwhile remit please draw on me for the balance [due to you] on my account. I should have remitted this balance long ago but the amount is so small that one can find no bills of exchange to match it.

I am grateful to you for the news about your East India Company's sale, together with the prices of these and other goods. Herewith goes a reciprocal note of the sale of goods by our Company, though I regret that very little opportunity arises for exchange since the trade between England and here is so limited that there seems nothing to be done in it. The principal dealers in most kinds of commodities, both in London and here, have their own agents both there and here so that for some time the reciprocal trade between England and here has been going very badly. I wish there might be some improvement so that we can find an opportunity to make a profit in something or other.

I must thank you for your recommendation to your friend, Mr Jean Gosselin. I hope to serve him to his satisfaction and in a similar case I shall not hesitate to recommend you. Please give him the enclosed, and if there is anything in which I can be of service you have only to command.

London—36s 1g at 2 usances.

Map 3. Sweden's iron and copper centres.

APPENDIX A

MARESCOE-DAVID LETTERS IN THE RIKSARKIV, STOCKHOLM

Scattered through the huge *Momma-Reenstierna Sammlung* in Section 3 of the Swedish National Archives are several groups of original letters complementary to those in the Marescoe-David archive.

(a) E.2525—62 letters to Abraham & Jacob Momma from John Buck & Charles Marescoe (May 1656 to December 1659).

(b) E.2513—18 letters to Jacob Reenstierna from C. Marescoe (March to August 1670);
    —7 letters to the same from Peter Joye (September to November 1670);
    —15 letters to the same from Leonora Marescoe (April 1674 to August 1675).

(c) E.2503—24 letters to Jacob Reenstierna from Jacob David (May 1674 to April 1678).

Also relevant are the following addressed to Jacob Reenstierna:

(d) E.2512—84 letters from Jacob Lucie & Cornelius van Bommell (October 1670 to April 1675);

(e) E.2498—210 letters from Jean & Hendrick Van Baerle (December 1666 to January 1676);
    —17 letters from David van Baerle (February 1674 to December 1676);

(f) E.2506—193 letters from Jan Jacob Hiebenaer (mainly January 1669 to October 1674).

Microfilm of items (a) to (e), kindly made available by the Riksarkiv, will be deposited with the Public Record Office, Chancery Lane, London.

(g) In addition, there are numerous copies of Momma-Reenstierna letters addressed to the London firm (of which some originals survive in the Marescoe-David papers) to be found in the letter-books of the Momma brothers, notably:

E.2479—letters of 1658;
E.2476—letters of 1659–60;
E.2477—letters of 1660–1;
E.2478—invoices of 1664–5;
E.2480—letters of 1667–9;
E.2475—letters of 1668–9;
E.2483—letters of 1670–1;
E.2595—letters and accounts of 1668, 1669.

Six representative letters selected from (a) and (b) are printed below in translation.

$$\frac{19\ Dec.}{27\ Dec.}1656$$

A1]   MARESCOE & BUCK to ABRAHAM & JACOB MOMMA

LONDON   14 NOVEMBER 1656

[D]   Our last letter to you was about a fortnight ago, with the sale-account of your 56 copper kettles, to which we refer ourselves. Since we have heard nothing from you this will serve to tell you that we have remitted on the 7th instant to David van Baerle for your account

£100 @ 35s 6g at 2 usances, dated 4 November in a bill of Guillaume Carbonnel drawn on Andre van Aenstenreeds;

£120 @ 35s 6g at 2 usances in a bill of Jacob Momma drawn on Pieter Trossen;

£100 @ 35s 5g at 2 usances in a bill of Herincook & Goschalck[1] drawn on John Tielens, for all which you will please credit us.

We have still had no news of the ship *Noort Pool*—God grant that it arrives safely![2] It seems to us that he is taking rather a long time, though he may have been waiting in the Sound for other ships to have as company. We wait to hear what iron you have since loaded for M. De la Bistrate. Please let us know if one could not have made in [Sweden] some copper bars of about 2½ feet long, weighing 2¼ to 2½ lb., and whether or not the export duty would amount to any more than on other wrought copper—i.e. what would it cost, free on board? Please give us prompt advice about this, for it might be that we shall order a substantial quantity for the spring.

We would also be glad to know, supposing we wanted to buy a substantial amount of iron for delivery in Stockholm, how much you would have to lay out for fine, square iron— 400 slb; for broad, flat fine-iron—400 slb; and for small, thin fine-iron—1,000 slb.[3] We believe there are iron-masters[4] who could quite easily undertake to provide such a consignment at a reasonable price with the certainty of making a profit. Also, tell us when their money will have to be available for payment. It would be advantageous if one could provide the money in specie via Hamburg, but the authorities[5] will not permit it.

We await your answer, particularly about the iron prices, so that we can act accordingly. Garcopper fetches £5 10s to 12s; copper plates £6 10s; copper-wire £6 8s to 9s; sheet copper £7 4s per cwt. Fine iron, £17 10s [per ton]; pitch £17½, tar £11, per last, for your information. With cordial regards, &c.

Hamburg: 34s 5g ⎫
Middelburg: 35s 7g ⎬ 2 usances.
Antwerp: 35s 2g ⎭

---

[1] I.e. Herringhook & Godschall.

[2] By 28 November Buck & Marescoe had learned that the *Noort Pool* had been wrecked off Yarmouth with the loss of all but 4 or 5 men.

[3] On 5 December Buck & Marescoe gave more precise specifications. The square iron was to be 1 inch thick, the broad flat-iron was to yield 6 bars per slb (i.e. 50 lb. a-piece) and be exactly 3 inches thick; the 1,000 slb of small, fine-iron was to yield 7 or 8 bars per slb (i.e. 43 to 37½ lb. a-piece).

[4] 'werck-meesters'.

[5] '. . . maer de Vorst sal het niet toe laeten.' In the context of Hamburg this means the Emperor.

$\dfrac{9\ Jan.}{31\ Jan.}$1657

[A2]   SAME TO SAME
LONDON   12 DECEMBER 1656

[D]   The above [of 6 December] is a copy of our last letter, to which we refer. We have since received your welcome letter of the 15th of November with the bill of lading for your rod-iron and the bar-iron from M. Ant. de la Bistrate, laden in [the ship of] Hendrick Claesen, with which we will supply ourselves. Neither he nor Adriansen have yet appeared.[1] For some days we have had a south wind (though it is at present westerly) so we hope to hear of them in a few days time. God bring them safely!

We have still not heard from Mr Focken about his settlement of the disagreement with the owners of the *Noot Muscatenboom*[2] but Mr Jacobsen has today shown us information in his own hand to that effect, sent to him by the captain who ordered him to take custody of the money into his own hands and keep it until he arrives here—whereupon we informed him that we had your order to receive your share and also Mr Radue's. We will come to an agreement with him and say no more about it.

If Capt. Hendrick Claesen arrives here we will advance him your one-eighth share of the freight money, which we will make over to Caspar Bruyn together with the proceeds of your goods sent by him aboard Capt. Adriansen.

You urge us to assist all the captains of any ships in which you have a part-interest. This we shall do to the best of our ability, as if for ourselves, but we do not understand whether the captains have orders from *all* the part-owners to address themselves to us. Meanwhile we will extend our help to any that come to our knowledge.

You will have seen our order to procure the purchase of 2,000 slb of iron—vizt. $\frac{1}{4}$-part broad, $\frac{1}{2}$ small, and $\frac{1}{4}$ square. Please get it at the keenest price and make sure it is in good, even and equal sizes—the square and small iron the lighter the better, of 9, 10, 11 or 12 feet long, but the broad ought to be according to the enclosed design[3] which is of a kind that comes from [Sweden] via Hamburg and is stamped with an 'F', which sells well here (if there is not too much of it) and is of the same type that we are asking for. As for the necessary purchase money, we have ordered you to draw at once *RD* 2,000 on Antoine de la Bistrate. If you have the opportunity of doing so profitably for us you can go up to six thousand rix-dollars and your bills will be promptly paid.

Concerning your proposal that we should accommodate you (here, as is customarily done in Amsterdam) with money advanced upon the goods shipped here, we say that it can be done, as long as it is not too much or too often. As you will have observed from our preceding letter, we could easily go up to four, five or six hundred pounds per ship, but we do not find it advisable to have the insurance done here as most of our insurers are not to our liking.[4] In case of a loss one has to wait, 3, 4 or 6 months, and then they deduct 15 or at least 10 per cent, as well as the premium, before they pay up. Therefore it is better to have it done in Hamburg or Amsterdam by those friends on whom you could draw the money, ordering them to reimburse themselves upon us. If you want the business to remain with us we shall arrange the insurance with the rest, remaining satisfied with $\frac{1}{2}$ per cent for any outlay. And iron, copper or copper-wire will always sell freely, so we are in no fear of over-supplying the market except at some times when for one or two months the market is somewhat quieter than at other times; but that is to be expected in all places.

We have written to Caspar Bruyn today, following your order, that he may draw £200 on us; wherewith our cordial regards, &c.

Amsterdam:	35s 4g	
Hamburg:	34s 2g	2 usances.
Paris:	52$\frac{1}{4}$d	
Antwerp:	35s	

[1] Both Claesen and Adriansen had arrived by 26 December; they were ready to depart again by 23 January.
[2] Hendrick Claesen's ship which, on an earlier voyage, had delivered a consignment short of its invoiced weight, over which this dispute arose.
[3] '. . . *volgens d'ingeslooten model* . . .'. Presumably this refers to a drawing, which has not survived.
[4] '. . . *alsoo meest van onse asseuradeurs ons niet aenstaen*.'

$$\frac{9\ Apr.}{11\ Apr.}1657$$

[A3]   SAME TO SAME
LONDON   13 MARCH 1657

[D]   The above [of 6 March] is a copy of our latest letter, to which we refer. We have since
received your welcome letter of 14 February and note what is happening with regard to our
commission—that the broad and square iron is being worked now—but we would hope that
you do not have to pay 26 dollars [per slb] for it, as that is much too high, all the more so in
view of the great danger it will run at sea if the Danes fall out with the Swedish Crown,
which is to be feared, so that 24 dollars would be quite enough. However, we shall rely on
your discretion to manage matters as if yourself, trusting that the iron will be evenly forged
from good material, according to our request. Speedy despatch is very important, so we urge
you to look out for Abr. Laurens or some other good skipper, and if the Sound should
become closed to your ships it would be best if you loaded everything aboard a Dutch ship
bound for Amsterdam, though the ship may come here for the decree forbidding that is not
much observed now, and the captain could give out (when he is here) that he is a Swede so
that there is no further dispute. Please give us timely advice of everything, and also to Ant. de
la Bistrate, so that we can act accordingly.
    We shall send you a sample of the copper rods at the earliest opportunity, as you requested.
We have already informed you about what we paid for your account to Capt. Hendrick
Claesen and remitted to Caspar Bruyn at Amsterdam, to whom we have today remitted in
our own bill £200 @ 34s 10g at 2 usances on Pilgrom & Arnout ten Groot Huysen, for
which you will please credit us.
    All kinds of commodities remain as in the copy above, only saltpetre is driven up to 80s per
cwt., great quantities having been bought up for sending to Holland and Hamburg, but on
the arrival of the ships from the Indies in May or June it will again fall to 73s or below. That
commodity is always bought here for cash, but as you ask for something in return for iron we
could accommodate you with the outlay of the money, or draw on Amsterdam; wherewith,
our cordial regards, &c.

Amsterdam: 34s 10g ⎱
Hamburg: 33s 6g ⎰ 2 usances.

[A4]   CHARLES MARESCOE TO JACOB MOMMA-REENSTIERNA
LONDON   18 MARCH 1670

[D]   My last to you was on the 4th of March, by which I advised you that I had remitted for your
account to Messrs Jean & David van Baerle £320 @ 35s 2g at 2 usances in two bills, as
follows:
        £220 on Jacobus Elison;
        £100 on Pieter de Lean.
Since then I have heard nothing from you, so this will serve to enclose your current account
by which a balance of £489 12s 7d remains due to me, which I have carried to your debt in a
new account, without prejudice to me for any debts which I have discounted. Below the
account is a specification of the interest placed to your debit. Please examine it and, finding it
correct, please note it and drop me a line about your findings.

Of the wire, I have sold to William Wathing 74 coils at £6 10s per cwt. payable in 6 months. I shall do my duty with the remainder and let you know what happens. Meanwhile I am extremely sorry that it is going so sluggishly,[1] but one cannot do more than one's best, and it is commonly the case that when one has brought a commodity up to a high price the retailers do all that they can to avoid buying anything and to discourage one, and if they do buy anything it is only because they have no more, either to sell or work with. That is what they are doing now, and what they buy is only in small parcels and that only when it is absolutely necessary. However, it is my intention to keep the price up and I think I have good reason for doing so for there is only a little in town and that is all in my hands, besides which the prospect is that it will be two months before any more comes from [Sweden]. A person has offered me £6 at 3 months for all which I have but I have refused him, considering it is better to do so and maintain the price in reputation until the first consignments arrive from [Sweden]. Thus, it is impossible to establish a new price-level unless there is an upsurge of demand, and then I shall be selling quantities all through the week, so that before long you can expect an account of it.

Meanwhile I would be glad to learn what amounts you intend to consign to me. You would do well to send some copper bars as soon as possible as several ships will soon be getting ready to sail for Guinea and this commodity will be in demand, for there is none of it in town and large amounts will be required. Hungary plates, £6 10s; garcopper £5 18s; sheet copper £6 18s. Iron is also in request—square, broad and small iron selling at 14s 6d [per cwt.]. Gothenburg deals are very dear, selling at £6 per cwt., and others accordingly.[2]

It has been said to me that you have agreed with our other friends in Sweden to consign all the copper-wire (which this place can consume) to one hand, but I believe that this has not yet been finally concluded for nothing has been written to me about it. If something like this has been decided I beg you to make me a participant. I have always sought every opportunity to procure your profit as if it were my own, and as the exchange has fallen so much I am very glad that I have remitted so much for your account at an advantageous price. Yours, &c.

Amsterdam:	34s 10g	
Hamburg:	35s	} 2 usances
Antwerp:	34s 8g	
Rouen:	56½d	

---

[1] '. . . dat het so traag voort gaet . . .'.
[2] To this point the letter is in Jacob David's hand; the next paragraph is in Marescoe's.

[A5]   SAME TO SAME
LONDON   1 APRIL 1670

[D]   My last letter to you was a fortnight ago accompanied by your current account, by which a balance of £489 12s 7d is due to me. With it I gave you news of the sale of 74 coils of copper-wire at £6 10s per cwt. to William Wathing. Since then I have received yours of the 28th of February from which I see that you have returned home in good health, which I am very glad to learn. God grant that you may long remain so.

I see that you have received the sale account of the 2,357 coils of wire, found it correct and thus made a record of it, which is good. Of the remaining copper-wire I have sold 150 coils to Nathaniel Humphreys and others at £6 6s per cwt., which you will please make a note of. I had thought of continuing the price at £6 10s but there is always someone who will interfere, be it well or badly. This certain person, who has received several consignments from [Sweden], has had 200 coils from Hamburg which, as soon as it arrived, he sent a barge alongside to fetch the 200 coils and went selling it at £6 5s per cwt, payable in 4 months according to what the buyer tells me, which is 5s below the market price. I cannot conceive what his purpose is in doing so but, meanwhile, that is the reason why I have had to sell at £6 6s. How would it have been if the consignment had been bigger? I fear it would have gone badly. Therefore I would be very glad if you gentlemen [in Sweden] could agree to send all your copper-wire to me here, so that with all of it in one hand the price could be maintained and our friends could make a profit. I am inclined to believe that that will come to pass (which I heartily wish for) for my Lord Cronström informed me in his letter of 19 February that, upon the return to Stockholm of Abraham Wolters from Hamburg, I shall be sent some terms of correspondence and that he has recommended me. Whatever may come of it I shall be glad to learn for I would be happy to see your trade flourish, of which there is a sufficient prospect as it would be of great advantage to those gentlemen. For me, that is the most important consideration, and I look out for any way of serving you better; and, in order to encourage our friends in this matter I shall be content (with regard to the trade in copper-wire and copper-wares) with $1\frac{1}{2}$ per cent commission and 5 per cent per annum for interest on money advanced upon current account. As regards discount, that would continue at 6 per cent as most of the debts only get paid in cash 1, 2 or 3 months after the due date. You could put this proposal (if it suits you) to our other friends and I have no doubt that it will greatly facilitate the business.

As regards the sale of goods, you will have no reason for anything but satisfaction, and the interests of our friends will always remain uppermost with me. Please now write to our friends to submit this proposal and let me know what success you have. I would not trouble you with this if it were not that the matter concerns you principally, so I hope you will forgive me. Yours, &c.

Amsterdam:	35s 2g	
Hamburg:	35s 3g	2 usances.
Antwerp:	35s 2g	
Rouen:	55d	

[A6] SAME to SAME

LONDON   20 MAY 1670

[D] My last letter to you was about a week ago, to which I refer. I have since had your very welcome letters of the 25th and 29th of April and 6th of May. With the first I see that I run a great risk of losing my good old correspondents; with the second you give me reason to hope that you will stand by me, and with the last you confirm that you will continue with me and thereupon order me to get insured for £5,000 the goods which you propose to consign to me in the ship called *t'Graffelycke Huys de la Gardie*, which I shall negotiate to have done at the best possible terms and will inform you when I succeed. Meanwhile, I am waiting for the bill of lading and beg God to bring the ship and its cargo in safety, and whenever it arrives I shall do the utmost within my powers to sell the goods for your greatest profit. One pays 2 per cent here for insurance from Stockholm, and I hope to be able to select good insurers at that price, for which I shall do my best.

By way of answer to your welcome letters I must say, truthfully, that your complaints have upset me not a little, for I have not been accustomed to hear such things from my friends, though my comfort has been that you would find me innocent of the intention which you charge me with. For the £200 formerly drawn by you on me, payable to the order of Antony Bruyn, has been fulfilled by me without the least delay or disrespect to your bill, and I shall reimburse myself from the effects which you will be sending me this spring. It is true that in passing I wrote a word about it to the Messrs Van Baerle asking, if they did not mind, if I might set it against the account of goods which I had in hand; but I never sought nor in the least intended to reimburse myself out of the goods which I had in hand, or to divert anything against their intentions or goodwill. They misunderstood what I wrote, and as soon as I had their answer about the bill (the £200 being by then already paid) I wrote back to them without a moment's loss that they had badly interpreted my letter and that—as I have said above—I only wanted to be reimbursed from the promised effects; and since they informed me that they had written to you about the matter as they understood it, so I begged you to forgive the blunder and to think no more about it, as I now do, hoping that no such error will recur again.

Now, I rejoice from the bottom of my heart that my proposal came in time to confirm our correspondence, and the conditions which I therewith offered I confirm with this, trusting that you and the other friends will be content with them and do nothing to reduce the commission. I can well believe that some people from other places may offer to serve you for 1 per cent commission (although that is very little for a person who wants to do his duty properly) but London differs considerably from other places, and I would say that a person can profit more in Hamburg by working for 1 per cent than here for 2 per cent, and one can do more there with one servant than here with two; for over there they have banks where most money is paid; the town is small, and thus all your debtors are under your eye; there are few difficulties in the Customs house; great quantities are bought, mainly for re-export elsewhere, and for cash. But here it is different. We have to receive and pay out all our money ourselves, and the town is large and many customers live 2 or 3 miles from the Exchange, to whom one has to run, which causes expense and for which several people have to be employed. The trouble we have with our customs officials is impossible to describe, for there is no question, quibble or quirk but they know how to torment the merchant with it; and then, in order to sell the goods, one has to deal with people who will only buy small quantities and then take pleasure in making me and my servants run after them for payment over 2 or 3 months; so, considering all that, I hope you will think and believe that my commission is very reasonable and be satisfied that, as regards the iron, the commission may also be reckoned at $1\frac{1}{2}$ per cent.

If you give orders to draw some sum on me at the same time that you send the bill of lading and instructions for insurance, as you are proposing, I shall follow your orders on the understanding that your intention will be to draw only a part of the value of the goods, for an insurance policy cannot be thought of as complete cover—firstly, because it is customary here in case of a loss (from which, may God preserve us!) for the insurers to deduct usually 10, 12 or 15 per cent of the principal, and thus the premium here is always smaller than at Amsterdam or Hamburg, &c; but if the goods have arrived here I shall be always ready to advance three-quarters or more of the value, either by remitting the money or having it drawn on me, as it suits you.

One reason which has impelled me to want to serve our friends for $1\frac{1}{2}$ per cent commission and 5 per cent per annum interest has been to be excused from advancing anything before I first have goods in hand, so that some of my clients—who entrust me with considerable sums—may be so much the easier in their minds. However, in order to demonstrate to you my affection and respect, I shall be happy to extend a thousand or twelve hundred pounds advance during the winter to be reimbursed by you in the spring, just as you have proposed, never in the least doubting your punctuality. I beg you to say or write nothing about this to anyone because I am not contemplating advancing anything to other friends in such a manner, and whenever they learn that one is allowing one friend such terms they think they have a right to demand similar ones.

I heartily wish you had informed me about your displeasure over what I wrote to Messrs Van Baerle concerning the aforementioned £200, and I thank you warmly for telling me about it now, begging you in our future friendship to write to me if it should ever happen that you have some occasion for displeasure; and I promise you that I shall respond in such a way as to remove all misunderstanding, for some time things can be said or done with the best of intentions (or, at least, without evil intentions) which being otherwise interpreted can turn out badly. Wherewith, cordial regards, &c.

Amsterdam: $35s$ $1g$
Hamburg: $34s$ $11g$
Antwerp: $34s$ $10g$ } 2 usances.
Rouen: $55\frac{1}{4}d$

APPENDIX B

ABRAHAM KOCK-CRONSTRÖM'S DRAFT
COMMISSION CONTRACT OF 1668

Among Marescoe's miscellaneous papers can be found this draft contract, endorsed by him 'Propositien van Sr Abraham Cock Cronstrom om in Correspondentie met mij te treeden, myn gesonden door Sr Johan Hanson—O[ntfangen] Xbre 1668 B[eantworden] 29 January noch beantwoort 26 February op een bysonder pampier als hier in te sien'. The terms of the contract have been summarized above in Chapter 3 and are reproduced here in the original Dutch (with contractions expanded).

[Side 1—a summary of terms, probably in Cronström's hand and initialled by him]

'1. 2 p.cent provisie van Incoop & vercoop en daer voor wordt de Asseurantie ook gedaen.
2. $\frac{1}{3}$ p.cent voor disponeering van gelde.
3. $\frac{1}{2}$ p.cent courtage te modereeren alsoo anders het genieten.
4. Op effecten gelden te verschieten a 5 p.cent soo inhanden en op die soo in der weegens a 6 p.cent als de cognossement aen hem gesonden en de asseurantie door hem gedaen is.
5. Sonder effecten in blanco te staen van soo veel als hij zall willen doen de somme te nomineeren.
6. Kort reekening te leeveren.

Daertegens obligeere mij met niemant andere te corresponderen als met hem en p. alle occasie zulke soortements te leveren als hij zall vinden te debiteeren—teweeten van draet, Ijzer en cooper.'

[Side 2—Marescoe's comments, in his own hand]

'1. Twee p.cent provisie van incoop & vercoop van goederen is well, maer de provisie voor d'asseurantie can daeronder niet loopen. Ick hebbe voor myn reekening goede sommen laeten verasseureerd tot Hamburg & Amsterdam ende noyt minder betaelt als $\frac{1}{3}$ p.cent provisie, ende het gemeynste dat hier genoomen wort daer voor is $\frac{1}{2}$ p.cent gelycke verscheyde vrinden van deese landen mij alloueeren, doch sall mij voor Ue met $\frac{1}{3}$ p.cent contenteeren.
2. $\frac{1}{3}$ p.cent voor disponeeren van gelden is well.
3. $\frac{1}{2}$ p.cent courtage voor vercoop van goederen is het minste dat ick oyt betaelt hebbe, maer men betaelt well somtyts $\frac{2}{3}$, ja 1 p.cent, doch sall niet meer in reekening brengen als $\frac{1}{2}$ p.cent courtage voor incoop van goederen wort niets betaelt, courtage van asseurantie is $\frac{1}{4}$ p.cent & van gelden p. wissell $\frac{1}{8}$ p.cent.
4. Op effecten in handen wort d'interest van verschooten penning altyt gereekent tot $\frac{1}{2}$ p.cent s'maents, doch indien het daer op aencompt om Ue daer mede te accomodeeren ick sall het tot 5 p.cent s'jaer doen, versoekende Ue belieft te notteeren dat Ue hier door ge-excuseert wort van groote schaede dat op trecken & hertrecken valt & ick misse mijn provisie—indien Ue iets begeert te hebben op goederen die onderweegens syn soo moet daer op d'asseurantie door my gedaen syn ende d'cognossement moet regel reght sonder indossement van Ue coomen.
5. Ick can niet well begrypen wat Ue hier mede segge will, doch als wij eens in kennis met

malcanderen coomen ende goede correspondentie houden sonder defidentie oft achterdencken ick sall well thien oft vyfthien hondert ponden will verschieten teegens $\frac{1}{2}$ p.cent s'maents in Marty om gereimbeurseert te worden tot goederen die Ue int voorjaer sall senden.

6. Vercoop oft incoop reekening sall ick Ue senden soo haest als de partyen gecompteert sullen syn & voorts een reekening courant alle jaer oft wanneer Ue sulcx sall begeeren.

7. Dit is in consideratie dat Ue met mij hier alleen sall believen te correspondeeren, ende mij met alle occasien senden sulcke sortimenten van iser, messingh-draet, cooper, etc als ick sall connen vinden te debitteeren oft vercoopen.'

[A further document, in a different hand and endorsed by Marescoe 'O[ntfangen] 16 Marty', sets out the following terms]

'Versoeck te weeten oft Ue volgende conditien soo ick ander weegen genoeten soudet gelieven integaen & t'accordeeren:

1. Op effecten tot de volle waerde sulke sommen t'avanceeren als noodig moogte syn, tegens intresse van 6 p.cent als de goederen in handen ende selve a prix courant vercoopen moogt.

2. Op effecten onderweegens synde waervan de cognossement afgesonden en d'asseurantie gedaen wisselbrieven t'accepteeren tot de $\frac{1}{2}$ oft $\frac{2}{3}$ vanden beloop.

3. Sonder effecten t'avanceeren, en op de naeste cargaisonen tot de somma van 5–6–7,000 RD, doch deese 2 puncten verstaen sig maer bij occasie en winter tyden oft andere casuelle toevallen.

4. De provisie soude men alsdan a 2 p.cent accordeeren en $\frac{1}{2}$ p.cent voor d'asseurantie, als de goederen niet arriveerden, maer arriveerende niet meer als 2 p.cent voor alles.

5. Dan soude men oock geobligeert syn niemandt anders tegebruycken en buyten dat meer andre commissien sien met handen tebrengen waer toe goede cause alsdan soude syn.'

APPENDIX C

THE IMPORTS AND EXPORTS

The Journals, Ledgers and Invoice book, supplemented by the letters and loose accounts, enable one to identify most of the Marescoe-David imports and exports between 1664 and 1678 by value and volume. Identification is less reliable after 1678. Within this period the firm received some 650 different shipments and despatched over 880, and a full list of their details would occupy some 40 pages.

Table A.1 summarizes the principal imports (almost all but the linen and dyestuffs exclusively from Sweden) by volume and value. Not tabulated, although included under the gross totals, are small amounts of wine and raisins from Malaga, some Spanish and Polish wool (from Bilbao and Hamburg respectively) and some £638-worth of hemp and cable from Gothenburg received in 1667.

Table A.2 summarizes the exports by destination and value. They include some 80 different commodities (even if cloth and calicoe are not differentiated by type) ranging from almonds, ambergris, aniseed and arsenic to vitriol, wax, whalefins and wine. However, Table A.3 lists the principal export commodities with an indication of their major destinations in percentage shares.

APPENDIX C—TABLE A.1. Principal Marescoe-David imports, 1664–1677, c.i.f.

Year	Iron		Copper		Latten,	Battery	Pitch & Tar			Timber	Linen	Dyes	Gross Totals
Jan.–Dec.	Cwt.	£	Cwt.	£	Cwt.	£	Lasts		£	£	£	£	£
							P.	T.					
1664	32,063	21,000	1,100	7,333	40?	242	289	755	11,702	—	558	667	41,790
1665	12,558	9,555	973	6,868	96?	579	127	420	7,039	—	816	—	25,098
1666	22,179	14,923	1,246	7,655	130?	784	294	212	7,043	1,601	324	—	34,208
1667	14,874	10,274	1,479	8,368	200?	1,198	172	109	3,582	5,583	2,556	904	34,136
1668	24,811	17,635	3,156	18,457	390?	2,273	276	724	10,290	3,441	—	159	53,558
1669	33,986	23,055	838	4,690	36	221	333	720	10,651	—	54	449	39,401
1670	12,621	9,876	1,614	9,508	312	1,875	274	855	10,436	1,844	65	244	34,734
1671	11,326	8,482	1,282	7,915	294	1,912	126	—	1,314	—	77	70	20,154
1672	29,160	20,783	1,201	7,250	251	1,542	156	67	2,184	201	—	—	32,684
1673	6,834	4,675	397	2,391	21	138	46	—	434	180	—	—	7,837
1674	19,000	13,658	2,984	17,458	226?	1,355	42	—	416	374	—	—	34,066
1675	6,708	4,695	440	2,306	—	—	2		25	86	—	—	7,133
1676	14,514	10,232	844	7,421	310	1,855	—	—	—	—	—	66	19,574
1677	5,182	3,444	222?	1,376	—	—	149	705	9,679	—	—	—	14,975

APPENDIX C—TABLE A.2. Marescoe-David exports by destination, 1664–1678, f.o.b.

Year	Sweden £	Hamburg £	United Provinces £	Spanish Netherlands £	France £	Spain £	Italy £	Levant £	E. Baltic £	Others £	Gross Totals £
1664	—	7,057	686	407	668	164	—	—	—	—	8,983
1665	—	152	42	1,114	292	440	—	—	—	—	2,039
1666	699	1,267	—	1,623	1,394	1,193	—	—	—	—	6,177
1667	—	779	1,842	74	6,783	2,755	887	—	—	—	13,118
1668	2,074	11,584	10,725	1,494	3,095	2,698	2,032	—	—	—	33,703
1669	—	4,293	2,767	2,744	1,628	743	4,638	—	—	—	16,812
1670	91	3,674	482	483	3,497	1,044	1,472	—	—	91	10,745
1671	—	5,824	318	—	2,104	414	741	—	—	—	9,400
1672	583	2,579	—	130	887	1,349	1,738	—	—	—	7,267
1673	—	1,517	—	—	1,160	1,210	81	—	—	—	3,967
1674	24	4,056	1,626	761	786	1,148	342	—	153	—	8,896
1675	2,612	2,704	—	—	2,033	135	863	769	53	—	9,170
1676	—	1,622	744	—	4,989	1,320	—	703	—	320	9,699
1677	659	4,577	458	—	3,674	1,914	—	—	—	105	11,387
1678	2,055	2,858	—	—	4,573	2,918	458	—	72	28	12,961
Totals	8,799	54,542	19,688	8,830	37,565	19,445	13,251	1,472	279	453	164,324*

* All totals have been rounded to the nearest £.

APPENDIX C—TABLE A.3. Principal export commodities, 1664–1678.

Percentage share of total exports	Commodity	Gross value (f.o.b.)	Principal destination	Percentage share
18.82	Sugar	£30,259.7	Hamburg	69.1
12.78	Cloth	£20,927.0	Spain	100.0
10.50	Lead	£17,221.9	France	35.5
			United Provinces	32.3
			Italy	30.1
6.80	Cottons: *Barbados* 60% *Turkish* 28% *E. Indian* 10%	£11,119.7	Sp. Netherlands	48.3*
			Hamburg	30.2
			France	11.2
5.24	Copper-wire	£8,575.8	France	95.5
4.90	Galls	£8,010.2	Hamburg	63.4
4.80	Indigo	£7,860.2	Hamburg	63.9
4.50	Ginger	£7,437.6	Hamburg	94.0
4.26	Tin	£6,979.0	Italy	33.9
			United Provinces	32.3
			France	27.5
3.52	Pepper	£5,765.4	Italy	61.8
3.18	Silk	£5,204.4	Hamburg	58.9
2.06	Oil	£3,365.0	Sp. Netherlands	58.2

* In this instance I have ignored the transfer of Lille to France in 1667–8 since both before and after its cession it was the major destination of the firm's exports of cotton.

APPENDIX D

SHIPPING

Notwithstanding the constraints of the Navigation Acts, there was nothing in the nature of the Marescoe-David firm's book-keeping which required full or accurate record of the nationality, let alone the tonnage, of the shipping it employed. Several hundred original bills of lading survive, notably for 1668, 1669, 1671, 1672, 1675, 1677, 1678, and 1679, but they do not always provide reliable evidence of a vessel's identity or size, or even proof that it was actually consigned to, or by, the firm. Fortunately, it was customary for the Journal entries to name the captain and ship responsible for goods imported or exported. The payment of customs and port charges, and the levying of commission on exports, tends to appear in the record at or near the departure date of a consignment. The dating of importing vessels is less easy, for freight, customs and unloading charges were often debited to the account only when the goods were sold and the account closed—sometimes months later. One may deduce from the warehousing charges (where they occur) just how long that interval has been, and the steady stream of shipping news in the incoming letters also provides corroboration of a vessel's movements. But the dating of imports and import-shipping is necessarily tentative, and the only reliable basis for establishing the seasonality of arrivals is provided for 1669–71 alone by the small pocket-book which belonged to Charles Marescoe and was completed by his successors. The few London port-books which survive for this period cannot, by their nature, provide a satisfactory alternative to the firm's own record.

The amalgamation of this imperfect evidence allows one to identify 315 captains, responsible for 423 of the 592 *export* voyages in which the firm participated between June 1664 and December 1678.

Of the 430 *import* voyages which brought goods to the firm between June 1664 and December 1679, 402 have identifiable captains representing 290 different individuals. Fifty-four of these also appear among the exporting captains. Thus, the total number of identifiable, individual captains employed by, or for, the firm over this period is 551, and of these 238 (or 43 per cent) are either ascertainably or probably English, drawn not only from London, Bristol, Newcastle, Hull or Yarmouth, but from Bridlington and Brighthelmstone, Colchester and King's Lynn, Whitby, Wivenhoe and Weymouth. The proportion of English skippers is, predictably, higher among exporting voyages (47.6 per cent) than among importing ones (37.9 per cent) where Dutchmen, Hamburgers and Swedes predominate. Several of the latter were veterans in the service of the Västervik Ship Company, appearing regularly year after year, but even they were eclipsed by Hamburg captains such as Willem Olofson (14 voyages), Andries Rump (11 voyages) or Dirck and Hendrick Roys (14 voyages between them) who combined the carriage of copper-wire across the North Sea with shorter cross-Channel export freights on the London firm's behalf. Indeed, the versatility of the Hamburg skippers is conspicuous and does much to explain why the English government was so suspicious of their possible Dutch identity.

APPENDIX D—TABLE A.4. Export voyages, 1664–1678.

Destination	64	65	66	67	68	69	70	71	72	73	74	75	76	77	78	Total
Dublin														1	1	2
Riga															1	1
Danzig											2	1			1	4
Stockholm					3		1		1		1	1		3	5	
Norrköping					2											19
SWEDEN			2													
HAMBURG	10	2	2	2	26	14	10	18	11	7	18	11	12	14	14	171
Amsterdam					24	11	3	1			5			3		
Rotterdam					4	1					1		2			
Middelburg					3											69
UNITED PROVINCES	3	1		7												
Antwerp					1	2	3		1		1					
Bruges					6	7	1		1							
Ostend											1					52
Nieuport					1	1										
SP. NETHERLANDS	2	7	16	1												
Dunkirk							3				2				5	
Calais						3	1		1							
St Valéry						5	8	7	6	6	7	6	1			
Abbeville							1	3	3	1	1					138
Rouen					9		1	2	1	3		3	11	7	10	
Bordeaux													8	1	1	
FRANCE	4		1	7												
Bilbao						1	1					3	6	8	9	
Cadiz					7	4	1½		3	5	4	1			3	
Malaga							1	2	2	1				1		81½
Alicante																
SPAIN	2	2	5	8												
Genoa														1		
Leghorn					2	10	4	1	3	1	1	2½				
Venice					6	11	3½	2	1							50
ITALY				1												
Aleppo												1½	2			3½
TOTALS	21	12	26	26	94	70	43	36	34	24	44	30	42	38	52	592

APPENDIX D—TABLE A.5. Export voyages, seasonality of departures, 1664–1678.

	Jan.	Feb.	Mar.	Apr.	May	June	July	Aug.	Sep.	Oct.	Nov.	Dec.	TOTAL
Ireland						2							2
East Baltic					1		2		1	1			5
Sweden			1	4		2	2	2	2	3	1		17
Hamburg	3	9	15	8	12	12	14	18	23	17	17	7	155
United Provinces	5	5	10	8	5	5	2	5	2	6	1	4	58
Sp. Netherlands		3	3		4	4	1	1	2	3	2	3	26
France	7	12	12	7	8	8	8	10	12	16	13	13	126
Spain	5	2	6	5	$4\frac{1}{2}$	9	2	8	8	8	4	3	$64\frac{1}{2}$
Italy	2	2		3	$5\frac{1}{2}$	2	7	6	7	$4\frac{1}{2}$	10		49
Middle East		1								$\frac{1}{2}$		1	$2\frac{1}{2}$
Totals	22	34	47	35	40	42	40	50	57	59	48	31	505
		27.3%				34.1%				38.6%			

APPENDIX D—TABLE A.6. Import voyages, 1664–1679.

Origin	64	65	66	67	68	69	70	71	72	73	74	75	76	77	78	79	Total
Riga				1													
Danzig		1															
Norway				6													
Sweden	15	12	19	19	36	26	28	14	18	4	18	8	?	?	17	17	
Hamburg	1		1	6	3	7	7	2	1	?	?	1	2	?	10	1	
United Provinces				2	2		2	8					?				
Sp. Netherlands	4	4	5	3													
France			2	2									?	3			
Spain	2			3	1	2		1	1	1			?	3	6	5	
Italy	1														?	1	
Middle East													1	?			
Totals	23	17	27	41	43	41	38	25	20	9	18	10	18	28	40	25	430

APPENDIX E

INSURANCE

Marine insurance formed an integral part of Marescoe's dealings with his Swedish suppliers. Under the terms of Article 5 of his 1668 Tar Company contract his obligation to advance credit upon goods in transit was conditional on their being properly insured in London,[1] and Willem and Jacob Momma likewise accepted the costs of insurance in London as the price for Marescoe's loans.[2] David similarly was frequently commissioned to place insurance of goods on the Baltic–London routes and, in addition, both men acted as brokers for, and participants in, a series of private insurances covering a wide range of Atlantic and Mediterranean routes.

The evidence left by these transactions confirms the picture, sketched long go by Violet Barbour,[3] of a comparatively mature European insurance market with its principal centres located in Hamburg, Amsterdam, London, Rouen, Paris and Genoa. On their relative merits Jacob Lucie was in no doubt that Hamburg was much to be preferred[4] and Marescoe admitted, more than once, that London's speciously cheaper premiums disguised the convention that the insured was expected to bear 10 to 15 per cent of any loss.[5] Thus, few of the firm's Hamburg or Amsterdam correspondents show much interest in the London market, and then only in the context of a war or blockade which rendered their own market inoperable.[6] Indeed, the limitations of London sometimes obliged additional cover to be sought in Amsterdam. Philip Botte's pitch and tar depots at Blackwall and Cuckold's Point were insured in this way[7] and in the winter of 1671–2 Jacob Reenstierna had to cover cargoes partly in London (at 5 and 6 per cent), partly in Amsterdam (at $4\frac{1}{2}$ per cent) and partly in Hamburg and Paris.[8]

Nevertheless, despite his disparaging verdict of 1656, Marescoe in the 1660s was evidently able to turn to a reliable if small group of London insurers to cover most of his needs. Between June 1664 and April 1668 his Journal records 108 policies, underwritten by 31 insurers. Participation tended to be concentrated in 10 individuals who account for nearly 84 per cent of the £40,000 covered by these policies, vizt.

53 policies	John Berry	£6,082 10s
40	Peter Lupart	£4,165
38	Nicolas Skinner	£4,900
29	John Sweeting	£3,150
25	Joas Bateman	£2,365
23	Thomas Fowke	£6,300
22	Edward Bouverie	£2,512 10s
17	Samuel Swynock	£1,500
15	Oliver Bowles	£1,225
10	Daniel Sochon	£1,000

It can be deduced from these figures that for most of the underwriters (with the exception of the wealthy Alderman Fowke) commitment to any one policy averaged about £100, although variations actually occurred within the range £25 to £400, vizt.

2 at £400	3 at £75
7 at £300	2 at £62 10s
2 at £250	2 at £60
37 at £200	63 at £50
26 at £150	1 at £40
208 at £100	3 at £35
5 at £80	2 at £25

The total 'lines' underwritten were thus 363, totalling £39,715.

A decade later, Jacob David's clientele exhibits some interesting differences. Between 1673 and 1677 he negotiated only 36 policies, but the total insured was £30,770 and the number of underwriters totalled at least 77.[9] Where four or five insurers had sufficed for most of Marescoe's policies, many of David's required more than ten. In one instance 33 subscribed to cover totalling £2,600. Although John Berry and Joas Bateman still appear among the leading underwriters there were several active newcomers, and among the minor participants one finds Michael and Benjamin Godfrey as well as Abraham, Isaac, John and Peter Houblon. Robert Knightley, Gerrard Lloyd, Daniel Andrews, George Marwood and George Sitwell (who figured in Barbour's sample policy of 1676)[10] all appear among Jacob David's enlarged circle. Its ten leaders include, with:

19 policies	John Berry	£2,200
17	Joas Bateman	£1,250
17	Geoffrey Nightingale	£1,575
15	Samuel Lethieullier	£1,475
15	George Torriano	£1,650
14	Richard Jenkinson	£1,350
13	Claude Hays	£950
12	Christopher Lethieullier	£1,150
12	Peter Paravicini	£750
12	George Sitwell	£1,100

With risks now more widely spread the average sum underwritten had fallen to £83.6, and the range had narrowed to £180, vizt.

15 at £200	11 at £75
1 at £175	146 at £50
8 at £150	3 at £33⅓
6 at £125	4 at £25
173 at £100	1 at £20,

making a total of £30,770 underwritten by 368 'lines'.

The greater caution implied by these figures may well reflect the painful experience of two decades troubled by wars and bad winters. Certainly by 1671 there had evidently been sufficient losses in foul winter weather to blunt London's appetite for North Sea insurance at any premium after September,[11] and one may deduce from the lengthy period which it took to procure signatories to some of David's autumnal policies that his clientele was a more reluctant and demanding one than Marescoe's. Commencing one Stockholm–London policy for £800 in October 1675 at 5½ per cent he had to re-negotiate in November at 6 per cent and by late December the last six of thirteen underwriters were successfully demanding 8 and 10 per cent.

The differential here is large enough to suggest that this policy may have been converted from 'risks of the sea alone' to 'all risks' (i.e. including enemy action) but since the ship in question was English this seems improbable. Regrettably, the Journal entries relating to insurance are rarely precise about the nature of the cover nor about its object, whether ship or cargo. In most cases it can be safely assumed to be the latter, and for 'risks of the sea alone' but occasionally the alternatives are specified. In August 1672 Willem Momma thought that the differential between 'all risks' at 4 per cent and 'risks of the sea alone' at 2 per cent was sufficiently small to justify taking the former,[12] and in a small number of instances insurance was sought on both ship and goods.

Yet, as Barbour noted, it was not unusual for cover to be incomplete, extending only to a portion of the cargo's value. This Marescoe's Journal confirms, for in three consecutive cases of loss incurred in 1666, valued at £600, £400 and £450, it was admitted that cover extended only to £270, £300 and £400 respectively. Settlements with the underwriters at 27 per cent, 85 per cent and 84 per cent of the principal insured were amicably reached over a business lunch—'op een middach maeltyt'—costing £2 7s.[13]

In the great majority of cases the Marescoe-David firm's exports and imports were evidently shipped uninsured, but—as the analysis of shipping movements reveals—a high proportion of the Swedish consignments and the largest percentage of the export voyages were commenced in the last and most dangerous third of the year.[14] The recorded policies, particularly on the Stockholm–London route, therefore tend to be concentrated in these months, but there are just sufficient examples in late summer to exhibit the seasonal movement by which premiums could double or treble between July and December.[15]

Marescoe's identifiable insurances are tabulated below according to roughly-defined areas; those of Jacob David between 1673 and 1679 are arranged in chronological sequence, and are made up of (A) those policies for which he acted as a broker, and (B) those policies in which he was underwriter. The latter series commenced in March 1677, and by April 1679 David had committed himself to insure £5,945 on 75 policies, vizt.:

1 at £300	1 at £70
5 at £200	1 at £60
2 at £150	23 at £50
1 at £125	16 at £25
25 at £100	2 at £20

The ventures were not rewarding ones: by 4 August 1679 David had to record a loss of £35 9s 3d to set against premiums totalling £315 15s.

---

[1] Tar Company Directors to CM, 11 December 1669.

[2] W. Momma to CM, 22 August 1669; CM to J. Momma-Reenstierna, 20 May 1670 (see Appendix A [**A6**]).

[3] V. Barbour, 'Marine risks and insurance in the seventeenth century'. *Journal of Economic and Business History*, I (1928–29) pp. 561–96.

[4] RA, Stockholm, E.2512, J. Lucie to J. Momma-Reenstierna, 11 June 1672.

[5] RA, Stockholm, E.2525, J. Buck & CM to A. & J. Momma, 12 December 1656 (see Appendix A [**A2**]; E.2513, CM to J. Momma-Reenstierna, 20 May, 1670 (see Appendix A [**A6**]).

[6] E.g. P. Berenberg to LM & PJ, 5 April 1672; F. Bostelman to JD, 5 October 1675; Marcus Fonck to JD, 16 December 1678.

[7] See p. 167.

[8] RA, Stockholm, E.2512, J. Lucie to J. Momma-Reenstierna, 24 November 1671, 15 March 1672.

[9] Three or four names are unclear.

[10] Barbour, op. cit. p. 594.
[11] RA, Stockholm, E.2512, J. Lucie to J. Momma-Reenstierna, 12 September 1671.
[12] W. Momma to LM & PJ, 18 August 1672.
[13] Journal (1664–68), 19 March 1666.
[14] See Appendix D, Table A.5.
[15] For detailed patterns of seasonality in eighteenth century marine insurance see F. C. Spooner, *Risks at Sea: Amsterdam insurance and maritime Europe, 1766–1780* (Cambridge, 1983).

TABLE A.7. CM's insurance policies, 1664–1669.

Date	No. of policies	From	To (i)	To (ii)	G(oods) & or S(hip)	Risks	Premium (%)
(A) BALTIC & NORTH SEA							
(i) 8 July 64	1	Archangel	Leghorn				9
(ii) 13 Dec. 66	1	Holland	Norway	London	S & G	Sea	5 & 7
23 Jan. 67	1	Holland	Norway	London	S	Sea & French	5
24 Jan. 67	1	Holland	Norway	London	S & G	All risks	8 & 9
(iii) 28 Dec. 67	1	Gothenburg	London		G	Sea	5
(iv) 6 July 64	1	Stockholm	London		—		2
16 Sep. 64	3	Stockholm	London		—		2
27 Sep. 64	2	Stockholm	London		G		2
21 Oct. 64	3	Stockholm	London		G		3
27 Oct. 64	1	Stockholm	London		G		3
11 Nov. 64	1	Stockholm	London		G		3
11 Nov. 64	2	Stockholm	London		G		$3\frac{1}{2}$
16 Nov. 64	3	Stockholm	London		G		$3\frac{1}{2}$
24 Nov. 64	1	Stockholm	London		G		$3\frac{1}{2}$
2 Dec. 64	2	Stockholm	London		—		5
21 Dec. 64	1	Stockholm	London		G & S		4 & 5
24 Dec. 64	1	Stockholm	London		—		6
3 Aug. 66	3	Stockholm	London		G	Sea	$2\frac{3}{4}$
24 Aug. 66	1	Stockholm	London		G	Sea	$2\frac{3}{4}$
26 Oct. 66	1	Stockholm	London		G		5
28 Dec. 66	1	Stockholm	London		G	Sea	$6\frac{1}{2}$
28 Dec. 66	1	Stockholm	London		G	Sea	5
25 Jan. 67	1	Stockholm	London		—		5
26 Aug. 67	1	Stockholm	London		G		3
31 Aug. 67	1	Stockholm	London		G		2
24 Dec. 67	3	Stockholm	London		G		3
(v) 26 Apr. 67	1	Norrköping	London		G		4
1 May 67	1	Norrköping	London		G		4
(vi) 4 Jan. 67	1	Leirvik	London				5
13 Dec. 66	1	Holland	Norway	London	S & G	Sea	5 & 7
24 Jan. 67	1	Holland	Norway	London	S & G	All risks	8 & 9

The following 9 draft policies survive among Marescoe's miscellaneous papers, partially underwritten:

Date	No. of policies	From	To (i)	To (ii)	G(oods) & or S(hip)	Risks	Premium (%)
(vii) 24 Dec. 68	1	Stockholm	London				4.4
12 July 69	2	Stockholm	London				$1\frac{1}{2}$

TABLE A.7 (*cont.*)

	Date	No.	From	To	To	Code	Notes	No.
	12 July 69	1	Stockholm	Bristol				2½
	6 Oct. 69	2	Stockholm	London				2
	21 Oct. 69	1	Stockholm	London				3½
	23 Nov. 69	1	Stockholm	London				3½
	24 Nov. 69	1	Stockholm	London				3½
	26 Nov. 69	2	Stockholm	London				3½
	15 Dec. 69	1	Stockholm	London				5
(viii)	28 Sep. 69	1	Gothenburg	London				1¼
(ix)	3 Dec. 69	1	Stockholm	Cowes, I.o.W.				4
(x)	8 May. 67	1	Setubal	Stockholm		S & G		5
	6 Sep. 67	1	Setubal	Gothenburg		G		4.4

B) CHANNEL AND ATLANTIC COASTS

Date	No.	From	To	To	Code	Notes	No.
28 Dec. 65	1	Dover	Amsterdam		G		2
13 July 67	2	Ostend	Amsterdam		G		2
19 Dec. 65	1	Hull	Amsterdam		G		10
21 Oct. 67	1	Plymouth	London		S		2
3 Mar. 65	1	La Rochelle	Amsterdam		G		6
26 Apr. 66	1	La Rochelle	London		G		12
30 Mar. 67	2	London	La Rochelle		G		7
13 Jan. 65	1	London	Charante		G		3½
18 Apr. 67	1	London	Newcastle	La Rochelle	G		8
31 May 67	2	Newcastle	La Rochelle		G		4 & 5
13 Apr. 68	1	Cadiz	London		G		2 & 2½
1 Oct. 64	1	Cadiz	Bristol		G	Turks & Moors	2
30 Mar. 67	1	Malaga	Bristol		G		12
24 Aug. 65	1	Cadiz	Limerick				10
22 May 65	1	Bristol	Setubal	Bristol			14
8 Feb. 65	1	Virginia	Bristol				7
10 Feb. 65	1	Virginia	Bristol				6
20 Feb. 65	1	Virginia	Bristol				6½
2 Mar. 66	3	Virginia	Bristol				16
12 Mar. 66	2	Virginia	Bristol				14
9 Aug. 64	1	Bristol	Virginia	Bristol			3
2 Feb. 65	3	Bristol	Virginia	Bristol			6
6 June 65	1	Bristol	Virginia	Bristol			8
30 Nov. 65	1	Bristol	Virginia	Bristol			16
4 Apr. 67	1	Bristol	Virginia	Bristol			17 & 18
18 Apr. 67	1	Weymouth	Virginia	Weymouth	G		14
8 Feb. 65	1	Nevis	Bristol				7
25 Feb. 65	1	New England	Virginia	England	S		9
22 Aug. 64	1	England	New Eng'd-Virginia-England				30
3 Mar. 65	1	Barbados	London		G		7
16 Mar. 65	1	Barbados	London		G		8
8 July 65	1	Barbados	London		G		9
21 Oct. 67	1	Barbados	London		G		3
8 May 67	1	London	Barbados		S & G		5
17 Jan. 65	1	London	Tangier	London			6
13 Apr. 68	1	London	Guinea				5½, 6 & 7
2 Feb. 65	1	London	India	London			12
6 Feb. 65	1	London	India	London			12

TABLE A.8. JD's insurance policies, 1673–1679.

Date	From	To	Premium (%)
(A)			
1 July 73	Stockholm	London	5
15 Aug. 73	Stockholm	London	5
29 Aug. 73	Stockholm	London	5
19 Sep. 73	Stockholm	London	$5\frac{1}{4}$
? Nov. 73	Stockholm	London	6
5 Dec. 73	Stockholm	London	$6\frac{1}{2}$
12 May 74	London	Rouen	2.3
31 July 74	Stockholm	London	$4\frac{1}{2}$
14 Aug. 74	Stockholm	London	$4\frac{1}{2}$
15 Aug. 74	Stockholm	London	$4\frac{1}{2}$
28 Aug. 74	Stockholm	London	$4\frac{1}{2}$
5 Sep. 74	Stockholm	London	$4\frac{1}{2}$
30 Sep. 74	London	St Valéry	2
9 Oct. 74	Stockholm	London	5
27 Nov. 74	Stockholm	London	5
18 Dec. 74	Stockholm	London	5
18 Dec. 74	Stockholm	London	7
1 June 75	London	Aleppo	2
? Oct. 75	Stockholm	London	$5\frac{1}{2}$
? Nov. 75	Stockholm	London	6
? Dec. 75	Stockholm	London	8 & 10
7 Sep. 76	Stockholm	London	$6\frac{1}{2}$
20 Sep. 76	London	Bordeaux	2
4 Oct. 76	London	Bordeaux	2
10 Oct. 76	Stockholm	London	7
13 Oct. 76	Stockholm	London	$7\frac{1}{2}$
19 Oct. 76	Stockholm	London	8
23 Oct. 76	London	Bordeaux	$2\frac{1}{2}$
27 Oct. 76	Stockholm	London	7
5 Dec. 76	London	Bordeaux	$2\frac{1}{2}$
4 Apr. 77	London	Stockholm	4
12 Apr. 77	London	Bordeaux	5
4 May 77	London	Bordeaux	4
17 July 77	London	Dublin	2
(B)			
8 Mar. 77	Scanderoon	London	3
12 Apr. 77	London	Rouen	2.3
19 May 77	Lisbon	Venice	2
19 May 77	Scanderoon	London	3
19 May 77	London	Leghorn	2
27 June 77	London	Bremen	$2\frac{1}{2}$
20 Aug. 77	Nevis	London	$2\frac{3}{4}$
20 Aug. 77	Genoa	Palermo	2
20 Aug. 77	London	Amsterdam	$1\frac{1}{2}$
24 Aug. 77	Lisbon	Naples	5

Date	From	To	Premium (%)
24 Aug. 77	Malaga	London	$2\frac{1}{2}$
6 Sep. 77	Venice	London	3
11 Sep. 77	Venice	London	3
5 Oct. 77	London	Rouen	$1\frac{3}{4}$
5 Oct. 77	Canaries	London	$3\frac{1}{4}$
8 Oct. 77	London	Rouen	$1\frac{3}{4}$
16 Oct. 77	Dublin	Lisbon	4
18 Oct. 77	London	Rouen	2
23 Oct. 77	London	St Valery	2
23 Oct. 77	London	Cadiz	3
23 Oct. 77	Scanderoon	Marseille	6
24 Oct. 77	Virginia	London	5
24 Oct. 77	Zante	London	5
31 Oct. 77	Oporto	London	5
1 Nov. 77	Venice	Cadiz	6
2 Nov. 77	Malaga	London	$4\frac{1}{2}$
2 Nov. 77	Venice	Amsterdam	$10\frac{1}{2}$
2 Nov. 77	Bordeaux	Rotterdam	4
6 Nov. 77	Smyrna	Amsterdam	11
6 Nov. 77	Scanderoon	Leghorn	6
6 Nov. 77	Venice	Cadiz	7
9 Nov. 77	Smyrna	London	$12\frac{3}{4}$
9 Nov. 77	Falmouth	Barcelona	10
9 Nov. 77	Gravesend	Cadiz	4
9 Nov. 77	Villa Nova	London	$5\frac{1}{4}$
10 Nov. 77	Newfoundland	The Straits	10
13 Nov. 77	Canaries	London	$3\frac{1}{2}$
13 Nov. 77	The Downs	Rotterdam	$1\frac{3}{4}$
13 Nov. 77	Scanderoon	Leghorn	$7\frac{1}{2}$
13 Nov. 77	London	Cadiz	2
21 Nov. 77	Amsterdam	Smyrna	5
21 Nov. 77	Hamburg	Cadiz	$5\frac{1}{4}$
21 Nov. 77	'Russia'	Leghorn	$12\frac{3}{4}$
21 Nov. 77	Canaries	London	$3\frac{1}{2}$
23 Nov. 77	Archangel	London	$33\frac{2}{3}$
24 Nov. 77	'Russia'	Leghorn	$12\frac{1}{2}$
24 Nov. 77	Malaga	Plymouth	4.4
28 Nov. 77	Oporto	London	$3\frac{1}{2}$
29 Nov. 77	London	Genoa	$3\frac{1}{2}$
3 Dec. 77	Zante/Cephalonia	London	$8\frac{2}{3}$
4 Dec. 77	Canaries	London	4
5 Dec. 77	Nantes	London	$2\frac{1}{2}$
5 Dec. 77	Oporto	London	$3\frac{1}{2}$
5 Dec. 77	London	Leghorn	4
29 Dec. 77	Cadiz	London	$2\frac{1}{2}$
3 Jan. 78	London	Cadiz	3
20 Feb. 78	London	Bordeaux	4
14 Mar. 78	London	Rouen	$4\frac{1}{4}$
26 Aug. 78	London	Dunkirk	1

TABLE A.8 (*cont.*)

Date	From	To	Premium (%)	Date	From	To	Premium (%)
19 Sep. 78	Cadiz	London	5	7 Apr. 79	London	Marseille	3
18 Oct. 78	London	Marseille	3	7 Apr. 79	London	Bordeaux	3
18 Dec. 78	London	Lisbon	2	10 Apr. 79	London	Oporto	$3\frac{1}{4}$
				10 Apr. 79	Majorca	London	$3\frac{1}{2}$
19 Mar. 79	London	Rouen	2	16 Apr. 79	London–Guinea–	Jamaica	10
20 Mar. 79	Alicante	Le Havre	4	16 Apr. 79	London	Nevis	3
20 Mar. 79	Marseille	Alicante	6				
21 Mar. 79	London	Rouen	$1\frac{1}{2}$				
4 Apr. 79	Madeira	Barbados	9				

APPENDIX F

FREIGHT RATES

Although there is abundant information on freight-rates scattered through the Journals, miscellaneous papers and in-letters, when it is broken down (i) by routes, (ii) by commodities, and (iii) by season, very little remains that can be presented as a long-run series. The only commodities and route which provide even a patchy sequence are, of course, iron and pitch and tar on the Stockholm–London run.

The rates for these were usually quoted in terms of the rixdollar at a given valuation in sterling—e.g. '8 rixdollars per last at 4s 6d sterling per rixdollar'. In 1667 the valuation rose to 4s 9d and in spring 1668 was still 4s 7d before returning to its customary 4s 6d. Supplementary to this freight-rate were three other rates expressed always in sterling—(i) *caplaken* or hat-money, a traditional gratuity to the captain, usually amounting to between 1s and 2s sterling per last, (ii) pilotage, also about 1s per last, and (iii) primage, a gratuity of 6d per last intended for the crew, though usually paid to the captain. These sterling items, which together could add between 2s 6d and 4s per last to the basic freight, oblige one to translate the total into shillings and pence in Table A.9 below. Uncertainty about departure dates allows one only to estimate the seasons to which the rates apply, whether (I) January–April, (II) May–August, or (III) September–December. But the resulting picture is quite distinct, of a trebling of freight-rates during the second Anglo–Dutch war, followed by a fall in 1668 to levels still somewhat higher than in 1664. The shipping depression of 1671 is followed by rising rates in 1672 but the peaks are not reached until the outbreak of the Scanian war in 1675. Thereafter Stockholm–London rates were at the mercy of English shipowners, but the Swedish–Dutch commercial treaty of 1676 seems to have relieved the pressure and allowed Philip Botte to secure English freights at £2 per last or less by 1678.

The significance of these rates becomes clearer when they are assessed as a charge on the gross sale-proceeds of the cargo. For high-value copper the freight burden was comparatively light, averaging about 1.7 per cent of the yield, but for iron it could amount to 19 per cent and for pitch and tar it often exceeded 21 per cent. These percentages dwarf the combined burden of customs duty, port charges and the $2\frac{5}{8}$ per cent commission which together averaged 10 per cent for iron and 7 per cent for pitch and tar. Furthermore, while customs and commission payments were simply an internal transfer, the freight payments (frequently handed over in cash at the firm's counting-house and signed for by the captain) were a significant sterling transfer in the settlement of England's deficits in the Baltic and a useful source of currency for Sweden in its purchases of French wine or Portuguese salt. One may estimate that 10 per cent of the value of Sweden's exports to England were transferred in this manner, 10 per cent absorbed internally, and 80 per cent transmitted across the European exchanges.

The burden of London–Hamburg freight-rates cannot be assessed as a percentage of the yield of commissioned exports for this is unknown, but the rates themselves suggest a pattern similar to those for Stockholm–London, stiffening in the late autumn and rising sharply in the years of war after 1672. However, comparison of unit-costs between commodities is rendered almost impossible, partly by the variety of accounting units used—rixdollars, schillings flemish, marks lüb. etc.—and by the imprecision of bulk units, such as sacks, bags,

APPENDIX F—TABLE A.9. Stockholm to London freight-rates (in shillings/pence).

		Iron	Copper	Pitch & Tar
1664	I	29/6	29/6	47/6
	II	38/0	35/0:42/0	50/0:55/0
	III	37/6:40/0	37/6:42/0	55/6:56/0
1665	I	39/9	46/6:47/6	56/0
	II	43/6:57/0	48/6:57/0	57/0:58/0
	III	56/6:78/6	81/6:90/0	82/6:93/0
1666	I	91/6:92/6	92/6	
	II	83/6:92/6	92/6	91/6
	III	83/6:87/7	92/6	65/9:81/0
1667	I			
	II	67/6:90/0	54/0:58/6	
	III	54/0:61/0	57/6:65/6	54/0:56/6
1668	I			50/0:54/0
	II	40/6:45/0	54/0	46/3:49/6
	III	31/6:39/6	33/0	49/6:50/6
1669	I	31/6:36/0	54/0	40/6:47/6
	II	40/6:43/10	54/0	46/0:50/7
	III			54/0
1670	nil			
1671	I		31/0:40/6	36/0:40/6
	II			
	III	27/0:31/6	36/0	
1672	I			
	II	42/9:54/0	54/0:58/6	
	III	40/6:45/0	36/0	
1673	nil			
1674	III	38/3:49/6		
1675	II	71/6:80/0		
	III	80/0:90/0		
1676	II	54/0		
	III	70/0		
1677	II	60/0	60/0	60/0
	III	40/0		40/0
1678	nil			
1679	II	35/0:40/0	45/0	

hogsheads and pieces. Averaging the known weights of Marescoe-David 'sacks' reveals that while sacks of galls weighed about 325 lb., and of pepper about 310 lb., bags of cottons averaged 220 lb. and ginger only 80 lb.—but variation could range between $+17\%$ and -5% around the mean. Thus the only commodity which yields even the semblance of a series is Barbados sugar, for which the freight-rate was given in rixdollars per last (Table A.10).

APPENDIX F—TABLE A.10. London to Hamburg: sugar freight-rates, 1668–1680, in rixdollars per last.

	1668	1669	1671	1672	1675	1679
Jan.	—	—	—	—	—	—
Feb.	6	—	—	—	—	—
Mar.	6	—	—	—	—	—
Apr.	6	—	—	10	—	—
May	—	—	—	11	—	—
June	6	—	—	—	—	—
July	—	$3\frac{1}{2}$	—	—	—	4
Aug.	6	4	—	—	—	—
Sep.	6	5	5	—	—	4
Oct.	—	—	3	—	7	5
Nov.	7	—	3	—	7	—
Dec.	8	—	—	—	—	—

APPENDIX G

EXCHANGE RATES

Good manners, if not explicit instructions, required merchants in most European centres to keep their customers informed of the current rates of exchange. The information was routinely placed at the close of a letter and appears there in much of the Marescoe-David correspondence from Hamburg, Amsterdam, Rouen, Paris and Venice. It is conspicuous by its absence in letters from Sweden or Spain for the sound reason that England's settlements with these countries were not usually made by a direct transfer across the exchanges. Hamburg and Amsterdam were the preferred routes for London's remittances on Sweden's account and it is the rates on these centres that Marescoe and David chose to quote in their letters to Stockholm (see Appendix A). As for Spain, transfers of value were usually in the form of the one-way traffic in clandestine bullion movements, and it is thus the premium on silver or gold which the firm's Seville or Bilbao agents have to record.

Yet, quotations of exchange rates hurriedly scribbled at the last moment on a busy post-day clearly lack the authority which accompanies the printed price-currents or exchange-courses prepared by the sworn brokers and patentees of the Amsterdam, Hamburg or London bourses. Slips of the pen were possible, and one cannot know at what time or on what range of evidence any quotation is taken. Few correspondents were as obliging as Abraham & Simon Vrouling of Rouen who, on 5 April 1678, noted that the rate on London was '$58\frac{1}{4}d$ ce matin, aprez $\frac{1}{2}$, a la fin $\frac{3}{4}d$'. Yet rates could move dramatically in a few days' trading. At Hamburg the response to the outbreak of the third Anglo–Dutch war in March 1672 was a 16-point fall in the rate on London within one week. On 6 June 1679 Danish menaces induced a 4-point fall, and there are occasional discrepancies of a similar scale between quotations sent at the same time from the same centre by different correspondents which must reflect the range of movement in the market that day.

Thus, with letters arriving from Hamburg, Amsterdam or Rouen at an average of four or five per week, it is possible to assemble a record of oscillations at these centres which is more sensitive than any that could be provided by the official weekly price-currents, even if they had survived in their entirety. As it is, space does not permit here more than a weekly indication of the lowest and highest rates reported, nor does it allow one to reproduce the running commentary on movements which several correspondents provide. It will have to suffice to say that while some writers shared the scepticism of the Parisian banker, Louis Froment—'quant aux changes, il est difficile de juger s'ils hausseront ou baisseront—on joue bien au hazard'—others offered firm predictions and confident analyses founded on ascertainable commercial and political prospects. The arrival of the *flota* or *galeones*, the holding of the English or Dutch East India Company sales, the size of the Bordeaux *vendange*, were conjunctures whose effects could be anticipated some weeks ahead. Less predictable were the movements of French subsidies to northern Europe, or the arrival in Hamburg of a Dutch convoy blown off course, but these could be quickly discounted by an adjustment in rates. Most feared were the paralysing consequences of a merchant bankruptcy which might trigger off a chain of failures in several centres. Such epidemics occurred at Amsterdam in the spring of 1669, in London in early 1676 and in Hamburg through the winter of 1677–8. For the exchanges their consequences were a curtailment of credit and a hardening of rates. But, even at the best of times, too much money could be chasing too few bills or, more rarely, too many bills could be chasing too little money as in Amsterdam during the welcome peace of late 1678. When such local disequilibrium occurred it was natural for the more adventurous dealers to practise arbitrage—dealing with a third centre where the rates on the second centre might prove more advantageous. The margins between Paris and Rouen, between Amsterdam and Antwerp were watched like hawks by dealers in London and Hamburg for some such opportunity. In June 1676 the rising rate on London at Amsterdam and the high premium on Antwerp bills made sense of Claude Hays' advice to David that he should use his credits in Amsterdam to secure short-dated bills on Antwerp. At other times a favourable Venice–Amsterdam exchange might encourage the London firm to settle its Hamburg debts by this round-about route. Thus the rates quoted in these letters were rarely confined to the bilateral terms between London and the correspondent's centre. One or two major dealers, such as Bartolotti & Rihel of Amsterdam, enclosed the full printed range of European exchange-quotations, from Danzig to Madrid, but this was exceptional. The principal centres for which quotations are frequent enough to justify weekly tabulation below are:

A. HAMBURG on (i) London; (ii) Amsterdam; (iii) Antwerp;
(iv) Paris; (v) Rouen; (vi) Venice.
B. AMSTERDAM on (i) London; (ii) Hamburg; (iii) Antwerp;
(iv) Paris (v) Rouen; (vi) Venice.
C. ROUEN & PARIS on (i) London; (ii) Amsterdam.
D. VENICE on (i) London; (ii) Amsterdam.

The tabulated figures require some explanation, although this is not the place for a detailed introduction to the technicalities of the early modern European exchanges. That task has been admirably performed by Professor John McCusker in his *Money and Exchange in Europe and America, 1600–1775: A Handbook* (London, 1978). The classic *Inquiry into the History of Prices in Holland* (Vol. I) by N. W. Posthumus (Leiden, 1946) also provides a full guide to Amsterdam's European exchange network. For the Paris exchange on London there are illuminating contemporary comments in John Locke's travel journals, cited in *Locke's Travels in France, 1675–1679*, ed. John Lough (Cambridge, 1953) pp. 180, 188, 190, 195, 200, 203, 204, 256, 259, 266, 267, 272. Locke's quotations have been incorporated, in square brackets, in Table A11 [c] below. The basic information required to interpret the figures below is, firstly, the nature of the monetary units in which the quotation of rates is given; secondly, the terms of 'usance' which the given rates assume; thirdly, the agio or premium between 'bank-money' (in which most quotations are made) and current money.

1. A. HAMBURG quotations on:
   (i) London are in schillings flemish (bank-money) per £1 sterling. The par of exchange was 32s flem. per £1 sterling but, as John Scarlett notes in his invaluable *The Stile of Exchanges* (London, 1682) the usual 'course' was 35s 6g.
   (ii) Amsterdam and (iii) Antwerp are in stuivers (bank-money) per Hamburg thaler (of 32 schillings-Lübeck per thaler). The par was $33\frac{1}{3}$ stuivers.
   (iv) Paris and (v) Rouen are in schillings-Lübeck per écu of 3 livres tournois.
   (vi) Venice are in grooten flemish per Venetian bank-ducat.
Note: 1 schilling flemish (or 12 grooten) was equivalent to 6 schillings Lübeck in Hamburg and to 6 stuivers in the Netherlands. The Hamburg thaler is not to be confused with its reichsthaler (or rixdollar) worth 48s lübs.

B. AMSTERDAM quotations on:

  (i) London are in schellings flemish (bank-money) per £1 sterling. 'The par betwixt London and [the Netherlands]' wrote Scarlett 'is reckoned generally to be 34s 4d for the Pound Sterling. But the course varies from 36s 3d Flemish to 37s and upwards'.

 (ii) Hamburg are as above, A (ii).

(iii) Antwerp are in percentage terms of the premium (or discount) payable in Amsterdam for a bill of exchange yielding £100 flemish in Antwerp. The par was $4\frac{1}{6}$ per cent—i.e. £96 flem. in Amsterdam procured £100 flem. in Antwerp.

 (iv) Paris and Rouen are in grooten flemish (bank-money) per écu.

  (v) Venice are in grooten flemish (bank-money) per Venetian bank-ducat.

C. PARIS and ROUEN quotations on:

  (i) London are in pence sterling per écu. The course in Scarlett's day was 54d or 55d.

 (ii) Amsterdam are as above, B (iv).

D. VENICE quotations on:

  (i) London are in pence sterling per Venetian bank-ducat. 'The course of Exchange for Venice from London is generally $50\frac{1}{2}$ to 50d sterling *in circa* for their Ducat in banco.' (Scarlett.)

 (ii) Amsterdam are as above, B (v).

2. The rates quoted also assume, or explicitly state, a 'usance' or customary interval between the date of a bill and the date when its payment falls due. Any bill could be made payable 'at sight' and those between Amsterdam and Hamburg invariably were, but the standard usance between many European centres was one month, and between London and continental centres it was usually double usance, or two months, expressed '2 usos'. In the tables below the rates quoted are at the following usance:

A. Hamburg on (i) London—at double usance, i.e. two months; (ii) Amsterdam, (iii) Antwerp, (iv) Paris, (v) Rouen—payable at sight; (vi) Venice—at 1 usance, i.e. two months.

B. Amsterdam on (i) London, (iv) Paris, (v) Rouen—at double usance, i.e. two months; on (ii) Hamburg, (iii) Antwerp—at sight; (vi) Venice—at 1 usance.

C. Rouen and Paris quotations are all at double usance.

D. The Venetian quotations are at single usance.

3. The final and most elusive qualification needed to interpret these figures is the agio, or premium payable in current money for bank money at Hamburg, Amsterdam or Venice. Although these agios fluctuated no less sensitively than the rate of exchange they are rarely quoted. The following instances have been noted:

A. HAMBURG:	1671	Week 37—$4\frac{1}{2}$%		1679	Week 2—$3\frac{1}{2}$%
		Week 45—$4\frac{1}{2}$-$4\frac{3}{4}$%			Week 36—4%

B. AMSTERDAM:	1668	Week 12—$3\frac{1}{4}$%		1672	Week 37—$5\frac{1}{2}$-6% loss
		,, 21—4%			,, 38—$6\frac{1}{2}$% loss
		,, 37—$3\frac{1}{2}$%			,, 40—5% loss
		,, 39—$3\frac{1}{2}$-$3\frac{3}{4}$%		1673	Week 9—3%
	1669	Week 6—$3\frac{3}{4}$%		1675	Week 8—$4\frac{1}{2}$%
		,, 29—3%			,, 25—$4\frac{1}{8}$-$4\frac{1}{4}$%
	1671	Week 15—$4\frac{3}{4}$-$4\frac{7}{8}$%		1676	Week 43—$4\frac{1}{4}$%
		,, 16—4%		1677	Week 1—4%
		,, 18—$4\frac{1}{4}$%			23—4%
		,, 21—$3\frac{3}{4}$%			27—$3\frac{3}{4}$%
		,, 23—$3\frac{3}{4}$%			
		,, 25—$3\frac{5}{8}$%		1678	Week 4—$3\frac{1}{4}$-$4\frac{1}{2}$%
		,, 29—$3\frac{5}{8}$%			,, 8—4%
		,, 36—$4\frac{1}{8}$%			,, 10—4%
		,, 39—$3\frac{7}{8}$-4%			,, 17—4%
		,, 41—$3\frac{7}{8}$%			,, 19—$3\frac{7}{8}$%
		,, 46—$3\frac{3}{4}$%			,, 23—$4\frac{3}{8}$%
	1672	Week 2—$3\frac{7}{8}$-4%			,, 33—$4\frac{1}{2}$%
		,, 26—$2\frac{1}{2}$-3% loss[1]			,, 37—4%
		,, 27—2-3% loss			,, 39—4%
		,, 32—3% loss		1679	Week 39—$4\frac{1}{4}$%
		,, 33—$1\frac{3}{4}$% loss			,, 48—$4\frac{1}{2}$%
		,, 34—$1\frac{7}{8}$% loss		1680	Week 13—$4\frac{1}{2}$%

[1] In the extraordinary conditions of June 1672, with its run on the Bank of Amsterdam, bank-money began to be sold at a discount for current coin—see [**197**]. J., D. & H. van Baerle to LM & PJ, 28 June 1672. On 12 September Huybert Huybertsen at Vlissingen reported the discount in Amsterdam to be 8 per cent, although the Van Baerles on the 16th put it at only $5\frac{1}{2}$-6 per cent. On 13 October Huybertsen invoiced LM & PJ with the proceeds and charges of exchanging £345 flemish bank-money at a 5 per cent discount, yielding £327 15s flem. *courant geld*, £325 net.

TABLE A.11. Exchange rates, 1668–1680.

[a] *Hamburg on London, Amsterdam, Antwerp, Paris, Rouen, Venice*

	1668		HAMBURG on:					
			London	Amsterdam	Antwerp	Paris	Rouen	Venice
1	Jan.	1– 7						
2		8–14						
3		15–21						
4		21–28						
5	Feb.	29– 4						
6		5–11						
7		12–18						
8		19–25	34/0	$32\frac{7}{8}$				
9	Mar.	26– 4	34/2–34/5	$32\frac{7}{8}$–33	$32\frac{1}{8}$–$32\frac{1}{4}$	$48\frac{3}{4}$–49	$48\frac{5}{8}$	$91\frac{1}{2}$–92
10		5–11	34/0–34/2	$32\frac{15}{16}$–$33\frac{1}{16}$	$32\frac{1}{3}$	$48\frac{3}{4}$		92
11		12–18	34/0–34/2	33	$32\frac{1}{4}$	$48\frac{3}{4}$		92
12		19–25	33/10–34/0	$33\frac{1}{16}$				
13	Apr.	26– 1	33/10–33/11	$33\frac{1}{16}$	$32\frac{1}{3}$–$32\frac{1}{2}$	$48\frac{1}{2}$–49		91
14		2– 8	33/9–33/10	33–$33\frac{1}{16}$				
15		9–15	33/10					
16		16–22	33/10–33/11	33	$32\frac{1}{3}$	49		91–$91\frac{1}{2}$
17		23–29	33/10–34/0	33–$33\frac{1}{16}$	$32\frac{1}{4}$	49	$48\frac{3}{4}$	91
18	May	30– 6	33/10–34/0	$33\frac{1}{16}$	$32\frac{1}{4}$	$48\frac{5}{8}$		91
19		7–13	33/9–33/10	33–$33\frac{1}{16}$	$32\frac{1}{4}$			91
20		14–20	33/8–33/10	$32\frac{15}{16}$–$33\frac{1}{16}$	$32\frac{1}{4}$–$32\frac{3}{4}$	$48\frac{3}{4}$		91
21		21–27	33/8–33/10	33–$33\frac{1}{16}$		$48\frac{3}{4}$		
22	June	28– 3	33/9–33/10	33–$33\frac{1}{16}$	$32\frac{1}{4}$			$91\frac{3}{4}$
23		4–10	33/10	$33\frac{1}{16}$	$32\frac{1}{4}$			92
24		11–17	33/10–34/0	$33\frac{1}{16}$–$33\frac{1}{8}$	$32\frac{1}{4}$–$32\frac{1}{3}$	$48\frac{3}{4}$		$91\frac{3}{4}$
25		18–24	33/10–34/0	$33\frac{1}{8}$	$32\frac{1}{8}$–$32\frac{1}{3}$			$91\frac{1}{2}$
26	July	25– 1	33/10–33/11	$33\frac{1}{8}$	$32\frac{3}{8}$–$32\frac{1}{2}$	$48\frac{3}{4}$–$49\frac{1}{4}$	$48\frac{1}{2}$–$48\frac{5}{8}$	$91\frac{1}{2}$
27		2– 8	33/10–33/11	$33\frac{1}{8}$	$32\frac{1}{2}$			91
28		9–15	33/10–34/0	$33\frac{1}{8}$–$33\frac{3}{16}$				91
29		16–22	33/11–34/0	$33\frac{1}{8}$	$32\frac{1}{4}$–$32\frac{3}{4}$	$49\frac{3}{8}$–$49\frac{1}{2}$		
30		23–29	34/1–34/3	$33\frac{1}{8}$	$32\frac{5}{8}$	$49\frac{1}{2}$		91
31	Aug.	30– 5	34/0	$33\frac{1}{8}$	$32\frac{5}{8}$–$32\frac{3}{4}$	$49\frac{1}{4}$–$49\frac{3}{4}$		91
32		6–12	34/0	$33\frac{1}{16}$–$33\frac{1}{8}$	$32\frac{1}{8}$–$32\frac{3}{4}$	$49\frac{3}{4}$		
33		13–19	34/0–34/1	$32\frac{7}{8}$–$33\frac{1}{16}$	$32\frac{1}{2}$	$49\frac{3}{8}$–$49\frac{1}{2}$		$91\frac{1}{2}$
34		20–26	34/0	$32\frac{15}{16}$–33		49		$91\frac{1}{2}$
35	Sep.	27– 2	34/0–34/2	$32\frac{7}{8}$–33	$32\frac{1}{2}$–$32\frac{7}{8}$	$48\frac{1}{4}$		$91\frac{1}{2}$
36		3– 9	34/0–34/3	$32\frac{15}{16}$–33	$32\frac{1}{2}$	49–$49\frac{1}{4}$		$91\frac{1}{4}$
37		10–16	34/2–34/5	$32\frac{7}{8}$–$33\frac{15}{16}$	$32\frac{1}{2}$	$48\frac{3}{4}$–49		$91\frac{1}{4}$
38		17–23	34/4–34/6	$32\frac{15}{16}$	$32\frac{7}{16}$–$32\frac{1}{8}$	$49\frac{1}{4}$–$49\frac{1}{2}$		$91\frac{1}{4}$–$91\frac{1}{2}$
39		24–30	34/6–34/7	$32\frac{15}{16}$	$32\frac{5}{8}$	49–$49\frac{1}{4}$		$91\frac{1}{4}$
40	Oct.	1– 7	34/6–34/7	$32\frac{3}{4}$–33	$32\frac{5}{8}$	$49\frac{1}{4}$		$91\frac{1}{4}$
41		8–14	34/6–34/7	$32\frac{3}{4}$–$32\frac{13}{16}$		$49\frac{1}{2}$		$91\frac{1}{4}$
42		15–21	34/6–34/7	$32\frac{3}{4}$–$32\frac{11}{16}$	$32\frac{1}{2}$	$49\frac{1}{2}$		
43		22–28	34/6–34/7	$32\frac{3}{4}$		$49\frac{1}{4}$		92
44	Nov.	29– 4	34/6	$32\frac{3}{4}$				
45		5–11	34/5–34/6	$32\frac{13}{16}$	$32\frac{1}{2}$	49		$91\frac{1}{4}$
46		12–18	34/4–34/5	$32\frac{13}{16}$	$32\frac{1}{2}$	$49\frac{1}{4}$		$91\frac{1}{4}$
47		19–25	34/5	$32\frac{7}{8}$	$32\frac{1}{2}$	$49\frac{1}{4}$		
48	Dec.	26– 2	34/5–34/6	$32\frac{13}{16}$	$32\frac{1}{2}$	49		$91\frac{1}{2}$
49		3– 9	34/4–34/5	$32\frac{13}{16}$	$32\frac{1}{2}$	49		92
50		10–16	34/6	$32\frac{13}{16}$	$32\frac{1}{2}$	49		
51		17–23	34/4–34/5	$32\frac{13}{16}$	$32\frac{1}{2}$			$92\frac{1}{4}$
52		24–31	34/5–34/7	$32\frac{3}{4}$	$32\frac{1}{4}$	49		92–$92\frac{1}{2}$

TABLE A.11 [a] (*cont.*)

	1669	HAMBURG on:					
		London	Amsterdam	Antwerp	Paris	Rouen	Venice
1	Jan. 1– 7	34/5–34/6	$32\frac{3}{4}$–$32\frac{13}{16}$				
2	8–14						
3	15–21					$49\frac{1}{2}$	
4	21–28	34/8	$32\frac{13}{16}$	$32\frac{3}{4}$	$49\frac{1}{4}$		
5	Feb. 29– 4					49	
6	5–11					49	
7	12–18	34/8	$32\frac{11}{16}$				
8	19–25	34/9	$32\frac{5}{8}$–$32\frac{11}{16}$			$49\frac{1}{4}$	$93\frac{1}{2}$
9	Mar. 26– 4	34/9	$32\frac{5}{8}$				$93\frac{1}{2}$
10	5–11	34/9	$32\frac{5}{8}$–$32\frac{11}{16}$				$93\frac{1}{2}$
11	12–18	34/7–34/8	$32\frac{5}{8}$	$32\frac{1}{4}$	$49\frac{1}{4}$–$49\frac{3}{8}$	49	$93\frac{3}{4}$
12	19–25					49	
13	Apr. 26– 1	34/8–34/9	$32\frac{5}{8}$				$93\frac{3}{4}$–94
14	2– 8	34/5–34/8	$32\frac{5}{8}$	$32\frac{3}{16}$	$49\frac{1}{4}$–$49\frac{1}{2}$	49	94
15	9–15	34/5–34/8	$32\frac{1}{2}$		$49\frac{1}{4}$–$49\frac{1}{2}$	49	94
16	16–22	34/8			$49\frac{1}{4}$	49	94
17	23–29	34/5–34/7	$32\frac{1}{2}$–$32\frac{9}{16}$				94
18	May 30– 6	34/6–34/7	$32\frac{1}{2}$				$93\frac{1}{2}$–94
19	7–13	34/5–34/8	$32\frac{1}{2}$		49	$48\frac{1}{2}$	94
20	14–20	34/8–34/9	$32\frac{1}{2}$	$32\frac{1}{2}$		$48\frac{1}{2}$	
21	21–27	34/8	$32\frac{1}{2}$		$48\frac{1}{2}$	$48\frac{1}{4}$	$93\frac{1}{2}$
22	June 28– 3						
23	4–10	34/8	32–$32\frac{1}{2}$		$48\frac{1}{2}$–49	$48\frac{1}{4}$	93–94
24	11–17	34/8	$32\frac{7}{16}$–$32\frac{1}{2}$				
25	18–24	34/8–34/10	$32\frac{1}{2}$		$48\frac{1}{2}$	$48\frac{1}{4}$	
26	July 25– 1	34/9	$32\frac{1}{2}$				
27	2– 8				$48\frac{1}{2}$	$48\frac{1}{4}$	
28	9–15	34/6–34/8	$32\frac{7}{16}$–$32\frac{1}{2}$	$32\frac{1}{2}$	$48\frac{3}{4}$	$48\frac{1}{2}$	
29	16–22	34/5–34/7	$32\frac{9}{16}$–$32\frac{5}{8}$	$32\frac{1}{8}$		$48\frac{1}{2}$	
30	23–29	34/5–34/6	$32\frac{5}{8}$–$32\frac{11}{16}$			$48\frac{1}{2}$	
31	Aug. 30– 5	34/5–34/6	$32\frac{11}{16}$–$32\frac{3}{4}$			$48\frac{1}{2}$	
32	6–12						
33	13–19	34/5–34/6	$32\frac{11}{16}$–$32\frac{13}{16}$	$32\frac{1}{8}$–$32\frac{3}{16}$	$48\frac{3}{4}$–$48\frac{7}{8}$	$48\frac{1}{2}$	93–$93\frac{1}{2}$
34	20–26	34/6–34/7	$32\frac{11}{16}$–$32\frac{3}{4}$			$48\frac{1}{2}$	
35	Sep. 27– 2	34/7	$32\frac{3}{4}$	$32\frac{1}{8}$	$48\frac{1}{2}$	$48\frac{1}{4}$	93–$93\frac{1}{4}$
36	3– 9	34/6–34/7	$32\frac{3}{4}$	$32\frac{1}{8}$			93
37	10–16	34/6–34/7	$32\frac{11}{16}$–$32\frac{3}{4}$	$32\frac{1}{8}$		$48\frac{1}{8}$	
38	17–23	34/8–34/9	$32\frac{5}{8}$–$32\frac{11}{16}$		48		93
39	24–30	34/7–34/10	$32\frac{1}{2}$–$32\frac{9}{16}$	$32\frac{1}{8}$	$47\frac{1}{4}$	47	93–$93\frac{1}{4}$
40	Oct. 1– 7	34/7–34/8	$32\frac{1}{8}$–$32\frac{7}{8}$	32	$47\frac{3}{4}$–48	$47\frac{1}{4}$	93
41	8–14					$47\frac{3}{4}$	
42	15–21	34/9–34/10	$32\frac{3}{8}$	32	$48\frac{1}{4}$	48	$93\frac{3}{4}$
43	22–28	34/9–34/10	$32\frac{3}{8}$		$48\frac{1}{4}$	48	
44	Nov. 29– 4	34/10	$32\frac{5}{16}$–$32\frac{3}{8}$	$32\frac{1}{8}$	$48\frac{1}{4}$	48	93
45	5–11	34/11	$32\frac{3}{8}$	32		$47\frac{3}{4}$–48	$93\frac{1}{2}$
46	12–18	34/8–34/10	$32\frac{1}{8}$–$32\frac{3}{8}$	$32\frac{1}{8}$	$47\frac{7}{8}$	$47\frac{1}{2}$–$47\frac{5}{8}$	$93\frac{1}{2}$
47	19–25	34/10–34/11	$32\frac{3}{16}$–$32\frac{1}{4}$	$32\frac{1}{8}$	47	47	
48	Dec. 26– 2	34/10–34/11	$32\frac{1}{8}$–$32\frac{3}{16}$	32–$32\frac{1}{8}$	$47\frac{1}{4}$–$47\frac{1}{2}$	$46\frac{1}{2}$–47	93–$93\frac{1}{4}$
49	3– 9	34/10–34/11	$32\frac{3}{16}$–$32\frac{1}{8}$	$32\frac{1}{2}$	$47\frac{7}{8}$–48	$47\frac{1}{4}$	93
50	10–16	34/9–34/11	$32\frac{3}{16}$	$32\frac{3}{16}$	$47\frac{5}{8}$–$47\frac{3}{4}$	$47\frac{1}{4}$	
51	17–23	34/8–34/10	$32\frac{1}{8}$	$32\frac{3}{16}$	$47\frac{3}{4}$	$47\frac{3}{8}$–$47\frac{1}{2}$	$92\frac{3}{4}$
52	24–31	34/7	$32\frac{1}{16}$			$47\frac{1}{4}$	

TABLE A.11 [a] (*cont.*)

1670			London	Amsterdam	Antwerp	Paris	Rouen	Venice
					HAMBURG on:			
1	Jan.	1– 7	34/6	$32\frac{13}{16}$	$32\frac{1}{16}$	$47\frac{3}{4}$	$47\frac{1}{2}$	92–$92\frac{1}{4}$
2		8–14						
3		15–21						
4		21–28	34/6–34/8	$32\frac{15}{16}$	$32\frac{1}{8}$	48	$47\frac{3}{4}$	$92\frac{1}{2}$–$92\frac{3}{4}$
5	Feb.	29– 4	34/7–34/8	$32\frac{7}{8}$–$32\frac{15}{16}$	$32\frac{1}{8}$	$48\frac{1}{4}$		$92\frac{1}{2}$
6		5–11						
7		12–18						
8		19–25						
9	Mar.	26– 4						
10		5–11						
11		12–18						
12		19–25						
13	Apr.	26– 1						
14		2– 8						
15		9–15						
16		16–22						
17		23–29						
18	May	30– 6						
19		7–13						
20		14–20						
21		21–27						
22	June	28– 3						
23		4–10						
24		11–17						
25		18–24						
26	July	25– 1						
27		2– 8						
28		9–15						
29		16–22						
30		23–29						
31	Aug.	30– 5						
32		6–12						
33		13–19						
34		20–26						
35	Sep.	27– 2						
36		3– 9						
37		10–16						
38		17–23	34/1–34/2	$32\frac{15}{16}$	$32\frac{3}{4}$			
39		24–30	34/3	$32\frac{15}{16}$	$32\frac{3}{4}$	$46\frac{3}{4}$	$46\frac{1}{2}$	
40	Oct.	1– 7						
41		8–14						
42		15–21						
43		22–28						
44	Nov.	29– 4						
45		5–11						
46		12–18						
47		19–25						
48	Dec.	26– 2						
49		3– 9						
50		10–16						
51		17–23						
52		24–31						

TABLE A.11 [a] (*cont.*)

1671		London	Amsterdam	Antwerp	Paris	Rouen	Venice
		HAMBURG on:					

	1671	London	Amsterdam	Antwerp	Paris	Rouen	Venice
1	Jan. 1– 7						
2	8–14						
3	15–21						
4	21–28						
5	Feb. 29– 4						
6	5–11						
7	12–18						
8	19–25						
9	Mar. 26– 4						
10	5–11						
11	12–18						
12	19–25						
13	Apr. 26– 1	34/7–34/9	$33\frac{1}{16}$–$33\frac{1}{8}$	33–$33\frac{1}{8}$	$47\frac{5}{8}$–$47\frac{3}{4}$	$47\frac{1}{4}$	
14	2– 8	34/7–34/8	$33\frac{1}{16}$	33	$47\frac{1}{2}$–$47\frac{3}{4}$		$90\frac{1}{4}$–$90\frac{1}{2}$
15	9–15	34/8–34/9	$33\frac{1}{16}$	33–$33\frac{1}{16}$	$47\frac{1}{2}$–$47\frac{3}{4}$		
16	16–22	34/8–34/9	$33\frac{1}{16}$	33–$33\frac{1}{16}$			$90\frac{3}{4}$
17	23–29	34/6–34/8	33–$33\frac{1}{16}$	33–$33\frac{1}{8}$	$47\frac{1}{2}$		$90\frac{1}{2}$–$90\frac{3}{4}$
18	May 30– 6	34/4–34/6	$33\frac{1}{16}$–$33\frac{1}{8}$	$33\frac{1}{16}$	$47\frac{1}{2}$		
19	7–13	34/3–34/6	$33\frac{1}{16}$–$33\frac{1}{4}$	$33\frac{1}{16}$			
20	14–20	34/4–34/6	$33\frac{1}{8}$	33	47		
21	21–27	34/5–34/6	$33\frac{1}{8}$–$33\frac{1}{4}$	33	$47\frac{3}{4}$		
22	June 28– 3	34/5–34/6	$33\frac{1}{16}$–$33\frac{5}{16}$		$47\frac{3}{4}$		
23	4–10	34/3–34/5	$33\frac{1}{8}$–$33\frac{1}{4}$		$47\frac{3}{4}$–$47\frac{7}{8}$		
24	11–17	34/3–34/4	$33\frac{5}{8}$		$47\frac{1}{2}$–$47\frac{3}{4}$		
25	18–24	34/3	$33\frac{1}{8}$–$33\frac{3}{8}$	33	$47\frac{5}{8}$–$47\frac{3}{4}$		
26	July 25– 1	34/1–34/3	$33\frac{1}{8}$–$33\frac{1}{4}$	33	$47\frac{1}{2}$–$47\frac{5}{8}$	$47\frac{1}{4}$	
27	2– 8	34/2	$33\frac{1}{8}$	33	$47\frac{1}{2}$–$47\frac{5}{8}$		
28	9–15	34/2–34/3	$33\frac{1}{8}$–$33\frac{3}{16}$	33	$47\frac{1}{2}$		
29	16–22	34/2–34/4	$33\frac{3}{8}$–$33\frac{7}{16}$	$32\frac{3}{4}$–33	$47\frac{1}{4}$		90
30	23–29	34/3–34/5	$33\frac{3}{8}$–$33\frac{7}{16}$	$32\frac{3}{8}$–$32\frac{7}{8}$	$47\frac{1}{4}$–$47\frac{1}{2}$	47	
31	Aug. 30– 5	34/4–34/5	$33\frac{1}{8}$–$33\frac{3}{8}$	$32\frac{3}{4}$–$32\frac{7}{8}$	$47\frac{1}{4}$	47	
32	6–12	34/5–34/6	$33\frac{3}{16}$–$33\frac{1}{4}$	$32\frac{5}{8}$–$32\frac{3}{4}$	47–$47\frac{1}{4}$		
33	13–19	34/4–34/5	$33\frac{1}{8}$–$33\frac{1}{4}$	$32\frac{3}{4}$–$32\frac{7}{8}$	47	$46\frac{3}{4}$	$89\frac{3}{4}$
34	20–26	34/4–34/6	$33\frac{1}{8}$–$33\frac{3}{16}$	$32\frac{3}{4}$–$32\frac{15}{16}$	47–$47\frac{1}{4}$		
35	Sep. 27– 2	34/4–34/5	$32\frac{15}{16}$–33	$32\frac{1}{2}$	$46\frac{3}{4}$–47		$89\frac{3}{4}$
36	3– 9	34/4–34/6	$32\frac{15}{16}$		47		
37	10–16	34/6–34/7	$32\frac{15}{16}$				
38	17–23	34/6–34/8	$32\frac{15}{16}$–$33\frac{1}{16}$		$46\frac{3}{4}$		
39	24–30	34/6–34/7	$33\frac{1}{16}$–$33\frac{1}{8}$		$46\frac{3}{4}$		
40	Oct. 1– 7	34/5–34/6	$33\frac{1}{8}$	$32\frac{7}{8}$–33	$46\frac{3}{4}$		
41	8–14	34/3–34/5	$33\frac{1}{16}$–$33\frac{1}{8}$	$32\frac{3}{4}$–33	$46\frac{3}{4}$–47	$46\frac{1}{2}$	
42	15–21	34/1–34/4	$33\frac{1}{8}$–$33\frac{3}{16}$	33	$47\frac{1}{2}$–$47\frac{5}{8}$	$46\frac{7}{8}$	
43	22–28	34/1–34/3	$33\frac{3}{16}$–$33\frac{1}{2}$	33–$33\frac{1}{16}$	$46\frac{3}{8}$–$47\frac{1}{2}$		
44	Nov. 29– 4	34/1–34/2	$33\frac{1}{16}$–$33\frac{1}{8}$	33–$33\frac{1}{16}$	46	46	$89\frac{1}{2}$
45	5–11	34/2	$33\frac{1}{8}$				
46	12–18	34/2–34/3	$33\frac{1}{8}$	$33\frac{1}{4}$	$46\frac{1}{4}$		
47	19–25	34/3–34/4	$33\frac{1}{8}$		$46\frac{1}{4}$–$46\frac{1}{2}$	46	
48	Dec. 26– 2	34/3–34/4	$33\frac{1}{16}$–$33\frac{1}{8}$	33	$45\frac{3}{4}$–$46\frac{1}{2}$	46–$46\frac{1}{2}$	$89\frac{1}{2}$
49	3– 9	34/3–34/4	$33\frac{1}{16}$–$33\frac{1}{8}$	$32\frac{15}{16}$	$46\frac{1}{4}$		
50	10–16	34/4	$33\frac{1}{8}$–$33\frac{1}{4}$				
51	17–23	34/3–34/4	$33\frac{3}{16}$–$33\frac{1}{4}$	$33\frac{1}{2}$	$45\frac{3}{4}$–$46\frac{1}{4}$		$89\frac{1}{2}$
52	24–31	34/3	$33\frac{1}{8}$				

TABLE A.11 [a] (*cont.*)

	1672	London	Amsterdam	Antwerp	Paris	Rouen	Venice
1	Jan. 1–7						
2	8–14	34/2	$33\frac{3}{16}$				
3	15–21	34/3	$33\frac{1}{4}$	33	$46\frac{3}{4}$		
4	21–28	34/3–34/4	$33\frac{3}{16}$	33	$46\frac{3}{4}$		$88\frac{1}{2}$
5	Feb. 29–4	34/3	$33\frac{1}{8}$		$46\frac{3}{4}$		$88\frac{1}{2}$
6	5–11	34/4–34/5	$33\frac{1}{16}$	$32\frac{7}{8}$–33	46–$46\frac{1}{2}$		
7	12–18	34/3–34/6	$32\frac{13}{16}$–$32\frac{15}{16}$				
8	19–25	34/5–34/6	$32\frac{3}{4}$		47		
9	Mar. 26–4	34/6–34/7	$32\frac{5}{16}$–$32\frac{1}{2}$	$32\frac{5}{8}$	47	$47\frac{1}{8}$	$88\frac{1}{4}$
10	5–11	34/8–34/10	$32\frac{1}{4}$–$32\frac{1}{2}$	$32\frac{1}{4}$	$46\frac{3}{4}$–47		
11	12–18	34/8–34/10	$32\frac{1}{4}$–$32\frac{5}{16}$		$46\frac{3}{4}$–47		
12	19–25	34/2–34/5	$32\frac{1}{4}$–$32\frac{1}{2}$	$32\frac{1}{4}$	$46\frac{1}{4}$–$46\frac{5}{8}$	46	
13	Apr. 26–1	32/8–33/0	$32\frac{9}{16}$–$32\frac{5}{8}$		$45\frac{3}{4}$–46	$45\frac{1}{2}$	
14	2–8	32/10–33/0	$32\frac{1}{4}$–$32\frac{5}{8}$	$32\frac{3}{8}$	$45\frac{1}{2}$	$45\frac{1}{2}$	
15	9–15	32/10–33/0	$32\frac{3}{8}$–$32\frac{5}{8}$		$45\frac{1}{2}$–46		$86\frac{3}{4}$–87
16	16–22						
17	23–29	32/10–33/0	$32\frac{1}{2}$	$32\frac{3}{8}$	$47\frac{1}{2}$	$47\frac{1}{4}$	$86\frac{1}{2}$
18	May 30–6	32/10–33/0	$32\frac{1}{2}$–$32\frac{5}{8}$	$32\frac{1}{2}$	47–$47\frac{1}{4}$	47	
19	7–13	33/0–33/1	$32\frac{7}{8}$–33	$32\frac{5}{8}$	47		87
20	14–20	32/9–32/10					
21	21–27	32/9–33/0	$32\frac{3}{8}$–$32\frac{7}{8}$	$32\frac{5}{8}$	46–$46\frac{3}{4}$	$46\frac{1}{2}$	$86\frac{1}{4}$
22	June 28–3	32/9	$33\frac{1}{4}$				
23	4–10	32/9	$34\frac{3}{4}$–35		46		86
24	11–17	33/0	$33\frac{1}{4}$–$33\frac{3}{4}$	$32\frac{7}{8}$	46		86
25	18–24	32/8–32/10	$34\frac{1}{2}$–35	$33\frac{1}{4}$	$46\frac{1}{4}$–$46\frac{1}{2}$		$86\frac{1}{2}$
26	July 25–1						
27	2–8	32/8–33/0	$33\frac{1}{2}$–$34\frac{1}{2}$	$32\frac{7}{8}$–33	46–$46\frac{1}{4}$		$86\frac{1}{2}$
28	9–15	32/9–33/0	34–$34\frac{1}{2}$	$32\frac{7}{8}$–33	46–$46\frac{1}{2}$		
29	16–22	33/0–33/1	$33\frac{3}{4}$	33	$46\frac{1}{4}$	$45\frac{3}{4}$	
30	23–29	33/0–33/1	$33\frac{1}{2}$–34	33			
31	Aug. 30–5	32/10–33/0	$33\frac{3}{4}$	$32\frac{1}{2}$–$33\frac{3}{4}$	$46\frac{1}{2}$–$46\frac{5}{8}$	$46\frac{1}{4}$	86
32	6–12	33/0–33/2	$33\frac{5}{8}$–$33\frac{3}{4}$				86
33	13–19	33/0–33/2	$33\frac{1}{8}$–$33\frac{1}{4}$	$32\frac{1}{2}$	$46\frac{3}{4}$–47		86
34	20–26	33/0–33/1	$33\frac{1}{8}$	$32\frac{1}{2}$	47		
35	Sep. 27–2	33/0	$32\frac{7}{8}$–33	$32\frac{1}{4}$–$32\frac{5}{8}$	47–$47\frac{1}{4}$		
36	3–9	33/0	$32\frac{11}{16}$–$32\frac{3}{4}$		$47\frac{1}{2}$		
37	10–16	33/0–33/1					
38	17–23	33/2–33/8	$32\frac{9}{16}$–$32\frac{3}{4}$	$32\frac{1}{4}$	$46\frac{1}{2}$–$46\frac{3}{4}$	$46\frac{1}{2}$	
39	24–30						
40	Oct. 1–7	33/6–33/8	$32\frac{1}{8}$–$32\frac{3}{8}$	$32\frac{1}{4}$			
41	8–14	33/8	$32\frac{1}{4}$	32	47		
42	15–21	33/6–33/8	$32\frac{1}{4}$	32–$32\frac{1}{8}$	$47\frac{1}{4}$–$47\frac{1}{2}$	47	
43	22–28	33/4–33/8	$32\frac{1}{4}$				
44	Nov. 29–4	33/0–33/4	$32\frac{1}{2}$	32	47–$47\frac{1}{4}$		$86\frac{1}{4}$
45	5–11	33/0–33/1	$32\frac{5}{8}$				
46	12–18	33/0–33/3	$32\frac{1}{8}$		47		
47	19–25	33/4–33/5	$32\frac{3}{8}$	$32\frac{1}{4}$	47		
48	Dec. 26–2	33/3–33/4	$32\frac{1}{4}$–$32\frac{5}{16}$				
49	3–9	33/6	$32\frac{1}{4}$	$32\frac{3}{8}$	$46\frac{3}{4}$	$46\frac{3}{8}$–$46\frac{1}{2}$	
50	10–16	33/6–33/7	$32\frac{1}{4}$		$46\frac{1}{2}$		
51	17–23	33/8	$32\frac{1}{4}$	$32\frac{3}{16}$	$46\frac{3}{4}$		$86\frac{3}{4}$
52	24–31	33/8–33/9					

TABLE A.11 [a] (*cont.*)

1673		HAMBURG on:					
		London	Amsterdam	Antwerp	Paris	Rouen	Venice
1	Jan. 1– 7						
2	8–14						
3	15–21	33/9	$32\frac{1}{2}$		$46\frac{7}{8}$		
4	21–28						
5	Feb. 29– 4	33/5–33/6	32	$32\frac{1}{8}$	$46\frac{1}{2}$	$46\frac{1}{4}$	$86\frac{1}{2}$
6	5–11						
7	12–18	33/6	$32\frac{5}{8}$	$32\frac{3}{8}$–$32\frac{1}{2}$			$86\frac{1}{2}$
8	19–25						
9	Mar. 26– 4	33/4	$32\frac{1}{2}$		$46\frac{1}{2}$		
10	5–11	33/3–33/4	$32\frac{5}{8}$				
11	12–18	33/2–33/3	$32\frac{5}{8}$–$32\frac{11}{16}$				
12	19–25						
13	Apr. 26– 1						

1674		HAMBURG on:					
		London	Amsterdam	Antwerp	Paris	Rouen	Venice
40	Oct. 1– 7						
41	8–14						
42	15–21						
43	22–28						
44	Nov. 29– 4						
45	5–11						
46	12–18						
47	19–25						
48	Dec. 26– 2						
49	3– 9	31/6	$34\frac{1}{2}$		46		
50	10–16	31/7	$34\frac{5}{8}$	$34\frac{1}{4}$			88
51	17–23	31/6–31/7	$34\frac{5}{8}$–$34\frac{11}{16}$				$88\frac{1}{4}$
52	24–31	31/6–31/7	$34\frac{5}{8}$–$34\frac{11}{16}$	$34\frac{1}{2}$	46–$46\frac{1}{2}$		$88\frac{3}{4}$–89

TABLE A.11 [a] (*cont.*)

	1675		HAMBURG on: London	Amsterdam	Antwerp	Paris	Rouen	Venice
1	Jan.	1– 7						
2		8–14	31/8	$34\frac{5}{8}$		$46\frac{1}{2}$		87
3		15–21	31/5–31/7	$34\frac{15}{16}$	$34\frac{1}{2}$	$46\frac{1}{2}$–$46\frac{3}{4}$	$46\frac{1}{2}$	87
4		21–28	31/4–31/5	$34\frac{7}{8}$–$34\frac{15}{16}$	$34\frac{1}{2}$–$34\frac{5}{8}$	47	$46\frac{1}{2}$	87–$87\frac{1}{2}$
5	Feb.	29– 4	31/4–31/7	$34\frac{3}{4}$–$34\frac{13}{16}$	$34\frac{3}{4}$	$47\frac{1}{4}$	47	87
6		5–11	31/6–31/7	$34\frac{9}{16}$–$34\frac{3}{4}$	$34\frac{1}{2}$			$86\frac{3}{4}$
7		12–18	31/8–31/10	$34\frac{9}{16}$–$34\frac{5}{8}$	$34\frac{1}{2}$	$46\frac{3}{4}$		$86\frac{3}{4}$
8		19–25	31/11–32/0	$34\frac{5}{8}$–$34\frac{11}{16}$	$34\frac{3}{4}$–$34\frac{1}{2}$	$46\frac{3}{4}$	$46\frac{5}{8}$	$86\frac{3}{4}$
9	Mar.	26– 4	31/10–32/0	$34\frac{1}{2}$				
10		5–11	32/0–32/1	$34\frac{1}{2}$	$34\frac{1}{4}$	47–$47\frac{1}{8}$	47	$86\frac{3}{4}$
11		12–18	32/1–32/2	$34\frac{7}{16}$–$34\frac{1}{2}$	$34\frac{1}{4}$	$47\frac{3}{8}$	$47\frac{1}{8}$	$86\frac{3}{4}$–87
12		19–25	31/10–32/2	$34\frac{7}{16}$–$34\frac{1}{2}$		47–$47\frac{1}{4}$		$86\frac{3}{4}$
13	Apr.	26– 1	32/1	$34\frac{7}{16}$				
14		2– 8	32/1	$34\frac{7}{16}$	34	$47\frac{1}{4}$		
15		9–15	32/1–32/2	$34\frac{9}{16}$		47		
16		16–22	31/10–32/0	$34\frac{5}{8}$–$34\frac{11}{16}$	$34\frac{1}{8}$	$46\frac{5}{8}$–47		$87\frac{1}{4}$
17		23–29	31/9–32/1	$34\frac{5}{8}$–$34\frac{11}{16}$	$34\frac{1}{8}$	47–$47\frac{1}{4}$		
18	May	30– 6	32/4	$34\frac{5}{8}$	$34\frac{3}{4}$	$47\frac{1}{2}$	$47\frac{1}{4}$	87
19		7–13	32/1–32/2	$34\frac{5}{8}$				87
20		14–20	32/3–32/5	$34\frac{3}{4}$–$34\frac{7}{8}$	$34\frac{5}{8}$	47	$46\frac{7}{8}$	$86\frac{1}{2}$
21		21–27						
22	June	28– 3	31/11–32/4	$34\frac{7}{8}$	$34\frac{5}{8}$	47	$46\frac{7}{8}$	87
23		4–10	31/11–32/1	$34\frac{13}{16}$–$34\frac{7}{8}$	$34\frac{5}{8}$	$46\frac{3}{4}$–$46\frac{7}{8}$		$86\frac{3}{4}$
24		11–17	32/–	$34\frac{3}{4}$	$34\frac{1}{2}$			
25		18–24	32/1–32/2	$34\frac{3}{4}$	$34\frac{1}{2}$	47		86
26	July	25– 1	32/0–32/4	$34\frac{3}{4}$–$34\frac{7}{8}$		47		
27		2– 8	32/2–32/3	$34\frac{11}{16}$–$34\frac{3}{4}$		47		
28		9–15	32/1–32/3	$34\frac{11}{16}$	$34\frac{1}{8}$	$46\frac{7}{8}$–47	$46\frac{7}{8}$	$86\frac{1}{2}$
29		16–22	32/2–32/4	$34\frac{5}{8}$–$34\frac{11}{16}$		47		87
30		23–29	32/2–32/3	$34\frac{5}{8}$–$34\frac{11}{16}$		47	$46\frac{3}{4}$	87
31	Aug.	30– 5	32/4	$34\frac{5}{8}$				
32		6–12	32/3–32/4	$34\frac{5}{8}$		$46\frac{1}{2}$		
33		13–19	32/3–32/5	$34\frac{1}{2}$–$34\frac{9}{16}$				
34		20–26	32/5	$34\frac{3}{8}$–$34\frac{1}{2}$	34	$46\frac{1}{4}$–$46\frac{3}{4}$	$46\frac{3}{4}$	$87\frac{1}{2}$
35	Sep.	27– 2	32/6–32/7	$34\frac{5}{16}$–$34\frac{7}{16}$				
36		3– 9	32/7–32/8	$34\frac{1}{4}$–$34\frac{3}{8}$	$33\frac{7}{8}$–34	47		
37		10–16	32/6–32/7	$34\frac{3}{8}$–$34\frac{7}{16}$				
38		17–23	32/6–32/7	$34\frac{1}{2}$				
39		24–30	32/6–32/7	$34\frac{1}{2}$–$34\frac{9}{16}$	34	47	$46\frac{7}{8}$	$87\frac{1}{2}$
40	Oct.	1– 7	32/6–32/7	$34\frac{9}{16}$–$34\frac{5}{8}$		$46\frac{3}{4}$		$87\frac{1}{4}$
41		8–14	32/6–32/7	$34\frac{5}{8}$–$34\frac{11}{16}$	$34\frac{1}{4}$–$34\frac{1}{2}$			
42		15–21	32/7–32/8	$34\frac{1}{2}$–$34\frac{9}{16}$				
43		22–28	32/7–32/8	$34\frac{1}{2}$–$34\frac{9}{16}$		$46\frac{3}{4}$		$87\frac{1}{4}$–$87\frac{1}{2}$
44	Nov.	29– 4	32/7–32/8	$34\frac{7}{16}$–$34\frac{1}{2}$	$34\frac{3}{4}$	$46\frac{3}{4}$–47		$87\frac{1}{4}$
45		5–11	32/9	$34\frac{3}{4}$	$34\frac{1}{8}$	47		$87\frac{1}{4}$
46		12–18	32/9–32/11	$34\frac{3}{4}$–$34\frac{1}{2}$	34–$34\frac{1}{8}$	$46\frac{3}{4}$–47		$87\frac{1}{4}$
47		19–25	33/1	$34\frac{1}{4}$				
48	Dec.	26– 2	32/11–33/1	$34\frac{1}{16}$–$34\frac{3}{16}$	$34\frac{1}{8}$	$45\frac{3}{4}$–46		87
49		3– 9	32/10–33/0	$34\frac{5}{16}$	$34\frac{1}{4}$	$45\frac{3}{4}$–46		
50		10–16	32/11–33/1	$34\frac{1}{4}$–$34\frac{5}{8}$		46		$86\frac{1}{2}$–$86\frac{5}{8}$
51		17–23	33/6–33/8			$46\frac{1}{2}$	$46\frac{1}{4}$	
52		24–32	33/1	$34\frac{3}{16}$				86

TABLE A.11 [a] (*cont.*)

1676			London	Amsterdam	Antwerp	Paris	Rouen	Venice
					HAMBURG on:			
1	Jan.	1-7	33/5	$34\frac{5}{8}$				
2		8-14	33/1-33/3	$34\frac{3}{4}$-$34\frac{9}{16}$	$34\frac{1}{2}$	$45\frac{3}{4}$-46		$85\frac{1}{2}$-86
3		15-21	33/3	$34\frac{1}{2}$-$34\frac{5}{8}$	$34\frac{1}{2}$	$45\frac{1}{2}$		$85\frac{1}{2}$
4		21-28	33/1-33/3	$34\frac{5}{8}$	$34\frac{5}{8}$	$45\frac{3}{4}$	$45\frac{1}{2}$	$85\frac{3}{4}$-86
5	Feb.	29-4	33/1-33/2	$34\frac{1}{2}$-$34\frac{9}{16}$				$85\frac{3}{4}$
6		5-11	32/11-33/0	$34\frac{1}{2}$	$34\frac{9}{16}$	$45\frac{3}{4}$	$45\frac{1}{2}$	$85\frac{3}{4}$
7		12-18	32/11-33/0	$34\frac{7}{16}$-$34\frac{1}{2}$	$34\frac{9}{16}$	$45\frac{3}{4}$		$85\frac{3}{4}$
8		19-25	33/0	$34\frac{7}{16}$-$34\frac{5}{8}$	$34\frac{1}{4}$	46		
9	Mar.	26-4	33/1-33/2	$34\frac{3}{8}$				86
10		5-11	33/2-33/4	$34\frac{1}{4}$-$34\frac{5}{16}$		$45\frac{3}{4}$		86-$86\frac{1}{4}$
11		12-18	33/3-33/4	$34\frac{1}{4}$-$34\frac{5}{16}$	$34\frac{1}{8}$			
12		19-25	33/2-33/3	$34\frac{1}{4}$-$34\frac{5}{16}$		$45\frac{3}{4}$-46		$85\frac{3}{4}$
13	Apr.	26-1	33/3	$34\frac{1}{4}$				
14		2-8	33/2-33/4	$34\frac{1}{4}$-$34\frac{5}{16}$		46		85
15		9-15	33/2-33/3	$34\frac{5}{16}$		46-$46\frac{1}{2}$		$85\frac{1}{4}$
16		16-22	33/2					
17		23-29	33/2-33/3	$34\frac{3}{8}$		46		$85\frac{1}{2}$
18	May	30-6	33/4	$34\frac{3}{8}$				
19		7-13	33/4	$34\frac{3}{8}$-$34\frac{7}{16}$				$85\frac{1}{4}$
20		14-20						
21		21-27	33/5-33/6	$34\frac{1}{4}$				
22	June	28-3	33/3	$33\frac{15}{16}$-34		$46\frac{3}{4}$		
23		4-10	33/5-33/6	$34\frac{1}{8}$		47		
24		11-17	33/7-33/10	$34\frac{1}{8}$-$34\frac{3}{16}$		47-$47\frac{1}{4}$		
25		18-24	33/8-33/9	$34\frac{1}{8}$		$47\frac{1}{4}$	47	$86\frac{1}{2}$
26	July	25-1	33/10-33/11	$33\frac{7}{8}$-34				$86\frac{1}{8}$
27		2-8	34/0	$33\frac{7}{8}$-$33\frac{15}{16}$				
28		9-15	34/2-34/3	$33\frac{13}{16}$-$33\frac{7}{8}$				
29		16-22	34/2-34/3	$33\frac{15}{16}$		47		87
30		23-29	34/2	$33\frac{13}{16}$-$33\frac{7}{8}$				87
31	Aug.	30-5	34/3	$33\frac{15}{16}$				$87\frac{1}{4}$
32		6-12	34/4	$33\frac{11}{16}$-$33\frac{3}{4}$		$47\frac{1}{4}$		87-$87\frac{1}{4}$
33		13-19	34/3-34/5	$33\frac{5}{8}$-$33\frac{13}{16}$		$47\frac{3}{8}$		87
34		20-26	34/4-34/5	$33\frac{7}{8}$-$33\frac{15}{16}$		$47\frac{1}{2}$		$87\frac{1}{2}$
35	Sep.	27-2	34/2-34/3	$33\frac{15}{16}$-$34\frac{1}{8}$		$47\frac{1}{4}$-$47\frac{3}{8}$	47-$47\frac{1}{8}$	88
36		3-9	34/3	$34\frac{1}{8}$-$34\frac{3}{16}$				
37		10-16	34/3-34/4	$34\frac{1}{8}$-$34\frac{1}{4}$		$47\frac{3}{8}$-$47\frac{1}{2}$	$46\frac{7}{8}$	$88\frac{1}{4}$
38		17-23	34/3-34/4	$33\frac{7}{8}$-$34\frac{1}{16}$				88-$88\frac{1}{2}$
39		24-30	34/4	$33\frac{15}{16}$				$88\frac{3}{8}$
40	Oct.	1-7	34/3	$33\frac{3}{4}$				
41		8-14	34/3-34/4	$33\frac{5}{8}$-$33\frac{11}{16}$				$88\frac{1}{4}$
42		15-21	34/3-34/4	$33\frac{5}{8}$-$33\frac{11}{16}$	$33\frac{3}{8}$-$33\frac{1}{2}$	$47\frac{1}{2}$		$87\frac{3}{4}$-88
43		22-28	34/4	$33\frac{5}{8}$				
44	Nov.	22-28	34/3-34/7	$33\frac{9}{16}$-$33\frac{5}{8}$	$33\frac{1}{8}$	$47\frac{3}{4}$		
45		5-11	34/8	$33\frac{5}{8}$				$88\frac{1}{4}$
46		12-18	34/7	$33\frac{5}{8}$				
47		19-25	34/7-34/8	$33\frac{5}{8}$-$33\frac{11}{16}$				$88\frac{1}{4}$
48	Dec.	26-2	34/8	$33\frac{9}{16}$-$33\frac{5}{8}$		$47\frac{1}{2}$		$88\frac{1}{2}$
49		3-9	34/8	$33\frac{9}{16}$				$88\frac{1}{2}$-89
50		10-16	34/8	$33\frac{9}{16}$	$33\frac{1}{8}$	$47\frac{3}{8}$	$47\frac{1}{4}$	$89\frac{1}{8}$
51		17-23	34/9-34/10	$33\frac{9}{16}$				$89\frac{1}{4}$
52		24-31						

TABLE A.11 [a] (*cont.*)

	1677		HAMBURG on:					
			London	Amsterdam	Antwerp	Paris	Rouen	Venice
1	Jan.	1– 7						
2		8–14						
3		15–21	34/4–34/5	$33\frac{9}{16}$				89
4		21–28	34/6–34/7	$33\frac{11}{16}$		$47\frac{1}{2}$		89
5	Feb.	29– 4	34/8–34/9	$33\frac{5}{8}$		$47\frac{1}{2}$		
6		5–11	34/6–34/8	$33\frac{9}{16}$–$33\frac{3}{8}$		$47\frac{3}{8}$–$47\frac{1}{2}$		89
7		12–18	34/5–34/7	$33\frac{1}{2}$–$33\frac{9}{16}$		$47\frac{3}{8}$		89
8		19–25	34/6–34/7	$33\frac{7}{16}$–$33\frac{9}{16}$		$47\frac{1}{4}$		
9	Mar.	26– 4	34/7–34/8	$33\frac{1}{2}$	$32\frac{7}{8}$–33	$47\frac{1}{4}$		
10		5–11	34/7–34/9	$33\frac{5}{16}$–$33\frac{9}{16}$				
11		12–18	34/7–34/8	$33\frac{7}{16}$–$33\frac{1}{2}$		$47\frac{1}{4}$		$89\frac{1}{4}$
12		19–25	34/8	$33\frac{1}{2}$		$47\frac{1}{2}$		$88\frac{7}{8}$
13	Apr.	26– 1	34/8	$33\frac{1}{4}$				$88\frac{7}{8}$
14		2– 8	34/9	$33\frac{1}{4}$		$47\frac{1}{2}$		89
15		9–15	34/9	$33\frac{3}{16}$–$33\frac{1}{4}$				$88\frac{3}{4}$
16		16–22	34/8–34/9	$33\frac{1}{4}$–$33\frac{5}{16}$	33			89
17		23–29						
18	May	30– 6	34/8–34/9	$33\frac{3}{16}$–$33\frac{1}{4}$	$32\frac{13}{16}$–$32\frac{7}{8}$	$47\frac{1}{2}$		89
19		7–13	34/8–34/9					
20		14–20	34/8	$33\frac{1}{4}$				
21		21–27	34/8–34/9	$33\frac{1}{4}$				
22	June	28– 3	34/8–34/9	$33\frac{1}{8}$–$33\frac{3}{16}$		$47\frac{1}{2}$–$47\frac{3}{4}$		89
23		4–10	34/8–34/9	$33\frac{3}{16}$				
24		11–17	34/9	$33\frac{1}{8}$–$33\frac{3}{16}$				$89\frac{1}{8}$
25		18–24	34/8	$33\frac{1}{16}$				
26	July	25– 1	34/8–34/9	33–$33\frac{1}{16}$		$47\frac{7}{8}$–48		
27		2– 8	34/9	$33\frac{1}{16}$		$47\frac{3}{4}$–$47\frac{7}{8}$		
28		9–15	34/8–34/10	$33\frac{1}{8}$	$32\frac{3}{4}$	$47\frac{7}{8}$		$89\frac{1}{4}$
29		16–22	34/8–34/9	$33\frac{1}{16}$–$33\frac{1}{8}$	$32\frac{3}{4}$–$32\frac{13}{16}$	$47\frac{3}{4}$–$47\frac{7}{8}$	$47\frac{1}{2}$–$47\frac{7}{8}$	89–$89\frac{1}{4}$
30		23–29	34/9	$33\frac{1}{16}$–$33\frac{1}{4}$				
31	Aug.	30– 5	34/8–34/10	$33\frac{1}{4}$		$47\frac{1}{4}$	$47\frac{1}{2}$	90
32		6–12	34/8–34/10	$33\frac{3}{8}$–$33\frac{7}{16}$	$32\frac{3}{4}$	$47\frac{1}{4}$	$47\frac{1}{2}$	90
33		13–19	34/8–34/9	$33\frac{3}{8}$–$33\frac{1}{2}$	$32\frac{3}{4}$–33	$47\frac{1}{2}$–$47\frac{5}{8}$		
34		20–26	34/9	$33\frac{3}{8}$–$33\frac{1}{4}$		$47\frac{5}{8}$		$89\frac{3}{4}$–90
35	Sep.	27– 2	34/8$\frac{1}{2}$–34/9	$33\frac{1}{4}$				90–$90\frac{1}{8}$
36		3– 9	34/8	$33\frac{1}{8}$				
37		10–16	34/7–34/8	$33\frac{1}{8}$–$33\frac{3}{8}$	$33\frac{1}{8}$	$46\frac{3}{4}$–$47\frac{1}{2}$	$46\frac{1}{2}$	$90\frac{1}{4}$
38		17–23	34/7–34/8	$33\frac{1}{8}$–$33\frac{3}{16}$	$33\frac{1}{8}$	$46\frac{3}{4}$–$47\frac{1}{2}$		$90\frac{1}{3}$–$90\frac{1}{2}$
39		24–30	34/7	$33\frac{3}{8}$	$33\frac{1}{8}$	46–$46\frac{1}{2}$	46	$90\frac{1}{2}$
40	Oct.	1– 7	34/7–34/8	$33\frac{1}{8}$–$33\frac{5}{8}$	33	$46\frac{3}{8}$–$46\frac{1}{2}$		$89\frac{3}{4}$–90
41		8–14	34/7	$33\frac{1}{8}$–$33\frac{3}{8}$		$46\frac{3}{8}$		89
42		15–21	34/7–34/9	$33\frac{1}{8}$–$33\frac{3}{8}$		$46\frac{1}{4}$–$46\frac{3}{8}$	$46\frac{1}{4}$	89–$89\frac{1}{4}$
43		22–28	34/7–34/8	$33\frac{1}{4}$		$46\frac{3}{8}$–$46\frac{1}{2}$		$89\frac{1}{4}$
44	Nov.	29– 4	34/7	$33\frac{1}{8}$–$33\frac{1}{4}$		$46\frac{3}{8}$		
45		5–11	34/6–34/7	$33\frac{1}{4}$–$33\frac{5}{16}$	33	$46\frac{1}{4}$		90
46		12–18	34/7	$33\frac{3}{16}$				
47		19–25	34/6	33–$33\frac{1}{8}$	33	$46\frac{1}{8}$–$46\frac{3}{8}$		90
48	Dec.	26– 2	34/5–34/6	$32\frac{7}{8}$–$32\frac{15}{16}$	$32\frac{3}{4}$	$46\frac{1}{4}$		
49		3– 9	34/4–34/6	$32\frac{7}{8}$–$32\frac{15}{16}$	$32\frac{3}{4}$	46		90
50		10–16	34/5–34/6	$33\frac{1}{8}$				
51		17–23	34/2–34/4	$33\frac{1}{8}$–$33\frac{3}{8}$	$32\frac{7}{8}$	46		
52		24–31	34/3	$33\frac{3}{8}$–$33\frac{1}{4}$	33–$33\frac{1}{8}$	46–$46\frac{1}{8}$		

TABLE A.11 [a] (*cont.*)

	1678		London	Amsterdam	Antwerp	Paris	Rouen	Venice
				HAMBURG on:				
1	Jan.	1– 7	34/2	$33\frac{1}{3}$		$46–46\frac{1}{4}$		$88\frac{3}{4}$
2		8–14						
3		15–21	34/0–34/3	$33\frac{1}{3}$		46		
4		21–28	33/10–34/0	$33\frac{3}{8}–33\frac{7}{16}$	$33\frac{1}{3}$	46		
5	Feb.	29– 4	33/4–33/11	$33\frac{7}{16}–33\frac{1}{2}$	$33\frac{3}{8}$	$45\frac{3}{4}$		88
6		5–11	33/3–33/4	$33\frac{1}{2}–33\frac{9}{16}$		45	$45\frac{1}{4}$	$87\frac{1}{2}$
7		12–18	32/6–33/2	$33\frac{9}{16}–33\frac{5}{8}$	$33\frac{1}{2}$	$45\frac{1}{2}$		87
8		19–25	32/5–32/7	$33\frac{1}{2}–33\frac{5}{8}$				87
9	Mar.	26– 4	32/0–32/2	$33\frac{7}{16}–33\frac{1}{2}$		$45\frac{1}{4}–45\frac{1}{2}$	$45\frac{1}{4}$	$86\frac{3}{4}–87$
10		5–11	32/5–32/8	$33\frac{7}{16}–33\frac{1}{2}$		$45\frac{3}{4}–46$		
11		12–18	32/6–32/10	$33\frac{1}{3}–33\frac{3}{8}$				
12		19–25	32/8–32/9	$33\frac{1}{3}–33\frac{3}{8}$	$33\frac{1}{4}–33\frac{3}{8}$	$46–46\frac{1}{2}$	$45\frac{3}{4}$	87
13	Apr.	26– 1	32/7	$33–33\frac{1}{3}$		$46\frac{1}{4}$		$87\frac{1}{2}$
14		2– 8	32/5–32/9	$33\frac{1}{4}$		$45\frac{3}{4}–46$	$45\frac{1}{2}$	$88\frac{1}{8}$
15		9–15						
16		16–22	$32/6–32/6\frac{1}{2}$					
17		23–29	32/6–32/7	$33\frac{1}{16}–33\frac{1}{8}$				$88\frac{1}{2}$
18	May	30– 6	32/7–32/8	33		46		
19		7–13	32/7–32/8	33		46		
20		14–20	32/7–32/8	$32\frac{15}{16}$		46		
21		21–27	32/7–32/8	33		46		$88–88\frac{1}{2}$
22	June	28– 3						
23		4–10	32/10–33/3	$32\frac{15}{16}–33\frac{1}{16}$		$45\frac{3}{4}$	$45\frac{1}{2}$	
24		11–17	33/3–33/6	$33\frac{1}{16}–33\frac{1}{8}$		$45\frac{3}{4}–45\frac{7}{8}$		
25		18–24	33/6–33/8	$33\frac{1}{16}$				
26	July	25– 1	33/9	33			$45\frac{1}{2}$	
27		2– 8	33/8	$32\frac{15}{16}–33$				
28		9–15	33/5–33/8	$32\frac{15}{16}–33$		46		$87\frac{1}{4}–87\frac{1}{2}$
29		16–22	33/6–33/9	$32\frac{15}{16}–33$		46	$45\frac{3}{4}$	$87\frac{1}{2}$
30		23–29	33/5–33/6	33		46		
31	Aug.	30– 5	33/6–33/8	$33–33\frac{1}{16}$				$89–89\frac{1}{4}$
32		6–12	33/8–33/9	$33–33\frac{1}{16}$		$46–46\frac{1}{2}$		
33		13–19	33/8–33/10	$33\frac{1}{16}–33\frac{3}{16}$			$46\frac{1}{8}$	$88\frac{1}{4}–88\frac{3}{4}$
34		20–26	33/11–34/1	$33\frac{3}{16}–33\frac{1}{3}$			$46\frac{1}{4}$	$87\frac{1}{2}$
35	Sep.	27– 2	34/0	$33\frac{1}{3}$		46	$46\frac{1}{4}$	$87\frac{1}{4}$
36		3– 9	34/0	$33\frac{1}{4}$				
37		10–16	34/0	$33\frac{3}{16}–33\frac{1}{3}$		46		$87\frac{1}{4}$
38		17–23	34/0	$33\frac{1}{3}$				$87\frac{1}{4}$
39		24–30	34/0	$33\frac{1}{3}–33\frac{3}{8}$		$46\frac{1}{4}$		$87\frac{1}{4}$
40	Oct.	1– 7	34/0–34/1	$33\frac{1}{3}$		$46–46\frac{1}{4}$		87
41		8–14	33/10–34/0	$33\frac{1}{4}$				
42		15–21						
43		22–28	33/7–33/9	$33–33\frac{1}{4}$		46		
44	Nov.	29– 4	33/8–33/9	33				
45		5–11	33/8–33/9	33		$45\frac{3}{4}–46$		$87\frac{1}{2}$
46		12–18	33/8–33/9	$32\frac{15}{16}–33$				87
47		19–25	33/7–33/9	$32\frac{15}{16}–33\frac{1}{8}$	33	$45\frac{1}{2}–45\frac{3}{4}$		$87\frac{3}{4}$
48	Dec.	26– 2	33/8–33/9	$33–33\frac{1}{8}$				
49		3– 9	$33/8\frac{1}{2}–33/10$	$33\frac{1}{16}–33\frac{1}{8}$		$45\frac{1}{2}$		$88–88\frac{3}{4}$
50		10–16	33/9–33/10	$33\frac{1}{16}–33\frac{1}{8}$		$45\frac{1}{2}–45\frac{3}{4}$		$88–88\frac{3}{4}$
51		17–23	33/9–33/10					
52		24–31	33/10–34/0	33		$45\frac{3}{4}–46$		

TABLE A.11 [a] (*cont.*)

	1679		London	Amsterdam	Antwerp	Paris	Rouen	Venice
			HAMBURG on:					

#	1679		London	Amsterdam	Antwerp	Paris	Rouen	Venice
1	Jan.	1– 7	$33/11$–$34/0$	33		$45\frac{3}{4}$–46		
2		8–14	$34/0$	$33\frac{1}{8}$–$33\frac{1}{2}$		$45\frac{3}{4}$		$87\frac{1}{2}$
3		15–21	$34/0$	$33\frac{3}{16}$		46		$87\frac{1}{2}$
4		21–28	$34/0$	$33\frac{1}{4}$				$87\frac{1}{2}$–$87\frac{3}{4}$
5	Feb.	29– 4	$34/1$	$33\frac{1}{8}$–$33\frac{3}{16}$		$46\frac{1}{8}$		$87\frac{1}{2}$
6		5–11	$34/0$–$34/2$	$33\frac{3}{16}$–$33\frac{1}{8}$		46–$46\frac{1}{4}$		$87\frac{1}{2}$
7		12–18	$34/1$	33–$33\frac{1}{8}$	$33\frac{1}{4}$	46		
8		19–25	$34/1$–$34/2\frac{1}{2}$	33–$33\frac{1}{16}$		46		
9	Mar.	26– 4	$34/1$–$34/3$	33–$33\frac{1}{16}$			$45\frac{7}{8}$	
10		5–11	$34/3$–$34/4$	$33\frac{1}{16}$–$33\frac{1}{8}$		$46\frac{1}{4}$		$87\frac{1}{2}$
11		12–18	$34/4$	$33\frac{1}{16}$		46		
12		19–25	$34/5$–$34/6$	$33\frac{1}{8}$				
13	Apr.	26– 1	$34/4$–$34/6$	$33\frac{1}{4}$–$33\frac{1}{8}$	$33\frac{1}{4}$–$33\frac{5}{16}$	$46\frac{1}{4}$		$87\frac{3}{4}$
14		2– 8	$34/4$–$34/5$	33–$33\frac{1}{8}$	$33\frac{1}{4}$–$33\frac{5}{16}$	$46\frac{1}{8}$–$46\frac{3}{8}$		87–$87\frac{1}{4}$
15		9–15	$34/4$–$34/5$	$32\frac{15}{16}$–33	$33\frac{1}{4}$	$46\frac{1}{2}$		$87\frac{1}{4}$
16		16–22	$34/4$–$34/5$	33				$87\frac{1}{4}$–$87\frac{1}{2}$
17		23–29	$34/5$–$34/6$	$32\frac{7}{8}$–$32\frac{15}{16}$		$46\frac{1}{2}$	$46\frac{1}{4}$	
18	May	30– 6	$34/5$–$34/7$	$32\frac{7}{8}$–$32\frac{15}{16}$		$46\frac{1}{2}$		
19		7–13	$34/6$–$34/8$	$32\frac{7}{8}$–33	33	$46\frac{3}{4}$		$87\frac{5}{8}$
20		14–20	$34/8$	$32\frac{15}{16}$–33		47		
21		21–27	$34/7$–$34/8$	33		$46\frac{1}{2}$–47		
22	June	28– 3	$34/6$–$34/7$	33				$87\frac{7}{8}$
23		4–10	$34/4$–$34/6$	33		$46\frac{3}{8}$–$46\frac{1}{2}$		88
24		11–17	$34/5$–$34/7$	$33\frac{1}{8}$				
25		18–24	$34/8$	$33\frac{3}{16}$		$46\frac{1}{2}$		$87\frac{1}{2}$
26	July	25– 1	$34/8$	$33\frac{3}{16}$–$33\frac{1}{4}$	$33\frac{1}{2}$	$46\frac{1}{2}$–$46\frac{5}{8}$		$87\frac{1}{4}$
27		2– 8	$34/8$	$33\frac{1}{4}$				
28		9–15	$34/8$–$34/9$	$33\frac{1}{8}$–$33\frac{3}{16}$		$46\frac{1}{2}$–$46\frac{3}{4}$		$87\frac{1}{4}$
29		16–22	$34/8$–$34/9$	$33\frac{3}{16}$				$87\frac{1}{4}$
30		23–29	$34/8$–$34/9$	$33\frac{3}{16}$				$87\frac{3}{4}$
31	Aug.	30– 5	$34/8$–$34/9$	33		47		
32		6–12	$34/9$–$34/10$	33				88
33		13–19	$34/9$	33		47		88
34		20–26	$34/9$	33–$33\frac{1}{16}$		$47\frac{3}{8}$		$87\frac{1}{2}$
35	Sep.	27– 2	$34/9$–$34/10$	33–$33\frac{1}{16}$		$47\frac{1}{4}$		
36		3– 9	$34/9$–$34/10$	$33\frac{1}{16}$		$47\frac{1}{4}$		$88\frac{1}{2}$
37		10–16	$34/9$–$35/0$	$33\frac{1}{8}$–$33\frac{3}{16}$		47		$88\frac{3}{4}$
38		17–23	$34/10$	$33\frac{1}{8}$				$88\frac{3}{4}$
39		24–30	$34/10$–$35/0$	$32\frac{15}{16}$–33		$47\frac{1}{8}$	47	$88\frac{3}{4}$
40	Oct.	1– 7	$35/1$–$35/2$	$32\frac{1}{4}$–$32\frac{1}{2}$		47		$88\frac{3}{4}$–89
41		8–14	$35/2$–$35/4$	$32\frac{1}{2}$–$32\frac{11}{16}$		$47\frac{3}{4}$		$89\frac{1}{4}$
42		15–21	$34/8$–$35/3$	$32\frac{3}{4}$–$32\frac{13}{16}$				
43		22–28	$34/7$	$33\frac{1}{16}$				$88\frac{1}{2}$
44	Nov.	29– 4	$34/5$	33–$33\frac{3}{16}$				
45		5–11	$34/4$–$34/6$	$33\frac{1}{16}$–$33\frac{1}{4}$	33	47–$47\frac{1}{8}$	$46\frac{3}{4}$	$88\frac{3}{4}$
46		12–18	$34/4$–$34/6$	$33\frac{1}{8}$–$33\frac{5}{16}$		47–$47\frac{1}{4}$		$89\frac{1}{8}$
47		19–25	$34/7$–$34/8$	$33\frac{1}{8}$–$33\frac{3}{16}$		$47\frac{1}{4}$		$89\frac{1}{4}$
48	Dec.	26– 2	$34/10$	33		$47\frac{1}{8}$		
49		3– 9	$34/8$–$34/9$	$33\frac{3}{16}$–$33\frac{1}{4}$		$47\frac{1}{4}$	47	$90\frac{1}{4}$
50		10–16	$34/7$–$34/9$	$33\frac{1}{8}$–$33\frac{5}{16}$		47		90
51		17–23	$34/7$–$34/8$	$33\frac{5}{16}$				$89\frac{3}{4}$
52		24–31						

TABLE A.11 [a] (*cont.*)

1680			London	Amsterdam	Antwerp	Paris	Rouen	Venice
					HAMBURG on:			
1	Jan.	1– 7						$88\frac{1}{2}$
2		8–14	34/7	$33\frac{1}{3}$–$33\frac{3}{8}$		$47\frac{3}{4}$		$88\frac{1}{4}$
3		15–21	34/4–34/6	$33\frac{5}{16}$–$33\frac{7}{16}$		$47\frac{1}{4}$–$47\frac{3}{8}$		$88\frac{1}{4}$
4		21–28	34/5–34/6	$33\frac{3}{8}$–$33\frac{7}{16}$				$88\frac{1}{2}$–$88\frac{3}{4}$
5	Feb.	29– 4	34/4–34/5	$33\frac{9}{16}$				$88\frac{1}{2}$
6		5–11	34/4–34/5					
7		12–18	34/6–34/7	$33\frac{7}{16}$–$33\frac{1}{2}$		$47\frac{3}{4}$		$88\frac{1}{4}$
8		19–25						
9	Mar.	26– 4	34/8					
10		5–11	34/9	$33\frac{1}{4}$	33	$47\frac{3}{8}$		
11		12–18	34/8–34/9	$33\frac{1}{4}$	33	$47\frac{3}{4}$–$47\frac{7}{8}$	$47\frac{5}{8}$	$88\frac{1}{3}$–$88\frac{1}{2}$
12		19–25						
13	Apr.	26– 1						

TABLE A.11 *(cont.)*
[b] *Amsterdam on London, Hamburg, Antwerp, Paris, Rouen, Venice*

	1668	London	Hamburg	Antwerp	Paris	Rouen	Venice
				AMSTERDAM on:			
1	Jan. 1– 7	35/7					
2	8–14	$35/5\frac{1}{2}$–35/6					
3	15–21						
4	21–28						
5	Feb. 29– 4						
6	5–11						
7	12–18						
8	19–25						
9	Mar. 26– 4	35/4					
10	5–11	35/4–35/5			$99\frac{3}{4}$–100		
11	12–18	$35/3$–$35/3\frac{1}{2}$		$2\frac{1}{4}$	100	$99\frac{3}{4}$	$93\frac{1}{4}$
12	19–25	34/11–35/1	$32\frac{7}{8}$	$2\frac{3}{8}$	$100\frac{1}{8}$–$100\frac{1}{4}$	$99\frac{3}{4}$	$93\frac{3}{8}$–94
13	Apr. 26– 1	34/11	$32\frac{3}{4}$		$100\frac{1}{2}$		
14	2– 8	34/6–34/7	$32\frac{7}{8}$	$2\frac{1}{8}$	$100\frac{5}{8}$	$100\frac{1}{2}$	
15	9–15	34/7–34/8	$32\frac{1}{8}$	$2\frac{1}{8}$	101		
16	16–22	34/11	$32\frac{1}{4}$		$100\frac{1}{2}$	100	
17	23–29	34/11–35/0	$32\frac{13}{16}$	$2\frac{3}{4}$	$100\frac{5}{8}$		
18	May 30– 6		$32\frac{7}{8}$	3	100		
19	7–13	34/7–34/8	$32\frac{15}{16}$	$2\frac{7}{8}$	$100\frac{1}{4}$–$100\frac{1}{2}$	100	
20	14–20	34/9	$32\frac{15}{16}$	$2\frac{1}{2}$	$100\frac{7}{8}$		
21	21–27	34/8–34/9	$32\frac{7}{8}$	$2\frac{1}{4}$	$100\frac{5}{8}$		
22	June 28– 3	34/11–35/0	$32\frac{15}{16}$	$2\frac{3}{8}$	101–$101\frac{1}{4}$	$100\frac{3}{4}$	$94\frac{1}{2}$–$94\frac{3}{4}$
23	4–10	34/10–34/11	$32\frac{15}{16}$–33	$2\frac{3}{8}$	$101\frac{7}{8}$		
24	11–17	34/10	$32\frac{15}{16}$	$2\frac{1}{8}$	$100\frac{5}{8}$–$100\frac{3}{4}$		
25	18–24	34/10–34/11	33		$100\frac{3}{4}$		
26	July 25– 1	34/9–34/10	33	$1\frac{7}{8}$–2	101–$101\frac{1}{4}$	$100\frac{3}{8}$	
27	2– 8	34/10	$32\frac{15}{16}$–33	$1\frac{1}{4}$–2	$101\frac{1}{4}$	$100\frac{1}{2}$	$92\frac{1}{4}$
28	9–15	34/11–35/0	33–$33\frac{1}{16}$	$1\frac{1}{4}$–$1\frac{7}{8}$	$101\frac{1}{4}$–$101\frac{1}{2}$	$100\frac{3}{4}$	94
29	16–22	35/2–35/3	33		$101\frac{1}{4}$–102		
30	23–29	35/2	$33\frac{1}{16}$	$1\frac{1}{4}$			
31	Aug. 30– 5	35/1–35/2	$33\frac{3}{8}$	$1\frac{5}{8}$–$1\frac{1}{4}$	$102\frac{1}{4}$	102	
32	6–12	34/11–35/0	$33\frac{1}{16}$–$33\frac{3}{8}$	$1\frac{3}{4}$–$1\frac{7}{8}$	$102\frac{1}{4}$–$102\frac{1}{2}$		
33	13–19	35/0–35/1	33	$1\frac{3}{4}$	101–$101\frac{1}{4}$		
34	20–26	$35/1$–$35/1\frac{1}{2}$	$32\frac{13}{16}$	$1\frac{3}{4}$	$100\frac{3}{4}$–101		
35	Sep. 27– 2	35/1	$32\frac{13}{16}$	$1\frac{5}{8}$	101–$101\frac{1}{4}$		
36	3– 9	35/1	$32\frac{13}{16}$	$1\frac{3}{8}$	$101\frac{1}{2}$		
37	10–16	35/5	$32\frac{13}{16}$	$1\frac{3}{8}$–$1\frac{1}{2}$	$101\frac{1}{4}$–$101\frac{1}{2}$		
38	17–23	35/6	$32\frac{13}{16}$	$1\frac{1}{4}$	$100\frac{3}{4}$	$100\frac{1}{4}$	
39	24–30	35/0–35/1	$32\frac{7}{8}$	$1\frac{1}{4}$	$100\frac{7}{8}$–101	$100\frac{3}{8}$	
40	Oct. 1– 7	35/2			$100\frac{3}{4}$–$100\frac{7}{8}$		
41	8–14	$35/0$–$35/0\frac{1}{2}$	$32\frac{5}{8}$–$32\frac{11}{16}$	$1\frac{1}{4}$	$100\frac{5}{8}$	$100\frac{3}{8}$	
42	15–21	35/1	$32\frac{5}{8}$	$1\frac{1}{8}$	$100\frac{3}{4}$		
43	22–28	35/2	$32\frac{5}{8}$	$1\frac{1}{8}$–$1\frac{1}{4}$	$100\frac{3}{4}$		
44	Nov. 29– 4	35/2–35/3	$32\frac{5}{8}$–$32\frac{11}{16}$	$1\frac{1}{4}$–$1\frac{3}{8}$	$100\frac{1}{2}$–$100\frac{3}{4}$	100	
45	5–11	35/2	$32\frac{5}{8}$	$1\frac{1}{4}$	$100\frac{3}{4}$		$94\frac{1}{4}$
46	12–18	35/2–35/3			$100\frac{1}{2}$–$100\frac{5}{8}$		
47	19–25	35/3–35/4	$32\frac{11}{16}$–$32\frac{3}{4}$	$1\frac{1}{4}$	$100\frac{1}{2}$–$100\frac{5}{8}$		
48	Dec. 26– 2	35/5–35/6	$32\frac{3}{4}$		$99\frac{7}{8}$–100	$99\frac{3}{4}$	
49	3– 9	35/6	$32\frac{11}{16}$–$32\frac{3}{4}$	$1\frac{1}{2}$	$99\frac{1}{2}$		
50	10–16	35/5	$32\frac{11}{16}$	$1\frac{1}{2}$	$99\frac{1}{4}$	$98\frac{3}{4}$	
51	17–23	35/2			99		
52	24–31	$35/2\frac{1}{2}$–35/3	$32\frac{11}{16}$	$1\frac{1}{2}$	$100\frac{1}{4}$		

TABLE A.11 [b] (*cont.*)

	1669		London	Hamburg	Antwerp	Paris	Rouen	Venice
			AMSTERDAM on:					

	1669		London	Hamburg	Antwerp	Paris	Rouen	Venice
1	Jan.	1– 7	35/4	$32\frac{11}{16}$	$1\frac{1}{2}$	$100\frac{5}{8}$		
2		8–14	35/3–35/4	$32\frac{11}{16}$	$1\frac{1}{2}$	$100\frac{1}{2}$–$100\frac{5}{8}$	$100\frac{1}{4}$	
3		15–21	35/3					
4		21–28	35/3–35/4	$32\frac{11}{16}$	$1\frac{5}{8}$	$100\frac{1}{4}$		
5	Feb.	29– 4	35/4–35/5	$32\frac{11}{16}$	$1\frac{7}{8}$–2	$100\frac{3}{8}$–$100\frac{1}{2}$		96
6		5–11	$35/4\frac{1}{2}$–$35/5\frac{1}{2}$	$32\frac{11}{16}$	$1\frac{3}{4}$	$100\frac{1}{4}$–$100\frac{3}{8}$		
7		12–18	35/4	$32\frac{3}{4}$	$1\frac{1}{4}$	$100\frac{1}{2}$		96
8		19–25	$35/4$–$35/4\frac{1}{2}$	$32\frac{11}{16}$–$32\frac{3}{4}$	$1\frac{5}{8}$	$100\frac{1}{2}$		96
9	Mar.	26– 4	$35/4$–$35/5\frac{1}{2}$	$32\frac{11}{16}$	$1\frac{1}{2}$	$100\frac{1}{4}$–$100\frac{1}{2}$		$96\frac{1}{2}$
10		5–11	35/6	$32\frac{5}{8}$	$1\frac{3}{4}$	$100\frac{1}{4}$		$95\frac{3}{4}$–96
11		12–18	$35/5$–$35/5\frac{1}{2}$	$32\frac{9}{16}$	$1\frac{5}{8}$	$100\frac{1}{8}$		
12		19–25	35/4–35/5					
13	Apr.	26– 1	35/4–35/5	$32\frac{1}{2}$	$1\frac{1}{2}$	$99\frac{3}{4}$–100		
14		2– 8	35/3–35/4	$32\frac{7}{16}$	$1\frac{1}{2}$	$99\frac{1}{2}$–$99\frac{3}{4}$		$95\frac{3}{4}$
15		9–15	$35/3\frac{1}{2}$–35/4	$32\frac{7}{16}$–$32\frac{1}{2}$	$1\frac{5}{8}$	$99\frac{3}{4}$		
16		16–22	$35/2$–$35/2\frac{1}{2}$	$32\frac{7}{16}$	$1\frac{5}{8}$	$99\frac{3}{4}$		
17		23–29	35/3–35/4	$32\frac{7}{16}$	$1\frac{5}{8}$	$99\frac{3}{4}$		
18	May	30– 6	$35/3\frac{1}{2}$–35/4	$32\frac{7}{16}$	$1\frac{1}{2}$–$1\frac{5}{8}$	$99\frac{7}{8}$		$95\frac{3}{4}$–96
19		7–13	$35/4\frac{1}{2}$	$32\frac{7}{16}$	$1\frac{3}{4}$	$99\frac{7}{8}$		
20		14–20						
21		21–27	$35/4\frac{1}{2}$–35/5	$32\frac{1}{2}$	$1\frac{5}{8}$	$99\frac{3}{4}$		
22	June	28– 3	$35/4\frac{1}{2}$	$32\frac{7}{16}$	$1\frac{5}{8}$	$99\frac{1}{4}$–$99\frac{3}{4}$		
23		4–10	35/4	$32\frac{7}{16}$	$1\frac{5}{8}$	$99\frac{5}{8}$		
24		11–17	35/3	$32\frac{7}{16}$	$1\frac{5}{8}$	$99\frac{1}{2}$–$99\frac{5}{8}$		
25		18–24	$35/2\frac{1}{2}$–35/3	$32\frac{7}{16}$	$1\frac{5}{8}$–$1\frac{3}{4}$	$99\frac{1}{2}$		
26	July	25– 1	$35/2\frac{1}{2}$–35/3	$32\frac{3}{8}$	$1\frac{5}{8}$–$1\frac{3}{4}$	$99\frac{3}{4}$		
27		2– 8	$35/2\frac{1}{2}$–35/3	$32\frac{3}{8}$	$1\frac{5}{8}$–$1\frac{3}{4}$	$98\frac{1}{2}$		
28		9–15	35/3			$98\frac{3}{4}$		
29		16–22		$32\frac{1}{2}$	$1\frac{5}{8}$–$1\frac{3}{4}$	$99\frac{1}{4}$		
30		23–29	$35/2\frac{1}{2}$			99		
31	Aug.	30– 5	$35/4\frac{1}{2}$–35/5	$32\frac{1}{2}$–$32\frac{9}{16}$	$1\frac{3}{4}$	99–$99\frac{1}{4}$		94
32		6–12	35/4–35/5	$32\frac{9}{16}$	$1\frac{3}{4}$	$99\frac{1}{4}$		
33		13–19	35/4	$32\frac{9}{16}$				
34		20–26	35/4	$32\frac{5}{8}$	$1\frac{3}{4}$	$99\frac{1}{4}$		94
35	Sep.	27– 2	35/4	$32\frac{9}{16}$–$32\frac{5}{8}$		99		
36		3– 9	$35/4$–$35/4\frac{1}{2}$	$32\frac{9}{16}$		$98\frac{3}{4}$–99	$98\frac{5}{8}$–$98\frac{3}{4}$	94
37		10–16	35/5	$32\frac{9}{16}$	$1\frac{5}{8}$	99–$99\frac{1}{4}$		
38		17–23	$35/4\frac{1}{2}$–35/5					
39		24–30	$35/5\frac{1}{2}$			$98\frac{1}{2}$		
40	Oct.	1– 7	35/4–35/5		$1\frac{1}{4}$	$98\frac{1}{2}$		$93\frac{1}{2}$
41		8–14	$35/2\frac{1}{2}$	$32\frac{1}{4}$–$32\frac{5}{16}$	1	$98\frac{1}{2}$	$98\frac{1}{4}$	$93\frac{3}{4}$–94
42		15–21	$35/2$–$35/2\frac{1}{2}$	$32\frac{1}{4}$–$32\frac{5}{16}$		98–$98\frac{3}{8}$		$93\frac{3}{8}$
43		22–28	35/2	$32\frac{1}{4}$	$1\frac{3}{4}$	$98\frac{1}{2}$		
44	Nov.	29– 4	$35/1$–$35/1\frac{1}{2}$	$32\frac{1}{4}$	$1\frac{3}{4}$	$96\frac{3}{4}$–$97\frac{1}{2}$		$93\frac{1}{4}$–$93\frac{1}{2}$
45		5–11	$35/1$–$35/1\frac{1}{2}$	$32\frac{1}{4}$–$32\frac{5}{8}$	$\frac{1}{2}$–$\frac{5}{8}$	$96\frac{3}{4}$–$97\frac{1}{4}$	97	$93\frac{1}{2}$
46		12–18	$35/1$–$35/1\frac{1}{2}$			$96\frac{1}{4}$	96	
47		19–25	35/1	$32\frac{1}{4}$	$\frac{3}{4}$	$95\frac{3}{4}$–96	$95\frac{1}{2}$	
48	Dec.	26– 2	$35/1\frac{1}{2}$–35/2	$32\frac{1}{4}$	$\frac{1}{4}$	97		
49		3– 9						$92\frac{3}{4}$
50		10–16	34/9–34/11	32–$32\frac{1}{16}$	$\frac{1}{4}$–$\frac{3}{8}$	$95\frac{3}{4}$–$96\frac{1}{8}$	$95\frac{5}{8}$	
51		17–23	34/8	32–$32\frac{1}{16}$				
52		24–31	34/4–34/5	$31\frac{7}{16}$–$31\frac{7}{8}$	$\frac{1}{8}$ loss	95		

1670		AMSTERDAM on:					
		London	Hamburg	Antwerp	Paris	Rouen	Venice
1	Jan. 1– 7	34/4–34/5	$31\frac{7}{16}$	$\frac{1}{8}$ loss	95		
2	8–14	34/4–34/5			$95\frac{1}{4}$		
3	15–21	34/6–34/7	$31\frac{13}{16}$	$\frac{1}{8}$ loss	$95\frac{7}{8}$		
4	21–28	34/8–34/10	$31\frac{13}{16}$	par	$95\frac{1}{2}$	$95\frac{1}{4}$	$92\frac{1}{2}$
5	Feb. 29– 4	34/9			$95\frac{1}{2}$		
6	5–11	34/9	$31\frac{7}{8}$	$\frac{1}{4}$ loss	$95\frac{7}{8}$	$95\frac{1}{2}$	
7	12–18	34/7	$31\frac{15}{16}$	$\frac{3}{8}$ loss	$96\frac{1}{4}$		
8	19–25	34/7–34/8	$31\frac{7}{8}$	$\frac{1}{2}$ loss	$96\frac{1}{8}$	96	$92\frac{1}{2}$–93
9	Mar. 26– 4						
10	5–11						

1671		AMSTERDAM on:					
		London	Hamburg	Antwerp	Paris	Rouen	Venice
14	2– 8						
15	9–15	$35/9\frac{1}{2}$–35/10	33	$\frac{1}{4}$–$\frac{1}{8}$	$98\frac{1}{4}$–$98\frac{3}{8}$		$93\frac{1}{2}$
16	16–22	35/9–35/10	$32\frac{15}{16}$	$\frac{3}{8}$ loss	$98\frac{1}{2}$	98	
17	23–29	$35/9$–$35/9\frac{1}{2}$			$98\frac{5}{8}$	$98\frac{3}{8}$	
18	May 30– 6	$35/7$–$35/8\frac{1}{2}$			$98\frac{3}{4}$–99	$98\frac{3}{4}$	
19	7–13	35/7–35/8	$32\frac{15}{16}$–33		99	$98\frac{5}{8}$	
20	14–20	35/7–35/8	$32\frac{11}{16}$	$\frac{1}{2}$–$\frac{5}{8}$	$99\frac{1}{2}$		
21	21–27	$35/9$–$35/9\frac{1}{2}$	$33\frac{1}{16}$–$33\frac{1}{8}$	$\frac{3}{4}$–$\frac{7}{8}$	$98\frac{3}{4}$–99		
22	June 28– 3						
23	4–10	35/9	$33\frac{1}{8}$–$33\frac{3}{16}$				$93\frac{5}{8}$
24	11–17	$35/8\frac{1}{2}$–35/9	$33\frac{1}{4}$	$1\frac{1}{8}$	$98\frac{1}{2}$–$98\frac{3}{4}$		$93\frac{3}{4}$
25	18–24	$35/9$–$35/9\frac{1}{2}$	$33\frac{1}{3}$	$1\frac{5}{8}$	$98\frac{1}{2}$		
26	July 25– 1	35/10	$33\frac{1}{3}$	$1\frac{5}{8}$	$98\frac{1}{2}$		
27	2– 8	$35/9\frac{1}{2}$–35/10	$33\frac{1}{4}$		98		$93\frac{1}{4}$
28	9–15	35/10	$33\frac{1}{8}$				
29	16–22	$35/10\frac{1}{2}$–35/11	$33\frac{3}{16}$–$33\frac{1}{4}$		99		
30	23–29	$35/10\frac{1}{2}$–35/11	$33\frac{3}{16}$–$33\frac{1}{4}$				
31	Aug. 30– 5	$35/10\frac{1}{2}$–35/11	$33\frac{3}{8}$				
32	6–12						
33	13–19						
34	20–26	35/10	$33\frac{1}{4}$		98		
35	Sep. 27– 2	35/9–35/10			$97\frac{1}{4}$–$97\frac{1}{2}$		
36	3– 9	35/9			96–$96\frac{1}{4}$		
37	10–16	$35/7\frac{1}{2}$–35/8			96–$96\frac{1}{4}$		
38	17–23	35/8	$32\frac{13}{16}$	$\frac{1}{2}$	$95\frac{1}{4}$–$95\frac{1}{2}$	95–$95\frac{1}{4}$	
39	24–30	35/9–35/10	$32\frac{3}{4}$–$32\frac{13}{16}$	$\frac{5}{8}$	$95\frac{3}{4}$–96	$95\frac{1}{4}$	$91\frac{1}{2}$–$91\frac{3}{4}$
40	Oct. 1– 7	$35/6\frac{1}{2}$–$35/7\frac{1}{2}$	$32\frac{3}{4}$–33		$96\frac{1}{2}$–$96\frac{3}{4}$		
41	8–14	35/7	$32\frac{15}{16}$–33		$96\frac{1}{2}$		
42	15–21	$35/6\frac{1}{2}$–35/7	$32\frac{15}{16}$	$\frac{3}{8}$	$96\frac{1}{4}$		92
43	22–28	35/4–35/7			$95\frac{3}{4}$		$91\frac{1}{2}$–$91\frac{3}{4}$
44	Nov. 29– 4	35/4–35/5	$32\frac{7}{8}$–$32\frac{15}{16}$		$94\frac{3}{4}$	$94\frac{1}{2}$	
45	5–11	35/4	$32\frac{15}{16}$				
46	12–18	35/3–35/4	$32\frac{7}{8}$–$32\frac{15}{16}$	$\frac{3}{8}$	$94\frac{1}{2}$–$95\frac{1}{4}$	$94\frac{1}{4}$	
47	19–25	$35/3\frac{1}{2}$–35/4	$32\frac{7}{8}$–$32\frac{15}{16}$	$\frac{1}{2}$	$95\frac{1}{4}$–$95\frac{1}{2}$		$91\frac{1}{4}$–92
48	Dec. 26– 2	$35/3\frac{1}{2}$–35/4	$32\frac{15}{16}$	$\frac{3}{4}$	$95\frac{1}{2}$–$95\frac{3}{4}$	$95\frac{1}{2}$	92
49	3– 9	$35/5\frac{1}{2}$–35/6	$32\frac{15}{16}$				
50	10–16	$35/6\frac{1}{2}$–35/7	$32\frac{7}{8}$–$32\frac{15}{16}$	$\frac{7}{8}$–1	$95\frac{1}{2}$–$95\frac{5}{8}$		
51	17–23	35/6–35/7	$32\frac{15}{16}$–33	$\frac{7}{8}$	95–$95\frac{1}{4}$	$94\frac{1}{2}$	
52	24–31	35/6–35/7	33–$33\frac{1}{8}$		$94\frac{1}{2}$–95	$94\frac{3}{4}$	

TABLE A.11 [b] (*cont.*)

	1672		London	Hamburg	Antwerp	Paris	Rouen	Venice
					AMSTERDAM on:			
1	Jan.	1– 7	35/6–35/8	$33\frac{1}{8}$–$33\frac{1}{4}$	$\frac{7}{8}$	$94\frac{3}{4}$–95	$94\frac{1}{2}$	
2		8–14	$35/7\frac{1}{2}$–35/8	33–$33\frac{3}{16}$	$\frac{3}{4}$–$\frac{7}{8}$	95	$94\frac{1}{2}$–$94\frac{5}{8}$	
3		15–21	35/6–35/8	$33\frac{1}{16}$	$\frac{3}{4}$	$94\frac{3}{4}$–95	$94\frac{1}{2}$	
4		21–28						
5	Feb.	29– 4	$35/8$–$35/8\frac{1}{2}$	33–$33\frac{3}{16}$	$\frac{5}{8}$	$95\frac{1}{2}$		
6		5–11	35/6–35/7	$32\frac{15}{16}$–33	$\frac{3}{4}$–1	96		$90\frac{1}{2}$
7		12–18	35/6	$32\frac{7}{8}$	1–$1\frac{1}{4}$	$95\frac{3}{4}$–96		90–$90\frac{1}{4}$
8		19–25	35/6	$32\frac{7}{8}$		$95\frac{3}{4}$		
9	Mar.	26– 4	$35/4\frac{1}{2}$–35/6	$32\frac{11}{16}$–$32\frac{3}{4}$	$\frac{7}{8}$	95		
10		5–11	35/6	$32\frac{1}{2}$				
11		12–18	$35/5$–$35/5\frac{1}{2}$	$32\frac{3}{16}$–$32\frac{1}{4}$				$87\frac{1}{2}$–88
12		19–25	$35/4\frac{1}{2}$–35/6	32–$32\frac{3}{8}$	$1\frac{1}{4}$	$93\frac{1}{2}$		$87\frac{1}{2}$–88
13	Apr.	26–1	34/0–34/10	$32\frac{3}{8}$–$32\frac{1}{2}$	$\frac{3}{4}$–1	$93\frac{3}{4}$	$93\frac{1}{2}$	$87\frac{1}{2}$–88
14		2– 8	33/1–33/2	$32\frac{3}{8}$	$\frac{1}{2}$	92		
15		9–15	33/5–33/6			92		
16		16–22	33/6			$92\frac{1}{2}$–$92\frac{3}{4}$		
17		23–29	33/6–33/8	$32\frac{1}{8}$–$32\frac{3}{16}$	par	95		
18	May	30– 6	33/8	$32\frac{3}{8}$–$32\frac{1}{2}$				
19		7–13	33/6–33/7	$32\frac{5}{8}$–$32\frac{3}{4}$	$\frac{1}{8}$ loss			
20		14–20	33/5–33/8	$32\frac{9}{16}$–$32\frac{3}{4}$	$\frac{1}{8}$ loss	$94\frac{1}{2}$–$94\frac{3}{4}$		$87\frac{1}{2}$–88
21		21–27	$33/7$–$33/7\frac{1}{2}$	$32\frac{3}{4}$				
22	June	28– 3	33/7	$32\frac{1}{2}$–$32\frac{5}{8}$				
23		4–10	33/6–33/8	$32\frac{1}{2}$–$32\frac{5}{8}$	par–$\frac{1}{2}$	94–$94\frac{1}{2}$		$87\frac{1}{2}$–88
24		11–17	34/6	34				
25		18–24	37/0–40/0	37–38	15–16	100–101	102	
26	July	25– 1	36/0–38/6	$36\frac{1}{2}$–37		100		
27		2– 8	35/0–35/8	33–$33\frac{1}{4}$		$97\frac{1}{2}$–98	99	
28		9–15	35/6	$33\frac{1}{2}$–$33\frac{3}{4}$	5	98		
29		16–22	35/4–35/8	$33\frac{1}{2}$–$33\frac{5}{8}$				
30		23–29	35/6	$33\frac{5}{8}$				
31	Aug.	30– 5	35/4–35/6	$33\frac{5}{8}$				
32		6–12	35/3	$33\frac{5}{8}$	$3\frac{1}{2}$	99	$98\frac{1}{4}$	
33		13–19	34/6–34/8	$33\frac{1}{4}$–$33\frac{3}{8}$		$98\frac{1}{2}$		
34		20–26	34/6–34/7	$33\frac{1}{4}$	3	$98\frac{3}{8}$–$99\frac{1}{2}$	$97\frac{1}{4}$	
35	Sep.	27– 2	33/8–33/9	33–$33\frac{1}{8}$	$2\frac{1}{2}$	98	$97\frac{1}{8}$	88–$88\frac{1}{2}$
36		3– 9	33/10–34/0	$32\frac{7}{8}$–$32\frac{15}{16}$	$1\frac{3}{4}$–2	97		
37		10–16	33/8–34/2	$32\frac{3}{4}$–$32\frac{7}{8}$	$1\frac{1}{2}$	$96\frac{1}{4}$–97		$87\frac{1}{2}$
38		17–23	34/2–34/4	$32\frac{3}{4}$		96		
39		24–30						
40	Oct.	1– 7	34/2–34/3	$32\frac{3}{8}$–$32\frac{1}{2}$		96		
41		8–14	34/3–34/4	$32\frac{3}{8}$	$\frac{3}{4}$	$96\frac{1}{2}$		
42		15–21	34/1–34/2	$32\frac{1}{8}$	$1\frac{1}{4}$	$96\frac{1}{2}$	96	
43		22–28	33/11–34/0	$32\frac{1}{16}$–$32\frac{1}{4}$	1	$94\frac{1}{2}$–$95\frac{3}{4}$	$95\frac{1}{2}$–$95\frac{3}{4}$	$87\frac{1}{4}$–$88\frac{1}{2}$
44	Nov.	29– 4	33/10	$32\frac{1}{4}$	1	$94\frac{1}{2}$–$95\frac{3}{4}$		
45		5–11	33/7–33/11	$32\frac{1}{16}$–$32\frac{3}{8}$	1	$94\frac{1}{2}$–$94\frac{3}{4}$		$86\frac{1}{2}$–$86\frac{3}{4}$
46		12–18	33/10	$32\frac{1}{4}$		94–$94\frac{1}{2}$		$86\frac{1}{2}$
47		19–25	33/10	$32\frac{1}{4}$	$\frac{1}{2}$	$94\frac{1}{2}$		86–$86\frac{1}{2}$
48	Dec.	26– 2	33/10	$32\frac{1}{4}$–$32\frac{3}{8}$	$\frac{3}{8}$	94–$94\frac{1}{2}$		$86\frac{1}{2}$–$86\frac{3}{4}$
49		3– 9	33/10–34/0		par	94		
50		10–16	33/11–34/0	$32\frac{1}{8}$	par	$93\frac{3}{4}$	$93\frac{1}{2}$	
51		17–23	33/11–34/0	$32\frac{1}{8}$–$33\frac{3}{16}$	$\frac{1}{4}$	$93\frac{3}{4}$		$87\frac{1}{2}$
52		24–31	34/1					

TABLE A.11 [b] (*cont.*)

1673			AMSTERDAM on:					
			London	Hamburg	Antwerp	Paris	Rouen	Venice
I	Jan.	1– 7	34/1–34/4	$32\frac{3}{8}$–$32\frac{1}{2}$	$\frac{1}{2}$	$94\frac{1}{2}$–$94\frac{3}{4}$	94	$88\frac{3}{4}$–89
2		8–14	34/2–34/2$\frac{1}{2}$	$32\frac{1}{8}$–$32\frac{5}{16}$	$\frac{1}{2}$			$88\frac{1}{2}$
3		15–21	34/1–34/3	$32\frac{5}{16}$	$\frac{1}{2}$–$\frac{3}{4}$	$94\frac{3}{4}$–95		$88\frac{1}{2}$
4		21–28	34/3					
5	Feb.	29– 4						
6		5–11	34/2–34/3					
7		12–18	34/2	$32\frac{1}{2}$	$\frac{7}{8}$	$94\frac{1}{2}$		
8		19–25	34/1			$94\frac{1}{2}$		$87\frac{1}{2}$
9	Mar.	26– 4	34/0			$94\frac{1}{2}$		$87\frac{1}{2}$
10		5–11						
11		12–18	34/0	$32\frac{1}{2}$		$94\frac{1}{2}$		
12		19–25	33/10–34/0	$32\frac{1}{2}$–$32\frac{5}{8}$	$\frac{5}{8}$	$94\frac{1}{2}$–$94\frac{5}{8}$		
13	Apr.	26– 1						
14		2– 8						
15		9–15						
16		16–22						
17		23–29						
18	May	30– 6						
19		7–13	33/10–33/11	$32\frac{3}{4}$	$\frac{1}{2}$			88–$88\frac{1}{4}$
20		14–20	33/11–34/0	$32\frac{13}{16}$–$32\frac{7}{8}$				
21		21–27						
22	June	28– 3	34/2–34/3	$33\frac{1}{16}$				
23		4–10						
24		11–17						
25		18–24						
26	July	25– 1						

TABLE A.11 [b] (*cont.*)

	1675		AMSTERDAM on:					
			London	Hamburg	Antwerp	Paris	Rouen	Venice
1	Jan.	1– 7	$34/2\frac{1}{2}$–$34/4$	$34\frac{1}{2}$	$\frac{7}{8}$	$100\frac{1}{2}$–101		$93\frac{3}{4}$–94
2		8–14	$34/4$	$34\frac{9}{16}$		$100\frac{1}{2}$		
3		15–21	$34/3\frac{1}{2}$–$34/4$			$101\frac{1}{2}$		
4		21–28	$34/4$–$34/5$	$34\frac{11}{16}$–$34\frac{3}{4}$	$1\frac{1}{4}$	$101\frac{1}{4}$–$101\frac{3}{4}$		
5	Feb.	29– 4	$34/4$–$34/5$	$34\frac{3}{4}$	$1\frac{3}{8}$	102–$103\frac{1}{2}$		$94\frac{1}{2}$–$94\frac{3}{4}$
6		5–11	$34/3$–$34/4$	$34\frac{5}{8}$	$1\frac{1}{8}$	$102\frac{1}{2}$		$94\frac{1}{2}$
7		12–18	$34/5$	$34\frac{9}{16}$–$34\frac{5}{8}$	$\frac{7}{8}$	$100\frac{1}{2}$–$103\frac{1}{2}$		$94\frac{1}{2}$–$94\frac{3}{4}$
8		19–25	$34/8$		$\frac{3}{4}$	$100\frac{3}{4}$	$100\frac{1}{2}$	
9	Mar.	26– 4	$34/6$–$34/8$	$34\frac{1}{2}$	$1\frac{1}{4}$	$101\frac{1}{2}$–102		$94\frac{1}{2}$
10		5–11	$34/6\frac{1}{2}$–$34/7$	$34\frac{7}{16}$–$34\frac{1}{2}$		$101\frac{3}{4}$		$94\frac{5}{8}$
11		12–18	$34/6$–$34/7\frac{1}{2}$	$34\frac{3}{8}$–$34\frac{7}{16}$	1	$101\frac{1}{2}$–$101\frac{3}{4}$		
12		19–25	$34/7$–$34/7\frac{1}{2}$	$34\frac{3}{8}$	$1\frac{1}{8}$	101–$101\frac{1}{4}$	$100\frac{3}{4}$	$94\frac{1}{2}$
13	Apr.	26– 1	$34/6$–$34/6\frac{1}{2}$	$34\frac{3}{8}$–$34\frac{1}{2}$	1–$1\frac{1}{4}$	$101\frac{1}{4}$		
14		2– 8	$34/6\frac{1}{2}$–$34/7$	$34\frac{5}{16}$	$1\frac{1}{4}$	$101\frac{1}{4}$	101	$94\frac{1}{4}$
15		9–15	$34/6$–$34/7$	$34\frac{5}{16}$–$34\frac{3}{8}$	$1\frac{1}{4}$	101–$101\frac{1}{2}$	$101\frac{1}{2}$	$94\frac{1}{4}$
16		16–22	$34/6$–$34/7\frac{1}{2}$	$34\frac{3}{8}$–$34\frac{7}{16}$	1	$101\frac{1}{4}$–$101\frac{5}{8}$		
17		23–29	$34/8\frac{1}{2}$			$101\frac{3}{4}$		
18	May	30– 6	$34/9$–$34/10$	$34\frac{9}{16}$–$34\frac{5}{8}$		$101\frac{3}{4}$–102	$101\frac{1}{4}$	94
19		7–13	$34/11$	$34\frac{5}{16}$				
20		14–20	$34/10$	$34\frac{1}{2}$		102		
21		21–27	$34/10$	$34\frac{1}{2}$	$\frac{1}{8}$	$101\frac{5}{8}$–102		
22	June	28– 3	$34/10$			$101\frac{5}{8}$		
23		4–10						
24		11–17	$34/9$–$34/10$		$\frac{7}{8}$			
25		18–24	$34/9$–$34/10$	$34\frac{11}{16}$–$34\frac{3}{4}$	$\frac{3}{4}$	$101\frac{1}{2}$–102		$94\frac{1}{4}$
26	July	25– 1						
27		2– 8	$34/10$–$34/11$	$34\frac{5}{8}$		102	$101\frac{3}{4}$	
28		9–15	$35/0$	$34\frac{5}{8}$		$101\frac{3}{4}$–102		$94\frac{1}{4}$
29		16–22	$34/11\frac{1}{2}$–$35/0$	$34\frac{5}{8}$		$101\frac{3}{4}$		
30		23–29	$35/0$	$34\frac{5}{8}$		$101\frac{3}{4}$		
31	Aug.	30– 5	$35/1$	$34\frac{5}{8}$		$101\frac{1}{2}$		
32		6–12	$35/1$			$100\frac{3}{4}$	$100\frac{1}{2}$	
33		13–19	$35/1$	$34\frac{1}{2}$	1	$100\frac{1}{2}$		$94\frac{1}{2}$
34		20–26	$35/1$	$34\frac{1}{2}$		101		
35	Sep.	27– 2	$35/0$–$35/1$	$34\frac{1}{4}$–$34\frac{5}{16}$	par	$101\frac{1}{4}$	101	
36		3– 9	$35/1$	$34\frac{1}{4}$		101–$101\frac{1}{2}$		
37		10–16	$35/2\frac{1}{2}$		1	$101\frac{1}{2}$		
38		17–23						
39		24–30	$35/2$–$35/2\frac{1}{2}$	$34\frac{1}{4}$	par	$101\frac{1}{4}$–$101\frac{3}{8}$	101	
40	Oct.	1– 7	$35/3\frac{1}{2}$	$34\frac{3}{8}$	1	$101\frac{1}{4}$		
41		8–14	$35/2$–$35/2\frac{1}{2}$	$34\frac{3}{8}$		$100\frac{3}{4}$–101		
42		15–21						
43		22–28						
44	Nov.	29– 4	$35/1\frac{1}{2}$	$34\frac{9}{16}$				
45		5–11						
46		12–18						
47		19–25	$35/2$–$35/3$		par	$99\frac{1}{8}$		
48	Dec.	26– 2	$35/3$–$35/4$	$34\frac{1}{16}$		$98\frac{3}{8}$–99		
49		3– 9						
50		10–16	$35/3$–$35/3\frac{1}{2}$	34	par	$98\frac{1}{4}$–$98\frac{1}{2}$		
51		17–23						
52		24–31	$35/8$	$34\frac{1}{8}$	$\frac{1}{8}$ loss	$99\frac{1}{2}$		

TABLE A.11 [b] (*cont.*)

	1676	— AMSTERDAM on:					
		London	Hamburg	Antwerp	Paris	Rouen	Venice
1	Jan. 1– 7						
2	8–14						
3	15–21						
4	21–28						
5	Feb. 29– 4	35/6	$34\frac{1}{2}$		$98\frac{1}{2}$		92
6	5–11	35/7	$34\frac{3}{8}$	par	$98\frac{1}{4}$–$98\frac{1}{2}$		
7	12–18						
8	19–25	35/8	$34\frac{3}{16}$	$\frac{1}{8}$–$\frac{1}{2}$	$98\frac{1}{2}$		
9	Mar. 26– 4	35/8–35/9	$34\frac{3}{8}$–$34\frac{7}{16}$	$\frac{3}{4}$–$\frac{3}{8}$			
10	5–11						
11	12–18	$35/8\frac{1}{2}$–35/9	$34\frac{7}{16}$–$34\frac{1}{2}$	$\frac{3}{8}$–$\frac{1}{2}$	$98\frac{1}{4}$–$98\frac{1}{2}$		$91\frac{3}{4}$
12	19–25	35/8–35/9	$34\frac{1}{4}$–$34\frac{5}{16}$	$\frac{1}{2}$–$\frac{5}{8}$	$98\frac{1}{2}$		
13	Apr. 26– 1						
14	2– 8	35/7–35/8					
15	9–15						
16	16–22						
17	23–29						
18	May 30– 6	35/8–35/9	$34\frac{1}{4}$–$34\frac{7}{16}$	$\frac{3}{4}$–$\frac{7}{8}$	$98\frac{7}{8}$–99		91–$91\frac{1}{4}$
19	7–13	$35/8$–$35/9\frac{1}{2}$	$34\frac{5}{16}$–$34\frac{7}{16}$	$\frac{7}{8}$	$98\frac{1}{2}$		
20	14–20						
21	21–27	35/10–35/11	$34\frac{3}{8}$–$34\frac{7}{16}$	$\frac{7}{8}$–1	$98\frac{1}{4}$–99		
22	June 28– 3						
23	4–10	$35/9$–$35/9\frac{1}{2}$		$1\frac{1}{2}$	$99\frac{3}{4}$–100		
24	11–17						
25	18–24						
26	July 25– 1						
27	2– 8						
28	9–15		$33\frac{7}{8}$				
29	16–22	36/2			$100\frac{1}{4}$–$100\frac{1}{2}$	100	
30	23–29						
31	Aug. 30– 5						
32	6–12	36/0–36/3	$33\frac{1}{4}$	$1\frac{1}{8}$	100	$99\frac{1}{2}$	
33	13–19	36/3	$33\frac{3}{4}$	$1\frac{1}{4}$	$100\frac{1}{4}$		
34	20–26	36/2–36/3	$33\frac{5}{8}$–$33\frac{11}{16}$	$1\frac{1}{8}$–$1\frac{3}{8}$	$100\frac{1}{4}$		
35	Sep. 27– 2	36/2	$33\frac{3}{4}$–$33\frac{13}{16}$		$100\frac{1}{4}$–$100\frac{1}{2}$		93
36	3– 9	$36/2\frac{1}{2}$			$100\frac{1}{2}$	$100\frac{1}{4}$	
37	10–16	36/4	$33\frac{7}{8}$	$1\frac{1}{8}$	$100\frac{1}{2}$–$100\frac{5}{8}$		
38	17–23	36/4	34–$34\frac{1}{16}$		$100\frac{5}{8}$		
39	24–30	36/3–36/4					
40	Oct. 1– 7						
41	8–14	$36/2\frac{1}{2}$	$33\frac{3}{4}$	1	$100\frac{1}{4}$		
42	15–21	$36/2$–$36/2\frac{1}{2}$			100	$99\frac{3}{4}$	
43	22–28	$36/2$–$36/2\frac{1}{2}$	$33\frac{9}{16}$	par	$99\frac{1}{4}$–100	$99\frac{3}{4}$	
44	Nov. 29– 4	$36/2\frac{1}{2}$	$33\frac{1}{2}$		$99\frac{1}{2}$–$99\frac{3}{4}$		
45	5–11	$36/2\frac{1}{2}$–36/3	$33\frac{1}{2}$–$33\frac{5}{8}$		$99\frac{1}{4}$–$99\frac{3}{4}$		
46	12–18	$36/2\frac{1}{2}$–36/3	$33\frac{1}{2}$		$99\frac{1}{4}$–$99\frac{1}{2}$		
47	19–25	36/3–36/4	$33\frac{1}{2}$–$33\frac{9}{16}$	$\frac{5}{8}$–1	$99\frac{1}{4}$–$99\frac{1}{2}$		
48	Dec. 26– 2						
49	3– 9	$36/5\frac{1}{2}$–36/6	$33\frac{9}{16}$	$1\frac{1}{4}$–$1\frac{3}{8}$	$99\frac{1}{2}$–$99\frac{5}{8}$		
50	10–16	$36/6\frac{1}{2}$–36/7	$33\frac{9}{16}$	$1\frac{1}{4}$–$1\frac{3}{8}$	$99\frac{3}{4}$		
51	17–23	$36/6$–$36/6\frac{1}{2}$			$99\frac{1}{2}$		
52	24–31	36/6	$33\frac{1}{2}$	$1\frac{1}{2}$–$1\frac{1}{4}$	$99\frac{3}{4}$		

TABLE A.11 [b] (*cont.*)

	1677		AMSTERDAM on:					
			London	Hamburg	Antwerp	Paris	Rouen	Venice
1	Jan.	1– 7	36/6	$33\frac{9}{16}$		$99\frac{3}{4}$		
2		8–14	$36/4\frac{1}{2}$–36/5	$33\frac{7}{16}$–$33\frac{1}{2}$				
3		15–21						
4		21–28	36/4–36/5	$33\frac{3}{8}$	$1\frac{1}{2}$	$99\frac{1}{4}$		
5	Feb.	29– 4	36/3–36/4	$33\frac{3}{4}$				
6		5–11						
7		12–18	36/3					
8		19–25	36/2	$33\frac{7}{16}$		$99\frac{1}{4}$		
9	Mar.	26– 4						
10		5–11	36/3	$33\frac{7}{16}$	$1\frac{1}{4}$	99		
11		12–18						
12		19–25	36/2	33–$33\frac{5}{16}$	1–$1\frac{1}{8}$	$99\frac{1}{2}$		
13	Apr.	26– 1						
14		2– 8						
15		9–15	36/2–36/3	$33\frac{1}{8}$–$33\frac{3}{16}$	$1\frac{1}{4}$	99–$99\frac{1}{2}$		
16		16–22	$36/2\frac{1}{2}$	$33\frac{3}{16}$–$33\frac{1}{4}$	$1\frac{1}{4}$	99		
17		23–29						
18	May	30– 6						
19		7–13	36/0	$33\frac{1}{8}$	$\frac{1}{2}$			
20		14–20						
21		21–27	$36/0\frac{1}{2}$–36/1		1	$98\frac{5}{8}$		
22	June	28– 3						
23		4–10	36/0	$33\frac{1}{16}$	$1\frac{1}{8}$–$1\frac{1}{4}$	99		
24		11–17	35/11					
25		18–24						
26	July	25– 1						
27		2– 8	35/11	$32\frac{15}{16}$		$99\frac{1}{4}$		
28		9–15	$35/11\frac{1}{2}$–36/0	$32\frac{15}{16}$	1			
29		16–22						
30		23–29	36/1			99		
31	Aug.	30– 5						
32		6–12	36/1–36/3	$33\frac{3}{16}$–$33\frac{1}{4}$	$1\frac{3}{8}$	$98\frac{3}{4}$		
33		13–19	36/1					
34		20–26						
35	Sep.	27– 2	36/1	$33\frac{1}{4}$	$1\frac{1}{4}$	99		
36		3– 9						
37		10–16	35/11–36/0	$33\frac{1}{8}$	$\frac{3}{4}$	$98\frac{1}{2}$		
38		17–23	$35/10\frac{1}{2}$–35/11	33	$\frac{5}{8}$	$98\frac{1}{4}$–$98\frac{1}{2}$		
39		24–30						
40	Oct.	1– 7						
41		8–14	35/11					
42		15–21						
43		22–28						
44	Nov.	29– 4	$35/9\frac{1}{2}$			$97\frac{1}{8}$	$96\frac{7}{8}$	
45		5–11						
46		12–18						
47		19–25						
48	Dec.	26– 2	35/6					
49		3– 9						
50		10–16	$35/6\frac{1}{2}$–35/7			$95\frac{1}{2}$		
51		17–23	$35/6\frac{1}{2}$–$35/7\frac{1}{2}$	$32\frac{13}{16}$	$\frac{3}{4}$	96	$95\frac{3}{4}$	
52		24–31	35/7–35/8	$33\frac{1}{8}$	$\frac{1}{2}$	$95\frac{3}{4}$–96		

TABLE A.11 [b] (*cont.*)

1678			AMSTERDAM on:					
			London	Hamburg	Antwerp	Paris	Rouen	Venice
1	Jan.	1– 7	35/9			$95\frac{1}{4}$		
2		8–14	35/8–35/9		$\frac{3}{8}$			
3		15–21	35/6–35/7	$33\frac{3}{8}$	1			
4		21–28	35/6–35/6$\frac{1}{2}$					
5	Feb.	29– 4						
6		5–11	34/10–34/11					
7		12–18	34/4	$33\frac{1}{4}$	$\frac{1}{4}$			
8		19–25	34/4–34/6	$33\frac{7}{16}$	$\frac{1}{4}$	$95\frac{1}{2}$		
9	Mar.	26– 4						
10		5–11	34/1–34/2		par			
11		12–18	34/2	$33\frac{3}{8}$	par			
12		19–25						
13	Apr.	26– 1	33/10–33/11					
14		2– 8	33/9–33/10					
15		9–15	33/10			96		
16		16–22	33/11–34/0		$\frac{1}{2}$	$95\frac{3}{4}$–96		
17		23–29	34/0–34/1	33	$\frac{1}{2}$	$95\frac{3}{4}$		
18	May	30– 6	34/3–34/4$\frac{1}{2}$	33	$\frac{3}{8}$			
19		7–13	33/11–34/0	$32\frac{15}{16}$				
20		14–20	33/11–34/0					
21		21–27						
22	June	28– 3						
23		4–10	34/4–34/5			$95\frac{1}{2}$–$95\frac{3}{4}$	$95\frac{1}{4}$	
24		11–17						
25		18–24						
26	July	25– 1						
27		2– 8						
28		9–15	34/9		$\frac{1}{4}$			
29		16–22	34/8–34/9	33		$95\frac{3}{4}$		
30		23–29	34/8–34/9	$32\frac{7}{8}$–$32\frac{15}{16}$	par	$95\frac{3}{4}$–96		
31	Aug.	30– 5	34/8–34/9	33	$\frac{3}{4}$	$95\frac{7}{8}$–96		
32		6–12	34/9	33		96	$95\frac{1}{2}$	
33		13–19						
34		20–26						
35	Sep.	27– 2						
36		3– 9						
37		10–16	35/2–35/3	$33\frac{3}{16}$–$33\frac{1}{4}$	$\frac{3}{4}$	$95\frac{7}{8}$–96		
38		17–23	35/2–35/3		$\frac{1}{2}$	$95\frac{3}{4}$		
39		24–30	35/2–35/3	$33\frac{3}{8}$	$\frac{1}{2}$–$\frac{5}{8}$	$95\frac{1}{4}$–$95\frac{3}{4}$		
40	Oct.	1– 7						
41		8–14						
42		15–21						
43		22–28						
44	Nov.	29– 4						
45		5–11						
46		12–18	34/10$\frac{1}{2}$–34/11	$32\frac{7}{8}$		$94\frac{3}{4}$	$94\frac{1}{2}$	$89\frac{3}{4}$
47		19–25	34/11	$32\frac{7}{8}$	$\frac{1}{4}$ loss	$94\frac{3}{4}$		
48	Dec.	26– 2						
49		3– 9						
50		10–16	34/11					
51		17–23	35/1–35/2	$33\frac{1}{16}$–$33\frac{1}{2}$		95–$95\frac{1}{4}$		
52		24–31	35/2	33		$95\frac{1}{4}$		

TABLE A.11 [b] (*cont.*)

1679			London	Hamburg	Antwerp	Paris	Rouen	Venice
			\<colspan: AMSTERDAM on:\>					

#	1679		London	Hamburg	Antwerp	Paris	Rouen	Venice
1	Jan.	1– 7	35/0–35/1	33				
2		8–14						
3		15–21	35/2	$33\frac{1}{16}$		$95\frac{1}{2}$		
4		21–28						
5	Feb.	29– 4						
6		5–11						
7		12–18						
8		19–25						
9	Mar.	26– 4	$35/4–35/4\frac{1}{2}$			$95\frac{1}{2}$	$95\frac{1}{4}$	
10		5–11	35/5–35/6	33		96		
11		12–18	35/6	33		$95\frac{1}{2}$		
12		19–25	35/5–35/6	33		$95\frac{3}{4}$		
13	Apr.	26– 1						
14		2– 8						
15		9–15	35/7	$33\frac{1}{16}–33\frac{1}{8}$				
16		16–22						
17		23–29						
18	May	30– 6						
19		7–13						
20		14–20						
21		21–27						
22	June	28– 3	35/8					
23		4–10						
24		11–17						
25		18–24	35/9	$32\frac{7}{8}–33$				
26	July	25– 1	35/9–35/10	$33\frac{1}{16}–33\frac{1}{8}$		$96\frac{1}{2}$	$96\frac{1}{4}$	
27		2– 8	35/10					
28		9–15						
29		16–22						
30		23–29	35/11				$96\frac{3}{4}$	
31	Aug.	30– 5	36/1					
32		6–12						
33		13–19	$36/0–36/0\frac{1}{2}$			$97\frac{3}{8}$		
34		20–26	$36/0\frac{1}{2}–36/1$					
35	Sep.	27– 2						
36		3– 9	$36/1\frac{1}{2}$					
37		10–16						
38		17–23	36/0					
39		24–30						
40	Oct.	1– 7						
41		8–14	36/0	$32\frac{3}{4}–32\frac{7}{8}$				
42		15–21	36/0–36/1	$32\frac{3}{4}$		$97\frac{1}{4}$	97	
43		22–28	35/10–35/11			$97\frac{1}{2}–97\frac{3}{4}$	$97\frac{1}{4}$	
44	Nov.	29– 4						
45		5–11						
46		12–18						
47		19–25						
48	Dec.	26– 2						
49		3– 9	35/11					
50		10–16						
51		17–23						
52		24–31	35/11					

TABLE A.11 [b] (*cont.*)

| | 1680 | | AMSTERDAM on: | | | | | |
			London	Hamburg	Antwerp	Paris	Rouen	Venice
1	Jan.	1– 7						
2		8–14						
3		15–21 ˙	$35/10\frac{1}{2}$–$35/11$	$33\frac{1}{4}$–$33\frac{5}{16}$		$98\frac{3}{4}$–99	$98\frac{1}{2}$	$92\frac{7}{8}$
4		21–28						
5	Feb.	29– 4	$35/11$			99		
6		5–11	$36/1$					
7		12–18						
8		19–25	$36/1$					
9	Mar.	26– 4						
10		5–11	$36/1$					
11		12–18	$36/0\frac{1}{2}$–$36/1$			$99\frac{1}{8}$	$98\frac{7}{8}$	
12		19–25	$36/0$					
13	Apr.	26– 1	$36/0$					

[c] *Rouen on London and Amsterdam; Paris on London and Amsterdam*

	1668		ROUEN on:	
			London	Amsterdam
1	Jan.	1– 7		
2		8–14		
3		15–21		
4		21–28		
5	Feb.	29– 4		
6		5–11		
7		12–18	$58\frac{1}{4}$	$102\frac{1}{4}$
8		19–25		
9	Mar.	26– 4		
10		5–11	58–$58\frac{1}{4}$	102
11		12–18		
12		19–25	$58\frac{3}{4}$–59	102–103
13	Apr.	26– 1	59	103
14		2– 8	59	$103\frac{1}{2}$
15		9–15	$59\frac{1}{4}$	$103\frac{3}{4}$
16		16–22	59	$102\frac{3}{4}$
17		23–29	59	102
18	May	30– 6	$59\frac{1}{4}$	$102\frac{1}{4}$–$102\frac{1}{2}$
19		7–13	59	$102\frac{1}{2}$
20		14–20	$59\frac{1}{4}$	$102\frac{1}{2}$–103
21		21–27	$59\frac{1}{4}$–$59\frac{3}{8}$	$103\frac{1}{4}$
22	June	28– 3	59–$59\frac{1}{4}$	103–$103\frac{1}{4}$
23		4–10	$58\frac{3}{4}$–59	103–$103\frac{1}{4}$
24		11–17	59	103
25		18–24	59	103
26	July	25– 1	$59\frac{1}{4}$	103–$103\frac{1}{4}$
27		2– 8		
28		9–15	$59\frac{1}{2}$	$103\frac{1}{2}$
29		16–22		
30		23–29	$59\frac{1}{2}$–$59\frac{3}{4}$	104
31	Aug.	30– 5	$59\frac{3}{4}$	$104\frac{1}{4}$
32		6–12		
33		13–19	$59\frac{1}{4}$–$59\frac{3}{8}$	$103\frac{3}{4}$
34		20–26	$58\frac{1}{2}$–59	$102\frac{3}{4}$–$103\frac{1}{2}$
35	Sep.	27– 2	$58\frac{1}{4}$–$58\frac{1}{2}$	$102\frac{1}{4}$–$102\frac{1}{2}$
36		3– 9		
37		10–16		
38		17–23		
39		24–30	$58\frac{3}{4}$–59	103
40	Oct.	1– 7	$58\frac{1}{4}$–$58\frac{1}{2}$	103
41		8–14	$57\frac{3}{4}$–$58\frac{1}{4}$	$102\frac{1}{4}$–103
42		15–21	$57\frac{3}{4}$	$102\frac{3}{4}$–103
43		22–28	$57\frac{3}{4}$	$102\frac{3}{4}$
44	Nov.	29– 4	$57\frac{3}{4}$	$102\frac{1}{4}$
45		5–11	57	$102\frac{1}{2}$
46		12–18	$57\frac{1}{2}$	$102\frac{1}{2}$
47		19–25	$57\frac{3}{4}$–58	$102\frac{3}{4}$
48	Dec.	26– 2		
49		3– 9	$57\frac{1}{4}$	$101\frac{3}{4}$
50		10–16	57	101
51		17–23	$56\frac{3}{4}$–57	101
52		24–31		

TABLE A. 11 [c] (*cont.*)

	1669		ROUEN on: London	Amsterdam
1	Jan.	1– 7	$57\frac{1}{2}$–$57\frac{3}{4}$	103
2		8–14	$57\frac{1}{2}$–$57\frac{3}{4}$	$102\frac{1}{2}$
3		15–21		
4		21–28		
5	Feb.	29– 4	$57\frac{1}{8}$–$57\frac{3}{8}$	$101\frac{3}{4}$–102
6		5–11		
7		12–18	$57\frac{1}{4}$	$101\frac{3}{4}$
8		19–25	$57\frac{1}{2}$	$101\frac{3}{4}$
9	Mar.	26– 4		
10		5–11	$57\frac{1}{4}$	$101\frac{3}{4}$
11		12–18	$57\frac{3}{8}$	$101\frac{1}{4}$
12		19–25	$57\frac{1}{4}$	$101\frac{1}{2}$
13	Apr.	26– 1	$57\frac{1}{4}$	$101\frac{1}{2}$
14		2– 8	$57\frac{1}{4}$	$101\frac{1}{2}$
15		9–15	57	$101\frac{1}{2}$
16		16–22		
17		23–29		
18	May	30– 6		
19		7–13		
20		14–20		
21		21–27		
22	June	28– 3	$56\frac{3}{4}$	101
23		4–10		
24		11–17		
25		18–24		
26	July	25– 1		
27		2– 8		
28		9–15		
29		16–22		
30		23–29		
31	Aug.	30– 5		
32		6–12		
33		13–19	57	$101\frac{1}{4}$
34		20–26	57	$101\frac{1}{4}$
35	Sep.	27– 2		
36		3– 9		
37		10–16	$56\frac{3}{4}$	$100\frac{3}{4}$
38		17–23	$56\frac{1}{2}$	$100\frac{1}{2}$
39		24–30		
40	Oct.	1– 7		
41		8–14		
42		15–21	$56\frac{1}{4}$–$56\frac{3}{8}$	100
43		22–28		
44	Nov.	29– 4	$55\frac{7}{8}$–56	$99\frac{3}{4}$
45		5–11		
46		12–18		
47		19–25	$55\frac{3}{4}$	$98\frac{3}{4}$
48	Dec.	26– 2		
49		3– 9	$55\frac{1}{2}$	$98\frac{1}{4}$
50		10–16	$55\frac{3}{8}$	$98\frac{1}{4}$
51		17–23	$55\frac{1}{2}$	$98\frac{1}{4}$
52		24–31	$55\frac{1}{2}$	$98\frac{1}{4}$

	1670	ROUEN on: London	ROUEN on: Amsterdam	PARIS on: London	PARIS on: Amsterdam
1	Jan. 1– 7				
2	8–14				
3	15–21	$55\frac{3}{8}$–$55\frac{1}{2}$	$97\frac{1}{2}$		
4	21–28	$55\frac{3}{4}$	$97\frac{1}{4}$		
5	Feb. 29– 4				
6	5–11				
7	12–18	$56\frac{1}{8}$–$56\frac{1}{4}$	$97\frac{3}{4}$–98		
8	19–25	$56\frac{1}{4}$	$97\frac{3}{4}$		
9	Mar. 26– 4	$56\frac{1}{2}$	$98\frac{1}{2}$		
10	5–11				
11	12–18				
12	19–25				
13	Apr. 26– 1				

	1671	ROUEN on: London	ROUEN on: Amsterdam	PARIS on: London	PARIS on: Amsterdam
14	2– 8				
15	9–15				
16	16–22	56	$99\frac{3}{4}$–100		
17	23–29				
18	May 30– 6				
19	7–13				
20	14–20				
21	21–27	$56\frac{1}{2}$	101–$101\frac{3}{4}$		
22	June 28– 3				
23	4–10	$55\frac{3}{4}$	$100\frac{1}{2}$		
24	11–17				
25	18–24				
26	July 25– 1				
27	2– 8				
28	9–15				
29	16–22	$55\frac{7}{8}$	100	$55\frac{7}{8}$–56	100
30	23–29			56	100
31	Aug. 30– 5	$55\frac{7}{8}$–56	100		
32	6–12				
33	13–19				
34	20–26				
35	Sep. 27– 2	$55\frac{1}{4}$	99		
36	3– 9	55			
37	10–16	$55\frac{3}{4}$			
38	17–23				
39	24–30	$54\frac{1}{4}$			
40	Oct. 1– 7	$54\frac{1}{4}$–$55\frac{1}{4}$	$97\frac{1}{2}$–$98\frac{3}{4}$	$55\frac{1}{2}$	
41	8–14	$55\frac{1}{4}$	$98\frac{1}{2}$–$98\frac{3}{4}$		
42	15–21				
43	22–28				
44	Nov. 29– 4				
45	5–11	$54\frac{1}{4}$	97		
46	12–18	$54\frac{1}{8}$	$96\frac{1}{4}$		
47	19–25	54–$54\frac{1}{4}$	$96\frac{1}{4}$–$96\frac{1}{2}$	$54\frac{1}{8}$–$54\frac{1}{4}$	$97\frac{1}{4}$–$97\frac{1}{2}$
48	Dec. 26– 2	$53\frac{7}{8}$–54	$97\frac{1}{4}$–$97\frac{1}{2}$		
49	3– 9	54	$97\frac{1}{4}$–$97\frac{1}{2}$	54	98
50	10–16	54	$97\frac{1}{2}$		
51	17–23				
52	24–31				

TABLE A.11 [c] (*cont.*)

			ROUEN on:		PARIS on:	
	1672		London	Amsterdam	London	Amsterdam
1	Jan.	1– 7	$54\frac{3}{8}$	$97\frac{3}{4}$		
2		8–14				
3		15–21	$54\frac{1}{4}$–$54\frac{3}{8}$	$97\frac{1}{4}$–$97\frac{1}{2}$		
4		21–28	$53\frac{3}{4}$	$96\frac{3}{4}$		
5	Feb.	29– 4	$54\frac{1}{4}$–$54\frac{3}{8}$	$98\frac{1}{4}$		
6		5–11				
7		12–18			54–$54\frac{1}{4}$	98
8		19–25				
9	Mar.	26– 4	$54\frac{1}{4}$–$54\frac{3}{8}$	$97\frac{1}{2}$–$97\frac{3}{4}$		
10		5–11				
11		12–18	$54\frac{3}{8}$	$97\frac{1}{2}$		
12		19–25				
13	Apr.	26– 1				
14		2– 8	55	96		
15		9–15				
16		16–22	$56\frac{1}{2}$			
17		23–29				
18	May	30– 6				
19		7–13				
20		14–20				
21		21–27				
22	June	28– 3				
23		4–10				
24		11–17				
25		18–24				
26	July	25– 1				
27		2– 8				
28		9–15	57	100		
29		16–22	$57\frac{1}{4}$	100		
30		23–29			56	100
31	Aug.	30– 5	$57\frac{1}{4}$	100		
32		6–12	$57\frac{1}{4}$	100		
33		13–19	$57\frac{1}{8}$–$57\frac{1}{4}$	$100\frac{1}{2}$		
34		20–26	57	100		
35	Sep.	27– 2				
36		3– 9				
37		10–16	$56\frac{3}{4}$	$99\frac{1}{2}$		
38		17–23				
39		24–30				
40	Oct.	1– 7				
41		8–14				
42		15–21				
43		22–28	56	$97\frac{3}{4}$	$56\frac{1}{4}$–$56\frac{1}{2}$	
44	Nov.	29– 4			$56\frac{1}{2}$	$97\frac{1}{2}$
45		5–11	$56\frac{3}{4}$	$97\frac{1}{2}$	57	97
46		12–18			$56\frac{1}{4}$–$56\frac{1}{2}$	97
47		19–25			56–$56\frac{1}{4}$	97
48	Dec.	26– 2			$56\frac{1}{4}$–$56\frac{1}{2}$	$97\frac{1}{2}$
49		3– 9			$56\frac{1}{4}$	96
50		10–16	$56\frac{1}{4}$	96		
51		17–23			$56\frac{1}{2}$	96
52		24–31			$56\frac{1}{2}$	96

TABLE A.11 [c] *(cont.)*

	1673	ROUEN on: London	Amsterdam	PARIS on: London	Amsterdam
1	Jan. 1- 7	$56\frac14$–$56\frac12$	96–$96\frac14$	$56\frac14$	$95\frac12$
2	8–14	56–$56\frac14$	$96\frac14$–$96\frac12$	$55\frac34$–$56\frac38$	
3	15–21	56–$56\frac14$	$96\frac12$		
4	21–28				
5	Feb. 29– 4				
6	5–11			$55\frac58$	$96\frac14$
7	12–18				
8	19–25				
9	Mar. 26– 4				
10	5–11	$56\frac14$	$96\frac14$		
11	12–18				
12	19–25	$56\frac18$	96		
13	Apr. 26– 1				

	1675	ROUEN on: London	Amsterdam	PARIS on: London	Amsterdam
27	2– 8			$58\frac78$–59	$103\frac14$
28	9–15	$59\frac18$–$59\frac58$	103	$58\frac78$	$103\frac14$
29	16–22			$58\frac12$	$102\frac12$
30	23–29	$58\frac14$–$58\frac12$	$102\frac12$–103	$58\frac38$–$58\frac12$	$102\frac12$
31	Aug. 30– 5			$58\frac14$–$58\frac38$	102–$102\frac14$
32	6–12	$58\frac38$	$103\frac18$		
33	13–19			58	$102\frac14$
34	20–26				
35	Sep. 27– 2	$57\frac12$–$57\frac34$	102	58	$102\frac12$
36	3– 9	$57\frac34$–$57\frac78$	102–$102\frac34$		
37	10–16	$57\frac34$	$102\frac34$		
38	17–23	$57\frac34$–$57\frac78$	102–$102\frac12$	$57\frac78$–58	$102\frac34$
39	24–30	$57\frac34$–$57\frac78$	$102\frac14$	$57\frac78$	
40	Oct. 1– 7	$57\frac58$–$57\frac34$	102–$102\frac14$	$57\frac12$	$101\frac34$
41	8–14	$57\frac18$–$57\frac14$	$101\frac12$		
42	15–21	$57\frac18$–$57\frac14$	$101\frac14$–$101\frac12$		
43	22–28	$57\frac12$–$57\frac58$	$101\frac12$–102		
44	Nov. 29– 4	$57\frac78$–58	$102\frac34$–103	58	103
45	5–11	$57\frac34$–58	103	$57\frac12$	$102\frac12$
46	12–18	$57\frac14$	102–$102\frac34$		
47	19–25	$56\frac34$–57	$100\frac12$–102		
48	Dec. 26– 2	$55\frac78$–$56\frac38$	100	$56\frac14$	$100\frac14$
49	3– 9	$56\frac18$–$56\frac14$	$100\frac14$		
50	10–16				
51	17–23	56–$56\frac38$	101–$101\frac12$		
52	24–31	$56\frac18$–$56\frac14$	$101\frac14$		

TABLE A.11 [c] (*cont.*)

#	1676		ROUEN on:		PARIS on:	
			London	Amsterdam	London	Amsterdam
1	Jan.	1–7				
2		8–14	$55\frac{1}{2}$–$55\frac{3}{4}$	$100\frac{1}{4}$		
3		15–21				
4		21–28	56–$56\frac{3}{8}$	$100\frac{1}{4}$–101		
5	Feb.	29–4	$56\frac{3}{4}$			
6		5–11				
7		12–18			$56\frac{1}{8}$–$56\frac{1}{4}$	101
8		19–25	56–$56\frac{1}{4}$	$99\frac{3}{4}$–100	56	100
9	Mar.	26–4	$56\frac{1}{8}$	$99\frac{3}{4}$	56–$56\frac{1}{8}$	100
10		5–11	56–$56\frac{1}{8}$	$99\frac{1}{2}$		
11		12–18	56	100	$56\frac{1}{8}$–$56\frac{1}{4}$	101
12		19–25	$55\frac{3}{4}$–56	$100\frac{1}{2}$–$100\frac{3}{4}$	$55\frac{3}{4}$	
13	Apr.	26–1				
14		2–8	$56\frac{1}{4}$	101		
15		9–15				
16		16–22	$56\frac{1}{4}$			
17		23–29				
18	May	30–6				
19		7–13	$56\frac{3}{8}$–$56\frac{1}{2}$	$101\frac{1}{2}$		
20		14–20	$56\frac{1}{2}$	$101\frac{1}{2}$		
21		21–27				
22	June	28–3	$56\frac{1}{4}$–$56\frac{1}{2}$	$101\frac{1}{2}$		
23		4–10	$56\frac{3}{8}$	$101\frac{1}{2}$		
24		11–17	56–$56\frac{1}{4}$	$101\frac{1}{2}$		
25		18–24	56	101–$101\frac{1}{4}$		
26	July	25–1	$56\frac{1}{4}$	$101\frac{1}{2}$		
27		2–8	$56\frac{1}{8}$–$56\frac{1}{4}$	$101\frac{1}{2}$		
28		9–15	$56\frac{1}{4}$–$56\frac{3}{8}$	$101\frac{1}{2}$		
29		16–22				
30		23–29	56	$101\frac{1}{2}$		
31	Aug.	30–5	$55\frac{7}{8}$–56	$101\frac{1}{2}$–$101\frac{3}{4}$	56	102
32		6–12	56	$101\frac{3}{4}$–102	$55\frac{7}{8}$	102
33		13–19	$55\frac{7}{8}$–56	$101\frac{3}{4}$–102	$55\frac{7}{8}$–56	102
34		20–26	$55\frac{3}{4}$			
35	Sep.	27–2	$55\frac{1}{2}$–$55\frac{5}{8}$	$101\frac{1}{2}$–$101\frac{3}{4}$	$55\frac{5}{8}$	102
36		3–9	$55\frac{1}{2}$	$101\frac{1}{2}$–$101\frac{3}{4}$		
37		10–16	$55\frac{1}{4}$–$55\frac{1}{2}$	$101\frac{3}{4}$	$55\frac{1}{2}$–$55\frac{5}{8}$	102
38		17–23	$55\frac{1}{4}$	$101\frac{1}{2}$		
39		24–30	$55\frac{3}{8}$–$55\frac{1}{2}$	$101\frac{3}{4}$–102		
40	Oct.	1–7	$55\frac{5}{8}$	102	$55\frac{1}{2}$–$55\frac{5}{8}$	$102\frac{1}{4}$
41		8–14	$55\frac{1}{4}$–$55\frac{1}{2}$	102	$55\frac{5}{8}$–$55\frac{3}{4}$	$102\frac{1}{4}$
42		15–21	$55\frac{1}{2}$–$55\frac{3}{4}$	$101\frac{3}{4}$–102	$55\frac{5}{8}$	102
43		22–28	$55\frac{1}{2}$–$55\frac{5}{8}$	$101\frac{3}{4}$	$55\frac{5}{8}$	$101\frac{3}{4}$
44	Nov.	29–4	$55\frac{1}{2}$	$101\frac{3}{4}$	$55\frac{1}{2}$	$101\frac{1}{2}$
45		5–11	$55\frac{1}{2}$	$101\frac{1}{2}$	$55\frac{1}{2}$	$101\frac{1}{4}$–$101\frac{1}{2}$
46		12–18	$55\frac{1}{4}$–$55\frac{1}{2}$	$101\frac{3}{4}$–$101\frac{1}{2}$	$55\frac{1}{2}$	$101\frac{1}{2}$
47		19–25	$55\frac{3}{8}$–$55\frac{1}{2}$	$101\frac{1}{3}$		
48	Dec.	26–2	$55\frac{3}{8}$–$55\frac{1}{2}$	$101\frac{1}{4}$–$101\frac{1}{2}$		
49		3–9	$55\frac{1}{4}$–$55\frac{1}{2}$	$101\frac{1}{4}$	$55\frac{1}{2}$	102
50		10–16	$55\frac{1}{8}$–$55\frac{1}{4}$	$101\frac{1}{2}$	$55\frac{3}{8}$–$55\frac{1}{2}$	$101\frac{3}{4}$
51		17–23	$55\frac{1}{8}$–$55\frac{1}{4}$	$101\frac{1}{2}$–$101\frac{3}{4}$		
52		24–31	$55\frac{1}{4}$	$101\frac{3}{4}$–102	$55\frac{1}{4}$–$55\frac{3}{8}$	$101\frac{3}{4}$–102

TABLE A.11 [c] (*cont.*)

1677			ROUEN on:		PARIS on:	
			London	Amsterdam	London	Amsterdam
1	Jan.	1– 7	$55\frac{1}{4}$–$55\frac{3}{8}$	102		
2		8–14	$55\frac{1}{4}$	$101\frac{3}{4}$–102	$55\frac{1}{8}$	
3		15–21	$55\frac{1}{4}$	$101\frac{1}{2}$–$101\frac{3}{4}$	55–$55\frac{1}{8}$	$101\frac{3}{4}$
4		21–28	$55\frac{3}{8}$–$55\frac{5}{8}$	101–$101\frac{1}{2}$	$55\frac{3}{8}$	$101\frac{1}{4}$
5	Feb.	29– 4			$55\frac{1}{2}$	
6		5–11	$55\frac{1}{4}$	$101\frac{1}{4}$	$55\frac{1}{4}$	$101\frac{1}{4}$
7		12–18	$55\frac{1}{4}$	$101\frac{1}{4}$	$55\frac{3}{8}$–$55\frac{1}{2}$	$101\frac{1}{2}$
8		19–25	$55\frac{1}{4}$–$55\frac{3}{8}$	$100\frac{3}{4}$		
9	Mar.	26– 4	$55\frac{1}{4}$	101–$101\frac{1}{4}$	$55\frac{1}{4}$	$101\frac{1}{2}$
10		5–11	55–$55\frac{1}{8}$	101		
11		12–18	$55\frac{1}{4}$–$55\frac{1}{2}$	101–$101\frac{1}{4}$		
12		19–25	$55\frac{1}{2}$	$101\frac{1}{4}$		
13	Apr.	26– 1	$55\frac{1}{4}$–$55\frac{3}{8}$	$101\frac{1}{4}$		
14		2– 8	$55\frac{1}{4}$–$55\frac{3}{8}$	$101\frac{1}{4}$–$101\frac{1}{2}$		
15		9–15	$55\frac{1}{4}$–$55\frac{3}{8}$	$101\frac{1}{4}$	$55\frac{3}{8}$	$101\frac{1}{4}$
16		16–22			$55\frac{3}{8}$	$101\frac{1}{4}$
17		23–29	$55\frac{3}{8}$	$101\frac{1}{4}$	$55\frac{1}{4}$–$55\frac{1}{2}$	$101\frac{1}{4}$
18	May	30– 6	$55\frac{3}{8}$	$100\frac{3}{4}$	$55\frac{3}{8}$	
19		7–13	55–$55\frac{1}{4}$	$100\frac{1}{2}$–$100\frac{3}{4}$		
20		14–20	55–$55\frac{1}{8}$	100–$100\frac{1}{2}$		
21		21–27	$55\frac{1}{4}$	$100\frac{1}{2}$		
22	June	28– 3	$55\frac{3}{8}$–$55\frac{1}{2}$	$100\frac{1}{2}$		
23		4–10	$55\frac{1}{2}$	$100\frac{3}{4}$		
24		11–17	$55\frac{1}{2}$	$100\frac{1}{2}$–102		
25		18–24				
26	July	25– 1				
27		2– 8	$55\frac{1}{2}$	101–$101\frac{1}{4}$		
28		9–15	$55\frac{1}{2}$	101		
29		16–22		$101\frac{1}{4}$		
30		23–29	$55\frac{3}{8}$–$55\frac{1}{2}$	$101\frac{1}{2}$–$101\frac{3}{4}$		
31	Aug.	30– 5	$55\frac{3}{8}$	$100\frac{1}{2}$	$55\frac{3}{8}$	
32		6–12	$55\frac{1}{4}$–$55\frac{3}{8}$	$100\frac{1}{4}$–$100\frac{1}{2}$	$55\frac{3}{8}$–$55\frac{1}{2}$	$100\frac{1}{4}$–$100\frac{1}{2}$
33		13–19	$55\frac{1}{4}$	$100\frac{1}{4}$		
34		20–26	55–$55\frac{1}{4}$	$100\frac{1}{4}$		
35	Sep.	27– 2	55	$100\frac{1}{4}$		
36		3– 9	$54\frac{3}{4}$–$54\frac{7}{8}$	100–$100\frac{1}{4}$		
37		10–16	$54\frac{7}{8}$–55	100–$100\frac{1}{2}$	$54\frac{7}{8}$–55	$100\frac{1}{2}$
38		17–23	$54\frac{7}{8}$	99–$100\frac{1}{4}$		$100\frac{1}{4}$
39		24–30	$54\frac{3}{4}$–$54\frac{7}{8}$	$99\frac{3}{4}$–100		
40	Oct.	1– 7	$54\frac{3}{4}$		$54\frac{1}{2}$	$99\frac{1}{2}$
41		8–14	$54\frac{1}{4}$–$54\frac{1}{2}$	$99\frac{1}{4}$	$54\frac{3}{8}$	99
42		15–21	$54\frac{3}{8}$	$99\frac{1}{4}$	$54\frac{3}{8}$	$99\frac{1}{4}$
43		22–28	$54\frac{1}{4}$	99	$[54\frac{3}{8}]$	
44	Nov.	29– 4				
45		5–11	$54\frac{1}{4}$–$54\frac{3}{8}$	$98\frac{3}{4}$–99	$54\frac{1}{4}$–$54\frac{3}{8}$	$98\frac{3}{4}$–99
46		12–18	$54\frac{3}{8}$–$54\frac{1}{2}$	99	$54\frac{3}{8}$–$54\frac{1}{2}$	$98\frac{3}{4}$
47		19–25	$54\frac{1}{4}$–$54\frac{3}{8}$	$98\frac{1}{2}$–99	$54\frac{3}{8}$	$98\frac{1}{2}$
48	Dec.	26– 2	$54\frac{1}{4}$	$98\frac{1}{4}$	$[54\frac{1}{2}]$	
49		3– 9	$54\frac{1}{4}$–$54\frac{3}{8}$	98		
50		10–16	54–$54\frac{1}{8}$	$97\frac{1}{2}$–98	54–$54\frac{1}{4}$	$98\frac{1}{4}$
51		17–23			$54\frac{1}{4}$	98
52		24–31	54–$54\frac{1}{4}$	$97\frac{1}{2}$–$98\frac{1}{4}$	$54\frac{3}{8}$	98

TABLE A.11 [c] (cont.)

	1678		ROUEN on:		PARIS on:	
			London	Amsterdam	London	Amsterdam
1	Jan.	1– 7	$54\frac{1}{8}$	$97\frac{1}{2}$–$97\frac{3}{4}$		
2		8–14	$54\frac{1}{4}$–$54\frac{1}{2}$	$97\frac{1}{4}$–$97\frac{3}{4}$	$54\frac{1}{8}$	$97\frac{1}{2}$
3		15–21	$54\frac{1}{2}$	$97\frac{3}{4}$	$54\frac{1}{2}$–$54\frac{5}{8}$	
4		21–28	$54\frac{1}{2}$–$54\frac{3}{4}$	$97\frac{1}{2}$–$97\frac{3}{4}$		
5	Feb.	29– 4			$54\frac{3}{4}$	$98\frac{1}{4}$
6		5–11	55	$98\frac{1}{4}$	$54\frac{3}{4}$	$98\frac{1}{2}$
7		12–18	56		$55\frac{5}{8}$–$55\frac{3}{4}$	$98\frac{1}{2}$
8		19–25	56	$98\frac{1}{4}$–$98\frac{1}{2}$	56–$56\frac{1}{4}$	99
9	Mar.	26– 4	$56\frac{1}{2}$	$98\frac{3}{4}$–99	56–$56\frac{1}{4}$	$98\frac{3}{4}$–99
10		5–11	$56\frac{1}{2}$–$56\frac{3}{4}$	$98\frac{3}{4}$–99	$56\frac{1}{4}$–$56\frac{1}{4}$	$98\frac{1}{4}$–$98\frac{1}{2}$
11		12–18	$56\frac{7}{8}$–57	$98\frac{1}{2}$		
12		19–25	57–$57\frac{1}{8}$	$98\frac{1}{2}$		
13	Apr.	26– 1	$57\frac{1}{2}$–$57\frac{7}{8}$	$98\frac{1}{2}$	$57\frac{7}{8}$	$98\frac{1}{2}$
14		2– 8	$58\frac{1}{4}$–59	$98\frac{3}{4}$	[58]–$58\frac{1}{4}$	98–$98\frac{1}{4}$
15		9–15	$58\frac{3}{4}$–$59\frac{1}{4}$			
16		16–22	$57\frac{1}{4}$	$98\frac{1}{2}$		
17		23–29	$56\frac{1}{4}$–$56\frac{3}{4}$	$97\frac{3}{4}$	57–$57\frac{1}{4}$	$97\frac{1}{2}$
18	May	30– 6	$55\frac{3}{4}$–$55\frac{7}{8}$	$97\frac{3}{4}$	56	$97\frac{1}{4}$
19		7–13	$55\frac{3}{4}$	$97\frac{1}{4}$	56–[$56\frac{1}{2}$]	$97\frac{1}{4}$–$97\frac{1}{2}$
20		14–20			$56\frac{7}{8}$–57	$97\frac{1}{2}$
21		21–27	$55\frac{1}{2}$–$55\frac{5}{8}$	97	$56\frac{3}{4}$–$56\frac{7}{8}$	97
22	June	28– 3		97		
23		4–10	56–$56\frac{3}{8}$	$96\frac{1}{2}$–$96\frac{3}{4}$	$56\frac{1}{4}$	$96\frac{3}{4}$
24		11–17	$55\frac{1}{4}$–$55\frac{3}{4}$	96–$96\frac{1}{2}$	$55\frac{3}{4}$–$55\frac{7}{8}$	$96\frac{1}{2}$
25		18–24	$55\frac{1}{2}$–$55\frac{5}{8}$	$96\frac{1}{4}$–$96\frac{1}{2}$	[$55\frac{3}{4}$]	
26	July	25– 1	$55\frac{5}{8}$–$55\frac{3}{4}$	$96\frac{1}{2}$–$96\frac{3}{4}$	$55\frac{3}{4}$	$96\frac{3}{4}$
27		2– 8	$55\frac{5}{8}$		$55\frac{3}{4}$–[56]	97
28		9–15	$55\frac{7}{8}$–56	$96\frac{3}{4}$	$55\frac{3}{4}$–56	97–$97\frac{1}{4}$
29		16–22	56	97	56	$97\frac{1}{2}$
30		23–29	56	97	$55\frac{7}{8}$–56	$97\frac{1}{2}$
31	Aug.	30– 5	$55\frac{7}{8}$–56	$96\frac{3}{4}$–97		
32		6–12	$55\frac{3}{4}$–56	97		
33		13–19	$55\frac{5}{8}$	97	$55\frac{3}{4}$	$97\frac{1}{4}$
34		20–26	$55\frac{1}{8}$	$97\frac{1}{4}$	55	
35	Sep.	27– 2	$55\frac{1}{4}$	$97\frac{1}{4}$	$54\frac{7}{8}$–55	$97\frac{3}{8}$–$97\frac{1}{2}$
36		3– 9	$54\frac{7}{8}$–55	$97\frac{1}{4}$–$97\frac{1}{2}$		
37		10–16	$54\frac{5}{8}$–$54\frac{3}{4}$	$97\frac{1}{4}$		
38		17–23	$54\frac{3}{4}$	97–$97\frac{1}{4}$	$54\frac{7}{8}$	97
39		24–30	$54\frac{5}{8}$–$54\frac{3}{4}$	97–$97\frac{1}{4}$		
40	Oct.	1– 7	$54\frac{3}{4}$–55	$97\frac{1}{4}$–$97\frac{1}{2}$		
41		8–14	$54\frac{7}{8}$–55	$97\frac{1}{2}$–$97\frac{3}{4}$	$55\frac{1}{4}$	98
42		15–21	55	$97\frac{3}{4}$–98	55	$98\frac{1}{4}$
43		22–28	$54\frac{7}{8}$–55	98		
44	Nov.	29– 4	$54\frac{7}{8}$	$97\frac{3}{4}$–98	55–$55\frac{1}{8}$	$98\frac{1}{4}$
45		5–11	$54\frac{7}{8}$			
46		12–18	$54\frac{3}{4}$	$97\frac{1}{2}$	$54\frac{3}{4}$	97
47		19–25	$54\frac{5}{8}$	$96\frac{1}{4}$–$96\frac{1}{2}$		
48	Dec.	26– 2	$54\frac{1}{2}$	$96\frac{1}{4}$–$96\frac{1}{2}$		
49		3– 9	54	96–$96\frac{1}{2}$		
50		10–16	$53\frac{3}{4}$–54	$96\frac{1}{2}$		
51		17–23	$53\frac{7}{8}$–$54\frac{1}{4}$			
52		24–31	$54\frac{1}{2}$	97		

TABLE A.11 [c] (*cont.*)

1679		ROUEN on:		PARIS on:	
		London	Amsterdam	London	Amsterdam
1	Jan. 1– 7	$54\frac{1}{4}$	$96\frac{3}{4}$–97		
2	8–14	$54\frac{1}{4}$	$96\frac{3}{4}$–97		
3	15–21	$54\frac{1}{2}$–$54\frac{5}{8}$	$96\frac{3}{4}$–97		
4	21–28	$54\frac{1}{2}$–$54\frac{5}{8}$	$96\frac{3}{4}$	$54\frac{1}{2}$–[$54\frac{5}{8}$]	$96\frac{1}{2}$–$96\frac{3}{4}$
5	Feb. 29– 4	$54\frac{1}{2}$	$96\frac{1}{2}$	$54\frac{1}{2}$	$96\frac{1}{2}$
6	5–11	$54\frac{5}{8}$	$96\frac{1}{4}$		
7	12–18	$54\frac{1}{2}$–$54\frac{7}{8}$	$96\frac{1}{4}$		
8	19–25	$54\frac{3}{8}$–$54\frac{1}{2}$	$96\frac{1}{4}$–$96\frac{1}{2}$		
9	Mar. 26– 4	$54\frac{1}{2}$	$96\frac{1}{4}$–$96\frac{1}{2}$		
10	5–11	$54\frac{5}{8}$–$54\frac{3}{4}$	$96\frac{1}{2}$–97	[55]–$54\frac{3}{4}$	$97\frac{3}{4}$
11	12–18	$54\frac{1}{2}$			
12	19–25	$54\frac{1}{2}$	$97\frac{1}{4}$		
13	Apr. 26– 1	$54\frac{1}{2}$	$97\frac{1}{4}$–$97\frac{1}{2}$	[$54\frac{3}{4}$]	
14	2– 8			$54\frac{5}{8}$–$55\frac{3}{4}$	$98\frac{1}{4}$
15	9–15	$54\frac{1}{4}$–$54\frac{1}{2}$	$97\frac{1}{4}$–$97\frac{1}{2}$	[$54\frac{5}{8}$]	
16	16–22	$54\frac{3}{8}$	$97\frac{1}{2}$–$97\frac{3}{4}$		
17	23–29	$54\frac{1}{2}$–$54\frac{5}{8}$	$97\frac{1}{2}$–98		
18	May 30– 6	$54\frac{1}{2}$	$97\frac{3}{4}$	[$54\frac{5}{8}$]	
19	7–13	$54\frac{1}{2}$	98–$98\frac{1}{4}$		
20	14–20	$54\frac{1}{2}$–$54\frac{5}{8}$	$98\frac{3}{4}$	$54\frac{3}{4}$	$98\frac{3}{4}$–99
21	21–27	$54\frac{1}{4}$–$54\frac{3}{8}$	$98\frac{3}{4}$		
22	June 28– 3	$54\frac{1}{4}$	$98\frac{1}{2}$		
23	4–10	$54\frac{3}{8}$–$54\frac{1}{2}$	$98\frac{1}{2}$–$98\frac{3}{4}$		
24	11–17	$54\frac{3}{8}$	$98\frac{1}{2}$	$54\frac{1}{2}$	
25	18–24	$54\frac{1}{2}$	$98\frac{1}{2}$		
26	July 25– 1	$54\frac{5}{8}$	$97\frac{3}{4}$		
27	2– 8	$54\frac{3}{8}$	$97\frac{1}{2}$–$97\frac{3}{4}$	$54\frac{1}{2}$	$97\frac{3}{4}$–98
28	9–15	$54\frac{1}{4}$–$54\frac{3}{8}$	$97\frac{3}{4}$		
29	16–22	$54\frac{1}{4}$–$54\frac{3}{8}$	$97\frac{3}{4}$–98		
30	23–29	$54\frac{3}{8}$–$54\frac{1}{2}$	98		
31	Aug. 30– 5	$54\frac{3}{8}$–$54\frac{1}{2}$	98		
32	6–12	$54\frac{3}{8}$–$54\frac{1}{2}$	$98\frac{1}{4}$–$98\frac{1}{2}$	$54\frac{3}{8}$–$54\frac{1}{2}$	99
33	13–19	$54\frac{1}{4}$	$98\frac{1}{2}$		
34	20–26	$54\frac{1}{4}$	$98\frac{1}{2}$		
35	Sep. 27– 2	$54\frac{1}{4}$	$98\frac{3}{4}$		
36	3– 9	$54\frac{1}{4}$	$98\frac{1}{2}$		
37	10–16	$54\frac{1}{4}$	99	$54\frac{3}{8}$	
38	17–23	$54\frac{1}{4}$	99		
39	24–30	$54\frac{1}{4}$–$54\frac{3}{8}$	$98\frac{1}{2}$–99		
40	Oct. 1– 7	$54\frac{3}{8}$	$98\frac{1}{2}$–$98\frac{3}{4}$		
41	8–14	54	98–$98\frac{1}{2}$	55	$99\frac{3}{4}$
42	15–21	$54\frac{1}{2}$–$54\frac{3}{4}$	99		
43	22–28	$54\frac{5}{8}$–$54\frac{3}{4}$	$99\frac{1}{4}$–$99\frac{1}{2}$		
44	Nov. 29– 4	$54\frac{3}{4}$	$99\frac{1}{2}$	55	$99\frac{3}{4}$
45	5–11	55	$99\frac{1}{4}$–$99\frac{3}{4}$		
46	12–18	55	$99\frac{1}{2}$–$99\frac{3}{4}$		
47	19–25	55–$55\frac{1}{8}$	$99\frac{1}{2}$		
48	Dec. 26– 2	$55\frac{1}{8}$	$99\frac{1}{2}$		
49	3– 9	55	$99\frac{1}{2}$		
50	10–16	55–$55\frac{1}{8}$	$99\frac{1}{2}$		
51	17–23	$55\frac{1}{4}$–$55\frac{1}{2}$	$99\frac{1}{2}$–$99\frac{3}{4}$		
52	24–31	$55\frac{3}{8}$–$55\frac{1}{2}$	$99\frac{3}{4}$–100		

TABLE A.11 [C] (*cont.*)

	1680		ROUEN on:	
			London	Amsterdam
1	Jan.	1– 7	$55\frac{1}{2}$	100
2		8–14	$55\frac{1}{2}$	
3		15–21	$55\frac{1}{2}$	100
4		21–28	$55\frac{3}{4}$–56	100–$100\frac{1}{4}$
5	Feb.	29– 4	$55\frac{3}{4}$–$55\frac{7}{8}$	$100\frac{1}{4}$
6		5–11	`56	$100\frac{1}{2}$
7		12–18	$55\frac{7}{8}$	$100\frac{1}{2}$
8		19–25	$55\frac{3}{4}$	$100\frac{1}{2}$
9	Mar.	26– 4	$55\frac{1}{2}$–$55\frac{5}{8}$	$100\frac{1}{2}$
10		5–11	$55\frac{1}{2}$	$100\frac{1}{2}$
11		12–18	$55\frac{1}{2}$–$55\frac{5}{8}$	$100\frac{3}{4}$–101
12		19–25	$55\frac{1}{2}$	$100\frac{3}{4}$
13	Apr.	26– 1	$55\frac{1}{2}$–$55\frac{5}{8}$	$100\frac{3}{4}$–101
14		2– 8	$55\frac{1}{2}$–$55\frac{5}{8}$	$100\frac{3}{4}$–101
15		9–15		
16		16–22		

TABLE A.11 *(cont.)*

[d] *Venice on London and Amsterdam*

	VENICE on	1668		1669	
		London	Amsterdam	London	Amsterdam
1	Jan. 1– 7				
2	8–14			$54\frac{3}{4}$	$96\frac{5}{6}$
3	15–21			$54\frac{7}{8}$	$96\frac{7}{8}$–97
4	21–28				
5	Feb. 29– 4			$55\frac{1}{2}$	$97\frac{3}{4}$
6	5–11			$55\frac{1}{2}$	$97\frac{7}{8}$
7	12–18				
8	19–25			$55\frac{3}{4}$	$98\frac{1}{2}$
9	Mar. 26– 4			$55\frac{1}{3}$–$55\frac{1}{2}$	$98\frac{1}{6}$–$98\frac{1}{4}$
10	5–11			$55\frac{2}{3}$	$98\frac{1}{6}$
11	12–18			55	$97\frac{3}{4}$
12	19–25			55	$97\frac{7}{8}$
13	Apr. 26– 1				
14	2– 8			$54\frac{7}{8}$–55	$97\frac{2}{3}$
15	9–15			$55\frac{1}{8}$	$97\frac{3}{4}$
16	16–22			$55\frac{1}{6}$	$97\frac{7}{8}$
17	23–29			$55\frac{1}{6}$	$97\frac{5}{8}$
18	May 30– 6			55	$97\frac{1}{8}$
19	7–13			$54\frac{7}{8}$	$96\frac{7}{8}$
20	14–20			55	$96\frac{7}{8}$
21	21–27			$54\frac{3}{4}$	97
22	June 28– 3	$54\frac{1}{3}$	96	$54\frac{2}{3}$	$96\frac{7}{8}$
23	4–10			$54\frac{3}{4}$	97
24	11–17			$54\frac{7}{8}$	$96\frac{7}{8}$
25	18–24	$55\frac{1}{3}$–$54\frac{3}{4}$		$54\frac{3}{4}$	$96\frac{2}{3}$–$96\frac{3}{4}$
26	July 25– 1			$54\frac{1}{2}$	$96\frac{1}{2}$
27	2– 8			$54\frac{1}{3}$	$96\frac{1}{3}$
28	9–15			$54\frac{1}{3}$	96–$96\frac{1}{3}$
29	16–22			$54\frac{2}{3}$	96–$96\frac{1}{8}$
30	23–29			$54\frac{1}{2}$	$96\frac{1}{6}$
31	Aug. 30– 5	$54\frac{5}{8}$	96–$96\frac{1}{8}$	$54\frac{2}{3}$	$96\frac{1}{8}$
32	6–12			$54\frac{5}{8}$	$96\frac{1}{8}$
33	13–19			$54\frac{5}{8}$	$96\frac{1}{8}$
34	20–26	$54\frac{5}{8}$–$54\frac{2}{3}$	96		
35	Sep. 27– 2	$54\frac{7}{8}$	96–$96\frac{1}{8}$		
36	3– 9			$54\frac{2}{3}$	$96\frac{3}{8}$
37	10–16			$54\frac{1}{3}$	96
38	17–23			$54\frac{1}{8}$	96–$96\frac{1}{8}$
39	24–30			54	$95\frac{3}{4}$
40	Oct. 1– 7	$54\frac{7}{8}$	96	$54\frac{1}{4}$	$95\frac{3}{4}$
41	8–14			$54\frac{1}{2}$	$95\frac{3}{4}$
42	15–21			$54\frac{2}{3}$	$95\frac{3}{4}$
43	22–28			$54\frac{3}{4}$	96
44	Nov. 29– 4			$54\frac{3}{4}$–$54\frac{7}{8}$	$95\frac{3}{4}$
45	5–11			$54\frac{3}{4}$–$54\frac{7}{8}$	$95\frac{7}{8}$
46	12–18	$54\frac{1}{4}$–$54\frac{1}{3}$	$97\frac{1}{2}$	$54\frac{1}{2}$	$95\frac{7}{8}$
47	19–25			$54\frac{1}{3}$	$95\frac{5}{8}$
48	Dec. 26– 2	$55\frac{1}{3}$	$97\frac{3}{4}$	$54\frac{1}{8}$–$54\frac{1}{4}$	$95\frac{1}{2}$
49	3– 9	55	97	54–$54\frac{1}{8}$	$95\frac{1}{4}$
50	10–16	$54\frac{1}{2}$	$97\frac{3}{4}$–$97\frac{7}{8}$	$54\frac{1}{8}$	95
51	17–23			$54\frac{1}{4}$	$94\frac{7}{8}$
52	25–31	$54\frac{1}{2}$	$96\frac{1}{4}$		

TABLE A.11 [d] (*cont.*)

	VENICE on		1670		1672	
			London	Amsterdam	London	Amsterdam
1	Jan.	1– 7	$54\frac{1}{6}$	$94\frac{1}{2}$	$51\frac{7}{8}$	$92\frac{1}{2}$
2		8–14	$54\frac{1}{6}$–$54\frac{1}{4}$	$94\frac{1}{2}$	52	$92\frac{5}{8}$
3		15–21	54	$94\frac{1}{2}$	52	$92\frac{1}{2}$
4		21–28	$54\frac{1}{4}$	$94\frac{3}{8}$		
5	Feb.	29– 4	$54\frac{1}{4}$	$94\frac{1}{6}$	$51\frac{1}{4}$	$92\frac{5}{8}$
6		5–11	$54\frac{1}{4}$	$93\frac{3}{4}$–$93\frac{7}{8}$	$51\frac{1}{2}$	92
7		12–18	$54\frac{1}{4}$	$93\frac{3}{4}$	$51\frac{1}{4}$	
8		19–25	*1671*		51–$51\frac{1}{6}$	91–$91\frac{1}{2}$
9	Mar.	26– 4	London	Amsterdam	$50\frac{5}{8}$–51	$90\frac{7}{8}$–91
10		5–11	53–$53\frac{1}{8}$	$95\frac{1}{4}$	$50\frac{7}{8}$	$90\frac{7}{8}$
11		12–18	$52\frac{3}{4}$	95		
12		19–25	$52\frac{1}{2}$	$94\frac{2}{3}$–$94\frac{3}{4}$	$50\frac{1}{2}$–$50\frac{2}{3}$	90
13	Apr.	26– 1	$52\frac{1}{2}$–$52\frac{5}{8}$	$94\frac{2}{3}$–$94\frac{3}{4}$		
14		2– 8	$52\frac{1}{2}$–$52\frac{5}{8}$	$94\frac{5}{8}$		
15		9–15	$52\frac{1}{4}$–$52\frac{5}{8}$	$94\frac{2}{3}$–$94\frac{5}{8}$	$50\frac{2}{3}$	$90\frac{1}{8}$
16		16–22	$52\frac{2}{3}$	$94\frac{5}{8}$		
17		23–29	$52\frac{3}{4}$	$94\frac{1}{4}$		
18	May	30– 6	$52\frac{2}{3}$	$94\frac{1}{4}$		
19		7–13	$52\frac{1}{2}$–$52\frac{5}{8}$	$94\frac{1}{4}$	52	89
20		14–20	$52\frac{2}{3}$–$52\frac{19}{24}$	$94\frac{1}{3}$–$94\frac{1}{2}$		
21		21–27	$52\frac{3}{4}$	$94\frac{1}{2}$	$52\frac{5}{6}$	$88\frac{7}{8}$
22	June	28– 3	$52\frac{3}{4}$	$94\frac{5}{8}$	53	$88\frac{1}{2}$–$88\frac{3}{4}$
23		4–10	$52\frac{5}{6}$	$94\frac{5}{8}$	53	$88\frac{5}{6}$
24		11–17	$52\frac{3}{4}$	$94\frac{1}{2}$	$52\frac{3}{4}$	89
25		18–24	$52\frac{1}{2}$–$52\frac{2}{3}$	$94\frac{1}{3}$	$52\frac{7}{8}$	89
26	July	25– 1	$52\frac{1}{2}$	$94\frac{1}{4}$	$52\frac{3}{4}$	
27		2– 8	$52\frac{1}{4}$	$94\frac{1}{4}$	53	100
28		9–15	52–$52\frac{1}{4}$	$94\frac{1}{3}$–$94\frac{1}{2}$		
29		16–22	$52\frac{1}{3}$	$94\frac{1}{2}$		
30		23–29	$52\frac{1}{4}$	$94\frac{2}{5}$	53–$53\frac{1}{2}$	
31	Aug.	30– 5				
32		6–12	$52\frac{1}{2}$	$94\frac{3}{8}$		
33		13–19			$53\frac{1}{2}$	$93\frac{1}{2}$
34		20–26				
35	Sep.	27– 2				
36		3– 9			53	$91\frac{1}{8}$
37		10–16	$52\frac{1}{2}$	$94\frac{1}{3}$		
38		17–23	$52\frac{1}{2}$	$94\frac{2}{5}$		
39		24–30	$52\frac{1}{3}$–$52\frac{2}{5}$	94		
40	Oct.	1– 7	$52\frac{1}{8}$–$52\frac{1}{6}$	$94\frac{1}{2}$–$94\frac{3}{4}$		
41		8–14			53	$89\frac{1}{2}$
42		15–21			$52\frac{7}{8}$	$89\frac{1}{6}$
43		22–28			$52\frac{3}{4}$	89
44	Nov.	29– 4				
45		5–11				
46		12–18	52	$93\frac{1}{2}$		
47		19–25	52	$93\frac{1}{4}$		
48	Dec.	26– 2	$52\frac{1}{8}$	$93\frac{1}{6}$		
49		3– 9	$52\frac{1}{6}$	93	$52\frac{1}{3}$	$88\frac{1}{2}$
50		10–16	52	$92\frac{3}{4}$		
51		17–23	52	$92\frac{3}{4}$	$52\frac{1}{2}$	$87\frac{2}{3}$
52		24–31	$51\frac{3}{4}$	$92\frac{5}{8}$		

APPENDIX H

PRICE-CURRENTS AND EXCHANGE-COURSES

Printed price-currents are frequently referred to in the Marescoe-David correspondence but regrettably few have survived among the letters. One must be grateful for those that have, for they make a significant addition to those known to N. W. Posthumus for Amsterdam, and to those being assembled by Professor John McCusker (to whom these examples have been communicated). Accompanied by a group of exchange-courses from Hamburg, Amsterdam and Venice, they are reproduced on microfiche (enquiries to The British Academy, as above, p. 220).

A. Price-currents:

(i)	Hamburg	1668	24 April
		1668	15 May
		1668	26 June
(ii)	Amsterdam	1668	16 April
		1668	28 May
		1668	23 July
		1668	1 October
		1669	21 January
		1669	18 February
		1669	25 February [2 copies, both fragile]
		1669	29 April
		1669	27 May
		1669	3 June
		1669	17 June
		1670	6 January
		1671	20 April
		1671	4 May
(iii)	Rouen	1668	17 February
		1668	6 April
		1668	13 April
		1668	4 May
		1668	1 June
		1668	8 June
		1668	16 November
		1669	25 January
(iv)	La Rochelle	1669	? February
		1669	30 May

B. Exchange-courses:

(i)	Hamburg	1676	12 December
(ii)	Amsterdam	1670	28 January
		1670	21 February

(iii) Venice	1668	7 December
	1668	23 December
	1671	8 May
	1671	22 May
	1671	29 May
	1671	5 June
	1671	25 June
	1671	3 July
	1671	17 July
	1671	7 August
	1672	10 June

APPENDIX I

WEIGHTS, MEASURES & MONEY

It may be some comfort to the reader to know that many of Marescoe's and David's correspondents found contemporary weights and measures totally confusing. Both men received pleas to explain, not merely English units but the relationship between Dutch and Swedish, German and Swedish, French and Spanish weights and measures. Several of the letters printed here [e.g. **14, 175, 253, 265, 267, 342, 415, 416, 462**] contain elementary advice on the English equivalents for local units, but it can be assumed that for much of the time men traded in comparative ignorance of what their goods would render in foreign currency, weights or measures. While this created the possibility of dispute it also enhanced the importance of the local agent or factor, and Marescoe's and David's seem to have honestly discharged the responsibilities placed upon them.

There are many detailed guides to early modern weights and measures, among them:

H. Doursther, *Dictionnaire des poids et mesures anciens* (Brussels, 1840);

E. F. Heckscher, *De svenska penning-, vikt- och mått systemen* (Stockholm, 1941);

W. C. Staring, *Maten, Gewichten en Munten* (Schoonhoven, 4th edition, 1902);

R. E. Zupko, *French Weights and Measures before the Revolution* (Bloomington/London, 1978).

I have also found P. Kelly *The Universal Cambist and Commercial Instructor* (London, 1835) and W. Beawes, *Lex Mercatoria Rediviva, or, The Merchant's Directory* (London, 1763, facsimile edition 1970) helpful guides to earlier usages, although they fall short of the admirable *Dictionnaire Universel de Commerce* of Jaques Savary des Bruslons (Amsterdam, 1733).

What follows is a brief guide to the basic units employed in this correspondence.

I. SWEDEN

Bulk commodities were freighted by the *last* of 4,800 lb., or the *great last* of 6,000 lb. Conventionally 12 barrels of pitch or 13 barrels of tar = 1 last.

Iron and copper were sold and invoiced by the *shippound* (slb). The metals shippound of Sweden consisted of 20 *lispound* each of 20 *pounds*. Thus 12 slb = 1 last; 15 slb = 1 great last. The Swedish metals shippound was estimated to be equivalent to 299–300 English pounds avoirdupois (or 2.68 cwt.) and samples of Marescoe's consignments confirm this ratio of 3 : 4 for English and Swedish pounds.

Iron and copper prices were usually quoted in dollars-copper-money (d.c.m.), although iron was sometimes given in dollars-silver-money (d.s.m.). The ratio between the copper and silver dollar (each of 4 marks of 32 öre) was revised in October 1665 from $2\frac{1}{2}$ copper öre: 1 silver öre to 3 : 1. However, for purposes of overseas payments the crucial ratio was that between the silver specie rixdollar and the dollar-silver-money. Up to May 1664 the ratio was 1 RD: $1\frac{1}{2}$ d.s.m; after May 1664 it was 1 RD: $1\frac{5}{8}$ d.s.m. The ratio between the rixdollar and the dollar-copper-money remained at 1 RD: $5\frac{1}{4}$ d.c.m. until 1674 but then changed almost monthly throughout the war to reach 1 RD: $6\frac{3}{4}$ d.c.m. by 1680.

The exchange rate on London was quoted in d.c.m. per £1 sterling, and although the rixdollar was conventionally rated at 4s 6d sterling the exchange could vary between 21 and 28 d.c.m. The rate on Hamburg was in marks per reichsthaler, and Amsterdam was quoted in marks per rixdollar (of 50 stuivers).

2. HAMBURG

W. Foxley correctly advised David [267] that the *last* in Hamburg was 10 per cent 'better than with you'. Doursther gives the ratio as 29.08 hectolitres for the English last to 31.65 hectolitres for Hamburg's.

Commodities were sold either by the shippound (of 280 lb.), by the centner (of 112 lb.), by the 100 lb. or the pound. J. A. Fonck was confused when he told Marescoe that 100 lb. English equalled 104 lb. in Hamburg; more correctly Claus Bene advised David that the English hundredweight 'must yield 104 lb. here' [475].

Prices were quoted either in *pfunds, schillings* and *grooten* flemish or in *marks, schillings* and *pfennigs* Lübeck (lübs.). 1 Mark lüb. (*ML*) = 16s lüb. (each *schilling* of 12 *pfennigs*) = 192d. £1 flem. = $7\frac{1}{2}$ Marks lüb. Some prices were quoted in reichsthalers (*RD*). 1 *RD* = 3 *ML*, thus $2\frac{1}{2}$ *RD* = £1 flem. But all these units of account had *two* values—either as current money or as bank money. The ratio (or agio) between the two varied constantly (see McCusker, *Money and Exchange . . . 1600–1775*, pp. 62–5) and while some prices were given in bank money others were in current money. For the quotation of key commodities see Table A.12.

3. AMSTERDAM

The conventional ratio between the early-modern English pound avoirdupois and the seventeenth-century Dutch *pond* is 100 lb. English:91.8 lb. Dutch (or 100 lb. Dutch:109 lb. English). Comparisons of weighings by Marescoe and the Van Baerles give a ratio of 100:91.285 on identical cargoes of lead and tin, but the Van Baerles were confused by the Hull lead fodder of $19\frac{1}{2}$ cwt. (each cwt. of 120 lb., not 112 lb.!). With that adjustment the ratio would have been 100:91.66.

Amsterdam prices were quoted either in guilders (or florins), each of 20 stuivers or 320 penningen, or in pounds flemish, schellings and grooten. £1 flem. = 6 guilders. Grain prices were quoted in gold guilders (ggl.). As in Hamburg, there was a variable agio between current money and bank money, but most prices were quoted in current money. For details of key commodities see Table A.12.

4. ROUEN

As Oursel had to explain to Marescoe [14], Rouen weights differed from Paris by about 4 per cent—i.e. 100 lb. Rouen = 104 lb. at Paris. The conventional ratio between the English and Rouen weight was 100 lb. English:88 lb. Rouen.

Prices are quoted in livres, sols and deniers tournois (£.t.s.d.), but the exchange on London was based on the silver écu (or crown), equivalent to 3 livres tournois. Thus, at a rate of 54d sterling per *W*, the livre was worth about 1s 6d.

5. LA ROCHELLE

The complications of weight-equivalents here were patiently explained to Marescoe by Jean Freyhoff in 1669 [66], and his account cannot be improved upon. Brandy was measured by the Amsterdam verge or viertel (of about 14 lb. avoirdupois) and conventional barrels varied between 27 viertels at La Rochelle (expressed $\frac{27}{v}$), 29 at Nantes and 32 at Bordeaux. Modern equivalents estimate 7.258 litres per verge, and for the thonneau, 900 litres.

6. SEVILLE

Weights figure less prominently here than money, but the conventional equivalents were 100 lb. Spanish:97 lb. English. Some commodities were weighed by the *arroba* (of 25 lb. Spanish) or the *quintal* (of 4 *arroba*). Bilbao weights seem to have differed: George Richards assessed the pound there at 10–12 per cent more than the English: thus 112 lb. avoirdupois = 100 lb., Bilbao.

Cloth lengths were given in *vares* which Upton & Bathurst correctly enough explain [2] as about 8 per cent less than 1 English yard, i.e. about 33 inches.

Prices are given either in *reals plata* (R. pta.), or *pesos* or ducats (D.) 8 R. pta. = 1 *peso* (the piece-of-eight, sometimes written '$\frac{8}{8}$'). 11 R. pta. = 1 ducat. Most English cloths were priced in *pesos* but the highly-prized Colchester bay was sold for ducats per piece.

Accounts were rendered in *reals plata* which Englishmen could conveniently value at 6d sterling each. But to arrive at the net yield for any parcel of cloth an extraordinarily complex series of duties had to be borne, involving nearly a score of calculations.

Each type of English cloth was notionally rated for customs purposes in *maravedis* (34 *mvs* per r. pta.). The following tariff can be deduced from Marescoe's sale-accounts:

Colchester bays:	9,740 *mvs* per piece
Ellbroad perpetuanas: ⎫ Serges: ⎭	5,200 ,, ,,
Lamparillas: ⎫ Hounscotts: ⎭	4,500 ,, ,,
Yardbroad perpetuanas: ⎫ Mohairs: ⎬ Chenies: ⎭	3,400 ,, ,,
Deribands:	700 ,, ,,

A concessionary abatement, or 'grace' of one-third was made on this tariff before the levy of the following duties on the remainder:

	%
1. Either (a) 15% ⎫ payable $\frac{1}{4}$ in silver ⎫	
or (b) (i) 5% ⎭ and $\frac{3}{4}$ in vellon ⎬	15.0000
plus (ii) 10% *alcavala major* in vellon ⎭	
2. Another $4\frac{3}{4}$% ($\frac{1}{4}$ paid in silver, $\frac{3}{4}$ in vellon)	4.6666
3. Another $\frac{3}{4}$%, plus a 5% premium, all in vellon	0.7875
4. $1\frac{1}{3}$% 'consulado' and 'lonja', plus a 5% premium ⎫	
(vizt. 1.3335 + 0.0666) all in vellon ⎭	1.3999
5. 1% 'for the Nation' and 'indulto', all in vellon	1.0000
6. 1% 'consumo'; 1% 'reventa'; $\frac{1}{4}$% 'donativo', and ⎫	
4% 'new alcavala', all payable in vellon ⎭	6.2500
totalling	29.1040

of which $2\frac{1}{2}$% was payable in silver, and $26\frac{1}{2}$% in vellon converted into *reals plata* at a variable premium which was at $137\frac{1}{2}$ in 1668–9 (i.e. 100 R. pta. = $237\frac{1}{2}$ r. vn).

7. LEGHORN

100 lb. at Leghorn = $75\frac{1}{2}$ lb. avoirdupois. Goods were sold by the *mille* (1,000 lb.) or *cento* (100 lb.) or pound. The quintal here was variable: for 'poor jack' (dried cod) it was 150 lb.

The *salm* of oil was a liquid measure of 35 gallons approximately.

Commodities were priced either in ducats, or in dollars (sometimes called 'crowns' or 'piastres') or in guilios, and accounts were kept in livres, soldi and denari. Conventionally, 1 ducat = 7 livres; 1 dollar = 6 livres, but the latter ratio was variable, and Death & Skinner converted at the rate of $5\frac{3}{4}$ livres to the dollar in 1669–70. 1 livre = $1\frac{1}{2}$ giulios; thus 1 dollar =

9 giulios; 1 ducat = $10\frac{1}{2}$ giulios. The exchange on London was given in pence sterling per dollar; on Amsterdam in grooten flemish per dollar, and on Venice in dollars per 100 Venetian ducats.

8. VENICE

100 lb. at Venice = $65\frac{3}{4}$ lb. avoirdupois. Here too commodities were sold by the *mille* or *cento* or *lb.* and were priced usually in current ducats (of 24 *grossi*) or livres (of 20 *soldi*). 1 ducat = 6 livres and 4 soldi. Accounts were kept in current ducats but the net proceeds were converted into bank ducats at a variable premium. The exchange on London was quoted in pence sterling per bank ducat and usually rated it at about 4s 4d–4s 6d.

9. ALEPPO & CONSTANTINOPLE

David's correspondents here obligingly explained the local weights, measures and currency with satisfactory accuracy. At Constantinople the *kintall* (of 100 *rottolo* or 45 *oques*) was considerably different from the *kintalls, rottolos, oques* and *drames* of Aleppo. At the former the *kintall* was about 118 lb. avoirdupois and thus the *oque* was indeed 2 lb. 11 oz. as Samuel Lannoy states [**322**]. But in giving the *rottolo* of 600 *drames* as just under 4 lb. English at Aleppo [**265**] Lannoy & Burkin seem to be referring to the 'Damassin' *rottolo* [Beawes, p. 896] rather than the heavier Aleppo *rottolo* used for silks, etc., which was little under 5 lb. avoirdupois.

APPENDIX I—TABLE A.12. Price quotations.

Commodities	LONDON	AMSTERDAM	HAMBURG
Iron	£.s.d. per ton/s.d. per cwt.	Guilders per 100 lb.	*ML* current per slb.
Copper	£.s.d. per cwt.	Guilders per 100 lb.	*RD* banco per slb.
Copper-wire	£.s.d. per cwt.	Guilders per 100 lb.	*ML* banco per 100 lb.
Garcopper	£.s.d. per cwt.	Guilders per 100 lb.	*RD* banco per slb.
Lead	£.s.d. per fodder.	Schellings per 100 lb.	*ML* banco per slb.
Tin	£.s.d. per cwt.	Guilders per 100 lb.	Schillings current per lb.
Pitch & Tar	£.s.d per last.	Guilders per last.	*RD* current per last.
Sugars	Shillings, pence per cwt.	Grooten per lb.	Grooten banco per lb.
Pepper	Pence per lb.	Grooten per lb.	Grooten banco per lb.
Ginger	Shillings, pence per cwt.	Guilders per 100 lb.	Grooten banco per lb.
Cottons	Pence per lb.	Grooten per lb.	Schillings flem. per lb.
Silk	Shillings, pence per lb.	Schellings flem. per lb.	Schillings flem. per lb.
Indigo	Shillings, pence per lb.	Stuivers per lb.	Schillings flem. per lb.
Campeachy	Shillings, pence per cwt.	Guilders per 100 lb.	*ML* banco per 100 lb.
Galls	Shillings, pence per cwt.	Guilders per 100 lb.	*ML* banco per 100 lb.
Currants	Shillings, pence per cwt.	Guilders per 100 lb.	*ML* current per 100 lb.
Tobacco	Pence per lb.	Stuivers per lb.	Schillings lüb. per lb.
Olive oil	£.s.d. per 236 gallons.	£ flem. per tun	*RD* banco per 820 lb.

INDEX OF COMMODITIES

INDEX OF PERSONS

Ships' captains are indexed collectively under Captains of ships, *and parties to bills of exchange under* Bills of Exchange. *Bold figures refer to letters by number, not page.*

INDEX OF PLACES

INDEX OF SUBJECTS